# MANAGING THE GLOBAL CORPORATION

## CASE STUDIES
## IN STRATEGY
## AND MANAGEMENT

**McGraw-Hill International Series in Business and Economics**

# MANAGING THE GLOBAL CORPORATION

## CASE STUDIES IN STRATEGY AND MANAGEMENT

## William H. Davidson

Associate Professor of Management and Organization
School of Business
University of Southern California

## José de la Torre

Professor of International Business Strategy
John E. Anderson Graduate School of Management
University of California, Los Angeles

**McGRAW-HILL PUBLISHING COMPANY**

New York   St. Louis   San Francisco   Auckland   Bogotá   Caracas   Hamburg
Lisbon   London   Madrid   Mexico   Milan   Montreal   New Delhi
Oklahoma City   Paris   San Juan   São Paulo   Singapore   Sydney   Tokyo   Toronto

This book was set in Times Roman by General Graphic Services, Inc.
The editors were Kathleen L. Loy and Larry Goldberg;
the production supervisor was Denise L. Puryear.
The cover was designed by Scott Chelius.
R. R. Donnelley & Sons Company was printer and binder.

**MANAGING THE GLOBAL CORPORATION**

**Case Studies in Strategy and Management**

1 2 3 4 5 6 7 8 9 0 DOC DOC 8 9 4 3 2 1 0 9

ISBN 0-07-015593-3

**Library of Congress Cataloging-in-Publication Data**

Davidson, William Harley, (date)
    Managing the global corporation: case studies in strategy and
    management/William H. Davidson, José de la Torre.
        p.   cm. — (McGraw-Hill international series in business and
    economics)
    ISBN 0-07-015593-3
    1. International business enterprises—Management.    I. De la
Torre, José R.    II. Title.    III. Series.
HD62.4.D39   1989
658'.049—dc19                                          89-2501

# About the Authors

WILLIAM H. DAVIDSON is Associate Professor of Management and Organization at the School of Business, University of Southern California. He holds the A.B., M.B.A., and D.B.A. degrees from Harvard University. He has been a visiting professor at INSEAD in France and at the Dalian Institute in the People's Republic of China. His other books include *Global Strategic Management, Revitalizing American Industry, U.S. Industrial Competitiveness,* and *The Amazing Race.*

JOSÉ DE LA TORRE is Professor and Director of the Center for International Business Education and Research at the John E. Anderson Graduate School of Management at UCLA. Previously, he was a professor at the European Institute of Business Administration (INSEAD) in France for 13 years and has been a visiting professor at various schools in Latin America as well as the U.S. Department of Commerce. He holds B.S.Eng. and M.B.A. degrees from Pennsylvania State University and a D.B.A. from Harvard University. His other books include *Clothing Industry Adjustment in Developed Countries, The Activities of IT-Multinationals in the European Community,* and *Exports of Manufactured Goods from Developing Countries.*

# Contents

# List of Contributors

## FACULTY

**STEPHEN A. ALLEN**
Professor of Management and International Business
Babson College, Wellesley, Massachusetts

**REINHARD ANGELMAR**
Associate Professor of Marketing
INSEAD, Fontainebleau, France

**CHRISTOPHER A. BARTLETT**
Associate Professor of International Business
Harvard Business School, Boston, Massachusetts

**DEAN BERRY**
Senior Partner
The MAC Group, London, England
and
Visiting Professor
London Business School, London, England

**DEBORAH SMITH COOK**
Assistant Professor of Business Administration
The George Washington University, Washington, D.C.

**WILLIAM H. DAVIDSON**
Associate Professor of Management and Organization
University of Southern California, Los Angeles, California

**YVES DOZ**
Professor of Business Policy
INSEAD, Fontainebleau, France

**KASRA FERDOWS**
Associate Professor of Technology and Operations Management
INSEAD, Fontainebleau, France

**THÉRÈSE FLAHERTY**
Associate Professor of Business Administration
Harvard Business School, Boston, Massachusetts

**FARIBORZ GHADAR**
Professor of International Business
The George Washington University, Washington, D.C.

**DOMINIQUE HÉAU**
Professor of Business Policy
INSEAD, Fontainebleau, France

**JAMES L. HESKETT**
Professor of Business Administration
Harvard Business School, Boston, Massachusetts

**JEAN PIERRE JEANNET**
Professor of Marketing and International Business
Babson College, Wellesley, Massachusetts

**CHARLES R. KENNEDY, JR.**
Associate Professor of Business Administration
The University of Virginia, Charlottesville, Virginia

**JOHN MCGEE**
Fellow
Templeton College, Oxford University, Oxford,
   England

**ARNOUD DE MEYER**
Associate Professor of Technology Management
INSEAD, Fontainebleau, France

**C. K. PRAHALAD**
Professor of Business Administration
The University of Michigan, Ann Arbor, Michigan

**GORDON SHILLINGLAW**
Professor of Accounting
Columbia University, New York City

**SERGIO SIGNORELLI**
Professor
Istituto Studi Direzionali SpA (ISTUD), Milan, Italy

**PAUL STREBEL**
Professor of Business Administration
IMEDE, Lausanne, Switzerland

**CHARLES SUMMER**
Professor of Business Policy
The University of Washington, Seattle, Washington

**GEORGE TAUCHER**
Professor of Business Administration
IMEDE, Lausanne, Switzerland

**DONALD H. THAIN**
Professor
University of Western Ontario, London, Ontario

**JOSÉ DE LA TORRE**
Professor of International Business
University of California, Los Angeles

**DAVID WEINSTEIN**
Professor of Marketing
INSEAD, Fontainebleau, France

**DAVID B. ZENOFF**
President, Zenoff and Associates
San Francisco, California
and
Visiting Professor
IMEDE, Lausanne, Switzerland

## RESEARCH ASSOCIATES AND ASSISTANTS

Armando d'Amico
Kenneth L. Delecki
Martin Flash
Claire Fortier
Robert S. Garrity
Catherine Gurling
David Harkleroad
Sandra Hom
Janet N. Hunter
André Khodjamirian
Anne Marden
Janette Marden
Susan Nye
Dr. Claudio Pitilino
Martine van den Poel
Deborah Rodgers
Alex Rottenburg
Mary Lou Scramm
Christopher Spray
Juliet Taylor

## INSTITUTIONS

INSEAD—The European Institute of Business Administration Fontainebleau, France

IMEDE—The International Management Development Institute Lausanne, Switzerland

The School of Business Administration, University of Southern California, Los Angeles, California

The Graduate School of Business Administration, Harvard University, Boston, Massachusetts

The Darden Graduate School of Business Administration, University of Virginia, Charlottesville, Virginia

Babson College, Wellesley, Massachusetts

The University of Western Ontario, London, Ontario, Canada

The School of Government and Business Administration, The George Washington University, Washington D.C.

# Preface

## OUR GLOBAL ENVIRONMENT

There is little doubt that the world is shrinking by the day. As distances and obstacles to international transactions diminish, producers and consumers expand their horizons. Regardless of the type of endeavor, the playing field is now the globe.

Modern advances in communication technologies and in transportation have brought distant lands and events into nearly everyone's field of vision and within the scope of personal experience. National cultural achievements, whether gastronomic, artistic, or literary, are rapidly shared by a world eager to savor humanity's inventiveness and to complement traditional domestic choices. Scientific discoveries spread widely at astonishing speed; often they are replicated across the globe within weeks of their first announcement. And no one can claim that sporting events, except for a few esoteric national pastimes, are any longer the domain of any one nation. But it is perhaps in the field of business that the transformation from a national to a global environment has been most dramatic.

In the immediate postwar period the ratio of world trade to world output (excluding the So-viet bloc countries and China) was considerably under 10 percent. By the late 1980s this ratio had surpassed 20 percent. In manufactured goods, world trade now represents more than 35 percent of total output of industrial products. Trade in minerals and agricultural products has also risen dramatically since the early 1950s. Thus, trade volume expanded at nearly 9 percent per annum during the last quarter of a century, far outpacing and significantly contributing to the unprecedented economic growth the world has experienced during this period.

Trade in so-called invisibles—tourism, the myriad of services from engineering to telecommunications that are critical to any modern society, dividend and financial flows, and other international transfers—grew at an even faster rate, to the point that they approached 50 percent of the value of merchandise trade in 1988. Led by the globalization of financial services and markets, this component of world trade promises to remain the fastest growing segment. In fact, the liberalization of trade in services and the international protection of intellectual property rights are two subjects of critical importance to the current Uruguay Round of trade negotiations under the auspices of the General

Agreement on Tariffs and Trade, which, if successful, may stimulate faster growth for many of the world's economies.

International capital flows, both portfolio investments by individuals and institutions as well as foreign direct investments (FDI) by corporations have also grown dramatically during the postwar period. In recent years, their growth has been accompanied by considerable diversification in the sources and destinations of investment. For example, whereas corporations based in the United States were responsible for nearly 60 percent of the total stock of FDI as recently as 1967, the rapid expansion of European and Japanese multinational corporations had reduced this figure to less than 40 percent by 1987. The United States, once the principal source of international investment capital, has become the major recipient. International investment activity in stocks, bonds, real estate, and other assets now plays a central role in securities markets, as greater integration of the world's major capital markets is driven by technological change. The recent frenzy of cross-border mergers and acquisitions within Europe and between Europe and the United States provides further evidence that the globalization of capital markets goes hand in hand with events in the real sector.

Yet, as direct investment continues to expand its organizational form and structure are rapidly diversifying. Joint ventures, licensing arrangements, as well as a multitude of non-equity collaborative agreements appear to be gaining ground relative to traditional investment patterns in wholly owned subsidiaries, as new companies and new countries enter the international arena. Partnerships and alliances represent one of the most dynamic dimensions of the global business environment in the 1980s.

Finally, the speed of technological diffusion has risen markedly since the early 1950s. Then, less than 20 percent of U.S. innovations would be transferred abroad within the first 3 years following their introduction to the domestic market. The figure today is closer to 65 percent.

Furthermore, although it used to be safe to predict an international life cycle that started in the United States and moved first to Europe, then to Japan, and eventually to the less developed countries (with a gap of maybe 5 to 10 years between each major stage), major innovations today have equal probability of emanating from any of the three major trading areas and are almost instantaneously adopted by the others. The rapid growth of Japanese and European firms among the top earners of U.S. patents corroborates this trend. And yet, the growing interdependence of world markets means that the source of innovation and the location of production are increasingly divorced both from each other as well as from the location of demand.

One ignores these trends only at one's peril. Business executives need to understand the factors driving industries and firms to compete on a global basis and to develop management strategies and policies to deal with this reality. Although the speed and degree of globalization will vary by industry according to a variety of technical and environmental factors, all modern executives, in any field of specialization, must incorporate knowledgeably a global perspective in the execution of their tasks.

## ORGANIZATION OF THE BOOK

We have written and designed this book to enrich the advanced student's understanding of business issues and problems encountered in managing global corporations. The field of international management encompasses a broad range of skills and disciplines. Case studies represent ideal vehicles for integrating the various perspectives needed to master typical international business situations. The cases printed in this volume reflect the authors' belief that international business is a cross-disciplinary field that can only be mastered through the integration of various skills, functions, and disciplines. The book is organized into ten parts with primary focus on individual areas of management concern.

## Part One: Defining a Global Competitive Strategy

Part One of the book deals with the broader environmental context of international business. The cases in this part emphasize technological and political dimensions of the international business environment. They also provide insights into the process and dynamics of industry globalization and the unique competitive interrelationships found in most industries subject to international competition.

Considerable debate and confusion surround the questions of what constitutes a global industry and what may be termed global, multinational, international, or transnational (if we accept the United Nations' terminology) companies. For our purposes, *global industries* are characterized by fairly homogenous market demand worldwide and exhibit minimum-scale requirements that exceed the size of any single national market. Global industry structures are derived from an overwhelming economic imparative to amortize R&D costs, exploit economies of scale, or take advantage of other firm-specific resources on a global basis. These industries (e.g., commercial aircraft or mainframe computers) are typically but not exclusively populated by *global companies,* that is, firms which optimize their activities as if the world were a single market, a definition rooted in their organizational and operating logic and not on industry association or international scope. In contrast, we define *multinational companies* as consisting of a loosely coupled network of national subsidiaries, enjoying varying degrees of self-sufficiency. These firms can successfully inhabit both global industries, where they pursue strategies of raising domestic barriers to the entry of global competitors, or *fragmented industries* (e.g., processed foods or retail banking), where they position themselves to compete against purely domestic firms by emphasizing certain advantages derived from their multi-country operations. Finally, *international companies* is a term we reserve to those mainly domestic companies which nonetheless participate in the international economy through exports and a few nonintegrated subsidiaries, licensees, and agents.

The transition from fragmented to global economic and technological conditions has characterized this last quarter of a century for many industries. How firms adapt or fail to accommodate to the new requirements of industries undergoing such a transition is the thrust of these first set of cases.

Case One (Tissot) serves as an excellent introduction to the set of issues that will preoccupy us throughout this collection. The electronic revolution has significantly altered the nature of competition in the watch industry. The case traces the results of this evolution from the perspective of a firm which is caught between the remnants of the traditional "craft" which made the Swiss industry world leaders for many years and the mass production and worldwide distribution strategies followed by the recent entrants from Japan and Hong Kong. Tissot's management must formulate a global strategy consistent with the industry's evolution and company's capabilities and previous experience.

In Cases Two through Four, the Michelin tire industry series takes us a step back in order to allow for a longitudinal analysis of the process of industry globalization. These cases permit extensive analysis of individual competitors in an industry experiencing rapid technological change and global market integration. The cases also address some public policy issues that often play a central role in determining the conditions for success in international business.

An additional industry analysis exercise is focused on the construction machinery industry in Case Five. The initial process of internationalization in this heavy manufacturing sector was led by a U.S. firm, Caterpillar, and a second wave of international activity was initiated by Komatsu, a Japanese producer of heavy construction equipment. The comprehensive note on the industry provides an opportunity to conduct a detailed analysis of industry economics, cost structure, market conditions, principal competitors, and a thorough environmental analysis. Complete case studies of Caterpillar and Komatsu in Case Six also permit a full analysis of the issues and options facing the two principal global competitors in this industry, as they move from an "international" to a more "global" strategy.

Case Seven (Heineken N.V.) is the last case in this part and describes the historical growth and development of a global company in a fragmented and domestically oriented industry. Contrary to the other sectors analyzed above, the economics of brewing do not call for extensive globalization. Yet, the company has been active in world markets for over a century. The case focuses on a reassessment of Heineken's international strategy with a view to increase the commitment of resources to fully owned subsidiaries in major markets.

## Part Two: Translating a Global Strategy into Local Action

While Part One focuses on global forces shaping industry environments, Part Two emphasizes the local dimension of managing a global corporation. Any global strategy still needs to be implemented through local operations, and although cold analytical reasoning may prevail in arriving at a clear and logical world design, personalities, historical commitments, and individual emotions enter the decision as soon as the specifics of a given proposal are on the table.

Cases Eight (Athenian Brewery S.A.) and Nine (J. J. Murphy's Brewery) exemplify two situations that put Heineken's new international strategy (discussed above) to the test and require it to be highly responsive to local conditions. The Greek market is growing, and Heineken's 98-percent-owned affiliate needs to expand its facilities. But its dominance of the local market, its competitors' lack of success, and its relatively poor profitability present a challenge in the face of a newly elected socialist government. The opposite is the case in Ireland,

where Heineken's licensee has just gone into bankruptcy, and the company holds a weak position in the face of a strong international competitor, Guinness. Here, however, local distributors and the government would welcome Heineken's involvement.

Two other case studies also focus on how multinational firms operate in relating global strategic considerations to local action in individual host countries. In Case Ten, Southland Bank and Trust Co. is a mid-size regional U.S. bank, headquartered in Atlanta, whose "turnaround" plan includes achieving a leading position in the international wholesale banking segment. The case is focused from the perspective of its London branch manager, who must translate these corporate objectives into a local strategy in one of the most competitive banking centers in the world. Case Eleven (The American Express Company in France) examines a proposal for the company's Traveler Cheques' group to enter into a joint venture with three leading French banks to issue French-franc-denominated traveler cheques. The venture raises many questions as to the structure of the arrangement and its impact on Amex's worldwide operations of one of its most successful global products.

## Part Three: Market Entry and Participation Policies

Corporations can participate in individual markets in a variety of ways. The firm may choose to enter a market by engaging the services of an agent or distributor, through a licensee, by undertaking a variety of joint venture forms, through acquisition, or by the formation of a wholly owned subsidiary. The issues and frameworks relevant to these decisions are the focus of Part Three.

Case Twelve (Patho-Control, Inc.) focuses on a small pharmaceutical venture only in its second year of operations. The company is approached to set up distribution in Europe through agents or a combination export management firm and to undertake a licensing agreement in Colombia. The management of the young company must assess its various options and choose the best strategy for expanding to foreign markets in the face of limited resources and knowledge. Case Thirteen (Copperweld Inc.) discusses a firm that successfully introduced a new welded-tube technology to the U.S. market in the 1960s, a market which was approaching saturation. Early export sales to Europe indicate that the same substitution process might occur there, but market and competitive conditions are very different. A proposal is made to invest in a $40 million facility to develop this market, but questions arise concerning joint venture partners, the possible reaction of competitors, and the most appropriate location.

Case Fourteen (Norman Machine Tool Company) provides a detailed analysis of a U.S. corporation's efforts to establish a joint venture in the People's Republic of China. Faced with severe competitive pressures from Japanese and European producers of machine tools, management believes they need a low-cost offshore operation to respond. The case describes Norman's negotiations with Chinese authorities over a 2-year period aimed at establishing a joint venture with the leading Chinese producer of machine tools; the case documents some of the key barriers and obstacles faced by firms attempting to establish a presence in the PRC.

## Part Four: Alliances, Mergers, and Acquisitions

A topic of great current interest occupies Part Four—the growth of a firm's international activities by collaborative alliances, mergers, and acquisitions. Traditionally, joint ventures and similar collaborations were undertaken by international investors only when they had been coerced by host country regulations, and these collaborations were typically limited to agreements with mostly silent partners in developing countries. Since the late 1970s we have seen a rash of collaborations and alliances between partners of equal technical or market standing, involving operations in the industrial countries.

Similarly, market entry or expansion by acquisition has been an increasingly favorite choice for firms coping with the structural rationalization that has accompanied the process of globalization in many industries.

The cases in this part deal with information technology and financial services, two industries that have undergone major technological and competitive challenges in the last 20 years. Case Fifteen (Italtel) examines the options facing the Italian Telephone Authority and its principal equipment supplier in establishing relationships with potential sources of critical technology as the industry shifts to digital switching and transmission. The case also deals with the choices of three major multinational companies operating in Italy—ITT, LM Ericsson, and GTE—as they too must decide whether to join forces with Italtel or risk going alone.

Cases Sixteen through Eighteen deal with the relationship between AT&T and Olivetti in the office automation industry and allow for a simulation of how to structure an international alliance in a complex and rapidly evolving competitive environment. Newly deregulated AT&T is transforming itself from a domestic monopoly to a competitive, high-tech company free to move into new world markets. It plans to enter the information processing field through the automated office equipment sector and to challenge IBM and the Japanese in the process. Olivetti has undergone a dramatic turnaround in office equipment and automation. Its U.S. position is still weak, however, and it lacks the capital strength to expand significantly there. The industry note (Case Eighteen) provides background data on markets, competitors, and technologies.

Case Nineteen (Midland Bank PLC) describes the early process of internationalization at Midland Bank through a series of acquisitions, the establishment of branches and affiliates in foreign countries, and a major international collaborative venture. By the late 1970s, Midland has changed its strategy to include greater direct participation in world financial markets under its own name. This leads to various attempts to enter the U.S. market and to a bid to acquire Crocker National Corporation in 1980. By 1982, as major management changes affect the upper echelons of the bank, Midland still faces the issue of how best to integrate Crocker in a global strategy.

## Part Five: Managing Political Risks at Home and Abroad

Assessing and managing the political environment is an integral part of the job of any senior international manager. Political constraints often make the best economic strategy unfeasible. Compromises which call for suboptimal economic performance may yield unexpected benefits in the form of political patronage, privileged access to markets, or procurement opportunities. But these advantages may be short-lived, requiring difficult trade-offs on the part of management. And when difficult political decisions cannot be postponed or avoided, the task of managing the possible negative fallout is critically important.

Part Five addresses the issue of political risk at home and abroad. Case Twenty in this series deals with the home environment and analyzes General Electric's decision to develop a rationalized production system for its world electric iron business. The case addresses how the corporation managed the political dimensions of this decision, specifically in California, while shifting to a new manufacturing configuration.

Case Twenty-One [Honeywell in France (A)] addresses the Honeywell Corporation's relationship with the public sector in France at a critical juncture. Following the electoral victory of the Socialist party in May 1981, Honeywell's partners in CII-Honeywell Bull, the main French computer manufacturer, were subject to nationalization. Honeywell's role in the joint venture was apt to change, and managing the relationship with its French partners would require significant political skills in the future.

Case Twenty-Two (Houston Machinery Inc.) deals with a U.S. corporation's attempt to es-

tablish a joint venture in Mexico. The joint venture requires the approval of a state-owned corporation and a government ministry. The management of Houston Machinery Inc. must structure the venture so that it is viewed attractively in the political arena in Mexico.

## Part Six: Managing the International Marketing Function

Among the most critical issues facing any manager with global marketing responsibilities are the selection of markets which the firm will enter and the extent to which product positioning and marketing strategies need to be adapted to local circumstances. In fact, the debate on the relative advantages of standardization versus adaptation has been at the core of the international marketing literature for nearly 20 years. Related to these issues, and often defining the choices, is how the internatinal marketing function is structured to balance these twin objectives of uniformity across markets and responsiveness to the idiosyncracies of domestic consumers.

Case Twenty-Three (General Electric Programmable Controllers) presents a situation in which a new business unit is attempting to develop a global marketing strategy for the introduction of a high-technology product. The company needs to develop a set of criteria and a process for assigning priorities to markets and for selecting entry strategies in each market so as to achieve the company's objective to become a global leader in this emergent industry.

Case Twenty-Four deals with Procter & Gamble Europe's decision to launch a new product, Vizir, in the European detergent market. The company's past success has been achieved through a number of national subsidiaries with strong local management and responsive to national differences in consumer habits and market structures. In June 1981, as P&G's German affiliate prepares to launch Vizir in its local market, questions arise as to whether a Europe-wide product roll-out would not be preferable, and, if so, should the company standardize its product formulation, packaging, advertising, and promotion. Case Twenty-Five [Kolbe Coloured Chemical Division (A)] presents a vehicle for analyzing international marketing coordination issues in an industrial product setting. The newly appointed divisional marketing manager with worldwide responsibilities must build a global segmentation and positioning strategy for the division's products and then sell it to its fairly autonomous operating units around the world.

## Part Seven: Managing the International Financial/Control Function

Part Seven treats the proper role of the financial and controller's functions in the strategic management of international operations. These functions are often viewed as discrete, stand-alone activities with their own specific skills and expertise. Our emphasis is instead on the linkages between the finance and control functions and general international management issues.

In Case Twenty-Six, the Argentine subsidiary of Gillette Corporation requires a major capital expansion to finance the introduction of the Trac II shaving system in the local market. The corporate treasurer's office must help in evaluating the attractiveness of the investment and, if the investment is approved, help arrange the necessary financing in a highly inflationary environment. The case develops the role of the corporate finance function in determining criteria for international project evaluation and implementation, subsidiary capital structure, exposure management, cash management, and capital budgeting. It also describes how the objectives of the treasury unit interact with those of general management in the field.

Case Twenty-Seven [Ford of Europe (A)] raises two basic issues: the role of financial control systems in implementing Ford's corporate strategy within a changing European automotive environment, and the contrast between Western and Japanese financial control systems. An internal company study has shown that comparable Japanese companies had 35 to 60 percent fewer finance people proportionally than Ford. The data in the case allow for examining the role of the control function in different multinational corporations.

## Part Eight: The Management of International Operations

Part Eight's five cases deal with the management of international operations. Two cases tackle the more traditional issues of technology transfer and the balance and coordination of international manufacturing facilities. Two others provide detailed insights into the product development process from an R&D and technology management perspective. The importance of integrated operations in support of global strategies is emphasized in these cases as well.

The series starts with a relatively narrow focus on the management of the manufacturing function in an international setting. Case Twenty-Eight (Applichem) provides extensive data on operating costs, raw material utilization rates, personnel, overheads, transportation costs, and exchange, inflation, and wage rates for six manufacturing plants around the world. At issue are problems such as how to compare productivity, facilitate learning, and transfer best practices across plants. Case Twenty-Nine (Honeywell Pace) examines the organization of production in a system where components are manufactured in a number of highly specialized plants in the United States, Japan, and Scotland. Changes in the European environment and excess inventories in Belgium force a reassessment of the company's global manufacturing strategy and organization.

Cases Thirty (Nestlé, S.A.) and Thirty-One (Ford of Europe—Product Research and Development) provide a detailed view into the management and organization of the product development process in these two very different organizations. The cases contrast the food industry, which requires significant levels of local adaptation and greater autonomy at the subsidiary level in terms of product development decisions, with the automotive industry, which, at least in terms of the European market, has been under increasing pressures to design and bring into market fairly universal products with broad appeal across countries. The different organizational and managerial issues raised by these two examples allow for some generalization on the role of the R&D function in multinational operations.

Finally, Case Thirty-Two [Benetton (A)] presents a more integrated view of the role of operations management in a global corporation. Benetton's success in the European market was accompanied by major innovations in manufacturing, logistics, and merchandising. By the end of 1982, Benetton's plans to expand further into the U.S. and Japanese markets require it to evaluate whether its unique methods of providing production and logistical support could be extended to these operations.

## Part Nine: Organization, Systems, People, and the Role of Top Management

Part Nine addresses the complex issues of implementation associated with global operations. How does the firm operating in a widely diverse set of environments achieve strategic unity of purpose while preserving the adaptability and motivation required for success at the local level? Cases Thirty-Three through Thirty-Eight tackle these issues on an increasingly complex scale, building from the general organizational-strategic interaction familiar to students of corporate strategy to introduce the additional difficulties of culture, language, and distance.

Case Thirty-Three (Republic-Telecom Inc.) describes the organization and management issues associated with the initial stages of internationalization of a company's business. The case describes a specific international venture opportunity and the process by which the company reviewed and acted on it. The roles of project champions, formal strategic planning systems, and senior executives can be analyzed in shaping international venture strategy. In Case Thirty-Four [A.B. Throsten (1)] a dispute be-

tween the management of the Swedish subsidiary of a diversified Canadian company and its headquarters' staff escalates and comes to the attention of top management. They must deal with an investment proposal of small financial importance but of great significance for the future structure and management culture of the entire organization. This case serves as an excellent bridge to the organizational problems typical of the transition from international to multinational structures.

The next two cases focus on the impact of rapid growth and international diversification on a company's management style and organization. A specific issue under study in Case Thirty-Five [Benetton (B)] is whether a separate U.S. subsidiary should be created to handle what could soon turn into Benetton's largest single market, including the question of what scope of activity such a subsidiary might have. Case Thirty-Six (Heineken Organizational Issues) presents some of the tensions which existed within the organization at the time of the strategic changes described in Case Seven. Essentially, the natural overlap of responsibilities between the geographic area coordinators and the worldwide functional managers leads to questions concerning their relative role and importance and whether the balance of power between areas and functions ought to be changed.

The last two cases in Part Nine deal primarily with people issues. Case Thirty-Seven (Suji-INS K.K.) presents a situation in which a U.S. and a Japanese firm are attempting to develop organizational and management systems that are mutually compatible in a joint venture in Japan. The case addresses the role of senior management in creating, designing, and implementing an international business relationship as well as the human resource requirements of effective joint venture management in the face of cultural conflicts. Case Thirty-Eight (Ciba-Geigy—Management Development) focuses on the human resources management function in a sophisticated global corporation. The triggering decision is the need to appoint a new pharmaceutical marketing manager for the French operating company. Top management of Ciba-Geigy France has one view, and the management development staff at headquarters has another. Detailed information on the company's strategy, organization, and management development system allow for a thorough discussion of the merits of each position and of the role of the human resource management function in a diversified global company.

## Part Ten: A Final Series—Managing Strategic Redirection

Part Ten's main objective is to integrate all the material covered in the casebook. Case Thirty-Nine (The European Paint Industry) provides detailed information on the evolution of cost structure, technologies, market segments, and industry structure. Case Forty (BOK Finishes) describes the paints and coatings business of a major European chemical firm based in Belgium, a business which has evolved from a series of mergers and acquisitions involving companies in the Netherlands, Germany, France, Italy, and Spain. The case ends with a proposal for some reorganization of the intercompany functional relationships designed to help face increasing problems of coordination in a more competitive environment. Cases Forty-One through Forty-Three describe situations prevailing in three of the division's major market areas: Automotive Products, Car Refinishes, and Decorative/Do-It-Yourself Markets.

This material lends itself very well to a role-playing exercise where the tasks assigned to the groups include a diagnosis of competitive trends in the industry, a definition of a competitive strategy for the division, and the design of an appropriate organization and management systems to implement such a strategy across what have been traditionally highly autonomous national operations. The diversity of requirements in each segment makes the task extremely difficult and the lessons more valuable.

## THE TEACHING AND PRACTICE OF INTERNATIONAL BUSINESS

Our intention in writing this casebook was to make more accessible for teachers and students of international business complex and current materials that reflect the reality of operating in a global competitive environment. Each case study reproduced here represents a set of problems or issues that are commonly encountered by managers who may be operating at various levels of responsibility in the global business arena. The cases were selected and arrayed to permit an effective application of current theory and knowledge in the area of international business management to problems ranging from the definition of competitive strategy to policy issues in all major functional areas.

The appropriate mix of case problems, and the theoretical readings and lectures which must accompany them, can best be determined by individual instructors based on their preferences and on the specific circumstances of their students' curriculum. These are, however, complex and advanced problems more suitable to students having considerable exposure to the full range of business courses required in a core business studies program as well as familiarity with the international economic issues which frame the environment in which trade and investment takes place. The number and sequence of cases presented in this casebook reflect a relatively comprehensive catalog of the issues we believe are most critical to the international manager. Obviously, it would be difficult, if not impossible, to use all these cases in any single course. The selection provided here is meant to offer a sufficient variety and a set of options from which each instructor can design his or her most effective course structure.

Although the cases were selected partly because of their focus on broad interdisciplinary issues, they also permit a rather narrow analysis of specific functional areas and issues, while encouraging a more integrated perspective on international management problems. We believe that analysis of the situations presented in these studies will yield significant insights into the general principles that underlie the successful practice of management in a global business environment.

## ACKNOWLEDGMENTS

First and foremost we wish to express our appreciation to all those who contributed materials to this casebook. Among many others, the following reviewers provided many valuable comments and suggestions: Benjamin Gomes-Casseres, Harvard University; Bruce Kogut, The Wharton School of the University of Pennsylvania; Edwin Miller, University of Michigan; Rosalie L. Tung, University of Wisconsin; and Heidi Vernon-Wortzel, Northeastern University. These individuals and institutions made significant commitments of time, effort, and financial resources to an activity not often rewarded in academic circles. For their dedication to pedagogical objectives and their willingness to allow us to use their material we are most grateful. Second, we would like to acknowledge the valuable collaboration of a large number of case writers who have assisted us over the years and across four continents in the preparation of international management cases. In particular, thanks are extended to Larry Ronan, Bob Garrity, Ken Delecki, and Sandy Hom for their past collaborations with Bill Davidson, and to Michel Bacchetta, Dana Dyas, Martin Flash, David Harkleroad, Andy Khodjamirian, and Martine van den Poel from José de la Torre.

The willingness of many leading international companies to allow these cases to be written also merits our sincere gratitude. Large and small, some more global than others, these firms have had the courage to have their strategies, policies, and decisions aired publicly. Whatever the circumstances or results, the frankness and honesty with which these firms have allowed others to learn from their experiences is indeed commendable. We thank them for their deep concern about the quality of management education.

The support of a number of institutions should also be acknowledged. For 13 years, the European Institute of Business Administration (INSEAD) in Fontainebleau, France, supported Professor de la Torre's case-writing efforts at great expense and graciously agreed to let us reproduce many of these and other INSEAD cases in this volume. We are also very grateful to the International Management Development Institute (IMEDE) in Lausanne, Switzerland, for its continued support of case writing on international issues and its generosity in allowing us to use many of the Institute's cases. Our thanks go also to our current institutions, the University of Southern California and the University of California, Los Angeles, for giving us time to complete this project. And to Bobbe Glick a special word of appreciation for her able administrative support and for serving as a live telecommunication relay.

Several colleagues have been particularly helpful in their efforts to further the development of effective international business case studies and teaching curricula. Among the many who have shared their insights with us over the years we wish to single out Yves Doz and Dominique Héau at INSEAD, and Bob Stobaugh and Mike Yoshino at the Harvard Business School. Finally, a word of thanks to our common mentor, teacher, and colleague, Ray Vernon, for all he has done to further the study of international business and for his relentless pursuit of knowledge and relevance.

*William H. Davidson*
*José de la Torre*

# MANAGING THE GLOBAL CORPORATION

## CASE STUDIES IN STRATEGY AND MANAGEMENT

# PART ONE

# Defining a Global Competitive Strategy

# Tissot

One sunny afternoon in May 1985 Dr. Ernst Thomke drove his Porsche through the Jura mountains; he was on his way to Bienne for a Tissot strategy session. After more than a decade of declining sales, layoffs, and factory closings, the popular business press was proclaiming the return of the Swiss watch industry. Much of the credit for the resurrection had been given to Thomke, president of Ebauches SA, one of the Asuag-SSIH companies, and initiator of a new, low-priced Swiss fashion watch: the SWATCH. Thomke believed that the predictions of a revived Swiss watch industry were premature. He had accepted the considerable task of giving the Asuag brands, and particularly Tissot, a hard look to formulate new strategies to bring the Asuag group profitability in the second half of the 1980s and beyond. Specifically, his goal was to increase Asuag-SSIH's total volume from 7 million to 50 million units. As his Porsche sped through the countryside he considered the past

and future trends for the global watch industry, and he asked himself, "How can Tissot grow and profit?"

In 1985, the future trends for the global watch industry were anything but clear. Over the past 15 years, the industry had experienced radical changes. Innovation in products, production, and marketing were all key factors in the volatility which marked a period of rapid entry (often followed by rapid exit) of new competitors and the departure of some established producers.

In 1970 the global watch industry was dominated by Swiss watch manufacturers. By 1975 the competitive field had expanded, and key players came from Switzerland, Japan, and the United States. By the early 1980s the United States had all but disappeared as a contender, and Hong Kong was the world's largest exporter in units in the industry with 326.4 million watches and movements in 1984. Japan ranked second in number and value of units produced. Between 1970 and 1984, the Swiss dropped to third place in unit volume as their assembled watch exports dwindled from 48 million to 17 million pieces. However, Switzerland continued to rank first in value of watch exports, SFr. 3.4 billion in 1984 (see Exhibits 1 to 7).

The case was prepared by Susan W. Nye under the direction of Visiting Professor Jean-Pierre Jeannet as a basis for class discussion rather than to illustrate either effective or ineffective handling of an administrative situation. Copyright 1985 by IMEDE, Lausanne, Switzerland. Reproduced by permission.

## EXHIBIT 1

**TOTAL PRODUCTION OF WATCHES AND WATCH MOVEMENTS
WORLDWIDE 1960–1984** (Million)

| Year | 1960 | 1970 | 1975 | 1980 | 1982 | 1983 | 1984 |
|------|------|------|------|------|------|------|------|
| No. | 98 | 174 | 220 | 300 | 330 | 370 | n.a. |

Note: Figures do not include other timepieces such as penwatches.
n.a. = not available.
*Source:* Swiss Watch Federation.

## EXHIBIT 2

**PERCENTAGE OF WORLDWIDE WATCH PRODUCTION BY COUNTRY,
1960–1983**

| | 1960 | 1970 | 1975 | 1980 | 1982 | 1983 |
|------|------|------|------|------|------|------|
| Switzerland | 43.0 | 42.0 | 32.0 | 18.4 | 10.8 | 9.3 |
| Japan | 7.2 | 13.7 | 14.0 | 22.5 | 24.7 | 26.1 |
| Hong Kong | — | — | — | 18.5 | 30.0 | 35.0 |
| USA | 9.7 | 11.5 | 12.5 | 4.0 | — | — |
| E. Germany | 20.5 | 14.5 | 16.7 | 15.7 | 14.8 | 13.2 |
| France | 5.6 | 6.3 | 7.6 | 3.3 | 2.9 | 2.2 |
| W. Germany | 8.0 | 4.7 | 4.3 | 2.2 | 1.2 | 1.1 |

*Source:* Swiss Watch Federation.

## EXHIBIT 3

**WATCH EXPORTS—WATCHES AND MOVEMENTS, 1960–1984** (Million SFr.)

| | 1960 | 1970 | 1975 | 1980 | 1982 | 1984 |
|------|------|------|------|------|------|------|
| Switzerland* | 1,159.2 | 2,383.7 | 2,764.3 | 3,106.7 | 3,091.9 | 3,397.3 |
| Japan | 16.4 | 399.3 | 835.1 | 1,911.1 | 1,908.5 | 2,876.2 |
| Hong Kong | — | 63.1 | 246.1 | 1,855.6 | 1,779.0 | 2,091.2 |
| France | 26.2 | 78.1 | 209.3 | 265.0 | 218.3 | 233.7 |
| W. Germany | 83.6 | 129.6 | 140.2 | 171.7 | 175.4 | 231.4 |

*Including nonassembled movements.
*Source:* Swiss Watch Federation.

**EXHIBIT 4**

### WATCH EXPORTS—WATCHES AND MOVEMENTS, 1960–1984 (Million)

|              | 1960 | 1970 | 1975 | 1980  | 1982  | 1984  |
| ------------ | ---- | ---- | ---- | ----- | ----- | ----- |
| Switzerland* | 42.6 | 73.4 | 71.2 | 51.0  | 45.7  | 46.9  |
| Japan        | 0.1  | 11.4 | 17.1 | 48.3  | 63.6  | 94.7  |
| Hong Kong    | —    | 5.7  | 16.1 | 126.1 | 213.7 | 326.4 |
| France       | 1.3  | 4.4  | 9.5  | 9.8   | 8.4   | 6.2   |
| W. Germany   | 3.8  | 4.1  | 9.5  | 4.5   | 4.7   | 5.5   |

*Including nonassembled movements.
*Source:* Swiss Watch Federation.

**EXHIBIT 5**

### EXPORTS AS A PERCENTAGE OF TOTAL PIECES PRODUCED, 1960–1984

|              | 1960 | 1970 | 1975 | 1980 | 1982 | 1984 |
| ------------ | ---- | ---- | ---- | ---- | ---- | ---- |
| Switzerland* | 97   | 97   | 97   | 97   | 97   | 97   |
| Japan        | 2    | 48   | 57   | 72   | 80   | n.a. |
| Hong Kong    | —    | 100  | 100  | 100  | 100  | 100  |
| France       | 24   | 40   | 57   | †    | †    | †    |
| W. Germany   | 48   | 50   | †    | †    | †    | †    |

*Estimation.
†Not available; because of reexports, exports are larger than production.
n.a. = not available.
*Source:* Swiss Watch Federation.

**EXHIBIT 6**

### VALUE OF ASSEMBLED WATCHES AS A PERCENTAGE OF VALUE OF WATCHES AND MOVEMENTS EXPORTED

|             | 1960 | 1970  | 1975 | 1980 | 1982 | 1984 |
| ----------- | ---- | ----- | ---- | ---- | ---- | ---- |
| Switzerland | 81.3 | 86.1  | 87.9 | 85.9 | 91.5 | 92.9 |
| Japan       | 51.6 | 83.6  | 92.1 | 90.6 | 87.6 | 85.0 |
| Hong Kong   | 97.1 | 100.0 | 96.6 | 95.4 | 96.9 | 96.7 |
| France      | 87.7 | 93.8  | 93.8 | 88.7 | 91.5 | 94.4 |
| W. Germany  | 91.1 | 88.7  | 90.6 | 89.0 | 92.0 | 94.8 |

*Source:* Swiss Watch Federation.

## EXHIBIT 7

**ASSEMBLED WATCHES AS A PERCENTAGE OF WATCHES AND MOVEMENTS EXPORTED**

|              | 1960  | 1970  | 1975  | 1980  | 1982  | 1984  |
|--------------|-------|-------|-------|-------|-------|-------|
| Switzerland  | 73.7  | 73.6  | 71.7  | 55.9  | 59.3  | 55.2  |
| Japan        | 29.0  | 64.8  | 78.1  | 75.5  | 67.5  | 60.6  |
| Hong Kong    | 98.2  | 100.0 | 98.1  | 94.4  | 95.6  | 92.1  |
| France       | n.a.  | 89.5  | 90.4  | 81.6  | 79.0  | 94.4  |
| W. Germany   | 89.3  | 88.9  | 85.5  | 69.0  | 74.4  | 72.6  |

n.a. = not available.
*Source:* Swiss Watch Federation.

## THE WATCH INDUSTRY IN SWITZERLAND

The Swiss watch industry was concentrated in the Jura along the western border of Switzerland. The Swiss had conquered the world market with mechanical watches and had developed a reputation for fine craftsmanship, elegance, and style. Swiss companies produced 80 percent of the watches selling for SFr 1,200 or more and virtually all top-priced watches. A large portion of these watches were still mechanical.

Until the early 1970s, Swiss watchmaking was intensely specialized and fragmented, with a rigid structure which had remained unchanged for centuries. Major changes began in the 1970s with several mergers involving sizeable firms and important initiatives in both horizontal and vertical integration.

The Swiss watch industry was essentially a group of industries. Traditionally, the Swiss had operated on a two-tier system: components manufacturing and assembly. In 1934 the Swiss government had instituted laws that made it illegal to open, enlarge, transfer, or transform any watchmaking facilities without government permission. Exports of components and movements were also illegal without permission, as was the export of watchmaking machinery. These regulations were instituted to protect the Swiss watch industry from foreign competition. The government began deregulating the industry in 1971, and in 1985 these laws were no longer in effect.

Swiss watch firms generally fell into one of three categories. First, there had been a large number of "one-man-and-a-boy" and other small enterprises which produced components or movements or put purchased parts into cases. These firms marketed on the basis of long-established personal contacts. Included in this category were the piece work assemblers. A significant portion of inexpensive mechanical watches were assembled by Jura farmers during the winter as in-home piece work. Second were the well-established, privately owned watchmakers which produced expensive, handmade watches. And finally, there was the Asuag-SSIH organization, which was a group of companies representing approximately 35 percent of total Swiss exports of watches and movements.

Watches and movements declined from 11.9 to 7.2 percent of total Swiss exports from 1970 to 1980. At the start of the 1970s there were 1,618 watchmaking firms in the industry; this figure had fallen to 634 by 1984. Between 1970 and 1984 the full-time labor force producing watches shrank from 89,500 to 31,000. Lay-offs due to the shrinking demand for mechanical watches were exacerbated by automation, rationalization, and concentration initiated throughout the Swiss watch industry.

## ASUAG-SSIH[1]

### Company Background

In an effort to resuscitate the industry, a consortium of seven Swiss banks orchestrated a merger between Société Suisse de l'Industrie Horlogère (SSIH) and Asuag in 1982. They provided Asuag-SSIH with capital and a cash infusion totaling more than SFr. 700 million. In return the banks gained 97 percent ownership of the new company and planned to sell shares to the public when it returned to profitability, estimated at 5 to 10 years. Turnaround began in 1984 with sales totaling SFr. 1,582.4 million and aftertax profits of SFr. 26.5 million. In February 1985, it was announced that control would be returned to private investors (see Exhibit 8).

Asuag, short for Allgemeine Schweizer Uhrenindustrie, had been the largest producer of watches and watch components in Switzerland, accounting for about one-third of total Swiss watch exports and 25 percent of production in Switzerland. Asuag had been founded in 1931 when the Swiss government orchestrated the consolidation of a wide variety of small watchmakers to strengthen the industry during the worldwide depression.

Movements were produced by the twelve subsidiaries of Ebauches SA, including ETA. ETA was the largest Swiss movement manufacturer. ETA produced a full range of movements but was best known as a producer of high-quality, expensive ultra-thin watch movements used for luxury watches. Ebauches companies sold 65 percent of their production volume to the Asuag-SSIH brands. Ebauches's sales had dropped from 51.1 million to 32.1 million pieces between 1973 and 1984. During this period the world market for movements had grown from 215 million to 350 units. Ebauches's world market share dropped from 23.8 to 9.2 percent.

Asuag's brands of finished watches included: Longines, Eterna, Certina, and Rado. Rado was the largest selling mid-priced Swiss watch with annual sales of about 1 million units. Fifty-five percent of Asuag's production was in finished watches. Asuag began losing money in 1977, reporting an accumulated net loss of SFr. 129 million in 1982.

SSIH had been the second-largest watch company in Switzerland, responsible for 10 percent of total output. SSIH was made up of a diverse group of companies producing watches and movements in all price categories. SSIH group companies included Omega, Tissot, and Economic Time.

SSIH had encountered severe financial problems in the late 1970s. In 1977 the Zurich-based trading group Siber Hegner & Co. AG, a major international distributor of Swiss watches, including Omega and Tissot, provided SSIH with a capital infusion of SFr. 32.5 million. A rescue plan was devised which deemphasized the lower price end of the market. Siber Hegner management concentrated on electronic quartz models which sold at prices above SFr. 235. Tissot watch prices were pushed upward, and Tissot models were sold in the SFr. 235 to 1500 range. Omega watches were priced above SFr. 600 at retail. Companies producing at the low-price end of the market were sold off, and inexpensive watch production was reduced from 69.2 to 19.7 percent of total. At the same time, the product mix was shifted, and electronic watches increased from 8.9 percent of total in 1976 to 47.9 percent of total sales in 1980. Siber Hegner provided a cash infusion for research and development and a worldwide advertising campaign. Acquisitions and joint ventures were arranged to improve integration, although management, production, marketing, and sales remained decentralized.

Initially, turnaround was successful, with profits in 1979 allowing for the first dividend payment since 1974. Profitability was short-lived, and in June 1981, SSIH announced a loss of SFr. 142 million for the year ending March 31, 1981, giving the company a net loss of SFr. 27.4 million. A consortium of Swiss banks in an effort to bail out the company provided cash and credit valued at almost SFr. 230 million in return for 96.5 percent equity in the recapitalized company.

---

[1]The company has since changed its name to SMH.

EXHIBIT 8

**ASUAG-SSIH ORGANIZATION 1983**

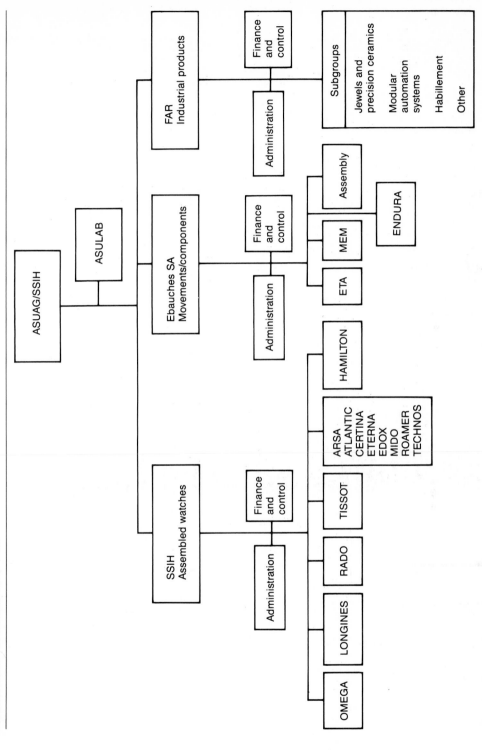

*Source:* Asuag-SSIH.

7

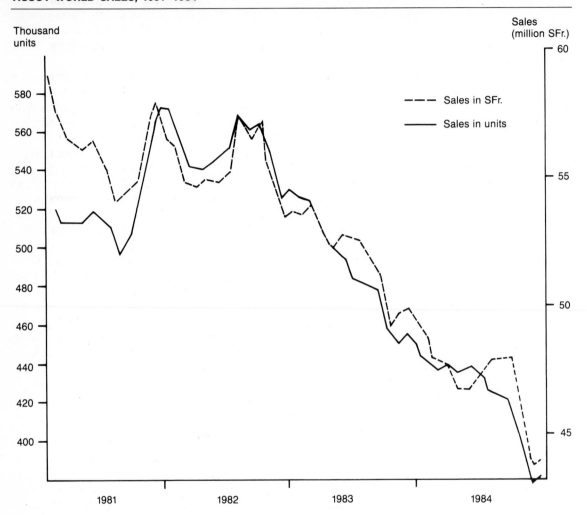

EXHIBIT 9

**TISSOT WORLD SALES, 1981–1984**

## Tissot SA

Thomke described Tissot, and most Asuag-SSIH watches, as a "branded commodity." The individual companies produced their products under recognized brand names, but Thomke felt that the watches had been poorly developed in terms of brand image and personality. Thomke believed the weak image had led to the decline in Tissot sales (Exhibit 9). His goal was to create a workable brand strategy and identity for Tissot. In May 1985, Thomke believed that Tissot had gained the reputation of an "inexpensive" Omega.

The company produced about 400,000 watches in 1984, for watch sales of SFr. 42 million. The average retail price for a Tissot watch was about SFr. 375. Strongest sales volume was from watches in the SFr. 300 to 700 range. Retail prices ranged from SFr. 175 to 800 for stainless steel and gold-plated watches. A second smaller line of gold watches sold for between SFr. 1,000 and 5,000. Tissot watches were sold in Europe: Switzerland, West Germany, Italy, Scandinavia and the United Kingdom. Tissot was also sold in Brazil, South Africa, Hong Kong, Singapore, and Japan. Tissot had been withdrawn from the U.S. market in the 1970s, but Thomke wanted to reintroduce it to the United States as soon as possible.

Tissot production was limited to assembly. Employment at the factory had declined from a high of 1,200 to 200. All components and movements were purchased from Asuag-SSIH or independent companies. At the start of 1985 Tissot workers were assembling a product line of some 300 styles, each produced in a woman's and man's model and in a number of different metals and combinations. Thomke had already assigned ten engineers at Tissot to review the product line and production process.

Tissot shared Omega's distribution at both the wholesale and retail level. Almost all Omega wholesalers were independent distributors. A total of 12,000 retail stores, mostly jewelry stores and a few ''high class'' department stores carried Tissot watches. The majority of its watch sales came from the top 3,000 stores. Ex-factory prices ranged from SFr. 60 to 2,000. Both wholesalers and retailers provided advertising and promotion support, but all promotion activities had to be initiated by Tissot.

Thomke was aware that if he wanted to build up a strong image for Tissot, he would have to increase his marketing and promotion expenditure. Asuag-SSIH set targets for marketing and profit margins (MPM) for each brand. Thomke felt that a 50 percent margin would give a brand adequate funds for marketing and profit. Only his latest product, SWATCH, came close to that figure, followed by Rado with almost 30 percent. A target MPM of 15 percent had been set for Tissot for 1984, but Thomke had learned that the actual margin had been closer to 10 percent.

Thomke believed that the MPM had been squeezed by wholesalers because of the slow turnover for Tissot watches. Wholesalers demanded a margin of 28 to 45 percent for Tissot watches. Explaining the situation, Thomke said, ''Tissot has never recovered the sales and market share it lost to Seiko and Citizen in the 1970s. Sales to retailers have slowed considerably, and consumer demand is down. To encourage wholesalers to keep Tissot in inventory, the company granted more liberal wholesaler margins, at the expense of marketing funds and profits.''

Thomke felt that it was still possible to build up the brand and reestablish a strong wholesale network. However, he realized that this was an expensive proposition. He was prepared to invest 18 to 20 percent of sales in promotion, but to have any effect he needed a promotion budget of SFr. 12 million for Europe alone. Thomke estimated that the company could spend SFr. 6 to 8 million in Germany, Tissot's largest market in 1985. This figure would be divided with one-half targeted for media advertising and the rest for point-of-sale promotion. If handled correctly, promotion activities would give Tissot the strong image which Thomke felt was essential to successful watch sales.

## WATCHMAKING TECHNOLOGY

### Designing a Watch Collection

Watches covered a broad spectrum in terms of style and price, ranging from sport watches for informal or daytime wear to luxury dress watches which were pieces of jewelry. It could take 3 years to bring a watch from the drawing board to the market. A watch collection was made up of as many as 30 to 40 lines. Each line had up to 1,000 models. A watch line was differentiated by case shape, design, and movement. The differences between models were cosmetic variations in color and types of materials or slight variations in technology, such as day/date calendars or self-winding mechanisms.

Watch cases were made in precious metals, standard steel, brass, and plastic. The cases of many expensive luxury watches were decorated with semiprecious and precious stones, such as lapis lazuli, diamonds, and sapphires. Watch cases were made in two or three pieces. Two pieces, the back and front, were standard and held the watch together. For better watches a separate rim held the crystal in place. The rim provided designers with more flexibility when developing new models and gave the watches a finer finish.

Watch crystals were pieces of thin glass or plastic which protected the hands and dial and came in three types. The most inexpensive were plastic, followed by mineral glass and sapphire glass. Sapphire glass was very hard and could not be scratched or chipped.

Straps or bracelets held the watch on the wrist and came in a variety of materials. Straps came in leather, plastic, and cloth ribbons. Bracelets were made from precious metals, standard steel, brass, and plastic. Precious and semiprecious stones were often set into the bracelets of luxury watches. Up until the 1970s most watches were sold with leather straps. In the past 15 years fashion had changed, and most watches were purchased with bracelets.

## Timekeeping Technology

Every watch was composed of four basic elements: a time base, a source of energy, a transmission, and a display. The movement was the watch's time base. Movements came in two major categories: mechanical and electronic. Mechanical movements were driven by the release of energy from an unwinding spring. Electronic watches ran on a battery. Energy was transmitted through a series of gears, a motor, or integrated circuits to the hands of analog watches. These hands moved around the dial to display time. Integrated circuits were used to transmit time to digital watches, and time was displayed numerically in a frame on the watch case (Exhibits 10 and 11).

## Mechanical Watch Movements

The movement was a complex set of 100 or more tiny parts. While all mechanical watch move-

ments operated on the same principle, there was a great deal of variety in watch quality. Friction and wear had to be minimized to insure long-term accuracy of the tiny moving parts. To minimize friction, jewels were placed at all the movement's critical pivot and contact points. Fifteen was the standard number of jewels, but high-quality movements might contain as many as thirty. Contrary to popular belief, adding more jewels did not necessarily indicate increased quality or cost to production. These internal jewels were synthetic and relatively inexpensive. It was the overall care and craftsmanship that went into the watches that created the expense and not the jewels themselves.

The precision and accuracy found in high-quality jewel-lever watches required micromechanical engineering expertise. A variety of modifications could be made to spring-powered watches which added to the complexity of the interior design but not the basic mechanism. Refinements, such as improved accuracy, miniaturization, water resistance, and self-wind technology, rather than radical new developments, had occurred. Calendars and chronographs, as well as watches with start-stop mechanisms were also possible.

Pin-lever watches, also called "Roskopfs" after their inventor, had metal pins instead of jewels on the escapement mechanism gear teeth. Roskopf's original goal in inventing this watch had been to make the movement so simple that watches could be made affordable to everyone.

## Electronic Movements

A Swiss engineer, Max Hetzel, invented the first electronic watch in 1954. This development was largely possible due to advances in miniature batteries and electric motors during World War II. Initially, electronics did not represent a big departure from mechanical technology, nor did it offer substantially better accuracy. Although the energy source was replaced with electronics, the transmission and regulating components remained unchanged.

The tuning-fork watch, developed in the 1960s, represented a significant change to the tradi-

E X H I B I T   1 0

**WATCHMAKING TECHNOLOGIES**

### Inside a mechanical watch

The time base is composed of a spiral balance wheel whose movement back and forth recurs, for instance 4 times per second. The source of energy is a taut spring. The transmission consists of a train of pinions and wheels. The display consists of hands moving around a dial.

### The movement blank

The Ebauche, the key part of the watch, serves to carry the main spring, the wheel pins, and the regulating parts. The cocks provide the support at the other end of the pins and pinions. Finally, the wheels and pinions intermesh to provide the transmission moving the hands. The plate, the cocks and the wheels together make up the movement blank of a watch in its unassembled stage.

In addition, the movement of a watch includes the regulating pieces. The whole assembly is inserted into a watch case with glass, dial, and crown for winding up the watch and setting the time; the whole thus constituting the finished product.

Despite the minute dimensions and the finishing and precision required for each unit, mass production reaches a rate of as much as 4,000 to 10,000 complete movement blanks (depending on caliber) per day and per assembly line.

### The regulating parts

The regulating parts carry out the function of time base. They include the balance wheels, the hairspring, and the assortment. These parts regulate the working of the watch, keeping constant control of the amount of energy provided by the main spring and transmitted to the display by the wheel assembly. Their production calls for extreme precision to micrometer* standards and a high degree of know-how for handling the tiny delicate pieces.

### The jewels

The jewels, synthetic rubies, are used to support the pins of the wheel and thus diminish friction and wear. Shaping them with the aid of a diamond paste has taken centuries to develop and achieve precision to a scale of a tenth of a micrometer. A new technology for doing this using laser beams has made it possible to speed up the predrilling of the holes in the jewels.

Inside an electronic watch (analogical or digital), the time base is composed of a quartz crystal vibrating at, for instance, 32,768 times per second. The source of energy is an electric battery. The transmission is provided by conductors and integrated circuits (analogical and digital watches) or a motor synchronized with a train of pinions and wheels (analogical watches). The display is provided by hands moving around a dial in the case of analogical watches or by figures appearing in a frame in the case of digital watches.

*1 micrometer, or micron, equals 0.001 millimeters.

---

tional principles of determining time. A small battery in the watch sent an electric current to the tuning fork and stimulated it to vibrate at 360 cycles per second. The vibrations were transmitted to a set of gears which drove the hands on the watch face. Tuning-fork watches if properly adjusted were accurate to within one minute per month.

The quartz crystal watch began appearing in the marketplace at the end of the 1960s. An electric current was passed through a quartz crystal to stimulate high frequency vibration which could be converted into precise time increments. Microcircuitry subdivided the crystal's frequency into an electric pulse which drove the watch. The pulse operated a tiny electric stepping motor or was transmitted through conductors and integrated circuits to drive the gears and watch hands.

In 1972, digital watches appeared for the first time. These watches had no moving parts, and the conventional face and hands were replaced

**EXHIBIT 11**

**INSIDE THREE WATCHES**

Mechanical watch

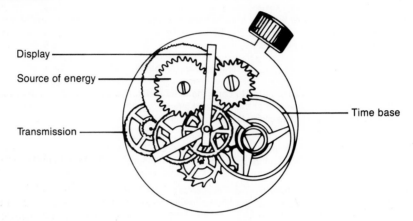

Electronic analogue

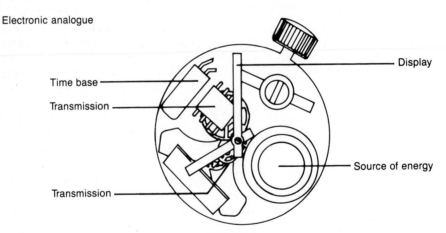

Electronic digital

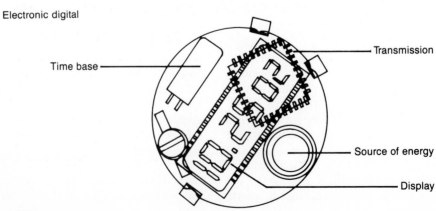

*Source:* Asuag-SSIH.

**EXHIBIT 12**

**MECHANICAL WATCH AND MOVEMENTS EXPORTS AS PERCENTAGE OF TOTAL EXPORTED, 1960–1984**

|             | 1960  | 1970 | 1975 | 1980 | 1982 | 1984 |
|-------------|-------|------|------|------|------|------|
| Switzerland | 100.0 | 99.6 | 98.1 | 80.4 | 50.8 | 29.4 |
| Japan       | 100.0 | n.a. | n.a. | 33.6 | 16.5 | 8.5  |
| Hong Kong   | —     | n.a. | n.a. | 28.7 | 15.1 | 7.6  |
| France      | 100.0 | 94.4 | 98.2 | 75.5 | 60.7 | 45.1 |
| W. Germany  | 100.0 | 85.8 | 84.7 | 50.7 | 29.2 | 16.8 |

n.a. = not available.
*Source:* Swiss Watch Federation.

with digital readouts. Early digital watches used light emitting diodes (LED) to show the time. With this technology, users pressed a button for time display. LED watches required a great deal of power, and batteries lasted no longer than one year. Liquid crystal diodes (LCD) came on the market in 1972; these watches displayed the time continually. These watches were considerably more conservative in energy usage, and batteries lasted from 3 to 5 years or longer.

Early electronic watches were not fully water- and shock-proof, and the batteries often malfunctioned in hot, humid climates. However, within a short period of time, technological advances led to electronic watches which were water-proof to depths of 30 meters, shock-proof and able to withstand tropical climates.

Designing electronic watches for women had initially created problems, as well as opportu-nities. To create models which fit a woman's smaller wrist required considerable miniaturization of the movement and battery. Creating smaller movements led to increased design flexibility. Improvements in miniaturization and advancement in large-scale integrated circuits (LSI) and battery technology allowed manufacturers to add special functions without excessive bulk. Watches began to take on the appearance of multifunction instruments. Runners, skin divers, sailors, and other sports enthusiasts bought watches which would provide them with water-proofing and sophisticated chronograph functions. Travelers were afforded the opportunity to buy watches with multi-time-zone functions and alarms. Watches were also available with calculators and radios, and progress was being made toward a television watch. Exhibits 12 through 15 show figures for exports on both me-

**EXHIBIT 13**

**ELECTRONIC WATCH AND MOVEMENT EXPORTS AS PERCENTAGE OF TOTAL PIECES EXPORTED, 1960–1984**

|             | 1960 | 1970 | 1975 | 1980 | 1982 | 1984 |
|-------------|------|------|------|------|------|------|
| Switzerland | —    | 0.4  | 1.9  | 19.6 | 49.2 | 70.6 |
| Japan       | —    | n.a. | n.a. | 66.4 | 83.5 | 91.5 |
| Hong Kong   | —    | n.a. | n.a. | 71.3 | 84.9 | 92.4 |
| France      | —    | 5.6  | 1.8  | 24.5 | 39.3 | 54.9 |
| W. Germany  | —    | 14.2 | 15.3 | 49.3 | 70.8 | 83.2 |

n.a. = not available.
*Source:* Swiss Watch Federation.

EXHIBIT 14

**VALUE OF MECHANICAL WATCH AND MOVEMENT EXPORTS AS PERCENTAGE OF TOTAL VALUE EXPORTED, 1960–1984**

|              | 1960  | 1970  | 1975  | 1980  | 1982  | 1984  |
|--------------|-------|-------|-------|-------|-------|-------|
| Switzerland  | 100.0 | 98.5  | 94.0  | 69.2  | 51.1  | 46.6  |
| Japan        | 100.0 | n.a.  | n.a.  | 22.2  | 11.4  | 9.8   |
| Hong Kong    | —     | n.a.  | n.a.  | 32.0  | 28.2  | 16.9  |
| France       | 100.0 | 91.1  | 96.2  | 56.2  | 34.3  | 24.0  |
| W. Germany   | 100.0 | 85.1  | 84.4  | 51.8  | 26.4  | 15.2  |

n.a. = not available.
*Source:* Swiss Watch Federation.

chanical and electronic watches. Exhibit 16 illustrates distribution of watch purchases in the United States.

## Producing Watches

Movements, hands, cases, and bracelets were assembled to produce a complete watch. Mechanical watch quality was dependent on the care taken in assembly as well as the quality of the individual components. High-quality mechanical movements were made by hand, and a combination of semiskilled and highly skilled workers was needed. Mechanical watch assembly was done in batches. Highly skilled workers were essential at the final stages of production, for finishing and adjusting to produce high-quality, finely finished, accurate movements and watches.

Although the term *pin-lever* refers specifically to the replacement of jewels with metal pins, Roskopfs were made from lower-quality materials. Labor requirements for Roskopfs were reduced with semiskilled or unskilled labor working in batch production.

Electronic movements for analog watches combined micromechanical and electronic engineering. The electronic regulating mechanism simplified the production process, which could be run in an automated setting with semiskilled labor. Movements for digital watches were radically different from analog watches. These watches had no moving parts, and time was programmed onto a silicon chip. Unskilled labor could be used to assemble digital watches, which were assembled in batches and on automated assembly lines.

Both mechanical and electronic watch relia-

EXHIBIT 15

**VALUE OF ELECTRONIC WATCH AND MOVEMENT EXPORTS AS PERCENTAGE OF TOTAL VALUE EXPORTED, 1960–1984**

|              | 1960 | 1970 | 1975 | 1980 | 1982 | 1984 |
|--------------|------|------|------|------|------|------|
| Switzerland  | —    | 1.5  | 6.0  | 30.8 | 48.9 | 53.4 |
| Japan        | —    | n.a. | n.a. | 77.8 | 88.6 | 90.2 |
| Hong Kong    | —    | n.a. | n.a. | 68.0 | 71.8 | 83.1 |
| France       | —    | 8.9  | 3.8  | 43.8 | 65.7 | 76.0 |
| W. Germany   | —    | 14.9 | 15.6 | 48.2 | 73.6 | 84.8 |

n.a. = not available.
*Source:* Swiss Watch Federation.

**EXHIBIT 16**

**WRISTWATCH PURCHASES
IN THE UNITED STATES***

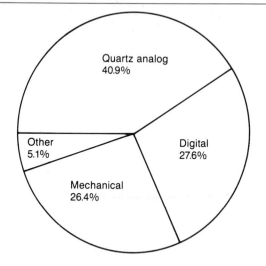

*Quartz analog
40.9%*

*Other
5.1%*

*Digital
27.6%*

*Mechanical
26.4%*

*Total number of surveyed buyers: 492
Source: National Jewelers/HTI, Consumer Survey 1983.*

bility was tied to the number of inspections the manufacturer made. For mid-priced and expensive watches, 100 percent inspection occurred at several points during the process. Tests were made for water- and shock-proofing as well as for accuracy.

Costs of production were a function of a company's degree of integration and automation and of material costs and the local wage rates. Material costs were based on the quality of the watch produced. With Roskopf watches labor constituted a significant portion of variable costs, but as the watches moved up-market, the materials—fine stainless steel, sapphire crystals and eventually precious metals and decorative jewels—played the major role in the watch's ex-factory price. Watchmakers could improve their variable costs by assembling at volumes above 10,000 pieces. Assemblers producing 100,000 to 500,000 units per year could benefit from component supplier discounts which were as high as 20 to 25 percent. Beyond this point, cost improvements could only be realized with new

production processes, automation, and robotics. Wages for the Swiss watch industry averaged SFr. 12 per hour. Most Swiss watchmakers sought a 30 percent gross margin. In Japan average hourly wages for factory workers were SFr. 7.20. Japanese producers had an average gross margin of 40 percent. In Hong Kong manufacturers kept their ex-factory prices low with inexpensive, but highly productive piece-work labor, averaging under SFr. 10 per day, fewer inspections, and cheaper materials. Gross margins of approximately 10 to 15 percent were typical for Hong Kong manufacturers (Exhibit 17).

## SEGMENTING THE GLOBAL WATCH INDUSTRY

### Price Segments

Price has been a traditional means of segmenting the watch market into three categories. The first group were low-price "C" watches and included all watches sold at retail for under SFr. 120. Roskopf watches and inexpensive digitals competed in this market. These watches accounted for 33 percent of total value of global watch sales and 86 percent of unit volume. The mid-price, or "B" watches, ranged from SFr. 120 to 700 at retail. This sector represented 25 percent of sales in Swiss francs and 12 percent of total units for 1984. Electronic watches dominated both the C and the B price segments.

The third category were the top priced watches. The retail price of "A" watches ranged from SFr. 700 to 5,000. Manufacturers of luxury watches—"AA" class—sold to a small exclusive group willing to pay several thousand Swiss francs for a special custom-design jeweled watch. Precious stones and/or metal used in the watch face and bracelet accounted for the major portion of the A and AA watch prices. This was particularly true for electronic watches where movements averaged SFr. 18. About 27 percent of the value of total watches and 2 percent of pieces sold worldwide were from the "A" tier. "AA" watches accounted for 16 percent of global

**EXHIBIT 17**

**BREAKDOWN OF PRODUCTION COSTS** (SFr.)

**Swiss watch with an ex-factory cost of SFr. 390**

| | |
|---|---|
| Materials | |
| Case | 70 |
| Bracelet | 90 |
| Dial | 50 |
| Crystal | 18 |
| Movement | 18 (50 for mechanical) |
| Hands | 5 |
| Total materials costs | 251 |
| Assembly and quality control | 25 |
| Margin | 114 |
| Ex-factory | 390 |
| Wholesalers' margin | 260 |
| Retailers' margin | 650 |
| Consumer price | 1,300 |

**Japanese watch with ex-factory cost of SFr. 250**

| | |
|---|---|
| Total variable costs | 150 |
| Margin | 100 |
| Ex-factory | 250 |
| Wholesalers' margin | 60–90 |
| Retailers' margin | 310–340 |
| Consumer price | 630–700 |

**Hong Kong watch with ex-factory cost of SFr. 80**

| | |
|---|---|
| Materials | |
| Case and dial | 15 |
| Bracelet | 15 |
| Crystal | 15 |
| Movement | 18 |
| Hands | 2 |
| Total materials costs | 65 |
| Assembly and quality control | 6 |
| Manufacturer's margin 10% | 8 |
| Ex-factory | 80 |
| Wholesalers' margin | 30 |
| Retailers' margin | 55–110 |
| Consumer price | 165–220 |

*Source:* Asuag-SSIH and interviews with industry experts.

watch sales in Swiss francs, but less than 0.5 percent of total units. Mechanical watches still dominated the high priced segments (Exhibit 18).

Evaluating timekeeping technology was difficult for consumers. When shopping for watches, consumers chose a particular price level and expected a certain level of technical proficiency, style, and intangibles such as prestige. Quartz technology had changed the price-accuracy ratio. Before the electronic watch, accuracy was bought with expensive, finely engineered jewel-lever watches. With the introduction of electronics, watches with accuracy of plus or minus 15 seconds per month could be purchased for as little as $9.95.

## Geographic Segments

Technologies and price have had an impact on the world markets for watches. Historically, the United States has been the major importer of finished watches. The United States was often the launching ground for new products, and success in this market indicated strong possibility of global success. The strong dollar and improving U.S. economy in 1984–85 had had a positive impact on the sales and profits of Swiss and Japanese watch companies. Europe and Japan were also strong markets for watches in all price categories. However, throughout the 1960s and 1970s, new opportunities for watch sales opened up in the oil-producing countries in the Middle East and in less developed countries (LDCs).

In the 1960s watch producers began to move into the LDCs with inexpensive Roskopf watches. This market was taken over by inexpensive digitals in the early 1970s. However, the initial success of the cheap digital in this market was short-lived, and consumers returned to mechanical watches. The miniature batteries in the quartz watch were very expensive in these regions, sometimes more than the original cost of the watch. By 1984, this problem had been solved, and inexpensive electric watches again dominated the LDC market.

A new opportunity for watch manufacturers developed in industrialized countries, with young children providing a new and growing market for inexpensive watches. Until the 1960s most children received their first watch in their mid- to late teens, often as a gift. Roskopf watches opened up the market to children in the 7- to

## EXHIBIT 18

### WATCH PURCHASES IN THE UNITED STATES AT RETAIL PRICES

| Cost of items | Watches (490)* | Quartz analog (200) | Digital (135) | Mechanical (130) |
|---|---|---|---|---|
| $1,000 or more | 0.8% | 0.5% | 0.7% | 1.5% |
| $300 to $999 | 2.4 | 4.0 | 0.7 | 1.5 |
| $100 to $299 | 23.5 | 38.0 | 8.9 | 14.6 |
| $50 to $99 | 33.5 | 33.5 | 31.9 | 35.4 |
| $25 to $49 | 39.8 | 24.0 | 57.8 | 47.0 |

*Total 490 responses for consumer survey.
Source: National Jeweler/HTI, *Consumer Survey 1983.*

## EXHIBIT 19

### TOTAL U.S. JEWELRY AND WATCH PURCHASES BY AGE GROUP (1,852 Items)

| Age | Percent |
|---|---|
| 55+ | 23.6 |
| 35–54 | 45.0 |
| 25–34 | 23.0 |
| 18–24 | 8.4 |

Source: National Jeweler/HTI, *Consumer Survey 1983.*

10-year range. A significant portion of these purchases were novelty watches, with cartoon and storybook characters which were sold as gifts for young children (Exhibits 19 and 20).

The market for expensive watches moved to the Middle East in the early 1970s. The rest of the world was caught in a recession, largely due to escalating oil and gas prices, and demand for high-price luxury items fell off. Buyers in the oil producing countries had both the money and the interest to purchase luxury goods. The Swiss were particularly adept at meeting the changing fashions and tastes of this new luxury segment and provided expensive, luxury watches with lapis-lazuli, coral, diamonds, and turquoise (Exhibits 21 to 26).

## TRENDS IN WATCHES DISTRIBUTION

### Wholesale Distributors

Watch distributors played an essential role in linking the manufacturer to the retailer. Distributors generally sold one or perhaps two noncompeting brands. Wholesalers expected exclusive distribution rights for the brand for a given

## EXHIBIT 20

### DISTRIBUTION OF U.S. WATCH AND JEWELRY PURCHASE PRICES BY AGE OF PURCHASER

| Cost of items | 18–24 yr (150)* | 25–34 yr (419) | 35–54 yr (821) | 55+ yr (431) |
|---|---|---|---|---|
| $1,000 and more | 1.3% | 1.5% | 3.3% | 1.2% |
| $300 to $999 | 11.3 | 8.8 | 9.0 | 10.4 |
| $100 to $299 | 27.3 | 25.3 | 26.7 | 27.6 |
| $50 to $99 | 20.7 | 24.8 | 25.3 | 28.5 |
| $25 to $49 | 39.4 | 39.6 | 35.7 | 32.3 |

*Number in survey.
Source: National Jeweler/HTI, *Consumer Survey 1983.*

## EXHIBIT 21

**MAJOR IMPORTERS OF SWISS WATCHES AND MOVEMENTS BY VOLUME**
(Million)

| Country | 1960 | 1970 | 1975 | 1980 | 1982 | 1984 |
|---|---|---|---|---|---|---|
| Hong Kong | 1.9 | 10.0 | 11.3 | 12.5 | 4.1 | 4.9 |
| United States | 12.4 | 19.2 | 12.0 | 5.9 | 3.6 | 4.6 |
| W. Germany | 1.3 | 2.9 | 5.0 | 4.9 | 3.6 | 4.0 |
| Italy | 1.2 | 2.6 | 2.6 | 2.5 | 2.3 | 3.0 |
| France | 0.2 | 0.7 | 0.8 | 1.6 | 1.9 | 2.2 |
| Japan | 0.2 | 1.0 | 1.6 | 0.7 | 0.7 | 2.0 |
| United Kingdom | 1.7 | 6.1 | 6.3 | 3.2 | 1.9 | 1.9 |
| Saudi Arabia | 0.2 | 3.4 | 1.1 | 1.0 | 1.2 | 0.9 |
| Arab Emirates | — | — | 1.4 | 1.9 | 1.3 | 0.8 |
| Spain | 0.8 | 2.5 | 1.9 | 1.3 | 1.1 | 0.8 |
| Total 10 largest markets | 19.9 | 48.4 | 44.0 | 35.5 | 21.7 | 25.1 |
| Total worldwide | 41.0 | 71.4 | 65.8 | 51.0 | 31.3 | 32.2 |

*Source:* Swiss Watch Federation.

region. Distributors maintained a sales force to sell to and service retailers. They purchased watches outright and maintained a local inventory.

Manufacturers expected their distributors to participate in promotion activities. Distributors attended trade fairs and contributed to advertising, mailing expenses, and point-of-purchase display materials.

The distributor had to find and oversee adequate watch repair services. Watch repair was a key issue for watches in the B, A, and AA categories. This service need had led to a close working relationship among the producer, distributor, and retailer. The distributor found and licensed watch repair services and jewelers with watch repair capabilities. For especially difficult repairs the distributor helped arrange for work to be sent back to the factory. With inexpensive, "throw-a-way" watches, repairs were less critical or nonexistent. Importers of C-level watches had greater freedom in channel selection. Mass

## EXHIBIT 22

**MAJOR IMPORTERS OF SWISS WATCHES AND MOVEMENTS BY VALUE** (Million SFr.)

| Country | 1960 | 1970 | 1975 | 1980 | 1982 | 1984 |
|---|---|---|---|---|---|---|
| United States | 250.6 | 482.2 | 348.6 | 379.7 | 407.8 | 598.7 |
| Hong Kong | 76.6 | 242.6 | 257.6 | 401.6 | 344.1 | 351.5 |
| Italy | 70.1 | 153.9 | 194.0 | 256.4 | 287.7 | 300.3 |
| W. Germany | 48.2 | 135.3 | 195.6 | 241.7 | 212.4 | 246.6 |
| Saudi Arabia* | 12.2 | 92.0 | 84.0 | 201.9 | 271.9 | 233.1 |
| France | 10.6 | 38.6 | 75.6 | 123.3 | 152.0 | 169.8 |
| Japan | 14.1 | 88.0 | 172.5 | 109.0 | 120.3 | 167.1 |
| Singapore | 38.3 | 45.1 | 58.3 | 79.7 | 106.2 | 150.3 |
| United Kingdom | 43.1 | 131.3 | 176.6 | 125.3 | 127.2 | 139.9 |
| Arab Emirates* | — | — | 59.4 | 71.7 | 94.9 | 82.1 |
| Total 10 largest markets | 563.8 | 1,409.0 | 1,622.2 | 1,990.3 | 2,124.5 | 2,439.4 |
| Total worldwide | 1,146.3 | 2,362.2 | 2,720.3 | 2,917.5 | 3,011.0 | 3,298.8 |

*Saudi Arabia with Arab Emirates in 1960 and 1970.
*Source:* Swiss Watch Federation.

**EXHIBIT 23**

**MAJOR IMPORTERS OF JAPANESE WATCHES AND MOVEMENTS BY VOLUME** (Million)

| Country | 1980 | 1982 | 1983 |
|---|---|---|---|
| Hong Kong | 14.2 | 23.0 | 28.3 |
| United States | 7.5 | 10.3 | 11.8 |
| Saudi Arabia | 2.1 | 2.8 | 3.9 |
| W. Germany | 3.4 | 2.7 | 3.1 |
| France | 1.1 | 1.9 | 2.6 |
| United Kingdom | 1.1 | 1.7 | 2.2 |
| Spain | 0.5 | 2.0 | 2.1 |
| Arab Emirates | 0.6 | 1.3 | 1.4 |
| Italy | 0.8 | 0.8 | 1.1 |
| Canada | 0.8 | 0.7 | 1.0 |
| Total 10 largest markets | 32.1 | 47.2 | 57.5 |
| Total worldwide | 48.3 | 63.6 | 76.0 |

*Source:* Swiss Watch Federation.

merchandisers, drugstores, and even supermarkets were used to distribute watches to end users. Some of these watches were sold with a guarantee, and rather than repair, a replacement was offered.

Most watch manufacturers had agreements with independent distributors. The Japanese and some of the private Swiss firms operated wholly or partially owned marketing and sales subsidiaries in their foreign markets. Twenty-five to 35 percent was the standard markup granted wholesalers and importers of Japanese and Hong Kong watches. This figure increased to 40 percent or more for importers of most Swiss watches.

## Retailers

A wide variety of retailers sold watches to the end user, including jewelry and department stores, mass merchandisers, and mail order catalogues.

**EXHIBIT 24**

**MAJOR IMPORTERS OF JAPANESE WATCHES AND MOVEMENTS BY VALUE** (Million SFr.)

| Country | 1980 | 1982 | 1983 |
|---|---|---|---|
| Hong Kong | 383.7 | 471.0 | 580.8 |
| United States | 316.9 | 372.9 | 403.4 |
| Saudi Arabia | 107.3 | 94.8 | 158.3 |
| France | 72.0 | 73.0 | 95.5 |
| W. Germany | 142.4 | 94.4 | 88.0 |
| Arab Emirates | 24.5 | 42.4 | 58.9 |
| United Kingdom | 54.3 | 56.0 | 56.7 |
| Canada | 44.6 | 39.6 | 51.1 |
| Italy | 40.9 | 33.3 | 47.6 |
| Singapore | 18.3 | 29.9 | 23.0 |
| Total 10 largest markets | 1,205.0 | 1,306.4 | 1,563.2 |
| Total worldwide | 1,918.5 | 1,925.4 | 2,224.7 |

*Source:* Swiss Watch Federation.

---

### EXHIBIT 25

**MAJOR IMPORTERS OF WATCHES AND MOVEMENTS FROM HONG KONG BY VOLUME** (Million)

| Country | 1980 | 1982 | 1983 |
|---|---|---|---|
| United States | 32.6 | 81.7 | 119.2 |
| W. Germany | 11.5 | 15.6 | 20.5 |
| Spain | 4.2 | 9.5 | 14.8 |
| United Kingdom | 9.7 | 10.4 | 12.6 |
| Japan | 5.9 | 8.2 | 12.4 |
| Canada | 2.9 | 8.6 | 10.2 |
| Italy | 4.6 | 5.2 | 8.0 |
| Saudi Arabia | 2.4 | 6.4 | 7.1 |
| Arab Emirates | 1.4 | 3.9 | 6.2 |
| France | 6.6 | 4.8 | 4.2 |
| Total 10 largest markets | 81.8 | 154.3 | 215.2 |
| Total worldwide | 126.1 | 213.7 | 284.1 |

*Source:* Swiss Watch Federation.

An estimated 40 percent of worldwide watch sales came from jewelry stores. Watch manufacturers benefitted from the jeweler's selling expertise and personal interaction with consumers. Watches sold in exclusive jewelry and department stores benefitted from the store's deluxe or fashion image. Fine gold, mechanical watches were a natural extension of the jeweler's product line, and most jewelers were capable of minor watch repairs and cleaning. When electronics were initially introduced, some jewelry stores resisted the new technology. Electronics were not within the jeweler's extensive training. Within a short period of time, however, customer demand and refinements to the technology moved quartz watches into jewelry stores worldwide.

Jewelry stores had been the traditional outlet for watch sales until the mid-1950s. The rapid growth in Roskopf and later in inexpensive dig-

---

### EXHIBIT 26

**MAJOR IMPORTERS OF WATCHES AND MOVEMENTS FROM HONG KONG BY VALUE** (Million SFr.)

| Country | 1980 | 1982 | 1984 |
|---|---|---|---|
| United States | 469.4 | 591.3 | 671.7 |
| W. Germany | 194.9 | 129.4 | 145.9 |
| Saudi Arabia | 58.9 | 102.3 | 100.5 |
| Japan | 69.5 | 65.1 | 84.7 |
| United Kingdom | 139.0 | 82.6 | 76.3 |
| Canada | 56.7 | 63.3 | 57.8 |
| Arab Emirates | 25.7 | 59.6 | 57.0 |
| Italy | 62.7 | 34.9 | 40.8 |
| France | 88.5 | 34.2 | 22.8 |
| Singapore | 43.8 | 46.8 | 34.2 |
| Total 10 largest markets | 1,209.0 | 1,209.4 | 1,291.5 |
| Total worldwide | 1,859.7 | 1,779.6 | 1,915.3 |

*Source:* Swiss Watch Federation.

EXHIBIT 27

**WATCH PURCHASES IN THE UNITED STATES BY OUTLET TYPE**

| Outlet | Analog | Digital | Watches (n = 485) |
|---|---|---|---|
| Jewelry store | 34.3% | 12.0% | 27.6% |
| Department store | 26.3 | 27.6 | 26.2 |
| Discount store | 14.7 | 23.1 | 16.7 |
| Catalog showroom | 14.7 | 10.4 | 10.3 |
| Mail order | 14.7 | 11.2 | 5.4 |
| Wholesaler | 2.5 | 1.5 | 3.1 |
| Drug store | 2.0 | 6.0 | 5.1 |
| Flea market* | — | — | 2.4 |
| Other outlets | 3.0 | 7.5 | 6.2 |

*Flea markets accounted for less than 1% of all categories.
n = number.
Source: National Jeweler/HTI. *Consumer Survey 1983.*

ital watch sales was accompanied by channel diversification, and watches moved into new outlets: drug stores, department stores, and supermarkets. Retail watch sales in the United States had been influenced by channel diversification, and in 1983 less than 30 percent of watches sold in the U.S. were purchased in jewelry stores (Exhibits 27 to 29).

Stock turn for a B, A, or AA watch could be as low as two times per year at retail, and phasing out older models and cleaning out the pipeline could take 2 to 3 years. C watches generally moved more quickly, with four to six stock turns per year.

Jewelry stores and department stores were accustomed to a 50 to 55 percent markup. Mass

merchandisers' margins varied and went as low as 25 percent.

## COMPETITORS IN THE GLOBAL WATCH INDUSTRY

### Timex

Timex, a U.S. company, began selling inexpensive, mechanical watches in the late 1950s. Most Timex watches fell into the C range, with prices ranging from under SFr. 15 to just over SFr. 250.

The company developed into a manufacturer of mass-produced, hard alloy pin-lever watches. Manufacturing was mechanized, simplified, and standardized. When the company's pricing plan called for a 30 percent markup at the retail level, jewelry stores refused to carry the watches. Timex moved into mass outlets such as drug, department, and hardware stores, and even cigar stands. The number of outlets for Timex watches in 1985 was estimated between 100,000 and 150,000. This figure was down from a high of 2.5 million in the 1960s. By the late 1960s, 50 percent of all watches sold in the United States were Timex. In 1985 Timex had capacity to produce 15 million watches.

Timex had an advertising budget of approximately SFr. 20 million, most of which was spent on television sports events. Timex produced a large number of styles but did not promote any single model or style. The company was known for its "takes a licking and keeps on ticking" slogan, promoting Timex durability.

EXHIBIT 28

**PRICE RANGES OF PURCHASES BY OUTLET TYPE**

| Outlet | $1,000+ (n = 40) | $300–999 (n = 173) | $100–299 (n = 485) | $50–99 (n = 466) | $25–49 (n = 657) |
|---|---|---|---|---|---|
| Jewelry store | 70.0% | 69.4% | 49.1% | 34.6% | 27.2% |
| Department store | — | 6.9 | 16.7 | 22.5 | 27.9 |
| Discount store | 2.5 | 1.7 | 5.8 | 9.7 | 10.5 |
| Catalog showroom | 5.0 | 5.2 | 8.9 | 9.4 | 7.3 |
| Other outlets | 22.5 | 16.8 | 19.5 | 23.8 | 27.1 |

n = number.
Source: National Jeweler/HTI. *Consumer Survey 1983.*

## EXHIBIT 29

**BRAND DISTRIBUTION OF WATCH PURCHASES IN THE UNITED STATES**

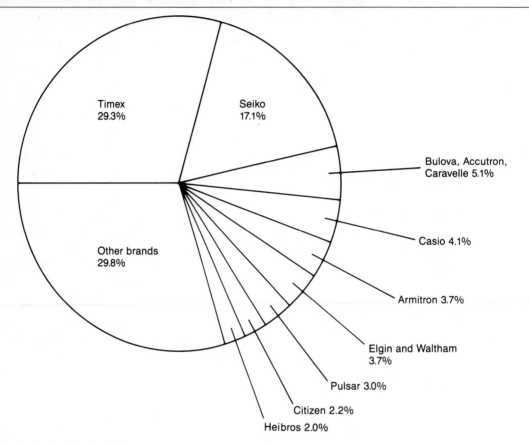

*Source:* National Jeweler/HTI. *Consumer Survey 1983.*

Timex began limited production of digital watches in 1972. By the mid-1970s the company was feeling pressure from new entrants from Japan and the United States. Sales support for mechanical watches was withdrawn, and Timex attempted to increase its digital capacity and to gain electronics capabilities rapidly. As a mechanical watch manufacturer Timex had been fully integrated, but used outside sources for electronic components. The company's initial entries to the digital market were poorly received, and sales declined to SFr. 1 billion in 1979. During the 1970s the company faced sig-

nificant losses which amounted to SFr. 260 million by the end of 1982. These losses were expected to escalate.

In the 1980s Timex moved into consumer electronics, computers, and home health care products and refocused its watch business to try to halt its profit slide and plant closings. In 1981 Timex invested in a British home-computer company founded by inventor Clive Sinclair. The computer had little capacity but had the lowest price on the market. In 1982, fierce price competition in the home-computer market squeezed margins, and the price was cut in half to approximately SFr. 100. The company also lost sales to competitors such as Commodore which offered more power for about SFr. 180. Timex management viewed the watch industry as splitting into two parts: jewelry and wrist instruments. Timex reported that its development plans would emphasize the wrist-instrument business with multifunction watches.

### Texas Instruments, Inc.

In 1975 a number of U.S. electronics companies entered the industry with digital watches and circuits for electronic movements. Finding themselves with excess capacity, an estimated 100 chip producers entered the watch market. Most started as suppliers of movements and components and integrated forward into production and assembly of complete watches. In the early days of digital watch sales, demand far outstripped capacity. In spite of this fact, the electronics companies continually pushed price down in a market share war which eventually destroyed this attempted entry into the watch business.

Texas Instruments (TI) was the largest of the semiconductor and computer companies to enter the watch industry. Its consumer electronics division began in the early 1970s with hand-held calculators. The company then broadened this line with watches, home computers, and educational products.

Watch manufacturing at TI began in 1976, when its first LED plastic-cased watch with a SFr. 40 price tag was introduced. One month later the price was cut in half. TI developed a digital watch that could be made from TI-built parts on automated equipment. Prices were set to undercut the mechanical watch competition with a goal to gain a large piece of both the U.S. and global markets. Prices were set to reflect budgeted, future volumes.

Although TI had surprised the competition with reduced prices, it was caught off-guard with advances in digital display readouts. To provide a full line of products the company imported 7 out of 13 of its basic lines from Hong Kong,

including its multifunction watches. The corporation reported SFr. 6.4 billion in sales in 1979, SFr. 800 million of which came from consumer goods. The division showed a pretax profit of SFr. 4 million down from pretax $28 million in 1978. Profits continued to slide, and TI moved out of the watch industry in 1982.

### Casio Computer Company

In 1974, Casio, a Japanese calculator company, entered the market and claimed 12 percent share of all Japanese watches sold within 5 years. Casio watches were sold in the C price range. Casio manufactured its watches in highly automated factories. Its product line was limited to digital watches, many of them multifunctional with stop watches, timers, and calculators. Casio management has been quoted as saying: "People should own at least three watches." In 1985 Casio was selling an estimated 30 million watches per year. The Casio name was clearly linked worldwide with multifunction watches.

Casio's first entry into the digital market was priced at SFr. 180, and initial sales were weak. As the company's watch prices began to fall, sales doubled annually from 1974–80.

Casio was among the first electronic watch producers to determine that the electronic watch's greatest appeal was technical rather than aesthetic. The company urged its department and mass merchandise store retailers to display its watches in the camera, calculator, or stereo department, rather than the jewelry department. Casio management felt that sales personnel at these counters understood electronic equipment better than jewelry salespeople and could therefore answer customer questions.

### The Hong Kong Watchmakers

Hong Kong entered the watch market in a major way in 1976, specializing in inexpensive electronic and mechanical watches. Hong Kong watch manufacturers did not sell under their own company or brand name. Private label watches were produced and sold in minimum lots of 1,000 to 2,000 pieces per model.

Ten major producers accounted for an estimated 70 percent of total volume, but as many as 800 "loft workshops" were also operating. These production facilities could be started at low cost and run with minimum overheads. Hong Kong was the world's largest watch exporter and was responsible for 326.4 million units in 1984; total value was SFr. 2,091.2 million.

Most watch production in Hong Kong was limited to assembly. Inexpensive components and movements were purchased in large lot sizes. Hong Kong manufacturers kept their design costs minimal or nonexistent by producing copies and near-copies of watches displayed at trade fairs and in jewelry stores. Average ex-factory prices were SFr. 25 for a mechanical, SFr. 60 for quartz analog, and SFr. 12 for electronic digitals. Hong Kong watch prices began to fall rapidly in the late 1970s. Simple watches selling for SFr. 18 to 20 in 1978 dropped to SFr. 12 in one year, and margins shrank to less than SFr. 1.

Counterfeiting was a fairly common practice among small Hong Kong manufacturers. A counterfeit copied the original watch design and was marked with the brand name. This practice was generally avoided by the large producers who beginning in the early 1980s were seeking entry into the international watch establishment. Counterfeiting was a significant problem faced by European and Japanese producers. Unlike technological innovations, it was very difficult to establish patents or copyrights on designs. Firms could try to protect their brand name by establishing a company or joint-venture within Hong Kong.

## SWATCH Watch SA

SWATCH was a plastic, quartz analog watch. SWATCH was sold at SFr. 15 ex-factory and SFr. 50 at retail in Switzerland. Prices outside of Switzerland were slightly higher, and the top price was $30 in the United States. The product was available in 12 styles, which changed twice per year, in a woman's and a man's model.

SWATCH Watch was an Asuag-SSIH company under the direction of Ernst Thomke. It was founded in 1985 when it was split off from its original producer ETA. SWATCH Watch remained within the Ebauches group of Asuag-SSIH. Within 2 years of its introduction in 1982, the brand had hit sales of 3.5 million units. Sales for 1985 were expected to reach 7.5 million units. In 1985 SWATCH management was concerned that the company's already constrained capacity could become an increasingly significant problem over the next few years. The product was produced on a fully automated and robotized assembly line, and the hands were the only component purchased from an outside source. The company had enjoyed rapid decline in production costs per watch. Thomke had met and surpassed his original target production cost of SFr. 10 per watch.

From introduction it had been positioned for active people, a sport or fashion accessory and not as a time piece. The watch sold in jewelry and department stores. The company had spent heavily on promotion and advertising, budgeting approximately SFr. 5 per watch for marketing expense and profits.

SWATCH invested SFr. 20 million in marketing efforts and was expected to spend SFr. 30 million in 1985. SWATCH was sold in 19 industrial countries, and approximately 50 percent of all SWATCHes were sold in the United States. In the majority of markets independent distributors were employed. However, SWATCH Watch USA was a wholly owned subsidiary which controlled distribution in the United States. SWATCH Watch USA played a significant role in the creation of marketing strategy and planning for the watch.

## Seiko

Seiko, part of the K. Hattori Company, began marketing an electronic, quartz watch in 1969 and emerged as the market volume leader in the global watch industry within 10 years. In 1984 the company reported annual sales of SFr. 3.8 billion for watches and clocks. Seiko watches fell within the B category, but the company competed in the C-segment watches with the Alba and Larus labels; high-C or low-B segment with the Pulsar label, and A segment with the

Jean Lassale brand. In 1984 the company sold 55 million watches, 22 million under the Seiko brand.

Seiko had been using assembly line production since the mid-1950s. Following the example of the Detroit automobile factories, its engineers designed assembly lines, and unskilled laborers were employed in most production. The firm was fully integrated, manufacturing key components, jewels, and even watchmaking machinery. Seiko was among the first to initiate large-scale production and sales of electronic watches.

Seiko had been protected from foreign competitors in its domestic market. Only expensive watches, about 5 percent of total units and 20 percent of total value of Japanese purchases, were imported. Almost all the low- to mid-price watches purchased in Japan were produced by Seiko or one of its two domestic competitors, Citizen and Casio. Japanese companies produced some low-priced movements for Hong Kong manufacturers. However, movements for B watch production were not exported to Hong Kong.

Seiko used the United States as a market for initial entry, where they gained a reputation which they then sold worldwide. The company offered fewer than 400 quartz and mechanical models in the United States but over 2,300 worldwide. These models included analog, digital, and multifunctions watches. Plans called for an expansion of the number of styles sold in the United States and a broadening of the price range at the upper and lower ends of the market.

Seiko owned sales subsidiaries in all its major markets. Seiko watches were sold in jewelry and department stores. It had also established service centers in all of its major markets. This service allowed the customer to bring or mail a repair problem directly to the company, bypassing the jeweler. Seiko spent as much as SFr. 80 to 100 million annually in worldwide advertising, mostly television, to sell its quartz watches. Seiko had created a strong brand image based on its quartz technology and accuracy.

Although Seiko was a formidable competitor for the Swiss watch industry, Japanese consumers were a major market for Swiss luxury watches. Throughout the 1970s and 1980s Swiss luxury watches were considered a status symbol in Japan. In 1981 Seiko moved into the luxury market, at home and abroad, when it purchased a small Swiss watch producer Jean Lassale. The company's plan was to combine Swiss design and elegance with Japanese engineering and technical skill in electronics.

By 1970 both Seiko and its Japanese competitor Citizen had diversified into new businesses with internal development, mergers, and acquisitions. Included in the expanded product line were: consumer electronic products such as computers, software, calculators, high-speed printers, miniature industrial robots, office equipment and machine tools and even fashion department stores. As Seiko faced the 1990s, these product lines were expected to become an increasingly important part of the company's total sales and profits. In 1970 clocks and watches represented 99 percent of Seiko sales, but by 1983 that share had dropped to 40 percent. Top executives at Seiko expected this figure to continue to decline to 30 percent by 1990.

## Longines SA

Longines was well-known internationally but losing money when it was acquired by Asuag in 1974. Longines was developed into the group's premiere, or top-priced, brand and began contributing to profits in 1976.

After joining Asuag, Longines' prices began to climb, as the company edged its way into the high-priced A watch segment. The first Swiss manufacturer to produce electronic watches in 1969, Longines' product mix was 50 percent electronic. In 1985 average ex-factory price for Longines watches was SFr. 450 to 500.

Longines produced at levels of about 500,000 watches per year. Investments were made in more efficient machines to reduce dependence on skilled labor, and the number of different types of movements and other precision parts was cut back. Longines continued to make about 30 lines, each with many variations.

Longines put all of its promotion money behind its leader model, the "Conquest." Management felt that the top-priced Conquest best represented the overall style of the collection. "The Longines Style" campaign was supported with an advertising and promotion budget of 10 percent of total sales, and this sum was matched by Longines agents. Advertisements were placed in international and local media.

In 1984 Longines introduced a new watch line, the Conquest VHP. VHP stood for "very high precision," and the watch promised accuracy within 1 second per month. The gunmetal-colored titanium and gold watch contained two quartz crystals. The first was the timekeeper and the second compensated for vibrations and effects of the weather. The watch sold for SFr. 1,650 at retail, and initial response from the marketplace was very positive. Advertising for the new line stressed the watch's Swiss origin with the heading "Swiss Achievement."

## Rolex

Rolex, with its prestigious "Oyster" line, was perhaps the best known of the Swiss luxury watch manufacturers. Rolex was a private company, owned by a foundation. The company was responsible for about 5.5 percent of Switzerland's watch exports by volume, with estimated annual export of 400,000 units, valued at SFr. 700 to 800 million. Rolex did not disclose its domestic sales.

Ninety percent of all Rolex watches were produced with mechanical movements housed in gold or platinum cases. The Oyster line was described as a premium sports watch. Retail Oyster watch prices ranged from SFr. 800 for stainless steel watches to SFr. 14,000 for solid gold watches. Production was semiautomated, and Geneva housewives made up a large part of the semiskilled labor. Skilled workers were required for hand assembly in the final stages of production. The company always allowed production to lag slightly behind demand.

Throughout the turbulent 1970s, the company had stayed consistently with the luxury sport watch market. Rolex limited advertising to the higher-priced Oyster line. Rolex also had a second line, "Cellini," of high-priced luxury dress watches. The company resisted entry into the electronic age; only 10 percent of the Rolex line was electronic. There was some speculation that in the next 3 to 5 years quartz watches would rise to 30 percent of total output. In 1983, quartz production was limited to watches under the Tudor brand, at the low end of Rolex's market and priced below SFr. 1,200. The Tudor watches were not advertised and did not bear the Rolex name. In 1985, the Rolex catalogue included three "Oysterquartz" models.

Rolex employed wholly owned, marketing subsidiaries in 19 countries. The Geneva headquarters worked through the subsidiaries to license jewelers to sell and service its watches. The subsidiaries provided sales and service support to local retailers and watch repairers. Maintaining adequate service coverage was important in an era of throw-away watches. For example, the New York subsidiary licensed 70 watch repairers to service Rolex watches. Distribution to retail outlets was based on a quota system. Subsidiaries were also used to maintain tight control over retail prices; Rolex did not permit any discounting. Promotion and advertising expenditures were estimated at 10 percent of sales. This expenditure was matched by the wholesalers and retailers.

## Piaget SA

Piaget SA was founded by George Piaget in 1874 and in 1985 was still a family business directed by the founder's grandsons and great-grandsons. The company's workshops produced approximately 15,000 handmade watches each year at prices ranging from SFr. 4,000 to 400,000. The company carried a large collection of luxury watches for both men and women, producing approximately 1,200 models.

Only gold and/or platinum were used to encase the watch movements, and many of the watches were decorated with precious stones. Both mechanical and quartz models were included in Piaget's collection. Piaget was the only producer of luxury dress watches which was fully integrated. The company produced the world's thinnest mechanical watches: 1.2mm for a hand-wind model, and 2mm for an automatic. Historically, the Piaget line was limited to dress watches, but the company entered the sports watch market in 1980.

Worldwide, Piaget watches were carried by 400 retailers. They tended to be the most prestigious stores in their areas and were located to be accessible to potential luxury watch buyers. Whenever possible, the watchmaker preferred retailers to carry only Piaget in their luxury dress watch line. Annual advertising expenditure for Piaget was estimated at SFr. 3 million, excluding the United States. About 55 percent of this expense was paid for by Piaget, and the rest was contribution from distributors and retailers.

Other Swiss manufacturers producing luxury dress watches included: Audemars-Piguet, Patek-Philippe, and Vacheron & Constantin. All three were smaller than Piaget, producing fewer than 15,000 watches per year and following similar strategies.

## Ebel

Ebel was founded in 1911 by Eugene Blum. The company described its transition in the 1970s as a renaissance.

In 1974 the third generation of Blums, Pierre-Alain, took over the company. When Pierre-Alain Blum became president, Ebel's 50 employees were making private label watches. With new management, Ebel began to take a closer look at the customers of its chief client Cartier. Within a short period of time, Ebel began branded watch production, and employment grew to 500 people; 1984 sales were estimated between SFr. 150 and 170 million.

The company's growth came about with the development of a unique one-piece watch case and bracelet construction which became the base for the Ebel collection. Ebel's goal was to design and maintain a "classic," timeless collection, and the company did not plan to make major annual changes to its line. Ebel watches sold at retail SFr. 1,000 to 15,000. The company had five models and realized 90 percent of its sales from the top three. The company's goal was to create a strong brand image. Using its leader model, Ebel promoted its watch lines with the slogan "architects of time."

Ebel moved into electronic movements in 1978. With that change in technology the company enjoyed a boost in sales. In 1985 Ebel was assembling 300,000 units per year. The company maintained tight control over its suppliers. Ebel had production and development contracts with its movement suppliers and partial ownership of its case and bracelet manufacturer. The company still assembled private label watches for Cartier. In 1975 sales to Cartier represented 90 percent of sales; 10 years later these sales represented less than 50 percent of total. It was estimated that Cartier sales provided about 25 percent of Ebel's profits in 1984.

Blum maintained close personal contact with the end customer with frequent visits to jewelry stores. His goal was to keep a close eye on stock levels at jewelry stores and avoid a build up of stocks in the distribution channels. He also wanted to ensure that the jewelry store's image was in line with the Ebel image.

In addition to its "architects of time" media advertising, Ebel used sports sponsorship as a means of building an image with the public. Ebel became one of the first watch companies to actively use sporting events for its watches' promotion. Ebel sponsorships included a soccer team in Geneva and tennis and golf matches.

In the 1980s Ebel was broadening its business activities. It expanded its product line by becoming the distributor for Schaeffer pens. Ebel also entered the clothing business with the American firm, Fenn, Wright and Manson. They opened a boutique in Geneva, and others were in the planning stages. Finally, Ebel was the agent for Olivetti computers for the French-speaking part of Switzerland. The distribution company employed 12 people, including programmers.

## Recent Entrants in the Watch Industry

A new group of "outsiders" and "newcomers" has entered the global watch industry. Many of these companies (or current ownership) have been operating for 10 years or less. With few exceptions, these "watchmakers" subcontracted all production and assembly, mostly in Switzerland. The watches were then positioned in the market as high fashion pieces.

Included in this group were Raymond Weil, founded in 1976. Within 10 years the company had reached annual sales levels of approximately 300,000 quartz watches, at prices ranging from SFr. 500 to 1,700. All work was subcontracted to companies and individual component manufacturers and assemblers in the Jura region of Switzerland. The company employed 15 people for design, marketing, and sales and administration. One-third of all wholesale activities were captively held.

Weil's success in the watch industry was attributed to the company's sense of style and fashion. A new collection was introduced each year with six woman's and six man's watches. Weil was constantly responding to changes in consumer tastes and the latest trend. His 1985 spring collection was named for a hit movie, *Amadeus*, a biography of the life of Mozart. Raymond Weil had a limited budget for its advertising and promotion expenditures, relying on a few well-placed messages and style to sell its products.

Cartier watches were classic in design and limited to 15 different models. Cartier subcontracted its watches from Ebel. The Cartier watch lines did include models which sold for as much as SFr. 100,000. Most Cartier watches sold at prices ranging from SFr. 1,200 to 25,000. Most Cartier watches were quartz. Selling at a level of 450,000 units per year, the watch was an addition to the company's collection of accessories and jewelry. The watches were sold through the company's specialized retail stores and independent boutiques and jewelry and fashionable department stores all over the world. Watch advertising and promotion expenses were minimized because the company's name was well recognized in the market place, and the watch fell under the umbrella of the company's other accessories.

Gucci watches were sold by an independent entrepreneur who licensed the Gucci name. These A watches were sold at Gucci shops and by independent jewelers and high-fashion department stores and boutiques. Annual volumes for Gucci watches were estimated at 400,000 units. The company did not advertise heavily and relied on the Gucci name for prestigious name brand identity.

## SUMMARY

Thomke knew that there were a number of options open to him to bring Tissot from its current status of a "branded commodity." He estimated that relaunch in Europe would be a minimum of SFr. 12 million. Costs for reintroducing Tissot to the United States would be even greater. To afford these marketing expenses, Tissot marketing and profit margins would have to improve, and sales volumes would have to grow. Thomke knew he could shift prices and was considering pushing Tissot prices downward to the bottom of the B group. A downward price shift would require a considerable increase in volume if the Tissot brand was to be profitable. The producer's margin decreased as watches moved down-market to the B and C segments. Thomke knew that producers of expensive watches which had a strong positive image with consumers could command high ex-factory prices. This provided the luxury watch firms with considerable margins for marketing expenditures and profit.

Thomke believed that to operate profitably a watch had to capture at least 10 percent of its market segment. He wanted to produce a workable brand strategy which would allow Tissot to gain at least 10 percent of its segment. Thomke had several key factors to consider. The fast-paced technological changes of the 1970s had slowed, and the traditional watch buying market was maturing. However, he saw that nontraditional approaches in the industry had allowed new entrants such as Raymond Weil and SWATCH to successfully gain footholds and profits in the global watch industry.

# Pneumatiques Michelin IA

In July 1969, the Michelin Tire Company announced it would establish production facilities in Nova Scotia, Canada. Approximately 85 percent of its production of steel-belted truck tires was reported to be for export to the United States, with the balance for Canada, the Caribbean, and South America. Local government officials and politicians were overjoyed at the news of the planned investment of nearly $100 million and the creation of 1,300 jobs. Their happiness was renewed in late 1971, when the plant began operating and the company announced an intended expansion of $40 million which would add a facility for making passenger car tires and could create another 1,300 jobs.

The Michelin investment in Canada was induced by major grants and other financial assistance by both federal and provincial govern-

This case was prepared by David Harkleroad, Research Assistant, under the supervision of professors Dominique Héau and José de la Torre at the European Institute of Business Administration (INSEAD), Fontainebleau, France. It incorporates material from a case series entitled "Michelin Tires Manufacturing Co. of Canada (A) through (D)," prepared by David E. Osborn under the supervision of Professor Donald H. Thain at the University of Western Ontario, Canada. Copyright © 1973 by The University of Western Ontario. INSEAD revision, 1982.

ments. In a discussion of the details before the Public Accounts Committee of the Nova Scotia Legislature on March 28, 1972, Finance Minister Peter Nicholson said there was "nothing new or strange in this day and age for international companies such as Michelin to be given incentives of various types. Countries all over the world were offering incentives, and few eyebrows were raised."

Nicholson's comments were made in response to the reaction of the powerful American tire and rubber lobby. On February 8, 1972, this organization had initiated a complaint with the U.S. Treasury Department of unfair export competition. The Treasury Department began an investigation to determine whether the Canadian government assistance to Michelin constituted a "bounty or grant" in violation of U.S. laws deserving of tariff retaliation. The outcome of the investigation threatened a new round in an international trade war, a chilling prospect to those concerned about Canada's chance for success in such a war.

## MICHELIN

Michelin was Europe's largest tire manufacturer and the third largest worldwide. Its history was inseparably linked with that of the pneumatic tire. The Michelin organization began in 1889 when the brothers Edouard and André Michelin made tires for horse-drawn carriages in Clermont-Ferrand, France, where the company headquarters were still located in 1972. In 1891, Michelin took out its first patent on the pneumatic tire, and, since that time, the company had constantly introduced innovations in the field. The most notable of these was the radial tire, which Michelin first introduced in France in 1948.

In 1959, François Michelin took command of the organization. His two main objectives were to reinforce Michelin's specialization in tire manufacture and to test the radial tire on European markets. From 1960 to 1965, the company increased the number of manufacturing plants from eight to ten in France and added five others in the rest of Europe. In 1963, it built a test center with 32 kilometers (km) of roads, second only in size to Goodyear's Nevada test track in the United States. In the same year, he created the Michelin Investment Holdings Company in Bermuda to serve as a focal point for the group's future activities in the western hemisphere.

A high priority was given at Michelin to technical research and development, and the resulting product improvements played a major role in the growing "radialization" of the European tire market. In addition, quality control and marketing planning were stressed. The Michelin radial tire enjoyed a reputation as one of the world's premier automobile tires and accounted for 80 percent of Michelin's production in 1971. The company's early commitment to the radial market put it at a great advantage relative to its European competitors, who did not begin radial tire production until the mid 1960s. By the end of the decade Michelin controlled over one-third of the total European tire market through its dominant position in the radial segments. This represented a total volume of about 200,000 tires per day.[1]

One characteristic of the Michelin organization was its penchant for secrecy, which led to many rumors and anecdotes about its real na-

ture. Complex security arrangements limited company personnel to their own departments or work areas, and all management personnel were required to take an oath of secrecy. Journalists, bankers, and academics received little information from the company even when it had a good story to tell. It was said that only two or three people outside the Michelin family knew all the company's organization.

The secrecy surrounding Michelin had not obscured its financial success. Although its reported figures were inadequate for complete analysis, Michelin's operating margins appeared to be 13 percent of sales. It had a record of steadily rising profits, unlike the four U.S. giants—Goodyear, Firestone, Uniroyal, and Goodrich—and unlike its chief European rival, Dunlop-Pirelli. In Europe, where it ranked first in tire sales, it employed over 70,000 persons, its 1971 sales were over $1.5 billion, and its cash flow that year was estimated at just under $200 million. These figures did not include Michelin holdings in Citroën automobiles or in Kléber-Colombes (the number-two French tire manufacturer), independently managed companies registered on the Paris Stock Exchange.

## THE CANADIAN TIRE INDUSTRY

The Canadian tire industry in 1972 was almost totally comprised of subsidiaries of foreign (mainly U.S.) tire manufacturers. Six companies, with a total of 10 plants, were engaged in the manufacture of tires; 7 of these plants were located in Ontario, two were in Quebec, and one was in Alberta. Goodyear Canada was the largest with four plants. Its U.S. parent was the world's largest rubber producer with total 1971 sales of $3.2 billion, 60 percent of which were tires. Other subsidiaries were: Firestone, Uniroyal, B. F. Goodrich, Dunlop, and Mansfield-

---

[1] In 1965, Sears and Roebuck, the world's largest retailer, had begun distributing Michelin's radials in the United States under its own private label. Total volume in this line represented fewer than 1 million units per year by 1971.

**EXHIBIT 1**

**SELECTED FINANCIAL INFORMATION: CANADIAN SUBSIDIARIES OF U.S. TIRE MANUFACTURERS**

| Year | Gross revenue (C$ million) | Goodyear Operating profit margin before taxes (%) | Net income (C$ thousand) |
|---|---|---|---|
| 1966 | 136.6 | 9.2 | 4,533 |
| 1967 | 149.8 | 8.6 | 4,128 |
| 1968 | 154.2 | 3.0 | 171 |
| 1969 | 175.8 | 4.8 | 1,232 |
| 1970 | 175.6 | 9.7 | 3,291 |
| 1971 | 185.4 | 13.3 | 7,753 |

| | B. F. Goodrich (C$ million) | | Firestone (C$ million) | |
|---|---|---|---|---|
| | 1970 | 1971 | 1970 | 1971 |
| Sales | 84.8 | 98.5 | 136.5 | 147.8 |
| Operating profit | 5.2 | 6.9 | 13.4 | 15.1 |
| Net income | 2.0 | 1.8 | 4.2 | 5.6 |
| Dividend | 0.3 | 0.3 | 2.7 | 0.8 |
| Operating profit margin before taxes | 6.1% | 7.0% | 9.8% | 10.2% |
| Current assets | 37.7 | 41.7 | 81.4 | 80.4 |
| Fixed assets | 20.6 | 19.7 | 61.0 | 60.0 |
| Other assets | 0.6 | 0.6 | 1.6 | 1.3 |
| Total assets | 58.9 | 62.0 | 144.0 | 141.7 |
| Equity | 27.9 | 30.4 | 54.6 | 59.4 |
| LT debt | 8.4 | 7.6 | 27.5 | 26.0 |

*Source:* Financial Post Corporation and company reports.

Denman General Ltd. Canadian subsidiaries, except Goodyear, did not publish financial information before 1972, when the government required federally incorporated companies to file certain financial information. Exhibit 1 summarizes available information.

Passenger car tires dominated the tire market (Exhibit 2), and subsidiaries of major U.S. auto manufacturers were the main consumers of the original equipment (OEM) tire production. Original equipment sales had been cyclical following the auto industry, despite the boost which the 1965 Auto Pact (see Appendix) gave to the Canadian segment of that industry.

Replacement tires accounted for approximately two-thirds of Canadian tire production by volume and for a higher portion by sales value and profits. Growth had been slow in recent years due to several factors: low auto production years in 1969 and 1970, the growth of foreign car imports, longer-lasting tires, and the increasing popularity of European radial tires, which were considered by many consumers to be technically superior to American tires.

Although domestic production tended to be roughly equivalent to domestic sales, the numbers and value of imported tires had increased markedly in recent years (Exhibit 3). At the same

## EXHIBIT 2

**CANADIAN TIRE PRODUCTION, 1962–1971**

| Year | Passenger car tires | Truck, bus & grader tires | Industrial tires | Tractors & implement tires | Airplane tires | Motorcycle tires |
|------|--------|--------|--------|--------|--------|--------|
| 1962 | 9,180,939 | 1,077,875 | 70,149 | 415,028 | 15,577 | 1,141 |
| 1963 | 10,545,390 | 1,207,215 | 75,944 | 515,205 | 13,340 | 1,154 |
| 1964 | 11,431,427 | 1,356,874 | 85,201 | 476,428 | 10,279 | 1,503 |
| 1965 | 12,052,428 | 1,491,641 | 133,924 | 458,261 | 11,907 | 1,320 |
| 1966 | 13,527,315 | 1,784,264 | 181,848 | 509,888 | 13,013 | 2,229 |
| 1967 | 13,998,051 | 1,849,185 | 176,740 | 488,769 | 18,268 | 1,579 |
| 1968 | 14,577,416 | 1,777,826 | 170,203 | 382,235 | 9,014 | 720 |
| 1969 | 16,614,725 | 2,006,635 | 239,744 | 332,522 | 9,775 | 1,650 |
| 1970 | 17,720,048 | 2,086,849 | 176,405 | 300,269 | 1,914 | 591 |
| 1971 | 16,891,603 | 2,213,828 | 206,093 | 327,050 | n.a. | 1,391 |

n.a. = not available.
*Source:* Rubber Association of Canada.

time, the Canadian industry had found it increasingly difficult to maintain its exports to foreign markets, where local productive capacity was greatly enlarged during the 1960s.

In the opinion of industry spokespeople, the import threat was likely to increase. Canada was bound, as a signatory to the General Agreement on Tariffs and Trade (GATT), to gradually lower her tariffs on a wide range of products, including tires and rubber products. This would create obvious difficulties for the Canadian tire industry, which had been created and developed behind a high tariff wall of 17.5 percent.

## FEDERAL-PROVINCIAL RELATIONSHIPS IN CANADA

In the early 1970s, Prime Minister Pierre Trudeau was at the height of his popularity because of his charisma and because of a booming econ-

## EXHIBIT 3

**CANADIAN TIRE PRODUCTION AND TRADE, 1967–1971**

| Year | Volume (thousands of units) | | | Value ($ million) | | | | |
|------|------|------|------|------|------|------|------|------|
| | | | | Imports | | | Exports | |
| | Production | Imports | Exports | Total | United States | France | Total | United States |
| 1967 | 16,535 | 2,767 | 825 | 17.4 | 10.5 | n.a.* | 15.5 | 11.1 |
| 1968 | 16,917 | 4,901 | 801 | 40.6 | 30.7 | 3.4 | 11.9 | 8.6 |
| 1969 | 19,206 | 6,237 | 529 | 51.6 | 38.9 | 3.7 | n.a.† | n.a.† |
| 1970 | 20,285 | 5,752 | 987 | 46.0 | 27.2 | 5.0 | n.a.† | n.a.† |
| 1971 | 19,640 | 3,623 | 634 | 69.4 | 41.9 | 7.7 | 18.7 | 14.7 |

n.a. = not available.
*Statistics for Europe not broken down by country.
†Statistics for exports given only for rubber industry, not broken down for tires.
*Source:* "Trade by Commodities," *OECD Abstracts;* D.B.S.

omy. He had been elected prime minister in 1969, and the ruling Liberal Party had been in power for a decade. Trudeau had a slim majority in the national legislature, but Canadian politicians almost always voted with the party, and even a majority of one would virtually ensure the passage of important legislation. The opposition was divided between the Conservatives and the New Democrats, a socialist party that had its roots in Western Canada. Robert Stanfield, the Conservative Party leader, was born in Nova Scotia, not far from the location of the Michelin plants.

Trudeau had increased the role of the federal government in economic affairs, and the federal assistance provided to Michelin was a direct result of his actions to channel money from the industrialized provinces into the more traditionally agricultural provinces. Previously, the national government had not played as large a role in internal matters as in the United States. The provincial governments had power over taxes, health, education, welfare, and natural resources.

Four of the provincial governments (Nova Scotia, New Foundland, Prince Edward Island, and Quebec) were controlled by Liberal governments, three by the Conservatives and three by the New Democrats. The Atlantic provinces had traditionally been a Liberal stronghold.

## NOVA SCOTIA AND
## THE ATLANTIC PROVINCES

Nova Scotia is one of Canada's easternmost provinces, almost an island, connected to the mainland by a narrow land bridge. Before the American Revolution, Halifax, the provincial capital, was one of the continent's main ports of call. As the years passed, however, the westward expansion moved industries inland toward the Great Lakes area. The province's major activities included coal mining, fishing, shipbuilding, and farming. There were few industries and a lack of a skilled industrial labor force. The coal industry was a major employer until the 1960s, when a major mine disaster and the gen-

eral trend away from coal as a primary fuel significantly reduced the importance of this industry for the region.

The Atlantic provinces, which included Nova Scotia, New Foundland, Prince Edward Island and New Brunswick, traditionally had been areas of low industrial development and high unemployment, as can be seen in Exhibit 4.

## BUSINESS-GOVERNMENT RELATIONS
## IN THE CANADIAN TIRE INDUSTRY

During World War II, industry members had been encouraged to cooperate to obtain maximum efficiency and effectiveness for the war effort. This cooperation continued until 1952, when all Canadian tire manufacturers, a distribution company, and the Rubber Association of Canada (RAC) were convicted of price fixing and prohibited from further cooperative activities with respect to the manufacture and sales of tires and tubes. Henceforth, competition was keen, and cooperation only occurred in areas of obvious common interest such as briefs to the government on such matters as legislation and freight rates.

In the early 1960s, discussions were held between industry executives and officials of the Federal Department of Industry on the question of including tires in the U.S.-Canada Auto Pact. Eventually, due in part to the apprehension among industry leaders about the wisdom of such a move, tires were excluded from the 1965 agreement. In 1966, a survey on the amount of value added in production by Canadian manufacturers was conducted with the implied intention of adding tires to the Auto Pact, but nothing concrete developed.

These events lingered in the minds of industry leaders, and as one later stated, they were "sick of playing 20 questions with the government." However, by the late 1960s, many executives were concerned about the low profitability and the ever-widening gap in productivity between U.S. and Canadian producers, particularly with respect to production of industrial products. A productivity gap was suspected in

EXHIBIT 4

**TRENDS IN INCOME, LABOR MARKETS, INVESTMENT AND PRODUCTION, EACH REGION COMPARED TO CANADA, 1950–1971** (Averages for Periods Shown, Canada = 100)

| Regions | Years | Earned income per head* | Unemployment rate | Labor force participation rate | In manufacturing per head | |
|---|---|---|---|---|---|---|
| | | | | | Total investment | Value added† |
| Atlantic | 1950–1959 | 63 | 176 | 88 | 44 | 35 |
| | 1960–1969 | 66 | 167 | 87 | 66 | 35 |
| | 1970–1971 | 69 | 132 | 86 | 131 | 35 |
| Quebec | 1950–1959 | 86 | 131 | 100 | 39 | 105 |
| | 1960–1969 | 89 | 134 | 98 | 88 | 102 |
| | 1970–1971 | 88 | 131 | 98 | 67 | 99 |
| Ontario | 1950–1959 | 120 | 74 | 105 | 142 | 153 |
| | 1960–1969 | 119 | 71 | 105 | 143 | 151 |
| | 1970–1971 | 120 | 77 | 104 | 137 | 150 |
| Prairie | 1950–1959 | 99 | 61 | 99 | 51 | 38 |
| | 1960–1969 | 95 | 63 | 102 | 42 | 40 |
| | 1970–1971 | 92 | 73 | 102 | 46 | 41 |
| British Columbia | 1950–1959 | 118 | 116 | 96 | 138 | 95 |
| | 1960–1969 | 110 | 117 | 99 | 129 | 92 |
| | 1970–1971 | 108 | 119 | 102 | 120 | 87 |
| Canada (actual levels) | 1950–1959 | C$1,169 | 4.2% | 53.5% | C$98 | C$537 |
| | 1960–1969 | C$1,177 | 5.1% | 54.6% | C$146 | C$691 |
| | 1970–1971 | C$2,653 | 6.2% | 55.9% | C$288 | C$920 |

*Earned income = Personal income *minus* government transfer payments (excluding interest) *minus* interest, dividends, and miscellaneous investment income of persons.

†The last two figures for each region and Canada apply to 1960–1967 and 1968–1969 respectively.

*Source:* Statistics Canada.

tire production as well, but there were no meaningful comparative figures due to the lack of cooperation within the industry. Some thought that the problems of the tire industry were those of distribution: Tires, due to their bulkiness, had high distribution and handling costs. Others thought that savings could be effected by rationalization with their U.S. parents, but one study by Goodyear indicated that the possible savings were not as much as expected. Nevertheless, the financial and labor resources of the tire companies in Canada were being stretched very thin. The number of tires (i.e., types of tires) had proliferated tremendously in the 1960s, and, in addition to their own brand names, the companies were producing private brands for a multitude of outlets. The resulting short runs, rising costs, and rising interest rates caused financial problems which were exacerbated in some companies by expensive union strikes.

In 1969, talk about rationalization resumed among industry executives, initiated by W. V. Turner, the president of the RAC. However, fear of antitrust caused them to go to the newly formed Department of Industry, Trade and Commerce (DITC), which appointed a study team. Despite a long-standing antagonism toward the government, industry executives agreed to provide cost figures on which a complete analysis of industrial rubber products could be based, even though they would not divulge such information to each other.

This third attempt at industry-government cooperation was to fare no better than the first two. At a meeting of the RAC board of directors in late 1969, the members reopened the question of some study on the tire industry to determine whether a program of rationalization should be analyzed in detail. Government officials scheduled a series of meetings with the presidents of each company, but these were later postponed. No explanation for the postponement was given until January 1970, when Turner was asked to come to Ottawa. At that meeting, he was informed that the federal government would allow Michelin to import radials not produced in its Nova Scotia plant dutyfree for a period of three years, in addition to other financial assistance. Turner listened in stunned silence, asked some questions to ensure that he understood completely, and reported back to the industry.

The industry was shocked by the news. It maintained that it had no opposition to the incentives offered to Michelin, especially since these grants were available to all. The contentious point was the remission-of-duty agreement. To the industry, the government, in addition to "bankrolling" Michelin with loans and grants, had by virtue of the dutyfree provision created an effective rationalization program which they had been seeking but which would not benefit them.

## THE ORIGINS OF THE MICHELIN DEAL

The story of Michelin's introduction to Canada was one of intrigue and political maneuvering on a complex, international scale. One of the central figures was Robert Manuge, the executive vice-president of Industrial Estates Ltd (IEL), a Crown Corporation which was the industrial development agency of Nova Scotia. On a flight from New York to Montreal in November 1967, Manuge shared a newspaper with a lady beside him. He discovered that she was the wife of the Canadian head of Citroën, and he met her husband upon landing at Montreal

airport. An appointment was arranged for Manuge with Maurice Sodoyer, the Michelin representative in Montreal, who suggested that Manuge contact Michelin headquarters in Clermont-Ferrand.

IEL had been organized in 1957 to introduce secondary manufacturing to Nova Scotia. It was empowered to lend as much as 100 percent of the cost of land and buildings, and at least 60 percent on machinery, all at current interest rates. Up to 1971, IEL's clients numbered 70 companies, 20 of which were already in business before they received any IEL grants. Of these, 17 either sold out to other companies or ceased operations entirely, but 80 percent of the new IEL-sponsored companies survived. The biggest blots on the IEL record were two bad investments in Clairtone Sound Corporation and Deuterium of Canada Ltd. IEL management participated in the initial project started by Clairtone costing roughly $4.5 million for a stereo hi-fi plant, and in the first phase of the Deuterium heavy-water plant which represented a $30 million investment. Expansion of these projects ultimately resulted in total investments of $20 million for Clairtone and $120 million for Deuterium. One newspaper report said: "it was no secret that the Michelin deal might go some way to getting IEL management off the hook." The same could undoubtedly have been said of many Nova Scotia politicians and business leaders who took part in these earlier decisions.

In December 1967, Manuge wrote a letter to Michelin setting out the advantages of a Nova Scotia location to serve both the U.S. and Canadian markets. He received a reply which stated that the company was interested but that negotiations must be carried out in secret. In February 1968, Manuge began a series of negotiations, involving over 40 trans-Atlantic flights, under the name Project Y. Almost all of his colleagues were unaware of the real nature of Project Y, and all visits of Michelin officials to Halifax were carefully disguised. At the same time, a New York lawyer was carrying on an investigation with IEL officials on behalf of an undisclosed client about the possibilities of locating in Nova Scotia. Manuge discovered much later that the lawyer had been retained by Michelin to establish independently IEL's veracity and competence.

On July 28, 1969, Frank H. Sobey, president of IEL, announced that the negotiations with Michelin had been successfully concluded. The company was to establish two plants in Nova Scotia: a steel cord plant in the town of Bridgewater, to employ 500 persons, at an estimated cost of $10.1 million; and a tire factory in the town of Granton, which would use the output of the steel cord plant to produce steel belted radial truck tires. Total output was estimated by industry sources to be between 5,000 and 8,000 truck tires a day. The tire factory would cost $41 million and would employ 800 persons. Cost overruns eventually brought plant costs to $22.5 and $62.2 million for Bridgewater and Granton respectively.

Disappointment about the IEL announcement was particularly evident in Quebec. A Quebec government source said that François Michelin was so bitterly opposed to Charles de Gaulle and his love affair with Quebec that it was almost impossible for Michelin even to discuss the possibility of locating a plant in Quebec.

## THE AGREEMENT AND INCENTIVES

The total package of financial incentives, as announced in January 1970, included provincial, local, and federal incentives:

1. IEL agreed to provide a $50 million, 6 percent loan to Michelin (Canada) to finance the construction of the two plants: a 10-year loan of $34 million and an 18-year loan of $16 million secured by a mortgage on the land, buildings, and machinery owned by Michelin in Nova Scotia.
2. IEL would grant a total of $7.6 million for capital costs ($5 million) and training of employees ($2.6 million).
3. The municipalities of Granton and Bridgewater reduced the taxes payable by Michelin to 1 percent of the real and personal property tax assessment, for a period of 10 years. In the absence of such agreements, the tax would have been 3.7 percent in Bridgewater and 2.1 percent in Granton.
4. The 40-acre plant site valued at $10,000 was donated to Michelin by the town of Bridgewater.
5. The first form of federal assistance offered was a cash grant of $8.07 million under the Area Development Incentives Act (ADIA).[2] The amount of the grant, which was based on the amount of investment and number of jobs, would be advanced once commercial production levels were achieved.
6. The second form of assistance, also provided under the ADIA, was an accelerated depreciation of capital costs. The company could write off building costs at 20 percent per year, and machinery at 50 percent per year, profits permitting.
7. Michelin was allowed to import much of its manufacturing machinery dutyfree.
8. The federal government would grant Michelin Canada the right to import tires into Canada free of duty for a period of 3 years. The imported tires had to be of a type and size not produced by Michelin in Canada, and the offer was conditional upon the dutyfree privilege not disrupting the operations of existing tire producers in Canada. The confidential letters of offer, written by then Finance Minister Edgar Benson, with the approval of his cabinet colleagues, were imprecise as to the date of commencement for the dutyfree priv-

---

[2]The ADIA was an outgrowth of a program begun in 1963 to attract industry to areas where there was an exceptionally high degree of unemployment. Under that early program, new industries locating in such areas were eligible for a 3-year tax holiday and accelerated capital cost allowances. The income tax benefits did not prove as great an incentive as had been expected, as the applicant companies often had little net income in their first few years of operation. To correct this deficiency, Parliament passed the ADIA in 1965, which provided cash grants to companies locating in areas designated by degree of unemployment, nonfarm family income and distribution of income.

ilege but suggested that it would occur no later than commencement of production in Canada.

The first three forms of federal assistance were available to all qualifying companies. The tariff remission was a form of assistance which the government of Canada had granted in the past in circumstances where it considered it to be appropriate. The tariff remission meant that Michelin would not have to pay the duty of 17.5 percent otherwise imposed on tires imported into Canada. Tires imported into Canada and subsequently exported to the United States would be subject to the U.S. duty on tires of 4 percent, as if they were imported directly from France. It was believed in some quarters that if Canada had not agreed to compensate Michelin for the amount of duty payable on imports of such tires, the company might have planned a different and less efficient product mix, or it would probably have produced a lower volume of tires of a greater variety of types and sizes, which might have reduced the employment opportunities offered by the project.

Michelin officials made it quite clear that they were not seeking any special treatment or benefit, that they would have no objection to the same arrangement being made with other Canadian manufacturers, and that they had no objection to the tariff on tires being reduced or removed. This latter course was not acceptable to the government as there was not sufficient time to assess its impact on the total industry. However, the chance for increasing employment in a region where unemployment was unusually high was of considerable interest, and the government was also attracted by the fact that it was an industrial development project rationalized to meet the standards of world competition. Michelin would manufacture certain types and sizes of truck tires in Canada and other types and sizes of truck, passenger, and light commercial vehicle tires would be supplied from European plants. Michelin's Canadian market was, of course, not large enough to warrant manufacture in Canada solely for the domestic market, but the import provisions would allow long production runs which would ensure that the Nova Scotia plant remained competitive on an international basis.

## CANADIAN INDUSTRY REACTION

Some Canadian government officials had formed the opinion that the tire industry was poorly managed and fraught with bickering and lack of direction. Events before and after Michelin's entry supported this.

The existing companies had different strengths and weaknesses and different commitments to the future. It was thus impossible to agree on any common action, since any suggestion invariably favored one company over another. Unanimity was reached only on the demand that government rescind the tariff agreement with Michelin. One proposal that received some support was that, as was the case under the Auto Pact, manufacturers could import tires dutyfree provided they maintained certain production levels in Canada and increased such production proportionately to the Canadian tire market. The agreement lasted two days, as one company immediately opposed it. Discussions continued through 1970 and into 1971, but nothing was accomplished. When Michelin's plant produced its first tires in October 1971, the issue arose again.

In late 1971, the executive committee of the Rubber Association of Canada met with government officials for further general discussion. The industry representatives discovered that one of their members, Uniroyal, had made a proposal to the government before their arrival, asking the minister of Finance for dutyfree entry of radial steel tires and equipment when imported by that company into Canada. This proposal was meant to equate Uniroyal with the arrangement made for Michelin. In addition, it was implied by Uniroyal that they would use whatever influence they had in the United States to get the Rubber Manufacturers' Association to back off its stand on countervailing duties. The proposal therefore had considerable appeal at that time to government officials. Although the proposal was not new, the break in ranks left the RAC executives with a bad taste in their mouths.

The government persisted, especially since dutyfree imports would permit increasing efficiency through specialization. The original proposal was later expanded into four:

1. Dutyfree entry of radial steel tires and equipment, when imported by manufacturers of radial steel tires in Canada.
2. Dutyfree entry of radial steel tires and equipment, when imported by manufacturers of tires generally.
3. Dutyfree entry of radial steel tires and equipment by any company doing business in Canada.
4. A reduction of the tariff from 17.5 percent to 4 percent on all tires on a most-favored nation basis.

The manufacturers rejected the third proposal, which would permit their customers to import directly from the United States. The fourth proposal upset the companies greatly, since it would radically change the nature of Canadian production. Dunlop, which did not plan to produce radials in Canada, favored the second proposal. However, Firestone had recently decided to invest in Canadian steel-cord production and would oppose any scheme that would eliminate what it thought was a competitive advantage. Goodyear wanted nothing less than the Michelin deal, though it preferred that the deal be dropped. The disagreement left most executives believing that their problems would have to be solved by themselves.

Growing U.S. opposition to Michelin was beginning to concern Canadian government officials. One company president felt that if one proposal were accepted, it would mean the companies would agree to dissuade their U.S. parents from opposing Michelin. However, the Michelin threat was different to each country in both nature and degree, and the Canadian government could not be sure how much influence the subsidiaries could have on their parents.

## U.S. INDUSTRY REACTION TO THE MICHELIN GRANTS

In bringing their complaint before the U.S. Customs Court, the U.S. industry requested that the government apply duties ranging from $41.60 a tire in 1972, to $1.06 a tire from 1982 to 1989. Though directed at Michelin, such action would bring the whole Canadian policy of regional development into question. This was happening at a time when the United States had suffered its worst balance-of-trade deficit in history (and the first since World War II), which had led to the Nixon "shock" of August 1971 and the subsequent devaluation of the dollar by 10 percent in December of that year. Facing growing subsidies and grants for industrial development in Canada, Europe, and the developing world, U.S. officials wondered where to draw the line. Section 303 of the Tariff Act provided that:

> Whenever any country . . . or other political subdivision of government . . . shall pay or bestow, directly or indirectly, any bounty or grant upon the manufacture or production or export of any article . . . manufactured or produced . . . in such country . . . , and such article is dutiable under . . . this Act, then, upon the importation of any such article . . . into the United States . . . whether . . . imported directly from the country of production or otherwise, there shall be levied and paid, . . . in addition to the duties otherwise imposed by this Act, an additional duty equal to the net amount of such bounty or grant.

There was obviously plenty of room for interpretation. The fact that 1972 was an election year in both Canada and the United States would probably influence the weight accorded to different factors in the final decision. Yet, countervailing duty was a strong weapon. It had first been used in the United States in the 1890s to protect the domestic sugarbeet industry from German producers who received direct export subsidies. The legislation had later been amended

---
**EXHIBIT 5**
---

**U.S.-CANADIAN TRADE, 1968–1971** ($ Million)

|  | 1968 | 1969 | 1970 | 1971 |
|---|---|---|---|---|
| U.S. exports to Canada |  |  |  |  |
| Agriculture | 462 | 527 | 556 | 544 |
| Minerals and fuels | 810 | 916 | 1,296 | 1,135 |
| Manufactures | 6,634 | 7,500 | 6,935 | 8,397 |
| Total | 7,906 | 8,943 | 8,787 | 10,076 |
| As percent of total U.S. exports | 23 | 24 | 21 | 23 |
| As percent of total Canadian imports | 73 | 73 | 71 | 70 |
| Canadian exports to United States |  |  |  |  |
| Agriculture | 504 | 568 | 669 | 659 |
| Minerals and fuels | 2,326 | 2,476 | 2,758 | 3,142 |
| Manufactures | 5,698 | 6,754 | 7,399 | 8,278 |
| Total | 8,527 | 9,798 | 10,826 | 12,079 |
| As percent of total Canadian exports | 68 | 71 | 65 | 68 |
| As percent of total U.S. imports | 27 | 29 | 28 | 28 |
| Net balance to United States | (621) | (855) | (2,039) | (2,003) |

*Source:* OECD trade statistics.

to provide relief from all bounties on exports to the United States but had been used sparingly and not at all from 1959 to 1967. Its application against Michelin would provide a further strain on already sensitive U.S.-Canadian trade relations (see Exhibit 5).

For the Canadian government, the issue was also crucial. Over 50 percent of Canada's manufacturing sector was in foreign hands, mostly U.S. hands. If U.S. laws were interpreted such that Canada's regional aid programs were declared subject to countervailing duty, the future effectiveness of such programs could be substantially reduced. The political fallout would be great if a negative decision were handed down.

---
**APPENDIX**
---

# The Automotive Products Trade Agreement of 1965[3]

In 1962, Canada established a rebate on duties paid on the import of certain automobile products. In 1963,

this was replaced by a new order allowing for dutyfree imports on car parts that would then be reexported. The response of the auto parts manufacturers in the United States was strong and unambiguous. They asserted that the Canadian rebate was a grant to stimulate Canadian exports. In such an instance, the Tariff Act required the U.S. secretary of the Treasury to apply countervailing duties.

In 1964, automotive products trade between the two countries was about $700 million, about 9 percent of the $8 billion in total annual trade between Canada and the United States. The two industries were very similar since consumers in both countries generally preferred the same types of cars and over 90 percent of Canadian auto products were made by subsidiaries of U.S. manufacturers. There was little scope for trade, particularly since Canada imposed a 17.5 percent duty on cars and up to a 25 percent duty on parts; U.S. duties amounted to 6.5 percent on cars and 8.5 percent on parts.

Canada's protective tariffs had stimulated indus-

---

[3]Taken in part from Lawrence A. Fouraker, "The Automotive Products Trade Act of 1965," in Raymond Vernon, *Manager in the International Economy*, Prentice Hall, 1968, p. 242.

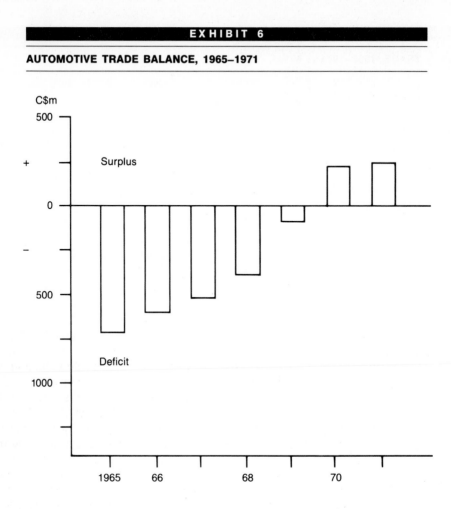

**EXHIBIT 6**

**AUTOMOTIVE TRADE BALANCE, 1965–1971**

try growth, but not efficiently. Canadian manufacturers were encouraged to include at least 60 percent Canadian value in their output. Most subsidiaries duplicated U.S. facilities and, because of the limited Canadian market, were unable to achieve similar economies of scale. As a result, Canadian autos cost about 10 percent more than those made in the United States.

The Johnson administration chose to negotiate the conflict with Canada rather than risk the possibility of retaliation in case countervailing duties were imposed. Also, security considerations required the installation of an early warning radar system along the Arctic Circle which needed Canadian consent. Eventually, an agreement was reached that provided for

- Dutyfree imports of automotive products into Canada only when imported by automotive manufacturers
- Canadian manufacturers to maintain existing production rates and to sign letters of intent to increase production to follow the growth of the Canadian market
- Remission of duties on all imports into the United States from Canada

Exhibit 6 shows the impact of the pact on the Canadian balance of automotive trade with the United States for 1965 to 1971.

# Pneumatiques Michelin IB

The world's tire industry was at a crossroads in the early 1970s. Long dominated by the five large U.S. manufacturers, new competitors and new technologies were rising to challenge their leadership position. Bridgestone and other Japanese tire manufacturers were making rapid inroads in many markets, targeting the Eastern bloc and third world nations as well as the lower end of the U.S. market with inexpensive, conventional tires. In the U.S. market alone, total Japanese share had grown from less than one percent in 1968 to over 4 percent in 1972. These imports appeared solely in the low price (under $20) segment. Michelin of France threatened on the opposite end of the spectrum with its high-quality radial tires, boasting longer tread life, improved handling, and increased gas mileage.

## THE U.S. TIRE INDUSTRY[1]

By the early 1970s, over 200 million tires a year were being sold in the United States, at a value of over $5 billion. Roughly 80 percent of the units and 65 percent of the value was for car tires; 15 percent of the units and about 25 percent of the value was for truck and bus tires; the remainder was for farm implement, specialty, and motorcycle tires. In the automobile market, roughly one-third of the tires were sold to automobile manufacturers and the remaining two-thirds were sold as replacement tires.

The U.S. tire industry began in the late nineteenth century when several firms began producing bicycle tires. Soon the industry became closely linked with automobile production, and, by 1920, there were over 175 different tire manufacturers making over 30 million tires a year. In the 1930s, falling demand and the resulting overcapacity, heightened by severe price competition between Goodyear and Firestone, forced many of the smaller manufacturers out of business. The cyclical nature of the industry had led many manufacturers to diversify to ensure more

This case was prepared by David Harkleroad, research assistant, under the supervision of professors Dominique Héau and José de la Torre at the European Institute of Business Administration (INSEAD), Fontainebleau, France. Copyright © 1982 by INSEAD.

[1]Much of the information in this case comes from *Economic Report on the Manufacture and Distribution of Automotive Tires,* U.S. Government Printing Office, March 1966. Industry observers thought the report's conclusions were still valid in the early 1970s.

**U.S. OEM PASSENGER TIRE MARKET SHARE BY TYPE OF CONSTRUCTION**

|  | Radial | Bias-belted | Conventional (4-ply) |
|---|---|---|---|
| 1968 | 2% | 6% | 92% |
| 1969 | 2 | 33 | 65 |
| 1970 | 3 | 65 | 32 |
| 1971 | 4 | 70 | 26 |
| 1972 (e) | 5 | 82 | 13 |

*Source:* Jules Pogrow, *The International Tire and Rubber Industry,* Cambridge, Mass., Harvard Business School, 1971.

steady profit growth, and only those companies with superior financial strength survived the decade. By 1945, there were only 23 tire manufacturers left, a number that was further reduced to 14 by 1965.

Significant quality improvements had been made in the first half of the century: The average tire life in 1910 was estimated at 9 months of normal use; by 1937, average tire life was nearly 3 years. The war years brought significant government subsidies to seek rubber substitutes and resulted in the discovery and introduction of synthetic rubber (butadiene) as a major raw material. Most of the subsequent improvements were the result of new materials and of better tread and rim design.

Beginning in the 1960s, manufacturers experimented with new tire types. Traditionally, tires consisted of four-cord plies laid at 45-degree angles to the tread (Appendix A describes the various types of tires). Early in the 1960s, in an attempt to reduce labor input,[2] manufacturers reduced the number of plies from four to two while keeping the overall thickness constant. However, customers rejected this change, partly due to quality problems, resulting in one of the industry's major marketing disasters. Undaunted, Armstrong Rubber Company, a rela-

tively small firm in the industry, introduced the bias-belted tire in 1966, which consisted of the traditional four-ply construction while adding a belt between the plies and the tread. This higher-quality tire, which improved safety and durability, was heavily supported by advertising when all major competitors entered the market in 1967. Bias-belted tire sales grew spectacularly, as witnessed by the figures in Exhibit 1.

By 1971, almost all U.S. manufacturers were producing at least one line of radial tires, but manufacturers were reluctant to abandon their concentration on bias-belted tires, which, in 1972, were expected to account for about 82 percent of the original equipment market and for 35 percent of the replacement market.

## INDUSTRY STRUCTURE

Manufacture of traditional tires was characterized by few technological barriers to entry. The production process consisted of rubber mixing, stock preparation, tire building, and tire curing and was not considered difficult to master (see Appendix B). Although significant advances in automation had been made, a substantial amount of labor input was still necessary in the tire building stage, particularly because of the large number of types and sizes of tires produced; U.S. census data indicated the breakdown of production costs in 1967 to be 51 percent materials, 20 percent labor, and 29 percent overheads. The industry in North America was also highly unionized. According to the United Rubber Workers (URW) union, a member of the AFL-CIO Federation, total membership covered nearly 190,000 workers in all rubber-related industries and included about 90 percent of U.S. and Canadian tire production.

The industry was characterized by limited economies of scale in production. A plant size of 5,000 to 8,000 tires a day, representing less than 1 percent of the U.S. market, was considered cost competitive, although this depended on the mix of models in production. Investment costs for such a plant were estimated at $7 to $10 million, plus $2 million for each 1,000 units

---

[2]The wrapping of layers of fiber cord around the tire mold was done entirely by hand and required significant expertise.

of daily capacity. Larger plants, over 10,000 units per day, with more automated production systems, would cost about $50 million plus $1 million per 1,000 units after the first 10,000. Lead times for construction and start-up of a new plant normally exceeded two years.

Given the high cost of molds and the set-up times involved, average length of production runs per model had a larger impact on unit costs than total plant size. Truck tires, which had to support heavier loads, required more plies and thus a greater labor input. They also required more expensive molds which were used to produce fewer tires. The additional steps necessary to produce belted tires also tended to reduce productivity by approximately 15 percent relative to conventional or bias-belted tires. Optimal plant size was also influenced by the need to be located close to volume buyers, since transport costs for the bulky tires were high. In highly competitive markets, where no tariffs were involved, the maximum radius for shipping tires overland was about 300 miles.

Few technological and production barriers to entry would seem to imply a low industry concentration level. Yet, according to the U.S. Federal Trade Commission, "the tire industry was one of the most concentrated in our economy." In 1971, the four largest manufacturers accounted for 71 percent of shipments and the eight largest for 90 percent.

In recent years, however, the industry was characterized by low profit margins. Large volume distributors often slashed retail prices in attempts to gain market share, forcing tire manufacturers to do the same or to provide lower-quality tires at competitive prices. Government antitrust action also had a role in keeping prices depressed. In 1959, the Federal Trade Commission charged the industry with price fixing, but the manufacturers cut prices by up to 19 percent 2 months later, and the case was settled out of court in 1962. Profitability in the tire industry was lower than that in most other industries with similar concentration ratios, as shown in Exhibit 2. As a percentage of sales, tire industry profits before tax averaged about

| EXHIBIT 2 | | |
|---|---|---|
| **AFTER-TAX ROI IN VARIOUS U.S. INDUSTRIES** | | |
| | **1947–1964** | **1959–1964** |
| Motor vehicles | 18.0% | 16.4% |
| Office equipment | 17.1 | 16.0 |
| Soaps and detergents | 13.6 | 14.0 |
| Cigarettes | 12.8 | 14.1 |
| Tires | 12.0 | 9.4 |
| Metal containers | 9.7 | 8.5 |

*Source:* Federal Trade Commission.

7.8 percent during the 1960s, which compared with 8.4 percent for all manufacturing industries.

The key to the industry's profitability was the automotive market; over 50 kilograms of rubber products other than tires went into every automobile manufactured in the United States. Thus, when automotive demand slowed down in the late 1960s, the industry suffered accordingly: It experienced an operating cash deficit of $1.1 billion for the 1965 to 1969 period; debt-to-equity ratios rose on the average from 0.3 in 1961 to nearly 0.75 in 1970; and corporate liquidity (the quick ratio) declined by two-thirds. It was estimated that "to support the present level [1971] of capital expenditures (7.5 percent of net sales) . . . the industry must realize a return on assets of 10.6 percent, nearly double what was actually achieved." The industry's hopes for recovery were closely related to the success of the higher-price, higher-profit bias-belted tires.

Tire manufacturers also attempted to defend their profitability through both vertical and horizontal integration, coupled with modest research and development programs. Backward vertical integration appeared in the form of rubber plantations, chemical plants, and textile mills, with forward vertical integration into wholesale and retail sales. Manufacturers also tended to integrate horizontally into associated products, such as mechanical rubber goods, foam products, and wheels.

---

**EXHIBIT 3**

---

**MANUFACTURER'S SHARE OF THE U.S. OEM MARKET,**
**1966/1972** (Estimate)

| | General Motors | Ford | Chrysler | American Motors | Total OEM |
|---|---|---|---|---|---|
| Goodyear | 8/20 | 30/18 | 77/68 | 70/70 | 30/n.a. |
| Firestone | 25/20 | 43/43 | 4/10 | —/25 | 25/n.a. |
| Goodrich | 20/10 | 16/10 | 19/9 | 30/5 | 16/n.a. |
| Uniroyal | 42/37 | 4/13 | —/— | —/— | 25/n.a. |
| General Tire | 5/13 | 7/10 | —/13 | —/— | 4/n.a. |
| Michelin | —/— | —/6 | —/— | —/— | —/n.a. |

n.a. = not available.
*Sources: Rubber World,* January 1966; *Modern Tire Dealer,* January 1973.

## MARKETS

The *original equipment market* (OEM) generally accounted for about one-third of total industry shipments of passenger car, truck, bus, and other tires. Automobile manufacturers set specifications on tire characteristics and durability and bought solely on the basis of price within these specifications. They would change suppliers if a tire manufacturer could offer a substantial price reduction, but since the market was highly competitive (OEM tires might be sold for as little as variable cost) only the large firms could compete in this market. The advantage of supplying OEM tires lay in the need to run plants at capacity and the fact that OEM suppliers could attract replacement sales. Only the top-five tire companies sold tires in the OEM market, and their shares of this market in 1966 and 1972 are shown in Exhibit 3.

While OEM market shares remained fairly stable over time, automakers used the semiannual price and supply reviews mainly as a penalty-reward system to keep price and service characteristics of the five suppliers in line with their needs. In addition, this was a highly cyclical industry. Although new car production had grown at 4.5 percent annually between 1961 and 1971, annual fluctuations were large. Estimated new car sales for 1972 were nearly 11 million, a 7 percent increase over 1971.

The *replacement market* typically accounted for two-thirds of the unit volume and a higher than proportionate share of sales and profits. In the replacement market, since one tire appeared much the same as another, consumers often could not determine quality differences and bought either the least expensive or the brand with which their cars had been originally equipped. A 1965 survey determined that price was the most important factor to consumers, followed by wearability and general quality. Brand was a factor only to 7 percent of respondents.

In addition to the three basic technology offerings, manufacturers were forced to provide an array of sizes, tread patterns, and cosmetic treatments to meet the buying public's demand. The general assortment of combinations offered by most major manufacturers included a range of features such as those shown in Exhibit 4. For a major tire producer such as Goodyear or

---

**EXHIBIT 4**

---

**TIRE CHARACTERISTICS**

| Physical characteristics | Tread patterns | Cosmetics |
|---|---|---|
| Height and width | All-season | White walls |
| Wheel diameter | Snow | Raised letters |
| Tubeless | Off-highway | Specialty stripes |

| EXHIBIT 5 | | | |
|---|---|---|---|

**PRICE SEGMENTS IN THE U.S. REPLACEMENT TIRE MARKET, 1972**
(Percent of Total Demand by Type)

| Price bracket | Conventional | Bias-belted | Radial |
|---|---|---|---|
| Over $50 | 4.5 | 4.2 | 68.6 |
| $42.50 to $50 | 6.8 | 10.5 | 21.3 |
| $37.50 to $42.49 | 10.5 | 20.4 | — |
| $32.50 to $37.49 | 16.5 | 30.2 | 10.1 |
| $27.50 to $32.49 | 26.3 | 20.1 | — |
| $22.50 to $27.49 | 22.1 | 8.5 | — |
| Under $22.50 | 13.3 | 6.1 | — |
| | 100.0 | 100.0 | 100.0 |
| Median price | $28.05 | $34.45 | $55.20 |

*Source:* National Rubber Tire Dealers' Association.

Firestone, offering a full line of tires meant maintaining a product line with over 8,000 distinct products. Prices for tires within the three basic categories reflected this wide range of products (see Exhibit 5).

Passenger-car tires accounted for about 85 percent of total replacement tire production. Demand fluctuated on the basis of the number of 2-year-old cars on the road, average annual mileage per vehicle, and prevalent tire life. Although the average annual miles driven per car remained relatively constant, the larger pool of cars on the road translated into a 4.4 percent annual increase in total vehicle miles driven. Despite improved tire construction, a faster rate of replacement occurred during the 1960s because of higher driving speeds, heavier cars, greater popularity of power systems, the imposition of federal and state tire-safety laws, including tread depth minima, and a generally more safety-conscious public. Annual increases in replacement shipments during the sixties averaged about 7 percent. The main uncertainty concerning future growth in the market centered on the tire-life of the new bias-belted tires.[3]

---

[3]One industry estimate was that, although conventional tires had an average life of 17,500 miles, bias-belted tires might average about 20,500. In contrast, radial tires would typically exceed 30,000 miles.

Producers were expecting both the OEM and replacement markets to converge on the bias-belted tire. Consumers had increased their spending on tires since 1964 (average unit price had gone up from $21.50 to nearly $30 in 1969), which had motivated producers to broaden their lines with many new styles and performance models.

## DISTRIBUTION

Since the early part of the century, replacement tires had been distributed through independent dealers. Some dealers sold a variety of brands, but many specialized in the tires of a single manufacturer. In 1926, 80 percent of replacement tires were sold through this channel. Retail margins on major brands averaged 25 to 30 percent, but independent dealers realized most of their profits on automotive service work.

In the 1930s, the large oil companies, in an effort to gain competitive advantages against each other, began offering automotive supplies, including tires, at their service stations. They were followed by large retail chain and mail order stores which, by buying in large volume, could offer attractive prices, usually under their own private brand names. By 1940, three chains accounted for about a quarter of the replacement market. Almost 90 percent of the major oil com-

## EXHIBIT 6

### REPLACEMENT SALES BY OUTLET TYPE

|  | 1965 | 1972(e) |
|---|---|---|
| Independent dealers | 36.5% | 52.4% |
| Chain, mail-order stores | 20.5 | 17.2 |
| Service stations | 25.6 | 13.7 |
| Tire company stores | 9.9 | 10.1 |
| Department, discount stores | 5.6 | 4.2 |
| Cooperatives | 1.5 | 2.1 |
| Direct | 0.4 | 0.4 |
|  | 100.0% | 100.0% |

pany tires came from one of the four major tire producers in 1962, and these were distributed through over 200,000 outlets nationwide. Sears, the largest of the retail and mail order chain stores, sold its tires through over 800 stores and, by the early 1970s, sold more tires than anyone but Goodyear and Firestone. By 1970, private label tires accounted for 40 percent of all tires sold in the domestic replacement market. The breakdown of automobile replacement tire sales by type of outlet is shown in Exhibit 6.

The oil companies' share of distribution had significantly eroded over the past few years with the advent of self-service gas stations and increasing competition from integrated automotive service centers. The oil companies behaved much like OEMs in their buying, in that they spread their business over several major manufacturers who would emboss the same name on the tire. For example, Atlas tires (Exxon) were made by Firestone, General, Goodrich, and Goodyear.

Chain and mail-order distribution had also eroded over the past 10 years. In this channel, chains such as Sears or Montgomery Ward contracted the manufacture of private brands for their exclusive use (e.g., Allstate, Riverside). They also exercised a certain amount of market power in their buying behavior. Discount chains were often included in the same category as mail-order distributors for planning purposes. Firestone and Armstrong accounted for 70 per-

cent of sales to chain and mail-order distributors.

Company-owned stores became popular as more manufacturers integrated forward to try to capture retail margins and associated service contributions. Manufacturers only offered their company brand and house brands in company stores but usually had better inventory selection due to close communication with warehouses. Companies felt direct retail exposure gave them added information on customer buying habits and helped to build brand loyalty via service. However, ownership of retail outlets did involve increases in fixed costs and overhead in a generally fragmented service market with varying degrees of overcapacity. Firestone and Goodyear had the largest number of company-owned stores with 1,950 and 1,750 respectively.

Truck tires were sold mainly through wholesalers who provided customer service such as balancing or alignment. Although there was some transfer of brand image from automobile tires, durability was the key selling point. Truckers often bought a specified number of miles or a specified number of retreads, rather than buying just a tire.

## INTERNATIONAL COMPETITION

The U.S. tire industry had faced economic problems which were usually attributed to low productivity, high labor costs and outmoded production facilities. However, the 1960s and early 1970s brought a new source of woe to them: severe competition from foreign-made goods. Between 1963 and 1970, imported tires went from 1.8 percent to 10.6 percent of the U.S. domestic market and would have been even higher in 1971 if the Nixon administration had not imposed a 10 percent import surcharge.[4] The growth of imports as a percentage of the large replacement tire market was occurring at an even faster rate. Over the same period, U.S. tire exports exhib-

---

[4]This measure lasted only 6 months and was eliminated after the dollar was devalued by 10 percent in December 1971.

| EXHIBIT 7 |
| --- |

**FINANCIAL INFORMATION ON MAJOR U.S. TIRE COMPANIES, 1966–1971**

| | Total sales ($ millions) | Operating profit (% margin before taxes) | Net income ($ millions) | Cash flow (% of sales) |
| --- | --- | --- | --- | --- |
| **Goodyear Tire and Rubber Co. Ltd.** | | | | |
| 1966 | 2,476 | 9.5 | 118.5 | 8.2 |
| 1967 | 2,638 | 9.2 | 127.1 | 8.4 |
| 1968 | 2,926 | 10.7 | 148.3 | 8.6 |
| 1969 | 3,215 | 10.5 | 158.2 | 8.4 |
| 1970 | 3,195 | 9.0 | 129.2 | 7.9 |
| 1971 | 3,602 | 10.4 | 170.2 | 8.4 |
| **Firestone Tire and Rubber Co. Ltd.** | | | | |
| 1966 | 1,815 | 10.6 | 101.8 | 9.0 |
| 1967 | 1,875 | 10.8 | 102.3 | 9.0 |
| 1968 | 2,131 | 12.1 | 127.0 | 9.4 |
| 1969 | 2,279 | 10.6 | 116.7 | 8.6 |
| 1970 | 2,335 | 8.1 | 92.8 | 7.8 |
| 1971 | 2,484 | 9.3 | 113.5 | 8.9 |
| **Uniroyal, Inc.** | | | | |
| 1966 | 1,324 | 7.1 | 45.3 | 6.2 |
| 1967 | 1,265 | 5.4 | 33.0 | 5.4 |
| 1968 | 1,429 | 8.5 | 57.0 | 7.0 |
| 1969 | 1,554 | 6.6 | 45.6 | 6.6 |
| 1970 | 1,556 | 4.1 | 24.1 | 4.8 |
| 1971 | 1,678 | 5.6 | 43.1 | 5.7 |
| **B. F. Goodrich Co. Ltd.** | | | | |
| 1966 | 1,039 | 8.6 | 48.6 | 8.7 |
| 1967 | 1,066 | 5.8 | 29.5 | 7.3 |
| 1968 | 1,140 | 8.3 | 44.9 | 7.9 |
| 1969 | 1,229 | 7.6 | 39.9 | 7.2 |
| 1970 | 1,205 | 5.2 | 12.3 | 5.6 |
| 1971 | 1,300 | 6.9 | 29.8 | 6.8 |

*Source:* Michelin Tires Manufacturing Co. of Canada (A), University of Western Ontario, 1973.

ited a declining growth rate, and the net effect was a constant year-to-year deterioration in the U.S. balance of trade in tires. By 1971, the Rubber Manufacturers' Association estimated the unfavorable balance of trade in the U.S. rubber industry at $163 million (Exhibits 7 to 11 summarize data on the U.S. tire industry).

The tire import threat was three-pronged. First, imported cars, with imported tires, had been taking around 16 percent of the U.S. auto market. Second, Japanese and other low-wage foreign producers had been shipping in millions of replacement tires, competing for sales mainly on a price basis in small size tires (less than 13 inches). In 1970, these imports took 5.7 percent of the replacement market, up from less than 1 percent in 1963. In the first 5 months of 1971, imports from Japan soared by 195 percent over

EXHIBIT 8

## U.S. TIRE PRODUCTION AND TRADE, 1963–1971

| Year | Total market* units (million) | | | Replacement market units (million) | | | Value ($ million) | | |
|------|--------|---------|-------------------------------|--------|----------|-------------------------------|---------|---------|-------------|
| | Market | Imports | Imports as percent of market | Market | Imports† | Imports as percent of market | Imports | Exports | Net balance |
| 1963 | 139.0 | 2.6 | 1.8 | 90.1 | 0.6 | 0.6 | 28.3 | 66.5 | 38.2 |
| 1964 | 152.0 | 4.0 | 2.6 | 101.2 | 1.4 | 1.4 | 40.4 | 74.2 | 34.0 |
| 1965 | 170.0 | 4.7 | 2.8 | 108.5 | 1.5 | 1.4 | 45.1 | 85.6 | 40.5 |
| 1966 | 176.0 | 6.8 | 3.9 | 116.9 | 2.3 | 2.0 | 61.1 | 79.7 | 18.6 |
| 1967 | 178.0 | 9.4 | 5.3 | 124.3 | 3.3 | 2.7 | 88.3 | 66.6 | −21.7 |
| 1968 | 206.0 | 13.4 | 6.5 | 139.2 | 5.2 | 3.7 | 125.7 | 88.2 | −37.5 |
| 1969 | 215.0 | 16.3 | 7.8 | 149.6 | 6.5 | 4.3 | 147.1 | 87.2 | −59.9 |
| 1970 | n.a. | n.a. | 10.6 | n.a. | n.a. | 5.7 | 215.0 | 75.0 | −140.0 |
| 1971 | n.a. | n.a. | n.a. | n.a. | n.a. | n.a. | 250.0‡ | 87.0‡ | −163.0‡ |

*Automotive and truck tires only; includes tires on imported vehicles.
†Over 85 percent of these were passenger car tires.
‡Estimates.
n.a. = not available.
Source: "Trade by Commodities," OECD Abstracts; Rubber Manufacturers Association.

**EXHIBIT 9**

**U.S. TIRE SHIPMENTS, 1966–1971** (Thousand)

| | Original equipment | Replacement | Export | Total shipments | Total production |
|---|---|---|---|---|---|
| | | Passenger car tires | | | |
| 1966 | 47,362 | 101,812 | 1,783 | 150,957 | 154,516 |
| 1967 | 40,827 | 108,499 | 1,653 | 150,979 | 141,896 |
| 1968 | 49,873 | 121,088 | 2,667 | 173,628 | 177,408 |
| 1969 | 46,172 | 129,112 | 1,850 | 177,134 | 180,480 |
| 1970 | 37,535 | 129,608 | 1,497 | 168,640 | 164,571 |
| 1971 | 48,610 | 135,009 | 1,558 | 185,177 | 187,725 |
| | | Truck and bus tires | | | |
| 1966 | 7,401 | 14,613 | 650 | 22,664 | 22,872 |
| 1967 | 6,873 | 14,418 | 465 | 21,756 | 21,165 |
| 1968 | 8,488 | 16,257 | 532 | 25,277 | 25,533 |
| 1969 | 9,430 | 17,439 | 569 | 27,438 | 27,211 |
| 1970 | 8,560 | 16,713 | 402 | 25,675 | 25,680 |
| 1971 | 10,251 | 18,386 | 391 | 29,028 | 28,428 |

*Note:* Years cited are calendar years.

1970 figures. The third part of the import threat was premium-priced, high-margin radial tires.

The major shares of the import market for replacement tires were estimated by industry sources in the early 1970s to be as follows:

France: 24%
Italy: 20%

Germany: 12%
Japan: 8%
Canada: 7%
United Kingdom: 5%

Imports from Canada were mainly brought in by U.S. parent companies to buffer domestic

**EXHIBIT 10**

**U.S. TIRE INDUSTRY STATISTICS**

| | Value of shipments ($ million) | Wages ($ million) | Value added ($ million) | Capital expenditures ($ million) | Total employees (thousands) | Production workers (thousands) | Value added per production worker-hour ($) |
|---|---|---|---|---|---|---|---|
| 1966 | $3,716 | $537 | $1,768 | $153 | 85.3* | 66.3* | 10.03* |
| 1967 | 3,734 | 574 | 1,823 | 199 | 92.7 | 68.7 | 13.35 |
| 1968 | 4,269 | 687 | 2,102 | 243 | 98.5 | 76.0 | 13.35 |
| 1969 | 4,717 | 754 | 2,304 | 342 | 103.0 | 80.0 | 13.51 |
| 1970 | 4,616 | 713 | 2,389 | 272 | 102.0 | 78.0 | 14.58 |
| 1971 | 5,322 | 797 | 2,767 | 220 | n.a. | n.a. | n.a. |

*Refers to 1963.
*Note:* Percentage change for first four columns for 1971/1970 were 15.3%, 11.8%, 15.8%, and (19.1%), respectively. Percentage change for those columns for 1971/1966 (ave.) were 7.4%, 8.2%, 9.4%, and 7.5%, respectively. Figures for last three columns for a 1963–1970 average are 2.6%, 2.3%, and 5.5%, respectively. The number of establishments was 182. The four (eight) largest manufacturers accounted for 71% (90%) of domestic production.
n.a. = not available.

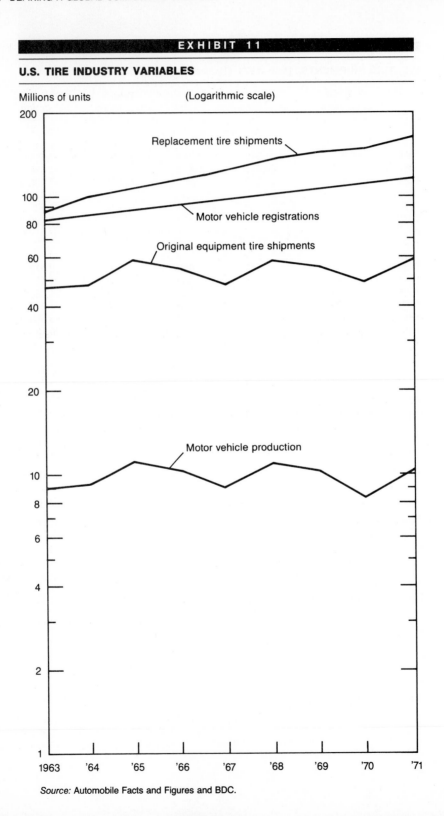

EXHIBIT 11

**U.S. TIRE INDUSTRY VARIABLES**

Millions of units          (Logarithmic scale)

Replacement tire shipments

Motor vehicle registrations

Original equipment tire shipments

Motor vehicle production

1963  '64  '65  '66  '67  '68  '69  '70  '71

*Source:* Automobile Facts and Figures and BDC.

inventories in periods of cyclical shortages. Michelin had become the major source of imported automobile tires in recent years, primarily due to its contract to supply private label radials to the Sears distribution network, and it was also a major factor in truck tire imports.

The RMA attributed the apparent loss of U.S. competitiveness to three factors: lower wage costs abroad (hourly compensation for production workers in the industry were estimated in 1970 to be $6 in the United States, $5 in Canada, $2.35 in France, and $1.75 in Japan); significantly higher tariffs in other markets (12.5 percent in Japan and 9 percent in the EEC); and unfair incentives granted exporters in other countries. Yet, the higher growth rate prevalent in overseas tire markets (113 percent versus 74 percent in the United States during the 1960s) was thought to limit foreign suppliers' capacity to expand sales to the U.S. market.

Nonetheless, the major U.S. companies were strongly represented in world markets through direct investments. Based on their dominant position in the home country and their ties to affiliates of U.S. car makers overseas, they had established a strong presence in foreign tire markets since the 1920s, as shown in Exhibit 12.

Exhibit 13 provides some estimates of the major market positions held by the largest five U.S. companies plus Michelin and Bridgestone in different world markets. Exhibit 14 shows relative market shares in the U.S. market for the same group of firms.

## POTENTIAL FOR RADIALS IN THE UNITED STATES

The future of the radial tire in the United States was, at best, uncertain in 1971. The radial tire offered some significant advantages such as longer life (Michelin offered a 40,000-mile guarantee in the late 1960s when other manufacturers were offering a 20,000- to 25,000-mile guarantee for conventional tires), 5 to 10 percent better gas mileage, and improved safety because of reduced distortion, friction, and tire heat and hence fewer blow-outs. Ralph Nader, the U.S. consumer advocate, had recently come out in favor of radial tires. However, radials were from 30 to 40 percent more expensive than other tires, and they were designed for European driving habits where the average car owner kept the car longer than the average U.S. car owner, where fuel was often double U.S. prices, where much of the driving occurred on winding roads not at all similar to the large U.S. superhighways, and where cars were designed with tougher suspensions. In Europe, by 1971, 65 percent of production was for radial tires, and some observers had been predicting since the late 1960s that as many as 70 million radials a year would be sold in the United States in the mid-1970s. However, Goodyear's chairman, Ralph de Young, predicted in 1971 that the radial would "remain a third choice for American motorists for many years to come."

De Young's statement about radials, though applicable to U.S. consumers' needs, undoubtedly also reflected resistance on the part of U.S. manufacturers to convert to radial production. The conversion from four-ply to bias-belted tires had been made, on the one hand, by expanding plant capacity to take account of lower productivity. Radial production, on the other hand, would require expensive new molds and ma-

---

### EXHIBIT 12

**COMPANY AND YEAR OF ENTRY**

| Country | Goodyear | Firestone | Goodrich |
|---|---|---|---|
| Canada | 1917 | 1919 | 1918 |
| United Kingdom | 1927 | 1928 | 1934 |
| Argentina | 1930 | 1930 | — |
| Brazil | 1938 | 1939 | 1953 |
| Sweden | 1938 | 1945 | 1939 |
| Philippines | 1956 | 1957 | 1975 |
| Japan | 1956 | 1962 | 1963 |
| France | 1959 | 1960 | 1967 |
| Portugal | 1960 | 1958 | — |
| West Germany | 1961 | 1960 | 1964 |
| Italy | 1963 | 1966 | 1972 |
| Taiwan | 1971 | — | 1973(e) |

*Source:* Company reports.

## EXHIBIT 13

### WORLD MARKET POSITION OF MAJOR TIRE PRODUCERS, 1971

| | Major producers' market share | | | | | | | Market size (millions of units) | Market growth rate (percentage of units)* |
|---|---|---|---|---|---|---|---|---|---|
| | Goodyear | Firestone | Uniroyal | Goodrich | General | Michelin | Bridgestone | | |
| Argentina | 29 | 26 | — | — | 8† | — | 4 | 5.64 | 6.1 |
| Benelux | 34 | 9† | 7† | 6† | — | 35 | — | 8.98 | 8.5 |
| Brazil | 32 | 28 | — | 8† | — | — | 5 | 10.99 | 9.3 |
| Canada | 33 | 26 | 3† | 17 | 3† | 14 | — | 26.68 | 6.4 |
| Costa Rica | 45 | 39 | — | — | — | — | 4 | .88 | (8.6) |
| France | 6 | 6 | 7 | — | — | 62 | — | 37.99 | 7.7 |
| India | 13 | 14 | — | 10† | — | — | 12 | 3.41 | 6.5 |
| Italy | 7 | 8 | 6 | — | — | 35 | — | 20.30 | (1.4) |
| Japan | — | — | — | — | — | — | 45 | 67.42 | 1.6 |
| Kenya | 31 | 80 | — | — | — | 3 | 8 | .31 | (4.1) |
| Mexico | 13 | 11 | 5 | 31 | 14 | — | 3 | 7.81 | 14.5 |
| New Zealand | 13 | 33 | — | — | 39 | — | 18 | 1.94 | 5.3 |
| Portugal | 8 | 26 | — | 14 | 9† | 15 | — | 1.91 | 3.0 |
| South Africa | 24 | 12† | 8† | — | — | — | — | 5.86 | (1.5) |
| Sweden | 13 | 22 | — | 9† | — | 18 | — | 5.86 | (1.5) |
| Thailand | 22 | 26 | — | — | — | — | 29 | 1.7 | 13.5 |
| United Kingdom | 20 | 8 | 7† | 6† | — | 20 | — | 29.39 | 1.4 |
| Venezuela | 31 | 20 | 15 | 11† | 16 | — | 6 | 2.98 | 10.5 |
| W. Germany | 9 | 7† | 6† | 5† | — | 33 | — | 43.20 | 4.3 |

*3-year average of annual compounded growth rate.
†Casewriter's estimate.

**MAJOR TIRE PRODUCERS' SHARE OF U.S. REPLACEMENT MARKET, 1966–1972 (%)**

| Year | Goodyear | Firestone | Goodrich | Uniroyal | General | Aggregate imports | Michelin | Bridgestone |
|------|----------|-----------|----------|----------|---------|-------------------|----------|-------------|
| 1966 | 27.5 | 25.3 | 9.2 | 11.0 | 2.6 | 1.0 | n.a. | n.a. |
| 1967 | 28.1 | 24.1 | 8.6 | 10.0 | 2.8 | 1.4 | n.a. | n.a. |
| 1968 | 28.1 | 24.5 | 8.8 | 10.0 | 2.7 | 2.0 | n.a. | n.a. |
| 1969 | 28.5 | 22.9 | 7.8 | 10.1 | 3.1 | 2.6 | n.a. | n.a. |
| 1970 | 28.6 | 21.6 | 7.6 | 9.9 | 3.6 | 3.6 | n.a. | n.a. |
| 1971 | 27.1 | 21.5 | 8.6 | 9.4 | 4.3 | 4.5 | n.a. | n.a. |
| 1972 | 27.2 | 22.2 | 9.0 | 9.7 | 3.8 | 5.6 | 1.6 | 0.46 |

n.a. = not available.

chines and a retraining of the labor force in the more exacting and more labor-intensive production process. Estimates of conversion costs ran as high as $2.5 million per 3,000 daily units of capacity. Though all the major U.S. manufacturers were producing limited quantities of radials, they had not yet perfected this production process. In fact, two U.S. manufacturers had introduced bias-belted tires into European markets to challenge the radials in their home ground.

# Types of Tires

Tires in 1971 consisted of three basic types: conventional four-ply tires, bias-belted, and radial tires:

*Conventional tires* or bias-ply tires were made of four-cord plies laid out at right angles to each other in a criss-cross fashion and at a 45-degree angle to the tread. In the early 1960s, manufacturers reduced the number of plies to two, while doubling ply thickness to reduce the amount of labor content in tire making, but the two-ply was less durable and consumers rejected the change.

*Bias-belted tires* were of essentially the same ply construction as conventional tires but were strengthened by the addition of a belt of rayon, polyester, or fiberglass between the plies and the tread.

*Radial tires* consisted of plies perpendicular to the

tread, following the radius of the tire, and had a belt of steel cord between the plies and the tread. Radial tires were more expensive to produce because of increased labor input needed to align exactly the plies and the steel belts and because of the higher cost of steel compared to textiles and fiberglass.

# Tire Production[5]

Tire production consisted of four production steps: preparation of materials, components subassembly, assembly, and curing. Tires were made of five components: plies of rubber-coated fabric or steel; an airtight safety liner for tubeless tires; an outer tread; sidewalls, which gave the tire strength and flexibility; and strands of steel wire called "beads," which formed the inner circumference of tires and allowed them to be tightly joined into a slat on the rim of the wheel.

*Preparation of materials:* Natural and synthetic rubber and other chemicals were blended in various combinations depending on the types of tire and the particular component involved. The rubber was then formed into a continuous sheet and laid on skids and stocked for component subassembly.

[5]This material is adapted from Jules Pogrow, *The International Tire and Rubber Industry*, Cambridge, Mass., Harvard Business School, 1971.

*Component subassembly:* Fabric (rayon, nylon or polyester), or steel in the case of radials, was dipped into a special solution and then dried. It was then passed between rolls which pressed warm and pliable rubber on to the sides and between the threads or strands. The resulting plies were then cut into standard widths and angles depending on the type of tire to be made. For tubeless tires, an airtight liner was then bonded on to what would then be the inner ply. Other machines cut tread and sidewall stock to the proper width. Some machines allowed the forming of tread and sidewall stock as single units. Beads were made of high tensile strength wire strands, which were bound together by a special insulating compound.

*Tire building:* Tire components were assembled on a semiautomatic precision machine with a collapsible drum. The worker wrapped the plies on the drum, layer by layer. If the tire were belted, a layer of rayon, fiberglass, or cord belt was wrapped over the plies. The machine automatically set the beads in place, turned the plies around the beads, and then stitched them together. The tread and sidewall units were then added and stitched to the rest. The worker then collapsed the drum, removed the tire, and checked it for appearance.

*Curing:* The tire was then placed in a mold, where it was vulcanized, or treated with sulphur and heat, to bond the components into an integral unit and to form the pattern on the tread. This process was entirely automated and tightly controlled as to time, temperature, and pressure.

# Pneumatiques Michelin II

At the time of its investment in a Canadian truck tire plant in 1969 (see Case Two), Michelin was estimated to have about a third of the European automobile tire market and more than half of the European truck tire market, though, typical of the company's penchant for secrecy, it stated that "present statistical methods [did] not permit the evaluation of [its] share of . . . the market with sufficient precision." Through its success in Europe, Michelin had grown from being the seventh largest tire manufacturer in the world in 1959 to the third largest in 1971. Its future performance, however, appeared to be linked to its ability to penetrate the large North American market, where, by 1971, the company's market share was less than 1 percent.

## THE KEYS TO MICHELIN'S SUCCESS

In 1959, François Michelin took command of the company with the goal of expanding the sales

This case was prepared from published sources by David Harkleroad, research assistant, under the supervision of professors Dominique Héau and José de la Torre at the European Institute of Business Administration (INSEAD), Fontainebleau, France, as a basis for class discussion. Copyright © 1980 INSEAD (revised, 1982).

of radial tires, which Michelin had introduced in 1948 in Europe. Like other tire companies, which had seen sales and profits fluctuate wildly during the first half of the century, Michelin had bought into unrelated companies, such as Citroën and Machines Bull, to ensure steady profit growth. After taking control of the company, François Michelin either sold off his nontire interests, as in the case of Machines Bull, or gave complete autonomy to the director, as in the case of Citroën, so that Michelin could concentrate exclusively on its tire business.

Michelin began by trying to dominate the French market. Marketing emphasis was on quality, at a high price. In addition, the company spared no expense in its research and development effort, with the result that Michelin had often led the competition in introducing new and superior products. Some of the company's innovations since its founding were:

1891—patent on a removable bicycle tire

1894—the first automobile tire

1899—the first tire able to withstand speeds of 100 km/h (60 mph)

1924—the removable steel wheel

1934—a nonskid tire

1937—the "metallic" tire, opening the use of steel cord in tire manufacturing

1948—the first steel-belted radial tire (the "X")

1965—the asymmetric tire, adapted to high performance automobiles

Most of Michelin's research was geared to radial tire technology, and there was little doubt in anybody's mind that in 1972 Michelin still had a clear technological lead in that area. Most of the specialized production machinery was developed in-house, and when the patent on the famous "X" tire ran out in 1967, such production know-how became a key protection against potential competitors. Voya Peters, head of Michelin's U.S. operations, explained: "Anybody can make a steel-belted radial tire; but to make 100 of them of uniform quality is our secret."[1] Michelin ensured that it would remain at the forefront of tire technology by devoting a large effort to R&D. In 1972, it employed about 4,000 R&D people, representing roughly 4 to 5 percent of the total workforce worldwide, and R&D expenses were estimated at around 3 to 4 percent of sales.

Until the 1960s, only French motorists seemed convinced of the value of Michelin's radials, which lasted longer and performed better than conventional tires. In the early 1960s, Michelin took a 27.8 percent interest in Kléber-Colombes, the number two manufacturer in France, a move interpreted by industry observers as an attempt by Michelin to prevent other tire manufacturers from buying into its home market. Michelin also obtained a one-fifth share in Semperit, the major Austrian tire producer, apparently intended to secure a position outside the EEC market.

Having established his market position in France, François Michelin was then free to devote his efforts to the rest of the European market, where the company had built a few plants before the war, and to the building of a strong dealer network. The number of Michelin tire

---

[1]*Forbes,* April 15, 1973.

| EXHIBIT 1 | | |
|---|---|---|

**MICHELIN GROUP SALES, 1969–1971** (Fr Million)

|  | 1969 | 1970 | 1971 |
|---|---|---|---|
| Domestic sales | 1,472 | 1,748 | 1,992 |
| French exports | 750 | 991 | 1,409 |
| Total | 2,222 | 2,740 | 3,402 |
| Group total | 5,500 | 6,700 | 7,900 |

*Source: Michelin Prospectus,* February 24, 1976.

factories increased from 8 to 10 in France and from 8 to 13 in the rest of Europe between 1960 and 1965. Michelin exported to countries where it had no plants, and, by 1971, about 75 percent of total group sales were outside of France, including about 40 percent of the output of the French manufacturing facilities (see Exhibit 1).

Michelin's investment in Canada was the first time the company had gone outside of Europe with large-scale production facilities. Sales of high-priced, high-quality radial tires to non-European markets, until then, had been secured largely through exports. In this respect, because of the high cost of shipping tires, Michelin was at a considerable disadvantage vis-à-vis other international manufacturers. Production capacity of U.S. manufacturers outside the United States (including minority participations in Japan) was three times that of Michelin's total capacity; their capacity in Europe alone was greater than that of Michelin, the largest European manufacturer (see Exhibit 2).

Another key to the company's success was its management style. François Michelin's prime concern was loyalty to the company, and job applicants were investigated to the extent that one publication called "draconian." Once hired, apprentices were taught "la sincérité vis-à-vis des hommes et vis-à-vis des faits, l'observation, l'esprit de progrès et par dessus tout, l'armour de l'ouvrage bien fait." Even managers with extensive prior experience underwent an 18-month training program, during which they learned the company philosophy and policies, their job requirements, and how to make tires by spending several weeks on the production

EXHIBIT 2

**ESTIMATED TIRE PRODUCTION CAPACITY, 1969** (Thousands of Daily Units)

| | U.S. companies | | | | | | Other | | | | Grand total |
|---|---|---|---|---|---|---|---|---|---|---|---|
| | Firestone | Goodyear | Uniroyal | Goodrich | Other | Total | Dunlop | Michelin | Pirelli | Other | |
| United States* | 206 | 246 | 123 | 91 | 308 | 973 | 23† | — | — | — | 997 |
| Canada | 21 | 31 | 16 | 8 | 5 | 81 | 8 | — | — | — | 89 |
| Western Europe | 73 | 82 | 36 | 20 | 8 | 218 | 100 | 201‡ | 72 | 123 | 714 |
| Asia‡ | 13 | 115 | 11 | 51 | 1 | 190 | 29 | — | — | 29 | 247 |
| Latin America | 17 | 25 | 3 | 7 | 9 | 61 | — | — | 11 | 1 | 73 |
| Rest of the world | 8 | 16 | 3 | 6 | 2 | 35 | 20 | 1 | 6 | 2 | 63 |
| Total | 338 | 515 | 191 | 182 | 332 | 1,558 | 179 | 202 | 89 | 154 | 2,183 |

*1968 figures.
†1970 estimates.
‡Includes production of minority-owned affiliates, e.g., Bridgestone (20% owned by Goodyear) and Yokohama (34% owned by Goodyear), Kléber-Colombes (28% owned by Michelin); and other smaller participations by Firestone (Japan and Germany), Uniroyal (Sweden and Japan), Goodrich (Sweden and New Zealand), and Dunlop (Japan and Australia).

Source: Jules Pogrow, *The International Tire and Rubber Industry*, Cambridge, Mass., Harvard, 1971.

line. The company had introduced Taylorized production lines before World War II, and increased salaries or gave bonuses to "ces 'bons ourvriers' qui (savaient) 'faire mieux et moins cher.' "[2]

Industry observers said that Michelin's workers were better paid than those in comparable jobs in other companies. This went hand in hand with François Michelin's strict antiunion stance, which came from his belief that unions had been formed only in reaction to bad management. Only about 8 percent of Michelin's employees belonged to unions, as opposed to a French national average of 20 percent.

"Monsieur François," as he was known to his employees, "éternellement vétu d'un costume et d'un imperméable sans âge," was aware that in the battle for world supremacy, he faced adversaries with strong financing and whose potential was underemployed. Cutting costs was essential, except for research and production: Rumor had it that "while factories are regularly modernized, the offices have not been refurbished since the turn of the century."

Michelin knew that he would be permitted no errors, and the danger of industrial espionage led him to restrict employees to their own work areas, which they could enter only with special badges. Outsiders were prohibited from entry:

> Michelin has an iron-clad rule that permits no visitors. As François Michelin puts it: "You need ten years to develop a machine and five minutes to understand it, and thus to copy it." Some years ago, when General de Gaulle visited Clermont-Ferrand (French company headquarters) a Michelin employee recalls: "We politely showed him the sales room, then we politely showed him the display room, then we politely showed him the executive offices, and then we politely escorted him to his limousine in the parking lot. No one but Michelin people ever goes into a Michelin plant."[3]

---

[2]Most of these quotes come from *Entreprise,* September 21, 1973.

[3]As quoted in *Business Week,* July 26, 1976.

The secrecy extended to all but the most senior managers, and even the organizational structure was unknown. One attempt at its description is shown in Exhibit 3. Managers' responsibilities were a function of the person rather than the position. "The theory is that without an organizational chart, executive responsibility can be shifted without hurting feelings."

The success of the strategy can be gauged from its market performance. Michelin had solidified its hold on the French car tire market (see Exhibit 4). In addition, Michelin was estimated to have 20 percent of the U.K. market, behind Dunlop, and 25 percent of the Italian market, behind Pirelli. It was among the market leaders in Germany, with 15 to 20 percent of the market, and was the leader in all other European countries. In terms of sales growth, Michelin had far outstripped its U.S. competitors in the years 1968 to 1970, achieving an average annual growth rate of 23 percent versus 7 percent for Goodyear, 5 percent for Firestone, and 3 percent for Goodrich.

This sales growth required large investments in plant, equipment, and inventories. The sales-to-total-assets ratio for the industry was between 1.1 and 1.2, and inventories represented about 30 percent of total assets. In 1970, when Michelin had 30 plants in the world, of which 13 were in France, it raised Fr110 million (Fr5 = $1) in capital in addition to its cash flow, estimated to be 10 to 12 percent of sales. In 1971, one new plant was added in France and seven elsewhere in Europe for a total investment in fixed assets of over Fr1.7 billion. The total uses of funds for the year was Fr2.2 billion (1.8 million in fixed assets and 400 million in inventory) of which Fr988 million came from internally generated cash. That year, the company issued its first bonds since 1963, providing another Fr664 million. It also reduced its cash balances by Fr321 million and raised another Fr251 million from other sources. On top of this, Michelin was planning on issuing Fr170 million of share capital in France in 1972. Exhibits 5 to 8 present available financial information about Michelin.

EXHIBIT 3

**MICHELIN'S ORGANIZATION**

Compagnie Générale des Etablissements Michelin: Clermont-Ferrand, France

Société d'Exportation Michelin

Compagnie Financière Michelin: Basle, Switzerland

N. V. Nederlandsche Banden-Industrie Michelin: Amsterdam

Société Anonyme Belge du Pneumatique Michelin: Brussels

Sociedad para la Fabricación en España de Neumáticos Michelin: Madrid

Michelin Reifenwerke A. G.: Karlsruhe

Societá per Azioni Michelin Italiana: Milan

Michelin Tyre Co. Limited: London

West Indies
Argentina
The Cameroons
Canada
Ivory Coast
Denmark
U.S.A.
Finland
Morocco
Norway
Sweden
Switzerland
Trading companies: Kenya Tanzania Uganda

Michelin Limited: Nigeria

Michelin Limited: Belfast

Manufacture Française des Pneumatiques Michelin: Clermont-Ferrand

Société d'Applications Techniques et Industrielles

Société des Matières Premières Tropicales: Malaysia

Société des Plantations et Pneumatiques Michelin au Sud-Vietnam

Manufacture Saigonnaise des Pneumatiques Michelin: Saigon

Michelin Tires Manufacturing Co. of Canada Ltd.: Nova Scotia

*Source:* Michelin Tire Co. of Canada, University of Western Ontario.

**EXHIBIT 4**

**MARKET SHARES IN THE FRENCH AUTOMOTIVE TIRE MARKET, 1972**

|  | OEM | Replacement |
|---|---|---|
| Michelin | 45–50% | 40–45% |
| Kléber-Colombes | 25–28 | 18–20 |
| Dunlop | 15–20 | 12–14 |
| Uniroyal | 3–4 | 8–9 |
| Firestone | 4 | 8 |
| Goodyear | 3–4 | 7–8 |

*Source: Entreprise,* September 21, 1973.

The Michelin family held about 50 percent of the shares of the Compagnie Générale des Etablissements Michelin, a nonlimited liability holding company, which owned virtually all the shares of the Manufacture Française des Pneumatiques Michelin, the French production arm, and all the shares of the Compagnie Financière Michelin, located in Switzerland, which was responsible for "coordinating and developing the industrial activities of the Michelin Group outside of France and [was] responsible for managing and coordinating such subsidiaries and for raising the funds required to meet their short, medium and long-term financial needs."[4] Fran-

---
[4]Michelin Prospectus, February 24, 1976.

çois Michelin was estimated to own about 3 percent of the holding company, but the family holdings gave him complete control.

In addition to these and its holdings in other tire companies, Michelin held 51 percent of the shares in Citroën, the third largest French car manufacturer. The remaining 49 percent had been acquired by Italy's Fiat when Michelin tried to sell off its interests to concentrate on the tire business. The French government, however, appeared determined to keep Citroën in French hands, and the arrangement between Fiat and Michelin was unsatisfactory to both. Michelin was considering reacquiring Fiat's shares, but Citroën was having financial difficulties (see Exhibit 9), and a large amount of time and money would be needed to restructure its finances and modernize its plants.

Michelin had integrated backward in the 1930s into rubber plantations and steel wire plants. Although the plantations were becoming less important as the use of synthetic rubber increased, the investment in steel wire plants had been an astute move. Thus, the company not only could control the quality of the wire used in its radials, but also could make it difficult for other companies, when they later began radial production, to obtain enough wire of the proper quality. Finally, the famous Michelin guides and maps, excellent publicity tools, represented about 1 percent of sales.

**EXHIBIT 5**

**MICHELIN FINANCES, 1968–1971** (Fr Million)

| Group (consolidated) | 1968 | 1969 | 1970 | 1971 |
|---|---|---|---|---|
| Sales | 4,380 | 5,500 | 6,700 | 7,900* |
| Sales of French subsidiary† | 1,900 | 2,200 | 2,750 | 3,402* |
| Cash flow | 525 | 670 | 724* | 988* |
| Net profit | 254 | 338 | 290 | 400 |
| Investment in plant | 420 | 600 | 1,200 | 1,700* |
| Cash flow/sales | 11.9% | 12.2% | 10.8% | 12.5% |

*Various Michelin publications.
†Before VAT.
*Source: Entreprise,* September 21, 1973.

---

**EXHIBIT 6**

---

**CONSOLIDATED BALANCE SHEETS, 1971** (Fr Million)

Assets
| | |
|---|---|
| Plant and equipment (net) | 3,652 |
| Interests in unaffiliated companies and goodwill | 661 |
| Inventory | 1,839 |
| Net cash, negotiable assets, and current liabilities | (191) |
| | 5,961 |

Liabilities
| | |
|---|---|
| Shareholders' capital | 450 |
| Retained earnings | 1,590 |
| Capital and other reserves | 1,985 |
| Minority interests | 67 |
| Medium- and long-term debt | 1,869 |
| | 5,961 |

---

*Note:* Although the figures given are thought to be representative by the source, they were pieced together from available information and should not be considered exact.
*Source:* Goy, Huvette et Cie.

## COMPETITION

In 1971, radial tires accounted for about 60 percent of the European tire market, up from 30 percent in 1965. European competitors had shifted production to radial tires to supply the growing demand, but none had been as successful as Michelin: 80 percent of Michelin's production was in radials, and the company

---

**EXHIBIT 7**

---

**GROUP CASH FLOW, 1971** (Fr Million)

Sources
| | |
|---|---|
| Internally generated funds | 361 |
| Depreciation | 627 |
| Operating cash flow | 988 |
| Increase in medium- and long-term debt | 664 |
| Increase in other liabilities | 169 |
| Exceptional items | 82 |
| Decrease in cash balances | 321 |
| | 2,224 |

Uses
| | |
|---|---|
| Investment in plant | 1,697 |
| Investment in other fixed assets | 142 |
| Increase in inventory | 385 |
| | 2,224 |

---

*Note:* Figures pieced together from available information and should not be considered exact.
*Source:* Goy, Huvette et Cie.

planned to phase out nonradial production completely. Other companies, notably Pirelli, had introduced radial tires with fiber belts, rather than with steel belts, but the quality was considered inferior to that of Michelin products by the company's own management. By 1968, all the European subsidiaries of U.S. manufacturers also had at least one production line of radials typically using fiberglass and polyester belts. Although not as strong nor as long-lasting as steel-belted radials, they were cheaper to produce.

The European tire market was very fragmented in the late 1960s, and increasing competition had led to numerous attempts at rationalization. The U.S. companies had expanded aggressively during the 1960s, and by 1969 they were operating 29 subsidiary plants in Europe. General Tire and Goodrich stressed minority participations with local producers, but the others had invested directly in major expansion programs. Their European plants were among the largest and most highly automated in the world. In addition to introducing their bias-belted tires, described as a cross between conventional and radial tires, they attacked the market aggressively, offering dealers large discounts and trying to secure broad distribution networks.

## EXHIBIT 8

**MICHELIN GROUP CASH FLOWS AND INVESTMENTS, 1970 AND 1971** (Fr Million)

| | Cash flows | | | | Investments | |
|---|---|---|---|---|---|---|
| | **1970** | **1971** | | | **1970** | **1971** |
| Générale des Etablissements | 36 | 62 | | — | — | — |
| Manufacture française | 193 | 278 | France | 443 | 534 |
| Great Britain (consolidated) | 72 | 99 | Great Britain (consolidated) | 146 | 237 |
| Italy | 123 | 149 | Italy | 223 | 329 |
| Spain | 128 | 164 | Spain | 188 | 213 |
| Germany | 29 | 69 | Germany | 165 | 375 |
| Belgium | (1) | 13 | Belgium | 1 | 5 |
| Low Countries | 0 | 9 | Low countries | 0 | 3 |
| Switzerland (year ending in June) | 131 | 160 | | — | — |
| Synthetic rubber plant* | 0 | 0 | Synthetic rubber plant* | — | 13 |
| Other | 13 | (15) | | | |
| Total | 724 | 998 | | 1,166 | 1,709 |

*50% owned by Goodyear.
*Note:* Figures pieced together from available information and should not be considered exact.
*Source:* Goy, Huvette et Cie.

They also sought agreements with the U.S. automotive companies operating in Europe to supply them with OEM tires.

As profitability among European manufacturers declined, a number of companies sought to create groups that would permit them to rationalize their operation. One such attempt was the so-called German solution, where Bayer, a large diversified German chemical firm, acquired 30 percent of Continental Gummiwerke, the fourth largest European tire manufacturer,

## EXHIBIT 9

**CITROËN, FINANCIAL RESULTS, 1966–1971**
(Fr Million)

| | Sales | Profits after tax | Fixed assets |
|---|---|---|---|
| 1966* | 3,777 | 22 | 1,048 |
| 1967* | 3,847 | 12 | 1,354 |
| 1968 | 3,326 | (119) | 1,823 |
| 1969 | 3,655 | (63) | 1,661 |
| 1970 | 4,390 | (373) | 1,808 |
| 1971 | 5,738 | 25 | 1,709 |

*S. A. André Citroën; *Automobiles Citroën* for the following years.
*Source:* Annual reports.

62 percent of Phoenix, the eighth largest, and 35 percent of Metzeler, the tenth largest. All of these manufacturers were located in Germany.

A second major group consisted of Dunlop, the major British tire manufacturer and the second largest in Europe, and Pirelli, the major Italian manufacturer and the third largest in Europe, who agreed to unite in 1970. Some 65 percent of Dunlop's sales and 35 percent of Pirelli's were in tires, and their union made them the second largest tire group in Europe, just behind Michelin. Dunlop was weak in radial tires, holding third place in the European radial market behind Michelin and Pirelli, but it had a wider geographical spread, covering Europe, the Commonwealth, Asia, and North America. Pirelli was strong in Southern Europe and South America. In only two areas, the United Kingdom and Germany, did production facilities overlap, but this did not seem to pose major problems. Together they controlled 45 percent of the British market, 35 percent of the Italian market, 18 percent of the German market, and 13 percent of the French market. Dunlop had decided to end its expensive racing support of Formula 1 cars in 1970, leaving the field to

Goodyear, Firestone, and Michelin, who began discreetly equipping Formula 1 cars that same year. Financially, the two companies were not particularly complementary, since both had high debt ratios. Because the merger had caused a decline in profitability, it was not clear that it could survive.

Exhibit 10 shows tire production capacity by company and country for Europe in 1964 and 1969. Exhibit 11 presents summary financial data for all major tire manufacturers for recent years.

All major competitors in Europe had strong R&D capabilities. Pirelli had just developed a triangular-section tire, and Dunlop had introduced its Donova, which was highly regarded by the market. Many manufacturers were working on puncture-resistant or run-flat tires, and, since Michelin had not modified its tire concept since 1948, these developments could be expected to give the steel-belted radial strong competition.

## MARKET TRENDS

During the 1960s, growth in the U.S. tire market was 74 percent compared to 113 percent elsewhere. The higher growth outside the United States was attributed to the increase in automobile usage and the expansion of highway systems in these countries. From 1957 to 1968, U.S. automobile production increased at a 4.5 percent annual rate, whereas production elsewhere increased at a 17.2 percent annual rate. Industry sources predicted that more than 60 percent of the tires sold in the world in the 1970s would be sold outside the United States. Exhibit 12 shows predicted growth in vehicle registrations and replacement passenger tires for the period 1968 to 1978.

The North American market was relatively mature, with sales growth at a 10 percent annual rate from 1957 to 1971 and expected to slow down considerably afterwards (see Case Three). Japan was the second largest tire-producing country in the world after the United States, and growth in production had averaged over 12 percent a year from 1967 to 1971. Demand

was predominantly for traditional tires, and approximately half the market was controlled by Bridgestone, in which Goodyear had a minority position, and another quarter was held by Yokohama, in which Goodrich held 34 percent. Japan's strict foreign investment laws had prevented foreign tire companies from investing there, except in minority ownerships or licensing agreements. Imports, representing about 2 percent of the market, were also strictly controlled. Dunlop was the only radial tire producer in Japan (in a joint venture), making tires for Toyotas destined for the European market. However, the investment laws had recently been liberalized, and several companies, including Michelin, were talking with Japanese companies about the possibility of creating additional joint ventures. But these investments would not take place before the mid-1970s, even if satisfactory agreements were achieved.

The European tire market had been growing at a fairly steady 9 percent a year rate in the 1960s, and the trend was expected to continue. The growth in radial tires was expected to be higher, approaching 13 percent. Already, 80 percent of the French and 60 percent of the European market was estimated to be "radialized" and though U.S. producers had introduced their bias-belted tires, these producers were shifting to radial production to meet demand. However, most sales in the less developed countries were for traditional tires, and radials for passenger cars were not expected to show much growth and would most likely be supplied through imports.

## MICHELIN'S OUTLOOK

**Europe** Over the next 4 years, to maintain its share of the French truck tire market at about 80 percent and its share of the car tire market at about 50 percent, Michelin planned to build three or four new plants, expand another three, and modernize the rest at a cost of Fr1.5 billion. To increase its penetration of other European markets, it would need another twelve plants in Italy, Spain, Great Britain, and Germany. Cap-

## EXHIBIT 10

**ESTIMATED TIRE PRODUCTION CAPACITY, WESTERN EUROPE, 1964 AND 1969** (Thousands of Daily Units)

### U.S. companies

| | Firestone | | Goodyear | | Uniroyal | | Goodrich | | Others | | Subtotal | |
|---|---|---|---|---|---|---|---|---|---|---|---|---|
| | 1964 | 1969 | 1964 | 1969 | 1964 | 1969 | 1964 | 1969 | 1964 | 1969 | 1964 | 1969 |
| United Kingdom | 11.5 | 18.3 | 17.8 | 29.0 | 3.8 | 4.0 | — | — | — | — | 32.1 | 51.3 |
| France | 4.0 | 6.5 | 3.5 | 9.0 | 6.0 | 9.0 | 16.0* | — | — | — | 29.5 | 24.5 |
| Germany | 9.3* | 14.3* | 9.3 | 16.0 | 4.5 | 10.0 | — | — | — | — | 23.1 | 40.3 |
| Italy | — | 5.3 | 1.9 | 5.0 | — | — | — | — | 17.5* | — | 19.4 | 10.3 |
| Sweden | 2.3 | 5.7 | 6.3 | 9.1 | 2.3* | 4.0* | 4.7* | 6.0* | — | — | 15.6 | 24.7 |
| Other | 11.8 | 23.3 | 7.5 | 13.8 | 4.7 | 8.5 | 6.0 | 13.5 | 7.8 | 7.6 | 37.8 | 66.7 |
| Total | 38.9 | 73.4 | 46.3 | 81.9 | 20.3 | 35.5 | 26.7 | 19.5 | 25.3 | 7.6 | 157.5 | 217.8 |

### European companies

| | Dunlop | | Pirelli | | Michelin | | Others | | Subtotal | | Grand total | |
|---|---|---|---|---|---|---|---|---|---|---|---|---|
| | 1964 | 1969 | 1964 | 1969 | 1964 | 1969 | 1964 | 1969 | 1964 | 1969 | 1964 | 1969 |
| United Kingdom | 53.4 | 56.5 | 2.9 | 5.7 | 10.0 | 30.0 | 4.5 | 7.5 | 70.8 | 99.7 | 102.9 | 151.0 |
| France | 19.0 | 18.5 | — | — | 48.0 | 104.0*† | 2.0 | 3.5 | 69.0 | 126.0 | 98.5 | 150.5 |
| Germany | 15.0 | 25.0 | 7.5 | 9.0 | 1.5 | 13.0 | 30.0 | 60.0 | 54.0 | 107.0 | 77.1 | 147.3 |
| Italy | — | — | 30.5 | 50.0 | 15.0 | 35.0 | — | 36.0 | 45.5 | 121.0 | 64.9 | 131.3 |
| Sweden | — | — | — | — | — | — | — | 0.1 | — | 0.1 | 15.6 | 24.8 |
| Other | — | — | 3.7 | 7.5 | 7.8 | 19.0‡ | 12.7 | 16.0 | 24.2 | 42.5 | 62.0 | 109.2 |
| Total | 87.4 | 100.0 | 43.7 | 72.2 | 81.3 | 201.0 | 49.2 | 123.1 | 263.5 | 496.3 | 421.0 | 714.1 |

*Minority interests.
†Including Kléber-Colombes.
‡Mostly Spain.
Source: Jules Pogrow, *The International Tire and Rubber Industry*, Cambridge, Mass., Harvard, 1971.

ital expenditures were expected to reach Fr600 to 700 million in each country. Other investments and increases in working capital, for all of Europe, were expected to require an additional Fr1.5 to 2.0 billion. An alternative to building its own new plants would be to reach an agreement with Bayer and the German group, and Michelin was rumored to be considering such a possibility.

**North America**  The North American market, representing over 40 percent of the world's total, was not unknown to the French firm. It had already built a factory in the United States in 1907 but was forced to close it during the depression. Its westward drive began anew in 1948 when it began exporting radials to the United States through a sales office. In 1963, it created a financial subsidiary in Bermuda to direct future U.S. activities, and in 1965 it agreed to supply Sears, Roebuck and Co., the world's largest retailer, with radial tires, to be sold under Sears' Allstate brand name: "Sears wanted a top-of-the-line tire. 'We had to convince Michelin to develop an American-sized tire; they were reluctant,' [said] a Sears official. 'But we saw the market developing, and we wanted the best. . . .' For Michelin, Sears represented a guaranteed demand base on which it could [later] build a U.S. tire business under its own name."[5]

By the 1970s, Sears was selling about a million premium-priced Michelin radials a year, representing about 0.5 percent of the market. In addition, Ford Motor Co. had begun equipping its luxury Lincoln Continental with Michelin radials, which, Ford believed, helped increase the sales appeal of the car. There were rumors that some Ford executives were considering offering radials as options on other cars. However, other automotive companies refused to consider Michelin's radials, since the company had no production facilities in the United States.

Michelin had been approached by several smaller competitors about the possibility of a joint venture, merger, or other similar agreement. Contacts had been made with General Tire and with Armstrong. Although an acquisition or merger would give Michelin a ready-made distribution network and access to capital markets, the cost of converting traditional tire plants to radial tire manufacturing was estimated to be more expensive than building a completely new plant, and Michelin's penchant for secrecy led many to believe it would never submit to SEC financial disclosure requirements. Finally, Ralph Nader had been attacking the safety of U.S.-produced tires, and had endorsed Michelin's radials. The publicity resulting from this was a tempting attraction to the French firm.

**Other Countries**  Michelin planned to continue to supply any LDC demand for radial car tires from France, but two countries showed some promise for the construction of truck tire plants: Brazil and Egypt. Michelin estimated that it would need to invest some $60 million in Egypt and $150 million in Brazil to supply the Middle East and South American demand for truck tires. In Japan, Michelin seemed to have no immediate interest, but was talking to a large trading group about a longer-term investment. Entry into the Eastern bloc countries would require investing there, but Michelin refused to consider this because of Fiat's experience in building a car plant in the Soviet Union. Shortly thereafter, Russian-made Fiats began appearing in Europe. Kléber-Colombes and Semperit, which did not share Michelin's secret radial technology, had filled the void by building plants in Bulgaria, East Germany, Yugoslavia, and Hungary.

**Motorcycle Tires**  In 1971, some 3 million motorcycles were sold in the world, and the market for motorcycle tires, though small, was attractive. Michelin completed an in-depth survey of the motorcycle tire market in 1971, but since most motorcycles were produced in Japan, it would have to produce there in order to tap the OEM market. Dunlop already supplied tires for all Japanese motorcycles exported to Europe.

---

[5]*Forbes*, April 15, 1973.

**EXHIBIT 11**

**SELECTED FINANCIAL DATA ON MAJOR TIRE COMPANIES, 1969** (US$ Million)

|  | Dunlop (U.K.) | Pirelli (Italy) | Continental (Germany) | Kléber-Colombes (France) | Trelleborg & Tretorn (Sweden) |
|---|---|---|---|---|---|
| Turnover (net) | 1,188 | 345 | 339 | 136 | 125 |
| Cost of goods sold | n.a. | n.a. | n.a. | n.a. | n.a. |
| Depreciation | 41 | 24.2 | 15.6 | 9.0 | 5.6 |
| Selling, general, & administrative | n.a. | n.a. | n.a. | n.a. | n.a. |
| Earnings before interest and taxes | 79.1 | (4.7) | 24.2 | 9.5 | n.a. |
| Interest | n.a. | n.a. | n.a. | n.a. | n.a. |
| Income taxes | n.a. | n.a. | n.a. | n.a. | n.a. |
| Other charges | n.a. | n.a. | n.a. | n.a. | n.a. |
| After tax profits | 34.4 | (3.7) | 10.8 | 2.4 | 1.7 |
| Cash flow | 75.4 | 20.5 | 26.4 | 11.4 | 7.3 |
| As % of turnover | 6.3 | 5.9 | 7.8 | 8.4 | 5.8 |
| Current assets | 598.3 | 324.6 | 121.0 | 65.4 | 66.7 |
| Fixed assets | 379.2 | 283.4 | 123.8 | 65.4 | 32.2 |
| Other | — | — | — | — | — |
| Total assets | 977.5 | 608.0 | 244.8 | 130.8 | 98.9 |
| Current liabilities | 331.0 | 157.2 | 74.7 | 47.2 | 29.5 |
| Long-term debt | 251.3 | 240.8 | 55.2 | 34.5 | 20.9 |
| Other | — | — | — | — | — |
| Equity capital | 395.2 | 210.0 | 114.9 | 49.1 | 48.5 |
| Capital investment | 82.1 | 42.6 | 21.1 | 16.1 | 8.4 |
| Employment (thousands) | 108.0 | 25.3 | 27.5 | 9.0 | 9.1 |
| Dividend payments | n.a. | n.a. | n.a. | n.a. | n.a. |

n.a. = not available.
*Source:* Annual reports and estimates.

**Materials** Rayon, the traditional material used in belting tires, was about half as expensive as polyester and fiberglass, though belts made of the latter lasted much longer. However, rayon's price was increasing while the price of the other two was declining, and all major U.S. manufacturers had at least one line of fiberglass and polyester belted tires in the early 1970s. Steel wire for radials, because of the technical difficulties of drawing it to the proper thickness, was found by U.S. manufacturers to be uneconomical. Yet, there was some speculation that a newly developed wire spinning process would allow U.S. producers to compete in the steel-belted radial market. Perhaps the most striking new material was Fiber B, developed by Dupont Chemicals for the Apollo space program, which had the same strength as steel while being much less dense. If tests were conclusive, Goodyear and Firestone seemed more likely to be able to obtain the fiber than Michelin since supply would be limited for at least several years due to Dupont's limited capacity. However, Fiber B was much more expensive than steel, and even if Michelin could obtain it, the company would need several years to test its application for tires before putting the product on the market.

## ORGANIZATION AND SOCIAL CONSIDERATIONS

As stated earlier, Michelin's centralized organization structure, reinforced by extensive training programs, created an "esprit de mai-

| Semperit (Austria) | Phoenix (Germ.) | Goodyear (U.S.) | Goodrich (U.S.) | Firestone (U.S.) | Uniroyal (U.S.) | General (U.S.) | Bridgestone (Japan) |
|---|---|---|---|---|---|---|---|
| 123 | 120 | 3,215 | 1,229 | 2,279 | 1,554 | 1,088 | 478 |
| n.a. | n.a. | 2,266 | 871 | 1,562 | 1,128 | 886 | 348 |
| 7.2 | 4.7 | 111 | 49 | 82 | 46 | 36 | 22 |
| n.a. | n.a. | 502 | 215 | 395 | 277 | 94 | 84 |
| 6.7 | 11.1 | 357 | 100 | 263 | 108 | 88 | n.a. |
| n.a. | n.a. | 54 | 30 | 31 | 22 | 16 | n.a. |
| n.a. | n.a. | 144 | 28 | 114 | 35 | 33 | n.a. |
| n.a. | n.a. | 2 | — | 4 | 4 | 4 | n.a. |
| 1.7 | 4.9 | 158 | — | 117 | 47 | 35 | 21 |
| 8.9 | 9.6 | 278 | 100 | 205 | 94 | 71 | 43 |
| 7.2 | 8.0 | 8.6 | 8.1 | 9.0 | 6.0 | 6.4 | 9.0 |
| 57.5 | 53.2 | 1,664 | 615 | 1,141 | 741 | 434 | 159 |
| 43.5 | 23.4 | 1,034 | 593 | 765 | 470 | 270 | 240 |
| — | — | 67 | 49 | 113 | 47 | 120 | — |
| 101.0 | 76.6 | 2,764 | 1,257 | 2,019 | 1,258 | 824 | 399 |
| 28.6 | 18.7 | 821 | 362 | 473 | 321 | 206 | 122 |
| 43.5 | 16.4 | 577 | 256 | 417 | 232 | 198 | 108 |
| — | — | 98 | 44 | 65 | 90 | 30 | — |
| 28.9 | 32.5 | 1,267 | 594 | 1,064 | 524 | 390 | 169 |
| 7.4 | 8.7 | 293 | 138 | 165 | 29 | 55 | n.a. |
| 10.8 | 8.2 | 134 | 53 | 100 | 67 | 34 | 11 |
| n.a. | n.a. | 59 | 25 | 47 | 23 | 18 | 6 |

son'' unmatched elsewhere in the industry. However, it was not clear that François Michelin could maintain his highly centralized, secretive, and paternalistic organization as the number of employees worldwide approached 100,000 and as the company competed in more diverse markets. Significant investments outside of continental Europe would certainly require more delegation of authority to managers in order for them to be able to respond quickly

**EXHIBIT 12**

**TEN-YEAR TIRE POTENTIAL OUTSIDE OF U.S. AND CANADA** (Thousands of Units)

| | Original equipment tires | | | Replacement passenger tires | | |
|---|---|---|---|---|---|---|
| | 1968 | 1978 | Growth (%) | 1968 | 1979 | Growth (%) |
| Western Europe | 59,300 | 105,100 | 77 | 62,300 | 112,500 | 81 |
| Latin America | 7,800 | 14,000 | 80 | 8,600 | 15,400 | 79 |
| Africa & Middle East | 5,000 | 9,500 | 89 | 5,000 | 9,300 | 86 |
| Far East & Oceania | 18,300 | 39,500 | 116 | 13,000 | 28,400 | 118 |
| Outside U.S. and Canada (Total) | 90,400 | 168,100 | 86 | 88,900 | 165,600 | 86 |

*Source:* Jules Pogrow, *The International Tire and Rubber Industry,* Cambridge, Mass., Harvard, 1971.

to the different and changing operating conditions.

Michelin's antiunion stance had led to the development in Clermont-Ferrand of a company town. The company had constructed housing for its employees and had provided hospitals, nurseries, and schools where, until recently, religious instruction was mandatory. It had been in advance of French government legislation by many years in providing social and welfare benefits such as free medical service, family allowance, paid vacations, and pensions. In addition, Michelin employees were reputedly better paid then their colleagues in similar positions in other companies. In fact, it was said that one of the reasons Michelin chose to invest in Nova Scotia was that unemployment was high and unionization was low in that area.

However, should the company decide to expand its investments abroad, it would have to deal with a workforce whose culture was different. For example, in the United States, Michelin would face the strong United Rubber Workers Union where periodical wage negotiations invariably resulted in high wage settlements or strikes. Michelin's workers had never gone on strike.

# The Construction Machinery Industry

This case describes the worldwide construction machinery industry during 1980 to 1985. It focuses on those industry segments in which Caterpillar Tractor, Komatsu Ltd., and their most important competitors operate.

## INDUSTRY OVERVIEW

Construction machinery can be viewed as falling into four general product categories—earthmoving machinery, cranes, forestry equipment, and a diverse group of special function machinery (e.g., asphalt and concrete pavers, mixers, spreaders, and finishing machines; compactors; air compressors, tools, and pumps; and hoists). The first two product categories were by far the largest sources of worldwide sales.

Earthmoving machinery comprised a broad range of equipment, including crawler dozers and loaders, wheeled dozers and loaders, motor graders, self-propelled scrapers, hydraulic excavators and backhoes, power shovels, trenchers, pipe layers, and off-highway trucks. List

prices of machines differed widely, depending on size and performance capabilities. For example, in 1984 U.S. list prices of bulldozers ranged from $30,000 to $800,000.

Building construction—residential, commercial, industrial, and governmental—represented a major source of demand for this equipment. Other important uses were in road and dam building projects, surface mining, mass transit construction, infrastructure repair and maintenance, and waste site management. Heavy cranes were employed on many of the same construction projects as well as for bridge building and in oil drilling. Self-propelled forestry equipment—fellers, skidders, transporters, loaders, harvesters—represented an application of heavy machinery technologies to the lumber and paper industries.

Buyers of these machines included construction companies, large and small contractors, state and local governments, mining and industrial concerns, logging companies, and farmers. Key elements in purchase decisions were performance-price characteristics of the product, service capability of manufacturers and their distributors, availability of rental and financing programs, delivery date, and general product

This note was prepared from public sources by Professor Stephen A. Allen as a basis for class discussion. Copyright © 1986 by Stephen A. Allen.

reputation. Yearly demand was sensitive to interest rates and various business cycles. Long-term demand and product mix in various national markets were driven by population growth, rate of economic development, demand and supply conditions in extractive industries, and government expenditures on public works. Product mix was also influenced by differences in equipment intensity for end-use applications. For example, in developed economies earthmoving equipment outlays ranged from 1 percent of total construction contract value for single-family homes to 8 percent for water management projects. Considerably higher equipment intensities were found in extractive industry applications. (See Exhibit 1.)

In 1984 worldwide sales of earthmoving equipment were approximately $16.4 billion, with U.S.-headquartered companies holding more than 55 percent of the market. Sales by product

### EXHIBIT 1

**EARTHMOVING EQUIPMENT INTENSITIES IN THE UNITED STATES**

| Application | Percent |
|---|---|
| Construction | |
| Residential buildings | 2 |
| Single-family homes | 1 |
| Nonresidential buildings | 2–3 |
| Nuclear power plants | 1 |
| Heavy construction | |
| Highway construction | 6 |
| Highway maintenance | 2 |
| Pipelines | 7 |
| Mass transit | 7 |
| Water management | 8 |
| Extraction | |
| Open-pit | 8 |
| Stripping | 17 |
| Logging | 25 |

*Note:* Equipment intensities for construction applications, defined as earthmoving equipment outlays as percent of total contract value, are representative of those found in developed economies. Intensities differ in less developed economies for light construction applications due to labor-machine cost trade-offs. Equipment intensities for extractive industries are defined as machinery costs (depreciation, rental) as percent of total product costs.
*Source:* Estimates from Wertheim & Co.

### EXHIBIT 2

**WORLDWIDE SALES OF EARTHMOVING MACHINERY BY PRODUCT SEGMENT** ($ Million)

| | 1980 | 1984 |
|---|---|---|
| Backhoes | | 1,600 |
| Excavators | 2,750 | 2,900 |
| Crawler tractors | | |
| Over 90 HP | 2,350 | 1,200 |
| Under 90 HP | | 1,700 |
| Wheel tractors | | 900 |
| Graders | | 800 |
| Crawler loaders | 1,400 | 1,000 |
| Wheel loaders | 4,400 | 1,900 |
| Off-highway trucks | | 1,000 |
| Scrapers | | 1,400 |
| Other (skidders, compactors, attachments) | | 1,400 |
| Paving equipment | | 600 |
| | 21,300 | 16,400 |

*Source:* Estimates from Wertheim & Co.

segment are shown in Exhibit 2. Sales of most classes of construction machinery reached a peak during 1978 to 1980 and fell precipitously during 1981 to 1983. Although worldwide data are not available, trends for U.S. shipments, shown in Exhibit 3, are indicative of the overall situation.

The construction machinery industry experienced three major periods of growth during the post–World War II era. From 1948 to 1952 pent-up demand in the United States and massive reconstruction activity in Europe and Japan stimulated sales. Growth accelerated once again in the 1960s due to the U.S. interstate highway program and emergence of developing countries as major markets. The 1970s witnessed completion of the U.S. interstate highway system and a slowing of real economic growth in most countries (partly due to OPEC oil shocks). However, equipment demand held up due to increased economic activity in OPEC and Pacific basin countries and accelerated development of energy resources (oil and coal) in North America. From 1967 to 1978 U.S. machinery shipments grew in real terms at a compounded annual rate of over 8 percent. The severe 1981

## EXHIBIT 3

**U.S. SHIPMENTS OF CONSTRUCTION MACHINERY INCLUDING EXPORTS** (Thousands of Units)

|  | 1970 | 1975 | 1980 | 1982 | 1983 | 1984 | 1985 |
|---|---|---|---|---|---|---|---|
| Excavators | 2.8 | 3.5 | 4.0 | 2.0 | 2.6 | 3.5 | 3.2 |
| Crawler tractors | 19.4 | 20.5 | 16.5 | 7.2 | 7.2 | 9.0 | n.a. |
| Graders | 6.8 | 7.8 | 7.2 | 4.0 | 3.4 | 4.8 | 4.9 |
| Crawler loaders | 7.4 | 5.0 | 4.4 | 1.4 | 2.2 | 3.4 | n.a. |
| Wheel loaders | 14.4 | 17.4 | 17.1 | 7.9 | 8.9 | 10.5 | 8.7 |
| Rear dump trucks | 2.1 | 3.1 | 2.0 | 1.0 | 1.0 | 1.1 | n.a. |
| Scrapers | 4.5 | 4.4 | 2.6 | 1.2 | 1.3 | 2.7 | 3.5 |
| Wheeled log skidders | 2.1 | 1.4 | 2.1 | 1.1 | 1.6 | 2.3 | 1.7 |

n.a. = not available.
*Source:* PREDICASTS, 1979–1985 annual industry shipment surveys.

to 1983 decline resulted from a combination of high interest rates, worldwide recession, a world oil glut, and debt problems of developing countries.

The construction machinery industry is highly competitive and relatively concentrated, as shown in Exhibit 4. Industry concentration has increased significantly over the past 25 years as leading companies have sought enhanced economies in distribution and service, R&D, and production both by high penetration of their traditional segments and by broadening segment coverage. In 1960 eight companies accounted for 40 percent of worldwide sales. By 1984 seven accounted for 73 percent.

Weak demand combined with high barriers to exit produced a difficult pricing environment during 1981 to 1985 (see Exhibit 5). In its 1984 annual report Dresser Industries noted,

The construction equipment industry continues to operate at approximately 25% below 1981 unit sales levels and at 50% of worldwide capacity. The problem of industry overcapacity has triggered severe price cutting in an effort to maximize volume. Moreover, the strength of the U.S. dollar against other world currencies has given foreign suppliers a cost advantage in domestic markets and penalized U.S. exporters.

The nature of the industry is undergoing significant structural change because a number of participants do not have the critical mass or a cost structure necessary to effectively compete in the world marketplace. Consequently, the trend of consolidations, divestments, downsizing, and strong competitive pressure will likely continue. The companies with the best chance of success over the balance of the 1980s will be those that can become world-class competitors in terms of cost, quality, performance, effective distribution, and scope of products.

The outlook is for continuing moderate improvement, with the U.S. market recovering to 1981 levels by 1987, but competitive pricing is expected to remain intense over the next several years.

The 1980s also witnessed important changes in the types of machinery purchased in the developed economies of North America, Europe, and Japan. In general, the composition of de-

## EXHIBIT 4

**ESTIMATED 1984 MARKET SHARES FOR EARTHMOVING MACHINERY (%)**

|  | United States | Worldwide |
|---|---|---|
| Caterpillar Tractor | 36 | 34 |
| Komatsu Ltd. | 4 | 14 |
| J. I. Case | 10 | 6 |
| Deere & Co. | 9 | 6 |
| Clark-Volvo | 4 | 6 |
| Dresser Industries | 4 | 4 |
| Fiat-Allis | 2 | 3 |
| All others | 31 | 27 |

| | EXHIBIT 5 | | |
|---|---|---|---|

**ESTIMATED PRICE AND VOLUME EXPERIENCE OF SEVEN LARGEST EARTHMOVING MACHINERY PRODUCERS (%)**

| | Increase (decrease) in $ sales | Change due to | | Change in U.S. wholesale price index |
|---|---|---|---|---|
| | | Price | Real growth | |
| 1972 | 21 | 5 | 16 | 4 |
| 1973 | 25 | 12 | 13 | 13 |
| 1974 | 24 | 10 | 13 | 19 |
| 1975 | 16 | 19 | (3) | 9 |
| 1976 | (1) | 6 | (7) | 5 |
| 1977 | 15 | 8 | 7 | 6 |
| 1978 | 27 | 9 | 18 | 8 |
| 1979 | 10 | 11 | (1) | 12 |
| 1980 | 3 | 12 | (9) | 14 |
| 1981 | 4 | 9 | (5) | 9 |
| 1982 | (25) | 5 | (30) | 2 |
| 1983 | (11) | (4) | (7) | 1 |
| 1984 | 13 | (4) | 17 | 2 |
| 1985 | 5 | (3) | 8 | 0 |

*Source:* Estimates by Wertheim & Co.

mand shifted away from large, specialized machines used in megaprojects toward smaller and more versatile equipment for inner-city renewal projects and infrastructure maintenance (e.g., excavators and loader/backhoes). This translated into lower-price (and in many instances, lower-margin) equipment and reduced replacement parts requirements.[1]

Prospects for improvement in equipment sales during the remainder of the 1980s were influenced not only by future activity levels in various user segments but also by changes in the population of used machinery. Industry observers estimated that the physical life of construction machinery averaged 5 years (versus a 25-year replacement cycle for farm equipment). However, decisions to rebuild equipment could extend life to 10 years. Assuming a conservative, 10-year replacement cycle, Wertheim & Co. estimated that the 1985 used equipment

population was 68 percent of that in the peak year, 1974. No one in the industry was certain how low the used population had to become before significant replacement demand began to develop.

Significant competitive contests were played out in a wide range of product-customer and regional market segments in this industry. Exhibit 6 provides an overview of current segment coverage by the seven largest producers. The Appendix profiles strategies of major participants other than Caterpillar and Komatsu.

Changing market conditions combined with increased competitive rivalry had a severe impact on producers' profitability during 1981 to 1985 (Exhibit 7). Results of U.S.-headquartered producers were particularly hard hit due to an appreciating dollar, which penalized competitiveness of exports and reduced the translated value of shipments from foreign plants.[2] During this period a number of companies exited the

---

[1]By way of contrast, a large crawler tractor used in mining would typically require replacement parts worth as much as the original price of the machine during its first two years of use.

[2]During 1980 to 1985 average U.S. dollar exchange rates appreciated 44 percent against the German mark, 4 percent against the Yen, 99 percent against the Cruzeiro.

EXHIBIT 6

COMPETITIVE POSITIONING OF MAJOR EARTHMOVING MACHINERY PRODUCERS, 1984

| | Caterpillar | Komatsu | Case | Deere | Clark-Volvo | Dresser | Fiat-Allis | Niche competitors | Worldwide segment sales ($ billion) |
|---|---|---|---|---|---|---|---|---|---|
| Backhoes | X | | XXX | XX | | | | Ford Tractor, Bamford (UK) | 1.6 |
| Excavators | XXX | XX | XX | XX | | X | X | AMCA; Poclain (France); Hitachi; Mitsubishi; O&K, Liebherr (Germ.) Bamford, Priestman (UK) | 2.9 |
| Crawler tractors | | | | | | | | | |
| Over 90 HP | XXX | XX | X | X | | XX | XX | | 1.2 |
| Under 90 HP | XX | XX | XX | XXX | | XX | X | | 1.7 |
| Wheel tractors | XXX | X | X | X | XX | XX | X | Ford, O&K, Bamford, Leyland | .9 |
| Graders | XXX | X | | XX | X | XX | X | | .8 |
| Crawler loaders | XXX | XX | X | XX | | | X | | 1.0 |
| Wheel loaders | XXX | XX | X | XX | XX | X | X | | 1.9 |
| Off-highway trucks | XX | X | | | XX | XX | | Unit Rig, IBH, Leyland | 1.0 |
| Scrapers | XXX | X | X | X | X | XX | X | | 1.4 |
| Other (skidders, compactors, etc.) | XXX | XX | X | X | XX | X | X | | 1.4 |
| Paving equipment | XXX | | | | | XX | | Barber-Greene, Blaw-Knox | .6 |
| | | | | | | | | | 16.4* |

XXX = leading position, XX = major participant, X = minor participant.
*U.S. market is $7.7 billion and non-U.S. market is $8.7 billion.

## EXHIBIT 7

### AGGREGATE RESULTS AND COMPANY SHARES OF TEN LARGEST PRODUCERS

| | Sales | | | | Operating profit | | | |
|---|---|---|---|---|---|---|---|---|
| | 1979 | 1981 | 1983 | 1985 | 1979 | 1981 | 1983 | 1985 |
| Aggregate results ($ million) | 14,889 | 16,036 | 11,418 | 13,591 | 1,481 | 1,410 | 116 | 733 |
| Company shares of aggregate results (%) | | | | | | | | |
| Caterpillar | 43.5 | 44.3 | 36.4 | 38.3 | 55.2 | 59.0 | (23.2) | 56.6 |
| Komatsu | 13.8 | 15.8 | 22.0 | 18.9 | 16.2 | 20.9 | 204.3 | 25.1 |
| Case | 10.0 | 9.4 | 9.5 | 7.9 | 5.6 | 3.0 | (36.2) | (11.7) |
| Deere | 6.7 | 4.9 | 5.7 | 6.9 | 4.5 | (2.8) | (56.0) | 3.0 |
| Clark-Volvo* | 6.3 | 4.9 | 5.8 | 7.0 | 4.4 | 2.6 | 37.1 | 8.9 |
| Dresser† | 3.9 | 3.6 | 6.5 | 7.5 | 3.1 | (0.7) | 6.0 | 6.7 |
| Fiat-Allis | 5.7 | 5.4 | 4.6 | 3.7 | 0 | 0 | (12.9) | 2.7 |
| AMCA(Koehring) | 2.1 | 1.9 | 1.8 | 2.0 | 3.1 | 3.4 | 4.3 | 3.0 |
| Ingersoll-Rand | 6.1 | 8.1 | 6.6 | 6.8 | 8.9 | 13.0 | (29.3) | 6.7 |
| Harnishfeger | 1.8 | 1.8 | 0.9 | 0.9 | (0.5) | 1.6 | 6.0 | (1.0) |

Table is based on construction machinery segment reporting, and does not include results of unconsolidated minority-owned subsidiaries or finance subsidiaries. Operating profits are before taxes, interest, corporate expenses, and major charges for restructuring.

*Based on combined results of Clark Equipment CM lines (Michigan and Melroe) and Volvo BM. Clark-Michigan and Volvo BM were combined in a 50-50 joint venture in 1985.

†Results for combined mixing and construction equipment segments. Reflect purchase of International Harvester (1983) and American Standard (1984) operations.

industry, typically by selling operations to other producers or spinning them off to employees. These included Allied-Bendix (Warner and Swasey-Gradhall), Allis-Chalmers, American Standard (WABCO), Eaton, General Motors (Terex), International Harvester, and Massey-Ferguson. The price of exit is exemplified by International Harvester, which sold operations with 1983 revenues of some $300 million to Dresser Industries for $82 million (roughly 25 percent of book value). Other producers sought to consolidate positions and reduce exposure by forming joint ventures (e.g., Clark-Volvo and Harnishfeger-Kobe Steel).

The remainder of this case focuses on the global rivalry between the industry's two largest broad-line companies, Caterpillar and Komatsu.

## CATERPILLAR TRACTOR

Headquartered in Peoria, Illinois, Caterpillar had long enjoyed the position of the world's largest and most broadly based producer of earthmoving machinery. It was also the world's second largest producer of diesel engines and occupied a second-tier position in the forklift truck market. Construction machinery accounted for roughly 75 percent of sales. The company was incorporated in California in 1925 to merge the original maker of crawler farm tractors, Holt Manufacturing Co., with C. L. Best Tractor Co., a maker of tracklaying tractors. Management soon elected to concentrate on construction applications of its equipment, where it saw the largest future volume.

Caterpillar's rise to global dominance in its field has been described as stemming from a combination of "good luck, shrewd judgment, and World War II":

> In retrospect, it seems clear that some U.S. company was foreordained to become the worldwide leader in the earthmoving field. The U.S. has a large land area and it was, of course, the first country to adopt the automobile on a truly mass scale. This virtually guaranteed that it would also

be first to develop superhighways and, therefore, machines to build them.

Caterpillar began staking out its gargantuan claim in its industry during the 1920s. Its first chief executive, Raymond Force, was committed to perfecting one line of machinery, and it was he who pulled Caterpillar almost entirely out of the overcrowded farm machinery business. By the time World War II came along, Caterpillar was already one of the finest producers of its kind in the country. The war created a tremendous demand for earthmoving equipment, and the U.S. Army decided to standardize on Caterpillar's bulldozers rather than those of competitors like International Harvester or Allis-Chalmers. By the end of the war it would have been difficult for other U.S. competitors to catch Caterpillar. As it happened, the competition was still not even trying very hard. IH, the second largest producer of earthmoving equipment, was still indecisive about what kind of company it wanted to be. Its net cash flow was larger than Caterpillar's until the early 1960s, but the funds were allocated among three principal divisions—farm machinery, on-highway trucks, and earthmoving equipment. Allis-Chalmers presented an even more fragmented picture, with more than half a dozen divisions competing for resources.[3]

Company executives cite two corporate policies which have directed Caterpillar's growth and development: *Focus,* the company produced only heavy machinery and engines and had steadfastly avoided diversification beyond these lines; *Preemptive market occupation,* management believed that Caterpillar should compete in all important national market segments, not only as a global profit seeker but to ensure that local producers would find it difficult to grow into world-class competitors. The press summarized Caterpillar's competitive thrust this way: "Most traditional competitors saw earthmoving equipment, diesel engines, and materials handling devices as mature businesses. Caterpillar consistently viewed them as great growth markets."[4]

[3]"The Going May Get Tougher for Caterpillar," *Fortune,* May 1972, p. 163.

[4]"Caterpillar: Sticking to Basics to Stay Competitive," *Business Week,* May 4, 1981, p. 74.

**EXHIBIT 8**

### CATERPILLAR TRACTOR SALES AND EARNINGS HISTORY

| Year | Sales ($ million) | Net income ($ million) | Return on sales (%) | Return on equity (%) |
|------|------------------:|-----------------------:|--------------------:|---------------------:|
| 1925 | 14 | 3 | 24 | 15 |
| 1930 | 45 | 9 | 20 | n.a. |
| 1935 | 36 | 6 | 17 | n.a. |
| 1940 | 73 | 8 | 11 | n.a. |
| 1945 | 231 | 7 | 3 | 10 |
| 1950 | 337 | 29 | 9 | 21 |
| 1955 | 533 | 36 | 7 | 17 |
| 1960 | 716 | 43 | 6 | 13 |
| 1965 | 1,405 | 159 | 11 | 24 |
| 1970 | 2,128 | 144 | 7 | 15 |
| 1975 | 4,964 | 399 | 8 | 25 |
| 1976 | 5,042 | 383 | 8 | 20 |
| 1977 | 5,849 | 445 | 8 | 20 |
| 1978 | 7,219 | 566 | 8 | 22 |
| 1979 | 7,613 | 492 | 7 | 17 |
| 1980 | 8,598 | 565 | 7 | 17 |
| 1981 | 9,155 | 579 | 6 | 16 |
| 1982 | 6,469 | (180) | — | — |
| 1983 | 5,424 | (345) | — | — |
| 1984 | 6,576 | (428) | — | — |
| 1985 | 6,725 | 198 | 3 | 7 |

A strong corporate culture also appears to have played an important role at Caterpillar:

Although Caterpillar is an intensely multinational company, its spirit has remained ethnocentric, even "Illinois-centric." Over two-thirds of Cat's top executives were actually born in Illinois or states bordering it. They tend to be straightlaced, with few eccentricities of manner or dress. And they are so dedicated to their work that they are sometimes described as having "yellow paint in their veins." As one top executive says, "At Caterpillar we make capital goods that change the face of the earth. We don't make consumer products that are here today and gone tomorrow."[5]

By nearly any financial standard Caterpillar was a premiere performer up through 1981 (Exhibit 8). During 1960 to 1981 net income ranged from 6 to 11 percent of sales and return on share-

holders' equity from 13 to 25 percent.[6] The only loss in the company's prior experience was one of $1.6 million in 1932. During 1982 to 1984 the company recorded cumulative net losses of $953 million as a result of industry conditions, a seven-month strike in the United States, and its own restructuring efforts.

## Products and Markets

In 1985 Caterpillar offered 131 basic models of construction machinery with a wide range of additional options in regard to horsepower, earthmoving capacity, and attachments (Exhibit 9). These machines were designed to achieve

---

[5]"The Going May Get Tougher," p. 162.

[6]These ratios are based on extremely conservative reporting practices, e.g., use of LIFO inventory valuation and accelerated depreciation for financial reporting. The spread in these ratios mainly reflects the inherent cyclicity of the construction machinery business.

**EXHIBIT 9**

## CATERPILLAR CONSTRUCTION MACHINERY PRODUCT LINE, 1985

### 1-10 . . . TRACK-TYPE TRACTORS — Standard Models

| Flywheel power 48 to 522 kW — 65 to 700 HP | D3B & D3B Custom 75 | D4E | D5B | D6D | D7G | D7H | D8L | D9L | D10 |
|---|---|---|---|---|---|---|---|---|---|

### LOW GROUND PRESSURE (LGP)

(Wider track, longer undercarriage) D3B LGP · D4E LGP · D5B LGP · D6D LGP · D7G LGP · D7H LGP

### SPECIAL APPLICATION (SA)

(Agricultural applications) D3B SA · D4E SA · D5B SA · D6D SA · D7G SA · D8L SA

### 12-20 . . . MOTOR GRADERS

| Flywheel power 93 to 205 kW 125 to 275 HP | 120B* | 140B* | 120G | 130G | 12G | 140G | 14G | 16G | *Brazilian sourced |
|---|---|---|---|---|---|---|---|---|---|

### 200-299 . . . EXCAVATORS

| Operating weight 13 018 to 64 910 kg — 28,700 to 143,100 lb | 205 LC | 206 | 211 & 211 LC | 212 | 213 & 213 LC | 214 | 215B LC & 215B SA |
|---|---|---|---|---|---|---|---|

### EXCAVATORS (cont'd)

| 224 | 225 LC & 225 SA | 235 | 245 & 245 MEH |
|---|---|---|---|

### FRONT SHOVELS

42 638 to 67 590 kg — 94,000 to 149,000 lb · 235 · 245

### LOGGER

31 661 kg — 69,800 lb **227**

      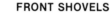  

### 400-499 . . . . BACKHOE LOADERS

Digging depth 4315 mm — 14'2" · 416

### 500-549 . . . SKIDDERS (Cable and Grapple versions)

| Flywheel power 96 to 130 kW — 130 to 175 HP | 518 | 528 | 518 Harvester |
|---|---|---|---|

### 550-599 . . . PIPELAYERS

| Lift capacity 18 100 to 90 700 kg — 40,000 to 200,000 lb | 561D | 571G | 572G | 583K | 594H |
|---|---|---|---|---|---|

### 600-699 . . . STANDARD WHEEL TRACTOR-SCRAPERS

| Heaped capacity 15.3 to 33.6 m³ 20 to 44 yd³ | 621B | 631D | 651E |
|---|---|---|---|

### TANDEM POWERED SCRAPERS

| Heaped capacity 15.3 to 33.6 m³ — 20 to 44 yd³ | 627B | 637D | 657E |
|---|---|---|---|

### ELEVATING SCRAPERS

| Heaped capacity 8.4 to 26 m³ — 11 to 34 yd³ | 613C | 615 | 623B | 633D |
|---|---|---|---|---|

**EXHIBIT 9 (cont.)**

## PUSH-PULL SCRAPERS

Heaped capacity
15.3 to 33.6 m³ —
20 to 44 yd³

627B

637D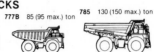

657E

## 700-799 . . . OFF-HIGHWAY TRUCKS

Capacity 31.8 to 117.9
(136 max.) metric ton —
35 to 130 (150 max.)
U.S. tons

769C 35 ton    773B 50 ton   777B 85 (95 max.) ton    785 130 (150 max.) ton

## OFF-HIGHWAY TRACTORS

Flywheel power
336 to 650 kW —
450 to 870 HP

768C    772B    776B

## ARTICULATED REAR DUMP TRUCKS

Capacity 22.7 to 49.9 metric ton — 25 to 55 U.S. tons

D25C 25 tons     D35C 35 tons    D35C-HP 35 tons    D350C 35 tons     D400 40 tons    D44 44 tons   D550 55 tons

## 800-899 . . . WHEEL TRACTORS

Flywheel power
157 to 336 kW —
210 to 450 HP

814B    824C    834B

## COMPACTORS

157 and 231 kW —
210 and 310 HP   815B    825C

## LANDFILL COMPACTORS

96 and 231 kW —
130 and 310 HP   816B    826C    518 Landfill
Compactor

## 900-999 . . . WHEEL LOADERS

Buckets 0.8 to 10.3 m³ —
1.0 to 13.5 yd³

*High lift arrangement
available.

910*    916    926    930**    936    950B    966C**    966D    980C*   **Brazilian
sourced

## WHEEL LOADERS (cont'd)

988B*    992C*

## TRACK-TYPE LOADERS

Buckets 0.8 to 2.8 m³ —
1.0 to 3.75 yd³

LGP arrangements
available.

931B    943    953    963    973*

*Steel mill arrangement available.

## INTEGRATED TOOLCARRIERS

Buckets 1.0 to 1.7 m³ — 1.25 to 2.25 yd³

IT12   IT18    IT28

## PAVEMENT PROFILERS . . . 6 Models

Cutting widths 305 to
3810 mm — 12" to 150"
Horsepower 67 to 746 kW —
90 to 1000 HP

PR-105   PR-275    PR-450    PR-1000

## CONCRETE SLIPFORM PAVERS . . . 7 Models

Paving widths 3.654
to 11.582 m —
12' to 38'

SF-175    SF-250   SF-450   SF-500   PS-28-300    TC-250    TF-250

## EXHIBIT 9 (cont.)

### FINEGRADERS ... 3 Models

Trimming widths
610 mm to 8.900 m —
24" to 29'2"

TR-500

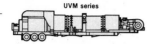

### ASPHALT PAVING EQUIPMENT ... 3 Models

Paving widths
2.438 to 8.534 m —
8' to 28'

AP-1200     WE-601B     WE-851B

### DRUM MIX ASPHALT PLANTS ... 19 Models

Portable and stationary plants
Production 38 to 794 metric t/hr —
42 to 875 ton/hr

UVM series     PVM series     SVM series

   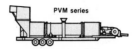  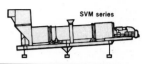

**Accessories to Asphalt Plants:**

— Emission Control Systems...
  Fabric filter particulate
  collection systems (stationary &
  portable)...40 models
  Wet-type particulate collection
  systems (stationary & portable)...
  12 models

— Aggregate Bins...
  Stationary...8 models
  Portable...11 models
— Inclined Conveyors...
  Stationary...4 models
  Portable...4 models

— Silo Storage Systems...
  Stationary...12 models
  Portable...4 models
  Highly Portable (self-erect surge
  bins)...2 models

— Asphalt Heaters...
  Stationary...6 models
  Portable...6 models
— Control Houses (stationary &
  portable)...3 models
— Portable Energy Centers...
  2 models

### COMPACTION EQUIPMENT ... 23 Models

Flywheel power
52 to 116 kW —
70 to 155 HP

Drum widths
1219 mm to 2134 mm —
48" to 84"

CS-551     CP-553

Wheel loads
1134 to 1814 kg —
2,500 to 4,000 lb

PS-110     PS-180     CB-514

Flywheel power
26 to 93 kW —
35 to 125 HP
990 mm to 1981 mm —
39" to 78"

CB-214     CB-224

### LIFT TRUCKS

**M prefix** ... Electric powered
with Cushion tires.
10 Models
Rated Capacity 1000-5000 kg
(2,000-10,000 lb)

**T prefix** ... Engine powered
with Cushion tires.
25 Models
Rated Capacity 1250-13 500 kg
(2,500-30,000 lb)

**R prefix** ... Rough terrain. Engine
powered with Pneumatic tires.
9 Models
Rated Capacity 2000-4000 kg
(4,000-8,000 lb)

**F prefix** ... Electric powered
with Pneumatic tires.
6 Models
Rated Capacity 1250-3000 kg
(2,500-6,000 lb)

**V prefix** ... Engine powered with
Pneumatic tires.
27 Models
Rated Capacity 1250-42 000 kg
(2,500-92,500 lb)

**Additional Identification:** Short Turn Radius (example: T60D Short Turn Radius or T60D STR). "C" as a prefix and numerical value indicates "compact" version with the same lifting capacity and load center as another model within the product series (example: MC30). Also, "SA" suffix identifies special application lift trucks.

**Lifting Capacity:** the nomenclature numerical value times 100. e.g., T30 = 1361 kg (3,000 lb), V180B = 8165 kg (18,000 lb) lifting capacity.

### ENGINES

Application configurations
include: On and off highway
trucks, stationary and mobile
industrial, marine, electric
power generation and
petroleum.

**3200 Series** ... 5
configurations
• 93 to 235 kW (125 to 355 HP)
  Diesel
• 60 to 154 kW (80 to 207 HP)
  Generator Sets

**3300 Series** ... 4 Models,
5 configurations each
• 64 to 250 kW (85 to 335 HP) Diesel
• 50 to 206 kW (37 to 154 HP)
  Diesel Generator Sets
• 62 to 164 kW (83 to 220 HP) Gas
• 70 to 150 kW (52 to 112 HP)
  Gas Generator Sets

**3400 Series** ... 3 Models,
5 configurations each
• 160 to 625 kW (215 to
  838 HP) Diesel
• 160 to 620 kW
  (215 to 831 HP)
  Diesel Generator Sets

**3500 Series** ... 3 Models,
5 configurations each
• 448 to 1492 kW (600 to
  2000 HP) Diesel
• 410 to 1690 kW
  (550 to 2266 HP)
  Generator Sets

**3600 Series** ... 4 Models,
4 configurations each
• 1500 to 4500 kW (1700 to
  6000 HP) Diesel
• 1240 to 4250 kW
  (1663 to 5699 HP)
  Generator Sets

**300 Series** ... 6 Models, 4 configurations each
• 373 to 1063 kW (500 to 1425 HP) Diesel
• 315 to 930 kW (422 to 1247 HP)
  Diesel Generator Sets
• 224 to 694 kW (300 to
  930 HP) Gas
• 170 to 650 kW
  (228 to 872 HP) Gas
  Generator Sets

*Last two digits of each series
(except 300's) indicate number
of cylinders; e.g., 04 = 4
cylinders, 12 = 12 cylinders.*

---
**EXHIBIT 10**
---

**CATERPILLAR SALES OF CONSTRUCTION MACHINERY AND RELATED PARTS BY DEALER OR CUSTOMER LOCATION** ($ Billion)

|  | 1979 | 1980 | 1981 | 1982 | 1983 | 1984 | 1985 |
|---|---|---|---|---|---|---|---|
| United States | 2.82 | 2.84 | 2.62 | 1.84 | 2.13 | 2.74 | 2.72 |
| Canada | 0.45 | 0.50 | 0.41 | 0.19 | 0.22 | 0.29 | 0.36 |
| Europe | 1.03 | 1.12 | 0.86 | 0.74 | 0.64 | 0.63 | 0.67 |
| Africa, Middle East | 0.86 | 1.14 | 1.63 | 0.85 | 0.57 | 0.58 | 0.52 |
| Latin America | 0.64 | 0.78 | 0.78 | 0.50 | 0.22 | 0.33 | 0.39 |
| Asia/Pacific: |  |  |  |  |  |  |  |
|   Caterpillar | 0.68 | 0.82 | 0.80 | 0.64 | 0.43 | 0.49 | 0.55 |
|   Joint ventures* | 0.80 | 0.75 | 0.72 | 0.65 | 0.47 | 0.50 | 0.48 |
|     Total | 1.48 | 1.57 | 1.52 | 1.29 | 0.90 | 0.99 | 1.03 |
|   Total outside U.S. | 4.46 | 5.11 | 5.20 | 3.57 | 2.98 | 2.82 | 2.97 |
| Total worldwide | 7.28 | 7.95 | 7.82 | 5.41 | 5.11 | 5.56 | 5.69 |

*Caterpillar-Mitsubishi and small Indian joint venture adjusted for sales to Caterpillar.

the maximum worldwide component standardization consistent with their intended functions. They covered a wide range of user applications and were offered in all major markets around the world (Exhibit 10).

The company enjoyed a strong reputation for high productivity machines which were reliable and supported by superior after-sales service (Exhibit 11). One important element in achieving this reputation had been continuous product and process development supported by large R&D expenditures. In recent years annual re-

---
**EXHIBIT 11**
---

**PERCEIVED PRODUCT QUALITY AND SERVICE SUPPORT: SURVEYS OF U.S. USERS**

|  | Product quality* | | Dealer service support* | |
|---|---|---|---|---|
|  | 1978 | 1983 | 1978 | 1983 |
| Caterpillar | 91 | 90 | 77 | 78 |
| Komatsu | 15 | 65 | 9 | 51 |
| J.I. Case | 47 | 52 | 35 | 38 |
| Deere | 59 | 58 | 44 | 48 |
| Clark | 49 | 48 | 36 | 33 |
| Dresser-IH | 47 | 52 | 38 | 40 |
| Fiatallis | 30 | 28 | 21 | 20 |
| WABCO† | 28 | 26 | 19 | 16 |
| Bucyrus-Erie | 53 | — | 24 | — |
| Terex (IBH) | 49 | 50 | 36 | 32 |
| Massey-Ferguson (IBH) | 21 | — | 16 | — |
| Average | 45 | 43 | 32 | 32 |

*100 = very good, 75 = good, 50 = average, 25 = below average or poor.
†Acquired by Dresser in 1984.
Source: Pit & Quarry magazine annual user surveys.

---
**EXHIBIT 12**
---

**ESTIMATED CATERPILLAR MACHINERY AND ENGINE PARTS SALES**

| Year | Reported sales ($ billion) | Estimated parts sales ($ billion)* | Parts as percentage of | |
| --- | --- | --- | --- | --- |
| | | | Total sales | Gross margin† |
| 1973 | 3.18 | 0.50 | 16 | 29 |
| 1974 | 4.08 | 0.55 | 13 | 29 |
| 1975 | 4.95 | 0.60 | 12 | 22 |
| 1976 | 5.04 | 0.63 | 13 | 22 |
| 1977 | 5.84 | 0.68 | 12 | 20 |
| 1978 | 7.22 | 0.74 | 10 | 18 |
| 1979 | 7.61 | 0.80 | 11 | 19 |
| 1980 | 8.60 | 0.82 | 10 | 17 |
| 1981 | 9.16 | 0.86 | 9 | 15 |
| 1982 | 6.47 | 1.00 | 15 | 35 |
| 1983 | 5.42 | 1.30 | 24 | 69 |
| 1984 | 6.58 | 1.70 | 26 | 69 |
| 1985 | 6.73 | 2.49 | 37 | 73 |

*Based on estimates by Wertheim & Co., which assume that machines stay in operation for 12 years and create parts demand valued at a percentage of their inflation-adjusted cost equal to one-half their age (e.g., a 12-year-old machine requires parts equal to 6% of its adjusted cost). Increases in parts sales from 1983 to 1985 reflect aging of machines sold in 1978–1981 peak years.
†Assumes estimated parts sales yield a 40% gross margin in all years.

search, development, and engineering expenditures have been $325 to $375 million (4 to 6 percent of sales), divided about one-third for process and product improvement and the balance for new product development. Nevertheless, Caterpillar had seldom been the first to market with radical new machines or technologies. *Business Week* has described the company's product development approach as follows:

The vast majority of Cat's research money is targeted directly toward product development, product improvement, and applied research. Caterpillar will undertake "pure" research only when it needs new materials or components that its suppliers cannot provide. With research geared heavily to existing products, Caterpillar is rarely the first to come up with a new offering in its markets. But being on the leading edge has never been one of the company's goals. It has built its reputation by letting other companies go through the trial-and-error process of introducing new products.

Caterpillar later jumps in with the most trouble-free product on the market.[7]

Replacement parts accounted for a significant portion of the company's sales and earnings (Exhibit 12). Industry analysts estimated Caterpillar's gross margin on parts at a stable 40 percent over the years. This compared with gross margins for finished machines and engines of 22 percent during 1979 to 1981, and 9 percent during 1982 to 1985. Most parts were proprietary, and Caterpillar had an estimated 75 percent share of the market for parts for its products. Sales of parts could reach $2.8 billion by 1990.

## Marketing and Field Service

Its large and financially strong worldwide network of independent dealers played a crucial role in Caterpillar's ability to sell and service

---

[7]"Caterpillar: Sticking to Basics," pp. 76–77.

its machinery. This network consisted of 82 full-line dealers in the United States and 127 abroad. In aggregate these dealers operated 992 branches and over 10,000 service bays, employed 72,000 people, and had a net worth of $2.7 billion (versus Caterpillar's net worth of $3.1 billion). Over the years Caterpillar had gone to considerable lengths to enhance dealer strength and to provide superior customer service. Important practices included:

- Maintaining a worldwide logistics and warehousing network which had the goal of delivering any part to any customer within 48 hours. Typically the company or its dealers met 97 percent of emergency parts orders within 24 hours and did not charge customers for many orders if they took longer than 48 hours to ship.
- Encouraging dealers to establish side businesses in rebuilding parts and engines. This increased dealer profitability and reduced customer maintenance costs.
- Repurchasing parts or equipment that dealers could not sell, thus encouraging them to maintain a full stock of all items.

Company-owned credit subsidiaries supported marketing efforts by financing customer purchases and dealer rental and leasing programs. These activities had tended to be less important for Caterpillar than for competitors such as Clark and Deere, because many Cat dealers either operated their own credit units or had ready access to external financing. In 1984 Caterpillar established a commodities trading subsidiary to engage in countertrade related to equipment sales.

High productivity, reliable machines, and excellent service had typically permitted Caterpillar to price its equipment at a premium. Under conditions of strong demand and short supply some machines have fetched prices 40 percent above those of the lowest-priced competitor. On bids for large projects or in markets where Cat had no dealer backup (e.g., the USSR) 10 to 15 percent premiums had been the maximum attainable. During 1982 to 1984, it appears that Caterpillar maintained its worldwide market share

by introducing several models aimed at smaller-equipment markets (which were more price sensitive) and by reducing its premium over competitors' prices.

Caterpillar had also followed a policy of differential pricing among regions of the world. Often this has meant setting lower dealer prices outside the United States—to gain market share during the 1970s and to hold it during the 1980s. Some analysts believed that Caterpillar had priced machines in Europe 20 to 25 percent below U.S. prices.[8] When the dollar strengthened after 1980, this translated into a price differential of as much as 30 to 40 percent in dollar terms and created a "gray market" for machines. As *Forbes* explained it,

> It's a classic case of arbitrage keeping markets efficient. A U.S.-built Caterpillar 215B hydraulic excavator lists in the U.S. for $120,000. A gray marketer can import an almost identical Belgian-made version for $74,000 (including insurance and freight) and sell it directly to a contractor for around $94,000—a 22% discount. Or, more likely, he will sell it to a Cat dealer for $85,000. That is around 15% less than Cat charges its dealers for equipment made in Peoria.[9]

One source estimated the overall U.S. gray market for construction machinery at $600 million during 1984 (about $400 million in Cat products). These activities had the effect of reducing U.S. profit realization for Caterpillar and disaffecting some of its U.S. dealers. This problem was expected to ease in 1986 with the weakening of the dollar.

### Manufacturing

Caterpillar's manufacturing policies straddled two potentially competing goals: maintaining maximum responsiveness to customer requirements *and* being the low-cost producer in the

---

[8]This practice did not elicit antidumping action by the EEC. The reasons seemed to be that it was limited to equipment manufactured in Europe and/or did not result in prices significantly below those of local competitors.

[9]"See the Nice, Gray Cat," *Forbes*, May 6, 1985, p. 31.

product-market segments in which it competed. The drive for customer responsiveness was reflected in the company's wide product line and in a bias for maintaining excess capacity. Prior to the 1981–1983 industry downturn, Cat typically maintained capacity 25 percent in excess of current demand. Management argued that the costs of carrying this excess capacity were preferable to losing orders or missing delivery commitments. The company's strategy for achieving cost leadership centered around concentrating component manufacturing in a few large-scale plants, high levels of backward integration, and heavy investments in automation.

In 1985 Caterpillar operated 25 manufacturing facilities around the world (excluding Solar Turbine units)—12 in the United States, 5 in Europe, and 8 in other regions (Exhibit 13). However, U.S. plants have typically accounted for some 80 percent of output and net plant and equipment (Exhibit 14). While non-U.S. sales have ranged from 42 to 54 percent of consolidated sales in recent years, non-U.S. production has ranged from 18 to 21 percent. This concentration of production in plants in and around Illinois, combined with a policy of maximum worldwide component standardization and factories focused by product, has permitted Caterpillar to achieve significant economies of scale and experience effects.

A policy of significant vertical integration has also enhanced Caterpillar's cost position. Some two-thirds of the manufacturing costs of construction machinery was in major components—engines, axles, transmissions, and hydraulics—the production of which was capital intensive and highly sensitive to economies of scale. As of 1984 Caterpillar fabricated an estimated 70 percent of its own components (versus 30 percent for Komatsu). Although Cat's costs were closely guarded information, the estimates in Exhibits 15 and 16 are indicative of the impact of integration on cost structure and profits under conditions of firm pricing and efficient capacity utilization (e.g., prior to 1981).

Concentrated production facilities have also allowed Caterpillar to derive maximum benefits

from investments in automation. The company has invested heavily in hard automation over the past decade and is believed to be relatively advanced in the use of flexible manufacturing systems.[10]

## Procurement

Vertical integration notwithstanding, Caterpillar purchased $4 to $5 billion of goods and services annually from some 23,000 external vendors. At its 1981 volume peak it was the second largest U.S. user of steel (GM being the first). As of 1981 25 percent of total purchases came from non-U.S. suppliers. Units in the United States purchased 7 percent of requirements offshore.

## Human Resources

Although Caterpillar has enjoyed a good reputation with regard to recruitment, development, and compensation of managerial and professional personnel, many observers viewed relations with hourly workers as a problem area.

A majority of the company's U.S. hourly workers was represented by the United Auto Workers (UAW). Union-management relations

---

[10]Traditional factory automation involves high-speed, high-volume production of a given item following a fixed production path or transfer line. Flexible manufacturing systems (FMS's) permit small-batch, multiple-item fabrication at costs equal to or better than traditional automation. An FMS consists of multipurpose computerized numerical control machining stations and automated inspection and support stations linked by automated handling systems. The overall system is controlled by a central computer which supervises parts routing, balances system loading, and alerts human operators to system problems. FMS cost advantages derive from reduced inventory and floor space requirements, lower labor requirements (most systems can run one or more shifts unattended), improved quality, major reductions in setup time, and reduced production lead times. These systems range in price from $4 to 20 million and take three to six years to design, build, and bring on stream. As of 1986 there were some 189 of these systems installed and operating worldwide. Caterpillar commissioned its first FMS in 1979 and had 16 systems operating by 1986 (6 in the United States and 10 in Europe. (See Exhibit 13.)

---

## EXHIBIT 13

**CATERPILLAR 1985 MANUFACTURING NETWORK**

| Location | Principal products |
| --- | --- |
| **United States** | |
| Aurora, Ill.* | Wheel loaders and tractors, compactors, excavators |
| Dallas, Ore.† | Lift trucks |
| Davenport, Iowa*† | Track-type loaders, parts for current and noncurrent products |
| Decatur, Ill.* | Motor graders, off-highway trucks, wheel tractor-scrapers, winches |
| East Peoria, Ill.* | Track-type tractors, pipelayers, power shift transmissions |
| Joliet, Ill. | Scrapers, bulldozers, rippers, hydraulic and hydrostatic controls and components |
| Lafayette, Ill. | Diesel engines |
| Mapleton, Ill. | Gray iron castings |
| Mossville, Ill. | Diesel and natural gas engines, hydraulic hose, marine transmissions |
| Peoria, Ill. | Rubber components |
| Pontiac, Ill. | Fuel systems |
| York, Pa. | Undercarriage parts, fuel injection components, oil coolers, screw machine parts |
| **Europe** | |
| Glasgow, Scotland*† | Track-type tractors, hydraulic controls and components |
| Gosselies, Belgium* | Wheel loaders and tractors, diesel engines, hydraulic components, excavators |
| Grenoble, France* | Track-type tractors and loaders |
| Leicester, England | Lift trucks |
| Vernon, France | Gray iron castings |
| **Canada, Latin America** | |
| Monterrey, Mexico | Parts and fabricated components |
| Piracicaba, Brazil | Wheel loaders, wheel tractor-scrapers, bulldozers, motor graders, track-type tractors, rippers |
| São Paulo, Brazil | Components, diesel engines |
| Toronto, Canada | Wheel loaders, lift trucks, skidders |
| **Asia/Pacific** | |
| Bombay, India (Tractor Engineers)‡ | Undercarriage components |
| Jakarta, Indonesia | Track-type tractors, wheel loaders, motor graders |
| Melbourne, Australia | Motor graders |
| Tokyo, Japan (Caterpillar-Mitsubishi)‡ | Track-type tractors and loaders, wheel loaders, diesel engines, transmissions, bulldozers, rippers, hydraulic controls, winches |

*Plants with one or more FMS's installed by 1985.

†In January 1987, the company announced plans to close the Davenport, Dallas, and Glasgow plants by the end of 1988, reducing factory floor space by further 3.8 million square feet.

‡50 percent owned. Manufacturing floor space is 2.7 million square feet for Caterpillar-Mitsubishi and 64,000 for Tractor Engineers.

*Note:* Entries exclude solar turbine plants (6 in North America) and remanufacturing facilities (6 plants). Manufacturing floor space of company-owned plants listed above is 41.3 million square feet. Net book value of properties located outside the United States represented 20.4% of consolidated net properties in 1985.

*Source:* Company publications.

---

had begun to deteriorate somewhat after 1978 as growth slowed and continuing automation began to shrink hourly jobs. However, except for an 80-day strike in 1979, there had been few work stoppages. This was believed to be due in part to management's relatively accommodative posture on wage rates (compensation per employee, adjusted for inflation, had risen faster than in the automobile industry during the 1970s).

In 1982 compensation per hourly U.S. employee, including fringe benefits, averaged $20 per hour as against $11 for Komatsu. Other as-

## EXHIBIT 14

**CATERPILLAR SOURCING PATTERNS—SALES BY MARKET AND BY PLANT LOCATION (%)**

|  | 1979 | 1981 | 1983 | 1984 | 1985 |
|---|---|---|---|---|---|
| **Sales by dealer location** | | | | | |
| United States | 46.2 | 43.4 | 54.1 | 58.1 | 56.0 |
| Europe | 15.2 | 10.8 | 14.2 | 11.4 | 12.0 |
| Africa, Middle East | 12.6 | 20.6 | 12.5 | 10.5 | 9.2 |
| Canada | 6.6 | 5.2 | 4.8 | 5.2 | 6.3 |
| Latin America | 9.4 | 9.9 | 4.9 | 5.9 | 6.9 |
| Asia, Pacific | 10.0 | 10.1 | 9.5 | 8.9 | 9.6 |
| **Sales by plant location** | | | | | |
| **United States** | | | | | |
| Domestic customers | 44.8 | 42.0 | 50.9 | 52.7 | 48.8 |
| Direct exports | 32.2 | 37.4 | 28.5 | 25.9 | 27.7 |
| Interregion transfers | 2.0 | 2.3 | 2.1 | 3.3 | 2.7 |
|  | 79.0 | 81.7 | 81.5 | 81.9 | 79.2 |
| **Europe** | | | | | |
| Unaffiliated customers | 14.3 | 12.0 | 12.3 | 11.5 | 12.8 |
| Interregion transfers | 0.1 | 0.1 | 0.1 | 0.4 | 0.4 |
| **All other** | | | | | |
| Unaffiliated customers | 6.6 | 6.2 | 6.1 | 6.0 | 7.4 |
| Interregion transfers | — | — | — | 0.2 | 0.2 |
| Total non-U.S. sales | 21.0 | 18.3 | 18.5 | 18.1 | 20.8 |
| **Direct exports of non-U.S.** | | | | | |
| plants to United States* | 0.4 | 0.4 | 1.9 | 3.2 | 5.3 |

*Included in sales to unaffiliated customers shown above.
*Note:* Figures include construction machinery and engines, exclude activities of joint venture companies. Interregion transfers are sales among CAT affiliates; all others represent direct sales to dealers or end users.
*Source:* Compiled from Caterpillar *Annual Reports,* 1979–1985.

pects of the labor agreement in force during 1982 included:

- An automatic 3 percent annual wage increase plus quarterly cost-of-living adjustments.
- Paid time off of 342 hours (nearly 43 working days) annually for an average employee. This came from vacations, holidays, a 50-hour personal allowance, and bonuses for good attendance (2 hours time-off credit for each full week on the job). The 342 compared with about 316 hours for GM and Ford workers.
- Complex seniority and work rules based on more than 500 job classifications. The business press outlined some of the issues surrounding these practices as follows: "A major sticking point is Caterpillar's desire to make

further productivity gains by changing some hallowed union work rules. Each time a job is eliminated, an average of five workers are bumped to new jobs as each one exercises seniority rights under the union contract. Playing musical chairs like that kills productivity. Caterpillar cites a recent example at an engine plant where a worker bumped down to a seemingly simple job of machining burrs off of connecting rods did $25,000 of product damage his first day in the new job."[11]

In October 1982, management went to the bargaining table with a long list of cost contain-

---

[11]"Caterpillar Faces Showdown with UAW," *Wall Street Journal,* March 5, 1986, p. 6.

---

**EXHIBIT 15**

---

**APPROXIMATE COSTS AND PROFITS FOR WHEELED FORESTRY EQUIPMENT (%)**

|  | Nonintegrated firms | Integrated firms |
|---|---|---|
| Selling price | 100 | 100 |
| Manufacturing cost |  |  |
| Direct labor | 6 | 8 |
| Purchased materials* | 58 | 30 |
| Overhead | 15 | 32 |
| Total | 79 | 70 |
| Manufacturing margin | 21 | 30 |
| Marketing, technical, and administrative costs | 12–15 | 12–15 |
| Operating profit† | 9–6 | 18–15 |

\*Steel represents approximately 15% of total manufacturing costs.
†Before interest and income taxes.
*Source:* Abell, Derek, *Defining the Business,* Englewood Cliffs, N.J., Prentice-Hall, 1980, p. 126.

ment proposals. Although the UAW had recently agreed to substantial "give ups" in bargaining with U.S. automobile companies and their suppliers, it drew the line at Caterpillar, which the union noted was profitable and the leader in its industry. A bitter, seven-month strike ensued—the longest companywide strike ever

waged by the UAW. A three-year contract was finally signed in April 1983. The settlement was described as follows:

> Caterpillar got far fewer concessions than it demanded, but it minimized damage by taking the strike at a time when demand was depressed. The company made a major concession in agreeing to a profit-sharing plan, but it did win union agreement for a three-year wage freeze. That means the cost to Caterpillar over the life of the contract appears to be considerably less than the 25% increase that would have occurred under a three-year extension of the old contract, which the union initially demanded.[12]

As Caterpillar implemented various cutbacks and restructuring programs, U.S. employment (both hourly and salaried) has fallen from 66,475 in 1980 to 37,750 at December 1985.

### Finance

The ratios in Exhibit 17 provide an overview of Caterpillar's financial management practices and

---

[12]"Caterpillar Well Positioned to Recover as UAW Ratifies 37-Month Contract," *Wall Street Journal,* April 25, 1983, p. 7.

---

**EXHIBIT 16**

---

**BREAKDOWN OF ESTIMATED MANUFACTURING COSTS FOR TWO TYPES OF MACHINERY FOR INTEGRATED PRODUCERS (%)**

|  | Wheeled forestry equipment | Medium-sized bulldozer* |
|---|---|---|
| Direct labor |  |  |
| Components and subassemblies | n.a. | 12.4 |
| Assembly | n.a. | 4.6 |
|  | 11.4 | 17.0 |
| Purchased materials | 42.9 | 49.6 |
| Overhead |  |  |
| Wage and salary related | n.a. | 18.0 |
| Other | n.a. | 15.4 |
|  | 45.7 | 33.4 |
|  | 100.0 | 100.0 |

\*Equivalent to a Caterpillar D-6D.
n.a. = not available.
*Source:* Estimates by Boston Consulting Group.

**EXHIBIT 17**

**COMPARATIVE RATIOS—CATERPILLAR VERSUS KOMATSU**

| | Caterpillar | | | | Komatsu | | |
|---|---|---|---|---|---|---|---|
| | 1979 | 1981 | 1984 | 1985 | 1979 | 1981 | 1985 |
| **Expenses (% sales)** | | | | | | | |
| Cost of goods sold | 77.7 | 76.7 | 83.4 | 78.0 | 67.1 | 68.5 | 69.7 |
| Selling, general, administrative | 8.7 | 9.5 | 13.1 | 12.6 | 17.6 | 19.0 | 20.3 |
| Research, development, engineering | 3.7 | 4.0 | 5.2 | 4.8 | 2.3 | 2.8 | 3.4 |
| Interest expense | 1.8 | 2.5 | 4.0 | 3.5 | 4.5 | 5.1 | 2.9 |
| **Operating ratios** | | | | | | | |
| Return on sales (%) | 6.5 | 6.3 | — | 2.9 | 4.2 | 4.7 | 2.8 |
| Sales ÷ assets | 1.4 | 1.3 | 1.1 | 1.1 | .7 | .8 | .8 |
| Return on assets (%) | 9.1 | 7.9 | — | 3.3 | 3.0 | 3.8 | 2.2 |
| Return on equity (%) | 16.9 | 15.9 | — | 6.5 | 10.9 | 11.9 | 5.9 |
| Employment (000) | 89.3 | 83.5 | 61.6 | 53.6 | 22.1 | 23.6 | 23.2 |
| Sales per employee ($000) | 85.3 | 109.6 | 106.8 | 125.5 | 115.2 | 135.3 | 146.0 |
| Gross machinery and equipment per employee ($000) | 27.3 | 38.9 | 63.7 | 70.6 | 28.3 | 31.3 | 46.7 |
| Inventory turn (mos.) | | | | | | | |
| Finished goods | 1.4 | 2.1 | 1.2 | 1.3 | n.a. | n.a. | 2.2 |
| Raw materials, supplies, work-in-process | 2.0 | 1.7 | 1.3 | 1.1 | n.a. | n.a. | 1.4 |
| Total | 3.4 | 3.8 | 2.5 | 2.4 | 4.1 | 3.6 | 3.6 |
| Accounts receivable turn (days) | 33 | 39 | 64 | 67 | 160 | 154 | 99 |
| **Financial ratios** | | | | | | | |
| Current ratio | 1.9 | 1.5 | 1.5 | 1.7 | 1.1 | 1.1 | 1.3 |
| Debt-equity ratio* | 0.5 | 0.5 | 0.7 | 0.5 | 1.6 | 1.2 | 1.1 |
| Short-term debt ÷ total debt (%) | 33 | 47 | 26 | 16 | 77 | 85 | 78 |
| Interest coverage † | 6 | 4.5 | neg. | 1.9 | 3.1 | 2.9 | 3.1 |
| Interest expense ÷ total debt (%) | 9.8 | 13.5 | 14.2 | 16.7 | 7.3 | 11.0 | 7.0 |
| Effective tax rate (%)‡ | 33.8 | 28.5 | (21.1) | 12.5 | 53.6 | 52.5 | 55.7 |
| Dividend payout ratio (%) | 37 | 36 | — | 25 | 24 | 18 | 30 |

*Total debt (short and long) to equity.
†Earnings before interest and taxes divided by interest expense.
‡Provision for income taxes (current and deferred) divided by income before taxes of consolidated subsidiaries.
n.a. = not available.
Source: Annual reports.

the financial impact of its operating policies versus those of Komatsu. Up through 1981 the company boasted a strong balance sheet. Losses from 1982 to 1984 resulted in deterioration of some ratios and a decision to cut quarterly dividends from $0.60 per share in 1982 to $0.375 in 1983 and $0.125 in late 1984.

## KOMATSU

In 1960 Komatsu, Ltd. had revenues equivalent to $78 million, the majority of which came from manufacture and sale of bulldozers in Japan. By 1985 its sales had reached ¥796 billion ($3.4 billion), and it was firmly established as the

### EXHIBIT 18

**KOMATSU SALES AND EARNINGS HISTORY**

| Year | Sales ($ million) | Net income* ($ million) | Sales in Japan (%) | Return on sales (%) | Return on equity (%) |
|------|------|------|------|------|------|
| 1960 | 78 | 4 | n.a. | 6 | n.a. |
| 1965 | 205 | 7 | 80 | 4 | 10 |
| 1966 | 232 | 14 | 90 | 6 | 15 |
| 1967 | 315 | 25 | 92 | 8 | 22 |
| 1968 | 431 | 31 | 91 | 7 | 21 |
| 1969 | 623 | 46 | 89 | 7 | 24 |
| 1970 | 734 | 37 | 86 | 5 | 16 |
| 1971 | 690 | 13 | 83 | 2 | 5 |
| 1972 | 896 | 29 | 83 | 3 | 10 |
| 1973 | 1,294 | 70 | 82 | 5 | 17 |
| 1974 | 1,379 | 50 | 68 | 4 | 11 |
| 1975 | 1,487 | 59 | 55 | 4 | 11 |
| 1976 | 1,360 | 51 | 59 | 4 | 9 |
| 1977 | 1,581 | 48 | 58 | 3 | 7 |
| 1978 | 2,280 | 93 | 62 | 4 | 10 |
| 1979 | 2,547 | 108 | 63 | 4 | 11 |
| 1980 | 2,857 | 122 | 57 | 4 | 11 |
| 1981 | 3,192 | 151 | 51 | 5 | 12 |
| 1982 | 3,254 | 131 | 42 | 4 | 10 |
| 1983 | 3,160 | 110 | 46 | 3 | 8 |
| 1984 | 3,004 | 96 | 55 | 3 | 6 |
| 1985 | 3,388 | 93 | 52 | 3 | 6 |

*Translated at ¥360 to $U.S. for 1960 to 1970 and at average annual exchange rates for years thereafter.
n.a. = not available.

world's second largest producer of construction machinery (Exhibit 18). Forty-eight percent of 1985 sales were outside Japan. Construction machinery accounted for 76 percent of revenues, the remainder coming mainly from metal forming equipment, robots, and diesel engines. Despite these achievements the company's 1985 annual report noted, "Since our founding, our record of growth has been marked with some turbulent moments in which Komatsu people wholeheartedly concerted their efforts for the survival of the company."

Founded in 1921 to produce machine tools and mining machinery, Komatsu gradually moved into manufacture of agricultural crawler tractors, cast steel products, large hydraulic presses, and bulldozers. The company's rebirth after World War II has been credited in considerable part to the vision and leadership of Hoshinari Kawai, who became president in 1947 after a distinguished career in government. Under his direction Komatsu focused its efforts on bulldozers, which enjoyed high growth due to Japanese reconstruction and the Korean war. By 1960 the company held 50 percent of the Japanese bulldozer market and had initiated a modest export program.[13] Nevertheless, Komatsu's position was precarious because it was based partly on tariff protection and because the com-

---

[13]Initial export orders came from Argentina, Spain (which was exporting rice to Japan at the time), and from Burma and the Philippines (both of which had war reparation agreements with Japan). Orders from the People's Republic of China, Brazil, Chile, Uruguay, Egypt, and New Caledonia soon followed.

pany's machines lacked the durability and reliability of those offered by large international producers. Mr. Kawai predicted (correctly) that it would be only a matter of time before major foreign competition appeared.

Within the next four years Japan significantly liberalized trade regulations for its machinery markets, permitting free import of bulldozers at low tariffs. Unlike autos and electronics, construction machinery was not viewed by Japan's Ministry of International Trade and Industry (MITI) as a priority sector which should receive continued protection as an "infant industry." Over bitter opposition from Komatsu and other domestic manufacturers, MITI also relaxed rules on foreign capital investment, paving the way for a joint venture between Caterpillar and Mitsubishi Heavy Industries in 1964. By 1965 Komatsu was about to witness Caterpillar's policy of preemptive market occupation in action. Komatsu's 1985 annual report recalled, "For us it meant a choice between a surrender and a do-or-die struggle for corporate survival."[14]

Komatsu's counteroffensive had actually begun in 1961 with a massive effort to redesign products and production processes. Dubbed Operation A, this effort was described as "total quality control." It started with a list of 1,657 problems to be corrected based on data compiled from user evaluations, warranty claims, and field site research.

During the next five years all employees—the president, line workers, engineers, managers, secretaries, and keypunch operators—were actively engaged in some aspect of the effort, ranging from training programs to over 1,100 quality circles. In 1964 the company was awarded the coveted Deming prize for outstanding quality programs. When the upgraded bulldozers reached the market in 1966, results were

spectacular. Durability of the new models was estimated to be twice that of the old, allowing Komatsu to double its warranty period. Actual customer claims under the new warranties turned out to be 67 percent lower than previous experience. After 1966 a successor to Operation A focused on a total approach to cost reduction. From 1965 to 1970 Komatsu increased its domestic market share for bulldozers from 50 to 65 percent despite growing competition from Caterpillar-Mitsubishi.

During the 1960s Komatsu also sought to broaden its technological base and to develop a full product line through joint ventures and licensing agreements with U.S. companies, including Bucyrus-Erie (excavators), International Harvester (wheeled loaders and off-highway trucks), and Cummins Engine (joint manufacturing and research agreements for diesel engines). The Bucyrus-Erie and International Harvester agreements barred Komatsu from selling excavators, trucks, and loaders in the United States for 17 years.

Although export sales grew steadily through the early 1970s, they took off after the oil shock of 1973. At that point Komatsu began to target OPEC and other rapidly industrializing countries (Exhibit 19). The company's export thrust was helped by aggressive pricing, by a relatively weak yen, by a willingness to use barter arrangements (in conjunction with Japanese trading companies) in cash-strapped developing countries, by significant government trade financing at rates sometimes lower than those provided by the U.S. Export-Import Bank, and by the Reagan Administration's unilateral trade sanctions against the Siberian natural gas pipeline.[15]

---

[14]In retrospect, Caterpillar-Mitsubishi appears to have played a superior "fighting unit" role (i.e., harrassing and tracking Komatsu as well as turning above-average profits). In 1979 it reported net income of $61 million on sales of $901 million. In 1985 sales were $675 and net income $7 million, although exchange rate translations somewhat distort comparisons across years.

[15]In 1981 the United States refused Caterpillar export licenses for pipelayers and other machinery ordered by the Soviets for this project. The company lost roughly $100 million in equipment sales (and up to $200 million in parts and follow-on business). Most of this business was picked up by Komatsu. It took Caterpillar until 1985 before it was again able to close significant orders for any of its products in the USSR. The company estimated its indirect loss of business after sanctions were lifted at $275 to $675 million.

---

## EXHIBIT 19

### KOMATSU SALES BY DEALER OR CUSTOMER LOCATION ($ Million)

|  | 1979 | 1980 | 1981 | 1982 | 1983 | 1984 | 1985 |
|---|---|---|---|---|---|---|---|
| **All products** | | | | | | | |
| Japan | 1,597 | 1,619 | 1,619 | 1,360 | 1,456 | 1,636 | 1,745 |
| Asia, Pacific (not Japan) | 416 | 521 | 719 | 996 | 963 | 579 | 524 |
| Europe, Africa | 222 | 378 | 479 | 642 | 504 | 337 | 507 |
| North and South America | 314 | 336 | 375 | 255 | 237 | 452 | 612 |
| | 2,547 | 2,854 | 3,192 | 3,253 | 3,160 | 3,004 | 3,388 |
| **Construction machinery** | | | | | | | |
| Japan | | | | 856 | 935 | 1,056 | 1,069 |
| Asia, Pacific (not Japan) | | | | 915 | 891 | 531 | 482 |
| Europe, Africa | | | | 590 | 467 | 308 | 466 |
| North and South America | | | | 235 | 219 | 415 | 555 |
| (U.S. portion) | | | | | (130) | (260) | (350) |
| Total worldwide | 2,061 | 2,270 | 2,526 | 2,596 | 2,512 | 2,310 | 2,572 |

## Products and Markets

Komatsu has steadily developed into a broad line producer with at least some offerings in most construction machinery categories (Exhibit 6). Product offerings differ significantly by geographic area. Until recently Komatsu has maintained its broadest coverage in Japan, the Pacific basin, and for large-scale projects anywhere in the world. Positions in other markets have involved a more targeted set of product categories (typically bulldozers and excavators).

Industry observers have estimated some of Komatsu's relative market positions as shown in Exhibit 20. An estimated 25 percent of Komatsu's export sales came from communist countries (USSR, East Bloc, PRC, Cuba), while about 33 percent came from developed market economies.

Komatsu's technology and product development thrusts differed in some important respects from those of Caterpillar. The company has invested heavily during the 1980s in an approach it calls "mechtronics," integration of mechanical and electronic systems to develop machines with unique performance capabilities or to enhance efficiency of traditional machines. It has introduced radio-controlled bulldozers, a laser-controlled autolevel motor grader, and large-scale microcomputer controls for several equipment models. Komatsu has also pioneered in developing specialty equipment for underwater and underground construction, including amphibious and swamp bulldozers, tunnel-boring machines and iron moles, and underwater rubble-leveling robots. The company had strong manufacturing process development capabilities. It was a significant producer of metal forming equipment and industrial robots, both for its own use and for external sale. R&D spending has risen from $58 million in 1979 to a peak of $139 million in 1983 before falling slightly (from 2.3 percent to rates of 3.5 to 4.5 percent of sales).

## EXHIBIT 20

### EARTHMOVING EQUIPMENT MARKET SHARES BY REGION, 1984

|  | Caterpillar | Komatsu |
|---|---|---|
| United States | 36% | 4% |
| Japan | 30 | 60 |
| Southeast Asia | 35 | 35 |
| Middle East | 45 | 30 |

## Marketing and Field Service

Most of Komatsu's sales in Japan were made directly by operating units or by company-owned distributors. Independent distributors and trading companies handled the remainder. Outside Japan sales were made by some 180 independent distributors covering 150 countries. In most major markets outside the Pacific basin Komatsu's dealer network was less well developed than Caterpillar's. For example, in the United States Komatsu had 50 distributors, most of which carry noncompeting models of other producers such as Clark and Dresser (versus 84 full-line dealers for Caterpillar, which sold only its equipment and which had capitalizations of up to ten times those of competing distributors). Industry observers predicted that as Komatsu broadened its product offerings in various regions it would move (with some success) to displace other producers in shared dealerships.

Komatsu supplied its overseas dealers through either trading companies or field marketing units located in ten countries (Australia, Belgium, Brazil, Germany, Indonesia, Mexico, Panama, Singapore, and the United States). These latter units provided dealers with technical assistance and logistical support for order and delivery of spare parts. Komatsu also maintained customer liaison offices in numerous cities (Havana, London, Paris, Warsaw, Moscow, Algiers, Nairobi, Johannesburg, Istanbul, Cairo, Amman, Baghdad, Jeddah, Dubai, Karachi, Bangalore, and Peking).

Aggressive pricing of machines played an important role in Komatsu's competitive battle against Caterpillar and others. Up through 1985 it had offered comparable equipment in some national markets at list prices 10 to 12 percent below those of Caterpillar. This pricing strategy seems to reflect a combination of willingness to accept lower margins, of low manufacturing costs, and of a yen which remained weak relative to the dollar until 1985. *Fortune* provided the following price comparisons in 1983:

A Komatsu D155A bulldozer with standard equipment lists in the U.S. for around $243,000 vs.

$276,000 posted for the Cat machine roughly comparable in size, the D8L. Were the yen to strengthen [from today's 238] to, say, 200 to the dollar, the U.S. price of the Komatsu machine, all other things equal, would rise to $290,000.[16]

Komatsu entered the United States in the late 1960s, gradually increasing its share of the bulldozer market to 8 percent in 1984. A negotiated termination of its agreements with Bucyrus-Erie and International Harvester during 1981 and 1982 permitted Komatsu to broaden its coverage from bulldozers to excavators and wheeled loaders. Total U.S. sales grew from $130 million in 1983 to $260 million in 1984, equal to about 4 percent of the U.S. earthmoving equipment market. Tokihiko Hasuo, executive vice president of Komatsu America, noted,

We got into the U.S. market very carefully. We brought our best quality machines first to see if they are accepted by U.S. customers. We didn't want to bring other machines in when we didn't have 100 percent confidence in them. After the crawler tractor and crawler loader were accepted, we started adding to the line. . . . Product support is one of the keys to whether or not we will be successful in America. If we expand our product line and don't have support, we will have done ourselves terrible damage.[17]

In mid-1984 Komatsu announced plans for a stepped up assault on the U.S. market, including establishing assembly operations during 1985. It publicly predicted that it would increase its U.S. market share to 15 percent by the early 1990s. Shoji Nogawa, the company's current president, outlined the plans as follows:

In the past, developing countries were potentially the most lucrative because their needs were so great. But the oil crisis and worldwide recession have taken the wind from their sails and we now consider the developed markets, particularly the U.S. with its vast natural resources and continuing urban development, as our major markets. Be-

---

[16]"High Stakes in the Cat Fight," *Fortune*, May 2, 1983, p. 80.

[17]"Komatsu in a Cat Fight," *Sales & Marketing Management*, April 1986, p. 50.

**EXHIBIT 21**

**KOMATSU 1985 MANUFACTURING NETWORK**

| Location<br>(floor space, thousand ft$^2$) | Principal products |
| --- | --- |
| Japan | |
| Komatsu (2,941) | Medium and small bulldozers, small hydraulic excavators, machine tools, presses, industrial robots, steel castings, rough-terrain cranes, transmissions |
| Hirakata (2,444) | Large bulldozers, large and medium hydraulic excavators, vibrating rollers, tunnel boring machines, steel castings, undercarriages |
| Oyama (1,598) | Engines, diesel generator sets, portable air compressors |
| Kawasaki (680) | Dump trucks, motor scrapers, hydraulic equipment |
| Himi (566) | Cast iron, sheet metal products, steel castings |
| Kawagoe (538) | Wheel loaders |
| Kashiwazaki (177) | Motor graders, road stabilizers |
| Hiratsuka (137) | High-purity silicon, amorphous silicon solar cells |
| Overseas | |
| Suzano, Brazil (319) | Bulldozers, cast iron |
| Chattanooga, Tenn.* | Hydraulic excavators, wheel loaders, dump trucks, small bulldozers |
| Gateshead (Newcastle), England* | Hydraulic excavators, wheel loaders |
| Mexico City, Mexico† | Bulldozers |
| Jakarta, Indonesia† | Bulldozers, excavators |

*Under construction.
†Joint venture companies.
*Note:* Manufacturing floor space totaled 9.4 million square feet in 1985, excluding US and UK facilities and joint venture companies.
*Source:* Company publications.

cause of that, we are planning to establish a production facility within a year or so.

It is necessary for us to embark on local production not only because of trade friction but also from the viewpoint of countermeasures against exchange fluctuations. We must devise a strategy based on international division of production. So in this sense, I think local production in the U.S. is a necessity.[18]

Shipping costs provided an additional motivation for U.S. production. Ocean freight, which depended both on weight and shape of machines, was 6 to 7 percent of total cost for bulldozers. For machines with long appendages (e.g., excavators) freight could be 10 percent or more.

---

[18]Japanese trade advertisement carried in *Fortune*, August 20, 1984, p. 94.

## Manufacturing

Komatsu's manufacturing strategy appeared to be similar to Caterpillar's in many respects. Like Caterpillar, it sought to balance responsiveness to customers with the need to be world competitive in costs and quality, and Komatsu also had concentrated production in a few large-scale plants and invested heavily in automation. In 1985 Komatsu had 11 factories, 8 of which were in Japan and accounted for some 95 percent of manufacturing floor space (Exhibit 21). Komatsu was believed to fabricate 30 percent of its own components (as against 70 percent for Caterpillar). This difference may be less significant than it appears because, like many Japanese companies, Komatsu probably had a number of closely tied outside suppliers. These arrangements provided many of the potential benefits of vertical integration without capital

| EXHIBIT 22 |
| --- |

**ESTIMATES OF 1979 COST STRUCTURE AND BREAKEVENS VERSUS SUBSEQUENT EXPERIENCE**

| | Caterpillar | | Komatsu | |
| --- | --- | --- | --- | --- |
| | $ million | % | $ million | % |
| **1979** | | | | |
| Net sales | 7,613 | 100 | 2,549 | 100 |
| Variable costs* | 4,949 | 65 | 2,039 | 80 |
| Contribution | 2,664 | 35 | 510 | 20 |
| Fixed costs | 2,053 | 27 | 384 | 15 |
| Operating margin | 611 | 8 | 126 | 5 |
| Other income† | 115 | 2 | 110 | 4 |
| Profit before taxes | 726 | 10 | 236 | 9 |
| $ sales breakeven‡ | 5,865 | | 1,920 | |
| **Subsequent experience** | | | | |
| 1980 sales | 8,598 | | 3,175 | |
| Operating margin | 658 | | 83 | |
| 1981 sales | 9,155 | | 3,184 | |
| Operating margin | 678 | | 140 | |
| 1982 sales | 6,469 | | 3,434 | |
| Operating margin | (587) | | 151 | |
| 1983 sales | 5,424 | | 3,207 | |
| Operating margin | (616) | | 128 | |
| 1984 sales | 6,576 | | 3,004 | |
| Operating margin | (378) | | 89 | |
| 1985 sales | 6,725 | | 3,388 | |
| Operating margin | 68 | | 86 | |

*Variable costs were estimated based on relationship between year-to-year changes in sales compared to year-to-year changes in total costs, excluding identifiable fixed costs (e.g., depreciation, interest, R&D, advertising).
†Includes license fees, interest income, income from finance subsidiaries, equity in income of unconsolidated subsidiaries, and other income.
‡Fixed costs divided by estimated percentage contribution margin.
*Source:* Annual report data, author's estimates.

investments and without assuming direct responsibilities for workers' employment security. Beyond these surface similarities, the manufacturing approaches of Komatsu and Caterpillar seemed to be quite different.

There is considerable evidence that Komatsu was not only a highly efficient manufacturer but that it had taken the lead as the industry's lowest cost producer. The comparative cost-profit structure estimates in Exhibits 17 and 22 suggest that this had happened as early as 1979. It is also noteworthy that while Komatsu's sales increased by 42 percent from 1979 to 1985, employment grew only 5 percent (see Exhibit 23 for an analysis of recent sales and cost trends).

A recent book by members of Boston Consulting Group's Tokyo office cites several reasons for Komatsu's manufacturing cost advantage[19]:

[19]James Abegglen and George Stalk, *Kaisha: The Japanese Corporation* (New York: Basic Books, 1985).

---

**EXHIBIT 23**

---

**INCREASE (DECREASE) IN KOMATSU SALES AND COSTS FROM PREVIOUS YEARS (%)**

|  | 1981 | 1982 | 1983 | 1984 | 1985 |
|---|---|---|---|---|---|
| Sales | 8.6 | 15.2 | (7.4) | (4.9) | 11.6 |
| Cost of sales* | 8.1 | 11.6 | (8.4) | (5.9) | 17.5 |
| Selling, general and administrative | 6.6 | 20.5 | (0.2) | 3.8 | (3.1) |
| Depreciation | 11.7 | 19.2 | 9.3 | 13.6 | 14.9 |
| Research and development | 17.7 | 56.1 | 6.5 | (9.6) | (8.7) |
| Interest | (0.5) | (11.2) | (16.6) | (27.8) | 21.6 |
| Number of employees | 4.4 | 4.2 | (3.2) | (1.7) | (0.9) |

*Excluding depreciation and R&D expenses.
*Note:* Figures are based on comparison of yen-measured results.

---

- Raw material costs. Lower costs of Japanese steel provided a 5 percent cost advantage in finished product for many types of machinery, including machine tools, autos, and bulldozers.
- Wage rates lower than those set by the UAW. The authors point out that although average wage rates in Japanese manufacturing were nearly the same as western averages, some western industries, such as autos and steel, had wages and benefits packages far higher than the national average and higher than justified by skill requirements.
- Superior labor productivity. The authors felt that the major causes for higher labor productivity were superior factory design and management, including more efficient material-handling environments, more "manufacturable" products, investments in quick changeover tooling (FMS's), and just-in-time scheduling.
- Asset productivity. The management approaches noted above also produced higher asset turns (and lower capital requirements per unit of output) due to higher utilization of equipment and lower inventory requirements.

The following quotes outline some of the reasoning behind the authors' assertions:

> The Japanese labor productivity advantage is enormous in high volume assembly processes where hundreds, even thousands, of interdependent steps must be coordinated. In simpler processes, such as a foundry, where perhaps thirty operational steps are required, the Japanese advantage is slight, and sometimes nonexistent. In process industries such as paper, chemicals, and metal refining, Japanese labor productivity in comparable plants is no better than can be found in western plants.

Higher labor productivity in complex manufacturing has only recently been achieved by Japanese firms. For example, in 1976 Caterpillar led Komatsu in labor productivity. By 1982 Komatsu had achieved a 50 percent labor productivity advantage despite continuing improvements by Caterpillar.

The Japanese attain their productivity advantages in both obvious and subtle ways. Obvious ways include heavier investment in capital equipment, product designs that are easier to manufacture, and more focused factories. In extreme situations these alone can result in productivity advantages of 20–30 percent. More subtly, in the last five years many Japanese manufacturers have modified their production process from batch and semicontinuous processing to near continuous processing. This has been implemented through just-in-time scheduling, different manning configurations, changes in material flows, and related techniques. These techniques are often described as inventory reducers and quality improvers; yet they are far more. Plants with these manufacturing systems require less labor (both direct and indirect) to operate, even when product variety is greater.

A Japanese or western competitor that has invested time and money in implementing the JIT manufacturing system can choose to use the cost savings in two ways—it can make the same variety of products at lower cost or higher quality (or both) or it can make a greater variety of products at similar, or even lower, cost. Komatsu provides examples of both choices. It first invested in quick changeover tooling for its engine plant. The production variety and the volumes of the plant have increased, but the number of employees at this plant remained almost constant. Initially, Komatsu may have benefited from its heavy investments in low setup tooling by making the same variety of products at lower costs. Beyond this, Komatsu has continued with investment in quick changeover tooling for its other plants. It is pursuing the benefits of making a greater variety at similar or lower costs. As a result, Komatsu has transformed itself from a short line manufacturer to a producer of a broad line of equipment. Such proliferation usually weakens the smaller competitor, yet Komatsu competes vigorously against Caterpillar.[20]

## Human Resources

Komatsu has a labor contract with the Komatsu Labor Union covering conditions of employment for a majority of its employees. This contract was renegotiated every two years and, among other things, required that all employees except those designated as managerial must become union members. In line with general Japanese practices, wages, benefits, and other remuneration were negotiated annually.

## Finance

Exhibit 17 compares Komatsu's balance sheet ratios with those of Caterpillar. In evaluating these data, one should note that Komatsu was engaged in direct sale of its products in Japan, whereas this was mainly an off-the-balance-sheet activity for Caterpillar.

[20]Ibid., pp. 60–63, 117–118.

# Profiles of Seven Significant Competitors

## J. I. CASE

Construction machinery sales were $1.51 billion in 1981 and $1.079 billion in 1985. A subsidiary of Tenneco, Inc. (nine major business groups, 1985 sales of $15.3 billion), Case manufactured agricultural equipment and light- and medium-sized construction machinery. Products sold through over 3,000 independent or company-owned dealers supported by company credit subsidiaries.

Case has long dominated the market for crawler and wheeled backhoes. Its 580E tractor backhoe/loader was the highest-volume model in the construction machinery industry and was believed to account for the bulk of its operating earnings. During the 1970s Case broadened its line through internal development and acquisitions—Drott (hydraulic excavators and cranes) and Davis (trenching and boring equipment). It also owned 44 percent of Poclain S.A., a large French manufacturer of excavators and cranes. In 1980 Case formed a joint venture with Cummins Engine to produce diesel engines for its construction equipment and farm tractors.

The company has held market share during the 1980s through aggressive pricing and because its emphasis on small and medium machines fits well with current U.S. demand. Its position could come under pressure from Caterpillar as it expands into smaller equipment segments. Less than 20 percent of sales were made outside the U.S. (excluding Poclain).

## DEERE & CO.

Deere's sales of industrial equipment in 1981 and 1985 were $782 and $943 million, respectively. Operating results for those years were a $39 million loss and a $22 million profit, respectively. Deere was the world's largest producer of farm tractors and implements. Industrial equipment segment accounted for 23 percent of 1985 sales. Two North American plants were devoted primarily to construction machinery. Roughly 12 percent of Deere's 3,500 dealers sold construction machinery and were supported by company credit subsidiaries.

Deere's products compete for about 40 percent of the estimated U.S. market for all types and sizes of industrial equipment. Its offerings fell into three broad categories: utility tractors and small earthmoving equipment, medium capacity construction and earthmoving equipment, and forestry machines. Deere's products enjoyed a high-quality reputation, and it held roughly 25 percent of the U.S. crawler market. Its main weaknesses were its low representation in overseas markets and in heavier machines.

Deere was the low-cost producer of agricultural equipment. Its industrial equipment business began with wheel and crawler tractors of a size and horsepower range similar to farm tractors, utilizing common componentry. The company was highly integrated, supplying most of its own engines, transmissions, and hydraulic components.

During the late 1970s Deere announced a strategy to become the number two worldwide producer of construction machinery in the 1990s. This strategy has come to naught due to heavy competition in both construction and farm equipment sectors and due to dealer resistance. New division management was emphasizing profitability rather than growth. The current strategy was to be the low-cost producer of small and medium machinery in the United States. In 1983 Deere announced a joint design and manufacturing venture for small excavators with Hitachi Construction Machinery Company.

## DRESSER INDUSTRIES

Dresser's figures for sales and profit (in $ million) were:

|  | 1981 | 1985 |
|---|---|---|
| Mining equipment sales | 344 | 436 |
| Construction equipment sales | 234 | 582 |
|  | 578 | 1,018 |
| Operating profit | (10) | 49 |

With sales of $4.1 billion and a net loss of $196 million for the year ending October 31, 1985, Dresser Industries operated in five business segments—products and services for the petroleum industry, energy processing and conversion equipment, refractory and mineral products and services, mining and construction equipment, and specialty industrial products.

Dresser's original position centered around its Marion line of walking draglines and giant power shovels and its Galion line of highway maintenance equipment. During the 1980s it filled out its product line through acquisition of troubled operations at bargain prices. In 1983 it purchased International Harvester's construction machinery business for $82 million (25 percent of book value). In late 1984 it purchased the WABCO off-highway truck business from American Standard for $66 million, at a similar discount.

Dresser management aspired to be the second- or third-ranked world-scale competitor. Its strategy centered around cost reduction (through automation and off-shore sourcing), upgrading the dealer network, and updating products. Industry observers were divided on the prospects for this strategy. The bears note that most of the products have been losing market share for several years, that the product line was skewed toward large machines and lacked a significant position in excavators, and that dealer coverage needed improvement. They also point out that recent operating profits were significantly impacted by liquidation of LIFO inventories resulting from rationalization of acquired units (and may not be repeated) and that 1985 profits were nearly wiped out by a $42 million write-down of mining equipment assets. The bulls point out that Dresser was getting high turnover on cheap assets, was providing stronger support for acquired units than their previous parents, and had the product breadth to succeed.

## CLARK-VOLVO

Clark-Volvo's construction machinery sales and operating profits (in $ million) were:

|  | 1981 | 1984 |
|---|---|---|
| Sales |  |  |
| Clark | 497 | 584 |
| Volvo BM | 285 | 345 |
|  | 782 | 929 |
| Operating profits |  |  |
| Clark | 29 | 42 |
| Volvo BM | 7 | 30 |
|  | 36 | 72 |

In 1985 A.B. Volvo and Clark Equipment Company formed a 50-50 joint venture to which Clark contributed its Michigan Company and Volvo its entire construction machinery line. The new company, VME Group N.V., reported sales of $772 million, a net loss of $7 million, and an equity base of $185 million for 1985. Volvo is Sweden's largest manufacturing company, with 1984 sales equivalent to $10 billion. Clark Equipment is a producer of material-handling equipment, construction machinery, and heavy-duty axles and transmissions with 1984 sales of $1.2 billion.

The Clark Michigan Company, which became part of VME, produced Michigan wheeled tractor shovels and dozers, Ranger woodland and logging equipment, and Euclid off-highway trucks (acquired in 1984). Estimated 1984 sales were $404 million and operating profit $10 million. Clark retained full ownership of another construction machinery operation, the Melrose Company, which produced small and medium loaders under the Bobcat name. Melrose had 1984 worldwide sales of $180 million and an operating profit of $32 million. The Volvo BM line consisted of wheel loaders, dump trucks, and front loaders. It was one of Europe's leading construction machinery companies and had a dominant worldwide share of the market for articulated dumpers.

Clark had never been a full-line producer in the construction machinery area—lacking coverage in crawlers, excavators, backhoes, and (until 1984) off-highway trucks. The Volvo joint venture provided added market share in traditional lines and in Europe. However, it did little in broadening product coverage, and neither company has a significant position in the Pacific basin. Lack of a full line increased the risks of dealer defections. In many instances current dealers had filled out their coverage with Komatsu or Dresser crawlers and excavators. As both of the latter companies push for wider coverage in various markets, dealers will be faced with the trade-off of retaining profitable parts and repair business from their Clark positions versus the longer-term attraction of signing on fully with potentially stronger competitors.

## FIATALLIS

Fiatallis's sales in 1981 and 1985 were $862 million and $497 million, respectively. Net loss in 1981 was $18 million, and net profit was $15 million in 1985. Fiatallis is a subsidiary of Fiat S.p.A., an Italy-headquartered producer of automobiles, trucks, agricultural tractors, and industrial equipment and services. In 1985 sales of construction machinery accounted for 3.5 percent of Fiat's Lit 27,101 billion ($14.2 billion) in sales.

Fiatallis was formed in 1974 as a 65-35 percent merger of the construction machinery operations of Fiat and Allis-Chalmers. In 1985 Allis-Chalmers sold its remaining 12 percent equity position to Fiat. Fiatallis's product line is skewed toward heavy equipment segments. In these segments it had a 1984 worldwide share of 7.4 percent (versus an estimated 3 percent share of the overall earthmoving machinery industry). Its heavy equipment market shares were 43 percent in Italy, 19 percent in the Middle East, and 4.6 percent in North America. Although the company claimed to have gained worldwide market share in heavy equipment since 1981, most industry observers believed it had experienced losses in overall share.

## AMCA INTERNATIONAL

AMCA's construction machinery sales in 1981 and 1985 were $309 million and $274 million, respectively. Operating profits for 1981 and 1985 were $48 million and $22 million, respectively.

A Canada-headquartered producer of industrial products and services with 1985 sales of $1.6 billion, AMCA's better-known companies are Gidding & Lewis, Dominion Bridge, Koehring, and Quonset Buildings. The construction machinery segment consisted of BOMAG, a Germany-headquartered company, which was a world leader in compaction equipment, and Koehring, headquartered in Waverly, Iowa. Koehring produced a broad line of hydraulic cranes, a full line of hydraulic excavators, specialty forklifts and loaders, and tree harvesting and pulp and paper equipment. Both companies were acquired in the 1980s.

## SAMSUNG HEAVY INDUSTRIES

Samsung turns out about 5,000 units of construction machinery annually, including excavators, loaders, dozers, cranes, and road rollers. The company held roughly 70 percent of the Korean market.

# Caterpillar and Komatsu in 1987

Case Six describes the competitive positioning and performance of Caterpillar, Inc. and Komatsu Ltd. during 1985–1987. Earlier developments in this competitive contest are covered in Case Five.

## INDUSTRY CONDITIONS

Medium-term prospects for the construction machinery industry were for modest growth at best. The *Economist* estimated that 1987 industry capacity exceeded demand by 40 percent and that worldwide sales would grow less than 2 percent annually through 1990. Sales of smaller machines were expected to grow 5 percent annually over the same period.

Prospects for the U.S. market looked much the same. Frost & Sullivan was forecasting annual growth in constant dollars at 1.5 percent through 1991, with flat demand during 1987–1988 and 3 percent annual growth for later years. Changes in U.S. tax law, which eliminated the

This case was prepared from public sources by Professor Stephen A. Allen as a basis for class discussion. Copyright © 1988 by Stephen A. Allen.

investment tax credit and lengthened depreciation schedules, were expected to have a mildly negative impact. Industry observers estimated that these changes would raise after-tax costs of new machinery purchases by up to 10 percent, pushing some potential buyers toward rental and lease arrangements of purchase of used machines.

Revenues and earnings of United States-based producers were expected to fare somewhat better than those of offshore rivals due to ongoing benefits from restructuring efforts and a major depreciation of the dollar. Between July 1985 and December 1987, the yen had appreciated 98 percent against the $U.S. (from 249 to 126). During the same period the Deutsche mark had appreciated 89 percent against the dollar.

## CATERPILLAR

During 1983–1985 Caterpillar undertook a massive program of consolidation and repositioning. Its immediate goal was to reduce its breakeven point permanently without taking actions detrimental to long-term success. Its longer-run goal was to become "the lowest cost producer in the industry based on value provided"; 1985 op-

---
**EXHIBIT 1**
---

**CATERPILLAR EXPORT ACTIVITY**

| Year | Gross exports ($ billion)* | Gross exports as % of U.S. factory shipments | Net exports ($ billion) | U.S. jobs supported by exports (thousand) | As % of U.S. employment | As % of total employment |
|------|------|------|------|------|------|------|
| 1981 | 3.7 | 48 | 3.3 | 31 | 46 | 36 |
| 1982 | 2.6 | 48 | 2.5 | 27 | 58 | 44 |
| 1983 | 1.6 | 38 | 1.3 | 16 | 37 | 28 |
| 1984 | 1.9 | 36 | 1.4 | 16 | 35 | 26 |
| 1985 | 2.1 | 38 | 1.4 | 15 | 40 | 28 |
| 1986 | 2.2 | 39 | 1.1 | 14.5 | 40 | 27 |

*Sales of U.S. manufactured product to non-U.S. customers plus U.S. transfers to other regions.
*Source:* Company annual reports.

erating expenses were reduced 22 percent below those of 1981. Management's objective for 1986–1990 was to reduce costs a further 15–20 percent below 1985 levels. Early cost reductions were accomplished in several ways:

- Plant closings. Six plants were closed by 1985, reducing factory floor space by 27 percent. In 1987, plans were announced to close three additional plants by the end of 1988, reducing floor space a further 9 percent. Nonrecurring charges related to these moves totaled $552 million (before taxes) during 1983–1987.
- Workforce reductions. The workforce was cut by 37 percent during 1981–1986 (from 85,922 to 53,731). This consisted of a 44 percent cut in hourly workers and a 26 percent reduction in salaried and/or supervisory jobs. The U.S. workforce was reduced 47 percent, non-U.S. workforce, 2 percent.
- Increased use of external suppliers and offshore sourcing. Actions included heavier loading of offshore plants and development of production agreements for finished machines with a variety of U.S. and offshore companies. Major production agreements included those for all forklift truck requirements (Daewoo of Korea and a Norwegian company) and several new products (paving equipment from CMI Corp. and a new excavator line from a German company). Make-buy decisions on components also underwent intensive review.

Company executives estimated that by 1990 Caterpillar would be making less than half of the number of parts items in-house than it did in 1980. The proportion of purchases from offshore suppliers increased during 1981–1985 from 7 percent to 16 percent of all U.S. purchases and from 25 percent to 38 percent for all worldwide units. Despite these moves Caterpillar remained a major U.S. exporter (Exhibit 1).

Chief executive officer (CEO) George A. Schaefer outlined Caterpillar's sourcing strategy as follows:

We once thought we should make virtually every part of every machine we produced. Today we shop the world for low cost, high quality goods and services.

Prior to 1981 only about 4% of our material consumed in U.S. facilities was received from overseas sources. By 1985 that figure had risen to 16%. We now expect that the pace of our move to overseas sources will slow—although there are still opportunities to find and develop more overseas suppliers.

Our byword in this whole effort is our determination to meet our target costs through our ability to remain flexible. With the change in the relationship of the dollar to foreign currencies, particularly those of Japan and Europe, our strategy to implement forward currency contracts to protect the value of selected significant long-term supply contracts has proven beneficial. Over 25%

of our goods received from overseas suppliers are now exchange rate protected, and we are continuing to apply this technique to areas that are still presenting opportunities.

With our multiple manufacturing locations within major currency sectors and our worldwide purchasing organization we have the capability to roll with the currency punches—enabling us to supply what is needed from wherever is advantageous. This sourcing flexibility provides us a real competitive advantage.[1]

During 1984–1985 the company more than doubled the number of models in its product line. This effort included extending product and geographic coverage in traditional segments and moving into new segments, particularly smaller machines. Mr. Schaefer noted,

> Historically new products have provided about a third of our growth. We are putting increasing emphasis on small machines, with appropriate design, cost effectiveness, and active training of dealers. Backhoe loaders are one major addition to our line. They're being made at our plant in Leicester, England. Production is already sold out through this year. These machines are the centerpiece of our small machine lineup: some 20 machines of about 100 horsepower and below. It is the broadest small machine line offered in the industry, and it will grow even further. It is aimed at a whole new breed of customer—smaller contractors and owner-operators who have not been traditional Caterpillar customers.[2]

In another speech, Schaefer stated:

> Many of our new products were developed in-house. Others were added to our line through joint ventures, license arrangements, and branding agreements. This strategy allows us to bring products to the marketplace quickly by taking advantage of other companies' manufacturing and engineering resources. It also allows us to expand

the product line without increasing industry capacity—and with relatively little capital investment.

One of the most significant arrangements of this type involves the hydraulic excavator market. Excavators represent 40% of the unit opportunity and 30% of the dollar opportunity for construction machines. That's a worldwide sales potential of more than $4 billion. Almost half of the world's excavators are sold in Japan, and up until now, Caterpillar has not been able to participate actively in that large market.

We have just expanded our joint venture with Mitsubishi Heavy Industries to include excavators. We have been partners with MHI for more than 20 years, but the original agreement did not permit Caterpillar-Mitsubishi to manufacture excavators. C-M has now acquired MHI's plant and will begin producing excavators there. We'll be able to meet the Japanese competition head on with a broad line of low-cost, high quality machines. We're enthused about the prospect of moving right into Komatsu's front yard.[3]

Major new product categories accounted for some $360 million of sales in 1986. According to *Business Week*,

> Cat has already grabbed about 11% of the backhoe-loader market. "They've made inroads into everybody's business in North America," admits John A. Borden, executive vice president for marketing at J.I. Case Co.[4]

By 1987 management felt that it had generally exhausted conventional approaches to cost reduction. Further performance improvements were expected to come from three initiatives: product engineering changes aimed at reducing manufacturing costs without compromising quality or value, plant modernization programs, and quality improvement. Mr. Schaefer described design programs as follows:

> A major portion of our research and engineering program is committed to projects that will allow more cost-effective manufacturing through better

---

[1]Remarks by George A. Schaefer to the Financial Analysts of Philadelphia, May 15, 1986. Company financial executives indicated to the case writer that planned offshore sourcing was hedged on a selective basis out as far as 3 years in currencies for which such forward contracts were available. At the end of 1986 Caterpillar had some $1.1 billion in forward contracts outstanding.

[2]*Ibid.*

---

[3]Remarks by George A. Schaefer to the Baltimore Security Analysts Society, September 16, 1986.

[4]"For Caterpillar the Metamorphosis Isn't Over," *Business Week*, August 31, 1987.

design and the use of new materials and technology. In October, 1987, we will begin production of a new line of smaller, more efficient, less costly engines in several products. The engines will appear in Caterpillar machines in early 1988 and will be used in more than 40 models—resulting in cost savings averaging $1,200 per unit. A new, more cost-effective transmission will replace the current design in some of our machines beginning in early 1988, producing cost savings averaging $1,000 per machine. Many such programs are underway. In some areas we are starting to get the benefits now, but the bulk of savings will be during 1989–91.[5]

In early 1986 management outlined plans for upgrading manufacturing activities. Dubbed the "Plant with a Future" (PWAF) program, this effort was described as follows by Schaefer:

PWAF is our game plan that combines more belt tightening measures with advanced technology and the just-in-time manufacturing philosophy. It will permit us to do more in less space with lower costs and greater manufacturing flexibility. Ultimately PWAF will produce factories in which computers will help with everything from the design of a product to its delivery. We envision our factories of the future being paperless because information will be stored in computers; inventories will be much smaller; and products will move through final assembly in much less time than it takes today. Production will be fine-tuned with products produced only as they are needed to fill orders, substantially reducing inventory at both ends.

The program will involve more than $1 billion in expenditures over the next five years alone, and it will be largely funded by savings generated as the program advances. We'll be using more robots, more automated welding equipment, and more flexible manufacturing systems. As we move closer to operating in a just-in-time mode, we have added to our electronic communication abilities and now have the worldwide ability to track incoming material so we know where the material is at any point in the transportation stream. As a result, we can precisely predict and control destination arrival times.[6]

Caterpillar executives emphasized that PWAF was not simply an automation project: PWAF represented a fundamental reformulation of the company's manufacturing strategy which emphasized significantly increased coordination among plants and with product engineering and marketing. PWAF encompassed redesign of components and products and of factory floor layouts as well as equipment investments. Factory floor space requirements were expected to fall from 45 million $ft^2$ in 1985 to 31 million in 1990. Coverage by the trade press cited some of the specific features of PWAF:

The five-year program to automate and integrate all of Caterpillar's plants will improve productivity and quality as well as cut production costs. Ray Adams, Director of Manufacturing, argues that it will also help other departments such as marketing by cutting the lead times in which marketing can promise a product. Product engineers will benefit by working with manufacturing to develop designs that can be produced with ease as well as help develop manufacturing systems that suit designs for which they are intended.

As an example of the benefits of the program, Adams notes that a bulldozer blade formerly had a production lead time of about 50 days. A target of five days has been set. Adams says this will provide invaluable aid to marketing representatives in selling bulldozers with a multitude of blade options available without having to inventory all the blades.

In hardware Adams says he expects the company to double the total number of flexible manufacturing systems from the current level of 15–20. Cells are expected to increase by a factor of four over the current 100–200. And while declining to give a specific number on robots, other published reports indicate that the number will increase four-fold from a current level of about 150.

Adams does not emphasize the hardware involved in the plans as much as the integration and redesign of production layouts for improved flow. For example, sheet metal fabricating and welding equipment will no longer be assigned to separate "functional" departments. Rather, it will be located on a "product" basis next to cutting machine tools.

Peter Donis, Caterpillar President, noted the

[5]Remarks by George A. Schaefer to the Dallas Association of Investment Analysts, May 13, 1987.
[6]Remarks to Financial Analysts of Philadelphia, May 15, 1986.

importance of this at the company's annual meeting when he pointed to motor grader front axle production at the Decatur, Ill., plant. There, he said, parts for axles move as much as 1.5 million feet through the facility. There are about 276 stops and delays in the plant, along with 130 setup hours per month. The PWAF plan will produce parts in a distance as short as 540 feet with two stops and delays with no setup hours.[7]

Caterpillar had begun a major program to train employees in basic quality concepts and tools in 1982. Mr. Schaefer noted,

We are now beginning to see results from that training effort. Since 1982 we have launched over 1,200 project teams whose goal was to improve the quality of existing processes. Almost 700 of these teams have completed work, and they have achieved some $64 million in cost savings. These are not one time only savings. They are ongoing. This amounts to an average savings per team of $92,000.

What is particularly exciting about these efforts is that we are gaining these benefits, in most cases, without incurring capital expenditures. We are doing it with present processes by using statistical analysis and teamwork to eliminate waste and by pursuing relentlessly opportunities to improve manufacturing processes. For example, in our Mossville, Illinois, engine plant a team of managers and hourly employees worked together to improve quality and reduce cost of connecting rods for one of our engine models. The cost of the product was reduced 47%, and annual savings exceeded $2 million. On top of that, warranty costs fell by 84%.[8]

Management claimed that relations with workers had improved considerably from the bitter days of 1982–1983. In July 1986, UAW members ratified a 28-month contract which included a continuing wage freeze, work rule changes, a job security pact, and a retraining program. While this contract involved no work stoppages, separate agreements with employees at plants in Joliet, Illinois (International Association of Machinists), and Toronto (Canadian Auto Workers) were preceded by strikes of 28 days and 16 days, respectively. Mr. Schaefer noted,

To fully achieve the potential of PWAF we absolutely need a flexible and participative work force. The new labor agreements with the UAW and the International Association of Machinists will help. These contracts sharply reduce the number of labor grades and job classifications. Also, the rules for assigning employees to jobs have been streamlined. The contracts will increase labor costs, but overall, we are pleased with the economics. . . . Our success in the economic and productivity provisions of the contract result largely from our willingness to address the job security concerns of employees and the UAW. While stressing continually that the only job security is a profitable company, we did provide an added measure of security through a new Protected Employee Group program. This provides that 90% of the current hourly work force is protected from layoff subject to only a few exceptions. Employment reductions through attrition can occur under the PEG program. . . . The IAM opted for a cash bonus in lieu of the job security program. Otherwise, the UAW and IAM agreements are similar.[9]

In another speech Schaefer noted:

We believe the agreement provides a base for a new direction in Caterpillar-UAW negotiations. One dimension of this new spirit is our UAW-Caterpillar Employee Satisfaction Process. Last year both Caterpillar and the UAW agreed that employees should participate more actively in matters that affect their jobs and their working relationships. The goal is to create an improved working environment and a means to tap the reservoir of employee ideas for work and quality improvement.[10]

Exhibit 2 traces cost and revenue trends from 1981 to 1986. During 1986 sales grew by 9 percent. However, net income fell by 62 percent,

---

[7]"Manufacturers on the Leading Edge," *American Metal Marketer,* September 1, 1986.

[8]Remarks to the Dallas Association of Investment Analysts, May 13, 1987.

[9]Remarks to the Baltimore Security Analysts Society, September 16, 1986.

[10]Remarks to the Dallas Association of Investment Analysts, May 13, 1987.

**EXHIBIT 2**

**INCREASE (DECREASE) IN CATERPILLAR SALES AND COSTS FROM PREVIOUS YEAR (%)**

|  | 1981 | 1982 | 1983 | 1984 | 1985 | 1986 |
|---|---|---|---|---|---|---|
| **Sales** | | | | | | |
| Due to price | 4.5 | 3 | (3) | (5) | 1 | 3 |
| Due to physical volume | (2) | (32) | (13) | 26 | 1 | 6 |
| **Costs (income statement categories)** | | | | | | |
| Cost of sales* | 4.3 | (24.0) | (17.6) | 22.4 | (4.4) | 12.9 |
| Selling, general, administrative expenses† | 13.0 | 1.5 | (8.7) | 2.1 | (1.5) | 11.0 |
| Depreciation and amortization | 21.1 | 12.7 | 0 | (2.8) | (3.3) | (8.4) |
| R&D expenses | 13.5 | 3.1 | (6.0) | 5.0 | (5.6) | (5.5) |
| Interest expense | 29.8 | 48.4 | (8.4) | (13.4) | (11.7) | (15.8) |
| **Other indicators** | | | | | | |
| Wages, salaries, and contributions for employee benefits | 8.1 | (15.0) | (13.4) | 13.3 | (10.4) | 0.5 |
| Materials, supplies, services purchased | 12.4 | (38.3) | (24.0) | 52.6 | n.a. | n.a. |
| Average number of employees | (3.4) | (12.2) | (20.3) | 4.8 | (8.9) | (3.2) |

*Excluding depreciation and R&D expenses.
†Excluding depreciation.
n.a. = not available.

due mainly to provisions for plant closings and lower LIFO inventory benefits (Exhibit 3). For the first nine months of 1987 the company reported net income of $180 million on sales of $5.9 billion. These results included $49 million of nonrecurring charges (including Caterpillar's share of a voluntary retirement program accepted by 1,200 hourly and salaried employees at Caterpillar-Mitsubishi Ltd.). In December 1987, Caterpillar raised its quarterly dividend to $0.1875 per share from $0.125.

## KOMATSU

For its part, Komatsu indicated continued commitment to its long-term goal of "encircling Caterpillar." However, appreciation of the yen from 250 in early 1985 to below 130 in late 1987 raised a host of problems. In 1986 the Japanese business newspaper, *Nihon Keizai Shimbun* estimated that a 150-yen rate would reduce Komatsu's profits by 52 percent. In its 1985 annual report company management stated,

> Komatsu is maneuvering with agility to tackle problems associated with the appreciation of the yen. For our short-term strategy, we are implementing all conceivable measures including a reasonable price boost of our products, further reductions in production costs, and expanded overseas parts procurement. To counterbalance the effect of the price hike on our customers' purchasing power, we are pursuing strategic marketing initiatives, including increased new product introductions and offshore assembly plants. We remain committed to making well defined, substantial investments in R&D and facilities enhancement.

Despite a 41 percent appreciation of the yen during 1985–1986 Komatsu raised prices in the United States by about 18 percent. *Fortune* noted,

## EXHIBIT 3

### CATERPILLAR OPERATING DATA

|  | 1985 | 1986 |
|---|---|---|
| **Sales ($ million)** | | |
| Machinery | 5,208 | 5,761 |
| Engines | 1,517 | 1,560 |
| United States | 3,763 | 3,984 |
| Europe | 804 | 1,077 |
| Africa, Middle East | 622 | 612 |
| Canada | 425 | 485 |
| Latin America | 467 | 543 |
| Asia, Pacific | 644 | 620 |
|  | 6,725 | 7,321 |
| **Income and expense ($ million)** | | |
| Operating profit | 302 | 249 |
| Nonrecurring items | (69) | (112) |
| Interest expense | (234) | (197) |
| Other income | 216 | 159 |
| Income taxes | (27) | (23) |
| Equity in profit of affiliated companies | 4 | (6) |
| Profit of finance subsidiaries | 5 | 6 |
| Net income—consolidated | 198 | 76 |
| Employment (thousand) | 53.6 | 53.7 |
| Return on sales (%) | 2.9 | 1.0 |
| Return on assets (%) | 3.3 | 1.2 |
| Asset turnover | 1.1 | 1.2 |
| Return on equity (%) | 6.5 | 2.4 |
| **Expenses (% sales)** | | |
| Cost of goods sold | 78.0 | 79.5 |
| Selling, general, administrative | 12.6 | 12.9 |
| R&D, engineering | 4.8 | 4.2 |
| Interest expense | 3.5 | 2.7 |
| **Operating ratios** | | |
| Sales per employee ($ thousand) | 125.5 | 136.3 |
| Inventory turnover (months) | | |
| Finished goods | 1.3 | 1.2 |
| Raw materials, supplies, work-in-process | 1.1 | 1.3 |
| Total | 2.4 | 2.5 |
| Accounts receivable (days) | 67 | 86 |
| **Financial ratios** | | |
| Current ratio | 1.7 | 1.5 |
| Debt-equity ratio* | 0.4 | 0.5 |
| Interest coverage† | 1.9 | 1.5 |
| Interest expense ÷ total debt | 16.7 | 12.5 |

*Total debt (short and long) to equity.
†Earnings before interest and taxes divided by interest expense.

━━━━━━━━━━━━━━ **E X H I B I T  4** ━━━━━━━━━━━━━━

**PARTNERSHIP ARRANGEMENTS DEVELOPED BY KOMATSU, 1985 TO 1987**

Dong-A Motor Ltd. (Korea)—licensing agreement for off-highway dump trucks

China National Technical Import Corp. (PRC)—agreement for joint assembly of heavy-duty dump trucks

ABG Werke GmbH (Germany)—OEM agreement for vibrating rollers to be marketed worldwide by Komatsu

Brown Group International PLC (UK)—OEM supply agreement for articulated dump trucks to be marketed worldwide by Komatsu

Clark Equipment (U.S.)—supply agreement under which Clark's Melroe Division will market Komatsu small hydraulic excavators under the Melroe name in North America

Samsung Heavy Industries (Korea)—collaboration agreement under which Samsung will produce and market Komatsu-designed small bulldozers, wheel loaders, and motor graders under the Samsung brand in Korea, using Komatsu components

Yanmar Diesel Ltd. (Japan)—cross-licensing agreement involving wheeled mini excavators from Komatsu and carrier dump trucks from Yanmar

Robbins Co. (U.S.)—technical licensing agreement for tunnel-boring machines to be used in the Euro Tunnel Project across the English Channel

*Note:* Arrangements developed for construction machinery only. Numerous agreements had been signed for other lines of business.

Donald Fites, Caterpillar's executive vice president, brands the announced increases a "public relations stunt." The price the customer pays for a Komatsu machine, Fites says, has hardly changed at all. Komatsu says prices actually charged vary by dealer, but have been rising gradually. Cat has continued to hold the line on prices in the U.S.[11]

Komatsu sales in the United States were $400 million in 1986, up 14 percent from 1985.

In 1985 Komatsu acquired and refurbished a former Koehring plant in Chattanooga, Tennessee. By 1987 this facility was producing 22 models of excavators, wheel loaders, dump trucks, and small bulldozers, accounted for an investment of $27 million, and employed 250. Production

was highly automated, and 1987 output totaled 1,300 units with plans to increase capacity to 2,500 units in 1988. U.S. value added was about 50 percent, with all steel, tires, hydraulics, and some engines purchased locally.

In a similar move the company acquired an idled facility in the United Kingdom, near Newcastle. This plant commenced production of wheeled loaders and excavators in late 1986. Output was projected to reach 2,400 units in 1988 with employment of 270. Management indicated that the plant expected to make significant use of local parts suppliers in EEC nations. Establishment of this facility was partly motivated by the EEC's levying antidumping duties against Komatsu's hydraulic excavators.

Management also announced several moves aimed at developing a coordinated overseas manufacturing network:

> In conjunction with production start-ups at plants in the U.S. and UK, Komatsu realigned operations of other existing overseas plants during 1986. Utilizing its cost-effective production of cast steel parts, Komatsu Brazil has begun to supply these parts to plants in Japan and to overseas locations as spare parts. From Dina Komatsu Nacional in Mexico, which is equipped with expertise in plate working technologies, such plate parts as buckets have been supplied to the U.S. plant. P.T. Komatsu Indonesia is also becoming further integrated into these arrangements.

In addition to increased sourcing of components from suppliers throughout the Pacific basin, Komatsu developed a number of partnership arrangements—licensing, coproduction, and marketing agreements—aimed at expanding its product-market scope and sharing product development efforts (Exhibit 4).

In 1986 Komatsu launched an additional product line targeted at differences in regional needs of users. Management noted,

> Beginning in the U.S. and Europe in 1986 Komatsu launched its New-Line Construction Equipment for Varied Regional Needs line. In order to supply such equipment we have divided the world marketplace into six regions for product specifi-

─────────────

[11]"Let Down by the Drooping Dollar," *Fortune*, June 9, 1986.

**EXHIBIT 5**

## KOMATSU OPERATING DATA

|  | ¥ measured | | $ measured |
|---|---|---|---|
|  | 1985 | 1986 | 1986* |
| **Sales (¥ billion, $ million)** | | | |
| Construction equipment | 604.5 | 567.5 | 3,398 |
| Metal forming machinery | 40.7 | 75.4 | 451 |
| Industrial machinery | 8.2 | 9.3 | 56 |
| Electronics, applied products, components | 79.5 | 74.0 | 443 |
| Other | 63.3 | 62.5 | 374 |
| Japan | 410.1 | 420.0 | 2,515 |
| Asia, Oceania | 123.2 | 96.7 | 579 |
| Americas | 143.7 | 125.4 | 751 |
| Europe, Africa | 119.2 | 146.6 | 878 |
|  | 796.2 | 788.7 | 4,723 |
| **Income and expense (¥ billion, $ million)** | | | |
| Operating profit | 43.2 | 26.7 | |
| Interest expense | (23.1) | (22.4) | |
| Interest and other income | 28.7 | 31.5 | |
| Income taxes | (27.2) | (20.0) | |
| Minority interests | (.1) | (.1) | |
| Equity in income of associated cos. | .4 | (1.0) | |
| Net income—consolidated | 21.9 | 14.7 | 88 |
| Employment (thousand) | 23.2 | 22.9 | |
| Return on sales (%) | 2.8 | 1.9 | |
| Return on assets (%) | 2.2 | 1.5 | |
| Asset turnover | .8 | .8 | |
| Return on equity (%) | 5.9 | 3.8 | |
| **Expenses (% of sales)** | | | |
| Cost of goods sold | 69.7 | 71.3 | |
| Selling, general, administrative | 20.3 | 20.8 | |
| R&D engineering | 3.4 | 3.7 | |
| Interest expense | 2.9 | 2.8 | |
| **Operating ratios** | | | |
| Sales per employee (¥ million) | 34.3 | 34.4 | |
| Inventory turnover (months) | | | |
| Finished goods | 2.2 | 2.1 | |
| Raw materials, supplies, work-in-process | 1.4 | 1.2 | |
| Total | 13.6 | 3.3 | |
| Accounts receivable (days) | 99 | 169 | |
| **Financial ratios** | | | |
| Current ratio | 1.3 | 1.4 | |
| Debt-equity ratio† | 1.1 | 0.8 | |
| Interest coverage‡ | 3.1 | 2.5 | |
| Interest expense ÷ total debt | 7.0 | 6.8 | |

*Dollar figures translated at average annual exchange rate of ¥167/$U.S.
†Total debt (short and long) to equity.
‡Earnings before interest and taxes divided by interest expense.

cations. Required quality standards are based on exhaustively analyzed market research data from all parts of the world. New models developed during 1986 were bulldozers, wheel loaders, and hydraulic excavators. These additional models have greatly widened customers' choices in accordance with their job-specific requirements, bringing about reductions in the total costs involved.

During 1985–1987 Komatsu moved to diversify its revenue base. Sales of metal-forming machinery and industrial equipment (e.g., robots, laser machines, machine tools) grew significantly. The company also entered a new line of business—plastics injection molding machinery and plastics component manufacturing.

In 1986 yen-measured net income fell 33 percent on a sales decline of 1 percent (Exhibit 5). Industry observers estimated that Komatsu's manufacturing cost advantage over Caterpillar had fallen to 15 percent in mid-1987 from more than 40 percent in 1984. The company was expected to report a further decline in earnings for 1987.

The Komatsu organization appeared to have suffered significant trauma related to rapid repositioning efforts. A rather unusual casualty of this situation was the company's president, Shoji Nogawa, who was asked by directors to resign his position in August 1987. Mr. Nogawa remains a director. A *Wall Street Journal* article commented,

> There are several examples of top Japanese executives who have responded to current pressures by standing tall and speaking with a strong voice, only to be sacked by directors. Earlier this year, Shoji Nogawa, the autocratic president of Komatsu lost his job for trying to impose too much, too fast from the top. Mr. Nogawa brought a decisive, strong-willed style of management to Komatsu. But after five years of increasing conflict between Mr. Nogawa and other Komatsu executives, he was removed as president.[12]

---

[12]"In Japan Breaking Step Is Hard To Do," *Wall Street Journal,* December 14, 1987,

# Heineken N.V.

During the early 1980s, the executive board of Heineken N.V., the famous Dutch beer and beverage company, had met a number of challenges to the basic strategy they had defined for the organization. Since the acquisition of the Amstel Brewery in 1968, Heineken had accelerated a process of diversification aimed at reducing its dependency on exports of Dutch beer. This had led to renewed efforts to be present in all European beer markets and to expand its activity in other continents, in addition to a growing commitment to nonbeer beverages. Presently, Heineken's management felt the need to evaluate the performance of the company in this respect and to make use of experience and forecasted market conditions to define a clear set of objectives that would guide the group's future geographical spread and product diversity.

## HISTORICAL BACKGROUND

Heineken N.V. was founded by G. A. Heineken in 1864, when he purchased for Df 48,000 one of the largest breweries of the time, *de Hooiberg* (the Haystack), which had been operating in the center of Amsterdam since 1592. In 1868 a new brewery was built in the meadows outside Amsterdam (now in the center of the city), and, as business was prosperous, a second Heineken brewery was inaugurated in Rotterdam in 1874. For a number of years, all Heineken beer was produced in these two breweries.

Modest export activities started as early as the 1860s, principally to India and the East and West Indies' markets, and developed rapidly to other countries. In 1927 Heineken acquired 100 percent of the shares of Brasserie Leopold, a family-owned brewery in Brussels. Shortly thereafter, the end of prohibition in the United States opened what was to become Heineken's largest single export market. Heineken's entry into Singapore, Indonesia, and Egypt were also of importance during this period.

This case was written by André Khodjamirian and Professor José de la Torre as a basis for discussion. The generous contribution of many Heineken executives is gratefully acknowledged, but the authors retain all responsibility for any errors or misinterpretation of facts. Copyright © 1985 by INSEAD, The European Institute of Business Administration.

Heineken's foreign interests expanded further in the early postwar years. In Singapore, the company bought a second brewery, which had been confiscated from the Germans, and expanded to Malaysia (a new brewery was established in Kuala Lumpur) and Australian New Guinea. Through a Belgian associate, Heineken obtained access to breweries in Zaire, Burundi, Rwanda, and Congo-Brazaville, and in West Africa, Heineken started operations with United Africa Company (a Unilever affiliate) on a ⁵⁰⁄₅₀ basis in Nigeria, followed later by Ghana, Sierra Leone, and Chad. In the Caribbean, the company acquired interests in Trinidad, St. Lucia, Martinique, and Jamaica.

Perhaps the most important event in the company's postwar expansion was the purchase of Amstel Brewery in 1968. The Amstel brand was second to Heineken in market share in the Netherlands with about 15 percent of the market and had recently expanded to a number of foreign markets in the Middle East, Africa, and the Caribbean. Conceived as a reactive move to a threat to its domestic market (see below), the merger gave Heineken a combined market share of 50 percent in the Netherlands, a broader product range with which it could stop further competitive threats, and a number of important affiliates in foreign markets.

In recent years Heineken continued its expansion into new and existing markets. A licensing agreement in 1968 with the United Kingdom's Whitbread proved to be a very successful operation. In 1972, Heineken acquired a financial participation in a French group of breweries which later led to a fully owned subsidiary in this large market. Two years later, Heineken entered into a joint venture in Italy with its British partner, Whitbread. Further expansion in South America and the Caribbean opened new geographical areas to Heineken. Since 1975, Norway, Sweden, and Ireland were added to the European countries where the Heineken or Amstel brands were produced under license. See Exhibits 1 and 2 for a summary of these developments.

## Financial Performance

Heineken could be qualified by any standards as a successful company. Besides being one of the largest beer exporters in Europe, and probably the world, the company enjoyed a solid image and followed a quality-conscious approach to producing beer that had won its product worldwide fame. Sales proceeds increased fourfold, from Df 1.1 billion in 1972, to over Df 4.2 billion in 1982. The company had increased trading profits 2.2 times during the same period, but overall profitability had declined in the last three years (see Exhibits 3 through 5 for details). Income from technical fees related to agreements with foreign operations contributed a small but important (in profit terms) fraction of total revenue. The rest originated from sales of beer, spirits and wine, and soft drinks.

Beer accounted for around 80 percent of Heineken's total income (see Exhibit 6). In fact, beer had increased its share of the company's business throughout the 1970s in spite of heavy investments in product diversification. Domestic sales in hectoliters rose from around 0.3 million in 1951, to over 7 million in 30 years (see Exhibit 7). Beer sales outside the Netherlands represented about 70 percent of total volume, and turnover in the Western Hemisphere, which included Heineken's major foreign market, the United States, grew from 5 percent of sales in 1973, to 15 percent in 1983 (see Exhibits 8 and 9).

Investments in plants and other installations increased by about four times in the 1972–1982 period. Asset turnover rate remained fairly constant, around 0.9, and the company had an average financial leverage (calculated on the basis of total debt to equity) of about 0.9.

## Organization and Planning

After the Amstel merger in 1968, the company operated through three major divisions: commercial, responsible for all Dutch sales; technical, handling all production and technical as-

EXHIBIT 1

**HEINEKEN'S INTERNATIONAL ACTIVITIES, 1863–1982**

| | |
|---|---|
| 1864–1885 | Limited exports to various countries such as France, Belgium, England, East and West Indies, Turkey, Egypt, and Spain. |
| 1878 | Brasserie Bavaro rented in Belgium, with an option to purchase; withdrew in 1879. |
| 1894 | Exports begin to the United States. |
| 1927 | Belgium: Acquisition of Brasserie Leopold; sold in 1964. |
| 1930 | Singapore: Joint venture and technical contract in Malayan Breweries (42 percent). |
| 1933 | Exports resume to the United States after prohibition. |
| 1936 | Indonesia: Minority participation taken in Surabaja Brewery; Heineken brand produced locally until 1963; holding later increased to 77 percent. |
| 1937 | Participation (via indirect holding) in some African countries, such as Egypt (nationalized under the Nasser regime) and the Belgian Congo (Zaire), and in Indo-China (sold in the 1950s). |
| 1940–1945 | Exports stopped due to World War II. |
| 1949 | Nigeria: Joint venture with United Africa Company (UAC) in Nigerian Breweries (first 50 percent, now 13 percent). |
| 1950 | Venezuela: Majority participation and Heineken license; divested in 1963. |
| 1952 | French Congo (Brazzaville): Indirect participation and technical contract in Brasserie de Brazzaville. |
| 1955 | Surinam: Amstel minority participation (now 38 percent and technical contract.<br>Belgium: Participation in Moutery Albert (malting plant), later fully owned. |
| 1956 | Burundi: Indirect participation (now 59 percent) and technical contract in Brarudi. |
| 1958 | Jordan: Minority participation and licensed production of Amstel. |
| 1959 | Rwanda: Indirect participation and technical contract in Bralirwa (now 70 percent). |
| 1960 | Netherlands Antilles: Amstel license and minority participation (now 52 percent) in Antillian Brewery.<br>Lebanon: Amstel license and minority participation.<br>Italy: Minority participation and technical contract in Dreher Beer; later fully owned. |
| 1961 | Ghana: Joint venture with UAC and technical contract in Kumasi Brewery Ltd.<br>Angola: Participation and technical contract in Nova Empresa de Angola (27 percent). |
| 1962 | Martinique: Minority participation in Brasserie Lorraine; later increased to 58 percent. |
| 1963 | Chad: Minority participation and technical contract in Brasserie du Logone.<br>Sierra Leone: Joint venture with UAC and technical contract in Sierra Leone Brewery Ltd. (now 22 percent).<br>Greece: Amstel minority participation, license and technical contract in Athenian Brewery S.A.; later increased to 98 percent. |
| 1964 | Papua New Guinea: Indirect participation via Malayan Brewery and technical contract. |
| 1965 | South Africa: Amstel license and technical contract.<br>Spain: Joint venture with UAC: sold in 1969. |
| 1969 | United Kingdom: Heineken license and technical contract with Whitbread. |
| 1972 | Sierra Leone: Heineken license.<br>France: Majority participation in Alsacienne des Brasseries (Albra).<br>Trinidad: Participation (38 percent), technical contract and Heineken license with National Brewing Co.<br>Jamaica: Heineken license and technical contract. |
| 1975 | Norway: Heineken license.<br>Portugal: Technical contract.<br>New Caledonia: Technical contract and later on participation (86 percent) via Albra.<br>Sweden: Heineken license to Falken; terminated in 1978. |

## EXHIBIT 1(cont.)

| | |
|---|---|
| 1976 | Haiti: Technical contract and Heineken license in 1977. |
| | St. Lucia: Participation (65 percent), Heineken and Amstel license and technical contract in Windward & Leeward Brewery. |
| | Tahiti: Technical contract, Heineken and Green Sands licenses. |
| | Italy: Heineken license. |
| 1978 | Ireland: Heineken license and technical contract with J.J. Murphy. |
| 1979 | France: Amstel license for low-calorie beer; terminated in 1982. |
| 1980 | Finland: Technical contract. |
| | Morocco: Heineken license. |
| | Nigeria: Green Sands license. |
| | Trinidad: Green Sands license. |
| 1981 | France: Heineken license. |
| | Italy: Amstel license to Peroni. |
| | South Korea: Heineken license and technical contract. |
| | Canada: Acquisition (100 percent) of existing brewery renamed Amstel Brewery, Canada. |
| 1982 | Sweden: Amstel license |
| | Central Africa: Doubling of participation in Zaire (60 percent), Rwanda (70 percent), Burundi (59 percent), the People's Republic of Congo (100 percent), and Angola (27 percent) by acquiring shares from Banque Lambert. |

*Source:* Company records.

sistance worldwide; and international, with line authority over exports, licenses, and participations. Each member of the executive board acquired direct operational responsibility for one division, and four regional groupings—Europe, Asia/Australia, Africa, and Western Hemisphere—were created at this time.[1]

During the 1970s, the corporate marketing, exports, and technical areas were given worldwide responsibility, but regional subgroups were established within each function. Simultaneously, four overall regional coordinators were given strategic and coordinating responsibility for their respective regions of the world and were placed under the direct supervision of one of the members of the board. The objective of this matrix structure was to balance the need for geographic focus and coordination with the requirement for close control of critical corporate functions. Exhibit 10 presents a simplified

version of the company's organizational structure in 1983.

Following the regionalization of foreign activities and their increased autonomy, the need for systematic planning was strongly felt. Beginning in 1980, a planning letter was sent by the Executive Board to all major affiliates early in the year. The letter would outline major objectives for the corporation and for the respective affiliate for the near future. This would then form the basis for a detailed subsidiary five-year plan that would be discussed with the board, the regional coordinator, and other key corporate executives. Such meetings were held at least once yearly but could be scheduled more frequently for certain critical activities.

Financial policy was highly centralized in Heineken. Retaining family control and avoiding falling "in the claws of the banks" were two important objectives. Headquarters would decide on how best to balance an affiliate's capital structure based on a number of criteria, the most critical of which was not to exceed an overall debt-to-equity ratio of 0.8 or 0.9 to 1. For this

---

[1]For a more detailed discussion of the company's organization, see Case Thirty-six.

# EXHIBIT 2

## LICENSING OPERATIONS AND PARTICIPATIONS WORLDWIDE, 1983 (THIRD PARTIES)

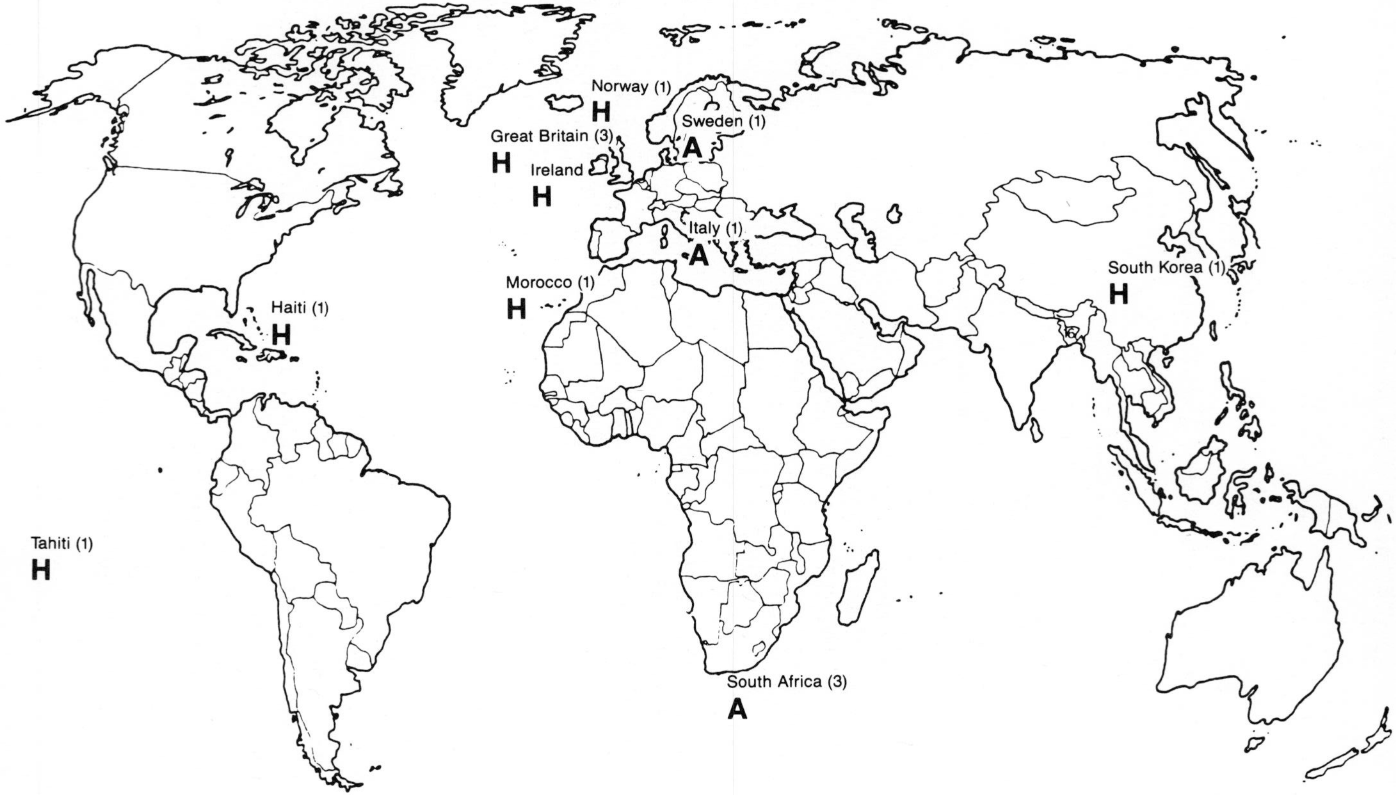

South Korea (1) **H**

Norway (1) **H**

Sweden (1) **A**

Great Britain (3) **H**

Ireland **H**

Italy (1) **A**

Morocco (1) **H**

South Africa (3) **A**

Haiti (1) **H**

Tahiti (1) **H**

(a) Licensing operations worldwide (third parties), 1983

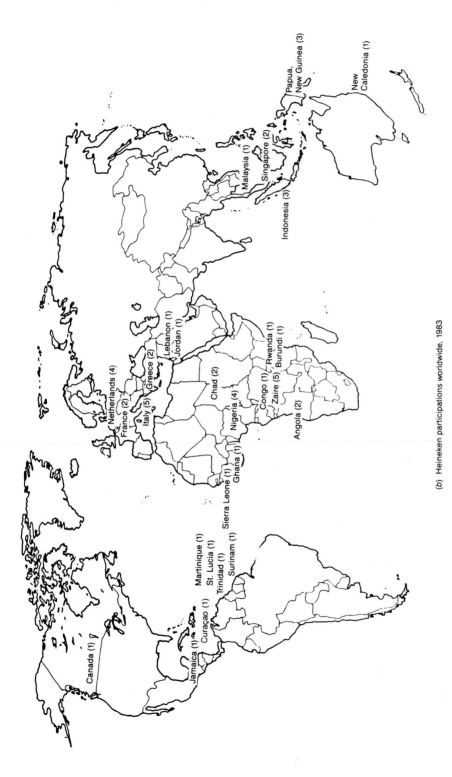

*(b)* Heineken participations worldwide, 1983

*Note:* **H** = Heineken; **A** = Amstel. Figures in parentheses represent number of breweries.
*Source:* Company records.

# EXHIBIT 3

## BALANCE SHEETS, 1974–1982 (Df Million)

| | 1982 | 1981 | 1980 | 1979 | 1978 | 1977 | 1976 | 1975 | 1974 |
|---|---|---|---|---|---|---|---|---|---|
| **Assets** | | | | | | | | | |
| Fixed assets | | | | | | | | | |
| Plants and installations | 2,174.0 | 2,113.5 | 2,088.1 | 1,776.9 | 1,571.8 | 1,397.0 | 1,154.3 | 1,071.3 | 901.9 |
| Other real estate | 73.5 | 61.5 | 61.8 | 58.8 | 57.7 | 57.4 | 51.2 | 55.7 | 48.6 |
| Participations | 67.6 | 69.0 | 60.3 | 60.1 | 56.6 | 59.8 | 56.9 | 59.6 | 57.3 |
| Miscellaneous | 89.1 | 78.6 | 76.2 | 69.6 | 77.0 | 74.9 | 61.7 | 73.0 | 69.3 |
| | 2,404.2 | 2,322.6 | 2,286.4 | 1,965.4 | 1,763.1 | 1,589.1 | 1,324.1 | 1,259.6 | 1,077.1 |
| Current assets | | | | | | | | | |
| Stocks | 605.0 | 504.8 | 480.3 | 403.1 | 375.1 | 358.3 | 278.5 | 278.7 | 231.4 |
| Accounts receivable | 343.7 | 325.9 | 286.2 | 277.0 | 261.8 | 227.6 | 179.6 | 167.7 | 177.3 |
| Cash & securities | 372.0 | 199.0 | 97.1 | 90.6 | 74.1 | 95.4 | 83.0 | 38.8 | 39.1 |
| | 1,320.7 | 1,029.7 | 863.6 | 770.7 | 711.0 | 681.3 | 541.1 | 485.2 | 447.8 |
| Total | 3,724.9 | 3,352.3 | 3,150.0 | 2,736.1 | 2,474.1 | 2,270.4 | 1,865.2 | 1,744.8 | 1,524.9 |
| **Liabilities** | | | | | | | | | |
| Group funds | | | | | | | | | |
| Share capital | 361.2 | 361.2 | 361.3 | 289.0 | 289.0 | 231.2 | 231.2 | 177.8 | 177.8 |
| General reserve | 673.7 | 572.4 | 497.8 | 557.7 | 465.1 | 459.2 | 382.7 | 392.1 | 350.4 |
| Revaluation reserve | 691.4 | 650.6 | 544.8 | 429.3 | 361.9 | 222.8 | 192.6 | 152.5 | 124.2 |
| Shareholders' equity | 1,726.3 | 1,584.2 | 1,403.9 | 1,276.0 | 1,116.1 | 913.2 | 806.5 | 722.4 | 652.4 |
| Minority interests | 74.8 | 51.1 | 33.9 | 23.6 | 39.6 | 37.6 | 27.5 | 47.6 | 44.5 |
| | 1,801.1 | 1,635.3 | 1,437.8 | 1,299.6 | 1,155.7 | 950.8 | 834.0 | 770.0 | 696.9 |
| Investment facilities equalization account | 101.9 | 98.4 | 90.8 | 48.8 | 27.1 | 14.5 | 8.4 | 5.5 | 4.6 |
| Provision for tax & | 485.8 | 428.8 | 427.3 | 307.1 | 272.3 | 360.8 | 251.2 | 177.9 | 164.8 |
| other | 587.7 | 527.2 | 518.1 | 355.9 | 299.4 | 375.3 | 259.6 | 183.4 | 169.4 |
| Debts | | | | | | | | | |
| Long-term debts | 341.8 | 326.3 | 330.9 | 227.5 | 239.1 | 214.5 | 202.9 | 201.6 | 205.7 |
| Current liabilities | 994.3 | 863.5 | 863.2 | 853.1 | 779.9 | 729.8 | 568.7 | 589.8 | 452.9 |
| | 1,336.1 | 1,189.8 | 1,194.1 | 1,080.6 | 1,019.0 | 944.3 | 771.6 | 791.4 | 658.6 |
| Total | 3,724.9 | 3,352.3 | 3,150.0 | 2,736.1 | 2,474.1 | 2,270.4 | 1,865.2 | 1,744.8 | 1,524.9 |

*Note:* Figures from 1971 to 1978 are as of 30 September and from 1979 onward are as of 31 December. Where necessary, figures have been rounded off.
*Source:* Annual reports.

EXHIBIT 4

**INCOME STATEMENTS, 1974–1982** (Df Million)

| | 1982 | 1981 | 1980 | 1979 | 1978 | 1977 | 1976 | 1975 | 1974 |
|---|---|---|---|---|---|---|---|---|---|
| Sales proceeds | 4,150.1 | 3,552.2 | 3,178.3 | 3,427.9 | 2,623.1 | 2,428.2 | 2,095.6 | 1,811.3 | 1,549.2 |
| Income from technical fees | 47.6 | 44.8 | 37.6 | 43.5 | 34.8 | 26.7 | 26.6 | 16.8 | 23.0 |
| Miscellaneous income | 17.1 | 16.2 | 14.0 | 17.8 | 13.8 | 15.3 | 14.7 | 14.0 | 12.0 |
| Turnover | 4,214.8 | 3,613.2 | 3,229.9 | 3,489.2 | 2,671.7 | 2,470.2 | 2,136.9 | 1,842.1 | 1,584.2 |
| Raw materials | 430.5 | 368.9 | 301.1 | 337.6 | 280.7 | 250.0 | 228.9 | 202.5 | 175.4 |
| Packing materials | 533.1 | 487.6 | 423.0 | 430.5 | 316.9 | 298.2 | 228.2 | 195.8 | 138.3 |
| Merchandise | 163.2 | 153.0 | 160.7 | 171.0 | 118.9 | 104.0 | 92.1 | 106.2 | 92.0 |
| Selling expenses | 332.9 | 301.2 | 269.8 | 265.4 | 232.0 | 212.0 | 190.6 | | |
| Other expenses | 516.3 | 470.5 | 433.2 | 419.0 | 284.1 | 273.4 | 248.8 | 361.0 | 283.3 |
| Excise duties | 909.6 | 627.7 | 594.5 | 662.1 | 505.2 | 477.6 | 444.1 | 381.0 | 352.1 |
| Salaries and social security | 766.8 | 676.7 | 623.3 | 687.6 | 513.5 | 451.4 | 378.4 | 344.0 | 285.5 |
| Depreciation | 268.4 | 267.7 | 227.3 | 228.3 | 164.3 | 155.6 | 128.1 | 105.0 | 94.6 |
| | 3,920.8 | 3,353.3 | 3,032.9 | 3,201.5 | 2,415.6 | 2,222.2 | 1,939.2 | 1,695.5 | 1,421.2 |
| Trading profit | 294.0 | 259.9 | 197.0 | 287.7 | 256.1 | 248.0 | 197.7 | 146.6 | 163.0 |
| Interest paid | 60.3 | 69.5 | 71.9 | 52.4 | 39.1 | 39.6 | 33.6 | 37.4 | 24.3 |
| Miscellaneous revenues & charges | 26.8 | 12.7 | 8.5 | 8.4 | 5.6 | 4.6 | 2.2 | 4.1 | 2.4 |
| Profit before Tax | 260.5 | 203.1 | 133.6 | 243.7 | 222.6 | 213.0 | 166.3 | 113.3 | 141.1 |
| Taxation on Profit | 108.9 | 82.2 | 53.9 | 104.0 | 105.0 | 106.9 | 84.9 | 55.3 | 65.9 |
| | 151.6 | 120.9 | 79.7 | 139.7 | 117.6 | 106.1 | 81.4 | 58.0 | 75.2 |
| Dividend from participations | 10.4 | 3.6 | 7.2 | 4.8 | 4.4 | 5.6 | 7.3 | 8.7 | 7.3 |
| Group profit | 162.0 | 124.5 | 86.9 | 144.5 | 122.0 | 111.7 | 88.7 | 66.7 | 82.5 |
| Minority interests | 8.8 | 4.1 | −3.8 | −0.8 | −3.3 | −2.2 | 3.4 | 3.9 | −1.5 |
| Net profit | 153.2 | 120.4 | 83.1 | 143.7 | 118.7 | 109.5 | 92.1 | 70.6 | 81.0 |
| Memoranda | | | | | | | | | |
| Dividends declared | 50.6 | 50.6 | 50.6 | 50.9 | 40.5 | 32.4 | 32.4 | 24.9 | 24.9 |
| Trading profit as percentage of turnover | 7.0 | 7.2 | 6.1 | 8.6 | 9.6 | 10.0 | 9.3 | 8.0 | 10.3 |
| Trading profit as percentage of total capital employed | 7.8 | 7.8 | 6.3 | 9.0 | 10.4 | 10.9 | 10.6 | 8.4 | 10.7 |
| Net Profit as percentage of shareholders' equity | 8.9 | 7.6 | 5.9 | 9.9 | 10.6 | 11.8 | 11.3 | 9.7 | 12.3 |
| Dividend as percentage of net profit | 33.0 | 42.0 | 60.9 | 35.4 | 34.1 | 29.5 | 35.1 | 35.3 | 30.7 |

*Source:* Annual reports.

---

**EXHIBIT 5**

---

**AVERAGE BREAKDOWN OF COSTS FOR RECENT YEARS AS PERCENTAGE OF TOTAL SALES**

|  | Labor | Materials | Capital | Other | Total |
|---|---|---|---|---|---|
| Production | 9.2 | 28.1 | 4.5 | 15.5 | 57.3 |
| Marketing and distribution | 6.9 | — | 0.4 | 7.4 | 14.7 |
| General and administrative | 2.8 | — | — | 0.6 | 3.4 |
| Total operations | 18.9 | 28.1 | 4.9 | 23.5 | 75.4 |
| Excise duties |  |  |  |  | 17.4 |
| Interest expense |  |  |  |  | 0.7 |
| Income taxes |  |  |  |  | 2.4 |
| Net profits |  |  |  |  | 4.1 |
| Total |  |  |  |  | 100.0 |

*Source:* Corporate records.

reason, affiliates were measured on a return on assets (ROA) basis, and cash flows were controlled centrally subject to legal and financial requirements. In this context, Dutch law was extremely generous in that profits earned abroad were not taxable in Holland when remitted as dividends; however, foreign losses were not deductible against Dutch income.

Human resource policy was also centrally determined. All major appointments at the affiliates were submitted to the board for approval by the director of Social Affairs with the concurrence of the appropriate regional coordinator and the local general manager. The technical function had traditionally been the most international at Heineken, since wherever the company was involved, and whether it participated in the equity or not, a Heineken brewmaster would be present. This had generated a cadre of expatriate technical personnel with significant international experience. Nontechnical functions tended to be staffed by nationals of each country, but Heineken's rapid international expansion in recent years had placed significant strain on the company's ability to provide sufficient human resources to meet its foreign operational requirements.

## THE MOVE INTO BEVERAGES

Heineken was first involved in nonbeer beverages as early as 1939, with the acquisition of a 20 percent share participation in Hoppe, an established Dutch manufacturer of *jenever* (a grain-based spirit similar to gin but flavored with juniper berries). Nearly 30 years later, in 1967, a British company, Allied Breweries, entered the Dutch market by acquiring two local medium-sized breweries. Allied's move was viewed as a significant threat by the management of Heineken, as Allied had been active in the local food and drink trade for years and had established a foothold in the Dutch distribution network.

Heineken's immediate response was to acquire the Amstel Brewery, the second largest in Holland. To many of Heineken's top executives, the entry of Allied Breweries into the Dutch market marked an important milestone in Heineken's overall strategy. The company's success in the beer business, both at home and abroad, had created a comfortable and secure feeling in the organization. The threat of losing market dominance to Allied and the subsequent merger with Amstel changed all that. Between 1967 and 1970, Heineken resolved to make up for lost time in nonbeer activities and proceeded to consolidate its operations on all fronts.[2]

---

[2] For a more detailed description of Heineken's nonbeer strategy and activities, see the case Distilled Trading International, Ltd. in this series, INSEAD, 1985.

# EXHIBIT 6

## TURNOVER BY PRODUCT GROUP, 1973–1982 (Df Million and Percent)

| | 1982 | 1981 | 1980 | 1978–1979 | 1977–1978 | 1976–1977 | 1975–1976 | 1974–1975 | 1973–1974 |
|---|---|---|---|---|---|---|---|---|---|
| In Df million | | | | | | | | | |
| Beer sales | 3,422.5 | 2,841.7 | 2,481.5 | 2,114.3 | 2,019.1 | 1,883.9 | 1,564.0 | 1,351.9 | 1,156.6 |
| Soft drinks | 326.6 | 288.1 | 279.7 | 241.0 | 203.3 | 183.7 | 179.0 | 167.2 | 134.5 |
| Spirits and wine | 300.1 | 317.6 | 308.6 | 336.0 | 282.0 | 264.2 | 154.3 | 205.9 | 179.9 |
| Other trading income | 100.8 | 104.7 | 108.6 | 134.6 | 118.7 | 96.4 | 88.9 | 86.3 | 78.2 |
| Total | 4,150.0 | 3,552.1 | 3,178.4 | 2,825.9 | 2,623.1 | 2,428.2 | 2,095.6 | 1,811.3 | 1,549.2 |
| In percent | | | | | | | | | |
| Beer sales | 82.5 | 80.0 | 78.0 | 74.8 | 77.0 | 77.6 | 74.6 | 74.6 | 74.7 |
| Soft drinks | 7.9 | 8.1 | 8.8 | 8.5 | 7.7 | 7.6 | 8.5 | 9.2 | 8.7 |
| Spirits & wine | 7.2 | 8.9 | 9.8 | 11.9 | 10.8 | 10.9 | 12.6 | 11.4 | 11.6 |
| Other trading income | 2.4 | 3.0 | 3.4 | 4.8 | 4.5 | 3.9 | 4.3 | 4.8 | 5.0 |
| Total | 100.0 | 100.0 | 100.0 | 100.0 | 100.0 | 100.0 | 100.0 | 100.0 | 100.0 |
| Exchange rate (Dfl/$) | 2.62 | 2.47 | 2.13 | 1.90 | 2.10 | 2.46 | 2.57 | 2.73 | 2.70 |

Note: Financial years 1972/1973 to 1977/1978 are from 1 October to 30 September.
Financial year 1978/1979 was for 15 months, but figures have been adjusted on a calendar-year basis.
Financial years from 1980 correspond to calendar years.
Source: Annual reports.

---

**EXHIBIT 7**

---

## BEER SALES OF THE NETHERLANDS BREWERIES

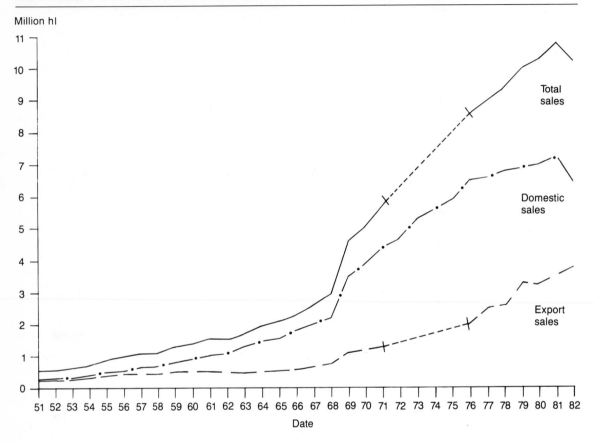

Million hl

*Source:* Annual reports.

## Growth by Acquisition

In a rush of acquisitions dating to the early 1960s, Heineken obtained equity positions in a series of companies manufacturing and/or distributing soft drinks, wine, and distilled products. Some of the rationale for these moves could be extracted from a study made by McKinsey and Co. in 1969, which suggested that "spirits and wines represent a significant portion of the 'drink' market not yet fully exploited by Heineken," and that important opportunities for "synergism" existed between these sectors, particularly in export markets.

By the end of 1973, Heineken's non-beer product portfolio included a number of established brands in the Dutch market:

| Soft drinks | *Jenevers* | Wine | Liqueurs |
|---|---|---|---|
| Vrumona (including Sisi, Royal Club, 7-Up, Pepsi Cola, etc.) Van Olffen | Coebergh Hoppe Bokma Hulstkamp Meder | Van Olffen Reuchlin | Hoppe Van Olffen |

Following the acquisition of Coebergh in 1972, Heineken's board commissioned an in-house team from the newly established corporate finance group to carry out a detailed study of the spirits and wine market in the Netherlands. The conclusion of the team's analysis was twofold. First, it confirmed that branded products would gain in importance as home consumption increased over time, although large-scale food distribution chains were increasing demand for "popular" staple products, particularly in the wine business. Second, the Dutch market for distillates was comparatively less promising than markets abroad. Therefore, it would seem that if Heineken wanted to continue a strategy of diversification into spirits, it would have to acquire simultaneously a brand image and access to foreign markets.

The board's internal debate on how best to proceed in the distillates business—"a Dutch base with some sales abroad versus a major international position in spirits"—remained unresolved after the company acquired a 30 percent interest in the English distiller Duncan, Gilbey and Matheson (DGM), early in 1975. DGM's relatively insignificant share in the distilled trade and lack of known brands led one Heineken Board member to describe the decision as follows: "The Board decided we would be a beer company with beverages in a supporting role, specially as a protection against further incursions into our home market. As far as international spirits were concerned, we would continue to do it the creepy-crawly way. DGM was an example of this; it was fun to do!" By March 1979, however, under the terms of the original agreement, Heineken was forced to take over the outstanding shares of DGM and gained full control of the company. The high investment in DGM signaled that the stakes in the game had increased significantly.

**The Bols Affair**

N. V. Koninklijke Distilleererijen Erven Lucas Bols produced a range of internationally known drinks, namely the Bols *jenevers* and liqueurs, had a dominant 20 percent share in the domestic spirits market, and had established distribution outlets in many countries. Bols was also the Dutch import agent for several prestige French wines, Courvoisier cognac, and a few whisky brands. Furthermore, Bols was the only distillery in the Netherlands that was backward integrated and distilled its own grain alcohol.

Heineken management believed that a merger of the two companies would have a number of very obvious advantages, namely the combination of Bols product range and brand image with Heineken's access to worldwide distribution, together with improved capacity utilization in distillates and lower capital requirements per unit of sales. In March 1976, the top executives of both companies discussed the possibility of a merger, but the Bols management did not appear enthusiastic. On April 3, 1976, a joint meeting of Heineken's supervisory council and executive board decided that a public offer should be made to the shareholders of Bols. A takeover bid was made the following week, but as a result of a share issue by Bols intended as a protective measure, the Heineken bid did not succeed.

Several other companies were then considered for acquisition. Even the possibility of starting up a distillery and yeast factory outside the Netherlands was considered. Faced with re-

EXHIBIT 8

## WORLDWIDE BEER SALES, 1973–1982

| | 1982 | 1981 | 1980 | 1978–1979 | 1977–1978 | 1976–1977 | 1975–1976 | 1974–1975 | 1973–1974 |
|---|---|---|---|---|---|---|---|---|---|
| Total sales (million hl) | | | | | | | | | |
| The Netherlands | 6.4 | 7.3 | 7.0 | 6.9 | 6.7 | 6.6 | 6.6 | 5.9 | 5.6 |
| Rest of Europe | 7.8 | 7.2 | 7.1 | 7.1 | 6.6 | 6.1 | 6.2 | 5.5 | 5.5 |
| Western Hemisphere | 4.0 | 3.8 | 3.6 | 3.1 | 2.4 | 1.9 | 1.5 | 1.1 | 0.9 |
| Africa | 6.3 | 6.0 | 5.8 | 5.3 | 5.7 | 5.7 | 5.6 | 6.0 | 5.8 |
| Australasia/Asia | 2.4 | 2.5 | 2.4 | 2.2 | 2.0 | 1.8 | 1.6 | 1.7 | 1.6 |
| | 26.9 | 26.8 | 25.9 | 24.6 | 23.4 | 22.1 | 21.5 | 20.2 | 19.4 |
| Percentage of Sales | | | | | | | | | |
| The Netherlands | 24 | 27 | 27 | 28 | 29 | 30 | 31 | 29 | 29 |
| Rest of Europe | 29 | 27 | 27 | 29 | 28 | 28 | 29 | 27 | 28 |
| Western Hemisphere | 15 | 14 | 14 | 13 | 10 | 8 | 7 | 6 | 5 |
| Africa | 23 | 23 | 23 | 21 | 24 | 26 | 26 | 30 | 30 |
| Australasia/Asia | 9 | 9 | 9 | 9 | 9 | 8 | 7 | 8 | 8 |
| | 100 | 100 | 100 | 100 | 100 | 100 | 100 | 100 | 100 |

*Note:* Figures are total sales of beer brewed under Heineken supervision.
*Source:* Annual reports.

EXHIBIT 9

## HEINEKEN AND AMSTEL SALES BY SOURCE

| | 1982 | | 1975–1976 | | 1970–1971 | |
|---|---|---|---|---|---|---|
| | Total sales (hl) | Percent exported from Holland | Total sales (hl) | Percent exported from Holland | Total sales (hl) | Percent exported from Holland |
| Europe except the Netherlands | 4,544,000 | 6.1 | 3,343,000 | 11.8 | 1,036,000 | 34.0 |
| Western Hemisphere | 3,220,000 | 90.2 | 1,312,000 | 88.7 | 641,000 | 86.1 |
| Africa | 499,000 | 37.1 | 414,000 | 71.3 | 393,000 | 42.0 |
| Australasia/Asia | 486,000 | 57.0 | 136,000 | 62.5 | 258,000 | 88.0 |
| Total | 8,749,000* | 41.7 | 5,205,000 | 37.2 | 2,328,000 | 55.7 |

*Excluding duty-free.
*Source:* Annual reports and company records.

EXHIBIT 10

## ORGANIZATIONAL STRUCTURE—1982

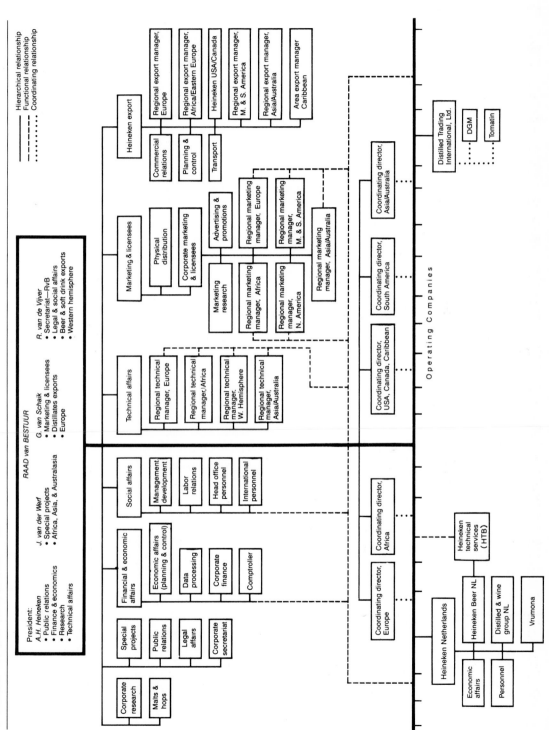

Hierarchical relationship
Functional relationship
Coordinating relationship

RAAD van BESTUUR

President:
A.H. Heineken
• Public relations
• Finance & economics
• Research
• Technical affairs

J. van der Werf
• Special projects
• Africa, Asia, & Australasia

G. van Schaik
• Marketing & licensees
• Distillates exports
• Europe

R. van de Vijver
• Secretariat—RvB
• Legal & social affairs
• Beer & soft drink exports
• Western hemisphere

peated failures in finding an external solution, the Heineken board turned to the construction of its own distillery in Zoetermeer.

The Zoetermeer plant was designed on a larger scale than the immediate market needed, no doubt to be prepared for the forecasted growth in distillates and Heineken's share in that business. In addition, the Hoppe and Coebergh distilleries were experiencing operational and environmental problems and needed to be relocated to new premises. Construction began in 1977, and the integrated plant became fully operational by mid-1979 at a cost of Df 60 million.

## The 1979 St. Moritz Review

Early in 1979, following the DGM takeover, an overview was made regarding Heineken's position in distillates. At issue was the search for ways to establish ties with a known international brand in spirits, an objective that might require larger-than-available capital outlays. At a meeting in the Swiss resort town of St. Moritz in the winter of 1979, Heineken's board considered a proposed company policy with regard to distillates. Some excerpts of that document are as follows:

> Heineken will not be interested in large takeovers of distilled companies because of financial restrictions. This policy, however, would not apply to companies producing whisky and cognac. The importance and authenticity of these spirits is such that it would provide Heineken with the independence and presence it seeks in the spirits trade.
>
> The U.K. being the centerplace of the spirits trade, Heineken's distilled products operation should ultimately relocate to that country.
>
> An active development program should be started to create an "own" brand franchise with high margins.
>
> Distillates companies within the Heineken group should be autonomous in canvassing markets but should be assisted by "signals" from the beer people. Distillates companies within the group should . . . seek out small local markets where Heineken is present and export there.
>
> An Executive Board member should be appointed to supervise the distillates operations.

The proposal was discussed and approved. Several months later, two possibilities for entering the whisky business came up: Bell's and Tomatin. Bell's, one of the top-selling brands in the business, was judged to be too expensive (over Df 100 million for a minority share). Instead, Heineken acquired 20 percent of Tomatin, a blender and exporter of bulk whisky without any major international brands for £1.55 million (Df 8 million). By the end of 1982, after two bad years of significant downturns in the spirit markets, the company was reassessing its position in distillates.

## THE MAJOR EUROPEAN BEER MARKETS

As evident from the company's chronology, Heineken's foreign involvement through the late 1960s was based essentially on the Far East, Africa, and the United States and represented limited commitment to European markets other than through some marginal export business. The United States was, of course, a very significant success story with exports reaching a volume of 320,500 hectoliters (hl) by the time of the Amstel merger in 1968. Elsewhere the company was involved with a large number of independent companies where it had small participations and/or technical assistance agreements, with or without licensing. This meant that the volume of beer brewed under Heineken supervision amounted to nearly as much as that brewed in Heineken-owned facilities (see Exhibit 8). This prompted one executive to comment: "Heineken has never been an empire; it has always been a commonwealth."

The questioning mood which followed the integration of Amstel into the Heineken group brought about a reassessment of this "low-profile" approach to foreign markets. First, Amstel had been more actively involved in foreign activities under its own name than Heineken, which had preferred small participations and technical agreements. Many of the key executives in the newly integrated company thus developed a more aggressive attitude toward foreign markets and were willing to argue forcefully for taking bigger risks with the promise of larger rewards. Also the Dutch beer market had stabilized since the relatively rapid growth in the immediate post-war period. With a market share of over 50 percent of its home market and little prospects for domestic sales growth, the joint Heineken-Amstel organization had the motivation and the availability of resources to consider significant expansion of its European activities.

The next few years saw the company responding to market or investment opportunities that came into Heineken's field of vision from a multitude of sources. This is perhaps best illustrated by the history of some of the various countries where Heineken took positions during this period.

## Belgium

After many years of low-level exports to Belgium, Heineken purchased a local family-run brewery in 1927 called Brasserie Leopold. After operating the business for over 30 years, urban renewal threatened to force Brasserie Leopold to move. Heineken, facing extensive relocation costs and given that Leopold had sales of only 200,000 hl (5 percent of the Belgian market), sold the brewery to its major Belgian competitor, Stella Artois.

## The United Kingdom

Traditionally, the U.K. beer market was a difficult one to enter. The close relationship between the brewers and the pubs, where nearly 90 percent of beer consumption took place, prevented outside brewers from entering. Only the shop trade was accessible without a connection with a local brewer. Heineken had been exporting beer to independent bottlers in the United Kingdom since the 1920s, but the volume had rarely exceeded 30,000 hl per year.

In the late 1950s, the lager market in Britain was showing signs of increasing growth. Whitbread, one of the "big six" British brewers,

approached Heineken to discuss the possibility of setting up a joint venture that would first handle Heineken imports into the United Kingdom and eventually build a lager brewing facility for the local market. An agreement was reached by which tankers of specially brewed Heineken (see below) were imported into Britain for distribution by Whitbread and other bottlers. Gradually, the local operation was rationalized to eliminate the independent bottlers and volume increased rapidly. In 1969, a technical contract and licensing agreement was concluded with Whitbread to produce Heineken locally. Ten years later, Heineken beer came to represent a significant share of Whitbread's volume (over 2 million hl per annum) and profits.

Heineken's market position in the United Kingdom was in many ways an anomaly. The Heineken formula was highly prized by the company, which had consistently resisted attempts to alter the beer in order to suit a particular market. The tax system and customer palate in the United Kingdom, however, demanded a change of policy. For the first time Heineken beer was brewed with a lower alcohol content than elsewhere in the world. Furthermore, the brand was positioned in the middle of the lager range, a marked contrast to other markets where it traditionally sold as a premium beer. Throughout Heineken, it was said, "the British exception confirms the rule."

## France

Other than exporting limited amounts of beer to France since 1875, Heineken's involvement in that market had been relatively minor. Imported by Moët-Hennessy and priced and sold as premium beer, Heineken's volume did not exceed 100,000 hl per year. In 1972, Heineken's involvement in the French market entered a new phase.

Four small regional French breweries had consolidated their operations by forming Alsacienne de Brasserie (Albra), which controlled about 6 percent of the French market. A proposal to acquire Albra revived Heineken's interest in the French market. Kronenbourg, the largest brewery in France, was discarded as a potential partner on the basis that cooperation could be overshadowed by competition. Union de Brasseries, a large but fragmented operation, did not appear to suit Heineken's objectives. Finally, Heineken's finance department was not overly enthusiastic about the Albra proposal on the grounds that the operation seemed too small.

In the summer of 1972, after several contacts were established between both firms, Heineken's board made a public offer for a controlling interest in Albra. By November, 76 percent of Albra's shares were in Heineken's hands. Over the next few years, the remaining minority shares were taken over and, in March 1981, Heineken France, a wholly owned subsidiary, was created.

Since 1973, Heineken's marketing staff had been concerned about their relatively low market share in France. Losses had been accumulating, and the general view in Amsterdam was that this could not be allowed to continue. The decision to produce Heineken locally came under study in 1977, and it presented an opportunity to possibly reposition the brand and increase volume considerably from 130,000 hl at the time. A forecast of 3 to 4 million hl was made provided Heineken was sold as a "deluxe" (i.e., standard) brand with a wider popular appeal. This option was rejected after much discussion, and a policy decision was made that the Heineken brand should not be used to compete with lower priced brands to gain volume.

Also in 1978, as part of its general review of the French market, Heineken reconsidered Union de Brasseries (UdB) as a vehicle to expand its market share by acquisition. UdB's product range, a combined market share of nearly 30 percent, and its distribution network were all attractive. But the French brewer's condition was not all that sound, with losses running at about Fr30 to 50 million per year. Most of its five breweries were old, to the point that two would have to be closed down (a difficult proposition for a Dutch company in France), and preliminary estimates showed a need for an investment of around Df 550 million over five years

to pull the company out of the red. After lengthy deliberations, Heineken decided not to bid for UdB (a separate deal was made to use their distribution system) and to concentrate on improving its position with Albra's facilities. By 1982, Heineken France was operating profitably for the first time.

## Italy

Heineken first entered the Italian market in 1960, when the second largest brewer in the country approached the company for assistance. Dreher's reputation and past performance, and the fact that Heineken had no presence in Italy, prompted the Dutch company to react favorably. Heineken offered Dreher a technical assistance contract which included a Heineken brewmaster to work in Italy, acquired a 7 percent token participation and appointed a representative to the board of Dreher.

In August 1974, Dreher's owners wanted out of the business altogether. The Dreher group was worth around Df 40 million and with seven breweries controlled nearly 20 percent of the Italian market. The offer interested Heineken, but the investment and risk were considered too large. They contacted Whitbread, its U.K. licensee, and eventually both companies acquired the Dreher operation on a 50/50 basis. Shortly thereafter, the two partners assumed full operational control over the business, and, Heineken being short of staff, Whitbread agreed to take over the financial and administrative management of the Italian operation. By May 1976, Heineken bottled beer was being produced locally and marketed together with the Dreher brand.

Internal problems and market difficulties since 1974 brought about accumulating losses for the Italian company. Whitbread, alarmed by this situation, refused to extend its commitment. Local management was hired, the organization was trimmed, marketing revamped and discounts cut, all of which helped to reduce losses partially, even though in the process Dreher lost around 8 percent in market share.

In 1979, the French BSN group acquired 30 percent of Wührer, the third largest brewery in Italy with a market share of about 10 percent, bringing increased competition to the market. The next year, Whitbread withdrew completely from Dreher, and Heineken assumed total control of the company. In order to streamline and consolidate the operation further, Heineken overhauled the Italian company's financial strategy and banking arrangements and closed two unprofitable breweries. By 1982 Dreher's market share was back up to 17 percent, and the operation was again profitable.[3]

## Norway

Heineken started brewing locally under license in 1975, following a period of limited imports. The beer was brewed by Arendals Bryggeri A/S, which was also the local Coca Cola bottler. Sales had grown satisfactorily, and production reached 80,000 hl per year by 1980. However, sales had declined perceptibly since then, causing headquarters marketing staff to reassess the wisdom of their position in the Norwegian market.

## Sweden

Exports to Sweden had been limited until the mid-1970s when a licensing agreement was reached with a local brewer, Falken Bryggeri AB. Sales of locally produced Heineken reached 100,000 hl per year, but stiff competition prevented the brand from increasing market share. In 1979, another major brewer in Sweden, Prypp, who produced Carlsberg under license, bought the Falken Brewery and assumed full control. Heineken was faced with the decision of whether to remain in the market in cooperation with a brewer that also carried a major competing international brand or to pull out. The European marketing regional manager felt that a termi-

nation of the licensing agreement would sacrifice their hard-earned market position. The executive board overruled him and terminated the agreement with Falken, thus resuming the importation of beer into Sweden.

The Swedish market was considered by many to be the most complicated in Europe. The government, in a drive to curb alcohol consumption, had decreed a complex system of beer categories by alcohol content and a fragmented distribution and import policy.

In 1982, Heineken granted an Amstel license to another Swedish brewer, Wärby-Bryggeri in Stockholm. Wärby was also to take over the distribution of the Heineken brand, but being a cooperative brewer, it had access only to cooperative outlets. This factor limited Heineken's market coverage and necessitated the setting up of a parallel distribution system. The different classes of beer, fragmentation of outlets, and multiple packaging needs resulted in high production costs in Holland and the loss of the bottles. Although Amstel sales surpassed Heineken's in 1982, volumes were insignificant. One senior marketing executive in Amsterdam stated: "The only possibility to survive is to go local. We need a partner in Sweden."

## Greece

In 1963, Amstel Brewery had begun negotiations to participate in a new brewery in Greece, Athenian Brewery, with a 25 percent share in partnership with local interests. Production started in 1965 in Athens with a capacity of 50,000 hl, and Athenian joined the Heineken family after the 1968 merger. A second brewery was built in Thessaloniki in 1974, after which market share rose rapidly to approximately 45 percent of the Greek market. Following the death of Athenian's founder in 1976, Heineken proceeded to expand its ownership position through various capital increases and complex negotiations, until it acquired complete control in 1979.

The rapid growth of the Greek beer market attracted significant competition in the late 1970s. Two local companies, Fix and Henninger (a German joint venture), were joined by Carlsberg

---

[3] In 1981, to the consternation of its Italian management, Heineken licensed the Amstel brand to their main competitor in Italy, the Peroni group, the largest brewery in the country with about 25 percent of the market.

(a United Breweries licensee) and Löwenbräu. Heineken responded by licensing its affiliate to produce Heineken locally in 1981, and by major increases in its advertising and promotion budgets. Both policies were aimed to maintain its dominant position in this relatively expanding market. After incurring severe losses during the first 18 months of operations, Carlsberg approached Heineken in late 1982 with an offer to sell its local brewery to Athenian.

### Ireland

Introduced to the Irish market by its U.K. licensee, Whitbread, Heineken licensed Ireland's third largest brewery, J.J. Murphy and Co. Ltd., in 1978. Murphy's had been looking for a lager brand to enter a market dominated by stout, where Guinness held a formidable 90 percent share. Lager sales were expanding rapidly, and the Heineken brand did well during its first three years, reaching 9 percent of the lager market or 51,000 hl by 1981. Murphy's, however, was encountering severe financial difficulties and made repeated pleas to Heineken for a significant financial contribution. In July 1982, Murphy's went into receivership, and Heineken's board was faced with the difficult decision of whether to acquire the failing company's assets or abandon the Irish market.

### Germany

The German beer market was characterized by its "purity law," establishing production standards that aimed to protect German barley growers. The market was also very fragmented, and many locally entrenched brewers "produced and sold beer around the church steeple." German beer was of high quality, and Heineken had for years thought hard as to how it could enter this large but difficult market where there were no national brands.

### Spain

Heineken had made an ill-fated attempt to enter the Spanish market in the 1960s, by setting up a joint venture with United Africa Co. in Burgos. After that venture failed, Heineken continued to export small quantities (8 to 10,000 hl per year) to Spain, but faced problems due to the high seasonality of sales (over 70 percent in the summer months), low stock rotation, and high luxury taxes on imported beer. The changing Spanish environment after 1975, and lower import duties permitted Heineken to drop its price premium to 67 percent above local competition by 1982. Volume rose to 25,000 hl, and a second distributorship was established to sell keg beer with estimated 1983 volume of an additional 25,000 hl. Corporate marketing staff advocated a fresh look at the Spanish market with the objective of establishing a major position through local production in the near future.

### AN EMERGING INTEGRATED BEER STRATEGY FOR EUROPE

The situations described above for the major European markets highlight the rather opportunistic nature of these major decisions during the decade following the Amstel merger. While there seemed to be a clear objective to establish Heineken as a premium brand in all major European markets, no explicit guidelines existed as to which markets should be given priority and what levels of commitment and risk were necessary or tolerable. This kind of approach frequently caused differences of opinion between the company's top management and its marketing, finance, or production executives. Perhaps a good illustration of this problem was the 1978–1979 proposal to acquire UdB.

The UdB acquisition would have given Heineken a major share of the French market, but at significant cost and risks. UdB was by no means an easy situation to handle, but lack of specific corporate guidelines on these issues prevented Heineken from making a broad evaluation of the situation, and the acquisition was seen only in light of its own value. As one senior staff member put it, "Heineken always tries to get a front row seat for 10 cents. The UdB acquisition would have required investments in excess of Df 500 million over five years. We settled instead for the third balcony.'' The internal debate on UdB and on the correct positioning for Heineken in the French market served as a catalyst, however, and prompted the executive board to propose a set of criteria in regards to marketing of Heineken beer with worldwide implications.

## The 1979 Review

Based on a study prepared at the request of the board by the Corporate Marketing Department in September 1979, corporate strategy was discussed extensively, particularly in the European context. It was decided that a number of countries—the Netherlands, France, Italy, Greece and the United States (because of its impact on European operations)—would be designated as ''primary markets'' where the company would have ''greater aspirations.''[4] Since Europe in general was of primary interest, a number of ''secondary priority'' markets—Belgium, Britain, Ireland, Germany, and Spain—were also identified.

The objectives of the company in primary markets were stated as follows:

- To obtain in each country a substantial long-term profitable position in the beer market;
- To assure an optimal exploitation of the Heineken brand, always in conjunction with its worldwide policy; and
- To aim for a positive contribution to corporate results by local brands and Amstel.

In addition, objectives for each country were also defined. For example, Athenian Brewery was to maintain its current market position in Greece while improving its financial results, and investigate the possibility of filling gaps in the ''high class'' beer niche with other beers such

as a special (export), a ''light,'' and Heineken. For Ireland, the objective was to reach 18% of the lager market without getting financially involved for the time being. For Spain, the short-term objective was to continue to expand turnover by way of exports and to explore the start of local production in the long term.

The document argued that in order to meet increasing market segmentation and product differentiation in world markets, Heineken was compelled to formulate logical and consistent product and brand policies. New markets could be entered by exporting or by setting up local production, either through licensing or by acquisition. Whenever local production was done through a licensee, the staff recommended that Heineken also assume a small financial participation. The criteria for selecting which entry strategy to use would depend on the following factors:

- Is the country designated a primary market?
- Brand and type of beer used.
- Import restrictions.
- Availability of interesting prospective partner.
- Market circumstances.
- Investment required.
- Legal restrictions on ownership.
- Price measures and controls.
- Restrictions on royalties.
- Transfer problems for dividends/cash flows.
- Nationalization risk.

The document also outlined a series of policy guidelines. Operating companies should be set up only in primary markets due to the limitation of available funds. Outside these areas, an entry by investment would have to be justified by expected or actual ROA, protecting existing volume, or the need to retain a licensing agreement. Furthermore, partnerships with ''like-minded,'' ambitious, international breweries should be avoided, and cooperation with weak partners nearly always produced bad results. When local production in any given market was envisaged, it should go hand in hand with technical assist-

---

[4]Although this document did not deal with them, Indonesia, Singapore and Malaysia were also considered by the company to be primary markets.

ance agreements which must extend to all the brands produced by the local "partner." Local beers should not affect corporate brands, and outlets where Heineken or Amstel beer was sold must have a certain image to appeal to the international consumer. Finally, it was suggested that all subsequent policies at lower levels of management should derive from the global policy of the corporation, that operating policies in the commercial and R&D area should be made more specific, and that executives should be encouraged to "stick their necks out and say, for example, by 1985 we want to be there."

### Licensing Policy

The Heineken executive board naturally extended its analysis to the company's approach to licensing. Throughout the years, Heineken had gained extensive experience in licensing agreements, but rarely had an in-depth evaluation of the relative merits of licensing as an entry vehicle into new markets been done. One member of the board described the tenor of their reflection as follows: "When we license, is it because licensing is good, or is it because we lack the necessary funds to participate financially? In other words, does the company look at these two operations separately or in conjunction with one another?"

The board saw a number of advantages in licensing, such as a smaller financial commitment, lower costs for higher volume, time gain in getting on stream, and flexibility, since its involvement could be increased as the market became better understood. Equally, a potential licensee stood to gain from having a "prestige" brand to "piggy-back" on its existing production and distribution systems, getting access to the technological know-how of Heineken, and tapping an additional profit source.

But there were also risks in licensing. Overflow of technical know-how could lead to local brands gaining quality parity with the Heineken brand, although this risk could partly be diminished by putting a Heineken brewmaster on the spot. Issues of "brand positioning" versus local

brands could be a possible source of conflict with the licensee. And there was a certain vulnerability vis-à-vis local government regulations in terms of royalties, prices, packaging quality, and reexports to neighboring markets.

It was agreed that the Heineken brand, being the flagship of the company, would be licensed with greater care and that market penetration strategies would be confined to Amstel. The executive board of Heineken wanted thus to further differentiate the "image" of the two brands.

### The European Beer Strategy

In November 1981, a study prepared by a multidisciplinary team of corporate executives laid the foundation for what was to become the European Beer Strategy. This study made a critical analysis of the position of Heineken and Amstel brands on the European scene and proceeded to make a series of recommendations. Brand pricing, positioning, and other details would be looked upon on a country-by-country basis, but they should not deviate from basic Heineken principles of price differentiation, quality, and image. The major conclusions of the study were as follows:

1. A viable long-term presence in the European beer market would require bulk production of beer due to factors such as economies of scale and price pressures. Also, in order to maintain its position with the trade and to absorb overheads, the company should carry small but profitable market segments.
2. The expansion capacity of the company must be quantified. This would depend on the financial norms of the group (e.g., debt/equity, profit/investment ratios), the possibility of disposing of unprofitable and strategically unimportant investments, and the ownership position required in existing subsidiaries.
3. Priorities must be set, taking into account these factors, to seek optimal return on operations in primary markets. Since a large proportion of the European market must be approached through licensing arrangements,

with or without participation, a policy should be established on potential partners in different markets.

4. Export activities should also be stepped up as an efficient means of assuming initial presence in a market.

5. The Heineken brand should be consistently priced 10 to 20 percent above local standard beer. The experience of downgrading Heineken in some markets shows a contribution loss not compensated by an increase of turnover.

6. Heineken subsidiaries should increase their efforts, where applicable, to develop standard local brands.

The study also identified a number of key environmental trends that would influence future strategic choices:

- Wine demand was increasing in beer markets, and, conversely, premium beer was becoming more popular in predominantly wine areas like France.
- The bulk beer segment was stagnating due mainly to overcapacity, brand proliferation, price competition, and lower profits.
- Market concentration was on the rise, especially among European companies and brands, following the American experience.
- An increasing trend toward price and product differentiation created contradictory demands for economies of scale and segment differentiation.
- "Everyone was entering everyone else's markets," and the aim seemed to be overall European brand leadership.
- Distribution was the key to growth and profits.

To "capture and control" distribution became of paramount importance. Local brewers, sensing this, were protecting themselves by forward integration, buying wholesalers. High-volume outlets provided a brewer with an important competitive advantage, namely for the sales of "bulk" or draft beer. Furthermore, the trend toward an increasing number of large "hyperstores" would affect a brewery's marketing and promotion approaches as well as the price structures of "premium" beers.

In view of these factors, the objective of the European Beer Strategy was to obtain in each major market "at least third place in market share, not less than 25 percent of the leader's share, and a minimum of 10 percent of the market. This would serve as the ground rule in evaluating the company's presence in each market, whether through exports, licensing or direct participation." Exhibits 11 and 12 present an analysis of Heineken's current position in selected markets and of its major competitors in Europe. Exhibit 13 shows 1981 production for the world's largest beer companies.

## Options and Implications

Exporting beer from the Netherlands was considered a definite means of growth but one that did not offer sufficient guarantees to Heineken to become a leader in the European market. Heineken's success in exporting beer to the United States, becoming over the years the highest selling imported beer in that country and to other markets in Africa or elsewhere, was not considered to be a valid model for Europe. The U.S. market was such that local production was believed to ruin a foreign brand's image, as was demonstrated by Löwenbräu and Tuborg. Elsewhere, conditions differed greatly from country to country, but the share of local production to total sales of Heineken and Amstel brands was generally on the rise (see Exhibit 9). Therefore, the European Beer Strategy was, as its name implied, almost exclusively related to European markets.

Increasing brand proliferation among breweries had diminished market price differences between imports and local production. In some countries, this factor put imported "premium" beer at a disadvantage, and continued profitability could not be expected from beer exports. Other factors mitigating against an export-based strategy were environmental restrictions, such as the mandatory use of one-way bottles, import

EXHIBIT 11

## CONSUMPTION AND MARKET SHARE IN MAJOR MARKETS, 1982

| | Beer consumption (thousand hl) | Population (million) | Per capita consumption (liters) | Number of breweries | Heineken company* | | |
| --- | --- | --- | --- | --- | --- | --- | --- |
| | | | | | Heineken (thousand hl) | Other brands (thousand hl) | Total share (%) |
| **Europe** | | | | | | | |
| Germany | 91,586 | 61.6 | 148.6 | 1,292 | — | — | — |
| United Kingdom | 61,780 | 56.1 | 110.3 | 138 | 2,084 | — | 3.4 |
| France | 24,302 | 54.2 | 44.8 | 63 | 402 | 1,332 | 7.1 |
| Spain | 21,519 | 37.9 | 56.7 | 39 | 22 | 4 | 0.1 |
| Belgium-Luxembourg | 13,213 | 10.2 | 129.3 | 134 | 38 | 1 | 0.3 |
| Netherlands | 11,728 | 14.3 | 82.0 | 22 | 4,935 | 1,469 | 54.6 |
| Italy | 11,624 | 56.6 | 20.5 | 30 | 352 | 1,744 | 18.0 |
| Switzerland | 4,605 | 6.5 | 71.2 | 40 | 11 | 6 | 0.4 |
| Sweden | 4,158 | 8.3 | 49.9 | 17 | 35 | 90 | 3.0 |
| Ireland | 3,761 | 3.5 | 108.0 | 5 | 49 | 114 | 4.3 |
| Portugal | 3,737 | 10.0 | 37.4 | 4 | — | — | — |
| Greece | 2,870 | 9.8 | 29.3 | 8 | 56 | 1,200 | 43.8 |
| Norway | 1,926 | 4.1 | 46.8 | 17 | 72 | — | 3.7 |
| **Americas** | | | | | | | |
| United States | 234,176 | 232.1 | 100.9 | 82 | 2,495 | 42 | 1.1 |
| Brazil | 29,500† | 126.8 | 23.3 | 32 | — | — | — |
| Mexico | 27,583† | 74.0 | 37.2 | 7 | — | — | — |
| Canada | 23,667† | 24.6 | 96.2 | 42 | 65 | 60 | 0.5 |
| Venezuela | 12,000† | 14.7 | 81.6 | 5 | 0.7 | — | — |
| Argentina | 2,237† | 28.4 | 7.9 | 9 | 0.8 | — | — |
| **Asia** | | | | | | | |
| Japan | 47,335† | 118.4 | 40.0 | 27 | 28 | — | — |
| Australia | 19,682† | 15.2 | 127.7 | 16 | 7 | — | — |
| Philippines | 7,700† | 48.4 | 15.9 | 4 | 0.3 | — | — |
| S. Korea | 5,988† | 38.1 | 15.7 | 2 | 45 | — | 0.8 |
| Taiwan | 2,825† | 17.6 | 16.1 | 1 | — | — | — |
| Singapore/Malaysia | 1,950† | 15.8 | 12.3 | 4 | 0.5 | 700 | 35.9 |
| Indonesia | 800† | 146.9 | 0.5 | 5 | 6 | 447 | 56.6 |
| **Africa** | | | | | | | |
| S. Africa | 12,000† | 30.1 | 39.9 | 5 | 0.2 | 299 | 2.5 |
| Nigeria | 10,380† | 77.1 | 13.5 | 25 | — | 2,322 | 22.4 |
| Egypt | 425† | 42.2 | 1.0 | 2 | — | — | — |

*Includes under "other brands" beer brewed under the supervision of Heineken.
†Production only.
Source: Company records.

---

**EXHIBIT 12**

---

**MAJOR EUROPEAN COMPETITORS**

---

1. *Norway-Sweden-Finland* In each of these markets, one or two groups controlled over 60 percent of local consumption. None, however, were of European scale or potential.

2. *Denmark* United Breweries Ltd. had a strong home market. They appeared to prefer licensing agreements except when defending existing subsidiaries. Otherwise, they did not seem inclined to take many risks or important participations, and their financial capacity was limited.

3. *Ireland* Guinness was strong, but its product had limited appeal and was not a potential European competitor.

4. *United Kingdom* Five groups controlled over 70 percent of the market. Some were looking to Europe for expansion, but their activities to date were limited.

5. *Germany* Highly fragmented market with three largest groups amounting to 20 to 25 percent of the local market. No German brewer had shown any intentions of launching a European strategy.

6. *Belgium* Stella and Pied Boeuf shared nearly 60 percent of their home market. Their growth was limited to about 300 km from Leuven/Liege, and they presented no major threat in Europe. Stella had a few arrangements in Africa and South America.

7. *France* BSN (Kronenbourg) and UdB dominated the market with over 70 percent. BSN had a clear international ambition that paralleled Heineken's. Given their late start, they were following a three-stage strategy: Succeed in Europe, follow with a "conquest of the New World" in the United States, and later expand overseas to "the four corners of the world." They had started by licensing third parties (e.g., in the United Kingdom) and by direct participations in Belgium, Spain, and Italy. BSN was strong financially and had an active acquisition program under way in food products.

   BSN was probably Heineken's most dangerous competitor on a European scale. How serious a threat they were in the near future would depend on what opportunities they got to buy market share, the relative investment priorities between food and beverages, and their experience in the United States.

8. *Portugal* Two state-owned groups controlled the market but should not be a factor elsewhere.

9. *Spain* Largest five companies shared about 65 percent of the local market. None were potential European competitors.

10. *Switzerland* Two groups dominated the market but were limited by their internal cartel rules. Not competitive outside their home market.

11. *Austria* Difficult to enter because of strict cartel rules, but not a factor outside.

12. *Italy* The five largest groups had 65 to 70 percent market share. Only Peroni was large enough to compete at the European level, but it had not shown any indications to do so.

13. *Greece* Both major groups with 75 percent of the market were related to foreign companies.

14. *United States* Anheuser Busch had begun to enter Europe by licensing third parties. Their choice has always been made on the basis of market leadership: BSN in France, Prypp in Sweden, Oëtker in Germany. Only if they were to shift to a strategy of direct participation would they become a credible threat. Philip Morris, in the meantime, was building up its relationship with Löwenbräu. They had good in-house European marketing know-how through their cigarette business.

---

*Source:* Casewriter estimates.

tariffs and custom duties protecting local brewers, and the fact that access to distribution channels was becoming increasingly dependent on having a high-volume "carrier" brand, usually one belonging to a major local producer.

Licensing made a "carrier" brand available and provided access to local distribution outlets. It allowed Heineken to concentrate on its corporate brands, as opposed to its own subsidiaries where the "carrier" brand was "owned" and required time and investment. Furthermore, licensing was less costly in terms of the consequences of a wrong choice of third-party "carrier," and a "pull out" option always existed. The study recommended that licensees should get more profit from a Heineken brand

| EXHIBIT 13 |
| --- |

**WORLD'S LARGEST BEER COMPANIES**

| Company | 1981 production (million hl) | Percent |
| --- | --- | --- |
| Anheuser Busch (U.S.) | 64 | 24.4 |
| Miller (U.S.) | 47 | 17.9 |
| Kirin (Japan) | 29 | 11.1 |
| Heineken (Netherlands) | 27 | 10.3 |
| B.S.N. (France) | 18 | 6.9 |
| United Breweries (Denmark) | 18* | 6.9 |
| Pabst (U.S.) | 16 | 6.1 |
| Allied Breweries (U.K.) | 14 | 5.3 |
| Bass Ltd. (U.K.) | 14 | 5.3 |
| Artois (Belgium) | 8 | 3.1 |
| Dub Schultheiss (Germany) | 7 | 2.7 |
| Total, 11 largest breweries | 262 | 100.0 |

*Estimated.
*Source:* Drexel Burnham Lambert, Inc.

than from their own. To compensate for its additional promotion and manufacturing costs, it was therefore a necessity for Heineken to be priced at least 10 to 15 percent above the standard local beer.

In order to implement the European Beer Strategy exclusively with fully owned subsidiaries, on the basis of an investment of D*f* 175 per hectoliter, D*f* 3,500 million would be required, a sum not within Heineken's present financial capabilities. Whatever cash flows might be made available for capital expenditures of this sort could be increased further by lowering current financial ratios, disposing of activities no longer fitting the overall strategy, or reducing some Heineken 100 percent participations to a lower percentage (but not below 60 percent).

### The 1983 Planning Letter

The executive board in its 1983 planning letter set out a series of objectives that should guide future strategic choices. The board once more asserted that Heineken should be ''an international beverage company with a strong accent on beer.'' Emphasis should be placed on improving investments already made in Europe and on the United States, although this should not exclude looking at other opportunities that might arise. ROA should be improved with an overall corporate objective of 10 percent. Guidelines were established whereby ROA should be 25 percent on new investments, 15 percent on expansion of existing operations, and 10 percent on replacement. The board also placed great emphasis on the need to be a good corporate citizen everywhere, to safeguard the quality and reliability of the company's products, and to let all employees know what their contribution should be to the achievement of these objectives.

# PART TWO

# Translating a Global Strategy into Local Action

# Athenian Brewery S.A.

In March 1984, the management of Athenian Brewery and its parent company, Heineken N.V., were evaluating several options that would allow them to meet expected capacity shortfalls in the near term. The rapidly expanding Greek market had attracted increased competition in the early 1980s, followed by a dramatic shake out of the brewing industry when growth expectations failed to materialize. Athenian Brewery's share expanded rapidly during this period, reaching 51.8 percent in 1983. Existing plants in Athens and Thessaloniki were fully utilized, and a decision had to be reached soon on what course of action to follow.

## BACKGROUND

During the 1950s the Amstel Brewery in Holland had reacted to the increasing competition it faced from Heineken in its home market by seeking

This case was written by André Khodjamirian, Research Associate, and Professor José de la Torre as a basis for discussion. The generous contributions of many executives in Athenian Brewery and Heineken are gratefully acknowledged, but the authors retain all responsibility for any errors or misinterpretation of facts. © INSEAD, The European Institute of Business Administration, 1984.

export and investment opportunities abroad. The KLM representative in Aman approached the company with the idea of building a brewery in Jordan, a project which was completed in 1958 with a small participation by Amstel (10 percent) and a license to produce Amstel for the local market. The contacts established at that time led two years later to the company being invited to join a group of business people in Beirut in a rescue of the Almaza Brewery. Amstel again assumed a small financial participation, licensed its main brand, and entered into a contract to provide Almaza with technical assistance and marketing support. One of the partners in the Lebanese venture was a Greek/Sudanese entrepreneur, Mr. Hadjivassiliou, who was later to assume a critical role in the company's involvement in the Greek market.

K. Fix A.E. Brewery and Winery was the sole producer of beer in the Greek market at the time. They produced two brands—Fix, which was available throughout the country, and Alfa, sold mainly in the rural areas—in four breweries in Athens and Thessaloniki. While wine was still the preferred drink among Greeks, beer consumption increased from about 200,000 hectoliters (hl) in 1950 to 463,000 hl in 1961, a level of approximately 6 liters per capita. Every summer, the Fix breweries could not supply peak demand, so quantities were rationed, quality was unstable, and advanced payments were often required from distributors. With import duties at 600 percent (except in the Dodecanese islands, where imports were permitted and Amstel was the leading brand), the market was effectively closed.

Early in 1962, Mr. Hadjivassiliou contacted Amstel on behalf of a group of Greek business people to explore the possibility of setting up a competing brewery in the country. Mr. Hoursoglou, a local soft-drink bottler, had obtained a permit to build a brewery in Athens and had been given until July of that year to show he was serious. A plan was developed to build a brewery with an initial capacity of 40,000 hl and a brewhouse designed to accommodate up to 120,000 hl if 6 brews were done per day.

The final proposal to Amstel's board was made in September 1962. It called for a total investment of 50.3 million drachmas (at the time, 8 drachmas = 1 Dutch guilder) of which Dr26 million would be in share capital and the remainder in short-term credits. Amstel would subscribe to Dr6 million of this, or 23 percent of the equity, provide technical assistance in the design and construction of the plant and later in brewing, and license the Amstel brand. For this, Amstel would receive a commission of Df5 per hectoliter of installed capacity, a fixed sum of Df24,000/year for help in starting production and a declining royalty which began at Df5 per hectoliter produced. Initial estimates were that the sum of commissions, dividends, and royalties would pay back the original investment in two years.

The economic and political climate was judged to be favorable. Greece was the first associate member of the EEC and was expected to become a full member by 1980. Capital flows were being liberalized progressively on a timetable that provided full convertibility by 1967. The government appeared stable after the defeat of the communists in the 1949 civil war, and it had shown a positive attitude toward foreign in-

vestment, including offering guarantees on the transferability of dividend payments. Finally, tourism was expected to develop rapidly as evidenced by the more than 600,000 American visitors to the country forecasted for 1962.

In 1965 the new Athenian Brewery plant was inaugurated by Prince Bernhard of the Netherlands. Under the watchful eye of Amstel's international director, Athenian jumped off to a quick start by selling 45,000 hl (7.6 percent of the market) in its first year of operations. A number of expansions to the brewing plant soon followed (total equity was increased to Dr60 million on a proportional basis), and by 1969, in spite of a strong counterattack by Fix which included an attempt to corner the market for bottles, Athenian produced 177,000 hl, or 21.3 percent of total consumption in Greece. Profits, however, were slow in coming. Partly due to the competitive reaction by Fix, which increased Athenian Brewery's costs, but also to Mr. Hadjivassilou's peculiar management style ("he did not believe in numbers, but preferred to manage with his eyes"), the company's cumulative results were still negative by the end of the 1960s.

Motivated by the rapid expansion in sales, Mr. Hadjivassilou had purchased a plant site in Thessaloniki with the idea of opening a second brewery in the north of the country. But the military coup d'état of 1967, a return to foreign exchange controls, the stagnation of the market which followed these events (total demand in 1970 was 867,000 hl or roughly similar to the 844,000 hl sold in 1967), and the poor profitability of the company did not encourage further investments by Amstel's board.

The high seasonality of the market (nearly two-thirds of annual sales took place in the May–September period) meant, however, that sales were being lost in the summer months to Fix and Alfa. This market opportunity was seized by a newcomer in 1971, much in the same fashion as Amstel had done earlier. A 50/50 joint venture between the German brewer Henninger and Greek interests, the new company established a brewery in the island of Crete which soon captured about 10 percent of the market. Its managing director, Mr. Tombros, had worked for Heineken in the Rotterdam brewery and had spent the last few years with the Fix brewery in Athens.

The merger of Amstel and Heineken in 1969 resulted in a number of organizational changes which delayed a response to the Greek situation. The Henninger entry, while initially discounted as insignificant, brought a new urgency to the analysis, and a decision was made to accelerate plans for a second brewery in Thessaloniki. Approved at the end of 1973, the new brewery with an annual capacity of 360,000 hl came on stream in a record time of 13 months. It was accompanied by a mandatory revaluation of existing assets and an expansion of the equity capital to Dr240 million, in which Heineken now held a 57 percent share.

## THE STRUGGLE FOR CONTROL

The following years (1973–1976) were characterized by a number of critical events:

- The total market again remained stagnant for four years, at a level of about 1.4 million hl (16 liters per capita).
- Henninger expanded by building a second brewery in the mainland in Atalanti and extended its market share to about 18 percent by 1976.
- Fix appeared to be in disarray, it suffered from poor management and its close connections with the deposed royal family; its share of the market dropped from 55 percent to 37 percent by 1976.
- Athenian's sales grew rapidly to the point where it surpassed Fix as the market leader with 45 percent market share.
- Democracy returned to Greece in 1974 bringing with it the prospects of an early entry into the European Community.

An internal debate on what to do in Greece continued to occupy Heineken's management; matters were made worse by a succession of personnel and organizational changes which shifted responsibility for European operations, and Greece specifically, no fewer than six times in six years. Some argued that it made no sense to commit further capital to such an uncertain market, particularly when the prospects of ever getting any money out seemed so remote. Others pointed to the gains made in market share and the prospects for growth and to the need to defend market leadership. Although stated profits were low, partly due to the accelerated depreciation of fixed assets, cash flows were adequate to support expansion (see Exhibits 1 and 2 for summary financial data). Finally, relations with the Greek partners had deteriorated considerably throughout the years, to the point where some action was deemed urgent in Amsterdam.

As a first step, a plan was put forth to increase the firm's capitalization to Dr336 million.[1] But a number of local shareholders banded together in order to extract a high price for consenting to Heineken's expansion plans, utilizing a minority protection clause that had been designed originally to protect Amstel's interests in 1963. In October 1976, Mr. Hadjivassiliou suffered a fatal heart attack. Faced with a sudden lack of leadership at the helm of the company, Heineken executives moved promptly, and a deal was reached with his survivors; the blocking strategy had failed. Mr. Miedema, formerly Amstel's international director, was immediately named general manager for Athenian Brewery and proceeded to devote the next eighteen months to sort out the company's financial affairs and to plan for his succession.

In the meantime, Henninger pursued an innovative and aggressive marketing policy with excellent results. They first introduced cans to the market in 1976 and, a year later, brought in a second brand, Kaïser, promoted as an international premium brand and sold at premium prices. These developments coupled with capacity and quality control problems in Athenian's Amstel line resulted in a slight erosion of

---

[1] Greek law prescribed a minimum ratio of equity capital to borrowed funds of 30:70 in a limited liability corporation.

EXHIBIT 1

**BALANCE SHEETS, 1969–1983** (Dr Million)

| | 1983 | 1982 | 1981 | 1980 | 1979 | 1978 | 1977 | 1976 | 1975 | 1973 | 1969 |
|---|---|---|---|---|---|---|---|---|---|---|---|
| Assets | | | | | | | | | | | |
| Current assets | 1,944.3 | 1,701.6 | 1,088.9 | 883.6 | 773.9 | 512.4 | 440.3 | 278.3 | 228.6 | 115.8 | 47.2 |
| Plant and equipment | 4,395.1 | 4,083.4 | 2,510.3 | 2,107.6 | 1,693.2 | 1,277.6 | 1,033.3 | 1,066.7 | 863.0 | 222.8 | 134.7 |
| Depreciation | 1,954.9 | 1,600.1 | 1,076.4 | 859.2 | 668.6 | 543.6 | 437.9 | 317.5 | 196.8 | 108.7 | 29.9 |
| Net fixed assets | 2,440.2 | 2,483.3 | 1,433.9 | 1,248.4 | 1,024.6 | 734.0 | 595.4 | 689.2 | 666.2 | 114.1 | 104.8 |
| Miscellaneous | 631.3 | 454.6 | 637.7 | 617.5 | 529.5 | 267.9 | 177.3 | 159.5 | 187.3 | 46.9 | 13.3 |
| Total | 5,015.8 | 4,639.5 | 3,160.5 | 2,749.6 | 2,328.1 | 1,514.2 | 1,213.0 | 1,127.0 | 1,082.0 | 276.8 | 165.3 |
| Liabilities | | | | | | | | | | | |
| Short-term obligations | 1,144.4 | 992.4 | 1,124.1 | 953.2 | 980.5 | 632.9 | 450.5 | 429.3 | 391.1 | 138.7 | 78.6 |
| Long-term debt | 1,801.5 | 1,561.4 | 1,214.6 | 1,084.9 | 640.8 | 445.5 | 342.7 | 405.5 | 425.1 | 48.3 | 28.4 |
| Total debt | 2,945.9 | 2,553.9 | 2,338.7 | 2,038.1 | 1,621.3 | 1,078.4 | 793.2 | 834.8 | 816.2 | 187.0 | 107.0 |
| Equity | 1,973.1 | 1,973.1 | 710.0 | 600.0 | 600.0 | 336.0 | 336.0 | 240.0 | 240.0 | 60.0 | 60.0 |
| Reserves | 34.5 | 34.5 | 33.8 | 33.5 | 31.4 | 29.6 | 27.5 | 24.4 | 31.8 | 4.5 | 0.5 |
| Retained earnings | 62.3 | 78.0 | 78.0 | 78.0 | 75.5 | 70.3 | 56.4 | 27.9 | (5.9) | 25.3 | (2.2) |
| Capital | 2,069.9 | 2,085.6 | 821.8 | 711.5 | 706.8 | 435.8 | 419.8 | 292.2 | 265.8 | 89.8 | 58.3 |
| Total | 5,015.8 | 4,639.5 | 3,160.5 | 2,749.6 | 2,328.1 | 1,514.2 | 1,213.0 | 1,127.0 | 1,082.0 | 276.8 | 165.3 |

*Source:* Company records.

EXHIBIT 2

**INCOME STATEMENTS, 1969–1983** (Dr Million)

| | 1983 | 1982 | 1981 | 1980 | 1979 | 1978 | 1977 | 1976 | 1975 | 1973 | 1969 |
|---|---|---|---|---|---|---|---|---|---|---|---|
| Net sales | 7,018.2 | 5,035.9 | 4,210.8 | 3,367.6 | 2,645.9 | 1,979.8 | 1,756.1 | 1,331.5 | 1,046.3 | 575.9 | n.a. |
| In thousand hl | 1,443.4 | 1,258.0 | 1,275.6 | 1,174.9 | 1,085.9 | 867.0 | 785.6 | 621.7 | 569.0 | 399.8 | 176.9 |
| In Dr/hl (thousand) | 4.86 | 4.00 | 3.30 | 2.87 | 2.44 | 2.28 | 2.24 | 2.14 | 1.84 | 1.29 | — |
| Gross profit | 1,970.1 | 1,667.3 | 1,393.2 | 1,065.4 | 829.6 | 642.5 | 602.3 | 419.2 | 268.4 | 144.3 | 57.3 |
| In percentage of sales | 28.1 | 33.1 | 33.1 | 31.6 | 32.6 | 32.5 | 34.3 | 31.5 | 25.7 | 28.0 | — |
| Sales and administration | 1,365.1 | 1,090.9 | 918.8 | 697.9 | 666.9 | 419.8 | 353.9 | 243.8 | 174.1 | 91.9 | 31.4 |
| Financial costs | 362.6 | 326.4 | 269.1 | 182.7 | 118.4 | 68.0 | 65.9 | 67.9 | 61.2 | 6.8 | 6.4 |
| Additional depreciation | 277.0 | 231.9 | 180.2 | 128.7 | 94.0 | 102.7 | 106.8 | 70.1 | 57.4 | 16.3 | 13.2 |
| Operating income | (34.6) | 18.1 | 25.1 | 56.1 | 50.2 | 52.0 | 75.7 | 37.3 | (24.3) | 29.2 | 6.3 |
| Other income (net) | 18.7 | (4.7) | 5.7 | — | 7.6 | 2.0 | (3.0) | 0.7 | (11.3) | 0.8 | 2.2 |
| Profit before taxes | (15.7) | 13.4 | 30.9 | 56.1 | 57.8 | 54.0 | 72.7 | 38.0 | (35.7) | 30.0 | 8.5 |
| Income tax | — | — | 0.2 | 1.4 | 3.6 | 3.5 | 8.9 | — | — | 3.6 | — |
| State taxes | — | — | 24.8 | 12.9 | 22.3 | 12.0 | 7.7 | 4.3 | 6.0 | — | — |
| Net profit | (15.7) | 13.4 | 5.9 | 41.8 | 31.9 | 38.5 | 56.1 | 33.7 | (41.7) | 26.4 | 8.5 |
| Memoranda | | | | | | | | | | | |
| Board fees | — | 0.7 | 0.6 | 1.1 | 1.4 | 2.4 | 4.4 | — | — | 3.2 | — |
| Dividend payments | — | 11.9 | 4.9 | 36.0 | 23.5 | 20.2 | 20.2 | — | — | 8.6 | — |
| Production depreciation | 312.7 | 260.2 | 196.3 | 171.3 | 108.7 | 72.0 | 69.0 | 64.2 | 39.5 | 20.2 | n.a. |
| Drachmas per Dutch guilder | 32.1 | 25.02 | 22.20 | 21.44 | 18.46 | 16.98 | 15.01 | 13.81 | 12.77 | 10.60 | 8.29 |

Source: Company records.

market share from 46 percent to 43 percent in 1978 (37 percent only during the summer months) while Henninger's share climbed to 28 percent (30 percent during the summer).

In response to this challenge, a local management team was appointed with Mr. M. Tanes as general manager and the equity capital in Athenian Brewery (AB) was increased to Dr600 million. This expansion, together with the acquisition of most of the shares held by various minority interests, required additional investments by Heineken in excess of D$f$20 million (by then, D$f$1 = Dr18.9), for slightly over 75 percent of the equity and thus the controlling interest. Subsequently, other minority partners were also bought out, giving Heineken the control of more than 90 percent of the equity by 1983.

## THE HEINEKEN DECISION

In June 1980, the board of management of Heineken examined a proposal advocating the introduction of the Heineken brand in the Greek market:

[A] second brand by Athenian Brewery has become a vital need in our efforts to defend our leading position in the Greek beer market under present and future expected developments. The main reasons justifying this action are:

(1) To strengthen Athenian Brewery's position in the A,B,C classes [the highest socioeconomic groups]. In this segment of the market, Henninger holds a slight edge over Amstel in customer preference and it is anticipated that the Kaïser brand, following its recent massive advertising, will move to capture the total of these classes. Reportedly, they intend to introduce cans and even 50 cl bottles.

(2) Athenian Brewery should be in a position to maintain a 45 percent share of the market in the next five years albeit the expected entry of Carlsberg and Löwenbräu in the near future.

(3) The introduction of Heineken will tend to block any new entries into the market other than those already on stream.

The objective was to achieve a volume of 65,000 hl for Heineken in 1981, corresponding to 2.5 percent of the market. The targeted volumes for subsequent years were:

1982: 80,000 hl or 2.9% market share
1983: 100,000 hl or 3.5% market share
1984: 120,000 hl or 4.0% market share
1985: 140,000 hl or 4.5% market share

Price would be set at 12 percent above Amstel. It was felt that a higher price premium would be difficult to sustain as the Greek consumer was becoming increasingly price conscious. Based on this price structure and sales volume, and the higher costs due to the use of imported materials, it was expected that operating profits would begin in 1983 and that cumulative cash flows associated with the launch would turn positive after 1985.

Initial distribution was to be limited to Athens, Thessaloniki, and other urban areas, which accounted for approximately 70 percent of the total Greek beer market, and strong merchandising efforts would be directed to the off-premise outlets (25 percent of overall sales but a higher proportion of the premium segment). Total advertising expenditures were planned at Dr20 million for 1981, or Dr308 per hectoliter. Major advertising objectives were to gain brand awareness during the first year (around 30 percent) and to differentiate the Heineken name from its main competitor, Henninger. Promotional expenses were earmarked at Dr2.7 million, or Dr41 per hectoliter. Finally, a Heineken brand manager was to be appointed.

At the same time, the beer market in Greece was growing at 6.5 percent, and projections for the following 5 years (1981–1985) were for an average growth of almost 5.7 percent per year. An improving economy and a rise in purchasing power had contributed to the increase of beer sales. The market, however, remained highly seasonal (see Exhibit 3), due to local custom and to the summer tourist trade. According to the Greek Institute for Consumer Protection, Mediterranean people drank beer in much the same way as they would other cold soft drinks and their popularity was on the rise. Relative

EXHIBIT 3

**SEASONALITY IN THE GREEK BEER MARKET (AVERAGE FOR 1981–1983)**

Annual consumption, %

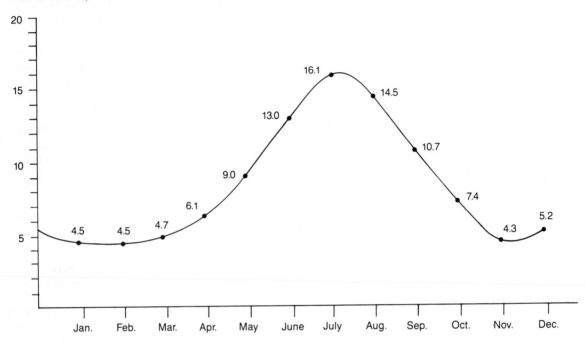

*Source:* Company records.

**THE BEER WAR**

In April 1981, Heineken was launched in the Greek market. Almost immediately thereafter, three other international brands, Spaten, Löwenbräu, and Carlsberg, entered the market, making 1981 a crucial year for the beer trade in Greece. The Fix brewery had licensed Spaten of Munich to develop a position in the premium brand segment, in the hope that this may assist them in halting their market share erosion. Löwenbräu was launched by Brewery of Greece A.E. in Patras, following an agreement between its owner, Greek shipowner G. Koumandros, and one of the oldest and most famous brewing houses in Munich. Carlsberg, a brand that enjoyed considerable presence in world markets, was introduced to Greece by the Catsiapis brothers under license from United Breweries of Denmark. The new plant built by them in Atalanti was thought to represent an investment of about Dr2 billion. These new plants significantly increased the production capacity in the country at a total investment estimated at Dr7.5 billion.

Greece had adopted the German *Reinheitsgebot* (or "purity law") tradition whereby only malt, hops, yeast, and water were allowed in the brewing process. Since prices were tied to the cost of production, competition among brands was based largely on access to distribution

price increases were also working in favor of the beer trade: In recent years, wine prices had increased at a rate of twice that of beer.

channels and advertising.[2] The entry of four new brands in 1981 meant that each company was forced to embark on a massive campaign to establish or increase its market share.

Fix was reported to be in considerable trouble, with a loss of Dr300 million in 1980. In order to hold on to its dwindling market share, the company placed its efforts on sales promotion through wholesalers and on advertising the Greek origin of the Fix brand. The launching of Spaten did not produce the expected results, and Alfa's distribution was limited to small villages where other brands were not available.

Henninger continued to increase its market share almost entirely at the expense of Fix. The company appeared to be well tuned to the shifting preferences of the Greek market and was first to realize the opportunity for a premium brand aimed at a growing number of image-conscious beer drinkers. Many industry observers argued that Henninger was the company that introduced real competition to the Greek beer market and credited its successful advertising as being a major factor in the growth of total consumption. Henninger was planning an expansion of its canning capacity to 4 million cans, and the company's strategy was to stress high standards of production and quality.

Carlsberg had entered the market at a lower premium level, slightly over the Amstel price, and aimed to establish an acceptable market share in the normal-priced beer sector, in spite of its being a premium-image brand. The company had organized a sales team according to international standards and was following an advertising campaign geared to create brand awareness.

Löwenbräu's entrance to the market had been delayed a few months owing to technical prob-

lems in production. Preceded by a dynamic advertising campaign, Löwenbräu was introduced as a premium brand with a traditional Bavarian heritage and was priced 25 percent higher than other standard brands. Plagued by distribution problems, however, it failed to achieve the expected results.

Athenian Brewery, in addition to launching Heineken with a massive advertising and promotional campaign, set out to increase the advertising budget for Amstel. Total AB expenditures for advertising rose from Dr18 million in 1980 (37.5 percent of industry total) to Dr39.6 million in 1981 (28.6 percent of total). Heineken's market share goals were soon attained, but Amstel continued to slip as other brands gained ground.

## THE SITUATION IN 1982

The socialist government elected in October 1981 adopted a considerably less liberal economic policy. In March 1982, a 100 percent increase in excise duty was announced, followed by a series of decisions that all brands of beer should be sold at the same price, that wholesalers should be allowed no more than 10 percent discount from selling price, and that companies should tone down their brand advertising.

The duty increase was particularly damaging to the industry, and after considerable lobbying and negotiation the government agreed to limit the increase to 40 percent.[3] The price freeze was also modified and applied to specific beer brands. As a result, Heineken and Kaïser were allowed to stay at a premium price level of up to 20 percent over standard brands because they were the only two brands that were recognised to be of superior quality and, more important, that had not engaged in discounting during the previous year's distribution war. Other brands were

---

[2] Prices were controlled by the government, which allowed a margin of 5 percent over ''full costs'' (defined to exclude depreciation, royalty payments, trade discounts and interest costs). Each brewery submitted its application for price increases independently, and the government selected one standard for the industry. Actual performance, however, was rarely controlled between price reviews. Athenian had succeeded in arguing that its higher cost structure in brewing Heineken justified a price premium.

[3] Excise duties on beer were imposed in Greece on the basis of malt consumption. Prior to 1982, the duty was fixed at Dr55/kg, which represented about 20 percent of the selling price of a bottle of beer. The increase to Dr77/kg was immediately reflected in selling prices.

all to be sold at approximately the same price, a move that mostly disadvantaged Löwenbräu and Carlsberg (these two plus Spaten were allowed a 2 percent premium). In order to break into the market they had allowed high margins to wholesalers and expected to make up for it through higher prices. The government argued that the higher margins were evidence of lower costs.

The government's new economic policies resulted in heavy losses for the industry in 1982, estimated by some observers to exceed Dr2,600 million. Labor costs had risen faster than the inflation level of 20 percent and taxes were expected to increase further in 1983. Furthermore, the government's urban planners were pushing for decentralizing industry. Not only was expansion no longer allowed in Athens, but some plants were going to be forced out into other locations. Other large cities like Thessaloniki might also be affected by similar regulations.

Market growth in 1982 dropped to 2.1 percent from a forecasted 5 percent, almost completely due to the volume effects of the tax increase. It was believed that Carlsberg ended 1982 with losses of Df40 million on an investment of Df75 million, and Löwenbräu lost Df60 million on an investment of Df115 million. Fix had been in difficulty since 1981 when a worker's council assumed management and the company started offering up to 30 percent discounts during the summer of 1982 to boost sales. Henninger was also affected, and production dropped 60,000 hl below forecasted level. Amstel held well, but Heineken sales also suffered. As a result, total monthly capacity of Athenian was underutilized by 30,000 hl.

Athenian's capital structure had changed substantially during the year. A mandatory asset revaluation of Dr563 million was reflected directly in the equity account. In addition, Heineken made new investments totalling Dr700 million (about Df28 million) in its Greek subsidiary, of which 80 percent were new funds injected into the company and 20 percent a capitalization of royalty payments. Both of these actions increased Athenian's financial capacity to face the working capital requirements which had resulted from the 1981–1982 beer war. Credit terms alone, for example, had doubled in this period.

## THE 1983 OPERATING PLAN

In September 1982, the management of Athenian Brewery drew their operating plans for 1983 with three objectives in mind:

- Remain market leader with 43 percent market share.
- Maintain financial health.
- Engage in some export activity to please the government.

Amstel production in 1982 had been 1.2 million hl, and a 5 percent increase was planned for 1983; this would yield a share of 43.2 percent of the bottle and can segment and 32 percent for draft beer. Advertising expenditures for Amstel were budgeted at nearly Df3 million in 1983 up from Df2.2 million in 1982. Over two-thirds of it were to be used on TV commercials. Promotional budget was also up by 15 percent to Df1.6 million.

One Heineken executive felt that Athenian had "missed the boat" in the draft beer segment. In 1981, there were 1,200 outlets for draft beer in the country, mainly in large urban centers. By 1982, this number had increased to 4,300. Athenian Brewery had entered this segment in late 1981 and had reached a 20 percent share by the end of 1982. Exhibit 4 shows the evolution of draft beer sales in Greece and Athenian Brewery's share expectations for 1983.

The Heineken brand was targeted to capture 65 percent market share in the premium segment, or a volume of 80,000 hl. This included 100 percent of the premium draft beer outlets, or 7,000 hl. Heineken's advertising budget was set at Df1.6 million versus Df1.5 million in 1982. Brand awareness was now evaluated to be at about 40 percent.

Exports of Marathon and Athenian brands (not sold domestically) were targeted to Middle

---
**EXHIBIT 4**
---

**DRAFT BEER SALES IN GREECE (1981–1983)**

| | All brands | | | Amstel | | |
|---|---|---|---|---|---|---|
| | No. of installations | Sales (thousand hl) | Percentage of total market | No. of installations | Sales (thousand hl) | Percentage of market |
| 1981 | 1,200 | 37 | 1.3 | 30 | 0.2 | 0.5 |
| 1982 | 4,300 | 160 | 5.5 | 800 | 32.5 | 20 |
| 1983(e) | 5,500 | 265 | 9.5 | 1,200 | 85 | 32 |

Eastern, African, and U.S. markets. This activity was intended to utilize excess capacity in low-demand months and develop goodwill with the government which was encouraging exports as a way to improve the country's balance of payments.

## EXCESS CAPACITY IN THE INDUSTRY

In March 1983, the Catsiapis brothers closed down the Carlsberg plant, and it was rumored that it might be put up for sale. The situation at Fix was not much better. Ever since the management of the company was taken over by the workers' council in 1981, matters had not improved, and the discounting strategy employed in 1982 barely got them through the peak summer months. By the end of the summer of 1983, Fix also closed its plants, and rumors of bankruptcy were circulating in the trade. The government had subsidized the company for part of 1981–1982 by offering them advantageous loans. In September 1983, the government was trying to interest other companies in the industry to take over the Fix workforce.

Published financial figures for Löwenbräu indicated that the company was "technically dead." Even if the massive investments were written off, the company was not even at a cash flow breakeven point (see Exhibit 5 for a financial analysis of all major competitors). Its owner, Mr. Koumandros, was a wealthy shipowner who lived in New York and had extensive flour-milling holdings in Nigeria. He only seemed re-

motely interested in the beer business and had delegated the management of the brewery to his son-in-law. A recent capital injection of Dr4 billion (about Df 160 million) would extend the life of the company for the foreseeable future.

Henninger was suffering from the financial strain of having overextended capacity (by 400,000 hl) by opening a third brewery in 1981 in Thessaloniki. There were also rumors of management problems, and the company failed to make any profit out of the closure of Carlsberg and Fix. Its capital base had also been increased in 1982 by about Dr1.2 billion (Df 48 million). Henninger Germany had not been keen to share in the additional investment and opted for granting its Greek subsidiary a 3-month revolving credit line. It seemed unlikely that the mother company was able or prepared to help if the situation deteriorated further.

The market was also erratic in 1983: Figures for the first half of the year showed a growth of over 10 percent in sales, whereas for the second half, a decline of 10 percent was observed. This phenomenon perplexed the trade, and many theories were put forward. Some felt it was a direct consequence of the 15 percent price increase that the government had authorized in September 1983, a move that many judged untimely as it had occurred just after the peak summer months and did not allow brewers to fully benefit from it. Others tied it to the general slowdown in the economy or to the bad publicity generated by the plant closings. Finally, some predicted an end to the rapid growth of previous

---
### EXHIBIT 5
---

**COMPARATIVE FINANCIAL ANALYSIS OF BEER COMPANIES IN GREECE, 1982**

|  | Athenian Brewery | Henninger | Carlsberg | Löwenbräu | Fix |
|---|---|---|---|---|---|
| Sales (thousand hl) | 1,258 | 787 | 206 | 322 | 312 |
| Results (Dr/hl) | | | | | |
| Gross margin | 1,325.3 | 1,377.3 | (138.5) | 336.6 | 1,614.3 |
| Administration | 122.2 | 104.3 | 524.1 | 2,291.6* | 107.7 |
| Selling expenses | 745.0 | 1,300.8 | 1,653.1 | 1,776.8 | 1,179.7 |
| Interest expense | 259.5 | 521.8 | 2,141.2 | — | 2,529.9 |
| Depreciation | 184.4 | 100.4 | 289.4 | 824.3 | 509.2 |
| Other expenses (income) | 3.7 | (19.0) | (10.7) | 48.1 | 677.0 |
| Net profit (Dr million) | 13.4 | (496.7) | (975.6) | (1,482.6) | (1,057.5) |
| Cash flow (Dr million) | 505.5 | 8.1 | (709.1) | (951.4) | (898.7) |
| Balances (Dr million) | | | | | |
| Fixed assets (net) | 3,013.2 | 2,344.5 | 2,820.2 | 6,460.6 | 2,100.4 |
| Current assets | 1,626.3 | 1,244.0 | 410.6 | 1,247.9 | 551.3 |
| Short-term debt | 992.4 | 2,155.0 | 1,659.9 | 1,667.6 | 555.4 |
| Long-term debt | 1,561.5 | 1,025.2 | 2,261.5 | 3,941.1 | 3,811.0 |
| Equity | 2,085.6 | 408.3 | (596.6) | 2,099.8 | (1,714.8) |
| Ratios | | | | | |
| Stocks (days) | 88 | 92 | 36 | 189 | 63 |
| Receivables (days) | 32 | 48 | 136 | 35 | 54 |
| Current ratio | 1.6 | 0.6 | 0.3 | 0.7 | 1.0 |
| Acid ratio | 0.2 | 0.1 | — | — | — |

*Includes interest expense.
*Source:* Company records.

years when per capita consumption had risen from 6 to 26 liters.

At the end of 1983, total capacity in the industry stood at 4.14 million hl (excluding Fix, which had an additional capacity of about 0.8 million) in a market that could only absorb 2.8 million hl. The major plants in 1983 are shown in Exhibit 6.

## ATHENIAN'S OPTIONS FOR EXPANSION

In order to analyze possible courses of action, a team was assigned from corporate headquarters to cooperate closely with the management of Athenian Brewery in what became known as the "Greek Production Capacity Project." It was agreed that the most desirable long-term objective was for Athenian Brewery to produce in breweries which they would own. Short-term decisions to solve capacity shortages, such as contract brewing with Henninger or Löwenbräu, or renting the Carlsberg plant, were not to be allowed to jeopardize this long-term consideration. The first step was to make total market forecasts for the next 10 years. As the position of Löwenbräu in the market was quite uncertain after 1984, share projections for Athenian Brewery with and without the presence of Löwenbräu were envisaged. Regional sales and different packaging requirements were also forecasted. Exhibits 7 and 8 show the historical and projected evolution of the Greek beer market and of Athenian Brewery's share.

There were a number of possible solutions to the long-term capacity problem. These are described in detail in Exhibit 9, and could be summarized in the following terms:

### EXHIBIT 6

**GREEK BREWING CAPACITY, 1983**

| Company | Location | Capacity (thousand hl) |
|---|---|---|
| Athenian Brewery | Athens | 600 |
| | Thessaloniki | 1,100 |
| | Subtotal | 1,700 |
| Henninger | Crete | 400 |
| | Atalanti | 600 |
| | Thessaloniki | 580 |
| | Subtotal | 1,580 |
| Löwenbräu | Patras | 460 |
| Carlsberg (closed) | Atalanti | 400 |
| Total | | 4,140 |

- Renovation and extension of the Athens brewery, undertaken independently from any other capacity extension solution
- Extension of the Thessaloniki brewery
- Building a new brewery close to Athens
- Purchase of available plants (Carlsberg and/or Löwenbräu)

Cash flow projections were first made for the building of a new plant near Athens. AB management knew that there was little chance that this option would be accepted by the government since it was contrary to both the prevailing urban plans, and the government's desire to increase capacity utilization in the industry; it was included in the analysis for comparative purposes only. Long-term purchase options were to include start-up costs only, as at the time the acquisition prices were not known. However, by calculating projected cash-flows based on estimated per-hectoliter production costs, a break-even investment cost could be identified for each relative to the other options.

Set up costs for short-term contract brewing or importation could also be estimated although projected cash flows for contract brewing would have to be made based on negotiations with the respective contracting parties. All these cash flow projections appear in Appendix A.

## FINAL CONSIDERATIONS

It was difficult to predict the attitude of the government if the Greek beer market were to be dominated by two foreign companies, Heineken and Henninger. The socialist government was taking on wide-ranging powers in handling the country's economic affairs, but the feeling was that the state had overextended itself in this matter and was, as a consequence, losing control of more fundamental problems. In 1984 the Greek Ministry of National Economy produced a report on the beer industry. This report contained a number of positive elements: recognition that beer prices should guarantee an adequate return on assets, although they would be fixed at the consumer level; allowance that Amstel might have a market share over 50 percent; and an implicit understanding that Fix was no longer viable and should be permanently shut down. There were also some negative aspects, however, namely the suggestion to form a Greek venture to absorb Carlsberg and Löwenbräu and to oblige Amstel and Henninger to produce and bottle beer on a contract basis with the new venture. A summary of the report appears in Appendix B. Finally, all price controls on other beverages (wine, soft drinks, etc.) had been progressively lifted since 1982. Industry executives expected beer price controls to follow this trend, but the timing of such a move was uncertain.

In evaluating the various options, corporate considerations and priorities would obviously need to be taken into account. The recent investments in France[4] were drawing considerably on Heineken's resources, and other current projects might place significant claims on the availability of corporate funds. Corporate policy would also need to be defined in regards to the

---

[4]In late 1983 Heineken had announced an agreement with the shareholders of Union de Brasseries (UdB) to combine their assets in France under a new holding company where Heineken would own 51 percent of the shares. An initial investment of Df100 million would be followed by important capital requirements for restructuring and modernization of their facilities.

EXHIBIT 7

## MARKET EVOLUTION AND MARKET SHARES, 1981–1983

| | Athenian Brewery | | Henninger | | Fix | | Löwenbräu | | Carlsberg | | Total market | |
|---|---|---|---|---|---|---|---|---|---|---|---|---|
| | Volume (thousand hl) | Share (%) | Volume (thousand hl) | Share (%) | Volume (thousand hl) | Share (%) | Volume (thousand hl) | Share (%) | Volume (thousand hl) | Share (%) | Volume (thousand hl) | Increase (%) |
| 1971 | 233.8 | 25.4 | 62.6 | 6.8 | 623.6 | 67.8 | — | — | — | — | 920.0 | — |
| 1972 | 276.0 | 27.1 | 108.7 | 10.7 | 634.3 | 62.2 | — | — | — | — | 1,019.0 | + 10.7 |
| 1973 | 400.0 | 31.9 | 162.8 | 13.0 | 689.8 | 55.1 | — | — | — | — | 1,252.6 | + 22.9 |
| 1974 | 501.8 | 34.1 | 190.2 | 12.9 | 779.6 | 53.0 | — | — | — | — | 1,471.6 | + 17.5 |
| 1975 | 572.1 | 40.2 | 213.7 | 15.0 | 637.8 | 44.8 | — | — | — | — | 1,423.6 | − 3.3 |
| 1976 | 624.1 | 44.6 | 251.2 | 18.0 | 522.8 | 37.4 | — | — | — | — | 1,398.1 | − 1.8 |
| 1977 | 788.0 | 45.8 | 380.0 | 22.1 | 551.7 | 32.1 | — | — | — | — | 1,720.0 | + 23.0 |
| 1978 | 870.0 | 43.0 | 563.7 | 27.8 | 591.3 | 29.2 | — | — | — | — | 2,025.0 | + 17.7 |
| 1979 | 1,089.0 | 46.7 | 680.0 | 29.2 | 562.0 | 24.1 | — | — | — | — | 2,331.0 | + 15.1 |
| 1980 | 1,179.3 | 47.5 | 759.0 | 30.6 | 544.0 | 21.9 | — | — | — | — | 2,482.3 | + 6.5 |
| 1981 | 1,279.0 | 45.3 | 860.0 | 30.4 | 407.0 | 14.4 | 121.0 | 4.3 | 158.0 | 5.6 | 2,825.0 | + 13.8 |
| 1982 | 1,258.0 | 43.6 | 787.0 | 27.3 | 312.0 | 10.8 | 322.0 | 11.2 | 206.0 | 7.1 | 2,885.0 | + 2.1 |
| 1983 | 1,450.0 | 51.8 | 845.0 | 30.2 | 135.0 | 4.8 | 357.0 | 12.7 | 13.0 | 0.5 | 2,800.0 | − 2.7 |
| 1984(e) | 1,640.0 | 55.0 | 985.0 | 33.0 | — | — | 355.0 | 12.0 | — | — | 2,980.0 | + 6.4 |

*Source:* Company records.

EXHIBIT 8

## TOTAL MARKET AND AB SHARE PROJECTIONS, 1984–2000 (Thousand hl)

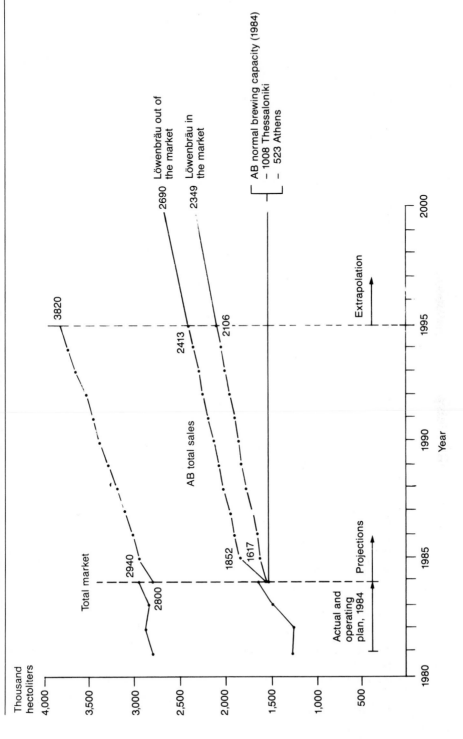

EXHIBIT 9

**DESCRIPTION OF OPTIONS**

| | Renovate Athens brewhouse | Extend Athenian's Thessaloniki brewery | Build new brewery |
|---|---|---|---|
| Plan | Put in new brewhouse, replace old cellars | Extend brewery in Thessaloniki | Build new brewery |
| Constraints | Government restrictions on building site<br>Building license requirements<br>Risk of withdrawal of building permit by government | — | Unlikely to obtain government permission—this option is merely a theoretical base |
| Capacity | Extra 150,000 hl brew capacity<br>Potential for extra lagering capacity<br>No bottling, kegging, or canning lines required | Maximum capacity of 280,000 hl | Capacity would cover requirements for next 20 years |
| Timing | In principle, two winters' work | 2 yrs. needed for completion of brewhouse and an additional year for the bottling line | n.a. |
| Location | Athens | Thessaloniki | n.a. |
| Set-up costs | Estimated at D$f$17.8 million. Some personnel cost savings are also expected | Estimated at D$f$16.4 million | n.a. |
| Purchase costs | n.a. | n.a. | n.a. |
| Distribution costs | Most advantageous: 40 percent of beer consumption takes place in Athens | High, due to distance from major market areas | n.a. |
| Personnel | n.a. | n.a. | n.a. |
| Subjective issues | Advantage of Heineken-built brewery | Advantage of Heineken-built brewery | n.a. |

n.a. = not applicable.
*Source:* Company records.

principle of brewing Heineken products in competitors' breweries.

Finally, market share objectives were still to be agreed. It was felt that Athenian Brewery should aim for a maximum share at a reasonable cost and refrain from overinvesting in a market where trends were subject to abrupt change. Appendix C provides information from the 1984 corporate guidelines for Athenian Brewery's 1985–1989 plan.

| Purchase Carlsberg | Purchase Löwenbräu | Contract brew with Henninger | Import bulk Heineken |
| --- | --- | --- | --- |
| Possibility to rent brewhouse prior to purchase | Purchase or rent for short-term contract brewing | Tactical move to cover peak season requirements | Tactical move to cover peak season requirements |
| Lengthy liquidation procedures<br>Maintenance work required | Willingness of company chairman to sell out. He is also receptive to contract brewing. | Willingness of local management to cooperate | Import license |
| Around 400,000 hl<br>Possible necessity to erect malting plant | Total 400,000 hl, 300,000 presently used<br>Malting plant exists | 600,000 hl | n.a. |
| Renting possible as of 2/1984<br>Purchase may take 2–3 years | n.a. | n.a. | n.a. |
| Atalanti, halfway between Athens and Thessaloniki | Patras, 180 kms. west of Athens | Probably Thessaloniki | n.a. |
| Estimated at D$f$400,000 | Less than Carlsberg option | Not defined | Extra cellars, duties |
| Estimated at D$f$65 million plus transfer tax of 5.2 million | Not defined | n.a. | n.a. |
| Saving of D$f$1.6 million compared to extending Thessaloniki brewery | Saving of D$f$1.9 million compared to extending Thessaloniki brewery | High, like option of extending Thessaloniki brewery | Transportation costs |
| 30 people (including AB technician) needed to brew 200,000 hl | Unknown | n.a. | n.a. |
| Quality control, supply continuity, personnel motivation | Company chairman unpredictability; possible quality, supply/delivery problems in contract brewing | Mistrust between AB & local Henninger management<br>Possible quality & supply problems | Principle of cross-company imports & attitude of Greek authorities |

# Excerpts from the "Greek Production Capacity Project" Report[5]

This project was set up to provide a framework to aid decision making regarding the potential undercapacity in Athenian Brewery. The objective is to set up good communication lines between Athens and Amsterdam and a solid data bank based on mutually agreed assumptions. This should facilitate quick and efficient decision making and thus obtain maximum advantage from long-term capacity extension opportunities that may appear suddenly.

Our basic scenario assumes that Löwenbräu stays in the market and permission is obtained to renovate and extend the Athens brewery in 1984. The first option is to extend the Thessaloniki brewery. In this case there would be no requirement for a new brewery before 1998. The other options in this scenario are to build a new brewery near Athens (at least in theory) or buy the Carlsberg brewery. The acquisition of the Löwenbräu brewery as a going concern is assumed to be not attractive financially.

Cash flow projections were prepared for each of these three options. An example of these for the extension of the Thessaloniki brewery is shown in Exhibit 10. Column 2 is taken from the market and market share projections shown in Exhibit 8 for bottles only (see below). This assumes Athenian Brewery will maintain a 55 percent market share throughout the period. Columns 3 and 4 give "normal" production figures (these understate "actual" capacity by about 10 percent) for both breweries including the renovation of Athens in 1984, the extension of Thessaloniki from 1987, and a new brewery near Athens from 1998. The short-term shortages (column 6) could be met from the capacity reserve of both existing breweries. The investments required (column 7) were assumed based on step-wise expansions at D$f$103 per hl of capacity and twice D$f$15 million for a completely new brewery near Athens in 1996–1997. Column 8 states the proportion of each annual investment (based

on an average life of 16 years) that goes into the residual value accounted for in the year 2000. Transportation costs (column 9) are based on the expected regional split of sales and other minor adjustments. The new brewery near Athens is also expected to increase fixed operating costs by D$f$3 million per year from 1998. Finally, column 11 summarizes all cash flows from costs and investments. Since sales revenues are assumed identical under all options, they are not included in the calculations.

The next step was to compare all three sets of cash flows. These figures are shown in Exhibit 11. The results are that the extension of Thessaloniki appears to be preferable to building a new brewery now. Also, the comparison with the purchase of the Carlsberg brewery yields a breakeven investment cost of D$f$32.5 million (including purchase price plus transfer costs, adaptations to Heineken standards, and extension of the bottling capacity), if a 15 percent discount rate is applied to the differential cash flows. This figure represents the maximum amount Heineken ought to be willing to pay for the Carlsberg brewery relative to pursuing the Thessaloniki expansion option.

A sensitivity analysis of these two options (Thessaloniki versus Carlsberg) indicated that the conclusions are heavily dependent on the sales forecast assumptions. For example, a 10 percent increase in sales volume yields a breakeven investment cost for Carlsberg of D$f$56.7 million, that is, almost twice the level calculated above.

A second set of calculations were carried out for the second scenario which assumes that Löwenbräu goes out of the market. In this case, Athenian Brewery's market share has been estimated at 63 percent throughout the period. The same options as for the first scenario are available to which one can add the possible purchase of Löwenbräu. The results are shown in Exhibit 12. Under these assumptions, the breakeven investment cost for Carlsberg amounts to D$f$67.8 million, while that for Löwenbräu is D$f$73.9 million.

Exhibits 10 through 12 consider only sales of bottled beer (in both 33- and 50-cl containers). This represented more than 90 percent of Amstel's projected volume, and over 80 percent for Heineken. Actual production capacities in thousand hectoliters for 1984 are shown in Exhibit 13. Expected demand for draft and canned beer could be met with existing facilities, except under the second scenario where a light increase in canning capacity in Athens would be required after 1994.

---

[5] Appendix A is derived from company records.

# EXHIBIT 10

## CASH FLOW PROJECTION RELATED TO THE EXTENSION OF THESSALONIKI

| | Thousands of hectoliters | | | | | Thousands of guilders | | | | |
| | | | | | | | | | | |
| Year | Sales (bottles) | Normal production Athens | Normal production Thessaloniki | Normal production total | Shortage | Investments | Contribution to residual value | Transportation costs | Additional operational costs | |
| (1) | (2) | (3) | (4) | (5) | (6) | (7) | (8) | (9) | (10) | (11) |
| 1985 | 1,446 | 533 | 881 | 1,414 | 32 | | | 10,460 | | −10,460 |
| 86 | 1,490 | | 881 | 1,414 | 76 | 12,463 | 2/16 | 10,853 | | −23,316 |
| 87 | 1,535 | | 1,002 | 1,535 | | 4,635 | 3/16 | 11,246 | | −15,881 |
| 88 | 1,580 | | 1,047 | 1,580 | | 4,532 | 4/16 | 11,639 | | −16,171 |
| 89 | 1,624 | | 1,091 | 1,624 | | 4,635 | 5/16 | 12,032 | | −16,667 |
| 90 | 1,669 | | 1,136 | 1,669 | | 4,635 | 6/16 | 12,426 | | −17,061 |
| 91 | 1,714 | | 1,181 | 1,714 | | 4,532 | 7/16 | 12,845 | | −17,377 |
| 92 | 1,758 | | 1,225 | 1,758 | | 4,532 | 8/16 | 13,264 | | −17,796 |
| 93 | 1,802 | | 1,269 | 1,802 | | 4,532 | 9/16 | 13,683 | | −18,215 |
| 94 | 1,846 | | 1,313 | 1,846 | | 4,429 | 10/16 | 14,102 | | −18,531 |
| 95 | 1,889 | | 1,356 | 1,889 | | 4,532 | 11/16 | 14,522 | | −19,054 |
| 96 | 1,933 | | 1,400 | 1,933 | | 19,532 | 12/16 | 14,816 | | −34,348 |
| 97 | 1,977 | 533 | 1,444 | 1,977 | | 19,429 | 13/16 | 15,110 | | −34,539 |
| 98 | 2,020 | 554 | 1,466 | 2,020 | | 4,532 | 14/16 | 15,404 | 3,000 | −22,936 |
| 99 | 2,064 | 598 | 1,466 | 2,064 | | 4,532 | 15/16 | 15,698 | 3,000 | −23,230 |
| 2000 | 2,108 | 642 | 1,466 | 2,108 | | 4,532 | 16/16 | 15,994 | 3,000 | +39,084 |
| | | | | | | 106,014 | 62,610 | 214,094 | 9,000 | 266,498 |

Note: Minus (−) is outflow; plus (+) is inflow.

**EXHIBIT 11**

**COMPARISON OF CASH FLOWS FOR ALTERNATIVE EXPANSION STRATEGIES WITH LÖWENBRÄU IN THE MARKET** (Df Thousand)

| | Extension Thessaloniki (A) | New brewery near Athens (B) | Purchase Carlsberg (C) | B – A | C – A |
|---|---|---|---|---|---|
| 1985 | – 10,460 | – 10,460 | – 10,460 | 0 | 0 |
| 1986 | – 23,316 | – 25,625 | – 10,853-X | – 2,309 | 12,463-X |
| 1987 | – 15,881 | – 42,888 | – 12,234 | – 27,007 | 3,647 |
| 1988 | – 16,171 | – 18,487 | – 12,614 | – 2,316 | 3,557 |
| 1989 | – 16,667 | – 18,755 | – 12,994 | – 2,088 | 3,673 |
| 1990 | – 17,061 | – 18,920 | – 13,374 | – 1,859 | 3,687 |
| 1991 | – 17,377 | – 19,040 | – 13,754 | – 1,663 | 3,623 |
| 1992 | – 17,796 | – 19,263 | – 14,134 | – 1,467 | 3,662 |
| 1993 | – 18,215 | – 19,486 | – 14,514 | – 1,271 | 3,701 |
| 1994 | – 18,531 | – 19,606 | – 14,894 | – 1,075 | 3,637 |
| 1995 | – 19,054 | – 19,932 | – 15,273 | – 878 | 3,781 |
| 1996 | – 34,348 | – 20,134 | – 15,595 | + 14,214 | 18,753 |
| 1997 | – 34,539 | – 20,233 | – 16,535 | + 14,306 | 18,004 |
| 1998 | – 22,936 | – 20,538 | – 20,771 | + 2,398 | 2,165 |
| 1999 | – 23,230 | – 20,740 | – 21,093 | + 2,490 | 2,137 |
| 2000 | + 39,084 | + 23,698 | – 7,885 | – 15,386 | – 46,969 |
| Cumulative | – 266,498 | – 290,409 | – 226,977-X | – 23,911 | 39,521-X |

*Note:* Net present value of (C – A) at 15 percent discount is equal to zero when X = 32,506.

EXHIBIT 12

**COMPARISON OF CASH FLOWS FOR ALTERNATIVE EXPANSION STRATEGIES WITH LÖWENBRÄU OUT OF THE MARKET**

(Df Thousand)

| | Extension Thessaloniki (A) | New brewery near Athens (B) | Purchase Carlsberg (C) | Purchase Löwenbräu (D) | B − A | C − A | D − A |
|---|---|---|---|---|---|---|---|
| 1985 | −22,858 | −22,858 | −22,858 | −22,858 | 0 | 0 | 0 |
| 1986 | −64,063 | −43,322 | −28,322-X | −28,322-Y | +20,741 | +35,741-X | +35,741-Y |
| 1987 | −18,539 | −89,880 | −14,407 | −13,932 | −71,341 | +4,132 | +4,607 |
| 1988 | −19,003 | −20,206 | −14,747 | −14,359 | −1,203 | +4,256 | +4,644 |
| 1989 | −19,467 | −20,453 | −15,087 | −14,786 | −896 | +4,380 | +4,681 |
| 1990 | −34,933 | −20,700 | −15,427 | −15,213 | +14,233 | +19,506 | +19,720 |
| 1991 | −35,294 | −20,844 | −15,767 | −15,640 | +14,450 | +19,527 | +19,654 |
| 1992 | −23,583 | −21,091 | −21,257 | −16,067 | +2,492 | +2,326 | +7,516 |
| 1993 | −23,834 | −21,338 | −21,597 | −16,494 | +2,496 | +2,237 | +7,340 |
| 1994 | −24,085 | −21,585 | −21,937 | −16,921 | +2,500 | +2,148 | +7,164 |
| 1995 | −24,336 | −21,831 | −22,279 | −17,350 | +2,502 | +2,057 | +6,986 |
| 1996 | −24,587 | −22,175 | −22,578 | −22,867 | +2,412 | +2,009 | +1,720 |
| 1997 | −24,838 | −22,519 | −22,877 | −23,234 | +2,319 | +1,961 | +1,604 |
| 1998 | −25,089 | −22,863 | −23,176 | −23,601 | +2,216 | +1,913 | +1,488 |
| 1999 | −25,340 | −23,207 | −23,475 | −23,968 | +2,133 | +1,865 | +1,372 |
| 2000 | +33,991 | +30,618 | +10,989 | −1,805 | −3,373 | −23,002 | −35,796 |
| Cumulative | −375,858 | −384,254 | −294,802-X | −287,417-Y | −8,396 | +81,056-X | +88,441-Y |

*Note:* Net present value of (C − A) at 15 percent discount is equal to zero when X = 67,755. Net present value of (D − A) at 15 percent discount is equal to zero when Y = 73,932.

EXHIBIT 13

**ATHENIAN BREWERY'S PRODUCTION CAPACITIES, 1984**

| | Brewing | Bottling | Canning | Racking |
|---|---|---|---|---|
| Athens | 523 | 533 | 163 | 81 |
| Thessaloniki | 1,008 | 881 | — | 52 |
| Total | 1,531 | 1,414 | 163 | 133 |

153

## APPENDIX B

# Excerpts from a Report of the Greek Ministry of National Economy Regarding the Beer Industry[6]

- The Greek beer industry should be competitive at the European level with regards to cost structure and product quality.
- Exports should be geared to Middle Eastern and Balkan countries due to lower transportation costs.
- Excise duties should not increase until they match the average EEC level [the implication appeared to be that prices would be allowed to rise with inflation while the duty would be kept constant].
- Prices of beer should be determined via competitive market forces at a level that provides the necessary income for an adequate return on assets as well as allow for self-financing. It should be noted that in the case of price fixing by the Ministry of Commerce, when long delays occur, it is mathematically proven that the beer companies will not be able to sustain accumulated losses.
- The government should intervene in fixing the final price that the consumer pays and not the factory price.
- New licenses for investment in the beer industry should not be granted, with the exception of bottling lines, productivity increases and new technology in the existing companies, until consumption absorbs total existing capacity including Carlsberg.
- Any proposal regarding restructuring of the beer industry should not endanger the viability of the financially and marketing sound Amstel brewery and the less problematic Henninger brewery.
- Fix and Alfa breweries should discontinue operations due to old technology and equipment.
- A new Greek venture could be built under the "Organization of Problematic Companies" to absorb Carlsberg and Löwenbräu. Production capacity will be 500,000 hl (18% market share).
- Amstel and Henninger could bottle beer in the new venture on contract basis after 1986 when their production capacity will be covered.
- Market share will then develop as follows: Amstel 52%; Henninger 30%; and "Greek company" 18%.

## APPENDIX C

# Excerpts from Corporate Guidelines for Athenian Brewery, 1985–1989[7]

In the coming five years, the Company appears to have several options available, for example:

- Product diversification (wines, soft drinks, etc.)
- A wider range of types of beer (Dark Beer, Murphy Stout)
- New packaging

May we ask that all aspects (commercial, technical and financial) of each available option be analyzed and briefly commented.

According to the current operational plan a decision on capacity must be taken in 1984. If this decision cannot be deferred, several alternatives are open to us (take-over, contract brewing, investment in installed capacity, or rental of installed capacity). If possible, we would appreciate a comprehensive analysis of each alternative from all angles, including the impact on the projected ROA calculations.

### MARGINS AND CONTRIBUTIONS

Referring to the current operational plan, it appears that the Heineken brand does not cover the global fixed costs which may be charged to it. This seems to be due to the high level of direct marketing costs. Bearing in mind the fact that our share of the premium market is about 65 percent, we are now in a position to plan for a contribution to profits, after coverage of all fixed expenditures.

### COST SAVINGS AND PRODUCTIVITY

Taking into account the prevailing high rate of inflation, and the tight government price controls, a squeeze on margins seems a probable if not inevitable risk. This, coupled with the overcapacity in the industry may have serious consequences. Would it be possible for each department to describe briefly under their corresponding functional chapter the cost-saving and productivity objectives they have set themselves?

---

[6]Appendix B is derived from company records.

[7]Appendix C is derived from company records.

# J.J. Murphy's Brewery

The beer market in Ireland was dominated by Guinness, who with their famous Stout, Smithwicks Ale, and Harp Lager, controlled nearly 90 percent of the market. Beamish and Crawford Ltd., producer of Beamish and Bass Ale and Carling and Carlsberg lagers, was the number two company with 6 percent of the total market. J.J. Murphy & Co. Ltd. of Cork was the only other brewer. Murphy's stout and Heineken lager, brewed under license, gave them 4 percent of the total beer market. In July 1982, Murphy's, as the company was known locally, went into receivership. Heineken had to decide what action to take with regard to its licensee, which represented 51,000 hectoliters (hl) in annual sales volume.

## MURPHY'S EARLY HISTORY

Murphy's was founded in 1852 and initially brewed porter, an old-fashioned dark ale. Sub-

This case was written by Ms. Marcelle Speller and Professor José de la Torre as a basis for discussion. The generous contributions of many Heineken executives is gratefully acknowledged, but the authors retain all responsibility for any errors or misinterpretation of facts. © INSEAD, The European Institute of Business Administration, 1984.

sequently, the company began to brew stout, and this remained its sole beer product until 1965. Throughout the years, Murphy's also acquired a number of licensed premises, mainly through defaults on payment of debts, and developed a wholesale spirits and soft drink bottling business.

In the early 1960s, the Irish beer market showed a trend away from stout toward lighter ales and lagers. Murphy's response was to form a joint venture with U.K.-based Watney's Brewery to brew and market Watney's Red Barrel ale in Ireland. Until this time Murphy's had distribution only in the Cork area, but plans were to sell Red Barrel nationally. New brewing and packaging facilities were built for ale in 1965, and annual sales grew to 40,000 hl in 1971. The cost of establishing national distribution, however, had been very high, and losses had plagued the venture since its inception, draining Murphy's cash resources. In 1971, the boards of both companies agreed to dissolve their joint operation, and Murphy's turned to Foir Teoranta, the Irish agency responsible for business rescues, for loans and equity capital. Another English brewer, Whitbread, was subsequently approached, and their ale, Trophy, was tested in Ireland. The Trophy test was not successful, and by early 1974 the losses were so great that Murphy's was offered for sale.

In April 1974, a consortium of about 1,200 pub owners bought 49 percent of Murphy's equity and, with the agreement of Foir Teoranta, who held the remaining 51 percent, set up a new management team to turn around the company and implement a long-term policy. The prime objective of the publicans was to ensure viable competition in the industry; they disliked having one supplier control 94 percent of the market. As viable competition could not be achieved with just one product, the new Murphy's management team set out to establish an ale and a lager alongside the existing stout and to develop a range of bottled beers, soft drinks, wines, and spirits supported, where appropriate, by a wholesaling operation. Since the equity base of the company was not sufficiently strong to finance this expansion, it was hoped that the sales of stout would generate the required cash.

As part of this policy of product diversification, Murphy's management decided to test the market's reaction to the Heineken lager which Whitbread brewed under license in the United Kingdom. This lager was a lighter beer than the standard Dutch Heineken, as strong beers paid very high excise duties in the United Kingdom. Heineken was tested in 19 pubs in Dublin from December 1974 to June 1975. The test showed that although the name was well accepted, there was only a small market for the weaker beer. A stronger product would be needed both to live up to the image of the Heineken name, and also to compete with Harp and Carlsberg which were already on the Irish market. Since Whitbread considered an investment in Murphy's too risky, Murphy's approached Heineken N.V. directly in February 1975, with a proposal to start a license operation for Heineken in Ireland.

## THE HEINEKEN LICENSING AGREEMENT

The relative success of the market tests encouraged Heineken to undertake a feasibility study for the granting of a license to Murphy's. Research showed that the lager market was small but growing and that a stronger lager could be exported from Holland for test purposes while the brewery was being brought up to standards under Heineken technical supervision. Murphy's financial position was weak but improving: The 1974 loss of £289,000 was turned into a profit of £108,000 in 1975.[1] The introduction of yet another ale, Schooner, appeared to be successful, and the new management seemed strong and effective. However, Murphy's location in Cork, on the south coast of Ireland, was not ideal for national distribution, especially when the Dublin market alone represented more than 40 percent of national consumption. But the support of the publicans, ever willing to protect themselves from a Guinness monopoly, was considered a major strength, and Heineken was prepared to take some risk.

The license agreement signed was a standard Heineken contract whereby a marketing company, Heineken Ireland, was set up as a wholly owned subsidiary of Heineken N.V. This company was given the exclusive right to use the Heineken trademarks and to market Heineken lager in Ireland. A separate agreement stipulated that Heineken Netherlands would be the technical adviser to J.J. Murphy's and have total responsibility for the production of Heineken beer. Heineken N.V. would also assume the direction of a marketing plan for the Heineken brand, advise on the selection and training of company marketing personnel, and retain control for advertising content and budget. The price, packaging, and positioning of Heineken lager was thus made subject to Heineken control. Finally, Heineken Ireland was required to report the progress of the brand and was restricted from exporting or handling any other beverage or soft drink without permission from Heineken N.V.

---

[1]Through 1978, the Irish pound was tied to the value of sterling. It has floated freely since January 1979. All values in this case are given in Irish pounds (£), or converted to Dutch guilders (Df) at prevailing rates.

## MURPHY'S PERFORMANCE, 1974–1980

The sales of J.J. Murphy's were £3.8 million in 1974, when the consortium of publicans started to manage the company. Their policy of expanding into a viable broad-based alternative to Guinness, using cash generated by increased stout sales, worked well at first. Large investments were needed for the new bottling plant as well as for improvements to the brewing plant. This was partly funded by bank loans, sales of tied houses, and retained profits. In 1976, the publicans bought out the shares held by Foir Teoranta and proceeded to issue £650,000 in additional share capital.

The financial performance of Murphy's was disappointing in 1977. This was attributed partly to government action in raising beer duty levels and, more significantly, to price restraint within the industry. Guinness had decided not to pass on the total price increase to the consumers, and the rest of the industry had had no choice but to follow.

In early 1978, however, the situation looked better. After an 18-month delay, Heineken lager was about to be launched. Youngers Ale (licensed from Scottish & Newcastle) was to be introduced with a heavy advertising budget (Schooner Ale having failed in the meantime due to quality problems). The new bottling plant would be fully commissioned by June 1, enabling the production of a full range of beer and mineral products. A license agreement with Canada Dry was about to be signed, and a wines and spirits division had been set up. Finally, the establishment of direct distribution and a national wholesale network for the Republic of Ireland was well advanced.

The midyear figures for 1978 were close to budget. Murphy Stout was on target, and Heineken was well above target—the import program from Holland was extended to the remainder of the year in spite of high transportation costs and it was decided to build additional fermentation capacity. However, Youngers Ale sales were down.

The first blow came in July 1978, when the government introduced very stringent legislation against drinking and driving. Murphy's sales declined below budget, losing £236,000 of expected profits. Heineken sales also declined to just above the original budget, but because the decision had been taken to continue imports from the Netherlands, a £188,000 loss of contribution against budget was achieved. A malfunction of the filler machinery caused the start up of the bottling line for Canada Dry to be delayed from June to October, which lost a further £111,000 in revenue. Finally, it became clear at this time that Youngers was not going to achieve its target, and there were both image and product difficulties which could not be solved in the short term. Advertising support for Youngers was therefore withdrawn.

The end result was that profits for 1978 were £540,000 below target (see Exhibit 1). The earlier expectations that profits from the sale of stout would finance expansion into lager, ale, and bottled product was obviously not working. The company again had a serious cash flow problem, and Heineken was asked for the first time to take a direct participation in the company. Heineken considered the sales projections optimistic and the 1979 plan and its funding implications too risky. Furthermore, Heineken was primarily interested in the development of Heineken lager in Ireland rather than in the total development of Murphy's. Thus, the proposal was rejected.

The results for 1979 showed a brief return to profitability, but after interest payments the net contribution dropped from £602,000 to £244,000, only 64 percent of budget. The 1980 budget was geared toward consolidation. The Heineken brand's continuing growth was the exception; it would be supported by heavy marketing expenditure and the addition of 100 outlets in Dublin. Since capital expenditures were to be limited to essential replacements and improvements of existing plant, Heineken's anticipated sales levels for 1980 would put the brewery at maximum capacity during the peak summer months. The development of the Heineken brand beyond 1980 was therefore very much dependent on the

EXHIBIT 1

**BUDGETED AND ACTUAL RESULTS, 1978–1981: PROFITS (LOSSES) BEFORE INTEREST BY PRODUCT GROUP** (£ Thousand)

|  | Draft Stout | Draft Ale | Draft Heineken | Bottled products | Wines & spirits | Total |
|---|---|---|---|---|---|---|
| **1978** |  |  |  |  |  |  |
| Budget | 936 | 6 | (130) | (393) | (19) | 400 |
| Actual | 700 | (76) | (318) | (504) | (58) | (140) |
| **1979** |  |  |  |  |  |  |
| Budget | 684 | 33 | 6 | (389) | 66 | 400 |
| Actual | 740 | 38 | (72) | (274) | 170 | 602 |
| 1980 budget | 889 | 28 | 26 | (247) | 210 | 854 |
| 1981 forecast | 1,026 | — | 10 | 123 | 167 | 1,326 |

*Source:* Company records.

expansion of brewing capacity. The need for increased capital was becoming more urgent.

An injection of £600,000 of short- to medium-term financing, preferably in the form of redeemable preference shares, was deemed necessary to develop brewing capacity and working capital requirements for Heineken to a level of 100,000 hl per year. In five years, the trading performance of the company might justify raising additional equity.

## HEINEKEN'S IRISH ACTIVITIES, 1979–1981

The 1979 European marketing review called for continuing the license agreement with Murphy's and reaching a target 18 percent of the lager market without any financial participation. Nonetheless, Murphy's request for a £600,000 contribution in May 1980 came as no surprise. The Heineken executive board requested that a joint working party be set up to examine the long-term viability of Murphy's. If the study indicated the possibility of an adequate return on investment, Heineken would be prepared to consider a substantial equity participation in Murphy's. The joint working party was constituted in August 1980, and its report was completed in November.

The report indicated that although Murphy's sales had increased from £3.8 million in 1974 to £19 million in 1979, profit performance was unsatisfactory in terms of return on capital. The main factors influencing this were considered to be:

- Heavy interest and depreciation charges resulting from the investment in plant and equipment
- Delays in commissioning the new brewing and bottling plant in 1978
- Shortage of capital to modernize the brewery, thereby affecting ability to maintain consistent quality and sales for Murphy's, and to expand capacity for Heineken
- Quality problems with the brewing of Youngers Ale resulting in the failure to capitalize on the initial launch success of the product

For the future, Murphy's stout was thought capable of regaining its 7.5 percent share of the stout market within three years by emphasizing quality, supporting this with increased marketing expenses directed at the young and more sophisticated drinker. Younger's Tartan Special Ale had been tested over a six-month period and it was considered that with proper marketing and good quality control it could reach 5 percent of the ale market by 1985, and 8 percent by 1988.

Heineken, already at 7 percent of the lager market by 1980, was thought capable of reaching 11 percent by 1985, and 20 to 25 percent by 1988. To achieve this, distribution, at that point confined to Dublin and Cork, would have to be developed, and a large marketing budget would be required. Total capital investments needed to sustain this growth over the next eight years were estimated to be £10.8 million.

The projected financial position showed trading profits (before interest, depreciation, and lease write-offs) of £1.1 million in 1980, rising to £5.7 million in 1988. Interest charges were excluded, since the capital structure had yet to be determined, but net cash flow was projected to be positive by 1984.

The joint working party proposed that Heineken should take a substantial share (i.e., not less than 20 percent) in Murphy's. However, in January 1981, Heineken's corporate staff rejected this recommendation on the bases that the sales projections were overly optimistic, the management of Murphy's too weak, and the financial return too low.

The only choice left to Murphy's appeared to be a merger with Beamish and Crawford, a subsidiary of Canada's Carling O'Keefe. Heineken's board was prepared to support this course of action as a last resort, despite the possible conflict of interest between Heineken and the Carling and Carlsberg lagers which were brewed by Beamish and Crawford, provided Heineken would be brewed in a different production facility from the other lagers.

Furthermore, rather than take a direct participation, Heineken would be prepared to invest a further Df 1 million[2] in technical assistance and marketing support. As it was, Heineken was already plowing back most of the license fees into marketing support in Ireland.

Negotiations between Murphy's and Beamish and Crawford stalled by July 1981. Murphy's tried to persuade Heineken to change its mind by proposing further cost savings, selling the mortgages to public houses, selling 50 percent of the wines and spirits agencies, and setting up a joint venture on the bottling line. Heineken was not impressed, and, in an effort to salvage what appeared to be the only viable solution, it even threatened to withdraw the Heineken license from Murphy's.

## MURPHY'S DETERIORATING POSITION

In spite of an increase in its overall turnover from £19.1 million in 1979 to £22.8 million in 1980, Murphy's pretax profits dropped from £244,500 in 1979 to a loss of £660,000 in 1980. High interest costs were responsible for much of this deterioration as the company was seriously undercapitalized.

In an effort to improve their financial situation, Murphy's undertook some basic restructuring during 1981. The bottling line which had been losing £640,000 per year was to be sold for an estimated £549,000, and the sale of stocks of packaging material was expected to raise an additional £560,000. (Only 7 percent of Murphy Stout and Heineken Lager sales had been in bottles.) This would reduce workforce levels by 79 workers. The malt house was also to be closed, which would save a further 25 workers. Redundancy payments would amount to £205,000 in 1982. The result of this restructuring was projected to contribute an extra £641,000 to the company's trading profit for the year and reduce the loan burden by £470,000.

In January 1982, Murphy's publican shareholders made a proposal for a merger with Beamish and Crawford (B&C), but B&C's counterproposal was not satisfactory to Murphy's shareholders and the deal fell through. Instead, the publicans planned to raise £1.5 million among themselves and continue to seek help from Heineken or any other source that would be willing to finance them. In the meantime, Foir Teoranta agreed that there would be no interest

---

[2] Most production and media costs for Heineken's introduction to the Irish market (about £225,000) had been advanced by Heineken against future royalties. Heineken had also guaranteed a £300,000 bank loan to Murphy's.

charges or repayments on their outstanding loan for three years.

Faced with the gravity of the situation, Heineken sent a member of the corporate finance department to conduct a detailed analysis of Murphy's situation. Simultaneously, contacts were reestablished with Guinness in order to explore their possible interest in taking up the Heineken license for Ireland within the context of a joint rescue operation.

The report concluded that Murphy's looked somewhat healthier after the restructuring. However, in order to make further necessary adjustments in the balance sheet, the planned injection of £1.5 million by the existing shareholders was absolutely essential. If Heineken lager sales grew as projected over the next three years the return on assets of the company was projected to grow from 6 percent in 1982 to 10 percent in 1984 (see Exhibit 2). For this to happen, Heineken would have to invest £650,000 immediately in additional share capital and be prepared to lend a further £500,000 for a new brewhouse in 1983. On a purely financial basis, the investment was not attractive. No dividends could be expected for the first few years, and the proposed loan would earn higher interest at lower risk in a bank.

Once again the issue of taking a participation in Murphy's, preferably with another company willing to share the risks, came under consideration. Guinness had shown no interest in Murphy's nor in a Heineken association. Irish Distillers and Associated Distilled Products, two national distributors of spirits, might be willing to participate but only if Heineken did the same. Existing shareholders were attempting to raise their £1.5 million contribution and Ireland's Industrial Development Authority had promised grants of £400,000, with the possibility of an extra £700,000.

In July 1982, the European marketing man-

---

**EXHIBIT 2**

**FINANCIAL RESULTS AND PROJECTIONS, 1981–1984: FEBRUARY 1982 REPORT**

| | Latest estimate— 1981 | Projections | | |
| --- | --- | --- | --- | --- |
| | | 1982 | 1983 | 1984 |
| Turnover (thousand hl) | | | | |
| Murphy's stout | 127 | 118 | 117 | 115 |
| Heineken | 58 | 70 | 86 | 106 |
| Other | 11 | 12 | 13 | 14 |
| Total | 196 | 200 | 216 | 235 |
| Results (£ millions)* | | | | |
| Gross margins | 6.8 | 6.4 | 6.8 | 7.4 |
| Fixed costs | 6.8 | 5.7 | 5.9 | 6.1 |
| Trading profits | 0 | 0.7 | 0.9 | 1.3 |
| Other income | 0.1 | 0 | 0.1 | 0 |
| Interest expense | 0.8 | 0.4 | 0.3 | 0.3 |
| Net profit | (0.7) | 0.3 | 0.7 | 1.0 |
| Ratios | | | | |
| ROA (%) | — | 6 | 9 | 10 |
| Profit/Interest | — | 1.8 | 3.2 | 4.8 |
| Debt/Equity | — | 0.3 | 0.4 | 0.6 |

*£1 equals Df3.8.
Source: Corporate report, February 1982.

ager wrote a memo to the executive board member responsible for Europe, alerting him to the worsening situation:

- Murphy's debts to Heineken included £29,000 in arrears on royalty payments plus the outstanding bank guarantee of £300,000.
- Corrections to the preliminary figures included in the February 1982 finance report, based on more recent audited data, resulted in a 1981 loss of close to £1.1 million.
- The sale of the bottling line would raise only £400,000, but no sale contract had yet been signed.
- The rate of increase of Heineken sales was slowing down considerably.
- The "fund raising" by the publicans would deliver no more than £500,000, one-third of the amount projected originally, and only £150,000 was on hand.
- Most other prospective buyers seemed to consider the risk of participation too great and the profit forecasts too optimistic.
- The Industrial Development Authority had not yet given any clear indication that it would give any grants to Murphy's.
- The current shareholders appeared not to have been told that their share capital would, for the greatest part, be written off due to the size of cumulative losses.

The memorandum went on to detail the latest proposal received from Murphy's managing director. This called for a minimum Heineken participation of £1 million in share capital and £400,000 in brand investments over the next three years. The final recommendation was that Heineken not invest in Murphy's on these terms; the current offer was no real improvement over the previous one and the situation had clearly deteriorated since February. If Murphy's went into liquidation, a real possibility, Heineken would have lost only £350,000.

On July 15, 1982, while negotiations were still under way to find a "knight in shining armor," Murphy's went into receivership.

## NEGOTIATIONS WITH THE RECEIVER

At this point, there was no room for further delays in reaching a decision on the Irish market. A multidisciplinary team including headquarters staff from finance, marketing, personnel, and technical control was sent to Ireland to conduct an in-depth analysis of the market and of Murphy's situation. Local solicitors and accountants were added to the team to advise on the feasibility of various options, particularly the labor relations aspects, and to verify the financial forecast for 1982. The Heineken team was headed by the European coordinating director reporting directly to the executive board.

As data was being gathered, negotiations began with the receiver. Heineken learned that two other firms, Beamish and Crawford and a second unnamed competitor, were also interested in acquiring Murphy's assets. As a first step, Heineken agreed that Murphy's could continue to produce Heineken lager under license in exchange for royalties until a final decision could be made on the disposal of the company, or until Heineken chose unilaterally to terminate the agreement.

A major factor in the analysis was, of course, the likely reaction of Guinness to a direct entry by Heineken into their home turf. The two companies were not strangers to each other. According to one executive:

We are fighting like hell in Malaysia, but we are their licensee in Indonesia; we have a close working relationship in Nigeria and Ghana, and even operate a joint brewery in Sierra Leone. We are very similar in many respects, and I have often thought that the complementarity of our two main products should have led us to closer cooperation worldwide. In fact, Whitbread once asked us to distribute their Mackeson stout throughout the world and we did not want to do so at the expense of alienating Guinness.

In Ireland, Heineken expected that this "live and let live" philosophy would continue, particularly given their limited marketing objec-

## EXHIBIT 3

### GUINNESS CHANGING STRATEGY

In October 1981, Arthur Guinness Son and Co. brought in Ernest Saunders as its new managing director. Saunders, whose previous experience included executive positions at J. Walter Thompson (advertising), Beecham (consumer products), and Nestlé, came into his new job with a mandate for change: "My brief is to undertake a thorough but rapid review of the business in all its aspects. . . . To examine what is we do well; what we can do better and be more profitable."

During 1981, Guinness made a record trading profit from its beer business but suffered losses in most of its other activities. While benefitting from "years of investment in its worldwide trade names, particularly Guinness Stout," diversification had been costly, and the company had begun to retrench by selling some of its losing affiliates. Recent financial results (in U.K. £ million) were as follows:

|  | 1981 | | 1980 | |
| --- | --- | --- | --- | --- |
|  | Sales | Profits | Sales | Profits |
| Brewing | 619.8 | 48.0 | 498.9 | 44.1 |
| General trading | 187.8 | 2.7 | 184.4 | 2.9 |
| Plastics and materials handling | 62.9 | 1.2 | 69.6 | 3.1 |
| Leisure | 7.4 | (1.6) | 7.2 | 0.1 |
| Confectionery | 19.5 | (1.3) | 17.1 | (0.3) |
| Films | 8.2 | (3.9) | 6.4 | (0.4) |
| Central costs | — | (3.1) | — | (2.5) |
| Total | 905.6 | 42.0 | 783.6 | 47.0 |

*Source: The Financial Times, January 21, 1982.*

tives. (See Exhibit 3 for a summary of recent information on Guinness.)

All the elements of the analysis were practically in place when Heineken received a call in early December from Murphy's marketing director claiming that Guinness appeared to be playing rough and trying to "push us out of our best Dublin outlets." As a result, two Heineken executives paid a visit to Dublin on December 14 and 15 in order to meet with a number of the major publicans in the area and with one of Guinness's key directors.

The interviews with eight pub owners confirmed the following points:

- While stout is declining, the trend is to lagers and lighter beers, especially among the young (see Exhibit 4), and away from spirits.
- Over 90 percent of beer consumption goes through the pubs and "it will continue to do so."
- "The pubs are an extension of the family sitting-room," and practically all are family-owned and operated; they wish to maintain

their independence and protect themselves from any monopoly supplier.
- The pubs are organized into a Licensed Vintners Association which is advising their members to gradually take over cleaning and servicing of pouring installations on a pro-rata basis from suppliers and which advocates multiple tap facilities (snakes) that would allow pub owners to offer different brands and types of beer from the same installation.
- Heineken is well accepted by consumers, supported by the publicans against a Guinness monopoly, and seen as a vehicle for the introduction of new products, e.g., ale and low-calorie beer.

The interview with the Guinness director was less clear. He stated that their major interest was to increase cost-competitiveness in general and that their "sales force is instructed to fight for every barrel." He indicated they would be willing to look at a Heineken proposal in light of profit contribution but it had to be done quickly. After the meeting, the visitors were left with the

| EXHIBIT 4 |
|---|

**POPULATION AND AGE STRUCTURE IN IRELAND, 1974 AND 1984 (PROJECTED)**

| Age group | 1974 | | 1984 | | |
| | Number | Percentage | Number | Percentage | Percentage increase |
|---|---|---|---|---|---|
| 0–14 | 961,000 | 31 | 958,000 | 28 | − 0.5 |
| 15–24 | 515,000 | 17 | 627,000 | 18 | 22.0 |
| 25–44 | 662,000 | 21 | 874,000 | 26 | 32.0 |
| 45–64 | 603,000 | 20 | 606,000 | 18 | 0.5 |
| Over 65 | 343,000 | 11 | 344,000 | 10 | 0 |
| Total | 3,084,000 | 100 | 3,409,000 | 100 | 10.5 |

*Source:* Company records.

impression that Guinness would consider Heineken as one more lager in their product range and that, as a consequence, they would be prepared to pay only a "token" royalty. The Heineken executives concluded:

> The trade would view Heineken very differently if distributed by Guinness. On the other hand, they will not accept special discounts from Guinness as an inducement to push Harp against an independent Heineken. The publicans would see this as providing them only a temporary advantage with disastrous long-term consequences if Heineken failed.

## A PROPOSAL FOR DIRECT ENTRY

One month later, on January 16, 1983, a proposal went to Heineken's Executive Board to invest about £6.6 million (D*f*25 million) immediately, and half as much over the next three years to acquire the assets of J. J. Murphy & Co. Ltd., and to establish a wholly owned operating subsidiary in the Irish market. The Appendix gives the detailed justifications and commitments for this proposal.

The decision would prove to be difficult. One board member felt that actual investment costs would be lower than projected by using old equipment and that Guinness would not fight due to anti-monopoly considerations: "Ireland contributes to our European image, and it may also help in the U.S. through the tourist trade." Another view was that, "Murphy's is a badly kept museum. It will cost a fortune and take

precious management time and effort to develop. . . . The possibility of exports is interesting, but in that case we should establish a new brewery with a minimum capacity of 500,000 hl." Another key executive felt that, "60,000 hl volume is not all that negligible. If you want to be the European brand you cannot give up a major market and come back later. In fact, as licensees . . . only Jamaica and Norway have done as well. Yet, I will admit that if it weren't lying on our doorstep, we wouldn't pursue it."

Finally, one board member summarized his views by saying: "If one accepts a negative or low return for the next few years, the biggest issue is what will the competitors do. If they fight, we are in trouble."

| APPENDIX |
|---|

# Investment Submission to Heineken's Board, January 16, 1983[3]

## PRODUCTS AND MARKETS

Heineken sales had developed quickly: From 21,000 hl in the last 8 months of 1978, to 36, 43, 51, and 48,000 hl for the years 1979 to 1982, respectively.

---

[3]Excerpts only. Figures have been disguised to protect confidentiality.

The brand had achieved 9 percent of the lager market in spite of the problems caused by Murphy's bankruptcy in 1982. It was projected that Heineken's market share would continue to improve in this growing segment. Murphy's Stout, while small, was considered an important carrier for Heineken and helped cover fixed costs (see Exhibit 5). The proposal argued that, "the only feasible alternative to an investment is to abandon the market. Neither Guinness nor Beamish & Crawford can be expected to support the brand and imports would be too expensive."

## CAPACITY AND FACILITIES

Given the current production mix, the brewery had a capacity of 200,000 hl per year. The facilities were old and in need of considerable maintenance. The value of the fixed assets was estimated at £1.5 million (about one-half of their book value) which took into account their current state. Other assets, such as stocks and receivables, had been estimated at £5.1 million after due consideration of their state and age.

Over the next four years, improvements to the brewhouse and filling and cleaning installations would require an additional investment of £4.6 million for a capacity of 300,000 hl. Investment in kegs and tap installations would require an additional £1.2 million.

## PERSONNEL

At the time, Murphy's employed 207 people: 26 in management and administration, 81 in production, and 100 in sales. It was estimated that 220 would be needed to sustain full operations.

Up to 1976, Murphy's had no funded pension plan; only its own system, established in 1912, to cover pension rights out of current income. There were 51 pensioners with rights under this old system as well as 9 current employees who had been ineligible to join the funded scheme in 1976. Under EEC regulations, incorporated into local law but never tested in Ireland, these 60 people had acquired rights amounting to £1.4 million (using standard actuarial estimates). In addition, the 1976 pension fund covering the remaining 196 employees was estimated to be underfunded by about £0.8 to 1.1 million.

After much discussion, it was agreed that the receiver would accept responsibility for the first 60 people and make a contribution of £0.5 million to correct the underfunding in the current scheme. Heineken executives felt this was a major victory as they did not want to expose themselves to industrial action or bad will in the Cork area were they to take over Murphy's without adequate provisions for pensions.

## INVESTMENT ASSISTANCE

The Irish Industrial Development Authority was charged with making grants available to new investors throughout the Republic. They had indicated a willingness to provide a 35 percent grant on the plant and equipment investments, which could amount to as much as £2.2 million over the 5-year period. Other subsidies for training and interest expense might total £0.4 million.

Foir Teoranta was also willing to provide an interest-free loan of £2 to 3 million to Heineken for a period of 2 to 4 years. Finally, the investment would benefit from accelerated depreciation, tax exemption on export production, and corporate taxes guaranteed at 10 percent or less until the year 2000.

## FINANCIAL REQUIREMENTS

Exhibits 6 and 7 summarize the financial projections. The total beer market was thought to remain stable through 1986 at about 4.3 million hl. Given the growth in lager relative to stout and the introduction of systematic marketing practices and quality controls, Heineken's share of 10 percent of the lager market by 1986 was thought conservative. Other assumptions included a slight decline for Murphy's stout, no change in gross margins per hectoliter, an investment of £160,000 per year in pension funds including contributions by the workers, depreciation calculated to Heineken norms, most IDA grants, and no specific royalty payments.

The relatively poor 1982 results in terms of Heineken's volume, were attributed to the bad publicity

| EXHIBIT 5 |
| --- |

**1981 MARKET SHARES**

|  | Stout | Lager | Ale | Total |
| --- | --- | --- | --- | --- |
| Guinness | 95% | 64% | 93% | 90% |
| Beamish & Crawford | — | 27 | 6 | 6 |
| Murphy's | 5 | 9 | 1 | 4 |

---

**EXHIBIT 6**

**PROFIT AND LOSS PROJECTIONS, 1983–1986**

|  | 1983 | 1984 | 1985 | 1986 |
|---|---|---|---|---|
| Turnover (thousand hl) |  |  |  |  |
| Murphy's Stout | 114 | 112 | 110 | 110 |
| Heineken Lager | 61 | 73 | 80 | 80 |
| Tartan Ale | 5 | 5 | 5 | 5 |
| Total | 180 | 190 | 195 | 195 |
| Profit and loss (£ thousands) |  |  |  |  |
| Turnover | 27,900 | 29,800 | 30,300 | 30,300 |
| Gross margin | 6,921 | 7,331 | 7,486 | 7,486 |
| Less: Direct costs |  |  |  |  |
| and overheads | 5,751 | 5,911 | 5,911 | 5,911 |
| Depreciation | 700 | 700 | 700 | 700 |
| Investment grants | (45) | (60) | (100) | (110) |
| EBIT | 515 | 780 | 975 | 985 |
| ROA (%) | 4.9 | 6.7 | 7.4 | 7.4 |

which followed the receivership decision in July 1982. Murphy's had had a trading loss of £228,000 (the total loss after interest payments had been £1.14 million) on sales of £26.6 million in 1981. The auditors engaged by Heineken estimated a trading profit of £628,000 on sales of £27.4 million for the year 1982, due in great part to significant savings obtained after the sale of the bottling plant in 1981. The Heineken team estimated the brewery's breakeven point (before interest payments) at 88 percent of current capacity. An

---

**EXHIBIT 7**

**USES AND SOURCE OF FUNDS** (£ Thousand)

|  | 1982 | 1983 | 1984 | 1985 | 1986 |
|---|---|---|---|---|---|
| Uses |  |  |  |  |  |
| Fixed assets | 1,600 | 1,700 | 1,300 | 2,000 | 800 |
| Stocks | 2,000 | 1,000 | 300 | — | — |
| Receivables | 3,000 | 1,900 | 400 | — | — |
| Total | 6,600 | 4,600 | 2,000 | 2,000 | 800 |
| Sources |  |  |  |  |  |
| Net earnings | — | 515 | 780 | 975 | 985 |
| Depreciation | — | 700 | 700 | 700 | 700 |
| IDA Grants | — | 855 | 240 | 700 | 90 |
| Creditors | — | 3,000 | — | — | — |
| Foir Teoranta | — | 2,000 | — | — | (2,000) |
| Total | — | 7,070 | 1,720 | 2,375 | (225) |
| Net annual requirements | 6,600 | (2,470) | 280 | (375) | 1,025 |
| Cumulative investment for Heineken* | 6,600 | 4,645 | 5,705 | 6,305 | 8,315 |

*Includes the initial £6.6 million required to purchase the existing assets, plus the net annual requirements and all reinvested profits.

increase of 15 percent (about 28,000 hl) in volume, however, would significantly increase trading profits.

Wine and spirits were expected to contribute to covering fixed costs. While margins were relatively low (12 percent on sales), they required no additional fixed expenses. The net contribution of the wine and spirits business could represent 60 percent of profits (EBIT) by 1986. Fixed costs were conservatively estimated, and all sales were domestic sales. The possibility of using Ireland as an export base had not been considered in the analysis. The Heineken team felt, however, that export potential was considerable, particularly to Northern Ireland, Britain, and the United States.

## FINANCIAL SOURCES

Local sources of subsidized finance (Exhibit 7) would be used to the extent possible. Heineken N.V. would need to put in share capital of no less than £2 million (Df7.6 million) and either provide directly or guarantee any additional long-term loans. Estimating Heineken N.V. cost of capital as 9 percent, the average cost of finance for the project would be 6.5 percent.

# Southland Bank and Trust Co.

"Our goal is to be the *premier bank holding company in the Southeast,* with a reputation for excellence in serving customers nationwide and throughout the world"; so stated Harrison Shaeffer, Southland Bank and Trust's (SBT's) CEO of three years. "We also will be the leader in bringing banking service to the Atlanta community. . . . Quantitatively: by the mid-1980's, our return on total assets (ROA) must be in the upper half of the 15 largest U.S. banks.[1] In this business, being unique is not achievable. What you want to do is to be very good . . . pick the areas where the markets are growing and where the returns look attractive . . . you're really dealing with the quality of people, with the training and development of those people, and with

how they are deployed." (H. Shaeffer, as quoted January 6, 1982, by a leading security analyst).

When Harrison Shaeffer assumed his responsibilities at SBT, one of the United States's 15 largest banks, the bank was suffering from:

1. Many nonperforming loans[2]
2. A $1-billion-plus short-term interest rate gap
3. A sense of "drifting" strategically
4. Five consecutive quarters of earnings decline
5. The loss of market share and market position with corporate customers
6. Poor morale, due largely to the five factors above, and a tough, autocratic previous CEO[3]

## GOALS, STRATEGY, MANAGEMENT STYLE

Shaeffer's "turnaround," long-term strategy, and management style had several key components. Among the bank's *goals,* were to: (1) position the bank for deregulation in the United States,

---

[1] In 1983, the bank ranked eighth among the top 15 in ROA; 1982 ROA was 0.37 percent, and the figure was 0.53 percent for the first five months 1983. Notably, the top-15 ROA target moved up each year as the competitors were increasingly successful.

The case was prepared by Professor David B. Zenoff with assistance from Ms. Janet Hunter, Research Associate, as a basis for class discussion rather than to illustrate either effective or ineffective handling of an administrative situation. Some disguise has been used. Copyright © 1984 by IMEDE, Lausanne, Switzerland. Reproduced by permission.

---

[2] In 1980, return on assets was at an all time low, and nonperforming assets were about 5 percent of loans, leases, and other real estate.

[3] In 1979, officer turnover reached 12.7 percent.

**167**

(2) maintain momentum beyond the "turn-around" phase, and (3) be among the leaders in every market in which the bank operated. As means to these and previous indicated goals, Shaeffer had:

- Built a new management team, recruiting 300 officers, including one-half of the senior management team
- Advocated more aggressive marketing
- Closed selected money-losing business units (e.g., the Bank's Madrid office and a Visa traveller's checks operation)
- Strengthened product development staffing, corporate planning staffs, and "relationship managers"
- Reorganized the bank into 100-plus strategic business units that were linked tightly through strong centralized management functions and coordinated strategies
- Placed more emphasis on geographic and specialty product units

The Bank's "philosophy" and driving themes were printed on small plaques, labelled "The Southland Bank and Trust Commitment." Officers displayed the "Commitment" on their desks or office walls. The plaque emphasized the following points about the bank:

- The customer is the bank's highest priority.
- The bank is strategically driven.
- The bank seeks to achieve excellence in all it does.
- The bank's people are the key to its success.

## BUSINESS SEGMENTS

In terms of pursuing its overall business goals, bank management identified six principal business segments and established objectives for each:

**Domestic Wholesale Banking Segment** The bank had established a relatively strong position. Its goals were to establish SBT as a premier wholesale bank through direct marketing programs that linked specialized industry expertise (e.g., service companies, retailing, energy, transpor-

tation) and a geographically organized distribution system. More specifically, the cornerstone of SBT's corporate strategy was "*becoming the 'premier' bank holding company in the Southeast.*"[4] ("Without demonstrating our excellence in our home market, it is unlikely that we can achieve our other goals.") Acquisition of banks in contiguous states, when permitted, was likely to be an important strategic element (e.g., the bank's 1982 acquisition of the Southern National Bank for $450 million cash).

Within the domestic wholesale lending realm, bank management further specified three customer categories, based on borrower's size (in annual sales):

1. *Companies with annual sales in excess of $1.5 billion.* The 250 largest companies qualified for this category. Typical lending spreads were very narrow; to receive adequate return on assets from these relationships, fee-based services (i.e., foreign exchange, letters of credit) were also sold. Many banks provided credit services to companies of this size, but only the lead banks (first tier) received the higher fee-based business. SBT claimed two-thirds of these companies as customers, but its relative market position with them was only modest. SBT intended to concentrate its energies on improving its standing with these companies rather than just increasing the number of relationships.[5]
2. *Companies with annual sales from $500 million to $1.5 billion.* Qualifying companies included those in the *Fortune* second 500. SBT did business with about 40 percent of these companies. For the most part, fee-based services were also sold with credit services to earn adequate returns. The bank intended to try to increase the number of relationships

---

[4] The "Southeast" has approximately 20 percent of the United States population and workforce and is the location for more than 2,500 companies whose total sales exceeded $30 billion. In 1983, these companies paid banks more than $1.3 billion in net annual revenues.

[5] SBT earned 250 to 300 basis point gross return on assets including fees where it was the lead bank. (A "basis point" is an interest rate; 100 basis points equal 1 percent.)

as well as increase its level of activity with clients in this category.

3. *Companies with annual sales $100 to $500 million.* Fewer than 400 of these companies were served by SBT, although customers of this size tended to be the most profitable. The bank had been working hard to increase its penetration, but progress was slow because this size company tended to find a large bank less responsive to its needs.

**Consumer Banking Segment**   Objectives for this segment were to build position as the premier consumer bank in Atlanta and establish a national leadership position in selected consumer markets and products.[6]

**Investment Banking Segment**   This segment's goal was to build global capability to meet customers' capital markets, trade finance, and leasing requirements—leading to status as a premier bank-affiliated investment bank.[7]

**Trading and Funding Segment**   SBT wanted to establish premier status in the trading business in which SBT could compete effectively and profitably; SBT also wanted to fund the bank at the lowest cost consistent with ensuring liquidity and solvency.

**Services Product Segment**   This segment's goal was to establish the bank as a premier operating bank by providing a range of high-quality innovative products which differentiated the bank and solidified relationships.[8]

**International Wholesale Banking Segment**   The last segment's goal was to position the bank as a leading international bank with local currency

capability in important developing countries and specialized expertise and scale in money centers to serve the needs of target customers on a global basis. Because International was, by definition, "riskier" than U.S. banking, and in 1982 had a lower profitability than the U.S. segments, important strategic elements for International were to decrease the market's perception of risk associated with SBT's international business and increase its ROA to at least equal the domestic bank.

By year-end 1983, SBT was perceived by most analysts and its executives as having achieved a "turnaround": officer turnover had decreased to 5 percent, return on assets had improved by 45 percent to put SBT in the top ten, earnings increased approximately 40 percent from a year earlier, the structural mismatching of assets and liabilities was eliminated, and asset quality had improved noticeably.

## THE STRATEGIC VIEW FROM LONDON

Mike Foote, SBT London branch manager, began 1984 in a reflective mood. The preceding year had been a challenging and largely satisfying one for him, his branch, and the bank in general:

1. The bank had refitted offices and consolidated all staff in one block, and his 250-person staff appeared happily and productively settled into the new work environment.
2. Mike, in his first full year as branch manager (and as a commercial banker), had made a successful transition from management consultant in banking to line manager.
3. The London branch had responded relatively well to headquarters' big push to improve significantly ROA but still was short of the goal by almost one-third.[9] This had been achieved through a major expense reduction

---

[6]For example, SBT had the highest level of credit card receivables outstanding among all U.S. banks, partly as the result of purchasing the business from a large money center bank.

[7]Investment banking was, by 1983, an autonomous unit. During the first six months of 1983 SBT ranked first among banks in private placements—from eleventh in 1981.

[8]For example, an SBT subsidiary did data processing for seven of the thirteen largest Atlanta savings and loans.

[9]In prior years, the London branch had experienced "downward drifting profitability"; it performed dramatically below SBT return standards and in 1982 had lost money—principally because of one large loan loss. 1983 results represented a dramatic improvement.

effort and a restructuring of the marketing program.

4. The bank's overall mood was optimistic, self-consciously proud, with great confidence in and loyalty to senior headquarters management.

Mike had just returned from an area head meeting at which the task for International had been reclarified and emphasized. To surpass the two national banks that had greater Southeast market share than SBT, SBT would have to grow through acquisitions paid for with its equity shares. Since its shares were selling at below book value, the bank as a whole had to increase its profitability to increase share price. International, with a below-bank-average ROA and higher-than-average risk, was charged with "significantly increasing profitability and reducing risk."

Mike Foote was perplexed about what to do now, since he had *already* focussed on what appeared to be the principal means to achieve such results. "I perceive us and the other banks here as being 'Single A' firms borrowing money and trying to lend the funds at a profit to 'double A' customers! How can we—or anyone—make decent money in this business? The fact is, and I have heard this said about many of our multinational competitors here, we make a sizeable percentage of our bottom-line through trading, serving as a foreign currency clearing center and providing other specialized services.[10] Yet, as a traditional commercial bank, much of our attention and our personnel development are elsewhere."

As a former consultant, Mike was notably adept at identifying priority management tasks and clarifying key strategic issues:

- "I worry about the inherent profitability of the traditional banking business; we have too many traditional commercial banks for a market of this size and with these types and numbers of segments. How can anyone make money?"

- "Complicating matters, noninterest expenses are relatively high and difficult to control; in foreign exchange we must do a *huge* volume to make interesting money, and disintermediation is growing (e.g., the increasing volume of sovereign floating rate notes is cutting into syndicated loan opportunities)."

- "How can we build a major position in those businesses where growth and profit opportunities may be greater outside the area of traditional banking, for example, in securities underwriting, trading, origination; specialized operational and computer-based services; specialized financing vehicles (leasing companies, finance houses); specialized merchant banking services (swaps); and middle-market commercial banking services?"

Over the past decade, SBT-London's business had shifted from approximately 20 percent *fee* and 80 percent interest *spread* revenues to 70 percent fee and 30 percent interest spread in 1983.[11] The customer base evolved *from* U.K. companies that were not well served by the clearing banks (which did not offer unsecured, term loans) and Atlanta-area headquarters companies doing business in the U.K. *to* UK-based regional headquarters of major U.S. multinationals, and specialized industries, principally commodities, transportation, and energy.

Although it was impossible to know precisely how SBT London ranked against other U.S. banks in the London market, its management assumed its relative market share position to be that shown in Exhibit 1.

Viewed from a *product* perspective, the London management made the assumptions shown in Exhibit 2.

Generally, SBT considered itself to be seventh in London among U.S. banks. It wanted to be the leading bank in London for companies with links to the Southeast United States and in the top five U.S. banks overall.

---

[10] SBT had one-half of the market for such clearings.

[11] Aside from Treasury, which fluctuated sizeably from year to year.

## EXHIBIT 1

### SBT's MARKET SHARE RELATIVE TO U.S. BANKS IN LONDON

| Segment | SBT London's share |
|---|---|
| U.K. MNCs | Less than 1 percent |
| U.S. MNC subs in U.K. | 5 to 10 percent* |
| Correspondent banking | 10 percent |
| Commodities financing | 10 percent |
| Transportation financing | 12 percent |
| Energy financing | 7 to 8 percent |

*SBT London estimated Citibank to have a 35 percent share among foreign banks.

## COMPETITION: CONSTRAINTS ON SBT

The bank felt several "pressure points" on the revenue-income side. First, it appeared that the clearing banks' international divisions were more readily accepting LDC sovereign risk exposures to win and/or hold U.K. corporate trade finance business—*without* asking for any special "rewards" or compensation from their customers. For SBT, the phenomenon seemed "crazy" and tended to rob it of a competitive resource. Since LDC sovereign lending was considered too risky and generally undesirable to SBT and other U.S. banks, the only circumstances that headquarters might approve would be: (1) *short*-term exposure, (2) associated with *winning* attractive trade finance deals, (3) where the client would *reward* the bank for making available a scarce resource. Hence, the clearers' (cunning? or unwitting?) "give-away" strategy was too competitive for SBT UK.

Another limit to SBT London's opportunities was that it did not have a scarce currency base (i.e., an inconvertible currency) on which to realize the most attractive spreads available from local currency lending. For example, in early 1984, French borrowers were not permitted to access the Eurofranc market; they could borrow

## EXHIBIT 2

### SBT RANK AND MARGINS BY PRODUCT

| Product | SBT rank* | Related profit margins |
|---|---|---|
| Credit services | | |
|     Lending | 20 | Low |
|     Trade finance | 10 | Medium |
| Trading, origination | | |
|     Foreign exchange | 7 | Medium |
|     Securities | 20 | Medium-high |
| Other merchant banking services | | |
|     Syndications | 12 | Low-medium |
|     Currency & interest rate swaps | 4 | Medium-high |
|     Merger & acquisitions & other advisory services | 20 | Medium-high |
| Operational, computer-based services | | |
|     Clearing services | 2 | Medium-high |
|     Cash management | 7 | Low-medium |
|     Other computer services | not participating | Medium-high |
| Consumer banking services | | |
|     Mass market services | not participating | |
|     Wealthy individual investments and trust services | 15 | Medium-high |

*Among the major "full-service" international banks operating in London.

"domestic francs" (for which banks earned attractive spreads). SBT could develop a "domestic franc" pool only by investing in a French equity base ("domestic franc" lending was tied by the government to the size of the local equity base, or through joint ventures with local financial institutions).

A third business opportunity constraint related to the London bank's concentration for years on the asset side of the business. It did not possess sufficient expertise or market position to sell liability products with which to fund itself at competitively low rates. It was, instead, very dependent on the rate-sensitive money market instruments.

Finally, SBT London found itself among approximately 400 competitors, many of which, in the opinion of Anthony Butler, SBT London senior relationship manager, did not operate on the same minimum ROA constraints as did SBT and other U.S. banks.[12] Whereas these agressive pricing competitors were in London to have a good name, and to fund themselves, seeking to earn sterling only to hedge their sterling expense stream, SBT was obliged to follow its global strategies and achieve profitability goals.[13]

In this competitive London market place, U.K. treasurers were "spoiled" by the aggressive bankers seeking their business, and thus they did not give rewards while expecting extremely thin pricing. "MNC treasurers are now their own central banks; they do much of their own foreign exchange trading, and they are good at it. Corporate dealers are *paid* to get the best price; therefore, their Treasurers do not interfere in transactions. Thus, we are dealt with on a *price* basis, with fewer "rewards" available to the banks. . . . With more skill in corporate treasuries, there are fewer companies that come to us and ask 'What should we do?' Rather, they come to us with the deal *already* designed and shop price." Exacerbating SBT London's con-

---

<sup></sup>[12]Exhibit 3 provides one view of the size of the U.K. banking industry in mid-1983.

[13]Which was expected to enhance the bank's opportunities to purchase other U.S. banks over time.

---

### EXHIBIT 3

**BANKING PARTICIPATION IN UNITED KINGDOM**

| Countries | Assets ($ billion) | Percentage of market share |
|---|---|---|
| United Kingdom | 642 | 26.9 |
| United States | 346 | 14.5 |
| Japan | 180 | 7.5 |
| France | 172 | 7.2 |
| Bahamas | 134 | 5.6 |
| Singapore | 103 | 4.3 |
| Swiss trustee accounts | 92 | 3.9 |
| Belgium | 78 | 3.3 |
| Netherlands | 69 | 2.9 |
| Switzerland | 67 | 2.8 |
| West Germany | 60 | 2.6 |
| Canada | 63 | 2.6 |
| Bahrain | 60 | 2.5 |
| Cayman Islands | 45 | 1.9 |
| Hong Kong | 43 | 1.8 |
| Italy | 40 | 1.7 |
| Panama | 39 | 1.6 |

*Source:* Quoted in the *International Herald Tribune*, June 20, 1983.

---

straints was their relative dearth of strong market connection in the United Kingdom. The market had long been influenced by existing strong ties of the "old boy" network. The London merchant banks, in particular, were thought to gain preferential access to numerous attractive deals through these ties. SBT, as a foreigner and relative newcomer, was not so fortunate.

Additionally, increasingly strong competition in the U.K. financial services realm was provided by U.S. investment banks and insurance companies that were attempting to expand into this segment.

On the positive side for SBT London, its management believed that the competitive benefits of operating as a responsive, manageable, large bank gave it a substantial edge versus the huge, slow-moving, bureaucratic clearing banks. SBT London perceived that its small London staff, effective matrix management process, and the availability of high-quality service products, trade finance, and foreign exchange expertise, were its competitive assets. In the latter regard,

SBT's U.S. cash management services, highly regarded in the U.S. market, were believed to be transferrable internationally. The bank's geographical spread and flexibility were also felt to be especially important advantages for competing for trade finance and commodity deals. The market in London was large, since 28 percent of the world's total international trade deals were put together there.[14] Being able to sell hard, coordinate both ends of a transaction, and decide quickly were requisite for competitive banks.

## MANAGING SBT'S LONDON BRANCH

SBT's London branch managership was a significant responsibility in the Bank's international operations (see Exhibit 4). Reporting to the London branch manager were:

- Account officers assigned to "traditional" commercial banking segments, namely, en-

---

[14]Other important centers included Geneva and Hong Kong.

ergy, commodities, U.S. multinationals, financial institutions, all other U.K. and other foreign companies, and a customer service and small account maintenance unit.

- Product specialists for cash management, securities clearing, and trade finance (wherein SBT assumed the buyer's risk).
- Functional staff, including: communications, computer systems, personnel, control, and accounting.
- An international consortium bank (SBT owned 22 percent) co-owned with U.S., German, Italian, and French banks, that had specialized in syndicating loans as a merchant bank. "We formed this before we had branches." In early 1984, it had considerable third-world debt on its book, and the syndicated loan market had dried up—although earnings were still acceptable because no LDC debt had been written off.
- A 20 percent SBT-owned, commercial bank in Scotland which operated an automobile finance company and did traditional commercial banking throughout Scotland. Its profit-

---

**EXHIBIT 4**

**SBT's INTERNATIONAL OPERATIONS**

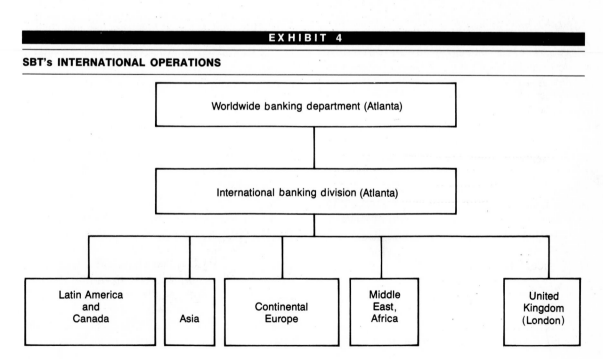

ability was acceptable. "It doesn't fit our needs or goals. Perhaps we should sell it or get its board's permission to review it closely and then bolster its management."

The London branch also "housed" several other SBT units, with whom Mike Foote "matrixed" and otherwise attempted to coordinate as appropriate: the heads of SBT's calling programs in Africa and Europe; the SBT Merchant Bank; the SBT's Treasury, which undertook foreign exchange trading, money market trading, and money market instruments trading (including U.S. treasuries, and bank CDs); and area product support specialists for trade finance, shipping, and energy. Foote explained,

> In considering the resources available to carry out our mission, we have 400 personnel, although we have significant gaps, principally in marketing, where our officers are trained traditionally. Some lack skills for clever marketing, and adequate technical product knowledge. It's hard to close the personnel resources gap. We had to transfer 10 account officers in 1983 to control noninterest expenses. As we became more successful, we required more skilled marketing officers. Raiding other multinational banks here would require us to pay more—and they aren't any better than we are. What we are attempting to do is recruit smart, local college graduates and train them (and our existing officers) in the appropriate credit and specialist skills . . . Attracting and retaining the best locals has its problems, too. Our competition is merchant banks that generally pay more and are less bureaucratic than commercial banks. Headquarters-based product specialists and planners, who are motivated to increase SBT's international business, can develop new products and respond to our requests for special situation support and counsel. At the levels of the branch manager, and the account and product managers, close and cooperative working relations between SBUs and different functional units are necessary. [The Appendix describes how part of SBT's matrix organization functioned.]
>
> What drives me? The themes we pursue are:
>
> • The customer is our highest priority.
> • We are strategically driven.
> • Maintain a standard of excellence in all we do.

> • Teamwork is the way we do things.
> • People are the key to our success.

> The International Banking Department has key performance targets. In 1983, they were: improve ROA, growth in loan volume, and increased demand deposits. In 1984, they were: improved ROA, greater profits, increased number of transaction "throughputs" using our existing products and capabilities—thus increasing total contribution to overhead.
>
> We are evaluated each year on how well we meet our objectives. In turn, our financial reward is tied to our performance/appraisal. My 1983 goals were fourfold:
>
> 1. Achieve an ROA target.
> 2. Ensure that our new central data processing system was operational.
> 3. Complete the refurbishment of offices and consolidation of staff in one location.
> 4. Divest a joint venture.
>
> Our formal appraisal system is reasonable and acknowledges the problem we have as managers . . . although it is difficult to measure results, because a few *big* good or bad results distort the overview.
>
> When I developed my 1983 ROA "budget" target, I wanted to beat it. I feel pressure to do better here than anyone else has done in this job. This is a high-profile position within the bank, and I want to demonstrate that a former consultant can be a high-performing banker and manager. It is difficult to do, because we have problems that are "invisible" to senior management, and this is a tough market. For me, an "invisible" problem arises when I am responsible for an area where I do not possess complete information or authority, e.g., the specialized units. If their performance is not good, it is difficult for me to correct it unless I work through their boss at headquarters.

## HOW TO PROCEED?

In the broadest sense, SBT London was charged by its Atlanta headquarters with raising its profitability so as not to detract from the bank's overall ROA. Within that broad mandate, various strategic ideas and questions were discussed by the London management team:

- How can we up-tier ourselves with major accounts?
- How can we obtain more volume throughput?
- How can we increase our visibility with attractive customers?
- Should we push hard on (U.S.-originated) cash management products as an important means of building desired relations in London—acknowledging that the payoffs from cash management *per se* would take years to accrue?
- Should we seek joint ventures with local partners possessing local currency capabilities and strong local contacts for business production purposes?
- What new businesses should we develop?

At a somewhat broader level of strategic perspective, Mike Foote, Anthony Butler, and several SBT London colleagues believed that the branch must be extremely good at the relatively few things it did, for the relatively few targeted companies—to decrease the expense base and upgrade its marketing effectiveness.[15] "And yet," sighed Foote, "I seriously doubt that even this would be enough to make a major positive contribution to the bank's overall goals and major strategies. We need to find further, significant opportunities."

---

**APPENDIX**

# Matrix Management

The relationship manager (RM) was responsible for worldwide strategic planning for key corporate accounts and set target objectives for the customer's operations globally. In tandem, the RM worked with a series of product managers (PM) who were responsible for identifying new product requirements and needs in the marketplace. The PM looked at possible products, "qualified them" to see if they were

---

[15]In Butler's words "Investment and merchant banks are staffed with one backup person for two sales personnel; we have three backups for each one in sales."

produceable, analyzed the costs and income possibilities, and kept information flowing between the RMs and PMs.

For example, in trade finance, PMs had to have technical expertise because the business was complicated. The London branch had a trade finance PM who reported directly (solid line) to Mike Foote, but had a dotted-line relationship to the trade finance coordinator for Europe/Middle East/Africa. The overall relationships were organized as shown in Exhibit 5. Depending on the branch size and expertise of the individuals, a trade finance product manager could be *dedicated* (i.e., responsible for trade finance products only) or *designated* (i.e., responsible for trade finance expertise/liason activities in addition to other responsibilities such as relationship management).

Generally, the success of this coordination effort depended on the expertise, interest, and personality of the product manager, if the PM were dedicated rather than designated, and how the PM structured and developed the job to be independent of, as well as interdependent with, relationship managers.

The London branch had the largest trade finance division outside of Atlanta, with four marketing and two support staff. Its customers fell into three categories:

1. Indigenous U.K. companies
2. Trading and commodity companies that used London as a major operations center
3. Customers from other parts of the bank that used London as a service center (e.g., a Chinese company buying from the London Metal Exchange)

The trade finance marketing officers called upon customers directly in some cases, prospected for new business, and followed up on business opportunities the relationship manager had qualified. In all cases, communication about customers and prospects had to flow freely between the RM and the PM.

Within the London branch, the trade finance function worked well because:

1. The branch manager had both the relationship managers and the trade finance product manager reporting directly to him. Therefore, he could ensure both sides worked together.
2. The branch manager was strongly committed to generating trade finance business.
3. The trade finance PM was dedicated to the trade finance area alone, possessed trade finance experience, and had developed good working relationships with the RMs.

### EXHIBIT 5

**MANAGEMENT RELATIONSHIPS**

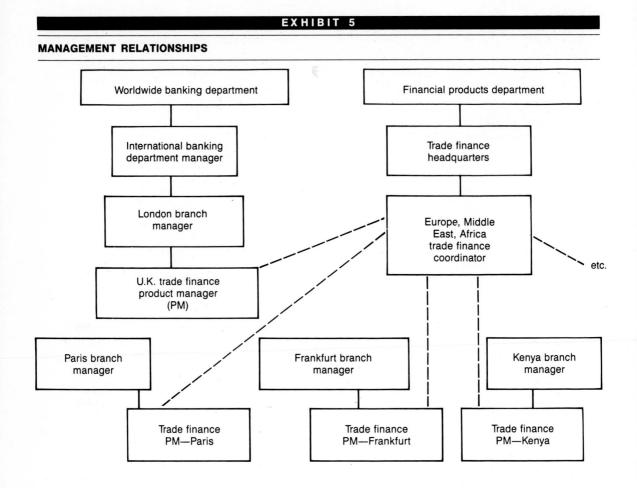

4. The Europe, Middle East, Africa trade finance coordinator resided in London and worked successfully with the trade finance offices.

When matrix management was first implemented at SBT, there was a minor problem in making it work. Relationship managers wanted to retain control over their customers and did not want the trade finance PM to call on the customer without the RM. However, this situation was soon rectified as explained above. In terms of new product development, ideas came from the line groups—both from the trade finance PMs and from the RMs. There were no product development managers at headquarters.

From an income standpoint, SBT's internal management information system identified trade finance income by customer. Therefore, both the relationship manager responsible for the customer and the trade finance PM received "credit." At annual employee reviews, performance was judged against commonly agreed upon objectives established at the beginning of the review period.

Because the London branch was a trade finance service center for other branches, it performed substantial work and booked business whose income went to other branches and not to the London branch. In 1983, $1.5 million in income booked by the London staff did not show on the London SBU's books. There were no internal accounting systems to transfer this income to the London SBU. Instead, the work was done "for the corporation's good" and narratively reported during the review process.

# The American Express Company in France

Late in September 1979, Mr. James Clark was formulating a final joint venture proposal which American Express would submit to a consortium of three French national banks to develop a French franc traveler's cheque. Mr. Clark, as Executive Vice President of the Traveler's Cheque and Money Order Division, part of American Express' Travel Related Services Group, was responsible for the joint venture negotiations for American Express. Although these had moved rapidly along in the last year, several specific points, including ownership interests, marketing rights, and servicing agreements, had yet to be established.

Mr. Clark appreciated the delicate nature of the project before him. Any final agreement would have to be acceptable to three different banks: Crédit Lyonnais and Banque Nationale de Paris (BNP), which were under the jurisdiction of the Ministry of Finance, and Crédit Agricole, which reported to the Ministry of Agriculture. He knew

This case was prepared by Mary Lou Schramm with Deborah Rodgers under the supervision of Professor Fariborz Ghadar as a basis for class discussion rather than to illustrate either effective or ineffective handling of an administration situation. © George Washington University School of Government & Business Administration, 1981.

that, in general, it was unusual for such large financial institutions, traditional rivals in the domestic market, to undertake cooperative dealings with one another. In addition, all three banks were eager to obtain the rights for administration of the traveler's cheques program, which consisted essentially of operating a clearing bank operation for the cheques, receiving settlement money from selling banks and paying for cheques tendered. To complicate matters further, a private French bank, Crédit Commerciale de Paris, had lately shown an interest in joining the agreement. Mr. Clark knew that a successful agreement would need to consider the interests of all of these parties.

## BACKGROUND

At the time, American Express, Crédit Lyonnais, and BNP were each issuing French franc traveler's cheques separately. The joint venture would enable them to expand their international business and to promote the French franc as a viable traveling currency. Moreover, the agreement would launch a close working partnership between American Express and the national French banks, a relationship that American Express had wished to cultivate for a number of years. The French banks, on the other hand, were eager to obtain access to worldwide markets and greater visibility in the traveler's cheque industry, and they would benefit from the economies of scale and global refund services offered by American Express.

Prior to the start of these negotiations, American Express had made some overtures to another consortium of European banks to aid in the development of a Euro-Traveler's Cheque (see discussion below). The banking group insisted on complete European control of the operation, which was unacceptable to American Express, and discussions were ended.

American Express then approached the French banks, in September 1975, about a joint business possibility regarding traveler's cheques, but nothing came of the offer. Several years later, however, Crédit Lyonnais suggested that they were interested in expanding their international business ties, and American Express repeated its interest. In June 1978, the two companies discussed the possibility of a joint business venture, examining general concepts involved in such a deal. Preliminary discussions were positive, and, by the fall of 1979, both companies had agreed to begin serious negotiations and invited the other French banks to join.

A new company, to be named Société Française du Cheque de Voyage (SFCV), was to be created to manage the project. It was not clear, however, who would have responsibility for the issuance of the cheques within France or abroad or who was to be responsible for SFCV's transactions and contacts with French banks selling the cheques. Should one of the local partners have sole responsibility for distribution of the cheques, it was then possible that the three banks would bid for that privilege. Another alternative would be to have responsibility for distribution rotate among the banks.

Also, the question arose as to where the cheques were to be printed. The banks preferred to contract out to French printers for the job; but since the cheques would resemble American Express traveler's cheques of other denominations in terms of basic design, format, and color, the company wished to maintain control over quality and security features. Mr. Clark had considered licensing SFCV to allow the joint venture to use its well-known design. However, American Express had never before entered into such an agreement with another party. Above all, it was important that the cheques reflected a high-quality product consistent with the image of American Express.

American Express was particularly qualified to perform inventory and administrative functions for SFCV. The joint venture would benefit from American Express's worldwide network of traveler's cheque operations, which included control over ordering and printing of traveler's cheques throughout the world, management of international marketing and advertising functions, and maintenance of loss and fraud control. In addition, American Express would be able to train the staff of French nationals that would operate SFCV. More importantly, American Express would aid the joint venture in cheque processing and acceptance, preparation of the company's financial reports, and administration of refunds through its worldwide refund service.

The French partners would be responsible for the "front end" operations—distribution of the cheques, maintaining contact with the selling banks, etc.—and for the investment of the "float," i.e., the funds that would be available to the issuers from the time a cheque was sold to the time the purchaser redeemed it. Because float constituted a major source of funds from traveler's cheque operations, the profitability of SFCV would depend upon the investment of such funds. It was possible that American Express could make investment recommendations based upon its financial expertise and previous experience in the area.

As Mr. Clark sat down to draft the joint venture proposal, several questions came to mind. What percentage ownership of SFCV should

American Express bid for, and how would the remaining equity be distributed among the French banks? Should all four parties have equal partnership in the joint venture, or should American Express have majority ownership? How should new entrants, such as Crédit Commerciale de Paris, be incorporated as partners in the company, and how would this be handled in the future if and when other banks demonstrated interest? Under such circumstances, how would profits be shared?

Questions also arose about the operations of SFCV. What proportion of SFCV management would be composed of executives on detachment from the parent companies, or should they be totally independent of them? In view of this, how and to what degree would American Express maintain control over their activities? Mr. Clark wondered about an appropriate promotional and advertising budget for SFCV, given the worldwide advertising budget for American Express. This led to the more general question of how SFCV would interface with the multinational operations of American Express.

## TRAVELER'S CHEQUE OPERATIONS

Revenue from the traveler's cheque business comes from two main areas: a share in the commission charged by the selling agents (banks or travel offices) and the interest earned in the investment of the float. Standard industry practice had been to charge 1 percent commission on the face value of the cheques sold, although this practice was frequently waived in the United States. American Express generally received one-third of the commission, Bank of America and Citibank collected one-tenth, while Thomas Cook took none of it. Visa would leave commission rates up to the issuing banks; large agents could negotiate lower fees or compensating forms of revenue related to sales.

The main source of revenue from traveler's cheques came from the investment of the float. The average float time or life of a traveler's cheque was 35 to 40 days. Increasing financial

sophistication on the part of consumers had diminished the practice of keeping cheques idle for a long period of time and could lead to shorter periods of float in the future. American Express estimated that, on average, 10 percent of their annual traveler's cheque sales were outstanding at any one time. Interest income from investment of these idle funds amounted to substantial revenues for the company. American Express had outstanding cheques for 1978, 1979, and 1980 in the amount of $2.1, $2.3, and $2.5 billion respectively (see Exhibit 1).

To rely on the revenue generated by the investment of these idle funds was profitable only when undertaken as a large-scale operation. Many small competitors of American Express and new cheque issuers risked suffering losses, particularly with the high costs associated with operating in the traveler's cheque industry. American Express, however, enjoyed an appreciable size advantage in this respect, benefiting from economies of scale in the following areas: production of a high-security medium of exchange; refunding services; writing off losses due to fraud, theft, or counterfeit; and marketing and advertising programs. Exhibit 2 shows the per-dollar cost of a traveler's cheque in 1977.

Although analysts had often predicted a decline in the traveler's cheque market, it had remained stable in recent years. Worldwide sales amounted to approximately $30 billion in both 1979 and 1980. However, competition in the worldwide credit field had increased noticeably during this time. For example, the growth of international cheque guarantee cards, including the Eurocheque card (see discussion below), enabled users to cash cheques at banks in various parts of the world. Increased use of travel and entertainment credit cards had also presented competition for traveler's cheques, and the growing popularity of prepaid package tours has partially eliminated the need for travelers to carry large sums of money. Finally, although traveler's cheque sales were likely to suffer from any decline in world travel that might result from depressed economic conditions, increased com-

## EXHIBIT 1

**AMERICAN EXPRESS COMPANY FINANCIAL STATISTICS, 1977–80** ($ Million)

|  | 1980 | 1979 | 1978 | 1977 |
|---|---|---|---|---|
| Operating results |  |  |  |  |
| Revenues | 5,504 | 4,667 | 4,076 | 3,431 |
| Profits on securities | — | — | — | 14 |
| Interest expense | 870 | 572 | 368 | 249 |
| Other expenses | 4,213 | 3,704 | 3,325 | 2,874 |
| Income taxes | 45 | 46 | 69 | 58 |
| Net income | 376 | 345 | 314 | 264 |
| Assets and liabilities |  |  |  |  |
| Time deposits | 1,084 | 976 | 891 | 858 |
| Investment securities | 7,089 | 6,594 | 5,810 | 5,121 |
| Accounts receivables/accruals | 4,887 | 3,597 | 2,705 | 2,155 |
| Loans and discounts | 3,690 | 3,369 | 3,320 | 2,571 |
| Total assets | 19,709 | 17,108 | 14,698 | 12,315 |
| Customer deposits/balances | 5,087 | 4,749 | 4,192 | 3,755 |
| Traveler's Cheques | 2,542 | 2,343 | 2,105 | 1,859 |
| Insurance reserves | 3,856 | 3,565 | 3,116 | 2,601 |
| Long-term debt | 1,099 | 689 | 479 | 329 |
| Preferred stock | 24 | 25 | 27 | 28 |
| Shareholder's equity | 2,162 | 1,833 | 1,593 | 1,379 |
| Shareholder's statistics |  |  |  |  |
| Net income per share | $5.27 | $4.83 | $4.39 | $3.68 |
| Dividends per share | $2.00 | $1.80 | $1.55 | $1.30 |
| Shares outstanding (million) | 71 | 71 | 71 | 71 |
| Other statistics |  |  |  |  |
| Number of employees | 44,031 | 40,732 | 37,856 | 35,399 |
| Percent outside U.S. | 34.5 | 32.8 | 32.2 | 32.3 |
| American Express offices | 751 | 741 | 715 | 693 |
| Representative offices | 782 | 798 | 654 | 477 |

*Source:* Annual reports.

petition within the industry in recent years demonstrated the continued strength of the product.

## MAJOR U.S. COMPETITORS

The *American Express Company* invented the traveler's cheque in 1891. In that first year $10,000 worth of traveler's cheques were sold. By 1901, sales had grown to $6 million. Since that time, American Express has established itself as a market leader of the industry, both in the United States and worldwide. As the largest issuer of international hard currency cheques, the company offered a choice of seven major currencies: British pounds sterling (since 1920), French francs

(since 1972), German marks (since 1972), Japanese yen (since 1974), Swiss francs (since 1969) and, of course, U.S. dollars (since 1891).

In order to increase its activities in the international arena, American Express had undertaken to develop business relationships with companies and financial institutions in other countries, particularly in Europe, through joint venture operations. This was exemplified by the recent negotiations for French franc traveler's cheques. If the French joint venture appeared to be a success, American Express would be encouraged to pursue similar discussions with institutions in other European regions, such as Scandinavia, Holland, and Switzerland.

EXHIBIT 2

## AVERAGE COSTS OF ISSUING A TRAVELER'S CHEQUE, 1977

| Cost categories | U.S. cents per $ |
|---|---|
| Production and distribution | 3.5–6.0 |
| Losses | 3.5–5.5 |
| Marketing | 5.0–7.0 |
| Processing and postage | 12.0–18.0 |
| Total (an average of the individual terms) | 27–32 |

*Source: The Banker,* December 1979, p. 25.

EXHIBIT 4

## TRAVELER'S CHEQUES ISSUED BY CURRENCY AND REGION, 1979

| By currency: | U.S. dollars | 75% |
|---|---|---|
| | Pounds sterling | 10 |
| | German marks | 10 |
| | Others | 5 |
| | | 100% |
| By region of issue: | North America | 65% |
| | Europe | 18 |
| | Rest of the world | 17 |
| | | 100% |

*Source: The Economist,* August 2, 1980, p. 72.

In recent years new competitors had attempted to capture some of American Express's world market share in the traveler's cheque industry. Much of the activity had centered around the growing European market. Exhibit 3 shows world market shares for 1978–79 by cheque issuer. Exhibit 4 shows the percentage of traveler's cheques issued in 1979 by currency and by major geographic region.

*Visa* introduced a large promotional operation for their traveler's cheques at the end of 1979. At that time, financial institutions that were or became Visa (credit card) issuers would also have an opportunity to issue Visa traveler's cheques. The issuing institutions would then make arrangements with other financial institutions and smaller agent banks within their market areas to sell the Visa cheques.

Visa planned to broaden its operations in the hope of capturing a 40 percent market share in the United States by the mid-1980s. Their international marketing alliances were already strong in bank cards (Visa/Bankamericard, Barclaycard, etc.). The Visa cheque was issued in four currencies: U.S. dollars, Japanese yen, British pounds sterling, and Spanish pesetas. It was issued by 24 institutions including Barclays Bank, First National Bank of Chicago, and Sumitomo Bank. Barclays incorporated their 5 percent of the world market share for traveler's cheques into the Visa operation, thereby expanding their own market and using Visa's worldwide communication network to provide better service. In May 1980, the Visa operation received added support when the Chase Manhattan Bank, the world's twelfth largest, announced that it would issue Visa cheques.

*Bank of America* was the founder of the Visa card but had refused to participate in its traveler's cheque operations. Bank of America had its own traveler's cheque operation, confined mainly to North America. Both Bank of America and *Citibank* issued U.S. dollar cheques only but were expected to expand into foreign currencies in the future.

## EURO-TRAVELER'S CHEQUE

A consortium of 56 European banks from 12 countries had set out in the late 1970s to challenge the domination of U.S.-based issuers of

EXHIBIT 3

## WORLD MARKET SHARE BY ISSUER IN 1978 AND 1979

| Issuer | 1978 | 1979 |
|---|---|---|
| American Express | 51% | 51% |
| Bank of America | 15 | 12 |
| Citibank | 15 | 13 |
| Thomas Cook | 7 | 9 |
| Barclay's | 5 | 5 |
| Others | 7 | 10 |

*Source: The Banker,* December, 1979, p. 34.

---

**EXHIBIT 5**

---

### THE TRAVELER'S CHEQUE LINKS OF 12 LARGE BANKS

| Bank | Country | Traveler's cheque |
| --- | --- | --- |
| Crédit Agricole | France | American Express via SFCV |
| Bank of America | United States | Bank of America |
| Citicorp (Citibank) | United States | Citicorp |
| Banque Nationale de Paris | France | American Express via SFCV |
| Deutsche Bank | W. Germany | European (ETC) |
| Crédit Lyonnais | France | American Express via SFCV |
| Société Génèrale | France | European (ETC) |
| Dresdner Bank | W. Germany | European (ETC) |
| Barclays | Britain | Visa |
| Dai-Ichi Kangyo | Japan | — |
| National Westminster | Britain | — |
| Chase Manhattan | United States | Visa |

*Source: The Economist,* August 2, 1980, p. 73.

---

traveler's cheques in the world market. The most influential members of the consortium were banks from Great Britain, France, and West Germany. Other participating banks represented countries such as Belgium, Denmark, Italy, the Netherlands, Norway, Portugal, Spain, and Switzerland. The consortium had previously set up an international cheque-guarantee card (Eurocheque card) which had attracted some 27 million holders and a travel and entertainment card (Eurocard). The proposal for a Euro-Traveler's Cheque would compliment this service line.

Britain's Midland Bank, owners of the Thomas Cook Traveler's Cheque, was leading the consortium with plans for a Euro-Traveler's Cheque (ETC). The plans involved building upon, and eventually replacing the Cook cheque. Their goal was to create a more "rational" and efficient European traveler's cheque industry. The industry in Europe was currently fragmented with dozens of cheque issuers in about 13 countries. In West Germany alone, for example, there were about 30 different traveler's cheques issued.

The ETC would be denominated in U.S. dollars and in various European currencies. Members in each participating country would hold shares in the consortium and would set up separate local companies to hold and invest the float

in that country's currency. These separate companies would be owned by each country's participating institutions.

The ETC partners also hoped to gain entry into the American market for traveler's cheques. They would offer Americans going to Europe a cheque denominated in the currency of the country they would be visiting, capitalizing on the fluctuating exchange rates of the dollar and in increasing demand for nondollar traveler's cheques.

The members of the ETC consortium expected to start with a 12 percent share of the European market and to increase this to 20 percent in their first year of operations. If they approached this goal, it would most likely be at the expense of American Express's 50 percent world share, and Citibank and Bank of America's combined 25 percent world market share. However, plans for the ETC had yet to reach the stages of implementation. Exhibit 5 indicates the linkages in traveler's cheques of twelve large international banks.

Mr. Clark knew that the proposed joint venture in France could be a crucial step in solidifying American Express's market position in Europe. Success or failure in this venture would significantly influence the company's global performance and prospects. His concern was finding the right formula to make such a venture work well for Amex and for its partners.

# PART THREE

# Market Entry and Participation Policies

# Patho-Control, Inc.

Late in 1983, Mr. Larry Mills, Vice President of Patho-Control, Inc. (PCI), was pondering an offer from Sr. Ismael Carrera to license PCI's product line for the Colombian market. Mr. Mills had among his various duties that of supervising any international operations that might develop for PCI. Complicating the picture were several requests from foreign and U.S. distributors for product information and a report prepared for PCI by an MBA student which recommended that certain policies be adopted regarding PCI's foreign involvement.

## BACKGROUND

PCI was founded in Dallas, Texas, in May 1979, by Mr. Andrew Light, a former district sales manager for a major international pharmaceutical firm. In 1975, Mr. Light conceived the idea of developing a series of aerosol disinfectant

products for medical use and began a laboratory research program in conjunction with a friend, a research chemist at another major drug company. Both these men, working on their own time, developed the formulae on which to base their product line. The effectiveness of the formulae was confirmed by some preliminary laboratory tests performed at a local university. These tests showed that the products were at least equal and generally superior to most competing products then on the market.

At this point, Mr. Light began to search for the necessary capital with which to launch an intensive R&D campaign. Early in 1979, he identified a small pharmaceutical laboratory heading for bankruptcy and began negotiations for the acquisition of the company's physical assets with the intention of making a subsequent public offering. Several months later Mr. Light was able to interest a group of investors in making a capital commitment of $300,000 to the new venture. A line of credit for $100,000 was obtained simultaneously from a Dallas bank. The funds were destined to purchase the laboratory facilities, and to cover product R&D activities, promotional expenditures, and administrative

This case was written by Professor José de la Torre and is not intended to illustrate either effective or ineffective handling of administrative matters. Most names, dates, and financial data have been disguised to protect the identity of the firm whose cooperation made this case possible.

expenses until sales reached satisfactory levels. Patho-Control was incorporated, and Mr. Light resigned his sales post to assume the presidency of the newly formed company.

Mr. Larry Mills, Mr. Light's brother-in-law, joined the company as Marketing Vice President in July 1980. Mr. Mills had just left his post as director of central services for a major metropolitan area in the eastern United States. In that position he had been responsible for the purchase and delivery of goods and services to all agencies and sectors of the metropolitan government.

One of Mr. Mills's early undertakings was to survey the market briefly and determine what marketing strategies were most appropriate. The survey revealed, among other things, that a few products dominated the market but that usage was not widespread. Also, the number of potential channels of distribution appeared to be very large.

During most of 1981 and part of 1982, PCI perfected its formulations and conducted more reliable independent tests. Manufacturing activities were subcontracted to a small local chemical firm which mixed the formulae and canned and packaged the products. Initially, Light and Mills set out to locate a number of wholesale distributors that could handle the Patho line. A hospital supply firm in Philadelphia was contracted to deal with that segment of the market. In mid-1982, a Dallas-based national pharmaceutical firm, Leighton Laboratories, took over as exclusive distributor of all PCI products in the United States. The contract stipulated that those regional distributorships already established would be placed under Leighton's control.

These activities were supplemented by extensive travel by Light and Mills, especially geared to major hospitals. A major marketing breakthrough came when one of the nation's leading medical schools adopted PCI's product line for their facilities. Sales in 1982 reached $45,000 and were expected to exceed $200,000 in 1983.

The relationship between PCI and Leighton, however, deteriorated rapidly throughout 1982–83. First, Leighton increased prices in certain products by more than 50 percent while cutting margins to regional distributors. This resulted in the loss of many distributorships, including several of those originally negotiated by Light. Also, a member of PCI's staff, hired on Leighton's recommendation, turned out to be working for the latter as an informer. The object of the intrigue was Leighton's determination to acquire PCI. Several offers to this effect had met with stern opposition from PCI's management-owners. Finally, in May 1983, the contract with Leighton was declared legally void.

Subsequently, PCI expanded its capital base through a limited issue of $125,000, placed among a few local investors, and by absorbing a local company in an unrelated line of business. In exchange for a limited number of shares, PCI acquired the assets of Volco Communications, Inc. (including a healthy liquidity position) and the services of Mr. John Sherman. Mr. Sherman was an aggressive entrepreneur with a proven record of turning small businesses into successful operations. He had been acting in a consulting capacity to Volco at the time the merger negotiations were begun. Once this was completed, he assumed the position of Chairman of the Board and Chief Executive Officer of PCI. Mr. Light remained as president of PCI, with Volco functioning as a semiautonomous division.

In the months that followed, PCI searched for an alternative distributor. In the fall of 1983 a tentative arrangement was reached with a major medical supplies firm, Franklyn Bros., Inc. While a final agreement was still a few weeks off, PCI was anxious to proceed quickly. Sales in the first nine months of 1983 had been less than $40,000, due in part to the problems with Leighton. PCI's R&D program required additional funds which would have to be generated internally. An attractive element in the negotiation was an offer by Franklyn's management practically guaranteeing an initial order of no less than $100,000, to be shipped to their regional warehouses throughout the United States.

## THE PRODUCT LINE

The company's product line consisted of five products able to provide a complete asepsis program in hospitals and other health care facilities. (See Exhibit 1 for additional product information obtained from a sample of PCI's advertising copy.) These products were:

1. *Pathofoam.* An aerosol germicidal foam for use as a hand-and-skin cleaner; this product was considered particularly suited to doctors, nurses, and others involved in handling large numbers of patients in sequence, as it provided for disinfectant action which limited the chance of contamination from one patient to the next. Pathofoam could also be used as a body rub and as a preparation for cleaning prior to a hypodermic injection.
2. *Pathospray.* A scented aerosol air sanitizer, Pathospray had germicidal properties capable of controlling germs, bacteria, and other atmospheric organisms. Its pleasant odor provided a feeling of freshness and cleanliness. One of its major virtues, as was the case with all other Patho products, was its nonflammable property.
3. *Pathokleen.* This aerosol foam cleaner was particularly designed for surface areas, beds, instrumentation, etc. Applied as a foam, it contained cleaning as well as germicidal elements.
4. *Pathowash.* A liquid cleaner for floors and other general cleaning purposes, this product contained a solution of the same germicidal ingredient above.
5. *Patho Swabs.* These were cotton swabs presoaked in the same basic solution.

In addition, the company was investigating other product possibilities deriving from the same general formulation. One of these was a fungicide product proved effective against athlete's foot and similar fungus infections. Other possible uses of the company's product under study

were impregnating carpets, wallpaper, and paints. The basic antiseptical properties of the general formulae could be applied to other materials in this fashion. In the case of carpets, for instance, it would prevent mildew and mold from forming due to dampness.

The company's major competitor was the Lehn and Fink Division (L&F) of Sterling Drug Company, producers of Lysol and its related products. Although Lysol spray was marketed in the United States and abroad directly to the consumer—and principally to the home user—it was often used in medical applications and distributed to hospitals under the name Amphil. PCI estimated that Amphil accounted for about 15–20 percent of L&F's total sales of about $100 million. It was also reported that L&F spent almost 30 percent of sales in promotion, although most of it was directed to the consumer market. L&F had its own production facilities and licensed its formulation and name in over 15 countries, including 8 in Latin America.

## INITIAL INTERNATIONAL ACTIVITIES

The news of PCI's new product line was reported in various trade journals. This publicity, together with relatively small advertising expenditures incurred during 1982, brought about a series of inquiries from abroad regarding the company's international intentions. Most often, the correspondence inquired about the nature of the products and stated the writer's willingness to undertake distribution of PCI's products in local or regional markets. At that time, PCI's management was totally preoccupied with matters relating to the start of U.S. operations and with securing such needed capital. Thus, most of the letters went unanswered.

Late in 1982, a call from PCI's local banker brought Mr. Light and Mr. Mills to a meeting with a visiting Colombian industrialist, Sr. Ismael Carrera. Sr. Carrera was President and part owner of Laboratorios Bio-Químicos, S.A. (Bioquim), a firm engaged in manufacturing and selling a wide array of pharmaceutical and cosmetic products. Although Bioquim had its own

## EXHIBIT 1

**SELECTED INFORMATION FROM PROMOTIONAL BROCHURE**

CROSS INFECTION . . . through the air, from surfaces and through human contact

- Cross infection, the transmission of infectious disease and a major problem confronting the medical field today, can now be effectively controlled with five new products in the pioneering *asepsis program* of Patho-Control.

- Today, as more is learned about infectious disease, great progress has been achieved in preventing its transmission.

- Infectious microorganisms exist in abundance, travel many paths in their migration, have the capacity to develop resistant strains to antibiotic therapy, and produce cultures with great rapidity. Infection can occur from many sources. Direct contact with institutionalized patients, staff, or visitors harboring bacteria in active lesions or as immune carriers, dust particles, inanimate surface reservoirs, fomites and surgical hypodermic or other percutaneous procedures are common routes of cross infection.

- The *asepsis program* of PATHO-CONTROL provides for effective control and reduction of the principal agents of infection—bacteria including bacillus fungi and protozoa. And through use of its complete program of asepsis effectively intercepts the broadest spectrum of cross infection factors—the many routes of pathogenic transmission.

- Product research and testing over a four-year development period have been accomplished in leading medical centers and in the most acute and routine areas of cross infection. Testing in connection with kidney transplant procedures at a leading university hospital has reduced infection to a level considered to be the most effective yet developed. The use of PATHO-CONTROL'S *asepsis program* in ordinary or less critical procedures should reduce the occurrence of cross infection in the medical field to an absolute minimum.

- Wherever the need for environmental asepsis—hospitals, nursing homes, doctors' offices, in the ophthalmic and dental fields, veterinary clinics, health and beauty salons, nurseries, and other infant-oriented fields— cross infection requires unrelenting efforts from those responsible for its prevention. The products of PATHO-CONTROL are unique in fulfilling the need for a *complete asepsis program* effective against a broad spectrum of pathogens—a new front line of defense against cross infection.

FIVE NEW PRODUCTS for an effective asepsis program:

1. **PATHOFOAM** PATHOFOAM is a highly effective germicidal foam reducing on contact infectious organism counts within a safe range. It is recommended for professional use on the hands between patient examinations to eliminate cross infection, effectively controlling bacteria, including bacillus fungus, and protozoa. Now the need for medical personnel to constantly immerse their hands in soap and water, found in most cases to be ineffective and a cause of dermatitis, is eliminated with the use of PATHOFOAM. Additionally, it contains the finest of skin conditioners and penetrating agents, leaving the skin soft and supple. An excellent body rub for the patient to prevent decubiti, PATHO-FOAM is packaged in a handy 6-oz. aerosol can, 10 per case, and contains a nonflammable propellant.

2. **PATHOSPRAY** A delightfully scented aerosol air sanitizer PATHOSPRAY will effectively reduce bacterial count in any room area, as well as deodorize and freshen the air with a pure extract of mint. Especially recommended for isolation areas, nurseries and doctors' offices, it should be sprayed toward the center of the room for one to two minutes to be most effective. Bactericidal and bacillicidal, protozoacidal and fungicidal, it is effective against a broad range of staph, strep, and other organisms that can cause strep throat, pneumonia, and other communicable diseases. Particularly recommended for carpeted areas to control further transmission of organisms over a greater area from vacuum exhaust by spraying at least two to three minutes prior to vacuuming. Packaged in 16-ounce aerosol cans, 10 per case.

3. **PATHOKLEEN** PATHOKLEEN is an aerosol foam cleaner that kills on contact a broad range of organisms, particularly those found on any surface area from dust fall-out. It is recommended for walls, tabletops, emesis basins, mattress covers, floors, cart wheels, and shoe soles in isolation areas or any area where a safe or total reduction of organism colonies is required. Bactericidal and bacillicidal, fungicidal and protozoacidal—PATHOKLEEN is nontoxic, pleasantly scented, and will leave areas clean bacteriostatically for hours. Packaged in 16-oz. aerosol cans, 10 per case.

4. **PATHOWASH** Packaged in 1-oz. individual polyethylene packets soluble in water over 120°F, PATHOWASH is a highly concentrated germicidal cleaner designed for use as an instant cleaning solution for walls and floors. It is highly effective in reducing on contact infectious bacteria and bacillus fungus and protozoa to a safe range and prevents pathogenic culture for sig-

**EXHIBIT 1(cont.)**

nificant periods of time. A 1-oz. packet, dropped into a cleaning solution container is sufficient for up to 3 gallons of heated water and is more than adequate for the standard 10-quart cleaning bucket.

5. **PATHO SWABS**  Ready for immediate use and proven by documentation as the fastest acting skin germicidal agent yet developed, PATHO SWABS is effective against bacteria and bacillus fungi and protozoa. Nonflammable and with practically no odor, it has proven to eliminate fungus nails, usually caused by constant use of alcohol and common to medical personnel performing prepping procedures often. Safe to

use with the fingers since it is almost immediate in action and destroys incubation by any outside organisms in the material, each swab contains a full cc of the formula and the desired amount on the prep area can be accomplished by pressure on the swab. PATHO SWABS can be used to prepare any site for injection by either needle or hypo gun and is ideal for swabbing stoppers of vials, IV bottles, blood bottles, and other containers prior to puncture. Empty plastic jars are ready for use in Pathology for specimens. Conveniently packaged in plastic jars of 100, 10 per carton, 6 cartons per case.

---

product lines, it also served as contract filler under license for a number of foreign firms such as Revlon and Bristol-Meyers. From the information provided by Sr. Carrera at the meeting, most of which was corroborated by PCI's bank, Bioquim appeared to be a solid company with extensive manufacturing and marketing experience, especially in over-the-counter and proprietary products with a major consumer orientation. The company also detailed certain products directly to doctors and hospitals, but to a lesser extent than it engaged in consumer activities.

The initial conversations with Sr. Carrera were based on the importation of PCI products into Colombia for distribution and resale by Bioquim. Sr. Carrera offered to do some market research upon his return and asked for a tentative export price schedule. Mr. Light, however, suggested that price considerations be reserved for discussion after Sr. Carrera had an opportunity to conduct his brief survey of the Colombian market.

## THE STUDENT PROJECT

In December 1982, PCI was contacted by the local field office of the U.S. Department of Commerce and invited to participate in an ''export-expansion'' program. Under the auspices of this program an MBA student from a nearby university was to collaborate with the firm for a

semester helping the company develop or expand its international marketing activities.

Mr. Lou Foster was assigned to PCI early in 1983. He was impressed by the large amounts of accumulated correspondence dealing with foreign inquiries about PCI's product line and proceeded to answer some of it. Product and company information was mailed to most of these firms. In addition, Mr. Foster sought to establish some criteria for determining which markets appeared most promising and for estimating potential demand in various areas. Finally, he undertook to contrast the net gains obtainable through several alternative strategies such as direct export, licensing, and indirect export.

In attempting to achieve some measure of market potential Mr. Foster began by establishing benchmarks of level of use in the United States. The firm, however, had little historical market data given its relative youth. In order to determine usage rates, Foster conducted several interviews in three local hospitals averaging slightly over 1,000 beds each. Each of these hospitals had between 9 and 12 operating rooms, and a staff which numbered in excess of 200 doctors, and each performed the full range of hospital services. The interviews, normally involving the chief of housekeeping services and other hospital personnel, yielded different results according to the particular views of each interviewee as to the effectiveness of the products. Nonetheless, the following conservative estimates for institutional usage rates were obtained:

- Pathofoam skin cleaner: 1.2 cans per bed per year
- Pathospray room spray: 2 cans per bed per year

- Pathokleen surface cleaner: 75 oz per bed per year

In addition, Mr. Foster determined that each can of Pathofoam could be used in 90 individual applications. Estimating a daily frequency of 5 usage doses per individual, he concluded that

---

## EXHIBIT 2

**HEALTH SERVICES DATA FOR SELECTED COUNTRIES, 1980 (OR NEAREST YEAR)**

| Country | Public health expenditures* ($ millions) | Expenditures as percent of national budget | Number of hospitals | Number of beds (thousands) | Number of doctors (thousands) | Other medical personnel (thousands) |
|---|---|---|---|---|---|---|
| North America | | | | | | |
| Canada | 3,674 | 10.5 | 1,226 | 182.8 | 43.2 | 140.4 |
| United States | 62,200 | 6.8 | 7,051 | 1,333.4 | 414.9 | 1,434.7 |
| Latin America | | | | | | |
| Argentina | 934 | 1.8 | 3,186 | 150.0 | 48.7 | — |
| Brazil | 2,485 | 6.8 | 5,426 | 445.8 | 62.7 | 43.0 |
| Colombia | 355 | 8.8 | 849 | 44.5 | 12.7 | 24.4 |
| Mexico | 765 | 2.4 | 1,575 | 67.4 | 31.6 | 43.6 |
| Venezuela | 1,147 | 8.9 | 444 | 41.4 | 14.8 | 45.6 |
| Europe | | | | | | |
| Belgium | 943 | 1.7 | 531 | 92.7 | 26.6 | 111.5 |
| France | 36,360 | 15.2 | 961 | 318.5 | 113.0 | 490.5 |
| W. Germany | 43,492 | 19.1 | 3,189 | 695.6 | 142.9 | 413.2 |
| Italy | 21,611 | 12.8 | 1,832 | 554.6 | 164.6 | — |
| Netherlands | 9,953 | 12.0 | 808 | 175.3 | 28.0 | 93.8 |
| Spain | 346 | 0.7 | 1,054 | 189.7 | 104.8 | 172.3 |
| United Kingdom | 21,618 | 12.9 | 1,937 | 351.5 | 125.0 | 235.6 |
| Africa | | | | | | |
| Egypt | 281 | 2.4 | 1,521 | 87.7 | 58.8 | 64.2 |
| Ethiopia | 34 | 3.8 | 86 | 11.1 | 0.4 | 7.7 |
| Ghana | 119 | 7.0 | 329 | 17.0 | 1.7 | 25.2 |
| Kenya | 141 | 8.3 | — | 24.7 | 1.5 | 14.8 |
| Morocco | 191 | 3.5 | 141 | 24.9 | 1.3 | 22.3 |
| Nigeria | 236 | 2.5 | — | 61.6 | 8.0 | 68.5 |
| South Africa | 354 | 2.0 | 788 | 156.2 | 14.5 | 111.0 |
| Zambia | 86 | 6.2 | 636 | 20.6 | 0.8 | 5.2 |
| Asia | | | | | | |
| India | 353 | 1.6 | 25,452 | 1,066.2 | 268.7 | 532.6 |
| Indonesia | 457 | 2.5 | 998 | 83.1 | 12.4 | 143.0 |
| Japan | — | — | 9,403 | 1,402.0 | 161.3 | 740.5 |
| Korea | 122 | 1.3 | — | 63.8 | 28.4 | 52.6 |
| Philippines | 195 | 4.9 | — | 93.4 | 7.4 | 20.7 |
| Thailand | 247 | 4.2 | 714 | 71.7 | 6.9 | 46.5 |

*These figures are not comparable due to differences in government accounting and health policies; they exclude social security and welfare payments and are converted at current exchange rates.

*Source:* United Nations *Statistical Yearbook.*

## EXHIBIT 3

**GNP, POPULATION, AND IMPORT REGULATIONS FOR SELECTED COUNTRIES, 1980**

| Country | GNP*<br>($ billions) | Population<br>(millions) | Tariff rate<br>applicable to<br>disinfectants<br>(*ad valorem*)<br>(percent) | Witholding or<br>remittance tax<br>on royalties<br>(percent) |
|---|---|---|---|---|
| **North America** | | | | |
| Canada | 260 | 24.0 | 7.5 (0 in bulk) | 25 |
| United States | 2,607 | 227.7 | 7 | 20 |
| **Latin America** | | | | |
| Argentina | 108 | 28.2 | 25 | 36 |
| Brazil | 250 | 121.3 | 37 | 25 |
| Colombia | 33 | 27.1 | 10 | 38 |
| Mexico | 186 | 69.3 | 10 | 42 |
| Venezuela | 59 | 15.0 | 80 | 50 |
| **Europe** | | | | |
| Belgium | 119 | 9.8 | 6 | 25 |
| France | 655 | 53.7 | 6 | 33.3 |
| W. Germany | 813 | 61.6 | 6 | 20 |
| Italy | 395 | 56.4 | 6 | 21 |
| Netherlands | 169 | 14.1 | 6 | 0 |
| Spain | 212 | 37.4 | 14 | 20 |
| United Kingdom | 534 | 55.9 | 6 | 27 |
| **Africa** | | | | |
| Egypt | 22 | 42.3 | 10 | 40 |
| Ethiopia | 4 | 31.0 | 0 | n.a. |
| Ghana | 5 | 11.5 | 10–25 | 50 |
| Kenya | 7 | 16.7 | 0 | 20 |
| Morocco | 18 | 20.1 | 30 (10 in bulk) | n.a. |
| Nigeria | 88 | 80.6 | 30 | 15 |
| South Africa | 80 | 28.6 | 20 (0 in bulk) | 15 |
| Zambia | 4 | 5.8 | 15 (0 in bulk) | n.a. |
| **Asia** | | | | |
| India | 163 | 663.6 | 100 | 52.5 |
| Indonesia | 72 | 146.4 | 30 | 20 |
| Japan | 1,040 | 116.8 | 10 | 20 |
| Korea | 62 | 56.0 | 20 | 25 |
| Philippines | 35 | 48.1 | 20 | 20 |
| Thailand | 33 | 46.5 | 30 | 25 |

*At current exchange rates.
n.a. = not available.

each doctor, nurse, or medical personnel represented a potential market of 10 to 15 cans per year.

The next step in arriving at some useful market estimates consisted of gathering data on the health care systems of the various countries under consideration. Mr. Foster selected those countries from which inquiries had been re-

ceived and added others of general interest in order to arrive at a cross-section that would allow applying his marketing criteria to a broad range of countries. Exhibit 2 (p. 189) presents, for those countries selected, various data such as number of medical personnel, hospitals, beds, and public health expenditures. He felt, however, that additional country information was needed to evaluate export potential more realistically. These data are given in Exhibit 3. Mr. Foster believed that by combining the results of the interviews with these data, a ranking system could be developed.

A major preoccupation of Mr. Foster was that no experience was available to translate U.S. usage rates to other areas of the world. As, and if, foreign business developed, it would become easier to assess potential demand in new markets, but at the present there were no assurances that even the U.S. rates were anywhere in line with reality.

## THE COLOMBIAN OFFER

In mid-March 1983, Sr. Carrera contacted Mr. Mills with a licensing proposal for PCI's products. Sr. Carrera claimed that his brief market test had been very encouraging and that, ". . . we believe that there is a good possibility of introducing [your products] in this market. However, initial sales volume will be limited given the need for extensive promotion of an institutional nature to acquaint hospitals and medical personnel with using this type of product." Furthermore, he felt that on quality and presentation PCI's line was "far superior to anything in the market at that time."

Unfortunately, Sr. Carrera continued, tariff duties were such (10 percent on most products under consideration) that importation of the cans would be expensive in terms of landed costs, although no estimates on transportation costs had been obtained. Sr. Carrera then suggested that both companies enter into an agreement for the production of PCI's product line by Bioquim under license from PCI.

One additional complication, according to Sr. Carrera, was the tendency of the Colombian government to be very strict on approving licensing agreements without show of need. Given that equivalent production was available in Colombia, the necessary approval for transferring funds arising out of royalty payments might not be obtainable. He continued: "Therefore, the only feasible alternative to operate would be

that we license your formulae and trademarks and agree to purchase our raw material needs from PCI. In this fashion, the corresponding royalties could be added to the export price of the raw materials." In his proposal, Sr. Carrera inquired whether PCI would be agreeable in principle to such an agreement. If so, he suggested a meeting either in Dallas or Bogota to work out the details.

## RECENT DEVELOPMENTS

Nearly six months had transpired since the last correspondence with Sr. Carrera. The domestic problems described above had occupied everyone at PCI to the exclusion of any international considerations. As the agreement with Franklyn Bros. appeared certain, the Colombian alternative reappeared in the company's view.

Mr. Mills was somewhat hesitant and confused. No one in PCI had any international experience on which he could rely. It appeared to him that the issue was more complex than just Colombia, since whatever PCI did in this instance might affect future operations elsewhere, or so he thought. For example, Franklyn had a Canadian subsidiary, as well as a network of relationships with European medical supply houses. However, their initial agreement was intended to cover only the United States and possibly Canada.

Mr. Foster had explained the relative merits and disadvantages of direct export, indirect exports through a combination export-manager (CEM) or the like, and licensing. Mr. Mills understood that the different alternatives were more or less appropriate depending on the level of foreign involvement of the firm. In fact, he had available some sample projections made by Foster based on various assumptions (see Exhibit 4). However, the dynamic nature of their business, its relative youth, and the lack of any significant experience made it impossible to predict what type of company they would be in a year's time, much less in three or four years. Nonetheless, Mr. Mills felt that a decision on Colombia could not be postponed any longer.

EXHIBIT 4

## COST AND REVENUE ESTIMATES FOR EXPORT BUSINESS

(Excerpted from Student's Report. All Figures Have Been Disguised.)

### A. Domestic costs

|  | Pathofoam ($ per case) | Pathospray ($ per case) | Pathokleen ($ per case) |
|---|---|---|---|
| U.S. manufacturer's price* | 8.00 | 10.50 | 12.50 |
| Variable costs |  |  |  |
| Manufacturing† | 3.45 | 5.17 | 6.90 |
| Packaging, etc. | 0.33 | 0.33 | 0.33 |
| Commission (8%)‡ | 0.64 | 0.84 | 0.96 |
| Contribution | 3.58 | 4.16 | 4.31 |

### B. Direct exports

In estimating landed prices to foreign locations, transportation, insurance, and additional packaging costs must be added to the base price figures. Tariffs would be calculated on the CIF value in order to obtain the final landed price. If direct exports were to be undertaken, the company would probably incur additional expenses in terms of administrative costs, travel, representation, telephone and telex, shipping, etc. These costs would have to be covered by export sales.

### C. Indirect exports

Preliminary contacts had indicated that employment of a combination export-management firm (CEM) could be arranged rather easily. These firms specialize in aiding smaller inexperienced manufacturers in developing export markets. As a general rule, CEMs handle all foreign marketing activities for the manufacturer. The latter simply packages the product according to certain instructions and ships it to a U.S. port location.

For these services, CEM's receive a fee that ranges from about 25% of gross sales to less than 10%. The actual figure depends on volume and length of association. A first-year contract is generally arranged at about a 20% level. As volume increases and economies of repetitive sales and scale set in, fees decline rapidly. The declining fee schedule is an attempt on the part of the CEM to discourage the manufacturer from going on its own as it gains international experience and as volume expands.

### D. Licensing

A normal licensing agreement would call for the provision of technical information and assistance in return for a fixed fee on sales. This fee may vary between 1 and 5 percent of sales, but it is commonly set at 2 to 3. There are, of course, certain costs involved in providing the necessary technical assistance, travel, supervision time, training, and so on.

Given the restrictions prevailing in Colombia, Sr. Carrera had suggested including the licensing fees in the raw material transfer price. Costs and yields were as follows:

|  | Pathofoam | Pathospray | Pathokleen |
|---|---|---|---|
| Raw materials' cost to Patho-Control ($/gal.) | 3.25 | 3.20 | 3.35 |
| Yield (cases/gal.) | 2.32 | 2.06 | 0.92 |
| Raw material cost per case ($) | 1.40 | 1.55 | 3.64 |
| Raw material cost as percent of manufacturing costs | 40.5 | 30 | 52.7 |

*Domestic prices varied with quantities ordered according to the following discount schedule: 10–24 cases—5%; 25–49 cases—10%; 50–99 cases—15%; 100 or more—20%.

†Raw materials represent about 40% of manufacturing costs (see section on licensing below). The remaining 60% includes labor, overhead charges, and profit accrued to the contract filler.

‡The local distributor, Franklyn, received a commission which varied with sales. At the time, it averaged 8%. Of course, this commission only applied to U.S. and Canadian (?) sales.

## Colombia—Selected Country Data

# COLOMBIA

*RELEASED OCTOBER 1983*

---

**CURRENCY** *The peso, subject to a crawling-peg system of minidevaluations, with an exchange rate of P84:$1 in October 1983.*

**SEE ALSO** *Latin America Introduction for Ancom-wide Rules, Basic Market Statistics and Comparative Taxation.*

---

### In the Past Twelve Months

•President Belisario Betancur Cuartas maintained widespread popularity despite the worst recession in 50 years. Betancur's amnesty program for guerrilla factions met limited success, and sporadic activity by these groups will continue (1.01).

•In 1982, GDP grew by a bleak 1.4%, while inflation remained high at 24.5%. The slumping industrial sector declined by 1.1%, and agricultural output fell for only the second time in 30 years (1.03).

•The Colombian peso was devalued by 19% vis-a-vis the US dollar during 1982 and by another 20% during first-half 1983 (1.04).

•To reduce both the fiscal deficit and dependence on central government revenue transfers, the government enacted a 1983 tax reform that will grant more autonomy to states and municipalities for setting taxes. To combat tax evasion, the reform increased the presumptive tax (whereby individuals and corporations are taxed on assumed revenues stemming from known assets at year-end) to 7% in 1984 and 8% in 1985 (8.01).

•In January 1983, the Monetary Board decided to eliminate the special reserve requirement by May. The move should help to stimulate the economy (11.01).

•The trend toward tariff liberalization has been slowed, with the government hiking import duties on thousands of products (13.03).

### In the Next Twelve Months

•Betancur's ability to attract support from outside his party should enable him to effectively reach agreements with the legislature on his most important policies (1.01).

•The government will focus on the construction industry to stimulate growth and employment during the next several years. Growth in GDP is targeted at 2.5%, and inflation should decline slightly (1.03).

•The Colombian peso will continue to be devalued in order to narrow the trade deficit. Foreign debt will grow significantly, reaching an estimated public- and private-sector debt of $14.65 billion in 1985 (1.04).

•Higher tariffs and nontariff barriers will become more prevalent as the government attempts to both slow import growth and protect domestic industries (13.02).

---

● ● ● ● ● ● ● ● ● ● ● ● ● ● ● ● ● ● ● ● ● ● ● ● ● ● ● ● ● ● ●

## 5.00 PRICE CONTROLS

The government's overall philosophy is to allow market forces to determine most price levels, and only a limited number of goods and services are regulated. However, the authorities are policing the price controls now in effect more strictly and could increase the number of products subject to controls if inflation does not abate.

A total of 36 products, all of which strongly influence the cost of living, are under direct control. They include beer and soft drinks, certain food items, dry-cell batteries, light bulbs, matches, cigarettes, a wide range of pharmaceuticals, cement, fertilizers, tires, metal and glass containers, and bottle caps. A freeze on urban housing rents was imposed in 1977, but an annual adjustment of 10% is now permitted. Also, automotive replacement products and spare parts are subject to a special and complex control system.

In 1979, the government tried a new tack in enforcing its price controls. It involved tying price-increase approvals to a formal commitment by the recipient firms to invest a percentage of sales in related or unrelated sectors. Such accords were negotiated with manufacturers of beer and soft drinks; the beer industry has agreed to invest up to 5% of its 1979 sales in new industrial expansion in exchange for a 15% price increase. However, there have been no subsequent cases in which this practice has been followed, and most firms believe the measure was temporary and limited in scope.

The Division of Control and Vigilance, under the Ministry of Development's Superintendency of Industry and Commerce (SIC), is in charge of price control enforcement. However, the actual establishment of prices for new products and price changes for products already under control is decentralized. For instance, the Ministry of Public Health is responsible for pharmaceuticals and the Ministry of Development for most other manufactures. Officials of the pertinent ministry first review the company's application, which should always include a detailed cost study.

There is no deadline on decisions from the ministries involved, and companies' prime complaint about the price control system stems from this unlimited review period. Another difficulty is the extensive paperwork; besides providing the relevant ministry with detailed price request applications and support studies, companies must give copies to the SIC. The aim is to centralize all information dealing with price movement in one agency, so as to help the SIC fulfill its watchdog function.

Controls are set at the producer level if there are few manufacturers, at the distribution level through maximum markups if distribution is highly concentrated and at the retail level if both production and distribution are concentrated. Several factors contribute to the determination of allowable price levels, including the comparative efficiency of production, the normal profitability of the industry in terms of return on assets, the ratio of profits to sales, the level of taxation, the ratio of turnover to capital, and the ratio of working capital to fixed assets. On a sectorial basis, the pharmaceutical and food industries will continue to encounter the greatest difficulty in obtaining adequate price relief.

Some 90% of the drugs produced in Colombia are subject to price controls. In August 1980, pharmaceutical firms were allowed a 20% price increase on 8,500 products in exchange for agreeing to withdraw approximately 3,000 other drugs from the market for reformulating purposes. In February 1981, another price adjustment was granted; this, though, was authorized only for laboratories that could prove that their costs had increased enough to warrant price relief. The ceiling for the price hike was set at 20%, and most authorizations fell below that mark.

In April 1983, the government granted another 20% price increase, and each laboratory was allowed to set hikes up to the limit. In addition, the government authorized price increases for various other products, including lightbulbs, cigarettes, urban and intercity transportation and fuels. In a related policy, the administration determined in Decree 3466 that all manufacturers and importers must register their products with the Superintendent of Commerce and Industry in order to inform the public about product guarantees.

## 6.00 LICENSING

**6.01 General.** Licensing is a method favored by many foreign firms for doing business in Colombia, largely because Ancom's foreign investment regulations make direct investment less attractive. Even if the constraints on licensing agreements become stricter, many companies will continue to license Colombian firms to maintain their market position.

**6.02 Patent and trademark protection.** Industrial property rights are protected under Art. 568 of the 1972 Commercial Code. The courts mete out stern penalties for infringement, including heavy fines, awards for damages and removal of machinery used to produce the goods from the defendant's premises. In some cases, the goods in question may be impounded, or the defendant may be prohibited from promoting the products until the matter is resolved. There are strict rules for obtaining patents to cover drug-manufacturing processes as well as working requirements and provisions governing compulsory licensing; these are detailed in the box.

When Stanley Works (US) filed an infringement claim against a local firm, the matter was directed to the Institute of Foreign Trade (Incomex). Incomex transferred the products under dispute (tape rules) from their free import status to the list of goods that require prior import licenses.

A serious obstacle to obtaining patents was removed in 1976. The Superintendency of Industry and Commerce (SIC) of the Ministry of Development had ruled that, under the Commercial Code, a patent was invalid if it was registered first in another country. In 1976, the ministry softened this stance in Resolution 391. It indicated that many applications for confirmation patents presented before the code's enactment in 1972 would be bound by Colombia's 1925 industrial property legislation, which does not stipulate that prior registration elsewhere results in the invalidity of a subsequent patent application in Colom-

# Patents and Trademarks In Colombia

**Conventions.** Pan American Convention 1929–69.

**Basic laws.** Industrial Property Act of 1925, amended 1931; Commercial Code 1972 and Decree-Law 1234, 1972; Law 14, 1979.

## PATENTS

**Types and duration.** Original patent valid for eight years from application date, renewable for four more years if it can be demonstrated that patent is being worked in Colombia. (Such working must be during the year preceding renewal.)

**Novelty.** Not sufficiently known in Colombia and abroad to be performed.

**Unpatentable** are creations not highly inventive or not having a significant effect on industry. For drugs, food and beverages, only process is patentable, and only if the process is used in Colombia within a year of application and if, as a result, a sufficient quantity of the product is supplied to the local market at a reasonable price. Also unpatentable are animal or vegetable varieties or strains and inventions contrary to health, hygiene, public security or morality.

**Application procedure.** Application must be made to the Office of Industrial Property of the Superintendency of Industry and Commerce. The application must include the name and address of the inventor and applicant; name of the invention; complete description of the invention, including drawings; statements as to its scope and industrial application; and an extract describing the invention for publication in the *Official Gazette*. Incomplete applications may be filed, as long as the application is completed within six months. Patents registered abroad must be registered in Colombia within six months of their prior registration; otherwise, they are invalid in Colombia.

After an application has been submitted, it is open to inspection, and the opposition has up to 70 days to present observations and objections. Applicant has 30 days to respond. Decision is made by judicial procedure. Any patent application may be examined and a copy made by anyone who wishes to do so.

**Examination procedure.** Once an application has been completed (and if there is no opposition), it is examined for novelty and usefulness. If these reports are positive, the patent is granted, but without guarantee as to novelty or usefulness.

**Fees.** Filing fees and stamps, P5,000; issuance fees and stamps, P3,000; renewal fees and stamps, P6,000.

**Compulsory licensing.** Anyone can apply for a compulsory license if a patent is not worked within four years after application or three years after granting (whichever is later); if working is suspended for a year or does not satisfy local demands as to quality, quantity or price; or if the patentee is unwilling to enter a licensing agreement on reasonable terms. Compulsory licensing may also be required in matters relating to public health or economic development, or if a product's price becomes abnormally high. Compulsory licenses are never exclusive.

## TRADEMARKS

**Duration.** Ten years from application, renewable for five-year periods.

**Legal effect.** Registration confers proprietary rights, but the uninterrupted use of a mark for three years confers the same rights as registration.

**Unregistrable.** Marks that portray the nature or the function of the product or that consist solely of a product's type, origin, quality, etc.; common names used to describe products; marks that are not distinctive, that imitate registered marks used or known in Colombia or another country or that are the same as marks withdrawn in the last three years; marks contrary to public morals or security; new marks containing foreign words or names (6.03), and signs and slogans of states or public organizations.

**Procedure.** Application is necessary for each class of goods (there are 34 in accordance with international classification) for which protection is sought. Application (including description in Spanish, power of attorney legalized by Colombian consul and five facsimiles) should be sent to the Office of Industrial Property. Next steps are examination as to registrability and publication in the *Gaceta de la Propriedad Industrial*. Opposition is due within 30 working days; if opposition, a decision is handed down by the courts.

**Fees.** Application fees and stamps P1,500; fees and stamps for renewal P1,500.

## INDUSTRIAL DESIGNS AND MODELS

Protection can be obtained for the same terms as patents; fees and stamps for application are P1,800; fees and stamps for renewal are P710. Novelty examination is not required.

---

bia. The ministry did let stand the code's requirement that to be accepted in Colombia a patent must be registered in the country within six months of its registry elsewhere. This requirement now applies to all patent requests submitted since the 1972 code went into effect.

Law 14 of 1979 restricts the use of foreign words in the names of products or companies and forbids the registration of new trademarks that contain foreign words. (Products sold under existing, untranslatable trademark names must now carry the proper pronunciation in parentheses; this would presumably be written phonetically.) The law's scope is limited, and in practice it is rarely enforced. Names, trademarks, public displays and advertisements of companies and products need not be changed to Spanish if they are proper names, nor must foreign industrial names that are either untranslatable or that would be damaged by a change because of the loss of goodwill that might result. Other foreign terms used commercially, however, must be translated. Municipal authorities are responsible for notifying firms that violate the law in writing, and for giving them reasonable time to comply. The ban on foreign words is aimed at preserving the Spanish language and protecting consumers.

**6.03 Legal and administrative limitations on licensing.** Companies must register all patent, trademark and similar agreements with the Exchange Office of the central bank to qualify for remittance rights. All such contracts must be approved by an interdepartmental Royalties Committee (Comite de Regalias), whether or not remittances are to be made abroad. The Royalties Committee, headed by the Minister of Development, makes detailed technical, legal and economic studies of each proposed contract and authorizes or denies registration of new and existing contracts, according to their importance to national development and the royalty rate requested. Committee officials commonly inspect the facility that will use the proposed technology.

The Royalties Committee must approve all contract requests, including those for modifications and extensions of existing contracts. Requests should be accompanied by the following: (1) a copy of the contract in Spanish, or an official translation, if warranted (for extensions, a duly authenticated photostatic copy of the original contract and accompanying modifications must be presented); (2) the STC's application form, properly filled out; and (3) the name of the legal representative, if one has been designated. Applications for extensions of existing contracts must be submitted at least three months prior to the expiration date.

The entire review should take no more than 45 days, according to official sources, but it usually takes longer. Royalties may not be paid in pesos if registration is denied by the Royalties

Committee. If an application is approved but the committee wants lower royalty payments, the difference between the requested and approved amounts may not be paid in pesos.

A 1972 law spells out the clauses in a licensing agreement that will not be accepted by the Royalties Committee. The agreement may not require the licensee to purchase equipment, raw materials or other know-how from a specified source; empower the licensor to set sale or resale prices; limit the licensee either in the use of competitive technology or in its plans to export; insist that the licensee pay royalties for trademarks or patents not utilized; or bind the licensee to minimum annual payments.

**6.04 Royalty and fee patterns.** Payments are ruled on by the Royalties Committee, whose decisions conform to no fixed regulations, but exports were the key to favorable terms. Two US cosmetics manufacturers in Medellin have been granted 7.5% royalties on products earmarked for export and 5% for those sold in the Colombian market; one contract is for two years, the other for one. A 2.5% payment for three years was authorized for a UK drug manufacturer that provides technical assistance to its Bogota-based operation, but the royalty was limited to the firm's export production. One US textile maker won a three-year contract providing for royalties of 3% on exports and 2% on domestic sales.

The terms of a few companies' original applications underwent some adjustments in 1980. A Brazilian company in the electrical equipment sector requested a 2.5% royalty plus a $3,000 payment for a trademark and technical assistance package. The final ruling came through with only a 2% royalty, and the additional payment was dropped. Another adjustment involved a European firm that accepted a 0.5% royalty instead of a 1% payment on a technical-assistance contract, but most applications came through essentially intact.

Partial data available for 1983 largely follow the wide-ranging approval pattern observed previously. Generally, the following rates are adhered to: automotive, 2.5% to 3.4% (Mazda has recently been allowed the latter rate); foodstuffs, 4% above net sales; capital goods, 2–3%; cosmetics, 4%; hotels, up to 20% above gross sales.

Some firms are finding ways to obtain extra payment via non-royalty-related routes. One food-processing firm that has been denied royalty payments since 1971 on the grounds that its technology is available in Colombia makes up the difference through technical-service fees ruled on by the central bank.

Companies frequently complain about the short duration of contracts. Capital-goods producers, who need longer periods to set up production, feel particularly vulnerable on this account. One US firm that recently asked for a 10-year term was forced to settle for five. The authorities, however, are usually willing to renegotiate at the end of contract terms.

In cases in which a trademark forms part of a broader contract involving technical assistance or know-how, linkage with a local trademark is usually not required. If a linked trademark is required, it is intended to ensure the local user's continued market share beyond the life of the contract. This protection includes export markets as well.

The government rejects contracts that call for royalties for production of goods already manufactured in Colombia without payment of royalties (e.g. televisions), although it will permit payments for know-how in such cases. It also will not approve royalty payments to parent firms that own 100% of the Colombian licensee's equity. Even payments to a foreign firm with a smaller equity share in the Colombian venture are discouraged. (These practices are in accordance with Ancom rules.) In the case of a 100% Colombian-owned enterprise, the royalty or other payment should represent the "price" of the technology distributed over the years of payment.

The government is reluctant to approve disclosure fees if royalties are also being paid. The same is true of fees for drawings. However, engineering supervisory fees are normally permitted.

## 7.00 REMITTABILITY OF FUNDS

**7.01 Exchange controls.** The basic legislation in this field was codified in Decree-Law 444 of March 22, 1967, and amended by Decree-Law 688 of April 20, 1967, Decree-Law 1900 of Sept. 15, 1973 and Decree-Law 170 of January 1977 (the last put Ancom's Decision 24 into effect in Colombia). All foreign exchange operations are subject to control.

Exchange policies are set by the Monetary Board, headed by the Minister of Finance and comprising the Ministers of Development and Agriculture, the directors of Planeacion and Incomex and the president of the central bank. The board is aided by two nonvoting monetary experts. The Monetary Board is authorized to draw up a foreign exchange budget periodically; however, in recent years it has not done so. Within this budget, it can establish priorities for the use of foreign exchange after setting aside enough to cover central bank obligations and to service the public foreign debt. The central bank implements and enforces the board's decisions. Incoming foreign equity and loan capital as well as reinvested earnings must be registered with the Exchange Office of the central bank.

Regulations implemented in 1977 require that companies use dollar-denominated exchange certificates (*certificados de cambio*), issued by the central bank and authorized credit institutions, when buying or selling foreign currencies. If a firm in Colombia receives payment in a foreign currency, it cannot legally convert the funds directly into pesos but must use the funds to purchase the certificates at officially quoted exchange rates.

An active open market for the certificates exists on the Bogota stock exchange, and many companies use their bankers or stockbrokers to sell certificates whose prices rise as the instrument approaches maturity. When firms want to buy foreign currencies, they reverse the process, purchasing certificates on the exchange and turning them in to the central bank on maturity for conversion into the appropriate currency. Thus, in the absence of exchange markets, much of the actual foreign exchange trading in Colombia is done on the stock market.

In 1980, the authorities offered some limited exchange control relief. Companies may open foreign-currency accounts to finance sending technicians and professional personnel abroad. In addition, they may pay stipends and fees outside the country in foreign currency. Regulations were also lifted from medical, food and communications expenses, payments to students abroad, the $6,000 limit for travelers, subscriptions to publications and expenses for books. In addition, the Monetary Board abolished the 20% reserve requirement formerly imposed on banks' foreign exchange accounts.

**7.02 Transfer of profits and dividends.** Under Ancom Decision 103 (incorporated into Colombian Decree-Law 170 of January 1977), annual remittances of dividends and profits are limited to 20% of the registered capital base. However, the government has recently raised the allowable remittance rate for dividends to 20% of registered capital plus the US prime rate for investments made after end-August 1983. (The mining, petroleum, natural gas and forestry sectors have been exempt from this requirement since 1973, and in April 1981 companies providing technical services linked to mining exploration or the establishment of a mining complex were added to this list. In addition, under Ancom's Decision 169, foreign investors participating in an Andean multinational company may remit 100% of profits.) Other investments regarded favorably include many types of manufacturing, agriculture and tourism. Higher remittances may be negotiated on an ad hoc basis with Planeacion (e.g. these have been granted to investments in the tourist industry), but for the most part the government maintains the 20% ceiling.

If a firm remits less than 20% in a given year, the difference can be made up in later years. Companies may, without prior authorization, set up special reserve funds to boost their registered capital bases; the amount thus reinvested annually is limited to 7% of the firm's capital.

Because of the remittance ceiling, many companies have blocked funds ("limbo capital") that they have invested in the intercorporate call loan market, lending mostly to foreign-owned firms that have parent guarantees. Under Resolution 29, implemented at end-1978, foreign companies may capitalize the limbo funds, provided that they invest 50% in Instituto de Fomento Industrial (IFI) bonds. Although the bond terms are not attractive (12% annual interest, five years' maturity), some investors interpreted the government's move as a harbinger of a more flexible attitude. Many firms are forgoing the IFI option and continuing to utilize their blocked funds in other ways, such as to finance working capital needs, company-to-company loans and real estate purchases. Xerox, for instance, bought a building a few years ago to avoid paying high rents for office space in Bogota. One corporate planner pointed out that the blocked funds will be capitalized at the prevailing exchange rate, not at the rate in effect when the funds were first accumulated. As a result, their capitalization may not substantially increase the remittance base of some companies.

During 1979, two firms took advantage of the IFI mechanism. International Paper invested P9.5 million, and Chrysler Colmotores (now owned by General Motors) purchased P225 million worth of IFI bonds. Later in 1979, Colmotores sold P40 million of its bond holdings at a P15 million loss and in January 1980 made another sale worth P45 million at an additional P14 million loss. In both cases, Colmotores worked out a buy-back agreement to repurchase the bonds after six months at the

## Corporate Taxation in Colombia, 1983

The following example indicates the aggregate burden of income and related taxes on a wholly foreign-owned Colombian corporation with net assets of P20 million that earned taxable income in 1982 of P4 million and declared a dividend of P1 million.

|  | **(P'000s)** |
|---|---|
| (1) Taxable income ...................................... | 4,000 |
| (2) Corporate income tax: 40% of (1) ...................... | 1,600 |
| (3) Net income after corporate tax ........................ | 2,400 |
| (4) Withholding tax on dividends (20% of P1 million) .................................... | 200 |
| (5) Total taxes ......................................... | 1,800 |
| (6) Total tax burden as % of taxable income* ................... | 45% |

* For firms that are more than 51% locally owned, a 24.4% discount on tax payable is available. This would bring the tax burden for a firm with the same assets and income as in the above example to 34%.

original selling price plus accumulated interest. In 1981, Olivetti, Chiclets Adamas and Colgate Palmolive all used the IFI mechanism. Companies purchasing IFI bonds in 1982 included Coca-Cola, Mobil, Thomas de la Rue and Nestle.

**7.03 Transfer of interest.** Payment of interest or principal on loans from abroad must be according to the terms stated in the original loan contract; otherwise, firms must obtain prior authorization from the Monetary Board and the Exchange Office. Exchange certificates are available at the prevailing rate.

**7.04 Transfer of royalties and fees.** Payment of royalties and related fees can usually be made without difficulty on agreements approved by the Royalties Committee and registered with the Exchange Office (6.03).

**7.05 Repatriation of capital.** The total amount of repatriated capital may not exceed the net value of the foreign investment (including authorized reinvestment), as registered with the Exchange Office.

**7.06 Repayment of principal.** Colombia imposes no restrictions on the repayment of loans that have been properly registered (see also 7.03). However, the Monetary Board regulates the terms, interest rates and general conditions of all external loans (11.01).

**7.07 Guarantees against inconvertibility.** None.

• • • • • • • • • • • • • • • • • • • • • • • • • • • • • • • • • • •

**8.11 Taxes on royalties and fees.** Royalties and technical-assistance fees of all types are taxed as normal income to the recipient. Such payments also face a 40% withholding tax, which may be credited against total income tax due. If the recipient has no agent or permanent establishment in Colombia, the withholding tax is considered final. Royalties paid to foreign companies face an additional 12% remittance tax, withheld at source.

Branches and foreign-controlled subsidiaries are not allowed to deduct technical assistance payments made to headquarter offices of offices outside Colombia. However, if the recipient has no legal residence in Colombia and is not required to be legally represented in the country, and if it is determined by the authorities that the technical services in question are not available in Colombia, the technical assistance payments are not subject to the 40% withholding tax or the 12% remittance tax.

• • • • • • • • • • • • • • • • • • • • • • • • • • • • • •

## 13.00 FOREIGN TRADE

**13.01 General.** In the past few years, Western Europe as a whole has displaced the US as Colombia's principal export market. Of the close to $3 billion generated by exports in 1982, Western European markets took 39.4%, while the US accounted for 23.24%; the Ancom countries and Japan took 16.5% and 4.23%, respectively. Eastern European countries accounted for 3.01% of Colombia's exports.

Colombia imported $6.1 billion worth of goods in 1982. The US supplied the largest share at 33.73%, followed by the EEC at 14.48% and the Ancom group with 13.28%. Japan contributed 9.09% of Colombia's imports.

Colombia is a good export base. The government fosters exports through incentives programs (13.06) and financial assistance (13.08). Foreign-owned firms are required to export a percentage of their output (3.02).

**13.02 Import controls.** The tendency toward trade liberalization has ground to a halt under the Betancur government. The administration has increased the number of goods requiring import licenses and raised tariffs by an average 20% in 1982 and by another 10% in June 1983 for some 2,000 products. The government is also combating smuggling and capital flight.

In addition, the government has introduced a tougher import payment schedule to help curb excess liquidity. The maximum payment terms, decreed in Monetary Resolution 45 of 1979, are five months for raw materials and consumer goods (extended to six months in early 1982), five years for capital goods imported under a global license and three years for other capital goods. Tough financial penalties are levied for noncompliance.

Moreover, prior import deposits are required before a foreign exchange license will be granted (13.04). Some manufacturers complain that the authorities respond to applications by granting most, but not all, of the licenses needed for parts and components, and that much persuasion is then necessary to get the one or two missing licenses—without which all the others may be useless. One company received an import permit for only 60% of the essential raw materials it required. The authorities claimed the company could obtain the remaining 40% locally if it "really looked around for it." On the other hand, the time required to get a license has been shortened; it now averages one to two weeks.

Importers receive nonnegotiable, non-interest-bearing certificates (*titulos de consignacion para la obtencion de licencias de cambio*) upon payment of the deposit. The certificates can in turn be used to cancel the obligation for which the foreign exchange license is sought.

Payment for imports is made through the exchange certificate market (7.01). The certificates are issued by the central bank and are freely negotiable among exporters, importers and commercial banks.

Several imports are subject to quotas. They include raw materials such as cocoa beans, natural rubber, raw cotton, cotton yarn and thread, uncombed wool, processed zinc, edible oils and oleaginous materials. In addition, importers must purchase a fixed percentage of similar local products. Vegetable oils are imported by the Instituto de Mercadeo Agricola (IDEMA), and IDEMA sometimes buys other foreign agricultural products to regulate local supply. There are no restrictions on the import of secondhand equipment.

**13.03 Tariffs and import taxes.** Colombia adheres to the NABALALC and Nabandina tariff nomenclatures. A few tariffs are prohibitively high, but manufactured goods as a whole face rates of about 25–30%. A preferential tariff system covers nearly 700 necessities traded between Peru and Colombia. In 1981, Colombia formalized its membership in GATT.

The present government has reversed a trend toward import liberalization and has raised import duties on thousands of products. The objectives of the administration's policy are to protect domestic producers, increase international reserves and obtain revenues through import tariffs in order to finance and stimulate exports. Nonetheless, an effort is made to adhere to the Ancom agreements.

The new tariff policy also brings an increase in the maximum automobile tariff from 150% to 180%, with the average duty being about 30%.

Products that bear low duties include farm and road-building machinery, engines, chemicals and newsprint. Leather products, wood and nonessentials carry high rates. Duties are almost all ad valorem, and value is calculated according to the average exchange rate in the certificate market during the preceding month.

Virtually all imports are subject to two additional ad valorem taxes: one to support the Export Promotion Fund (5% of c.i.f. value) and the other for the government's general expenditures (1.5% of the duty payable). LAIA and Ancom goods are exempt. Consular duties of 1.2% of the net f.o.b. value of the goods apply to all imports but may be dropped in the future. Finally, special taxes are levied on such goods as cigarettes, cotton, wheat and playing cards. Sales tax is also charged (8.14); however, imports incorporated into goods destined for export are exempt from such taxes (13.06).

When packaged together, goods subject to different rates are assessed at the highest applicable rate. Therefore, exporters often package different types of goods separately when shipping to Colombia.

**13.04 Nontariff barriers.** In addition to higher tariffs, it is expected that nontariff barriers will be used more frequently in Colombia. Although the prior import deposit law was gradually trimmed and subsequently eliminated, it may be restored as an import control.

In addition, all companies and individuals must now make a deposit *before* they can obtain foreign exchange licenses for payments abroad. The only overseas payments exempt from this requirement are import shipping charges, which are subject to a special regime. Under Monetary Board Resolution 19 of 1979, the additional deposit, which is made in local currency, must equal 95% of import value.

Foreign suppliers have faced greater competition from local firms in bidding for public-sector purchases (including purchases by partially state-owned ventures) since the "Buy Colombian" Decree 2248 was passed in 1973. This law gives Colombian companies various advantages, including permission to import duty-free any goods needed to meet a public-sector contract. The decree states that, for purposes of a public-sector tender, participating producers are considered foreign if the cost of their imported raw materials and/or intermediate products exceeds 50% of the value of foreign suppliers' bids. In assessing cost, public-sector purchasers must add to the price of foreign suppliers' products the costs of transportation, financing, insurance, import duties, etc. In contrast, when calculating the true cost of locally made products, they must subtract the amount of local sales tax.

Additional legislation was passed in 1983 to help domestic producers. Decree 222/83 gives the government the right to modify contracts if warranted in the public interest, and also states that all insurance contracts of less than P120 million must be arranged through La Previsora, the state insurance company.

Colombian authorities closely monitor imports by state entities and government agencies. In January 1978, a local-content formula was devised to guide state agencies in determining when a product is "locally manufactured." (A local product is one with more than 50% local value added.) State concerns are required to give preference to local producers over foreign manufacturers when purchasing.

Imported goods that fail to meet quality and technical standards established for comparable local products are banned. Mining and petroleum companies may not import goods (including machinery and equipment) if Colombian producers can provide items of equivalent quality by a specific delivery time; however, the government sometimes grants exceptions.

To lessen delays in customs procedures, in 1979 the government issued a decree requiring that customs officials and importers adhere to strict deadlines. The state-owned port agency, Empresa Puertos de Colombia, must notify customs in writing within 24 hours of the quantity, condition and location of landed merchandise. Importers must present the import manifest to customs within 12 working days. Customs, in turn, must endorse the manifest or return it to the importer for corrections and additions within 24 hours. Once the Verification Division has approved the manifest, it must be cleared by the other customs departments within eight working days. Importers may get their merchandise out of customs even sooner—within two days—without satisfying all customs requirements if they certify they will fulfill them subsequently and make a prior deposit toward the import duties due. If there is disagreement on merchandise valuation and duties owed, customs must resolve such questions within 60 days; meanwhile, the merchandise can be released if the importer makes an additional refundable deposit. Importers were given more time to appeal customs decisions. Lastly, duties may be paid to any of the official banks, so that opportunities for fraud have been reduced.

Under Law 14 of 1979, all products sold in Colombia, whether manufactured locally or abroad, must bear a label stating where they were produced, and any literature accompanying products sold locally must be in Spanish.

# Copperweld Inc.

Throughout the latter half of 1979 and the early months of 1980, Copperweld, an American steel company, was actively considering an investment proposal for a steel tube producing plant in Europe. Although Copperweld already had some sales in Europe of the type of tubes it intended to fabricate at the new site, the company had no direct operating experience outside the United States. Evaluations of the threats and opportunities presented by the proposed investment was consequently a particularly challenging task for the company's Board and its management. This case describes the issues confronting those ultimately responsible for committing some $40 million to the investment.

## EARLY HISTORY

The history of the Copperweld corporation dated back to the early twentieth century when a plant was established to produce conductors for electrical transmission. These conductors were made by dipping hot steel bars into molten copper and then drawing down the resulting composite bi-metallic bar (hence the company name) to the required diameter. In some cases the final cable was no larger than a human hair, but more frequently they were larger in size and intended for use as power cables.

By the 1930s the company integrated backward by entering production of special steel bars. Most of these bars, but not all of the grades made, were an input to the manufacture of electrical cable. A second possible outlet for steel bars was the manufacture of seamless tubes, and Copperweld diversified further in the 1950s by purchasing its major customer, the Ohio Seamless Tube Company (OST). A second tube company, Regal Tube of Chicago, was purchased later in 1972.

By 1980, the Copperweld company, with headquarters in Pittsburgh, Pennsylvania, had three main operating groups: Copperweld Bi-metallics, Copperweld Steel Company, and Copperweld Tubes. Although Bi-metallics had developed some sales overseas and was involved in a joint venture in Japan, steel and tube sales were almost exclusively oriented toward

This case was prepared by Mr. Martin Flash under the direction of Professor José de la Torre at the European Institute of Business Administration (INSEAD), Fontainebleau, France. The generous cooperation of Copperweld Corporation and its senior executives is gratefully acknowledged. Certain figures have been disguised to protect their confidential nature. © INSEAD, 1984.

the American market. The company was run by a central corporate leadership responsible essentially for financial, control, and personnel functions. Each of the company's various production facilities was run as a profit center, retaining its separate identity. Within the Tube group, OST and Regal operated in this way, and sales and marketing for both facilities were handled by another profit center, the Copperweld Tubing Group. Exhibit 1 summarizes corporate financial data for recent years.

## THE TUBE DIVISION

The Ohio Seamless Tube Company, founded in 1890 in Shelby, Ohio, originally made its tubes from hollow billets imported from Sweden. These billets were then drawn down to required size. (See the next section for a description of all main processes and products.) By the end of the century, the business had expanded into other drawn seamless products such as gun barrels and rotors, and OST was considered a world leader in seamless tube manufacture. The *Kitty Hawk,* the Wright brothers' aeroplane which first flew in 1903, was made partially with OST tube as was Charles Lindbergh's *Spirit of St. Louis* in its historic flight across the Atlantic in 1927.

During the next three decades, OST diversified its production into tubes made of different steel alloys and into high-pressure applications. In 1937, OST became the first American manufacturer of electrically welded tube. Sales of welded tube began to complement those of seamless tube, and research and development efforts were increasingly directed toward an experimental variant of welded tube achieved by drawing called the drawn over mandril (DOM) tube. Research on this process had started in 1938 but was discontinued during the war.

In 1952, when OST was acquired by Copperweld, initial investments were devoted to improving seamless production. Soon thereafter, however, R&D in DOM production was reinstated, and commercial quantities were produced after 1961. By 1968, demand for welded tube in the company exceeded for the first time that for seamless. Continued growth in demand for DOM

tube persuaded Copperweld management to erect a second plant at Shelby exclusively for DOM production. When this plant came on stream in 1978, total annual capacity at Shelby was 60,000 tons of seamless and 185,000 tons of welded tube (approximately two thirds in DOM tube), with tube sizes ranging from ½-inch to 12¾-inch outside diameters, and from 0.028-inch to 0.625-inch wall thickness.[1]

Regal Tube Company in Chicago was founded in 1946 and was a pioneer in heavy welded structural tubes. When acquired by Copperweld in 1972, Regal expanded into DOM through additional investment. Its emphasis, however, remained on the heavy end of tubing (large diameter, and/or thick walls), Regal possessing one of the world's biggest drawbenches at 800,000 pounds of pull. Its annual capacity was 120,000 tons of structural tube and 45,000 tons of DOM tube in sizes from 4 to 12 inches and wall thickness up to 0.58 inch.

## TECHNOLOGY AND PRODUCTS

Most steel products could be made by starting from any one of three basic forms:

- *Slabs* were large rectangular shapes which were rolled to make flat products such as steel sheet, steel strip, or shipbuilding plates. Any of these products could then be rolled into tubes.
- *Blooms* consisted of heavy bar-shaped forms which were generally rolled into large structural (i.e., load carrying) shapes such as beams.
- *Billets* were lighter, round forms which were rolled into smaller products such as bars, rods, and wire, or which could be pierced and rolled to make tube.

A diagram of the principal steel-product-making processes can be found in Exhibit 2. From the above it can be seen that tubes were made by two distinct processes; either by piercing billets to make seamless tube or by bending

---

[1]The steel industry was essentially an "inch" industry, although conversion to the metric system was under way in many areas; 1 inch = 2.54 centimeters.

## EXHIBIT 1

### CORPORATE FINANCIAL PERFORMANCE, 1969–1978

| Year ended | Gross revenues ($ million) | Net income* ($ thousand) | Equity† ($ thousand) | Common shares (thousand) | Per common share ($) Earnings* | Dividend | Price range High | Low | Book value | Return on equity† (%) |
|---|---|---|---|---|---|---|---|---|---|---|
| 1978‡ | 421.4 | 11,276 | 136,539 | 5,713 | 2.00 | 1.24 | 22½ | 16¼ | 23.90 | 8.3 |
| 1977 | 349.0 | 16,307 | 130,640 | 5,615 | 2.91 | 1.20 | 25¾ | 17½ | 23.16 | 12.5 |
| 1976 | 298.5 | 18,904 | 120,716 | 5,548 | 3.39 | 1.20 | 26½ | 18⅜ | 21.58 | 15.7 |
| 1975 | 283.0 | 18,435 | 107,097 | 5,216 | 3.32 | .943 | 21 1/16 | 9⅝ | 19.56 | 17.2 |
| 1974 | 321.9 | 16,799 | 89,641 | 5,167 | 3.06 | .786 | 13⅞ | 9 | 17.32 | 18.7 |
| 1973 | 223.1 | 12,691 | 76,644 | 5,142 | 2.30 | .686 | 15¼ | 9⅝ | 14.88 | 16.6 |
| 1972 | 184.4 | 9,733 | 67,278 | 5,115 | 1.77 | .557 | 16¼ | 9 5/16 | 13.11 | 14.5 |
| 1971 | 147.3 | 6,818 | 60,096 | 5,100 | 1.25 | .476 | 10 | 6 1/16 | 11.78 | 11.3 |
| 1970 | 131.6 | 2,212 | 55,706 | 5,100 | .42 | .500 | 9¼ | 5 | 10.92 | 6.8 |
| 1969 | 142.3 | 5,298 | 56,043 | 5,100 | .97 | .571 | 14 | 8¼ | 10.99 | 9.0 |

*Net income and earnings per share are after taxes and after extraordinary credits or charges as shown on the income statement, fully diluted.

†Equity for this purpose is defined as the sum of capital stock, surplus, and retained earnings at the company's year-end.

‡Includes nonrecurring charge of $7,921,000 ($1.41/share).

*Note:* Copperweld Corporation was a manufacturer of welded and seamless tubing (44 percent of sales); bimetallic rod, wire, and strand (11 percent); and specialty alloy and carbon steel bars (45 percent). Imetal, a unique holding company domiciled in France, with interest in basic metals, owned 66 percent of the outstanding stock of Copperweld. The company had 4,960 stockholders and 3,972 employees.

---

**EXHIBIT 2**

## PRINCIPAL PROCESSES IN STEELMAKING

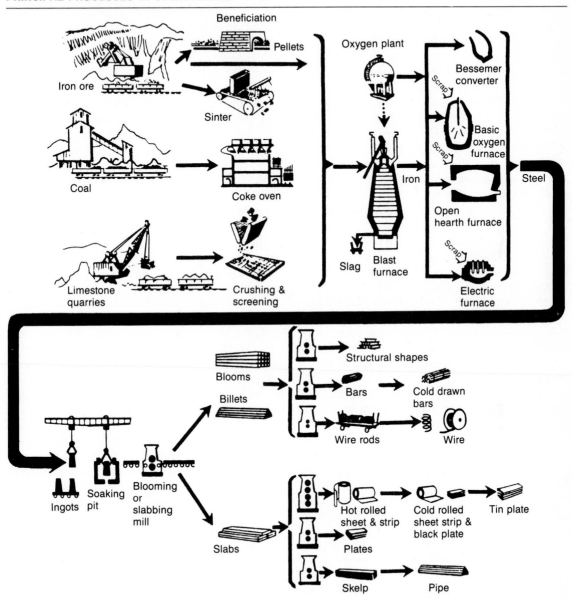

*Source:* American Iron and Steel Institute (AISI), *The Picture Story of Steel.*

sheet or plate and welding the seam thus obtaining welded tube.

*Seamless tube and pipe* were made from solid round billets which were heated to red heat and then pierced to produce a hollow billet. The hollow billet was then rolled to produce a tube, during which considerable elongation of the billet took place. Piercing could be done by drilling or by ramming a rod through the hot billet; rolling was done on lines of shaped rollers. The most common process for seamless tube production combined piercing and rolling in one operation and is shown in Exhibit 3. An alternative process (also illustrated) was to extrude the solid billet and then roll it to its final size.

The resulting tube from either operation was known as hot finished seamless (HFS) and had certain characteristics which were intimately related to its manufacturing process. Because it was hot finished, the surface of the steel inside and out was of low surface quality, since oxidation inevitably took place. This did not affect the steel quality, but for most applications surface oxidation had to be removed by machining. Because the tube was seamless it could be made from a wide variety of steels (only a few alloys could be welded), in a wide range of wall thicknesses (there was a limit to weld thickness of about one inch or less) and in many internal and external diameters. But the process had certain dimensional limitations: small diameters were difficult to make; internal and external diameters were subject to some dimensional variation; and it was difficult to obtain good concentricity between inside and outside diameters. There were two consequences of these limitations. Customers who needed accurate outside diameters had to machine the outside of the tube in order to obtain the required tolerances, while those customers who required good concentricity had to machine inside and outside to obtain the desired final dimensions. A diagram of the variations inherent in the process may be seen in Exhibit 4.

In order to overcome some of the dimensional variations of HFS and to obtain other dimensions and/or mechanical properties, HFS tubes could be drawn (i.e., pulled through a die of a diameter smaller than the HFS tube) in order to produce cold drawn seamless (CDS). Because this was a cold process, some stress relieving by heat treatment was sometimes needed subsequently. Some improvement vis-à-vis HFS was achieved on the surface finish as

well as on the tolerances of external and internal diameters but not on concentricity. The advantages of CDS were similar to those of HFS, except CDS had better tolerances and a much wider downward range of diameters. Its applications ranged from hypodermic needles to oil well casings. The disadvantages for customers requiring accurate outside or inside diameters, or both, were similar to those of HFS.

*Welded tube* was made from bending sheet and welding the edges. This could be done longitudinally or spirally, the latter being used chiefly for very large pipeline pipe (for a distinction between pipe and tube, see below). The welding process produced a residue on the weld called "flash" which was later cut off both from the outside and inside of the tube to produce a flush surface. The nature of the welding process restricted the applications as only certain grades of steel and up to certain thicknesses ($\frac{5}{8}''$) could be welded. Also, although the use of steel sheet to make the tube gave better dimensional control, the welding process did not produce a perfectly round tube. For most welded pipe applications (e.g., water, gas pipe) this was not important, and the tube had the advantage over CDS that it is was much cheaper and faster to make.

*DOM tube* was simply a welded tube which was later drawn by passing it through a die and over a mandril held inside the tube. This gave a tube of great concentric accuracy (see diagram in Exhibit 4). It should be noted that a drawn seamless tube was also drawn over a mandril, but this did not remove any concentricity inaccuracies inherent in seamless. Equally the advantage of DOM arose not least from the fact that it was made from accurate flat strip which resulted in even thickness and good surface finish inside and outside. Exhibit 5 illustrates the manufacturing process for DOM tube.

The drawing process in DOM tube necessarily accentuated any dimensional inaccuracies, and it was therefore important to achieve accurate flash removal in the welding process. Consequently, line speeds on a weld mill producing DOM tube were about half those used for producing ordinary welded pipe. For this

EXHIBIT 3

## PROCESSES FOR MAKING SEAMLESS TUBE

PIERCING OPERATION

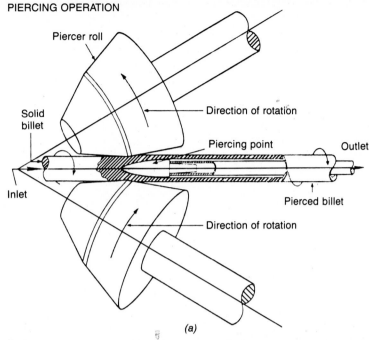

*(a)*

The *piercing* process (*a*) employs two barrel-like or cone-shaped rolls with their axes inclined at opposing angles, 6° to 12° from the horizontal line of the mill. The rolls rotate in the same direction, squeezing the heated billet between their largest diameters. This action rotates the billet at high speeds and drives it forward over a piercing point held between the rolls by a stationary bar. As the steel "flows" around the point, a hole forms through the length of the rotating billet. Wall thickness is initially regulated by the space between the shoulder of the piercing point and the rolls. The pierced billet is slightly larger in diameter and much longer than the solid billet from which it was made. It also has a relatively heavy wall and is not particularly smooth or accurate in any dimension. Following the piercing operation, and usually while still at rolling temperature, the hollow billet is given its finished wall thickness and outside diameter by one or more hot or cold finishing operations.

EXTRUSION PRESS

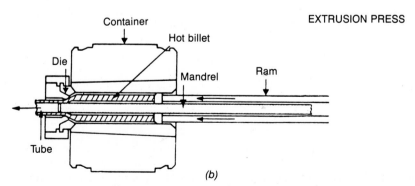

*(b)*

The *extrusion* (*b*) process consists of ramming the hot billet over a rod or mandrel and through a die which reduces it to the desired size. For large reductions in size several passes through the die are needed. Finishing operations are similar to those in the previous process, although drawn tubes generally exhibit closer tolerances on external dimensions than pierced tubes.

## EXHIBIT 4

## TUBE CHARACTERISTICS UNDER ALTERNATIVE PROCESSES

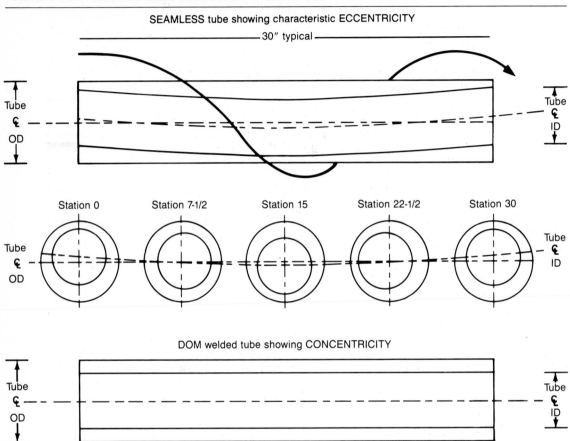

SEAMLESS tube showing characteristic ECCENTRICITY

DOM welded tube showing CONCENTRICITY

SPIRALING ECCENTRICITY OF SEAMLESS TUBING AND CONCENTRICITY OF COPPER-WELD DOM TUBING: To some degree, spiraling eccentricity occurs in all seamless steel tubing as a natural consequence of the rotary piercing process. The effect may be compared to gun barrel rifling. The eccentric spiral makes a complete revolution in approximately every 30″ (approximately 76 cm) of tube length. In contrast, Copperweld DOM tubing is concentric, with uniform wall thickness throughout its length. For illustrative purposes, degree of eccentricity is exaggerated.

reason, DOM tube was not competitive with ordinary welded pipe, and its cost structure was such that the most direct competitor was CDS.

Advances in welding technology in the United States had eliminated worries about weld integrity in DOM, but in contrast proportionally greater research had been devoted in Europe to improving seamless technology, particularly with reference to tolerances. For certain applications, particularly hydraulics, this development had not eliminated the inherent advantage of DOM in terms of its closer tolerances.

Direct cost comparisons among different tube technologies could be made bearing in mind that the different mechanical and chemical properties inherent in the various methods made each

## EXHIBIT 5

### DOM MANUFACTURING PROCESSES

1. From hot roll to coil

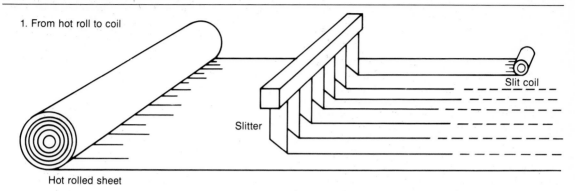

Hot rolled sheet
Slitter
Slit coil

2. Weld line

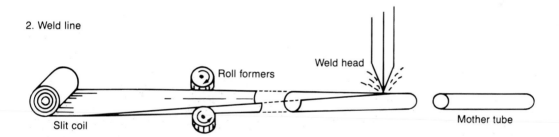

Slit coil
Roll formers
Weld head
Mother tube

3. Draw bench

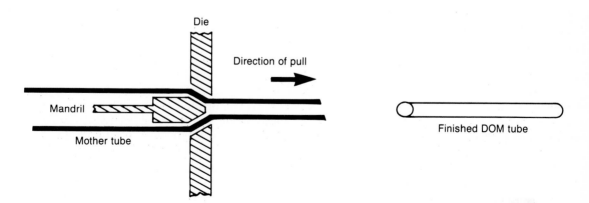

Die
Direction of pull
Mandril
Mother tube
Finished DOM tube

type of tube more suitable for certain markets. Indicative full costs (in dollars per ton) in manufacturing were as follows:

Welded pipe: $600

HFS: $800

CDS: $1,100

DOM: $1,000

The steel input, whether billets or steel coil, accounted for approximately $400–$450 of these figures in all cases.

## MARKETS AND MARKETING

The different processes of manufacture described above and the associated costs and mechanical properties meant that different tube types found different uses and applications. Within the whole tube market, overlaps of use only occured in certain applications and depended not only on relative mechanical properties, or the importance of different tolerances, but also on relative prices for the alternative tubes and for the related finishing processes. For example, when machining was required to achieve the desired final shape, the price of the tube would be important in relation to the price of machining it. Alternatively if something had to be welded onto the tube, different tubes might give different welding characteristics, and the resulting deformations might be more or less expensive to remove. Suffice it that the combinations of utility and cost were many and complex.

In the marketing of tubes there were some generally accepted categories of classification. First, it was common to distinguish between pipe and tube. Pipe was generally made in a small range of standard sizes and in very large batches. It was essentially a commodity product. Tube was made in small batches and in a large variety of sizes, frequently nonstandard, and in a large variety of grades. It was a customer-oriented product with very different marketing and production requirements from pipe.

Second, tube markets could be divided further into three main categories: structural, mechanical, and hydraulic. A fourth category, oil

country tubular goods (OCTG), used mainly in well casing and tubing, was considered a special case. As these were end-user categories, precise limits to each segment were difficult to define. Even with a production-based definition, such as pipe and tube, the boundary between the two was not always clear.

*Structural tube* was used in load-bearing applications ranging from buildings to ships, bridges, cranes, etc. and was overwhelmingly (90 percent) HFS.[2] *Mechanical tube* was used for all machining stock, and one of its major end users was the automotive industry. Although a lot of precision tube (CDS) was used, the majority of mechanical tube (80 percent) was HFS. *Hydraulic tube* (which includes pneumatic tube) consisted of a specialized sector, dominated in Europe by CDS (45 percent), but using a lot of HFS (40 percent) and some DOM (15 percent). The proportions of these types of tubes in the different European markets and their geographic distribution is shown in Exhibit 6.

All tube users received supplies from two sources. One source was direct shipments from the mill, which prevailed whenever delivery times tended to be long or, alternatively, requirements were large and regular. Mills would tend to limit direct sales to quantities of at least 50 tons and require up to 12 weeks lead time. Occasionally, shortages would push these figures higher as was currently the case in the OCTG market. Alternatively, customers could turn to any one of a small number of local stockists or warehouses, which were frequently either owned by a mill or had a special relationship with one, and which supplied small quantities in wide varieties. In every country independent stockists operated in competition with tied stockists. Users in the structural market tended to buy largely from the mill, their requirements being generally infrequent, involving long deliveries and special applications. While most structural tube was delivered ex-mill, structural pipe was often supplied by stockists.

---

[2]Note that structural *pipe* (as opposed to tube), used primarily in scaffolding and noncritical structural applications, was overwhelmingly made from welded pipe.

| EXHIBIT 6 |
|---|

**EUROPEAN SPECIALTY TUBE MARKETS—1981 PROJECTION**

**A. By type of tube**

| | Tons (thousands) | Percent |
|---|---|---|
| HFS | 378 | 72 |
| CDS | 127 | 24 |
| DOM | 21 | 4 |
| | 526 | 100 |

**B. By major user**

| | Tons (thousands) | Percent |
|---|---|---|
| Automotive | 111 | 21 |
| Structural engineering | 88 | 17 |
| Cranes, etc. | 68 | 13 |
| General industry | 259 | 49 |
| | 526 | 100 |

**C. By country and application (thousands of tons)**

| | Structural | Mechanical* | Hydraulic† | Total |
|---|---|---|---|---|
| United Kingdom | 25 | 45 | 25 | 95 (18%) |
| Germany | 35 | 105 | 45 | 185 (35%) |
| France | 20 | 30 | 22 | 72 (14%) |
| Italy | 20 | 30 | 16 | 66 (13%) |
| Sweden | 10 | 30 | 18 | 58 (11%) |
| Others | 10 | 30 | 10 | 50 (10%) |
| Total | 120 (23%) | 270 (51%) | 136 (26%) | 526 (100%) |

*About 20–25 percent of this market calls for precision tubes, mostly served by CDS tube but amenable to DOM substitution.

†Over 60 percent of the hydraulic market was thought to be of potential interest for DOM tube.

*Note:* European production of pipe and tubing amounted to over 12 million tons (see Exhibit 7) of which about one-third was exported. The specialty tube markets shown above were much smaller but sold at higher prices.

In contrast, the mechanical market was very fragmented in each country, except for one or two large bearing and automotive part companies, with a very large variety of requirements which changed frequently. Consequently, supply by stockist was the dominant feature in this market.

The hydraulic market lay between these two extremes. The users were few in number and often had regular production schedules. They tended therefore to be mill supplied. However those producers who acted as subcontractors to major producers of earthmoving equipment or mechanical handling products, frequently had changing work loads and hence relied on stockists to supply these variations. In total, some 10–20 percent of hydraulic tube consumption passed by the stockist route.

## DOM MARKETING

DOM had a number of market advantages over both HFS and CDS. It was made from accurate strip which could be cleaned on both sides before welding. As a result, it exhibited excellent surface finish, uniform thickness, and accurate concentricity. Making DOM was inherently a more flexible process than producing either HFS or CDS because of the relative ease with which sizes could be changed on a weld mill compared with a seamless plug and rolling mill. It was also an inherently cheaper process than CDS, requiring less capital investment and giving bigger throughputs of steel for a given diameter. The actual DOM manufacturing process was cheaper and required less energy, but the billets utilized to make HFS or CDS were a cheaper raw material per ton of steel than hot rolled sheet for DOM. An exact economic comparison was, therefore, extremely difficult to obtain, and it was further complicated by the different positions in tube manufacturing of companies with different levels of vertical integration and, therefore, with different pricing strategies. In general, DOM could be competitive with HFS and CDS for certain applications, of which the most important was hydraulic.

The advantages offered by DOM to hydraulic tube producers lay largely in the finishing process. The better internal surface quality required a quicker and lighter finishing (machining) operation than CDS or HFS. Also because tolerances were tighter, less metal needed to be removed to achieve a true internal diameter. Better concentricity meant less differential strains under pressure (because of different wall thickness), and better concentricity enabled finishing machines to work off the external diameter, which could greatly increase the speed of finishing operations. Better concentricity was also particularly important in the manufacture of telescopic tube "nests," where internal and external diameters needed to be accurately machined.

The net effect of using DOM tube was to reduce the cost of the finished tube. This reduction could be in the order of 50 percent of the value added to the tube through machining, which in itself could amount to from 50–100 percent of the original value of the tube. However, to achieve this level of saving it was necessary to invest in new and different finishing equipment which was tailored to DOM characteristics but used less men and produced more tube. Such equipment, however, could not handle CDS or HFS, thus requiring an irreversible capital spending decision of important propor-

tions. Since DOM offered the potential of large process savings and implied reorganization and reinvestment in production, marketing of DOM tube was directed to the technical director level at the plant and not the company's buyer or materials purchasing officer.[3]

Copperweld started marketing DOM in the United States in the early sixties and for ten years was virtually unchallenged in the American market. The first major customer to convert was Caterpillar. They took three years to evaluate the product and to decide to incorporate it into their production. Within the two following years, Caterpillar converted 90 percent of their hydraulic tube to DOM. Early growth rates were of the order of 20–25 percent per year, and by 1975, the U.S. market consumed over 150,000 tons of DOM tube. Copperweld's share was over 35 percent; the rest being held principally by two companies, Babcock and Wilcox and Lone Star, each with about 20 percent market share in DOM. Although Copperweld was the market leader and pioneer of the technology, it was not protected by any important patents. The secret of success was more in production know-how and marketing expertise. Although the size of investment ($40–$50 million for a 40,000 ton integrated plant) was a significant barrier to entry, many weld mills and draw benches existed in various steel mills (not always both in the same mill) for pipe and CDS production, making an entry by diversification at least a possibility. Technical factors however, particularly but not only in terms of the weld mills, usually mitigated against such an approach. Copperweld was unchallenged in its ability to make the heavier sizes of DOM.

By the end of the 1970s, annual market growth

---

[3]DOM tube could be used with standard (i.e., CDS or HFS) finishing equipment, but in such a case cost savings rarely exceeded 10–20 percent of value added. A typical hydraulic tube customer might consume 400 tons of tube per year. In order to handle DOM tube on existing production equipment, such a customer would need to spend $50–$100,000 in modifications. If, however, a customer were to invest in new specialized equipment tailored to DOM tubes and able to yield full productivity benefits, the necessary investment would range from $250–$500,000.

in the United States had slowed to about 6 percent in volume (relatively high for a steel product), and total market size was about 320,000 tons. The company's management felt that the most likely growth opportunities were outside the United States, particularly in Europe.

## THE EUROPEAN MARKET

The total mechanical tube and pipe market (including hydraulic) in Europe was approximately the same size as that of the United States. In 1972, however, the hydraulic sector in Europe was approximately 40 percent of the comparable U.S. level, and not one manufacturer used DOM.

There were two essential reasons for this. One reason cited earlier was that European steel tube manufacturers had devoted relatively more effort to improving seamless technology. But also the relatively low level of international competition in the end product markets had shielded hydraulic manufacturers from the stimulus to reduce production costs. Throughout the 1970s, increased market penetration in Europe by the U.S. construction equipment multinationals (first importing and later manufacturing locally), and a growing internationalization of the hydraulic industry provoked an increased interest in cost reduction and an appreciation of the advantages offered by DOM. Although differences in specifications for hydraulic use meant that the potential in Europe for conversion was slightly less than in the United States, it appeared that the short and medium-term DOM potential was very attractive.

In 1972, on the advice of Arthur D. Little (ADL), the international consultants, one of whose partners was a Copperweld board member, Copperweld entered into a sales and distribution agreement with a Dutch distributor aimed at serving European markets. By 1975, a modest sales level (800 tons) had been achieved by selling essentially only to U.S. multinationals operating in Europe. In order to go further a direct marketing effort was initiated to attempt to convert the market to DOM. This was done by establishing local agents and distributors in three countries (United Kingdom, Germany, and

Sweden) and by a personal intensive marketing effort made by Rick Barclay, head of the marketing unit in Copperweld Tubing Group, Pittsburgh. Whenever good agents were established, success was threefold. The customer base was broadened, accounts of major cylinder producers were converted, and supply lines were improved by better local stock levels. Sales continued to grow through the late seventies, and in 1978, ADL undertook a second study of the market.

The conclusion drawn from this closer look at the market confirmed many of the early ideas. First, the market had much in common with the United States, in spite of some national differences, and it appeared there was good DOM sales potential. Second, there was by now some European production of DOM but only in small diameters and not always successful. The stronger companies in seamless production did not appear interested in DOM. Copperweld, clearly dominating the U.S. market and unchallenged in large diameters, had the beginning of a customer base built in Europe and demand was both present and growing. Third, sufficient sales to justify a plant in Europe seemed a real possibility. ADL recommended that a local sales manager be appointed, that a sales organization be established to support the local dealers, that the customer base be strengthened, and that the potential of the market be confirmed by further sales prior to considering a plant. A minimum plant capacity of 40,000 tons per year was given as a working figure based on the line speed of a 3-shift weld mill. The sales level in 1978, was only 5,000 tons per year.

## INITIAL STEPS

Following receipt of the report from ADL, the idea of a European plant was given careful scrutiny inside Copperweld. Outline capital estimates were made and returns on investment (ROI) calculated. They were not encouraging, however. In September 1978, the corporate comptroller wrote to the Tubes Division Vice President, Mr. H. Breedlove (who was also Vice President of the corporation), that on a capital estimate of $47.4 million, ROI was only 5.3 percent, and that an arbitrary reduction of capital investment by $16 million would only raise ROI to 11.5 percent. He went on: "Upon further review of the profitability forecast, we are inclined to believe that the figures portrayed are, if anything, optimistic."

Tube Division management was not dismayed by this view; it was after all an early opinion based on very rough calculations. Encouraged by Breedlove, Rick Barclay pushed ahead establishing a good sales organization in Europe. An expatriate American, Ted Eves, with good European experience, was hired as Sales Manager, and he set about consolidating the dealer network and employing his own area marketing personnel. Independent dealers specializing in tubes had been enlisted in the United Kingdom, Sweden, and Germany; new dealers were added in France, Spain, and Italy; and the company's "own" workers were employed in all these markets.

Sales growth, Copperweld's leading position in DOM technology, and the knowledge that investment incentives could improve the profitability of a plant, persuaded Breedlove and Barclay to broach the subject of a European plant informally with the board in 1979. The chair of the board was Tony Bryan, an American who had been partly educated in the United Kingdom and had flown for the RAF in the war. Like Breedlove, he had worked for the chemical industry early in his career and had been with Copperweld fewer than ten years. Indeed it was a matter of note that the great majority of senior vice presidents in Copperweld had started their careers outside the steel industry and had joined the company after Bryan. Only Rick Barclay among senior executives had had a long career with the company (7 years) and with steel (14 years).

The major shareholder of the company, owning 66 percent of the capital, was a French investment company, IMETAL. A subsidiary of the Banque Rothschild, IMETAL had holdings in a number of basic metals companies, most notably Penarroya, a Spanish lead and zinc company, and Le Nickel, a French company which was 50 percent owned by Elf-Aquitaine, the French national oil group. IMETAL was represented on Copperweld's board by two directors, one of whom was Bernard de Villemejane, IMETAL's chairman.

The reaction of Villemejane to the idea of a European plant was very positive. He suggested that initial work be directed to the United Kingdom, which was offering at the time some of the most attractive financial incentives in Europe. It was also the home of a newly elected Conservative government which promised to develop a favorable climate for business. And a new investment in the United Kingdom would fit the logic of IMETAL's investment in the United States by further widening its portfolio.

## THE SECOND CONSULTANTS

The encouragement given to Barclay, however, left him in somewhat of a dilemma. His responsibility was for all marketing; Europe was only a small fraction (5 percent) of total sales. His European sales manager was busy developing sales. Only he, Barclay, of those in the United States, knew Europe's steel markets well, and even he would be the first to admit only passive knowledge of some of Copperweld's competitors there. Furthermore, the structure of the European market and the relationships between the various European producers was very different from the American scene. To compound this, his knowledge of the investment incentives in Europe and the minutiae of investment analysis was sufficient to convince him of his need for assistance. It arrived from a most unexpected direction.

In April 1979, Rick Barclay received a letter from a small London-based consulting company which apparently had learned of Copperweld's European developments via work they had done themselves in the hydraulic sector. Barclay soon ascertained that they knew Copperweld's main markets and had good experience in the European steel industry. Their understanding of DOM potential was remarkably strong, and by being in London they could provide local analytical and "leg-work" assistance. Barclay decided to engage them.

The brief given to the consultants was a wide one. First, they were to establish a profile of the incentives and benefits available for the three most attractive locations within the United Kingdom. Copperweld's sales were strongest in the United Kingdom, and the whole management was anglophilic. Second, the consultants were to draw up a list of possible joint venture partners. There were two reasons for this. One was a desire to keep the investment down, and for this it seemed logical to build a plant without a weld mill. The latter was an expensive piece of equipment, and pipe weld mills were in plentiful supply in Europe. With some reeducation a joint venture partner with a weld mill could supply Copperweld with "mother-shells," welded tubes suitable for drawing to DOM. Also, as a newcomer to Europe, Copperweld could benefit from the availability of finance, institutional access, management, and local knowledge that a local partner could provide. The third task for the consultants was to run all preliminary negotiations with interested parties, to develop primary options for Copperweld, and to exploit all incentive opportunities. Finally, they were to advise on overall strategy for all the important aspects of the investment.

## THE MARKET POTENTIAL

The market for application of hydraulic and precision mechanical tube in 1979 in Europe was valued at over $200 million, about 190,000 tons, of which 120,000 tons were suitable for DOM applications. Copperweld's sales were then 8,000 tons and rising; 15,000 tons or more in two years' time seemed quite feasible. The largest market by far for hydraulic and precision mechanical tube was Germany (70,000 tons), followed by the United Kingdom (40,000 tons), and France (25,000 tons). Hydraulic tube accounted for approximately the same proportion, around 25 percent of all tube sales, in each market (see Exhibits 6 and 7). About two-thirds of the hy-

draulic market was estimated to be suitable for DOM conversion. A smaller portion of the mechanical market, where precision tube was used, was also thought to be suitable for converting to DOM.

Copperweld's sales in 1979 were 4,200 tons in the United Kingdom, 1,400 tons in Sweden, 800 tons in Italy, 700 tons in France, and 500 tons in Germany (see Exhibit 8). Growth of the "potential" DOM market was expected to be 6 percent per annum, linked as it was to a rising level of mechanization (and hence a greater use of hydraulic systems), and to particular growth in the range of sizes and steel grade types which could be covered by DOM. The actual growth of DOM sales could be much higher, depending on the conversion rate from CDS.

The rate at which the market would convert from CDS was something of an imponderable. On the one hand European producers of CDS were dominant national producers, and their product was better than that of the American producers. On the other hand, hydraulic producers were competing more and more on an international basis, which meant a constant downward pressure on production costs. Finally, the change to DOM, while spearheaded by Copperweld, would depend to some extent on the reaction of a few European producers, notably Hoesch in Germany, Rothrist in Switzerland, and Teksid in Italy, all of which were producing some small-diameter, thin-wall DOM.

## EUROPEAN TUBE PRODUCERS

The pattern of European seamless tube production was that each major country had one dominant supplier of tubes in any particular quality, and export sales occured largely outside Europe in third markets. In Germany, Mannesmann was by far the largest European tube producer, with production in excess of 2 million tons a year of both commodity seamless tube and pipe and precision-finished tube. While Mannesmann was clearly the industry leader in both prices and technology, a second German manufacturer, Bentler, played an important role with a yearly

<table>
<tr><td colspan="5" align="center">**EXHIBIT 7**</td></tr>
</table>

**EEC PRODUCTION OF PIPE AND TUBING, 1979–1980** (Thousands of Tons)

| | Seamless pipe and tube | | Welded pipe and tube* | |
|---|---|---|---|---|
| | **1979** | **1980†** | **1979** | **1980†** |
| Germany | 2,009 | 1,999 | 2,952 | 2,748 |
| France | 603 | 646 | 1,527 | 1,455 |
| Italy · | 824 | 880 | 2,260 | 2,525 |
| Netherlands | — | — | 240 | 265 |
| Belgium | 53 | 60 | 192 | 166 |
| Luxembourg | — | — | 122 | 113 |
| United Kingdom | 501 | 373 | 874 | 697 |
| Ireland | — | — | — | — |
| Denmark | — | —. | 64† | n.a. |
| EEC | 3,990 | 3,958 | 8,231 | 7,969 |

*The overwhelming majority consists of pipe.
†Estimates.
n.a. = not available.

production of about 500,000 tons. The only company with a comparably wide product range was Vallourec in France, with production of nearly 1 million tons and a bias toward commodity tube and OCTG. In the United Kingdom, there were two producers, British Steel Corporation (BSC) and Tube Investments (TI), but BSC had largely excluded itself deliberately from the precision quality tube sector which was served by TI. TI and Vallourec had a joint company in France, Valti, for production of mechanical precision tube. In Italy, Dalmine was a producer of CDS with a patchy record in precision tubes, mainly because of competition from Falk, a specialist in Italy in precision bearing and mechanical tube. Outside the EEC, two important Swedish producers of tube were Sandvik, Europe's biggest maker of carbides, and SKF, Europe's leading manufacturer of industrial bearings. Both were producers of specialty steels and tubes, with concentration on the special heavy-duty areas of tube usage. Development of DOM would affect the CDS business of all these producers, but only in two cases, TI and to a lesser extent Valti, did hydraulic tube form a significant (about 10 percent in the case of TI) part of their volume.

<table>
<tr><td colspan="8" align="center">**EXHIBIT 8**</td></tr>
</table>

**COPPERWELD EUROPEAN SALES OF DOM TUBE, 1972–1979 AND 1980 FORECAST** (Thousands of Tons)

| | 1972–1974 average | **1975** | **1976** | **1977** | **1978** | **1979** | **1980*** |
|---|---|---|---|---|---|---|---|
| United Kingdom | n.a. | 200 | 600 | 1,000 | 2,400 | 4,200 | 5,500 |
| Sweden | n.a. | 100 | 300 | 500 | 1,300 | 1,400 | 1,800 |
| Italy | n.a. | 0 | 700 | 500 | 800 | 800 | 1,000 |
| France | n.a. | 400 | 200 | 300 | 300 | 700 | 1,000 |
| W. Germany | n.a. | 800 | 500 | 300 | 300 | 500 | 1,500 |
| Others | n.a. | 0 | 0 | 0 | 0 | 400 | 700 |
| Total | 600 | 1,500 | 2,300 | 2,600 | 5,000 | 8,000 | 11,500 |

*1980 figures are estimates.
n.a. = not available.

The importance of the hydraulic business, how-ever, laid on its higher prices and margins and not on its volume. In general, the market for seamless tubes of all types was three to four times that of hydraulic tubes (not counting pipe, which was practically all seamless), and only a portion of the hydraulic market was suitable for DOM as a replacement for CDS.

Producers of welded pipe were far more nu-merous, the barriers to entry being much lower than for CDS. Frequently, but not always, welded and seamless tube producers were different companies. Exceptions to this were TI and BSC. There were only two important producers of DOM tubes in Europe, Hoesch in Germany and Teksid in Italy. Both were producers of small-diameter DOM tube sold on the local market, in Teksid's case largely to its mother company Fiat for use in manufacturing shock absorbers. A third producer, Rothrist, sold most of its out-put to the pneumatic market. As with CDS pro-ducers, they had limited or nonexistent sales elsewhere in Europe. TI had at one stage started DOM production, using mother shells from Hoesch, but had been unable to master the tech-nology and had withdrawn. In theory, of course, any producer with access to a weld mill and a draw bench could produce DOM, but in practice only a dedicated plant would ensure mastery of the technological details and provide the ability to respond to a market the dominant character-istic of which was tailor-made small lots. For example, in the United States, OST could re-ceive, produce, and deliver an order for DOM tube in less than 3 weeks. As a comparison, ex-mill deliveries of CDS usually took 10–12 weeks. Although delivery from stockists was much quicker it was also more expensive, and gen-erally they catered only to standard sizes.

Competition between the different tube mak-ers in Europe took place along several dimen-sions, the most obvious being technology and relative prices. While DOM was priced above CDS in view of its advantages, it was not di-vorced from the CDS price level. Another fea-ture of competition was that major customers avoided relying on one source. In any one ter-ritory, the major producer usually had the lion's share of orders, but there was often a second, and sometimes a third, supplier. However, the supply networks of tube producers outside their own territories were generally very weak.

In building up its market in Europe, Copper-weld had thus far met with little reaction from the domestic producers. Despite its growing sales, the impact in each country was relatively small perhaps partly because Copperweld was work-ing with independent distributors, which as a group rarely if ever had a majority share of the market. Copperweld's sales record was uneven among European markets, but even in the United Kingdom, where the largest volume sales had been achieved, there had been no reaction from TI, the producer most affected. It appeared that TI's long-term strategy was to move away from a dependence on steel products and British mar-kets; hence some marginal loss of market to DOM, whose arrival appeared inevitable, seemed acceptable.

## THE JOINT VENTURE PARTNERS

The qualities required of any joint venture (JV) partner were financial strength, management skills and vitality, and institutional position and access in Europe. An additional requirement was familiarity with engineering and industrial mar-keting. Potential U.K. companies which could fill these criteria were not numerous.

TI was one obvious partner but was dis-carded because of potential conflict of interests and because their apparent long-term strategy was leading them away from tubes. BSC, not directly involved in the hydraulic sector al-though a supplier of billets to TI and an obvious source of "mother shells," was interested both because of the increased strip demand that DOM would create and because a DOM plant could bring employment to depressed steel areas. They were invited to show interest at two levels, as JV partner and as mother shell supplier on a commercial basis. Another possibility on this dual basis was Natural Gas Tubes (NGT), owned by the Indian entrepreneur Swraj Paul and a producer of gas pipe in South Wales, although

EXHIBIT 9

**PLANT LOCATION ALTERNATIVES**

| | RDG* (%) | BSC aid | Land prices (£/acre) | Labor | | Inward traffic | |
| --- | --- | --- | --- | --- | --- | --- | --- |
| | | | | Availability | Work ethic | U.K. | International |
| **Main sites** | | | | | | | |
| Cardiff Dockland: imposing site, adjacent to large GKN works, on the sea and prominent | 15 | yes | 30,000 | 3 | ID | 3 | 3 |
| Washington New Town: quiet, out of the way, small and successful new town beyond the suburbs of Newcastle | 22 | no | 12,000 | 3 | ID | 2 | 2 |
| **Secondary sites** | | | | | | | |
| Peterlee | 22 | yes | 15,000 | 3 | ID | 2 | 2 |
| Shotton | 15 | yes | 20,000 | 3 | ID | 2+ | 3+ |
| Wrexham | 22 | yes | 18,000 | 3 | ID | 2 | 3 |
| Ebbw Vale | 22 | yes | 12,000 | 3 | ID | 3 | 2 |

*Regional development grant in percent of investment.
1 = unsatisfactory.
2 = satisfactory.
3 = good.
ID = insufficient data.

with a capacity (both in output and size range) far below that of BSC.

Three companies whose role could only be as JV partner were considered: GKN, a motor vehicle components and steel bar group; Acrow, a scaffolding and metal fabrication company; and Johnson Firth Brown (JFB) a special steels and engineering products group. Acrow declined, but the other two companies showed interest in discussing details with Copperweld. Hence Copperweld obtained expressions of interest to move discussions to a more detailed level from four companies: BSC, NGT, GKN and JFB.

## TECHNICAL CONSIDERATIONS

Without a weld mill, a supplier of mother shells was imperative. Some shells could be, and in the cases of heavier sizes would be, supplied from the two American plants. But with a two-to three-month delivery period it was obviously desirable to keep these purchases to a minimum. To assess the capabilities of different suppliers, the technical expert of Copperweld, Jim Seastone, undertook a tour of the plants which seemed most appropriate as potential suppliers: BSC, NGT, and Alessio in Italy, a producer of welded pipe for the local market of similar size to NGT.

Mr. Seastone was impressed by Alessio's general technical ability and willingness to accommodate the exigencies of DOM production into its production program. Alessio had modern equipment in the required size range and was excited at the prospect of export sales. Alessio was nonetheless, primarily a pipe producer, and DOM production for them would be a new experience. Although it was not Seastone's primary concern, they were also some distance from a U.K. location, and the Italian record of strikes was a worry.

| Exit time | Proximity to domestic market | Attraction to staff | Site attraction | Physical characteristics | Utilities | Site delivery speed | Ease to visit |
|---|---|---|---|---|---|---|---|
| 2+ | 2+ | 3 | 2 | ID | 3 | 2+ | 3 |
| 3 | 2 | 2 | 3 | 3 | 3 | 3 | 2 |
| 3 | 2 | 2− | 1 | 3 | 3 | 1 | 2 |
| 2+ | 3 | 2+ | 1+ | 2 | 3 | 3 | 2+ |
| 2+ | 3 | 2+ | 2+ | 3 | 3 | 3 | 2 |
| 2+ | 2+ | 1 | 1− | 1− | 3 | 3 | 2 |

NGT was equally enthusiastic but unlike Alessio its technical ability was weak, partly a function of emphasis on commodity gas pipes. The major disadvantage of NGT was the range of the pipe mill, which could not in Seastone's opinion be extended easily.

BSC gave Jim Seastone a rather reserved welcome for reasons that were not clear. However their plant and staff were evidently capable of DOM production, although the fit with pipe production did not look easy. Both NGT and Alessio had spare capacity, but BSC was working flat out, and accommodating the slower line speeds needed to produce DOM looked problematical.

For all three companies there were common considerations for Copperweld affecting its choice of a mother shell supplier. First, all would have to be taught the production techniques for DOM. There was nothing particularly arcane or difficult about this except that it was one of the "arts" of DOM. Second, although the American plants would supplement some mother shell supply and could obviously produce all requirements, a second European source was imprac-

ticable on the volumes of DOM projected. Hence price, and the guaranties going with it, was of vital importance. The initial discussions covered only general feasibility and price areas; detailed agreement would come later.

## LOCATION AND GRANTS

The climate for investment in the United Kingdom in 1979 was notably favorable. The previous Labour government had developed a system of grants which were generous and, equally important, easy to obtain and almost without equal in Europe. The new Conservative government provided an attractive business environment, and although likely to avoid some of the more notorious funding operations of its predecessor, seemed unlikely to change the basic grant structure.

Incentives for investment in the United Kingdom were basically of three forms. A statutory grant of a fixed percentage of the investment varied with the locality chosen and was restricted to designated areas of the country. An additional discretionary grant was possible given certain criteria such as the degree of international mobility (i.e., the need to "attract" the investment to the United Kingdom rather than see it go elsewhere), the fit with the local industrial scene, the need to make the investment viable, or indeed any criteria that the government deemed appropriate. Finally, financial assistance was available at the European level for investments in particularly disfavoured areas, notably declining coal and steel areas.

This last source of finance was also partly discretionary, depending on a recommendation of the local host government and approval by the European Community's own industrial committees. An important addition to this basic package was provided by BSC, which in an effort to provide new work for its redundant steel workers, had started BSC (Industry), an entrepreneurial organization to help inward investment with front end help (site visits, small studies, etc.) and institutional guidance for the various local, national, and international authorities involved.

With the active help of BSC (Industry) the consultants prepared a list of possible sites, visited some with Copperweld staff, and prepared a matrix of all the options (see Exhibit 9 on pp. 216–217).

## FINANCIAL ANALYSIS

Although the raw numbers would be gathered in Europe, the financial analysis was to be car-ried out in Pittsburgh on a model developed by the corporation. There was uncertainty concerning the numbers to be fed in, inevitable at such an early stage, and the precise method of analysis. The new plant would evidently take business away from the American plants, so the loss of income probably had to be accounted for. Also, even though sales in Europe would include large diameters supplied from the United States, the proposed plant was probably best assessed on the returns from its own output, as this was considered a true measure of investment return. A further complication was caused by Rick Barclay presenting two sales forecasts for European sales, one based on a new local plant and the other on continued ex-U.S. sourcing. It seemed logical to evaluate the new plant then only on the incremental sales that would be generated.

One aspect of the analysis was made easier by the fact that the plant envisaged for Europe was almost a mirror image of the new plant built in 1978 at OST. Although initial ideas were to start with an independent European mother shell source, it was always intended that with sufficient sales volume the European affiliate would justify investment in a weld mill of a size similar to that of OST, probably some four years after the initial investment. The similarities with Plant 2 at OST were relevant on several counts. First, equipment estimates and specifications were easily updated. Second, manning requirements

---

### EXHIBIT 10

**SALES FORECAST, 1981–1985** (Thousands of Tons)

|  | 1981 | | 1982 | | 1983 | | 1984 | | 1985 | |
|---|---|---|---|---|---|---|---|---|---|---|
|  | Market | Sales | Market | Sales | Market | Sales | Market | Sales | Market | Sales |
| United Kingdom | 33 | 6.5 | 34 | 8.5 | 36 | 10.0 | 37 | 12.0 | 38 | 13.0 |
| France | 16 | 2.0 | 16 | 3.0 | 17 | 4.0 | 17 | 5.0 | 18 | 5.0 |
| Scandinavia | 18 | 2.5 | 19 | 3.5 | 20 | 5.0 | 21 | 5.5 | 22 | 5.5 |
| Italy | 16 | 2.0 | 16 | 3.0 | 17 | 3.5 | 17 | 4.5 | 18 | 5.0 |
| W. Germany | 46 | 2.5 | 48 | 5.0 | 49 | 6.5 | 50 | 7.5 | 52 | 8.0 |
| Others | 5 | 1.5 | 5 | 2.0 | 6 | 2.5 | 7 | 2.5 | 7 | 2.5 |
| Total | 134 | 17.0 | 138 | 25.0 | 145 | 31.5 | 149 | 37.0 | 155 | 39.0 |

*Note:* Shares for the years were: 1981, 13%; 1982, 18%; 1983, 22%; 1984, 25%; 1985, 25%.

| EXHIBIT 11 |
| --- |

**DOM TUBE PRICES, 1980** ($ per Ton)

|  | Diameter | | | |
| --- | --- | --- | --- | --- |
|  | 1–2½″ | 2½–4¼″ | 4–6″ | Over 6″ |
| Book price FOB U.S. mill | 1,208 | 1,103 | 1,103 | 1,129 |
| Current freight | 180 | 180 | 180 | 180 |
| Total | 1,388 | 1,283 | 1,283 | 1,309 |
| Duty at 10% | 139 | 128 | 128 | 131 |
| Net book price delivered | 1,527 | 1,411 | 1,411 | 1,440 |

Note: Minimum order was currently 20,000 pounds, or about 10 tons. Discounts of 13.5% on average were common throughout Europe depending on competitive and market conditions.

were clearly identified, even though there was some doubt in everyone's mind as to whether any U.K. plant could emulate the very high productivity of its American sister. Third, the process costs were known and hence, by simply allowing for the different raw material and scrap costs in Europe, running costs were identified. But allowances for differences in production efficiency, that is, in terms of the amount of steel lost in the process of going from either sheet or shell to tube, was unknown. The U.S. experience was for a "yield" of 72 percent from sheet, or 85 percent from shell, of the initial tonnage input.

The variables fed into the analysis were relatively few. Sales volume was obtained from Rick Barclay's forecasts (see Exhibit 10) based on his own and his European manager's views, cross-checked many ways. Sales price was estimated from the prices Copperweld was getting for its fast rising sales volume (Exhibit 11). Material prices were taken from quotations for mother shells from BSC and NGT and, for the eventual weld mill, from BSC for strip. One difficulty was that the shell prices were only based on initial quotations, and the strip prices were only based on currently ruling Davignon prices, although everyone knew that a customer of Copperweld's importance would get a discount even if it had to remain unpublished.[4] La-

bor costs were based on prevailing U.K. rates, as were scrap prices and costs relating to the various consumables of the process. Perhaps the two most important variables were the amount of discretionary grant likely to be received, which Copperweld could not know definitely before entering into detailed negotiations, and the exchange rate for the dollar, which was assumed as $2.10 = £1.00, not without some misgivings. No allowance for differential inflation was made, and all costs and prices were assumed to rise proportionately.

The range of returns with and without the weld mill was prepared in comparative form as shown in Exhibit 12. Also shown are two comparable income statements with and without the weld mill for a sample year (Exhibit 13).

The most likely returns to be developed by the European plant were of the order of 20–25 percent ROI if good grant conditions were achieved. Although this was considerably above the corporation hurdle rate of 8–10 percent, recent investments, which had been devoted entirely to internal additions and improvements in various Copperweld U.S. plants, had shown re-

---

[4]Prices were fixed for most steel products throughout the EEC under the Davignon Plan for restructuring the steel industry. These were not uniformly applied. For example, hot-rolled coil prices were not fixed if used for tube making.

---

**EXHIBIT 12**

---

**ROI CALCULATIONS ON EUROPEAN PLANT**

| | ROI (%) | | | |
|---|---|---|---|---|
| | No RDG, No SFA* | RDG +50% SFA | RDG +75% SFA | RDG +100% SFA |
| Plant without weld mill | 9.9† | 17.5 | 19.2 | 21.3 |
| Plant with weld mill from 1/86 | 13.5‡ | 21.5 | 23.0 | n.a. |
| Plant with weld mill from 1/83 | 15.2 | 23.6 | 24.7 | n.a. |

*RDG = Regional development grant, assumed at the statutory level of 22% of the investment; SFA = Selective financial assistance, a discretionary grant variable up to $4 million.

†Sensitivity analysis for a plant without weld mill, no RDG and no SFA: 5% increase in sales price—12.6% ROI; 5% decrease in shell price—11.7% ROI; both—14.3% ROI.

‡Sensitivity for plant with weld mill from 1/86, no RDG and no SFA: worst sales forecast—10.5% ROI; best sales forecast—15.3% ROI.

---

turns of 35–40 percent. Currently, however, there were no competing projects being prepared for the board, which had earmarked some $40 million per annum for the next few years as available for investment.

## BOARD PRESENTATION

In order to get the outline approval from the board and to benefit from their comments it was decided to make a presentation to the board in October 1979. If approval was given, then the management would prepare a formal investment proposal, an exhaustive internal document called PAR (program analysis and review) which would be considered by the board at some subsequent meeting after all aspects of the investment had been settled and a capital committment was required. The presentation was to take the form of an explanation of the underlying sales logic, buttressed by the financial details as they were known at the time.

The meeting was opened by H. Breedlove who explained how from small beginnings in 1972, largely due to Rick Barclay's efforts, sales had grown in Europe to a point where a European plant was the next logical step. Barclay filled in with greater detail. He expected the

European market for hydraulic tube in 1986 to be some 160,000 tons suitable for DOM. Copperweld had led development of DOM in Europe as they had in America but were now faced with a dilemma. The market was ripe for large-scale conversion but unlikely to buy more from Copperweld unless production could be brought closer to consumption. If Copperweld did not put up a plant then sooner or later an indigenous producer would take the plunge, others would follow, and Copperweld would have to retreat, if not completely, then to the large sizes in which it was unrivalled. On the other hand, by creating a plant Copperweld could continue to develop the market to its advantage.

Rick Barclay went on to discuss the competition, and how despite their extensive investments in tube their interest in DOM had been slight. There were in his view a number of reasons why Copperweld had been unchallenged: a broad customer base, an efficient target accounts approach (i.e., only selling to customers to whom DOM was particularly appropriate), good product quality and good technical support from the United States, excellent distribution and local sales support, and, not least, the advantage of offering an alternative supply source to European producers.

---
**EXHIBIT 13**
---

**PROJECTED INCOME STATEMENTS FOR FIFTH YEAR OF OPERATIONS (1986) WITH AND WITHOUT A WELD MILL**

|  | Without weld mill | | With weld mill | |
|---|---|---|---|---|
|  | $ thousand | % | $ thousand | % |
| Total sales | 42,904 | | 42,904 | |
| (in tons) | (35,000) | | (35,000) | |
| Less freight | 215 | | 215 | |
| Net sales | 42,690 | 100.0 | 42,690 | 100.0 |
| Cost of sales | | | | |
| Material | 24,721 | 57.9 | 15,177 | 35.6 |
| Labor | 1,093 | 2.6 | 1,255 | 2.9 |
| Salaries | 405 | 0.9 | 435 | 1.0 |
| Fringes | 320 | 0.7 | 360 | 0.8 |
| Utilities | 2,004 | 4.7 | 2,004 | 4.7 |
| Supplies | 1,110 | 2.6 | 1,366 | 3.2 |
| Maintenance | 939 | 2.2 | 1,622 | 3.8 |
| Total | 30,592 | 71.7 | 22,219 | 52.0 |
| Gross profit | 12,097 | 28.3 | 20,471 | 48.0 |
| Selling expenses | 1,030 | 2.4 | 1,030 | 2.4 |
| General & administrative costs | 225 | 0.5 | 225 | 0.5 |
| Depreciation* | 240 | 0.6 | 323 | 0.8 |
| Income before taxes | 10,602 | 24.8 | 18,892 | 44.3 |
| Taxes | 5,725 | 13.4 | 10,202 | 23.9 |
| Income after taxes | 4,877 | 11.4 | 8,690 | 20.4 |

*In either instance, almost all investments in building, machinery and equipment ($28 million in the first case and $41 million in the second) would have been depreciated in full against income during the first four years of operations.

•

H. Breedlove then took up the discussion and gave the board four options. The first was to continue exporting to Europe but to expect a shrinking market share. The second was to draw and finish in Europe from U.S.-made shells. The third option was to draw and finish locally from European-made shells, and the fourth was to weld, draw, and finish in Europe. In his view the third and fourth options were the most attractive. In round terms the last of these options would involve an investment of $40 million, take 24 months to achieve, give an internal rate of return of 23 percent, a return on invested capital of 16 percent, and a 4-year pay back. The preferred site was the United Kingdom, and calculations presented assumed this, although several locations within the United Kingdom were possible. There was also an option to take on a joint venture partner, which might reduce the risk.

# Norman Machine Tool Company

Charles Jones, president of Norman Machine Tool Company, and Ronald Jepson, vice-president for business and development, were seated in Mr. Jones's office in the early spring of 1982:

"You've been at this almost a year now, Ron," said Charles Jones.

"I know, Chuck. We're getting close," replied Ronald Jepson.

"That's what you said last November about getting the land for the plant," said Jones.

"We're better at it now. We've learned so much."

"That's fine, Ron, but I'm the CEO. What do I tell the board? We're not a training center. We're a manufacturing company. All we're doing is pouring money down a well. The monthly reports from this operation are becoming an embarrassment."

"China doesn't live by monthly reports. Things take time."

"Time," said Jones, "You've had 10 months, and the joint venture doesn't exist yet. We don't even have it structured on paper."

"Other firms are experiencing the same delays," said Jepson.

"That doesn't help our monthly earnings," Jones said and paused. "Ron, . . . is it worth it?"

"I hope so. I've never been through this before. But then few have. China is so promising. The modernization policy has to work. With Mao gone and these new people at the top, the China market can finally become a reality. Being one of the pioneers isn't easy. You agreed when we started, Chuck. You knew it would take a while."

"I knew. You knew. But the Board didn't know. Did you bring that report from Dave Thomas and the new financials?"

"Yes," answered Jepson, handing him the folder. (See Appendix.)

"Good. I hope it helps."

This case was prepared by William H. Davidson, Associate Professor of Business Policy, with the assistance of Robert S. Garrity. Copyright, 1985 by the University of Southern California Graduate Business School sponsors. The case is a fictitious composite of data gathered from a confidential survey and interviews with officers of some 50 U.S. firms engaged in negotiations or operations of joint ventures in the Peoples Republic of China. Interviews were conducted in the United States and the PRC.

## BACKGROUND

The Norman Machine Tool Company of East Rutherford, Indiana, had seen declining sales in the late 1970s. Competition from Japan and Europe had put a strain on U.S. tool builders. Japan had grabbed a significant share of the U.S. market with high-quality, low-cost machine tools. The effect on the U.S. industry was traumatic. By the late 1970s, closings and mergers were occurring frequently.

Norman had experienced major growth in the 1940s as the United States began producing war equipment for lend-lease to Britain and Russia and then for direct involvement in World War II. The Marshall Plan and Korean War kept demand for machine tools up. The 1950s and 1960s saw continued growth. By the 1970s, however, the Japanese and Germans had rebuilt their industry and began to challenge the U.S. machine tool builders. Norman did not feel these pressures as much as other producers because it served the custom tool market primarily. Customers would tell Norman their needs, and machines would be developed to their specifications. Orders from the Pentagon also comprised an important part of Norman's business. However, Norman's sales to industrial customers, which represented half of Norman's $420 million in revenues, had slipped sharply.

Donald Jepson came to Norman in 1965 following a career in the military. He had been a lieutenant on General MacArthur's staff during the occupation of Japan and had followed Japan's reconstruction effort ever since. Jepson felt at the time that Japan's prewar industrial strengths would eventually be renewed and that Japan would be a major competitor during his business career.

The 1970s were the turning point. When the 1973 oil shock caused a need to retool the U.S. auto industry, the Japanese were ready with standard machines, low prices, quick delivery, and good service. Since then, Japanese tool venders had continued to grab a greater share of the market in numerical controls, computer-aided design and test equipment, and computer-aided manufacturing systems.

Jepson believed that Norman's best hope lay in setting up less costly operations abroad. Joining in a U.S. Department of Commerce Trade Mission to China, he visited several machine tool builders. One of these firms was of particular interest to Jepson. The Zhonhei Manufacturing Co. was the leading Chinese producer of machine tools. It produced a low-cost, standardized line of tools that would perfectly complement Norman's existing line of specialty, custom products.

In addition to providing a source of low-end tools, Jepson believed that China's modernization represented a tremendous market opportunity for Norman's products. He returned to Indiana with a convincing report. Letters were exchanged, and a meeting was set up for June 18, 1981, in Beijing.

Norman assembled a team of negotiators to go to Beijing. Mr. Jepson led the team, which included an attorney, a finance officer, David Thomas, and a construction engineer, Michael Fletcher. Since none of the team spoke Chinese, a translator was contracted to accompany the team. Mr. Jepson had met, on his previous trip, a Hong Kong Chinese who was available for such duty. The translator, Mr. Lin, made a visit to Norman in April. A second strategy meeting would be held in Hong Kong prior to entering China.

In the three months prior to June, all the team members began to read a little about China. Visas were secured through letters of invitation issued by Zhonhei. These letters were sent with passports to the Chinese Embassy in Washington and returned with visas after six weeks. The group arrived in Beijing as scheduled, after a two-day planning session in Hong Kong.

## THE INITIAL MEETING

The two sides were to gather in a conference room of the Tianmen Building, an old hotel near the Temple of Heaven, that had taken on the function of an office building. The lobby was plain and small. The Norman team was greeted in the unfurnished lobby by an English-speaking Chinese in a blue Mao jacket. Ronald Jepson and his colleagues glanced around as their host led the way to the third floor. There was no elevator. At the third floor, they were led down a poorly lit hallway to a large reception room. The conference room of the hotel was plain— four white walls, a long wide table draped with a white cotton cloth, seven chairs on each side, a second row behind the Chinese side and a third row which encircled the room. The Norman team was met at the door by Director Lao of Zhonhei Manufacturing, who was the senior officer of the potential partner. The Chinese negotiators stood up to greet the Americans as did the people in the second and third rows. No one sat behind the Norman chairs. Handshakes, smiles, and a feeling of cautious enthusiasm filled the room. The Chinese studied the suits, white shirts, and ties. The Americans eyed the Mao jackets. Introductions were made through the translators. Soon everyone was seated, and two fellows from the second row were pouring hot water into the glasses at each place at the table. The steamy liquid from a tall aluminum thermos stirred up the tea leaves that rested at the bottom of each glass.

On the Chinese side of the table in the center seat was Mr. Zien, an officer of the People's Republic of China's Ministry of Machine Builders. Also with him at the table was Director Lao, an officer from the Ministry of Finance, an officer from the Ministry of Land Use, the Mayor of Zhonhei, the Governor of Xinhei province, the Provincial Director of Transportation, and Mr. Hua, director of personnel and head of the Zhonhei Plant Communist Party Council. The other 19 Chinese were not introduced. They sat quietly, usually attentively with pad and pen in hand. Ages at the table were 55–70. In the secondary seats, 30–50.

On the U.S. side in the center seat was Mr. Jepson flanked by the lawyer and translator, flanked by the finance officer and engineer, flanked by two empty chairs. Ages ranged from 28 to 61.

The first day was filled with long Chinese orations on the New Economic Policy, the quest for modernization, the fine Zhonhei company, the beginning of a new era for China, Zhonhei, and Norman. The first day achieved some getting to know each other and a recognition that translation requirements were going to cut by at least 50 percent the volume of accomplishment per session. Tea glasses were constantly being filled, and the back rows saw frequent departures and arrivals.

The Americans were staying at the Beijing Hotel. They had booked four rooms, for a period of nine days. The nine days went much like the first with long speeches, some interruptions, and frequent changes of personnel on the Chinese side. The front row stayed the same, but in the 19 other chairs some 43 different people came and went. The word-for-word translations made it slow going, but a familiarity was building. After nine days, the Americans found themselves heading for the airport with only one thing in hand, the date of the next round, September 12, 1981.

When Mr. Jepson had addressed production planning, marketing, market share, building sites, etc, the Chinese responses were "we are considering this," "the amount will be determined after further study," etc. He had laid out to the partner some of Norman's goals, methods, and expectations for the joint venture. He was going back to Indiana with little to report.

Jepson decided that nine days would not be enough next time. So David Thomas, the finance officer, was asked to secure five rooms for one month. The team would return to Beijing with a written plan, specific questions, a request for a visit to the Zhonhei plant, and orders to stay until there was something to report. After the first two weeks of meetings in September, Mr. Jepson extended the rooms for another four weeks and secured invitations to Beijing for the spouses of the American negotiators. Jepson himself came and went from Beijing. He could not afford the time to stay straight through and left Dave Thomas in charge. Thomas had set up an office with facilities for a secretary at the Beijing Hotel across from his room. Two rooms were held for incoming Norman people and the fifth as an investment in the future. Companies from Europe, Japan, and the United States were clamoring for space, so the extra room seemed a sensible move.

## THE SECOND PHASE

Dave Thomas, age 41 and a senior finance officer with Norman, oversaw the primary negotiations at the Tianmen Hotel. He met regularly with a group headed by Director Lao, age 52. In early October, Michael Fletcher, Norman's chief engineer, began a series of separate engineering discussions with a group headed by Mr. Hua, director of personnel, a man of 63 years who had been specially assigned to the joint venture negotiations. Fletcher, age 39, had an MS in engineering and 11 years experience with Norman. Hua brought a group of six engineers to each meeting at the hotel. They were usually the same people. Mr. Lin translated for Fletcher when he was available. Madame Zhou of the Foreign Trade Ministry translated for Hua and his team, and for both sides in Lin's absence. The agenda for the first meeting was one of generalities. As in the primary negotiations, the opening remarks by Hua were long. He spoke of China, America, Communism, Zhonhei, Norman, and the promising future. It took place on a Monday morning at 9 a.m., with a break from noon to 2, and concluded at 5 p.m.

Fletcher had been with the negotiating team since the beginning so the day did not surprise him. He had requested two engineering colleagues from the United States but told them to arrive on Monday afternoon, since he would not need them that first day.

After the day's meeting, Fletcher returned to the Norman rooms to have dinner with Dave Thomas in the restaurant at the hotel. They had not tired of the menu yet. The food was authentic and quite good. The selection was a bit more extensive and intriguing than the Golden

Dragon Inn back home. The desk clerk had a message for him. It was a long distance call from his engineers who were now in Hong Kong. The call had been placed at 11:07 a.m. and received in Beijing at 3:21 p.m. It read, "Rain around Beijing has cancelled our CAAC flight. No flights tomorrow. We think we are booked for Wednesday noon. Should arrive 3:00."

Fletcher's first emotion was frustration, but a couple of days delay would be standard fare for his Chinese counterparts. He could help Dave Thomas and have a few chats with some of the other U.S. firms in town. He dispatched Mr. Lin to request the postponement. The group did arrive on Wednesday. Fletcher met his associates, Linda Jenkins and Henry Anderson, at the airport. Jenkins had been trained at MIT, Anderson at the University of Texas. Linda had been with the company 8 years, Henry, 6 years. They gathered in the Norman receiving room with its beautiful Tianjin carpet and comfortable furniture. Ron Jepson had felt it necessary to provide well for his people, although he received ceaseless challenges to the bill he was running up in China.

A week later the group gathered again after supper.

"Linda, how have you found your people?" Fletcher began.

"They are very pleasant. Mr. Zhen speaks no English, so perhaps that accounts for his shyness. On the other hand, Mr. Bin speaks well and has no qualms about sharing thoughts or asking questions. Madame Wu is good. Modest English but good engineering," reported Jenkins.

"Henry, how about your people?" asked Fletcher. "Fine. No problems. Workable English and satisfactory engineering. Not quite up to their titles, but satisfactory," Anderson said.

"Any thoughts on Mr. Hua?" Fletcher asked.

"Not much English." Anderson spoke up. "Didn't you say he was specially chosen for this job?"

"Yes." Fletcher answered, "Linda?"

"He seems to lack a good engineering background."

"Is that so necessary?" asked Fletcher.

"To select experts, one must be able to ask proper questions."

"Where was Hua before the joint venture?" asked Thomas.

"Beijing," said Fletcher.

"In a machine tool factory?"

"No. Last week I asked Director Lao the same questions. He was from the Bureau of Machine Building. The CCP overseer in his division."

"A Party guy?"

"Yes. He started in Harbin at age 18. Kept his nose clean, by Mao's standards. Pushed the party line."

"So he's not an engineer."

"No."

"And he's not a manager."

"So where did Lao come from?" asked Anderson.

"Zhonhei I guess," said Linda.

"No," said Thomas. "He was out near Xian."

"The Terracotta sculpture town?" asked Anderson.

"Not in it but near it. On a farm." reported Thomas.

"A farm near Xian. What was he doing there?" asked Fletcher.

"Planting rice."

"Cultural Revolution?" asked Anderson.

"I think so."

"Must have been a good plant manager in 1966," Fletcher conjectured.

Fletcher and Hua met together frequently to discuss recruiting, and the general plans for the joint venture.

"The Zhonhei Municipal Construction Company has three new Mitsubishi cement trucks, ample labor, and all the engineer talent they need. We will not need to purchase any trucks or hire construction engineers," said Fletcher.

"We can hire our own construction people with RMB," said Hua.

"We are not creating a construction company, we're establishing a joint venture to build machine tools."

Hua also pushed hard for the production of more sophisticated machine tools by the joint venture. Fletcher reminded him that the joint venture's initial intent was to produce a low-cost, standardized unit to be called the Model 10. He suggested that Hua talk to Jepson about importing other Norman models into China.

Fletcher asked about the process of selecting engineers. Hua explained that he would provide a list of candidates for each position.

"That will be fine for many of the less skilled jobs, but we would like to advertise for the senior technical spots," said Fletcher.

"I will provide you with a list of candidates from which to choose for all positions," replied Hua.

"An open competition for the senior people will give the joint venture the best opportunity to succeed. Not only will they be the best technicians in the province, but we can select people, who when trained in Indiana, can teach colleagues and subordinates well. I'm sure you will provide an excellent list of candidates, but consideration by Norman of the candidates for that list might assist you," said Michael Fletcher.

"I will provide you with a list of candidates for all positions," said Mr. Hua.

The land use document, establishing a site for the JV facility, had been signed by Jepson and Lao in December. Mr. Lao said he would submit it for approval. By telex, Jepson periodically questioned Dave Thomas about the status of the approval. Each time Thomas answered, "Not yet."

When Jepson arrived in February 1982, Beijing sat under a gray cloud of coal smoke created by the heating and cooking facilities throughout the city. The cold was piercing, and the frequent winds carried dust everywhere.

Ronald Jepson entered the office at the Beijing Hotel. Thomas used a white cloth to wipe the thin gray dusting from the coffee table before setting the tea before his guest.

"The land use approval?" Jepson asked as he set down his glass.

"Not yet," Dave reported.

"What is the delay?"

"The system. The bureaucracy."

"Yes, I know, but it's beginning to be a bit ludicrous," Jepson retorted.

"Director Lao submitted it to the Land Use Bureau. It entered at a rather low level. It then must follow the switch-back trail of Chinese bureaucracy. The paper must zigzag its way to the top to the final decision makers. The top people put their chop (name stamp) on it for final approval. Everyone gets a crack at it first. It takes time."

"Well, who has it now?" asked Jepson trying to keep his tone steady.

"We don't know."

"Who doesn't know—we Norman, or we Zhonhei and Norman?"

"The latter."

"Can we find out and get Lao to speed things up?"

"I'm not sure."

"That's not like you, Dave. You always have a way to get things done. That is why you're here."

"I built that reputation in Indiana."

"What has stopped you?"

"The routing system. Since the paper entered the Bureau, it has been lost."

"Lost?"

"Not lost. It's there. But for all practical purposes it's temporarily gone. Reviewers do not initial what they see. There isn't a definitive route for documents. It may be far along, or it may be at the bottom of a stack in someone's in-basket."

"Are you being gentle with me, or could it have gone out in last month's trash?" asked Jepson cautiously.

"I wouldn't say that yet," Thomas answered as his eyes studied the ring his glass left on the table.

"Then let's send it through again."

"Well, we will, if need be. But not yet."

"It's been three and a half months, Dave."

"I know."

"That doesn't bother you."

"It would, back home. But here, we're still within the standard waiting period."

"It took us six weeks to get a phone," lamented Jepson. "We had a time securing a driver.

I thought we'd only have these problems at the beginning. Over time things should move along. It's not like we won't pay. We have the dollars. They want the dollars."

"That's irrelevant. No matter what you want here, you have to get in line. The line is long and slow. Mr. Lao reminded me, in one of my moments of haste, that it took 2000 years to build the great wall, and it's still standing. We're the visiting team, Ron. We don't know whether the Chinese rule book and ours are the same. Though we may be playing what we perceive as the same game, it seems to be quite different . . . sorry for the lecture, Ron."

"No, no. You have to deal with this everyday. I have to realign my thinking each time I get off that plane. Things are actually going well. You've settled in, haven't you Dave? I appreciate the way you attend to and learn about China and the Chinese. You're doing a good job. Now tell me, where do we stand on buying steel?"

"I spoke with Zhao the finance officer two weeks ago. Yesterday I pressed him for an answer. He said he had not yet spoken with Director Lao," Thomas reported.

"Why Lao? Who's the purchasing officer?"

"Ms. Li."

"Did he ask her?"

"No. He said he must ask Director Lao."

"Seems a waste of time to go to his boss when it would be easier to go to purchasing," Jepson pondered aloud. "I don't quite comprehend the rules around here. Perhaps you could talk with Li. I'll speak with Lao."

"This is a tougher game than we thought," Jepson added after a pause.

"It's completely new. Can you imagine having to clear everything with the mayor of East Rutherford or constantly get approval from Indianapolis? Or better yet, be in constant contact with Washington? Imagine a central government that plans and manages everything from offshore oil drilling all the way down to the toilet paper at a construction site? Slow, everything is slow. Duplication, redundancy, excessive bureaucracy, the red tapes."

"You mean red tape."

"No, 'tapes.' The Chinese who speak to me

in English say 'red tapes.' It's an appropriate description. We use red tape to mean bureaucratic holdups. Consider it as a plural, one after another. That's China."

The next day Jepson met with Mr. Lao.

"Mr. Thomas has asked Mr. Zhao about purchasing steel. He's received no reply since Zhao hasn't spoken to you," Jepson began.

"What do you need to know?" asked Lao encouragingly.

"Where can we get it? What grade? How much volume? How much time? What price? etc."

"I'll ask Ms. Li."

"She's in purchasing?"

"Yes."

"Why didn't Zhao ask her instead of waiting to see you?"

"Standard procedure is to go through senior managers to get information from other divisions. Departments are afraid to communicate directly for two reasons. They fear reprisals from above for mistakes. They also do not want to release information. Each division's realm is sacred. If they give away material, info, etc. they no longer control it. So Zhao was afraid of me and thought Li wouldn't help him directly."

Jepson sat back in his chair.

"I'll see what I can do," Lao offered.

One of the reasons for Jepson's visit was a second look at the plant site in Zhonhei. The Americans spent nine hours on the train to Zhonhei. Ronald Jepson was accompanied by Dave Thomas and Michael Fletcher. Arriving at the station, their escorts led them to waiting cars. They were timeless Shanghai models: a Chinese version of a Russian imitation of an American Studebaker. Inside, the group was struck by the nylon curtains over the back door windows and rear windshield. They had noticed them in Beijing on similar cars and a few Mercedes Benz vehicles.

The factory was a pair of large concrete block houses. After passing through the fence gate, the cars pulled up to a long low building. They entered to find an austere receiving room. They sat on the sofa. Their host walked across the gritty concrete floor to a small refrigerator in the corner of the room. From it he produced four bottles of an extremely sweet, bright orange soft drink. The Americans nursed the beverages during the waiting period.

Director Lao entered the room with three associates, and everyone proceeded on the tour. Walking toward the first building they passed a storage yard stacked with rusty sheets of metal.

"A large inventory," Jepson observed.

"I try to order to meet my needs and keep these stacks down, but there is no predicting delivery," explained Director Lao. "Some months we have not enough. Other months too much. We are only a manufacturing center. Distribution of materials is directed by city, province, or state officials depending on the item. The state planning council determines our production quotas and delivery schedules. We are assigned supplies, prices, and customers by the state.

That's on paper. In practice there are the priorities. We may be assigned to receive 1200 tons of steel. In January the first 100 tons arrive, 12 days late mind you. February snows stop deliveries, and March 5 we get 2 shipments totalling 175 tons. By now the military has syphoned off a little extra. April rains wash out roads so April 22, we get 65 tons. Higher-priority projects, such as high rises in Beijing, auto manufacturing in Shanghai, etc., have gotten extra allocations. So we end up short of steel."

"Where did all of this steel come from?" asked Fletcher.

"The mayor of Xinhei is an avid trader trying to modernize his municipality. He is always in the market for concrete. We buy concrete from my brother-in-law's plant, and ship it to Xinhei for steel."

"You can't use it in this condition," stated Fletcher, "it needs to be cleaned."

"There are many Chinese in this province who are waiting for work," Lao began.

"You mean unemployed?" said Jepson.

"There is no unemployment in China," answered Lao. "I send a request to the job assignment bureau for 200 workers. The bureau sends 400, because there are many people waiting for work. We give them solvent, steel wool, or steel brushes, and they scrub the stock. We get clean steel.''

"We won't be able to operate that way in the JV,'' said Jepson. "We'll need to keep inventory low and protected from the elements. It's too costly to hire crews to clean materials.''

"Fine,'' said Lao. "I hope you are right.''

The Zhonhei enterprise was a self-sufficient, vertically integrated operation. It manufactured or produced everything it needed: parts for machinery; washroom fixtures; garden vegetables. Services were also provided: meals, childcare, laundry. All was provided by the factory. Nothing was contracted out.

In the factory, the Americans noted the equipment, safety standards, numbers of people per task, use of space, etc. After the tour they agreed that the equipment was adequate. Chinese made, much of it looked like it was built in 1959, although many items carried a 1975 stamp. But it worked. It performed the necessary functions. Mr. Hua was calling for new Japanese or German tools, but the Chinese products would do. The machines would have to be rearranged on the floor, though. There was no safe or logical traffic pattern for workers or materials. Housekeeping was needed. Floors, machines, and materials needed a good scrubbing and logical arranging.

"Perhaps we should add housekeeping to the job descriptions. Make it a criteria for earning a bonus,'' said Jepson.

Lao smiled and nodded.

Before returning to the States, Jepson asked Thomas to write a brief on the Chinese style of doing business. He needed something for Charles Jones's presentation at the April board meeting when he got home. (Thomas's report appears in the Appendix.)

After Jepson's visit, negotiations continued in earnest. The table was headed by the Vice Minister Xin, of the PRC's Ministry of Machine Building, Director Lao, and Mr. Hua. When Xin was absent, Lao or Hua chaired the meetings.

Translation was satisfactory most of the time. There were often conceptual misunderstandings. The major impediments were the Chinese side's lack of experience in profit-oriented business and the Norman's translator's lack of experience in the industry.

On one occasion, after eight months of meetings, the talks stalled over the use of foreign exchange. Norman indicated the need for sending profits home to shareholders. The Americans explained this point very carefully and calmly. At one point during the morning session the Chinese looked quite surprised by Jepson's statement. They quickly conferred among themselves and waited. No one spoke for two minutes. Then Mr. Hua asked if, perhaps, there had been some mistake. Mr. Thomas asked Mr. Lin what had happened. The translator said he had relayed the message of Mr. Thomas to the Chinese. Mr. Thomas asked why that would cause such a stir. Mr. Lin guessed it was the firm words he had used to press the point with the Chinese. Mr. Thomas asked Mr. Lin to repeat the statement without added emphasis. Director Lao perceived the source of confusion, nodded confidently to Thomas, and suggested the morning session adjourn.

In a discussion of startup costs, Fletcher explained that Norman's contribution to construction of the plant would be billed at Norman's cost. Director Lao said that he would consider it. Two days later, he told Dave Thomas that Zhonhei would accept it. The following week Mr. Xin returned to chair the meetings. He praised the Americans for their generosity in handling the bill for the renovations.

"I beg your pardon,'' said Thomas.

"Yes,'' said Mr. Xin. "Director Lao reported that renovation would be handled at your expense.''

"At our cost,'' said Thomas.

"Yes, cost, expense. It's very generous.''

Dave Thomas turned to Michael Fletcher, "When did we discuss this point?''

"Last Tuesday."

"Was Lin here then?"

"I think so," replied Fletcher.

Turning back, Thomas said, "Excuse me, Mr. Xin. When we said cost, we did not mean expense."

Xin conferred with his translator. "In our language they are synonomous," explained Xin.

"Can you help us here Lin?" asked Jepson, who then gave a brief lecture on the difference between standard transfer costs and normal billing arrangements.

It had been agreed that each side would contribute $1.5 million to the joint venture: Norman in the form of foreign exchange, equipment, technology transfer, and training; Zhonhei in the form of land, organizational fees, plant, equipment, local currency, and foreign exchange. Dave Thomas questioned the $0.87 million assessment for the proposed site property. Director Lao questioned the need to purchase the blueprints for the machinery which Norman would provide. Both sides held fast to their positions.

Realizing that land was one of China's great resources and its use could be very profitable for Norman, Dave Thomas agreed to the valuation of the site. Thomas spoke at some length privately to Lao about the effort required to create the blueprints, and the custom of technology transfer. After much discussion, Lao agreed to support Norman's valuation of the blueprints.

Dave Thomas conferred with Lao on the subject of personnel. The director explained the policy that the joint venture managers could select whomever they pleased from the list provided by the director of personnel. Thomas said that such a list might not provide access to the best people. Acknowledging that the personnel department would know who is available for the positions, he suggested that the joint venture advertise the openings to ensure that the best candidates apply.

"After all," said Thomas. "It is easier for a good engineer to find a factory than for a factory to find an engineer."

"Is this the way it is done in your country?"

"Yes."

"But you do not have a system of party work-groups, and your government agencies do not direct your factories."

"Yes, and this joint venture is a blending of our two systems with the goal of manufacturing high-quality machine tools in a cost efficient way to earn maximum profit. To do this, we need the best people."

"We will use Norman's modern machinery and methods."

"Yes. But a machine or method is only as good as the people who use them. I think you agree."

Taking a moment of silence, Director Lao replied, "You are correct. I do agree."

In June of 1982, Ronald Jepson returned to Beijing with a renewed spirit. Jones's report to the board had gone well, and they were willing to continue the effort. The negotiations picked up again.

"The electronic control units for the Model 10 will have to be imported," said Jepson.

"That will take foreign exchange," answered Lao.

"Yes, but the quality required is not available in China," added Jepson.

"I see."

"We can produce it," interrupted Hua.

"In five or six years perhaps," said Jepson. "But for the JV we'll import. We should also import specialty steel."

"We have the steel," insisted Hua.

"Yes, but the grade is not right."

"China can produce it."

"Our reports show that availability will be unreliable."

"China has the steel," Hua reiterated.

"Delays will be costly," explained Jepson.

"It is not necessary to import steel. China is a powerful industrial society. Workers make very good steel."

The discussion moved on to royalties and dividends.

"A joint venture requires investment. It must provide a return," said Jepson.

"You may have it in the form of imported machines," said Hua.

"We also require a financial return on our investment."

"Where will we get foreign exchange for your capitalists in America? If you send foreign exchange home to your stockholders we will be weak. You Americans are rich. You do not need to take our reserves," said Hua.

"Perhaps we can exchange the RMB generated by domestic sales at the Bank of China."

"That is difficult," explained Lao. "We can apply, but it is not guaranteed. If we sell to domestic users as an import substitute we can request payment in foreign exchange."

"I see," said Jepson.

"But that takes foreign exchange from other People's factories. We must not do that. We must export," said Hua.

"The joint venture will not be ready to export to third parties for two or three years."

"Can you wait two years to extract foreign exchange, Mr. Jepson?" asked Lao. "After all you have taught me the American way of going into debt at the beginning to gain profit in the end."

"Two years will be fine if it is stipulated in the agreement," answered Jepson.

"Thank you," said the Director.

Hua then introduced the question of staffing levels. He proposed that the joint venture hire 1800 workers initially at an annual wage equivalent to U.S. $4,000. The list of candidates was ready for review.

Mr. Jepson said, "We won't need 1800 people. At $4000 per employee, the labor costs would be too high. With the level of automation we'll be using and the goal of cost-effective production, 600 employees is more than adequate.

"Additionally, your candidate list will be excellent for less skilled positions. Let's advertise for the senior engineer jobs."

"Excuse me," said Lao. "The lunch hour is upon us. So let us leave this topic for the afternoon."

After lunch, Lao began with a discussion of training requirements. He requested an extensive training commitment from the Norman corporation.

"That is probably more than we can handle," replied Jepson.

"Part of the spirit of the JV is to have you train us," said Lao.

"We can take the top managers and engineers to Indiana for training," said Jepson. "They can return to China to teach their colleagues and subordinates."

"The training would be more complete if we sent more people."

"That would be very expensive," explained Jepson.

"Expensive," said Director Lao. "We hear that every day. You come to China to use our labor to sell to our Chinese factories. You want to use our foreign exchange without earning it through export. The capitalists come to the greatest nation in the world and expect to run things like the foreign devils of the last century. China will not permit it. Chairman Mao led us out from under the oppression of foreign exploitation. He created the great People's Republic of China. We are beginning to open our door to let the running dogs in, and they expect to take from us again. Not so, American capitalist. You are not dealing with China's past. We do not need your company. There are many others who will come to us. We do not even need them because, in all things, the will of the people will prevail.

"We are giving you our land, our resources, our precious labor. You see it only as a place and means to extract profit with as little investment and effort as you can employ. We ask you for patience, and you cry of stockholders. We provide steel, and you insult us by saying it is below standard. We ask for training and you speak of expense. Your money, your precious dollar is nothing. Our land, our labor, those are the truly valuable things on the Earth.

"Go back to your stockholders. Go back to your banks. Take your whole group and go. China will not be pushed, insulted, exploited."

In their suite of rooms the Americans sat quietly. They gathered at 6:30 before heading for the hotel dining room. Ron Jepson looked around at each of his compatriots, his eyes finally resting on Dave Thomas. "What do we do now Dave?"

# Joint Venture Report from China

To: Ronald Jepson
Re: Norman MT Co. experience with PRCJV to date,
2/3/82

The following is a description of the negotiating conditions here in China. I begin with a little bit of history in order to explain the environment into which we have stepped. That is followed by a list of observations and an editorial conclusion.

## HISTORY

China's New Economic Policy (NEP) and America's improved relations make China a very attractive market. Deng Xiao-ping's leadership has enjoyed broad support among China's cadres. After Chairman Mao died in 1976, the purge of the Gang of Four indicated the beginning of significant changes in China. The Joint Venture Law of 1979 and other commercial laws are tangible evidence of Deng's efforts to institutionalize the NEP. Putting laws on paper is an effort to give confidence to foreign investors in China.

After decades of war and turmoil before the 1949 Liberation and the 27 years of isolation under Mao, the new leadership is implementing practical steps to modernize China. In 1960, after the disastrous Great Leap Forward, Deng Xiao-ping and Liu Shao-chi, senior officials under Mao, attempted a similar pragmatic economic policy. Their efforts began to get China back on steady economic footing. But in 1966, Party Chairman Mao, feeling threatened by Deng's and Liu's growing influence, initiated a political movement to regain personal power. What became known as the Cultural Revolution imposed 10 years of near anarchy on the People's Republic of China. Factory managers and educators were purged from their offices. Manufacturing suffered, and schools closed. For 10 years, experience in production and formal schooling were very limited.

In 1976, Mao died, and the pragmatists moved back toward seats of power. Madame Mao and her Gang of four were purged as a statement that impractical political zeal would no longer guide the People's Republic of China. In 1978, Hua Guo-feng led China and initiated a new economic plan. It was a mixture of the Great Leap Forward and practical economic management. But in 1979 Deng Xiao-ping, who had been operating behind the scenes, moved Hua out to avoid another economic disaster. Deng initiated the three-Year Readjustment Plan which reined in all of Hua's overzealous policies. Many international contracts were cancelled, and it appeared on the surface to be another of China's policy reversals. Instead, it was a more careful reassessment of the same theme.

The adoption of commercial law, Chinese trips abroad for technical and management training, and invitations to investors have been indications of the focus on pragmatism and efficiency. Deng's own pronouncements have been verbal statements of a move from Mao's "politics in command" to "economics in command." Mao believed that political will was more important than scientific expertise. Deng favors expertise in economic modernization.

## OBSERVATIONS

Despite these shifts, doing profitable business in China remains a difficult goal. Exhibit 1 shows a Pro Forma Financial Statement. The Chinese management system is quite different from our own. The Chinese manager is bound by the experience of the past twenty years. Business and production in China are characterized by:

1. Factories are fully integrated. Each factory wants to produce each and every component of its final product.
2. Self-sufficient provinces or municipalities, not national integration, are the rule. For example, there are something like 400 truck factories in China producing a total of about 200,000 trucks per year. These are small, inefficient plants.
3. Rules change quickly. The open-door policy is brand new. The Chinese have little or no experience with international business, profit-oriented business, performance-based management, autonomy of provinces, municipalities, industries. The government loosens the reins on initiative for awhile then pulls them in again. The

| | | | | EXHIBIT 1 | | | | |

## PRO FORMA FINANCIAL STATEMENT: CHINA JOINT VENTURE, NORMAN MACHINE TOOL, JULY 1982

Projected Revenues and Expenses, as Incurred in Renminbi and Dollars (Thousands)

| | 1983 | | 1984 | | 1985 | |
|---|---|---|---|---|---|---|
| | RMB | US$ | RMB | US$ | RMB | US$ |
| Revenues | 12,000 | 0 | 24,000 | 5,000 | 48,000 | 10,000 |
| Costs of goods | | | | | | |
|   Materials | 4,000 | 1,800 | 12,000 | 4,700 | 24,000 | 9,400 |
|   Labor | 3,000 | 0 | 6,000 | 0 | 9,000 | 0 |
|   Factory overhead | 1,000 | 0 | 1,000 | 0 | 1,000 | 0 |
|   Salaries/benefits | 460 | 180 | 500 | 190 | 600 | 200 |
|   General & administrative costs | 600 | 25 | 650 | 30 | 700 | 35 |
|   Depreciation | 400 | | 400 | | 400 | |
|   Interest expense | 1,500 | 0 | 1,500 | 0 | 1,500 | 0 |
| Net income | 1,040 | (1,995) | 1,950 | 80 | 10,800 | 335 |
| Taxes (Chinese) | 520 | 0 | 975 | 40 | 5,400 | 162.5 |
| Dividends | 260 | 0 | 487.5 | 20 | 2,700 | 83.75 |
| Retained earnings | 260 | (1,995) | 487.5 | 20 | 2,700 | 83.75 |

Key assumptions are: (1) Shipments are of Model 10 units only, (2) Prices are RMB 30,000 and U.S. $10,000 for Chinese and export market, respectively. (3) Norman will purchase 500 units in 1984, 1000 units in 1985. (4) Straight-line depreciation of plant and equipment is taken over a 20-year schedule. (5) RMB = 2.4 per U.S. $1. (6) Interest rate on RMB loan is 10 percent.

legal, managerial, and commercial infrastructures (as well as the physical) are still evolving.

4. The Chinese cannot say "No." It is a problem for us. Discussions may proceed without a yes or no from the Chinese. They end the discussion with: "We will consider it," "We will see about the arrangements," etc. No commitment either way. They do not come back with a "no," even if they knew from the start they cannot meet the deadline. This seems to be done to save personal face, departmental face, or national face.

5. Creativity and initiative are nonexistent. A worker gets no notice or reward for a job well done but will surely suffer consequences for an error. Chinese are very risk-averse as a result.

6. Sourcing is unreliable and relies a great deal on barter. If factory A orders parts from B through the government resource agency, it may take some time. So A may trade cement (a material which C needs and A can get at low cost) to C for parts.

7. Quality control is not an integral part of production. A quota system puts primary emphasis on 200 items not 200 good items.

8. Prices are controlled by the state. They do not reflect production costs. Accountability for a cost-revenue ratio rests nowhere in the factory.

9. Distribution is a series of delays, overruns, and deficits. When I asked one manager why there was such a large inventory of finished goods in the yard, he answered, "My job is production. Moving this out is transportation's job," and "transportation" is a provincial agency.

10. The wage standard is based solely on date of hiring and level of education. Merit and performance have had little to do with compensation and clout.

11. Everyone is on a payroll. During sluggish times, some may not work while in the plant. They may not even come to the plant. But the privilege of socialism is that everyone has a "job." Everyone is guaranteed a wage.

12. Chinese enterprises are top-heavy. There is an excessive collection of managers and bureaus which oversee the operation. Managers are implementors of others' policies. They do not participate in planning the budget, production, hiring, etc. They merely carry out orders like sergeants or line supervisors. They must serve not only the state, municipal and provincial ministries and bureaus but also the Workers' Party Committee in their plant. Recently, the state ordered that supervisors and managers be elected by their fellow workers. This seems to be an effort to make management more performance-

**EXHIBIT 2**

## CHINESE GOVERNMENT STRUCTURE

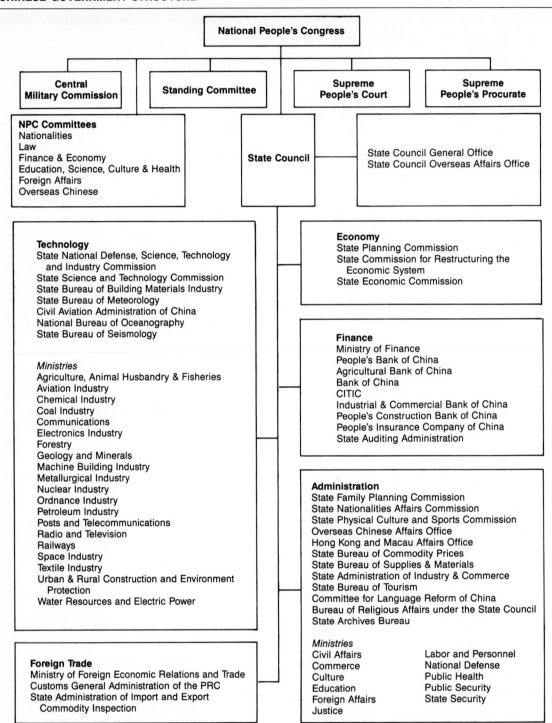

**National People's Congress**

**Central Military Commission**

**Standing Committee**

**Supreme People's Court**

**Supreme People's Procurate**

**NPC Committees**
Nationalities
Law
Finance & Economy
Education, Science, Culture & Health
Foreign Affairs
Overseas Chinese

**State Council**

State Council General Office
State Council Overseas Affairs Office

**Technology**
State National Defense, Science, Technology
   and Industry Commission
State Science and Technology Commission
State Bureau of Building Materials Industry
State Bureau of Meteorology
Civil Aviation Administration of China
National Bureau of Oceanography
State Bureau of Seismology

*Ministries*
Agriculture, Animal Husbandry & Fisheries
Aviation Industry
Chemical Industry
Coal Industry
Communications
Electronics Industry
Forestry
Geology and Minerals
Machine Building Industry
Metallurgical Industry
Nuclear Industry
Ordnance Industry
Petroleum Industry
Posts and Telecommunications
Radio and Television
Railways
Space Industry
Textile Industry
Urban & Rural Construction and Environment
   Protection
Water Resources and Electric Power

**Economy**
State Planning Commission
State Commission for Restructuring the
   Economic System
State Economic Commission

**Finance**
Ministry of Finance
People's Bank of China
Agricultural Bank of China
Bank of China
CITIC
Industrial & Commercial Bank of China
People's Construction Bank of China
People's Insurance Company of China
State Auditing Administration

**Administration**
State Family Planning Commission
State Nationalities Affairs Commission
State Physical Culture and Sports Commission
Overseas Chinese Affairs Office
Hong Kong and Macau Affairs Office
State Bureau of Commodity Prices
State Bureau of Supplies & Materials
State Administration of Industry & Commerce
State Bureau of Tourism
Committee for Language Reform of China
Bureau of Religious Affairs under the State Council
State Archives Bureau

*Ministries*

| | |
|---|---|
| Civil Affairs | Labor and Personnel |
| Commerce | National Defense |
| Culture | Public Health |
| Education | Public Security |
| Foreign Affairs | State Security |
| Justice | |

**Foreign Trade**
Ministry of Foreign Economic Relations and Trade
Customs General Administration of the PRC
State Administration of Import and Export
   Commodity Inspection

oriented. It has yet to filter through the entire economy.

13. Hiring and selection at all levels for the joint venture is in many ways out of our hands. Top managers are provided by Zhonhei. Engineers and mid-level managers are to be selected by the joint Zhonhei-Norman management. The pool of candidates is provided by Hua, the director of personnel. From that pool, we can choose freely, but the candidates are not always the best experts which we know are available.

14. The key to productivity is job descriptions. Write jobs descriptions for each and every position. Chinese workers are not productive in a typical factory because of the structure. Given a clear picture of their responsibilities and criteria for earning bonuses and promotions, productivity soars. They are motivated and industrious given the proper structure.

## EDITORIAL

We're not doing business with Zhonhei Manufacturing Co., we're negotiating with the whole of China.

Look at the attached organization chart by the Chinese government (Exhibit 2). We now know someone from virtually every agency of the federal government. They are all involved, and its worse at the provincial and municipal levels. The people at the table are not the decision makers. They are thorough questioners, following an idea until they've exhausted their lists. The point is settled. The next day or week they return with another battery of questions on what we thought was a settled point. It's as if they are reporting each session to a higher authority. Those authorities then grill them on each point. Where they fail to answer, new questions are developed for us. This happens again and again. Director Lao is a fine fellow with a keen awareness of the proper means of running a profitable operation but doesn't have the clout we associate with his title. The decision makers are elsewhere. They must be the authorities who oversee the area, or the industry. Lao is constantly reporting to the Mayor, Provincial Governor, Beijing Ministry, officials, etc. It is very frustrating and time consuming. I hope we won't have to run the joint venture in the same fashion, if we are able to establish it in the first place.

# PART FOUR

# Alliances, Mergers, and Acquisitions

# Italtel

In early 1982, Marisa Bellisario, the new Managing Director of Italtel, the Italian state-owned producer of telecommunication equipment, was facing difficult decisions. In particular she had to decide whether to seek a collaborative agreement with a foreign partner to codevelop and market digital switching systems. Marisa Bellisario had already moved quickly on several fronts. A former Executive Vice President of Olivetti, with a good track record as an operating manager at General Electric and Honeywell, and a former general manager of Olivetti's North American operations, Bellisario had taken responsibility of a company plagued by huge losses ($200 million in 1981, on sales of about $500 million), overemployment (almost 29,000 employees), bureaucratic stultified management structures and processes, and a difficult technological predicament.

Italtel was a 98-percent-owned affiliate of STET, a large state holding company controlling the bulk of Italian telecommunication services and related electronic industries. STET also owned 60 percent of SIP, the principal telephone services company in Italy, accounting for over 80 percent of all national purchases of telecommunication equipment.

Upon joining Italtel in the Spring of 1981, Bellisario had taken responsibility for labor relations and strategic planning, starting a frank and open dialogue with the unions about needed employment cuts and developing a strategic plan for the company with the help of outside consultants. Soon afterward, Bellisario was promoted to Managing Director as part of a general management shakeup affecting STET and its many affiliates. Immediately upon her appointment, Bellisario began to put in place a new executive team, hiring outsiders she had known in her prior career and promoting new managers within Italtel.

STET was committed to bail out Italtel from its current predicament and agreed to refinance the company, converting most of its debt into equity. Bellisario expected these various measures would allow Italtel to break even in 1984 and to make substantial profits in 1985. Two difficult issues remained, however: technology

This case was written by Professor Yves Doz, with the assistance of Ing. Armando d'Amico, Research Associate, at INSEAD, the European Institute of Business Administration, Fontainebleau, France. © INSEAD 1985. Revised June 1988.

and export sales. Although Italtel had been working on digital switching systems for over 10 years, success in these areas had been modest so far.

In their initial strategic survey, the external consultants (Arthur D. Little) had praised Italtel's efforts to develop a new system. But they had also suggested that Italtel should consider some form of collaborative agreement with another telephone equipment supplier. The potential goals of such an agreement would be:

1. To share future R&D costs incurred in developing a new system. While Italtel's own efforts had led to the development of a small second-generation system (up to 14,000 lines), developing a larger one for urban locations would cost at least another $150 million.
2. To increase their market share in Italy. Italtel supplied about half of the Italian market for switching systems. Three foreign multinationals (MNCs) shared the other half. Various ministries and political parties had suggested that the number of suppliers be reduced from the current four to two, either via the elimination of some suppliers (as had been done in France in 1975–76) or by encouraging suppliers to join efforts. Italtel could increase its market share by teaming up with one of the other suppliers.
3. To gain access to export markets. Even under the best development hypotheses, the Italian domestic market would hardly provide Italtel with a sufficient sales volume to spread R&D and other fixed costs. Exports were necessary to complement domestic sales and achieve efficient production volumes.

The company's planning staff had forecast yearly domestic sales of 500,000 lines and export sales of 250,000 lines by 1986–87. Both figures were seen as optimistic, as was the $150 million hypothesis for further R&D expenses.

Italtel was also subject to serious constraints. STET's support was predicated on the understanding that Italtel would provide the nucleus for a successful Italian effort to develop a complete digital switching system network—one independent from foreign licenses and free of export restrictions. Bellisario was also concerned with the need not to demotivate competent R&D teams during the turnaround of the company. She knew that the MNC suppliers were lobbying with the various ministries, and with STET, to get their systems approved and to speed up the signing of initial purchase orders. Both ITT and LM Ericsson, two major international suppliers with large subsidiaries in Italy, already had trial exchanges in operation in Italy, and the trials were reportedly successful. The third multinational supplier, GTE, was adapting a large U.S. system of advanced design to Italian standards.

Doubts were expressed in some circles about Italtel's capability to develop a successful system within reasonable costs and delays. Some, including several managers within the company, were advocating buying licenses from Siemens (whose own digital switching system was under development), from one of the three multinational manufacturers in Italy, or yet from another company, such as the French manufacturer CIT-Alcatel which had close ties with Olivetti, the Italian office equipment and information technology company.

## ITALTEL'S POSITION IN DIGITAL SWITCHING[1]

Italtel's research project for digital switching was launched in 1971, under the code name "Proteo," with the support of STET, which wanted to reduce its dependence on foreign technology. A small, first-generation digital switch (designated as "CT"), with a maximum capacity of 2,000 lines, was introduced into the Italian telephone network in 1975. By 1981, 25 of these CT-based local and transit exchanges, and 6 operators' control exchanges were already

---

[1] See Appendix A for a summary discussion of the major technological, cost, and competitive issues surrounding the development of the public switching industry in the early 1980s.

installed and in operation in the public network. This early operational experience with first-generation equipment had been helpful in guiding the development of a second more advanced generation. Nonetheless, Proteo's development process was longer and more costly than anticipated. In 1978, when the first products were being installed, a broad review of the project had taken place which stressed the need to accelerate development.

After this review, Italtel management decided to maintain production and installation of the proven CT exchanges and to continue development of a large local exchange (60,000 lines) as well as a transit exchange (16,000 lines) of the same technology. They also decided to start work immediately on a new generation of equipment by setting up a joint venture for the design of the system in the United States with an independent research group. A new company, called ABC, was created in Dallas, Texas, in early 1979, and given the task of developing a prototype in two years. Ready access to telecommunication and electronic engineers and to microelectronic components, as well as the existence of a skilled design group, were used to justify the U.S. location.

Proteo development was thus continuing along two main paths. First, the transit exchange (TN 16), whose development involved about 500 people (300 in R&D and 200 in production planning), was centered in the Castelletto laboratories near Milan, where Italtel was based. The second generation local/transit exchange (designated "UT 10/3") was being developed in Dallas, with about 60 people, 22 of whom were Italtel engineers on detachment.

The TN 16 project was fully integrated into the company's organization. The UT 10/3 organization in Dallas, however, was kept separate and autonomous, and had its own staff functions (personnel, control, information systems, and quality control) as well as two line functions in R&D and manufacturing. Most UT 10/3 engineers were young and highly motivated, communication was easy, resource problems were few, and the project enjoyed maximum priority.

In this privileged environment, development proceeded quickly, and the first prototype was shipped to Milan in early 1981. Work then began on the difficult task of transferring the know-how to Italy and on bringing the project to the manufacturing phase. The first network installation was scheduled for 1983.

In summary, Italtel's technical position in digital electronic public switching by 1981 consisted of *first generation* equipment based on centralized architecture (initiated in 1971) including:

- Local switch CT2 (2,000 lines); 39 exchanges to be delivered by end-1981, with a larger CT60 version (60,000 lines) under development.
- International transit/operator-assistance switch TI-2/CIMA2; three TI-2s to be delivered and 11 CIMA2s installed by end-1981.
- Transit switch TN 16 (16,000 trunk lines); one exchange to be delivered by end-1981. The TN 16 introduced pulse code modulation (PCM) and was fully compatible with digital local switches and PCM transmission.

The *second generation* under development was based on decentralized, distributed architecture (initiated in 1979) and included local/transit switch UT 10/3 (10,000 lines or 3,000 trunks).

The first-generation technologies, although performing well and necessary for meeting the network modernization schedule of SIP, were not intended to be pursued for future local switching needs. While progress on the TN 16 was satisfactory, its future was somewhat unclear since it remained a first-generation system. Italtel planned to start series production around 1982–83, but the TN 16 was too small for some large cities. The fact that transit lines were operated directly by a PTT agency (ASST) rather than SIP, complicated the issues.[2]

However, the technical concept of UT 10/3 was very modern and competitive, according

---

[2] See Appendix B for details of the institutional environment in Italy, which had a major determining role in the future of the industry.

EXHIBIT 1

## STRUCTURE OF THE ITALIAN PUBLIC SWITCHING NETWORK, 1979

| Exchange size (number of lines) | Number of exchanges | Exchanges as percent | Percent of subscribers | Average annual segment growth (%) | | Italtel market share (%) |
|---|---|---|---|---|---|---|
| | | | | 1970–80 | 1983+ | |
| Less than 100 | 920 | 10 | 1 | 9 | 9 | 44 |
| 100 to 500 | 5,060 | 55 | 9 | 9 | 9 | 52 |
| 500 to 2,000 | 2,200 | 24 | 14 | 7 | 9 | 48 |
| 2 to 10,000 | 690 | 7.5 | 26 | 7 | 9 | 49 |
| Over 10,000 | 320 | 3.5 | 50 | 4 | 8 | 55 |
| Totals | 9,200 | 100 | 100 | 6 | 9 | 52 |

*Note:* Total lines exceeded 2.9 million; the last three figures at bottom are weighted averages for all categories.

to qualified external consultants. The UT 10/3 represented a compact solution (i.e., it obtained more lines in a given size than most other switches) and used up-to-date memory and microprocessor technology. Contrary to first-generation exchanges, it was based on a distributed architecture which allowed easy growth into larger size ranges.

The UT 10/3 already covered small-capacity local exchanges; its modular structure allowed it to grow steadily in increments of 1,000 lines up to 14,000 lines. For local switching requirements below 1,000 lines, remote units could be used, which worked in practice as smaller local switches, utilizing the switching capabilities of a remote UT 10/3. This was an important advantage in Italy, since a large percentage of local switches handled fewer than 1,000 subscriber lines. The UT 10/3 also covered most of the needs for urban switches in Italy. As shown in Exhibit 1, 97 percent of all local switches, accounting for 51 percent of the market in terms of number of lines, required fewer than 10,000 lines of capacity.

The UT 10/3 was to be only the first product of a family. If Italtel were to develop a complete line of digital electronic public switches, it would also need a large transit switch (designated TN 60) with up to 60,000 trunk lines capacity, a large local switch (UR 100), up to 100,000 local lines,

some small local switches (concentrators), and data packet switches (ACP).

Italtel had started to study these products and was planning their development, as illustrated in Exhibit 2, on the basis of the UT 10/3 technology. Globally, only about Lit 200 billion (about $150 million) had been spent by Italtel on Proteo up to 1980, considerably less than the amounts spent by most competitors. But the total development costs for a complete family of electronic public switches was estimated at well over Lit 500 billion (nearly $400 million).

Furthermore, Italtel's R&D engineers knew that the public switching exchanges recently introduced in the market, or about to be introduced, would have a lifetime of about 10 years and would need to be replaced in the 1990–95 period. The development of a new line of public switches encompassed a series of steps in terms of timing and resource allocation that could take 8–10 years and require over 3,000 man-years of development effort before entering production and with no shortcuts possible. Therefore, any new product development effort had to be launched no later than 1983–84 if Italtel wanted to continue to develop its own technology. In 1981, the R&D department numbered 1,850 people, 1,250 of whom were in Castelletto, 500 in the TN 16, UT 10/3, and other special projects, and 100 distributed among the plants. Exhibit 3

EXHIBIT 2

## PRODUCT DEVELOPMENT SCHEDULE, 1980–96

| | 80 | 81 | 82 | 83 | 84 | 85 | 86 | 87 | 88 | 89 | 90 | 91 | 92 | 93 | 94 | 95 | 96 |
|---|---|---|---|---|---|---|---|---|---|---|---|---|---|---|---|---|---|
| **Local switches** | | | | | | | | | | | | | | | | | |
| CT-2 | | | | | | Fading out | | | | | | | | | | | |
| UT 10/3 | | | | | | | | | | | | | New generation likely | | | | |
| UR 100 | | | | | | | | | | | | | | | | | |
| **Transit switches** | | | | | | | | | | | | | | | | | |
| TN-16 | | | | | | | | | | | | New generation likely | | | | | |
| TN-60 | | | | | | | | | | | | | | | | | |
| **International transit switches** | | | | | | | | | | | | | | | | | |
| TI 2 | | | | | | | | | | | | | | | | | |
| **Packet switches** | | | | | | | | | | | | | | | | | |
| ACP | | | | | | | | | | | | | | | | | |

Legend:

- Preliminary development
- Development
- Field trials & preliminary production
- Commercialization

**EXHIBIT 3**

**ITALTEL: R&D COSTS AND EMPLOYMENT BY PRODUCT CATEGORY, 1980**

| Product category | Percent of sales | R&D employment | R&D costs (Lit billions) | | |
| --- | --- | --- | --- | --- | --- |
| | | | Internal R&D work | External R&D & royalties | Total |
| Public switches: | | | | | |
| Electromechanical | ⎫ 55.0 | 175 | 5.5 | 2.2 | 7.7 |
| Electronic | ⎬ | 860 | 27.2 | 3.6 | 30.8 |
| Transmission equipment | 12.5 | 300 | 9.5 | 2.6 | 12.1 |
| Radio equipment | 4.2 | 215 | 6.8 | 0.6 | 7.4 |
| Subtotal | 71.7 | 1,550 | 49.0 | 9.0 | 58.0 |
| Private communications systems | 19.7 | 190 | 6.0 | 1.4 | 7.4 |
| Military equipment | 2.7 | 100 | 3.2 | 0.6 | 3.8 |
| Other | 6.0 | 60 | 1.8 | — | 1.8 |
| Total | 100.0 | 1,900 | 60.0 | 11.0 | 71.0 |

provides a breakdown of R&D resources and cost allocations for 1980.

## THE ITALIAN MARKET FOR TELECOMMUNICATION SWITCHING SYSTEMS

The evolution of the Italian market for telecommunication equipment had raised difficult issues for manufacturers. In the late 1960s and early 1970s, under pressure from government and public opinion, SIP employed its abundant resources to invest massively in network development (although in doing so it brought into the network a large number of less profitable residential customers) and in automation of the switching systems. Since electronic switches were not yet available in Italy for mass production, such expansion had to rely on well-proven electromechanical switches. Although SIP's expansion coincided with a period of technical transition from electromechanical to digital electronic systems, it forced equipment manufacturers to increase their capacity to produce a labor-intensive, already obsolete, electromechanical technology. Italtel's employment thus doubled from about 15,000 in 1970 to nearly 30,000 by 1975, and the 1973 corporate plan called for nearly 36,700 employees in 1978.

In 1974, the 10-year expropriation payment schedule from the state to SIP ended. Following the oil crisis, inflation suddenly accelerated in Italy. Yet, SIP was unable to raise its telephone rates to keep pace with inflation. Caught between rapidly rising costs and stable operational revenues, SIP had to cut its investment programs to remain solvent. By the end of 1974, it had cut its purchases of new switching equipment from a planned 850,000 lines to 649,000. The situation worsened in 1975 with orders barely exceeding 500,000 lines. Subject to a political battle between supporters and opponents of state-owned enterprises, the process of rate increase for SIP was particularly slow.

With no rate increases being granted between 1977 and 1979, SIP registered huge losses, could not honor its commitments to suppliers, and was forced to stretch its payment delays. With a production capacity of 550,000 lines per annum, much of it in new plants, Italtel suffered heavy losses throughout the period. Furthermore, Italtel's export capability was severely limited under the terms of its licensing agreements with Siemens. Exports accounted for only about 2 percent of sales, mainly to Malta and Somalia.

Some important changes started in 1980, when Giovanni de Michelis, the Socialist Minister of State Shareholdings presented a government

---

**EXHIBIT 4**

---

**DEMAND AND SUPPLY OF TELEPHONE LINES IN ITALY, 1975–79** (Thousands)

|  | 1975 | 1976 | 1977 | 1978 | 1979 |
|---|---|---|---|---|---|
| Demand for telephones | 792 | 951 | 1,087 | 1,255 | 1,431 |
| Number of new lines installed | 570 | 511 | 612 | 678 | 716 |
| Net increase in the number of new subscribers* | 930 | 867 | 964 | 1,039 | 1,115 |
| Unsatisfied demand at year end | 241 | 285 | 315 | 463 | 794 |

*Including existing lines returned to SIP and allocated to new subscribers.

White Paper on the reform of state-controlled enterprises. On the whole, it concluded that the internationalization of state companies was an essential need for the 1980s. The White Paper also outlined the main guidelines of a long-term strategy, pointing out sectors to restructure (steel, petrochemicals, automobile, shipbuilding, and mining), sectors to develop because of their strategic importance (electronics, energy, transportation, food, specialty steels, construction, plant engineering, and space activities), and others in which the state should not invest any further.

The section on electronics pointed to the deficient state of telephone services in Italy as evident by pent-up demand, low telephone density compared to other European countries, insufficient telephone penetration and poor service to rural areas, etc. (see Exhibit 4). It suggested an acceleration of network expansion to 1.2 million new subscriber lines per year for the next 10 years, and a rapid changeover to electronic technologies to forgo the need for later reconversion from electromechanical to electronic equipment.

In the same period, the Ministry of Posts and Telecommunications (PTT) published a draft plan with the objective to develop the Italian telecommunication network into an integrated services data network to include telegraph, telephone, telex, and packet switching services. So far as telephone equipment was concerned, the plan recommended a gradual adoption of digital electronic switching and expressed concern with full utilization of analog equipment within depreciation limits, the pace of conversion versus that of technological progress, quality requirements, and the impact on installations, operations and maintenance, as well as on employment levels. In the end, the PTT forecast the installation of 11 million new lines between 1981 and 1990, with gradual changeover to electronic technology throughout the period (see Exhibit 5).

Ministry officials also strongly recommended taking advantage of the technological changeover to reduce the number of systems used in the Italian network from four to two. Instead of the current market-sharing arrangement giving roughly half the market to Italtel and splitting the other half among three multinationals, a "two-pole" policy was recommended:

- The first pole would be Italian, and probably state-owned, and would supply about half the market for digital switching. Control of the technology would be in Italian hands, and it was expected that this "pole" would also export Italian-designed and -made systems.
- The second pole would be constituted around an MNC supplier, providing state-of-the-art technology and manufacturing in Italy.

The ministry recommended further that these two poles be set up and their participants chosen before large firm order commitments were made for new digital switching systems, following the system trials currently being performed.

The PTT plan also expressed strong employment concerns, with a forecast decrease of manufacturing employment in the industry from

**ITALIAN MINISTRY OF PTT, 1981 DEVELOPMENT PLAN**

| Years | New local lines (thousands) | | | New trunk lines (thousands) | | |
|-------|-------------------|---------------------|-------|-------------------|---------------------|-------|
| | Electromechanic | Digital electronic | Total | Analog electronic | Digital electronic | Total |
| 1981 | 710 | 40 | 750 | 5.7 | 3.0 | 8.7 |
| 1982 | 850 | 60 | 910 | 7.0 | 10.3 | 17.3 |
| 1983 | 840 | 110 | 950 | 1.8 | 27.9 | 29.7 |
| 1984 | 760 | 210 | 970 | 0.9 | 18.0 | 18.9 |
| 1985 | 650 | 350 | 1,000 | 0.9 | 18.7 | 19.6 |
| 1986 | 450 | 650 | 1,100 | — | 17.5 | 17.5 |
| 1987 | 300 | 900 | 1,200 | — | 17.5 | 17.5 |
| 1988 | 150 | 1,150 | 1,300 | — | 17.5 | 17.5 |
| 1989 | 100 | 1,300 | 1,400 | — | 17.5 | 17.5 |
| 1990 | 50 | 1,450 | 1,500 | — | 17.5 | 17.5 |
| Totals | 4,860 | 6,220 | 11,080 | 16.3 | 165.4 | 181.7 |

*Note:* An "accelerated" development rate hypothesis included an extra number of about one million new lines to be supplied in the period 1987–90.

70,000 to about 46,000, as a result of the switch from electromechanical to electronic products, only partly offset by a 10,000 to 15,000 employment increase in the provision of new services. A number of offsetting measures were suggested for reducing these negative employment effects:

- The expansion of the domestic market and an acceleration of the rate of replacement of existing equipment
- Product diversification and development of new services
- Higher penetration of export markets, with Italian products not subject to license restrictions
- Transfer of workers from the manufacturing companies toward the service carriers

Yet, the actual rate of network expansion, and therefore the size of the Italian market for new telephone lines, depended largely on SIP's ability to finance its growth, and SIP had little control over its rate structure. Local services, in particular, were unprofitable, and SIP did not favor the growth pattern suggested in the plan, based on connecting large numbers of private new subscribers who would most likely be light users of the profitable long-distance services but heavy users of the unprofitable local services. The Italian network was already geographically scattered with many small exchanges, and further penetration of rural areas would only reinforce this costly dispersion of equipment.

Four main companies supplied the Italian network, with a fifth one (Fiat's subsidiary Telettra) supplying a few transit switches and transmission equipment (see Exhibit 6). In their work for Italtel, the ADL consultants hired by Bellisario had carried out an analysis of key success factors on the Italian switching market and compared Italtel to major competitors according to these. Exhibit 7 provides a summary of their conclusions. Each of the three main foreign competitors is described briefly below, and relevant information on their parent companies is also provided.

## FACE AND ITT

FACE was a fully-owned subsidiary of ITT, regrouping most of ITT's industrial operations in

| EXHIBIT 6 |
|---|

**MARKET POSITIONS OF MAJOR COMPETITORS IN ITALY, 1981**

| | Market shares | | Estimated capacity (lines) | Estimated capacity utilization |
|---|---|---|---|---|
| | Local | Trunk | | |
| Italtel | 52% | 51% | 470,000+ | 65% |
| FACE (ITT) | 18 | 19 | 170,000 | 75 |
| FATME (LME) | 16 | 17 | 150,000 | 75 |
| GTE | 14 | 13 | 110,000 | 75 |
| Telettra | — | minor | 15,000 | 50 |
| | 100% | 100% | 915,000 | |
| Total (Lit billion) | 500 | 180 | | |

*Note:* Most production capacity was for electromechanical switches.

Italy.[3] FACE controlled 23 different subsidiaries, each with technological and managerial autonomy but closely related to FACE on a financial and strategic basis. Together, their total investment reached Lit 222 billion and had a turnover (net of intragroup trade) of nearly Lit 500 billion in 1980. At the end of 1980, the FACE group employed 12,389 people, about 6,000 of whom were in the south, and most of the others were around Milan, Turin, Florence, and Bologna.

Research was carried out in four main locations (Florence, Milan, Pomezia, and Salerno), employing about 940 engineers and technicians of whom fewer than 500 worked on telecommunication products. Over the 3 years 1978–80, R&D expenditures totalled nearly Lit 80 billion, or approximately 7 percent of sales.[4] Research efforts had been concentrated on three areas: (1) contribution to the development of System 12

(ITT's new digital switch) for introduction in Italy, (2) cooperation with other ITT subsidiaries to develop terminals and PABXs, and (3) work on microelectronics and fiber optics.

FACE had been created in 1909 and, after entering the ITT Group, had grown rapidly in the 1960s and early 1970s. Like other Italian telecommunication equipment manufacturers FACE was hit by the 1975 crisis, to which it had responded in three ways:

1. FACE increased its exports from 10 to 40 percent of its total turnover. FACE had exported exchanges to a wide range of countries (Greece, Brazil, Colombia, Chile, a number of African countries, Sri Lanka, and others) directly or, most often, as a subcontractor to other ITT subsidiaries. In 1980–81, the bulk of switching system exports were being delivered to Nigeria. Despite some recent setbacks there, exports still accounted for 26 percent of sales in 1981, and orders currently under negotiation were promising. For the 1978–80 period, FACE had contributed, on average, Lit 70 billion annually to Italy's balance of trade.

2. FACE engaged in a vigorous diversification effort toward new related areas, such as automated mail-sorting equipment, car components, and railway signaling systems. While some of these activities were in mature sectors, others offered attractive growth oppor-

---

[3] In addition to FACE, ITT had various activities in Italy. It was a major car component manufacturer and a significant hotel operator (via the Sheraton chain). A large expansion of the Sheraton chain in Italy was under consideration, and car component operations not only supplied Fiat, but also exported a large share of their production to other automotive manufacturers. Italy was a sourcing platform for such components as shock absorbers for the whole of ITT.

[4] Part of the research work performed in Italy under FACE's legal umbrella was paid for by other ITT units outside of Italy and did not show as R&D expenditures on FACE's financial accounts.

---

**EXHIBIT 7**

**COMPETITIVE ANALYSIS OF ITALTEL IN THE ITALIAN SWITCHING MARKET, 1980\***

| Key success factors | Relative weight of success factor | FACE | FATME | GTE | Telettra |
|---|---|---|---|---|---|
| Price/performance | 3 | 0 | 0 | − | |
| Ability to influence standards | 3 | − | − | = | |
| After-sales service | 2 | − | + | 0 | |
| Size of local manufacturing | 2 | = | − | − | |
| Generation of technology available | | | | | |
|   Electromechanical | 2 | + | + | 0 | |
|   Electronic | 2 | 0 | − | − | |
| Total cost advantage | | | | | |
|   Electromechanical | 1 | + | + | 0 | |
|   Electronic | 1 | 0 | − | − | |
| Manufacturing flexibility | 1 | + | + | + | |
| Commitment/Financial resources | 1 | − | − | − | |
| Management systems | 1 | + | + | 0 | |
| Union relationships | 1 | 0 | 0 | + | |
|   Total (unweighted) | | −1 | 0 | −5 | |
|   Total weighted score | | −5 | −2 | −13 | |

\*Data for Telettra was insufficient for scoring.
*Note:* All competitors were rated against Italtel on the basis of their performance in a number of key success factors. Weighted scores are used to arrive at an overall assessment. Rating codes are as follows: + +: much better than Italtel; +: better than Italtel; 0: equal to Italtel; −: worse than Italtel; =: much worse than Italtel.

tunities. Yet, telecom-related activities still accounted for 64 percent of FACE's sales in 1981.

3. FACE had tried to stabilize employment and then decreased it by attrition between 1974 and 1980, with a slight increase in the South while decreasing in the North.[5] The growth in export sales, new Italian orders in 1977–78,

and the efforts to diversify yielded significant productivity gains without major redundancies, allowing the company to remain profitable throughout the period. In 1980, FACE's group profits had reached Lit 10.5 billion, but real sales volume stagnated.

In 1980 FACE was preparing the introduction of System 12 in Italy. Following an experimental

---

[5]FACE's management was hoping to avoid drawing significantly on the "Cassa Integrazione" or having to lay off permanently large numbers of workers. "Cassa Integrazione" was a government scheme designed to combat unemployment. Companies could lay off workers temporarily (so they would not be registered as unemployed), and the workers would receive about 85 to 90 percent of their wages,

with most of the cost picked up by the state. This gave Italian companies much leeway in varying employment levels without having to lay off or rehire people formally. FACE still employed several thousand people making electromechanical switches and was attempting to manage the process of reducing employment as smoothly as possible.

---

**EXHIBIT 8**

**WORLDWIDE SALES AND ORDERS OF SYSTEM 12 SYSTEMS (END OF 1981)**

| Country/standard* | Subscriber lines | Trunk lines |
|---|---|---|
| **Lines in service** | | |
| Belgium/1240 | 1,000 | — |
| Italy/1240 | — | 6,000 |
| Taiwan/1210 | 4,000 | — |
| United States/1210 | 374,000 | 3,950 |
| Total | 379,000 | 9,950 |
| **Lines on order or being installed** | | |
| Belgium/1240 | 2,880 | 2,000 |
| Denmark/1240 | 66,000 | 17,000 |
| Finland/1240 | 1,000 | 1,500 |
| Germany/1240 | 5,200 | 8,400 |
| Italy/1240 | 960 | 12,360 |
| Mexico/1240 | 422,000 | 38,100 |
| Philippines/1210 | 6,000 | — |
| Spain/1240 | 10,000 | — |
| Taiwan/1210 | 52,000 | — |
| United States/1210 | 230,116 | 3,179 |
| Venezuela/1240 | 140,000 | — |
| Total | 936,156 | 82,539 |

*The "1210" system is specified to the North American standard, whereas the "1240" system is specified to the CCITT standard used in Europe and most other countries.

installation of a prototype system in Rome in 1977, FACE's laboratories in Pomezia and Salerno were working on the adaptation of System 12 to Italian requirements and on gearing up the manufacturing process in Italy. With a total of about 100 R&D engineers and technicians, Pomezia also contributed to the overall Europewide development of System 12. The first commercial installation of a System 12 exchange in Italy was planned in Bologna for 1981–82.

The adoption of System 12 by SIP and ASST was very important to FACE and to ITT. For FACE this represented an opportunity to remain a significant public switching systems supplier, polish its high-technology image, and lessen somewhat its employment problems. To ITT, any new market for System 12 was critical. Although System 12 had registered sales in a number of countries (see Exhibit 8), it was late, compared to competitors' systems. Every possible sale was needed to contribute toward the recovery of the heavy R&D investments already made and to reinforce ITT's image as a world leader in telecommunication equipment.

## ITT-EUROPE AND TELECOMMUNICATIONS

ITT had traditionally allowed considerable autonomy to its telecommunication equipment subsidiaries, and FACE was one of the main ITT "system houses" representing all related ITT interests in Italy. Traditionally, ITT had been very responsive to national governments' requests and priorities. Key decisions in Europe were often made as a result of consensus among the country managers rather than based on top management edicts. A worldwide telecommunication equipment business group did exist in New York, but its role had been one of coordination and of integration between U.S. and European operations rather than one of line management. With ITT's growing stake in the U.S. telecommunication equipment business, however, this worldwide business group might take a more prominent role in the future.

Under the strong leadership of Harold Geneen, ITT had developed tight management systems, organized around planning and control functions. Top management devoted a lot of attention to developing business plans and negotiating them between corporate, regional, unit, and product management. A powerful controllers' hierarchy exercised considerable influence in the planning and budgeting process, and product line managers in Brussels and New York provided secondary sources of information. National subsidiaries therefore were autonomous, but only with the counterweight of strong central management systems and product executive accountability (see Exhibit 9).

Following Geneen's retirement, the five New York–based product group executives constituted the Office of the Chief Executive and took a more active role in developing coordinated

EXHIBIT 9

## ITT EUROPEAN ORGANIZATION, 1981

Reporting to ITT Controller, N.Y.

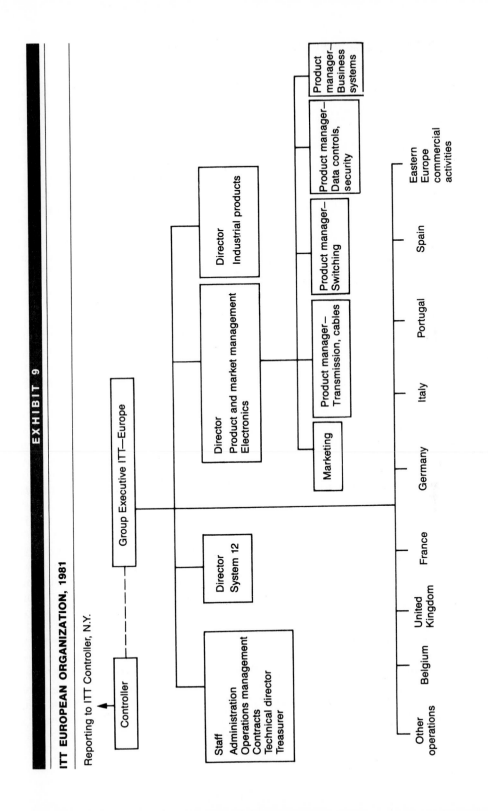

---

**EXHIBIT 10**

**ITT'S TELECOMMUNICATION RESEARCH CENTERS IN EUROPE**

| Country | Technical staff | Technologies |
|---|---|---|
| Spain (Madrid) | 300 | Software, networking, systems |
| Germany (Stuttgart) | 200 | Data systems, software, advanced materials, voice recognition, fiber optics |
| Italy (Pomezia) | 100 | Fiber optics, systems, avionics |
| Norway (Oslo) | 50 | Small digital systems, optical cables, LSI designs |
| Belgium (Brussels) | 60 | LSI, MOS circuits |
| United Kingdom (Harlow) | 300 | Multiple programs |

*Note:* This table does not include automotive research activities (about 500 technicians and scientists) nor semiconductor and materials research activities.

---

worldwide business strategies. They did not, however, set out to build larger staffs, beyond a few product line managers, and relied instead on the staff and management groups of the various geographic operating units and subsidiaries.

Altogether, ITT-Europe counted over 2,000 research scientists and engineers working in diverse areas, including advanced VLSI circuits and fiber optics. ITT spent about $600 million per year on R&D in Europe, as illustrated in Exhibit 10.

Over the years, ITT-Europe had decreased its commitment to the telecommunications equipment business. It sold its Le Materiel Telephonique subsidiary to Thomson in France in 1976. A year later, it sold 30 percent of its German subsidiary, Standard Electric Lorenz, on the German stock market, and was considering a similar move for its Standard Telephones and Cables (STC) subsidiary in the United Kingdom. In 1978, the British government had briefly considered, and then dropped, a plan to merge STC with Plessey. The question of STC's continuing participation in the System X project in the United Kingdom was openly raised, and it was rumored that STC might withdraw from the

U.K. digital switching market. In 1981–82, ITT was also negotiating the nationalization of its remaining French telecommunication equipment subsidiary, CGCT, with the French government. These partial divestitures were seen by some observers as a sign of a possible loss of commitment on ITT's part toward the European telecommunication equipment business. Others, on the contrary, interpreted them as ITT's way to contribute funding to the escalating expenditures associated with System 12 development.

Altogether, telecom and electronics products accounted for almost one-third of ITT's worldwide sales of $23.2 billion (the other main businesses were engineered products with 25 percent of sales; insurance and finance, also 25 percent; and consumer products and services with 15 percent). European sales exceeded $9.8 billion in 1981 (42 percent of total revenues), with Germany and the United Kingdom being the major markets (36 and 22 percent, respectively, of European sales), and Italy accounting for 8.3 percent. Profits in Europe were well above average for the ITT group and accounted for about two-thirds of ITT's worldwide profits. The telecommunication and electronics group was relatively more important to the European organization (47.5 percent of sales) than to the parent company.

## FATME

Headquartered in Rome, where it was the largest industrial employer, FATME was LM Ericsson's main Italian affiliate. FATME operated exclusively in the telecommunication equipment sector, and close to 80 percent of its work force was involved in switching equipment manufacturing. Total employment was almost 5,700 people, 4,200 of whom were manufacturing workers. In the late 1970s, FATME had managed to remain profitable throughout the crisis.

LM Ericsson controlled FATME via a 51 percent equity ownership in a holding company, SETEMER, which in turn owned the totality of FATME's shares. The other 49 percent of SETEMER's capital was owned by Italian private investors. The wide diversity of FATME's telecommunication products, as well as its relatively small size, required much flexibility in the manufacturing process. The Rome plant had 2,550 workers and 357 other employees in 1981 and

was the main plant active in electronic switching (the AKE and AXE systems), transmission equipment, and telematics. Smaller plants in the South employed about 750 people. Installation employed a few hundred people in various locations.

FATME had a small R&D lab (about 50 people) working on digital transmission and digital switching. R&D expenditures grew, in current lire, from 5.9 billion in 1976 to 11.9 billion in 1980. Yet, FATME's overall R&D effort remained quite limited in size, particularly when compared to its parent company. Contrary to ITT, which decentralized its R&D activities into multiple subsidiaries, LM Ericsson carried out the bulk of its R&D efforts in Sweden.

FATME had successfully introduced in Italy earlier versions of its AXE system and was planning to begin deployment of its digital derivative, the AXE 10-D, in the early 1980s. In 1979 FATME had already installed a digital trunk exchange in Naples, which proved satisfactory in trials through 1980. Exhibit 11 provides a breakdown of FATME's sales by product line; 25 percent of its production was already in electronic technologies.

---

### EXHIBIT 11

**FATME: SALES BREAKDOWN BY TYPE OF PRODUCT** (Lit Billions)

| Product Category | 1976 | 1977 | 1978 | 1979 | 1980 | 1981 |
|---|---|---|---|---|---|---|
| Telephone sets, accessories | 1.7 | 1.7 | 3.5 | 4.8 | 5.5 | 6.4 |
| Electromechanical PBXs | 0.3 | 1.6 | 2.3 | 2.3 | 3.3 | 1.3 |
| Electronic PBXs | — | — | — | 0.1 | 1.5 | 9.4 |
| Electromechanical public exchanges | 51.9 | 51.1 | 57.7 | 55.1 | 60.4 | 70.1 |
| Electronic public exchanges (AKE/AXE) | 2.5 | 16.1 | 17.6 | 24.5 | 20.9 | 24.7 |
| Manual systems | 0.2 | 0.2 | 2.6 | 0.1 | 7.4 | 1.0 |
| Installation charges | 15.8 | 24.3 | 22.3 | 27.0 | 28.8 | 34.1 |
| Power supply equipment | 0.3 | 0.5 | 0.5 | 0.3 | 0.4 | 0.4 |
| Data transmission equipment | 1.7 | 1.7 | 0.9 | 2.5 | 2.4 | 2.9 |
| Terminals | 5.6 | 6.6 | 8.4 | 10.8 | 11.5 | 24.2 |
| Railways signalling | 0.2 | 0.1 | 0.2 | 0.4 | 1.0 | 1.9 |
| Others | 0.6 | 0.9 | 0.9 | 1.6 | 1.7 | 2.3 |
| Total sales | 80.8 | 104.7 | 116.9 | 129.5 | 144.7 | 178.7 |

PBX = private branch exchanges.

The shift toward electronic technologies called for FATME to decrease manufacturing employment. The company was already using the "Cassa Integrazione" facilities for temporary lay-offs, and management expected that FATME would have to decrease employment by a few hundred workers in the early 1980s, possible mainly through early retirement in the main Rome factory. In keeping with LM Ericsson's overall diversification policy, FATME had begun introducing office automation equipment in Italy. This new activity employed slightly more than 300 people in 1981, but its growth was expected to partly offset the jobs lost in the transition from electromechanical to electronic switching. Since 1977, however, the total number of workers had decreased slowly at FATME.

In 1980, SETEMER bought 81 percent of FIAR, a former General Electric subsidiary involved in the manufacture of laser and radar systems, air navigation control equipment, and other advanced electronic systems. FIAR had sales of $25 million in 1980 and orders of $80 million but was unprofitable. LM Ericsson could complement FIAR technically, and increased sales could return the company to profitability. To some, the acquisition of FIAR was seen as a gesture of goodwill on the part of LME toward the protection of key industrial competencies in Italy, since short of the LME acquisition, FIAR's future might have been compromised.

## LM ERICSSON

Since its creation in 1875, LM Ericsson had been among the leading manufacturers of telecommunication equipment. It had manufacturing affiliates in about 25 different countries and sales subsidiaries in another 25. Over the 1970s, its performance, both in sales volume growth and profitability measures, had been excellent, and its international position was extremely strong. Of total 1980 sales of $2.8 billion (93 percent of which were in telecommunication-related fields), 38 percent were in public switches and exchanges. Sweden accounted for only 22 percent of sales, with the rest of Europe, Latin America,

and Asia coming next in importance (34, 16, and 14 percent, respectively). Total employment numbered 65,900, of which Sweden accounted for about 60 percent. Its strong position (a sales backlog of more than $3 billion in 1981) was bolstered by the success of its AXE system (see Exhibit 12).

Traditionally, LM Ericsson had kept centralizing and decentralizing forces in balance in its organization. Technology and manufacturing were centrally coordinated in Stockholm, and most R&D was performed in Sweden, with the exception of a few product lines, such as ship PABXs and interphone systems which were being developed in Holland. Manufacturing was coordinated centrally but largely managed at the national level within the various subsidiaries. Sales and service organizations were essentially locally managed. Although the company had an elaborate management control and planning system, its main influence on the subsidiaries was exercised through pride and loyalty. LM Ericsson usually sent trusted Swedes to occupy key positions in its various subsidiaries to ensure consistency with corporate goals and culture, and tried to foster a high-commitment climate throughout the organization.

According to company executives, Italy was among the most independent subsidiaries, partly because until recently it had concentrated on production of electromechanical switches which did not call for much integration with the rest of the organization. The introduction of AXE had brought closer links with headquarters, but mostly on an informal basis. Other subsidiaries of LM Ericsson had been more closely controlled as they shifted from electromechanical to electronic technologies. But the Italian office automation business was expected to be more centrally coordinated than had been the case for telecommunication equipment.

Throughout its history, LM Ericsson had been sensitive to the need to adjust to differences in requirements among countries. In several locations, such as Mexico, it had managed to disengage partially from ownership in various operations and yet to retain a major share of the

---
**EXHIBIT 12**

---

## WORLDWIDE SALES AND ORDERS FOR LM ERICSSON'S AXE 10-D SYSTEMS (END OF 1981)

(Lines in Thousands)

| Countries | In service | | | On order | | |
|---|---|---|---|---|---|---|
| | Number of exchanges | Local lines | Trunk lines | Number of exchanges | Local lines | Trunk lines |
| Argentina | 24 | 187.0 | 116.6 | 31 | 224.1 | 59.2 |
| Australia | 1 | 4.0 | — | 3 | 11.0 | — |
| Bahrain | 1 | 10.0 | 6.0 | — | — | — |
| Brazil | — | — | — | 5 | 50.8 | — |
| Cayman Islands | — | — | — | 1 | 2.8 | — |
| Colombia | 2 | 10.0 | 12.3 | 26 | 295.0 | — |
| Costa Rica | 1 | — | 8.0 | — | — | — |
| Denmark | 4 | — | 16.3 | 40 | 259.4 | 22.1 |
| El Salvador | — | — | — | 6 | 30.4 | 5.0 |
| Finland | 2 | 4.0 | 0.5 | 12 | 78.8 | 33.4 |
| France | 41 | 393.8 | — | 58 | 469.2 | — |
| Holland | 18 | 55.8 | — | 17 | 84.5 | — |
| Hong Kong | — | — | — | 1 | — | 5.1 |
| Ireland | — | — | — | 5 | 9.6 | 30.2 |
| Italy | 4 | — | 13.3 | 1 | — | 2.6 |
| Kenya | — | — | — | 1 | — | 1.0 |
| Kuwait | 3 | 40.0 | — | 3 | 70.0 | — |
| Lebanon | — | — | — | 3 | — | 14.8 |
| Malaysia | 3 | 40.0 | — | — | — | — |
| Mexico | 6 | 17.5 | 12.0 | 11 | 33.1 | 15.8 |
| Norway | 1 | — | 1.0 | 1 | — | 1.0 |
| Panama | 3 | 10.0 | — | 3 | 15.0 | — |
| Saudi Arabia | 24 | 187.0 | 116.6 | 31 | 224.1 | 59.2 |
| Seychelles | — | — | — | 1 | 3.4 | — |
| Spain | 2 | 20.0 | — | 7 | 53.0 | 8.7 |
| Sweden | 15 | 160.4 | 1.0 | 10 | 310.0 | 9.0 |
| Tunisia | — | — | — | 8 | 74.5 | 10.0 |
| United Arab Emirates | 2 | 4.0 | 3.0 | 6 | 72.6 | 8.5 |
| Venezuela | 1 | 5.0 | — | 40 | 277.3 | 8.2 |
| Yugoslavia | 1 | 10.0 | — | 20 | 115.6 | 22.6 |
| Totals | 135 | 971.5 | 190.0 | 325 | 2,577.2 | 257.3 |

market for equipment. In many host countries, the fact that Sweden was a small neutral country could be an advantage when competing against U.S.-based or European companies. Only in France, following the 1976 forced divestiture of its subsidiary, had there been conflict between LM Ericsson and host country authorities on the exact terms of the transaction and on the financial situation of the subsidiary.

## GTE-TELECOMMUNICAZIONI S.P.A.

GTE had long been present in Italy, with the manufacture of public switching systems, and transmission and station equipment. GTE-T (Italy) was a technology leader in the field of transmission equipment but less so in switching, where it manufactured conventional electromechanical equipment. GTE had about 8 percent of the

Italian market for public switches in 1977, although its share had risen slightly since then. Altogether, state-owned Italian customers accounted for 57 percent of total GTE-T sales. The main Italian plant was in a suburb of Milan, where about 3,500 persons were employed, including 2,000 workers.

Italy was GTE's main production center for transmission equipment outside North America, and exports were substantial. Transmission equipment accounted for over half of GTE-T's sales, public switching for 31 percent, and station equipment and PABXs for the remaining. Over 60 percent of the transmission equipment GTE made in Italy was exported to a number of countries, in particular to Spain, Portugal, Turkey, Nigeria, the United States (communication satellite subsystems), Greece, the Netherlands, Belgium (where GTE had a local manufacturing subsidiary ATEA), and Australia.

GTE-T was active in the development of digital switching systems and participated in five projects outside of Italy. It had contributed to a joint project with GTE's U.S. affiliate manufacturing switching equipment (Automatic Electric) to adapt GTE's electronic analogue systems (n°1 and n°3 EAX), which were used for transit exchanges. A special laboratory had been set up for this purpose in Waltham, Mass., staffed partly with Italian engineers and partly with engineers from Automatic Electric.

Automatic Electric had developed a highly successful, partly distributed, large local digital exchange in the United States called GTD 5. In 1981, this system was being tried on GTE's own network, and it was expected to be mass-produced starting in 1982–83. In order to be used in the international networks, however, GTE needed to adapt this system to the CCITT standards prevalent in Europe and most of the world. That would involve about $50 million in additional expenditures, a significant amount, relative both to the initial GTD 5 development cost and to its potential markets abroad.

GTE had had mixed success in its international sales of electronic switching systems. A massive Iranian contract had been brought to a halt after the 1978 revolution, and the company was entangled in a major suit with the revolutionary Iranian government for payment of the work and equipment provided. GTE had registered some sales in Korea, Taiwan, and the Philippines, countries which had standards more easily compatible with the United States, and where American suppliers were welcome. The Italian subsidiary had participated in some of these export orders, particularly those with Iran.

## GTE-USA

GTE's organization was divided into two large units: Telephone operations was responsible for 28 operating companies in the United States, Puerto Rico, and Canada and accounted for 62 percent of total 1981 revenues of $11 billion; manufacturing was responsible for all other activities. Manufacturing consisted of five major groups, including all domestic affiliates—Information Systems, GTE-Sylvania (lighting and components), GTE Laboratories (research and military work), and Automatic Electric/Lenkurt (U.S. telecommunication equipment)—and an international group. The latter, with total 1981 revenues of $2 billion, was in itself divided into four divisions, one of which was responsible for telecom manufacturing operations outside the United States.

In the late 1970s, GTE's top management was making several major strategic moves. First, it was divesting, both in Europe and in the United States, its consumer electronics activities. European consumer product units were sold to German and French interests, and the U.S. operations were sold to Philips. Second, capitalizing on U.S. deregulation, GTE was showing great interest in value-added and data networks in the United States, as well as in information systems and data processing equipment. GTE also committed resources to its lighting and lamp business in the United States and internationally (e.g., by acquiring French lampmaker, Claude). These changes were implemented mainly by a group of senior executives recruited from General Electric. They were driven simultaneously by strong strategic thinking and short-term pressures to shape up the operations.

Traditionally, international operations at GTE had been quite autonomous, organized by regions and countries. The head of the European region was a well-experienced Italian, based in Milan, who was also quite close to the Italian subsidiary. There was little experience with, and moderate interest and understanding of specific European and Italian issues within staff groups in the United States. Up to 1980, therefore, the autonomy of the international subsidiaries had, by and large, been preserved. See Exhibit 13 for a summary of GTE's major manufacturing and sales affiliates outside the United States.

Things began to change dramatically in 1981. The remaining manufacturing businesses were reorganized into three worldwide groups, and all telecommunication equipment activities were brought together into a newly created "communications product (CP) group," headed by a senior ex-GE executive who started to take a global view of the businesses and to analyze their potential. With total revenues of $2.2 billion and operating income of only $112 million (16 percent of corporate total), the CP group was second in importance in GTE, after the telephone companies.

According to some, GTE's international telecommunication operations were too small to yield good returns and to warrant corporate attention. Therefore, the argument went, GTE would have to either divest most if its international operations, or make a major resource commitment to their development. With the GTD 5, GTE clearly had an excellent system, yet it lacked the necessary market presence (e.g., well-established subsidiaries) and the internationally experienced managers to undertake a major drive to gain world market share.

## OTHER OPTIONS

In addition to cooperating with one of the three suppliers currently present in the Italian market, Italtel had a number of other options. First, it could continue to develop Proteo on its own and encourage STET, SIP, and the various ministries to force divestment by the MNCs, along the lines of what had been negotiated by the French PTT in the mid-1970s. Second, Italtel could negotiate with other European partners. The EEC commission often lamented the lack of cooperation among the European suppliers of telecommunication equipment. CIT-Alcatel, General Electric (U.K.) and Plessey with their

---

## EXHIBIT 13

**GTE'S INTERNATIONAL TELECOMMUNICATION REVENUES, 1981**

| Countries | Total ($ million) | Public switching ($ million) | Exports | Station equipment ($ million) | Exports | Transmissions ($ million) | Exports |
|---|---|---|---|---|---|---|---|
| Canada | 135 | 95 | | 20 | | 20 | 10% |
| Italy | 76 | 35 | 55% | 3 | 10% | 38 | 60 |
| Belgium | 24 | 18 | 20 | 6 | 70 | — | — |
| Germany | 6 | — | | 6 | | — | — |
| Spain | 9 | — | | — | | 9 | 30 |
| Brazil | 25 | 13 | | 4 | | 8 | 20 |
| Mexico | 15 | 12 | | 1 | | 2 | — |
| Argentina | 5 | 5 | | — | | — | — |
| Philippines | 4 | 3 | | 1 | | — | — |
| Taiwan | 3 | 3 | | — | | — | — |
| Totals | 302 | 185 | | 41 | | 77 | |

System X, Philips, or Siemens—with a long international tradition in the industry and its previous ties to Italtel but lagging in efforts to develop a new system—were all potential candidates.

An alliance with another Italian supplier, Telettra, also deserved careful consideration. Telettra was the leading Italian supplier of transmission equipment, a business in which Italtel was not very strong and ran extremely high losses. Telettra, however, had almost no market presence in switching but did have a large and competent R&D group working not only on digital PCM transmissions but also on advanced digital switching software.

Telettra belonged to the FIAT group, with whom IRI (the state holding controlling STET) had engaged in a complex industrial restructuring effort. In the main, this would involve the transfer of certain activities from one group to the other, and their consolidation in one company per sector. Under discussion were the transfer of FIAT's steel and aeronautical activities to IRI, FIAT's support to IRI-owned Alfa Romeo (to develop new models), rationalization of the shipbuilding industry, and cooperation between Telettra and STET.

Marisa Bellisario and her management team were keenly aware that any option selected would involve difficult trade-offs. SIP and STET had to be satisfied that they would have a viable system (including large exchanges) within the time frame of the new telecommunication development plan, although its actual implementation might be delayed somewhat. The state might contribute some R&D funds, but, unlike the French PTT or the British Post Office, it would not underwrite and fund a major R&D program from public budgets.

Italtel had been criticized by many for its dependency on Siemens, but in some political circles they were quite skeptical about Proteo's development, given the delays incurred in the 1970s, and advocated either a return under Siemens' wing (when their own digital system would be ready), or closer cooperation with another

foreign supplier and the acquisition of manufacturing rights under license by Italtel. Old-guard Italtel employees were quite willing to join forces with Siemens. Yet, given the efforts demanded by the reorganization and reductions in labor and staffs implied by Dott. Bellisario's turnaround program, an abandonment of Proteo's research (even in disguise) might have devastating effects on morale within Italtel. A bright and able, large research group had been constituted in Castelletto and in the United States, and losing the bulk of its researchers might also cripple the company for a long time and negate the major investments made since 1970. STET, with a clear mandate to develop advanced electronic technologies in Italy, could hardly let digital switching become a missing link in its overall strategy.

---

**APPENDIX A**

# A Note on Competition in Digital Switching Systems, 1982

In the early 1980s, the world's telephone switching equipment industry was in the midst of a major transition. Its technological base was shifting from electromechanical systems to electronics, while transmission modes were changing from analogue to digital coding. Both developments had far-reaching implications for the structure and evolution of competition in the industry. This appendix summarizes some of the most important elements of this technological revolution.

## TECHNOLOGY

When a telephone call is connected through an exchange to the telephone of the person being called, a direct current flows through a "transmitter," a device containing packed carbon granules whose resistance to the current fluctuates under the pressure of sound waves from the speaker's voice. The resulting signal is, therefore, an "analogue" of the sound waves. The "receiver" at the other end of the system, reverses the process and recreates sound from an electric signal.

Each telephone "station" needs two wires to connect it to an exchange from which the call is forwarded to its destination. In the earliest systems, lifting the telephone from its cradle completed the electric circuit and notified an operator at the exchange to join the caller's line. She would ascertain the number required and complete the connection, either in the same exchange or by passing it to the corresponding operator in another exchange, thus manually "switching" the call.

The first automatic switching system to become commercially available was patented in 1879 by Almon Brown Strowger. As an undertaker in Kansas City, Mr. Strowger complained that telephone operators were diverting his calls to competitors and thus set out to devise a system that could not be misused. A Strowger exchange (as it developed after much modification) provides switching on a "step-by-step" principle. The rotation of the dial produces electrical impulses in a control circuit that moves a "selector" to a position corresponding to the digit being dialled. This completes a circuit through to a second selector where the process is repeated, and so on for as many digits as required. Since each stage involves the physical movement of mechanical selectors, the speed of the process has to be carefully regulated so as to not overwhelm the system.

The main alternatives to the Strowger exchange appeared in the 1920s and were designed as a series of matrices where every telephone in a system was connected both to one of a set of horizontal wires and to one of a set of vertical wires. Any connection could then be made by searching for the "cross-point" corresponding to the caller's number and connecting it to the cross-point of the telephone being called, either in the same matrix or in another. The lifting of the receiver would connect the subscriber to a "common control," which allocates pieces of equipment called a "register" and a "supervisory" to the call and directs a coded version of the calling number to the register. The latter sets up a path from the caller through the switching matrices to the supervisory, which returns a dialing signal (tone) to the caller. The caller then dials a number, which is stored by the register, before it contacts the common control and asks for a path through the switching matrices that will join the supervisory to the number being called.

This operation completes the connection, and the supervisory remains in the circuit for the duration of the call supplying current to the telephones and reporting when the call is concluded.

The electromechanical version of matrix switching is the "crossbar" exchange, which in its present form dates to the early 1940s. The crossbar selector is simply a set of horizontal bars placed against a set of vertical bars, with a system of electromagnets which, by a two-stage process, will set up a contact at any point of the matrix of cross points within the bars. In the "reed relay" version, the contacts are made between gold-plated reeds in a gas-filled tube, actuated by magnetic attraction generated by a current in a coil wound around the tube.

All these switching systems are used to complete circuits carrying analogue current. In fact, the voice signal can be converted, either at the local exchange (that is, before feeding it into the trunk network that connects different exchanges) or at the telephone itself, to a digital form, such as the binary code used by computers. Variations in the amplitude of the sound waves are converted into a series of "1" and "0" digits, packaged together into the trunk network, and transmitted in groups separated by a code from other conversations so that each caller uses a path for only a fraction of time.

Solid-state switching systems have emerged in the last 20 years as an alternative to electromechanical switches, particularly when coupled with new transmission technologies such as microwaves and optical fibers. Stored program control (SPC) switches developed as the most flexible and powerful control system, and the large economies characteristic of the manufacturing processes of solid-state devises in integrated circuits make them the obvious choice for future switching systems. Yet the SPC concept itself was going through significant change in the early 1980s. Initially, it used centralized computers for complete control, requiring at least two machines in parallel for reliability. This was replaced by decentralized concepts where multiple processors were used to handle smaller numbers of subscribers, and a hierarchy of processors was established for switching purposes. Decentralized control allowed for the division of hardware and software into modules, where each could be optimized for particular exchange characteristics and facilitate gradual expansion of the network. Most recently, design efforts focused on the use of powerful microprocessors to provide fully dis-

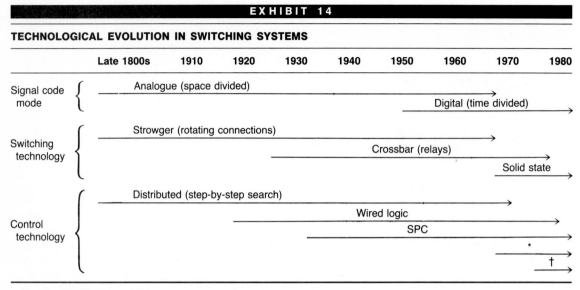

**EXHIBIT 14**

**TECHNOLOGICAL EVOLUTION IN SWITCHING SYSTEMS**

\* = Decentralized, hierarchical.
† = Distributed (microprocessor-controlled).

tributed real time control of all telephone functions. Exhibit 14 summarizes the technological evolution of the industry.

## THE ECONOMICS OF SUBSTITUTION

The first use of digital technology occurred in long-distance trunk lines. Quality improvements possible by digitalization of transmission, as well as the implications that a more efficient form of transmission had for the capacity of the network to accommodate volume increases without major additional investments, led the industry to begin the process of introducing digital pulse code modulation (PCM) for long-distance transmission in the 1970s. In spite of the penalties incurred by converting analogue signals to digital codes as they entered the trunk lines and back again at their destination, PCM coding was economically attractive.

Combining digital transmission with digital switching provides even greater economic advantages. Savings on investment can be substantial, since digital systems require smaller buildings, less power, less infrastructure, etc. An analysis of the investment costs associated with three main alternatives by which the Brest region in eastern France could extend its ser-

vices from 13,500 to 35,100 subscribers in a period of 10 years (1975–85), yielded the following results (as a percent of the most expensive alternative):

1. Analogue transmission and switching: 100.0
2. Analogue switching and digital transmission: 84.2
3. Digital switching and transmission: 62.0

Thirty percent of the cost of the first alternative involved the acquisition and installation of additional cables for transmission, unnecessary under the other two alternatives. Also, the mixed-technologies solution required expensive multiplexing equipment not necessary in an all-digital network.

But whereas digital switching equipment was originally more expensive on a per-line basis than the available analogue equivalent (about 15 percent in the example above of an early conversion), both systems were subject to very different long-term cost behavior. First, digital switches depended on solid state microelectronics, the real cost of which was on a steep decline compared with electromechanical devices. Second, successive generations of digital switches employed fewer and less varied components, which increased reliability while decreasing the cost of inventories, spare parts, and maintenance. Third, the cost mix associated with digital switches

| EXHIBIT 15 |
|---|

**WORLD MARKET FOR SWITCHING SYSTEMS**

|  | 1982 | 1985 | 1990 |
|---|---|---|---|
| Total volume (millions of lines) | 31 | 38 | 48 |
| By region (%): |  |  |  |
| North America | 38 | 37 | 36 |
| Europe | 31 | 30 | 28 |
| Middle East and Asia | 16 | 17 | 18 |
| Latin America | 9 | 10 | 11 |
| Oceania | 3 | 3 | 4 |
| Africa | 3 | 3 | 3 |

included relatively few elements subject to large price increases (e.g., less labor, installation, and maintenance costs). Only software development might be subject to cost increases over time, and this accounted for nearly 50 percent of the cost of a new digital system (including R&D amortization), but the trend toward modularization and distributed systems would affect these costs positively. Finally, digital switches required less maintenance and service, and rendered many network tasks, such as a change in a subscriber's number, very easy to perform centrally.

## MARKETS AND COMPETITION

The total market for telecommunication switching systems, excluding the Eastern European countries, was estimated at about $10 billion in 1982, representing the equivalent of 31 million local subscriber lines of switching equipment. The market was expected to grow at a 6–7 percent annual rate, in volume, and to reach 50 million lines per annum by 1990. During the 1980s, the average real price per line was expected to fall by about 3 percent per annum, for the reasons indicated above. Therefore, the total size of the market in 1990 would be of the order of $14 billion in constant money.

Digital switching was expected to take a rapidly growing share of the total market. In 1982, less than one-third of the world demand for switching systems would be digital. By 1985, digital technologies were expected to account for 50 percent of the market, and this proportion was forecast to reach 95 percent of all shipments of switching equipment by 1990. Local exchanges accounted for 80 percent of the total market. Of these, small rural exchanges of less than 500

lines accounted for 10 percent, while larger (up to 150,000 lines) local exchanges would account for the other 70 percent. The size mix of local exchanges varied with the geography and population density of each country, but medium-size exchanges (8–35,000 lines) represented the bulk of demand in most developed countries. Trunk and transit exchanges accounted for 15 percent of total demand, while special exchanges (e.g., data, telex, mobile, military) accounted for the remaining 5 percent. Exhibit 15 provides data on the forecast geographic distribution of this market through 1990.

In practically all countries (the major exception being the United States) the provision of telephone services was a regional or national monopoly, administered or regulated by a ministry of post, telegraph, and telecommunications (generally known as "PTTs"). By the 1960s almost all telephone networks were in national hands. Most countries had also required multinational manufacturers of telecommunication equipment to produce locally to local standards. Early industry leaders (ITT, LM Ericsson, Siemens, Plessey, etc.) had quickly established many foreign manufacturing subsidiaries to meet these requirements (see Exhibit 16).

Competition in switching equipment was generally limited by the PTTs to a few suppliers (usually two to five) and administered either through the allocation of regions (as in Italy) or by public purchasing policies (as in France). The PTTs tried to balance a natural desire to standardize all equipment in the network with the maintenance of a competitive environment conducive to price and service efficiency and technical progress. Over the decades, a stable competitive system developed whereby each national market

---

**EXHIBIT 16**

**ESTABLISHED POSITIONS IN PUBLIC SWITCHING** (Selected Markets, 1970s)

| Countries | Major suppliers (%) | | | | | | | |
|---|---|---|---|---|---|---|---|---|
| | Local | ITT | LME | Siemens | Plessey | GEC(UK) | GTE | Philips |
| Austria | 50 | 25 | — | 25 | — | — | — | — |
| Belgium | — | 80 | — | — | — | — | 20 | — |
| Denmark | — | 8 | 70 | 22 | — | — | — | — |
| Finland | — | 6 | 76 | 17 | — | — | — | — |
| Portugal | — | 51 | — | — | 49 | — | — | — |
| Switzerland | 50 | 30 | — | — | 20 | — | — | — |
| Argentina | — | 60 | — | 40 | — | — | — | — |
| Colombia | — | 5 | 70 | 10 | — | 15 | — | — |
| Mexico | — | 20 | 80 | — | — | — | — | — |
| Peru | — | 75 | — | — | — | — | — | 25 |
| Venezuela | — | 10 | 40 | 25 | — | — | — | — |
| S. Africa | — | — | — | 20 | 50 | 30 | — | — |

was open only to those firms implanted locally (either as foreign affiliates or in joint venture with local interests, often including the PTT itself).

Conversion to digital switching put these relationships in question. The economic characteristics of the industry were drastically modified, and the justification for a company to maintain many manufacturing centers and local operations was no longer as evident. Simultaneously, the penalty for a PTT to maintain different switching equipment in the network would rise, as software compatibility was essential to efficient operations while an increasing proportion of the equipment costs represented software development. The competitive environment of the industry would, as a result, be subject to increasing pressures over the next decade, as the data below illustrate.

Digital switching developments had imposed major R&D expenditures on most competitors and drastically changed the cost structure of the equipment industry relative to that of electromechanical technology. While simple systems with restricted size ranges and features (e.g., Stromberg Carlson's Century) might cost as little as $100 million to develop, including all necessary system software, a leading-edge, second-generation system would require in excess of $1 billion to develop. Exhibit 17 presents some estimates of the cumulative R&D costs associated with some of the main digital switches on the market or expected by the mid-1980s.

Manufacturing processes had also changed drastically for equipment producers. One way to handle the transition to electronic switches was to rely on outside vendors for many components. This could range from subcontracting component manufacturing to the lowest-cost, most efficient semiconductor suppliers, to using off-the-shelf computers and microprocessors as central processors. Intel had thus become a major manufacturer of telephone circuits, while Digital Equipment had sold some of its PDP minicomputers as main exchange processing units. Although allowing the telecommunication equipment companies to benefit from learning curves typical of the electronics industry, value added per line was significantly reduced (see Exhibit 18). The implication of these trends for industry employment were of concern to many governments.

These factors also opened the industry to competition from new quarters. Computer and semiconductor companies were obvious candidates, as were firms from industries with system design and software capabilities. The number of suppliers of digital switching had increased to 26 by 1981. The most successful were those which not only had led in technological innovation but had supported their products with major marketing efforts and attractive financing programs, and enjoyed, in many cases, some degree of home government assistance. They also benefitted from a strong domestic market requiring rapid modernization, the only exceptions being LM Ericsson

**CUMULATIVE R&D COSTS OF MAJOR DIGITAL SWITCHING PROJECTS**

(1981 Constant U.S. $)

| Company (switch) | Estimated cumulative costs |
|---|---|
| Stromberg Carlson* (Century) | 120 million |
| CIT-Alcatel (E-10) | 200 million† |
| Northern Telecom (DMS) | n.a. |
| GTE (GTD-5) | 300 million |
| Siemens (EWS-D) | 400 million (until 1983) |
| LM Ericsson (AXE-10) | n.a. |
| Philips (PRX-D) | 900 million |
| ITT (System 12) | 1.2 billion (until 1986) |
| Plessey/GEC/STC (System X) | 1.8 billion (until 1986) |

*Acquired by Plessey in 1982.

†Does not include research performed by the state research institute, the Centre Nationale d'Etude des Télécommunications.

n.a. = not available.

*Note:* These estimates were compiled by the authors from various sources and expert interviews. The figures do *not* correspond to those officially published by PTT and manufacturers, since they tend to understate R&D expenditures in most cases.

(with a small domestic market) and Nippon Electric (Japan had not yet committed to digital switching). The rise of new competitors such as Northern Telecom (Canada) or CIT-Alcatel (France) had intensified competition and forced many companies into complex technological and coproduction agreements in order to maintain market presence, particularly in developing countries (e.g., NEC in Syria and CIT-Alcatel in India and Poland). Exhibit 19 summarizes the order book of most competitors in digital switches.

The rising front-end costs associated with new switching systems forced competitors in two directions—to expand sales revenues to amortize past R&D expenditures and to fund further development. It was generally accepted that at least a 5 percent share of the world market was needed to recover typical investments in a new system over an eight-year period, before new technologies would render it obsolete. Most national markets were too small to justify these investments. Therefore, a capacity to generate export sales would become a critical competitive advantage.

A second approach was to share the development burden by entering into cooperative agreements among manufacturers, or between manufacturers and state

**LABOR CONTENT OF MAIN EXCHANGE SWITCHES OF DIFFERENT TECHNOLOGY**

(Man-Years per 1,000 Line-Equivalent)

| | Technology | | | |
|---|---|---|---|---|
| | Electromechanical | Space-divided electronic | Digital electronic (1981) | Digital electronic (1985 forecast) |
| Manufacturing | 5.9 | 2.2 | 1.8 | 1.0 |
| Installation | 2.9 | 1.3 | 0.8 | 0.4 |
| Total | 8.8 | 3.5 | 2.6 | 1.4 |
| (Index) | (100) | (40) | (30) | (16) |

---

**EXHIBIT 19**

---

**CUMULATIVE ORDERS BY MAJOR SUPPLIERS OF DIGITAL SWITCHING SYSTEMS** (Thousands of Lines)

| | As of December 1979 | | Forecast (end-1982) |
| --- | --- | --- | --- |
| | Installed | Cumulative orders | cumulative orders |
| CIT-Alcatel | 1,164 | 2,900 | 8,500 |
| Western Electric | n.a. | 4,500 | n.a. |
| Northern Telecom | 650 | 1,500 | 5,200 |
| LM Ericsson | 73 | 1,200 | 4,100 |
| Nippon Electric | 40 | 450 | 4,000 |
| Thomson CSF | — | 500 | 3,000 |
| GTE | n.a. | 1,300 | n.a. |
| ITT | 100 | n.a. | 1,000 + |
| GEC-Plessey | — | — | 1,000 + |
| Siemens | — | 120 | 600 |
| Stromberg Carlson | 142 | n.a. | n.a. |
| TRW-Vidar | 28 | n.a. | 300 + |
| Italtel | — | 15 | 350 |

n.a. = not available.
*Note:* Figures are estimates.

---

research agencies. However, the experience of System X in Britain (jointly developed by General Electric, Plessey, and Standard Telephones and Cables), the NTT-supported DTS-D60/D70 system in Japan, and the Tropico system in Brazil suggested that cooperative agreements and the direct involvement of PTTs in system development significantly increased R&D costs.

---

**APPENDIX B**

---

# Italian Government Agencies Concerned with Telecommunication Policy

The history of the Italian telecommunications industry is a turbulent one. In 1925, after a long period of instability, the government auctioned five 30-year concessions to private companies to provide local telephone services in each of the country's five major regions. As no private bidder was found for the long-distance service concession, a state agency, the Azienda di Stato per i Servizi Telefonici (ASST), was created to provide interregional services. During the depression years, the Istituto per la Ricostruzione Industriale (IRI) was established by the Mussolini government to finance Italian industry. IRI became the majority stockholder in three of the five regional telephone operators and conferred these shares to a new holding company, Societá Torinese Esercizio Telefonico (STET), with the mandate to coordinate their activities. In 1957, STET acquired a controlling interest in the remaining two telephone companies.

The Societá Idroelettrica Piemontese (SIP) was a successful operator of hydraulic power generation activities in the north of Italy until 1964, when these were nationalized by the government. The need to redeploy its resources, particularly the large expropriation payments received from the state, led SIP to acquire the remaining shares of the five regional telephone companies associated with STET. Following a series of mergers and restructuring, SIP became the almost exclusive concessionaire of local telephone services in Italy, and STET became its principal stockholder with nearly 60 percent of its shares. ASST remained in the business as an agency of the Ministry of Post and Telecommunications (the Italian PTT), responsible for most trunk line service in Italy. Throughout the years these two agencies had divided their orders for telecommunication switching gear

---

**EXHIBIT 20**

---

**SHARING OF THE ITALIAN MARKET FOR PUBLIC SWITCHING EQUIPMENT
ON THE BASIS OF FIXED TERRITORY ALLOCATION**

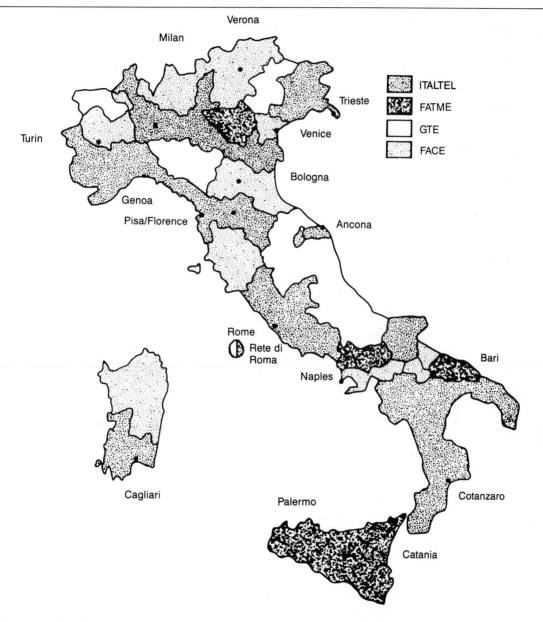

among the four main suppliers along regional basis corresponding to the original operating companies (see Exhibit 20).

Italtel (or its predecessor) was first established in 1921, in Milan, as a sales agency of the German telecommunications giant Siemens A.G., later expanded to include manufacturing operations in 1927. After World War II, the company was nationalized and

EXHIBIT 21

**ITALIAN PUBLIC AGENCIES CONCERNED WITH TELECOMMUNICATION POLICY**

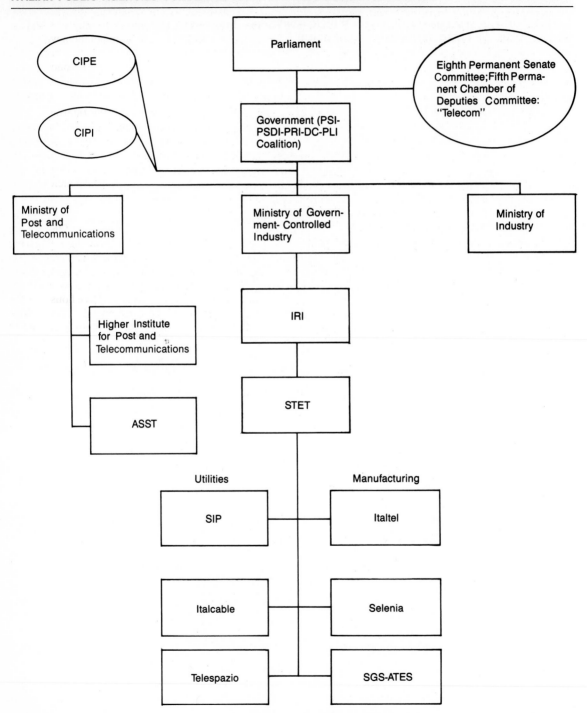

added to STET's portfolio of related businesses, but it retained a licensing agreement with Siemens to produce traditional electromechanical switching equipment for the local network. In the late 1960s, STET diversified further into electronics, acquiring companies in semiconductors, and space communication systems and cables, among others, to become the largest electronics group in Italy.

As of 1981, the major players influencing telecommunications policy in Italy included the following agencies and state holding companies (see Exhibit 21):

*The Ministry of Post and Telecommunications* had overall responsibility for postal, telephonic, radio-telegraphic and television and radio broadcasting services. Through ASST it operated long-distance telephone services directly. Also reporting to the ministry was the Higher Institute for Post and Telecommunications with a consulting and think-tank role on future sectoral policies.

*The Ministry of Industry* had oversight responsibility for all decisions concerning industrial and commercial activities, including telecommunications.

*The Ministry of State Shareholdings,* created in 1956, was in charge of monitoring the activities of the three main state-owned holding companies, IRI, ENI and EFIM, and supplied them with guidance relating to industrial policy and coordination. In principle, these holdings were autonomous in designing strategies for their companies and in stimulating their competitiveness and efficiency.

*CIPE and CIPI* (respectively, the Interministerial Committee for Economic Planning and for Industrial Planning) were constituted by various economic ministers and chaired by the Prime Minister. Their main purpose was to design and coordinate economic and industrial policies for the nation, particularly in terms of development priorities and plans.

The *Eighth Permanent Commission of the Senate* and *Fifth Permanent Commission of the Chamber of Deputies on Transportation and Telecommunication* were constituted by parliamentary representatives in rough approximation to their parties' representation in the respective houses of the Italian Parliament. They exercised a consultative role and intervened mainly in matters related to pricing of public services.

# The American Telephone & Telegraph Co.

In the summer of 1983, Mr. Charles Brown, Chairman of AT&T, was approached by Mr. Carlo de Benedetti, CEO of Ing. C. Olivetti, S.p.A. As a regulated company, AT&T had largely refrained from actively engaging in overseas activities, but now with divestment formally effective on January 1, 1984, the company would be free to compete on a world scale. Mr. Brown was therefore interested in discussing possible business with Olivetti.

AT&T had established a joint venture with Philips, the Dutch electronics company, in the same year. That venture was limited to telecommunications switching and transmission gear and did not include computers and office automation, an area AT&T knew had enormous potential and where Olivetti was active. Beyond the Philips venture and a minor investment in Ireland, AT&T had no active relationships in Europe. Mr. Brown felt that AT&T's potential

in Europe was substantial. AT&T not only had the technology of Bell Labs, it also dominated the world's largest telecommunications market.

## COMPANY BACKGROUND

From the moment Alexander Graham Bell patented the telephone in 1876, the Bell Telephone Company moved quickly ahead of its would-be competitors to become "the long distance phone company of America." Because phone services were considered to be "natural monopolies," they were usually either state-owned or government regulated (as in the United States). These national monopolies controlled what happened in their own countries and negotiated with one another on international services. They produced their own equipment or obtained it through suppliers of their choice. Equipment down to the simple telephone was leased rather than sold to users.

By the middle of the century, Bell Telephone had become the world's largest regulated company. AT&T had been incorporated as a subsidiary of Bell as early as 1885, dominating the telecommunications industry of America until the sixties by its sheer size. The enormous in-

The case was prepared by Ms. Juliet Taylor under the supervision of Professor George Taucher as a basis for class discussion rather than to illustrate either effective or ineffective handling of an administrative situation. The case was prepared entirely from published reports and data. Copyright © 1986 by IMEDE, Lausanne, Switzerland. Reproduced by permission.

vestments required for R&D and equipment coupled with regulation had protected AT&T from all competition except from small local independent companies.

In 1982 AT&T was the world's largest corporation. A study comparing its growth with that of the gross national product of the United States revealed that, from 1947 to 1981, AT&T grew three times as rapidly as the U.S. economy. With assets of $145.5 billion, 1 million employees, 3 million shareholders, and almost every household in America as a customer, it was more like a nation than a company. Its revenues of $66 billion were the same size as Austria's GDP. (See Exhibit 1 for financial data.)

The Bell System comprised a holding company, AT&T, that owned Western Electric, Long Lines, and most of the stock of the 22 Bell local telephone companies. AT&T also shared the ownership of prestigious Bell Telephone Laboratories with Western Electric. The separate subsidiary, American Bell, which due to FCC (the U.S. Federal Communications Commission) regulations was required to operate at arm's length from regulated AT&T, is covered in more detail under the section "Information Systems."

## CHANGES LEADING TO DEREGULATION

Rapidly changing technology, starting in the 1960s, began to put into doubt the "natural" monopoly argument. Whereas in the "good old days" equipment sometimes lasted 30 years without a change, new systems became obsolete almost as soon as they were installed. For years, simple copper wires and electromechanical switching relays sufficed to carry and distribute information (phone calls, telegrams or telex messages). The arrival of digitalization, optical fibers, microwave radio transmission, and communication satellites permitting the simultaneous transmission of diverse data revolutionized the telecommunications business.

The greatest impact on telecommunications was made by the digital computer. As these computers proliferated throughout the business world, faster and more efficient transmission equipment was needed. Telecommunications became a vital strategic weapon to all companies. Instead of using telephone equipment merely for phone calls or telex messages, suddenly it was in demand for sending large amounts of computer data at high speeds, for facsimile transmission, videoconferencing, and so forth. The efficiency of the communications systems available to customers could affect their competitiveness in world markets.

These developments in the 1960s and 1970s forced many governments to review their PTTs (Post office, Telephone and Telegraph). The FCC had already started chipping away at the AT&T monopoly position as early as the 1960s, when microwave communication was opened to limited competition. Space satellites, also excluded from the AT&T monopoly, offered tremendous scope for development and competition to traditional transmission methods. For the first time, competitors had access to the profitable long-distance market as well as equipment sales to customers, both at the heart of the AT&T monopoly. Meanwhile, AT&T was increasingly left with "dead-end" technology in its regulated business while inhibited by the same regulation from competing in the new technological areas.

By the mid-1970s, it was clear that the U.S. government was accelerating the trend toward deregulation, and competitors were gradually encroaching on AT&T's formerly protected domain. AT&T's response to the new competition provoked a series of private legal actions for alleged antitrust violations. In 1974, the U.S. Justice Department brought its own antitrust case against AT&T. Years of discussion ensued as both the Bell System and the Justice Department attempted to settle without a trial. After six years of abortive negotiations, the antitrust trial started at the Federal Courthouse in Washington, D.C., on January 15, 1981. One year later a settlement was announced. The Justice Department had proposed a break-up of monopolistic AT&T by splitting off Western Electric and Bell Laboratories. AT&T instead agreed

| EXHIBIT 1 |
|---|

**AT&T RESULTS IN BRIEF: SELECTED FINANCIAL AND OPERATING DATA**

| | 1982 | 1981 | 1980 | 1979 | 1978 |
|---|---|---|---|---|---|
| Revenues, ($ million) | | | | | |
| Local service | 28,986 | 25,553 | 22,449 | 20,208 | 18,685 |
| Toll service | 33,257 | 30,189 | 26,051 | 23,371 | 20,770 |
| Other (including other income) | 3,514 | 3,339 | 3,049 | 2,604 | 2,289 |
| Total | 65,757 | 59,081 | 51,549 | 46,183 | 41,744 |
| Expenses ($ million) | | | | | |
| Operating | 45,025 | 39,346 | 34,305 | 30,236 | 26,527 |
| Income taxes on operations | 4,931 | 4,119 | 3,581 | 3,607 | 3,826 |
| Other operating taxes | 4,879 | 4,430 | 3,928 | 3,602 | 3,439 |
| Interest | 3,930 | 4,363 | 3,768 | 3,083 | 2,690 |
| Total | 58,765 | 52,258 | 45,582 | 40,528 | 36,482 |
| Income before cumulative effect of a change in accounting principle ($ million) | 6,992 | 6,823 | 5,967 | 5,655 | 5,262 |
| Prior years cumulative effect of a change in accounting for deferred income taxes ($ million) | 287 | | | | |
| Net income ($ million) | 7,279 | 6,823 | 5,967 | 5,655 | 5,262 |
| Preferred dividend requirements ($ million) | 142 | 146 | 150 | 156 | 164 |
| Income applicable to common shares ($ million) | 7,137 | 6,677 | 5,817 | 5,499 | 5,098 |
| Earnings per common share | 8.40 | 8.47 | 8.04 | 8.01 | 7.73 |
| Based on average shares outstanding (thousands) | 849,550 | 788,178 | 723,516 | 686,109 | 659,843 |
| Total assets ($ million) | 148,186 | 137,750 | 125,553 | 113,444 | 103,025 |
| Long- and intermediate-term debt ($ million) | 44,105 | 43,877 | 41,255 | 37,168 | 34,203 |
| Preferred shares subject to mandatory redemption ($ million) | 1,550 | 1,563 | 1,575 | 1,588 | 1,600 |
| Convertible preferred shares subject to redemption ($ million) | 301 | 336 | 385 | 433 | 501 |
| Dividends declared per common share | 5.40 | 5.40 | 5.00 | 5.00 | 4.60 |
| Ratio of earnings to fixed charges | 3.64 | 3.26 | 3.34 | 3.76 | 4.10 |
| Toll messages for the year ended December 31 (million) | 19,275 | 18,643 | 17,457 | 16,193 | 14,639 |
| WATS messages for the year ended December 31 (million)* | 6,615 | 5,655 | 4,874 | 4,244 | 3,631 |
| Network access lines in service at December 31 (million)† | 85 | 84 | 82 | 79 | 76 |

*Charges for toll messages and WATS messages for the year ended December 31, 1982 account for about 36% and 9%, respectively, of total billed operating revenues.

†Recurring charges for network access lines in service for the year ended December 31, 1982 account for about 24% of total billed operating revenues.

to divest itself of its 22 Bell Operating Companies in return for release from the restrictions of a consent decree which, since 1956, had prohibited its entry into nontelephone markets.

The new AT&T (Exhibits 2 and 3) would be made up of two parts, managed as one business by AT&T Corporate, which was responsible for overall corporate strategy and policy. The two parts were to be:

*AT&T Technologies,* an umbrella group organized along a line-of-business structure and comprising Bell Laboratories (R&D), AT&T Network Systems, AT&T Consumer Prod-

**EXHIBIT 2**

**AFTER THE BREAKUP: AT&T ORGANIZATIONAL UNITS, 1983**

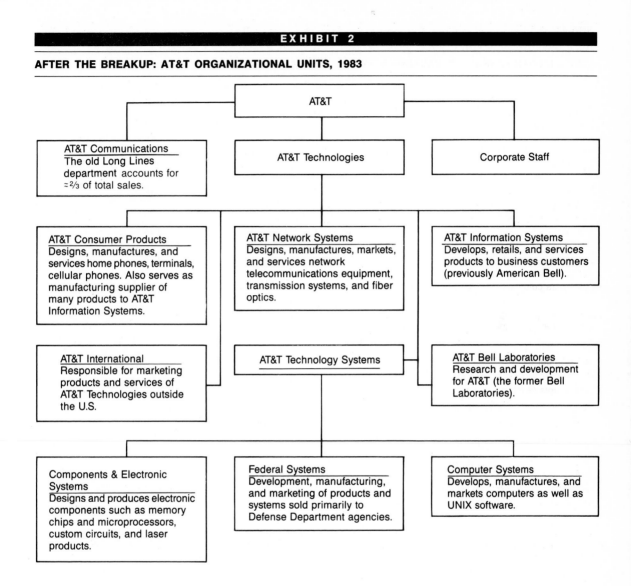

ucts, AT&T Technology Systems, AT&T International, and AT&T Information Systems, known as ATTIS, the new deregulated marketing organization.[1] (See Exhibit 4.)

*AT&T Communications,* a regulated entity and expanded version of the Long Line Division of the old AT&T offering intercity and overseas telecommunication services. (See Exhibit 5 for a divisional sales breakdown.)

The former 22 wholly-owned Bell Operating Companies were to be regrouped into seven regional companies: NYNEX, Bell Atlantic, Bell South, Southwestern Bell, Pacific Telesis, U.S. West, and Ameritech. Each of these companies would be independent of AT&T and of each

---

[1]The manufacturing plants of Western Electric were to be assigned to the various lines of business.

---

### EXHIBIT 3

**AT&T—BEFORE AND AFTER BREAKUP**

**January 1982: Breakup announced**

| | Number of employees |
|---|---|
| AT&T corporate headquarters | 13,302 |
| Long Lines (interstate long distance) | 42,834 |
| AT&T International | 530 |
| Bell Labs | 24,000 |
| Western Electric | 159,862 |
| 22 operating companies | 798,000 |
| Total | 1,038,528 |

**January 1984: Breakup takes effect**

| | |
|---|---|
| AT&T corporate headquarters | 2,000 |
| AT&T Communications (interstate and some intrastate long distance) | 120,000 |
| AT&T International | 900 |
| Bell Labs | 19,000 |
| Western Electric | 135,000 |
| Seven independent regional companies | 580,000 |
| Central Services Organization (research and systems engineering group owned by the seven regionals) | 8,800 |
| AT&T Information Systems (unregulated subsidiary formed Jan. 1, 1983, with 28,000 people) | 110,000 |
| Total | 975,700 |

*Source:* Data from American Telephone & Telegraph Co. AT&T estimates.

---

other. Nonetheless, it was unlikely that the equipment and technology links with Western Electric and Bell Labs would be totally severed—at least for the foreseeable future.

In a complex restructuring process along with "the most enormous task of reorienting managers that any company has had to face," AT&T geared itself for the future. With divestiture, data processing—the fastest growing and most competitive industry in the business world—had become accessible to them. Furthermore, as a nonregulated company, AT&T was in a position to set its sights on markets outside the United States.

---

### EXHIBIT 4

**AT&T INFORMATION SYSTEMS BREAKDOWN**

| Product | Revenues ($ million) | Percent |
|---|---|---|
| PBX | 815 | 7.9 |
| Key | 865 | 8.4 |
| Station apparatus | 550 | 5.3 |
| Workstations | 125 | 1.2 |
| Minicomputers | 250 | 2.4 |
| Rental revenues | 6,487 | 62.7 |
| Service | 721 | 7.0 |
| Other | 531 | 5.1 |
| Total | 10,344 | 100.0 |

## AT&T PRODUCTS AND STRATEGY

AT&T pursued its global goals, developing its strategies to meet its objectives. An ambitious line of products was announced ranging from small home devices to large minicomputers and all the network links between them. AT&T hoped to market a telephone as a terminal with a personal computer attached and a larger computer into which the desktop setup would be hooked. This whole system would plug into AT&T's ACCUNET Digital Network, or SKYNET satellite telecommunications systems, permitting conversation between cities or countries concerning the data displayed on the screen.

---

### EXHIBIT 5

**AT&T SALES BREAKDOWN—ESTIMATED 1984**

($ Million)

| | |
|---|---|
| Gross revenues | 35,036 |
| Access charges (payments to regional AT&T companies) | (20,633) |
| Net revenues from long-distance telecommunication | 14,403 |
| AT&T Information Systems | 10,344 |
| AT&T Technologies (Western Electric sales to outsiders) | 7,639 |
| AT&T International | 650 |
| Miscellaneous | 15 |
| Total sales | 33,051 |

AT&T's Components and Electronic Systems organization produced silicon chip products and other components basic to telecommunications, information processing, and computers, including advanced electronic memory chips and integrated circuits. Bell Labs had been first to develop the 256K dynamic random access memory chip.

With its move into the information processing sector, AT&T would challenge industry giant IBM, whose revenue from data processing was $34.7 billion in 1983 (Digital Equipment, in second place, had sales of $4.8 billion). AT&T's computer sales were an estimated $850 million. Yet AT&T was also a giant and a force to be reckoned with. (Its operating revenues, including access charges, were forecast at $56.5 billion for 1984.) Not since the 1950s when GE, Sperry, RCA, and Honeywell entered the computer race, had IBM been challenged by a company of anywhere near its own size. AT&T had made significant contributions to developing the computer age. In the forties, Bell Labs had more patents and expertise than any other firm in the field. If any company in the early days could have successfully challenged IBM, it would have been AT&T. However, AT&T's agreement with the U.S. Justice Department to manufacture computers solely for its own operations after 1956 stopped any hope of its competing in this field. When this restriction was lifted in January 1983, AT&T was free to sell computers, software, and services.

In computers, AT&T's top-of-the-line offering was its 3B family of minicomputers. The 3B 20D (for duplex, with dual central processing units) was still being developed and would be used in network switching equipment. The 3B 20D was roughly comparable to Digital's supermini VAX 11-780 (which sold for half a million dollars). AT&T's 3B 20S (for simplex or single central processing unit) was designed to handle a wide range of general purpose applications. A smaller and less expensive member of the 3B family, the 3B 5, which (like the 3B 20) used AT&T's own 32-bit microprocessor and ran on Bell Labs' operating system, was to be

part of AT&T's office strategy. Smaller desktop versions of these models were in development.

In software, AT&T had a potentially good offering (outside of telecom technology); this was its UNIX, a multiuser operating system developed 10 years before by Bell Labs. UNIX had never been fully exploited commercially due to AT&T's limits in the computer area, yet those who had used it both inside AT&T's own companies as well as in universities and training centers all over the United States rated it highly. In 1983, Intel, Motorola, and National Semiconductor, three major chip makers, agreed that their most advanced microprocessors would conform to AT&T's Unix version-5. This agreement meant that the AT&T design would become a standard for 16- and 32-bit microprocessors. After months of debate in the industry concerning standard operating systems for 32-bit multiuser microcomputers (PCs), IBM put its seal of approval on UNIX. With IBM setting the example, other manufacturers followed. NCR and Hewlett Packard both designed microcomputers and personal computers around UNIX. Ironically, even though Bell Labs had invented the UNIX system, AT&T was unable to make further developments, due to its isolation from the market. In fact, licensors such as IBM had developed far greater capability in the use of UNIX than AT&T.

For AT&T, after nearly 30 years of exile from manufacturing and selling computers, the real door opener to its new target market, information processing, was to be through its telephone technology. By 1983, telephones were no longer headsets and cradles; telephones meant digital multiline PBX (private branch exchange) systems enabling an office to become its own in-house phone company. Switching calls could be done internally instead of at the external central switching station. In these new PBX systems, voices were carried in discrete units or bits rather than in waves as was done by the previous generation of analog exchanges. PBX systems could be connected to other digital equipment such as terminals, personal computers, or even large mainframe computers. Voice and data could be transmitted over a single telephone line. This merging of voice and data was to make the PBX the hub of the automated office of the future and the target of every equipment manufacturer wishing to stay in the race.

In 1983, AT&T launched its first digital PBX System 85 that would compete with the two main suppliers in the segment, Rolm and Northern Telecom. In addition, the plan was to introduce, over the next two years, 30 or so products, such as word processors, workstation terminals, a desktop computer, printers and data terminals. All of these products were designed to communicate with each other through Dimension System 85. AT&T was therefore well placed to compete in the field.

## INFORMATION SYSTEMS DIVISION

In 1982, AT&T had formed a deregulated subsidiary called American Bell that would supply equipment and services and spearhead its entry into the computer industry, linking this effort to AT&T's massive telecommunications strength.

American Bell comprised two divisions:

*Consumer Products* was to provide home and small business communications and information systems.

*Advanced Information Systems,* the larger of the two divisions, was to market information movement and management systems for business and government customers.

In June 1983, American Bell learned that it could no longer use the Bell name. It then became known as AT&T Information Systems (ATTIS). ATTIS was AT&T's marketing arm whose main function was to establish itself in the new market areas it coveted and was now free to penetrate. Although ATTIS was given some manufacturing and development capability, it was still heavily dependent on Bell Labs and AT&T Technologies for its new product development and supply.

One of ATTIS' first tasks was to reestablish AT&T's market position in PBXs. By 1975 the PBX market had been liberalized, and the PBX was growing in importance. It had started to look and act more and more like a computer. As a result of this evolution, twenty or so companies were now competing for market share. By 1982, AT&T's share had dropped from almost 95 percent of the large and medium PBX market in the mid-1970s to only about 25 percent.

As far as computers were concerned, ATTIS had a three-pronged approach:

1. Business customers would be sold enhanced computer and office automation devices to be used compatibly with existing communication equipment.
2. Residential customers would be sold personal computer telephone devices to be used as home information terminals.
3. AT&T would integrate the systems, connecting all computers, desktop devices, and communications equipment into a common network.

To achieve its objectives, ATTIS had considerable resources beyond its impressive line of products. It had a 3,500-person sales force and an extensive customer base. ATTIS also had a $4 billion line of credit from AT&T.

## AT&T'S INTERNATIONAL BUSINESS

Although described in 1983 as a pygmy abroad, AT&T was once quite active outside the United States. In the 1920's, AT&T had dominated the world telecom market with 14 Western Electric plants around the globe making telephone equipment, electric fans, and household products. In 1925, AT&T made its goal to supply every American home and office with a telephone. Its interest in business abroad declined, and it sold its overseas business to a tiny company for $30 million. The company was ITT. Ironically, Bell Telephone of Antwerp and the other companies that later formed the ITT empire had started as AT&T subsidiaries. During the next 40 years, AT&T concentrated mainly on America, leaving the phone business of the rest of the world to ITT, GTE, Northern Telecom, NEC, Ericsson, and others.

In 1965, the U.S. Defense Department asked AT&T to carry out some overseas surveys. Then, in the mid-1970s, Western Electric set up a division to sell products abroad, quickly obtaining contracts in Saudi Arabia and South Korea. The company also signed a contract with the Iranian government to provide advice and equipment to improve Iran's civilian telecommunications network. When the Shah fell, AT&T initially lost $65 million because the Khomeini government did not honor the agreement until several years later.

AT&T International, headed by Bob Sageman, was created as a wholly owned subsidiary in 1980. During the first two years of operation, there was not much activity. Then, in 1983, Western Electric International linked up with Gold Star Semiconductor Ltd. in South Korea to manufacture electronic switching equipment. That venture accounted for roughly half of AT&T's international sales of about $600 million, still a small fraction of AT&T's consolidated sales of over $50 billion.

Also in 1982, AT&T attempted to enter the European Common Market through the purchase of Telectron, a manufacturer of transmission equipment in Ireland. This venture subsequently turned sour due to union disputes and slow production, and most of the company's plants were closed in 1984.

In that same year, during a routine meeting between AT&T and Philips to renegotiate licenses, a top Philips executive noted that Philips was spending a lot to develop a digital switch to route calls on public telephone systems. He was talking to the right people, for AT&T's Bell Labs was bursting with this type of development work. The discussion led to a joint venture proposal whereby AT&T's 5ESS (a digital electronic switching system) would be manufactured in Europe. Philips would save money on development in exchange for providing AT&T with a worldwide sales and manufacturing network as well as help in adapting ATT's digital switch to the world market. Philips was delighted. AT&T's 5ESS, which cost some $400 million to develop, was a world-class product. It was capable of serving telephone central offices of over 100,000 lines. It could supercede Philip's own PRXD switch which had also cost several hundred million dollars to develop but had not been very successful.

On paper this new joint venture looked ideal; yet for AT&T it was far from perfect. A question arose concerning the limits of the agreement with Philips. In the initial discussion, there was a possibility that PBXs might be included, but the final contract agreed only on distribution of computerized public exchange equipment and digital switching and transmission systems. Philips, whose diverse product range included electronic hospital equipment, records, shavers, household appliances and various consumer products, was not a major player in communications with only $1.2 billion of its previous year's sales of $16.4 billion coming from this segment. Philip's presence in 70 countries should have given AT&T more clout abroad than it could have had on its own, but AT&T may have lacked confidence in Philip's office automation and PBX experience. The agreement, based on AT&T's 5ESS, which would be converted to CCITT[2] specifications for Holland and Germany, served only part of AT&T's requirements. The company still needed a suitable distribution and sales network for its System 85 and 75 PBXs, products it hoped would lead into the office automation market in Europe. However, it was improbable that any of the telecom giants such as ITT or Siemens would link up with AT&T at the time.

## AT&T'S MANAGEMENT CULTURE

The massive changes surrounding divestment caused wide speculation in the press, Wall Street,

---

[2]CCITT—International Consultative Committee for Telegraph and Telephone, Geneva, the standards body for telecommunications of the U.N. specialized agency, ITU, determined telecommunication standards employed outside North America and Japan.

and the business community. Opinion was divided on AT&T's future. "AT&T is a great big company that has the attitudes of a monopoly entrenched in it," remarked Richard M. Moley, marketing vice president from Rolm Corp. "AT&T's transformation is a corporate gamble to top all corporate gambles," said a well-known N.Y. firm of communications consultants. Quoted an analyst: "AT&T's pronouncements on marketing may be more wishful thinking than reality. Evidence abounds that the company's much-touted new marketing culture is at odds with AT&T's older, entrenched operations mentality, and that marketing executives and operations veterans are locked in a power struggle for control of the company in which operations were gaining the upper hand." AT&T's struggles with marketing versus operations had been ongoing for many years before deregulation took place.

In the early 1970s, when AT&T started facing competition from other companies, an IBM "whizzkid" named Archie McGill was hired to head AT&T's marketing. McGill, the youngest group vice president in AT&T's history, created a stir. He hired a group of dynamic young marketing executives for AT&T, many of them from IBM. Thereafter, the operations versus marketing battles started, and the rivalry that developed never subsided. "Manufacturing had never been asked to hurry with their products before," said impatient marketing personnel. Operations executives, "bred in an environment of extensive planning, detailed corporate manuals and endless memos," were startled by McGill's new team. Stated McGill, "AT&T has had a difficult time understanding that the customer is the company's reason for being. Marketing at AT&T faced a tough mental and cultural barrier." "There's so much mistrust and anxiety among executives that the ranks feel it now," quoted a former marketing manager.

Some experts claimed that internal strife, in which marketing lost ground to operations, hampered AT&T's adjustment to deregulation.

One major problem facing management was whether certain products should be produced internally, a slow process, or manufactured outside more rapidly. Marketing obviously preferred the latter solution, and they scored an apparent victory when an agreement was made with Convergent Technologies in California to manufacture minicomputers and desktop computers for AT&T. An analyst at Dean Witter Reynolds predicted in 1983, "IBM will flatten AT&T in the automated office unless the marketing types can gain more control."

It was true that operations managers rather than marketing managers had moved into the corporation's pivotal jobs after a top-level reorganization. For a company which had always been strong in R&D, technological and product supremacy, it was understandable that manufacturing prowess should continue to be a major preoccupation. In 1983, a fierce battle between the two sides centered around AT&T's entry into computers. One manager involved in the dispute stated, "when the battle ended, the manufacturing side had won control of computer pricing policy, distribution channels, and even marketing's product task forces." This conflict led to the exodus of some of AT&T's top marketing talent, including Archie McGill. Departing executives explained that a clash in corporate culture had produced battle after battle between operations and marketing.

When announcing AT&T's new strategy in 1983, vice chair James E. Olson stated, "We are market driven . . . everybody will be part of marketing in the new AT&T." No longer protected by regulation, nor able to count on its own divisions for customers, AT&T needed marketing clout. Enabled at last to enter the data processing business where its main competitor, IBM, and other heavyweights such as DEC were already deeply entrenched, marketing talent was the number-one criterion for success of AT&T's information systems. Yet, in spite of Olson's statement, experts were not so sure about marketing at AT&T.

# Ing. C. Olivetti & Co. S.p.A.

## COMPANY BACKGROUND

Until 1976, Olivetti was best known as the family-owned Italian typewriter company, famous for the elegant design of its products. The company had been run with panache, and its history had been colorful. The Olivetti family had devoted considerable attention to developing the company's image, and this was reflected in its typically Italian attitude to everything aesthetic, the architecture of its buildings, and the stylish appearance of its products. The Olivetti family was also renowned for its exemplary treatment of personnel and factory workers.

Camillo Olivetti, the son of a northern Italian real estate broker, founded the company in 1908 and built its first headquarters in Ivrea in the foothills of the Italian Alps, just over the border from Switzerland. The headquarters are still there today. Camillo had an electrical engineering degree from Turin University and before starting work in Italy spent two years as a research assistant at Stanford.

Olivetti's first typewriter, the M11, was displayed at the Turin fair in 1911. The Italian Navy ordered 100 machines, and from then on the company never ceased to expand. By 1924, a workforce of 400 was turning out 4,000 typewriters per year, and by 1929 output had increased to 13,000. The product line was broadened to include first teleprinters and teletype machines, office furniture, and filing cabinets; in 1946 adding machines and calculators were included in the mix.

Olivetti's first foreign company, Hispana Olivetti, was founded in Barcelona in 1929, followed by a Belgian branch in 1930. In the same year, Olivetti's successful M40 typewriter was launched.

The most influential of the Olivettis, Adriano, joined the firm as Advertising Manager and in 1933 became General Manager. After some years of traveling in the United States to gain insights on the U.S. market, products, and business

The case was prepared by Ms. Juliet Taylor under the supervision of Professor George Taucher as a basis for class discussion rather than to illustrate either effective or ineffective handling of an administrative situation. The case was prepared entirely from published reports and data. Copyright © 1986 by IMEDE, Lausanne, Switzerland. Reproduced by permission.

techniques, Adriano succeeded his father as President of Olivetti in 1938.

The depression years were hard in Italy, but Adriano kept Olivetti in business, maintaining the workforce and increasing orders. Olivetti continued to prosper under Adriano, who was making a name for himself as a social reformer, philosopher, and patron of the arts. One of his main interests was urban planning. He rebuilt the Olivetti complex in Ivrea to include special living accommodation for his workers, turning it into a model village. His deep interest in design led him to solicit the help of such world-renowned architects as Mies van der Rohe and Walter Gropius and of artists such as Klee and Kandinsky, all of whom helped contribute to what was to become known as the "Tocco Olivetti" or the Olivetti touch. Adriano's desire to create an image combining functionality with beauty was reflected in the advertising which he introduced for Olivetti's products, long before advertising came into common use.

## GROWTH—THE FIFTIES AND SIXTIES

During the fifties and early sixties, Olivetti consolidated its position, and between 1951 and 1961, increased its total labor force from 6,000 to 39,000 (including foreign sales organizations). By 1961, there were 39 sales branches and 250 exclusive distributors in Italy alone, and 22 Olivetti associated sales branches throughout the world. Factories had been built in Scotland, South Africa, and South America as rising labor costs in Italy forced Adriano to reexamine his manufacturing policy.

After a period of such rapid growth on all levels, Olivetti became preoccupied with increasing costs and the company's liquidity. Retained earnings and additional loans kept Olivetti going into the early sixties, but when Adriano died in 1960, he left the company in an alarming state of indebtedness.

One of the turning points in the history of Olivetti, its first serious foray into the United States, also contributed to its debt after Adriano's death. In 1959, Adriano had masterminded the takeover of a majority holding in the Underwood Company. The prestigious U.S. office machinery manufacturer was almost bankrupt when Olivetti came to its rescue. The objective of the acquisition was to secure Olivetti's entry into the U.S. market. It succeeded. Olivetti/Underwood's share of the typewriter market rose from 1.7 percent in 1950 to 21.5 percent in 1966. However, the price paid was high. It took four years to turn Underwood around, and the process cost Olivetti dearly in investment and administrative problems.

With the Underwood deal, Olivetti's sales rose by 204 percent in 1963, but long-term debt increased even more (from $21 million to $66 million). Sales were around $420 million. Bank loans increased from $7.6 million to $32.5 million within a few years.

For the next 10 years, Olivetti continued to expand, in spite of its problems, at a rate unprecedented in Italian industry. By 1966 it was the sixth largest company in Italy with almost 80 percent of its sales abroad. By then, 35 percent of its total sales was in calculators, 28 percent in manual and electronic typewriters, and the rest spread amongst accounting machines, office furniture, and various other allied items. There were no more Olivettis suited to the role of president, although family members remained in some executive positions. After Adriano's death, disagreements developed between the Olivetti family and its nonfamily presidents. With mounting debt and a recessive economy, the early sixties were fraught with problems for the company. Reinvested profits and increased loans were no longer enough to sustain Olivetti's rapid growth, so capitalization was increased and reached almost $100 million by 1962. No longer able to face the pressure from the banks, the Olivetti family was forced to sell almost half its stock to a consortium, which was formed to provide both funds and new management. Short-term debt was consolidated, the management overhauled, and Dr.

Bruno Visentini, then Vice President of Italy's huge state-controlled conglomerate, IRI, became president of Olivetti.

Seriously undercapitalized due to the family's insistence on retaining control, by the late seventies Olivetti's debt situation was more acute than ever. In 1978, it looked as though the once so buoyant and stylish typewriter manufacturer would either go bankrupt or fall into the hands of the Italian government. Just when Olivetti most needed funds to finance expansion and automate production, in order to meet the greatest challenge in the industry's history (i.e., the electronic office), the company was paralyzed, unable to pay even its managers' salaries. Not only did Olivetti need money, but it also badly needed a new and dynamic leader to turn the company around. Radical action was essential to Olivetti's survival.

## NEW TOP MANAGEMENT

In April 1978, Olivetti's chairman, Bruno Visentini took the necessary steps to find a new leader. He approached Carlo de Benedetti, an Italian industrialist of stature, who had a substantial fortune of his own. He had spent a few months as Managing Director of Fiat before leaving abruptly, presumably after differing with the Agnellis who ran the company. As part of his agreement with Fiat, de Benedetti had obtained 6 percent of Fiat's common stock, thus making him the largest single shareholder after the Agnellis. He sold his share back to Fiat when he left. This money, plus income from his various other business activities, gave de Benedetti plenty of funds to invest, so that when he was approached by Visentini, the proposition looked like the perfect challenge.

De Benedetti agreed to rescue Olivetti by investing over $17 million of his personal fortune (thus making himself majority shareholder) and by moving in as Vice Chairman and CEO. Olivetti reported substantial losses in 1978. De Benedetti took immediate steps to reverse the trend.

The electronic age had arrived, and he wanted to be right in at the start.

Mechanical typewriters were no longer to be produced by Olivetti, although the company did plan to continue selling mechanical typewriters produced in Asia under license and contract manufacturers. De Benedetti replaced the mechanical model with a new line of electronic machines, soon to be Olivetti's star product and to make it the number one typewriter company in the world, ahead of IBM. The industry, including the market leader IBM, had been working on the electronic typewriter for a number of years. De Benedetti was able to accelerate the development process and beat IBM to the market by several months. It was rumored that Olivetti's research establishment believed that another five years would be needed to enter the market—a process that de Benedetti was able to reduce to a few months. Despite product innovations, Olivetti's workforce was reduced from 61,500 to 47,600 within a few years after de Benedetti's arrival. Initial resistance from unions was finally overcome when they became convinced that a labor reduction was essential for the organization's survival. All in all things looked much rosier for Olivetti.

However, the problem of capitalization persisted as de Benedetti pursued his goal of competing in the electronic equipment race. After only one year as head of the company, de Benedetti had incurred debts of over $1 billion to pay for retooling Olivetti's plants and boosting output of electronic-based equipment. In three years, R&D costs had soared from less than $30 million when he took over to more than $100 million.

To support these outlays, de Benedetti undertook a series of venture capital moves in the United States, spending $60 million to assume minority interests in 22 small high-tech companies. It was hoped that this move would give Olivetti early access to new developments and keep it abreast of market and new product trends in the United States. During the seventies, Olivetti had often been too late in the market with new products, a failing that had weakened its position in the office equipment market. De Benedetti was a confirmed America watcher. He believed that tracking progress in the United States would enhance Olivetti's position in Europe and would ensure that his strategy anticipated market demands.

Carlo de Benedetti searched relentlessly for ways to improve performance, cut costs, reduce debt, while maintaining Olivetti's forward momentum toward the integrated office market. New accounting systems were introduced, control tightened, low-profit products discontinued, and plants closed or revamped. De Benedetti promised that R&D costs would not exceed 3 percent of sales over the next five years. Since R&D investment is so crucial to the survival of manufacturers in the electronics field, this latter pledge was the most radical of all. Competition in office automation from such giants as IBM, DEC, and Xerox was the greatest threat to a small contender such as Olivetti. These giants spent heavily on R&D in the early eighties, having the financial resources to do so. The top three electronics companies in Europe in 1982 (Philips, IBM, and Siemens) spent more than 6 percent of sales on R&D, while others in the top twenty spent as much as 14 percent of sales. Olivetti, with an R&D budget of 4 percent of sales in 1982, held thirteenth position in sales among European electronics producers but was one of the lowest spenders on R&D. By the following year, however, Olivetti's R&D budget had climbed to 6 percent of sales.

Fortunately, de Benedetti's successful turnaround of the company enabled Olivetti to raise new capital in Italy, to reduce its heavy debt, and to produce substantial profits by 1982 (102 billion lire on sales of 3,341 billion lire). According to de Benedetti, this 3 percent aftertax profit was "fantastic in Italy, and acceptable for Europe, but was not satisfactory on an international level." He intended to change this state of affairs as well. News of de Benedetti's spectacular handling of the Olivetti situation had made him one of the most talked about top executives

in Europe. He was pleased with the success so far, but still determined to attack Olivetti's main competitors in the emerging office automation field. They were, in his opinion, IBM and the Japanese. Olivetti needed more global thrust.

When de Benedetti took over Olivetti in 1978, 56 percent of sales were made to European customers and less than 12 percent came from the United States. Even in electronic typewriters, where Olivetti was the world leader, the company was unable to penetrate the U.S. market significantly. This problem frustrated de Benedetti, who believed that penetration of the United States was essential to his global strategy and Olivetti's long-term survival.

In 1982, Olivetti entered into a joint venture with a U.S. manufacturer of automatic bank teller machines, Docutel Corporation. Docutel had an outstanding record of growth, having risen from near bankruptcy to sales of $53 million and profits of almost $5 million by 1981. Chairman B. Meredith was looking for diversification into office equipment. In 1982, he achieved this objective by purchasing the marketing and distribution operations of Olivetti U.S., which included electronic typewriters, calculators, copiers and PCs, and should have opened doors to large bank customers for these products. One year after the deal, however, Docutel was in the red, having lost $1.5 million in the first half of 1983 on sales of $110 million. After 13 consecutive years of losses by Olivetti U.S. in office equipment (totaling $164 million), the Docutel experience was an unwelcome setback. A stronger hold on the United States had to be secured.

Nevertheless, by 1982, the Olivetti empire had extended all over the world, through takeovers and increased local marketing and distribution networks (see Exhibit 1). Olivetti had taken over Hermes Precisa International of Switzerland, Logabax of France (whose large sales to the French government made France Olivetti's number two market), and Data Terminal Systems of West Germany (a subsidiary of the U.S. firm).

By 1983, Olivetti was established as the

## EXHIBIT 1

**SUBSIDIARIES INCLUDED IN THE CONSOLIDATED FINANCIAL STATEMENTS
AS OF DECEMBER 31, 1983**

| Company name | Registered office | Currency | Share capital | Percentage of ownership Group | Third parties |
|---|---|---|---|---|---|
| Parent company | | | | | |
| Ing. C. Olivetti & Co., S.p.A. | Ivrea | Lire | 344,189,624,000 | | |
| Italian subsidiaries | | | | | |
| Finbes, S.p.A. | Ivrea | Lire | 20,000,000,000 | 100.0 | |
| OCN, S.p.A. | Marcianise | Lire | 27,000,000,000 | 100.0 | |
| Esercizio Pietro Pontiggia—PPL, S.p.A. | Ivrea | Lire | 2,000,000,000 | 100.0 | |
| OCN Sistemi, S.p.A. | Ivrea | Lire | 2,000,000,000 | 100.0 | |
| OSAI A-B, S.p.A. | Ivrea | Lire | 2,613,636,000 | 68.0 | 32.0 |
| Olivetti Synthesis, S.p.A. | Ivrea | Lire | 8,000,000,000 | 100.0 | |
| Olivetti Accessori, S.p.A. | Ivrea | Lire | 14,000,000,000 | 100.0 | |
| Motori ed Apparecchiature Elettriche, S.p.A. | Ivrea | Lire | 2,000,000,000 | 100.0 | |
| Eleprint, S.p.A. | Ivrea | Lire | 5,600,000,000 | 100.0 | |
| Olivetti Peripheral Equipment, S.p.A. | S. Bernardo d'Ivrea | Lire | 10,000,000,000 | 100.0 | |
| Tecsinter, S.p.A. | Ivrea | Lire | 2,500,000,000 | 100.0 | |
| Manifattura Valle dell'Orco, S.p.A. | Ivrea | Lire | 2,000,000,000 | 100.0 | |
| Olivetti Leasing, S.p.A. | Ivrea | Lire | 5,000,000,000 | 51.0 | 49.0 |
| La Zincocelere, S.p.A. | Ivrea | Lire | 1,750,000,000 | 51.0 | 49.0 |
| Nord Elettronica, S.p.A. | Altare | Lire | 900,000,000 | 51.0 | 49.0 |
| Olivetti Tecnost, S.p.A. | Ivrea | Lire | 3,000,000,000 | 100.0 | |
| Elea, S.p.A. | Ivrea | Lire | 500,000,000 | 100.0 | |
| Syntax, S.p.A. | Ivrea | Lire | 1,500,000,000 | 100.0 | |
| Immobiliare Ivrea San Giovanni, S.p.A. | Ivrea | Lire | 10,500,000,000 | 100.0 | |
| Ivrea San Giovanni Leasing, S.p.A. | Ivrea | Lire | 2,000,000,000 | 100.0 | |
| Software Sistemi, S.p.A. | Bari | Lire | 1,000,000,000 | 100.0 | |
| Publisystem—Sistemi di Software per la Pubblica Amministrazione, S.p.a. | Bari | Lire | 200,000,000 | 100.0 | |
| Olivetti Finanziamenti Commerciali, S.p.A. | Ivrea | Lire | 3,750,000,000 | 83.26 | 16.74 |
| Ages Italia, S.p.A. | Borgoticino | Lire | 1,830,000,000 | 51.0 | 49.0 |
| Mael Computer, S.p.A. | Carsoli | Lire | 2,500,000,000 | 70.0 | 30.0 |
| Edizioni di Comunità, S.p.A. | Ivrea | Lire | 200,000,000 | 100.0 | |
| Eurofly Service, S.p.A. | Turin | Lire | 1,000,000,000 | 62.0 | 38.0 |
| Olteco-Olivetti Telecommunicazioni, S.p.A. | Ivrea | Lire | 6,000,000,000 | 100.0 | |
| Foreign subsidiaries | | | | | |
| Olivetti International, S.A. | Luxemburg | ECU | 412,400,000 | 100.0 | |
| Austro Olivetti GmbH | Vienna | A.Sh. | 38,800,000 | 100.0 | |
| Olivetti Belge, S.A. | Brussels | B.Fr. | 50,000,000 | 100.0 | |
| Olivetti A/S | Copenhagen | D.Kr. | 64,000,000 | 100.0 | |
| Olivetti France, S.A. | Paris | F.Fr. | 130,000,000 | 100.0 | |
| Ruf France, S.a.r.l. | Paris | F.Fr. | 16,887,000 | 100.0 | |
| Sadga, S.A. | Paris | F.Fr. | 401,500 | 79.85 | 20.15 |
| Olivetti Lorraine Informatique, S.A. | Nancy | F.Fr. | 1,000,000 | 66.63 | 33.37 |
| Société Nouvelle Logabax, S.A. | Paris | F.Fr. | 50,000,000 | 64.99 | 35.01 |
| British Olivetti Ltd. | London | £ | 12,000,000 | 100.0 | |
| Olivetti (Suomi) O.Y. | Helsinki | M.F. | 3,600,000 | 100.0 | |
| Olivetti Hellas, A.E. | Athens | Dracme | 42,400,000 | 100.0 | |

| EXHIBIT 1 (cont.) | | | | | |
|---|---|---|---|---|---|

| | | | | Percentage of ownership | |
| Company name | Registered office | Currency | Share capital | Group | Third parties |
|---|---|---|---|---|---|
| Olivetti Norge, A/S | Oslo | N.Kr. | 25,610,000 | 100.0 | |
| Deutsche Olivetti D.T.S. GmbH | Frankfurt | D.M. | 50,100,000 | 100.0 | |
| Olivetti Portuguesa, S.a.r.l. | Lisbon | Esc. | 19,000,000 | 100.0 | |
| Hispano Olivetti, S.A. | Barcelona | Pts | 983,125,300 | 99.90 | 0.10 |
| Rapida, S.A. | Barcelona | Pts | 154,560,000 | 73.45 | 26.55 |
| Olivetti Corporation of Japan | Tokyo | Yen | 2,600,000,000 | 100.0 | |
| Olivetti (H.K.) Ltd. | Hong Kong | $ H.K. | 500,000 | 100.0 | |
| Olivetti Pacific Distributors Ltd. | Hong Kong | $ H.K. | 100,000 | 100.0 | |
| Olivetti (Malaysia) Sdn. Bhd. | Kuala Lumpur | Ringgit | 1,000,000 | 100.0 | |
| Olivetti (Singapore) Pte. Ltd. | Singapore | $ S. | 7,000,000 | 100.0 | |
| Olivetti Australia (Pty.) Ltd. | Sydney | $ Aus. | 3,600,000 | 100.0 | |
| Olivetti Africa (Pty.) Ltd. | Johannesburg | Rand | 2,100,000 | 100.0 | |
| Lole (Pty.) Ltd. | Johannesburg | Rand | 3,600 | 100.0 | |
| Olivetti Canada Ltd. | Toronto | $ Can. | 7,134,000 | 100.0 | |
| Olivetti Argentina, S.A. | Buenos Aires | Ps.A. | 10,802,000 | 100.0 | |
| Olivetti do Brasil, S.A. | São Paulo | N. Cruz. | 8,411,000,000 | 100.0 | |
| Oliund C. & R. Ltda | São Paulo | N. Cruz. | 1,538,217,143 | 100.0 | |
| Olivetti de Chile, S.A. | Santiago | Ps.Cil. | 217,329,050 | 100.0 | |
| Olivetti Colombiana, S.A. | Bogotá | Ps.C. | 15,000,000 | 100.0 | |
| Olivetti Mexicana, S.A. | Mexico City | Ps.M. | 1,238,625,000 | 100.0 | |
| Olivetti Peruana, S.A. | Lima | Soles | 1,483,923,000 | 100.0 | |
| Olivetti Uruguaya, S.A. | Montevideo | Ps.Ur. | 25,000 | 100.0 | |
| Olivetti de Venezuela, C.A. | Caracas | Bol. | 5,000,000 | 100.0 | |
| Olivetti Management, S.A. | Lugano | S.Fr. | 50,000 | 100.0 | |
| Olivetti International (Service), S.A. | Lugano | S.Fr. | 50,000 | 100.0 | |
| Euroimport Trading, S.A. | Panama | $ US | 100,000 | 100.0 | |
| Risk Insurance Corporation, S.A. | Panama | $ US | 100,000 | 100.0 | |
| Olivetti New Properties N.V. | Curaçao | $ US | 10,000 | 100.0 | |
| Olivetti Investment N.V. | Curaçao | $ US | 10,000 | 100.0 | |
| Hermes Precisa, S.A. | São Paulo | N. Cruz. | 662,212,800 | 100.0 | |
| Olivetti Realty N.V. | Curaçao | $ US | 50,000 | 100.0 | |
| Olivetti Supplies Inc. | Middletown (N.Y.) | $ US | 1,000 | 100.0 | |
| Olivetti Nederland B.V. | Gravenhage | Dfl. | 9,862,000 | 100.0 | |
| Olivetti Holding B.V. | Amsterdam | Dfl. | 30,410,000 | 100.0 | |
| Olivetti de Puerto Rico Inc. | San Juan | $ US | 1,000 | 100.0 | |
| Olivetti Advanced Technology Center Inc. | Cupertino (Cal.) | $ US | 1,000 | 100.0 | |
| Hermes Precisa International, S.A. | Yverdon | S.Fr. | 16,000,000 | 48.35 | 51.65 |
| Olivetti (Suisse), S.A. | Zurich | S.Fr. | 5,000,000 | 100.0 | |
| Precisa, S.A. | Yverdon | S.Fr. | 500,000 | 100.0 | |
| Japy Hermes Precisa, S.A. | Paris | F.Fr. | 26,518,800 | 100.0 | |
| S.A. Hermes Precisa Belgium | Brussels | B.Fr. | 26,100,000 | 100.0 | |
| Hermes Precisa B.V. | Rotterdam | Dfl. | 1,500,000 | 100.0 | |
| Hermes Precisa Ltd. | Colchester | £ | 100,000 | 100.0 | |
| Hermes Products Inc. | Linden | $ US | 500,000 | 100.0 | |

*Note*: Certain minor subsidiaries and nonoperating companies included in the consolidation have not been listed here due to their immateriality in the consolidated financial statements.

strongest European competitor to IBM in office automation (although the gap between IBM and Olivetti was still enormous). This resurgence was due to several good products, such as upgraded typewriters and a line of microcomputers and minicomputers, that had been brought quickly and effectively into the market. Most observers concluded that Olivetti's marketing and distribution organization—continually being upgraded—was the key factor to Olivetti's success, particularly in Europe.

Computer-based office information systems gradually replaced the older equipment and calculators, although the typewriter remained the core of Olivetti's business. The thrust toward the so-called office of the future brought a new range of sophisticated electronic office equipment onto the market. Olivetti's first word processor appeared in 1976, followed by an improved version the next year. Success with computers had eluded Olivetti after it developed one of the first desktop PC-like machines, known as Programma 101, back in the early sixties, which was quite an innovation at the time. The failure of the P101 has been a matter of considerable speculation. The product was remarkable but rather "user unfriendly." Furthermore, some felt that the typewriter-oriented sales organization was not prepared to sell complex office systems. The machine was able to use as many as 500 different programs supplied by Underwood Olivetti. Olivetti also dabbled in the mainframe market but, finding the effort unprofitable, sold its computer division to General Electric in 1968.

The company's next entry into the computer field was with a mini, developed in 1974. In the spring of 1979, Olivetti planned to launch several new models at the lower end of the minicomputer market. De Benedetti meanwhile had established a Silicon Valley research base and was intent on designing the new Olivetti products with the very latest U.S. features. This venture paid off. De Benedetti launched Olivetti's first personal computer, the M20, in 1982. Olivetti's total sales in personal computers in 1982 was estimated at $56 million worldwide,

compared to PC industry leader, Apple, with $850 million. IBM sold $630 million. By 1983, Olivetti's market presence in the sector was consolidated by an enhanced version with improved software and increased local storage capacity. An attempt to sell the M20 in the United States had been unsuccessful due to its inability to run programs designed for IBM machines. However, the launch of the IBM compatible M24 desktop PC was a turning point for Olivetti and rounded off its comprehensive office equipment line. Already world leader in electronic typewriters, in spite of heavy Japanese competition, Olivetti soon became a leading European manufacturer of data processing equipment (other than mainframes). Despite this relative success, Olivetti was unable to achieve significant worldwide results (40,000 sold in the first year, with an estimated capacity of 200,000 units per year), or to penetrate the U.S. market with its PC.

Thus Olivetti entered the eighties with considerable ambition and impressive success. However, for de Benedetti to sustain this growth, increasingly large amounts of capital would be required.

At about this time, the huge French steel-and-glass conglomerate, St. Gobain Pont-à-Mousson, was nationalized by Mitterand's government. In the spring of 1980, St. Gobain had paid $230 million for 20 percent of Olivetti, which was subsequently increased to 30 percent. St. Gobain had been moving energetically into information processing, and the plan was to combine Olivetti's office equipment know-how with that of St. Gobain's computer affiliate CII-Honeywell Bull, forming a powerful team which would be able to take over the European office systems market. Unfortunately, the two sides could not agree, and de Benedetti withdrew his team. The French investment in Olivetti, however, remained. When the French government withdrew St. Gobain from data processing, negotiations started for reacquisition of the investment, and the 100 million shares were sold to various other European organizations. De Benedetti would have liked to repurchase this stock, but the Italian capital market was either too thin or conservative to support repurchase.

Pondering these issues facing him and Olivetti, de Benedetti received a phone call from Gianni Agnelli, Chairman of FIAT. Agnelli had been serving on an international advisory board for AT&T. In a private discussion with Brown, Chairman of AT&T, Mr. Agnelli casually suggested that it would be a good idea for Brown to meet de Benedetti on an informal basis. Brown immediately expressed interest and asked Agnelli to arrange a meeting.

Exhibits 2 through 6 summarize Olivetti's financial performance for recent years.

---

### EXHIBIT 2

**OLIVETTI ANNUAL REPORT: FINANCIAL HIGHLIGHTS**

|  | Estimated 1983 | 1982 | Percent change |
|---|---|---|---|
| Net revenues (L billion) | 3,736.2 | 3,341.4 | 11.8 |
| R&D expense (L billion) | 187.2 | 162.2 | 15.4 |
| Operating profit | | | |
|   L billion | 468.3 | 337.1 | 38.9 |
|   Percentage of average invested capital | 20.6 | 17.0 | |
| Net income | | | |
|   (L billion) | 295.3 | 102.8 | 187.3 |
|   Percentage of revenues | 7.9 | 3.1 | |
|   Percentage of average shareholders' equity | 27.4 | 13.4 | |
| Earnings per common share (L) | 857 | 318 | 169.5 |
| Cash dividends per share (L) | | | |
|   Common and preferred | 240 | 200 | 20.0 |
|   Savings | 260 | 220 | 18.2 |
| Working capital provided from operations (L billion) | | | |
|   Total | 616.6 | 380.8 | 70.9 |
|   Excluding research contributions | 507.9 | 360.7 | 40.8 |
| Total assets (L billion) | 5,121.1 | 4,345.0 | 17.9 |
| Invested capital (L billion) | 2,341.2 | 2,200.0 | 6.4 |
| Shareholders' equity (L billion) | 1,202.1 | 954.8 | 25.9 |
| Net financial indebtedness (L billion) | 726.0 | 862.9 | (15.9) |
| Stock exchange capitalization (total shares) | 1,290.1 | 658.7 | |
| Price/earnings ratio for common shares | 4.5 | 6.2 | |
| Number of employees | 47,800 | 49,763 | (3.9) |

*Note:* Figures in parentheses indicate percentage change. Exchange rate (1983 average) was $1 = L1,500.

EXHIBIT 3

**OLIVETTI ANNUAL REPORT: CONSOLIDATED STATEMENTS OF INCOME FOR THE YEARS ENDED DECEMBER 31, 1983 AND 1982** (Translation of Original Prepared in Italian)

| | Estimated 1983 (L million) | Percent | 1982 (L million) | Percent |
|---|---|---|---|---|
| Net revenues | 3,736,219 | 100.0 | 3,341,360 | 100.0 |
| Cost of goods sold and services provided | 2,049,909 | 54.9 | 1,807,525 | 54.1 |
| Gross profit | 1,686,310 | 45.1 | 1,533,835 | 45.9 |
| Selling, general, and administrative expenses | 1,030,821 | 27.6 | 1,034,536 | 30.9 |
| R&D expenses | 187,182 | 5.0 | 162,184 | 4.9 |
| Operating profit | 468,307 | 12.5 | 337,115 | 10.1 |
| Other income (expenses) | | | | |
| Interest expense, net | (151,022) | 4.0 | (194,559) | 5.8 |
| Losses on foreign currency transactions, net | (32,212) | 0.9 | (9,681) | 0.3 |
| Translation gains (losses), net | 46,398 | 1.2 | (1,553) | 0.1 |
| Research contributions received during the year in suspension of taxes | 108,664 | 2.9 | 20,091 | 0.6 |
| Other expenses, net | (39,194) | 1.0 | (10,125) | 0.3 |
| Group share of net earnings (losses) of nonconsolidated companies | (19,933) | 0.5 | 3,071 | 0.1 |
| Income before taxes and minority interests | 381,008 | 10.2 | 144,359 | 4.3 |
| Income taxes | (96,263) | 2.6 | (42,466) | 1.3 |
| Minority interests | 10,590 | 0.3 | 915 | 0.1 |
| Net income | 295,335 | 7.9 | 102,808 | 3.1 |

*Note*: Exchange rate (1983 average) was $1 = L1,500.

EXHIBIT 4

**OLIVETTI ANNUAL REPORT: FIVE-YEAR COMPARISON OF FINANCIAL DATA**

| | 1979 | 1980 | 1981 | 1982 | Estimated 1983 |
|---|---|---|---|---|---|
| Net revenues (L billion) | 1,852.7 | 2,180.2 | 2,887.9 | 3,341.4 | 3,736.2 |
| Net income (L billion) | 33.3 | 87.6 | 95.6 | 102.8 | 295.3 |
| Dividends paid (L billion) | 11.1 | 22.7 | 48.4 | 65.6 | 84.2 |
| Shareholders' equity (L billion) | 50.5 | 360.8 | 582.4 | 954.8 | 1,202.1 |
| Net financial indebtedness (L billion) | 859.2 | 753.7 | 844.4 | 862.9 | 726.0 |
| Number of employees (at year end) | 55,931 | 53,339 | 53,471 | 49,763 | 47,800 |

*Note*: Exchange rate (1983 average) was $1 = L1,500.

| EXHIBIT 5 |
| --- |

**OLIVETTI ANNUAL REPORT: CONSOLIDATED GROSS PROFIT**

| | Gross profit (L billion) | | Percentage of revenues | |
| --- | --- | --- | --- | --- |
| | 1983* | 1982 | 1983 | 1982 |
| Italy | 674.7 | 547.0 | 48.9 | 48.4 |
| Other European countries | 634.8 | 572.6 | 43.7 | 44.9 |
| Total Europe | 1,309.5 | 1,119.6 | 46.3 | 46.6 |
| North America | 86.7 | 112.9 | 33.1 | 39.9 |
| Latin America | 97.3 | 133.9 | 46.7 | 46.0 |
| Far East and Africa | 192.8 | 167.4 | 44.3 | 46.2 |
| Group total | 1,686.3 | 1,533.8 | 45.1 | 45.9 |

*1983 figures are estimates.
*Note*: Exchange rate (1983 average) was $1 = L1,500.

| EXHIBIT 6 |
| --- |

**OLIVETTI ANNUAL REPORT: CONSOLIDATED NET REVENUES (PERCENTAGE INCREASE OVER PREVIOUS YEAR)**

| | Estimated 1983 (L billion) | 1982 (L billion) | Change | |
| --- | --- | --- | --- | --- |
| | | | Value | Percent |
| Italy | 1,378.4 | 1,129.9 | + 248.5 | + 22.0 |
| Other European countries | 1,452.4 | 1,275.1 | + 177.3 | + 13.9 |
| Total Europe | 2,830.8 | 2,405.0 | + 425.8 | + 17.7 |
| North America | 262.0 | 282.8 | − 20.8 | − 7.4 |
| Latin America | 208.4 | 291.0 | − 82.6 | − 28.4 |
| Far East and Africa | 435.0 | 362.6 | + 72.4 | + 20.0 |
| Group total | 3,736.2 | 3,341.4 | + 394.8 | + 11.8 |
| Group total (on a comparable basis) | 3,736.2 | 3,276.5 | + 459.7 | + 14.0 |

*Note*: Exchange rate (1983 average) was $1 = L1,500.

# Note on the Office Automation Industry

*World revenue for the information processing industry grew 15% per year from about $55 billion in 1973 to $230 billion in 1983. The high demand for information related products and services is expected to continue and produce an annual revenue likely to exceed the $1 trillion mark by 1993.*

*IBM Annual Report 1983*

Many estimates were being made in 1983 as to expected market size for information processing products and services 10 or 20 years hence. However, the vastness and complexity of the business and the many disparate forecasts available produced a wide range of guesses. IBM, undisputed industry leader with revenues of $34.7 billion in 1983 (almost seven times as much as its nearest competitor, Digital), was probably the best authority on the subject.

The pace of technological development and

This industry note was prepared by Ms. Juliet Taylor under the supervision of Professor George Taucher for use with the AT&T and Olivetti cases (Cases sixteen and seventeen). Copyright © 1987 by IMEDE, Lausanne, Switzerland. Reproduced by permission.

the arrival of microchips and semiconductors led to the appearance of a vast array of computers and computer-based equipment which gave birth to an industry growing in size and complexity with dizzying speed. Information processing encompassed every aspect of compiling, storing, accessing, manipulating, and communicating data.

Traditionally, the equipment for the various communication and processing functions was supplied by three types of manufacturer who specialized in telecommunications, electronic data processing, or office equipment. Companies such as AT&T, IBM, and Olivetti fell into these respective categories. However, as offices became increasingly automated, and more text-processing workstations were installed, the distinction between data processing and office equipment became less clear. Furthermore, the need to connect mainframe computers with workstations placed more emphasis on telecommunications. This link-up of pieces of stand-alone equipment would play a major role in creating the so-called office of the future market, sometimes referred to as "the integrated office," "the automated office," etc. The convergence of previously separate industries was

**285**

**EXHIBIT 1**

**PERSONAL COMPUTER INDUSTRY 1978–1982: ESTIMATES FOR WORLDWIDE SALES** ($ Million)

| Supplier | 1978 | 1979 | 1980 | 1981 | 1982 |
|---|---|---|---|---|---|
| Apple Computer | 26.5 | 109.1 | 242.9 | 566.0 | 852.7 |
| Commodore BMI | 52.7 | 96.4 | 161.6 | 158.8 | 146.9 |
| Digital Equipment Corp. | | | | | 27.2 |
| Eagle Computer | | | | 2.0 | 13.3 |
| Franklin | | | | | 56.9 |
| Hewlett-Packard | | | 71.5 | 138.6 | 72.0 |
| IBM (PC 5150) | | | | 75.9 | 630.9 |
| Intertec Data | | 2.2 | 12.1 | 19.8 | 16.1 |
| Morrow Designs | | | | | 31.5 |
| Kaypro Corp. | | | | | 27.7 |
| Osborne Computer | | | | 15.8 | 232.0 |
| Otrona Corp. | | | | | 21.1 |
| Tandy/Radio Shack | 89.4 | 140.0 | 174.7 | 206.4 | 321.4 |
| Xerox Corporation | | | | 88.6 | 90.7 |
| Zenith/Heathkit | 7.5 | 18.2 | 24.6 | 36.9 | 53.6 |
| Other U.S. | 156.0 | 96.0 | 75.9 | 46.8 | 169.7 |
| Subtotal U.S. | 332.1 | 461.9 | 763.3 | 1,355.6 | 2,863.7 |
| Olivetti | | | | | 56.0 |
| Philips Data | | | 3.6 | 10.2 | 18.2 |
| Triumph/Adler | | | | 34.8 | 32.3 |
| Other European | | | 14.8 | 57.0 | 93.0 |
| Subtotal European | 0.0 | 0.0 | 18.4 | 102.0 | 199.5 |
| Epson Inc. | | | | | 15.0 |
| Fujitsu | | | | 22.0 | 30.8 |
| Hitachi | 0.5 | 2.2 | 4.7 | 9.8 | 21.0 |
| NEC | 3.3 | 7.7 | 35.6 | 91.5 | 215.3 |
| OKI Electric | | | 4.4 | 9.5 | 20.3 |
| Panafacom Ltd. | | | | 21.0 | 52.2 |
| Sanyo Business Systems | | | | | 46.3 |
| Sharp Electronics | 1.7 | 3.3 | 19.6 | 105.0 | 189.7 |
| Sony Corporation | | | | | 22.5 |
| SORD Computer | 5.0 | 8.2 | 12.8 | 32.3 | 90.0 |
| Other Japanese | 0.5 | 1.3 | 1.9 | 7.5 | 74.3 |
| Subtotal Japanese | 11.0 | 22.7 | 78.9 | 298.6 | 777.4 |
| Grand Total | 343.1 | 484.6 | 860.7 | 1,756.2 | 3,840.6 |

*Source:* Dataquest, 1983.

inevitable, and indeed, such evolution had been forecast and carefully plotted by the main protagonists. However, the frequent difference between vendors' concepts of customers' integrated office needs and the customers' actual needs tended to cause confusion in the industry. By the early 1980s, vendors and customers were beginning to sort themselves out, and more co-

herent plans for information systems were being created.

The information processing market was still technology driven. In 1983, manufacturers developed and sold products because the technology was there, rather than to meet the needs of the consumer. The customer tended to purchase these products randomly instead of following an overall plan for office automation, which meant that equipment was often incorrectly used or not used at all. It was into this rather unstructured office-of-the-future market that suppliers pitched themselves.

In 1978, Apple Computer of California had aggressively thrust a microcomputer onto the market, an event that was to revolutionize the industry. The personal computer (PC) had arrived, and the waves it caused never subsided. By 1983, the full impact of the PC penetrated all levels of the industry.

At first the PC was not taken really seriously in the industry but was regarded as a toy or a gimmick. However, when Apple's sales in 1980 reached $242 million and more than doubled to $566 million in 1981, IBM was forced to react. Realizing the PC's potential, although it was a stand-alone and did not fit into existing systems, IBM prepared to enter the race. Breaking its own tradition in order to gain time, IBM purchased off-the-shelf components for its PC, contracting subassembly work to outside companies. Between 1981 and 1982, IBM increased its sales of PCs from $138 million to $630.9 million and took second place behind Apple, which had $852 million in sales by 1982. Other suppliers joined in, but it was IBM's entry into this segment that confirmed the trend and gave the PC respectability and a rapidly growing share of the computer market. In 1983, European PC market leader, Olivetti, had sales of $56 million in the segment. See Exhibit 1 for estimates of worldwide sales of PCs in 1978–1982.

The proliferation that followed, referred to by A. D. Little's Leon Jackson as "the PC orgy," was to shake the foundations of data processing. Formerly, computers had been used by specialists, whose knowledge of the workings of a mainframe gave them an aura of mysticism that the PC would dispel forever. PCs were accessible to anyone. Now managers had their own hands-on tool with which to forecast, calculate, and communicate.

With the data processing market flooded by more than 1 million PCs by 1983, a number that would swell to 6 million within the next two years, strategic plans for convergence were temporarily sidetracked. The incompatibility of the PC with other systems was frustrating as it was hard to fit into the plans for integration. Then, as a wider range of software appeared, the PC could be used in place of machines that were already installed or anticipated for use in an overall system. This overlap was particularly felt in the word processing field, an area that was overwhelmed by PCs using text processing software. From the organizational standpoint, more confusion resulted.

Convergence gave the telecommunications industry (dominated in the United States by AT&T at the time) a new importance and a vital role to play. It was telecom technology that would provide all the networks and links between computers in the office and between offices all over the world. Telecommunications was at the heart of office automation. The chief contenders in the office-of-the-future market realized that to offer a full range of products, they needed telecommunications expertise.

IBM hoped that its purchase of 15 percent of Rolm Corporation in 1983 (later to become a total takeover), would give it the private branch exchange (PBX) and local area network (LAN) technology it would need to offer the total automated office package.

## THE INTEGRATED OFFICE[1]

### Introduction

The multifunctional, integrated office system is increasingly exhibiting the three following characteristics:

- The ability to perform several tasks, such as access to information, communications, document generation, personal computing, and personal information management

---

[1] The balance of this case is extracted from a study prepared by Leon Jackson and Norman Weizer, of Arthur D. Little Decision Resources, Acorn Park, Cambridge, Massachusetts 02140, USA. January 1985. Reproduced with permission.

- The ability to support the manipulation of information in several formats (text, data, images, graphics, and voice)
- The ability to be used by different departments within an organization, such as manufacturing, engineering, accounting, R&D, and sales

Over the past year, office automation market dynamics have revealed that large, medium, and small organizations have similar functional needs but that solutions for these needs vary. Within a user organization, there are both "suppliers"—often the data processing department—and "users." The decision-making process of these suppliers is changing as financial justifications are yielding to global concerns of strategic impact. Also, senior management is increasingly being drawn into the office system planning process as investment increases.

The personal computer proliferation has focused attention on the need for comprehensive planning, which is heavily influenced by corporate culture. The concept of information resource management is beginning to be recognized, as is the crucial importance of education, awareness building, and training before, during, and after office systems are installed. Approved vendor lists are increasingly used to overcome standards and compatibility problems. An additional technological planning consideration for user organizations is the influence a PBX investment decision has on the structure of the final office system.

In the industry, several changes are also taking place. Segmentation into vendor types—total systems suppliers, niche vendors, and commodity vendors—continues.[2] The differences between the data processing, office systems, and telecommunications industries continue to blur, aided by accelerating mergers and cooperative relationships among suppliers. Personal computing companies, finding it harder to compete

with systems suppliers for the business of large organizations, are concentrating on medium and small businesses and educational applications. As a result of the AT&T breakup, new distribution channels have appeared through the regional operating companies, and a new major competitor in the office systems market (AT&T itself) has emerged.

Several technological aspects are receiving increased attention. There is a heavy emphasis on multifunctionality and comprehendable user interfaces by software developers, urged on by users. Relational databases and decision-support systems are becoming realizable tools. The PBX-versus-LAN debate is being to some extent resolved with hybrid systems. Image and voice integration are evolving, and low-cost, high-quality hardcopy output devices are generally available.

## Industry Structure

There will be basically two major industries developing over the next five years: the integrated information systems industry and the intelligent network service industry. This second industry will serve the information processing, computing, programming, and communications needs of smaller companies. Communications services are already becoming more valuable as the AT&T breakup proceeds. The "battle of the giants" (AT&T and IBM) takes place at the intersection of these two industries. AT&T has inherent communications strengths and is currently introducing a new line of office data processing products; IBM is a natural information processing equipment supplier and is active in communications-oriented joint ventures.

The office systems industry is going through a massive transition (see Exhibit 2) with a large number of products having to move forward to integrated systems at all levels and types of businesses. Few vendors will be able to become total-systems suppliers, and the rest will have to find a niche.

Vendor realignment will be the rule, resulting in market focus changes and increasing numbers of associative relationships. Vendors are al-

---

[2] See Leon Jackson and Norman Weizer, *The U.S. Office Automation Market, 1983–1988: The Evolution toward Integrated Information Processing*, R830703, July 1983, for background.

## EXHIBIT 2

**THE INDUSTRY IN TRANSITION 1983–1989 (ESTIMATE)**

|  | 1983 | Transition | 1989 |
|---|---|---|---|
| Products | Standalone systems<br>Clustered systems<br>Early multifunctional systems<br>Mainframe solutions | Gradual movement to integrated systems supporting workstations with multifunctional capability<br>System architecture expands to include PBXs, LANs, and computers<br>Increasing commodity nature of hardware subsystems<br>Increasing software integration | Integrated systems becoming predominant |
| Standards | Frameworks established | Gradual market-driven adoption of a few comprehensive standards | A few official and *de facto* families of standards being widely accepted |
| Vendors | Product-oriented vendors from DP, office systems, and telecommunications industries<br>PC vendors facing uneven market "bunch," concentrating on existing bases | Few vendors able to grow into total system suppliers<br>Other vendors forced to accept niche or commodity vendor role to protect market share or customer base | Vendors have become:<br>  Total systems vendors<br>  Niche vendors<br>  Commodity vendors<br>  Defensive vendors<br>Differentiation of DP, office systems, and telecommunications vendors is disappearing |

*Source:* Arthur D. Little, Inc.

ready beginning to realize that synergy is possible: Each others' strengths can be combined to provide the most effective systems for end users. See Exhibit 3 for a list of the largest worldwide manufacturers of information processing products.

**Multifunctional Systems and Subsystems**  Vendors in this subcategory provide systems that support all office automation functions with data, text, image, and graphics information. These systems follow the standards of the total system supplier and are compatible with LANs and PBXs. They may also have limited interactive data processing capabilities. This subcategory also includes vendors of voice mail subsystems.

**Multifunctional Workstations**  Vendors in this subcategory provide hardware and software packages that are fully compatible with those of

total system or multifunctional system suppliers. These devices handle all office automation functions but are tailored for *user types* (e.g., financial, executive) in terms of size of screen, colors, dimensions, portability, amount of storage, etc.

**Specialized Workstations**  These vendors provide hardware and software packages that are fully compatible with those of total system or multifunctional system suppliers, but which are designed for *specialized functions,* e.g., engineering, CAD/CAM, typesetting, animation. They offer special processors, special I/O, special interfaces to external equipment, etc.

**File Servers**  These vendors provide mass storage subsystems, including the required interface to networks and the necessary software. They

EXHIBIT 3

**TWENTY LARGEST WORLDWIDE MANUFACTURERS OF INFORMATION PROCESSING PRODUCTS, 1982 AND 1983 (ESTIMATE)**

| Rank | | | Estimated revenues ($ billion) | |
|------|------|------|------|------|
| 1982 | 1983 | | 1982 | 1983 |
| 1  | 1  | IBM | 28.9 | 34.7 |
| 2  | 2  | Digital Equipment | 4.0 | 4.8 |
| 3  | 3  | Burroughs | 3.8 | 4.0 |
| 5  | 4  | NCR | 3.2 | 3.5 |
| 4  | 4  | Control Data | 3.3 | 3.5 |
| 7  | 4  | Hewlett-Packard | 2.2 | 3.5 |
| 7  | 7  | Fujitsu | 2.2 | 2.8 |
| 6  | 7  | Sperry Computer Systems | 2.8 | 2.8 |
| 10 | 9  | NEC | 1.5 | 2.1 |
| 12 | 10 | Wang | 1.3 | 1.7 |
| 11 | 10 | Hitachi | 1.4 | 1.7 |
| 9  | 10 | Honeywell Information Systems | 1.7 | 1.7 |
| 17 | 13 | Bull | 1.1 | 1.3 |
| 12 | 13 | Olivetti | 1.3 | 1.3 |
| 12 | 13 | Siemens | 1.3 | 1.3 |
| 12 | 13 | Xerox | 1.3 | 1.3 |
| 16 | 17 | ICL | 1.2 | 1.2 |
| 20 | 18 | Apple | 0.7 | 1.1 |
| 18 | 19 | Nixdorf | 0.9 | 1.0 |
| 19 | 20 | Data General | 0.8 | 0.8 |

*Sources:* Arthur D. Little, Inc., estimates, and company reports.

are fully compatible with the equipment of total systems or multifunctional systems suppliers. They provide low cost per storage increment, flexible electronic filing and retrieval, or both.

**Print Servers** These vendors provide hardcopy subsystems, including the required interface to networks and the necessary software. They are fully compatible with the systems of total systems or multifunctional systems suppliers. They provide combinations of low cost, high speed, and high reliability, or comprehensive printing/copying/facsimile capabilities.

**Communications Products** Vendors of communications products and systems, notably PBXs and LANs, will offer communications frame-works for integrated systems, thus providing opportunities for cooperating niche vendors to compete with total systems suppliers.

**Commodity Suppliers** These are vendors who provide commodity components of the systems. Vendors in this category will provide basic devices with total plug-in compatibility into specified standard networks, workstations, or systems. Software typically will be limited to emulation or control programs. Devices will include:

• Terminals
• Workstations, including communicating personal computers
• Mass storage devices

- Printer/copier/fax devices
- Facsimile devices
- Components

Many of the components of the integrated office information system are becoming commodity products. For example, low-cost printers for the personal computer can be considered a commodity product. Companies will specialize in the development and manufacture of low-cost highly reliable components that are totally compatible with the offerings of the other vendor types. While many of these devices will be sold on an original equipment manufacturer (OEM) basis, the user will have the opportunity to buy them directly from the commodity vendors.

## AT&T

### Product Line Description and Evaluation

The AT&T product line is a study in extreme contrasts. The many communications-related products include some of the most advanced in the industry. However, their computer-related products, although technically at the state-of-the-art, do not yet have the mature software "glue" to make them major competitors in the integrated office information system market.

AT&T has numerous communications terminals, services, and network products. Its sales in the office equipment market are concentrated in the PBX segment, however (see Exhibit 4). Many of these products are primarily intended for use as a part of a large public networking offering, but they can also be adapted for use in private networks as a part of an integrated office information system.

Some of the newest networking products, such as the AT&T Information Systems Network, are designed for use in integrated office information system networks. These systems compare very favorably with other products now on the market.

In the computer area, AT&T offers a relatively complete line of microcomputer and minicomputer systems. They range from single-user personal computers to midrange superminicomputers.

At the current time, AT&T has priced these systems somewhat higher than their major competitors. It will probably have to reduce these prices to a competitive level within the near future in order to gain market momentum.

### Product Line Evaluation

We provide our subjective relative assessment of each vendor's product line. On a scale of 0 to 10 we evaluate how each vendor provides major aspects of a multifunctional integrated of-

---

**EXHIBIT 4**

**MAJOR VENDORS' SALES BY PRODUCT SEGMENT, 1983** ($ Million)

| Product Segment | AT&T | IBM | DEC |
|---|---|---|---|
| Mainframes | | 11,434 | |
| Minicomputers | | 2,827 | 2,688 |
| Microcomputers | | 2,600 | 300 |
| Office systems | | 1,600 | 290 |
| Data communication | | 500 | |
| Peripheral | 107 | 9,953 | 1,400 |
| Software and services | 75 | 6,879 | 148 |
| PBX and CPE* | 7,888 | | |
| Total revenues | 8,071 | 35,603 | 4,826 |

*Private branch exchanges and customer premise equipment.
*Source:* Datamation, June 1984.

fice system as compared to the level we believe will be generally available in 1989. The multifunctionality measure indicates how well each system provides the five functional tools of office automation in a convenient and easy-to-use manner. These five tools are access to information, communication, document generation, personal computing, and personal management. The other measures indicate the level of integration of each form of information—text, data, graphics, image, and voice—into the multifunctional system (see Exhibit 5).

## Strengths and Weaknesses

AT&T has enormous strengths with which to focus on the integrated office information system market. The premier technological resource of Bell Labs, AT&T's enormous financial resources, and its unparalleled experience in the telecommunications field provide it with major advantages over other vendors in the industry.

The company is well known by all of its potential customers, and there is no question that AT&T will remain in business. Therefore, AT&T does not suffer from the major problems which face most firms when they enter a new business.

The Unix operating system also provides AT&T with a major potential strength in the data processing and office automation areas of the market. As Unix becomes more widely adopted, increasing amounts of third-party software will be produced, making AT&T's systems more attractive to potential customers. In addition, AT&T has announced its Information Systems Architecture (ISA), which defines how its system components are to be linked together. The ISA includes provisions to integrate voice and data services in the office environment.

AT&T's major weaknesses primarily stem from its lack of experience in the integrated office information system industry. Although its line of PBXs, data communications equipment, processors, and some terminals have been used internally by the AT&T organization, AT&T is starting from scratch in the end-user office automation market. As previously mentioned, AT&T has also not yet developed a full line of systems and application software, which is needed to develop its products into a multifunctional, integrated office information system.

The company has to establish its identity in this new market and train its people how to market in an unregulated environment. In addition, the company has to learn how to operate its business with the lean, productive workforce required by the very competitive integrated office information system industry.

## Strategy and Prognosis

AT&T is aggressively pursuing a strategy of becoming one of the major total-systems suppliers of integrated office information systems. Leading with its telecommunications strengths, it is expanding its product lines as rapidly as possible to produce the total variety of products required.

Emphasizing Unix and its increasing standardization in the information processing industry is an integral part of AT&T's strategy. It is through the increasing popularity of Unix with third-party software vendors that AT&T intends to obtain the application software that it requires.

Over the next two to four years, AT&T will face tough competition in the integrated office information system market. The lower cost

---

| EXHIBIT 5 |

**EVALUATION OF VENDOR PRODUCT LINES ON A 0 TO 10 SCALE**

| Attribute | AT&T | IBM | DEC |
|-----------|------|-----|-----|
| Multifunctionality | 2 | 6 | 7 |
| Text | 3 | 7 | 7 |
| Data | 5 | 9 | 9 |
| Graphics | 5 | 6 | 6 |
| Image | 4 | 4 | 2 |
| Voice | 9 | 3 | 4 |

*Note:* 10 is highest positive ranking.
*Source:* Arthur D. Little, Inc.

structure enjoyed by its competitors and their installed bases will pose significant barriers to AT&T's penetration of these markets. We therefore forecast that AT&T will continue to develop value-added networks, applications to run on these networks, and network service offerings, but it will also increase its communications-based office automation efforts considerably. AT&T is acknowledged to have unparalleled expertise in the network area and hence should experience greater success in network markets than in the hardware markets.

Beyond the two- to four-year horizon, AT&T cannot be overlooked as a potential major contender in the total-systems market. Its success will greatly hinge on its ability to market effectively in the increasingly competitive environment and to develop the organizational and management structures required to support this marketing effort.

## DIGITAL EQUIPMENT CORP.

### Product Line Description and Evaluation

Using its large base of installed VAX computers, which are very often used in technical computing applications, Digital Equipment Corporation has had considerable success in introducing its office automation system into major corporations. Outside of the technical areas, Digital has encountered more difficulty because of its somewhat confused workstation policy. The confusion, now being addressed, stems from the multiplicity of workstations offered and the lack of communication to the market as to the options that are available and their best uses. Digital still intends to market computers with a range of price performance characteristics to match users' requirements.

Digital offers a range of terminals as workstations for its office automation systems. The most integrated are the Professional Series, Decmate, VT 200 series of terminals, and dumb terminals. However, the most competitive microcomputer, the Rainbow, has not as yet been well integrated and has reduced Digital's competitive position in markets requiring multifunctional workstations having both personal computer and fully integrated capabilities. The terminals can be connected to the department-level system using an Ethernet LAN with optional terminal servers or directly connected by twisted wire pairs. The company has developed extensive relationships—most importantly with Northern Telecom—with PBX vendors and intends to provide PBX wire as an alternative connection in the near future.

Department-level systems are limited to the VAX family (excluding the PDP 11). Digital's office system framework is the All-In-One system, which allows use of the many powerful programs available on the VAX. Communication between Digital's systems is done by Decnet under DNA, a comprehensive and powerful communication architecture. Communication with IBM mainframes and other devices can be via SNA or X.25. In those organizations that will use Digital for mainframe systems, the choice is between a VAX or a VAXCLUSTER. The product line standards of the Digital office automation system are Decnet/DNA, VMS operating system, and SNA. Digital recently announced three IBM interconnect products that support IBM's DIA and DCA document interchange architectures and DISOSS. The Distributed Host Command Facility allows access by an IBM-host-controlled 327X terminal to any application resident on a VAX; the DISOSS Document Exchange Facility allows bidirectional participation between a VAX system and an IBM office system network; and the VAX VMS Printer Emulator allows IBM print files to be transferred to the VAX and viewed, manipulated, and/or printed using the VAX system.

Overall, the All-In-One system has a good level of multifunctionality. As far as integration is concerned, we believe that the system handles data very well and text and graphics reasonably well, but to date there has been no integration of image capability. Version 2.0 of the All-In-One system, announced in December 1984, incorporates an electronic mail feature that provides integrated voice and text messaging and can be accessed from any touch-tone telephone worldwide.

## Strengths and Weaknesses

Digital's major strength is its solid reputation in data processing, particularly in technical areas. The company is also strong in communications capabilities. It has an extensive base of VAX users, who are good prospects for expansion to office automation capabilities. The All-In-One system is competitive, and considerable penetration of the customer base is taking place. Digital has always shown a willingness to associate with other companies to achieve its objectives. This policy was shown in its decision to become an early participant in the Ethernet program and its excellent relationships with PBX vendors.

The company still exhibits organizational problems, which make it a difficult company with which to do business unless the user attains national account status. The confusing workstation approach is an indication of the internal competition, which has cost the company momentum despite its technology leadership in many areas.

## Strategy and Prognosis

Digital plans to build on its position as the number two company in the computer business by providing comprehensive integrated office systems to the customer base and to new business. Its strategy is specifically to associate with other companies to achieve a total-systems-supplier status or to provide department-based systems as a major niche vendor.

Despite some recent disappointing financial results, Digital's enormous strengths ensure that the company will indeed be a successful major niche vendor with particular strengths in the technical and scientific areas of major corporations. Its chances of becoming a total-systems supplier and hence to compete more directly with IBM depend upon its ability to overcome internal competition so as to take advantage of all its strengths in this highly competitive marketplace.

## IBM

### Product Line Description and Evaluation

IBM has the largest product line of any of the vendors in the industry. Until recently, IBM has had two separate, major solutions: One was the mainframe-based solution, built around VM/CMS and PROFS, and the other was the departmental-system-based solution, built around OS/MVS and DISOSS. In past months, IBM has made several announcements which describe their intentions to integrate these two solutions into one overall solution. These announcements involve increasing the communication links and compatibility between DISOSS-based systems and PROFS-based systems.

At the present time, IBM still lags some of its major competitors in terms of the ease of installation and use of its office automation systems. It is likely that forthcoming announcements will help rectify these problems.

IBM's purchase of one of the major U.S. PBX suppliers, Rolm Inc., will, in the near future, also have the effect of strengthening its product line in the critical voice communications and LAN product areas.

### Strengths and Weaknesses

IBM's major strength is that it is IBM. Its presence as the major mainframe vendor in a majority of large businesses in the United States provides it with an increasing advantage in the overall office automation market as its customers perceive the need for additional integration between data processing and office automation. IBM also has extensive experience in the office markets where its simpler products (e.g., the Selectric typewriter) are often the industry standards. Another major strength is its workstations, especially those based on the IBM Personal Computer family. Its 3270/PC and the recently announced PC/AT have set new price and performance standards for the remainder of the industry. These systems are not only becoming pervasive in IBM accounts but are also very popular in accounts dominated by the other vendors.

IBM's architecture and statement of direction announcements have provided it with significant strengths in the market. Some of its architectural standards (e.g., DIA and DCA) are likely to become international standards, in effect requiring its competitors to modify their systems to meet IBM-generated standards. Its statements of direction allow its customers to plan their long-range strategies with confidence by providing them with sufficient knowledge of IBM's long-term product strategy.

These statements of direction and architectures also compensate for some of the weaknesses in IBM's current product lines. In the past, IBM has made anticipatory announcements of future products to forestall customer frustration with problems in its current product lines. These statements sometimes delay the development of a market until IBM actually produces a product. For example, the IBM cabling system announcement and its description of IBM's eventual LAN design, has had a significant negative impact on the development of the LAN market.

IBM's major weakness stems from its lack of a single integrated office system framework such as DEC's All-In-One or Data General's CEO systems. The equivalent functions are now distributed between DISOSS and PROFS in the IBM product line. These two software systems are not compatible and do not fully interoperate at the current time.

IBM also lacks a competitive departmental system. It has multiple candidate systems including the small 43XX systems, the S/36, S/38, B100, and the S/1 systems. However, none of these systems has all the functions and ease-of-use attributes required of a modern departmental system in an integrated information processing system.

## Strategy and Prognosis

IBM's short-range strategy has been to alleviate the compatibility and communications problems which currently plague its product line. It has been announcing hardware and software products at a very rapid pace. These newly announced products serve two purposes. At least temporarily, they patch its existing problems to give it time to develop permanent solutions. They also sufficiently meet users' current needs to limit the penetration of other vendors' products into IBM's customer base.

IBM's long-term strategy is to integrate its entire product line using the several communications, data processing, and document architectures that it has been promulgating over the past several years. Its goal is to allow a compound document (one consisting of data, text, graphics, images, and voice information) to be composed on an IBM workstation and to be revised and printed on any other properly equipped IBM workstation or system. It is IBM's intent to develop a totally integrated system which encompasses all of its products.

There is little question that IBM will remain the strongest total-systems supplier in the industry. Its aggressive pricing strategies, significant R&D activities, investments in and purchases of suppliers of significant technologies (e.g., Intel and Rolm), and most importantly its marketing skills will serve to keep it at the top of the heap.

# Midland Bank PLC

On July 15, 1980, the Midland Bank announced its bid for 57 percent of Crocker National Corporation, a deal worth more than $820 million and destined to fulfill a major objective of Midland's international strategy. Crocker was the thirteenth largest bank in the United States and was based in the sophisticated banking market of California. The Crocker acquisition vaulted Midland Bank into the ranks of the top dozen banks in the world, with combined assets, on paper at least, of £41 billion. It was the largest in a series of acquisitions by the major British clearing banks in the decade of the 1970s and was designed to well and truly launch Midland into the world of international banking, matching and indeed overtaking the other members of the UK "Big 4" (Barclays, National Westminster, and Lloyds).

One of the early steps toward this interna-

This case was prepared by Alex Rottenburg, Janette Rutterford, and Catherine Gurling under the supervision of Professor Dean Berry and Dr. John McGee, at the London Graduate School of Business Studies. The case is intended for class discussion and not to illustrate correct and incorrect handling of administrative situations. Copyright © 1982 by London Business School. Revised by José de la Torre, 1988.

tionalization process originated in 1974 with the appointment of Malcolm Wilcox as one of Midland's two Chief General Managers to lead the International Division. The other, S. T. Graham, would lead the Domestic Division. Wilcox's appointment saw the emergence of an international strategy with the explicit objectives of expansion overseas by means of direct representation, entering the wholesale banking market in every significant world currency center and being present in other important country markets as well. Wilcox believed that size was an essential ingredient of this strategy, with the obvious corollary that substantial investment in assets overseas would be required. At the time, the strategy was subjected to considerable internal debate by senior executives at the Midland as it marked an important departure from the traditional methods of international operations at the bank, that is, a primary reliance on cooperative ventures.

Even after the acquisition of Crocker was consummated in October 1981, debate continued inside and outside the bank. The *Financial Times* noted that, "There is speculation in London Banking Circles whether the Crocker Tail (a very big tail admittedly) might not proceed to wag the Midland dog.'' Others thought that, ''Indeed it looks as though Crocker National is rather a bigger mouthful than Midland would ideally have liked, and it is having to digest it slice by slice.'' There were many who found the advertising placed in *Fortune Magazine* in 1982 (see Exhibit 1) provocative in that it suggested important unresolved issues still persisting at Midland.

## INDUSTRY CHANGES

The functions of the U.K. clearing banks had traditionally been regarded as the safeguarding of liquid assets, the transmission of money on customers instructions, and the provision of credit facilities, in particular corporate working capital and bridging finance. However, the 1950s and 1960s saw profound changes in both the domestic and international markets. For example, the role of sterling in international trade had declined and with it the importance of London as the preeminent world banking center. Companies were becoming increasingly multinational with requirements for project financing throughout the world and demanding specialized corporate finance services in many countries. Also, the Eurocurrency markets were fast developing in line with these requirements.

Not only were the international markets expanding but competition in the United Kingdom increased considerably in the 1960s and 1970s with the arrival of many foreign banks. By 1979, some 390 foreign banks had a presence in London. Foreign bank operations in the United Kingdom consisted frequently of small units, fast and flexible, with low overheads and high-caliber staff. By March 1979, one-quarter of the $2.6 billion put up under the E.C.G.D.[1] foreign currency scheme in the United Kingdom came from foreign banks, an indication of their ag-

gressive marketing. For the British clearing banks these developments meant that they would have to make considerable efforts if their businesses were to continue to grow.

## MIDLAND'S EARLY HISTORY

The Birmingham and Midland Bank Ltd. was established in 1836 in Birmingham and remained small in size and regional in scope for the next 50 years. Under the guidance of Sir Edward Holden, the architect and builder of the modern Midland Bank from the 1890s until his death in 1919, the bank began to grow by means of an aggressive series of acquisitions and by the establishment of new branches, extending its geographical coverage across England, Wales, Scotland, and Northern Ireland.

The bank's head office was moved to London in 1891 in order to provide better access to money markets with which to finance an increasing level of trade and manufacturing activity and to supply central services for the branches, which grew from 45 in 1890, to 280 in 1900, and 2,140 in 1939. Deposits grew correspondingly from £5.6 million in 1890, to £37.8 million in 1900, and £349 million in 1925. And a range of new products and services was developed including safe deposit facilities, travellers cheques, and night safes, aimed at the smaller consumer. Branch facilities were also opened in trade fairs, universities, ocean liners, and industrial estates during this period.

The war and its aftermath saw a reduction in the number of branches, but a new phase of branch expansion commenced in 1957 along with the refurbishment, relocation, and extension of existing branches to meet the increased demand for current accounts and other services. This expansion brought with it a measure of decentralization with the initial appointment of four Regional Managers to liaise with the head office. This was later expanded in 1967 to a structure with 24 regional head offices, managed by Regional Directors where decision making could be devolved from the center.

---

[1]E.C.G.D. stood for the Export Credit Guarantee Department of the Bank of England, which has as its major mission to finance foreign trade and investment by British-based firms.

## EXHIBIT 1

### FORTUNE MAGAZINE AD (January 11, 1982)

# MIDLAND BANK WELCOMES ITS ALLIANCE WITH CROCKER.

## (SO WILL YOU. AND HERE'S WHY.)

The recent alliance with Crocker National Corporation marks an exciting new development, starting from a business relationship which began in 1909.

At the present time Midland provides a range of international services offered by no other bank. The Group strengths include Samuel Montagu, one of the world's leading merchant banks; Thomas Cook, the world's largest travel organisation; and London American Finance Corporation, which provides a complete export finance service. In France, BCT Midland Bank, with Midland Bank France S.A., makes Midland the largest independently-owned foreign bank in that country. In West Germany, the Group is represented by Trinkaus and Burkhardt, a leading private bank. In the United Kingdom, Forward Trust is well established in the provision of asset finance. In Australia, Associated Midland offers industrial and consumer finance facilities. These organisations are supported by Midland's own branches and offices.

Crocker will give added strength to an already thriving Midland Bank Group, which is also a major force in correspondent banking, in the Eurocurrency markets, in the provision of finance for aerospace, shipping, oil energy and other specialist industries.

The Group also has considerable experience in foreign exchange dealing in London and in other major financial centres throughout the world.

Midland's total investment in Crocker National will be US$830 million, of which US$495 million will be represented by new capital, and Midland's shareholding will reach 57%. The combined asset base of this powerful alliance will be US$80 billion, making it one of the most influential banking groups in the world—justifiably able to look to the future with great confidence. Together, we make a great team.

**Midland Bank Limited**
Head Office, 27-32 Poultry, London EC2P 2BX.

# CROCKER BANK WELCOMES ITS ALLIANCE WITH MIDLAND BANK, LTD.

## (SO WILL YOU. AND HERE'S WHY.)

You may already know that our new banking relationship increases Crocker's capital base and expands our presence around the world.

But behind those facts is something more important: How this alliance increases our ability to serve the world's business.

To borrowers, Crocker can now provide a major new source of credit because of increased legal lending limits. What's more, this infusion of capital allows us to become a more potent lending force to more industries. And it allows us to become a more active manager of large loan syndications.

By combining our resources with Midland in international and merchant banking, we'll now be able to handle nearly any banking need anywhere in the world.

And as your business becomes more concerned with the international flow of money, we can offer an expanded, worldwide network to expedite it.

In an age when large-scale technological innovations are revolutionizing the banking industry, this new relationship lets us share the costs of developing the systems, hardware, and people we need. The result will be even greater efficiencies for our customers.

Crocker and Midland have been doing business together for over 70 years. Now, we're combining the best managerial talent, financial thinking, and advanced resources from both sides of the Atlantic—a synthesis of banking expertise that will do more for your business.

**Crocker Bank**
Doing more for your business.™

Competition for individual deposits from other institutions, the high cost of maintaining branch networks, and government restrictions on lending in the late 1950s and early 1960s led the Midland to embark on a program of diversification into related financial services, expanding its activities away from those of a pure commercial bank. Midland moved successively into credit finance and leasing (Forward Trust), factoring[2] (Griffin Factors), merchant banking and venture capital (Samuel Montagu), insurance (Bland Payne), and travel services (Thomas Cook), as indicated in Exhibit 2. These interests were maintained as separate and autonomous subsidiaries, turning Midland into a holding structure with many companies with diversified interests. Subsequent reorganization following the acquisition of the Drayton group in 1974 led to the creation of a new money market division and to a consolidation of the merchant and investment banking activities as well as corporate finance, as described below.

## INTERNATIONAL ACTIVITIES, 1913–1963

International trade had trebled in value from 1875 to 1913. Companies were consolidating their domestic operations (e.g., in the tobacco, brewing, iron and steel industries) and beginning to develop their trading activities overseas. Business banking requirements at home and abroad were expanding at a greater rate than those of individual depositors.

In 1918, under Holden's guidance, the London Joint Stock Bank was acquired with the express intention of developing the international business of the bank. The London Joint Stock Bank had extensive connections overseas in the form of correspondent links developed initially in its relationship with national banks in foreign

countries.[3] Correspondent banking became the cornerstone of Midland's foreign expansion with the development of a huge network of correspondent links, increasing to more than 20,000 banks in 200 countries by 1970. This expansion gave Midland the status of the world's largest bank, with £1,635 million in total assets in 1948, before the 1949 sterling devaluation.

Midland considered the indirect representation of correspondent banking the most suitable approach to international markets, preserving flexibility and noninvolvement in the legal, political, and business constraints internal to those markets. In this fashion, neither the bank's shareholders nor its customers' capital was committed overseas, nor was competition set up with foreign banks in their own territory. B. T. Smith, then General Manager for International Banking, described Midland's international business:

> We were not involved in foreign investment, but in foreign trade letters of credit, foreign government loans and so on, which really depended on sterling being a world currency. You don't need overseas branches for that sort of thing. . . .
>
> We had, and still have, a considerable number of talented middle managers that enable us to deliver an exceptional personal service to our correspondents by taking care of all the problems they encountered in London. The whole thing was built on personal relationships forged by people going out from London to the correspondents, Midland "graduates" who were and are loyal to the Midland and the way we do things. This is what banking is all about.

A central Foreign Banks Department was set up in 1902 to deal with these correspondent links,

---

[2]Factoring was a service with various aspects. First, an accounting service was provided for the issuing of invoices and debt collections. Second, there was an insurance service against bad debts. And third, it could include a system by which 80 percent of the value of the invoice could be made available to the client as cash advances.

[3]An overseas bank with a correspondent bank in London would keep its sterling balances with that bank. In turn the London bank would maintain its foreign currency reserves with the overseas bank (all interest-free). Each bank would act as the other's banker in that country, serving the other bank's customer with letters of credit and currency drafts, drawing on each other to agreed limits at an agreed rate. Deposits so held at home or abroad could be put out on the money market and provided a useful income as well as an asset base to both banks.

---

**EXHIBIT 2**

---

## MAJOR MIDLAND BANK ACQUISITIONS, ESTABLISHMENTS, AND PARTICIPATIONS FROM 1902 TO 1981

| Year | Venture | Structure |
|------|---------|-----------|
| 1902 | Foreign Banks Department | Established |
| 1905 | Foreign Exchange Department | Established |
| 1917 | Belfast Banking Co. Ltd. | Acquired |
| 1918 | London Joint Stock Bank Ltd. | Acquired |
|      | Overseas Branch | Established |
| 1919 | Clydesdale Bank Ltd. | Acquired |
| 1924 | North of Scotland Bank Ltd. | Acquired |
| 1945 | Finance or Industry Ltd. | Established* |
| 1958 | Forward Trust Ltd. | Acquired |
| 1963 | Cooperation agreement among Midland Bank, Deutsche Bank, Amsterdam Rotterdam Bank, and Société Générale de Banque | Established |
| 1964 | Midland & International Banks Ltd. | Established (45%) |
| 1965 | Northern Bank | Acquired |
| 1966 | Check Card introduced | |
| 1967 | Midland Bank Finance Corp. Ltd. | Established |
|      | Banque Européenne de Crédit S.A. | Established (Belgium, 14%) |
|      | Montagu Trust Ltd. (parent company of Samuel Montagu & Co. Ltd. and Bland Payne Holdings Ltd.) | Acquired (33%) |
| 1968 | European American Banking Corp. | Established (New York, 20%) |
|      | Midland Montagu Industrial Finance Ltd. | Established |
| 1969 | Forward Leasing (U.K.) Ltd. | Established |
| 1970 | European Banks International Co. S.A. | Established (Belgium)* |
|      | Euro-Pacific Finance Corp. Ltd. | Established (Australia, 15%) |
| 1971 | The Joint Credit Card Co. Ltd. | Established* |
|      | Term Loan Division | Established |
|      | Insurance Advisory Services | Established |
| 1972 | Europarisch-Asiatische Bank A.G. | Established (Germany, 14%) |
|      | UBAF Bank Ltd. | Established (London, 25%) |
|      | Controlling interest in Thomas Cook Group Ltd. | Acquired |
| 1973 | Holdings in Montagu Trust Ltd. | Increased (100%) |
|      | Shield Factors Ltd. | Established* |
|      | European Banking Co. Ltd. | Established (London, 14%) |
|      | Iran Overseas Investment Bank | Established (London, 6%) |
| 1974 | Overseas Branch becomes International Division Banque Européenne pur l'Amerique Latine S.A. | Established (Brussels, 16%) |
|      | Drayton Corp. Ltd. | Acquired |
|      | Drayton Montagu Portfolio Mgmt. Ltd. | Established |
| 1975 | London American International Corp. Ltd. | Established |
|      | Corporate Finance Division | Established |
|      | Midland Financial Services Ltd. | Established (Canada) |
|      | Shareholding in Standard Chartered Bank Ltd. | Increased (16%) |
| 1977 | Holdings in Thomas Cook Group Ltd. | Increased (100%) |
|      | Moracrest Investments Ltd. | Established* |
|      | Midland Bank Industrial Equity Holdings Ltd. | Established |
| 1978 | Midland Bank France S.A. | Established |
| 1979 | Banque de la Construction et des Travaux Publiques | Acquired (67%) |
| 1980 | Trinkhaus & Burkhart | Acquired (60%) |
| 1981 | Crocker National Corp. | Acquired (57%) |

*Joint venture.

which was succeeded in 1918 by the Overseas Branch handling both the correspondent links and foreign exchange transactions.

The international business of Midland grew rapidly, representing the largest share of overseas banking passing through London. By 1949, foreign exchange transactions reached a volume of £27 million, growing to over £135 million by 1954. The number of transactions handled on the instructions of overseas banks doubled to 1.23 million between the years 1952 and 1962, with the result that by 1963 the Overseas Branch was the largest head office branch of Midland, employing more than 1,000 people. Midland became very much a "banker's bank" as a result of this international expansion, with business transactions that did not require direct representation overseas, that could be built up on the basis of personal relationships between the banks involved, and which operated on a worldwide basis from one single division based in London.

## INTERNATIONAL DEVELOPMENTS, 1964–1974

From the mid-1960s, competition was more intense in wholesale banking and corporate finance than in retail banking. The nature of this business had changed radically with the emergence of multinational companies. The U.S. commercial banks were quickest off the mark in following the multinationals abroad, making a virtue of necessity, and achieving, through the establishment of branches in London, a level of total assets of £33.6 billion, representing approximately 50 percent of all foreign-owned assets in London by 1975. The U.K. clearing banks' share of these assets amounted to only £31.6 billion, with the Midland representing £10.1 billion (32 percent). In 1974, 62 percent of Citicorp's profits for the year ($193 million) came from overseas earnings. Midland's total profit for that year was £122 million, of which approximately 12 percent was attributable to international business.

U.S. banks were driven overseas by several factors. One was the nature of U.S. banking regulations, which limited a bank's ability to operate branches in more than one state within the United States and prohibited mixing commercial and investment banking activities under one corporate roof. An added attraction was the growing Eurodollar market, which rose from capital export restrictions imposed by the Johnson administration in the United States in the late 1960s and which was centered in London. As U.S.-based multinationals demanded more corporate financial services from Eurodollar sources (exempt from restrictions), the U.S. banks moved to London to provide them.

European banks met the challenge of increasing international competition in a variety of ways. One preferred option was to establish banking clubs which were loose cooperative groupings in the same tradition of correspondent links. The principal groups were ABECOR, EBIC, InterAlpha and Europartners. Midland was at the forefront of this movement, signing a cooperation agreement in 1963 with Société Générale (one of the three largest French commercial banks), Amro Bank (Netherlands), and Deutsche Bank to form the European Advisory Committee. This was later formalized in 1970 with three more members—Banca Commerciale Italiana, Creditanstalt-Bankverein (Austria), and the Société Générale de Banque (Belgium)—as the European Banks International Company (EBIC).

These clubs or consortia were largely based in London to take advantage of the growth in Eurocurrency markets. Their objectives were to allow banks to participate in international capital markets, to develop and gain skills in a particular product or geographical area from association with other members, and in some cases to circumvent national regulation and legislation. Foreign markets provided "off-balance-sheet" opportunities for medium- and long-term lending in markets other than their own. Jack Hendley, Senior General Manager at Midland, explained the development of these consortia:

> The Euromarkets required quite different forms of expertise and a different set-up. Basically consortia and syndicated lending allowed us to pen-

etrate markets in a much bigger and efficient and effective way than we could possibly have done on our own. It has minimized our investment costs and put us in a position to benefit from the knowledge and expertise of the other members. Such consortia need less capital and protect the territories of the members while enabling them to lend overseas. They are highly profitable. There is no way that we could have done so well with the capital invested elsewhere.

Participating banks agreed not to compete in domestic banking against each other. In the words of Jack Hendley,

We would not even consider establishing extensive branch networks overseas. It only pays to establish an independent presence in really big financial centers. Otherwise it only makes sense to go either through another bank in the form of a correspondent relationship or through a partnership with their major banks.

Almost simultaneously with the establishment of EBIC, Midland, in collaboration with the Commercial Bank of Australia, the Toronto-Dominion Bank, and the Standard Chartered Bank (a U.K.-based bank operating mainly in former British colonies), formed Midland and International Banks Ltd., commonly known as MAIBL in 1964. This consortium had a distinctly Commonwealth flavor as opposed to EBIC's European orientation. The Midland's international expansion by the use of consortia continued in 1967 with the creation by the EBIC partners of the Banque Européenne de Crédit (BEC) based in Brussels, and the European American Bank and Trust Corporation (EAB) in New York in 1968. This last venture provided an important representation in the United States for international trade and commercial banking services. Further geographical coverage came with the formation of the Euro-Pacific Finance corporation in 1970. EBIC went on to extend its activities into South-East Asia with the European Asian Bank in 1972 (directly owned by EBIC) and again into the United States with the European Banking Company of London and Chicago in 1973.

Other ventures took place outside the activities of MAIBL and EBIC, including the foundation of UBAF (Union de Banques Arabes & Françaises) a consortium between Arab and French banks and Midland. Midland also increased its shareholding in the Standard Chartered Bank in 1975, which covered the geographical areas of the Far East, Middle East, and Africa. Standard Chartered had its own retail banking branches across the world (1,400 branches in 1976) and participated in various joint ventures as well. See Exhibit 2 for a listing of all Midland Bank's participations.

## ORGANIZATIONAL DEVELOPMENTS

In the early 1940s the top management team was relatively small and decision making, especially on lending and international business, was highly centralized and remote. The management style was characterized by many committees and shared responsibility among senior executives. There was little contact between the top executive group and the local branches in this respect. To quote a senior General Manager, "It was a very rules-centered operation, hierarchical and very centralized. At one time branch managers required head office permission to lend over £50."

Branch managers were encouraged to relate to the local community, with little discussion with the head office, leading to a feeling of a compartmentalized and fragmented bank on the part of employees. The board was traditionally nonexecutive, consisting of chairpersons of the bank's major clients or members of the aristocracy, people with no banking experience who generally did not become involved in the running of the bank.

In 1964, a Scottish industrialist and accountant, Sir Archibald Forbes, was appointed Chairman. Although maintaining the tradition of nonbanking chairmen, Sir Archibald believed that the board should run the bank and executives should execute their wishes. He recruited more industrialists to the board and began to install systematic financial controls. The administration of the bank was reorganized in 1965, followed by an overhaul of accounting procedures in 1967, which introduced new systems for capital and departmental budgeting, corporate planning, and financial strategy.

## THE INTERNATIONAL DIVISION

In 1974 the Midland took a significant step by changing the Overseas Branch into the International Division, creating a strategically autonomous unit responsible for all the international activities of the bank including correspondent banking, foreign exchange, project finance, bond issues, and joint ventures. General Manager W. G. Barrett commented on the change, "The Overseas Branch was pure banking. It had no corporate finance and didn't really capitalize on the correspondent network; the old established personal links are now dying away. It was the growth in Eurocurrency lending that stimulated the bank to have an international division."

The decision to set up a division rather than a separate subsidiary, as most of Midland's competitors had done, was not arrived at without considerable debate amongst the senior executives of the bank. Those in favor of a subsidiary felt that it would give international operations greater control of such things as staff and new products. They also felt that total autonomy would give the flexibility and speed of response that international banking was seen to require. Those in favor of the bank's international operations being a division argued that the complexities involved in transferring assets from the domestic side were too many; that senior management would be reluctant to move to a new and small subsidiary. Furthermore, a new company would be unable to raise capital as easily as the parent, and the capital base of any new subsidiary would not be as large as Midland's own capital base, thus restricting the scope of its international operations. Commenting on these arguments, a junior executive in the International Division observed that, "Size is important, both to be trusted and to get capital.

There is a certain emotional hankering after a separate company, but after all, we are autonomous—we have our own balance sheet, our own personnel, our own flexibility. I also believe that the group approach is important—we all try to sell each other's services."

Another executive discussed some of the drawbacks: "In some ways our international operations are run as if it were a domestic branch. No doubt the domestic branch rules are excellent, but the problem is that these have infused themselves throughout the organization, leaving the management culture constrained and poorly adapted to the complex international environment. In international you need speed, flexibility and coherence. But throughout the Division there are 'identity islands' that are sealed off from each other on an informal basis."

## CORPORATE FINANCE

In 1975 Midland reorganized its internal operations by setting up a Corporate Finance Division, dealing with major corporate clients and split between the domestic and international sides of the bank. Previously, corporate clients had been handled by the regional and branch network. The International Division saw the creation of the new division as being helpful to the bank's international business. A General Manager commented: "Executives thought of corporate finance as an afterthought, because all were either domestic or correspondent bankers. We did not have an investment mentality or commitment, for example we did not invest in personnel to develop the business, but only bought personnel after the business materialized."

Midland was rather late relative to many of its competitors, particularly the U.S. banks, in separating major corporate customers from other activities. By 1979, the reorganization of these activities was completed following the abolition of exchange controls in the United Kingdom, bringing both domestic and international corporate finance under the same roof.

## DUAL LEADERSHIP

Shortly before the creation of the International Division in 1974, Midland had taken the unusual step of appointing two Chief General Managers. Stuart Graham was made responsible for domestic operations and Malcolm Wilcox for the International Division and other activities. Stuart Graham observed: "Maybe the board wanted vigorous change; maybe the amount of change it wanted was thought to be too much for one man."

The split was not universally considered a good idea on the bases that it did not promote synergy and made the functional managers' task more difficult and that it enforced the split between domestic and international, for instance, in corporate finance. Both men, Wilcox and Graham, were 53 years old on their appointment and both came from middle-class backgrounds and grammar school. In each case they joined the bank early at the age of about 16. Stuart Graham's path through the bank was very traditional; he had worked his way through branches in the West End and the City, moving out briefly to Leicester and then returning to head office, progressing through the posts of General Manager's Assistant, General Manager for the City, and Assistant Chief General Manager in 1970.

Malcolm Wilcox had also followed a traditional route through the bank's branches until, in 1966, his career took an unconventional turn into the related financial services and other activities of the Midland. After an appointment to Forward Trust, during which the subsidiary was restructured, Malcolm Wilcox became involved in the reorganization of the Midland's installment finance, merchant banking, leasing, and factoring activities. The revitalization of Thomas Cook was also his responsibility and represented a considerable achievement. Malcolm Wilcox's image, said an executive, "is that of the entrepreneurial type but possessing, at the same time, a keen eye for the important details."

Both Stuart Graham and Malcolm Wilcox, with their distinctive personalities, reported to the Chairman, then Lord Armstrong, who had succeeded Forbes in 1975. Lord Armstrong, previously head of the British Civil Service for many years, was a strong leader, and the board continued its active role under his leadership as it had done under Forbes.

## PERSONNEL

The type of person that Midland recruited and the career pattern that they could expect had, in common with other British clearing banks, barely changed in the last 50 years. An entrant to the bank, usually at age 16, could expect a lifetime career that started as a teller in a local branch, hopefully progressing through a spell acquiring "back room skills" and passing the Institute of Bankers' exams, to a period moving around the branches before becoming a supervisor. The next step would be an appointment to Assistant Manager and, finally, to Branch Manager. If aspirants showed exceptional ability or an unusual talent, such as languages, they would be moved to the London head office, where loyalty, reliability, and being a "Midland Bank person" was an important asset. An almost tribal sense of loyalty existed within the bank but did not extend to the group of subsidiary companies where, to quote a manager, "a Midland banker remains part of an inner club, set apart from the locals in the subsidiary."

This system had as a consequence a very low turnover in staff and engendered strong opinions among executives. One General Manager in International Banking, for example, commented, "Most of the top executives in the bank today were recruited as clerks from grammar schools, with 'O' or 'A' levels.[4] They wanted a good solid job and came from the kinds of families where parents emphasized conformity and loyalty. Often their fathers were themselves in secure banking jobs. Don't forget that Midland was not

---

[4]The British equivalent of junior or senior high school levels, although "A" level exams would be comparable to honors courses in the U.S. system.

a family-dominated bank like Barclays. This consistency of background of the executives of the bank is very important.'' Another executive added, ''You were more likely to be promoted if you had a not-very-profitable loan portfolio with no bad debts than if you had a more profitable portfolio with some bad debts. The best way to get ahead was to keep your nose clean and not make bad judgments.''

Graham and Wilcox were strong believers in counterbalancing the risk of ''tunnel vision'' by using outside expertise and set out to change the culture of the bank by recruiting specialists such as lawyers, chartered accountants, and systems analysts. As Malcolm Wilcox observed, ''the days when the grammar school boy could do everything are past.''

The difficulties involved in changing such a large organization were not underestimated by the senior executives of Midland:

> You need the right personnel in the right places. In international banking you need young, aggressive, market oriented types, and they are not cheap. But because the bank is one single bargaining unit, we can't pay international more than domestic for similar grades. Also the extreme centralization and long hierarchy leads to an outlook that makes change very difficult. You can't persuade people that a different approach will lead to a successful career when they see how everybody else has made their way to the top. They find it difficult to believe that it will be that different for them.

## PLANNING AND GENERAL PROCEDURES

By 1972, the Midland was concerned about its position in the banking world (it ranked fourth among British clearing banks), in particular with regard to its international strategy. The Stanford Research Institute (SRI) was commissioned to carry out a competitor comparison during 1973 and 1974. This was followed by an International Division Conference in November 1974 at Betchworth, Midland's own staff college, to consider the bank's future international strategy

in the light of the SRI report. As a result, Midland declared its intention of being a major international bank making at least 40 percent of its profit overseas.

The Betchworth conference was seen by many Midland executives as a critical turning point. Said one,

> There was some degree of formal planning before Betchworth and there have been conferences since, but Betchworth is the key. It was Malcolm Wilcox's idea; it was he who brought SRI in. It set a new direction and began a building process that is still going on. For example, in early 1979, a Strategic Planning Working Party was set up to review the Bank's strategic priorities, and SRI was again commissioned for a study. This time they were to review the organizational structures of a range of international banks to see if there were any lessons applicable to Midland's own structure.

## THE COMMITTEES

Most decisions in Midland were made by a series of committees chaired by top executives. The most important of the many committees that existed was the Credit Control Committee (CCC), with separate domestic and international subcommittees reporting to it. This committee, which met daily, was critical since the Midland was, in the words of a senior manager, ''a lending-led credit organization. The CCC actually took decisions, and often other noncredit-related decisions went to it in default.''

The Group Coordinating Committee handled domestic business predominantly but was mandated also to coordinate the activities of the Chief General Managers. The Group International Coordinating Committee met monthly, chaired by Malcolm Wilcox. It had been established to coordinate the international activities of the banking and nonbanking subsidiaries, and tried to provide marketing orientation to the bank's international activities. It also helped formulate strategy. The Standing Committee of the Board was the final committee consisting of the Chair, the two Deputy Chairs, and the two

Chief General Managers. It had received delegated authority from the board to examine and coordinate the major policies of the bank. The Standing Committee decided capital expenditures and had the authority to modify board proposals. Observed one Midland executive, ''In some ways it is just a talking shop. Armstrong uses it to bring any differences of opinion between the two CGMs into the open where he can then moderate it. Like the PA system [see below], it is a very Civil Service way of doing things.''

## THE PERSONAL ASSISTANTS

The Chairman and the senior executives of the bank all had one or more Personal Assistants (PAs). Many of today's senior executives had served as PAs in their day. The PAs' function was to interpret and clarify instructions, acting as intermediaries, and as such were important to the organization. They also served to reinforce personal loyalties, although their role varied from area to area:

> PAs were less important for Graham, who has a classic pyramidal structure, and more important for Wilcox, who has a large number of unintegrated small entities, each separate and with its own traditions. The PAs help keep him in touch but they are becoming less important as the Division's own people are put in power. The PAs are also an important means of getting resources from Central Services which, because of relative size, tend to devote more time to the clearing side of the bank's activities.

## ORGANIZATIONAL CHANGE

In July 1980, a few days before his sudden death, Lord Armstrong discussed change at Midland: ''You go along on an even keel. It looks ponderous but it doesn't actually capsize. You cannot change a clearing bank very quickly any more than you can change the Inland Revenue or the Department of Social Security.''

In spite of a legacy that might have ossified any organization, change had taken place at Midland. Much of the credit belonged to Malcolm Wilcox and Lord Armstrong. Wilcox was seen as a man with vision, who believed in an orderly and detailed exposition and rationale for all proposed activities and used whatever aids to management decision making were available. Lord Armstrong's knowledge of politics and his concern for the international market had also contributed greatly to Midland's development.

According to then Assistant Chief General Manager, Geoffrey Taylor, ''We are improving. We now have group-wide corporate planning and departmental five-year plans. France [see below] is an example of the new planning—it was the end result of management decisions built into the planning process some years ago.''

## THE NEW INTERNATIONAL STRATEGY

David Montagu, former chief executive of Orion Bank, once stated: ''Consortium banks can take on a life of their own provided the shareholders' commitment is there for expansion. Once these banks have established an identity of their own they need to expand, not only for commercial reasons, but to develop the careers of the people that work for them.'' Despite the broad geographic and product coverage available to it through its various consortia, Midland began to feel an increasing need to grow internationally through direct representation. Malcolm Wilcox said, ''with the advantage of hindsight it would have been preferable if we had linked our consortia development with more expansion in our own name . . . [but] we have made it increasingly apparent to the other members [of EBIC] that our own initiative is growing stronger and stronger.''[5]

By 1974, Midland under Wilcox developed a two-pronged international strategy: to continue with consortium banking and strengthen its global correspondent ties, and to increase growth by

---

[5]In fact, another EBIC member, Deutsche Bank, had already opened a branch in their own name in New York.

exploiting new opportunities by means of direct representation in key markets.

## FRANCE

In January 1977, the Group Coordinating Committee met to discuss the means by which these goals would be achieved. Feasibility studies for direct representation in France were subsequently carried out, and in October 1977 Geoffrey Taylor submitted a memo to the committee (Exhibit 3) in which he argued for the creation of a subsidiary which would employ local personnel from outside the International Division. It was argued that a person different from the traditional domestic banker was required. The memo was submitted to and discussed by the board and the Chairman's Policy Committee in November 1977, whereupon the board agreed to establishing a French subsidiary with an initial capital of FF20 million.

Midland was assisted in its entry into the French market by the pro-competition attitude of the French government, keen to develop Paris as a major financial center. A major stroke of luck was the almost accidental recruitment of Hervé de Carmoy in January 1978 to spearhead this effort. A graduate of one of France's prestigious "Grandes Ecoles," with an MBA from Cornell University, de Carmoy had 16 years of experience with the Chase Manhattan Bank, most recently as Head of European Operations.

De Carmoy recruited key people using his extensive contacts in Paris and persuaded Midland to increase the total number of staff to 40 and initial capitalization to FF100 million. This

---

**EXHIBIT 3**

**MEMORANDUM ON PROPOSED FRENCH INVESTMENT (CONDENSED)**

To:  Group Coordinating Committee
From:  Geoffrey W. Taylor
Date:  October 1977

Three years ago Paris was identified as a financial center in which we should have a presence, but we could not find a suitable representative and nothing was done.

Since then we have concluded that we need a presence in the major financial centers of Europe, by means of branches or subsidiaries, whichever is most appropriate. The requirement is for a sophisticated and flexible approach which should combine local custom with present-day financing trends.

Defining the resource needs for a complete European network is at the moment not possible, as we lack the necessary information.

Paris is now the second largest Euromarket center outside London and the time seems right to consider investing there in the form of a subsidiary active in the wholesale market. Taxation reasons and the opportunity of coopting well connected locals to the board suggest that this would be the most appropriate form of representation.

The general acceptance by EBIC members not to open up in each other's countries has been undertaken by the concept that wholesale banking operations in money centers in each other's countries would not be against the spirit of the EBIC philosophy. Local soundings suggest that the correspondent banks would be very helpful.

Domestic corporations usually have several banks, which will mitigate the initial impact of our arrival. The main business opportunities have been identified as being of a merchant banking nature, namely in the foreign exchange and wholesale markets, including investment and merger advise, securities, Euromarket trading and portfolio management. Such a subsidiary would not be able to obtain adequate retail deposits and would have to rely on the inter-bank market for its funds. A wholesale operation of this type would represent a radical departure from the traditional style of our overseas operations. The initial cost is expected to be £2.5 million, and 18 staff are regarded as sufficient. Projections are:

|  | Year 3 | Year 5 |
|---|---|---|
| Return on assets | 7% | 8% |
| Return on capital | 13.3% | 23.7% |
| Net profits | £314,000 | £558,000 |

would give the subsidiary greater lending capacity in French francs and avoid losses in the first year until fully operational. The activities of Midland Bank France S.A. (MBFSA) were to include money market operations, corporate finance, syndicated loans, correspondence banking, bullion dealing, and fee earning activities—all of them profitable parts of the wholesale sector. Later that year, Midland Bank also opened its own branch in Paris, using the same premises and staff as MBFSA, so as to increase the lending capabilities of the French operation.

At the end of 1979, Midland purchased a 38 percent shareholding in the Banque de Construction et Travaux Publiques (BCT), a publicly quoted bank with large construction and residential mortgage investments. With fifteen branches of its own, BCT still had lending capacity under the French system of encadrement.[6] BCT also had excellent connections; Midland's partners in BCT were an insurance company and France's three largest commercial banks, Société Générale, Crédit Lyonnais, and Banque Nationale de Paris.

Discussing the French venture, John Harris, then General Manager, Related Services, commented,

> The French experience has been critical. We succeeded because there was a Board commitment to make the funds available and buy the right people. We have established a way of growing into key international markets, combined with the choice of an excellent international entrepreneur. We have a segmented strategy that draws upon our correspondent network, which has been very helpful, and we have avoided businesses with high overheads. Equally, with the acquisition of BCT we are in a position to move into related services in France. What really distinguishes the whole thing is that we started off by saying "Where can we make a profit?" rather than, "What should we be doing as an international bank in France?"

---

[6]This was a French regulation by which a bank's lending limits were controlled as a function of its previous loan portfolio and the government's overall credit policy. It allowed for credit rationing to be used as part of monetary and fiscal policy.

## THE UNITED STATES

It had been widely expected that Midland would move directly into the United States following a series of acquisitions there by the other British clearing banks. National Westminster had acquired the National Bank of North America, Standard Chartered the Los Angeles–based Union Bancorp, and Barclays the American Credit Corporation. Up to the late 1970s, Midland had relied on the European American Bank (EAB) for its participation in the U.S. market. A proposal to merge with Standard Chartered, in which Midland had a 16 percent share, was turned down by Lord Armstrong, who objected to Standard's connections to South Africa. Instead, Wilcox targeted California, Texas, and Illinois as locations for a possible acquisition.

In late June 1979, Midland Bank made its move to acquire Walter E. Heller International, a Chicago-based financial conglomerate. The bid of $520 million was the largest made so far by a British bank in the United States, and it was for "a finance house with a bank tagged on," unlike other U.K. banks who had purchased more traditional banking houses. According to management, "this gives us a foothold in North America which will be of long-term benefit to the Midland group."

The bid for Heller raised questions over Midland's holdings in Standard Chartered as well as EAB. Under U.S. bank regulations, banks were not permitted to enter related fields nor operate deposit-taking branches in more than one state. European American Bank, of which Midland owned 20 percent through its membership of EBIC, owned Franklin National Bank with many branches in New York. Midland's holding in Standard Chartered was also likely to come under scrutiny by federal and state banking authorities, given the latter's California operations (although the authorities had broad discretion in the 5 percent to 25 percent ownership range) as would Thomas Cook's travel interests in the United States.

By mid-October the shareholding in Standard Chartered had been sold. Yet, a week later the bid for Heller was called off. No reasons were given by Midland, but there was speculation that Heller's debt portfolio held an unacceptable level of risk. This was a disappointment to Geoffrey Taylor who had personally negotiated the Heller deal, and a mounting sense of frustration, together with a fear of missing a window of opportunity that may soon disappear with a congressional ban on foreign bank takeovers, was shared by the International Division's top management.

## THE NEXT CANDIDATE

Midland continued to build up financial resources by selling off interests such as Sedgewick Forbes and Bland Payne Insurance and borrowing in the Eurodollar markets in order to finance its £1 billion acquisition spree in Europe and Australia. It was widely considered just a matter of time before Midland made another attempt to enter the U.S. financial market.

For years, Malcolm Wilcox had maintained a friendly relationship with the chairman of Crocker National, his namesake Thomas Wilcox. They had discussed various cooperative schemes in the past, and, following the Heller affair, Malcolm decided to press the issue. Taylor led once more the negotiations and returned from the United States with a proposal by Tom for a share of Crocker in exchange for cash, but the proposal refused to yield control over any aspect of Crocker's management to Midland.

Midland's first offer was to buy nearly 50 percent of Crocker's shares at their book value of about $50 per share (market price was $36 at the time) and inject an additional $500 million in cash for 6.6 million shares at $75 each. Tom Wilcox agreed to the first half of the proposition but insisted on a price of $90 for the new shares on the basis of Crocker's rising profit prospects. Following some tough negotiations which significantly strained the relationship between the two Wilcoxes, Midland essentially agreed to Crocker's terms.

On July 15, 1980, the bank announced a plan to acquire 57 percent of Crocker in two stages. The first stage would consist of the purchase by Midland of 6.5 million shares from existing Crocker shareholders at $50 per share, plus 3 million new shares at $90 each, a total investment of $595 million for a 51 percent equity stake. The second stage would allow for a second allotment of 2.5 million new shares also at $90 each, to be purchased over a period of three years from the date of acquisition of the first shares.

This was the largest attempted foreign takeover of a U.S. bank. Crocker ranked fourth in its home state of California and had assets of more than $16 billion at the end of 1979. It operated 382 branches in California and had representative offices in 12 countries as well as in New York and Chicago. Crocker also operated subsidiaries in the areas of credit insurance, trust and investment, property and mortgage banking, leasing and factoring, and consumer and commercial finance (see Exhibit 4 for financial details on Crocker). In fact, Crocker was very similar to Midland in that it consisted of a general commercial bank, with a strong domestic orientation, and a number of subsidiary companies providing specialist financial services (unlike Heller whose principal interests were in wholesale banking).[7] Malcolm Wilcox saw the Crocker acquisition as ''providing the Midland with an opportunity to participate in one of the world's most rapidly growing markets in partnership with an American institution whose roots are in that market and whose strength and confidence are recognized throughout the bank business community.'' To the chairman of Crocker, Tom Wilcox, ''the most important of many advantages to Crocker is the infusion of nearly half a billion dollars of additional equity capital.''

As part of the agreement, the transaction was to be called an alliance and not a merger. Furthermore, Midland agreed to grant Crocker

---

[7]Shortly thereafter, Midland announced the purchase of Citibank's 60 percent holding of a large private bank in Germany, Trinkhaus and Burkhardt, for $50 million, thereby gaining entry into Germany's domestic money market and corporate banking sector.

| EXHIBIT 4 |
| --- |

**CROCKER NATIONAL CORPORATION—SELECTED FINANCIAL INFORMATION, 1977–1980** ($ Thousand, Except Where Indicated)

|  | **1977** | **1978** | **1979\*** | **1980** |
| --- | --- | --- | --- | --- |
| Net interest income and other operating income | 468,530 | 596,053 | 687,880 | 786,663 |
| Net interest income | 397,312 | 518,083 | 592,514 | 660,749 |
| Income before securities transactions | 53,799 | 75,242 | 89,357 | 95,100 |
| Net income | 53,839 | 71,831 | 89,228 | 95,735 |
| Primary earnings per common share: Income before securities transactions ($) | 4.35 | 5.95 | 6.69 | 6.72 |
| Net income ($) | 4.35 | 5.66 | 6.68 | 6.76 |
| Cash dividends per common share | 1.66 | 1.80 | 2.00 | 2.20 |
| Net assets at year end | 474,868 | 568,609 | 659,998 | 738,622 |
| Loss from the purchasing power of net monetary assets (constant dollar) | 1,318 | 4,436 | 28,855 | 52,062 |
| Market price of common stock at year end ($) | 25.13 | 24.38 | 29.00 | 37.13 |
| Average CPI (index) | 181.5 | 195.4 | 217.4 | 246.8 |

\*1979 income statement numbers exclude the gain on sale of the Los Angeles headquarters building of $40,114 pre-tax and $27,670 after-tax, equal to $2.26 primary earnings per common share.

"maximum operating autonomy" for at least five years, except only should Midland's investment be "in jeopardy." Crocker would be granted two places in Midland's board in exchange for yielding three seats on its board to Midland. When Midland politely requested to locate its San Francisco representative office in the Crocker building, they were told that there was no room in their 38-story corporate headquarters.

The bid caused some consternation within the United States as opposition to the growing number of bank takeovers became more vociferous. A waiting period commenced as Midland submitted its case for retaining its interests in Thomas Cook and EAB to the Federal Reserve Board, which proceeded to hold hearings on the merits of the case. The situation was complicated further by the existence of two rival bids from the Hong Kong and Shanghai Bank along with that of Standard Chartered for the Royal Bank of Scotland. It was thought that the Bank

of England's decision on this case could influence the U.S. regulators' decision on Crocker. The Bank of England was in a sense in the same position vis-à-vis the Royal Bank of Scotland as the Federal Reserve Board was relative to Crocker in considering bids from overseas banks.

## THE OUTCOME AND FUTURE

In October 1981, Midland was allowed to complete the first stage of the Crocker acquisition provided they disposed of their Thomas Cook Travel interests in the United States and reduced their holding in EAB to less than 5 percent.

Midland's international activities for 1981 contributed only 38 percent of total profits of £299 million. The Crocker acquisition would change this significantly, but much remained to be done as evidenced by the chairman's statement to the stockholders in its 1981 *Annual Report* (see Exhibit 5).

**EXHIBIT 5**

**STATEMENT ON INTERNATIONAL BANKING BY THE CHAIRMAN OF MIDLAND BANK, 1981\***

Shareholders are aware that, in recent years, it has been our wish to develop and enlarge our international activities and interests in order that a greater proportion of Group profits should emanate from operations outside the United Kingdom. The action which was taken in the 1960s to enter consortium relationships to specialized international business has been followed by a period in which we have sought a direct presence in the principal international financial centers, in order both to diversify our interests and to service better the needs of our rapidly growing clientele. In this respect we have identified the United States of America and Western Europe as priority areas for the continuing expansion of our trading activities overseas.

Against this background the major developments of 1980 have been the preliminary agreement, announced in July, for Midland to acquire a majority interest in Crocker National Corporation of California, and our purchase also, during October, of a majority shareholding in Trinkaus and Burkhardt, one of the largest private banks in West Germany.

Our proposed investment in Crocker National Corporation has been overwhelmingly endorsed by the shareholders of both companies and we must now await the deliberations of the United States regulatory authorities. Our application is currently being examined by the Federal Reserve Board and it would be premature to predict the final outcome but we remain very hopeful of success. Our alliance with Crocker will preserve their operational autonomy and the infusion of capital will ensure that they are in a strong position to take advantage of any changes in the structure of banking in the United States, whilst also being able to introduce new services and continue their development of technologically advanced systems.

In Europe, the acquisition of a controlling interest in Trinkaus and Burkhardt has enabled us to increase our involvement in the German corporate market. With its branches in major cities in Germany and operating subsidiaries in Switzerland and Luxembourg, this bank has provided us with a good foothold in the German domestic money market and in loan syndication and private portfolio management activities, as well as strengthening our links with the major West German corporations. This development complements our earlier moves in France, where the progress of Midland Bank France and BCT Midland Bank continues to be highly satisfactory. Elsewhere in Europe the nature of our representation is under continuing review, and, in addition to opening an EEC Representative Office in Brussels in 1980, we have now received official permission to convert our successful representative office in Madrid into a full branch during 1981.

In the Far East we have achieved a significant local presence with the most recent developments being the opening of new branches in Hong Kong and Singapore. A particularly important event in 1980 has been the establishment of our representative office in Beijing. . . .

Our other international subsidiary and associated companies have also continued to develop satisfactorily. Midland Financial Services in Canada has grown rapidly and is now seeking full chartered bank status under new Canadian legislation. The London American Group achieved substantially higher business volumes and increased profits in an exceptionally difficult world trading environment. Midland and International Banks Limited (MAIBL) showed steady and profitable growth, whilst our associations with European Banks' International Company (EBIC) and its successful trading operations have continued to prosper.

Despite the current difficult conditions of high international liquidity and resultant low lending margins, income earned through our International Division—which remains the core of our international business—has increased considerably in 1980. The volatility of interest and exchange rates during the year, coupled with increasing political uncertainties, have provided a less-than-ideal environment for business expansion. The appreciation in sterling's exchange rate during the year (an average increase of 10 percent against the dollar) served to depress the growth in international earnings expressed in sterling terms. Despite this, the profit contributing from International Division itself in 1980 showed a rise over 1979 in excess of 40 percent.

\**Annual Report 1981.*

Opinions among Midland's senior executives varied widely. Said one:

International banking needs very sophisticated communications and is very competitive. You often get local chauvinism giving the domestic lender the advantage, and the decline in sterling has given U.S. banks the edge. . . . There are too many banks chasing the multinationals. We are better off sticking to our own customers and governments. . . . Our strategy is eclectic, a mix of representative offices, consortia, etc., fitted into our existing correspondent network. We have excellent personal relationships throughout the world with the important banks. There is our strength.

---

**EXHIBIT 6a**

---

## A CONSULTANT'S DIAGNOSIS OF CROCKER'S CULTURE

---

In 1982 Midland commissioned an in-depth study of the current strategic direction and corporate culture at Crocker National Bank. The comments below are excerpted from the findings of the study as reported to Midland's top management by the consultants and do not necessarily reflect Midland's own assessment of the situation.

1. Crocker is a collection of many businesses and individual management styles. This is partly the result of frequent changes in the bank's market focus and its senior management. Exhibits 6b and 6c trace some of these historical relationships.

2. There is a lack of institutionalized systems and processes at Crocker. For example, strategic planning fosters brainstorming and creativity not directly related to the bottom line. Financial systems reward agility with numbers, conservatism, and no errors, which tend to limit risk, defer strategic expenditures, and foster incrementalism. Human resource policies result in an insular style, where good news is rewarded and bad news penalized, personal relations are cultivated, and autonomy is sought. Finally, the prevailing marketing philosophy is that each customer must be satisfied, that all markets must be served, and that relationships are what is important.

3. Crocker has a leader-dependent organizational culture.

4. The organization's decision style is reactive and internally focused. Formal decision-making is highly centralized, and there is no broadly shared decision process among top managers. Turf issues make compromise difficult, and formal committee structure is not used effectively. The result is that information and requests for decisions flow up the ladder, while downward communication of decision criteria is poor.

5. Three subcultures can be identified at different organizational levels. For the Holding Company:
   - Short-term investment criteria
   - "Stand alone" evaluations
   - Make easy decisions first
   - Few constraints and risk aversion
   
   For the Bank:
   - Bottoms-up market direction
   - Deal-making orientation
   - Individual turfs protected
   - Firefighting
   
   For the SBUs (strategic business units into which the bank was divided):
   - Follow the market
   - Push decisions to the top
   - Manage based on personal relationships and "good effort"

6. Crocker's long-range objectives (6.5% asset growth rate, increases in market share, and a 27.3% growth in ROE) are ambitious. So are its declared strategies of focusing on high profit market segments, creating value through relationships, and being market and service oriented. But Crocker's short-term strategies and policies reinforce dysfunctional elements of the historical culture.

| Historical behavior | Desired behavior |
|---|---|
| • Bureaucratic | • Bias for action |
| • Poor communication | • Effective communication |
| • Incrementalism | • Long-term vision |
| • Averse to risk | • Aggressiveness |
| • Limited long-term commitment | • Loyalty |
| • Self-interest | • Accountability |
| • Cultivation of personal relations | • Market orientation |
| • High departmental loyalty | • Collaboration |
| • Autonomy | • Autonomy |
| • Process orientation | • Profit orientation |

7. In summary, the bank will be unfocused and adrift until a new leader is positioned or fundamental changes in culture and process occur.

## EXHIBIT 6b

### CROCKER'S KEY DECISIONS AND PERFORMANCE

Percent return on equity

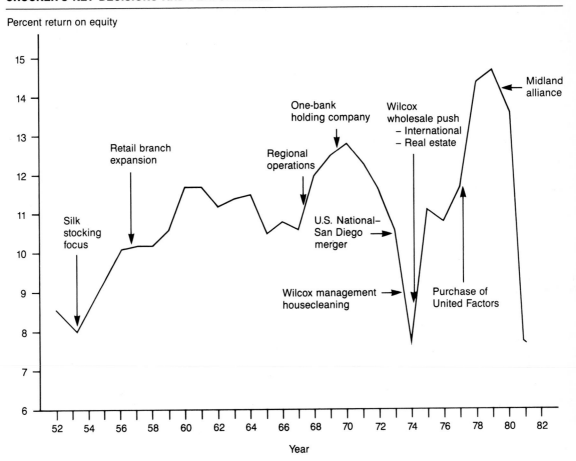

Year

Another executive argued that

[the banks] are entering into a period when expansion of international business through lending will slow down. We are not going to see anything approaching the expansion rate of the last five years in the next five. A new caution has been developing over recent months.

Commenting on the International Division's general strategy at the time, Geoffrey Taylor observed:

We must ride three horses at once—correspondent banking, EBIC, and our own international op-

erations, such as France. We must get bigger but we can't do it organically, therefore acquisition is the only route.

Malcolm Wilcox concluded:

I want to see the fulfillment of some of our main international ambitions, so that the Midland Bank will be seen as one of the world's major international banking groups. I want to see us providing a more comprehensive range of services for British industry, especially in the exporting area. On top of this, of course, we must be in America in a significant way. I don't really think there are

EXHIBIT 6c

**MANAGEMENT CONTROL PHILOSOPHY AT CROCKER OVER TIME**

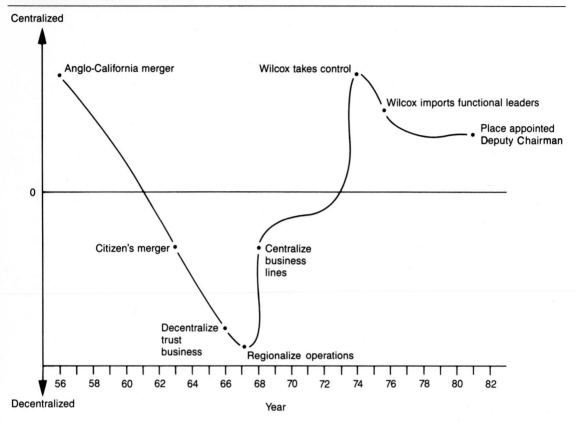

priorities. All the things referred to earlier must be done if we are to become truly international, and we will need the right people if we are to do it. There is much to be done.

The acquisition of Crocker marked a new era for the Midland Bank. Malcolm Wilcox, the guiding hand behind much of this strategy retired in July 1981, followed not long after by Stuart Graham in April 1982. Geoffrey Taylor became sole Chief Executive in 1982, with two Deputy Chief Executives, John Brooks, responsible for Domestic Banking, and John Harris, responsible for International. It was their responsibility to integrate the new acquisitions into a cohesive group and to tackle any unresolved issues. Crocker in particular would present a major challenge to Midland's new management, as it represented a significantly different managerial culture to that of Midland's (see Exhibit 6 for a view on this culture).

Exhibits 7 and 8 present additional information on the Midland's accounts and its organizational structure in 1981. Exhibit 9 lists the largest banks in the world by asset size in 1970 and 1980.

**EXHIBIT 7**

**STATISTICAL SUMMARY OF MIDLAND BANK, 1976–1980**

|  | 1976 | 1977 | 1978 | 1979 | 1980 |
|---|---|---|---|---|---|
| **Income statement (£ million)** | | | | | |
| Group profit before tax | 167 | 197 | 231 | 315 | 232 |
| Taxation | 68 | 85 | 88 | 123 | 62 |
| Profit attributable to operations | 93 | 106 | 119 | 166 | 169 |
| **Assets and liabilities (£ million)** | | | | | |
| Shareholders' funds | 676 | 766 | 960 | 1,286 | 1,349 |
| Shareholders' funds and loan capital | 907 | 1,049 | 1,286 | 1,582 | 1,789 |
| Current, deposit, other accounts | 10,441 | 11,754 | 13,826 | 18,042 | 22,906 |
| Customers' accounts, advances etc. | 7,261 | 8,425 | 10,094 | 13,137 | 17,040 |
| Total assets | 11,843 | 13,283 | 15,554 | 20,205 | 25,343 |
| **Miscellaneous** | | | | | |
| Shareholders* | 98,059 | 94,072 | 96,126 | 93,541 | 90,442 |
| Earnings per share (pence) | 71.3 | 81.3 | 88.8 | 117.4 | 102.7 |
| Dividends per share (pence) | 12.5 | 14.6 | 16.4 | 20.0 | 21.5 |
| Branches in the United Kingdom | 3,578 | 3,537 | 3,298 | 3,352 | 3,353 |
| Employees worldwide† | 63,200 | 65,100 | 69,400 | 72,000 | 77,900 |
| Average remuneration per employee (£/year) | 3,325 | 3,659 | 4,139 | 4,702 | 5,880 |
| Average base interest rate (%) | 11.10 | 8.86 | 9.09 | 13.68 | 16.30 |

*Number of shareholders registered at year end.
†Average weekly number of staff employed.

**EXHIBIT 8**

**MANAGEMENT STRUCTURE CHART AT APRIL 1979**

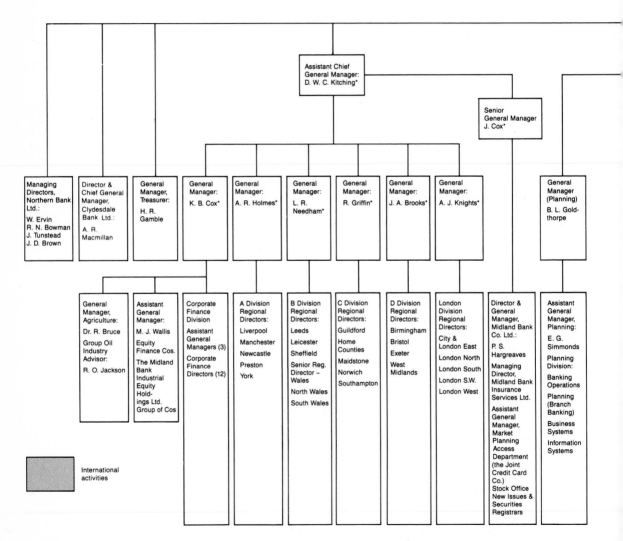

| | |
|---|---|
| | Assistant Chief General Manager: D. W. C. Kitching* |
| | Senior General Manager J. Cox* |

**Managing Directors, Northern Bank Ltd.:**
W. Ervin
R. N. Bowman
J. Tunstead
J. D. Brown

**Director & Chief General Manager, Clydesdale Bank Ltd.:**
A. R. Macmillan

**General Manager, Treasurer:**
H. R. Gamble

**General Manager:**
K. B. Cox*

**General Manager:**
A. R. Holmes*

**General Manager:**
L. R. Needham*

**General Manager:**
R. Griffin*

**General Manager:**
J. A. Brooks*

**General Manager:**
A. J. Knights*

**General Manager (Planning)**
B. L. Goldthorpe

**General Manager, Agriculture:**
Dr. R. Bruce
**Group Oil Industry Advisor:**
R. O. Jackson

**Assistant General Manager:**
M. J. Wallis
Equity Finance Cos.
The Midland Bank Industrial Equity Holdings Ltd. Group of Cos

**Corporate Finance Division**
Assistant General Managers (3)
Corporate Finance Directors (12)

**A Division Regional Directors:**
Liverpool
Manchester
Newcastle
Preston
York

**B Division Regional Directors:**
Leeds
Leicester
Sheffield
Senior Reg. Director – Wales
North Wales
South Wales

**C Division Regional Directors:**
Guildford
Home Counties
Maidstone
Norwich
Southampton

**D Division Regional Directors:**
Birmingham
Bristol
Exeter
West Midlands

**London Division Regional Directors:**
City & London East
London North
London South
London S.W.
London West

**Director & General Manager, Midland Bank Co. Ltd.:**
P. S. Hargreaves
Managing Director, Midland Bank Insurance Services Ltd.
Assistant General Manager, Market Planning
Access Department (the Joint Credit Card Co.)
Stock Office
New Issues & Securities Registrars

**Assistant General Manager, Planning:**
E. G. Simmonds
Planning Division:
Banking Operations
Planning (Branch Banking)
Business Systems
Information Systems

International activities

*Member of Credit Control Committee.

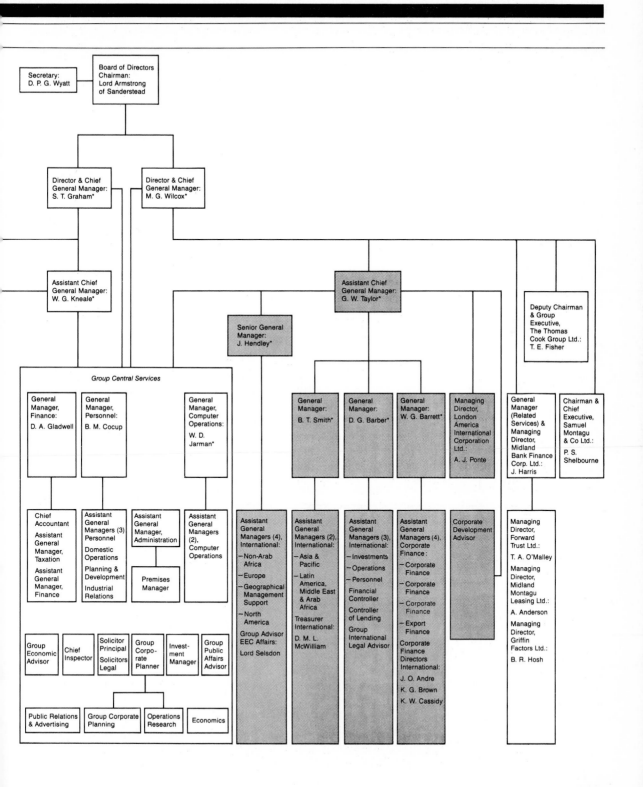

Secretary:
D. P. G. Wyatt

Board of Directors
Chairman:
Lord Armstrong
of Sanderstead

Director & Chief
General Manager:
S. T. Graham*

Director & Chief
General Manager:
M. G. Wilcox*

Assistant Chief
General Manager:
W. G. Kneale*

Assistant Chief
General Manager:
G. W. Taylor*

Senior General
Manager:
J. Hendley*

Deputy Chairman
& Group
Executive,
The Thomas
Cook Group Ltd.:
T. E. Fisher

*Group Central Services*

General
Manager,
Finance:
D. A. Gladwell

General
Manager,
Personnel:
B. M. Cocup

General
Manager,
Computer
Operations:
W. D.
Jarman*

General
Manager:
B. T. Smith*

General
Manager:
D. G. Barber*

General
Manager:
W. G. Barrett*

Managing
Director,
London
America
International
Corporation
Ltd.:
A. J. Ponte

General
Manager
(Related
Services) &
Managing
Director,
Midland
Bank Finance
Corp. Ltd.:
J. Harris

Chairman &
Chief
Executive,
Samuel
Montagu
& Co Ltd.:
P. S.
Shelbourne

Chief
Accountant
Assistant
General
Manager,
Taxation
Assistant
General
Manager,
Finance

Assistant
General
Managers (3)
Personnel
Domestic
Operations
Planning &
Development
Industrial
Relations

Assistant
General
Manager,
Administration

Premises
Manager

Assistant
General
Managers
(2),
Computer
Operations

Assistant
General
Managers (4),
International:
—Non-Arab
Africa
—Europe
—Geographical
Management
Support
—North
America
Group Advisor
EEC Affairs:
Lord Selsdon

Assistant
General
Managers (2),
International:
—Asia &
Pacific
—Latin
America,
Middle East
& Arab
Africa
Treasurer
International:
D. M. L.
McWilliam

Assistant
General
Managers (3),
International:
—Investments
—Operations
—Personnel
Financial
Controller
Controller
of Lending
Group
International
Legal Advisor

Assistant
General
Managers (4),
Corporate
Finance
—Corporate
Finance
—Corporate
Finance
—Corporate
Finance
—Export
Finance
Corporate
Finance
Directors
International:
J. O. Andre
K. G. Brown
K. W. Cassidy

Corporate
Development
Advisor

Managing
Director,
Forward
Trust Ltd.:
T. A. O'Malley
Managing
Director,
Midland
Montagu
Leasing Ltd.:
A. Anderson
Managing
Director,
Griffin
Factors Ltd.:
B. R. Hosh

Group
Economic
Advisor

Chief
Inspector

Solicitor
Principal
Solicitors
Legal

Group
Corpo-
rate
Planner

Invest-
ment
Manager

Group
Public
Affairs
Advisor

Public Relations
& Advertising

Group Corporate
Planning

Operations
Research

Economics

**317**

**EXHIBIT 9**

**LARGEST 25 BANKS IN THE WORLD BY ASSET SIZE, 1970 AND 1980**

| 1970 | | | 1980 | | |
|---|---|---|---|---|---|
| **Bank** | **Country** | **Total assets ($ billion)** | **Bank** | **Country** | **Total assets ($ billion)** |
| Bank of America | U.S. | 28.9 | Citicorp | U.S. | 109.6 |
| Citicorp | U.S. | 25.3 | Bank of America | U.S. | 106.8 |
| Chase Manhattan | U.S. | 24.0 | Crédit Agricole | France | 106.6 |
| Barclays | U.K. | 15.8 | Banque Nationale de Paris | France | 105.6 |
| National Westminster | U.K. | 13.0 | Crédit Lyonnais | France | 98.8 |
| Manufacturers Hanover | U.S. | 12.3 | Société Générale | France | 90.8 |
| Banca Nationale del Lavoro | Italy | 12.1 | Barclays | U.K. | 88.5 |
| Morgan Guaranty | U.S. | 11.8 | Deutsche Bank | Germany | 88.2 |
| Western Bancorp | U.S. | 11.3 | National Westminster | U.K. | 82.5 |
| Royal Bank of Canada | Canada | 11.0 | Dai Ichi Kangyo | Japan | 79.5 |
| Chemical Bank | U.S. | 10.8 | Chase Manhattan | U.S. | 75.7 |
| Banque Nationale de Paris | France | 10.6 | Fuji Bank | Japan | 70.3 |
| Canadian Imperial | Canada | 10.5 | Sumitomo Bank | Japan | 68.7 |
| Westdeutsche L. | Germany | 10.5 | Sanwa Bank | Japan | 64.2 |
| Deutsche Bank | Germany | 10.5 | Dresdner Bank | Germany | 62.8 |
| Crédit Lyonnais | France | 9.8 | Mitsubishi Bank | Japan | 62.2 |
| Bankers Trust | U.S. | 9.7 | **Midland Bank** | U.K. | 60.4 |
| Fuji Bank | Japan | 9.7 | Westdeutsche L. | Germany | 58.1 |
| Sumitomo Bank | Japan | 9.4 | Norinchukin | Japan | 55.7 |
| Mitsubishi Bank | Japan | 9.4 | Manufacturers Hanover | U.S. | 53.4 |
| Sanwa Bank | Japan | 9.2 | Cie. Financière de Paris et de Pays Bas | France | 52.6 |
| **Midland Bank** | U.K. | 8.8 | | | |
| Continental Illinois | U.S. | 8.7 | Banco de Brasil | Brazile | 52.2 |
| Banca Commerciale Italiana | Italy | 8.6 | Royal Bank of Canada | Canada | 51.1 |
| Bank of Montreal | Canada | 8.3 | Algemene Bank | Germany | 51.1 |
| | | | Commerz Bank | Germany | 50.7 |

*Source: The Banker.*

# PART FIVE

# Managing Political Risks at Home and Abroad

# General Electric and the Electric Iron Industry in 1982

In February 1982, General Electric was scheduled to close its plant in Ontario, California, and transfer all manufacturing responsibility for its electric iron business to facilities in Singapore, Brazil, and Mexico. Local reaction was strong, with the unions leading an effort to keep the plant open and local government and community groups seeking to put pressure on the company to reconsider. A church-backed group had introduced a stockholders' resolution accusing the company of "exporting jobs" and calling for a reversal of the decision. To aggravate matters further, Mike Wallace of CBS's *60 Minutes* began filming on a program to air in the coming months dealing with the problem of "run-away" plants and foreign sourcing and focusing on the Ontario plant closing.

## BACKGROUND

The story of the lightweight, or "ironless," iron began with an industrywide squeeze on margins

This case was written by Professor José de la Torre from public sources. Sections of it draw extensively from a study of the Worldwide Kitchen Electric Industry, prepared by Professors C. K. Prahalad and Gary Hammel at the University of Michigan, 1982.

in the middle 1970s. This squeeze produced a natural reaction: vigorous programs by all manufacturers to reduce costs. General Electric (GE), facing the most severe cost problems, was the leader in the fight to trim costs. In the early 1970s, GE had begun a program to redesign its electric iron. Its then-current product line was based on a very complex basic iron design which was interdependent with an obsolete manufacturing process. Although competitors produced irons in highly automated plants in the southern states, GE's irons were made in an increasingly inefficient California plant. Component manufacture and subassembly at GE's Ontario facility were highly mechanized, but final assembly was not. In the final assembly operation, workers manually inserted subassemblies containing more than 140 parts into the small body of the iron. As features had been added to the basic design through the years, this problem had become magnified. A gravity-fed, die-casting process for soleplates was also regarded as quite inefficient.

GE's response to these problems was a massive investment program (rumored to have cost between $15 and $20 million), to find a new, more producible iron. Out of that effort came an entirely new iron technology. Instead of an iron made essentially of metal, with a plastic handle, GE's F200 iron, as it was called, was made primarily of plastics—phenolic, polypropylene, and Lexan. The only metal visible on the compact iron was the cast aluminum soleplate. As compared to GE's metal iron, the redesigned plastic iron had a third fewer parts and subassemblies, weighed about a third less, and required one third fewer labor hours per thousand units produced. In manufacturing, the iron required fewer operations, which made it possible to use standardized processes for several production functions, and reduced indirect costs, material spoilage, and rework.

Production of the F200 commenced in 1977, a year behind GE's initial schedule. The iron was produced in an automated plant in North Carolina that housed production facilities for other GE housewares appliances. The F200 was GE's first entry in the compact-appliance market segment, previously the domain of Sunbeam. GE hoped that the F200 would provide experience in the new production technology and would yield better data on consumer acceptance of a plastic iron, thus reducing the risk of the full-size redesign program.

The delay in production start-up and product introduction for the F200 came in part as GE redirected its engineering talent and investment toward a renewed cost reduction program at its Ontario facility. During this time, with the company facing a severe cash crunch, the redesign program was halted to protect short-term cash flow. The delay of the F200 program also caused postponement of the F200's successor program—a redesign of GE's full-size iron. In 1979, GE began producing a full-size lightweight iron, the F300 series, in Singapore, and in early 1982 it was scheduled to open production facilities in Brazil and Mexico.

## CONSUMER PREFERENCES

From the beginning, consumers were quick to accept the new iron technology. The plastic iron's light weight was perhaps its best selling point. Although some people remained unconvinced that it was heat and moisture, and not weight, that removed wrinkles from clothes, most consumers appreciated the labor- and effort-saving benefits of the new irons. Other salient customer benefits of the plastic iron included attractive molded-in colors and streamlined, unified appearance; a skirt that stayed cool to the touch during ironing; a resistance to scratches, dents, and chipping; and a surface that didn't show fingerprints.

Demand for the new lightweight irons turned out to be greater than either GE or Proctor-Silex had anticipated. In 1979, lightweights captured about 15 percent of the market. Over 2 million lightweight irons were sold in 1980, up 50 percent from 1979, and for 1981, expectations were that 4 million plastic irons would be sold in the United States.

Of course, not all consumers or retailers accepted the switch to plastic with complete equanimity. One discount retailer said, "People still perceive metal irons as higher value, and many also see them offering a better quality than the plastic version." Another retailer termed the move to plastics "dumb." Nonetheless, consumers had clearly voted in the marketplace, and the plastic iron was an acceptable alternative to the 100-year-old metal iron. In 1981, GE and Proctor-Silex announced plans to discontinue the manufacture of metal irons for the U.S. market. Sunbeam, however, said it would continue to offer a metal iron, as well as plastic models.

## THE MARKET AND COMPETITION

The U.S. market for electric irons had seen significant changes in competitive conditions during the 1970s. Price pressures had been considerable, as evidenced by the fact that discount houses and mail-order chains had taken 52 percent of retail sales in the product. Between 1972 and 1980, manufacturers' prices increased by only 27 percent, while retail prices of irons rose by 46 percent, and the overall price index for personal consumption jumped by 78 percent. The high levels of saturation (99.9 percent in the United States and 95 to 98 percent in Europe) meant that nearly 90 percent of sales were for replacement in 1982. Exhibit 1 shows sales figures for recent years.

One result of these pressures was a rise in import shares in most countries; U.S. imports rose from 62,000 units in 1977, to nearly 2 million (18 percent of consumption) in 1980. In that year, the equivalent import shares in other countries were 48 percent in France, 43 percent in Germany, 24 percent in Italy, 48 percent in Spain, and 47 percent in the United Kingdom (see Exhibits 2 through 4).

By 1980, U.S. market shares were as follows:

| | |
|---|---|
| General Electric | 55% |
| Proctor-Silex | 24 |
| Sunbeam | 14 |
| Hamilton Beach | 4 |
| Others | 3 |
| | 100% |

## PRODUCTION COSTS

Industry executives generally agreed that the minimum economic plant size for manufacturing electric irons was in the range of 1.5 to 3.0 million units per year. The U.S. plants of Sunbeam and Proctor-Silex fell within this range, as did GE's foreign plants. Scale benefits were not thought to increase significantly above the 3 million unit mark. A GE executive remarked that even though the company's Ontario plant had produced almost twice as many irons as competitors' plants, GE had enjoyed no special learning curve or scale-derived cost advantages.

Outside the United States there were many manufacturers with relatively small plants. In Italy, Spain, Sri Lanka, Malaysia, Argentina, and other countries, manufacturers operated plants with as few as 300,000 units of annual capacity. Some industry executives believed these producers to be subsidized by their governments, but it was also true that the capital intensity of iron production could be reduced in low-wage countries and with it, minimum economic plant size. For example, it seemed likely that manufacturers producing irons in the Far East would use less automation than would manufacturers in high-wage countries. Thermostats and cordsets would be assembled by hand, soleplate assembly would be less automated, and so on. For most manufacturers, wherever they were producing, an upper limit of labor intensity was imposed by a need for consistent and high-quality production.

Efficiencies in iron production were not, then, primarily a function of the capital intensity of production, i.e., the capital costs of production machinery. The optimum volume for a single machine stamping soleplates, or molding handles, for example, was about 300,000 units per year. These were the most capital-intensive pieces of equipment required to produce irons. The minimum efficient increment of volume for a manufacturer was thus about 300,000 units.

But there were other scale benefits that accrued at production volumes above 300,000 units per year. Volume buying of materials was probably the most important. There was also the ability to automate processes at larger volumes, and in some cases this made it possible to reduce costs per unit for materials handling and certain production operations. Finally, it was also argued that a plant could not be efficiently operated at less than 70 percent capacity.

## WORLD SOURCING

GE executives argued that the high costs that would have been incurred in refitting and retooling its Ontario facility necessitated selection of another site for the production of the plastic irons. In selecting a production site for the new full-sized "world iron," the F300, GE considered Asheboro, North Carolina, Shannon, Ireland, and Singapore. The Singapore location looked as if it offered the greatest cost reduction benefits. It was estimated that product costs could be cut by 15 to 30 percent by manufacturing in Singapore.

The value-added structure for a typical elec-

EXHIBIT 1

## SALES OF ELECTRIC IRONS IN SELECTED COUNTRIES, 1976–1980

| | Units (thousands) | | | | | Percentage change from 1976 to 1980 |
|---|---|---|---|---|---|---|
| | 1976 | 1977 | 1978 | 1979 | 1980 | |
| North America | | | | | | |
| United States | 8,003 | 7,329 | 9,426 | 9,681 | 11,184 | 39.7 |
| Canada | 890 | 1,046 | 1,174 | 1,213 | 1,114 | 25.2 |
| Europe | | | | | | |
| Austria | 449 | 432 | 498 | 432 | 357 | (20.5) |
| Belgium | 739 | 684 | 681 | 650 | 682 | (7.3) |
| Denmark | 250 | 180 | 152 | 178 | 152 | (32.3) |
| Finland | 176 | 152 | 158 | 144 | 158 | (10.2) |
| France | 2,698 | 2,895 | 2,917 | 2,888 | 2,623 | (2.8) |
| West Germany | 3,535 | 3,833 | 3,696 | 3,365 | 3,047 | (13.8) |
| Greece | 171 | 228 | 273 | 279 | 310 | 81.3 |
| Italy | 2,929 | 3,155 | 3,410 | 2,844 | 2,839 | (3.1) |
| Netherlands | 598 | 596 | 680 | 650 | 670 | 12.0 |
| Norway | 66 | 93 | 78 | 121 | 100 | 51.5 |
| Portugal | 220 | 211 | 225 | 194 | 200 | (9.1) |
| Spain | 530 | 460 | 500 | 635 | 740 | 39.6 |
| Sweden | 468 | 362 | 346 | 320 | 376 | (19.7) |
| United Kingdom | 2,618 | 2,359 | 2,710 | 2,983 | 2,874 | 9.8 |
| Other developed countries | | | | | | |
| Australia | 747 | 882 | 784 | 679 | 767 | 2.7 |
| Japan | 2,894 | 2,723 | 2,513 | 2,794 | 3,100 | 7.1 |
| South Africa | 112 | 140 | 84 | 228 | 351 | 313.4 |
| South America | | | | | | |
| Argentina | 832 | 844 | 856 | 1,081 | 1,211 | 45.6 |
| Bolivia | 32 | 42 | 67 | 61 | 66 | 106.3 |
| Brazil | 1,350 | 1,498 | 1,648 | 1,796 | 1,958 | 45.0 |
| Chile | 105 | 119 | 136 | 156 | 179 | 70.5 |
| Colombia | 179 | 189 | 194 | 196 | 197 | 10.1 |
| Costa Rica | 41 | 64 | 90 | 68 | 61 | 48.8 |
| Guatemala | 33 | 54 | 60 | 67 | 75 | 127.3 |
| Mexico | 1,366 | 1,448 | 1,552 | 1,674 | 1,791 | 31.1 |
| Panama | 18 | 21 | 35 | 35 | 43 | 138.9 |
| Venezuela | 449 | 392 | 413 | 415 | 432 | (3.8) |
| Africa | | | | | | |
| Ethiopia | 10 | 10 | 11 | 5 | 4 | (60.0) |
| Liberia | 8 | 8 | 11 | 13 | 12 | 50.0 |
| Zaire | 14 | 18 | 15 | 18 | 16 | 14.3 |
| Middle East | | | | | | |
| Egypt | 61 | 68 | 77 | 86 | 99 | 62.3 |
| Iraq | 87 | 107 | 129 | 163 | 204 | 134.5 |
| Kuwait | 74 | 99 | 105 | 131 | 145 | 95.9 |
| Qatar | 9 | 14 | 8 | 6 | 5 | (44.4) |
| Far East | | | | | | |
| Hong Kong | 220 | 312 | 345 | 478 | 428 | 94.5 |
| Indonesia | 117 | 184 | 299 | 237 | 223 | 90.6 |
| Malaysia | 76 | 85 | 102 | 125 | 144 | 89.5 |
| Pakistan | 0.4 | n.a. | 0.5 | 0.4 | 0.6 | 50.0 |
| Philippines | n.a. | n.a. | 0.1 | 1.6 | 8.2 | n.a. |
| Singapore | 70 | 68 | 74 | 87 | 102 | 45.7 |

*Source:* Economic Research Council Statistics.

EXHIBIT 2

## TEN LARGEST IRON-EXPORTING COUNTRIES, 1976 AND 1980

|  | 1976 | | 1980 | |
|---|---|---|---|---|
|  | Exports (thousands) | Rank | Exports (thousands) | Rank |
| West Germany | 1,807 | 1 | 2,459 | 1 |
| Netherlands | 1,464 | 2 | 871 | 8 |
| United States | 1,251 | 3 | 1,458 | 4 |
| Italy* | 954 | 4 | 1,492 | 3 |
| Singapore* | 848 | 5 | 2,420 | 2 |
| France | 737 | 6 | 947 | 7 |
| Brazil* | 660 | 7 | 1,256 | 6 |
| United Kingdom | 605 | 8 | 280 | 10 |
| Spain | 560 | 9 | 516 | 9 |
| Japan* | 332 | 10 | 1,272 | 5 |
| Total | 9,218 | | 12,971 | |

*Countries whose volume growth was greater than mean growth for all countries.
*Note:* Does not include Eastern European countries.
*Source:* Economic Research Council Statistics.

EXHIBIT 3

## TEN LARGEST IRON-PRODUCING COUNTRIES, 1976 AND 1980

|  | 1976 | | | 1980 | |
|---|---|---|---|---|---|
|  | Production (thousands) | Rank |  | Production (thousands) | Rank |
| United States | 8,003 | 1 | United States | 9,780 | 1 |
| West Germany | 4,090 | 2 | Japan* | 4,344 | 2 |
| Japan | 3,435 | 3 | West Germany | 4,206 | 3 |
| Italy | 3,418 | 4 | Italy | 3,650 | 4 |
| United Kingdom | 2,671 | 5 | Brazil* | 3,179 | 5 |
| France | 2,528 | 6 | France | 2,300 | 6 |
| Brazil | 2,082 | 7 | Singapore* | 1,990 | 7 |
| Mexico | 1,371 | 8 | Mexico | 1,883 | 8 |
| Netherlands | 1,352 | 9 | United Kingdom | 1,813 | 9 |
| Spain | 870 | 10 | Argentina* | 989 | 10 |
| Total | 29,820 | | Total | 34,134 | |

*Countries that increased their rank between 1976 and 1980.
*Note:* Of 25 (noncommunist) countries reporting iron production for the years 1976 and 1980, the ten largest producing countries accounted for over 85% of total production.
*Source:* Economic Research Council Statistics.

**EXHIBIT 4**

## IRON IMPORTS TO THE UNITED STATES BY COUNTRY OF ORIGIN, 1978 TO 1981

|  | 1978 (thousands) | | 1979 (thousands) | | 1980 (thousands) | | 1981* (thousands) | |
|---|---|---|---|---|---|---|---|---|
|  | Units | Value | Units | Value | Units | Value | Units | Value |
| Canada | 8 | $ 73 | 17 | $ 169 | 29 | $ 262 | 9 | $ 109 |
| France |  |  | 7 | 120 | 16 | 122 |  |  |
| Germany |  |  |  |  |  |  |  |  |
| Hong Kong |  |  |  |  |  |  | 65 | 594 |
| Japan | 42 | 191 | 12 | 81 | 10 | 106 | 15 | 169 |
| Mexico |  |  |  |  |  |  | 22 | 169 |
| Singapore |  |  | 480 | 5,452 | 1,244 | 12,345 | 2,040 | 23,812 |
| Taiwan | 169 | 437 | 263 | 801 | 306 | 881 | 350 | 1,088 |
| Other | 22 | 134 | 19 | 111 | 16 | 144 | 14 | 132 |
| Total | 241 | 835 | 798 | 6,734 | 1,621 | 13,861 | 2,515 | 26,073 |

*Estimated from past year data.
*Source:* U.S. General Imports Schedule A (FT-150), U.S. Dept. of Commerce.

tric iron manufacturer in the United States was as follows:

| Manufacturer's net sales billed | 100% |
|---|---|
| Variable costs | 50 |
| Fixed costs | 25 |
| Merchandising | 15 |
| Net contribution margin | 10% |

In a U.S. plant, labor constituted from 30 to 40 percent of variable costs. By moving to a low-wage offshore production site, it was possible to decrease the labor component of the variable cost to around 10 percent (see Exhibit 5 for relative labor costs in a sample of countries). By reducing variable costs by 30 percent, it was

**EXHIBIT 5**

## LABOR COSTS FOR LIGHT ASSEMBLY (UNSKILLED) WORKERS IN SELECTED COUNTRIES AND LOCATIONS, JULY 1982

|  |  | Benefits | | |
|---|---|---|---|---|
| Location | Hourly rate | % | $ | Total labor costs |
| Pittsfield (U.S.) | $7.98 | 52 | $4.15 | $12.13 |
| Shannon (Ireland) | 2.99 | 33 | 1.00 | 3.99 |
| Milan (Italy) | 3.48 | 141 | 4.91 | 8.39 |
| Stratford-on-Avon (U.K.) | 3.49 | 30 | 1.06 | 4.55 |
| Hong Kong | 1.06 | 37 | 0.39 | 1.45 |
| Singapore | 0.87 | 48 | 0.42 | 1.29 |
| Manila (Philippines) | 0.46 | 70 | 0.32 | 0.78 |
| Bogota (Colombia) | 0.86 | 119 | 1.02 | 1.88 |
| Cerro Gordo (Mexico) | 1.27 | 69 | 0.88 | 2.15 |
| Sao Paolo (Brazil) | 1.01 | 83 | 0.84 | 1.85 |

*Note:* Monetary figures are U.S. $ at current exchange rates.

possible to cut the overall cost of the iron by 15 percent.

Singapore, unlike Ireland, had been granted tariff preferences by the United States and the European Community (EEC) under the Generalized System of Preferences (GSP), which allowed designated products from less-developed countries to enter the U.S. and EEC markets dutyfree. At the time GE decided on the Singapore location, the U.S. duty on irons amounted to 17 percent and the EEC tariff was about 11 percent. Another point in Singapore's favor was the fact that GE already had a plant there producing audio equipment. In 1978, GE installed 1.5 million units of F300 capacity in Singapore and began shipping the first F300 models to the United States in 1979.

In planning for the Singapore facility, GE executives realized that if consumers accepted the new plastic iron, a second production site for the F300 would become necessary. Although the Singapore facility could and would be expanded (to 3 million units, eventually), the terms of the tariff preferences granted by the GSP limited any manufacturer's imports into the United States from one country to 50 percent of industry volume in the preceding year.

Another issue was the danger of supply interruptions inherent in single-site manufacturing. After looking at several other sites, Brazil was selected. GE had been doing business in Brazil for most of the century and had a Brazilian affiliate which manufactured low- and medium-technology consumer and industrial products, including metal irons for the local market. In addition, many of GE's domestic-based businesses exported to Brazil.

In the last analysis, the decision to manufacture in Brazil turned on a package of export incentives offered by the Brazilian government. To participate in the "BEFIEX" program, as it was called, a company had to commit itself to a positive trade and international payments balance over a period of several years. At the time negotiations for entry into Brazil began, GE as a company was a net importer into Brazil. Yet company executives realized that exports from Brazil could be increased with the selection of Brazil as the second production site for the redesigned iron, plus the transfer of U.S. manufacturing capacity from California to Brazil. If export commitments from other GE businesses operating in Brazil could also be obtained, General Electric could easily become a net exporter from Brazil. On this basis, GE applied for BEFIEX incentives.

Progress toward the BEFIEX agreement was slow. During the course of negotiations, GE became concerned that if the agreement fell through, the company would find itself without a second production site and with inadequate capacity to serve a U.S. market that was rapidly converting to plastic. As a hedge, Mexico was chosen as a third site for the production of the F300. As in Brazil, GE had a Mexican affiliate as well as a border assembly operation that could easily handle the additional business.

GE's initial plans called for it to enter the European market with the redesigned iron. In late 1980 and early 1981, as capacity became available for such a move, the dollar was higher against most European currencies than it had been in many years, and the competitive situation in Europe was more intense than it had been in some time. GE had always had a relatively weak position in the European electric appliance markets and would need to rely on independent importers and distributors, which added another stage to the distribution channel and markup structure.

GE found it difficult to gain retail space with an unknown brand and a limited product line. Retailers looked for broad product lines, and other manufacturers gained shelf space for their irons on the basis of other, high-margin products they could offer the retailers. So, although the redesigned iron had seemed to offer an opportunity to penetrate new markets with an adaptable and cost competitive product, the project's major accomplishment (and still its first objective) was to provide a very cost competitive sourcing base for the U.S. market. The World

Iron Project, as it came to be known within General Electric, did not so much lead to irons for world markets as it led to world sourcing of irons for the U.S. market.

## GENERAL ELECTRIC IN 1982

In December of 1980, GE announced the retirement of its legendary chairman Reginald H. Jones and the appointment of John F. Welch, Jr., as chairman and CEO effective April 1, 1981. The changing of the guard at GE came as the U.S. economy headed into recession. Jones was leaving the helm of a very successful company, the tenth largest industrial corporation in the United States, highly diversified in consumer products and high-technology fields, with a AAA bond rating, a 19.5 percent return on equity, and $2.2 billion in cash reserves and securities.

Jack Welch was 45 years old on the day of his appointment. Having received a Ph.D. in chemical engineering from the University of Illinois in 1960, he joined GE's chemical development operations as a process development specialist. He rose through the technical ranks, becoming general manager of the Plastic Department in 1968. Five years later, he was named vice president and group executive of the Components and Materials Group, senior VP and executive for Consumer Products and Services Sector in 1977, and vice chairman and executive officer in 1979.

GE was known as a well-managed company. It was generally recognized as the birthplace of modern strategic management, having pioneered in the introduction of strategic business unit analysis and portfolio management techniques. GE probably had one of the most extensive and sophisticated strategic planning systems anywhere. But this excellent reputation and past performance was no guarantee of future success. Jack Welch would be challenged to meet the company's long-term objectives of increasing earnings per share 25 percent faster than the rate of growth in GNP in the face of

tougher competition and a continued slowdown in the growth of GE's traditional businesses.

## PROSPECTS FOR THE 1980s

In a presentation to the financial community at the Hotel Pierre in New York City on December 11, 1979, Jones pointed to how GE was "positioned to achieve the objective of sustained earnings growth, faster than the growth of the U.S. economy, in the 1980s."[1] He added: "General Electric is embarked on a course of large-scale innovation, productivity improvement, and business development for the 1980s, and we have built up the financial resources to bring that bold and entrepreneurial strategy to a successful conclusion."

The public promise of rapid growth carried major implications for strategic planning. At the annual general management conference in Belleair, which took place a month later, Daniel Fink, the newly appointed senior vice president for Corporate Planning and Development, questioned the adequacy of the existing strategic plans to meet Jones's growth challenge. He began by reviewing the recent and projected changes in business mix, and relative earnings as summarized in Exhibit 6. Armed with these figures, Fink then argued:

> Our implied strategy seems to be one of slowing, or even halting, the aggressive and successful diversification of the past decade. The vision of GE in 1984 that we get from the long-range forecasts is very much like GE in 1979. Same product mix, same international mix, same strategy of leveraging earnings over sales growth. How can that be? And, more important, do you believe it?
>
> It's that contradiction of a steady-state GE and a rapidly changing world that gives us, I think, the key strategic issue as we enter the '80s. How do we attain the vision now to reject that static fore-

---

[1] Parts of this section are taken from "General Electric— Strategic Position: 1981," Harvard Business School (9-381-174), 1981.

**EXHIBIT 6**

**GENERAL ELECTRIC BUSINESS MIX**

|  | 1968 | 1979 | 1984 | Projected change |
|---|---|---|---|---|
| Electrical equipment | 80% | 47% | 44% | −3% |
| Materials | 6 | 27 | 27 | 0 |
| Services | 10 | 16 | 19 | +3 |
| Transportation | 4 | 10 | 10 | 0 |
| International | 16 | 40 | 43 | +3 |

cast and then to take the strategic actions that will move us forward in the '80s, just as we did in the '70s?

The GE that Jack Welch took over in 1981 was in the midst of actively probing a panoply of new technology businesses. Lively discussions were being held in offices throughout the company on what GE should do about the factory of the future, the office of the future, the house of the future, the electric car, synthetic fuel, and the like. The list of opportunities seemed endless. Clearly, GE would have to make some hard choices. In this connection, Welch was reported to have said: "My biggest challenge will be to put enough money on the right gambles, and to put no money on the wrong ones. But I don't want to sprinkle money over everything."

## THE BUSINESSES IN 1982

In early 1982, General Electric was organized into seven major product groups and an international unit managing multi-industry operations. These groups were constituted as follows:

1. *Technical systems*—electronic and other high-technology products and services primarily for aerospace applications and defense; medical and communications equipment; and data processing, microelectronics and robots.
2. *Services and materials*—information services, engineering; main companies: General

Electric Credit Corporation, General Electric Venture Capital, and General Electric Information Services Company
3. *Power systems*—steam turbine-generators, gas turbines, nuclear power reactors and nuclear fuel assemblies, transformers, switchgear, meters, and installation and maintenance engineering services
4. *Industrial products*—components (appliance controls, small motors, and electronic components); industrial capital equipment (construction, automation, and transportation); maintenance, inspection, repair and rebuilding of electric, electronic, and mechanical apparatus; main company: General Electric Supply Company
5. *Consumer products*—major appliances, air-conditioning equipment, lighting products, housewares and audio products and services, television receivers, and broadcasting and cablevision services
6. *Natural resources*—mining of coal, principally in Australia (Utah International, Inc.); uranium (Pathfinder Mines Corporation); iron and copper, oil and natural gas production (Ladd Petroleum Corporation); ocean shipping; and land acquisition and development
7. *Aircraft engines*—jet engines, defense electronics, missiles, nuclear-propelled engines, radars, etc.
8. *Foreign multi-industry operations*—foreign affiliates which manufactured products primarily for sale in their respective home mar-

kets (Canadian General Electric Company Ltd. was the largest of the multi-industry affiliates)

Sales and net earnings at GE increased by 9 percent in 1981 over 1980; return on equity was 19.1 percent, and total borrowings fell to less than 20 percent of capital (see Exhibit 7 for more detailed financial statements). Against this background, Welch, in his annual message to the stockholders, described four programs launched during the preceding year destined to "position" the company for the future:

1. A major reorganization (the first since 1977) realigned the business sectors as described above. The main objective was to focus managerial attention and responsibility in growth areas such as electronics and the service businesses. GE's domestic employment increased to 289,000 in 1981 from 285,000 in the previous year, with worldwide employment growing from 402,000 to 404,000 in the same years. Employee training and development was highlighted as a major corporate activity. Over 30,000 employees participated

---

### EXHIBIT 7

**SUMMARY OF FINANCIAL RESULTS, 1977 TO 1981**

| | 1981 | 1980 | 1979 | 1978 | 1977 |
|---|---|---|---|---|---|
| **Operating results ($ million)** | | | | | |
| Sales | 27,240 | 24,959 | 22,461 | 19,654 | 17,519 |
| Cost of goods sold | 18,945 | 17,751 | 15,991 | 13,915 | 12,288 |
| Selling, gen., & adm. | 4,966 | 4,258 | 3,716 | 3,205 | 3,011 |
| Depreciation, etc. | 882 | 707 | 624 | 576 | 522 |
| Operating margin | 2,447 | 2,243 | 2,130 | 1,958 | 1,698 |
| Other income/charges | 213 | 250 | 261 | 195 | 191 |
| Income taxes | (962) | (958) | (953) | (894) | (773) |
| Minority interest | (46) | (21) | (29) | (29) | (28) |
| Net earnings | 1,652 | 1,514 | 1,409 | 1,230 | 1,088 |
| **Balance sheet results ($ million)** | | | | | |
| Current assets | 10,804 | 9,883 | 9,384 | 8,755 | 7,865 |
| Current liabilities | 8,734 | 7,592 | 6,872 | 6,175 | 5,417 |
| Net working capital | 2,070 | 2,291 | 2,512 | 2,580 | 2,448 |
| Short-term borrowing | 1,171 | 1,093 | 871 | 960 | 772 |
| Long-term debt | 1,059 | 1,000 | 947 | 994 | 1,284 |
| Minority interests | 166 | 154 | 152 | 151 | 132 |
| Shareholders' equity | 9,128 | 8,200 | 7,362 | 6,587 | 5,943 |
| Total assets | 20,942 | 18,511 | 16,644 | 15,036 | 13,697 |
| **Per-share values ($)** | | | | | |
| Net earnings | 7.26 | 6.65 | 6.20 | 5.39 | 4.79 |
| Dividends declared | 3.15 | 2.95 | 2.75 | 2.50 | 2.10 |
| Market price range | 70–51 | 63–44 | 55–45 | 58–44 | 57–47 |
| **Other figures** | | | | | |
| Earnings as % of sales | 6.1 | 6.1 | 6.3 | 6.3 | 6.2 |
| Earnings as % of equity | 19.1 | 19.5 | 20.2 | 19.6 | 19.4 |
| Number of shares (million) | 227.5 | 227.5 | 227.2 | 228.0 | 227.2 |
| Investment ($ million) | 2,025 | 1,948 | 1,262 | 1,055 | 823 |
| Total employment (thousands) | 404 | 402 | 405 | 401 | 384 |

*Source:* Annual reports.

## EXHIBIT 8

**FINANCIAL RESULTS BY INDUSTRY SEGMENT, 1979 TO 1981** ($ Million)

| | Revenues | | | Operating profit | | | Assets | | |
|---|---|---|---|---|---|---|---|---|---|
| | 1981 | 1980 | 1979 | 1981 | 1980 | 1979 | 1981 | 1980 | 1979 |
| Services & materials | 2,593 | 2,230 | 1,991 | 606 | 518 | 475 | 3,224 | 2,766 | 2,278 |
| Consumer products | 6,643 | 6,342 | 5,990 | 549 | 615 | 617 | 2,926 | 2,656 | 2,500 |
| Industrial products | 4,871 | 4,690 | 4,375 | 495 | 438 | 335 | 2,074 | 2,031 | 1,916 |
| Natural resources | 1,722 | 1,374 | 1,260 | 493 | 404 | 431 | 2,359 | 2,109 | 1,679 |
| Power systems | 5,982 | 5,815 | 5,124 | 446 | 366 | 349 | 3,718 | 3,702 | 3,381 |
| Technical systems | 3,979 | 3,252 | 2,761 | 249 | 230 | 215 | 2,309 | 1,713 | 1,328 |
| Aircraft engines | 2,950 | 2,660 | 2,190 | 322 | 275 | 185 | 1,951 | 1,703 | 1,225 |
| | 28,740 | 26,363 | 23,691 | 3,160 | 2,846 | 2,607 | 18,561 | 16,680 | 14,307 |
| Intercompany accounts | (886) | (840) | (711) | (99) | (39) | (42) | 2,381 | 1,831 | 2,337 |
| Financial charges | — | — | — | (401) | (314) | (258) | — | — | — |
| Total | 27,854 | 25,523 | 22,980 | 2,660 | 2,493 | 2,391 | 20,942 | 18,511 | 16,644 |

*Note:* Products and services of multi-industry foreign affiliates are classified by appropriate industry segments.
*Source:* Annual reports.

## EXHIBIT 9

**FINANCIAL RESULTS BY GEOGRAPHIC SEGMENTS, 1979 TO 1981** ($ Million)

| | Revenues | | | Net earnings | | | Assets | | |
|---|---|---|---|---|---|---|---|---|---|
| | 1981 | 1980 | 1979 | 1981 | 1980 | 1979 | 1981 | 1980 | 1979 |
| United States | 22,697 | 20,750 | 18,859 | 1,373 | 1,175 | 1,120 | 16,004 | 13,732 | 12,693 |
| Far East including Australia | 1,624 | 1,277 | 1,183 | 228 | 169 | 174 | 1,187 | 1,090 | 842 |
| Other areas of the world | 4,798 | 4,459 | 3,814 | 68 | 181 | 120 | 3,902 | 3,808 | 3,207 |
| Elimination of intracompany transactions | (1,265) | (963) | (876) | (17) | (11) | (5) | (151) | (119) | (98) |
| Total | 27,854 | 25,523 | 22,980 | 1,652 | 1,514 | 1,409 | 20,942 | 18,511 | 16,644 |

*Note:* U.S. revenues above include export sales to unaffiliated customers of $3,681 million in 1981, $3,781 million in 1980, and $2,772 million in 1979, and royalty and licensing income from unaffiliated foreign sources.
*Source:* Annual reports.

in courses organized by the GE Management Development Institute in Crotonville, N.Y., and hundreds of local programs were conducted by GE affiliates throughout the world. The aim was to select the best people and structures to fit the strategic needs of growth opportunities and problem businesses and to reward successful performance.

2. Portfolio repositioning was undertaken to strengthen the core businesses, which must provide the cash-generating capacity to finance future growth and diversification, and to develop key positions in "engineered materials, information and financial services, construction services, medical systems and natural resources."

3. Program investments were being undertaken to provide the infrastructure (e.g., computer software and electronics technology) with which to tackle the "megamarket of factory automation" in the future.

4. A major effort was launched to establish three concepts as part of the GE culture: "reality" (an awareness of the requirements of the marketplace and an understanding of corporate social responsibilities); "excellence" (quality in products, services and performance); and "ownership" (responsibility for one's actions and decisions).

Exhibits 8 and 9 summarize industry segment and geographic segment financial information as reported by GE for 1979–1981.

# Honeywell in France (A)

In November 1981, Edson Spencer, chairman and chief executive officer of Honeywell, Inc., was contemplating the start of negotiations between Honeywell and St. Gobain, the two principal joint venture partners in CII-Honeywell Bull (CII-HB). Spencer had become increasingly pessimistic about the general business climate in France since the election of Socialist Party leader François Mitterrand to the presidency in May 1981; however, he had also been recently informed by high French government officials that Honeywell's role in the Bull joint venture could yet be rewarding. This was possible in spite of the fact that St. Gobain was being nationalized and that the role of Honeywell in the joint venture would have to change as a result. Given these recent conversations, Spencer decided to explore the possibility of a mutually beneficial relationship through negotiations.

In this context, a number of questions were weighing on Spencer's mind: What should Honeywell's negotiating strategy be? What were the relative bargaining strengths between Honeywell and the French side? What were the intentions and options of French government officials, who were always in the background behind St. Gobain? How should Honeywell's negotiation effort be organized, and what should its negotiating tactics be? Answers to these questions required analysis of CII-HB's importance to and position within Honeywell, the history of the computer industry in France, and the backgrounds of the individuals involved in the actual negotiations.

## HONEYWELL, INC.

Honeywell was formed as the Minneapolis Honeywell Regular Co. after a 1927 merger between Minneapolis Heat Regular Co. and Honeywell Heating Specialties Co. (Its present name was adopted in 1964.) Originally, therefore, Honeywell was a specialist in thermostatic controls. Over time and through subsequent acquisitions, Honeywell broadened its activities into measuring instrumentation, pneumatic controls, and avionics. Control systems, however, remained its core business, comprising 46 percent of total

This case was written by Charles R. Kennedy, Jr., Associate Professor of Business Administration. Copyright © 1984 by The Colgate Darden Graduate School Sponsors, Charlottesville, Virginia. Revised December 1987.

sales and 59 percent of total profits as the company moved into the 1980s. Edson Spencer and past Honeywell chairmen, in fact, had all been the previous heads or executive vice presidents of Honeywell Control Systems.

Diversification into the computer business started in 1955 and was furthered by the 1965 acquisition of Computer Control Company. International activity followed immediately afterward with the formation of Honeywell Europe in 1966. Computers or information processing systems remained a minor part of Honeywell, however, until the 1970 purchase of General Electric's Information Systems Equipment Division. Nevertheless, Honeywell Information Systems (HIS) never surpassed control systems in relative sales or profits. As the company entered the 1980s, computers and information systems comprised 34 percent and 32 percent of sales and profits, respectively. Increasingly, however, Honeywell saw a major area of future competitive strength as being based in the synergy between control and computer systems, with one of the main battlefields focused on the rapidly growing office automation market.

## BACKGROUND OF THE COMPUTER INDUSTRY IN FRANCE: BEFORE CII-HB

CII-HB had its roots in a French computer company called Compagnie des Machines Bull (CMB), which started as a small punch-card machine producer in the 1930s. By the late 1950s, CMB had become a relatively large and prosperous computer firm, with an average annual increase in sales of 25 percent between 1953 and 1960. In fact, by 1960 CMB employed 11,000 workers, making it one of the top 30 employers in France, and held about one-third of the French computer market, which was the largest share of any domestic firm. CMB also held about 10 percent of the computer market in Western Europe. CMB was such a success and stimulus to French national pride that it was often called "the Brigitte Bardot of French industry."

During the early 1960s, however, serious problems for CMB began to emerge, most no-

tably the challenge posed by International Business Machines (IBM), who along with other U.S.-based computer firms expanded very rapidly in Europe during the post–World War II period. IBM in particular offered European computer customers new, technologically advanced mainframes that CMB lacked. In response, CMB had no choice but to develop a "state of the art" mainframe in order to compete with the Americans. Such product development, however, was difficult to achieve technologically and enormously expensive.

These obstacles to product development were greatly aggravated by CMB's relationship with the French "Gaullist" government. CMB was largely a family-owned and -managed corporation that had had strong ties to the Vichy government during World War II. As a result, the French government under the leadership of Charles de Gaulle refused to give CMB any financial support or special development contracts. In fact, several large loans to CMB that required Ministry of Finance approval were turned down during the early 1960s, a time in which research and development capital was critical. In order to survive in an increasingly competitive world, CMB was forced to look for other sources of capital.

General Electric had decided to enter the computer market in 1959 and began selling computers in France via limited export sales in 1962. Given GE's general lack of international experience, particularly in the computer business, they preferred to expand their operations in Europe through acquisitions or joint ventures with established firms. GE had offered to buy a 20 percent equity position in CMB in 1962 at the prevailing market price, along with promises of massive financial and technical support. CMB initially refused, but by the end of 1963, CMB's competitive position relative to IBM had deteriorated to such an extent that negotiations with GE were renewed. An agreement that largely duplicated the 1962 offer was then reached.

Before the deal could be consummated, however, Ministry of Finance approval, which in actuality meant President Charles de Gaulle's approval, was needed. The French President's decision, which came in early 1964, was an emphatic rejection of an "American solution" to CMB's problems, primarily because computers were perceived to be a vitally important strategic industry. Of course, de Gaulle was also generally concerned with the growing American business presence in Europe, which he felt was aided by the U.S. government's international monetary policies, but he was particularly angered by the U.S. government's recent embargo on computer sales to the French military-nuclear industry. In other words, U.S. business dominance of the computer industry had political-military implications that de Gaulle was unwilling to accept.

CMB was then forced to try a "French solution" by increasing its ties to domestic banking and electronic firms. This attempt proved futile, however, since French banks refused to back CMB with the funds it needed because of the company's weak financial and technological position. As a GE negotiator observed: "They [CMB] felt that even if necessary financing were forthcoming from French sources, this still wouldn't have been enough to make the company safe in the face of the onslaught of IBM competition. They had to have some stronger backing than that."[1] CMB still needed the capital and technical support that only a major firm like GE could offer.

By April 1964 the French government had apparently come to the same conclusion; it reversed its earlier decision, which it had termed "irrevocable", and now accepted "in principle" a GE-CMB joint venture. During the summer of 1964, a final agreement was struck and approved by the French government on terms much more favorable to GE than before. Instead of a 20 percent minority equity share, GE purchased 51 percent of the marketing and 49 percent of the manufacturing arms of GE-Bull (two

separate corporate entities were created) for a price that was 25 percent less per share than had been offered six months earlier. Such a corporate structure and equity share were very much to the advantage of GE, for the company was mainly interested in CMB's extensive European marketing network (as was Honeywell six years later). Most of GE's computer manufacturing and product development would be centered in Phoenix, Arizona. As one GE executive stated about the 1964 merger, "the main point is that we are acquiring a first class distribution system. We will integrate production and distribution to make the best use of the strengths of both companies."[2]

In spite of favorable entry terms, GE's computer business in France, and worldwide, did not prove very successful. Between mid-1964 and early 1967, for example, GE invested around $200 million in Bull's operations. Each and every quarter in that time period showed negative operating profits. GE's reaction was retrenchment: Headquarters recommended a 25 percent reduction in Bull's labor force, or the lay-off of 2,500 workers, and the dropping of the Gamma 140 computer line, which had been designed by CMB before the GE merger. French protests over "foreign domination" ensued and were aggravated by a renewed U.S. computer embargo to the French nuclear industry. The French government reacted to these developments by announcing that it no longer considered GE-Bull even a quasi-French computer firm (in fact GE now held 66 percent of the equity as a result of capital contributions in the 1964–1967 period), and thus GE-Bull would no longer receive preferential treatment in government purchases or R&D assistance. Labor and product cuts were also implemented by the fall of 1967, and it was in this atmosphere that William R. Hart became managing director of Bull's operations.

GE-Bull's retrenchment policy proved financially successful under Hart's management. By

---

[1]"Business around the Globe," *Fortune*, September 1964, p. 59.

[2]*Ibid.*

1969, Bull reported its first net profit, $650,000. Nevertheless, GE finally decided in February 1970 that the company should withdraw from the computer business worldwide and focus its resources on nuclear, jet engine, and other "core" electrical products instead. Although GE's chairman denied it, IBM simply proved to be too strong a competitor to warrant the risks and massive capital infusions required in the computer industry.

By May 1970, GE and Honeywell announced what many analysts regard as a "textbook" merger. It combined GE's mainframe technology and European marketing network with Honeywell's compatible computer line and management experience. Together, GE's and Honeywell's computer businesses held a 10 percent worldwide market share, making it the "undisputed number 2" behind IBM. In France, Honeywell Bull had around 20 percent of the market versus IBM's 52 percent. Of course, French government approval was needed for the Honeywell arrangement. Such approval was quickly given after Honeywell agreed to merge much of its other European operations into Bull's orbit. In fact, such a merger was gladly accepted by Honeywell, because Bull's marketing and manufacturing network dwarfed what Honeywell already had in place within the Common Market.

In October 1970 the GE and Honeywell merger was finalized with the creation of Honeywell Information Systems, 81.5 percent owned by Honeywell and 18.5 percent by GE. (GE's 18.5 percent was to be sold to Honeywell by 1980, which in fact occurred.) HIS represented the entire computer operations of both Honeywell and GE and included GE's 66 percent ownership of Bull.

HIS quickly proved a financial success. As Honeywell's *1971 Annual Report* stated, "Earnings of the company were up 12 percent on a sales increase of 1 percent. . . . Improved earnings in our worldwide computer business contributed significantly to this performance. This was due in part to the fact that we have begun

to realize the benefits we foresaw in merging GE's computer operations with ours." HIS revenue in 1971 had climbed to $950 million or 47 percent of total Honeywell revenue, versus a premerger (1969) level of $763 million in computer-related sales and revenue, which was only 24 percent of the corporate total. Over half of 1971 HIS revenues, moreover, came from foreign computer operations, primarily those of Honeywell Bull. The French joint venture, in fact, marketed over half of its production in 38 countries outside France.

Clearly Honeywell had taken a huge step toward establishing a major multinational presence. As Honeywell's *1970 Annual Report* stated, "We stepped up our evolution as an international company through the merger. We now employ 42,000 people outside of the U.S. (versus under 20,000 before 1970) and our volume there was $662 million or 34 percent of total sales (versus under 20 percent in pre-merger years). About two-thirds of the computer operations that we acquired from GE are (in fact) overseas."

The internationalization of Honeywell continued to bear fruit in subsequent years, although the recession years of 1974 and 1975 crimped sales and earnings for HIS and Honeywell in general, as revealed in Exhibit 1. It was within this financial backdrop that intensive negotiations concerning the future status of Honeywell Bull took place in France during 1975.

During the 1960s, in conjunction with the falling out between the French government and GE-Bull, another "national champion" in the computer industry had been created, Compagnie Internationale pour l'Informatique (CII). The French government had merged three small computer firms and provided CII massive infusions of capital and preferential purchases in the hope of challenging the U.S. multinationals. By 1973 the effort was clearly faltering, as CII had not gained above 10 percent of the French market. There was some discussion within the Gaullist government of President Pompidou to merge CII with Honeywell Bull, but an "all-

### EXHIBIT 1

**TOTAL REVENUE AND EARNINGS BEFORE TAXES**

|                              | 1972  | 1973  | 1974  | 1975  |
| ---------------------------- | ----- | ----- | ----- | ----- |
| Revenue                      |       |       |       |       |
| HIS ($ million)              | 1,061 | 1,177 | 1,233 | 1,324 |
| Increase (%)                 | 12    | 11    | 5     | 7     |
| Honeywell Inc. ($ million)   | 2,125 | 2,391 | 2,626 | 2,760 |
| Increase (%)                 | 9     | 13    | 10    | 5     |
| HIS as percent of total      | 50    | 49    | 47    | 48    |
| Earnings before taxes        |       |       |       |       |
| HIS ($ million)              | 54    | 75    | 53    | 57    |
| Honeywell Inc. ($ million)   | 169   | 209   | 188   | 173   |
| HIS as percent of total      | 32    | 36    | 28    | 33    |

*Source:* Honeywell, Inc., *10-K Annual Report,* 1973, p. 8; 1974 and 1975, pp. 9–11.

European solution" was attempted instead. Consequently, with government prodding, CII in mid-1973 formed a French-German-Dutch combine called Unidata, with Siemens of Germany and Philips of Holland as partners.

Unidata did not meet French expectations or interests. CII sold virtually no machines in its partners' home countries, while Siemens and Philips made substantial inroads into the French market. As a result, the French government withdrew from Unidata and negotiated a merger of CII and Honeywell Bull by mid-1975, thus effectively ending the attempt for an all-European solution.

Honeywell's *1975 Annual Report* listed the benefits of this agreement: (1) a substantial increase in its share of the French computer market from around 20 to 25 percent; (2) French government subsidies of $270 million over four years; (3) French government promises of preferential purchases totaling $1 billion; and (4) a $58 million payment to Honeywell for decreasing its equity share from 66 to 47 percent in the newly merged company, which represented a net gain of $14.8 million.

Other benefits, which the *1975 Annual Report* did not mention, were significant as well. Honeywell retained certain specific management rights, including a veto power over capital increases, mergers, acquisitions, and other significant investments. Honeywell also had the right to appoint the chief executive officer, although the managing director would, by subsequent practice, always be a French national. In addition, Honeywell obtained a comprehensive set of security guarantees designed to protect the value of its equity share, namely a French legal commitment to buy Honeywell's 47 percent in CII-HB at book value in the event of nationalization. This provision was particularly important because in the 1974 presidential elections, François Mitterrand had campaigned for the nationalization of the French computer industry and lost by only 400,000 votes. The concept of a common product line was also agreed to and would be implemented by a technical committee, the chair and majority of which were assigned to Honeywell. Common product line development was augmented by a royalty-free, cross-licensing agreement and by a "mirror-image" distribution system arrangement in which each party agreed to market each other's products based on the present status quo. From the view of Honeywell and the French government, the result of this merger was a big plus for both parties.

## THE PRE-1981 HISTORY OF CII-HB: FINANCES, PRODUCT DEVELOPMENT, AND POLITICS

As the 1975 negotiations were underway, Bill Hart, the old managing director of the GE-Bull joint venture in the late-1960s, was lured away from GE to become HIS's senior vice president. One of his principal responsibilities was to oversee CII-HB relations. CII-HB's performance and importance to HIS are reflected in Exhibit 2.

Honeywell's earnings per share rose $1.60 in 1980. As Edson Spencer, Honeywell's chairman and CEO noted, "In 1980 our equity share in the French company's operating profit increased Honeywell earnings by $1.45 per share."

In the area of product development, a major dissimilarity between HIS and Bull was found in the large-scale mainframe business (memory capacity of over 1 million bytes or at least 1 megabyte). Bull's large mainframes were based on the old CII Iris 80 line, which was a product development undertaken during Unidata days. As a replacement for the Iris 80, Bull was developing two new large mainframes, the so-called Y4 and Y5. These two large-scale systems, however, were viewed as a halfway step in the project to develop a completely common product line between HIS and Bull by the mid-1980s. While politically and commercially viewed as necessary, potential product competition and incompatibility existed in the interim between Bull's large mainframes and HIS's systems.

At the medium-scale mainframe level, similar differences between HIS and Bull were present. Bull was the sole manufacturer of the Level 64 line, which had a memory size of between 192K bytes and 768K bytes, depending on the particular model. HIS produced instead a Level 66 line of machines that had a memory size that started at the upper end of the Level 64 but reached a top capacity of four megabytes. The Level 66 thus included a large-scale and medium-size mainframe. Potential competition, therefore, existed at the upper end of the 64s with the lower end of the 66s.

Attempts to avoid such competition leading to HIS-Bull conflicts were based on two policies or actions. First, Bull by 1980 was producing and marketing Level 66s as well as Level 64s within its own sales territory. Second, marketing guidelines were established for selling Bull 64s in the United States and other HIS markets. For mid-range systems, a Level 64 would be sold if that customer did not need greater expansion capacity in the future. If such expansion was highly probable, then Level 66s were sold instead.

The minicomputer business also experienced close cooperation. In 1975 the Level 6 system was introduced by HIS, with manufacturing extended to France in 1978. Although Bull called these the "mini-6s," they were the same machines as produced by HIS. These minicomputer systems were becoming increasingly crit-

---

**EXHIBIT 2**

**SELECTED FINANCIAL RECORDS OF CII-HB**

|  | 1976 | 1977 | 1978 | 1979 | 1980 |
|---|---|---|---|---|---|
| Totals in $ millions |  |  |  |  |  |
| Net assets | 230 | 250 | 293 | 354 | 450 |
| Total revenue | 655 | 765 | 1,486 | 1,215 | 990 |
| Net income | 8.5 | 5.6 | 21.1 | 29.9 | 32.4 |
| Net Income in % |  |  |  |  |  |
| CII-HB's percent of HIS | 40.7 | 15.1 | 38.6 | 36.0 | 31.2 |
| CII-HB's percent of Honeywell, Inc. | 7.5 | 3.9 | 10.5 | 11.5 | 11.0 |

*Source:* Honeywell, *Annual Reports,* 1977–1980.

**EXHIBIT 3**

**R&D EXPENDITURES AND INTERCOMPANY SALES, CII-HB AND HIS**

|  | 1976 | 1977 | 1978 | 1979 | 1980 |
|---|---|---|---|---|---|
| R&D expenditures |  |  |  |  |  |
| CII-HB ($ million) | 69.4 | 91 | 108 | 127.9 | 129.6 |
| Total HIS ($ million) | 331.5 | 397.7 | 431.7 | 551.4 | 720.6 |
| CII-HB as percent of HIS total | 20.9 | 22.9 | 25.0 | 23.2 | 18.0 |
| Intercompany sales ($ million) |  |  |  |  |  |
| HIS sales to CII-HB | 74.1 | 89.9 | 93.6 | 113.5 | 131.1 |
| CII-HB sales to HIS | 66.6 | 69.6 | 51.3 | 48.2 | 48.8 |

*Source:* Honeywell, *Annual Reports,* 1977–1980.

ical to HIS and Bull as add-ons to medium-scale and large-scale mainframes.

This high degree of product development and marketing cooperation can be seen in the relative R&D expenditures and product flows between HIS and Bull, shown in Exhibit 3. All these financial and product/market factors were critical ingredients of negotiating strategy between Honeywell and the French government in 1981–1982.

Political pressures on Honeywell's role in Bull had been mounting well before the 1981 presidential election. Protests had been heard since the inception of the 1975–1976 merger between CII and Honeywell Bull. The French Communist Party termed the deal "sabotage," while the Gaullist party (UDR) called it a deception. These criticisms were in large part, of course, political posturing against President Valery Giscard d'Estaing and his UDF coalition, a French conservative but internationally minded party. In another sense, however, these criticisms reflected a genuine debate over who, the French nation or Honeywell, had benefited most from the deal. Giscard and Honeywell naturally argued that both parties had benefited to a substantial degree—after all, IBM was the common threat to the aspirations of each side.

IBM certainly saw the Honeywell-French government relationship as a coalition formed against its interests. Since the CII merger with Honeywell, "IBM's share of government com-

puter orders [in France] had dropped steadily, from 37 to 26 percent, according to IBM officials. They attribute the decline to French government support of CII-Honeywell Bull." In addition to government controls, IBM asserted that they had lost some private contracts "because of government pressure." IBM decided not to protest this alleged favortism formally because as an IBM spokesman remarked, "as they say in the French Foreign Legion, things could always get worse."[3]

In spite of possible Honeywell–French government collusion against IBM, the French political challenge to CII-HB increased substantially during the parliamentary elections of 1978, when Giscard's moderate-conservative coalition narrowly defeated the leftist alliance. As the Honeywell president stated afterward, he "was very relieved" by the election results because "we would have lost our business" if Mitterrand and the leftists had won. The 1978 elections, however, did not end or reduce the threat to Honeywell's French operation. During 1979, for example, St. Gobain (with tacit government approval) bought out Compagnie Général d'Electricité's 20 percent share in the French majority side of the CII-HB group and began to negotiate the full or partial purchase of the government's 20 percent share as well. The threat

---

[3] *Wall Street Journal,* April 7, 1980, p. 24.

to Honeywell was that St. Gobain would begin to "dominate the otherwise fragmented French side, achieving effective control of CII-HB".[4] These efforts continued into 1980 because "now the French want to squeeze out American Honeywell's remaining minority stake."[5]

In short, the potential threat to Honeywell's position in CII-Bull had a long history that predated the socialist election victory in May 1981. It was rooted in French national pride, which transcended the political ideologies of the right and left, and was made worse by the fact that 75 percent of the roughly $8 billion of computers installed in France were sold by U.S. companies. Many Gaullists, out of the nationalistic tradition of their founder, General Charles de Gaulle, had pressed for the nationalization of the French computer industry, and this conservative-nationalistic policy goal dovetailed quite nicely with the Socialist Party objective of "recapturing the domestic market."

## THE POST–MAY 1981 ENVIRONMENT

On May 10, 1981, Edson Spencer received a phone calls from Roger Fauroux, head of St. Gobain, informing him that Mitterrand's election was imminent and that the nationalization of St. Gobain (now the majority French partner in CII-HB) was a near certainty. Its exact impact on Honeywell, however, was far less certain.

The Socialist government moved quickly on its election platform in all respects. Minimum wage and social security benefits were increased 10 percent and 20 percent respectively. In addition, paid vacation benefits were extended, and the workweek was reduced from 40 to 39 hours. Presidential decrees also added 210,000 new jobs to the public sector. More fundamentally, a nationalization plan affecting 11 major industrial groups, including St. Gobain, was approved by the National Assembly in July 1981

by a 302 to 107 vote margin. Three firms with large foreign ownership (CII-HB, ITT-France, and Roussel-Uclaf) were targeted for intensive negotiations on their future status. The compensation bill flowing from the government to private stockholders of the 11 industrial groups was initially $5.5 billion, but it increased to $7 billion after French court pressure and rulings.

These policies had been implemented within an economic climate that had been deteriorating during the last year or two of Giscard's presidency. The primary cause of these economic reversals was not domestic policies but the consequences of the second oil shock, which followed the Iranian revolution. Many analysts were wondering if Mitterrand's domestic policies would help or aggravate the situation.

Spencer and other Honeywell executives visited Paris frequently to assess the situation. Commercially, CII-HB was suffering and on its way to a 1981 operating loss that would reduce Honeywell's corporate earnings by $14 million or 61 cents per share, which represented 5 percent of Honeywell's total earnings per share in that year. Politically, Spencer found the overall business climate less than desirable. Thus, as Spencer commented, "Every indication was negative. We had only one viable option—to take our assets and get out."[6] Spencer's pessimism, however, obviously did not extend to all Honeywell business interests in France, because in July 1981 Honeywell expanded its French control systems subsidiary with an infusion of $6 million in cash. The sell-out option for Honeywell's stake in Bull was made possible by the 1976 agreement, which gave Honeywell the right to sell those assets at book value and be paid in dollars from an escrow account in a London bank if nationalization occurred. Based on the 1981 CII-HB balance sheet, Honeywell would be entitled to around $200 million, slightly more than the amount it had invested in 1970. With the nationalization of St. Gobain, CII-HB was also technically nationalized, which gave

---

[4] *The Economist,* November 17, 1979, p. 81.

[5] *The Economist,* April 5, 1980, p. 63.

[6] *Fortune,* June 28, 1982, p. 97.

Honeywell the legal option to pursue or demand the implementation of the 1976 agreement.

Before taking this course of action, however, Spencer during an early November visit to Paris "began to hear from high Ministry of Industry officials that France was determined to become a world-class computer power and that Honeywell's role could be interesting and rewarding."[7] Shortly thereafter, Spencer was invited to the Elysée Palace for a discussion with Jacques Attali, Mitterrand's special counselor. Spencer reported that "Attali made it clear that he was speaking for the President and that *le President* wanted Honeywell to stay in France."[8] Spencer then decided to explore what possibilities existed between Honeywell and the French government.

Within days of the Attali-Spencer meeting, negotiations between Honeywell and the French

---

[7] *Ibid.*
[8] *Ibid.*

were scheduled to begin. The French side was to be represented by executives of St. Gobain. The Honeywell negotiating team was to be composed of three individuals: William R. Hart, the senior vice president (second in charge behind the president) of HIS; David Louis, Honeywell's chief financial officer; and John Karis, Honeywell's assistant general counsel. Of the three, Bill Hart, of course, had the greatest experience with Bull and the French government. He had been involved with Bull since the late 1960s, was a Bull board member during the present negotiations, and had known many of the St. Gobain negotiators in that capacity for several years. The other two individuals had never been intimately involved in Honeywell-French relations.

The central questions for the negotiators remained: Given Bull's importance to Honeywell and the history of the computer industry in France, what should Honeywell's negotiating strategy be? How should Honeywell's negotiating effort be organized?

# Houston Machinery Inc.

Jerry Crosby, Vice-President of Houston Machinery Inc. (HMI), sat in his office on November 21, 1986, rereading a telex from his prospective joint venture partner. The company, Petroleum Services S.A., had rejected HMI's latest proposal. After three months of negotiations, Crosby wanted to finalize an agreement establishing a joint venture to assemble and sell oil-recycling machinery to oil distributors in Mexico. HMI's discussions with the President of Petroleum Services, Rafael Lunada, had been positive and friendly. The two parties agreed on everything except the price to charge for the joint venture's product. Petroleum Services wanted to establish a price of $25,000 per unit, whereas Crosby felt that $25,000 was too high and wanted to charge $19,000 per unit. Although the negotiations had been friendly up to this point, the disagreement on pricing was beginning to strain the relationship. Crosby knew that his boss, Gene Nelson, wanted to reach an understanding before a December 5 meeting in the host country with Petroleum Services and representatives of the state-owned national petro-

leum corporation, PEMEX. If there was to be any chance of concluding a final agreement during Nelson's visit to the host country, Crosby would have to move fast. If he was unable to establish an acceptable price, he would have to recommend that the venture be scrapped or renegotiated. Crosby also knew that PEMEX's approval of the agreement would be critical in influencing government permission to establish the joint venture. He turned to his desk to review the analysis once again.

## HMI AND THE TEXAS OIL RECYCLER

Gene Nelson invented the Texas Oil Recycler (TOR) in the late 1960s while working as an engineer for a major U.S. oil corporation. When the oil crisis caused a surge in oil prices in the early 1970s, Nelson decided to start his own company to produce and market the TOR. He later convinced Jerry Crosby, then a marketing manager with the same major oil firm, to join in this venture. With the help of Crosby and money from a San Francisco–based venture capital firm, Houston Machinery reached annual sales of $40 million by 1980. After establishing a domestic base, he decided to expand internationally.

The TOR took used motor oil and reprocessed it to produce a lower-quality grade of oil. One TOR unit could process up to 1,000 barrels of used oil per year, and the unit had a useful life of approximately ten years. Reprocessed oil sold for about a 30 percent discount off benchmark prices for high-grade crude oil. There were many applications for recycled oil, such as asphalt production, low-grade motor oils, chemical feedstocks, and other uses.

TORs were mobile "mini-refineries" that oil distributors installed at their main distribution points. Large gasoline stations, automotive service centers and truck, taxi and car fleet owners were also important customers. About $5.00 in variable costs were incurred in reprocessing a barrel of oil, including $2.50 in chemicals and filters supplied by HMI. By virtue of being located at the distributor's site, TORs saved on transportation costs. They also allowed the distributor a much higher price for used oil, thereby increasing the distributor's margins. The benefits of the TOR were so compelling that even major oil companies used them in their own distribution systems. Several oil companies used TORs to preprocess low-grade crude oil, as well as used motor oils, prior to introducing those materials into their refineries.

U.S. oil distributors had responded positively to the TOR's introduction in 1974, and TORs had successfully captured the U.S. oil-recycling market. By 1985, HMI had sold over 8,000 units in the United States and Canada. Although sales of new units had peaked, sales of filters, chemicals, replacement parts, and processing units provided a source of ongoing revenues. Sales of chemicals and parts exceeded $15 million in 1985. With the U.S. market approaching saturation, HMI began to actively search for foreign markets. In 1978, HMI had begun exporting to agents in European markets. HMI expected to achieve cumulative sales of over 10,000 units in Europe, and the company was well on its way to achieving that goal. More than 6,000 units had been sold by the end of 1985. In 1980, HMI further expanded its international operations by entering into a licensing

agreement in Brazil with expected cumulative sales of 1,000 units or more.

These agreements had proved to be profitable for the company, but Crosby felt that HMI had further opportunities. In developing an international marketing plan, HMI had originally focused on oil-importing countries that could use TORs to reduce their reliance on imported oil. Nelson had recently decided to widen his scope to include oil-exporting countries facing foreign exchange pressures. Countries such as Indonesia and Mexico looked especially appealing, because of their foreign exchange shortages and because of their large markets and ambitious economic development programs. He also hoped to take a more direct stake in developing these markets. The European agent relationships and the Brazilian licensing agreement had been satisfactory, but Nelson felt that direct ownership would provide more control and profit. However, given the company's lack of international operations experience and conditions in markets such as Mexico and Indonesia, he had concluded that joint venturing would provide the best vehicle for market entry.

At an international oil convention in Dallas, Nelson was able to meet several prospective joint venture candidates from these countries. He and Crosby had followed up these initial contacts in efforts to negotiate agreements to sell the TOR in foreign markets. Petroleum Services was the primary joint venture candidate in Mexico.

Crosby had assumed responsibility for negotiating the joint venture with Petroleum Services. He had concluded that the joint venture would be most attractive to his Mexican partner and the Mexican government if the TOR was assembled in the host country. He had concluded that it would cost HMI $5,000 per unit to supply the joint venture with the components needed to assemble the TOR. He calculated that it would cost the joint venture $8,000 per unit to assemble and distribute each TOR, approximately $5,000 for assembly and $3,000 for sales and installation costs. Since TORs sold for $20,000 in the United States, Nelson felt that the venture looked very attractive, especially when he considered the host government's ambitious road building program. Demand for asphalt was so high that the government used high-quality oil for asphalt production.

Crosby had full authority for negotiating the terms of the joint venture agreement. The only restriction placed on him was an acceptable return on investment over the life of the project coupled with a $10 million before-tax minimum return over five years. Crosby felt he was close to concluding an agreement with Petroleum Services that would meet these objectives.

## PETROLEUM SERVICES

Petroleum Services had been active in the petroleum business in Mexico for more than 50 years. It originally manufactured storage tanks for gasoline distributors and gas stations but had expanded to include gas pumps, meters, and related equipment. The current President of the company, Rafael Lunada, was the son of the founder and had aggressively taken the firm into new lines of business. Despite diversification efforts, all the company's sales were in the petroleum industry, and more than 50 percent of sales were to the national oil company, PEMEX. Petroleum Services had felt that the proposed joint venture was an excellent opportunity, and the company had responded to Crosby's initial proposal with enthusiasm.

## THE INITIAL AGREEMENT

Crosby flew to the host country in August 1986 and met the senior management of Petroleum Services. The meeting proved fruitful, and the two negotiated a skeleton agreement. Negotiations continued, and by mid-November the parties had agreed to the following:

- HMI would provide assembly machinery valued at $3 million for a 40 percent equity position in the company.
- HMI would receive a 5 percent royalty on sales for its expertise and technical assistance.

- HMI would provide necessary components for the machines at a 30 percent markup, totalling $6,500 per TOR kit.
- Sales of parts and chemicals to the joint venture would be priced at a 30 percent margin to HMI.
- Petroleum Services would provide property and plant valued at $2 million for a 60 percent equity position.
- Other investments, start-up costs, and working capital requirements would be met by local bank financing.

Lunada felt that demand for TORs followed the curve shown in Exhibit 1, and Crosby agreed with him. Lunada expected government approval of the agreement to take three months. If the agreement was endorsed by PEMEX, government approval would be virtually guaranteed. The plant could be up and running in April of 1987 if the agreement were signed in December. PC and HMI just had to agree on the price and the production quantity.

Crosby kept looking at his pro forma statement (shown in Exhibit 2). He knew the joint venture would be profitable for both parties. He just wondered why he and the local partner could not agree on a price for the TOR. Also, if it were possible to reach an agreement with Petroleum

| EXHIBIT 1 |
|---|

**LUNADA'S TOR DEMAND PROJECTIONS**

| Cumulative units over 5 years | Price per unit |
|---|---|
| 800 | $28,000 |
| 1,200 | 26,000 |
| 1,400 | 25,000 |
| 1,600 | 24,000 |
| 1,800 | 22,000 |
| 2,100 | 20,000 |
| 2,300 | 19,000 |
| 2,400 | 18,000 |
| 2,600 | 16,000 |
| 2,600 | 14,000 |
| 2,600 | 12,000 |

EXHIBIT 2

**CROSBY'S PRO FORMA INCOME STATEMENT** ($ Thousand)

|  | 1987 | 1988 | 1989 | 1990 | 1991 | Total |
|---|---|---|---|---|---|---|
| Sales |  |  |  |  |  |  |
| TORs | 1,900 | 5,700 | 11,400 | 13,300 | 11,400 | 43,700 |
| Parts and chemicals | 100 | 500 | 1,200 | 2,500 | 3,800 | 8,100 |
| Cost of goods sold |  |  |  |  |  |  |
| Components | 650 | 1,950 | 3,900 | 4,550 | 3,900 | 14,950 |
| Assembly | 500 | 1,500 | 3,000 | 3,500 | 3,000 | 11,500 |
| Parts and chemicals | 70 | 350 | 840 | 1,750 | 2,660 | 5,670 |
| Gross margin | 780 | 2,400 | 4,860 | 6,000 | 5,640 | 19,680 |
| Selling, general & administrative expenses | 635 | 1,200 | 2,100 | 2,400 | 2,100 | 8,435 |
| Royalties | 100 | 310 | 630 | 790 | 760 | 2,590 |
| Pretax income | 45 | 890 | 2,130 | 2,810 | 2,780 | 8,655 |
| Tax | 18 | 356 | 852 | 1,124 | 1,112 | 3,462 |
| Net income | 27 | 534 | 1,278 | 1,686 | 1,668 | 5,193 |
| HMI's pretax share | 18 | 356 | 852 | 1,124 | 1,112 | 3,462 |
| Royalties | 100 | 310 | 630 | 790 | 760 | 2,590 |
| Component and parts markup | 166 | 530 | 1,094 | 1,454 | 1,514 | 4,758 |
| Total HMI return | 284 | 1,196 | 2,576 | 3,368 | 3,386 | 10,810 |

*Note:* Units sold were projected at: 1987, 100; 1988, 300; 1989, 600; 1990, 700; 1991, 600, for a total of 2,300.

Services, he also wondered how PEMEX and the host government would react. He knew that Nelson hoped to show a formal agreement to senior PEMEX officials during his December trip to Mexico. Crosby wondered if there were any other pitfalls that might threaten the successful formation and management of the joint venture.

Crosby also was highly concerned about the health of the Mexican economy. Racked by massive inflation and devaluation, Mexico's economic outlook was uncertain (see Exhibits 3 through 7). The possibility of political instability worried him. In addition, a Mexican joint venture would raise financial management issues that HMI had not faced before. Crosby felt that if HMI could find a way to make this joint venture work, the knowledge gained in the process would be invaluable in creating other joint ventures in a number of markets.

**EXHIBIT 3**

**MEXICO: SELECTED TRADE, PETROLEUM, AND ECONOMIC DATA**

| Year | Exports (billions of pesos) | Imports (billions of pesos) | Trade balance (billions of pesos) | Oil exports (billions of pesos) | Oil production* (thousand tons) | Foreign exchange rate (Pesos/$) |
|------|------|------|------|------|------|------|
| 1972 | 21.24 | 33.98 | (12.74) | 0.27 | — | 12.50 |
| 1973 | 28.27 | 47.67 | (19.40) | 0.31 | — | 12.50 |
| 1974 | 37.34 | 75.71 | (38.37) | 1.54 | 33,540 | 12.50 |
| 1975 | 36.30 | 82.13 | (45.83) | 5.75 | 41,413 | 12.50 |
| 1976 | 53.52 | 90.90 | (37.38) | 8.40 | 45,690 | 15.43 |
| 1977 | 102.05 | 132.99 | (30.94) | 23.23 | 54,350 | 22.57 |
| 1978 | 135.65 | 172.03 | (36.38) | 41.42 | 66,436 | 22.77 |
| 1979 | 204.86 | 275.65 | (70.79) | 89.32 | 80,000 | 22.81 |
| 1980 | 357.50 | 447.00 | (89.50) | 225.67 | 106,775 | 22.95 |
| 1981 | 480.90 | 590.10 | (109.20) | 338.35 | 120,000 | 24.52 |
| 1982 | 1,231.80 | 774.70 | 457.10 | 941.87 | 150,390 | 56.40 |
| 1983 | 2,632.00 | 972.40 | 1,659.60 | 1,822.04 | 149,000 | 120.09 |
| 1984 | 4,082.40 | 2,010.80 | 2,071.60 | 2,754.25 | 151,065 | 167.83 |
| 1985 | 5,705.10 | 3,597.50 | 2,107.60 | 3,799.90 | 150,500 | 256.87 |

| Year | Current account balance (millions of dollars) | Money supply (billions of pesos) | Gross domestic product (billions of pesos) | Consumer price index (1980 = 100) | Annual inflation rate (%) |
|------|------|------|------|------|------|
| 1975 | (4,042) | 122.4 | — | — | — |
| 1976 | (3,409) | 258.0 | 1,371.0 | 44.2 | — |
| 1977 | (1,854) | 208.2 | 1,849.3 | 57.0 | 29.5 |
| 1978 | (3,171) | 270.2 | 2,337.4 | 67.0 | 17.5 |
| 1979 | (5,459) | 360.9 | 3,067.5 | 79.1 | 19.4 |
| 1980 | (8,162) | 477.2 | 4,276.5 | 100.0 | 26.5 |
| 1981 | (13,899) | 635.0 | 5,874.4 | 127.9 | 27.9 |
| 1982 | (6,218) | 1,031.0 | 9,417.1 | 203.3 | 60.1 |
| 1983 | 5,419 | 1,447.0 | 17,141.7 | 410.2 | 101.8 |
| 1984 | 4,240 | 2,315.0 | 28,748.9 | 679.0 | 65.5 |
| 1985 | 540 | 3,462.0 | 45,588.5 | 1071.2 | 57.8 |

*The figure quoted is the estimated production of crude petroleum.
*Source:* Compiled from *International Financial Statistics,* 1981 and 1987, and *Petroleum Economist,* January 1980 to January 1987.

## EXHIBIT 4

## MEXICO AT A GLANCE

### GEOGRAPHY

Mexico, the United Mexican States, is the third largest country in Latin America with an area of 760,000 square miles (1,970,000 square kilometers).

### CLIMATE

Approximately 50 percent of Mexico is arid or semiarid. The rainy season occurs between May and October, with very little rainfall during the rest of the year. The annual rainfall does increase towards the southern part of the country. The climate does vary in part due to the wide variation in altitudes in the country and the effect of the Pacific Ocean and the Gulf of Mexico on the coastal area. Mexico City and many other regions in the central part have a temperate or semitropical climate.

### POPULATION

In recent years, the population growth rate of Mexico has averaged 2.54 percent annually, based upon midyear estimates. This represents a tripling of the population since 1940. Additionally, there has been a substantial movement of people to urban from rural areas. It is now estimated that 60 percent of the population lives in urban areas.

### GOVERNMENT

Independence was granted in 1821 to Mexico from Spain, after 400 years' rule as a colony. However, decades of struggle for political power slowed economic development. Peace was achieved under Porfirio Diaz at the end of the last century, and it was at this time that huge lands were used for cattle raising and farming. A revolution in 1920 led to 10 years of civil war, almost completely destroying the agricultural economy of the country. The Mexico of today is only 60 years old, resulting from reforms in the 1920s.

The government is now a federal, democratic republic divided into a federal district and 31 states. The federal government's powers are greater than those of the U.S. counterpart. Areas which they are particularly strong are:

1. The federal government may remove from office any state governor for specified but broad reasons.
2. The principal types of tax revenues are reserved for the federal government, which distributes certain revenues to the states.
3. Public education, except at the preparatory and university levels, is provided, managed, and financed by the federal government.

The chief executive is the president, and there is a bicameral legislature as well as a judicial branch. The president's term is for six years, and he or she may not be elected again.

### GENERAL ECONOMY

The economy of Mexico is a mixed economy, with the government, its agencies, or government-owned or controlled companies dominant in the areas of public utilities, petroleum, banking, and certain basic manufacturing industries. Government financing of cooperative farms (*ejidos*) and purchases of crops at supported prices also dominate a large part of the agriculture of the country. Private enterprise is the principal factor in manufacturing, mining, commerce, entertainment, and the service industries, including construction, although large government-owned companies now exist in all these areas. Foreign investment is most frequently found in manufacturing and mining and with less frequency in other areas.

The principal government investments are in the national railroads, the electric utilities, water supply and irrigation, the telegraph system, the petroleum and basic petrochemical industries, and, since its nationalization on September 1, 1982, the banking system. The government is also the principal or sole owner of three of the four largest steel companies, holds a large majority of the shares of the telephone company, and is the largest producer of sulphur. It owns a manufacturer of heavy trucks under license, as well as a marketing company called CONASUPO, which distributes basic necessities to low-income groups, and it operates a chain of supermarkets. The government also owns a number of sugar mills, as well as a considerable number of enterprises financed by the government development bank, Nacional Financiera, S.A. Many of these companies were acquired to avoid imminent bankruptcy and the consequent loss of sources of employment. In addition, government agencies have subscribed to substantial minority interest in the equity shares of a number of companies in mining and other industries, often as a prerequisite for authorizing tax or other benefits.

Private investment and reinvestment in many industries, as well as in industrial securities, modern supermarkets, and department stores, have increased so much as to indicate that Mexican savings formerly invested abroad were being returned in substantial amounts. However, the flow of this type of capital was reversed during the years from 1974 to 1978 and again since 1981.

Net foreign direct investment has also been a factor of major importance in expanding the economy but represents, nevertheless, only about 5 percent of total public and private investment. New foreign investment increased substantially in the years from 1979 to 1981 but has continued at a considerably reduced rate since then.

Very substantial new oil fields have been brought into production during the last seven or eight years, principally in the southeastern part of the country and in the territorial waters of the Gulf of Mexico, with the result

EXHIBIT 4 (cont.)

that Mexico has become one of the world's five or six most important exporters of crude oil. Proven reserves were estimated at 72 billion barrels as at both September 1, 1981 and 1982, about 33 percent of which represents natural gas equivalents. Oil production and exports averaged about 2.8 million and 1.5 million barrels per day, respectively, during the latter part of 1983. These rates are expected to continue in 1984, in part because of the rather unstable world market. Moreover, Petroleos Mexicanos (PEMEX), the government-owned oil company, has been obligated to reduce its rate of drilling new wells, in line with general reductions of government expenditures. The principal benefits of the oil industry to the country arise from its export earnings (approximately 76.5 percent of total exports in 1982) and the very substantial amounts transferred to the federal government as payment of taxes, aggregating 29.6 percent of the total tax collections from all sources for the year 1982.

The rapidly increasing population of Mexico and improvements in the average standard of living have created an increasing local market for goods and services other than base necessities; however, this growth has been limited by the large percentage (about 36 percent) of the population that is dependent on agriculture, cattle ranching, and other rural occupations. Efforts to improve productivity and standards of living in many agricultural areas have been hindered by a lack of modern agricultural equipment and know-how. Privately owned farms are usually small because of the strict limitations in the Mexican Constitution regarding the maximum area that may be owned by a single individual (in the case of irrigated land, for example, 250 acres). Much of the arable land has been expropriated for the establishment of collective farms (ejidos). Mexico is almost self-sufficient in the production of staple foods.

## MAJOR INDUSTRIES

Over 36 percent of the economically active population is still dependent on agriculture, livestock, and other rural occupations, although this percentage continues to decline each year. These occupations were responsible for only 7.4 percent of the gross national product in 1982. Services, including resorts, hotels, restaurants, and other aspects of the tourist industry, employ over 22.5 percent of the economically active population, about the same percentage occupied in manufacturing.

The oil and basic petrochemical industries, entirely in the hands of PEMEX (the government-owned, fully integrated oil company, which has a complete constitutional monopoly in these areas), have been increasing at rates well ahead of industry in general. The huge new oil and gas fields that have been located and brought into production in recent years indicate that these two

industries, as well as the manufacture of secondary petrochemicals by private enterprise, will be responsible for an increasing share of the gross national product in the future.

The largest manufacturing industries are automobile assembly plants; steel manufacturers; the textile industry, including processing of synthetic fibers; food processing; and breweries. Mining has been an important industry in Mexico for centuries, and Mexico is the world's largest producer of silver. The construction industry in all its phases must be considered as a major industry, although the construction industry, together with the automobile and capital goods industries, were those most affected by the recession that began in 1982.

## BASIC RESOURCES

In addition to its very large oil reserves mentioned previously, Mexico is well-endowed with other mineral resources, including quantities of silver (the world's largest producer), cooper, lead, zinc, sulphur, and fluorite, and deposits of coal and iron ore.

Only a small portion of the land can be considered as first-class agricultural land, particularly because of lack of rainfall in the northern part of the country. However, irrigation has increased considerably the amount of land under cultivation, and in a normal crop year, Mexico is largely self-sufficient in food, except for recurring deficiencies of wheat and corn in recent years. The principal agricultural exports have been coffee, cotton, and vegetables.

The extensive coastlines of Mexico include many lovely bays. There are numerous archaeological sites being developed as attractions for several million tourists a year, largely from the United States.

## POTENTIAL GROWTH AREAS

Because of the tremendous increase in the population, the demand for all types of consumer goods, including durables and particularly necessities, is expanding very rapidly. Priority status for purposes of tax incentives has been granted to the production of many types of basic consumer goods, including economy lines of household items.

The two largest unsatisfied local markets are those for agricultural equipment and for housing, particularly low-cost units. Moreover, as the market for locally manufactured consumer goods has expanded, the government is now attempting to encourage private industry to invest in the production of capital goods for existing and additional factories in Mexico, in order to reduce dependence on imported machinery and equipment. As a result of the devaluation of the peso, the reduction in the already low labor costs, when converted to U.S. dollars, has also made increasingly attractive the establishment

**EXHIBIT 4 (cont.)**

of in-bond processing plants near the U.S. border or elsewhere to handle labor-intensive operations.

The government also wishes to stimulate industries which can export locally manufactured goods.

The discovery of substantial additional petroleum and natural gas reserves, particularly in the southeastern part of the country, has converted Mexico into an oil-exporting country. Moreover, a 48-inch gas pipeline has been laid by PEMEX, the government-owned petroleum company, from the southeastern fields to the northern and central parts of the country. Major additions to two oil-refining complexes are being built, as well as substantial additional facilities for the production of petrochemicals. Coatzacoalcos, Veracruz, and its immediately surrounding areas has become a major population and industrial center and within a few years may well rank as the fourth such center in size in the country. Although in accordance with the Mexican Constitution the petroleum and basic petrochemical industries may be operated only by the government or its agencies, growth in these industries and in offshore drilling in the Gulf of Mexico and the Caribbean Sea provide substantial opportunities for construction, supply and service companies, both foreign and Mexican.

### TRANSPORT AND COMMUNICATIONS

The system of paved highways in Mexico has been expanded considerably in recent years. It now exceeds 37,000 miles (60,000 kilometers) in total and connects all major cities in the country and most of the smaller urban areas, as well as several points on the borders with the United States and Guatemala.

The two major airlines, both of which are government-owned, also have numerous flights that connect most of these cities. These airlines and many of the larger international airlines maintain regular service between Mexico City, some of the other large cities and principal resorts, and many cities in the United States and the rest of the world.

The National Railroad Network has been operated by the federal government for many years and is still the largest freight carrier in the country. However, the combination of low rates, inefficient operation, and the inability to use modern, heavy equipment because of inadequate roadbeds has resulted in large annual losses and in inefficient service. Present plans call for improvement of this service and increased freight rates. Nevertheless, because of the relatively long distance involved, the capital investment that would be required to improve the roadbeds and acquire heavy equipment is probably beyond the means of the government in the near future. Considerable amounts of freight are carried by the many licensed truck lines, a business limited by law to Mexican

nationals operating as individuals or cooperatives, but shortages of equipment are threatening to produce serious supply bottlenecks. The many intercity bus lines now carry far more passengers than the railroads, and large modern bus terminals have been opened in Mexico City.

### EMPLOYMENT AND STANDARD OF LIVING

Mexico's biggest problem is to find gainful employment for its rapidly increasing population. Government officials estimate that something over 800,000 jobs a year must be provided. Unemployment and underemployment are considerable and increased substantially in 1982 and 1983, although no comprehensive statistical information is available. The unskilled labor pool is very large in most parts of the country, particularly outside Mexico City, where the labor force has proved to be easily trained for semi-skilled and skilled jobs. The in-bond processing plants near the U.S. border are obtaining 20 to 30 percent higher productivity rates than in the United States. There is, however, a shortage of white-collar workers, inasmuch as the increasing industrial development of the country has resulted in a demand for capable, well-trained personnel and, particularly, for executives, a demand that has exceeded the available supply.

Legal minimum wages have been increased very considerably since 1973 in an effort to match inflation, with somewhat lower rates of increases in other wages and salaried positions. Nevertheless, the average earnings of Mexican labor are far below those in the United States and Europe when converted to U.S. dollars at current exchange rates. The legal minimum wage in effect in Mexico City since January 1, 1984 amounts to about $29 per week. Per capita income for Mexico as a whole for 1982, converted at the average rate of exchange in effect during the 12 months, amounted to about $2,252. However, in the case of a large proportion of the population, particularly in rural areas, per capita income was well below the national average. In general, except for executives and owners, standards of living in Mexico are considerably lower than in the developed countries.

### MEMBERSHIP IN TRADE BLOCS

Mexico is a member of the successor organization to the Latin American Free Trade Association (LAFTA), now called the Latin American Integration Association (LAIA-Asociación Latinoamericana de Integración), which includes most countries of Latin America. As a result of this membership, merchandise exports of Mexican source products to other members receive favorable treatment; this has somewhat increased the market available to enterprises established in Mexico.

*Source: Doing Business in Mexico,* Price Waterhouse, 1984.

EXHIBIT 5

## MEXICO: GROSS DOMESTIC PRODUCT BY ACTIVITY (Current Prices in Billions of Pesos)

| | 1970 | 1975 | 1976 | 1977 | 1978 | 1979 | 1980 | 1981 | 1982 | 1983 | 1984 | 1985 |
|---|---|---|---|---|---|---|---|---|---|---|---|---|
| Industry | | | | | | | | | | | | |
| Agriculture, hunting, forestry and fishing | 54 | 123 | 46 | 195 | 240 | 281 | 357 | 477 | 693 | 1,359 | 2,479 | — |
| Mining and quarrying* | 11 | 31 | 34 | 60 | 77 | 129 | 288 | 366 | 930 | 2,042 | 2,880 | — |
| Manufacturing* | 105 | 258 | 317 | 443 | 553 | 717 | 988 | 1,315 | 2,005 | 3,876 | 6,866 | — |
| Electricity, gas, and water | 5 | 10 | 14 | 22 | 24 | 31 | 42 | 52 | 77 | 155 | 277 | — |
| Construction | 24 | 66 | 85 | 104 | 139 | 194 | 276 | 409 | 590 | 878 | 1,433 | — |
| Wholesale and retail trade restaurants and hotels | 115 | 277 | 338 | 446 | 560 | 743 | 1,000 | 1,361 | 2,146 | 3,822 | 6,549 | — |
| Transport, storage and communication | 21 | 63 | 82 | 114 | 150 | 200 | 279 | 389 | 604 | 1,139 | 2,003 | — |
| Finance, insurance, real estate and business services | 51 | 107 | 133 | 168 | 215 | 269 | 349 | 487 | 737 | 1,236 | 1,970 | — |
| Community, social and personal services | 38 | 90 | 119 | 160 | 204 | 273 | 377 | 538 | 869 | 1,516 | 2,526 | — |
| Total industries | 425 | 1,024 | 1,268 | 1,711 | 2,164 | 2,838 | 3,956 | 5,395 | 8,653 | 16,023 | 26,982 | — |
| Producers of government services | 25 | 88 | 119 | 159 | 199 | 263 | 368 | 551 | 872 | 1,263 | 2,118 | — |
| Other producers | — | — | — | — | — | — | — | — | — | — | — | — |
| Subtotal | 450 | 1,112 | 1,387 | 1,870 | 2,363 | 3,101 | 4,324 | 5,945 | 9,524 | 17,286 | 29,101 | — |
| Less imputed bank service charge | 5 | 12 | 16 | 21 | 26 | 33 | 48 | 71 | 107 | 145 | 352 | — |
| Plus import duties | — | — | — | — | — | — | — | — | — | — | — | — |
| Plus value-added tax | — | — | — | — | — | — | — | — | — | — | — | — |
| Gross domestic product | 444 | 1,100 | 1,371 | 1,849 | 2,337 | 3,068 | 4,276 | 5,874 | 9,417 | 17,142 | 28,749 | — |

*Basic petroleum manufacturing is included in item "Mining and quarrying."
Source: *National Accounts Statistics*, International Monetary Fund 1985.

## EXHIBIT 6

## MEXICO: PRINCIPAL CENTRAL GOVERNMENT ACCOUNTS (Billions of Pesos)

| | 1978 | 1979 | 1980 | 1981 | 1982 | 1983 | 1984 | 1985 |
|---|---|---|---|---|---|---|---|---|
| **Revenue** | | | | | | | | |
| Budgetary receipts | | | | | | | | |
| Federal taxes | | | | | | | | |
| Individual income | 64.5 | 74.6 | 103.2 | 137.6 | 246.3 | 334.8 | 538.8 | 895.2 |
| Wages & salaries | 52.3 | 56.6 | 79.0 | 103.1 | 181.7 | 227.5 | 356.5 | 637.3 |
| Corporate income | 66.3 | 98.3 | 142.8 | 182.6 | 213.0 | 376.5 | 631.4 | 994.9 |
| Social security | 54.7 | 70.5 | 94.7 | 129.1 | 215.0 | 354.1 | 578.0 | 1,012.6 |
| Payroll or labor | 3.3 | 4.2 | 5.9 | 7.9 | 12.0 | 18.0 | 28.8 | 48.8 |
| Property | — | — | 2.0 | 3.7 | 1.6 | 1.5 | 0.2 | 0.2 |
| Domestic taxes on goods & services | 116.1 | 157.5 | 196.5 | 283.8 | 442.6 | 2,036.7 | 3,349.8 | 5,237.5 |
| Taxes on hydrocarbons | — | — | — | — | — | 1,016.2 | 1,700.2 | 2,790.1 |
| International trade transactions | 36.0 | 63.7 | 184.8 | 260.1 | 502.3 | 221.0 | 130.1 | 312.7 |
| Other taxes (migration, stamps, etc.) | 4.0 | 5.3 | 19.1 | 2.7 | 0.9 | 1.4 | 1.9 | 1.6 |
| Total federal taxes | 397.2 | 530.7 | 828.0 | 1,110.6 | 1,815.4 | 3,571.5 | 5,615.5 | 9,140.8 |
| Nontax receipts | | | | | | | | |
| Lottery profits | 0.5 | 1.1 | 2.2 | 4.5 | 3.9 | 4.1 | 14.4 | 9.3 |
| Dividends | 0.4 | 1.0 | 0.7 | 0.6 | 1.4 | 1.6 | 2.2 | 4.5 |
| Bank of Mexico profits | 0.1 | 0.1 | 0.2 | 0.6 | 0.3 | — | — | — |
| Interest | — | 0.1 | 0.1 | — | 0.2 | 16.0 | 7.0 | 52.5 |
| Dividends & interest | 0.6 | 0.6 | 4.2 | 13.0 | 14.1 | 261.6 | 220.9 | 278.5 |
| Other royalties | 0.2 | 0.9 | 2.7 | 1.8 | 6.4 | 12.5 | 38.4 | 33.9 |
| Other property income | 6.5 | 8.3 | 11.9 | 17.4 | 40.2 | 74.5 | 67.6 | 140.7 |
| Administrative fees & charges | 2.4 | 3.6 | 5.1 | 6.6 | 9.1 | 17.1 | 27.9 | 39.3 |
| Fines & forfeits | 2.3 | 3.1 | 5.2 | 7.0 | 15.1 | 29.6 | 40.2 | 61.3 |
| Other nontax receipts | 2.2 | 1.9 | 2.9 | 4.4 | 32.3 | 42.3 | 15.8 | 65.0 |
| Total nontax receipts | 15.2 | 20.7 | 35.2 | 55.9 | 123.0 | 459.3 | 434.4 | 685.0 |
| Adjustments* | (74.4) | (92.1) | (153.0) | (216.3) | (295.5) | (349.8) | (841.9) | (1,320.6) |
| Net revenue | 322.8 | 438.6 | 675.0 | 894.3 | 1,519.9 | 3,221.7 | 4,773.6 | 7,820.2 |

**Expenditures**

| | | | | | | | |
|---|---|---|---|---|---|---|---|
| Budgetary payments | | | | | | | |
| General public services | 8.4 | 7.8 | 158.8 | 105.6 | 179.0 | 329.3 | 572.4 | 919.5 |
| Defense | 11.0 | 14.5 | 17.3 | 29.3 | 45.4 | 87.2 | 181.4 | 296.9 |
| Education | 72.3 | 94.3 | 134.5 | 215.1 | 369.5 | 489.5 | 833.9 | 1,361.0 |
| Health | 14.6 | 19.7 | 17.8 | 22.0 | 36.6 | 53.7 | 102.4 | 162.7 |
| Housing & sanitary | 0.0 | 0.0 | 19.3 | 48.4 | 66.0 | 100.7 | 160.7 | 202.7 |
| Economic services | 94.7 | 124.6 | 233.5 | 430.4 | 705.3 | 1,171.5 | 1,833.4 | 3,023.8 |
| Agriculture | 42.7 | 55.2 | 81.7 | 102.6 | 173.6 | 213.2 | 345.7 | 591.9 |
| Mining & manufacturing | 0.0 | 0.0 | 0.1 | 12.4 | 87.9 | 203.0 | 282.6 | 528.0 |
| Utilities | 11.3 | 10.4 | 0.1 | 0.4 | 73.3 | 312.7 | 364.8 | 647.9 |
| Roads | 5.0 | 7.7 | 9.9 | 22.0 | 38.6 | 85.7 | 130.1 | 152.3 |
| Other Transport | 7.0 | 13.2 | 34.2 | 40.1 | 62.4 | 109.8 | 203.6 | 260.1 |
| Other | 28.7 | 38.1 | 107.5 | 252.9 | 269.5 | 247.1 | 506.6 | 843.6 |
| Social security & welfare | 73.4 | 95.1 | 119.8 | 173.8 | 298.8 | 457.5 | 642.3 | 1,141.0 |
| Public debt interest | 41.2 | 52.5 | 75.1 | 168.6 | 417.3 | 1,603.2 | 2,259.2 | 4,363.0 |
| Other budget payments† | 69.9 | 132.0 | 32.5 | 93.4 | 855.6 | 292.0 | 282.0 | 327.7 |
| Net expenditures | 385.5 | 540.5 | 808.6 | 1,286.6 | 2,973.5 | 4,584.6 | 6,867.9 | 11,798.3 |

**Other expenditures and financing**

| | | | | | | | |
|---|---|---|---|---|---|---|---|
| (Deficit)/surplus | (62.7) | (101.9) | (133.6) | (392.3) | (1,453.6) | (1,362.9) | (2,094.3) | (3,978.1) |
| Domestic financing | | | | | | | | |
| Monetary authorities | — | 103.6 | 145.3 | 263.1 | 1,278.3 | 662.7 | 1,473.2 | 2,317.6 |
| Deposit money banks | — | — | — | — | 4.5 | 16.1 | (0.6) | — |
| Other domestic | — | 5.4 | (8.4) | 5.5 | (57.4) | 122.8 | 35.4 | 1,352.0 |
| Other Fin. institutions | — | 3.0 | (7.5) | 7.5 | (45.3) | — | — | — |
| Nonfinance (private sect) | — | (0.7) | (0.7) | — | — | — | — | — |
| Other | — | (2.3) | 8.2 | (7.5) | 45.3 | — | — | — |
| Total domestic | n.a. | 109.0 | 136.9 | 268.6 | 1,225.4 | 801.6 | 1,508.0 | 3,669.6 |
| Foreign financing | | | | | | | | |
| Int'l development inst | — | 2.3 | (0.2) | 6.6 | 14.1 | 23.2 | 75.4 | 161.8 |
| Foreign governments | — | (0.3) | (0.4) | — | — | — | — | — |
| Other | n.a. | (9.1) | (2.7) | 117.1 | 214.1 | 538.1 | 510.9 | 146.7 |
| Total foreign | n.a. | (7.1) | (3.3) | 123.7 | 228.2 | 561.3 | 586.3 | 308.5 |
| Total financing | n.a. | 101.9 | 133.6 | 392.3 | 1,453.6 | 1,362.9 | 2,094.3 | 3,978.1 |

*Adjustments are made for the following: net taxes paid to the social security system, tax refund payments, and taxes collected for states.
†Includes debt repayment.
*Note:* Years end December 31.
*Source:* Compiled from *Government Finance Statistics Yearbook,* 1981 and 1987, and *National Accounts Statistics,* International Monetary Fund, 1985.

# EXHIBIT 7

**WORLD ESTIMATED OIL PRODUCTION** (Thousands of Tons)

| | 1975 | 1976 | 1978 | 1979 | 1980 | 1981 | 1982 | 1983 | 1984 | 1985 |
|---|---|---|---|---|---|---|---|---|---|---|
| North America | 481,428 | 466,022 | 556,197 | 565,000 | 565,155 | 552,000 | 560,400 | 563,200 | 571,840 | 576,750 |
| USA | 411,402 | 403,041 | 481,461 | 479,000 | 482,205 | 477,000 | 486,200 | 486,700 | 488,500 | 492,000 |
| Canada | 70,026 | 62,981 | 74,736 | 86,000 | 82,950 | 75,000 | 74,200 | 76,500 | 83,340 | 84,750 |
| Caribbean | 182,714 | 183,189 | 200,993 | 223,300 | 237,482 | 252,850 | 267,912 | 263,550 | 265,148 | 258,450 |
| Mexico | 41,413 | 45,690 | 66,436 | 80,000 | 106,775 | 120,000 | 150,390 | 149,000 | 151,065 | 150,500 |
| Venezuela | 122,075 | 118,249 | 115,734 | 125,000 | 112,855 | 115,000 | 100,175 | 97,500 | 95,520 | 88,500 |
| Trinidad | 11,124 | 11,570 | 11,854 | 11,500 | 10,982 | 10,500 | 9,104 | 8,500 | 8,800 | 9,400 |
| Colombia | 8,102 | 7,680 | 6,774 | 6,500 | 6,465 | 6,950 | 7,326 | 7,550 | 8,650 | 8,900 |
| Guatemala | — | — | 43 | 125 | 250 | 300 | 340 | 355 | 250 | 150 |
| Cuba | — | — | 115 | 115 | 105 | 60 | 540 | 600 | 775 | 900 |
| Barbados | — | — | 37 | 60 | 50 | 40 | 37 | 45 | 88 | 100 |
| Other Latin American countries | 44,090 | 44,254 | 51,109 | 55,950 | 57,615 | 58,800 | 61,111 | 65,100 | 71,519 | 75,800 |
| Argentina | 20,227 | 19,704 | 22,945 | 24,500 | 25,200 | 25,500 | 24,390 | 24,650 | 23,797 | 22,800 |
| Brazil | 9,440 | 8,710 | 8,285 | 8,500 | 9,360 | 11,000 | 13,355 | 16,500 | 22,776 | 27,000 |
| Ecuador | 7,765 | 9,070 | 9,730 | 10,750 | 10,810 | 10,200 | 10,688 | 12,150 | 13,065 | 14,000 |
| Peru | 3,657 | 3,700 | 7,722 | 9,850 | 9,550 | 9,400 | 9,465 | 8,700 | 9,119 | 9,300 |
| Bolivia | 1,855 | 1,990 | 1,587 | 1,250 | 1,135 | 900 | 1,210 | 1,100 | 962 | 1,000 |
| Chile | 1,146 | 1,080 | 840 | 1,100 | 1,560 | 1,800 | 2,003 | 2,000 | 1,800 | 1,700 |
| Middle East | 980,573 | 1,101,728 | 1,089,851 | 1,131,700 | 947,455 | 811,800 | 640,453 | 569,712 | 561,631 | 506,162 |
| Saudi Arabia | 352,029 | 428,659 | 421,975 | 510,000 | 496,360 | 490,000 | 323,330 | 246,000 | 228,720 | 165,000 |
| Iran | 266,676 | 293,906 | 260,850 | 145,000 | 76,600 | 65,000 | 120,396 | 124,000 | 109,135 | 110,000 |
| Iraq | 110,096 | 104,378 | 128,925 | 175,000 | 130,000 | 44,000 | 49,566 | 46,000 | 58,740 | 70,000 |
| Kuwait | 104,791 | 108,029 | 108,905 | 130,000 | 81,440 | 58,000 | 41,615 | 54,000 | 57,305 | 50,000 |
| Egypt | 11,700 | 16,060 | 24,440 | 27,500 | 30,083 | 32,500 | — | — | — | — |
| Syria | 9,637 | 9,760 | 10,008 | 8,500 | 8,498 | 8,500 | 8,200 | 8,400 | 8,963 | 9,000 |
| Bahrain | 3,041 | 2,840 | 2,656 | 2,500 | 2,414 | 2,300 | 2,187 | 2,100 | 2,090 | 2,100 |
| Other | 122,603 | 138,096 | 132,092 | 133,200 | 122,060 | 111,500 | 95,159 | 89,212 | 96,678 | 100,062 |
| Africa | 231,555 | 263,430 | 276,055 | 305,250 | 267,798 | 192,740 | 215,866 | 216,750 | 231,225 | 237,185 |
| Nigeria | 87,982 | 101,417 | 93,995 | 114,000 | 101,750 | 68,000 | 63,468 | 60,000 | 68,015 | 73,000 |
| Libya | 72,390 | 92,052 | 96,205 | 101,000 | 85,935 | 55,000 | 55,167 | 52,000 | 51,670 | 50,000 |
| Other | 71,183 | 69,961 | 85,855 | 90,250 | 80,113 | 69,740 | 97,231 | 104,750 | 111,540 | 114,185 |

| | | | | | | | | | | |
|---|--:|--:|--:|--:|--:|--:|--:|--:|--:|--:|
| Western Europe | 24,167 | 33,702 | 83,972 | 110,450 | 117,656 | 124,670 | 141,900 | 161,860 | 178,492 | 185,450 |
| United Kingdom | 1,551 | 10,580 | 54,006 | 79,000 | 80,468 | 89,000 | 103,387 | 114,500 | 125,940 | 128,500 |
| Norway | 9,277 | 9,832 | 16,800 | 18,000 | 24,381 | 23,000 | 24,480 | 30,000 | 34,954 | 38,000 |
| W. Germany | 5,741 | 5,570 | 5,056 | 4,800 | 4,631 | 4,470 | 4,234 | 4,160 | 4,030 | 4,000 |
| Austria | 2,037 | 1,950 | 1,815 | 1,825 | 1,475 | 1,300 | 1,303 | 1,200 | 1,206 | 1,150 |
| Spain | 1,745 | 1,960 | 980 | 1,100 | 1,597 | 1,400 | 1,533 | 3,000 | 2,318 | 2,100 |
| Netherlands | 1,572 | 1,500 | 1,520 | 1,550 | 1,567 | 1,500 | 1,895 | 2,800 | 3,381 | 4,000 |
| France | 1,070 | 1,060 | 1,890 | 2,000 | 1,414 | 1,700 | 1,638 | 1,600 | 2,064 | 2,500 |
| Italy | 1,017 | 1,070 | 1,473 | 1,725 | 1,825 | 1,500 | 1,744 | 2,200 | 2,285 | 2,400 |
| Denmark | 157 | 180 | 432 | 450 | 298 | 800 | 1,686 | 2,400 | 2,314 | 2,800 |
| Far East | 109,075 | 122,224 | 243,333 | 251,375 | 240,867 | 235,285 | 230,875 | 242,745 | 272,482 | 277,475 |
| China | 77,000 | 84,700 | 104,050 | 108,000 | 105,950 | 100,000 | 102,120 | 105,000 | 115,210 | 125,000 |
| Australia | 19,277 | 20,346 | 20,876 | 21,000 | 17,990 | 18,350 | 17,530 | 19,500 | 23,391 | 27,000 |
| Indonesia | 65,527 | 74,848 | 82,415 | 80,000 | 78,540 | 79,000 | 64,646 | 63,000 | 71,850 | 60,000 |
| Brunei | 9,531 | 11,080 | 10,980 | 12,000 | 12,485 | 9,000 | 8,015 | 8,750 | 8,575 | 7,500 |
| India | 8,090 | 8,610 | 10,993 | 13,000 | 9,404 | 15,000 | 19,712 | 24,000 | 28,004 | 31,000 |
| Malaysia | 4,709 | 5,460 | 10,840 | 13,000 | 13,156 | 11,000 | 15,200 | 18,050 | 21,030 | 20,200 |
| Burma | 1,032 | 980 | 1,410 | 1,500 | 1,395 | 1,200 | 1,350 | 1,300 | 1,500 | 1,500 |
| Japan | 607 | 600 | 542 | 450 | 430 | 390 | 398 | 420 | 403 | 500 |
| Pakistan | 302 | 300 | 448 | 500 | 494 | 475 | 582 | 600 | 900 | 1,650 |
| Taiwan | — | — | 220 | 250 | 180 | 180 | 175 | 175 | 175 | 175 |
| Philippines | — | — | — | 1,300 | 513 | 250 | 470 | 1,000 | 570 | 1,750 |
| New Zealand | — | — | 559 | 375 | 330 | 440 | 677 | 650 | 874 | 1,200 |
| Thailand | — | — | — | — | — | — | — | 300 | 1,100 | 2,500 |
| USSR and Eastern Europe | 513,458 | 544,530 | 595,511 | 608,170 | 625,032 | 630,850 | 635,740 | 641,350 | 634,597 | 617,310 |
| USSR | 489,800 | 521,000 | 572,500 | 585,000 | 603,000 | 609,000 | 613,000 | 618,000 | 613,000 | 595,500 |
| Romania | 14,637 | 14,850 | 13,724 | 13,500 | 11,500 | 11,000 | 11,700 | 12,500 | 12,000 | 11,600 |
| Yugoslavia | 3,691 | 3,710 | 4,077 | 4,100 | 4,244 | 4,300 | 4,324 | 4,200 | 4,034 | 4,100 |
| Albania | 2,310 | 1,870 | 2,000 | 2,000 | 3,500 | 3,800 | 4,000 | 4,000 | 3,000 | 3,500 |
| Hungary | 2,005 | 2,100 | 2,200 | 2,050 | 2,033 | 2,000 | 2,026 | 1,950 | 2,008 | 2,050 |
| Other | 1,015 | 1,000 | 1,010 | 1,520 | 755 | 750 | 690 | 700 | 555 | 560 |
| Total world production | 2,644,060 | 2,843,779 | 3,097,021 | 3,251,195 | 3,059,060 | 2,858,995 | 2,754,257 | 2,724,267 | 2,786,934 | 2,734,582 |

Source: Compiled from the *Petroleum Economist*, January 1980 to January 1987.

# PART SIX

# Managing the International Marketing Function

# General Electric Programmable Controllers

In early January 1984, Dave Shea was privately reviewing his first three months at General Electric (GE). As Manager of Worldwide Distribution and Sales for the Programmable Controls Department, he had been given an ambitious mandate to market programmable controllers (PCs) on a global scale. Although he had hoped to spend the first three or four months easing into the organization and overcoming the natural scrutiny that a new manager faced, Dave was forced to hit the ground running. He had previous experience in marketing PCs at Texas Instruments (TI), where he had been responsible for PC distribution activity, but in the presence of a complex and rapidly changing domestic organization and a limited international presence, his task at GE seemed challenging indeed.

The worldwide introduction of programmable controllers was a first step in the Factory Automation Products Group's broader strategy to achieve a position of worldwide leadership in the field of factory automation. If Dave Shea was to distribute GE's PC products on a world-wide basis, it would also be the first attempt at implementation of a global strategy in the industry. Such a strategy would certainly test GE's sales and marketing organizations. It would also send signals to other competitors in PC sales. Shea's main challenge was to enlist company-wide support for his plans. As he reflected upon his progress to date, he wondered how quickly he could get the GE organization to respond to his plans.

## GE DOMESTIC ORGANIZATION

Dave Shea was under great pressure to meet the high expectations set forth by GE. In one respect, he was fortunate to have the tremendous resources of the corporation available, yet the complex matrix organization that he faced was overwhelming. He commented, ''With no direct reports, different ways of motivating people are necessary. . . . Understanding the dotted-line relationships are just as important. This is quite a change from an organization (TI) where the lines were solid. . . . This is another world!'' Furthermore, the company's organization was changing so rapidly it was difficult to stay current with the lines of authority.

Sales of PCs were managed by the Manufacturing Automation Sales Division (MASD), which had been formed in 1984. The organization was based in Charlottesville, Virginia, the site of the Factory Automation Group headquarters. MASD was the combination of two previous selling organizations, the Contractor Equipment Sales Division (CESD) and the Industrial Sales Division (ISD)—both located at Bridgeport, Connecticut. Previously, CESD was responsible for selling to independent distributors, and ISD was responsible for direct sales to end customers. The management infrastructure for MASD was presently being built to oversee the merged sales force. Fifteen full-time sales representatives and three engineers came from CESD, and fifty-four sales representatives and fourteen application engineers came from ISD. MASD was divided geographically into eight districts. Each district manager was a generalist supervising all the sales force in that area. Each sales rep would sell a range of industrial products, although Dave was in the process of training six sales reps to focus solely on PCs. In addition to dedicated PC sales reps, other sales representatives of the Factory Automation Group, particularly those selling robots, vision, and general purpose controls, were to be incorporated into this structure over time.

Highlighting the unique situation that faced Dave Shea was dependence on PC sales staff who were technically part of the U.S. sales organization in New York. They did not report directly to him; yet, without their support, Shea's implementation plans would be impossible to achieve. The dedicated MASD PC sales representatives, however, were to be funded directly by Charlottesville.

Exhibit 1 provides an organization chart for the Factory Automation Products Division, and Exhibit 2 depicts the U.S. sales organization for the Programmable Controls Department.

## DOMESTIC COMPETITION

Industrial controls could be segmented into process control systems and discrete control products. Companies that focused on control systems for continuous process facilities typically did not offer discrete control devices for manufacturing applications. In addition, process control systems vendors tended to concentrate on specialized process applications, such as chemical, petroleum, electricity, and metals industries, whereas discrete devices often were general purpose products.

### Process Control Systems Market

Honeywell and Foxboro accounted for more than two-thirds of the total market for process control systems. After these two leading firms, Fisher Controls led Leeds and Northrup, Fischer and Porter, Taylor, and EMC Controls in a closely bunched group comprising 25 percent market share. Bailey Controls, Bristol, and Beckman Instruments accounted for a combined share of about 3 percent. Thirty other suppliers captured 5 percent of the business. The domestic U.S. market for process control systems slightly exceeded $1 billion in 1984, representing almost half of the total world sales.

*Honeywell* was a broad-based manufacturing and service company with annual worldwide sales of process control systems over $800 million in 1983. Honeywell's process control products included instruments and computer-based systems for indicating, recording, and automatically controlling process variables such as flow, humidity, liquid level, temperature, and pressure.

*Foxboro* reported 1983 process control sales of more than $600 million. Products included sensors, transmitters, analytical instruments, controllers, and associated accessories.

*Fisher Controls* was a subsidiary of the Monsanto Company. Fisher had total sales of about $600 million in 1983. The company was the leading manufacturer of process control valves and had built on this strength during the past decade to become a prominent supplier of control room and field instruments.

*Taylor Instruments* was a division of Sybron Corporation. Taylor was a major manufacturer of process instruments. The company had mar-

EXHIBIT 1

**GE PROGRAMMABLE CONTROLS DEPARTMENT: 1984 ORGANIZATION CHART**

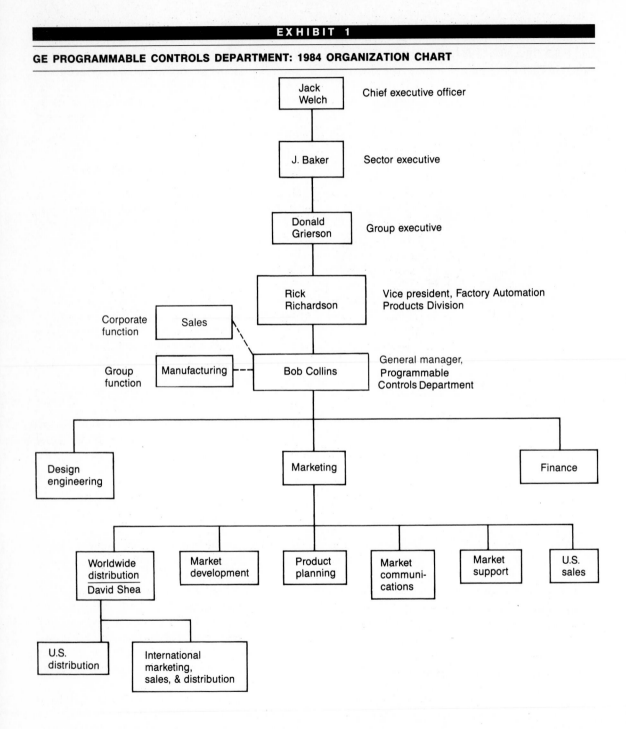

EXHIBIT 2

**PC SALES ORGANIZATION, 1984**

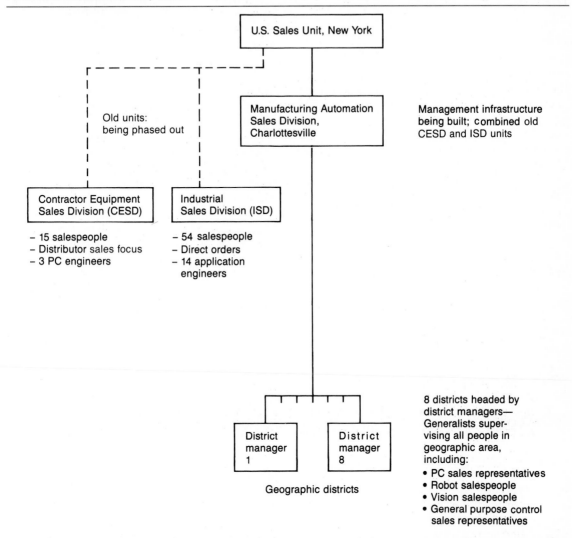

ket strengths across the process industries, with particular recognition in the food and beverage and pulp and paper sectors.

*Leeds and Northrup* was a division of General Signal. Leeds and Northrup had sales in excess of $200 million in 1983. The company marketed successfully across most process industry segments and had particular strengths in the utilities industry.

*Beckman Instruments* was acquired by Smith Kline Corporation in 1981. An estimated $220 million was generated through sales of process control equipment. Products included air-quality test and measuring instruments, moisture measuring instrument, and materials analysis instruments.

*Bailey Controls* was a division of Babcock and Wilcox, a McDermott company. Annual sales for Bailey were over $150 million. Bailey manufactured a full line of industrial instrumentation but enjoyed its greatest success in systems associated with combustion control in power utilities. International sales represented 35 percent of the total.

## The Programmable Controller Market

Programmable controller suppliers focused on the possibility that general purpose, distributed control systems would become a critical part of factory automation efforts. A number of manufacturers had begun to implement distributed control systems using PCs. These systems were usually preferred in small batch plants and were attractive to users because they facilitated strategies more flexible than those permitted by existing factory control systems.

In many cases, a set of PCs at individual work stations could be linked together to emulate a larger central process control system. In other cases, PCs were used in stand-alone systems such as those that might be used to control compressors, chillers, mixing tanks, or other relatively autonomous work stations. In some cases, it was possible to link these dedicated controllers to existing central plant control systems.

In 1984, the U.S. PC market totalled about $450 million. Allen-Bradley and Gould-Modicon were the dominant players with 36 percent and 31 percent market share, respectively. TI had a 12 percent market share, and GE followed with a 7 percent share. A number of other companies, including Westinghouse, Square D, Reliance, Eagle Signal, and ISSC, comprised the remaining 14 percent of the market.

*Allen-Bradley* had 1983 sales of about $900 million. Chief products were a full line of PCs, electrical distribution and control equipment, precision gears, and specialty plastic products for manufacturing plants. Allen-Bradley was a privately owned corporation.

*Eagle Signal* was a division of Gulf and Western. Eagle manufactured a line of PCs oriented toward process applications and linkage to large central process control systems.

*Modicon* was a subsidiary of Gould. Modicon was solely focused on the PC industry and possessed the largest installed base of PCs in the United States.

*Industrial Solid State Controls* (ISSC) had sales of $13 million in 1983. ISSC was one of the original suppliers of PCs to the process industries and was a subsidiary of IPC (Germany).

*Square D* had sales of more than $1 billion in 1983. The company was primarily a supplier of electrical control and distribution equipment. Square D manufactured a network-oriented PC system.

*TI* manufactured a wide range of electronic components and products. Its Industrial Controls Division produced PCs. TI's products were most typically used in discrete stand-alone applications.

## INDUSTRIAL CONTROL SYSTEMS

Almost all industrial processes were operated under some form of automatic control. In some instances, the systems were open-loop and simply provided commands to initiate various production phases. More often, manufacturers required closed-loop control, in which measurements or conditions were recorded, and the control system initiated commands for actions that corrected or compensated for deviations or initiated a process only after another was completed.

## DISTRIBUTED VERSUS CENTRALIZED CONTROL

In a centralized system a single computer was programmed to perform all the control and monitoring functions for the process. In a distributed system a central computer, if one existed, would provide only supervisory support to a number of remote microprocessors which performed the actual process control functions.

Future trends in computerized process controls were expected to heavily favor distributed controls over centralized systems. Among the most important reason was reliability. If one computer in a distributed system failed, the effect was much less drastic than if a central computer failed. Other advantages of distributed systems were: (1) enhanced digital signal transmissions to the supervisory computer from remote process computers; (2) lower hardware costs; (3) greater process or control flexibility; and (4) easier expansion of the system.

## PROGRAMMABLE CONTROLLERS

PCs were first developed in the mid-1960s. They were used by both discrete and process manufacturers to control simple machining tasks and to regulate temperature and pressure. The first PCs were designed to replace electromechanical relay switches in the automotive industry. A relay was a circuit connecting device. When the relay was closed, the circuit was completed and a work function was initiated. Like electromechanical relay controls, PCs controlled machining operations depending on the open or closed status of relay switches connected to points of a machining center. PCs cause events to occur through a series of if/then statements: if a part is in place, then close the clamp; if the clamp is closed, then start the drill motor; etc. Input to the programmable controller was the open or closed status of a relay connected to the clamp, for instance, and output was the action that caused the clamp to close.

Until PCs were developed, modifications and repairs on relay systems were time consuming and costly. For example, in the automotive industry, relay systems had to be scrapped when car models changed because the relay logic also changed. PCs provided a more versatile control system. PCs also allowed users to access data that was previously unavailable. Such data included cycle counts, the number of parts that passed through a machine, how long a machine had been operating and the time lapse between tool changes. To extract this information, however, users had to add higher-level computer languages to their systems.

Each PC typically consisted of the same basic components—a microprocessor, memory, I/O devices, and a power supply. Available options included terminals to program the controllers and monitor the status of a machine during operation, as well as network interfacing. Products differed in terms of memory size and in the number of machine parameters that could be controlled.

PCs served as a basis for a limited number of continuous process control systems. Because of the more restrictive nature of PCs, however, these systems had inherent cost, power, and flexibility disadvantages when implementing continuous or advanced control functions, in contrast to central process control systems.

Rather than controlling a factory with one high-end programmable controller, users controlled individual machine stations with smaller, local PCs. PCs were noted for their use in dedicated, discrete manufacturing processes. An example would be in batch manufacturing applications, where a variety of products were produced in limited quantities. Other examples of PC use included work stations along an automobile assembly line, batch food and drug applications, blending controls in food and beverage plants, detergent formulations, and material handling applications. Most applications appeared in discrete stand-alone uses. PCs in distributed systems could be linked together. Integrated PC systems, however, were currently the exception rather than the rule.

## GE PRODUCT LINE

To best meet the needs of the total PC market, GE developed a family of products designed to maximize commonality and range of applications. Manufacturers generally specified the complexity of a PC by the number of relays (I/O points) it could manage. The typical ranges of I/O points for PC's were as follows:

- Small—50–100 relays
- Medium—150–500 relays
- Large—500–3000 relays

GE was represented in each of these size categories. The Series One units featured up to 112 I/O points. Internal functions included tim-

ers, counters, master control relays, shift registers, and sequencers. A hand-held programming panel allowed the operator to monitor logic,
timer, and counter values. These units sold for
as little as $500 and typically less than $2,000
per station. Series Three PCs were optimized
for medium-scale applications up to 400 I/O
points. These units had full detachable key-
boards with cassette recorders and printers for
program storage and documentation. Programmable diagnostics enabled users to monitor and
indicate specific machine or process faults or
sequence errors. Prices for this series ranged
from $1,000 to $6,000. Series Six large-scale PCs
were available in models with up to 6000 I/O
points. CRT terminals were available for stand-
alone units that could be used on-line or off-
line. The off-line mode allowed any existing program to be monitored or changed without disturbing the control operation. Series Six systems sales typically entailed extensive customized
hardware and software, and sold for an average
of $20,000 or more.

## SEGMENTATION

Suppliers typically segmented their customers
by industry and by type of operation, process
or nonprocess (discrete). The following is a list
of PC user industries, segmented in this manner:

| Process | Nonprocess |
| --- | --- |
| Food | Machinery |
| Paper | Electrical equipment |
| Chemicals | Fabricated metals |
| Petroleum and coal | Transportation equipment |
| Rubber and plastic | Electronic devices |
| Glass | Consumer electronics |
| Utilities | Aerospace |
| Primary metals | Instruments |

A breakdown of the U.S. programmable controller market by major industry user segments
appears in Exhibit 3. While process industries
often exhibited highly sophisticated control sys-

tems, factory automation was more a concept
than a market in 1984.

## FACTORY AUTOMATION

Factory automation was typically approached
on a piecemeal basis. Individual operations or
production lines were automated using diverse,
often incompatible equipment such as PCs, robots, and computerized machine tool controls
(CNCs). Automation efforts were hampered by
the multiplicity of vendors and equipment. Few
firms or even facilities had achieved full, integrated automation.

Manufacturing firms generally had not demonstrated a willingness to fully automate existing facilities because of changeover costs. In
addition, automated facilities were only effective when supported and supplemented by sophisticated computer-aided engineering, design
and manufacturing systems (CAE, CAD, CAM),
automated materials handling, and a range of
operations management software systems. Few
firms were willing to make the large investments
necessary to develop a fully automated manufacturing system. As a result, the factory of the
future marketplace had yet to demonstrate any
of its promise. GE's commitment to the market
had not wavered, but the financial performance
of the factory automation group had been highly
disappointing. GE management hoped that programmable controllers might provide a vehicle
for market development and short-term financial results. Dave Shea had been hired to generate these results.

## DISTRIBUTORS

An integral part of the sales organization for
electrical and electronic products was the independent distributor. The typical distributor
was an independent business owner who sold
electrical equipment for use on the factory floor.
Customers would tell distributors what they
needed and provide specifications. The PC,
however, presented a far more difficult sales

**EXHIBIT 3**

**U.S. PROGRAMMABLE CONTROLLER MARKET SIZE AND SEGMENTATION**

| | 1983*<br>($ million) | 1984*<br>($ million) | 1986†<br>($ million) | Annual growth rate<br>1983–1986 (%) |
|---|---|---|---|---|
| **Process** | | | | |
| Food | 27 | 35 | 50 | 23 |
| Paper | 14 | 18 | 25 | 21 |
| Chemicals | 22 | 28 | 39 | 21 |
| Petroleum & coal | 10 | 12 | 17 | 19 |
| Rubber & plastic | 14 | 18 | 24 | 20 |
| Glass | 9 | 12 | 16 | 20 |
| Utilities | 17 | 22 | 33 | 25 |
| Primary metals | 18 | 23 | 27 | 15 |
| Total | 131 | 168 | 231 | 21 |
| **Discrete** | | | | |
| Nonelectrical machinery | 27 | 35 | 45 | 19 |
| Electrical and electronic | 46 | 60 | 79 | 20 |
| Fabricated metals | 23 | 30 | 38 | 18 |
| Transportation equipment | 72 | 85 | 105 | 13 |
| Other | 61 | 82 | 92 | 15 |
| Total | 229 | 292 | 359 | 16 |
| Grand total | 360 | 460 | 590 | 18 |

*Estimates; †Projection.

task. The customer typically had to be educated about the product, sold on the product's economics, and given specific applications and software support.

Allen-Bradley, long established in traditional product lines, had been particularly successful in adapting its distributors to the new selling requirements of the PC. They looked for distributors with advanced engineering or technical backgrounds who could understand PC technology and identify applications. The company provided them with much educational and sales support and, as a result, Allen-Bradley's distributors were as effective as most companies' direct sales representatives.

There were, however, great differences in the distribution policies of the top PC manufacturers. GE and Westinghouse had their own in-house distributors. GE Supply Company (GESCO) was a major distributor of electrical equipment to industrial customers. However GE frequently used independent distributors for its electrical equipment. TI had recently developed a set of independent distributors to market its PCs. Gould/Modicon and Siemens sold only through direct salesmen.

## INTERNATIONAL COMPETITION

Allen-Bradley was the world leader in PC sales, although its sales were concentrated in the United States. Siemens, on the other hand, had 20 percent of the European market but limited sales outside of Europe. The former number one seller in the United States, Gould/Modicon, had approximately 32 percent of domestic sales but limited presence overseas. TI had declined from 35 to 13 percent of market share since the 1970s in the United States, but it was beginning to expand its foreign market share. Despite the fact that GE was recognized to have all the technological pieces in place for factory automation, it had less than 10 percent of domestic PC sales and a smaller share abroad. GE's small market share was deceiving, however, since sales had doubled in the last two years and were expected to grow 50 percent in 1984.

Although the PC market was fragmented, some worldwide players were emerging. Gould/Modicon, TI, and Allen-Bradley were all strong competitors, capable of competing worldwide, but only Allen-Bradley had a broad product line beyond PCs (i.e., numeric control and general purpose controls). Allen-Bradley also had probably the strongest distribution system among the PC manufacturers. Approximately 80 percent of its sales went through distributors, who were supplemented with PC experts and direct salesmen. Only Siemens, however, rivaled GE in sheer size and scope. They had recently started a new affiliate based in Boston, Siemens Factory Automation, to offer PCs and factory automation systems. Siemens appeared to have plans for a strong presence in the U.S. and global PC markets. Unlike GE, they did not sell through distributors. All their sales were made through a direct sales force.

## EUROPEAN MARKETS

PC markets were highly localized and fragmented. Each country was viewed as a different market with different competitors and selling requirements. For example, distribution channels often varied among countries. Because of this range of market conditions, few companies were able to excel in more than one country. Although Siemens was dominant in Germany, they did not have similar status in any other country. Since Europe's market size, approximately $380 million, was second only to the U.S. market, it was of prime interest to Dave Shea. GE's commitment to a global strategy required them to develop a presence in Europe. The following provides an analysis of the major European markets (see Exhibit 4).

**United Kingdom** The U.K. PC market was estimated to reach approximately $30 million in 1984. Allen-Bradley was the leader with 24 percent of the market followed by GEC Ltd. with 17 percent market share. Other significant competitors were TI with 13 percent share and MTE with 10 percent share. IPC/ISSC and Omron had 6 percent and 5 percent market share, respectively, and others comprised the remaining 25 percent. The UK market was significant for suppliers of process control systems, primarily Fisher, Foxboro, and Honeywell. The U.K. PC market was expected to grow annually by 20 percent through 1989.

**Germany** The German PC market was expected to total about $227 million in 1984. It was forecast to grow by almost 19 percent annually through 1989. Siemens was the dominant PC manufacturer, holding 30 percent of the market in Germany. Unlike most other European countries, distributors were not significant in Germany. Siemens, for example, sold only directly through their sales force. If GE was to enter this market, they might have to acquire a local company to distribute their products or develop a local selling organization.

**Italy** Italy's market size was approximately $37 million. The dominant companies were Allen-Bradley, TI and Siemens with 22%, 19% and 14% market share, respectively. IPC/ISSC, Gould/Modicon and COGEMAC (a GE affiliate), were also significant participants.

**France** France represented almost $80 million of the European market. Historically, Telemechanique dominated the French market with about a 25 percent market share. The recent merger of SMC Renault and Merlin-Geri, the number two and five companies, respectively, had formed a new leader in PC sales. Together, they represented approximately 35 percent of French sales. The French market was estimated to grow at 16 percent annually through 1989.

**EXHIBIT 4**

**INTERNATIONAL PC MARKET SIZE** ($ Millions)

| | 1983 | 1984 | 1985 | 1986 | 1987 | 1988 | 1989 |
|---|---|---|---|---|---|---|---|
| **Europe** | | | | | | | |
| Germany | 218 | 227 | 278 | 353 | 415 | 470 | 539 |
| France | 83 | 78 | 89 | 105 | 124 | 144 | 164 |
| Italy | 31 | 37 | 48 | 66 | 74 | 79 | 84 |
| United Kingdom | 27 | 30 | 38 | 50 | 60 | 70 | 75 |
| Total | 359 | 372 | 453 | 574 | 673 | 763 | 862 |
| **Asia** | | | | | | | |
| Japan | 130 | 128 | 151 | 168 | 184 | 202 | 214 |
| Australia | 17 | 17 | 22 | 28 | 34 | 41 | 47 |
| Taiwan | 16 | 17 | 23 | 30 | 39 | 45 | 51 |
| Korea | 8 | 9 | 13 | 17 | 22 | 30 | 39 |
| P.R.C. | 6 | 6 | 9 | 12 | 17 | 22 | 28 |
| Other Asia | 12 | 13 | 16 | 20 | 25 | 2 | 39 |
| Total | 189 | 190 | 234 | 275 | 321 | 372 | 418 |
| **Other** | | | | | | | |
| Mexico | 9 | 9 | 11 | 13 | 16 | 22 | 27 |
| Canada | 28 | 30 | 40 | 49 | 59 | 69 | 79 |
| South America | 35 | 34 | 41 | 47 | 58 | 69 | 81 |
| Middle East | 16 | 17 | 22 | 28 | 34 | 40 | 43 |
| Total | 88 | 90 | 114 | 137 | 167 | 200 | 230 |
| **Total** | 636 | 652 | 801 | 986 | 1,161 | 1,335 | 1,510 |

*Note:* 1983 figures are estimates; 1984–89 are projections.

## EUROPEAN DISTRIBUTION PLANS

Since GE would have to compete in each country on the terms dictated by that environment, Dave Shea knew he would have to adapt his global strategy on a market-by-market basis. In evaluating each international market, he also had to consider different methods of participation. The four modes of entry he considered were agreements with local distributors, acquisitions, development of local selling units, and joint ventures with either local companies or GE subsidiaries.

Acquisition was attractive for several reasons; speed of market entry, installed base, and direct control were primary benefits of such an approach. However, there were very few attractive acquisition candidates in the European PC industry, and those that did exist were quite expensive. Local distributors could provide ex-

tensive market knowledge and relationships without significant capital investment, but they often were less effective than a direct sales force and were difficult to control. Joint ventures exhibited many of the same characteristics but required greater financial and organizational investments. A direct sales force could provide Shea with perhaps the strongest presence in European markets, but it would take time and money to create a strong, dedicated PC field sales organization in Europe.

### Industrial Automation Europe

As an example of GE's worldwide resources, Industrial Automation Europe (IAE), the company's foreign factory automation arm, was available to manage the PC sales organization in Europe. IAE reported directly to Charlottes-

---

**EXHIBIT 5**

---

**INDUSTRIAL AUTOMATION EUROPE: 1984 ORGANIZATION CHART**

---

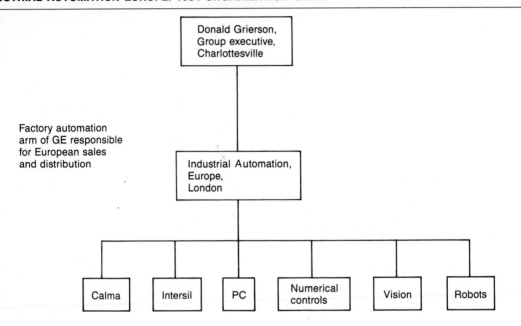

ville and was responsible for Calma (CAD/CAM systems), Intersil (semiconductors), programmable controls, numeric controls, robots and vision products (see Exhibit 5). All direct PC sales personnel would be employed through this organization, as would the European PC Manager, when selected. The entire European PC field sales force would report to this new manager. Funding of $2 million to build a PC sales organization was being supplied by Charlottesville for 1984. The Programmable Controls Department was receiving these funds from corporate venture funding sources as a testament to the importance GE headquarters placed on this business venture.

Through IAE, GE planned to hire a direct sales force and develop selected distributors in each European country. By using IAE to manage European market development, GE would be better able to control the marketing process and the dissemination of technology. However, there were two exceptions to this approach. In

Italy, COGEMAC would be responsible for building the PC sales and marketing organization. COGEMAC was a subsidiary of COGENEL, which was part of the Technical Systems Group. Since COGEMAC was a GE subsidiary, there was no concern for outside control; however, the fact the COGENEL was part of a different GE group highlighted the complexity of managing reporting relationships. In France, Shea felt that GE must sacrifice client control and find a suitable joint venture partner in order to meet the unique needs of that market.

## Use of Distributors

Dave Shea felt that in addition to IAE's direct sales force, distributors would play a critical role in most if not all markets. In some customer segments, distributors would fill the primary selling role. In others they would be secondary or nonexistent participants.

Potential distributors were screened in Europe for final selection by Dave Shea. The selection process was straightforward, since there were specific attributes necessary for approval:

- Local organizations were favored over global organizations, since separate distributors were being selected for each market.
- Distributors must have an established industrial customer base.
- They must have established reputations for industrial sales rather than construction business.
- They must have a strong high-technology orientation: competitive PC products, companion products to PCs, or process control equipment.

PC sales required an organization with technical sales competency. PC products were already selling in international markets, but GE needed to develop distributors that would market not only PCs but the factory automation product line of the future. Over the long term, distributors would have to be capable of adding value through functions such as software development, programming, and systems and technical support.

Another question Dave faced was which GE products should be emphasized in each market. He was aware that there were vastly different efforts required to sell a Series Six PC product as compared to a Series One. Ideally, distributors that could market GE's full family of PCs were desirable. Dave wondered, however, if sales of the Series Six line should be limited to direct sale.

## ASIA MARKETS

In addition to the United States and Europe, GE also hoped to build a presence in Asia. Asia represented about $190 million in sales; Japan alone accounted for almost $130 million of this market. GE's target markets included Taiwan, Korea, Hong Kong, Singapore, and the Philippines. Although small, Taiwan and Korea were expected to grow by almost 25 percent and 35 percent annually over the next five years.

While Dave Shea was formulating his distribution strategy for the Far East, GE Trading Company (GETC) proposed an association to help market PCs. GETC, which exported both GE and other companies' products totaling about $260 million in 1983, had just completed a change in strategy resulting in a more aggressive approach and a greater emphasis on GE-sourced products. Upon reaching an agreement with the PC group, GETC established an Electronic Programs Marketing Manager in New York to be responsible for PC sales in Asia. Shea now had an organization around which to plan distribution strategy in Asia.

Since the total Asian market was small, and individual countries represented only $3 to $5 million in PC sales to GE, a strategy similar to the one planned in Europe was not viable. A direct sales force was uneconomic; an intermediary between the company and distributors was necessary. As a solution, one person in each targeted country was picked from within GETC to promote PCs. They were given initial training on the product, applications, competitors, and selling techniques so that they could provide the necessary interface with the distributors, and were paid a commission based on distributor sales. The candidates for distributors were picked by GETC people subject to final approval by Dave Shea. Because of the small size of the local markets, only one distributor was planned for each country. GE was requesting that the distributors share some of the initial investment. Subject to the achievement of mutually defined sales goals, the exclusive sales agreement would last at least three years.

The major country missing from the list of target countries was Japan. Since GE sourced two of its three major PC products, the Series One and Three lines, from a Japanese firm, Koyo K.K., GE had agreed not to sell in Japan. In Koyo, GE found low-cost electronics manufacturing expertise that it did not have. GE added much design input into the Series One and Three lines. Koyo produced these products under a private label to GE specifications.

## SUMMARY

As Dave Shea glanced at his watch, he realized he had lost track of the time as he contemplated the challenge that awaited him. He knew his strategy for PC distribution was sound, but he felt distracted by the sheer number of obstacles that he would confront. Strong international competitors pursuing global strategies, a complex internal matrix organization which would limit Shea's direct control, and an ambitious mandate from corporate headquarters added up to a complex situation. At this stage, not only was Dave directing the strategy and implementation, but he was also making the merchandising decisions and approving distributors. He commented, "The risk is great, but that is what

makes this job so exciting. GE has distribution knowledge, but not high-technology distribution. . . . This is why I was hired." At TI, Dave had gained this type of experience by developing their distribution program. He also had experience in sales management which would be valuable at GE.

In spite of all the difficulties associated with this assignment, Dave Shea knew he had some power which was not written in his job description. This business venture was much different from normal GE operations; he had a green light from management. Bob Collins, the General Manager for Programmable Controls, was running interference for planning and budgeting; and Jack Welch, the CEO, repeatedly emphasized the importance of this business. The PC Department was a showcase, a model of the future for GE. As Dave thought about this, he felt a surge of confidence that he would succeed.

# Procter & Gamble Europe

There were three critical decisions facing Procter & Gamble's (P&G) senior management in June 1981 as they reviewed the German test market results for Vizir, the new heavy duty liquid (HDL) detergent:

- Should they follow the recommendation of Wolfgang Berndt and his German team and authorize a national launch on the basis of four months of test results? Or should they wait until final test market results were in, or perhaps even rethink their entire HDL product strategy?
- If and when the decision was taken to launch Vizir, to what extent could this be considered a European rather than just a German product? If a coordinated European rollout was planned, to what degree should the company standardize its product formulation, packaging, advertising, and promotion?
- Finally, what organizational implications would these decisions have? For example, to what

extent should individual country subsidiary managers retain the responsibility to decide when and how this new product would be introduced in their national market?

## PROCTER & GAMBLE: COMPANY BACKGROUND

To understand anything in P&G, one had to appreciate the company's strong and long-established culture that was reflected in the corporate values, policies, and practices. The following paragraphs outline how the company saw itself in each of these areas.

### Corporate Values

Established in 1837 by two men of strong religious faith and moral conviction, P&G soon had developed an explicit set of corporate standards and values. From their earliest contact, prospective employees were told of P&G's firm belief that the interests of the company were inseparable from those of its employees. Over the years, this broad philosophy had been translated

---

This case was prepared by Associate Professor Christopher A. Bartlett. Proprietary data have been disguised, but key relationships are preserved. Copyright © 1983 by the President and Fellows of Harvard College. Revised September 1987.

into a variety of widely shared management norms such as the following:

- P&G should hire only good people of high character.
- P&G must treat them as individuals with individual talents and life goals.
- P&G should provide a work environment that encourages and rewards individual achievement.

The shared beliefs soon became part of the company's formal management systems. General managers would tell you they were evaluated on the achievements in three areas: volume, profit, and people. P&G also tried to attract people willing to spend their entire career with the company. Promotions were made from within, and top management was chosen from career P&G people rather than from outside the company.

## Management Policies

Over its almost 150-year history, P&G had accumulated a broad base of industry experience and business knowledge. Within the company, this accumulated knowledge was seen as an important asset, and a great deal of it had been formalized and institutionalized as management principles and policies. In the words of Chairman Ed Harness, "Though our greatest asset is our people, it is the consistency of principle and policy which gives us direction."

It was in the marketing area that these operating principles and management policies were the most strategically important for a company with reputation as a premier consumer marketer. One of the most basic policies was that P&G's products should provide "superior total value" and should meet "basic consumer needs." This resulted in a strong commitment to research to create products that were demonstrably better than the competition in blind tests. (In the words of one manager, "Before you can launch a new brand, you must have a win in a white box.")

Furthermore, P&G believed strongly in the value of market research. In a business where poorly conceived new product launches could

be very expensive and sometimes not very successful, continuous and detailed market research was seen as insurance against major mistakes. Chairman Ed Harness had described their market research objectives as being "to spot a new trend early, then lead it."

For similar reasons, P&G also believed in extensive product and market testing before making major brand decisions. Having spotted a trend through market research, the company typically spent two or three years testing the product and the marketing strategy it had developed before committing to a full-scale launch. One paper goods competitor said of them: "P&G tests and tests and tests. They leave no stone unturned, no variable untested. You can see them coming for months and years, but you know when they get there, it is time for you to move."

Finally, P&G believed that through continual product development and close tracking of consumer needs and preferences, brands could be managed so that they remained healthy and profitable in the long term. Their rejection of the conventional product-life-cycle mentality was demonstrated by the fact that Ivory Soap was over 100 years old, Crisco shortening was more than 70, and Tide detergent more than 35, yet each was still a leader in its field.

## Organization Practices

In addition to strong corporate values and clear management principles, the P&G culture was also characterized by well-established organization practices and processes. Its internal operations had been described as thorough, creative, and aggressive by some, and as slow, risk-averse, and rigid by others. There was probably an element of truth in both descriptions.

Perhaps the most widely known of P&G's organizational characteristics was its legendary brand manager structure. Created in 1931, the brand management system was designed to provide each brand with management focus, expertise, and drive at a low level in the organization. By legitimizing and even reinforcing the internal competition that had existed since Camay Soap was launched in competition with Ivory in 1923, the brand manager system tended to restrict lateral communication. This resulted in a norm among P&G managers that information was shared on a "need to know" basis only.

Although the brand manager system may have impaired lateral communication, vertical communication within P&G was strong and well established. Proposals on most key issues were normally generated at the lower levels of management, with analysis and recommendations working their way up the organization for concurrence and approval. In P&G, top management was intimately involved in most large decisions—e.g., all new brand launches, capital appropriations in excess of $100,000, and personnel appointment and promotion decisions three levels down. Although the approval system could be slow and at times bureaucratic (one manager claimed that a label change on Head and Shoulders shampoo had required 55 signatures), it was designed to minimize risk in the very risky and expensive consumer marketing business. Once a project was approved, it would have the company's full commitment. As one manager said, "Once they sign off [on the new brand launch], they will bet the farm."

A third characteristic of the P&G management process was that proposals were committed to paper, usually in the form of one- or two-page memos. The purpose was to encourage thoroughness and careful analysis on the part of the proposal originators and objectivity and rationality on the part of the managers who reviewed the document. Written documents could also flow more easily through the organization, building support or eliciting comments and suggestions.

## P&G INTERNATIONAL: EUROPEAN OPERATIONS

### Expansion Principles

Although P&G had acquired a small English soap company in 1926, it was not until the postwar years that the company built a substantial European presence. In 1954 a French detergent company was acquired; two years later, a Bel-

gian plant was opened; and by the end of the decade P&G had established operations in Holland and Italy. A Swiss subsidiary served as a worldwide export center. In the 1960s, subsidiaries were opened in Germany, Austria, Greece, Spain, and the Scandinavian countries. The European Technical Center (ETC) was established in Brussels in 1963, to provide R&D facilities and a small regional management team.

By 1981 Europe represented about 15 percent of P&G's $11 billion worldwide sales, with almost all that substantial volume built in the previous two-and-a-half decades. The German and U.K. subsidiaries were the largest, each representing about one-fifth of the company's European sales. France and Italy together accounted for another 30 percent, and Belgium, Holland, Spain, Austria, and Switzerland together made up the balance.

As international operations grew, questions arose as to how the new foreign subsidiaries should be managed. As early as 1955, Walter Lingle, P&G's Overseas vice president, laid down some important principles that guided the company's subsequent development abroad. Recognizing that consumer needs and preferences differed by country, Lingle emphasized the importance of acquiring the same intensive knowledge of local consumers as was required in the United States. Lingle said, "Washing habits . . . vary widely from country to country. We must tailor products to meet consumer demands in each nation. We cannot simply sell products with U.S. formulas. They won't work—they won't be accepted."

But Lingle insisted that the management policies and practices that had proven so successful for P&G in the United States would be equally successful overseas. He said: "The best way to succeed in other countries is to build in each one as exact a replica of the U.S. Procter & Gamble organization as it is possible to create."

### European Industry and Competitive Structure

From their earliest exposure to the European market for laundry detergents, U.S. managers realized how important the first of these principles would be. Washing habits and market structures not only differed from the familiar U.S. situation but also varied from one country to the next within Europe. Among the more obvious differences in laundry characteristics were the following:

- Typical washing temperatures were much higher in Europe, and the "boil wash" (over 60°C) was the norm in most countries. However, lower washing temperatures were commonplace in some countries where washing machines did not heat water (e.g., the United Kingdom) or where hand washing was still an important segment (e.g. Spain, Italy).
- European washing machines were normally front loading with a horizontal rotating drum—very different from the U.S. norm of an agitator action in a top loaded machine. The European machine also had a smaller water capacity (3 to 5 gallons versus 12 to 14 gallons in the United States) and used a much longer cycle (90 to 120 minutes versus 20 to 30 minutes for the United States).
- Europeans used more cottons and fewer synthetics than Americans and tended to wear clothes longer between washes. Average washing frequency was 2 to 3 times per week versus 4 to 5 times in the United States. Despite the lower penetration of washing machines, much higher detergent dosage per load resulted in the total European laundry detergent consumption being about 30 percent above the U.S. total.

Market structures and conditions were also quite different from those in the United States, and also varied widely within Europe, as illustrated by the following examples:

- In Germany, concentration ratios among grocery retailers were among the highest in the world. The five largest chains (including coops and associations) accounted for 65 percent of the retail volume, compared with about 15 percent in the United States. In contrast, in Italy, the independent corner store was still

very important, and hypermarkets had not made major inroads.
- Unlimited access to television similar to the U.S. market was available only in the United Kingdom (and even there was much more expensive). In Holland, each brand was allowed only 46 minutes of TV commercial time per annum; in Germany and Italy, companies had to apply for blocks of TV time once a year. Allocated slots were very limited.
- National legislation greatly affected product and market strategies. Legislation in Finland and Holland limited phosphate levels in detergent; German laws made coupons, refunds, and premium offers all but impossible; elsewhere local laws regulated package weight, labeling, and trade discounts.

The competitive environment was also different from P&G's accustomed market leadership position in the United States. In Europe, P&G shared the first-tier position with two European companies, Unilever and Henkel. By the early 1970s each company claimed between 20 percent and 25 percent of the European laundry detergent market. P&G's old domestic market rival Colgate had a 10 percent share and was in a second tier. At a third level were several national competitors. Henkel was present in most European markets but strongest in Germany, its home market; Unilever was also very international, dominating in Holland and the United Kingdom; Colgate's presence in Europe was spottier, but it had built up a very strong position in France. National companies typically were strong at the lower end of their local markets.

Each company had its own competitive characteristics. Unilever had long been a sleeping giant but was becoming much more aggressive by the mid-1970s. Henkel was a strong competitor and could be relied on to defend its home market position tenaciously. Colgate was trying to elbow its way in and tended to be more impulsive and take bigger risks, often launching new products with only minimal testing. As a result, P&G's market share varied by national market (see Exhibit 1).

EXHIBIT 1

**LAUNDRY DETERGENT MARKET** ($ Million)

|  | Total market | P&G share |
|---|---|---|
| Germany | 950 | 200 |
| United Kingdom | 660 | 220 |
| France | 750 | 160 |
| Italy | 650 | 140 |
| Spain | 470 | 90 |
| Total Europe | 3,750 | 950 |

By the mid-1970s, the rapid growth of the previous two decades dropped to a standstill. Not only did the oil crisis add dramatically to costs, but almost simultaneously, washing machines approached the 85 percent penetration rate many regarded as saturation point. In the late 1970s, volume was growing at 2 percent per annum. As market growth slowed, competitive pressures increased.

## P&G Europe's Strategy and Organization

These differences in consumer habits, market conditions and competitive environment, led to the development of strong national subsidiaries with the responsibility for developing products and marketing programs to match the local environment. Each subsidiary was a miniature Procter & Gamble, with its own brand management structure, its own product development capability, its own advertising agencies, and typically, its own manufacturing capability. The subsidiary general manager was responsible for the growth of the business and the organization.

Most subsidiaries faced a major task of establishing P&G in the basic detergent and soap business in their national market. The general manager typically tried to select the best volume and profit opportunity from the more than 200 products in the company's portfolio. The general manager of the Italian subsidiary described the choices he faced when he took over in 1974:

> Given the limits of P&G Italy's existing brands (a laundry detergent, a bar soap, and a recently ac-

quired coffee business), we had to build our volume and profit, and broaden our base. The choices we had were almost limitless. Pampers had been very successful in Germany and Belgium, but Italy couldn't afford such an expensive launch; Motiv, a new dishwashing liquid was being launched in France and Germany, but we were unconvinced of its potential here; Mr. Propre [Mr. Clean in the United States] was successful in three European countries, but competition in Italy was strong; finally we decided to launch Monsavon, the French bar soap. It represented an affordable new product launch in a traditionally good profit line.

Each of the country general managers reported to Tom Bower, an Englishman who had headed up P&G's European operations since 1961. Bower had a reputation as an entrepreneur and an excellent motivator. He believed that by selecting creative and entrepreneurial country general managers and giving them the freedom to run their business, results would follow. The strategy had been most successful for P&G, and sales and profits had grown rapidly throughout the 1960s and into the early 1970s. Growth had been aided by P&G's entry into new national markets and new product categories and by the rapid growth of the core detergent business with the penetration of washing machines into European homes.

Bower made sure that his small headquarters staff understood that they were not to interfere unduly in subsidiary decisions. Primarily, it was the subsidiary general manager's responsibility to call on ETC if there was a problem.

When Tom Bower retired in 1975, his successor, Ed Artzt, was faced with a situation quite different from that in the 1950s and 1960s. As growth slowed, competition intensified, prices weakened, and profits dipped. Artzt felt that if profit and sales growth were to be rekindled, the diverse country operations would have to be better coordinated.

Over the next five years, under his leadership, the role of ETC took on new importance. (Exhibit 2 shows an abbreviated organization chart). If increased competition was leading to declining margins, more emphasis must be placed

## EXHIBIT 2

### ABBREVIATED ORGANIZATION CHART: P&G EUROPE

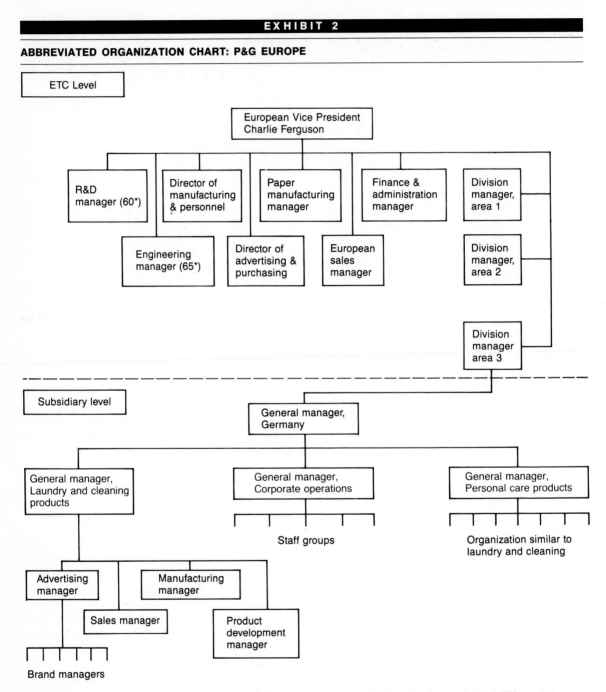

*Number of managerial and technical/professional staff. Total number of managerial/technical/professional staff at ETC was 175.

on controlling costs, and Artzt moved to strengthen the ETC finance manager's role. The finance manager described the problems:

> Largely because of duplication of marketing and administrative groups in each subsidiary, our overhead expense per unit was almost 50 percent higher than in the U.S. parent. We needed to get it under control. Our problem was that we couldn't get meaningful or comparable costs by subsidiary. Our introduction of better cost and reporting systems helped put pressure on subsidiaries to control their costs. It had a very beneficial effect.

Artzt was also concerned about the slowing of innovation in P&G Europe and felt that part of the sales and profit problem was due to the fact that too few new products were being developed, and those that were, were not being introduced in a coordinated manner. Under the strong leadership of Wahib Zaki, Artzt's new R&D manager, ETC's role in product development took a dramatic shift.

Previously each subsidiary was responsible for initiating its own local product development. These groups drew on the company's basic technology from the United States, as modified by ETC. The R&D group in a subsidiary the size of France was around 30, whereas Germany's technical staff was perhaps twice that size. Responding to its own local market, the subsidiary defined and developed products with the appropriate characteristics, perhaps calling on ETC for specialized technical support or backup. There was no requirement for a subsidiary to use standard formulations or technology. As a result, Ariel detergent had nine different formulas Europewide, having been positioned diversely as a low- and a high-suds powder, and for low- and high-temperature usage, depending on the country.

The problem with developing products in this way, concluded Zaki, was that there was insufficient focus, prioritization, or strategic direction for the work. As a result, the strong technical capabilities housed in the European Technical Center as well as in the United States were not being fully or effectively utilized. Fur-

thermore, their efforts were not being appreciated by local country management, who tended to view the technical center as a high-cost, perfectionist group that did not respond rapidly enough to market needs.

Zaki aimed to change this by having ETC take a stronger leadership role in R&D and by assuming responsibility for coordinating the new product development efforts among the subsidiaries. He felt the time had come where this was possible. His analysis indicated that habit differences between countries were narrowing and no longer justified product differences of the type that then existed from one country to another. He felt the need to establish priorities, to coordinate efforts, and, to the extent possible, to standardize products Europewide. To achieve these goals he needed the involvement and cooperation of the subsidiaries.

In 1977, Zaki reorganized European R&D, creating European Technical Teams to work on products and technologies that had Europewide importance. In his vision, European products would be superior to existing local national products but without compromising performance or increasing cost. The objective was to focus the resources of the total European R&D community around key brands and to define a long-term European approach to product development.

As roles became clearer, the ETC technical groups were seen as being the developers of new technologies ("putting the molecules together" as one described it), while the subsidiaries took responsibility for testing and refining the products in the field. After a couple of painful years, the new process seemed to be working. "Lead countries" were named for each of the key products, thereby giving more local subsidiary responsibility and ownership for the development process, and ensuring ongoing coordination among subsidiaries. Transfer of technical staff between ETC and subsidiaries further encouraged the interdependence and cooperation.

An experimental attempt at "Europeanization" in marketing, however, had been less successful. In a break from the philosophy of product adaptation, a group of managers in Cincinnati had concluded that "a baby is a baby" worldwide and that the laborious market-by-market evaluations necessary for cleaning products would not be needed for disposable diapers. In line with this decision, it was decided to gain experience by managing key elements of Pampers (such as product and copy strategy) on a Europewide basis. A senior manager was transferred from the German subsidiary where Pampers had been launched in 1973 to ETC where he was given responsibility for leading key activities on Pampers in all subsidiaries.

The brand promotion manager responsible for Pampers in France at the time recalled the experiment:

> As soon as it was known I would be principally working with the European Pampers manager in ETC and not the subsidiary GM, my local support dried up. I couldn't get a brand manager or even an assistant to work with me. The French subsidiary manager was preoccupied with the Motiv (dishwashing liquid) launch and was trying to regain leadership with Ariel (laundry powder). The Pampers situation was a disaster. Eventually Pampers was given back to the subsidiaries—it was the only way to get their support.

This experience conveyed a very important lesson to P&G's top management. It appeared that while coordination and planning could be effectively centralized and implemented on a European basis, the day-to-day management of the business had to continue to be executed at the local subsidiary level.

In 1980, Ed Artzt was transferred back to Cincinnati as executive vice president of P&G, and Charlie Ferguson was named Group Vice President, Europe. Ferguson had a reputation as an energetic, creative, and intelligent manager who got things done. Impressed by the effectiveness of the European approach to technical development, Ferguson was convinced that a similar approach could succeed in product marketing.

With the encouragement and support of his boss, Ed Artzt, who remained a strong advocate of Europeanization, Charlie Ferguson began to test the feasibility of developing Europewide brand and marketing strategies. In pursuing the Eurobrand concept, as it was becoming known, Artzt and Ferguson saw Vizir, the new heavy duty liquid being prepared for launch in Germany, as being a good test case.

## THE VIZIR PROJECT

### Product Development

Following Lever's success in the United States with a product called Wisk, in 1974 P&G launched Era as their entrant in the fast-growing HDL detergent segment. As a late entrant, however, they were unable to match Wisk's dominant share. P&G managers watching developments from Europe realized that if the HDL product concept was transferable to their market, the first company to stake out the territory would have a major advantage. The success of liquids in other product categories (e.g., household cleansers), the trend toward low-temperature washes, and the availability of liquid product plant capacity, all provided additional incentives to proceed with the project.

ETC initiated its HDL project in late 1974, and as a first step tested the U.S. product Era against European powders in a small-scale test panel. Given the differences in laundry habits on either side of the Atlantic, it was not surprising that Era was evaluated poorly. The problems reported by the panel related not only to the product's washing performance (e.g., whitening ability, suds level), but also to its form. European washing machines were built with drawers that allowed different powdered products (pretreatment, main wash detergent, fabric softener) to be activated at different times in the typical 90-minute cycle. To win acceptance of a laundry liquid would be difficult. First consumers would have to be convinced that this product would achieve similar results; then their established usage behaviors would have to be changed.

Undeterred, a group at ETC began to work on a HDL product that would be more suited to European laundry practices. It was with high hopes and considerable corporate visibility that the modified European HDL product was placed in six full-scale blind tests in Germany, France, and the United Kingdom. The results were disastrous in all tests. Given the high level of internal expectations that had been created, many P&G insiders felt that the product was dead since it would be impossible to rebuild internal support and credibility.

However, the scientists at ETC were convinced that they should be able to capitalize on the intrinsic ability of a liquid detergent to incorporate three times the level of surfactants compared to a powder. (The surfactant was the critical ingredient that removes greasy stains.) The challenge was to compensate for the shortcomings of the HDL that offset this important advantage. Unlike U.S. products, European powdered detergents normally contained enzymes (to break down proteins), and bleach (to oxidize stains), in addition to builders (to prevent redisposition of dirt), phosphates (to soften water), and surfactants. Unfortunately, it was not then possible to incorporate enzymes and bleach in a liquid detergent, and it was this limited capability that was behind the new product's blind test failure in Europe.

The challenge of overcoming these deficiencies excited P&G's scientists at ETC and in the United States. Eventually they were able to patent a method to give enzymes stability in liquid form. Soon afterward, a bleach substitute that was effective at lower temperatures was developed. The product modifications showed in improving consumer blind test results. In late 1976, the new HDL product won a blind test against the leading French powder, Ariel; the following year it won against Persil, the German market leader.

Although the project was still on shaky ground within P&G, the successes resulted in the establishment of a HDL brand group in Germany. The group reported to Germany's newly appointed advertising manager for laundry and cleaning products, Wolfgang Berndt, a 34-year-old Austrian who was recognized as one of the promising young managers in Europe. He had started his career 10 years earlier in the company's Austrian subsidiary, and after gaining training and experience in brand management in Austria, the United Kingdom, and Germany, had spent two years in Cincinnati as a brand manager in the parent company's Toilet Goods Division. He returned to Europe in 1973 as brand promotion manager in P&G Italy, before transferring to Germany a year later. He was appointed advertising manager in 1977, and having been in this new position only a few months, Berndt was keen to ensure he gave appropriate attention to this important but delicate new HDL responsibility.

In early 1977, Colgate began test marketing Axion, an HDL formula that was similar to its U.S. product Dynamo. Axion showed excellent initial results, gaining almost 4 percent share in three months. However, sales declined from this peak, and within 18 months Colgate closed down the test market and withdrew Axion.

Meanwhile, P&G's research team had developed three important additional breakthroughs: a fatty acid that provided similar water softening performance to phosphate, a suds suppressant so the product would function in European drum washing machines, and a patented washing machine anticorrosion ingredient. By 1979, European development efforts had shifted to product aesthetics, and the search began for perfumes compatible with the newly formulated *HDL-Formula SB* as it was known.

Meanwhile, during this period Henkel had been working to reformulate their leading powder and relaunched it as New Persil. Blind tests against New Persil in early 1980 were a breakeven. Finally, in October 1980 with a new fragrance, Procter's Formula SB won a blind test against New Persil by 53 to 47. The product's superiority was confirmed in subsequent tests against the main competitive powders in France (58 to 42 win for Formula SB) and in the United Kingdom (61 to 39 win).

Now, Berndt and his German brand group were ready to recommend a full-scale test market. During the previous 18 months they had cleared the proposed brand name (Vizir), appointed an advertising agency (Grey), designed packaging (bottles and labels), and collected and analyzed the masses of consumer and market data that were necessary to justify any new product launched in P&G. Management up to the highest level was interested and involved. Although an initial capital approval had been received for $350,000 to buy molds and raw materials, the test market plan for Berlin was expected to involve a further investment of $1.5 million plus $750,000 for original advertising production and research. A national launch would involve an additional $1.5 million in capital investment and $16 million in marketing costs and would pay out in about 3 years if the product could gain a 4 percent market share. A Europewide launch would be 5 or 6 times that amount.

While Berndt and his team had decided to proceed with the test market, a great deal of uncertainty still surrounded Vizir. There were some in the company questioning whether it made sense to launch this product at all in Germany, particularly with the proposed marketing positioning and copy strategy. Others were less concerned about the German launch but were strongly opposed to the suggestion that Vizir be made a Eurobrand and launched in all key European markets.

## Vizir Launch Decision

One issue that had resulted in some major concern in P&G's senior management related to Vizir's positioning in the detergent market. Its strength was that it gave superior cleaning performance on greasy stains at low temperatures and (following the product improvements) matched powder performance on enzymatic stains and whiteness. The problem was that P&G's Ariel, the leading low-temperature laundry powder in Germany, made similar performance claims, and it was feared that Vizir would cannibalize its sales. So close were their selling propositions that two separate agencies operating independently produced almost identical commercials for Vizir and Ariel in early 1981 (Exhibit 3).

The German brand group argued that Vizir had to be positioned in this way, since this was the promise that had resulted in high trials during the Axion test. To position it as a pretreatment product would severely limit its sales potential, while to emphasize peripheral benefits like fabric care or softness would not have broad appeal. They argued that it had to be seen as a mainwash product with superior cleaning performance at lower temperatures.

Another concern being expressed by some managers was that P&G was creating a product segment that could result in new competitive entries and price erosion in the stagnant heavy-duty detergent market. Liquids were much easier to make than powders and required a much smaller capital investment. ("For powders, you need a detergent tower—liquids can be made in a bath tub" according to one manager.) Although P&G had patented many of its technological breakthroughs, they were a less effective barrier to entry than might be expected. One product development manager explained:

> Our work on Vizir was very creative, but not a very effective barrier to competition. Often it's like trying to patent a recipe for an apple pie. We can specify ingredients and compositions in an ideal range or a preferred range, but competitors can copy the broad concepts and work around the patented ranges. And, believe me, they are all monitoring our patents! Even if they don't (or can't) copy our innovations, there are other ways to solve the problems. If enzymes are unstable in liquid form, you could solve that by dumping in lots of enzymes so that enough will still be active by the estimated usage date.

If capital costs were low, and products could be imitated (at least partially), the concern was that new entrants could open up a market for "white labels" (generic products). Without the product or the market development costs of P&G they probably could undercut their prices. The German's proposed pricing strategy had been to price at an equivalent "cost per job" as the leading powders. This pricing strategy resulted

**EXHIBIT 3**

**COMPARATIVE SCRIPTS: VIZIR AND ARIEL COMMERCIALS**

| *Vizir*—"Peter's Pants"— Woman in laundry examining newly washed pants on her son | *Ariel*—"Helen Hedy"—Woman in laundry holding up daughter's blouse |
|---|---|
| *Announcer:* Hey, Peter's things look pretty nice. | *Announcer:* Looks beautifully clean again, doesn't it? |
| *Woman:* Thanks. | *Helen:* Yes, sure. |
| *Announcer:* Too bad they're not completely clean. | *Announcer:* Also close up? |
| *Woman:* What? | *Helen:* Well, no. When you really look up close—that's gravy. A stain like that never comes out completely. |
| *Announcer:* There's still oily dirt from his bicycle. | *Announcer:* Why is that? |
| *Woman:* I can't boil modern fabrics. And without boiling they don't get cleaner. | *Helen:* Because you just can't boil these modern things. I can't get Barbel's blouse really clean without boiling. |
| *Announcer:* Oh yes! Here is Vizir, the new liquid detergent Vizir, the liquid powder that gets things cleaner. Without boiling! | *Announcer:* Then use Ariel. It can clean without boiling. |
| *Woman:* Bicycle oil will come out? Without boiling? | *Helen:* Without boiling? Even these stains? That I want to see. |
| *Announcer:* Yes, one cap of Vizir in the main wash and on tough soil pour a little Vizir on directly. Then wash. Let's test Vizir against boil wash powder. These make-up stains were washed in powder at 60°—not clean. On top we put this unwashed dirty towel, then pour on Vizir. Vizir's liquid powder penetrates the soil and dissolves it, as well as the stain that boil wash powder left behind. | *Announcer:* The test: With prewash and mainwash at low temperature we are washing stubborn stains like egg and gravy. The towel on the right had Ariel's cleaning power. |
| *Woman:* Incredible. The bicycle oil—gone! Without boiling. Through and through cleaner. | *Helen:* Hey, it's really true. The gravy on Barbel's blouse is completely gone. Even against the light—deep down clean. All this without boiling. |
| *Announcer:* Vizir—liquid power to get things cleaner. | *Announcer:* Ariel—without boiling, still clean! |

in a slightly higher gross profit margin for Vizir compared to powders. The pricing decision was justified on two grounds: A premium price was required to be consistent with the product's premium image and to avoid overall profit erosion, assuming that Vizir would cannibalize some sales of the company's low-temperature laundry detergent brands.

At this time P&G was a strong number two in the German detergent market—the largest in Europe. Henkel's leading brand, Persil, was positioned as an all-temperature, all-purpose powder, and held a 17 percent share.[1] P&G's entrant in the all-temperature segment was Dash, and this brand had 5½ percent share. However, the company's low temperature brand, Ariel, had a

share of 11 percent and was a leader in this fast-growing segment, far ahead of Lever's Omo (4½ percent) and Henkel's new entrant Mustang (2½ percent).

The final argument of the opponents was that even ignoring these risks there were serious doubts that this represented a real market opportunity. P&G's marketing of its HDL in the United States had not been an outstanding success. Furthermore Colgate's experience with their

---

[1]These share data related to the total detergent market (including dishwashing liquid). The heavy-duty segment (i.e., laundry detergent) represented about two-thirds of this total.

European test market had been very disappointing.

In early 1981, Wolfgang Berndt's attention was drawn to an interesting article that concluded that it would be difficult for a liquid to compete in the European heavy duty detergent field. The paper, presented to an industry association congress in September 1980 by Henkel's director of product development and two other scientists, concluded that HDLs would continue to expand their penetration of the U.S. market, due to the less demanding comparison standard of U.S. powder detergents and to the compatibility of HDLs with U.S. washing practices. In Europe, by contrast, the paper claimed that liquids would likely remain specialty products with small market share (1 percent compared to 20 percent in the United States). This limited HDL market potential was due to the superiority of European powder detergents and the different European washing habits (higher temperatures, washing machine characteristics, etc.).

While managers in Brussels and Cincinnati were wrestling with these difficult strategic issues, Wolfgang Berndt was becoming increasingly nervous. He and his Vizir brand group were excited by the product and committed to its success. Initial test market readings from Berlin were encouraging (see Exhibit 4), but they were certain that Henkel was following Vizir's performance in Berlin as closely as they were. The product had now been in development and testing for seven years, and the German group felt sure that Henkel knew their intentions and would counterattack swiftly and strongly to protect their dominant position in their home market. By the early summer, rumors were beginning to spread in the trade that Henkel was planning a major new product. Henkel sales reps had been recalled from vacation, and retailers were being sounded out for support on promotional programs.

On three separate occasions Berndt or a member of his group presented their analysis of the test market and their concerns about a

preemptive strike; but on each occasion it was decided to delay a national launch. Senior management on both sides of the Atlantic explained it was just too risky to invest in a major launch on the basis of three or four months of test results. Experience had shown that a one-year reading was necessary to give a good basis for such an important decision.

## Eurobrand Decision

Another critical issue to be decided concerned the scope of the product launch. Within P&G's European organization, the budding Eurobrand concept, whereby there would be much greater coordination of marketing strategies of brands in Europe, was extremely controversial. Some thought it might conflict with the existing philosophy that gave country subsidiary managers the freedom to decide what products were most likely to succeed in their local market, in what form, and when.

The primary argument advanced by Artzt and Ferguson and other managers with similar views, was that the time was now ripe for a common European laundry detergent. While widely differing washing practices between countries had justified, up until now, national products tailored to local habits, market data indicated a converging trend in consumer laundry habits (see Exhibit 5).

Others were quick to point out that despite the trends there were still huge differences in washing habits that were much more important than the similarities at this stage. For example, Spain and Italy still had a large handwash segment; in the United Kingdom and Belgium top loading washers were still important; and in Southern Europe, natural fiber clothing still predominated. Besides, the raw statistical trends could be misleading. Despite the trend to lower-temperature washing, even in Germany over 80 percent of housewives still used the boil wash (over 60°C) for some loads. In general, they regarded the boil wash as the standard by which they judged washing cleanliness.

EXHIBIT 4

**SELECTED TEST MARKET RESULTS—VIZIR BERLIN TEST MARKET**

**Total shipments and share**

| Month | Shipments: MSU (volume index) | | Share (%) | |
|---|---|---|---|---|
| | Actual | Target | Actual | Target |
| February | 4.6 | 1.8 | | |
| March | 5.2 | 2.5 | 2.2 | 1.8 |
| April | 9.6 | 4.5 | 5.2 | 2.7 |
| May | 3.1 | 3.1 | 3.4 | 3.4 |

**Consumer research results**

| Use and awareness (at 3 months; 293 responses) | | | Attitude data (at 3 months; including free sample only users) | | |
|---|---|---|---|---|---|
| | Vizir | Mustang* | | Vizir | Mustang† |
| Ever used (%)† | 28 | 22 | Unduplicated comments on: | | |
| Past 4 weeks | 15 | 9 | Whiteness, brightness, cleaning or stain removal | 65/11‡ | 58/8‡ |
| Ever purchased† | 13 | 15 | | | |
| Past 4 weeks | 8 | 6 | Cleaning or stain removal | 49/8 | 52/4 |
| Twice or more | 4 | n.a. | Cleaning | 12/2 | 17/n.a. |
| Brand on hand | 15 | 11 | Stain removal | 37/6 | 35/n.a. |
| Large sizes | 3 | 5 | Odor | 30/4 | 15/3 |
| Advertising awareness | 47 | 89 | Effect on clothes | 7/– | 13/6 |
| Brand awareness | 68 | 95 | Form (liquid) | 23/11 | n.a. |

*Mustang was a recently launched Henkel low temperature powder on which comparable consumer data were available. It was judged to have been only moderately successful, capturing 2½% market share compared to Ariel's 11% share as low-temperature segment leader.
†Difference between use and purchase data due to introductory free sample program.
‡Number of unduplicated comments, favorable/unfavorable about the product in user interviews (e.g., among Vizir users interviewed, 65 commented favorably about whiteness, brightness, cleaning, or stain removal, while 11 commented negatively about one or more of those attributes).
n.a. = not available.

Some subsidiary managers also emphasized that the differences went well beyond consumer preferences. Their individual market structures would prevent any uniform marketing strategy from succeeding. They cited data on differences in television cost and access, national legislation on product characteristics and promotion tool usage, differences in distribution structure and competitive behavior. All these structural factors would impede standardization of brands and marketing strategies Europewide.

The second point Artzt and Ferguson raised was that greater coordination was needed to protect subsidiaries' profit opportunities. (However, they emphasized that subsidiary managers should retain ultimate profit responsibility and a leadership or concurrence role in all decisions affecting their operations.)

Increasingly, competitors had been able to imitate P&G's new and innovative products and marketing strategies and preempt them in national markets where the local subsidiary was

**EXHIBIT 5**

## SELECTED MARKET RESEARCH DATA

### Selected washing practices

| | Germany | | U.K. | | France | | Italy | | Spain | |
|---|---|---|---|---|---|---|---|---|---|---|
| | 1973 | 1978 | 1973 | 1978 | 1973 | 1978 | 1973 | 1978 | 1973 | 1978 |
| Washing machine penetration: Percent of households with drum machines | 76 | 83 | 10 | 26 | 59 | 70 | 70 | 79 | 24 | 50 |
| Washing temperature: | | | | | | | | | | |
| Up to 60° (including handwash) | 51 | 67 | 71 | 82 | 48 | 68 | 31 | 49 | 63 | 85 |
| Over 60° | 49 | 33 | 29 | 18 | 52 | 32 | 69 | 51 | 37 | 15 |
| Fabric softener use: Percent of loads with fabric softener | 68 | 69 | 36 | 47 | 52 | 57 | 21 | 35 | 18 | 37 |

### Selected consumer attitude data (German survey)

| Laundry cleaning problems (% respondents claim)* | Grease based | Bleach sensitive | Enzyme sensitive |
|---|---|---|---|
| Most frequent stains | 61 | 53 | 34 |
| Desired improvement | 65 | 57 | 33 |
| In washes to 60° | 78 | 53 | 25 |
| In washes above 60° | 7 | 36 | 65 |

*Do not add to 100% because multiple responses allowed.

constrained by budget, organization, or simple poor judgement from developing the new product category or market segment. For example, Pampers had been introduced in Germany in 1973 but was not launched in France until 1978. Meanwhile in 1976, Colgate had launched a product called Calline (a literal French translation of Pampers) with similar package color, product position, and marketing strategy and had taken market leadership. Late introduction also cost Pampers' market leadership in Italy. The product was just being introduced in the United Kingdom in 1981. An equally striking example was provided by Lenor, a product similar to Downy in the United States. This new brand was launched in 1963 in Germany, creating a new fabric softener product category. It quickly became an outstanding market success. Nineteen years later, Lenor made its debut in France as the number three entrant in the fabric softener category and consequently faced a much more difficult marketing task.

Artzt and Ferguson were determined to prevent recurrences of such instances. Particularly for new brands, they wanted to ensure that product development and introduction was coordinated to ensure a consistent Europewide approach and, furthermore, that marketing strategies were thought through from a European perspective. This meant thoroughly analyzing the possibility of simultaneous or closely sequenced European product introductions.

At the country level, many were quick to point out that since the company wanted to keep the subsidiary as a profit center, the concept was not feasible. To establish a new brand, and particularly to create a new product category such as disposable diapers, was an incredibly expensive and often highly risky proposition. Many country general managers questioned whether they should gamble their subsidiary's profitability on costly, risky new launches, especially if they were not at all convinced their local market was mature enough to accept it. In many cases they had not yet completed the task of building a sound base in heavy and light duty detergents and personal products. They felt that

their organization should not be diverted from this important task.

The third set of arguments put forward by the advocates of the Eurobrand concept related to economics. They cited numerous examples: the fact that there were nine different Dash formulas in Europe; Mr. Clean (known as Mr. Propre, Meister Proper, etc.) was sold in nine different sizes Europewide. To go to a single formula, standard-size packs, and multilingual labels could save the company millions of dollars in mold costs, line downtime for changeovers, sourcing flexibility, reduced inventory levels, etc.

Other managers pointed out that the savings could easily be offset by the problems standardization would lead to. The following represent some of the comments made at a country general managers' meeting at which Charlie Ferguson raised the Eurobrand issue for discussion:

> We have to listen to the consumer. In blind tests in my market that perfume cannot even achieve breakeven.
>
> The whole detergent market is in 2 kilo packs in Holland. To go to a European standard of 3 kg. and 5 kg. sizes would be a disaster for us.
>
> We have low phosphate laws in Italy that constrain our product formula. And we just don't have hypermarkets like France and Germany where you can drop off pallet loads.

One general manager put it most forcefully in a memo he wrote to ETC management:

> There is no such thing as a Eurocustomer so it makes no sense to talk about Eurobrands. We have an English housewife whose needs are different from a German hausfrau. If we move to a system that allows us to blur our thinking we will have big problems.
>
> Product standardization sets up pressures to try to meet everybody's needs (in which case you build a Rolls Royce that nobody can afford) and countervailing pressures to find the lowest common denominator product (in which case you make a product that satisfies nobody and which cannot compete in any market). These pressures probably result in the foul middle compromise that is so often the outcome of committee decision.

## Organization Decision

The strategic questions of whether to launch Vizir and if so on what scale also raised some difficult questions about the existing organization structure and internal decision-making processes. If product market decisions were to be taken more in relation to Europewide strategic assessments and less in response to locally perceived opportunities, what implications did that have for the traditional role and responsibility of the country general manager? And if the Eurobrand concept was accepted, what organizational means were necessary to coordinate activities among the various country subsidiaries?

By the time Charlie Ferguson became vice president of P&G Europe, the nontechnical staff in ETC had grown substantially from the 20 or so people that used to work with Tom Bower in the early 1970s. Ferguson was convinced that his predecessor, Ed Artzt, had been moving in the right direction in trying to inject a Europewide perspective to decisions and in aiming to coordinate more activities among subsidiaries. He wanted to reinforce the organizational shift by changing the responsibilities of the three geographic division managers reporting to him.

In addition to their existing responsibilities for several subsidiaries, Ferguson gave each of these managers Europewide responsibility for one or more lines of business. For example, the division manager responsible for the U.K., French, Belgian, and Dutch subsidiaries was also given responsibility for packaged soaps and detergents Europewide. Although these roles were clearly coordinative in nature, the status and experience of these managers meant that their advice and recommendations would carry a good deal of weight, particularly on strategic and product planning issues.

Following this change, for the first time clear Eurowide objectives and priorities could be sent by line of business, product group, or brand. Not surprisingly, some country subsidiary managers wondered whether their authority and autonomy were being eroded. Partly to deal with this problem, and partly because the division managers had neither the time nor the resources to adequately manage their product responsibilities, Ferguson created a new organizational forum he termed the Euro Brand Team.

Borrowing from the successful technical team concept, each key brand would have a team with a "lead country." Typically the country subsidiary with the most resources, the leading market positions, or the most commitment for a product would be given the lead role so it could spread its knowledge, expertise, and commitment. The charter of the lead country would be to coordinate the analysis of opportunities for the standardization of the product, its promotion, and packaging. It would also be asked to facilitate the simplification of the brand's management by coordinating activities and eliminating needless duplication between subsidiaries.

The main forum for achieving this responsibility would be the Euro Brand Team meetings. It was envisioned that various managers from the regional office and the subsidiaries would be invited to these meetings. From ETC, the appropriate European division manager and European functional managers (e.g., technical, manufacturing, purchasing, advertising) would be invited. Advertising and brand managers from all countries selling the product would also be invited. It was proposed that the meeting be chaired by the brand manager from the lead country. Thus, a typical team might have more than twenty invited participants.

At the subsidiary level, the proposal received mixed reviews. Some saw the teams as a good way to have increased local management participation in Eurobrand decisions. These individuals saw the European technical teams as evidence such an approach could work and felt it represented a far better solution than having such decisions shaped largely by an enlarged staff group at ETC. Another group saw the Euro Brand Teams as a further risk to the autonomy of the country manager. Some also saw it as a threat to intersubsidiary relations rather than an aid. One general manager from a smaller country subsidiary explained:

When a big, resource-rich subsidiary like Germany is anointed with the title of Lead Country, as it probably will be for a large number of brands, I am concerned that they will use their position and expertise to dominate the teams. The rich will become more powerful, and the small subs will wither. I believe this concept will generate further hostility between subsidiaries. Pricing and volume are the only tools we have left. The general manager's role will be compromised if these are dissipated in team discussions.

Another concern was that team meetings would not be an effective decision-making forum. With individual subsidiaries still responsible for and measured on their local profitability, it was felt that participants would go in with strongly held parochial views that they would not be willing to compromise. Some claimed that because the teams' roles and responsibilities were not clear it would become another time-consuming block to decision making rather than a means to achieve progress on Eurobrands. A subsidiary general manager commented:

The agenda for the Euro Brand Teams is huge, but its responsibilities and powers are unclear. For such a huge and emotionally charged task, it is unrealistic to expect the "brand manager of the day" to run things. The teams will bog down and decisions will take forever. How many of these meetings can we attend without tying up our top management? Our system is all checks and no balances. We are reinforcing an organization in which no one can say yes—they can only veto. With all the controls on approvals, we've lost the knack to experiment.

At least one manager at ETC voiced his frustration directly: "If we were serious (about standardization), we would stop paying lip service, and tell everyone 'Like it or not, we're going to do it.' "

Charlie Ferguson remained convinced that the concept made sense, and felt that *if* Vizir was to be launched and *if* it was to be considered a Eurobrand, it might provide a good early test for Euro Brand Teams.

# Kolbe Coloured Chemicals Division (A)

Thomas Kessler, head of Marketing Center Coloured Pigments in Kolbe's Coloured Chemicals Division, sighed with relief as he finished writing the Strategic Plan 1983–93 in May 1983. The neat 37-page document represented almost nine months of work by the seven-member "Permachrome 90" team.

Thom was convinced that the plan would be well received by his superiors. But during his career in several companies he had often seen strategic plans obtain official blessing yet trigger no further action. He wondered how he could contribute to transform the ideas of the Permachrome 90 team into reality.

## COMPANY BACKGROUND

Coloured Chemicals (CC) was one of ten business areas of Kolbe, a diversified multinational corporation with headquarters in Essen, West Germany. The division's activities covered the production of colors for all uses.

This case was prepared by Anne Marden, Research Associate, under the direction of Professors Reinhard Angelmar and David Weinstein. Copyright © 1986, INSEAD, Fontainebleau.

Like many chemical companies, Kolbe's distant origins were in dyestuffs. Hence, being in CC had long been special, like being on the Mayflower. But the newer parts of the company had grown much faster, in part thanks to the cash provided by CC. By 1982, with worldwide sales of DM4.9 billion (13 percent of total corporate sales) the CC division occupied only the sixth rank among Kolbe's ten business areas. The stagnation in CC sales and declining profits, due primarily to industry maturity, had even led to discussions about withdrawing from the industry.

Morale was low during the early 1980s. Because of the poor sales performance, little hiring had occurred during the past years. The average age of managers and scientists was around 45 years, and the average seniority with Kolbe, 20 years. People from other divisions considering a transfer into CC were told by their colleagues that they would be going into "a dying part" of the company.

But in mid-1983, the mood was again one of quiet optimism, thanks to a series of recent changes. A "rejuvenation" program involving early retirement allowed recruitment of a few young managers. In 1982, the division produced its first worldwide strategic plan. In what was seen to be "a huge break with Kolbe tradition," selective price aggressiveness based on cost reduction efforts was for the first time accepted as a legitimate competitive tool alongside the traditional product differentiation.

Also in 1982, corporate management undertook a strategic analysis of the entire corporation. Each of the seven product areas within the CC division was designated a profit center. Four out of the seven were assigned a mission as "cash cow" and the remaining three as "turnaround" business units. The mission of a cash cow was defined in a corporate strategic planning document as follows: "These businesses will be run to maximize productivity and minimize the use of financial resources."

The functionally oriented organizational structure of CC headquarters was adjusted to the profit center approach. At the level below the heads of the functions, a team comprising a representative from marketing, R&D, and production was created for each of the seven profit centers, with team leadership intended to rotate annually. The aim was to integrate the functional efforts toward a common strategic goal.

This structural innovation created considerable anxiety, mainly because the job responsibilities and reporting relationships were rather vague. It also upset the prevailing pattern of blaming, whereby each function saw the others as sources of the division's problems. For R&D and production the profit center teams were overlays on their existing internal structure, which remained functionally oriented. Only marketing was organized according to distinct profit centers (see Exhibit 1).

Marketing also took other initiatives. Beginning in 1981, a series of intensive one-week marketing seminars led by consultants from a leading U.S. consulting firm exposed more than 200 managers from all CC functions around the world to fundamental marketing concepts. In 1982, Marketing carried out its first market research studies, designed to measure customers' needs and their perceptions of Kolbe's offering compared to competitors. Not everybody was convinced of the value of such studies. A frequently heard reaction of experienced salespeople from the countries was: "Why don't they ask us? We know everything about the customers." It turned out that there were significant differences between the customers' own perceptions of their needs and the assessment of these needs by CC sales personnel. In particular, CC staff tended to value technical aspects more than did most customers, who showed great concern for flexibility in logistics and other areas.

All the recent changes in CC had been engineered by managers who had been with CC for many years, as no senior position in the division was held by a newcomer. Ralf Brudel, who was appointed as head of CC in 1982 from the position of Marketing Manager Food Colours, was seen as the driving force behind many of the changes. As head of the division, he used every conceivable occasion to communicate his conviction that a market-oriented way of thinking and behaving in all functions held the key to CC revival.

## THE COLORED PIGMENTS MARKET

### The Products

Colored pigments are chemical products used in industry for coloring human-made materials. Several hundred organic and inorganic chemical compositions are the basis for about 1,500 different trade form products that satisfy thousands of potential uses. For example, lovers of "red" can choose from among 20 to 30 different rubine pigments. The specific red to be used will depend upon the desired properties in the end application.

Besides their color, products are also differentiated by form: basic pigment or prepared product. The required form depends on the end application and varies according to the type of material and the stage of processing at which the coloration is made.

Application technology was evolving toward high-temperature processes which result in improved resistance to heat. Another area of

**EXHIBIT 1**

**SIMPLIFIED CC ORGANIZATION CHART (1982)**

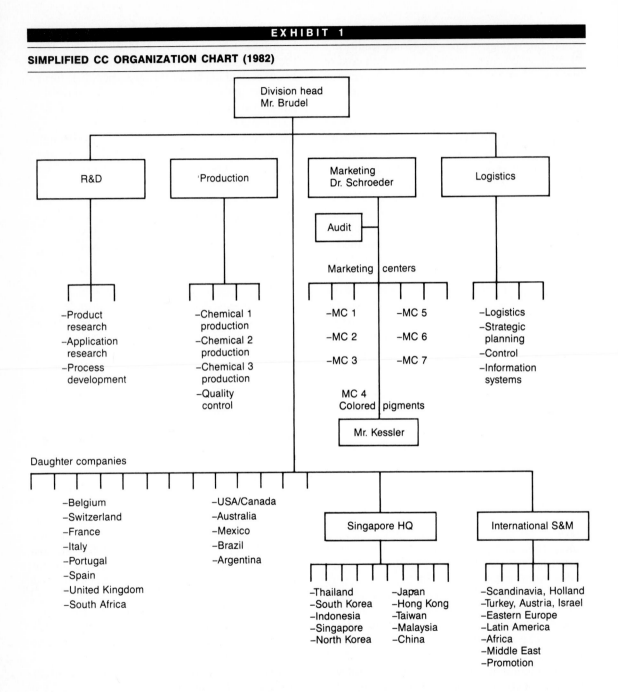

innovation was continuous process technology, in which color application became part of an integrated, nonstop materials manufacturing facility.

Adjustment of the basic pigment to fit a specific application technology could be performed during the final stages of pigment production or by supplier technical forces both in local labs

EXHIBIT 2

**EVOLUTION OF COLORED PIGMENT AND PERMACHROME SALES WORLDWIDE, 1960–1982**
(DM Billion—Nominal)

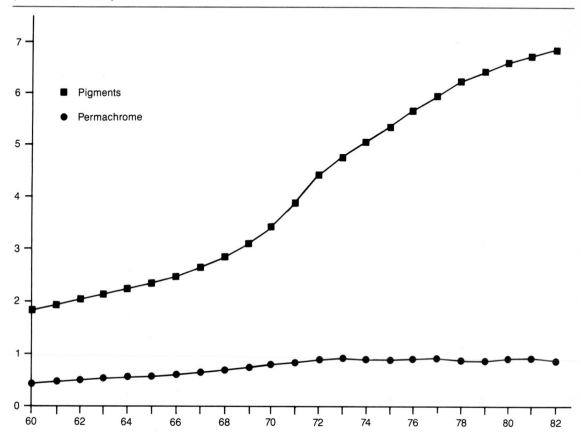

and at the customer's plant. Large-volume users tended to prefer suppliers who could supply the basic pigments at competitive prices.

No major breakthrough in colored pigment technology had occurred during the previous ten years, nor was any expected in the future. The bulk of product R&D consisted of "fine-tuning" in response to changing applications requirements. It took about six years to go from initial chemical synthesis to market introduction of a new product.

## Colored Pigments Demand

Rapid changes in technical requirements started to take place in the late 1950s. High-tech plas-

tics, brilliant colors for automobile paints, and pigments with a "shimmering" quality for cosmetics are examples of changing coloration needs. Growth slowed down during the late 1970s (Exhibit 2), with 2 percent annual growth projected through the 1980s and 1990s. In addition, stringent ecological regulations were causing substitution of older colored chemicals by new and costly elaborations.

In 1982, Europe was still the largest single market for colored pigments, but the United States was a not-too-distant second, followed by Japan (Exhibit 3). Colored pigment demand in the Far East had grown dramatically during the 1970s as a consequence of the shift of in-

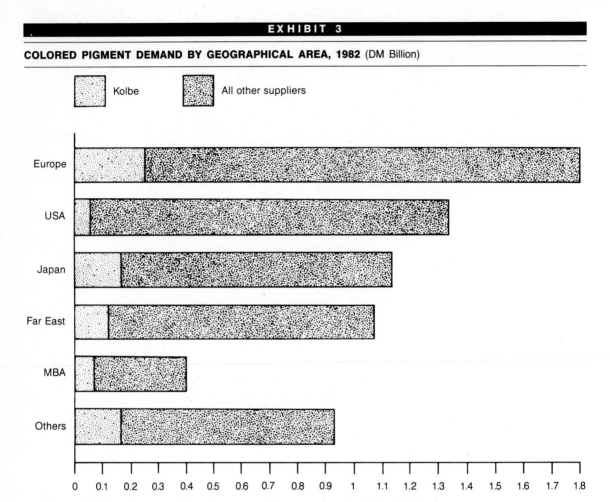

EXHIBIT 3

**COLORED PIGMENT DEMAND BY GEOGRAPHICAL AREA, 1982** (DM Billion)

☐ Kolbe          ▨ All other suppliers

*Europe* includes Belgium, France, West Germany, Italy, Portugal, Spain, and the United Kingdom.
*USA* includes the United States and Canada.
*Far East* includes Hong Kong, Indonesia, South Korea, Malaysia, Singapore, Taiwan, Thailand, North Korea, and China.
*MBA* includes Mexico, Brazil, and Argentina.
*Others* include Australia, South Africa, India, Scandinavia, Holland, Austria, Switzerland, Turkey, Greece, Israel, the Middle East, Eastern Europe, and African countries.

dustrial production to this region. Most industry observers expected future growth in North America and the Far East to remain above average. In contrast, weaker growth was forecast for the large established markets in Europe.

## Competition

The rapid growth of the colored pigment segment during the 1960s had attracted many chem-ical manufacturers. The oil shocks of the 1970s resulted in industrywide overcapacity. Although some smaller manufacturers were driven out of business, a good many remained and created considerable competitive instability.

In 1982, the six major European producers (Becker, Kolbe, Hamann, Bürgin, Royal, and Lüthi) accounted for 58 percent of worldwide colored pigment production. The dramatic growth of the Far East market had led to the emergence

EXHIBIT 4

**WORLDWIDE MARKET SHARES (VALUE) IN COLORED PIGMENTS, 1982**

| Competition | Market share (%) |
|---|---|
| Becker | 14.2 |
| Kolbe | 12.6 |
| Hamann | 9.5 |
| Bürgin | 8.3 |
| Royal | 7.7 |
| Klenk | 5.3 |
| Sunn | 5.1 |
| Japanese | 17.2 |
| All other | 20.1 |
| | 100.0 |

of a strong Japanese colored chemical industry which dominated the region and was becoming well established in the North American market (see Exhibit 4).

All major competitors produced other colored chemicals besides colored pigments. Becker, the market leader in colored pigments, relied heavily on this segment. For Kolbe, the largest producer of colored chemicals overall, colored pigments represented only 15 percent of total production, compared to 45 percent for Becker. Significant synergies between the different colored chemicals existed in all functional areas.

Competition through product differentiation, which prevailed during the market growth phase in the 1960s, had given way to the use of other competitive tools. The significant overcapacities, the differing profitability objectives of large and small suppliers, and the often doubtful allocation of joint costs and resulting profitability indicators all contributed to a climate of intense price competition. Other important marketing instruments were technical service and logistics.

## KOLBE'S COLORED PIGMENT OPERATIONS

### Overall Position

Kolbe's 1982 colored pigment sales amounted to DM859 million, 17.5 percent of total CC sales.

Profitability for colored pigments was always lower than for other colored chemicals. The Permachrome pigment line showed stagnating sales and sharply decreased margins in the years following 1973. Sales increased somewhat after 1979, thanks to the acquisition of a competitor, only to decline again in 1982, as can be seen in Exhibit 5. Kolbe's worldwide market share, in decline since the late 1960s, was 12.6 percent in 1982. Kolbe's market share in other colored chemical product segments was between 20 and 25 percent.

Colored pigments had been designated a cash cow by Kolbe's corporate management in 1982.

### Products

With more than 600 different items, Kolbe's product line was the broadest among all competitors. While Kolbe fielded products in the top four selling color indices (Exhibits 6 and 7), its sales were spread over many products. Kolbe's largest item, Red 104, accounted for a mere 3 percent of its sales. By comparison, Becker derived 18 percent of its sales from Yellow 34. Exhibit 8 summarizes the concentration of sales for the five largest European competitors.

### Markets

Kolbe colored pigments were available around the world, yet the European market alone accounted for about one-third of its sales. The company drew an above-industry share of its sales from its growing Far Eastern markets (including Japan) as well as from a diverse group of small countries, but lagged behind in the United States and Canada (see Exhibit 3).

Although no systematic worldwide data existed about its position in various customer size segments, it was believed that Kolbe's strength was with medium-sized and small customers where its technical service and broad line were highly valued.

---

### EXHIBIT 5

**EVOLUTION OF SALES, GROSS MARGIN, AND PRICE IN PERMACHROME**

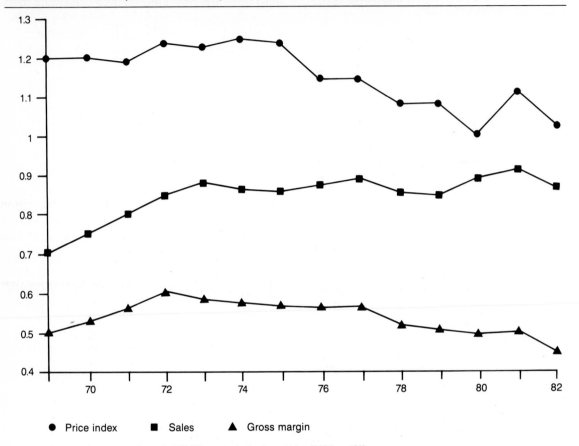

● Price index    ■ Sales    ▲ Gross margin

*Note:* Sales and gross margin are in DM billions, and price is an index (1980 = 100).

---

### EXHIBIT 6

**THE LARGEST SELLING COLOR INDICES IN COLORED PIGMENTS, 1982**

| Color index | Tons (thousands) | DM/kilo |
|-------------|------------------|---------|
| Yellow 34   | 150              | 5.00    |
| Red 104     | 30               | 9.00    |
| Blue 15     | 30               | 17.00   |
| Yellow 12   | 5                | 19.00   |

*Note:* Total market = 400,000 tons.

## Colored Pigments Organization at Headquarters

Because of CC's functional structure, relevant resources for colored pigments were spread throughout many different units.

**R&D** R&D expenditures accounted for about 5 percent of colored pigments costs, but no R&D staff was specifically dedicated to colored pigments. In the past, scientists had been rather free to choose problems of interest to them. Little coordination existed between scientists

EXHIBIT 7

**THE SEVEN LARGEST SELLING PRODUCTS IN COLORED PIGMENTS, 1981**

| Supplier | Color index | Tons (thousands) | Percent of market (volume) |
|----------|-------------|------------------|-----------------------------|
| Becker | Yellow 34 | 34.9 | 8.7 |
| Becker | Red 104 | 5.2 | 1.3 |
| Kolbe | Red 104 | 3.0 | 0.75 |
| Hamann | Blue 15 | 3.6 | 0.9 |
| Becker | Blue 15 | 2.8 | 0.7 |
| Bürgin | Yellow 12 | 2.4 | 0.6 |
| Kolbe | Yellow 12 | 2.4 | 0.6 |

working on different technical problems related to the same product.

**Production**   Variable production costs (raw materials) accounted for about 50 percent, and fixed production cost (depreciation, personnel, etc.) for 25 percent of total pigment costs. Production took place in two steps—chemical synthesis and finishing. In some cases, further preparation into "prepared form" was carried out.

EXHIBIT 8

**SHARE OF COLORED PIGMENT SALES OF THE TOP 15 PRODUCTS, 1982** (DM Billion)

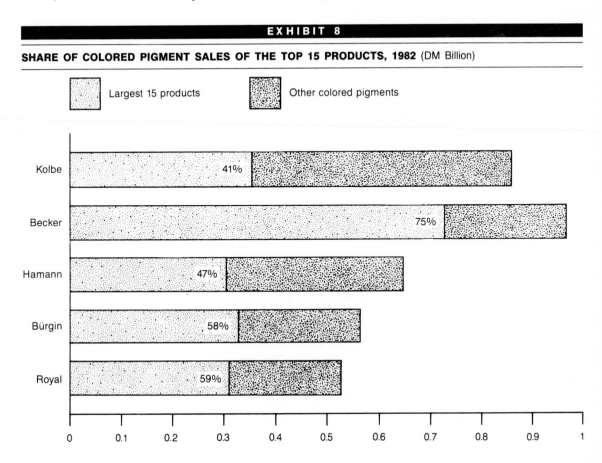

Colored pigment production was concentrated in two major production sites, the largest of which was located in nearby Duisburg. Partially processed "intermediate" materials, some of which were manufactured in another Kolbe division, were synthesized into raw pigment in batch processes in these plants, which also housed facilities for other coloured chemicals and even products from other divisions. The sequence from raw pigment to basic or prepared form involved a complex materials flow. As much as four months might pass between synthesis and packing for sale. This created quality problems in addition to transportation and inventory costs. The production system in use allowed the production of many different products, but changeover from one production run to the next was costly.

In 1980, visits by two production engineers to competitors' factories triggered a review of Kolbe's production costs. The review focused on two of the large volume Permachrome products on account of the large observed price differences. It was concluded that Kolbe's production costs were about 50 percent above those of the leading competitive products and that significant opportunity for materials cost savings existed through higher volume purchasing or integration.

Based on these results, one group developed options for improving the Permachrome production process using the existing production lines. Another group looked into possibilities of using highly advanced, continuous process technology to achieve important cost reductions while maintaining some product variety. In addition, corporate management reviewed the possibility of intermediate production in other company divisions. A proposal for implementing process changes for Permachrome and other products at a total cost of $30 million was accepted by division management in 1982.

**Marketing**  Costs of worldwide marketing, logistics and sales accounted for about 20 percent of total colored pigment costs. Until 1982, colored pigments were handled at headquarters by a product manager for colored pigments. The manager's main functions consisted of recommending a product assortment to each country, transmitting technical and logistical information between Essen and the local daughter companies (DCs), and setting prices. DCs were not allowed to purchase products from third parties for resale or rounding out of the line, but they were free to pick and choose from among the available Kolbe range. Prices were in principle negotiated between Essen and the DCs, taking into account competitors' prices. In practice, product managers in Essen tended to apply a cost-plus formula with little regard to differences in market conditions.

### Colored Pigments Organization in the Countries

Colored pigments were handled differently from country to country. The large daughter companies such as Brazil, France, Italy, and the United Kingdom had their own local CC division with marketing, technical, and sales resources, among others. Exhibit 9 shows the structure of the U.K. CC operations as an example.

The U.S. subsidiary (Exhibit 10) was a bit of an exception. Kolbe sales centers were located in New York and Chicago, while other geographic regions, including Canada, were covered by "sales agents" who sold the Kolbe products under local trade names. Technical and marketing resources were centralized in the New York Headquarters.

In 1982, the countries with CC divisions accounted for 60 percent of total worldwide demand and 50 percent of Kolbe's colored pigments sales.

The Far Eastern countries, including Japan, were handled through a Regional Headquarters in Singapore. The Regional Headquarters provided technical support and sales training for the 10 countries that were under its responsibility. Colored pigments were grouped together with all other colored chemicals in the "Marketing Center Colour Products."

**EXHIBIT 9**

**U.K. ORGANIZATION: COLOURED CHEMICALS DIVISION, 1982**

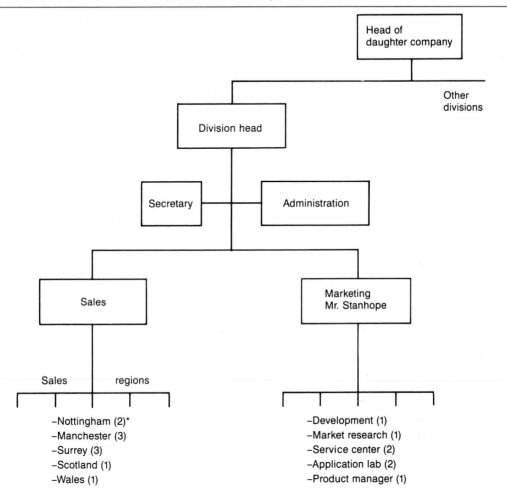

*Figures in parentheses represent number of people in function.

Each Far Eastern country typically had a marketing and a sales unit. The marketing unit would often have one product manager (called "promoter") for each profit center and a sales force responsible for the entire CC product range. Promoters attempted to "sell" their products to the sales force. In 1982, the Far East countries generated 16 percent of worldwide demand for colored pigments and 15 percent of Kolbe's colored pigments sales. The more developed Japanese market, 17 percent of worldwide demand, accounted for 20 percent of Kolbe's sales.

Finally, 121 countries around the world were managed by International Sales and Marketing (ISM). All ISM staff was located in Essen. Sales and product management, handling the entire

---

### EXHIBIT 10

**U.S. ORGANIZATION: COLOURED CHEMICALS DIVISION, 1982**

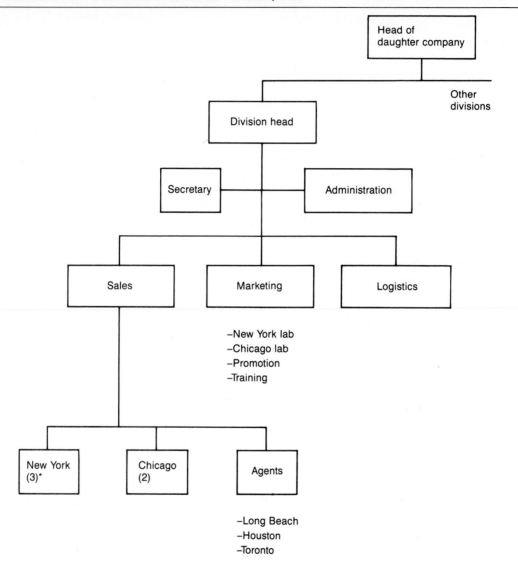

*Figures in parentheses represent numbers of sales representatives.

CC product range, was organized by region and subdivided by countries or country groups (Exhibit 1). Sales methods varied widely between regions such as Turkey/Austria/Israel and the Middle East; 14 percent of 1982 industry colored pigment sales were generated in the ISM countries, compared to 20 percent of Kolbe's colored pigments sales.

## Information and Planning Systems for Colored Pigments

Information on Kolbe's sales of colored pigments was provided by the countries at quarterly intervals. Information on market activity, including total colored pigments market evolution, competitive behavior, and the like, was infrequent and inconsistent. Country forecasts and plans existed only at the level of the entire CC product range.

During 1982, in an attempt to implement the corporatewide portfolio approach at the country level, CC management in Essen had developed the "key SBU" program. Each country was asked to single out for special attention some of the seven CC product areas. Countries were then expected to submit, once every two years, annual market and sales forecasts for each of these key SBUs.

In mid-1983, no key SBU country assignments existed yet for colored pigments, contrary to the other product groups. The choices had been held back until development of a pigment product strategy.

## Attitude Toward Colored Pigments in the Daughter Companies

Daughter company managements enjoyed considerable discretion for country operations. The heads of the country CC divisions were mainly evaluated on CC profitability, whereas marketing and sales staff on all levels were judged primarily on overall CC sales performance. In the absence of differentiated product and segment objectives, the tendency had been to allocate resources to existing areas of strength, where maximum short-term sales results could be achieved.

Kolbe's marketing and sales staff was accustomed to dealing with technically differentiated products for which customers required technical assistance. In the maturing colored pigments market, product performance by and large ceased to be a differentiating factor, and prices and logistical services increased in importance. As larger customers became more technically knowledgable, there was a noticeable trend away from prepared products toward basic pigments. Kolbe's prices tended to be significantly above competitors' prices, especially on the larger-volume products such as Yellow 34 and Red 104. With Kolbe being less willing to compete in the high-volume, low-margin items, it tended to become a supplier for specialities and prepared products.

Over the years, interaction between the countries and Essen on the subject of colored pigments had become limited to phone calls and telexes dealing with logistical and pricing issues. As Essen tended to be unresponsive on price issues, sales forces in many countries became demoralized and reduced their efforts in colored pigments.

## MARKETING CENTER COLORED PIGMENTS

### The Marketing Center (MC) Concept

In parallel with the creation of the seven multifunctional profit centers in CC, seven separate marketing centers (MCs) were set up during the second half of 1982 in Essen, each with responsibility for one product area. MC heads reported to Dr. Schroeder, the CC Marketing Manager.

The idea behind the creation of MCs was to foster stronger functional integration by making MC heads responsible for worldwide sales, market share, and net contribution (sales minus production, R&D, logistics, sales, and marketing costs) of their product area. It was also hoped that the MC approach would enhance implementation of the key SBU program. Yet the head of MC had no formal power over production, R&D, logistics, the countries, or any other organizational units.

The resources of the MC colored pigments consisted of the MC head, a product manager (Stephan Ullrich), the head of an application lab (Carl Ertel), several other members, one secretary, and an annual budget for expenses such as travel, the organization of conferences, and production of sales and technical aids. Budget overruns were to be authorized by Schroeder.

In view of the limited power and resources of the MC units, there was considerable scepticism regarding their capacity to effectively assume strategic responsibility.

## The Head of MC Colored Pigments

Thomas Kessler was appointed head of MC colored pigments in the fall of 1982. He had joined Kolbe in 1978 after marketing experience with several plastics companies. His initial assignment as CC Strategic Planner resulted in the 1982 CC strategic plan. Its development had required intense interaction with senior divisional managers, both in Essen and in key countries. Kessler was also responsible for the market research initiated in 1981 and for running the worldwide marketing seminars. The latter brought him into contact with managers from all functional units around the world.

The appointment of Kessler to head of MC colored pigments was seen by many as an important test for the new orientation within CC which Ralf Brudel was promoting, and a critical challenge for Thom Kessler.

## Building the P90 Team

Kessler's background in industry operations and his marketing philosophy convinced him that colored pigments needed a segmentation approach. To develop it, Thom sought inputs from all functional areas.

Formal meetings were held with researchers, planners, and members of MC colored pigments to discuss the idea of segmentation and a long-term strategy. Kessler's plan was to foster motivation and commitment to colored pigments by getting everyone involved in analyzing the data. He wanted to build the strategy and the team together. Gradually these meetings became more frequent, about once a week, as participants began to gain enthusiasm and confidence in marketing concepts. This activity led to the institutionalization of the group into the

P90 team, "the Permachrome strategy for the 90s."

Along with Thom Kessler, Stephan Ullrich, and Carl Ertel from MC colored pigments, the seven-member team included one chemist from synthesis research and another from physical form development for all colored chemicals. An engineer from production and a logistics manager from divisionwide planning and control rounded out the multifunctional group (Exhibit 11).

In addition to the weekly meetings, research members of P90 found themselves working more and more on colored pigments. The multifunctional approach gave the chemists a chance to see how their work related to the actual market place. They felt they were being given a chance to show that R&D had an important role to play even in a mature industry.

The interaction between the marketing center and R&D was unusual in the division. The chemists were exhilarated by Kessler's outspoken leadership. As one commented, "he can motivate people and convince people. He can push people but in a way that makes them feel like they are doing it themselves."

Ralf Brudel, the CC head, liked this style. It was known that he favored a marketing orientation. Yet he was concerned that people outside marketing should not feel forced to follow directions from marketing. They should be motivated to develop this approach on their own.

Besides this core group of people, Kessler drew on expertise in a number of other functional groups within the division. The marketing auditor for all colored chemicals helped provide marketing data. The production engineers working on the Permachrome cost reduction projects provided cost estimates and eventually joined the actual team.

## The Segmentation Scheme

After considering numerous segmentation schemes, the P90 team came up with a scheme involving 10 end uses. The scheme was based on the idea that performance of a colored pig-

---

### EXHIBIT 11

**FUNCTIONAL HOMES OF THE P90 TEAM, 1982**

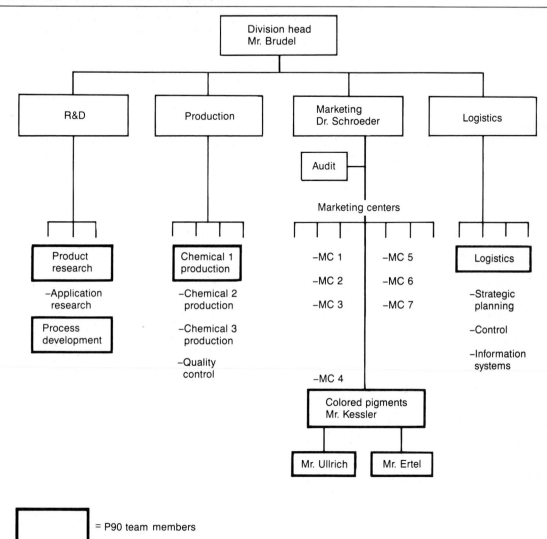

= P90 team members

---

ment product varied mainly as a function of three parameters:

1. The end application: the type of material to be colored varied from high-strength plastics to paints, inks, and cosmetics.
2. The required performance of the end product: The end product could require high re-

sistance to heat and cold, various textures, and degrees of color strength and opaqueness.

3. The dispersion method: This varied according to the polymer and the sophistication of the customer. Some pigments were ground into the raw material before it was processed.

Others were dispersed into the material with a chemical dispersing agent.

It was rare for a product to perform well in all kinds of applications. In the past, R&D had tried to develop ''universal'' products, particularly in prepared forms. This was now recognized to be impossible. Results from a 1981 survey carried out by Stephan Ullrich, and summarized in Exhibit 12 were used to estimate segment sizes, growth rates, and Kolbe shares.

After eight months it was time to pull together the information gathered and to come to preliminary conclusions about future directions. Ralf Brudel and others were getting impatient.

## The Strategic Plan

The Strategic Plan 1983–93 analyzed systematically the product and market position of Kolbe and the various competitors. The finding that Kolbe held the number two world market share, in spite of a weak position in many large markets, came as a big surprise to many in CC.

The plan expected the market to grow at an average 2 percent per year with a trend toward higher growth in products suited for new materials technology. The mission of the colored pigments business was defined as holding on to this number two position.

Five strategies were proposed that would provide Kolbe competitive advantage in both cost and quality in specific end use segments:

1. *The first strategy* encompassed segments 1, 4, and 5 (printing ink paste, industrial paint, and PVC plastics). The main thrust of this option was to use plant modernization and economies of scale to achieve 50 percent cost reduction in Permachrome Yellow 34. Market share would be sustained or increased by competing on price. Major responsibility for implementation would rest with production, where the plant modernization project was already underway. Schroeder would have to support a flexible pricing policy to ensure the volume necessary to achieve the cost reductions.

2. *The second strategy* targeted the high-tech plastics segment. An acquisition of a competitor active in this segment was proposed. Implementation of this option depended on

---

### EXHIBIT 12

**SEGMENTATION SCHEME, 1982**

| End use segment | Market tons | Market growth | Kolbe share | Strategies | | | | |
|---|---|---|---|---|---|---|---|---|
| | | | | 1 | 2 | 3 | 4 | 5 |
| 1. Printing ink paste | 60,000 | Low | Above average | √ | | √ | | |
| 2. Printing ink liquid | 30,000 | Medium | Average | | | | | |
| 3. Trade paint | 30,000 | Low | Below average | | | | | |
| 4. Industrial paint | 75,000 | Low | Below average | √ | | | √ | |
| 5. PVC plastics | 36,000 | Zero | Above average | √ | | | | √ |
| 6. Polyolefine plastics | 28,000 | High | Below average | | | √ | | |
| 7. High-tech plastics | 5,000 | High | None | | √ | | √ | |
| 8. Colored mass fiber | 33,000 | High | Below average | | | √ | | |
| 9. Office equipment | ? | High | None | | | | | |
| 10. Cosmetics | ? | ? | None | | | | | |

*Note:* Total market = 400,000 tons; overall Kolbe market share = 12.6%; market growth = 2% p.a. Figures are estimated based on 1981 market survey.

divisional and corporate management for its approval and coordination. The acquisition proceedings were expected to take place in 1984.

3. *The third strategy* encompassed three segments: It was thought that production experience and a strong market position in printing ink paste could be used to boost Kolbe's presence in segments 6 and 8: polyolefine plastics and mass colored fibers. With the high-production volume expected from the strategy, cost reductions through integration into intermediates would be possible. This would be combined with research in both product and process technology that was expected to develop improved product forms around 1987. Implementation required cooperation with other divisions and with other CC marketing centers.

4. *The fourth strategy* was specific to segments 4 and 7: industrial paints and high-tech plastics. Although industrial paints comprised a low-growth segment, the faster growing automotive subsegment presented a considerable opportunity. The key element in this option was the development of new chemistry for pigments that would perform well in high-performance automotive paints and high-strength plastics. Research projects addressing this problem had just started. New products were not expected before 1987.

5. *The fifth strategy* focused on PVC plastics. Thanks to segment-specific products, Kolbe already had a good position in this segment. Daughter company support was needed to hold this position in the low-growth segment until the expected launch of new products within two to three years.

The expected results of each strategy varied, but overall the plan proposed to gradually increase worldwide market share to 14 percent over the 10-year period. Net contribution would continue to decline until 1985 and would increase significantly thereafter.

## ISSUES

The colored pigments strategic plan was completed. There was little question about the acceptance of the plan by division management. Kessler was eager to get going with implementation.

In order to implement the plan, colored pigments would have to become a key SBU in the important markets. But colored pigments was over a year behind the other marketing centers in approaching the daughter companies.

At the same time, there was a great deal of work to be done in Essen for carrying out the strategies. It would not be easy to manage such a complicated process.

# PART SEVEN

# Managing the International Financial/Control Function

# Gillette Corporation

John Chapman frowned as he examined the monthly exposure statement of Gillette Argentina S.A. As president of the Argentine subsidiary, his duty was to sign and submit the statement to corporate headquarters in Boston. John was worried about the impact this statement might have on his request for capital to finance introduction of the TRAC II shaving system in Argentina.

## THE FINANCING DECISION

In January of 1978, Chapman sent a $3 million capital expenditure request to his superior in Gillette International Division. This money was needed to finance the introduction of the TRAC II shaving system in Argentina.

Chapman felt that introduction of TRAC II in 1978 was crucial for Gillette's future in Argentina. Although Gillette was the sole local manufacturer of razors and blades, reductions in tariffs had made imports increasingly competitive in recent years. Although Gillette held 95 percent of the Argentine razor and blade mar-

ket, Shick and BIC had made preliminary advances into the market in 1977. Chapman expected increased competition in 1978.

In addition to the threat of increased competition, Chapman felt that 1978 would be a turning point for the Argentine economy. The military government had made significant progress in reducing inflation and building up the country's reserve position. Argentina's economic prospects were better than they had been in a decade.

Chapman had developed an extensive promotional campaign to accompany the introduction of TRAC II. The theme would be: "Gillette has faith in Argentina." Chapman felt that a substantial Gillette investment in Argentina at this time would have tremendous public relations value.

Chapman had calculated a need for $3 million on the following basis. Half of the request would cover importation and installation of machinery. About $1 million was budgeted for additional working capital requirements. The remainder would be applied to the promotion campaign.

The need for additional working capital was partially due to increased unit volume, but because of continuous high inflation in Argentina, ever-increasing sums were required to finance accounts receivable. In addition, stiffer competition in recent months had forced Chapman to extend more liberal credit terms to the 6,000 outlets in Gillette Argentina's distribution network.

Chapman knew that his request involved two separate issues which would be decided independently. The first issue was whether the capital request would be approved. This decision would be made within the International Division, although final approval of the board of directors would be required. The second issue was the method of financing. This would be determined by the Treasurer's Office at corporate headquarters.

There were two principal sources for the needed capital. One was through extension of intercompany receivables from the parent company to the Argentine subsidiary. This credit would be denominated in dollars at an annual interest cost of 10 percent. The second source of finance was local debt. At present, interest costs on Argentine loans were running at an annual rate of 220 percent.

## BACKGROUND—GILLETTE COMPANY

King C. Gillette patented the safety razor with disposable blade in 1898. The Gillette Company was formed in 1901 to produce and market this invention. The new product was an immediate success. Gillette was selling 250,000 razors a year by 1905. Although razor sales quickly stabilized at about 400,000 units, annual sales of blades multiplied annually to over 5 million packages per year by 1910. In 1910, a package of one dozen Gillette blades sold for $1.

When the United States entered World War I, each U.S. soldier was equipped with a Gillette razor and blade set. The government had placed an order with the company for 3.5 million razors and 36 million blades. This order not only established a whole generation of Gillette shavers but allowed the company to expand its scale of manufacturing and significantly reduce unit costs.

As a result, Gillette was well-prepared for the arrival of competitors when its principal patent expired in 1921. In addition to its edge in manufacturing, Gillette had diligently built up an extensive distribution network, primarily in drug stores. The company also employed an aggressive advertising and promotion program.

In more recent years, the firm had successfully diversified into cosmetics and toiletries, writing instruments, and cigarette lighters. Toni Corporation, a home permanent producer, was acquired in 1948. Toni's product line was expanded to include shampoos and hair spray. In 1953 Gillette's Toiletry Division introduced Foamy shaving cream, which was followed by Right Guard aerosol deodorants in 1960. The Papermate Pen Company was acquired in 1955. Gillette acquired Braun A.G., a West German manufacturer of audio equipment, appliances, and electric razors in 1967.

Gillette's policy of diversification and acquisition resulted in dramatic growth. Sales rose by over 400 percent between 1967 and 1977. The growth rate for the previous decade had been less than 200 percent. Sales exceeded $1.5 billion for the first time in 1977.

The dramatic growth in sales did not yield a similar increase in profits. Although diversification had reduced blade and razor sales to less than a third of the total by 1977, this line still contributed almost three-quarters of total profit (Exhibit 1). After excellent results in the early 1970s, net income had declined for three consecutive years before a modest increase in 1977. The company's stock had been depressed during this period, falling from $38 per share in 1976 to a low of $23 in 1977. It stood at $25 in January 1978.

Profit margins had been squeezed by rising interest costs and foreign exchange losses. Total interest expense had increased from $1,587,000 in 1966 to over $35 million in 1977 (Exhibit 2). The effects of foreign exchange losses were cited in the 1976 *Annual Report:*

> Net income for 1976 was affected significantly by lower foreign exchange rates in virtually all of the

| EXHIBIT 1 |
| --- |

**GILLETTE COMPANY SALES AND PROFITS BY PRODUCT LINE, 1977**

|  | Net sales (%) | Contribution to profits (%) |
| --- | --- | --- |
| Blades and razors | 31 | 75 |
| Toiletries | 26 | 13 |
| Writing instruments | 8 | 6 |
| Braun | 23 | 13 |
| Other | 12 | 7 |

countries in which the company does business. In addition to lowering the operating results of Gillette International, net exchange losses charged to pretax income were $9.5 million higher than in 1975 ($19,081,000).

The effective income tax rate increased from 42.3% in 1974 to 45.6% in 1975 and 48.0% in 1976. The increases were due primarily to a rise in exchange losses, most of which have no tax benefits. Net income decreased by $5.0 million (6%) in 1975 and by $2.5 million (3%) in 1975.

The effect of foreign exchange fluctuations on net income had become a vexing problem for U.S. multinational firms since the advent of floating exchange rates and the introduction of Financial Accounting Standards Board Ruling 8 (FASB 8) in 1974. This ruling had eliminated the

use of special reserve accounts for handling foreign exchange gains and losses and required that foreign exchange gains and losses now be entered directly to the income statement. Volatile foreign currency fluctuations now directly affected corporate earnings.

## INTERNATIONAL OPERATIONS

The Gillette Company exhibited an international orientation almost from its inception. Its first sales subsidiary was established in England in 1905. Formal distribution arrangements were secured in a dozen countries in 1906. Manufacturing operations commenced in Montreal in 1906 and Leicester, England, in 1909. Gillette's foreign business was seriously curtailed during World War I, but the company vigorously expanded its foreign operations after the war. Sales branches were opened in Milan, Brussels, Geneva, Copenhagen, and nine other cities by 1920. From 1920–1923, foreign sales more than tripled. Foreign revenues accounted for 30 percent of total company sales in 1923.

International markets were a principal source of growth in the post–World War II era. In the 1940s and 1950s, new plants were opened in West Germany, Mexico, Switzerland, Argentina, Brazil, South Africa, France, and Australia. By 1953, foreign operations were con-

| EXHIBIT 2 |
| --- |

**GILLETTE COMPANY FINANCIAL STATISTICS, 1967–1977** ($ Thousand)

| Year | Sales | Net income | Income per share* | Interest expense |
| --- | --- | --- | --- | --- |
| 1968 | 553,174 | 62,278 | 2.14 | 5,205 |
| 1969 | 609,557 | 65,532 | 2.25 | 5,739 |
| 1970 | 672,669 | 66,075 | 2.26 | 7,750 |
| 1971 | 729,687 | 62,399 | 2.13 | 9,519 |
| 1972 | 870,532 | 75,018 | 2.54 | 9,810 |
| 1973 | 1,064,427 | 91,065 | 3.06 | 14,908 |
| 1974 | 1,246,422 | 84,995 | 2.83 | 23,481 |
| 1975 | 1,406,906 | 79,954 | 2.66 | 30,314 |
| 1976 | 1,491,506 | 77,557 | 2.58 | 26,348 |
| 1977 | 1,587,209 | 79,720 | 2.65 | 35,415 |

*In dollars.

tributing half of total profits. In 1978, Gillette had manufacturing plants in 20 countries, direct marketing operations in another 22, and distribution arrangements in virtually all the rest.

The largest single foreign operation was Braun. Braun had foreign operations of its own in Europe and Latin America as well as a substantial export business, but its principal market was West Germany. Braun's 1977 sales were $365 million or 23 percent of Gillette's consolidated sales.

The remainder of Gillette's foreign sales were primarily in razors and blades. This principal product line accounted for over 75 percent of Gillette's remaining international sales. Major international markets for the company were France, Italy, Spain, Argentina, Brazil, Canada, and the United Kingdom. Each of these markets generated in excess of $25 million in annual sales volume.

## THE INTERNATIONAL DIVISION

Gillette's primary product lines were managed in international markets by the International Division. This division was divided into four main groups—Australia, Europe, Latin America, and a fourth group headquartered in London which served Africa and the Middle East. Braun A.G. was a separate group which reported directly to the president of Gillette (see Exhibit 3).

The product lines managed by the International Division were razors and blades, toiletries, and writing instruments. These lines had several similar characteristics. They yielded high gross margins and offered tremendous financial leverage above breakeven sales levels. Consequently, there was a strong emphasis on volume and market share. Since these products were convenience purchases, mass promotion and distribution were essential. The development and maintenance of extensive distribution channels was an important objective. Credit terms to retailers were one competitive weapon used in acquiring distribution.

The potential leverage implicit in these products encouraged a strategic willingness to buy market share. By acquiring market share, a firm could take advantage of the leverage factor and eventually establish a dominant position in the market. Gillette's policy emphasized market share and a long-term approach in building a dominant market position. The extension of credit to expand distribution was one element in this strategy.

Credit terms varied considerably in different countries; the differences were due primarily to local conditions and levels of competition. Gillette, like most U.S. firms, generally offered better terms than those normally available in the local economy. As the dominant firm in most of its markets, Gillette rarely initiated liberalization of terms to the trade. However, company policy was to liberalize credit to the extent necessary to meet competition.

## THE TREASURER'S OFFICE

Although operating policies for foreign subsidiaries were generally determined within the International Division, the corporate Treasurer's Office also played an important role in international financial decisions. A separate International Finance Department within the Treasurer's Office was responsible for managing this role.

Within the International Finance Department, there were three separate functional units:

1. Subsidiary financial planning and dividends
2. Exposure management
3. Intracompany pricing and royalties

The International Finance Department also maintained close ties with the Tax Department, since most financial decisions were affected by tax factors.

In September of 1977, a new manager was appointed to head the International Finance Department. Lloyd Swaim, who had been responsible for Gillette's domestic treasury functions, was appointed senior assistant treasurer in charge of International Finance. Although Swaim would now be responsible for all international finance

---

**EXHIBIT 3**

**THE GILLETTE COMPANY ORGANIZATION CHART, 1977**

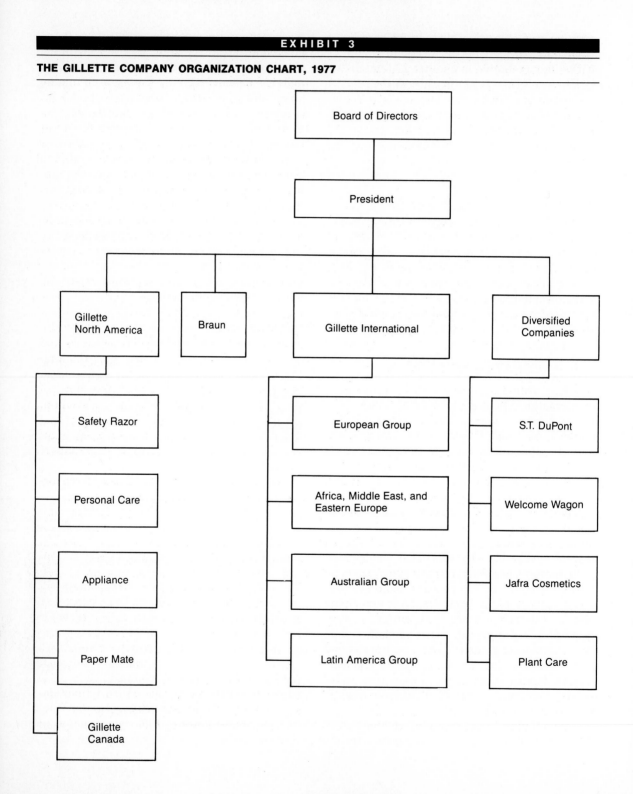

functions, the domestic treasury units would continue to report directly to him.

This organizational change reflected an increased emphasis on international financial issues within the Treasurer's Office. Swaim was particularly concerned with the performance of the subsidiary financial planning and exposure management units.

## SUBSIDIARY FINANCIAL PLANNING

The level of corporate investment in a given foreign subsidiary was determined within the International Division. Each subsidiary manager prepared an annual budget with detailed balance sheet, cash flow, and profit/loss accounts. This budget established performance goals for subsidiary managers and provided the basis for comparison with actual results. This comparison was the principal method of evaluating management performance. A capital spending budget was also developed by each subsidiary manager. Requests for capital expenditures in excess of $500,000 had to be approved by the company's capital expenditure committee and voted upon by the board of directors. Budgets were first submitted in person to regional group headquarters. The group reviewed the budget and negotiated any modifications with the country manager. After approving the budget, the group consolidated all country budgets under its jurisdiction and submitted an aggregate budget to the International Division.

Once budgets were approved, the Treasurer's Office directly managed any international capital flows required by the budget. Although levels of capital flows were determined in the International Division, the form of such flows was determined by the Treasurer's Office.

The treasurer moved funds across borders primarily through the use of intracompany pricing, dividend and royalty payments, new equity investment, and intracompany loans. In determining how funds were transferred, the Treasurer's Office assessed the overall capital structure of individual subsidiaries.

There were several guidelines which the treasurer attempted to apply to subsidiaries' capital structure. In general, the level of equity investment in a country should be equivalent to the level of fixed assets within the subsidiary. Net working capital should be offset by short- or long-term debt. In addition, subsidiary managers, who were otherwise free to arrange subsidiary finance, were to secure debt in local currency only. Although subsidiary capital structure varied considerably, there were few exceptions to this last rule. The intention was to offset any asset exposure in a given currency by an equivalent amount of local debt.

These policies had very important effects on international operations. Subsidiary managers were evaluated both on operating and legal entity results—that is, on dollar results before interest charges and foreign exchange losses and on legal entity performance measures which included interest expense and translation losses. As a result, managers were very conscious of the effects of foreign exchange translation. However, in attempting to adhere to the optimal capital structure cited above, subsidiary managers had to weigh two important operational factors.

Much of Gillette's growth had come from foreign markets, and the more rapidly growing subsidiaries often had great need for working capital. In many of these markets, it was difficult and expensive to finance working capital through local long-term debt. As a result, many of Gillette's subsidiaries were financing working capital needs with new equity, retained earnings, and credit from the parent system. Gillette's repatriation policy was such that earnings were generally not remitted from fast-growing subsidiaries. The fact that fixed assets depreciated in value over time while retained earnings accumulated also contributed to the tendency to deviate from the optimal capital structure developed by the Treasurer's Office.

The second operational factor which affected

capital structure was the extremely high cost or unavailability of local debt in many countries. Subsidiary managers were often reluctant to take on high-cost local loans. Since these managers had some autonomy in arranging sources of finance, they attempted to utilize other sources before relying on local debt. The Treasurer's Office was continually involved with requests by subsidiary managers to allow them to take on low-cost loans in hard currency. These requests were almost always denied.

Subsidiary managers had to consider several other factors in determining local capital structure. The strategic importance of growth and market share encouraged the extension of credit to the channel. In addition, the International Division favored high-growth subsidiaries in its capital allocation process. A subsidiary with a record of rapid growth could secure financing from the parent company, whereas a subsidiary with slower growth had more limited access to internal sources of finance. However, the financial staff of the International Division kept a close eye on credit terms and average account receivable maturities in each subsidiary.

The extremely high cost of local debt in many countries resulted in heavy interest expense. As a result of the policy requiring the use of local debt, Gillette showed an average interest cost of 23 percent for short-term debt totaling $114.3 million on its 1977 consolidated financial statements. This interest cost was incurred despite the fact that Gillette had over $130 million in cash, time deposits, and marketable securities on its balance sheet as of December 31, 1977. The high rate was justified by management in that local debt eliminated potential foreign exchange losses. In addition, interest expense was deductible for tax purposes, whereas most foreign exchange losses were not.

The use of dual performance evaluation criteria also presented a conflict to subsidiary managers. Both measures were considered by the International Division, although it was felt that local operating results were given more emphasis within the division. With an increasing corporate emphasis on profitability, however, the International Division was becoming increasingly sensitive to legal entity results.

## EXPOSURE MANAGEMENT

The exposure management unit was closely related to subsidiary financial planning. Every month, the Treasurer's Office received a monthly exposure statement from each of Gillette's foreign subsidiaries. These exposure sheets (see Exhibit 4) summarized the current assets and financial liabilities of each subsidiary in local currency. Gillette's reporting system took into account intrasystem payables and receivables and dollar or other currency-denominated assets or liabilities. After factoring these amounts out of totals, liabilities were subtracted from assets to yield a net exposure position. If this exercise resulted in a positive number, the company was vulnerable to foreign exchange loss should the local currency depreciate in value. These exposure statements were evaluated by the senior assistant treasurer and staff, often in conjunction with the financial staff of the International Division.

The head of the exposure management unit received daily foreign exchange information and advice from Morgan Guaranty's foreign exchange advisory service. This information was used to stay abreast of likely currency movements. If Gillette had a net asset position in a currency, the first step would be to use future markets to cover part of the exposure, if such a market existed for the currency in question.

Future markets existed for about a dozen major currencies. This technique could not be used to offset exposed positions in other currencies. The bulk of Gillette's exchange/losses were incurred in currencies for which no future market existed.

For weak currencies such as the Argentine peso, a net asset position could not be offset with future contracts. In such a situation, Gillette's treasurer would consider several alternative means of reducing exposure. One technique would be to repatriate the maximum

---

**EXHIBIT 4**

---

## GILLETTE MONTHLY SUBSIDIARY EXPOSURE STATEMENT

COUNTRY: _____
EXPOSURE CALCULATION
Month of _____ 19 ___

|  | Local Currency | U.S. Dollar Value |
|---|---|---|
| Total current assets, per B/S |  |  |
| Less:   Accounts receivable, Gilcon |  |  |
| Add:   Other noncurrent assets |  |  |
|     Deferred assets |  |  |
|  |  |  |
| Subtotal |  |  |
|  |  |  |
| Less:   Cash and securities |  |  |
|     Net receivables |  |  |
|     Other (specify) |  |  |
|     Amounts denominated in |  |  |
|         other foreign currency |  |  |
| *Total assets exposed* |  |  |
|  |  |  |
| Total current liabilities, per B/S |  |  |
| Less:   Accounts payable, Gilcon |  |  |
|     Dividend payable |  |  |
|     Advance advertising provision |  |  |
| Add:   Deferred income taxes |  |  |
|     Long-term debt |  |  |
|     Other liabilities |  |  |
|  |  |  |
| Subtotal |  |  |
|  |  |  |
| Less:   Loans payable |  |  |
|     Accounts payable |  |  |
|     Accrued liabilities |  |  |
|     Other (specify) |  |  |
|     Amounts denominated in |  |  |
|         other foreign currency: |  |  |
| *Total liabilities for exposure* |  |  |
|  |  |  |
| Net exposed assets |  |  |

---

amount of retained earnings permissible under local law. A second would be to have the subsidiary pay royalties or fees to the parent or other subsidiaries. A third would be adjustment in the terms of intrasystem transactions between the subsidiary and the rest of Gillette. Another alternative would be the use of swap arrangements. If all else failed, the subsidiary could convert any liquid assets into hard inventory commodities. The use of these latter techniques, however, impinged upon the normal operations of the subsidiary, and the Treasurer's Office was generally reluctant to impose itself in this manner. The normal procedure in such cases was to take a long-run approach which emphasized maximum repatriation and an increase in local debt to offset any net exposure. This procedure could be overruled by the International Division if it restricted the expansion of a rapidly growing subsidiary.

## GILLETTE ARGENTINA

The Argentine subsidiary, formed in 1942, was Gillette's first manufacturing operation in Latin America. Despite difficulties in procuring imported supplies during World War II, the company grew rapidly and was highly profitable at an early date.

In 1947, the Argentine government imposed foreign exchange controls which prohibited the repatriation of local profits to the United States. As a result, the subsidiary's earnings accumulated in Argentina.

Foreign exchange restrictions were lifted in 1955, and Gillette was able to repatriate earnings for the first time since 1946. Repatriation of profits and dividends had been allowed since 1955, although limitations and restrictions on such remittances had been increasing. As of 1978, all payments of royalties and fees, dividends, and profits were subject to government approval. If approved, up to 12 percent of registered capital could be remitted annually without payment of remittance taxes.[1] A progressive tax was levied on all remittances in excess of 12 percent of registered capital. This tax was levied as follows:

| Remittance | Tax (%) |
| --- | --- |
| Less than 12 percent of registered capital | 0 |
| 12–15 percent of registered capital | 15 |
| 15–20 percent of registered capital | 20 |
| Greater than 20 percent of registered capital | 25 |

Shortly after foreign exchange controls were limited in 1955, Gillette announced it would expand production in Argentina. Expansion was delayed for four years until government permission to import machinery was granted. The

[1] Registered capital was the official equivalent of paid-in-capital plus retained earnings. Remittance Taxes were levied on distributed funds after payment of normal income taxes.

plant expansion took place in 1959, and Gillette invested an additional quarter of a million dollars in working capital in 1960. As a result of this investment, sales grew rapidly in the 1960s, topping $20 million in 1965.

Argentina was the most vital and prosperous economy in Latin America during the 1950s and early 1960s. By the late 1960s, however, the economy began to falter. Inflation, fueled by rising government expenditures, began to gather momentum. At the same time, government policymakers opted to maintain a fixed exchange rate from 1967 to 1969. This severely affected the country's balance of trade. Argentina's principal exports were price-sensitive commodities which suffered from overvaluation of the peso.

Inflation increased by 400 percent between 1975 and 1977 alone. In response to economic and social disintegration, a military junta composed of the three commanders-in-chief of the armed forces came to power in 1976.

Economic projections for the Argentine economy predicted a reduced rate of inflation for 1978. The First National Bank of Boston's Argentine newsletter summarized these predictions:

> The Ministry of Economy has publicly advised that inflationary expectations of a 107% annual rate for 1978, derived from a survey of leading companies, is out of touch with the reality of the budget and monetary policy for next year.
>
> Both private and public sectors agree that inflation will fade away gradually, but they differ in figures. While the former contemplates an inflation rate of over 100%, the latter bases its calculations on a rate ranging from 60% to 80%. This conflict is not new, but for the first time in many years it would appear that the government is in a position to reach its monetary goals.

The rapid inflation of the 1970s has been accompanied by frequent devaluations of the peso. In 1975, the peso was officially devalued 11 times. The inflation/devaluation cycle in Argentina has made life very difficult for businesspeople with international links. It has also resulted in significant foreign exchange losses for multinational firms with local subsidiaries. See the Appendix for a summary of the latest "Country Report" on Argentina prepared by the subsidiary's controller in 1978.

Gillette has experienced major foreign exchange losses in Argentina. Yet the Argentine subsidiary remained in a dominant market position, with over 90 percent of the local market. Gillette Argentina had shown consistent profits,

both in pesos and dollars (Exhibit 5). John Chapman, who had been president of Gillette Argentina since 1972, intended to maintain that market position and achieve his budgeted level of sales and profits for 1978. In order to do so, however, he would need additional capital to finance introduction of TRAC II and high working capital requirements. He hoped the financing decision would be resolved soon in his favor.

---

### EXHIBIT 5

**GILLETTE ARGENTINA FINANCIAL STATEMENTS** ($ Million)

| | 1976 | 1977 | Budget 1978 |
|---|---|---|---|
| **Profit and loss statement** | | | |
| Sales | 20.0 | 26.0 | 30.0 |
| Cost of goods | 10.0 | 14.0 | 15.0 |
| Gross margin | 10.0 | 12.0 | 15.0 |
| Interest expense | 1.0 | 2.5 | 2.0 |
| Marketing & other expenses | 5.0 | 5.2 | 7.0 |
| Profit before tax | 4.0 | 4.3 | 6.0 |
| Profit after tax (Argentina) | 2.0 | 2.2 | 3.0 |
| Profit after translation loss | 1.0 | 1.1 | 1.7 |
| **Balance sheet** | | | |
| Current assets | | | |
| Cash | 1.5 | 3.0 | 3.5 |
| Accounts receivable | 7.0 | 7.8 | 9.0 |
| Inventories | 3.0 | 4.2 | 5.0 |
| Other | .2 | .2 | .2 |
| Fixed assets (net) | 2.5 | 2.5 | 4.0 |
| Total assets | 14.2 | 17.7 | 21.7 |
| Current liabilities | | | |
| Loans payable | 2.0 | 3.2 | 4.0 |
| Accounts payable | 4.0 | 4.5 | 5.0 |
| Intercompany payable | 1.0 | 2.0 | 3.5 |
| Other | 1.2 | 1.2 | 1.1 |
| Long-term debt | — | — | — |
| Capital stock | 3.0 | 3.0 | 3.0 |
| Retained earnings | 3.0 | 3.8 | 5.1 |
| Total liabilities | 14.2 | 17.7 | 21.7 |

*Note:* Numbers have been disguised.

# APPENDIX

## GILLETTE ARGENTINA CONTROLLER'S DEPARTMENT COUNTRY REVIEW

### General data

*Area:* (continental) 1.1 million square miles
       (total)       1.4 million square miles

*Climate:* runs from subtropical in the extreme north to frigid in the extreme south.

*Population:* 25.4 million

| | |
|---|---|
| Urban | 80% |
| Annual growth rate | 1.4 |
| Economically active | 45 |

*Gross domestic product per capita:* Approx. $2,000

*Total production:* Approx. $46.9 billion

| | |
|---|---|
| Crop, farming, and livestock | 15% |
| Manufacturing | 38 |

*Primary production* (principal products):

| | |
|---|---|
| Wheat | Sorghum |
| Corn | Beef |

*Industrial production* (principal products):

| | |
|---|---|
| Steel | Ships |
| Tractors | Machine tools |
| Diesel locomotives | Petroleum |

*Exports*

| | |
|---|---|
| 1970 | $1.0 billion |
| 1974 | 3.9 |
| 1977 | 5.7 |

### Economic program—basic objectives

On March 24, 1976, when the Armed Forces took over, Argentina was living its worst economic crisis.

The economic situation was marked by:

1. Cessation of foreign payments, which was leading to a stoppage of imports and, subsequently, to the closing down of industries.
2. Hyperinflation.
3. Massive devaluations.
4. Important recession, black market and product shortages.

To fight the above chaos, the Military Junta adopted an economic program, the guiding principles of which are:

1. Pragmatism. The plan is not tied to any dogmatic pattern. This gives it the necessary flexibility to be adapted to the different situations that may arise.
2. Gradualness.
3. The plan is based on the idea that a speculative economy has to become a productive one.
4. It considers private enterprise as fundamental for the economy, and the state handles the general management of the economy but is not directly involved in industry.

The basic objectives of the economic program are:

1. To reverse the conditions of the foreign sector.
2. To control the inflationary process.
3. To accelerate the rate of growth of the Argentine economy.

The measures taken to achieve these objectives are summarized below.

*Foreign sector*

- Maintain a realistic peso/dollar parity
- Free the exchange rate
- Eliminate export duties
- Promote traditional and nontraditional exports
- Obtain foreign financial assistance

*Inflation*

- Decrease monetary expansion
- Free the price system
- Control salary increases
- Reduce the fiscal deficit
- Improve the financing system

*Economic growth: short term*

- Solve the foreign sector situation
- Reduce inflation rate
- Encourage enterprise profitability
- Stimulate investments and savings

*Economic growth: long term*

- Pass an industrial promotional law
- Pass a foreign investment law
- Pass a transfer of technology law

**APPENDIX (cont.)**

### Balance of payments—trade

The Argentine Foreign Trade situation shows a significant negative figure for 1975 of $1.32 billion. The decline began by mid-1974 primarily due to:

1. Overvaluation of the peso, thus encouraging imports.
2. Uncertainty and permanent fluctuations in the different exchange rates.
3. Rising inflation with its distorting effects on markets and stocks.
4. Growing costs and declining volumes of manufactured goods.
5. EEC ban on meat imports.

The crisis in this sector was gradually overcome in 1976 showing a favorable figure of $602 million. Main points of the plan put in force to stabilize the foreign sector were:

1. Realistic peso/dollar parity, maintaining a higher rate for farming products, thus favoring exports of this kind of goods.
2. Promotion of exports of goods which could be profitably sold at international prices.
3. Elimination of export duties.
4. A 27 percent drop in imports basically due to the industrial recession the country was experiencing.

Continuing with this positive trend, 1977 balance of payments amounted to $1.7 billion with a record export figure of $5.7 billion and imports of $4.0 billion.

### Central Bank reserves

In March 1976 Central Bank reserves were almost exhausted. The country was virtually bankrupt. The Foreign Trade situation together with the paying off at due dates of heavy foreign financial commitments and the great expenditure incurred in travel and tourism abroad were the main reasons for this.

In addition to the commercial transactions improvement, several international credits were immediately renegotiated while new financial assistance was rapidly obtained from the IMF and other international credit institutions.

Previous government encouraged short-term period loans with exchange insurance coverage (swaps), which were continually renewed. At the end of March 1976, when the volume of short-term operations amounted to double the existing gross reserves, swap rates were significantly increased, and exchange coverage was eliminated. By the end of that year short-term loans were reduced by more than 50 percent, while at the end of 1977 they were practically nil. Free reserves grew from $200 million in March 1976 to $1.4 billion in December, $2.2 billion in July 1977, and $2.7 billion in September last year. Unofficially, total reserves at 1977 year-end reached almost $4 billion from less than $1 billion in 1975.

### APPENDIX (cont.)

#### Devaluation

The peso-dollar parity suffered a tremendous jump in 1975, a year in which devaluation reached 768 percent. This was due to:

1. Political instability.
2. Loss of confidence in the country's capability to pay the foreign debt, as a consequence of the balance of payments situation.
3. Seven years of artificial exchange rates which, generally low, have done nothing but discourage exports and encourage imports.

The new government gradually changed the exchange system throughout 1976 without producing upheavals. 1976 devaluation was almost 220 percent. The unification of the different exchange rates was reached by the end of 1976. It is now practically free and regulated only by the Central Bank through its official purchases in the free market, adjusting the rate on a daily basis to maintain the parity in accordance with theoretical parity.

1977 devaluation was 116 percent, and an 84 percent increase in the peso-dollar parity has been estimated for 1978.

#### Inflation

The reduction of the inflation rate was one of the main problems that the economic team had to solve. Back in 1975 total year inflation reached almost 335 percent. The first quarter of 1976 showed a record level of 89 percent with an extraordinary rate of 38 percent for March only. If we project this rate during a 12-month period we arrive at a figure of 4,700 percent, which is comparable only to the German inflation of the 1920s.

As of the second quarter of 1976, we can appreciate a significant declining trend: 57 percent for the second quarter and 23 percent for the third and fourth quarters, respectively, leaving a total year increase of 348 percent, especially due to the impact of the first semester rates.

This tendency has continued in 1977, which ended with a 160 percent rate, while we estimate that 1978 will reach a 100 percent inflation rate.

The tools that have and are being used in order to reduce inflation are:

1. Reduction of the fiscal deficit and public expenditures.
2. Reduction of the monetary expansion.
3. Elimination of price controls in the private sector and of public services' unrealistic fares.
4. Official control over salaries.
5. Financial reform, which virtually implies a free-banking system thus stimulating competition among financial institutions while assuring positive interest rates in real terms.

# Ford of Europe (A)

As he read the report of the Finance trip to Japan in February 1981, Bud Marx, the Financial Vice President of Ford of Europe Incorporated (FOE), began to realize that the finance function in the European Ford companies was facing a challenge to its role more serious than any since the formation of FOE in 1967. At the time of the report 30,000 salaried employees were working for Ford companies in Europe of which 5,000 were in Finance. The report indicated that the Japanese companies visited (Toyo Kogyo, Nippondenso, and Nissan) had 35 to 60 percent fewer finance people proportionately than Ford. To make matters worse, this conclusion was surfacing against the backdrop of a $1,200 to $1,700 small car cost advantage in favor of the Japanese and a $1.5 billion 1980 loss by Ford Motor Company in the United States (Ford US).

This case was prepared by Professor Paul Strebel as a basis for class discussion rather than to illustrate either effective or ineffective handling of an administrative situation. The sections on the industry and Ford reflect the IMEDE consulting reports prepared for FOE under the supervision of Professor George Taucher. Copyright © 1984 by IMEDE, Lausanne, Switzerland. Reproduced by permission.

## EUROPEAN AUTOMOBILE INDUSTRY

In common with the worldwide picture, the Western European auto industry was already mature and relatively concentrated in 1981. The annual growth rate was about 2.5 percent, with Renault, Peugeot, Fiat, Volkswagen, and Ford each holding between 12 to 14 percent market share. Owing to the technical sophistication of the average European customer, the market was highly segmented not only by country but also by car size with the principal growth coming from the medium car sector (see Exhibit 1 for the main segments).

Apart from the oil price shocks which accentuated the demand for fuel-efficient cars, the main event of the 1970s was the arrival of the Japanese (Exhibit 2). The initial strategic focus of the Japanese was on productivity and the exploitation of a 30 percent cost advantage. The Japanese advantage, which was based mainly on cheaper labor, higher productivity, and cheaper sourcing (approximately $2,200 in total per car), would have been even greater in the absence of a shipping and selling cost disadvantage (approximately $800 per car) relative to domestic manufacturers (see Exhibit 3).

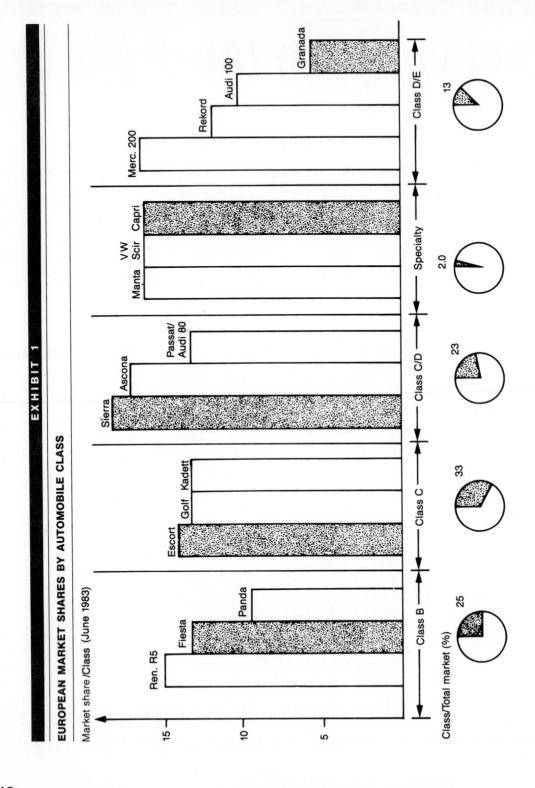

EXHIBIT 1

**EUROPEAN MARKET SHARES BY AUTOMOBILE CLASS**

Market share /Class (June 1983)

EXHIBIT 2

**EUROPEAN CAR SALES AND IMPORTS**

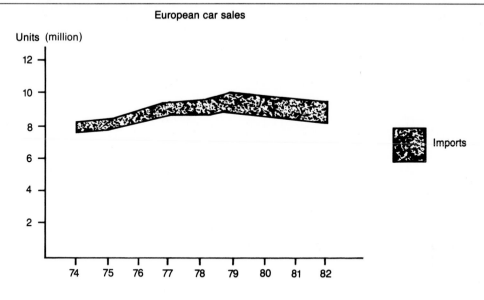

European car sales

European car imports

Source: Ford reports.

A key response to the increasing Japanese market share came from the European governments. The auto industry was politically important in Europe with an approximate 8 per-cent contribution to GNP and 5.5 percent of total labor employed. To protect employment, governments subsidized the auto industry in times of crisis and in the process took larger shares

EXHIBIT 3

## JAPANESE COST ADVANTAGE OVER U.S. MANUFACTURERS

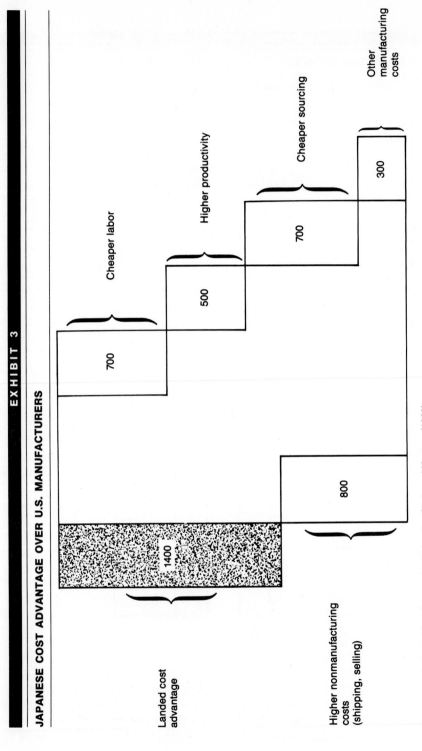

Landed cost advantage

Cheaper labor 700

Higher productivity 500

Cheaper sourcing 700

Other manufacturing costs 300

1400

Higher nonmanufacturing costs (shipping, selling) 800

*Source: Industrial Renaissance by Abernathy, Clark, and Kantrow (1983).*

of ownership. The result was that, in the United Kingdom British Leyland was 95 percent owned by the government; in Spain the government owned 56 percent of Seat; in France 100 percent, of Renault; in West Germany, 40 percent of Volkswagen; in Italy, 100 percent of Alfa Romeo; and in the Netherlands, 45 percent of DAF.

To protect the domestic industry from the Japanese, the governments imposed tariffs, import quotas, and other nontariff barriers. Consequently, in many countries, local operations were essential to ensure access to the national market. Moreover, early creation of local operations tended to result in market dominance. The Japanese, not surprisingly, penetrated most rapidly in the smaller countries without domestic auto industries.

Government intervention spawned an inconsistent set of regulations across countries, which restricted design flexibility and accentuated the segmentation of the European market. The consequent small size of most markets, coupled with the difficulty of building a Europe-wide market share, made economies of scale difficult to achieve. This fact had a critical impact on profitability, because the capital intensity of the industry required a high sales volume to break even.

Europe-based manufacturers responded to the Japanese challenge by increasing R&D to maintain their traditional lead in innovation. Renault, for example, spent 2.5 percent of sales or FF1.3 billion on R&D in 1981, compared to FF800 million or 2 percent of sales in 1979.

In addition to increasing emphasis on innovation, cost reductions were being pursued through shared economies of scale, supply system rationalization, and increased use of robots in manufacturing. But increasing automation and investment in flexible production systems to meet the fragmented and changing demand raised fixed costs and lowered variable costs, resulting in higher operating risk. Another consequence was greater capital costs and increased effective capacity when demand was projected to grow by only 2 percent annually. The rationalization process, also going on in the United States, generated excess global capacity, which was particularly marked in the mature European market where plants were running at only 80 to 85 percent capacity in 1981.

With some exceptions, the European industry was also hampered by low productivity. Labor absenteeism was high, running at 20 percent rate in France and Italy, compared with 10 percent in Germany, 6 percent in the United States, and 1 percent in Japan. In 1981, for example, Japanese workers produced 5 times more cars per employee than the European average.

## FORD'S EUROPEAN POSITION

Taken as a whole, the Ford group of companies in Europe was one of the most profitable European auto manufacturers. With average net profits of $600 million over the years 1979 to 1981, the Ford companies in Europe did much better than GM (an average loss of $200 million) or Renault (average profit of $100 million), for example, and was second only to Volkswagen which had average profits of $1 billion. The 1981 return on sales was just under 3 percent; the 1981 return on assets was 7 percent compared to Volkswagen's 0.5 percent. In addition, Ford's European Operation had become the cash generator for the whole of the Ford worldwide group of companies; whereas, the consolidated Ford Motor Company without the Ford European Operation made losses in 1980 and 1981, and barely made a profit in 1979, the Ford European companies in total reported profits in all three years.

Ford had a reputation for producing popular cost-effective automobiles. Coordination of manufacturing had contributed to productivity, which was a good 10 to 15 percent above the European average since 1976. Centralized design produced vehicles with wide market appeal. The millionth Escort, an all-time sales record in Europe, was produced in 1971; in 1981, the Escort was the European car of the year.

Market surveys showed that, in recent years, customers perceived Ford to be more innovative than either Volkswagen or Opel. (But the overall opinion of the Ford make among new car buyers was still well below that of its two key rivals.) In Europe, Ford also had a high-quality distribution network. Although it had fewer dealers (2601) than Volkswagen (3306), Ford's network sold more cars per dealer (467 versus 339 for Volkswagen). In addition, only 5.54 percent of its dealers serviced other major manufacturers, the lowest percentage among the European major automotive companies.

The emphasis on popular cost-effective products put Ford in a leadership position in some of the largest Europe-wide market segments as defined by automobile size, but the competition was very close. The total market share of Ford held steady between 11 and 13 percent throughout the 1970s into the 1980s, except for a slight drop in 1974. Ford Motor Company Limited (Britain) had a strong U.K. market share, 30 percent versus 18 percent for its nearest rival, British Leyland. Ford Germany had a significant domestic market share, 11 percent versus 30 percent for Volkswagen. However, the highly competitive Southern European markets, where Ford companies averaged only an 8 percent share, were becoming increasingly important owing to their higher growth rates (see Exhibit 4).

In response to the threat of Japanese imports and the developing excess industry capacity, the major players were all reducing costs and attempting to develop distinct manufacturing strategies. Fiat had a centralized manufacturing base but was developing flexible manufacturing methods designed to increase its response to different market conditions. Fiat's delivery time, for example, was 7 days compared to Ford's 21 days. Peugeot was also concentrating on flexible manufacturing methods based on dispersed but integrated operations. General Motors was cutting costs by standardizing manufacturing in its integrated operations, and Volkswagen was standardizing methods within a centralized manufacturing base. On the marketing side, competitors were employing aggressive strategies, some of which are summarized in Exhibit 5.

## FINANCE FUNCTION IN FOE

FOE was incorporated in 1967 to act as a coordinating body for Ford's European operations as well as to provide a better local market perspective in anticipation of the evolution of a European Common Market. Previously this coordination function was performed at the Ford Head Office in Dearborn, Michigan and a Ford US branch office in Brussels. See Exhibit 6 for FOE's organization chart.

FOE attributed its relative success to thorough application of Ford's basic philosophy which emphasized production efficiency ("you can dismantle any Ford vehicle and not a single part can be produced in a more efficient way") and the application of strict financial controls. The manufacturing and the national sales companies were tightly coordinated on the basis of separate profit plans, and the component sources, R&D, and service centers were evaluated on their budgets.

The establishment of European headquarters resulted in a highly coordinated functional organization (Exhibit 6). FOE's internal culture, which reflected its organization, rewarded reliability and stability. Its management style could be described as reactive rather than proactive. Typical comments about its style included the following: "Historically Ford has been a follower offering good value for the money." "You won't find many rebels at Ford." "Ford has a centralized management style." "The bottom line is all that is important."

The finance function played a major role in implementing the Ford philosophy. The financial staff at the field-plant and operation-component levels had a strong liaison relationship to the Vice President of finance who reported directly to the FOE Chairman. Apart from its budgeting, planning, and capital appropriation roles, finance provided advice to line management with respect to other decisions such as pricing and marketing expense.

Finance acted as intermediary between marketing and production in the manufacturing programming process, which matched demand with

**EXHIBIT 4**

**MARKET SHARES IN MAJOR EUROPEAN AUTO MARKETS, 1982**

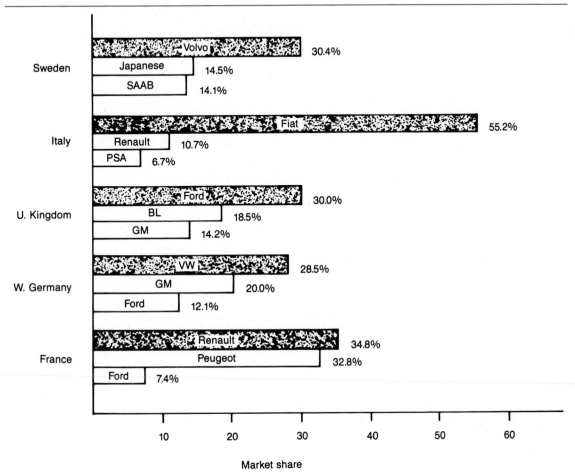

Market share

capacity. Ford's manufacturing was "order driven" with the orders coming from the sales departments' forecasts. The marketing people preferred to update their demand forecasts as frequently as possible, whereas the manufacturing side preferred a more stable production schedule with long runs. At this "traditional point of friction," FOE's finance department acted as an honest broker, recommending schedules and setting transfer prices which balanced off the preferences of sales and manufacturing.

When Bud Marx was reading the report on the finance trip to Japan, the finance function had a good reputation both within and outside FOE as a key instrument in building and maintaining FOE's efficiency and profitability. It saw itself as a "well oiled and tightly manned" department. There were, of course, some problems with Ford's tight financial controls (for example, 15 months were required to process a request to recommend the release of the funds for an $11.7 million investment in a vertical

---

**EXHIBIT 4 (cont.)**

---

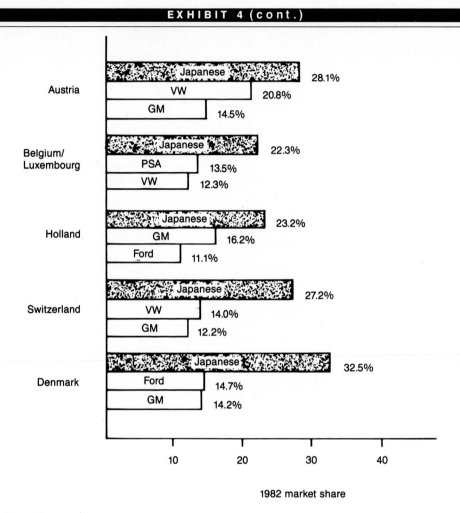

1982 market share

*Source:* Ford of Europe report.

flaskless molding facility), but nothing like the potential problems Bud was beginning to see on the horizon if no action was taken on the report's findings.

The report had its genesis in a trip to Japan by Bill Hayden, the FOE Vice President of manufacturing during the fourth quarter of 1979. Up to that point, almost everyone at Ford, both in Europe and the United States, believed that the Ford Werke A.G. (Ford Germany) plants in Saarlouis and Genk were some of the most efficient anywhere and that the low price of Jap-

anese cars was due to "dumping." When Hayden visited Toyo Kogyo and Toyota to investigate a power train sourcing issue, he was struck by the virtual absence of inventory on the factory floor and the apparent invisibility of indirect overhead staff. In his view, the Japanese were not dumping, they were making a handsome profit. Their prices were low, because their costs were "quantum jumps" below Ford's best plants.

On his return, Hayden wrote a confidential report to the Chairman over the weekend and subsequently briefed several senior manage-

EXHIBIT 5

STRATEGIES OF FORD'S EUROPEAN COMPETITORS

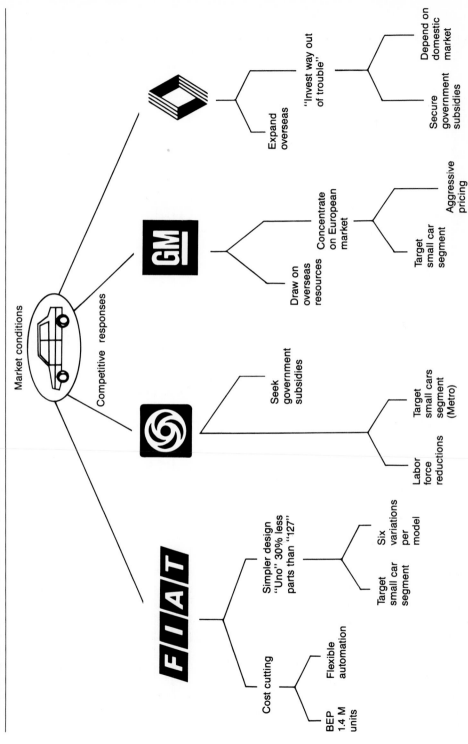

**EXHIBIT 6**

**FORD OF EUROPE'S ORGANIZATION CHART**

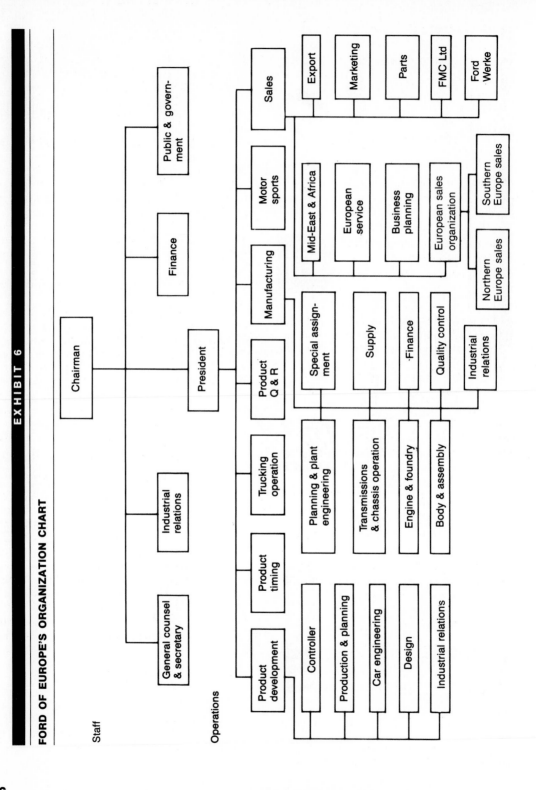

ment meetings, including one in the United States. Hayden's presentations were strong and to the point. The questions at these meetings were frequently aggressive, with the sceptics arguing that "you haven't counted right." In January 1980, Hayden sent a group of his manufacturing staff over to Japan to see for themselves. This was followed by another group in February 1980, which included several financial controllers but still concentrated its efforts on understanding the Japanese manufacturing process.

Ford had a small finance staff attached to its sales organization in Japan which had never made any comments about the relative roles of finance in Ford and Japan. As the size of the Japanese cost advantage became clear, however, Bud Marx decided to have a group of European financial people investigate the finance and control process in Japanese auto manufacturers. Their main observations were that:

1. The Japanese control process is *simple*.
2. Control is *shared* through all functional areas of the organization and is not dominated by finance.
3. Japanese companies are organized for *cost reduction*.
4. Overall, the Japanese operate their financial systems with *fewer people*.

The report (see Appendix for a summary) did not explain, however, why FOE's financial systems, which were once a key strength, now seemed to be a weakness. Nor was it clear, whether Japanese systems were appropriate in a European context. Or whether the finance group should make the personnel cuts implied in the report. And if not, what should be done?

## APPENDIX

# Ford of Europe's Japan Finance Business Study

Several recent studies have suggested that the Japanese cost for a small car delivered to the United States is $1,200 to $1,700 lower than ours. Importantly, this advantage results from more than labor rates—it includes labor productivity and lower overhead costs. Based on our observations in Japan, it appears that our finance function is substantially more costly than Japan's.

On a relative basis (ignoring any inefficiencies in the base and making generous adjustments for integration levels and for the use of administrative people to perform what we consider to be finance functions), the Japanese companies that we visited (Toyo Kogyo, Nippondenso, and Nissan) have fewer finance people than Ford (35 to 60 percent less). In our judgment, these Japanese efficiencies result principally from:

1. The Japanese system is simple—they control their businesses with less data.
2. Control is shared through all the organization:
   • Appropriations projects are prepared and reviewed largely by operating management.
   • Project expenditures are controlled by engineering and manufacturing administrative departments.
   • Product changes are estimated and controlled by product and manufacturing engineering.
   • Purchasing objectives are established by the purchasing function; purchasing also controls and approves supplier prices.
   • Industrial relations provides the timekeeping function.

3. There is a high level of responsibility, accountability, cooperation and trust, resulting in fewer controls and less auditing; there are very few "police" in the system. All the firms we visited have audit fees that are substantially less than Ford's, and they either have no internal auditing functions or ones that conduct management audits only. The Japanese companies also have excellent supplier relations that permit them to reduce the controls over the receipt of goods and the payment of bills.
4. There is a greater computerization of accounting functions—most notably accounts payable and receivables—and these functions are highly centralized.
5. The Japanese companies are strongly committed to cost reductions. Every company we visited had a vigorous cost reduction committee at a very high corporate level supported by subgroups in all the operations.

Some of the Japanese efficiencies are intrinsically simple, mechanical differences in the things we control that we can adopt, such as increased computerization of accounting (though these changes may require time to accomplish). Others are differences in approach and management style that may be appropriate for us, such as shared control and a simpler, less sophisticated, financial control system.

Changes such as these can be adopted only with the agreement and support of operating management—agreement to require less support from the finance people and agreement that it is appropriate for other functional activities to share control responsibilities. Some of the Japanese style, however, is a result of cultural differences, and these efficiencies may be harder (or impossible) for us to adopt. We could not get entirely out of our coordinating role nor could we dispense with *all* our internal auditors.

We did not become experts on the Japanese financial system in one week's time. There is still a great deal that we do not know about the Japanese financial controls, and there is considerable judgment included in this report. We believe, however, that our overall impressions are accurate. Furthermore, we believe that our recommendations identify areas that need to be examined carefully, whether they were inspired by Japanese efficiencies or by our own understanding of what can be done to improve the efficiency of the Ford finance system.

We cannot, nor would we want to, adopt all the Japanese concepts. Mr. Okino, the Director of Finance at TK, admitted in private discussions that he is not entirely pleased with his financial control systems and wanted to make certain "improvements" after visiting and talking with Matsushita Electric Industrial. Toyota declined to talk to us because "We are embarrassed with our system and plan to make changes." This may or may not be true; the point is the Japanese systems are not perfect. The one overriding thing that we did learn was that the Japanese system is simple and that a simple system can work. It is this simplicity that must be pursued as a way to reduce costs.

We recognize that the central challenge, as we examine our system, will be "how to make the system more simple and less costly, without compromising essential controls."

The attached report summarizes our key observations regarding the Japanese finance system, and suggests a number of changes that we recommend:

1. Establish a study group to review our financial control system, with the objective of identifying workload reductions of 25 percent by year-end 1981 and making further improvements over the 1982–1983 period.
2. Consider shifting some of the control responsibilities into other functions.
3. Organize the company to emphasize cost reduction efforts.

## THE JAPANESE CONTROL SYSTEM IS *SIMPLE*

### Discussion

The physical concentration of Japanese facilities in a few domestic sites simplifies the overall management task and contributes to simplification of the accounting and analytical functions. (We have more than 60 U.S. locations responsible for payables; Toyo Kogyo has 1.)

The Japanese appear to focus on fewer fundamental corporate goals (for example, volume, quality, productivity), and they do not further subdivide these goals into multiple, detailed, operating and financial objectives.

Unlike Ford, where we have much financial data, the Japanese companies operate with fewer and less frequent financial reports (available reports are largely accounting documents).

The Japanese system tends to emphasize physical concepts rather than profit or cost measures only. For example, labor minutes replace labor cost as a principal focus in manufacturing. At TK, the plants receive only one financial budget performance report monthly.

Budgets, prepared for six-month periods, are fundamental operating plans developed to a great extent by operating people. The emphasis is on "bottom line" results. The budget process takes about three months of which approximately one week is involved in reaching a management consensus on whether the operating plans are sufficient to permit achievement of corporate objectives. Release of the budget is considered authority to act.

Decision making is accomplished through a system called "*Ringi*." The Ringi form is a 1-page summary (generally without attachments) used to review all appropriations actions, major programs, and overruns to the budget. The Ringi form is circulated to all functional areas and is approved by a high-level person in each area after being reviewed by the workers.

The forecast is made only for the six-month budget period; at Nissan, the first forecast for the budget period is not made until midway through the budget period. The forecasts are prepared centrally. The operating activities are assumed to be meeting budget targets unless an activity has requested an approval for a budget overrun. Profit reporting is simplified because all variance explanations are broad, normally limited to two or three major explanations. We saw no evidence of differentiating between performance and nonperformance factors. We saw no evidence of condition adjustments. Forward-year plans, like Ford's, are prepared annually, generally with three- to five-year horizons for detailed plans. They focus, however, on broad strategy and policy issues and do not rely on financial data. The budget is closely linked to the first year of the forward-year plan. Like the budget, the business plan is largely prepared by operating personnel.

Very limited detail is used to support appropriations requests. The Japanese finance people play a minor role in the preparation and approval process. Pay-back is the only financial measurement used. Once approved, project control is maintained by the engineering and/or manufacturing activities; finance approval is not required to revise line-item detail within a project.

Product program cost objectives concentrate on fundamental elements such as variable costs and facility/tooling investment. Product cost control in all three companies is the direct responsibility of product engineering, not finance. Product program approvals are covered in 1- to 2-page documents; a limited number of status reports are reviewed by top management during the product development stage.

Product quality is one of the three basic ingredients of their business, but we saw no evidence of a sophisticated system to track quality or to financially justify quality decisions.

Accounting is highly centralized; consolidated income statements and balance sheets are not required. Payables, receivables, general ledger, assets accounting, timekeeping, and payroll either are mechanized or have the responsibility assigned to other company activities. External audit fees are very low—less than $200,000 (6,000 hours) at all companies visited. TK was the only company with internal auditors (20 people), and they performed only management audits (no assistance is given to external auditors).

The systems activities are centralized; there are no interfacing systems activities in the operations. There is widespread mechanization accomplished with minimum programming resources probably because the systems that are mechanized are simple.

## Recommended Items for Study

To simplify Ford's system the following steps should be considered:

- Reduce emphasis on multilevel objectives and increase emphasis on net "bottom line" results.
- Reduce the number of presentations and meetings. Reduce presentations to key decision data with a minimum of attachments to help eliminate the "backup-book" mentality.
- Reduce analysis of labor and overhead.
- Simplify budget process/procedures, while concentrating on a limited number of basic financial objectives. For example, demand less budget detail and focus on bottom line results; use the cost reduction committee concept (discussed later) to establish achievable tasks and plans; give operating activities within profit centers more responsibility for development of profit budget detail; restrict time for negotiation of budgets—negotiate only major operating objectives; evaluate potential benefits of six-month budgets.
- Reduce forecast detail and the frequency of forecasts required from the operating divisions (rely on forecasts developed at the group and staff levels for interim periods). Reduce forecast analysis. Cover only those elements that have a major impact on bottom-line operating results. Require forecasts from operating activities only for budget variances; do the rest of the forecast centrally. Compare forecasts against the budget only—not prior year actuals, unless done centrally.
- Reduce the level of detail required to support appropriations and product program requests. Simplify multiple profit analysis evaluations (accounted profit, TAR, payback period, incremental profit, etc.) and shift emphasis to the "basics" (variable cost and F&T). Reduce status report frequency and detail for product programs. Allow operating activities to control projects to the bottom line.

- Simplify the product quality tracking system.
- Simplify, centralize, and mechanize accounting functions where possible.
- Implement procedures to reduce internal auditing requirements. As the Japanese would do, invite the outside auditors to participate in reducing the cost and improving efficiency by suggesting ways that they can reduce their audit requirements.
- Review the most effective organization of the systems function; place increased emphasis to modernize, simplify, standardize, and mechanize financial reporting and analysis.

## SHARING CONTROL

Control is shared through all functional areas of the organization and is not dominated by finance.

### Discussion

Because the Japanese do not have our concept of a dominant finance function, their operating people seem to have accepted more responsibility for the financial results of their actions. Our "operating staff" role is unknown to finance people in Japan; thus, their executives appear to be more directly involved in the operating detail. In general, their finance functions are centralized, and the operations have either limited or no "pure finance" people to serve as controllers. Examples of financial control responsibilities that are assigned to operating activities in Japan include:

- Pricing—pricing is controlled by the sales activities.
- Scheduling—product schedules are controlled between sales and manufacturing and approved by the management committee/executive committee.
- Payroll—payroll and timekeeping systems are mechanized with the initial input controlled by the industrial relations activity.
- Product variable cost—product costs are estimated and controlled by the engineering units without finance involvement.
- Appropriations—manufacturing and engineering units run the approval system. Requests are brief, less detailed, and prepared by operating managers.
- Project control—control of approved appropriations actions also is performed by the operating activities, with concentration on achieving the net approved investment level, rather than line-by-line project control—without finance involvement.

## Recommended Items for Study

After the controls are simplified, investigation should focus on which control responsibilities can be performed as well by operating activities as by finance. Where possible, control should be shifted to other activities, and accountability requirements should be tougher.

## COST REDUCTION

Japanese companies are organized for cost reduction.

### Discussion

The Japanese have a strong focus on cost reduction as a positive function. All three companies employ a high-level cost reduction committee to focus on efficiency improvements. At Nissan, the Vice Presidents of manufacturing and engineering control this committee, and all activities are represented, including product engineering, manufacturing engineering, purchasing, and accounting.

Within each finance activity, a function was established to support the company's cost-reduction effort. Major emphasis in Nissan and Nippondenso is placed on a value engineering organization which reviews all designs for lowest-cost, best-function approach—Nissan has a 30-person value analysis department (0.5 percent of their total engineering headcount, or equivalent to a 70-person department based on NAAO engineering headcount).

Manufacturing and purchasing personnel regularly visit suppliers to "rationalize" vendor production processes.

## Recommended Items for Study

We should establish a high-level, operational cost reduction committee, with joint operating and staff participation. The purpose of the committee would be to stimulate cost-reduction efforts throughout the company, to ensure the involvement of all activities, and to facilitate the implementation of cost-reduction ideas. The finance role should not be more than supporting; the ideas must be generated by the operating people.

A major value-engineering activity should be established to provide formalized training throughout engineering. Also, we should substantially increase

**EXHIBIT 7**

## FINANCE HEADCOUNT ANALYSIS

### Toyo Kogyo (Annual sales are $4.5 billion—1.1 million vehicles.)

| | |
|---|---:|
| Finance personnel (including systems) | 517 |
| Less nonfinance personnel and keypunch operators | (125) |
| Subtotal | 392 |
| Administrative support personnel performing finance functions | |
| Project control (TK estimate) | 40 |
| Budgeting (TK estimate) | 50 |
| Business research department | 20 |
| Subtotal | 502 |
| Allocation (Ford estimate—30% × 502) | 150 |
| Total estimated finance personnel | 652 |
| Total personnel | 24,600 |
| Finance personnel as a percentage of total personnel | 2.65 |

### Nissan (Annual sales are $13 billion—2.6 million vehicles.)

| | |
|---|---:|
| Finance personnel | 400 |
| Systems | 250 |
| Subtotal | 650 |
| Administrative support personnel performing finance functions | |
| Allocation (Ford estimate—50% × 650) | 325 |
| Total estimated finance personnel | 975 |
| Total personnel | 56,000 |
| Finance personnel as a percentage of total personnel | 1.70 |

### Nippondenso (Annual sales are $2.3 billion.)

| | |
|---|---:|
| Finance personnel (including systems) | 249 |
| Administrative support personnel performing finance functions | |
| Allocation (Ford estimate—50% × 249) | 125 |
| Total estimated finance personnel | 374 |
| Total personnel | 24,000 |
| Finance personnel as a percentage of total personnel | 1.60 |

### Ford (Annual sales are $37.1 billion—4.4 million vehicles.)

| | |
|---|---:|
| 1979 | |
| Finance personnel | 19,639 |
| Less estimated nonfinance personnel | (1,000) |
| Total estimated finance personnel | 18,639 |
| Average personnel (hourly and salary) | 494,579 |
| Finance personnel as a percentage of total personnel | 3.80 |
| 1980 | |
| Finance personnel | 18,539 |
| Less estimated nonfinance personnel | (1,000) |
| Total estimated finance personnel | 17,539 |
| Average personnel (hourly and salary) | 426,735 |
| Finance personnel as a percentage of total personnel | 4.10 |

EXHIBIT 8

**ORGANIZATION CHARTS**

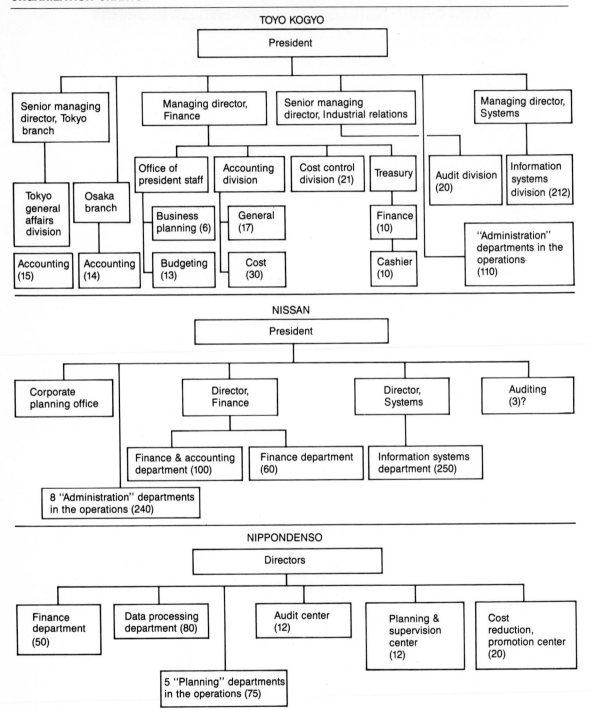

---

**EXHIBIT 9**

---

**CONTACT LIST**

---

Sofia University, Tokyo
R.J. Ballon — Professor

Coopers & Lybrand
Michael R. Fielding — Partner in Charge
Raymond J. Yonke — Managing Partner
Etsuo Sawa — Partner
Hal H. Oishi — Executive Partner
Howard K. Hiroki — Associate Director Far East

IBM
Mototsugu Nakatsu — Manufacturing Controller
J. Fujieda — Manager of DP Marketing Plans
Noboru Ueda — Manager of Development Office
Yukichi Arao — Manager of Product Forecasting, Market Research & Forecasting

Toyo Kogyo
Sadao Okino — Managing Director
Ichiro Maeda — Director and Manager, Office of the President's Staff
Toshiaki Kakimoto — Deputy Manager, Office of the President's Staff
Makoto Miyaji — Director and Manager, Accounting Division
Yoshio Mizobuchi — Manager, Cost Control Division
Osamu Nobuto — Director and Manager, Office of International Business Development
Mitsuji Muraoka — Manager, Information Systems Division
Kazutomo Tsuchiya — Staff Manager, Office of International Business Development
Tadashi Fujino — Manager, Budget Planning Department
Shoji Shimonaka — Section Chief, Mazda

Nissan
Ken Ohmori — General Manager, Finance & Accounting Department
Masanori Kobayashi — Manager, Finance & Accounting Department
Takehiro Kasai — International Division
Kushida — Deputy General Manager, Accounting Department
Kotana — Manager, Corporate Planning Office
Hotta — Corporate Planning Office

Nippondenso
Masao Tsukamoto — General Manager, Planning & Supervision Center
Shigeru Miyasaka — Manager, Finance & Accounting Department
Takashi Shioya — Overseas Sales Division, Original Equipment Sales
Nobuhiro Sugawara — Assistant Manager, Management Control Section, Planning & Supervision Center

---

manufacturing and purchasing review of vendor production processes to improve efficiency.

## FEWER PERSONNEL

Overall, the Japanese operate their financial systems with *fewer people*. Exhibit 7 provides direct comparisons of headcounts for Toyo Kogyo, Nissan, Nippondenso, and Ford.

## Discussion

It is very difficult to compare finance functions between Ford and the Japanese companies because of the different organizational structures (Exhibit 8). It seems clear, however, that on any basis Ford has substantially more finance personnel. The number of finance people at Nissan and Nippondenso represented about 1.7 percent of total employment and at Toyo Kogyo about 2.6 percent. This compared with over 4 percent at Ford.

The Japanese utilize fewer finance people because (1) they do most things more simply than we do, (2) they have operating activities share some control functions that the Ford finance department performs (thus avoid duplication) and (3) they run their business with less financial data. The finance role at the Japanese companies is one of coordination of the corporate goals, the collection of data, and the reporting of actual results. The role does not appear to be that of "police." There was no evidence of finance people controlling or reviewing data and recommendations prepared by other finance people within the organization.

## Recommended Items for Study

We should evaluate the possibility of reducing by year-end 1981 finance workload by 25 percent and reducing finance headcount as soon thereafter as possible without compromising the control system. Accomplishing this objective will require the support of operating management and finance personnel. Obtaining the support of finance personnel will require personnel policies that arrest fears as jobs and grades within finance are eliminated. Over the longer term (1982 and 1983), we should make additional reductions as systems improvements and changes in operating responsibilities permit.

---

*Note:* The sources used in this study appear in Exhibit 9.

# PART EIGHT

# The Management of International Operations

# Applichem

The Gary [Indiana] plant had had obvious problems for years. It was an ineffective operation. It had a fiefdom type of management. The people had grown complacent and inefficient. They had lost their technical curiosity. And the state-of-the-art technology was in Frankfurt. In the late 1970s, when I was business manager, I tried to get them to invite Ari (the Frankfurt manufacturing and technology expert) to Gary. After months of talking, they finally invited him to get me off their backs.

In the Fall of 1981, we [top management] had a meeting reviewing our 10-year plan. After my part, I said that I was going to shift production of Release-ease and another product from Gary to Frankfurt as fast as possible. I almost got punched in the mouth for that. We had been working on it [the Gary plant] for years. But we were not doing anything! At Gary there were still 1300 people putting out 300 million pounds of material a year. At Frankfurt, 600 people put out about 10 percent less material.

This case was prepared by Associate Professor M. Thérèse Flaherty as the basis for class discussion rather than to illustrate effective or ineffective handling of an administrative situation. Names of individuals and certain financial data have been disguised. Copyright © 1985 by the President and Fellows of Harvard College. Revised July 1986.

J. S. (Joe) Spadaro, Vice President and Director of the Plastics Business, was discussing the conditions in Release-ease manufacturing which led him to request a study comparing productivity at six Release-ease plants. He had requested the study in June 1982, and it had been finished in September 1982.

Spadaro had joined Applichem in 1956 when he was 27. His bachelor's degree was in mechanical engineering, and he had held several jobs before that, including managing a machine shop but not including anything related to the chemical industry. His first assignment had been in Italy where he spent 10 years; then he had spent 5 years in the United Kingdom before returning to work at corporate headquarters in Chicago.

## BUSINESS BACKGROUND

Release-ease was a specialty chemical. Applichem developed it in 1952 in response to a customer's request for help in formulating a plastic molding compound which released easily from metal molds after compression molding. It was sold as a dry powder.

Making molded plastic parts is much like

making molded gelatin. Both gelatin and the plastic molding compound are hot and liquid when put in the mold; both harden as they cool. Both tend to leave residue on the mold after they are unmolded. Washing a gelatin mold is easy, and the mold is rarely needed again immediately. But molds for plastic parts are precision stainless steel; they can be difficult to clean, and they are used repeatedly, with unmolding and cleaning being the bottleneck.

When a customer requested help in cleaning molds quickly, Applichem applications engineers came up with Release-ease. It was a chemical to be added in low concentration to the plastic molding compound during its manufacture so that the molded parts would be easier to separate from the mold and would leave the mold cleaner. Release-ease was widely used in molding plastic parts.

Applichem had held the patent, and the product family had been a steady sales and profit generator for the company through 1982. Applichem had done no research on the Release-ease product or process after about 1953. What product and process changes there had been were made by manufacturing people in the plants. And most of those had been made by Aristotle (Ari) Pappas, Manager of Release-ease manufacturing at the Frankfurt plant.

The specifications of Release-ease varied slightly among regions. Over the years as customers encountered problems in their molding processes, Applichem's applications engineers had worked with them to identify aspects of Release-ease or other aspects of the customer's process which could relieve the symptoms. The process was one of trial-and-error. Customers were also continually finding ways to use lower concentrations of Release-ease to achieve the same results. In 1982 Applichem's market research group expected little net increase in demand for Release-ease during the next 5 years.

In Europe suspendability of the particles in liquid came to be an important property, and most promotional literature stressed this property. Competition was fiercer in Europe than in the United States; quality and product specifi-

cations were more closely monitored there. Several managers told the casewriter that they were convinced that Release-ease made in the Frankfurt plant met specifications better than that made in other plants. There were two other important differences in customers' uses in Europe and the rest of the world. First, European customers used their Release-ease within 1 year of purchase, whereas some final customers in the United States would use it as long as 3 years after manufacture, and customers in other regions varied between the two extremes. Second, European customers purchased Release-ease in 50-kilo bags, but customers in the United States and Japan used packages in many sizes from ½ kilo on up.

Release-ease sold at an average price of $1.01 a pound. Applichem's Release-ease sales by region, production by each of the six plants, as well as exports and imports by region are shown in Exhibit 1.

Applichem's strongest competitor was a large United States–based chemical company whose only plant for making a close substitute for Release-ease was located in Luxembourg. Its sales in Europe were strong, and it made some export sales to the United States and Latin America. But Applichem had by far the largest market share and the mystique associated with having patented the earliest available form of the product. A third United States–based company provided some competition in the United States, but J. (John) Benfield, who was Operations Manager for the Plastic North American Business Team in 1982, said that he thought that the latter company was not seriously committed to the business for the long run. They had a plant with some excess capacity, and in 1982 they were using it to produce another close substitute for Release-ease.

In Japan Applichem was the only company whose product had been approved by the regulators. Joe Spadaro said that eventually there would be some other products sold in Japan, even if only exports from Europe. And the Plastics Operations Manager of the Pacific Area told the casewriter that he had heard that someone

---
**EXHIBIT 1**
---

**RELEASE-EASE SALES, PRODUCTION AND TRADE BY REGION** (Millions of Pounds)

| | Sales | Plant | Actual 1982 production | Exports by region | Imports by region |
|---|---|---|---|---|---|
| North America (incl. Mexico and Canada) | 32 | Gary<br>Canada<br>Mexico | 14.0<br>2.6<br>17.2 | 14.2 | 12.4 |
| Western Europe (incl. Middle East and Africa) | 20 | Frankfurt | 38.0 | 18.0 | 0 |
| Latin America | 16 | Venezuela | 4.1 | 0 | 11.9 |
| Pacific and rest of world | 11.9 | Sunchem | 4.0 | 0 | 7.9 |
| Total | 79.9 | | 79.9 | 32.2 | 32.2 |

in the Japanese government had been approached with the idea of approving a Release-ease-type product.

## COMPANY BACKGROUND

Applichem was a manufacturer of specialty chemicals founded in Chicago just before World War II. Most of its products were devised by Applichem's applications engineers as solutions to a specific customer's problems. Applichem's research department subsequently refined the product and process—in successful cases—to arrive at a product with broader application.

Applichem had a strong functional orientation, even though some matrix elements had been introduced to the organization during the mid-1970s. There is evidence of this in the June 1982 organization chart presented in Exhibit 2. There were Business Managers for two businesses reporting to a Group Vice President and four Area Vice Presidents reporting to the Chief Operating Officer. Each Business Manager led four business teams, one for each of the four areas. Each area business team was headed by one full-time manager. On each team were a Financial Manager, a Marketing Manager, an R&D Manager (who usually focused on new product introductions), and an Operations Manager. The functional managers also held line jobs in their respective Area organizations. The Op-

erations and Marketing Managers, like employees in the manufacturing plants and sales and marketing organizations, reported up through the Area organizations. Finance and R&D reported up through the functional organizations. For example, John Benfield, Operations Manager for the Plastics North America Business Team in 1982, reported through two boxes on the organization chart in Exhibit 1: directly to Joe Spadaro and through several people to the Vice President of the North American area.

## TECHNOLOGY

Release-ease was manufactured by a four-step process. In the reaction step the raw materials (several of which were hazardous, flammable, and therefore not transportable internationally) were combined in a precise sequence under pressure and heat to form the Release-ease. The Release-ease was then precipitated out to form a slurry. The timing of introducing materials into the pressurized vessel (or kettle)—as well as the temperature and pressure which prevailed, the feedrates, heat removal, and agitation—affected the size and composition of the forming Release-ease particles. The quality of the Release-ease, the amount of raw materials, and the characteristics of the process were unaffected by the source of energy used in the plant. So steam, natural gas, oil, and electricity were

EXHIBIT 2

**APPLICHEM ORGANIZATION CHART, JUNE 1982**

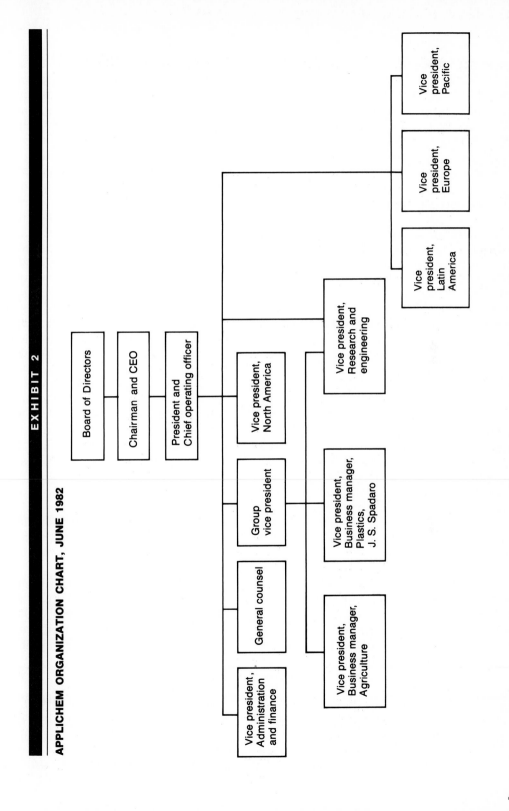

combined differently at different plants to minimize local cost.

The second step was to clean, or isolate, the Release-ease particles from the slurry. This was done by moving the slurry on a conveyor belt made of mesh so that the liquid fell through the belt to the trough below, leaving wet Release-ease particles on the belt. In the third step, Release-ease particles were dried; and in the fourth step the Release-ease powder was packaged in bags on an automated filler line.

Laboratory samples were taken for analysis at the end of the reaction, cleaning, and drying steps. It usually took 4 hours for operators to get the laboratory results. Since waiting between the cleaning and drying steps impaired product properties, Release-ease particles moved continuously between cleaning and drying. The information was used to classify the material after it was processed. Material that was off-spec was reworked in some plants; in other plants some of it was reclassified as QC-3 (QC-1 was the category for product which conformed to specs) and sold for a lower price.

Throughout the process there were possibilities for yield loss. For example, in the reaction step some of the raw materials were added in powder form, and they could be lost as dust on the floor and in the air. In the cleaning step, particles might be filtered out with the liquid and impurities. Recapturing waste materials was an important source of yield increases; the manufacturing people typically improved recapture gradually over years of work. Waste could also be an important health and safety measure.

The average yield of Release-ease on raw material A was a key indicator of the overall performance of the Release-ease manufacturing processes at different plants. The yield was defined by dividing the actual number of pounds of active ingredient in the final product by the number of pounds of active ingredient which would be in the Release-ease if all the key raw material A were converted to active ingredient. Yields were usually expressed in percentages. Benfield explained, "Plants designed for larger volumes of output generally have higher yields.

Raw material A might not wind up in the final product for one or both of two reasons: (1) There might be physical losses (waste) during the process. For example, raw material A per pound of Release-ease left in a drum container (used in low-volume processes) would be greater than that left in a railroad tank car (used in high-volume processes). (2) The available raw material A might not be converted during the process. Larger-scale processes would have less waste than smaller-scale processes. But the proportion of available raw material A converted to Release-ease would be determined by how well the process was run, regardless of scale. A well-run, low-volume (around 5 million pounds a year) process would have an average yield on A of 91 or 92 percent; a well-run, medium-volume plant would have an average yield on A of 94 to 95 percent; a well-run, high-volume plant would have an average yield on A of 98 to 99 percent."

Usually, the manufacturing process was run 24 hours a day, 7 days a week. This was because shutting down the process required expensive cleaning of the reaction kettles and the driers where Release-ease particles stuck. Similarly, changing the size of bag in the packaging line frequently took a day.

One of the main quality measures for the final product performance was the percent of active ingredient in the powder, since high amounts of active ingredient correlated well with good application properties, especially for U.S. markets.

The Plastics North America Business Team estimated that in 1982 it would cost about $20 to $25 million to build another plant like that in Gary, Indiana. And they expected that the plant would have a useful technical life of about 20 years if properly maintained.

## THE MANUFACTURING PLANTS

The *Gary* plant was managed by the North American area. It supplied Release-ease to customers located in that area. The plant was located in Gary, Indiana (just outside Chicago), and in a neighborhood where immigrants from Eastern Europe had settled during the early twentieth century. The plant was founded in 1905 and purchased in 1951 by Applichem as the company's first large manufacturing facility. Many people who worked in the Gary plant in 1982 had followed 6 to 10 other members of their families who had worked there over the generations. They were loyal to the plant and to the plant manager, who had grown up in the neighborhood and called himself the "Gary kid."

Release-ease was the first product Applichem manufactured there, and the process had changed incrementally with the market for Release-ease. Most equipment for the process used in 1982 had been installed between 1959 and 1964. It was designed to run a wide range of product formulation and package types. In 1982 Gary ran eight formulations of Release-ease and about 80 package sizes, whereas the Frankfurt plant, for example, ran only two formulations of Release-ease and one 50-kilo package.

The plant manufactured 19 product families in addition to Release-ease. It had a total of 1,000 nonunion employees, down from about 2,000 during the mid-1960s. It had a Release-ease design capacity of 18.5 million pounds a year, and around 60 people manufactured 14 million pounds of Release-ease in 1982.

The *Canadian* plant, located in Southern Ontario, had been started in 1955. It was managed by Canadian nationals who reported to the North American area. It had a nonunion work force, and in 1982 it supplied four products in addition to Release-ease.

The plant was generally well-regarded within Applichem for its efficiency and the quality of its product. It had a "no-frills" design and had been well-maintained since its inception. It had a rated annual capacity of 3.7 million pounds of Release-ease, and it manufactured 2.6 million pounds of Release-ease in 1982. It supplied Release-ease only in 50-kilo packages.

The *Frankfurt* plant was managed by German nationals who reported through the Europe area, and it supplied customers located in Europe, the Middle East, and Africa as well as other Ap-

plichem plants. It made 12 product families in addition to Release-ease. The plant had 600 employees in 1982. It made about 38 million pounds of Release-ease a year in 1982, and its design capacity was 47 million pounds a year. It had two processes for manufacturing Release-ease: one installed between 1971 and 1974 and one installed in about 1961, with later major modifications to increase capacity. The processes featured computer control of the first process step and extensive solids recovery and waste treatment. Frankfurt bulk-shipped Release-ease to other company plants which then packaged it and shipped it to customers.

Release-ease manufacturing was managed by Ari Pappas. He was a Greek national who had headed Release-ease manufacturing at Frankfurt since the mid-1960s. He had become acquainted with Joe Spadaro and several other members of Applichem's top management team when they had worked in Europe during the 1960s. Pappas had a technical bent; and he had worked with customers, the Applichem Technical Center in Europe, and his own employees to improve the yields and reliability of the Release-ease he made.

The *Mexican* plant was part of a wholly owned subsidiary of Applichem. It was managed by Mexican nationals, who reported to the Vice President of the Latin American area. It supplied the Mexican market and in early 1980s the Far East. The plant processed about 17.2 million pounds of Release-ease during 1982 and had a design capacity of 22 million pounds a year. All its Release-ease was packaged in 50-kilo bags. The process had been installed in 1968 with extra drying capacity introduced in 1978. It was similar in design to the Gary plant and manufactured six product families in addition to Release-ease.

The *Venezuelan* plant was started up in 1964. It had a no-frills design, and no improvements had been made between 1964 and 1982. Its rated annual capacity was 4.5 million pounds, and it produced 4.1 million pounds of Release-ease in 1982. Its Release-ease was packaged only in 50-kilo bags. The plant had old equipment, and the only dryer was in poor repair. It was managed by Venezuelan nationals, who reported to the Vice President of the Latin American area, and it manufactured one product family in addition to Release-ease.

The educational levels of the Mexican and Venezuelan operators were significantly below those of operators in the other plants. Benfield explained that the Mexican operators had some technical depth and were able to maintain process improvements suggested by Ari, while the Venezuelans were not. The Venezuelans had not improved process yield or capacity.

*Sunchem* was Applichem's 50 percent Japanese joint venture in Japan which owned and operated a manufacturing plant for Release-ease and one other product for the plastics industry. It was managed by Japanese nationals and reported to Applichem's Pacific area. It was founded in 1957 and had supplied the Release-ease requirements of Japanese customers after that. The process had been redesigned in 1969. Some automation and waste recovery had been introduced. Its volume was constrained by low dryer capacity in 1982. The Japanese plant processed many ½-kilo and 1-kilo packages. The plant had a rated capacity of 5 million pounds a year, and it produced 4 million pounds in 1982. Within Applichem the Japanese plant was generally thought to be technically excellent. Employees there did more development work than the other plants: They had a product test laboratory, a plastics engineering lab, and a workers' dormitory for single men. Japanese managers said that they required more environmental protection measures than the other plants. Theirs was, for example, the only plant with scrubbers for processing gaseous wastes.

There was no union at this plant, although there generally were industry—as opposed to company—unions in the Japanese chemical industry. In 1979 the plant manager wrote to U.S. management to explain why an unusually large number of employees was needed in Japan relative to similar Applichem plants elsewhere. He wrote:

Work rules and regulations seem to be more severe than those in other countries. For example, the Japanese Fire Prevention Law prescribes that the work of handling flammable raw materials must be performed by those having a license for doing such work. Among the works requiring a similar license are those of wide variety in which we handle high-pressure gas, as in refrigerators, toxic substances and organic solvents, and drying works being performed where oxygen is not sufficient. A number of plant operators will have to attend training courses to acquire such licenses. . . .

We know that one operator has been taking care of running of several kettles at the Gary plant. Only one operator would not be enough to handle all kettles here because our workers do more work with the kettles. . . .

In accordance with a strong recommendation by the Shift Work Committee of the Japan Industrial Hygiene Institute, manufacturers are required to allow a temporary sleeping time for 2 hours a day to all who are engaged in midnight works.

## THE CROSS-PLANT PRODUCTIVITY STUDY

Benfield had managed the study comparing productivity at different plants. Talking in retrospect about it, he said:

The report got things on an even keel. It set the agenda. Until then our report managers at one plant rarely encountered managers from sister plants. And they never gave much attention to improving their process on the basis of what other plants had done.

Although the standard costs and volumes of Release-ease were easily available for each plant, the technical information needed for the Study was not available. Allocating indirect labor over products was a major problem. The Japanese and Gary employees, for example, complained throughout that they simply had low volumes which caused their overhead to be too high. Yield information was available, but only the technical people in the plants had it. The Study was able to identify precise labor productivity differences among plants and to set an agenda for improvement.

It was important that financial and technical people in all the plants worked together developing the numbers. We argued back and forth during the process, trying to ensure that everyone in the plants agreed with the numbers. For example, to satisfy some concerns at Gary, where a lot of time was spent packaging Release-ease in small packages, packaging was studied separately for all plants. And the Japanese overestimated their material usage in their standards because they did not want to be caught short. So we took their usage numbers from their actual experience year-to-date.

Over the 4 months that we worked on the report before it was published in September 1982, prob-

ably 4 man-years went into it. The individual plants were not interested in repeating the comparison project. In fact, some said that they hoped it was never done again. It was a pain.

Exhibit 3 presents the breakdown and comparison of manufacturing costs for Release-ease at Applichem's six plants in 1982 as it appeared in the study. Exhibits 4 through 7 present some of the data which Benfield's group used in defining and computing the cost figures presented in Exhibit 3. The costs in Exhibit 3 are manufacturing, as opposed to delivered, costs. An-

## EXHIBIT 3

**COMPARISON OF WORLDWIDE RELEASE-EASE MANUFACTURING COST** ($/100 lb of Release-ease)

| | Plants | | | | | |
|---|---|---|---|---|---|---|
| Expense | Mexico | Canada | Venezuela | Frankfurt | Gary | Sunchem |
| Raw materials | | | | | | |
| A | 27.00 | 28.32 | 24.67 | 24.02 | 27.96 | 29.62 |
| B | 14.57 | 15.26 | 26.82 | 11.69 | 13.52 | 20.41 |
| C | 16.39 | 11.19 | 19.18 | 9.03 | 6.92 | 24.68 |
| D | 5.89 | 7.45 | 9.52 | 3.75 | 6.48 | 5.50 |
| Other | 11.20 | 6.48 | 7.10 | 4.51 | 5.95 | 11.65 |
| Subtotal | 75.05 | 68.70 | 87.29 | 53.00 | 60.83 | 91.86 |
| Raw material overhead | — | — | — | — | 2.65 | — |
| Operating costs | | | | | | |
| Direct labor, salary, & fringes | 2.38 | 7.03 | 4.68 | 5.78 | 8.46 | 12.82 |
| Depreciation | 0.95 | 0.97 | 0.94 | 1.05 | 1.60 | 3.23 |
| Utilities | 5.08 | 5.50 | 5.96 | 5.54 | 5.45 | 10.49 |
| Maintenance | 1.60 | 2.75 | 2.17 | 1.34 | 3.71 | 3.77 |
| Quality control | 0.64 | 1.30 | 1.81 | 0.57 | 1.54 | 2.77 |
| Waste treatment | 1.37 | 0.96 | — | 0.64 | 1.02 | 10.61 |
| Plant administration | 1.11 | 3.62 | 4.58 | 2.91 | 1.22 | 4.07 |
| Development | — | — | — | 0.38 | 0.97 | 2.48 |
| Supplies | 2.25 | 0.98 | 3.65 | — | 0.77 | 0.56 |
| Building expense | — | — | — | 1.12 | 0.64 | 0.36 |
| Other | 2.20 | 1.44 | 1.23 | 1.01 | 0.29 | 6.22 |
| Subtotal | 17.58 | 24.55 | 25.02 | 20.34 | 25.67 | 57.38 |
| Subtotal: cost before packaging | 92.63 | 93.25 | 112.31 | 73.34 | 89.15 | 149.24 |
| Package, load, & ship | 2.38 | 4.10 | 4.03 | 3.35 | 13.78 | 4.56 |
| Total cost | 95.01 | 97.35 | 116.34 | 76.69 | 102.93 | 153.80 |

*Note:* Operating costs include indirect labor and associated material costs other than raw materials; raw material overhead in the Gary plant included incoming inspection, handling, and inventory carrying costs related to raw materials. For other plants those costs were included in operating costs.

---
**EXHIBIT 4**
---

**NUMBER OF PEOPLE AT EACH OPERATION AT EACH PLANT**

| | Plants | | | | | |
|---|---|---|---|---|---|---|
| | **Mexico** | **Canada** | **Venezuela** | **Frankfurt** | **Gary** | **Sunchem** |
| Direct labor | | | | | | |
| Reaction | 5.5 | 3.1 | 3.4 | 13.9 | 6.3 | 5.0 |
| Clean | 1.8 | 2.0 | 1.7 | 11.8 | 2.5 | 3.4 |
| Dry | 1.8 | 2.0 | 1.7 | 5.6 | 3.6 | 3.4 |
| Package | 10.4 | 5.0 | 6.2 | 14.6 | 11.3 | 2.7 |
| Subtotal | 19.5 | 12.1 | 12.9 | 45.9 | 23.7 | 14.4 |
| Indirect Labor | | | | | | |
| Maintenance | 5.6 | 2.0 | 1.5 | 14.6 | 6.4 | .3 |
| Quality control | 1.8 | 2.1 | 1.8 | 4.9 | 3.2 | 2.4 |
| Production supervision | 2.1 | 1.6 | .6 | 7.3 | 3.4 | 2.5 |
| Plant administration | 3.1 | 3.7 | 4.3 | n.a. | 1.5 | 3.4 |
| Development | .6 | — | — | 1.7 | 2.2 | 3.2 |
| Waste treatment | 1.8 | 1.4 | — | .8 | .1 | 2.5 |
| Utilities | 1.3 | 1.0 | 1.3 | 2.8 | 1.1 | .8 |
| Raw materials handling | — | .6 | — | 2.4 | 4.1 | — |
| Shipping | 3.1 | 1.9 | 1.5 | 5.7 | 9.2 | — |
| Miscellaneous | 5.5 | 1.3 | — | n.a. | 3.4 | 1.5 |
| Subtotal | 24.9 | 15.6 | 11.0 | 40.2 | 34.6 | 16.6 |
| Total | 44.4 | 27.7 | 23.9 | 86.1 | 58.3 | 31.0 |

n.a. = not available.

nual volume of Release-ease was a plant's fore-cast volume of Release-ease for 1982. Indirect costs were allocated over all the products in each plant; the standard cost of Release-ease included the allocated indirect costs. The operating costs were derived by dividing a plant's annual budget for the corresponding element of expense for all Release-ease production by the annual volume. Raw material prices and exchange rates were those used in the plants' 1982 business plans. Benfield said,

> Although exchange rate changes have a significant impact on comparative raw materials costs stated in dollars, the impact is lessened due to the fact that more than half of the raw materials are available in competitive international markets. We estimate that over the long haul only 30 to 40 percent of the raw material cost is directly influenced by exchange rate changes. A variety of energy sources are used by the plants depending on local price and availability. We expect the overall utility costs per pound of Release-ease to continue to be roughly equivalent for all plants except Sunchem where high local electricity costs reflect Japan's generally high energy cost.

Two employees from the Gary plant spoke with the casewriter about the study. T. E. (Tom) Schultz was a project manager in development engineering at the Gary plant when Benfield was assembling the productivity study. He had joined Applichem in 1978 just after completing his bachelor's degree in chemical engineering. And in the period before Applichem's U.S. controller took over, Schultz and Gary's Production Manager for Release-ease began work to improve productivity in the Release-ease area. By the time John Benfield requested information for the productivity study, they had it close to ready. The entire process of getting the data ready for

## EXHIBIT 5

**MISCELLANEOUS INFORMATION**

| | Plants | | | | | |
|---|---|---|---|---|---|---|
| | **Mexico** | **Canada** | **Venezuela** | **Frankfurt** | **Gary** | **Sunchem** |
| Utility usage (per million pounds product) | | | | | | |
| Steam (metric ton) | 2.09 | 3.06 | n.a. | 3.18 | 2.74 | n.a. |
| Natural Gas (cubic meter) | — | 84.31 | 277.20 | — | 78.40 | — |
| Oil (liter) | 98.00 | — | — | 74.20 | — | 214.20 |
| Electricity (kilowatt hours) | 298.20 | 360.12 | 387.80 | 245.00 | 344.40 | 463.40 |
| Utility costs (dollars per unit purchased) | | | | | | |
| Steam (metric ton) | 25.00 | 19.50 | 5.21 | 20.56 | 23.43 | n.a. |
| Natural Gas (cubic meter) | — | 0.12 | 0.05 | — | 0.18 | — |
| Oil (liter) | 0.32 | — | — | 0.35 | — | 0.31 |
| Electricity (1000 kilowatt hours) | 40 | 40 | 71 | 45 | 56 | 79 |
| Raw material usage (pounds per hundred pounds of Release-ease) | | | | | | |
| A | 20.04 | 19.53 | 19.27 | 18.90 | 20.75 | 19.14 |
| B | 51.21 | 51.15 | 50.60 | 47.82 | 53.8 | 48.23 |
| C | 55.97 | 50.96 | 52.00 | 50.28 | 53.6 | 49.49 |
| D | 26.40 | 26.09 | 26.00 | 24.21 | 28.77 | 25.07 |
| Active ingredient (A.I.) in product as shipped (average percent) | 85.6 | 84.7 | n.a. | 84.4 | 84.6 | 85.4 |
| Average yield on raw material A (percent) | 94.7 | 91.1 | 91.7 | 98.9 | 90.4 | 98.8 |
| Volume (million pounds) | | | | | | |
| Annual production volume in 1982 | 17.2 | 2.6 | 4.1 | 38.0 | 14.0 | 4.0 |
| Annual design capacity | 22.0 | 3.7 | 4.5 | 47.0 | 18.5 | 5.0 |

*Note:* Average yield on raw material A is actual pounds A.I. ÷ theoretical pounds A.I.; multiplied by 100 for percent.
n.a. = not available.

## EXHIBIT 6

**TRANSPORTATION COSTS AMONG PLANTS** (Cents/lb)

| | Destination plant | | | | | |
|---|---|---|---|---|---|---|
| **Source plant** | **Mexico** | **Canada** | **Venezuela** | **Frankfurt** | **Gary** | **Sunchem** |
| Mexico | 0.0 | 11.4 | 7.0 | 11.0 | 11.0 | 14.0 |
| Canada | 11.0 | 0.0 | 9.0 | 11.5 | 6.0 | 13.0 |
| Venezuela | 7.0 | 10.0 | 0.0 | 13.0 | 10.4 | 14.3 |
| Frankfurt | 10.0 | 11.5 | 12.5 | 0.0 | 11.2 | 13.3 |
| Gary | 10.0 | 6.0 | 11.0 | 10.0 | 0.0 | 12.5 |
| Sunchem | 14.0 | 13.0 | 12.5 | 14.2 | 13.0 | 0.0 |

*Note:* It cost 11¢ to transport a pound of Release-ease from Canada to Mexico and 11.4¢ to transport a pound of Release-ease from Mexico to Canada. The price of transport depended on distance, type of transport and the volume transported. Where there were differences in transport costs between two locations, they were due to differences in the volumes Applichem had historically shipped in each direction between the locations.

These costs exclude duty into each country. In 1982 the duty into each country was the following percent of the value of Release-ease imported: Mexico, 60%; Canada, 0%; Venezuela, 50%; Germany, 9.5%; United States, 4.5%; Japan, 6%.

### EXHIBIT 7

## HISTORY OF EXCHANGE, INFLATION, AND WAGE RATES

| | Mexico | Canada | Venezuela | Germany | United States | Japan |
|---|---|---|---|---|---|---|
| | Average annual exchange rates (currency/$1) | | | | | |
| 1982 | Ps.96.5 | C$1.23 | Bs.4.3 | DM2.38 | 1.0 | ¥235.0 |
| 1981 | 26.2 | 1.18 | 4.3 | 2.25 | 1.0 | 219.9 |
| 1980 | 23.2 | 1.19 | 4.3 | 1.96 | 1.0 | 203.0 |
| 1979 | 22.8 | 1.17 | 4.3 | 1.73 | 1.0 | 239.7 |
| 1978 | 22.7 | 1.19 | 4.3 | 1.83 | 1.0 | 194.6 |
| 1977 | 22.7 | 1.09 | 4.3 | 2.10 | 1.0 | 240.0 |
| | Average annual price indexes (1980 = 100) | | | | | |
| 1982 | 194.2* | 116.8 | 123.0† | 114.1‡ | 113.7‡ | 103.2* |
| 1981 | 124.4 | 110.2 | 113.8 | 107.8 | 110.6 | 101.4 |
| 1980 | 100.0 | 100.0 | 100.0 | 100.0 | 100.0 | 100.0 |
| 1979 | 80.3 | 88.1 | 83.3 | 93.0 | 86.1 | 84.9 |
| 1978 | 67.9 | 77.0 | 76.3 | 88.7 | 76.3 | 79.1 |
| 1977 | 58.6 | 70.5 | 71.0 | 87.7 | 71.0 | 81.2 |
| | Average gross money wages before income taxes, social security contributions, and benefits (local currency per hour) | | | | | |
| 1982 | 99.42 | 10.25 | 14.37 | 14.64 | 8.50 | 1424.86 |
| 1981 | 63.46 | 9.17 | 13.08 | 13.92 | 7.99 | 1372.77 |
| 1980 | 48.11 | 8.19 | 11.26 | 13.18 | 7.27 | 1292.66 |
| 1979 | 39.91 | 7.44 | 10.42 | 12.36 | 6.69 | 1203.80 |
| 1978 | 34.17 | 6.84 | 9.88 | 11.73 | 6.17 | 1134.00 |
| 1977 | 29.70 | 6.38 | 8.74 | 11.14 | 5.68 | 1061.00 |

*Wholesale prices.
†Home and imported goods.
‡Industrial prices.
Source: For exchange rates and price indexes: *International Financial Statistics,* International Monetary Fund. For wages: Business International Corporation, *Worldwide Economic Indicators,* New York. The values for Venezuela were estimated by Benfield using Applichem sources because the complete series was unavailable in *Worldwide Economic Indicators.*

the study took about 2 man-years. But Schultz had been enthusiastic about the study because he had believed that corporate managers were seeking to identify the best process ideas from all the plants and to implement them wherever they were relevant throughout the Applichem manufacturing network. Tom Schultz said:

There were several difficulties in comparing cost, usage and yield statistics across plants—even data assembled as carefully as that gathered by Benfield. For example, the Gary plant was designed to manufacture prototype samples for customers, and most products in the Release-ease family had first been manufactured in Gary. Also, being an old product, Release-ease had folklore in Gary. There was also a body of opinion to the effect that older product [greater than 2 years] suffered some degradation in applications performance. As it was not unusual for product in the United States to be in the distribution channel for 2 years, Gary placed great emphasis on achieving high A.I. at time of manufacture. We were also very leery about implementing some of the changes that the Frankfurt plant had made because we were afraid that our product shelf-life might be adversely affected. As Frankfurt's product stayed in the distribution channel for at most 1 year, their emphasis on high

A.I. product was less than ours, and they were more adventuresome in adopting process changes.

You know, when I joined the Gary plant it seemed that we had the lowest costs of any plant. But then the exchange rates changed a lot. And the productivity study came along just when we looked bad . . . I wonder when the exchange rates will swing back and make Gary look good again.

W. C. (Wanda) Tannenbaum was Financial Analyst at the Gary plant during the productivity study. She had joined Applichem in 1981, after completing an undergraduate degree in business from the University of Illinois. She noted that the study was very technically oriented, that she was involved only to "look it over." She explained:

At Applichem we use fully allocated standard costs for operations management. For sourcing we used out-of-pocket costs. The data needed for the study were available but not in accessible form. For example, we had many monthly reports, but no data were cumulative. And standard costs were redefined only once or twice a year, so it was just about impossible to get actual costs for Release-ease by month.

In Finance we did a lot of computer work to get the reports we wanted. In fact, we installed an Apple III in 1982, the first PC [personal computer] in Applichem.

The allocation of indirect costs was a big problem for the study—especially for a plant like Gary. It was not designed to be a real streamlined operation. It was designed to be a batch operation for research and specialty products. Its equipment is unique. It is spread out all over the place. You just can't compare it with plants that make commodities.

# Honeywell PACE

Until January 1982, Bob Naylor, factory manager of Honeywell's High Technology Unit (HTU) in Newhouse, Scotland, had been concerned with ensuring firm orders for his products so that he could manufacture in the high-volume stable quantities for which his plant was designed. During two years of steady growth, he had succeeded in persuading Honeywell's Process Automation Center Europe (PACE) in Brussels, the only outlet for HTU's products, to place firm orders six months before production, and had permitted only a 20 percent variation on orders placed for the second quarter and no variance for the first quarter.

But when in January 1982 he became the first operations manager of PACE, reporting to its director, John Dickens, Naylor saw the issue from a different perspective. One of his first tasks had been to review PACE's 1982 inven-

tory plan. Controller[1] usage, as shown in Exhibit 1, had grown steadily since 1978, and he knew from an earlier meeting held in October 1981 to plan HTU's production schedule that PACE had expected demand to rise to 2,500 units in 1982. Before becoming operations manager of PACE, he had laid plans to increase controller production at HTU from 35 to 50 units per week.

However, the decline in world commodity prices and demand had suddenly begun to affect investment levels in PACE's customer industries, and expected orders had failed to materialize. The January business forecast revised projections downward to 2,120 controllers, but checks with sales subsidiaries made Naylor suspect that even this figure was optimistic, and he settled for a revised plan of 2,000 units. The February forecast reduced expected usage yet again to 1,700 units. Because at this point Naylor had already accumulated an excess inventory of 380 controllers, more than enough to meet his total needs for three months, he realized that drastic action was called for. He telephoned Jack Fraser, HTU's new factory manager. "Get ready to close and take a vacation," he warned, only half-joking. "I won't be need-

---

This case was prepared by Associate Professor Kasra Ferdows and Christopher Spray. Certain names and figures have been disguised. Copyright © 1985 by INSEAD, the European Institute of Business Administration, Fontainebleau, France.

[1]Controllers, manufactured at HTU, were a major component of the process control systems sold by PACE, the TDC 2000.

| EXHIBIT 1 |  |
|---|---|

**PACE CONTROLLER USAGE**

| Year | Usage |
|---|---|
| 1978 | 537 |
| 1979 | 1106 |
| 1980 | 1479 |
| 1981 | 1791 |

ing any more deliveries for three months." A few hours later he received a telephone call from Peter Williams, president of Honeywell Europe, who insisted that HTU could not close and that Naylor would have to accept deliveries from HTU.

Quite apart from the immediate problem, Naylor wondered how he could prevent similar problems from occurring in the future. He determined that one of his first tasks as operations manager at PACE would be to establish a better system for inventory planning and control.

## HISTORY OF HONEYWELL

In 1906 Mark C. Honeywell founded the Honeywell Heating Specialities Company in Wabash, Indiana, to build water-heating equipment. Through a series of mergers and acquisitions, the company developed expertise in manufacturing automatic temperature controls for industrial processes and later for heating regulation in office buildings. Prewar experimental work in electronics led to the development of the first successful electronic autopilot in 1941, which was used on U.S. bombers in World War II.

After the war, Honeywell continued to expand its control system operations, developing domestic, commercial, industrial, and military applications. Much of the expansion was overseas, including the establishment of the Belgian subsidiary in 1946, and the first factory in Newhouse, Scotland, which was opened in 1950. Sales grew rapidly in the postwar period from $13.5 million in 1946 to exceed $100 million for the first time in 1950 and $1 billion by 1957.

At the same time Honeywell developed interests in the new data processing industry, purchasing Raytheon's interests in Datamatic Corporation in 1957 and merging with General Electric's computer division in 1970. In 1971 Honeywell reorganized into two large worldwide operating units, Control Systems and Information Systems. By 1982, Honeywell earned net profits of $273 million on worldwide sales of $5.49 billion and employed 100,000 people.

Over the years, Honeywell Control Systems divided into five groups, each specializing in products for different markets: Commercial Buildings, Residential Components, Industrial Products, Aerospace, and Defense. A sixth group, International Operations, controlled overseas operations for the product groups and was divided into four large geographic segments—Europe, Far East and Australia, Latin America, and Canada (see Exhibit 2).

## THE TDC 2000

Within the Industrial Products Group (IPG) were several divisions, including the largest, the Process Control Division (PCD), which manufactured a range of 2,400 instruments to measure and control industrial process variables.

In 1975 PCD launched a product that represented a new approach to industrial process control systems, the TDC 2000. A first attempt to offer industrial users a complete package of control instruments organized into a coherent system, it consisted of instruments to measure process variables such as flow, pressure, and temperature that were linked to "controller" units. The systems could contain several controllers, each of which measured up to eight variables, and presented information about them in a digestible form to operators. In most cases the system also regulated automatically the processes it measured. Because complete reliability was essential to users for whom even a brief breakdown could mean serious safety hazards and costly production losses, all systems contained backup units to take over if any part of the system failed.

**EXHIBIT 2**

HONEYWELL ORGANIZATION CHART, 1982

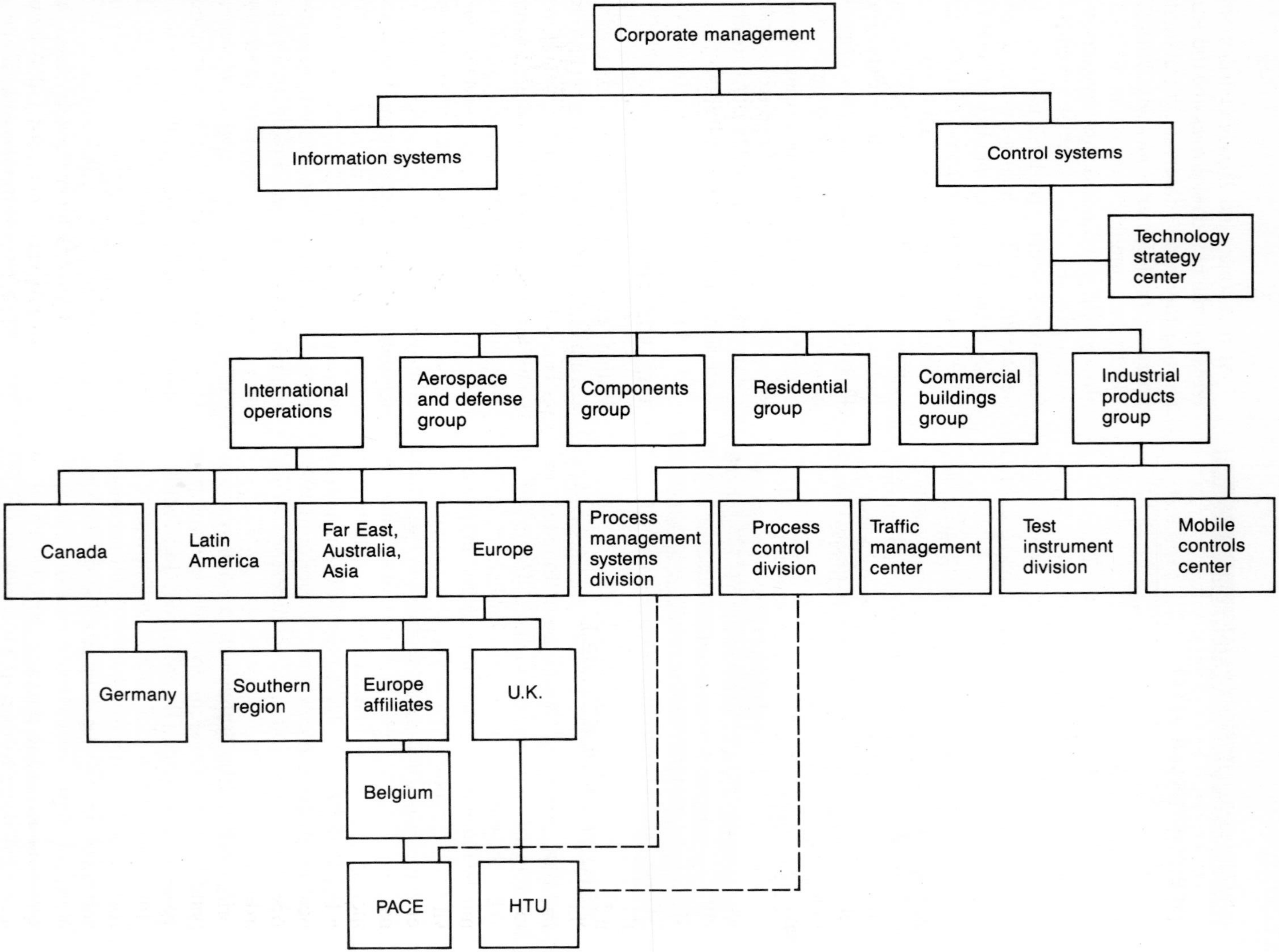

- Corporate management
  - Information systems
  - Control systems
    - Technology strategy center
    - International operations
      - Canada
      - Latin America
      - Far East, Australia, Asia
      - Europe
        - Germany
        - Southern region
        - Europe affiliates
          - Belgium
            - PACE
        - U.K.
          - HTU
    - Aerospace and defense group
    - Components group
      - Process management systems division
    - Residential group
      - Process control division
    - Commercial buildings group
      - Traffic management center
    - Industrial products group
      - Test instrument division
      - Mobile controls center

Because the number and combination of variables that users wished to measure differed considerably, until the launch of TDC 2000 the users or their contractors had designed their own systems based on the range of components offered by Honeywell and other competitors.

Design of a highly reliable low-cost system that was flexible enough to meet the very different needs of users in a wide range of industries had required five years of intensive research and development effort. The final product consisted of a hundred or so different modules that could be mass-produced as standard items from which Honeywell systems engineers could select in consultation with customers to design a custom-built system that met the customer's exact requirements.

The PCD recognized that module production and system assembly required very different skills and decided from the outset to keep the two steps of the manufacturing process completely separate. Units to manufacture standard modules were established in existing PCD factories at PCD's Fort Washington headquarters and in Phoenix. A few low-volume models were also made at the Kamata/Isehara plant in Japan, but no module was made in more than one location.

Because systems design and assembly of modules required close contact and cooperation with customers, a network of five systems centers was established from the outset near the main user markets. A headquarters center was opened in Phoenix, a second U.S. center was in Fort Washington, and overseas centers were located in Canada, Australia, Japan, and Europe. Each center served its local market only, ordering the modules it required from PCD factories. In 1979 a separate Process Management Systems Division (PMSD) was formed to manage the systems centers worldwide (see Exhibit 3 for details of the PCD and PMSD factory networks). While overseas manufacturing and sales were managed by the International Operations Division, PCD and PMSD retained control of key areas such as future product research and development and determined the international transfer prices at which PCD sold standard modules to PMSD.

TDC 2000 found an immediate market among the large petroleum and petrochemical companies in refining and distilling plants throughout the world, which accounted for half of its sales. Other users were producers of major processed commodities such as steel, sugar, cement, wood pulp/paper, and electricity (for a profile of major European purchasers see Exhibit 4).

Half of the sales were for new plants. The system accounted for only a fraction of plant cost—a $500 million plant would require typically a system costing $1 million. Other sales were to replace existing instrumentation, because it was obsolete or because installation could be justified on the basis of cost reduction through process optimization. In later years, a further important source of sales was existing TDC 2000 users who wished to expand their system.

When Honeywell launched TDC 2000 in 1975, it had defined a new product market, which its ability to demonstrate a track record for reliability and a strong international customer base made it difficult for other companies to enter. When competition did arrive in the early 1980s, it was accompanied by a sudden decline in investment levels in the process industries, and both these factors contributed to lower order levels during 1982. Nevertheless TDC 2000 still accounted for about 40 percent of world sales. There were two or three international competitors and a few national competitors in each of the major OECD (Organization for Economic Cooperation and Development) countries that normally enjoyed an advantage in bidding for their government contracts. A new generation of TDC 2000s in development, which involved the introduction of higher-order computer controls for total plant management, was due in 1983–1984 and was expected to strengthen Honeywell's technical leadership of the market.

## TDC 2000 IN EUROPE

In 1975, John Dickens, formerly head of Systems Development Engineering at Honeywell's U.K. subsidiary, was given responsibility for establishing the European Systems Center for design and assembly of TDC 2000. The Process

**EXHIBIT 3**

**PCD/PMSD FACTORY NETWORK, 1982**

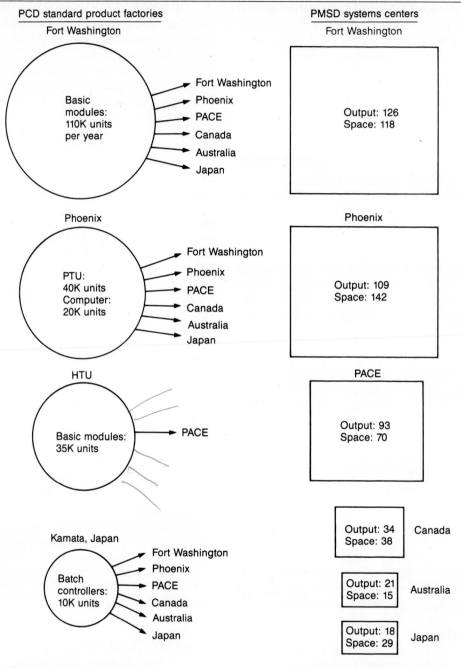

PCD standard product factories

Fort Washington

Basic modules: 110K units per year
→ Fort Washington
→ Phoenix
→ PACE
→ Canada
→ Australia
→ Japan

Phoenix

PTU: 40K units
Computer: 20K units
→ Fort Washington
→ Phoenix
→ PACE
→ Canada
→ Australia
→ Japan

HTU

Basic modules: 35K units
→ PACE

Kamata, Japan

Batch controllers: 10K units
→ Fort Washington
→ Phoenix
→ PACE
→ Canada
→ Australia
→ Japan

Total floor space: 250,000 sq. ft.
Total employees: 750

PMSD systems centers

Fort Washington

Output: 126
Space: 118

Phoenix

Output: 109
Space: 142

PACE

Output: 93
Space: 70

Output: 34
Space: 38    Canada

Output: 21
Space: 15    Australia

Output: 18
Space: 29    Japan

Output: Revenue units in 1982
Space: Thousands of square feet
Total employees: 850

**452**

## EXHIBIT 4

### PACE MULTINATIONAL ACCOUNTS FOR TDC 2000

| Company* | Projects | Loops |
|----------|----------|-------|
| A | 9 | 1,152 |
| B | 3 | 800 |
| C | 7 | 1,936 |
| D | 7 | 618 |
| E | 5 | 448 |
| F | 7 | 902 |
| G | 34 | 3,876 |
| H | 15 | 2,430 |
| I | 64 | 13,202 |
| J | 31 | 3,440 |
| K | 5 | 228 |
| L | 4 | 608 |
| M | 6 | 2,904 |
| N | 22 | 1,742 |
| O | 8 | 380 |
| P | 18 | 3,600 |
| Q | 65 | 4,024 |
| R | 23 | 3,804 |
| S | 10 | 2,030 |
| T | 28 | 3,214 |

*These are very large multinational companies such as BASF, Dow, Mobil, BP, Shell, Union Carbide, Exxon, Alcoa, Dupont, and ICI.

Automation Center Europe (PACE) was established in Belgium in vacant office and factory space within Honeywell Europe's headquarters on the outskirts of Brussels.

Company documents defined PACE's basic charter as follows:

It is a prime objective of Honeywell to supply digital control systems of high quality in cost effective configurations and with delivery lead times to meet customer schedules. PACE is a central source for such systems and the activities which relate to them, including: pre-sales support, technical consultation, system design, project management, assembly, test and commissioning/service back-up. It was founded to provide the efficiency of a single high-volume operation, concentrated direct lines of communication with the factory sources and management, and a central pool of product and application knowledge.

Dickens believed that PACE had a twofold role:

For logistic reasons, PACE acts as a coordination center between the sixteen European sales subsidiaries. Since most of our customers are multinational in size and scope, it is important that there is coordination on design standards and pricing.

There are also considerable economic advantages from having a centralized organization. For example, by having only one central Guest Center where the system can be demonstrated to potential customers there is a substantial reduction in investment required in demonstration systems.

Additionally by centralizing the systems design and engineering function, we can maintain specialized expertise that could neither be developed nor justified economically on a country by country basis.

Between 1975 and 1980, sales of TDC 2000 in Europe grew rapidly from a few thousand dollars to over $100 million (see Exhibit 5). Throughout most of this period of steady growth, PACE successfully achieved both sales and profit targets while meeting customer delivery schedules for more than 95 percent of orders. This required a constant expansion of PACE's manufacturing floor space and personnel. After renting additional space locally, PACE finally moved into its own permanent offices and factory adjacent to the Honeywell Europe headquarters in mid-1982.

Growth of PACE was matched by the other systems centers, and by 1978 the PCD recognized that the level of future expected worldwide sales could not be met by the production of modules from the existing PCD plants.

In considering how to increase production, PCD reviewed its original policy of making each module in only one location, which it felt made TDC 2000 particularly vulnerable to sudden stoppages in one of the plants: shortages of a single module could delay shipment of an entire system. In particular, there was concern that any labor unrest in the United States could affect assembly operations in Europe. The PCD therefore decided to establish a special plant in Europe to provide a duplicate source for PACE

EXHIBIT 5

**PACE GROWTH, 1975–1982**

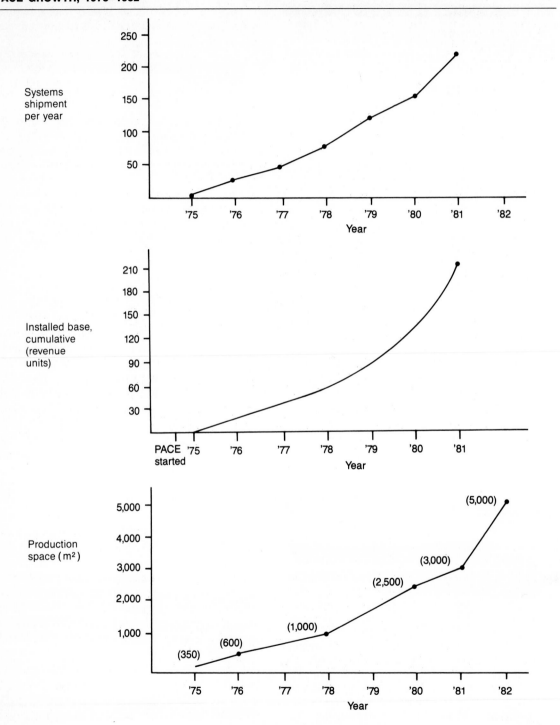

of the main modules, thereby reducing its dependence on the U.S. factories. The new factory would supply none of the other assembly centers, because it was feared that this would be seen by the U.S. plant unions as a threat to their continued existence.

Newhouse in Scotland was chosen as the most appropriate site for the factory, called the High Technology Unit to distinguish it from other local firms using older electronic technologies. Honeywell's own plant at Newhouse had been established in 1950 to manufacture analog instruments and pen recorders, but the market for them had declined by 1978 as they neared the end of their life cycle. Numbering 7,000 at its peak, the work force had fallen to 1,500, and further reductions were planned. Although HTU was able to use the administrative services (personnel, finance, et cetera) of the main factory, HTU required different manufacturing skills and was therefore able to include only a few existing Honeywell employees in its 100-strong work force.

Bob Naylor, formerly a production manager in Burroughs' U.K. subsidiary, was recruited as a factory manager of HTU, reporting to Honeywell's Scottish factories manager based at Newhouse. He established HTU from scratch in an unused 26,000 sq. ft. building adjacent to the main factory and began manufacturing TDC 2000 modules that had the highest volume usage, gradually duplicating more of the products previously made only in the United States. When HTU reached capacity it was intended to supply about 80 percent of PACE's long-term needs. In this way HTU would be protected from variations in PACE's demand, which would be met from other PCD plants, so that it could manufacture in high-volume stable quantities. In most cases, HTU used similar or identical production machinery and techniques to those used in the United States, and its performance was judged against cost standards set for the U.S. factories. Because HTU's transfer prices to PACE were the same as those fixed for the U.S. factories, matching U.S. cost standards was essential for profitable operations.

About 60 percent of HTU's total costs were for raw materials, half of which were purchased locally and the rest from other Honeywell divisions or from Honeywell-approved vendors. Lead times varied considerably but could be up to 3 months for circuit boards and 12 months for integrated circuits.

These constraints meant that HTU had to plan its production schedules a year to 18 months in advance and could not respond quickly to sudden increases or decreases in demand from PACE. Therefore Naylor insisted on firm orders six months in advance from PACE. The HTU held no finished goods inventory, shipping all modules to PACE as soon as they were completed and invoicing PACE for them on the dispatch date.

## ORGANIZATION OF HONEYWELL EUROPE

Honeywell Europe was split into four geographic regions—West Germany, United Kingdom, European Affiliates, and Southern Region—each with approximately equal sales (see Exhibit 6). The latter two divisions were further subdivided by country. Each country was a separate profit center, responsible for both local selling activity and manufacturing operations, and its performance was evaluated on the basis of its success in maximizing sales profits and minimizing factory costs.

PACE reported directly to the managing director of the Belgian subsidiary; HTU reported to the manager of Honeywell's Scottish factories, who in turn reported to the chairman of Honeywell U.K. The structure of the 16-country selling organizations varied according to their size, but TDC 2000 sales were normally a responsibility of an Industrial Products Group (IPG) sales manager, to whom several salespersons reported, some of whom would be TDC 2000 specialists.

Honeywell Europe also had vice presidents of finance and administration, of technology and operations, and of marketing and a director of employee relations, to whom PACE and HTU

**EXHIBIT 6**

HONEYWELL EUROPE ORGANIZATION

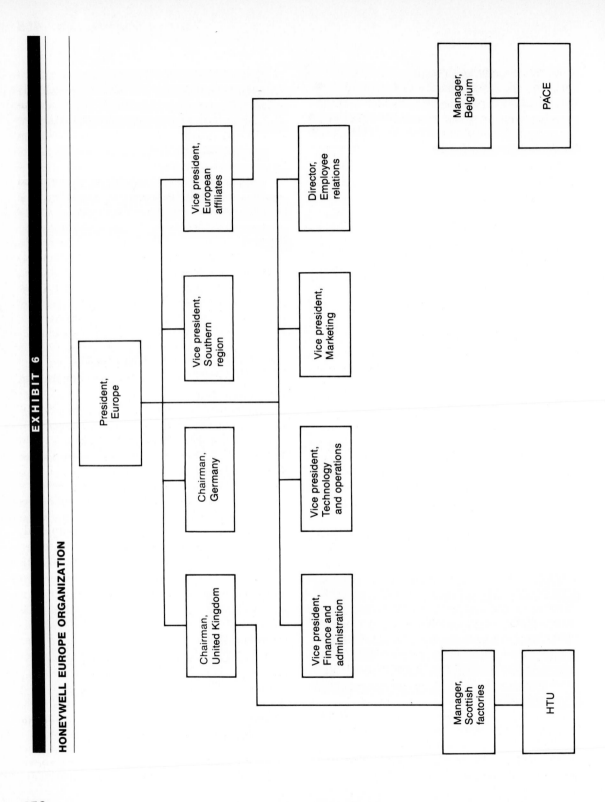

reported in a matrix structure, drawing on services and specialist expertise they provided. The functional vice presidents provided important links between countries, coordinating aspects of strategy and policy between them and resolving intercountry disputes. They were the only formal link between PACE and HTU below the president of European operations.

## PACE IN 1982

In 1980 sudden sales growth had for the first time led to problems in meeting delivery dates, with inventory shortages causing delays in 25 percent of deliveries. To resolve the problem and to prepare for expected continuing expansion in sales, Dickens decided to recruit an operations manager. Bob Naylor, with his intimate knowledge of HTU's operations, was considered an ideal person to manage the important relationship with HTU, and Dickens recruited him to fulfill the new role. After working closely with PACE during 1981, he finally moved to Brussels in January 1982.

After Naylor's arrival, Dickens restructured PACE as shown in Exhibit 7. Besides an important support staff providing technical, financial, and administrative services, the organization was designed to focus on three key areas: management of individual projects, management of day-to-day operations, and strategic planning of future development.

### Project Management

Serge Dupont was responsible for systems engineering. Reporting to him were four project managers, each of whom was in charge of a team of four or five engineers. The project manager was assigned to a project at an early stage, often before the order was confirmed, and he was responsible for all stages in coordination with the appropriate department (see Exhibit 8 for details of a typical project flow through PACE). During early discussions with a potential purchaser, the project manager and PACE team in general provided technical support and coordination with the sales subsidiary, particularly where projects were for multinational companies, were large (e.g., over $750,000), had new or complex process applications, or had intrinsic safety requirements.

With advice from PACE, the sales subsidiary then prepared a final job quotation that included a general system specification, a price, and a delivery date. At this point, the project manager reserved the bulk materials required for assembly and a slot in the production schedule. As soon as the order became firm, the project manager issued a project plan and a project milestone schedule (see Exhibit 9) specifying the freeze dates by which customers had to approve progressively more detailed aspects of the system's design. The systems engineers then designed the detailed system layout, confirmed the materials requirements, and prepared detailed drawings for use by the production department during assembly.

In production, 17 assembly workers with general fitting skills were managed by a supervisor who assigned specific orders to small teams that completed all phases of the assembly operations. The system was thoroughly tested at PACE before shipment to the subsidiary and delivery to the customers. Customer acceptance was either at the PACE test station or when installation at the customer's plant was completed. A project took from three to nine months to complete according to size, and the customer was billed progressively via the country sales subsidiary as costs were incurred.

### Operations

While project managers coordinated the progress of individual projects through production, Naylor oversaw overall operations and worked on development of standards and systems for all stages of the design, assembly, and testing procedure. Commenting on his role, Naylor said:

> I'm a great believer in having adequate information, and then analyzing it to extract useful data.

EXHIBIT 7

PACE PARTIAL ORGANIZATION CHART, 1982

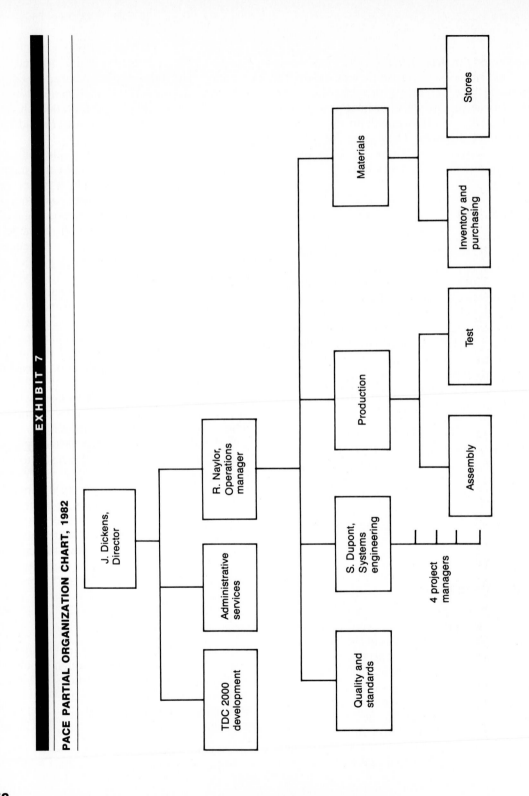

EXHIBIT 8

## PROJECT FLOW THROUGH PACE

EXHIBIT 9

## PROJECT MILESTONE SCHEDULE

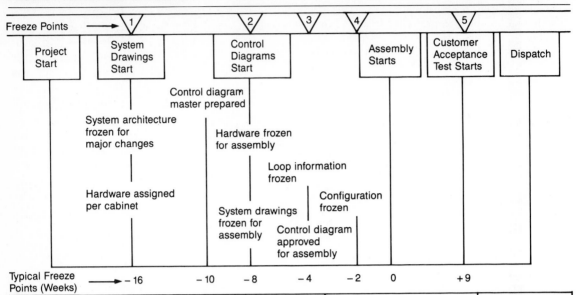

| Freeze Point | Information | Situation before Freeze | Situation after Freeze | Effect of Changes after Freeze on: | |
|---|---|---|---|---|---|
| | | | | Delivery | Cost |
| 1 | System architecture/ content fixed to within ± 10% | Equipment ordered in bulk quantities. Modifications to quantities and types permitted. | Bulk equipment is assigned to special cabinet layouts. Changes to equipment content accepted if less than ± 10%; similarly, minor changes to cabinet layout can be incorporated. | None | None |
| 2 | System layout/ assignment frozen for assembly purposes | Changes to system drawings can be implemented. Limited changes to hardware content (± 10%) and rearrangement can be accepted (stock levels should avoid delivery delays). | Any modifications to system drawings will not necessarily be included in system assembly. Hardware changes will be implemented either after acceptance test or on site. | Yes | Yes |
| 3 | Loop data frozen | Modification to loop/process data will be incorporated in drawings and assembly (unless magnitude or impact of changes prevents this). | Modifications will only be accepted for implementation in documentation and system after acceptance test. | Yes | Yes |
| 4 | Configuration data frozen | Configuration data will be checked and discussed etc. but will not be entered into system. | Configuration data will be entered. Modification and corrections will be inserted during acceptance test. | None | None |
| 5 | Documentation | Changes accepted for modification to drawings and print-out of configuration made if required. | No changes accepted (transparencies provided to customer print-out of data case if required). | None | None |

This is not only for my sake, but for the benefit of those reporting to me as well. As I often explain to them, they need good data as much as I do. Without it they cannot justify their actions and the productivity of their departments.

At the same time, computer printouts are no substitute for practical knowledge of the job. For example, I insist that my schedulers know not only part numbers, but the function of the part as well. This means that if one part is out of stock they can make sensible suggestions to the systems engineers about possible substitutes.

He believed that it was important to instill these attitudes in all his subordinates. With these attitudes, he wished to establish formal performance standards to introduce what he described as "the disciplines of a real factory." In 1982 he was considering which were the key parameters he should set out to measure.

### Strategic Planning

Naylor's arrival allowed Dickens to devote more of his time to the longer-term planning of PACE's development, leaving day-to-day operating concerns to Naylor. In particular he was able to coordinate future sales strategy with the country subsidiaries and to work on the development of TDC 2000.

Recently Naylor was appointed to represent Europe on the Industrial Products Group Worldwide Manufacturing Council, which met two or three times a year to consider the future management of PMSD and PCD factories and products throughout the world, and he was also a member of the Worldwide Systems Centers Council, which considered operating issues and future strategy for the PMSD system centers. Because of the complexity of Honeywell's formal reporting structure, these were valuable opportunities to discuss important issues for PACE and to coordinate the activities of system centers worldwide.

Dickens also spent much of his time developing PACE's formal strategic and operational plans, which in 1982 it presented separately from the Belgian subsidiary to the European Board.

The two-stage cycle began in April with a strategic review. Dickens reviewed PACE's past strategy and presented his view of PACE's future mission and his proposed methods for achieving goals in specific areas. The plan was discussed, amended, and approved by July. The approved strategy provided the basis for developing an operational plan that defined detailed financial objectives for the following year. The plan was first presented in mid-September and discussed during the next six weeks before final acceptance.

### SOLVING THE INVENTORY PROBLEM

Naylor felt that inadequate forecasting was at the root of PACE's inventory problems. "One of the difficulties," he explained, "is that we have long lead times in this business, but we can see only a few months ahead."

The forecasting unit at Honeywell's European headquarters at that time provided predictions of overall dollar sales revenue for the year ahead, divided into quarters. It based its forecasts on overall economic variables such as capital spending levels in PACE's customer industries. Recently these forecasts had failed to foresee the downturn in sales. Naylor decided to supplement this overall business view with his own review of expected sales levels at each of the subsidiaries. To compile these forecasts Dickens recruited Veronique Meister, who had worked for Honeywell Europe for 12 years and knew well the people working in the sales subsidiaries.

Veronique Meister made monthly telephone calls to all 16 sales subsidiaries to review all likely orders for the forthcoming year with sales managers, asking them to assign a booking date, and a probability that the job would be booked. Using her own knowledge and judgment to assess the accuracy of their predictions, she included in her forecast any order she thought had a more than 60 percent probability of being placed. The forecasts provided aggregate data concerning value of sales at customer prices, which Naylor converted into controller usage because these were a main determinant of system cost. In 1982 Naylor estimated that one controller was used per $22,000 of sales. By analyzing past data, Naylor had developed a simple computer model that gave him an average usage of each module per 1,000 controllers. Thus he could convert sales data into an expected usage of each standard module per month.

In this way, Naylor managed to tap the large amount of hard information available in the sales subsidiaries and use it to adjust his assembly schedule, which he planned by week for the six months ahead. Because the schedule for the first quarter was based substantially on actual orders, it usually required little change, but demand for the rest of the year was less certain, and Naylor found the forecasts helpful to develop rough assembly plans that he changed as the booking picture developed. Naylor also used the forecasts to develop his inventory plan, which he discussed monthly with Jack Fraser, HTU's manager, who used PACE's inventory plan to plan his production schedule and materials ordering.

Materials ordering for HTU was a more complex process because each module contained several thousand components, some of which had to be ordered up to a year in advance. These lead times were a major constraint on HTU's flexibility. HTU used a computerized MRP schedule to produce data for component requirements.

Business forecasts indicated that sales would show no improvement until the end of 1983. While PACE was flexible enough to withstand the slump in sales reasonably well, the consequences were more serious for HTU, which was preparing plans to move to a four-day work week in 1983 and was concerned that if short-time working continued it would lose its highly trained work force to new factories that were opening nearby, leaving it unable to meet the upturn in demand predicted for 1984.

By the end of 1982, despite substantially improved forecasting methods, PACE had not been able to resolve its inventory problems. The substantial cost of holding unused modules, running to several years' supply of some low-usage models, had depressed PACE's profits in 1982. Both Dickens and Naylor had become convinced that the problem would not be resolved until HTU shared with PACE responsibility for meeting inventory holding costs. Accordingly, they requested a meeting of senior Honeywell Europe staff so that they could make recommendations for changes in the formal relationship between PACE and HTU. Shortly before Christmas 1982, they met to discuss how they would present their case.

# Nestlé, S.A.

With worldwide sales of SFr35.2 billion in 1987, Nestlé was the second largest food company in the world and the largest Swiss company. Although it had diversified into cosmetics, pharmaceuticals, and pet foods during the previous decade, Nestlé's core business still remained the processing of agricultural raw materials into food products. A summary of the company's financial results for recent years is provided in Exhibit 1.

Beginning in the early 1970s, Nestlé had embarked on an ambitious acquisition program which included, among others:

1973: Stouffer (U.S.): frozen foods, ice cream, food service, hotels

1977: Alcon (U.S.): ophthalmic products

1978: Chambourcy (France): refrigerated products, desserts

1979: Beech-Nut (U.S.): baby foods

1984: Warner Cosmetics (U.S.): perfumes and cosmetic products
Ward Johnson (U.S.): chocolate and confectionery products

1985: Carnation (U.S.): food products
Hills Bros. (U.S.): coffee

1986: Herta (Germany): cold cuts

In addition, many smaller companies were acquired in recent years, and Nestlé held important interests in a few other companies, most notably a substantial minority participation in L'Oréal, the French-based multinational cosmetic products company. In 1988, Nestlé was back on the acquisition trail with its bids for Buitoni, the Italian pasta and food products company, and Rowntree, one of Britain's premier confectionery manufacturers.

The pattern of acquisitions over the past 15 years displayed certain important characteristics. First, although Nestlé had entered new industries via this route, e.g., pharmaceuticals with Alcon, the thrust of its acquisition program had been the consolidation and expansion of its presence in the food industry. Second, although Nestlé had acquired companies worldwide, it had spent a disproportionate amount on pur-

This case was written by Associate Professor Arnoud de Meyer. Copyright © 1987 by the European Institute of Business Administration (INSEAD). The generous cooperation of Nestlé executives is gratefully acknowledged. Revised by José de la Torre, 1988.

**463**

EXHIBIT 1

## SUMMARY OF FINANCIAL PERFORMANCE AND ACTIVITIES, 1983 TO 1987

| | 1987 | 1986 | 1985 | 1984 | 1983 |
|---|---|---|---|---|---|
| **Operating results** (SFr million) | | | | | |
| Consolidated sales | 35,241 | 38,050 | 42,225 | 31,141 | 27,943 |
| Cost of sales & distribution | 21,625 | 24,447 | n.a. | n.a. | n.a. |
| Marketing, administration, and R&D | 9,965 | 9,932 | n.a. | n.a. | n.a. |
| Trading profit | 3,651 | 3,671 | 4,315 | 3,206 | 2,883 |
| Net profit after taxes | 1,827 | 1,789 | 1,750 | 1,487 | 1,261 |
| Cash flow (PAT + depreciation) | 3,011 | 2,946 | 3,081 | 2,491 | 2,171 |
| **Balance sheet items** (SFr million) | | | | | |
| Current assets | 16,241 | 15,820 | 15,236 | 16,407 | 13,868 |
| Fixed assets | 8,902 | 9,275 | 9,952 | 8,067 | 6,621 |
| Short-term liabilities | 7,547 | 8,119 | 8,858 | 7,651 | 6,092 |
| Other liabilities | 4,939 | 4,775 | 5,092 | 3,834 | 3,277 |
| Shareholder's equity | 12,657 | 12,201 | 11,238 | 12,989 | 11,120 |
| **Per-share values** (SFr) | | | | | |
| Net profit | 537 | 526 | 515 | 480 | 430 |
| Dividend | 150 | 145 | 145 | 136 | 125 |
| Price range (thousands) | | | | | |
| Bearer shares | 11.4–7.2 | 9.9–7.3 | 9.2–5.6 | 5.6–4.5 | 4.9–3.7 |
| Registered shares | 5.5–3.9 | 5.1–3.9 | 5.0–3.3 | 3.3–2.8 | 3.0–2.3 |
| **Other figures** | | | | | |
| Trading profit/sales (%) | 10.4 | 9.6 | 10.2 | 10.3 | 10.3 |
| Net profit AT/sales (%) | 5.2 | 4.7 | 4.1 | 4.8 | 4.5 |
| Net profit/equity (%) | 14.7 | 15.3 | 14.4 | 12.3 | 11.9 |
| Number of shares (millions) | 3.2 | 3.2 | 3.2 | 3.1 | 2.9 |
| Total employment (thousands) | | | | | |
| Administration and sales | 65 | 66 | 63 | 57 | 59 |
| Factory personnel | 98 | 96 | 92 | 81 | 81 |
| Average exchange rate (SFr/$) | 1.49 | 1.79 | 2.45 | 2.36 | 2.10 |

### Geographical distribution of sales and personnel, 1987 (%)

| | Sales | Personnel |
|---|---|---|
| Europe | 43.1 | 43.3 (9.5 in Switzerland) |
| North America | 28.5 | 23.2 |
| Asia | 13.0 | 8.0 |
| Latin America & Caribbean | 10.0 | 17.8 |
| Africa | 3.0 | 4.4 |
| Oceania | 2.4 | 3.3 |
| | 100.0 | 100.0 |

### Subdivision of sales by product group, 1987 (%)

| | |
|---|---|
| Drinks | 30.1 |
| Dairy products | 17.9 |
| Culinary products | 11.7 |
| Frozen foods & ice cream | 10.5 |
| Chocolate & confectionery | 7.9 |
| Refrigerated products | 7.9 |
| Infant foods & diet products | 5.7 |
| Pet foods | 4.3 |
| Pharmaceutical & cosmetics | 2.2 |
| Subsidiary products/activities | 1.0 |
| Hotels & restaurants | 0.8 |
| Total | 100.0 |

### Sales in main markets, 1987 (SFr million)

| | |
|---|---|
| United States | 9,298 |
| France | 4,160 |
| West Germany | 3,827 |
| Japan | 2,266 |
| United Kingdom | 1,852 |
| Brazil | 1,628 |
| Spain | 1,522 |
| Italy | 939 |
| Switzerland | 872 |
| Canada | 760 |
| Total | 27,124 (77% of total sales) |

*Source:* Annual reports.

EXHIBIT 2

**NESTLÉ'S WORLDWIDE POSITIONS IN 1987**

# Manufacture and sale of products

Position in 1987 in markets manufacturing and selling products under Nestlé processes and trademarks

● Local production[1]
◐ Local production and imports
○ Imports[2]

| Country | Number of factories Total 383 | Condensed milk | Milk powder | Other milk products | Infant formulae | Cereal food for infants | Baby foods | Coffee extracts | Roast and ground coffee | Other preparations for drinks | Liquid drinks | Chocolate, confectionery and biscuits | Dehydrated and canned culinary products | Frozen food | Ice-cream | Refrigerated products | Products for the Foodservice trade | Pet food | Pharmaceutical products |
|---|---|---|---|---|---|---|---|---|---|---|---|---|---|---|---|---|---|---|---|
| Austria | 3 | ● | ○ | ○ | ◐ | ● | ○ | ○ | ● | ○ | | ○ | ◐ | | | ◐ | ○ | ○ | ○ |
| Belgium | 5 | ○ | | ○ | ○ | ● | ○ | ○ | | ○ | ○ | ◐ | ◐ | ◐ | | ◐ | ○ | ○ | ◐ |
| Denmark | 4 | ● | ● | ● | ◐ | ◐ | ○ | ○ | | ◐ | ○ | ○ | ◐ | ● | | ○ | ◐ | ○ | ○ |
| Spain | 23 | ● | ● | ● | ● | ● | ● | ● | ● | ● | ● | ◐ | ◐ | ◐ | ● | ◐ | ◐ | ◐ | ○ |
| France | 31 | ● | ● | ● | ● | ● | ◐ | ● | | ● | ○ | ◐ | ◐ | ● | ● | ● | ● | ● | ◐ |
| Greece | 4 | ◐ | | ◐ | ○ | ○ | ○ | ○ | | ● | | ◐ | ◐ | | | | ● | ○ | ○ |
| Italy | 13 | ◐ | | ◐ | ◐ | ● | ◐ | ○ | | ◐ | ○ | ◐ | ◐ | | | | ◐ | ◐ | ○ |
| Norway | 5 | ● | ● | | ● | ● | ◐ | ○ | | ● | ○ | | ○ | ◐ | | | ● | ◐ | ○ |
| Netherlands | 7 | ● | ● | ● | ● | | | ◐ | | ◐ | | ○ | ◐ | ○ | | | ◐ | ○ | ○ |
| Portugal | 6 | ● | ● | ◐ | ◐ | | | ● | | ● | ○ | ◐ | ● | ○ | | | ◐ | ○ | ○ |
| Fed. Rep. of Germany | 31 | ● | ● | ◐ | ◐ | ● | ● | ● | ● | ● | ● | ◐ | ◐ | ○ | | ● | ○ | ○ | ○ |
| Republic of Ireland | 1 | ○ | | ○ | | | | ○ | | ○ | | ◐ | ○ | | | ○ | ○ | ○ | ○ |
| United Kingdom | 19 | ● | | ◐ | ◐ | ○ | | ◐ | ○ | ◐ | ○ | ● | ◐ | ◐ | | ◐ | ● | ○ | ○ |
| Sweden | 6 | | ● | | ● | | ● | ◐ | ○ | ● | ○ | | ◐ | ● | | ● | ○ | ○ | ○ |
| Switzerland | 13 | ● | ● | ● | ● | ● | | ● | | ● | ○ | ◐ | ◐ | ◐ | ● | | ● | ◐ | ○ |
| Turkey | 1 | ○ | ○ | | ○ | | | ○ | | ○ | | ◐ | | | | | | | |
| Canada | 15 | ● | ● | ◐ | | | | ◐ | ● | ◐ | ● | ◐ | ◐ | ◐ | | | ◐ | ◐ | ◐ |
| United States | 66 | ● | ● | ◐ | | ● | ● | ◐ | ● | ◐ | ● | ◐ | ◐ | ● | ● | ● | ◐ | ● | ● |
| Saudi Arabia | 1 | ○ | ○ | ○ | ○ | | ○ | ○ | | ○ | | ○ | ● | | | | ○ | ○ | ○ |
| South Korea | 1 | | | | | ● | | | | ● | | | ● | | | | | | |
| India | 2 | ● | ● | | ● | ● | | ● | | | | | ● | | | | ● | | |
| Indonesia | 2 | ● | ● | ● | ● | ● | | ◐ | | ● | | | ◐ | | | | ◐ | | |
| Japan | 4 | ● | ● | | | | | ◐ | ○ | ◐ | ◐ | ◐ | ◐ | ○ | | | ◐ | ◐ | ○ |
| Malaysia | 5 | ● | ◐ | ◐ | ◐ | ● | | ◐ | | ● | | | ● | ● | | | ● | ○ | ○ |
| Philippines | 3 | ◐ | ◐ | ◐ | ◐ | ● | | ● | | ● | | | ● | | | | ● | ○ | ○ |
| Singapore | 1 | ● | ○ | ○ | ○ | ○ | | ○ | | ● | ○ | ○ | ◐ | ○ | | | ◐ | ○ | ○ |
| Sri Lanka | 2 | ● | ◐ | ○ | ◐ | ● | | ○ | | ● | | | ○ | | | | ◐ | | |
| Taiwan | 1 | ○ | ○ | ○ | ○ | ● | | ◐ | | ● | | | ○ | | | | ○ | | ○ |
| Thailand | 4 | ● | ○ | ◐ | ○ | ● | | ◐ | | ● | | ● | ◐ | | | | ● | | ○ |
| Argentina | 6 | ● | ● | ● | ● | ● | | ● | ● | ● | | ● | ● | | ● | | ● | | ◐ |
| Belize | 1 | ○ | ○ | ○ | ○ | ○ | ○ | ○ | | ○ | ● | | ○ | | | | | | |
| Brazil | 17 | ● | ● | ● | ● | ● | ● | ● | ● | ● | | ◐ | ● | ● | ● | ● | ● | | ◐ |
| Chile | 7 | ● | ● | ● | ● | ● | | ● | | ● | | ◐ | ● | | | | ● | | ○ |
| Colombia | 3 | ● | | ● | ● | ● | | ● | | ● | | ● | ● | | | ◐ | ● | | ○ |
| Ecuador | 3 | | ● | ● | ◐ | | | ● | ● | ● | | ● | ● | | | ◐ | ● | | ○ |
| Guatemala | 1 | ○ | ○ | ○ | ○ | ● | | | | ● | | | ● | | | | | | |
| Jamaica | 2 | ● | | ● | | ○ | ○ | | | ● | ○ | | ● | | | | | | ○ |
| Mexico | 12 | ● | ● | ● | ● | | ● | | ● | | | | ● | ● | | ● | ● | | ◐ |
| Nicaragua | 1 | | ● | | | | | | | | | | | | | | | | |
| Panama | 2 | ● | | ◐ | ○ | ○ | ○ | ● | | ○ | | ○ | ◐ | | | ◐ | | | ○ |
| Peru | 2 | ● | ● | | ◐ | ● | | ● | | ● | | | ● | | | | ● | | ○ |
| Puerto Rico | 1 | ○ | ○ | ○ | | ○ | ○ | ○ | | ○ | ● | ○ | ◐ | ○ | | | ◐ | ○ | ◐ |
| Dominican Republic | 2 | ● | ● | | ○ | ○ | ○ | | | ● | | | ● | | | | ● | | ○ |
| Surinam | 1 | | | | | | | | | | | | ◐ | | | | ● | | ○ |
| Trinidad and Tobago | 1 | ◐ | ○ | ◐ | ○ | ○ | ○ | ◐ | | ◐ | ◐ | | ○ | | | | ● | | ○ |
| Uruguay | 1 | | ○ | | ○ | ○ | | ● | ● | ● | | ○ | ○ | | | | ● | | ◐ |
| Venezuela | 2 | | | ● | ● | ● | | ● | | ● | | | ● | | | | ● | | ○ |
| South Africa | 12 | ● | ● | ● | ◐ | ◐ | | ◐ | ● | ● | | ◐ | ◐ | | | ● | ◐ | ○ | ○ |
| Ivory Coast | 2 | ○ | ○ | | ○ | ◐ | | ● | | ◐ | | | ◐ | | | | | | |
| Ghana | 1 | ● | | | | ● | | | | ● | | | ● | | | | ● | | |
| Kenya | 1 | | | | ● | ● | | ○ | | ● | | | ● | | | | | | |
| Nigeria | 1 | ○ | ○ | | ○ | ● | | | | ● | | | ◐ | | | | | | |
| Senegal | 1 | ● | ○ | | ○ | ○ | | ○ | | ○ | | | ○ | | | | | | |
| Tunisia | 1 | ○ | | | ○ | ● | | | | ● | | | ● | | | | | | ○ |
| Zimbabwe | 1 | ● | ● | | ● | ● | | ○ | | ● | | | | | ● | | | | |
| Australia | 14 | ● | ● | ● | ● | | | ◐ | | ● | ● | ● | ◐ | ● | ● | | ◐ | ● | ○ |
| Fiji | 1 | ○ | | | ○ | ○ | | ○ | | ○ | | | ○ | ◐ | | | ○ | ○ | |
| New Zealand | 3 | ● | | ● | ● | | | ◐ | | ● | | ● | ◐ | ○ | | | ● | ○ | ○ |
| Papua New Guinea | 1 | ○ | ○ | ○ | ○ | ○ | | ◐ | | ○ | | | ◐ | | | | ○ | ○ | |

[1] May represent production in several factories.
[2] May, in a few particular cases, represent purchases from third parties in the market concerned.

Countries within the continents shown according to the French alphabetical order.

465

chases in the United States, consistent with Nestlé's desire to expand its presence in the American market. The purchase of Carnation in 1985, for example, was Nestlé's largest single acquisition, following which North America's share of Nestlé's sales climbed from 24.1 percent in 1984, to 37 percent in 1985. The Carnation acquisition contributed largely to Nestlé's 1985 total revenue growth of 35.7 percent over 1984.

With 383 production facilities in over 50 countries (see Exhibit 2) and no more than one-third of its sales from any one continent, Nestlé could be categorized as a truly global company.

## THE EARLY DEVELOPMENT OF R&D AT NESTLÉ

Since the end of the World War II, research and development (R&D) activities at Nestlé evolved from being highly centralized to form a dispersed international research and technology development network. The origins of this transformation could be traced to the merger with Maggi of Switzerland in 1947.

Prior to that time, Nestlé's R&D efforts were limited to basic scientific research and some process development work centralized at their laboratory in Vevey, Switzerland. The merger with Maggi raised the issue of integrating the R&D work being carried out at Maggi with similar efforts at Nestlé. An initial attempt to transfer all R&D efforts to the central facilities in Vevey was not successful in that Maggi's research potential was lost in the larger facility. As a result, R&D activities at Maggi were returned to its original center in Kempttal, where they were allowed to proceed, subject to control of headquarters in Switzerland.

Following this experience, as new companies with their own R&D facilities were acquired, the practice of allowing their R&D efforts to remain in the "home" environment was continued. Thus, a number of new Nestlé-controlled R&D centers emerged throughout Europe. Although financed from Switzerland, these centers did not always enjoy the same visibility or prestige as Vevey and were left much to their own devises.

The turning point for R&D at Nestlé came in 1969, with the creation of the Department of Technological Development. The importance of other corporate R&D units as sources of product technology was recognized and supported. Thus, Nestlé undertook an active role in developing and enhancing the expertise of these centers and in coordinating their activities.

The Department of Technological Development as well as the central research center were incorporated into Nestec Ltd. (Nestlé Products Technical Assistance), a wholly owned subsidiary, headquartered in Vevey, with a 1988 staff of over a thousand people active in providing assistance in all aspects of corporate activities (R&D, marketing, production, engineering, personnel training, etc.) to all Nestlé companies worldwide.

With a staff of fewer than 20 people, Nestec's Technological Development Department had a mandate to provide technological assistance to all food production centers throughout Nestlé and to develop technological know-how for the group as a whole. As General Manager, R&D, Brian Suter explained, "the role of Nestec is to manage a portfolio of projects for the corporation as a whole, participate in the establishment of corporate strategy, and ensure that R&D will respond to the requirements of that strategy."

As a result of the success of the policy of enhancing R&D facilities attached to new acquisitions, coupled with Nestlé's international expansion, Nestec took an active role in establishing new Technological Development Centers around the world that would develop products based on raw materials available locally. The number of these centers, mostly known by the suffix "Reco" (for *re*search *co*mpany), had doubled since 1975, to reach a total of 16 centers, operating 21 facilities in 10 countries (see Exhibit 3). Of these, seven were established directly by Nestlé (not including the soon-to-be-opened AfriReco in Abidjan, Ivory Coast), and most others had been obtained as a result of acquisitions.

In addition to this emphasis on technology development, basic scientific research remained an important element of Nestlé's R&D strategy, as was evident from the inauguration of the new Nestlé Research Center (NRC) above Lausanne, Switzerland in 1987. The NRC combined all scientific research under one roof, with the exception of a small operation in Tours, France, which was part of FranceReco and carried out research in plant genetics. The company's rationale for this move to centralize basic research (as opposed to product development) was that it was consistent with the nature of research in the nutritional sciences. According to this view, there was a close interdependence among the various relevant disciplines, and proximity of activities would greatly enhance the effectiveness of overall nutritional research efforts.

Whatever diversity might exist in the system, Nestlé placed great emphasis on avoiding R&D duplication. Each center was specialized in a particular Nestlé product line or technology, and any R&D related to a product was carried out by the center best qualified for that activity. Given the geographical dispersion of the Technological Development Centers, one of Nestec's most important roles was in coordinating these many activities.

## ORGANIZATION OF R&D AT NESTLÉ

Exhibit 4 depicts the structure of R&D management at Nestlé. One of the functional responsibilities of the Managing Director of Nestlé was R&D, for which he was directly accountable to the Board of Directors of the corporation. Furthermore, the General Manager of R&D at Nestec was a member of the General Management body of the Nestlé group (equivalent to an executive committee). This high-level representation in the executive and top decision-making offices of Nestlé was a sign of the importance attributed to R&D by the corporation. In fact, Nestlé considered itself (and was considered by competitors) as being strong in technology. The company did not provide public data on R&D expenditures or employment, so it was difficult to obtain any quantitative measure of Nestlé's dedication to R&D.

**Nestec** Headquartered in Vevey, Switzerland, Nestec's R&D Department played the key role of coordinating Nestlé's worldwide R&D efforts. The heads of all the Recos and the NRC were considered part of the R&D management team. All technology assistance requests from Nestlé's operating companies throughout the world were channeled through Nestec to the appropriate Reco. It was Nestec's responsibility to ensure that duplication of R&D efforts did not take place and that new projects were assigned to the most qualified centers. It was possible, however, for Nestec to assign certain projects to more than one center if they were to complement each other's activities. As S. Brengou, the Director of FranceReco, explained, "even if two centers work on the same product, they often approach the problem in two different ways, using different technologies."

**Nestlé Research Center** NRC was Nestlé's central research laboratory in Lausanne, engaged in basic research in all major areas of biological and nutritional sciences. The activities of this center could be categorized into three broad areas:

- Enlarge its knowledge of nutritional science through in-house research and collaboration with nutritional and medical research institutes around the world
- Find better uses for raw materials of vegetable and animal origin, and reduce the use of additives through basic knowledge of composition, functional, and sensory properties
- Use of plant and molecular biology for obtaining new and improved raw materials and nutrients

---

**EXHIBIT 3**

---

**NESTLÉ'S GLOBAL RESEARCH AND DEVELOPMENT NETWORK**

**SCIENTIFIC RESEARCH**

The center at La Tour-de-Peilz, near Lac Leman, was moved to the new Nestlé Research Center, above Lausanne, at the end of 1986, while the satellite center in Orbe remained at its original geographic location. The main fields of scientific research at Nestlé were:

- Basic research in nutritional sciences, biochemistry, immunology, and toxicology
- Biological studies in the areas of microbiology, molecular biology, biochemistry, and fermentation to develop an understanding of future human nutritional needs and assist technological process developments
- Nutritional evaluations to understand the physiological effects of products on the human metabolism
- Fundamental scientific research on the composition and physical and sensory properties of nutrients

The Tours center in France, managed under the FranceReco umbrella, carries out research in plant genetics.

**TECHNOLOGICAL DEVELOPMENT**

The role of the Technological Development Centers (or Recos) was to develop new products from locally available raw materials for worldwide use. To avoid duplication of efforts, each center had been assigned unique missions in terms of products and technologies.

  1. **Linor, Orbe, Switzerland.** Established by Nestec in 1958, expanded in 1965 and 1978.

    *Areas:*  Instant coffee, decaffeination technology, cocoa-based instant drinks, cereal-based dehydrated products, fermentation technology, packaging

  2. **Alpura-KoReco, Konolfingen, Switzerland.** Dates from 1974.
    *Areas:*  Long conservation dairy products, powder milk, soya-based products, aseptic filling technology, dietetic products for infants

  3. **VitoReco, Kempttal, Switzerland.** Originates from the Maggi merger. Developed in 1958; renamed VitoReco in 1975, and moved to new facilities in 1980.
    *Areas:*  Dehydrated culinary products, pasta, culinary aids, meat aroma, bouillion

  4. **Food Technology Group, La-Tour-de-Peilz, Switzerland.**
    *Areas:*  Food service products (for hotels and restaurants), bakery products, microwave processing technology

  5. **Chocolate Technology Group, Broc, Switzerland.**
    *Areas:*  Chocolate and confectionery

  6. **DeReco, Germany.** There were two centers within this organization.
    *Ludwigsburg:*  Cold sauces, instant desserts, drinks, coffee mixtures
    *Weiding:*  Baby foods in jars, fresh dairy products, desserts

---

**Recos**   The Recos were Nestlé's centers for the development of technology into products and processes. The area of specialization of each center was generally predetermined to prevent duplication of efforts. In the case of the seven centers directly established by Nestec, their specialization had been partly a function of the local climate and raw materials availability, but the specialization of the acquired centers had evolved historically.

For example, FranceReco's two centers at Beauvais and La Meauffe had developed from the Maggi merger and the Claudel acquisition, respectively. Thus, it was natural that the Beauvais center specialized in culinary products and

La Meauffe in cheese, their respective areas of specialization under Maggi and Claudel. Similarly, the work on ice cream at Beauvais was a development of the activities of Gervais after its acquisition.

Although all the Recos were managed under the Nestec umbrella, there was no hard and fast "Nestlé model" of an R&D center. All Recos followed certain Nestlé norms in terms of layout, communication, planning, and reporting, but the internal operations of each center were very much determined by historical and cultural influences particular to it. Sometimes local requirements would lead the Recos to fulfill more than an R&D function. In EastReco in Singa-

EXHIBIT 3 (cont.)

7. **FranceReco, France.** Besides the Tours research facility mentioned above, there were three other centers. The Beauvais center was developed from the Maggi merger and the Gervais acquisition. The center at La Meauffe originates from the Claudel acquisition.
   *Beauvais:* Frozen foods and ice cream, dehydrated culinary products, sterilized products
   *La Meauffe:* Fresh cheese, refrigerated milk-based products
   *Béziers:* Specialty vegetable oils

8. **DomeReco, Corbie, France.** This center belonged to Gloria pet foods and was obtained as a result of Carnation acquisition.
   *Area:* Pet foods

9. **LondReco, Hayes, England.** This center developed from Crosse & Blackwell's research facility, purchased in 1960.
   *Areas:* Sterilization technology, pickles, refrigerated culinary products, liquid sauces, aseptic filling technology

10. **NordReco, Bjuv, Sweden.** Developed from the center obtained through the Findus acquisition in 1962.
    *Areas:* Frozen food, refrigerated culinary products, agronomy research, dietetic and baby foods, culinary products, fish and meat sourcing and handling

11. **NovaReco, Robbio, Italy.**
    *Areas:* Long conservation cheese, processed cheese, semihard and hard cheese

12. **HispaReco, Badajoz, Spain.** Established by Nestec.

*Areas:* Agronomy research (fruit and vegetables), vegetable-based frozen and sterilized products

13. **CalReco, California, USA.** Calreco was Carnation's R&D center, which was integrated into Nestec in 1985.
    *Areas:* Chocolate-based drinks, nutritional drinks, culinary products, food industry product, ice cream, pet foods

14. **WestReco, USA.** Three centers established by Nestec in the USA under WestReco.
    *Marysville, Ohio:* Coffee (instant, roast and ground), tea, soya-based products
    *New Milford, Conn. (established in 1981):* Refrigerated and dehydrated culinary products, fruit juices and drinks, meat aromas, dietetic products for adults
    *Fulton, N.Y. (established in 1984):* Chocolate and confectionery, chocolate-based drinks, cocoa

15. **LatinReco, Quito, Ecuador.** Established by Nestec in 1983.
    *Areas:* Dehydrated culinary products, infant cereals, malnutrition studies, agronomy research

16. **EastReco, Singapore.** Established by Nestec in 1983.
    *Areas:* Dehydrated culinary products, soya-based products, fermentation products, agronomy research

17. **AfriReco, Abidjan, Ivory Coast.** In the process of being established by Nestec.
    *Areas:* Mainly dehydrated culinary products

pore, for example, the task of the technological center included also quality assurance activities for the whole of the Far East region, ensuring that all products in all factories were produced to Nestlé's standards. Somewhat unexpectedly, this side activity provided a lot of very useful information about product performance and market needs to the Reco. The knowledge thus acquired, for example, on the level of pesticides in Thai raw materials, would help the Reco to devise products and processes for such a situation.

Two characteristics of the corporate R&D organizational structure at Nestlé were of special interest. First, although most Technological

Development Centers were located at or near production facilities run by a national operating company, they were managed separately through Nestec. This separation of management was seen as overcoming the danger of a short-term R&D mentality that could result from local control. The Reco manager and the local country manager were thus hierarchical equals, and a high level of informal contact was encouraged between them.

Second, all the Recos were managed as profit centers. Their revenues came from a "fees plus percent margin" that these centers charged for activities undertaken at the request of Nestec, whether in terms of their R&D missions or of

**EXHIBIT 4**

**NESTLÉ ORGANIZATIONAL CHART**

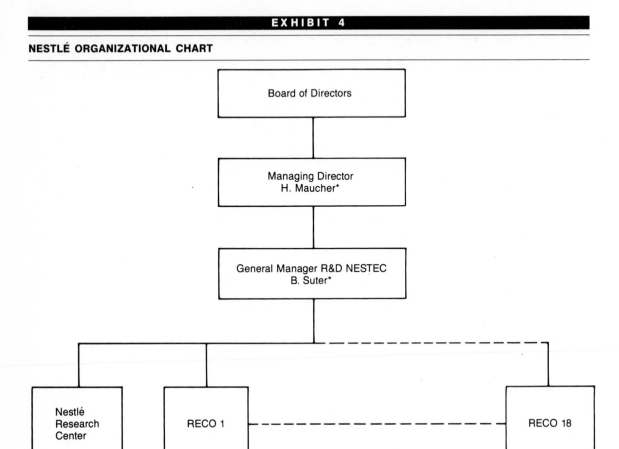

Basic research      Technological development

\* Member of Nestlé group general management.

their rendering technical assistance services. Thus, in addition to its support of long-term projects or investments such as the new NRC, Nestec played the role of a broker by putting customers (operating units) in contact with the appropriate suppliers (the Recos, NRC or other providers of technical assistance services), and charging the customers a fee for services rendered.

The objectives of Nestlé's R&D activities were twofold: (1) to develop basic scientific know-how in all aspects of the nutrition field, one of the main tasks of NRC, and (2) to develop technological know-how in food processing and pro-

duction for continuous improvement of existing products as well as for the development of new products, the task of the Recos. It was up to Nestec R&D to orchestrate the multiple sites and resources to deliver on both counts.

## SITE SELECTION AND SPECIALIZATION

For those R&D centers that were inherited as part of an acquisition, their previous expertise in a given field and proximity to a production facility usually determined the mission assigned to them in the corporate R&D portfolio. An example could be seen in NordReco, which was developed from the initial facilities of Findus in Sweden, a specialist in frozen foods acquired in 1962. Similarly, DomReco in France, which was obtained as a result of the Carnation acquisition, was assigned work mainly in the development of pet food products, its area of specialization under Carnation management.

The issue of site selection and specialization became more critical in those centers directly established by Nestec. According to Suter, one of the most important factors in site selection was proximity to a production facility. Since a principal function of these centers was the development of new products, constant communication between the development center and production was considered essential for efficiency.

Another factor of more recent importance to Nestlé was the establishment of development centers in regions of strategic interest to the company. This explained the creation of LatinReco in Ecuador and the new center under development in the Ivory Coast. Given the differing tastes and eating habits of the people in these regions, it was important to develop products based on local preferences and raw materials as these markets developed.

Geographical and environmental factors played a role in site selection as well. For example, the fact that three different climatic regions existed in Ecuador (dry coastal, high-elevation temperate, and central tropical) was an important factor in the location of LatinReco. Within a relatively small area, different types of vegetables and cereals could be grown and developed for production and later introduced in practically any Latin American country. Another example was the presence of an extensive irrigation system near the site in Spain selected for HispaReco, which became known as the "California" of Europe.

Also important to site selection were local restrictions on work permits for foreign nationals. Nestlé relied heavily on expatriates in the initial staffing of management positions in new centers. Less restrictive work permit regula-

tions were cited as a factor in selecting Singapore over competing locations as the site for EastReco.

Site specialization was also related to these factors. The different climates in Ecuador, once again, made it a prime candidate for developing special expertise in the area of vegetable-based culinary products. Local raw materials also played an important role in site specialization. Given the importance of soya in Southeast Asia, Singapore had been given the mandate to develop soya-based culinary products. A farm in neighboring Malaysia had solved the problem of limited agricultural land in Singapore.

Although in certain areas, such as dehydrated culinary products, more than one center was engaged in R&D activities, this did not necessarily imply duplication of efforts. Each center in these cases typically had developed an expertise in specific types of raw materials or technology, which it developed for worldwide utilization. Also, on projects where Nestec assigned tasks to more than one center, a project leader was usually selected and given overall responsibility.

Sales volume did not seem to play a significant role in either the site selection or specialization decision. Ecuador and Singapore, for example, were not sources of sales revenue for Nestlé. Japan and Brazil, however, were countries which were major revenue earners for the company (fourth and sixth in 1987, respectively) but had no Recos.

A critical issue in the decision whether to establish a new center or expand an existing one concerned the relationship between the size of an R&D facility and its effective management. According to Suter, efficiency was at maximum with a size of 60 to 150 people. W. Zettl, Director of EastReco, was also of the opinion that a Reco of 150 people was about the maximum which could be handled efficiently. At Nestlé the size of Recos ranged from 20 in the smallest, to 250 in the largest.

Four of the Recos (FranceReco, WestReco, CalReco, and Linor) had more than 200 employees. Of these, however, FranceReco and

WestReco comprised a number of independent centers, while CalReco was obtained as a result of the Carnation acquisition and was not under the control of Nestec until late 1985. The 450 people at NRC in Vevey constituted a much larger center than thought optimal, but the company argued that it was composed of various groups arrayed by disciplines, and, as such, it could be considered as several centers operating under one roof.

Cooperation with external organizations was a complementary part of the global R&D mission at Nestlé. Aside from the links between the Nestlé Research Center and various institutes around the world, some Recos had developed working relationships with local research organizations, as was the case with universities in Ecuador and Singapore. Any such cooperation, however, was based on specific needs or the requirements of a given project. Nestlé rarely supplied funds to external research centers for general scientific research.

## BUDGETING, PLANNING, AND CONTROL OF R&D

The global R&D budget was developed at Nestec with input from all parties. The most important element of the budget was people. It was, therefore, not surprising that the Director of Technological Development at Nestec had final authority to fix the number of total employee-hours for each center in a given year. This decision was reached after consultation with all center directors and a review of R&D plans and projects for each center. Within this budget, there was an allowance of 3 percent (in hours) for "free creative activities," to be used for nondirective work at the center directors's prerogative.

The decision to use employee-hours as a unit of measure was noteworthy. Given international variations in the cost of scientific personnel and the rate of currency fluctuations, employee-hours were a readily comparable unit of measure for R&D activities against which output and efficiency could be evaluated at all centers, re-

gardless of their location. Furthermore, since 60 to 65 percent of the cost of R&D was labor, control over the number of employee-hours provided an effective means of control over the budget. However, although the total number of employee-hours was fixed by Nestec, the mix of people at each center (i.e., the relative number of scientists, engineers, and technicians) was left to the center directors. Faced with a trade-off between obtaining a uniform unit of measure for all centers and full budget control, Nestlé opted for the former.

Since most of the R&D at the Recos was of an applied nature, planning of R&D projects was very important to the success of product development at Nestlé. In its capacity as the supervising body, Nestec played an important role in defining and assigning R&D projects to various centers. In addition to handling requests from operating companies for technical development, Nestec had the responsibility of setting priorities based on corporate objectives in the face of limited resources. Consequently, an extensive planning process was put in place to define each center's activities for the year.

Through a series of meetings with the operating and geographic units, marketing and production staffs, and the Reco directors, Nestec developed a full R&D program which was finalized along with the budget in August of each year. The plan took into account requests from the operating units and established priorities based on corporate objectives for the coming year. Furthermore, Nestec would attempt to balance short- and long-term projects at each center. The final proposal for each Reco was drawn up by the director of the center in close cooperation with Nestec coordinators, whose responsibility was to ensure the fit between Reco R&D plans and corporate objectives.

A preliminary draft of the plan was circulated to various departments for review and comment. Most often it was approved without much change, an indication that the Nestec coordinators had ensured beforehand that the R&D plans met corporate objectives for the coming year as identified by all interested parties.

One participant in the R&D planning process called it an example of "participative centralization." The central body, Nestec, interpreted corporate objectives and market requirements, evaluated projects, set up priorities, and developed R&D plans with inputs from all parties. The unique aspect of this arrangement was that, unlike the classical centralized system, the corporate staff constituted a small organization which carried out no research. Market data were obtained through discussions with the operating units; thus effective communication became a crucial element in the functioning of the planning system.

To keep track of the status of all projects, each center maintained a standard project file through which information was communicated to Nestec. The file contained data such as project status, expenditures, milestones, completion time, and other vital data. In addition, each center supplied a full report on its activities and progress every 4 months. Nestec gathered these reports and provided a summary to the General Management body.

Centers were also requested to submit a "Special Report" once on each project, generally at its conclusion. This report contained all major research findings, the reasons for the project's failure if unsuccessful or manufacturing specifications if successful. These reports were also used to evaluate the quality of the work carried out at different centers, and, in certain situations, they could provide some protection against patents claimed by others. On average, between 100 and 200 special reports were submitted to Nestec each year.

Another element of control at Nestlé was the frequent visits by Nestec staff to R&D centers. Each center was visited at least twice a year by either the director or the director's deputy, in addition to numerous visits by the project coordinators. Although the main purpose of these visits was to keep communication lines open and reinforce personal contacts within the R&D organization, the visits also served to provide first hand information about center operations. The staff at Nestec also controlled what information from the various reports it received would be of interest to different centers and transmitted the findings accordingly. Glossaries (annotated lists) of important notes and communications that each center submitted during the years were also made available to all centers which could then use them to request additional data from the appropriate center. Proper diffusion of these reports was an important element of communicating technical information around the world.

## COMMUNICATION POLICIES

The view at Nestlé was that a system of centralized R&D management and independent research centers could not succeed unless it was supported by extensive communication between all interested parties (Nestec, the Recos, the operating companies' production and marketing staffs, etc.). A number of policies had been introduced to achieve this despite the geographic dispersion.

The main element of this policy was the collection and distribution of activity reports from the centers by Nestec as described above. The efficient distribution of information contained in these reports was a major concern to most center directors. A second element was the twice yearly Nestec staff visits to each center. For example, the centers were encouraged to arrange from time to time special functions to familiarize the Nestec staff with the culture of each country and environment.

A yearly meeting of all Reco directors was held in Switzerland to discuss general issues and ideas. This not only enhanced Reco-Nestec communications, but it also provided opportunities for inter-Reco contact and familiarization. In fact, telephone conversations, discussions, and visits between managers in different Recos were always encouraged and seemed to be a common practice. For example, Zettl, director of EastReco, stated that he normally took advantage of being in Europe for the yearly directors' meeting to visit one or more European Recos and factories, and he stressed the fact that most of his colleagues had already visited EastReco, although it had been in operation for only 4 years.

More technical meetings (analytical, microbiological, etc.) were also held frequently, which brought together technical specialists from around the world on a regular basis. Discussions of new ideas and products between marketing, production, and R&D staffs were also strongly encouraged by Suter, a practice enshrined with a special name: "Trialogue."

Job rotation was another element of Nestlé's policy to promote communication within the company. Employee transfers between the Recos and production facilities supported the efficiency of R&D activities. Furthermore, periodic visits by key production personnel to different R&D centers developed their awareness of R&D and vice-versa.

Communication at Nestlé, however, went beyond these formal meetings and visits. Directors of Recos which shared common areas of research were in constant contact with one another. For example, the staff at NordReco, HispaReco, FranceReco, and VitoReco (all centers working on frozen and/or culinary products) met regularly outside formal channels. At times, samples of new products were sent to interested centers by the center that had developed it. Nestlé's policies encouraged this type of contact. For travel within Europe, for example, no higher approval than the Reco director was required. This multitude of contacts, reinforced through telephone communication and the fact that most of the directors had known each other for some time, greatly contributed to the efficiency of information diffusion within Nestlé R&D.

The open communication style had filtered down to the internal operations of the Recos as well. In FranceReco, extensive formal and informal arrangements existed by which people at the various local centers met to discuss R&D issues or even to taste and rate products. For example, various project leaders at Beauvais gathered two or three times a year to carry out what had been termed as "cross work." They listed issues that had to be solved against the technologies that might be used. This often pro-

vided a guideline about technologies which FranceReco needed to master and those which it could obtain from other centers. Sometimes a certain technique or approach from one domain was applied to another, as was the case when a design technique employed for making ice cream was successfully applied to some frozen food products.

Brengou emphasized that FranceReco worked mostly on the basis of informal communication, "there is a conflict between structure and the flexibility required in this domain [food research]." A similar statement was made by Zettl: "R&D requires teamwork and a team can only work if everybody works more or less at the same level. A natural hierarchy will establish itself on the basis of competence."

## HUMAN RESOURCE MANAGEMENT ISSUES

The international nature of R&D at Nestlé posed special problems in human resource management which required careful attention. Issues ranging from salary compensation in different countries, to training of local researchers, the hiring of expatriates, and motivation of researchers in remote sites had led Nestlé to follow deliberate human resource management practices designed to eliminate or minimize any problems associated with international R&D.

**Recos** As Nestlé considered itself an international company although some importance was attached to the basic Swiss character of the group, it had no specific rules about the nationality of R&D center directors. There was no deliberate attempt to assign only local nationals to project leader or director positions, nor was there a practice of only hiring Swiss nationals for these positions. Aside from competence, human and technical skills, two major criteria were considered in staffing these positions: language skills and work experience in at least two or three different countries. It was thought that these requirements would provide managers with an appreciation of different cultures and make them more effective in dealing with local researchers.

A common practice encouraged by Nestec was to fill technical position vacancies at Recos with new graduates in order to develop personnel. Exceptions were made for those areas where a Reco did not have expertise in a field, and experienced professionals were sought from outside. In general, the proportion of expatriate personnel at most R&D centers ranged from 5 to 10 percent for most European centers, to about 25 percent for centers in Singapore and Ecuador.

These guidelines had to be seen in a dynamic context. EastReco, for example, was started mainly by expatriates. Their number peaked at 22 and was subsequently reduced to 13 (out of about 120 employees) by 1987. Eventually, it was expected to drop to about 6 to 8. The replacement of expatriates by local personnel had gone somewhat slower than expected in this case. For many Singaporeans, Nestlé was viewed as a reference and not as a long-term career. The loyalty to the company which existed in other Nestlé sites had not yet flourished, and there were few role models of successful Singaporeans who had a long period of service with the company because of EastReco's recent founding. The opposite was the case in France, where Brengou expressed his regret at not being able to attract more qualified foreign nationals to FranceReco.

**Nestec R&D Corporate Staff**   Certain qualities were deemed essential for anyone aspiring to a position in this group, given the key role it played in the system. Interpersonal skills, considerable experience within Nestlé, age (maturity), willingness to travel, and competence in a domain in which Nestlé was active were among the most important qualifications. Age and experience were related to both know-how and credibility; competence in a specific domain ensured that all areas of critical knowledge were represented in Nestec. Yet, as the staff at the center was small and the fields of R&D at Nestlé were many, extreme specialization was less important than a broad technical competence.

Nestec corporate staff were expected to be in constant communication with R&D centers.

This involved at least two yearly visits to each center and annual or semiannual seminars with directors and project leaders. Furthermore, since they performed coordinating as well as supervisory roles, the Nestec staff were on call should any problems arise on a project. In general, it was felt that only people with intimate knowledge of the company through many years of experience in various production or R&D capacities were capable of performing this role.

**Remuneration**   Salary proposals for R&D staff at the centers were typically made by the local directors and sent to Nestec for approval. Since it was recognized that headquarters could not often judge the appropriateness of these salary recommendations, the country managers were consulted. In fact, R&D center directors were required to discuss and coordinate employee salary levels with the respective country managers. The compensation of the directors were determined by the Nestec General Manager after consultation with the country managers.

**Training and Continuing Education**   The training and development of local researchers and staff were left to the center director, whereas project leaders were required to attend initial training courses at the training center in Switzerland. Thus, the center directors were free to influence their employees' professional development according to their own priorities. For example, new technical recruits at FranceReco were sent to work in a production facility during the first 3 months of their employment. Brengou believed that a satisfactory performance in a production center was a prerequisite to a satisfactory performance in R&D. Zettl, on the other hand, was concerned that a training stint in Switzerland could be used as a reference to apply for a job in other Singapore companies.

## CORPORATE CULTURE

It appeared that a major reason for Nestlé's R&D success was the existence of a "Nestlé family culture." Despite the great distances that separated the sites, the open communication policy implemented in the company had contributed to the development of a closely knit network of R&D centers. This identification with Nestlé was best summed up by Brengou when he said that "here one becomes Nestlé."

In spite of this corporate identification, there was no "standard" Nestlé R&D center. National characteristics and the historical background of each center were often evident in its internal operations. FranceReco, for example, employed its chefs in positions of project leadership and as heads of product development teams, whereas in other centers chefs were employed only to produce prototypes. At the Beauvais center, there were a few "tasting rooms" where employees gathered to taste and rate new recipes, and the chefs often presented their daily experiments with recipes to the employees at 11:30 a.m. (there were typically about fifteen recipe experiments at Beauvais every day).

Perhaps the best description of the Nestlé R&D environment was that it consisted of a multicultural society with common goals and values. The motivation to develop products for worldwide use and Nestlé's policy of reinforcing personal contacts reduced nationalistic barriers. At the same time, however, individual Reco cultures were reinforced through activities such as the get-togethers organized by Recos during the Nestec staff visits.

## SOME CONCERNS ABOUT THE FUTURE OF R&D AT NESTLÉ

The main concern of Nestec executives and Reco directors was improving the efficiency of R&D at Nestlé. Although there were no convincing methods of measuring R&D efficiency, there were constant discussions about how to improve it. This included a consistent effort to see that R&D projects were linked to clear business objectives, while striving not to lose the "creative touch."

Extensive use of electronic and data processing equipment was one approach to improve

efficiency. Brengou mentioned that he felt FranceReco was slow in adopting information systems. His center, however, was moving ahead with this process, and he expected to see computer terminals in most services within 5 years. Although computers were used for technical support (e.g., statistical analyses), even some chefs had begun to employ computers to obtain data such as calorie values and product costs for the recipes they developed. Suter felt that although use of information systems has spread gradually at Nestec R&D, experimentation with electronic conferencing was under consideration. Yet, he felt this could not replace personal contacts.

Two areas of concern brought up by Brengou were more efficient use of the Nestlé Research Center and better management and distribution of the extensive technical reports generated worldwide. There were concerns also on the future ability of Nestlé to maintain its R&D culture and style. Nestec was constantly involved in preserving a delicate balance between centralized control and motivating the R&D centers to develop their own "personality." According to Zettl, there was a basic attitude of trust between the central organization in Vevey and the Recos. "They don't jump on us all the time," he said. "We get the necessary freedom, but on the other hand we have to perform according to Nestec's standards. Nestec's management is very gentle, but it can become very tough if something goes wrong."

The issue was particularly important when dealing with R&D centers obtained as a result of acquisitions. How could a center that had previously operated autonomously, within a different culture, be integrated into Nestec? A case in point was the ongoing integration of CalReco, obtained as part of the Carnation acquisition, into Nestec's policies and procedures. Under Carnation's management, the R&D center was engaged in activities spanning a greater part of the food world. This was inconsistent with Nestlé's policy of center specialization. Some R&D activities at Calreco would, therefore, have to be adapted to a new mission, a difficult task to impose without affecting national sensitivities and motivation.

Similar problems had already occurred at the time of the integration of the German centers. Suter acknowledged the seriousness of these issues and cautioned that the integration or establishment of a new R&D center into the "Nestlé family" would take about 5 years before it became effective. Brengou added that "[R&D coordination] at Nestlé works because people know each other, because most of them have made their entire career at Nestlé," a situation not shared with new companies or other countries. Zettl agreed and warned that it might require more than a decade to create this culture in EastReco. As Nestlé's acquisitiveness continued, the complexity of the company's R&D management system would rise accordingly.

# Ford of Europe— Product Research and Development

Ford of Europe was the result of a long evolutionary process by which the European subsidiaries created by the Ford Motor Company since before the turn of the century were integrated into a single operating company. The first Ford plant in Europe was established in Manchester, England, in 1911. The first German plant was built in Cologne in 1930. By 1987, Ford had component factories and assembly plants in the United Kingdom, the Federal Republic of Germany, Belgium, France, Spain, and Portugal and a sales organization that covered all European countries.

For many years, Ford's German and British subsidiaries led an almost independent life, each with their own product development and production units and with separate marketing territories. Beginning in 1967, a major effort began to fuse the several parts of Ford in Europe and, in effect, to forge a truly European company. See Exhibits 1 to 4 and the Appendix for summary statistics on Ford Motor Company and its principal worldwide activities.

Ford of Europe's product development organization consisted of two development centers and a proving ground. Traditionally, the first center, located in Laindon (United Kingdom), had served mainly the needs of the British subsidiary, and the second one in Merkenich, near Cologne, had been associated with Ford of Germany. The test site in Lommel (Belgium) was principally linked with the German product development group. In 1984, the structure of the product development group at Ford of Europe was changed from a vertical and functional organization into one with multiple horizontal reporting relationships. The adoption of this matrix structure came following comparisons with some of Ford's Japanese competitors, and in particular Mazda, in which the Ford Motor Company had a 25 percent stake. The new structure's stated objectives included to become a more customer-responsive, resource-effective organization and to reduce the length of the development cycle.

By the end of 1987, Ford of Europe executives were evaluating the results of the new organization and questioning to what extent the

This case was written by Associate Professor Arnoud de Meyer at the European Institute of Business Administration (INSEAD). The generous cooperation of Ford of Europe executives is gratefully acknowledged. © INSEAD, 1987. Revised by Professor José de la Torre, 1988.

---

**EXHIBIT 1**

**FORD'S FINANCIAL PERFORMANCE BY GEOGRAPHIC SEGMENTS, 1982–1986** ($ Millions)

| | 1986 | 1985 | 1984 | 1983 | 1982 |
|---|---|---|---|---|---|
| **Sales to unaffiliated customers** | | | | | |
| United States | 42,790 | 36,779 | 36,788 | 28,375 | 20,541 |
| Canada | 3,158 | 2,901 | 2,445 | 1,953 | 1,282 |
| Europe | 12,481 | 8,745 | 8,423 | 9,518 | 9,541 |
| Latin America | 2,401 | 2,402 | 2,187 | 2,226 | 3,307 |
| All others* | 1,886 | 1,947 | 2,523 | 2,385 | 2,396 |
| Total | 62,716 | 52,774 | 52,366 | 44,455 | 37,067 |
| **Net income (loss)** | | | | | |
| United States | 2,460 | 1,988 | 2,391 | 1,516 | (1,118) |
| Canada | 167 | 148 | 317 | 177 | (153) |
| Europe | 559 | 326 | 147 | 281 | 451 |
| Latin America | 66 | (57) | (110) | (193) | 10 |
| All others | 33 | 110 | 162 | 86 | 152 |
| Total | 3,285 | 2,515 | 2,907 | 1,867 | (658) |
| **Assets at December 31** | | | | | |
| United States | 22,701 | 19,396 | 17,648 | 13,229 | 11,410 |
| Canada | 2,938 | 2,667 | 2,215 | 1,737 | 1,551 |
| Europe | 11,179 | 9,107 | 6,539 | 7,736 | 7,765 |
| Latin America | 2,501 | 2,131 | 2,173 | 2,147 | 2,505 |
| All others | 2,224 | 1,820 | 2,095 | 2,103 | 2,506 |
| Less: intercompany receivables | (3,610) | (3,517) | (3,184) | (3,083) | (3,775) |
| Total | 37,933 | 31,604 | 27,486 | 23,869 | 21,962 |
| **Capital expenditures** | | | | | |
| United States | 1,966 | 2,553 | 2,442 | 1,096 | 1,470 |
| Canada | 174 | 180 | 127 | 160 | 73 |
| Europe | 720 | 620 | 641 | 789 | 837 |
| Latin America | 295 | 256 | 213 | 205 | 455 |
| All others | 198 | 128 | 92 | 83 | 133 |
| Total | 3,353 | 3,737 | 3,515 | 2,333 | 2,968 |

*Primarily activities in the Asia-Pacific region.
*Source:* Annual reports.

European experience in product development should be extended worldwide.

## THE NEW ORGANIZATIONAL STRUCTURE

In 1983, Ford of Europe (FOE) launched a study of its administrative and managerial practices in various fields relative to its major competitors, especially the Japanese. A number of areas in product development were singled out as requiring improvement: the design approval process, preprogram development, vendor participation, cost and feasibility studies, prototype procurement, and development and testing.

More generally, it was recognized that key attitudinal and behavioral changes were required to achieve the desired objectives of more effective communication, a greater problem-solving orientation, working relationships based on consensus and trust, more flexible working arrangements, and a closer customer focus. A matrix structure was chosen as the catalyst that would facilitate these changes; it was intended that such an organization would maintain tech-

**EXHIBIT 2**

**FORD'S VEHICLE SALES BY REGION AND TYPE, 1982–1986**
(Thousands of Units)

|  | 1986 | 1985 | 1984 | 1983 | 1982 |
|---|---|---|---|---|---|
| North American cars and trucks |  |  |  |  |  |
| United States cars | 2,094 | 1,941 | 2,048 | 1,672 | 1,271 |
| Canadian cars | 189 | 195 | 167 | 143 | 119 |
| U.S. trucks | 1,404 | 1,260 | 1,239 | 994 | 803 |
| Canadian trucks | 127 | 120 | 95 | 69 | 70 |
| Total | 3,813 | 3,515 | 3,548 | 2,879 | 2,263 |
| Other markets' cars and trucks |  |  |  |  |  |
| W. Germany | 862 | 770 | 790 | 833 | 798 |
| Britain | 438 | 422 | 372 | 414 | 423 |
| Spain | 268 | 266 | 269 | 228 | 230 |
| Brazil | 183 | 185 | 169 | 165 | 145 |
| Australia | 143 | 177 | 156 | 138 | 142 |
| Mexico | 44 | 70 | 51 | 48 | 90 |
| Argentina | 33 | 33 | 50 | 57 | 79 |
| All others | 132 | 112 | 180 | 172 | 124 |
| Total | 2,102 | 2,036 | 2,036 | 2,056 | 2,005 |
| Tractors |  |  |  |  |  |
| United States | 29 | 36 | 32 | 28 | 24 |
| All other markets | 39 | 48 | 51 | 39 | 49 |
| Total | 68 | 84 | 83 | 67 | 73 |
| Total world vehicle sales | 5,984 | 5,634 | 5,667 | 5,002 | 4,341 |

*Source:* Annual reports.

nical specialization while improving product focus and encouraging a team approach.

Exhibit 5 summarizes FOE's new organization for the product development group. Ken K. Kohrs, vice president of Product Development, was responsible for the coordination of all R&D operations, and all related divisions reported to him directly. Alex Goldberg was in charge of Finance and Business Strategy, a staff department reporting to Kohrs, which played a significant role in supervising the medium- and long-term business strategy and product development at Ford. The horizontal lines represent the five offices whose directors were responsible for all major products and components, i.e., powertrain, small, medium, and large passenger cars, and commercial vehicles. The total R&D program management at Ford of Europe was organized through these offices. The vertical lines represent the technical or engineering departments, each responsible for technical development in a specific field (powertrain, body, chassis, and electrical) as well as product design. Each technical group had its own research staff. A powertrain systems group linked both major engineering divisions.

The technical departments were put in charge of technical execution and development, and the program departments were charged with the tasks of program planning and control, financial budgeting and followup, and timing control in terms of product development and launch. As Dr. Werner Kalkert, director of Powertrain Engineering in Germany put it, "the vertical lines are responsible for who and how, the horizontal lines for what and when."

Not all employees were directly involved in the matrix. Services such as Personnel, Fi-

## EXHIBIT 3

**FORD'S MARKET SHARE BY REGION AND VEHICLE TYPE, 1982–1986 (%)**

|  | 1986 | 1985 | 1984 | 1983 | 1982 |
|---|---|---|---|---|---|
| Cars |  |  |  |  |  |
| United States | 18.2 | 19.0 | 19.2 | 17.2 | 16.9 |
| Canada | 17.2 | 17.0 | 16.9 | 15.2 | 15.8 |
| W. Germany | 10.6 | 10.9 | 12.5 | 12.0 | 11.3 |
| United Kingdom | 27.5 | 26.6 | 27.9 | 29.0 | 30.5 |
| Other European markets | 8.0 | 8.3 | 8.7 | 8.1 | 8.2 |
| Mexico | 12.1 | 15.7 | 12.3 | 14.3 | 12.9 |
| Brazil | 19.6 | 20.1 | 21.2 | 19.3 | 17.6 |
| Argentina | 14.2 | 15.3 | 21.8 | 28.6 | 33.9 |
| Other L. American markets | 9.3 | 8.3 | 10.8 | 12.9 | 15.9 |
| Australia | 30.8 | 28.8 | 29.1 | 28.2 | 26.0 |
| S. Africa | n.a. | n.a. | 14.3 | 14.2 | 14.5 |
| All other markets | 2.4 | 2.0 | 2.0 | 2.1 | 2.0 |
| Worldwide total | 13.3 | 13.6 | 14.0 | 12.9 | 12.5 |
| Trucks |  |  |  |  |  |
| United States | 28.1 | 26.8 | 28.0 | 31.3 | 30.6 |
| Canada | 29.7 | 29.2 | 28.4 | 28.7 | 26.7 |
| W. Germany | 7.6 | 5.8 | 6.5 | 6.7 | 8.1 |
| United Kingdom | 25.9 | 29.2 | 30.8 | 32.2 | 36.6 |
| Other European markets | 5.4 | 4.9 | 5.1 | 4.8 | 6.1 |
| Mexico | 21.4 | 24.1 | 21.6 | 25.3 | 27.7 |
| Brazil | 24.4 | 25.0 | 26.8 | 25.8 | 23.2 |
| Argentina | 39.3 | 54.3 | 61.0 | 66.3 | 54.1 |
| Other L. American markets | 13.9 | 13.5 | 17.3 | 15.4 | 17.5 |
| Australia | 16.3 | 13.8 | 11.2 | 11.1 | 13.0 |
| S. Africa | n.a. | n.a. | 11.0 | 13.0 | 10.3 |
| All other markets | 1.1 | 1.2 | 0.8 | 0.9 | 1.0 |
| Worldwide total | 16.5 | 15.6 | 15.6 | 15.5 | 14.6 |

*Source:* Annual reports.

## EXHIBIT 4

**FORD'S EMPLOYMENT BY GEOGRAPHIC REGION, 1982–1986** (Thousands)

|  | 1986 | 1985 | 1984 | 1983 | 1982 |
|---|---|---|---|---|---|
| United States | 181.5 | 172.2 | 173.7 | 163.4 | 155.9 |
| Canada | 18.7 | 18.9 | 18.8 | 16.5 | 15.8 |
| Europe | 111.8 | 110.9 | 117.7 | 124.8 | 130.5 |
| Latin America | 54.7 | 50.8 | 50.6 | 50.4 | 50.3 |
| Asia-Pacific | 15.5 | 16.4 | 16.9 | 18.2 | 19.7 |
| Other | 0.1 | 0.1 | 6.0 | 6.8 | 7.0 |
| Total | 382.3 | 369.3 | 383.7 | 380.1 | 379.2 |

*Source:* Annual reports.

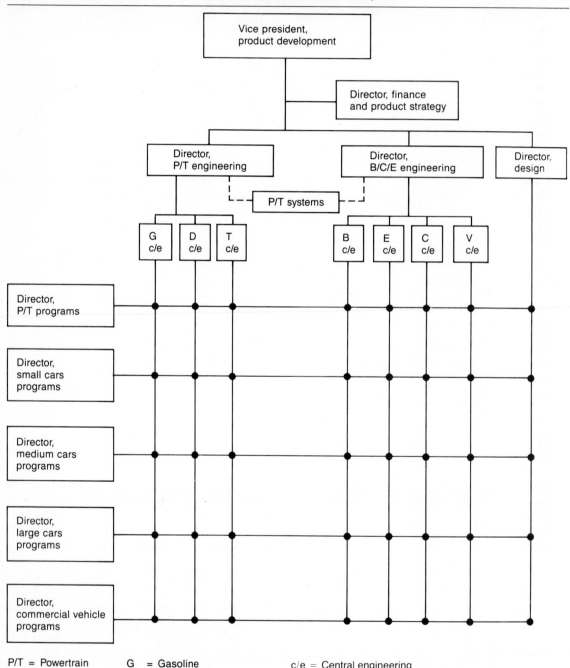

**EXHIBIT 5**

**FORD OF EUROPE SIMPLIFIED R&D ORGANIZATIONAL STRUCTURE, 1987**

P/T = Powertrain    G = Gasoline       c/e = Central engineering
D   = Diesel         T = Transmission
B   = Body          C = Chassis
E   = Electrical     V = Vehicle development

nance, and Systems remained as central activities, though management believed that the very existence of a matrix would sensitize everyone to the need for a greater customer focus. The same was true at the engineer level. The structure and organization of individual technical groups and the nature and content of their work had remained largely unchanged, except to the extent that the supervisor now established priorities via dialogue with managers on both sides of the matrix.

Implementation of the new structure had not been easy. Intensive and regular communication and discussion between the program directors and the technical managers had helped to resolve the many conflicts that emerged. Kohrs described the process by which the responsibilities of programs and technical directors were determined:

At the Program Director/Chief Engineer level within the organization, responsibilities were established clearly and quickly. The Functional Chiefs maintained authority over their area and total engineering responsibilities for their products. In essence, this did not represent a significant change, although their approach now had to take into account the conflicting demands made on their resources by the newly appointed program directors.

The program directors' responsibilities were defined by the organizational substructure assigned to them, which consisted of the planning function, program finance, and vehicle engineering (later to disappear as a separate entity).

A much broader perspective was encouraged with the appointment of two directors from outside the product development area, one from Manufacturing and one from Sales and Marketing. However, it was still necessary to clarify and consolidate these roles, and a great deal of internal cooperation was generated through this exploratory process. We focused extensively on team building training to achieve the behavioral changes and the broader business approach to problem solving. The most important question we asked of the teams was, "What do we have to change in order to ensure the success of the Program Management approach?"

Further down in the organization it was antic-

ipated that some role confusion would result from the matrix structure, and all management personnel were prepared for this. A simple guideline was provided suggesting that program activities focus on execution, i.e., how it should be done and who should do it. In the end, after many expected difficulties, all parties have agreed that the responsibility for defining the "what, when, how, and who roles" be shared among them.

## TASKS SPECIALIZATION

One important feature of the new organization at FOE was the fact that duplication of efforts were to be eliminated within Europe. As Kohrs said, "the structure does not allow it." Ford management believed this was necessary, but they admitted that, "as such we do not have a financial yardstick that 'proves' the case either way, we just keep pushing to reduce duplication to a minimum. Line managers would quickly react if they believed our action would result in inefficiencies."

As a result of this policy, a conscious allocation of technologies between the British and the German divisions was instituted. The U.K. group became responsible for body interiors and hardware, interior design, engine installation and calibration, chassis design, and electrical systems. The German subsidiary's product development group was assigned body structure, exterior design, basic engine development, some electrical components, transmissions, and the vehicle development office. Component testing activities operated at both sites, while vehicle testing was based in Germany and at the proving grounds in Belgium. Of a total employment of 3,500 in Product Development, about 60 percent were in Britain and most of the remainder in Germany and Belgium.

This breakdown of tasks between Ford of Britain and Ford of Germany was partly historical, dating to the initial attempts in 1967 to integrate operations for the whole of Europe. Kohrs believed that, "Ford of Britain had a better reputation in engineering the chassis items, while Ford of Germany had a better reputation for engineering the transmissions. In general terms, however, the principle behind the 1967 split was that both companies should retain a wide range of expertise, and they were to avoid major redundancies at the start-up. That is clearly no longer the case.''

## RELATIONSHIP WITH FORD IN THE UNITED STATES

Although the European product development groups coordinated some of their work with their U.S. counterparts, duplication of efforts was common. Ford's efforts to build a world car, or to build at least world components, was thought to require closer collaboration between both companies. Previous attempts in this direction (the Escort), however, had not yielded major benefits in terms of degree of standardization. But management emphasized that these previous efforts had taught Ford a lot about communication and that in the future the commonality of parts would definitely increase.

Given the interdependency of technologies within the automobile industry, Ford Motor Company felt that it would need to develop a more efficient organization where technological tasks were allocated to the most capable development centers worldwide. To begin this process and promote more effective coordination between these units, two concepts had been developed. One was the establishment of a technical planning process through nonhierarchical groups, and the second was the improvement of communications.

## THE ROLE OF GROUPS

Prior to 1983, there was a small but permanent staff of experts in the corporate research group in Detroit which had overseeing responsibilities for the broader development of corporate technology. They were responsible for coordination and overview of R&D, would carry out the task of technological forecasting, and would advise senior management on strategic choices with respect to technology. The disadvantage of this system (as expressed by Kohrs, who had been at the head of this group in the past) was that there was no ''ownership'' of the recommendations made by this group; operating management would seldom ''buy into'' these recommendations.

The *theme groups* were Ford's approach to organize all strategic technologies under one roof. Their job was to develop an R&D plan for the long-term competitiveness of the entire Ford Motor Company. Four theme groups encompassed related technologies: body interior and electronics; body structure, vehicle design, and chassis; powertrain; and manufacturing. The importance attached to these groups, whose members were drawn from throughout the company, was evident from the fact that senior Ford executives were at the head of each. The vice president for European Product Development (Kohrs) was in charge of the first group, the vice president for North American Product Development headed the second, the corporate vice president for Research the third, and the vice president for European Manufacturing the fourth. Although these groups did not have their own staff, there were a number of ad hoc operational and corporate staff working parties created which reported to them and which could carry out specific studies at their request.

In February of each year, the U.S. corporate research staff met to analyze the external environment, discuss the advances of the competition, and review future technical requirements. Broader societal trends were also taken into account. The staff presented their ideas to the different constituencies in Europe and North America as a way to arrive at technical, market, and societal references used to guide advanced R&D development. By April, the four theme groups presented their five-year analyses about the direction of technological change in their respective areas and forecasted resource needs to senior management. Their outlook was based on information gathered during the first 4 months of the year and through extensive study group meetings. Finally in November, each group presented its recommendations to Ford top management for the R&D budget for the following year. These recommendations formed the basis of the R&D budget for the entire Ford Motor Company.

The integration between the different theme groups was forged through meetings between the four group chairs twice yearly. Although the theme groups had no direct responsibility to carry out R&D work, they were constituted by operational and staff personnel in the different subsidiaries who would later on be called upon to execute the necessary work. In this manner, commitment to the recommendations was built into the organization.

A second structural innovation was the creation of *working groups,* which, contrary to the technically oriented theme groups, were systems oriented. These groups were multifunctional (and multiaffiliate if a worldwide program was involved) and were the focal point of program development. As such they operated for a limited time. At times there could be as many as 23 working groups involved in a single complex vehicle project. The participants in these groups typically represented engineering, finance, service, manufacturing, and supply. They had no formal staff and were a way of involving everybody who must contribute to the success of a project without creating a bureaucratic structure. Once all the parameters of design, process, and cost had been developed and agreed upon, the groups were disbanded, and individual members returned to their area to execute the program.

The working groups were chaired by program managers from each engineering department. Like the program managers themselves, the groups had a dual reporting structure, i.e., to the heads of each engineering department and to the program director. In practice, the working groups were directed and coordinated by a central steering group made up from program managers, marketing and manufacturing personnel, and chaired by the program director or her or his representative.

The third and most important operational group was the *program team,* headed by the program director. The team was the control group for the total project including design (style), engineering, finance, marketing, and manufacturing. Close communications and consensus within this group were critical to project success. For whole programs, key areas of North America or other end user markets manufacturing locations would be represented on the teams.

The existence of these groups and their structure signalled a direction toward what Kohrs termed, "a worldwide consolidation of Ford development." Both U.S. and European personnel were involved in these groups. Key groups were led by high-level executives, and most others were led by the logical technical expert.

## COMMUNICATION

Close and constant communication between all relevant parties was judged essential to R&D efficiency at Ford of Europe. In order to achieve this goal, impressive means of communication had been established.

The company operated two daily flights between the United Kingdom and Germany with its own planes. All R&D personnel with appropriate approval from their superior could use these flights to visit the centers in Britain, Germany, and other Ford facilities in Europe. As an example, Dr. Kalkert, whose main office was in Germany, visited the U.K. headquarters once every week. Program directors often divided their workweek between both sites.

The most impressive aspect of Ford's communication network, however, was its video-conferencing facilities. The video conference rooms in Britain and Germany were equipped with the latest state-of-the-art technology, some of it being of Ford's own development or improvement. Various cameras enabled constant visual contact between the two sides, while others were especially set up for close caption of products. During a meeting, the parties on either side had the opportunity to observe detailed mechanical features of any product on display at the other end. Special cameras allowed for magnification and zoom of the objects on display.

There was also an electronic drafting board in each video center. Any drawing on one board would simultaneously appear on a video screen on the other side. Furthermore, either party could modify the drawing in real time. At the end of the session, the drawing could be stored for common access by both the U.K. and German staffs.

The video-conferencing network was heavily used, with a utilization rate in excess of 85 percent of capacity. Although communication was also possible between either European center and Detroit, this seemed to work less efficiently. One possible reason was the fact that the U.S. side of the installation was not "owned" by the U.S. product engineering group, but by corporate staff. And there was considerably less integration (and therefore need) of design and components between North America and Europe than within European operations. To the extent that "world cars" were to increase in relative importance, European management felt that North America would have to expand their facilities.

Video conferencing was still evolving. Plans were discussed to equip some individual managers' offices with small monitors and cameras, and to provide them with parallel office-to-office communication with their counterparts anywhere in Europe, although with a lower resolution than in the main system. Management stressed, however, that video conferencing could never completely replace the need for physical presence and that meetings had to be organized for personal contact.

Office automation was progressing very rapidly at Ford as well. A plan was underway to supply a full workstation for every two engineering personnel at Ford R&D. These workstations were to have a multifunctional capacity, and the users would have access to limited computer-aided engineering (CAE), telex transmission, word processing, as well as viewing engineering drawings. One of the most recent tools developed by Ford was a worldwide engineering release system called WERS, by which world standards and a common database for engineering changes and releases were to be established.

Ford was also well known for its extensive use of an integrated computer-aided design (CAD) system. Since 1982, all drawings were created electronically and made available worldwide through a common database. Some of the components which were designed before 1982 were still on paper but would eventually be transcribed to the database.

Communications in general were taken very seriously at Ford's product development units. According to Kohrs: "Video-conferencing, integrated CAD/CAM databases, electronic mail and intensive jet travel all contribute to lowering the communication barriers. All things considered, however, the most effective communications, especially in the beginning, is a handshake across a table to build mutual trust and confidence. Then the electronics can really be effective."

## HUMAN RESOURCE MANAGEMENT ISSUES

Since Ford of Europe covered a limited geographic area, some of the problems associated with extensive global R&D organizations did not exist to the same extent. Yet, the complexity of the product development matrix structure demanded managers of a special calibre, whose performance, particularly at the nodes intersecting program and technical responsibilities, was the key to the success of the organization's R&D efforts.

The qualifications most valued in the choice of these people were (1) breadth and length of experience, (2) an engineering background, (3) a demonstrated ability to work in teams, and (4) a good understanding of the business decision process. Of these characteristics, the teamwork requirement was perhaps the most important factor, since all groups required that individuals be able to work in teams and perform efficiently under pressure. Though not specifically included in formal career planning at FOE, many in senior management felt that a rotation between Germany and the United Kingdom, and between engineering, manufacturing, and marketing, would favor the development of managerial competence (and career prospects) in Ford of Europe.

With respect to personnel management, Ford of Europe complied strictly with the spirit and letter of national British and German legislation and codes of practice in matters pertaining to remuneration, social security, and worker participation. But they also tried to develop a "single team" culture among all European employees and instituted English as the company's working language. Where differences might exist in training between a British and a German engineer, management stressed that Ford methods and operating procedures guaranteed that the work was carried out with the same Ford standards of quality. This strong FOE culture allowed for easier collaboration between German and British development engineers.

## TRAINING

Training had always played an important role in the development of R&D activities at Ford of Europe. Annual training plans were developed with line management with the emphasis determined by perceived need, and these varied from year to year.

At the time, a five-point training strategy had evolved which embodied a number of long-term objectives. The emphasis was on raising the technical competence and skill levels of the engineering employees, in CAE as well as in core engineering skills, e.g., electronics. There was also a Ford-specific masters program in advanced automotive engineering, which was run in collaboration with a British university and which was open to both British and German engineers. These programs were consistent with Ford's move towards high-technology-based products and process development. In a typical year, each engineer would receive more than a week of training.

## CONCLUSION

As Kohrs emphasized, the Ford Motor Company was moving toward a greater global rationalization of its R&D activities. In some ways, Ford was reducing the national focus of its product development. Rather than having several laboratories working independently, and in parallel, the approach was to manage an international network of product development activities that would eventually cover the world.

Ford of Europe had led in this direction, and its relative success was being promoted as a harbinger for the entire worldwide Ford organization. The program teams and the theme groups were clear displays of Ford's global intentions in the management of R&D, and the commitment of top-level management at Ford to this cause was evident from the fact that many of these groups were headed by Ford executives from the parent company.

Yet, many Ford executives argued that the world car was an illusion. Consumer preferences and market conditions differed widely between markets. Even within Europe, significant differences existed in terms of required product attributes and the determinants of success among its major market areas, for example, between Germany and Italy. Excessive homogenization was raised as a possible and dangerous result of this integration process.

**APPENDIX**

# Additional Information on Ford's Worldwide Activities

## FORD OF EUROPE

Ford operated 26 industrial sites in Europe, ranging from major vehicle assembly plants to component manufacturing facilities. The major operating units and their principal plants are shown in Exhibit 6.

Ford of Europe consisted of 15 national companies, each of which produced its own financial state-

| EXHIBIT 6 | | | |
|---|---|---|---|
| **FORD OF EUROPE MAJOR OPERATING UNITS, 1987** | | | |
| Company | Location | Employees | 1986 Production |
| United Kingdom | Dagenham | 26,300 | 281,000 vehicles |
| | Halewood | 9,700 | 181,000 vehicles |
| | South Wales | 3,100 | components |
| | Southampton | 3,100 | components |
| | Midlands | 2,100 | components |
| | N. Ireland | 800 | components |
| | Others | 100 | various |
| W. Germany | Cologne | 25,900 | 177,000 vehicles |
| | Genk (Belgium) | 9,700 | 267,000 vehicles |
| | Saarlouis | 7,700 | 301,000 vehicles |
| | Duren | 1,600 | components |
| | Wulfrath | 850 | components |
| | Lommel (Belgium) | 200 | testing |
| | Others | 400 | various |
| Spain | Valencia | 7,900 | 266,000 vehicles |
| France | Bordeaux | 4,200 | components |

ments. For 1986, the German company reported sales of DM16.7 billion and profits of DM587 million. The British operation had a turnover of £5.2 billion in 1986, and profits of £217 million. In both cases these figures included cars, trucks, and tractor operations.

The year 1986 was very good for FOE, with record unit sales and major profit improvements, in spite of some erosion in market share to Fiat, Volkswagen, and the Japanese. Ford of Britain and Fiat joined forces in heavy trucks in 1986; they created a joint venture, Iveco Ford Truck Ltd., where Ford and Fiat each owned 48 percent of the new company and the remaining shares were held by Credit Suisse-First Boston.

## LATIN AMERICAN OPERATIONS

The extremely difficult economic conditions prevailing in Latin America had a major negative impact on operations there, although some improvement was obtained in 1986. In November 1986, Ford and Volkswagen announced the creation of a joint venture to manage their automotive operations in Brazil and Argentina, Autolatina. Although separate product lines and dealer networks would be maintained, Autolatina was expected to achieve major economic efficiencies in manufacturing by rationalizing both companies' production facilities in the two countries.

## ASIA-PACIFIC OPERATIONS

Ford maintained its leadership position in the Australian and New Zealand markets and announced a possible joint venture with Mazda to set up an assembly operation in New Zealand. In Taiwan, Ford Lio Ho began shipment of vehicles to the Canadian market, and Ford acquired 10 percent of Korea's Kia Motors Corporation, the company building the Ford Festiva model introduced in the United States in 1987. In February 1986, a Northern Pacific Business Development office was set up in Tokyo to coordinate Ford's activities in Japan (including its 25 percent holding in Mazda), South Korea, and the People's Republic of China.

# Benetton (A)

Luciano Benetton leaned across his desk in an office decorated with frescoes carefully restored to their original beauty in the splendid eighteenth-century Villa Minelli in Ponzano Veneto near Treviso, the soft light of the early winter Italian sun providing a contrast to the forcefulness of his voice: "When speaking of the 'second generation' Benetton, I am thinking of a new business reality which is extra-European in scope. But we have to take into account the diverse requirements of the markets we are planning to enter."

In particular, decisions were being made in late 1982 about how the Benetton Group should best carry out its plans to enter the U.S. and Japanese markets for casual wear garments. In addition to questions as to how best to present its products to consumers in such markets, Benetton's management was reviewing alternative methods of providing production and logistical

support for new markets. It was hoped that some of or all the unique features of the company's marketing and operating strategies could be preserved to provide it with the advantages it would need in these new, highly competitive markets.

## COMPANY BACKGROUND

The Benetton[1] Group was one of several entities comprising the INVEP Group, an organization that encompassed all the business activities controlled equally by three brothers, Luciano, Gilberto, and Carlo Benetton, and their sister, Giuliana. By specializing in the production and retailing of casual wear clothing items, particularly woolen sweaters, cotton T-shirts, and jeans, Benetton had, by 1982, become the world leader in the field of knitwear. In that year it had sold 26.9 million units of clothing, of which nearly half were for export from Italy. It supplied more than 1,900 shops, nearly all of which

---

This case was prepared by Professor Sergio Signorelli of the Istituto Studi Direzionali SpA (ISTUD) and Professor James L. Heskett of the Harvard Graduate School of Business Administration. Selected data in the case were based on estimates or are disguised. Copyright 1984 by the Istituto Studi Direzionali SpA and the President and Fellows of Harvard College. All rights reserved. Revised June 1986.

---

[1] Pronounced be-net-ón. Many people mistakenly pronounced the name as if it were spelled b-e-n-e-l-t-o-n. Names ending in consonants, while not typical of Italy in general, were quite common in the region in which Treviso was located.

**489**

were operated with the understanding that the shops would stock only Benetton products. As a result, Benetton was thought to be the largest consumer of wool in the world, purchasing nearly 9 million pounds in 1982. About 60 percent of all garments sold through Benetton stores were of wool.

The Benettons had grown their business from rather meager beginnings. Their father, a truck driver in Treviso, a town situated north of Venice, had died just after World War II when the eldest, Luciano, was 10 years of age, requiring that he and his siblings find work at an early age. Nineteen years later, in 1965, they formed their company when Luciano and Giuliana decided that their complementary skills could provide the basis for a venture. At the time, Giuliana was sewing woolen sweaters of traditional somber colors and scratchy wool for one of the region's many textile artisans while developing much more colorful and fashionable designs in her own time. Luciano, a wholesaler who sold the output of a number of artisans to department stores, remarked: "I saw Giuliana's designs and I was sure I could sell them."[2]

Soon the pair had their first success with a violet pullover made of a soft blend of wool, angora, and cashmere. Other colorful sweaters achieved similar success, and the two youngest Benetton brothers joined the partnership. Gilberto, formerly employed by the Crafts Association of Treviso, was put in charge of administration, and Carlo, the youngest and a draftsman in a small local engineering company, assumed responsibility for production.

The Benettons initially sold their products through leading Italian department stores. But in 1968, as soon as their product line was sufficiently extensive to permit it, they opened their first shop in Belluno. It occupied only about 400 square feet, in part because of limited Benetton product line at the time. But it set the pattern for the stores to follow. By 1975 they owned or franchised some 200 shops throughout Italy.

In 1978, the company realized $78 million in sales, 98 percent of it in Italy. The decision to launch a major export program to the rest of Europe at that time provided the basis for even more significant growth. By 1982, Benetton's sales had grown to roughly $311 million,[3] or about two-thirds of that for the INVEP Group. The latter included revenues from Benetton Cotone (cotton) (20 percent), as well as three manufacturing operations. Financial statements for the Benetton Group are presented in Exhibits 1 and 2.

## THE KNITWEAR INDUSTRY

The knitwear industry generally was considered to comprise basic categories of knitted underwear, hosiery, and knitted overwear. Its development in Italy and the United States had followed distinctly different paths.

In Italy, knitted overwear represented about two-thirds of the industry production. In general, knitted overwear production involved more steps, more labor, less expensive equipment, and lower levels of technology than either underwear or hosiery production.

Starting with low-level industrialization of knitting between 1870 and 1890, the industry extended from the Biella area across northern Italy. It was concentrated in areas in which small subcontractors, specializing in one or more of the several steps in production shown in Exhibit 3, were located. This so-called externally decentralized system of production had evolved from the original system based on homework that prevailed into the 1950s.

Reliance on homework offered significant labor cost savings, often involving low wages and no responsibility for fringe benefits. It limited investment in fixed assets to that required for relatively simple knitting machines. It allowed a company to smooth its workload while passing

---

[2] Kenneth Labich, "Benetton Takes on the World," *Fortune,* June 13, 1983, p. 114.

[3] Actual sales figures for Benetton were 404 billion lire and for INVEP 624 billion lire. An approximate average exchange rate of $1 = 1,300 lire has been assumed throughout the case for 1982.

## EXHIBIT 1

### INCOME STATEMENTS FOR THE BENETTON GROUP, 1981 AND 1982

| | 1981[a] | | 1982 | |
|---|---|---|---|---|
| | Billions of lire | Percent of adjusted billings | Billions of lire | Percent of adjusted billings |
| Net consolidated billings | 373.7 | 92.9 | 404.1 | 100.6 |
| Minus adjusted | +28.4 | +7.1 | −2.4 | −.6 |
| Adjusted billings | 402.1 | 100.0 | 401.7 | 100.0 |
| Expenses | | | | |
| Purchases | 157.4 | 39.1 | 134.5 | 33.5 |
| Labor costs | 21.1 | 5.2 | 26.4 | 6.6 |
| Other costs[b] | 148.0 | 36.7 | 175.4 | 43.7 |
| Balance | 75.9 | 19.0 | 65.5 | 16.3 |
| Less financial charges | (15.1) | (3.8) | (20.7) | (5.2) |
| Plus interest income | 2.4 | 0.6 | 3.5 | 0.9 |
| Less miscellaneous charges | (5.2) | (1.3) | (6.3) | (1.6) |
| Plus miscellaneous income | 6.5 | 1.6 | 7.4 | 1.8 |
| Less depreciation of multiannual charges[c] | (9.1) | (2.3) | (6.3) | (1.6) |
| Less equipment and plant write-offs | (10.4) | (2.6) | (12.6) | (3.1) |
| Gross profit before reserves and transfers | 45.1 | 11.2 | 30.4 | 7.6 |
| Less various reserves | (9.8)[d] | (2.4) | (1.7)[e] | (0.4) |
| Less losses on transfers of assets | (0.1) | — | (0.1) | — |
| Plus gains on transfers of assets | 0.7 | 0.2 | 0.3 | 0.1 |
| Plus capitalized financial charges | — | — | — | — |
| Gross profit before taxes | 35.9 | 8.9 | 29.0 | 7.2 |
| Less taxes | (16.3) | (4.1) | (12.6) | (3.1) |
| Net profit | 19.6[f] | 4.8 | 16.4[f] | 4.2 |

[a]In evaluating 1981 data, please note that they cover 18 months for the main operating company (Benetton S.p.A.).

[b]Of which royalties of 10 billion in 1981 and 13 billion lire in 1982 were paid to INVEP. Roughly 80 percent of these costs represented payments to Benetton's manufacturer-contractors.

[c]Including depreciation of start-up costs.

[d]Of which 4 billion lire was placed in reserves for future risks and 4 billion lire was placed in reserves for reinvestment funds. (According to Law No. 675-1977.)

[e]Of which 1.4 billion lire of exchange fluctuation reserves were increased by Benetton and Benetton Lana.

[f]For purposes of rough calculations, the average exchange rate for the dollar against the lira was about $1 = 1,150 lire in 1981 and $1 = 1,300 lire in 1982.

fluctuations on to individual homeworkers. And it provided surprisingly high productivity.

In the 1950s, institutions called "groupers" began to appear. They were owned by artisans who acted as intermediaries between a company and homeworkers, collecting orders and in some cases material from contracting companies, organizing work by distributing it to various individuals paid directly by the grouper, and guar-anteeing the final product. Relationships between companies, groupers, and homeworkers seldom were exclusive.

By the 1970s, the small artisanal subcontractor companies had replaced many of the homeworkers. Among factors accounting for this were: growth in the sector requiring subcontractors with greater production capability; more complex products; the passage of a new law on

## EXHIBIT 2

**CONSOLIDATED BALANCE SHEETS OF THE BENETTON GROUP, AT DECEMBER 31, 1981 AND 1982** (Billion Lire)

| Account | December 31, 1981 | December 31, 1982 |
|---|---|---|
| Cash | 12.8 | 3.4 |
| Net commercial credits | 85.5 | 140.1 |
| Remainders of the period | 52.0 | 49.6 |
| Financial credits to the Holding Society | 9.7 | 6.7 |
| Other current active accounts | 11.5 | 25.6 |
| Gross current assets (1) | 171.6 | 225.4 |
| Suppliers (accounts payable) | 65.3 | 72.6 |
| Negative balances with banks | 23.2 | 47.3 |
| Financial debits to the Holding Society | 1.7 | — |
| Other current debits | 18.8 | 16.9 |
| Current debits (2) | 109.0 | 136.8 |
| Current net assets (1 − 2) = (3) | 62.6 | 88.6 |
| Gross technical investments | 57.8 | 71.9 |
| Less depreciation | (10.4) | (22.6) |
| Net technical investments | 47.5 | 49.3 |
| Preemptions for investments | .4 | 8.4 |
| Financing for third parties | — | — |
| Net investments (4) | 47.9 | 57.7 |
| Multiannual charges (5) | 1.2 | 2.5 |
| Start-up charges (6) | 16.3 | 10.5 |
| Medium- and long-term passive funds | | |
|    Guaranteed loans | 5.1 | 4.6 |
|    Nonguaranteed loans | 0.1 | 47.7 |
|    Employees' pension fund | 2.8 | 3.7 |
|    Tax fund | 16.2 | 0.3 |
|    Currency fluctuation fund | 1.1 | 2.0 |
| Total, medium- and long-term passive funds (7) | 25.3 | 58.3 |
| Net capital (3) + (4) + (5) + (6) − (7) | 102.6 | 100.9 |

*Note:* Exchange rates were $1 = 1,212 lire, December 31, 1981 and $1 = 1,382 lire on December 31, 1982.

homework introducing standards and making use of homework more expensive and less flexible; and the introduction of tax reform in 1973 to discourage the hiding of income. As a result, the importance of the grouper had declined.

Nevertheless, in 1981, according to an estimate by Databank, the knitted overwear sector of Italy consisted of approximately 17,500 companies (consisting in turn of 27,000 local units) employing a total of 130,000 people, other than homeworkers. There were thought to be only 17 companies with 250 employees or more. Among these, Benetton was dominant, with more than three times the sales volume of the next largest manufacturer in the industry.

As a nation, Italy had become the largest producer of knitted overwear in Europe, producing 60 percent of all European Economic Community (EEC) output in 1977 followed by the United Kingdom with 16 percent. Of its production, 47 percent was for export, with Germany (38.5 percent of Italian exports) representing by far the

**EXHIBIT 3**

**FLOW OF WORK THROUGH BENETTON'S FACTORIES AND SUBCONTRACTORS**

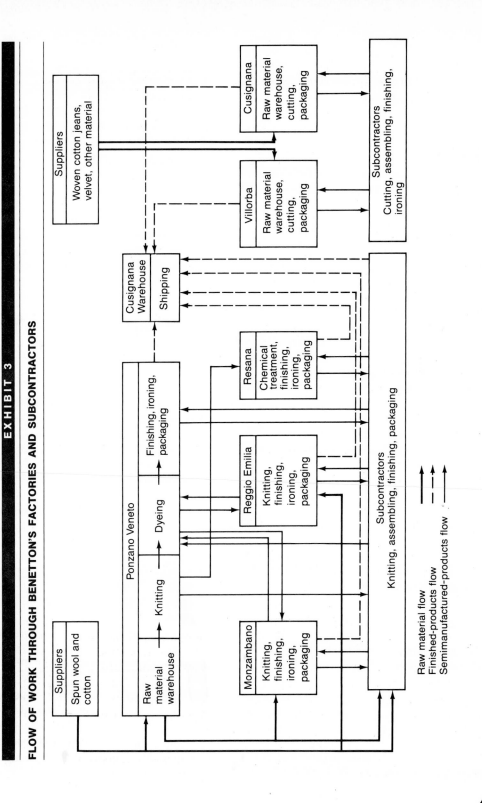

largest market followed by France and the Benelux countries. In total, EEC countries took 80 percent of Italy's exports. In contrast to major exporters in the Far East, most Italian exports of knitted overwear were marketed abroad under the trademarks of the producing companies.

Imports of knitted overwear garments in the EEC had been restricted by a series of so-called Multifiber Agreements which imposed strict limits on the growth of imports of such items from non-EEC countries. The most recent agreement extended such controls to 1986. By 1982, only 19 percent of the 810 million items of knitted overwear sold in the EEC originated from outside the community. Twenty-seven percent originated from EEC countries other than Italy, with Italian firms commanding a 54 percent share of total sales.

In contrast, the knitwear industry in the United States had become concentrated in its early stages of development on the production of knitted underwear and hosiery. The need for high productivity in these sectors had resulted in relatively high investments, factories employing hundreds of persons, and vertically integrated companies engaged in many stages between the spinning of yarn to the production of finished garments. The largest of these firms was Burlington Industries, with 1982 sales of more than $2.5 billion. The strong promotion of, and preference for, garments of synthetic yarns had, if anything, accentuated the trend toward investment and industry consolidation. Manufacturers of knitted overwear, in contrast, had steadily declined in importance. The proportion of the total of nearly 1 billion knitted overwear garments sold in the United States in 1982 that were imported, primarily from the Far East, had climbed to roughly 40 percent in 1982 and was significantly higher in lower-priced categories.

## MANUFACTURING

The basic process for the production of knitted overwear garments from wool and cotton is shown in Exhibit 3. Traditionally, it had involved the spinning or purchase and dyeing of yarn, the warehousing of spun material in finished or unfinished form, finishing operations such as mercerizing (immersion in caustic soda to produce a shinier material), waxing (to improve gliding properties and reduce friction during manufacturing and cleaning), and the removal of residual oil.

For women's garments, for example, first a prototype and sample collection was prepared. At Benetton, this generally was done four times per year under the direction of Giuliana Benetton, twice for the major spring/summer and fall/winter collections and twice for "integrative" collections for Christmas and for sport. Including woolen and other garments, a major collection contained typically 450 items, while the integrative collection following it featured perhaps 50 fashion-oriented items. The same line was created for all countries. It was estimated that about half of the items contained in the two main collections represented about 90 percent of sales.

Once designed, garments were then manufactured by machines producing parts of garments in their correct shapes or woven materials that had to be shaped. The next stage, assembly, involved joining the basic parts of each garment, such as front, back, and sleeves for sweaters. This could be accomplished in a visible manner with the edges of two parts sewn together, or a remeshing process associated with higher-quality garments that produced an invisible seam. The latter was used for most Benetton garments. Finishing operations included those of making buttonholes, sewing buttons, ironing, labelling, and final inspection prior to packaging for shipment.

In contrast to operations required for knitted products of natural materials, those made from synthetic fibers which dominated the U.S. market could be shaped and assembled with highly machine-intensive operations. This ranged from hosiery, which could be produced nearly totally by machine in several operations, to knitted underwear, for which finishing operations often were simple and performed in the least expensive manner.

## Putting Fashion on an Industrial Level

Benetton had, over the years, been an innovator in the production of knitted overwear products. Ten years before the development of machinery for making hard and rough wool soft and pliable, for example, Luciano Benetton had improved on a crude process that he had observed in Scotland for achieving the effect produced by rudimentary machines with wooden arms that battered the raw knitwear in water. Similarly, in order to avoid the use of centrifugal dryers that shrank the wet knitwear, at Benetton a process was developed by which it was placed in a bag on a stick and rotated vertically in the air.

At a time when women's seamless stockings became popular, hosiery knitting machines that could only produce seamed stockings were made obsolete. One of Benetton's employees had recommended buying and converting the equipment for the production of overwear. Machines providing 90 percent of Benetton's knitting capacity in its early years were thus purchased for approximately $1,000 per machine, converted for an additional $4,000 each at the time and performing the work of machines valued at much more. They since had been replaced by more modern knitting machines, some of them driven by magnetic tape programmed to provide intricate knitted designs.

But perhaps the most significant development in Benetton's operations occurred when the company began dyeing assembled garments rather than yarn in 1972. It required that garments first be treated in a strong chemical solution for about 20 minutes to soften them and increase their receptiveness to dye. Next, garments were "cooked" for 40 minutes and then stirred in dye-filled vats. Including time for softening, the vat time required for the entire process was about two hours.

The dyeing rooms at the Ponzano plant contained 10 smaller vats in which batches with an average size of about 300 garments were processed. They required careful loading and checking of dyes to ensure desired colors. The room also contained four newer dyeing machines with automatic dye control and water extracting capability with capacities of 530 garments each per batch.

Dyeing represented a bottleneck at the Ponzano factory. As a result, for much of the year the dyeing machines were operated on a three-shift basis. Even though the process was critical to product quality, Benetton was able to dye only about 35 percent of its total production at the Ponzano factory and an additional 20 percent at other company plants. The remaining 45 percent was dyed by contractors, with more than half of it dyed by two large contractors owned by the Benetton family.

It was estimated that labor and production overhead costs for garments dyed after manufacture were 10 percent higher than those for garments knitted from dyed thread. Benetton, it was thought, was the only manufacturer of woolen garments that dyed them from grey stock.

The garment-dyeing capability allowed more popular items in Benetton's line to be produced in response to requests for changes in preseason orders from agents serving retail outlets. As a result of this development, it was estimated that Benetton's inventory turnover for cotton and woolen items at the factory and warehouse was no more than the typical industry figure of 4.5 times per year in spite of the fact that its product line for knitted wear contained nearly 500 different color and style combinations. As Luciano Benetton had remarked in an interview with an American business journalist: ". . . we have kept the same strategy all along—to put fashion on an industrial level. Most of the rest of Italian fashion is still on an artisan level."[4]

## Manufacturing Organization

The company relied heavily both on internally and externally decentralized operations in the language of the industry. Its internal decentralization involved nine Benetton facilities, seven in Italy, one in France, and one in Scotland,

---

[4]Labich, "Benetton Takes on the World," p. 116.

employing about 1,700 people. Operations performed at the seven Italian locations, along with the associated flow of material, are shown in Exhibit 3.

All thread was received at the Cusignana warehouse (about 12 miles from Ponzano) and subsequently shipped to various factories. Textile fabrics were shipped by suppliers directly to Benetton's plants, including those of two of its contractors. Each factory in the group differed in size and functions performed.

For example, some woolen knitwear was produced in Ponzano (all processes), some in Resana (chemical treatment and finishing), and some in Reggio Emilia and Monzambano (knitting and finishing). Some manufactured items (those in "tintura d'al greggio" or undyed form) were then returned to Ponzano for dyeing and reshipment to the warehouse in Cusignana.

Ready-made material for cotton garments was shipped to the Cusignana factory, assembled there, and stocked in the central warehouse. Summer cotton shirts, however, were produced in Fontane, where only a part of the manufacturing was done internally.

Jeans were the only product category manufactured nearly totally outside Benetton's factories. However, final stages providing necessary controls were centralized in the Cusignana factory.

Functions performed and products made at Benetton's foreign factories differed as well. For example, the plant in Scotland manufactured only items knitted of cashmere for distribution through some 20 shops operated under the name Casa di Hogg, in Italy, with no association with Benetton's name. Another plant at Troyes, France, produced only woolen garments for distribution to a portion of the French retail stores. Constituting only about 5 percent of Benetton's total sales, none of these garments required dyeing. (Selected data on Benetton's factories are contained in Exhibit 4.)

In addition, Benetton utilized a network of about 220 production units, either subcontractors or groupers, employing a total of about 10,000

---

**EXHIBIT 4**

**SELECTED DATA FOR BENETTON'S FACILITIES, DECEMBER 1982**

| Company name | Location | Land and building surface (square meters)[a] | | Number of employees | Product (processes) |
|---|---|---|---|---|---|
| Benetton Lana | Ponzano Veneto | 39,720[b] | 19,901[b] | 346 | Wool knitwear |
| Benetton Lana | Rosana | 20,440 | 3,233 | 138 | Wool knitwear |
| Benetton Lana | Mozambino | 6,500 | 4,751 | 180 | Wool knitwear |
| Benetton Lana | Quattro Castella | 23,542 | 3,523 | 77 | Wool knitwear |
| Benetton Cotone | Fontane | 16,852 | 5,794 | 94 | Cotton overwear |
| Benetton Cotone | Villorba | 13,865 | 14,100 | 130 | Cotton overwear |
| Benetton Jeans | Cusignana | 65,665[c] | 40,417[c] | 274 | Trousers, jeans |
| Benetton[d] | Castrette | — | —[e] | — | |
| Benetton | Ponzano Veneto | — | — | 247[f] | Control, management |
| Benetton | Cusignana | — | — | 51 | Control, management |
| Totals | | 186,584 | 91,719 | 1,537 | |

[a]1 square meter = approximately 10 square feet.
[b]Includes the area of the technical offices in Ponzano Veneto rented by Benetton.
[c]Includes the area of the factory rented by Benetton.
[d]The company also owned the Villa Minelli located in Ponzano Veneto. This was an historical building used for management offices situated on 37,935 square meters of land with a floor space of 5,049 square meters.
[e]This was a piece of land on which the building of an industrial complex was started in 1982. Warehousing for finished products now located at Cuisignana in the factory owned by Benetton Jeans was to be moved here.
[f]Including the employees at Villa Minelli.

people. These were located mostly near Benetton's production facilities in northeast Italy at Ponzano Veneto, Cusignana, and Fontane but increasingly were being developed near other plants as well. Subcontractors and groupers performed about 40 percent of the company's knitting of wool, 60 percent of the work of assembling garments, and 20 percent of the finishing operations. Typically, the more complex garments were produced internally in Benetton's factories. Cutting and dyeing of nearly all wool was performed in Benetton's plants.

The contracting network on which Benetton relied represented a kind of "parallel empire" to the company itself. Many of the contractors were owned in whole or in part by managers of Benetton. According to one trade article: "The system is now established, and one can say that there is no head or manager from Benetton who is not at the same time owner, president, or director of a leading contracting company in the whole Lombardia-Veneto area (northern Italy)."[5]

According to the head of the textile section of the trade union, the production rates among contractors were superior to those of Benetton's factories for comparable jobs. There was a second tier to this system of external decentralization as well, consisting of subcontractors. It was alleged by one trade unionist that trade union rules and working hours were adhered to only at the first level of decentralization. There was no doubt that subcontractor costs included lower employment tax payments to the state than those incurred by Benetton. In addition to other benefits, the contracting network provided Benetton with a flexible production capacity that absorbed most of the fluctuations in demand. It provided work for many relatives of the company's full-time employees as well.

However, the production processes required a constant shuttling of work in process from one location to another, a function performed largely by subcontractors. While this reduced cost savings from external decentralization, it resulted in total production costs for woolen items that were perhaps 85 percent of those producers of garments of comparable quality in Europe and on a par with those in the Far East. More important, it reduced Benetton's risk from business fluctuations.

Still other functions were centralized at the company's headquarters. Technical research and planning, for example, were carried out at Ponzano Veneto. Under the supervision of Giuliana Benetton, product planning and design as well as the acquisition and exploitation of necessary patents and rights were managed.

All purchasing was done at Ponzano Veneto. Wool was purchased in spools from Italian producers. Material for newer items in the product line was purchased in more nearly finished form. Cotton was purchased already woven. Velvet arrived already dyed and ready for cutting. And the predyed cloth for jeans, introduced by the company first in 1972, was totally imported from the United States. Cutting was done on the basis of layouts produced by computer at Ponzano.

## The Supply Cycle

The large volume of business done by the company required that production planning for woven cotton and woolen items be begun far in advance of shipment to the stores. For example, for the spring-summer major line to be introduced in the stores early in January, final designs were prepared in February and early March, as shown in Exhibit 5. Samples of each of the 600 items in the total collection were assembled. In April about a fourth of the items were eliminated in a "prepresentation" meeting between Giuliana Benetton, Benetton's product and manufacturing managers, and several of the company's 70 agents. The remaining were then produced in small quantities for presentation by area managers to agents and by agents to their individual clients (store owners) in a process that extended from mid-May to mid-July. Within two weeks after the collection of the first orders from fran-

---

[5]Giuseppe Cosentino, "The Benetton Case—The Top of the Iceberg," *Panorama*, December 15, 1982.

**EXHIBIT 5**

## OPERATING CYCLE, BENETTON GROUP

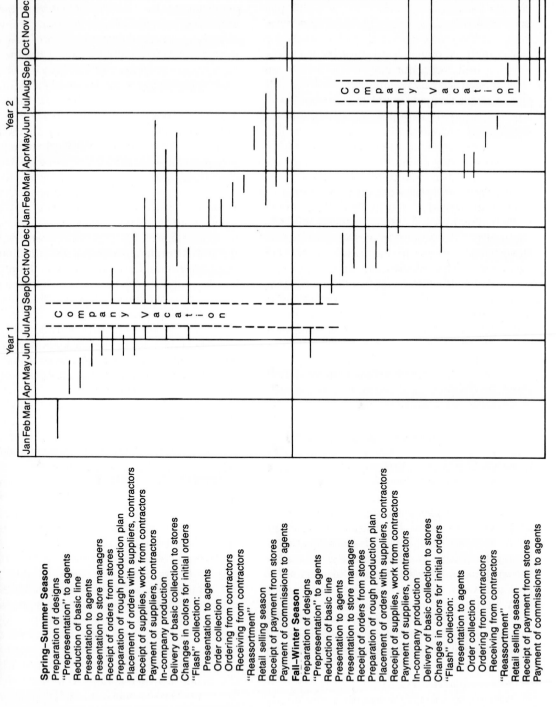

chisees by agents in early June, a rough production plan for the season, by fabrics and styles, was "exploded" from the first 5 to 10 percent of total orders. This allowed time for the placement of final orders for purchased threads and garments as well as negotiations with subcontractors for necessary increases or decreases in subcontracted volumes prior to the start of production of so-called basic retail stocks early in July, in advance of the company's three- to four-week vacation in August.

As orders for basic stocks were received from agents, they were assigned reserved slots in the rough production plan by fabric, style, color, and individual store. These orders were produced for delivery to stores from early November through late May for a sales season beginning early in January in the stores. They were scheduled so that each store could present 80 to 90 percent of all items (fabrics, styles, and colors) in its basic collection to its customers at the outset of the selling season. Other items and remaining quantities ordered arrived at the stores during the selling season.

Because Benetton required its clients to commit themselves to specific orders seven months in advance of the start of the selling season, it provided several opportunities to franchisees to adjust the actual items presented to their customers. From August through early December, as they gathered more information about color preferences, clients and agents were allowed to specify colors for woven items held in "greggio" up to that point, with a limit of 30 percent of the total orders for woolen items on such orders. During this period, Benetton's product managers negotiated with agents to encourage them to concentrate their orders on items achieving the highest order popularity.

A second process, called the "flash collection," involved the addition of about 50 items to each season's product line based on early customer requests for fabric-style-color combinations not found in the store. This occurred for the spring-summer collection in January and required the analysis of requests by Benetton's product and manufacturing managers and a sub-set of agents prior to the presentation of the flash collection by agents to the stores.

A third process, "reassortment," involved the acceptance of additional orders for rapid delivery later in the selling season, approximately March for the spring-summer collection. Fill-in reassortment orders were processed for store delivery roughly five weeks from the date of their receipt at Benetton. It was made available only for a small number of items determined through a process of negotiation between Benetton's product managers and agents. Because of its process of dyeing "grey" garments, Benetton's plant at Ponzano had the capability to fill an order within seven days of its receipt from an agent. This practice, occasionally requested by agents through Luciano Benetton and product managers, was not encouraged, because it often resulted in dye batches smaller than vat capacity and interfered with long-standing production plans.

Major collections were planned so that about 80 percent of a season's total sales volume was represented by the basic collection, less than 10 percent by the flash collection, and less than 10 percent by reassortment. The remaining sales were realized from a small "cruise" collection presented in the spring and a small "Christmas" collection presented in the fall. In total, sales of the fall-winter collection approximated 60 percent of a typical year's sales volume.

Production of the basic spring-summer collection ended in late April for final deliveries to stores by late May, by which time production for the following season's fall-winter collection was well underway.

Payments to subcontractors, representing a major cash outflow, were made 70 days after the end of the month in which production occurred or, in the case of the spring-summer collection, in October. Collections from retail franchisees were based on a season beginning date of March 30 for the spring-summer season, with one-third of payment due 30, 60, and 90 days after that date or the date of actual receipt of merchandise. This was designed to minimize retailers' investment in inventories.

The construction of a company-owned wool-spinning mill which could supply about 20 percent of Benetton's needs was in the planning stage.

## MARKETING

From the beginning, Benetton's marketing strategy had been based on the development of fashionable but casual knitted garments featuring bright colors, in contrast to much of the available product in European stores at the time. Colors such as pink and turquoise were staples at the time only in Benetton's product line and continued to be popular items.

### Product Development

The basic philosophy behind the design of products had varied little over the years. According to one recent report:

> The company has no plans to vary the design philosophy behind its product line. Though Giuliana has hired designers from top firms all over the world and follows major fashion trends, she contends that she has merely enlarged on her original insight that young, free-spending customers will always be attracted to brilliant reds and greens and a variety of pastels. "You never discover a new design," she says. "You merely make small changes in the old ones."[6]

The number of product lines had, however, been expanded in conjunction with efforts to retail Benetton products under different labels and store names. Thus, a "012 Benetton" line of children's wear had been developed for presentation in shops decorated with stuffed animals and rainbows carrying the same name. "Jeans West" shops carried Benetton knitwear and trousers targeted to the youth market. Stores carrying Benetton knitwear and trousers with higher fashion content for men and women were named "My Market." A line of items was produced for the "Sisley" label, directed to so-

phisticated men and presented in stores carrying that name. Although there was no direct equivalent to Sisley for women, shops with the "Mercerie" name stocked some items aimed at a similar market segment but bearing the Benetton label. Shops under all these names were intended for center city locations in European cities. In addition, recently a number of shops named "Tomato" had been opened in outlying urban areas to carry knitwear and trousers aimed at the youth market. They featured flashing lights and rock music.

In fact, for each trade name, the appropriate style of furniture and equipment, color of lighting, type of music, and appropriate sex, age, and dress style for salespeople was studied and selected to attract the targeted clientele.

Overall, Benetton shops were identified by more than 10 different names, most of which were not known outside Italy. In spite of the multiplicity of names for stores, it was estimated that during 1982, 70 percent of total sales were made under the Benetton label and 25 percent under the 012 Benetton label. However, in total, the Benetton catalogue listed more than 2,000 different item-label combinations.

### Pricing

The median retail price of Benetton garments in 1982 was about $20. Prices ranged from under $10 for a pair of socks to $120 for a high-fashion denim jacket. While opinions differed, prices generally were considered lower than competition for the quality of product, nearly always offered in natural wool or cotton. The price-quality combination, high-fashion content, and the multiplicity of bright colors were at the core of the company's retailing strategy.

### Distribution

Concurrent with the development of their product line, Benetton began searching for ways of gaining control over their channels of distribution.

Benetton had achieved its retail distribution through an unusual arrangement with "agents"

---

[6]Labich, "Benetton Takes on the World," p. 115.

in Italy and other countries of Europe. According to one company marketing executive, the use of the term "franchising" in describing Benetton was a misnomer. Largely through verbal agreement, agents of the company were assigned large territories in which to encourage the development of Benetton retail outlets. They would in turn find smaller investors and store operators with the "Benetton mentality" (according to Benetton's director of communications) with whom they established individual partnerships at the level of the individual outlet. An individual agent might thus supervise and hold an interest in a number of stores. Late in 1982, Benetton conducted its business with 70 such agents. Agents were compensated by Benetton on the basis of a commission of about 4 percent of the factory sales of goods sold through their retail outlets, in addition to their share of the profits of the stores in which they held ownership.

For their part, agents found and helped train individual store operators, displayed the Benetton collection to store operators in their regions, assembled orders for the initial stock and stock reordered during each season, and generally supervised the merchandising and pricing at the stores.

Store owners were not required to pay Benetton a fee for use of its name or a royalty based on a percentage of sales or profits. Among other things, they were required to carry only Benetton merchandise, maintain a minimum sales level (equivalent to orders for about 3,500 garments per year), adhere to suggested mark-ups of about 80 percent from cost, pay for their orders according to a preset schedule, and in the words of one Benetton manager, develop "an understanding of Benetton's way of doing business."[7]

---

[7]Payment terms calling for one-third of payment within 30, 60, and 90 days each of the beginning date of the season (for goods received prior to that time) could result in payments on average being made to Benetton in about 80 days, depending on the relation between the date the merchandise actually was received and the date set for determining payment dates.

In a recent interview, Luciano Benetton had provided some insight into the company's strategy for developing shopowners: "We have caused a (new) type of retailer to become important, who until the day before was perhaps a florist or a hairdresser. His prior career was of no importance, but he had to have the right spirit to work in a Benetton shop." The ideal Benetton retailer was relatively young and thought to have good potential for "growing with Benetton."

All Benetton outlets were required to use Benetton fixtures and follow basic merchandising concepts, the most important among them being that all merchandise was to be displayed on open shelves accessible to customers who could touch it and try it on. The open displays in an otherwise undecorated space created an impression of great color and fashion to the window-shopping customer. This was thought to be especially effective with the 19- to 25-year-old market toward which Benetton had directed its European marketing efforts.

Benetton clients were expected to maintain storage facilities which, in combination with their store shelves, could accommodate 30 to 40 percent of a season's sales in addition to merchandise still being sold from the preceding season. Typically, such storage consisted of small basement rooms under the retail outlets. However, the company's written agreement with a client, when it existed, typically was limited to the use and protection of Benetton's trademark.

Benetton's relationship with agents was managed largely on a verbal basis of trust. Agents rarely had to be replaced for failure to meet expectations.

Benetton had given a great deal of attention to store location, emphasizing areas of high traffic for young adults. Most important, European locations had been selected by Luciano Benetton and his assistants, according to a pattern of market development in which the first store in a given market often was sited in a high-prestige location. According to one legend in the company, it had taken Benetton six years to find the proper location for one shop in Turin. Once the site for a lead store had been selected and developed, an effort was made rapidly to blanket the area around it with shops offering Benetton's merchandise.

As many as six different shops, of which no more than two might be called Benetton, could be located within several city blocks of one another. The company had 46 shops in Milan, Italy, alone. While they were adapted in layout to fit desirable sites, all were much smaller and had several characteristics that set them apart from other young women's casual apparel shops, as suggested by the comparative profiles shown in Exhibit 6. The layout of a typical Benetton shop is shown in Exhibit 7.

By the end of 1982, shops were being opened in Europe at the rate of one every working day. Of the more than 1,800 shops in operation at the time in Europe, 1,165 were located in Italy alone. (See Exhibit 8 for a tabulation of shops by type and by location.) According to one company executive, while many shops had been moved, "none had been closed."

While Benetton retail shops differed, depending on available real estate, they all had one thing in common. They carried only Benetton products, in spite of the fact that only 20 of Benetton's stores outside Italy were owned by the company.

Retailers were expected to follow guidelines for offering sale merchandise. These were established and managed by agents in each region, who also moved merchandise among shops as sales patterns developed. As a result, the typical level of mark-downs as a percentage of sales for a Benetton retail outlet was relatively low, ap-

---

**EXHIBIT 6**

**COMPARATIVE PROFITS FOR TYPICAL BENETTON STORE, EUROPEAN YOUNG WOMEN'S APPAREL STORE, AND AMERICAN SPECIALTY CHAIN STORE FOR YOUNG WOMEN'S APPAREL**

| Item | Typical Benetton store* | Store of European competition | American specialty chain store* |
|---|---|---|---|
| Annual sales ($) | 305,000 | 150,000 | 400,000 |
| Selling space (sq. ft.) | 500 | 1,200 | 2,700 |
| Storage space (sq. ft.) | 200 | 300 | 300 |
| Type of location | Downtown street | Downtown street | Suburban shopping mall |
| Initial margins (% of sales price) | 44 | 50 | 57 |
| Realized margins (% of sales price) | 37 | 45 | 45 |
| Median sales price per unit ($) | 18 | 40 | 23† |
| Average size per transaction ($) | 26 | 50 | 35† |
| Employee hours per week | 90 | 200 | 230 |
| Selling hours per week | 45 | 45 | 76 |
| Average store inventory, at cost ($)‡ | 40,000 | 30,000 | 50,000 |
| Expense categories (% of sales) | | | |
|   Cost of goods sold | 61 | 55 | 55 |
|   Labor | 7 | 29 | 13 |
|   Occupancy (rent and utilities) | 5 | 7 | 10 |
|   Other (including overhead) | 8 | 6 | 10 |
| Net profit before taxes (%) | 19 | 3 | 12 |

*Based on case writers' estimates.

†These figures had risen with the introduction of designers' clothing for casual wear. Stores not carrying such clothing realized average prices of perhaps $18 per garment. Stores featuring such clothing averaged as much as $55 per item for lines of clothing comparable to those sold by Benetton.

‡Estimated on the basis of a store capacity of 2,000 pieces plus a back-up stock varying between 500 pieces toward the end of one season and 2,500 pieces at the beginning of the next.

# EXHIBIT 7

## TYPICAL LAYOUT OF A BENETTON RETAIL STORE

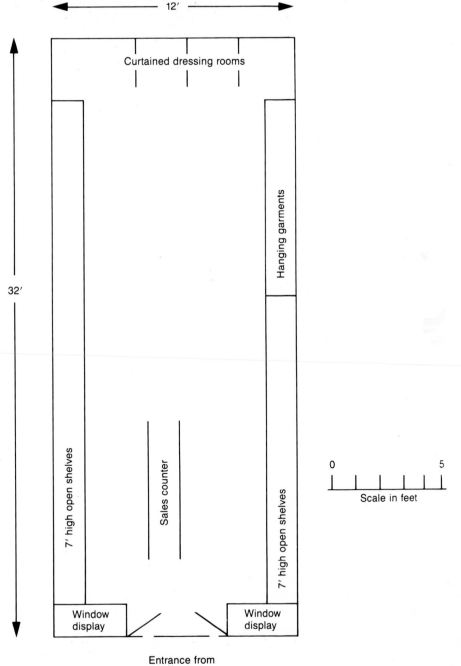

*Note:* In cases where a Benetton and Benetton 012 store were located next to one another, they might be connected by an interior doorway.

| EXHIBIT 8 |
| --- |

**LOCATION OF BENETTON STORES, BY COUNTRY AND PRODUCT LINE, DECEMBER 1982**

| Country | Number of stores, by product line | | | |
| --- | --- | --- | --- | --- |
| | Benetton* | 012† | Sisley‡ | Total |
| Italy§ | 659 | 380 | 126 | 1,165 |
| France | 198 | 80 | 5 | 283 |
| Germany | 138 | 30 | — | 168 |
| Switzerland | 53 | 10 | 3 | 66 |
| United Kingdom | 35 | 8 | 1 | 44 |
| Austria | 28 | 8 | — | 36 |
| Belgium | 12 | 2 | — | 14 |
| Ireland | 8 | 5 | 1 | 14 |
| Sweden | 9 | 4 | — | 13 |
| Holland | 8 | 3 | — | 11 |
| Spain | 9 | — | — | 9 |
| Other | 79 | 15 | — | 94 |
| Total | 1,236 | 545 | 136 | 1,917 |

*Figures only for Benetton in Italy included stores operated under the names of Tomato, Mercerie, My Market, Fantomex, Jeans West, Pulloveria, and several others.
†The 012 stores carried children's clothing.
‡The Sisley stores specialized in fashion-oriented casual wear for men.
§Figures for Italy included "franchised affiliates," store sites developed and supervised by agents in the manner described in the case, and "third-party shops," which, although not bound by agreements, adopted the same sales formula as the affiliates. Many of the latter had been converted to franchised affiliates, leaving only about 400 third-party shops by the end of 1982. At its peak in 1978, the number of company-owned shops reached 58. By 1982, there were none in Italy.

proximating 7 percentage points of a retailer's prescribed initial margin. The "model" for Benetton retail store operations was that a store would have no more than 15 percent of a season's merchandise as it entered the last two weeks of a season. This could then be sold at cost to allow the retailer to present a newly merchandised store to the customer at the outset of the new season. Benetton did not accept merchandise returns from its agents or retailers.

## Promotion

Benetton relied on location and bright, inviting store appearance as a cornerstone for its promotional effort. Window displays often were spare and allowed a clear view of the open shelves of colorful merchandise from the street. In addition, it used mainly three media in Europe to advertise its name: television, press, and the sponsoring of sports events.

On television, spots were placed that concentrated on the "sport" and "youth" image of the Benetton name. Magazine advertising was used for institutional campaigns and emphasized color and the Benetton "life-style."

Benetton management had invested in the sponsoring of sports events throughout much of the company's existence, reflecting the interests of the Benettons themselves. Thus the company sponsored a rugby team which had moved into the top league in Italy, later adding the sponsorship of a handball team as well. It had already committed what was estimated to be well over $2 million for the sponsorship of a race car for the 1983 season of World F-1 auto racing.

All these efforts were put forth on behalf of the Benetton name, the only Benetton trade name with enough volume and outlets to support a multinational campaign, and were intended to support the image of a product line aimed at the active young adult or child. Benetton had spent over twice as much for advertising in Italy as its nearest European competitor, Maglificio Piave, manufacturer of the Stefanel brand of clothing. Over two-thirds of Benetton's 1981 advertising budget for Italy, 955 million lire, was spent for magazine advertising.

## LOGISTICS

Logistics played an important role in the Benetton strategy. Starting at the retail level, stores carrying Benetton products were designed with limited storage space for back-up stocks. Upon arrival at the store direct from Benetton, merchandise often was checked and placed directly on the display shelves. This required that shipments to stores be planned and executed according to a carefully prepared schedule.

Agents managed the replenishment process by collecting and assembling orders from individual stores and relaying them electronically to Villorba, where directions were given for orders to be manufactured to order. In principle, Benetton did not manufacture anything without an order in hand. From receipt of a replenishment order, the company could have merchandise at the retail site in Europe no more than five weeks from the transmission of an order from an agent. (This contrasted with the shipment of a season's initial assortment, for which production began six months and ended 40 days in advance of the display of merchandise in the stores.)

All merchandise was premarked in the currency of the country of destination with tickets coded to be processed electronically at the time of the sale. To facilitate replenishment, Benetton had under design two major improvements in the logistics system. An elaborate new information network, relying on automatic cash registers in clusters of ten shops each hooked into Benetton's three large Siemen's 7865 computing units in Italy and an Olivetti 5330 unit in Paris,

recently had been proposed by Elio Aluffi, managing director of internal operations. It would be capable of instantly recording individual sales in Benetton's European shops. Its cost was estimated to be roughly $7.5 million. Although proposed for possible implementation by the summer of 1983, there was some question about its acceptance by agents, several of whom had indicated that the new system was not needed.

In addition, Luciano Benetton had on his desk a proposal for the construction of a new 200,000-square-foot central warehousing facility at Castrette, about 12 miles from the Ponzano headquarters, at a cost of about $20 million. The core of this facility would be ten robot stacker cranes capable of stowing and picking cartons from its stocking capacity of nearly 250,000 boxes of merchandise. Its daily total handling capacity was estimated to be 15,000 boxes (either in or out of the warehouse). With the new warehouse operating by the end of 1984, plans called for a reduction in minimum lead time required for the distribution of orders for each collection from 40 to 35 days.

The number of items per box to be handled at Castrette would vary, but it was thought to average 28. It depended on the size of the order directed to an individual factory where the items would be boxed and shipped to Castrette. No boxes would be opened while at the Castrette warehouse. All were labelled at the factory for use with optical scanners which routed the merchandise through the warehouse. Prices to retailers did not vary on the basis of the number of items shipped per box.

In addition to service improvements, the new warehouse offered the possibility of savings of perhaps 20 percent on transport costs for finished products. Not only could orders be consolidated for an individual store at Castrette but they could be loaded in sequence for store delivery by truck. (All orders were sold at a "store delivered" price. This price did not vary by destination.) While a detailed analysis of current transportation costs had not been completed, the casewriters estimated that they could be as high as 5 percent of sales.

With the opening of the Castrette facility, the current warehouse at Cusignana would be closed and all items produced in Italy moved through Castrette.

## EUROPEAN COMPETITION

Benetton had experienced increasing competition in Italy and Europe, primarily from firms emulating elements of its strategy. For example, other Italian manufacturers recently had instituted programs of direct selling by franchising local retailers. Both had had to abandon gradually their wholesale customers and launch new trademarks.

One, Maglificio Torinese, had, since 1980, been opening shops for the exclusive sales of the Kappa Sport product line specializing in casual sportswear. It now had more than 100 outlets in Italy with plans to extend its sales network to other countries. Maglificio Piave, launching its ''Stefanel'' trademark in 1979 to replace the Sigma brand formerly sold to wholesalers, already sold through 150 exclusive outlets in Italy and some 30 others throughout Europe.

It was apparent to Benetton's management that its current product lines were reaching the saturation point in the Italian market. As a result of this as well as increasing competition from emulators, a growing amount of competitive imported merchandise, and a stagnant economy, Benetton's billings in Italy had levelled out in real terms.

There had been some debate about the importance of other European markets in Benetton's future strategy. As Elio Aluffi, a long-time Benetton employee recently moved to his new post as head of internal operations, had said: ''We haven't completed our work yet in Europe. We have to consolidate that market.''[8]

But while there still appeared to be significant potential for Benetton in the rest of Europe, with expected annual increases in sales of 15 percent resulting from expanded efforts in England, Belgium, and the Netherlands, it was generally concluded that potential margins to be obtained from incremental sales in Europe were lower than those that might be realized in totally new markets like Japan and the United States. As a result, the Benettons and their senior managers were studying alternatives for developing the U.S. market, where it was felt there might be a potential for 1,000 or more retail outlets.

## THE U.S. STRATEGY

Many issues had been raised at Benetton in the process of developing alternatives for serving the U.S. market. They reflected questions among managers whether the formula so successful in Italy could be applied in the United States, and if it couldn't, whether Benetton would enjoy the competitive advantage that was responsible for its success in Europe.

Several elements of the U.S. market were particularly worrisome. First was its sheer size and the ability of Benetton to accommodate the volumes of potential sales it might enjoy. Second, the Benetton name and its associated labels were unknown except among those who had travelled in Europe. There was already formidable U.S. competition, primarily in the form of well-established manufacturers and retailers of casual wear. Several of these manufacturers carried on their own extensive consumer advertising program. Levi Strauss, with 1982 sales of about $2.3 billion, not only manufactured jeans and related items but also operated retail stores, budgeting more than $100 million each year for advertising and promotion. In addition, several large retail chains carried a great deal of merchandise aimed at Benetton's prime markets, including The Limited (with approximately 750 retail stores), Charming Shops (260 stores), Petrie (nearly 800 stores), and Miller-Wohl (nearly 300 stores). Although none of these competitors manufactured garments, many offered products produced with their labels. And several had engaged relatively heavily in media advertising to solidify their position; The Limited alone was thought to have an annual advertising budget of $20 million. All owned and controlled their own stores, mostly in modern shopping malls (largely nonexistent in many parts of Europe), with a

---

[8]Labich, ''*Benetton Takes on the World*,'' p. 118.

size and sales volume per store considerably larger than Benetton's.

Nevertheless, it was thought that Benetton could capitalize on the strong image of Italian design and the upsurge of popularity of Italian fashion in the United States. And its nontraditional (for the United States) approach to retailing might provide advantages in finding good store locations that competitors couldn't utilize.

A debate had arisen concerning the product line and its presentation. Basic among the issues discussed was whether the product mix should be altered significantly. For example, there was some support for upgrading the target market, average sales points, and dollar margins per item for a U.S. strategy. This could be centered around the Sisley and Mercerie merchandise lines for men and women. Consistent with this long-term target, the INVEP Group recently had acquired a 50 percent interest in an Italian fashion house, Fiorucci. Although the company was not highly profitable, the acquisition gave the Benettons entry into higher fashion markets, with potential benefits for the image of other of the group's labels.

However, it was argued that the company could gain maximum penetration by maintaining its European price points, adjusted only for U.S. import tariffs of 35 percent of manufactured cost. If this were done, however, little or no additional budget could be devoted to the development of designs especially for the U.S. market.

American preference for easy-to-care-for garments raised questions about the potential attraction of Benetton's natural fibers. Also, tastes seemed to be changing more rapidly than in the past. New products made of "plush" (velvet) and heavy knitted cotton had replaced wool among some consumers' preferences. As Luciano Benetton pointed out, however: "Heavy knitted cotton items have played an important part in all our recent collections. In cases such as this a company must be adaptable and ready to respond to the demands of the market."

In the process of developing an appropriate retailing strategy for the United States, several questions had been raised. Should Benetton de-

velop markets as they had in Europe, relying on agents to develop and control a retailing network? Twenty regions for U.S. development had been identified on the basis of population and per capita clothing purchase data. In addition, the question had been posed as to whether Benetton should rely on existing or new agents. Nearly all its current agents were from Europe or the Middle East. But they knew the company and its policies and were trusted by Benetton's management. In addition, an opportunity to participate in the development of the U.S. market could increase their loyalty to the company. However, many of the existing agents did not know the U.S. market well. Several were thought already to be getting overloaded with work.

Whether or not agents were used, a decision had to be made whether "lead" stores displaying the Benetton name at prestigious addresses should be opened prior to blanketing a metropolitan area with numerous outlets or whether Benetton could rely on department stores to provide space for Benetton products until the name could become better known in the United States. At least two leading U.S. department store organizations, Macy's and Associated Dry Goods, had approached Benetton with proposals to open small Benetton boutiques in their department stores, if necessary under the agent arrangement. However, both had desired an exclusive agreement with Benetton or its agents. Or should a new type of retailing outlet be designed altogether? In addressing this last question, Luciano Benetton commented:

> The idea we are looking for would represent a new era in the point-of-sale development. For instance, instead of small structures, we would have larger retail areas in which we would present more diverse merchandise. . . . Small shops like our conventional points of sale cannot serve as points of reference where people meet or listen to music. Today the necessity is felt, abroad as in Italy, for large spaces where consumers can meet.

Even Benetton's small shops required an investment estimated to average about $70,000 each for the United States. This assumed preliminary work to condition the space for Benetton's fixtures of $15,000 to $20,000, about $40,000 for the fixtures, and from $5,000 to $15,000 for transportation of the fixtures from Italy, depending on whether surface or air transport were used. It assumed no investment, for well-run stores, in inventory and the payment of no "key money" to obtain desirable retail locations.

It was clear to everyone concerned that it would be impossible to launch a full-scale advertising program for the Benetton name in the United States similar to that already existing in Europe. But it was thought that some promotional effort would be expected by Benetton's retailers. One estimate of the minimum annual advertising budget required just to achieve visibility and begin to build awareness for the name in the United States was $2 million. Questions remained, however, as to how a budget of that size should be allocated to various media.

How would a new U.S. market be supported operationally? Alternatives under consideration were: (1) the development of a new plant with dyeing facilities and a warehouse in the United States; (2) the opening only of a new warehouse to stock finished product shipped from the Ponzano factory; or (3) direct distribution to U.S. retail sites from Europe, either using conventional forms of communication or an extended computer linked up with product shipment by air.

The first of these would require a capital investment of perhaps $10 million and labor costs perhaps 50 percent higher than at the Ponzano plant. Of more importance would be the difficulty of managing the crucial dyeing operation at a foreign site. Regardless of whether a new dyeing facility were opened in the United States, it was assumed that the company could not afford to source "grey" garments in the United States at anywhere near the cost it experienced in Italy. Thus, added costs of shipping such garments by surface or air would be incurred anyway, with the difference in total transit time for the two methods being about three weeks. It was estimated that delivery by air to the United States in semifinished or finished form would add perhaps 50 percent to the current average of transportation costs for garments shipped in Europe or by surface means across the Atlantic Ocean.

The second alternative would make an investment in U.S. plant capacity unnecessary for the time being. But Benetton would lose inventory savings of the kind enjoyed in Europe, and its new warehouse at Castrette already could provide sufficient capacity to serve both the U.S. and European markets.

The third alternative would allow Benetton to delay significant commitments of capital to either plant or inventory but would require increased transportation costs even if no computer link-up were attempted. The latter would, it was thought, pay for itself in perhaps three years by providing more timely information.

Nor was entry into the U.S. market the only new venture confronting Benetton's management. Plans were underway to develop the Japanese market as well. And in one move apparently aimed at enhancing Benetton's image further, the family was reported to be considering a joint venture with a French manufacturer of perfumes to produce a new line of Benetton perfumes and cosmetics.

Benetton was reported to be having difficulties with its recent acquisition of an Italian shoe manufacturer, Calza Turificio di Varese, manufacturing one million pairs of shoes per year with 86 retail shops and 1982 sales of about $40 million. Benetton had bought a 70 percent interest in it for $12 million in June 1982. Although this had not dimmed management's enthusiasm for adding Benetton shoes to its retail lines, Luciano Benetton commented that "as an experience, it has been quite interesting. But the factory is old and there have been many problems."[9]

In response to an interviewer who had questioned the acquisition of the shoe manufacturer, Luciano Benetton replied:

---

[9]Ibid., p. 119.

I don't agree, because there are too many logical relationships. We are known for woolen knitwear. And when we started making trousers, we thought this already might be a different sector. Instead, it was coordinated exactly as we can coordinate the shoes. . . . If the common denominator is clothing, we will also have to produce evening dresses. But we don't because ours is the "cas-ual" market segment comprising clothing without too much elegance for specific hours of the day.

By the end of 1982, action had been taken on a number of the issues concerning the development of the U.S. market. But others remained, several of which could greatly affect the company's U.S. strategy.

# PART NINE

# Organization, Systems, People, and the Role of Top Management

# Republic Telecom Inc.

John Gates, manager of business development for Republic Telecom Mobile Services International Division, reviewed his material one more time in preparation for the Corporate Management Committee meeting. "Think we missed anything?" he asked his boss, Tom Reizer, head of the international unit.

"That should do it. After six months, we've finally reduced this to a two-hour presentation," Tom said.

The two international division managers were discussing a report defining market priorities and plans for their group in anticipation of a formal presentation the next day. April 5, 1987 had been circled on both men's calendars for months since it would be on that day their view of Mobile Services International's future would be presented to the Corporate Management Committee.

"When did you last talk to the Hong Kong people?" asked John.

"Yesterday. I told them that I would be calling within a week with our decision, after the big committee meeting. They weren't too pleased with the fact a decision still hasn't been made."

"How long have we been working on the Hong Kong deal now?"

"Seventeen months," said Tom.

"It would be great to finally give them the go or no go. However, the delay has certainly been a plus for them—this project's price has been increasing daily for the last two months. Will everyone be there tomorrow?"

"Yes, they're all scheduled to attend. The CEO, head of corporate planning, the chief financial officer . . ."

"Think they'll be surprised at our recommendation?" asked Tom.

"Perhaps. In any case, it will be a very interesting meeting."

## COMPANY HISTORY

The Republic Telecommunications Corporation (RTC), one of seven regional Bell operating companies (RBOC's) born from the AT&T divestiture, existed as a holding company providing strategic planning, financial, legal, and human resource services for its group companies. These group companies consisted of three reg-

This case was written by William H. Davidson and Sandra Hom. Copyright © 1988 by University of Southern California.

ulated Bell operating companies and five unregulated companies (see Exhibit 1).

In addition RTC had established an international subsidiary in September 1984. The international affiliate's mission was to facilitate international projects for both regulated and unregulated subsidiaries. Among RTC's lines of business, mobile telecom and particularly paging services appeared to have immediate overseas potential.

## THE PAGING INDUSTRY

Radio-based paging can be traced back to military applications in World War II. The Federal Communications Commission (FCC) first allocated mobile radio frequencies for commercial use in 1949, and a number of telephone companies and independent vendors began offering paging services to the general public. In 1987 there were 700-plus Radio Common Carriers (RCCs) offering public paging services. Many RCCs were family-owned local businesses, and many operated telephone answering services as an added service for paging customers. However, the trend was toward larger national firms acquiring local paging operations.

Subscribers to paging services initially consisted primarily of doctors, emergency professionals, construction workers, and field sales and service workers. The first page is said to have been sent to a doctor in New York on October 15, 1950, while he was playing golf.

Paging was a relatively inexpensive way to keep in touch, unlike mobile cellular technology. Cellular telephones service cost $1,000 or more for the phone unit, plus a hefty monthly service fee and a per-minute usage charge. Paging devices cost $100 to $300, and the only additional fee was a monthly service charge, which could run as low as $10 per month.

The U.S. paging industry experienced tremendous growth in 1980 to 1986, averaging 25 to 30 percent annually. By 1987 there were nearly 5 million pagers in operation on both private and common carrier systems in the United States.

The total world market for paging exceeded 10 million users.

A paging system operated as a one-way radio system transmitting information to the person being paged (Exhibit 2). Each pager had its own phone number and when the number was dialed, information was received on the pager from a radio relay service. Information could be received by one of three primary methods: tone-only, tone-and-voice, and numeric display. These three carrier systems served over 85 percent of the market. Alphanumeric pagers (transmitting text and data), introduced in 1985, had only begun to appear in 1987.

In 1987, tone-only pagers had the capacity to produce two or more tones, each signaling a specific calling source. Tone-only was the least expensive service, as subscribers with their own units could obtain service for as little as $10 per month. This basic service required that the user call a predetermined number to receive any messages.

Tone-and-voice service allowed users to hear short messages. However, since they required much more airtime than the other two technologies, they had not been heavily promoted and were being phased out in some locations. Numeric display pagers informed the users what number to call to directly contact the person paging them. Alphanumeric pagers had the capacity to receive paragraph-length messages.

Although the paging industry had demonstrated continued growth, it had not achieved subscriber penetration as rapidly as some experts had predicted. Mobile communications was a $2 billion industry as a whole in 1986, yet only 4 out of every 100 people utilized paging services, and only 1 out of every 1000 subscribers used mobile phone service. The growth of the paging industry had been hindered by wave-length supply limitations.

Inadequate spectrum availability had historically limited supply for not only paging but mobile radio, mobile telephone, and other services relying on radio frequencies. This resulted in fierce bidding for these frequencies. Paging and cellular franchises were awarded by the FCC.

EXHIBIT 1 °

REPUBLIC TELECOMMUNICATIONS GROUP ORGANIZATIONAL CHART

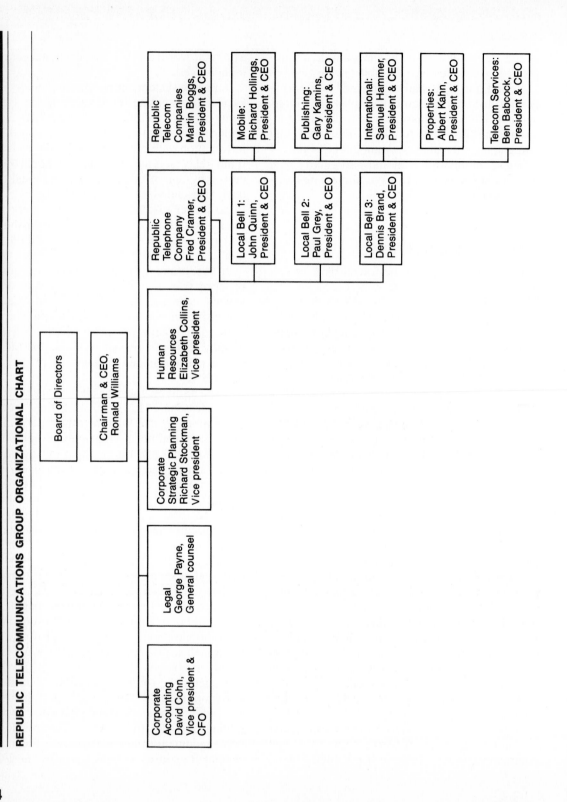

Board of Directors

Chairman & CEO, Ronald Williams

Corporate Accounting
David Cohn, Vice president & CFO

Legal
George Payne, General counsel

Corporate Strategic Planning
Richard Stockman, Vice president

Human Resources
Elizabeth Collins, Vice president

Republic Telephone Company
Fred Cramer, President & CEO

Local Bell 1:
John Quinn, President & CEO

Local Bell 2:
Paul Grey, President & CEO

Local Bell 3:
Dennis Brand, President & CEO

Republic Telecom Companies
Martin Boggs, President & CEO

Mobile:
Richard Hollings, President & CEO

Publishing:
Gary Kamins, President & CEO

International:
Samuel Hammer, President & CEO

Properties:
Albert Kahn, President & CEO

Telecom Services:
Ben Babcock, President & CEO

**A TYPICAL PAGING SYSTEM**

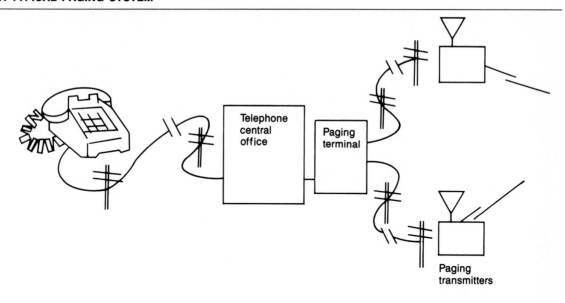

Telephone central office

Paging terminal

Paging transmitters

Pocket paging unit

. . .*OFFICE*. . .

# Republic
# Paging Services

® A Republic Telecommunications Company

Paging service and equipment sales operated as two separate sectors. The six major paging services operators included: Graphic Scanning Inc., Metromedia Inc. (Southwestern Bell), MCI Air Signal (BellSouth), Communications Industries Inc. (Pactel), Mobile Communication Corp of America, and Lin Broadcasting. The six leading equipment manufacturers were: Motorola Inc., Nippon Electric Co., Multitone Electronic Inc., General Electronic Co., Panasonic Corp., and Harris Corp.

Overseas, market development in Europe was not far behind that in the United States. Other areas were significantly less developed, although the paging market in Japan was relatively advanced in 1987 (see Exhibit 3).

## THE INTERNATIONAL DIVISION

The new freedoms given to the RBOCs after the AT&T divestiture spurred the creation of RTC's international division in 1984. RTC's goal of being a major player in the international telecommunications market by 1995 would be achieved by offering consulting, management, and operational services through the new international division.

No plan existed. Rather, an opportunistic approach would be adopted, with an emphasis on partnerships, primarily in the form of joint ventures. Through this form of cooperative relationship, RTC could spread its R&D costs while reaping the benefits of technological advances made by joint venture partners.

Samuel Hammer was named the first president of the international division. He was an engineer by training but started with Republic as a field service representative installing telephones in 1962. In 1981 Hammer was promoted to head the Corporate New Ventures Group. One project he developed during this period was the idea of selling used telecom switches to third-world countries.

International's strategic thrust originally focused on activities in newly developing countries, where two-thirds of the world's population were served by less than 10 percent of its telephones. This original focus had since shifted to include opportunities in fully developed countries such as Japan and Great Britain, where telecom markets were opening up to competition.

## PAGING INTERNATIONAL

The promise of international business opportunities was also addressed at the operating subsidiary level. Reizer was hired by International and given the task of determining whether Republic Telecom could play a role in the overseas paging market. When it was determined that untapped foreign markets existed in this area, Mobile International (MI) was created to find and pursue potential opportunities. This new

---

**EXHIBIT 3**

**NIPPON TELEGRAPH AND TELEPHONE: PAGING, CELLULAR, AND TELEPHONE SUBSCRIBERS IN JAPAN**

|  | Auto telephone subscribers | Radio pagers | Subscriber lines |
|---|---|---|---|
| 1984 | 40,392 | 1,885,961 | 44,435,000 |
| 1985 | 62,103 | 2,155,894 | 45,300,000 |
| 1986 | 95,131 | 2,487,946 | 46,800,000 |
| 1987 (estimated) | 141,000 | 2,700,000 | 48,400,000 |

*Source:* Compiled from *NTT Annual Reports,* 1987–1988, and the 1987 *White Paper on Communications in Japan.*

unit was formally established by the Mobile Services subsidiary and staffed with a skeleton crew. This new unit reported to and followed the Mobile Services subsidiary guidelines. Reizer left the Corporate International Unit to head MI. John Gates, 31, was asked to transfer into Mobile International from the Corporate Planning division. He was induced with the offer that he would share the responsibility for running and developing MI with Reizer. He would also receive a hefty increase in salary. Funding for this unit came from Mobile's budget and was initially limited to $450,000, which would include salaries and benefits, office and travel expenses, and consulting fees.

Mobile's president was Richard Hollings, a rising and visible executive. Under his direction, the Mobile Services subsidiary had exceeded its five-year sales and market penetration goals in just under two years.

The Mobile International team came from diverse backgrounds. Although Reizer reported to Hollings, International's president Hammer had personally selected and hired Reizer. Reizer was young, entrepreneurial, and had international exposure—prior to joining the unit, he was employed with IBM. Also, as a child, he spent many years in Argentina as his father was the former CEO of the Latin American division of a major pharmaceuticals firm. Gates came from a liberal arts background. After several years with a major consulting company, he joined Republic Telecom as a corporate planner. George Johnson provided the technical support for the group. Experience gained during his 30 years with Republic as an engineer provided technical and maintenance resources to the group. Carlos Hernandez joined the unit several months after it was formed. His area of expertise was finance, and he was in charge of developing the Latin American market.

## BUSINESS DEVELOPMENT

As manager of International Business Development for the paging division, Gates's major responsibilities included identifying and analyz-

ing business opportunities and implementing projects. These activities were pursued toward a sole purpose—to position Republic International and Mobile International as a single, long-term force in the global market. Implementing MI's mission of becoming the "door to the world" for Republic left many avenues open.

Republic Telecom's corporate planners had identified two priority markets: Western Europe and Asia. Entry into these key markets would be achieved through projects, joint ventures, or acquisitions.

Results from a corporate external consultancy study stated that the best opportunities for the Republic Telecom Group existed in the paging arena and recommended a strategy of direct investment positions and strategic alliances.

In pursuing international business activities, Gates wrestled with two major issues. First, project selection involved the input of many players and perspectives and consequently, achieving consensus on opportunities was difficult. Gates commented:

> Effective business development assumes a commitment to follow through in a timely fashion and no second guessing. If we (MI) commit to a project, we'll take the responsibility. But we'll need support from the line of business, from corporate functional areas and senior management. The decision-making process and corporate support are critical.

Second, business development required not only a financial but also a human resources base. Staffing had been difficult. As Gates observed:

> My job is to generate business, but if we can't support the business, we will look foolish if we can't follow up and then deliver. So far, the operating companies have been reluctant to provide those resources.

## BUSINESS DEVELOPMENT PHASES

When business development opportunities were identified, the next phase of activity for the MI group depended on the type of venture being pursued. If it were a project where no capital investment was involved, MI could proceed with the project without corporate review. However, where a long-term operational role was involved and a large capital investment was to be made, as in the case of joint ventures and acquisitions, MI could only recommend action for approval by the Corporate Management Committee.

Once the MI unit identified an attractive project, an initial analysis was prepared. This analysis was presented in bullet format, outlining all the potential opportunities, the markets, the players, the opportunities, and the required investment. This initial outline was submitted to the business development unit in Corporate Planning. It was this unit's responsibility to write a formal proposal and present it to the Corporate Management Committee.

After initial discussions, the preliminary project statement would later be supplemented by a more detailed analysis done within MI. This analysis touched on all aspects of a potential market assessment:

1. *Country/economic analysis:* A brief description of country location, size, population, cultural, and economic conditions was prepared to obtain a better understanding of the perspective market.
2. *Financial issues:* A cost-benefit analysis, projected cash flow, sales projections, etc. were made.
3. *Technical issues:* Specifics on the technical aspects of the potential venture were developed.
4. *Legal and tax issues:* Pertinent legal and taxation issues were discussed.
5. *Foreign exchange:* Types of exposure were analyzed and ways to minimize risks were identified.
6. *International cash management:* Methods of cash management and timing were addressed.

The Corporate Business Development unit would supplement this analysis, requesting additional inputs from MI in preparing its presentation to the Corporate Management Committee.

The Committee essentially consisted of three individuals; the Chairman and CEO, Ronald Williams; VP-Planning, Richard Stockman; and the CFO, David Cohn. These members, as in the case of most RTC senior officers, were selected for those positions from the AT&T management team in place prior to divestiture. The CEO and planning executive came from similar backgrounds—engineers with the AT&T system for 30-plus years. The CFO had joined AT&T only 10 years ago.

## THE BRAZIL PROJECT

MI had initiated several projects since its creation. In 1984 the Brazilian government issued a tender for construction of a telecommunications system in a rural area of Brazil. Nine firms submitted a bid, and ATS, a major Japanese telecommunications equipment maker, emerged as the winner. Although the Brazilian government awarded the contract to the Japanese because of their lower equipment prices, they did not feel that the Japanese firm could adequately manage the telecom network once it was installed. After the bid was accepted, the Brazilian government insisted that ATS only build the system and hire a telecom services company to run the network and train the staff.

MI submitted a bid for the network management contract. The initial proposal called for a management contract for a staff of 15 at a price of $10.5 million for a two-year period. The 15 people qualified to handle the contract were to be a mixture from both sides of the Republic Group—the regulated Bell companies and the unregulated side. However, the state public utilities commission (PUC) stepped in and said that regulated and unregulated personnel could not work together. Gates was originally assured by the corporate human resources department that the selected individuals would be available when needed. This turned out not to be the case. To circumvent the problem with the PUC, people from the regulated Bell company took a leave of absence and were hired by the unregulated side—at the same salary. More importantly, the

Bell company committed that these individuals would not lose their seniority. Although MI won the contract for network services, ATS soon discovered that they had not included sufficient funds in the contract to pay for management services. In the end a separate agreement between RTC and the Brazilian government was negotiated and signed. A staff of 11 was finally negotiated at a price of $5.7 million. Despite all these problems, this project had proved to be profitable for Republic.

## THE HONG KONG PROJECT

Republic had a prime opportunity to enter one of their targeted markets, Hong Kong, when they were approached by a local firm to purchase an interest in Struan Telecom (ST).

ST commenced operations in 1985 as a paging and cellular services company. The firm was a joint venture owned by three partners: Struan-Phillips (Hong Kong), 50.5 percent; Comco (United States), 27.5 percent; and Wireless Communications (United Kingdom), 22.0 percent. ST initially started operations by selling and leasing alphanumeric pagers. Although these paging units were generally not popular elsewhere, ST managed to achieve monthly sales levels exceeding their best sales projections in their first year of operations. ST was the third largest and fastest growing paging vendor in the fragmented Hong Kong market with a share of 9.6 percent in 1986. Golden Tone Paging, the leading vendor, held a 21 percent share, and Monarch Paging, the second leading firm, held a 14 percent share of the $40 million paging market. Thirteen other firms offered paging services (Exhibit 4).

To achieve its goal of becoming the dominant vendor of mobile services in Hong Kong, ST wanted to affiliate with a major telecommunications company such as Republic. ST hoped not only to gain share in the rapidly growing paging market but to establish a leading position in the emerging cellular phone business. Although there were over 300,000 paging subscri-

bers in Hong Kong in 1986, cellular phones had not yet achieved significant penetration. See Exhibit 5 for Hong Kong telecommunications market statistics.

Struan proposed that Republic could purchase the 22 percent interest held by Wireless Communications for $2.7 million. The joint venture would pay Republic $1.5 million per year in management fees to operate the network. In addition, Republic would receive options to buy an additional 20 percent of the company's equity at book value. Finally, Republic would also receive options to participate in the cellular telephone franchise in Macao and two cellular franchises in the People's Republic of China owned by ST.

The majority partner in the Struan-Phillips Group was an old established investment holding and trading company operating in Hong Kong since 1842. The Group was involved in five major areas: trading, property development and management, retailing, China trade, and telecommunications. In 1986, sales exceeded $3.7 billion, and the firm was involved in over 100 cooperative ventures. Sir Alexander Guinness, a managing director and senior board member of the Struan group, was responsible for managing the potential relationship with Republic.

In approaching the discussions with Struan, Gates realized he would have a difficult challenge ahead of him. Since Republic Telecom's support staff was very limited, he hired an independent consultant to provide additional assistance with this project. Since the Hong Kong project would be Republic Telecom's first foreign joint venture, Gates asked the consultant to summarize the issues associated with international joint ventures. A summary of the consultant's report is shown in the Appendix.

During the preliminary negotiating stage, it was decided that a group consisting of Gates, Hammer, and two technicians would fly out to meet the Struan-Phillips people. This team visited Hong Kong in November 1985. Original plans called for the group to meet Guinness at his office. Hammer did not like this idea and asked that Guinness come to the hotel and start

---

### E X H I B I T   4

---

**THE HONG KONG MOBILE SERVICES MARKET**

| | 1985 | 1986 | 1987* |
|---|---|---|---|
| **Paging** | | | |
| Total subscribers | 270,000 | 305,000 | 330,000 |
| Market share (%) | | | |
| 1. Golden Tone Paging | 18.0 | 21.0 | 26.4 |
| 2. Monarch Paging | 13.0 | 14.0 | 14.1 |
| 3. Struan Telecom | 2.7 | 9.6 | 12.5 |
| 4. 21st Century Communications | 11.0 | 8.0 | 9.0 |
| 5. Pedigree Paging | 9.0 | 7.0 | 6.5 |
| 6. Worldwide Systems Inc. | 7.6 | 6.5 | 6.2 |
| 7. Luk-Yee Communications | 7.0 | 5.8 | 5.1 |
| 8. Hong Kong Paging | 6.0 | 5.5 | 5.0 |
| 9. NCC Communications | 5.5 | 5.4 | 4.5 |
| 10. Splendour Systems Inc. | 5.0 | 4.3 | 3.5 |
| 11. Monotone Communications | 3.5 | 2.5 | 2.0 |
| 12. BEEP Inc. | 3.0 | 2.5 | 1.0 |
| 13. Crown Communications | 2.4 | 2.0 | 1.0 |
| 14. Grand Systems | 2.1 | 2.0 | 0.9 |
| 15. Universal Paging | 1.3 | 1.2 | 0.9 |
| 16. Kep Paging | 1.0 | 0.9 | 0.5 |
| 17. International Telecom Services | 1.0 | 0.9 | 0.5 |
| 18. New Age Communications | 1.0 | 0.9 | 0.5 |
| **Cellular phone** | | | |
| Total subscribers | 29,000 | 40,000 | 53,000 |
| Market share (%) | | | |
| 1. Chinatel | 39.0 | 43.0 | 41.0 |
| 2. Hong Kong Cellular | 37.0 | 40.0 | 44.0 |
| 3. Struan | 24.0 | 17.0 | 15.0 |

*Figures for 1987 are forecast estimates.
*Source:* Company records

the meeting there. This meeting led into a dinner where the negotiating teams could discuss the venture on a more informal basis. Gates found himself seated next to Hammer, with Guinness seated on Hammer's left. During the second course, Gates heard Hammer say to Guinness, ". . . been in this business for 25 years and never did much traveling when I was younger. For the past 5 years I have been doing a lot of traveling and haven't really enjoyed it . . . can't seem to adjust to time changes and don't really enjoy exotic foods. . . ."

### INTERNAL ISSUES

For the project to have any type of life expectancy, both Hammer and Hollings needed to push the project along. Although Hollings endorsed the trip to Hong Kong, he did not appear really interested and said, ". . . we've got plenty to do here. Besides, I can't put a lot of time and resources into this." Gates found it difficult to secure both men's strong support for the project. As a result, it did not receive high priority from the Corporate Business Development unit. Nine

---

**EXHIBIT 5**

---

**HONG KONG TELECOMMUNICATIONS TRAFFIC STATISTICS, 1977, 1981, 1987**

| | 1977 | 1981 | 1987(e) |
|---|---|---|---|
| International telephone circuits | 638 | — | 6,367 |
| International telegraph circuits | 1,811 | — | 3,608 |
| International leased circuits | | | |
| Voice grade | 67 | — | 1,886 |
| Exchange capacity (thousands) | 1,203 | 1,636 | 2,206 |
| Annual growth (thousands) | 58 | 148 | 136 |
| Annual increase (%) | 5.0 | 10.0 | 6.6 |
| Exchange lines connected (thousands) | 156 | 227 | 288 |
| Exchange lines ceased (thousands) | 72 | 123 | 175 |
| Exchange lines in service (thousands) | 994 | 1,384 | 1,877 |
| Annual growth (thousands) | 84 | 105 | 112 |
| Annual increase (%) | 9.3 | 8.2 | 6.4 |
| Telephones in service (thousands) | 1,251 | 1,823 | 2,507 |
| Annual growth (thousands) | 119 | 147 | 159 |
| Annual increase (%) | 10.5 | 8.7 | 6.8 |
| Exchange lines, business (%) | 23.1 | 24.8 | 27.3 |
| Exchange lines, residential (%) | 76.9 | 75.2 | 72.7 |
| Exchange lines, per 100 people | 21.8 | 26.6 | 33.9 |
| Telephones, per 100 people | 27.4 | 35.1 | 45.3 |

*Source:* Compiled from *Country Market Survey,* 1981 and the *Hong Kong Annual Report,* 1987.

months passed before the project was formally presented for review to the Corporate Committee. During this period, it was reviewed twice by Corporate Business Development and both times returned to MI with more questions. First the business development office wanted to review the financial conditions of the potential majority partner. When Gates requested the information from Guinness, he replied "Before I release any financial details to you, I need to know if Republic Telecom is seriously interested." A letter of interest was drawn and sent.

Gates could feel what started as a comfortable negotiating relationship with the Hong Kong people slowly turn into a tense one. He was constantly on the phone with them, requesting and re-requesting information.

## THE REVIEW MEETING

Prior to entering the review meeting, Gates had contacted Guinness for some final inputs. ST was reporting outstanding results for the first quarter of 1987, had increased its market share to more than 15 percent during this quarter, and was considering the acquisition of Monarch Paging to assume a leadership position in the market. In addition, Struan's share of the cellular telephone business had risen sharply in the first quarter of 1987.

After informing Gates of these developments, Guinness continued, "We are ready to go ahead on this and I should inform you that we are now looking at two other bids, one submitted by a British firm and the other by a Canadian one. We have to make a decision on this soon and I need to know if you still want or do not want this deal. By the way, the price has gone up. They now want $15 million for the 22 percent interest.''

Gates whistled under his breath. That was the third increase in six months.

When Gates approached the Business Development unit again about making a final decision, they postponed any action until the project could be discussed again at the corporate plan-ning meeting already scheduled for Mobile International on April 5. The future direction of MI would be discussed at that time. Gates had been asked to present the Hong Kong proposal at this meeting by Reizer.

On April 5, 1987 Gates found himself in the waiting area of the board room at corporate headquarters. He looked at his watch, he paced the floor. Ten minutes later he was ushered into the board room and the doors closed.

# AB Thorsten (1)

By late July 1986, Anders Ekstrom awaited with a certain amount of impatience for a decision from corporate headquarters in Montreal, Canada, on his proposal to begin manufacturing XL-4 in Sweden within the next year. After several months of preparation, Ekstrom was anxious to finalize this matter and return his attention to his many responsibilities as President of AB Thorsten, a wholly owned subsidiary of Roget Industries Ltd., a large diversified Canadian company.

## ROGET'S HISTORY AND OPERATING PHILOSOPHY

Roget Industries Ltd. was one of the largest industrial companies in Quebec, Canada. Founded in the 1920s, the company originally produced a simple line of chemical products for sale in Canada. By 1986, it had expanded to produce more than 200 complex chemicals in 21

The case is based on a series entitled AB Thorsten (A through C) prepared by Professors Gordon Shillinglaw and Charles Summer at the International Management Development Institute (IMEDE), Lausanne, Switzerland. Copyright © 1988 by IMEDE. Reproduced by permission.

factories located throughout Canada, the United States, and a few European countries.

André Juvet, Chairman of the Board and President of Roget, believed that the company's organization (see Exhibit 1) was the result of careful planning:

> Until the mid-1960s, we were organized with one large manufacturing division here in Canada, and one large sales division with a small department devoted to export markets. However, exports grew so fast, and domestic markets became so complex, that we were forced to create three main product divisions, each with its own manufacturing plants and sales organizations.
>
> At first, the United States had been our largest foreign market, but beginning in 1975, we integrated all North American operations into one organization and gave each division direct responsibility for its international operations. As sales to other markets expanded, each division gradually set up foreign subsidiaries to manage the business in specific areas. For example, in Industrial Chemicals we have two European subsidiaries—one in the United Kingdom serving the EEC markets, and one in Sweden, which serves all Scandinavia. The U.K. and Swedish companies account for 9 percent and 5 percent of divisional sales, about half of which originates in Canada. The domestic department of the Industrial Chemicals Division

**EXHIBIT 1**

## ROGET INDUSTRIES LTD.—ORGANIZATION CHART

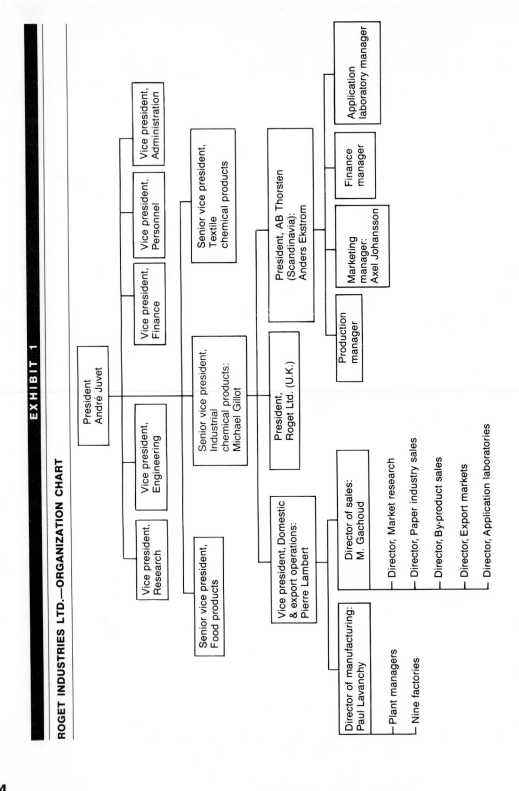

handles all exports, whether they go to our subsidiaries or to independent agents.

Another thing we achieved in the new organization is individual profit responsibility of all executives at all levels. Gillot is responsible for profits for all industrial chemicals; Lambert is responsible for profits from North American operations (manufacturing and sales) and from export sales, and Ekstrom is responsible for profits in Scandinavia from both imported and locally made products. We also utilize a rather liberal bonus system to reward executives at each level, based on the profits of their divisions.

This, together with a policy of promotion from within, helps stimulate managers in Roget to a degree not enjoyed by some of our competitors. It also helps to keep executives in an industry where experience is of great importance. Most of our managers have been in the starch chemicals business all of their lives. It is a complex business, and we feel that it takes many years to learn it.

We have developed certain policies—rules of the game—that govern relationships with our subsidiary company presidents. These are intended to maintain efficiency within the whole Roget complex, and at the same time they provide subsidiary managers with sufficient autonomy to run their own businesses. For example, subsidiary managers can determine what existing Roget products they want to sell in their part of the world market. Export sales will quote the managers the same price as they quote agents in all countries. The managers are free to bargain, and if they don't like the price they needn't sell the product. Second, we encourage subsidiaries to propose to division management in Montreal the development of new products. If these are judged feasible we would proceed to manufacture them in Canada for supply to world markets. Third, subsidiary presidents can build their own manufacturing plants if they can justify the investment in their own market.

## COMPANY BACKGROUND

AB Thorsten was acquired by Roget in 1978. Since that time the same team had constituted Thorsten's Board of Directors: Michael Gillot, Senior Vice-President in charge of Roget's Industrial Chemical Products Division; Ingve Norgren, a Swedish banker; Ove Svensen, a Stockholm industrialist; and the current president of Thorsten. Swedish corporation law required any company incorporated in Sweden to have Swedish directors, and the Roget management felt fortunate in having found two men as prominent as Norgren and Svensen to serve on the Thorsten Board.

During the first four years of Roget's ownership, Thorsten's sales fluctuated between Skr50 and Skr70 million but hit a low at the end of that period. The Board of AB Thorsten decided at that time that the company was in serious trouble, and that the only alternative to selling was to hire a totally different management team to overhaul and streamline the whole company. On advice of the Swedish directors, Anders Ekstrom, a 38-year-old graduate of the Royal Institute of Technology, was hired. He had a total of 16 years of experience in production engineering for a large machinery company, as marketing manager of a British subsidiary in Sweden, and, more recently, as division manager in a large paper company. As Ekstrom described his experience:

> Working for the paper company, the European subsidiary of a large U.S. firm, was particularly valuable to me. I knew little of modern financial methods and strategic planning prior to my working with them. As I came into contact with executives who had attended many top U.S. business schools, I came to realize that these were the kind of tools I needed to be successful, those that Sweden needs to operate our industry with maximum productivity. Sure enough, they have been invaluable to me and to Thorsten. A few men in Roget know them, but even there such methods are relatively unknown among many managers. One day, everyone here will know these methods, and we will be competitive or even superior to the United States in management. I am proud to have learned such management techniques and they give me confidence in managing Thorsten—for the benefit of the company and for the benefit of Sweden's productive capacity.

Ekstrom had been president of AB Thorsten since early in 1982. During that time, sales had increased to Skr200 million, and profits had reached levels that Roget's management found highly satisfactory. Both Ekstrom and Norgren attributed this performance to: (1) an increase in industrial activity in Scandinavia since the 1982 recession; (2) changes in production methods, marketing strategy, and organization structure made by Ekstrom; (3) the hiring of competent staff; and (4) Ekstrom's own ambition and hard work. Ekstrom's knowledge of modern planning techniques—sophisticated market research methods, financial planning by use of discounted cash flows and incremental analysis, and, as Ekstrom put it, "all those things I learned from my former American employer"—had also contributed to the successful turnaround in Thorsten.

Ekstrom recognized that at the time he joined Thorsten, there were many risks:

> I like the challenge of building a company. If I do a good job here, I will have the confidence of Norgren and Svensen as well as of the Roget management in Montreal. Deep down inside, succeeding in this situation will teach me things that will make me more competent as a top executive. So I chose this job even though I had at the time (and still have) offers from other companies.

## INITIAL PROPOSAL FOR MANUFACTURE OF XL-4

In September 1985, Ekstrom informed the Thorsten Board of Directors that he proposed to study the feasibility of constructing a facility in Sweden for the manufacture of XL-4, a product used in paper converting. He explained that he and his customer engineers had discovered a new way of helping large paper mills adapt their machines at little cost so that they could use XL-4 instead of traditional substitute products. Large paper mill customers would be able to realize dramatic savings in material handling and storage costs and to shorten drying time substantially. In his judgment, Thorsten could develop a market in Sweden almost as big as Roget's present worldwide market for XL-4. XL-4 was then being produced in Roget's In-

dustrial Chemicals Division at the rate of 600 tons a year, but less than 2 percent of this was going to Sweden. According to Ekstrom, Gillot and the other directors seemed enthusiastic. Gillot reportedly said, "Of course, go ahead with your study and when you have a proposed plan, with the final return on investment, send it in and we will consider it thoroughly."

During the next six months, we did the analysis. My market research department estimated the total potential market in Sweden at 800 tons of XL-4 per year. We interviewed important customers and conducted trials in the factories of three big companies. These proved that with the introduction of our machine designs the large cost saving would indeed materialize and would overwhelm the small investment costs associated with making the necessary changes. We determined that if we could sell the product for Skr18.50 per kilogram, we could capture one-half of the market within a three-year period.

At the same time, I called the head of the Corporate Engineering Division in Montreal and asked for his help in designing a plant to produce 400 tons of XL-4 per year and in estimating the cost of the investment. This is a routine thing. The central staff divisions are advisory and always comply with requests for help. He assigned a project manager and four other engineers to work on the design of factory and machinery and to estimate the cost. At the same time I assigned three men from my staff to work on the project. In three months this joint task group reported that the necessary plant could be built for about Skr7 million.

Our calculations, together with a complete written explanation, were mailed in early April 1986 to Gillot. I felt rather excited, as did most of my staff. We all know that introduction of new products is one of the keys to continued growth and profitability. The yield on this investment (15 percent) was well above the minimum 8 percent established as a guideline for new investments by the Roget Vice-President of Finance. We also knew that it was a good analysis, done by modern tools of management. In the covering letter, I asked that it be put on the agenda for the next Board meeting.

The Board meeting was held in Stockholm on April 28, 1986. The minutes show on the agenda "A Proposal for Investment in Sweden"

---

### EXHIBIT 2

**AB THORSTEN PROPOSAL TO MANUFACTURE XL-4 IN SWEDEN— FINANCIAL SUMMARY** (Skr Thousand)

| Year | Description | After-tax cash flows* | Present value at 8% |
|------|-------------|----------------------:|--------------------:|
| 0 | Equipment | −7,000 | |
| | Working capital | − 560 | |
| | Total | −7,560 | −7,560 |
| 1 | Cash operating profit | +1,050 | |
| | Working capital | − 20 | |
| | Total | +1,030 | + 954 |
| 2 | Cash operating profit | +1,600 | |
| | Working capital | − 70 | |
| | Total | +1,530 | +1,312 |
| 3 | Cash operating profit | +2,150 | +1,708 |
| 4 | Cash operating profit | +2,150 | +1,580 |
| 5 | Cash operating profit | +2,150 | +1,463 |
| 6 | Cash operating profit | +1,450 | + 914 |
| 7 | Cash operating profit | +1,450 | |
| | Recovery value of equipment and working capital | +2,150 | |
| | Total | +3,600 | +2,100 |
| | Projected grand total | +6,500 | +2,470 |

#### Financial conclusions

| | |
|---|---:|
| Net present value to the corporation (Skr) | 2,470,000 |
| Payback period (years) | 4 |
| Internal rate of return (%) | 15.7 |

*From Exhibits 3, 4, and 5.

---

to be presented by Ekstrom. They also quote from his remarks as he explained the proposal to the other directors:

You will see from the summary table (Exhibit 2) that this project is profitable. On an initial outlay of Skr7 million for plant and equipment and Skr560,000 for working capital, we get a rate of return of 15.7 percent and a present value of Skr2.47 million.

Let me explain some of the figures underlying this summary table. My second chart (Exhibit 3) summarizes the operating cash flows that we expect to get from the XL-4 project. The sales forecast for the first seven years is shown in the first row. The forecast was not extended beyond seven years because our engineers estimated that the technology of starch manufacture will improve gradually, so that major plant renovations will become necessary at about the end of the seventh year. Actually, we see no reason why demand for XL-4 will decline after seven years, as we shall see in a minute.

The estimated variable cost of Skr10 per kilogram represents the full operating cost of manufacturing XL-4 in Sweden, including out-of-pocket fixed costs such as plant management salaries but excluding depreciation. These fixed costs must be included, of course, because they are incremental to the decision.

We feel certain that we can enter the market initially with a selling price of Skr20 per kilogram, but full market penetration will require a price reduction to Skr18.50 at the beginning of the sec-

---

**EXHIBIT 3**

---

**ESTIMATED OPERATING CASH FLOWS FROM MANUFACTURE AND SALE OF XL-4 IN SWEDEN**

| | Year | | | | | | | |
| | 1 | 2 | 3 | 4 | 5 | 6 | 7 | Total |
|---|---|---|---|---|---|---|---|---|
| 1. Sales (tons) | 200 | 300 | 400 | 400 | 400 | 400 | 400 | 2,500 |
| | **Skr per kg** | | | | | | | |
| 2. Sales price | 20.0 | 18.5 | 18.5 | 18.5 | 18.5 | 18.5 | 18.5 | |
| 3. Variable costs | 10.0 | 10.0 | 10.0 | 10.0 | 10.0 | 10.0 | 10.0 | |
| 4. Profit margin | 10.0 | 8.5 | 8.5 | 8.5 | 8.5 | 8.5 | 8.5 | |
| | **Thousand Skr** | | | | | | | |
| 5. Contribution | 2,000 | 2,550 | 3,400 | 3,400 | 3,400 | 3,400 | 3,400 | 21,550 |
| 6. Promotion costs | 1,300 | 750 | 500 | 500 | 500 | 500 | 500 | 4,550 |
| 7. Before-tax profit | 700 | 1,800 | 2,900 | 2,900 | 2,900 | 2,900 | 2,900 | 17,000 |
| 8. Depreciation | 1,400 | 1,400 | 1,400 | 1,400 | 1,400 | 0 | 0 | 7,000 |
| 9. Taxes payable | (350) | 200 | 750 | 750 | 750 | 1,450 | 1,450 | 5,000 |
| 10. Net cash flow | 1,050 | 1,600 | 2,150 | 2,150 | 2,150 | 1,450 | 1,450 | 12,000 |

ond year. The variable contribution resulting from these figures is shown on the fifth line. The next two rows list the market development and promotion expenditures that are needed to launch the product and achieve the forecasted sales levels, and the resulting net operating cash flows before tax.

The cost of the plant can be written off for tax purposes over a five-year period, at the rate of 20 percent of original cost each year. Subtracting this amount from the before-tax cash flows, and mul-

tiplying by the tax rate (50 percent), yields the payable tax in row 9. When this is subtracted from the before-tax cash flow, it yields the after-tax cash flow in the last line.

A proposal of this kind also requires some investment in working capital. Our estimates on this element (Exhibit 4) is that we will need about Skr800,000 to start with, but some of this can be deducted immediately from our income taxes. Swedish law permits us to deduct 60 percent of the cost of inventories from taxable income. For

---

**EXHIBIT 4**

---

**ESTIMATED WORKING CAPITAL REQUIRED FOR MANUFACTURE AND SALE OF XL-4 IN SWEDEN**

(Skr thousand)

| | (1)<br>Inventory<br>at cost | (2)<br>Other current<br>assets less<br>current<br>liabilities | (3)<br>Working<br>capital<br>[(1) + (2)] | (4)<br>Change<br>from<br>previous<br>year | (5)<br>Tax credit<br>[30% of<br>change<br>in (1)] | (6)<br>Net funds<br>required<br>[(4) − (5)] |
|---|---|---|---|---|---|---|
| Year 0 | 800 | 0 | 800 | +800 | 240 | 560 |
| Year 1 | 900 | −50 | 850 | + 50 | 30 | 20 |
| Year 2 | 1,000 | −50 | 950 | +100 | 30 | 70 |
| Years 3+ | 1,000 | −50 | 950 | 0 | 0 | 0 |
| Total | 1,000 | −50 | 950 | 950 | 300 | 650 |

**EXHIBIT 5**

**ESTIMATED END-OF-LIFE VALUE OF SWEDISH ASSETS** (Skr)

| | | |
|---|---:|---:|
| Plant | 3,000,000 | |
| Less tax on gain if sold at this price | 1,500,000 | |
| Net value of plant | | 1,500,000 |
| Working capital | 950,000 | |
| Less payment of deferred tax on special inventory reserves | 300,000 | |
| Net value of working capital | 650,000 | |
| Net value of Swedish assets after 7 years | | 2,150,000 |

this reason, and given a tax rate of 50 percent, we can get an immediate reduction of Skr240,000 in the taxes we have to pay on our other income in Sweden. We'll need small additional amounts of working capital in the next two years, so that altogether our requirements will add up to Skr650,000 (net of taxes) by the end of our second full year of operations.

Now let's come back to the issue of what happens after 1994. Seven years is a very conservative estimate of the life of the product. If we limit the analysis to seven years, we would overlook the value of our assets at the end of that time. At the very worst, the plant itself should be worth Skr3 million after seven years (Exhibit 5). We'd have to pay tax on that, of course, because the plant would be fully depreciated, but this would still leave us with a value of Skr1.5 million for the plant. The working capital should also be fully recoverable. After paying the deferred tax on inventories, we'd get Skr650,000 back on that. The total value at the end of seven years would thus be Skr2.15 million.

As I said earlier, however, we have chosen to be conservative in these calculations. It is quite probable that with a small additional investment the plant could be refurbished and XL-4 sales to Scandinavia could continue for many years.

Ekstrom ended this opening presentation by saying, "Gentlemen, it seems clear from these figures that we can justify this investment on the basis of sales to the Swedish market. Our Group Vice-President for Finance has laid down the policy that any new investment should yield at least 8 percent. This particular proposal shows a return of 15 percent. My management and I

strongly recommend this project." (The Thorsten vice-presidents for production, sales, and finance had been called into the Board meeting to be present when this proposal was made.)

Ekstrom told the case writer that while he was making this proposal he was sure that it would be accepted and that Gillot had said "that it seemed to him to be a clear case." The minutes of the Board meeting show that Gillot asked a few questions, mainly about the longer-term likelihood for sales of more than 400 tons a year, about sales to other Scandinavian countries, and about sources of funds. Ekstrom added:

> I explained that we in Sweden were very firm in our judgment that we would reach 400 tons a year even before one year, but felt constrained to show a conservative estimate of a three-year transition period. If sales to other countries took off in the future, an expansion of the plant's capacity could be undertaken at a fraction of the total costs now envisaged. We also showed him how we could finance any expansion by borrowing in Sweden. That is, if Roget would furnish the initial capital requirements from Canada, and if our 400 tons were reached quickly, any funds needed for further expansion would easily be lent by local banks. The two Swedish directors confirmed this. The Board then voted unanimously to approve the project.

## DISAGREEMENT BETWEEN PARENT AND SUBSIDIARY

About a week later, Gillot telephoned Ekstrom. "Since my return to Montreal I have been through

| EXHIBIT 6 | | |
|---|---|---|

**ESTIMATE OF WORLD MARKET FOR XL-4 AND CURRENT SALES (1985)**

| | Potential market (percent of world paper production) | Current sales of XL-4 (percent) |
|---|---|---|
| Sweden | 12 | 1.7 |
| Finland | 7 | 0.5 |
| Norway | 3 | 0.2 |
| USSR | 10 | 0.0 |
| Rest of Europe | 20 | 8.6 |
| Canada | 15 | 54.8 |
| United States | 13 | 28.5 |
| Rest of the world | 20 | 5.7 |
| Total | 100 | 100.0 |

some additional discussions with the production and marketing people here. They think the engineering design and plant cost are accurate but that you are too optimistic on your sales forecast. It looks like you will have to justify this more.'' Ekstrom related his reaction:

I pushed him to set up a meeting the following week. This meeting was attended by me and my marketing and production directors from Sweden, and four people from Canada—Gillot, Lavanchy [Director of Manufacturing], Gachoud [Director of Sales], and Lambert [Vice-President for Domestic and Export]. It was one of the worst meetings of my life. It lasted all day. Gachoud argued that they had sales experience from other countries and that in his judgment the market potential and our share were too optimistic, that the whole world market for Roget was only 600 tons a year (see Exhibit 6), and that it was inconceivable that Sweden alone could take 400 tons. I told him over and over how we arrived at these figures, but he just kept repeating the overoptimism argument.

Lavanchy then said that the production of this product was very complicated and that he had difficulties producing it in Canada, even with trained workers who had years of experience. I told him I only needed five trained production workers and that he could send me two men for two months to train Swedes to do the job. I impressed on him that ''if you can manufacture it in Canada, you can manufacture it for us in Sweden until we learn,

that is, if you don't have confidence in Swedish technology.'' He repeated that the difficulties in manufacturing were great. I stressed that we were prepared to learn and take the risk. Somehow I just couldn't get through to him.

At 6 p.m. everyone was tired. Lambert had backed up his two production and sales officials all day, repeating their arguments. Gillot seemed to me to just sit there and listen, occasionally asking questions. I cannot understand why he didn't back me up. He seemed so easy to get along with at the earlier Board meeting in Stockholm—where he seemed decisive. Not so at this meeting. He seemed distant, indecisive, and an ineffective executive.

He stopped the meeting without a solution and said that he hoped all concerned would do more investigation of this subject. He vaguely referred to the fact that he would think about it himself and let us know when another meeting would be held.

## OBJECTION FROM A SWEDISH DIRECTOR

Ekstrom returned to Stockholm and reported on the meeting to his own staff and to the two Swedish members of his Board. ''They, like I, were really disgusted. Here we were operating with initiative and with excellent financial techniques. Roget management had often emphasized the necessity for decentralized profit responsibilities, authority, and initiative on the part of foreign subsidiary presidents. One of my men told me that they seem to talk decentralization and act like tin gods at the same time.''

Norgren, the Swedish banker on Thorsten's Board, expressed surprise: ''I considered this carefully. It is sound business for Thorsten, and XL-4 will help to build one more growth company in the Swedish economy. Somehow, the management in Montreal has failed to study this, or they don't wish the Swedish subsidiary to produce it. I have today dictated a letter to Mr. Gillot telling him that I don't know why the project is rejected, that Roget has a right to its own reasons, but that I am prepared to resign as a director. It is not that I am angry, or that I have a right to dictate decisions for the whole worldwide Roget group. It is simply that, if I spend my time studying policy decisions, and those decisions do not serve the right function for the business, then it is a waste of time to continue.''

Ekstrom added, ''while I certainly wouldn't bring these matters out in a meeting, I think those Canadian production and sales people simply want to build their empire, and make the money in Roget Canada. They don't care about Thorsten and Sweden. That's a smooth way to operate. We have the ideas and the initiative, and they take them and get the payoff.''

## FURTHER STUDY

After Gillot received Norgren's letter, he contacted Lavanchy, Gachoud, and Bols (Vice-President, Finance, Roget corporate staff). He told them that the Swedish XL-4 project had become a matter of key importance for the whole Roget Group, because of its implications for company profits and for the morale and autonomy of the subsidiary management. He asked them to study the matter and report their recommendations in one month. He also wrote Ekstrom, ''Various members of Corporate Staff are studying the proposal. You will hear from me within about six weeks regarding my final decision.''

## REPORT OF ROGET'S DIRECTOR OF MANUFACTURING

A month after he was asked to study the XL-4 project, Lavanchy gave Gillot a memorandum explaining his reasons for opposing the proposal:

At your request, I have reexamined thoroughly all of the cost figures that bear on the XL-4 proposal. I find that manufacture of this product in Sweden would be highly uneconomical for two reasons: (1) overhead costs would be higher; and (2) variable costs would be greater.

As to the first, suppose that Thorsten does sell 400 tons a year so that our total worldwide sales

| EXHIBIT 7 |
| --- |

**ESTIMATED VARIABLE COST OF MANUFACTURING XL-4 IN CANADA FOR SHIPMENT TO SWEDEN** (SKr)

| Variable costs per ton | |
| --- | --- |
| Manufacturing | 9,300 |
| Shipping from Canada to Sweden | 2,500 |
| Swedish import duty | 2,000 |
| Total | 13,800 |

rise to 1,000 tons. We can produce the whole 1,000 tons in Canada with essentially the same capital investment we have now. If we produce 1,000 tons, our fixed costs will decrease by C$218 (Skr1,200) a ton.[1] That means Skr720,000 in savings on production for domestic and export to countries other than Sweden (600 tons a year), and Skr1.2 million for worldwide production including Sweden.

Second, if we were to produce the extra 400 tons in Canada, we could schedule longer production runs, have lower set-up costs and larger raw material purchases, thus allowing mass purchasing and material handling and lower purchase prices. My accounting department has studied this and concludes that our average variable costs will decrease from C$1.75 to C$1.70 (Skr9.50 to Skr9.30) per kilogram as indicated in Exhibit 7. This difference means a saving of nearly C$22,000 (Skr120,000) on Canadian domestic production or Skr200,000 for total worldwide production, assuming that Sweden takes 400 tons a year. Taxes on these added profits are about the same in Canada as in Sweden, about 50 percent of taxable income.

In conclusion, the new plant should not be built. Ekstrom is a bright young man, but he does not know the adhesives business. He would be head over heels in costly production mistakes from the beginning. I recommend that you inform the Thorsten management that it is in the company's interest, and therefore it is Roget policy, that he must buy from Canada.

---

[1]Total fixed costs in Canada were C$327,300, the equivalent of Skr1.8 million a year. Divided by 600, this equals Skr3,000 a ton. If it were spread over 1,000 tons, the average fixed cost would be Skr1,800.

## REPORT OF VICE-PRESIDENT OF FINANCE

A few days later, Gillot received the following memorandum from Eric Bols, Roget's financial Vice-President:

I am sending you herewith a complete economic study of the two alternatives which have been raised for producing XL-4 within the Roget group. The Swedish management has proposed constructing a plant in Sweden, while Lavanchy and Lambert on our Canadian staff have proposed producing here in Canada.

First of all, I should state that I agree that this kind of matter must be resolved by highest authority. Industrial Chemicals is not the only group within the company which has such location problems, and Juvet [President of Roget Industries Ltd.] is concerned that any precedent set would also apply to the food and textile divisions.

After thorough analysis by the most advanced financial methods, it is clear that the Roget Group will benefit substantially by producing total world requirements for XL-4 in Canada, including the 400 tons per year which Swedish management estimate it will need over the next seven years. Not only will the Roget group of companies gain the Skr173,000 difference between the net present values of both proposals, but the really important factor is that we would have to furnish only C$130,000 (Skr720,000) in initial capital funds, while

in Sweden it would cost Skr7.64 million (C$1.4 million) to build a new plant and stock it (see Exhibit 8).

The importance of this factor can be demonstrated. The internal rate of return on invested capital is 60 percent for the Canadian project because of the low initial investment, while it is only 15.7 percent for the costly Swedish investment. Stated in another way, Sweden is asking us to invest Skr6.92 million more than necessary (their initial investment less ours). If this amount were invested in Eurodollar bank certificates, which have averaged 8 to 9 percent over the last 10 years, it would grow to more than Skr12 million after seven years. This shows the opportunity cost of committing needless money in Sweden. Such money is, in effect, wasted, because the internal rate of return is so much lower in Sweden.

Another way to see the importance of initial capital is to look at the payback period. It would take the group four years to get its money back in Sweden but only two and one-half years in Canada. Exhibits 10 through 12 are constructed exactly as Ekstrom performed his analysis and provide the subsidiary figures that are summarized in Exhibit 9. They show operating profits, working capital requirements, and the salvage value of assets at the end of seven years, expressed in Swedish kroner at current exchange rates to facilitate comparison. You already have from Paul Lavanchy the variable cost of manufacture and shipping, which are incorporated into Exhibit 7. There is,

---

**EXHIBIT 8**

**COMPARISON OF ECONOMIC GAINS BETWEEN TWO ALTERNATIVE PROPOSALS FOR THE MANUFACTURE OF XL-4**

|  | Made in Sweden | Made in Canada |
|---|---|---|
| Present value of investments (Skr) | 7,640,000 | 720,000 |
| Present value of operating profits (Skr) | 8,760,000 | 2,930,000 |
| Present value of residual assets (Skr) | 1,340,000 | 420,000 |
| Net present value (Skr) | 2,470,000 | 2,643,000 |
| Payback period (years) | 4 | 2.5 |
| Internal rate of return (%) | 15 | 60 |
| Best economic and financial alternative: manufacture in Canada | | |

*Note:* An 8% discount rate is assumed.

EXHIBIT 9

## ROGET'S PROPOSAL FOR MANUFACTURE OF XL-4 IN CANADA FOR EXPORT TO SWEDEN AND OTHER WORLD MARKETS (Skr Thousand)

| Year | Description | After-tax cash flows* | Present value at 8% |
|------|-------------|----------------------:|--------------------:|
| 0 | Working capital | − 540 | − 540 |
| 1 | Cash operating profit | + 30 | |
| | Working capital | − 100 | |
| | Total | − 70 | − 65 |
| 2 | Cash operating profit | + 390 | |
| | Working capital | − 100 | |
| | Total | + 290 | + 249 |
| 3 | Cash operating profit | + 750 | + 595 |
| 4 | Cash operating profit | + 750 | + 551 |
| 5 | Cash operating profit | + 750 | + 510 |
| 6 | Cash operating profit | + 750 | + 473 |
| 7 | Cash operating profit | + 750 | |
| | Recovery value of working capital | + 740 | |
| | Total | +1,490 | + 869 |
| | Projected grand total | +4,170 | +2,643 |

### Financial conclusions

| | |
|---|---:|
| Net present value to the corporation (Skr) | 2,643,000 |
| Payback period (years) | 2.5 |
| Internal rate of return (%) | 60.0 |

*From Exhibits 10, 11, and 12.

EXHIBIT 10

## ESTIMATED OPERATING CASH FLOWS FROM MANUFACTURE OF XL-4 IN CANADA FOR SHIPMENT TO SWEDEN

| | Year | | | | | | | |
|---|---|---|---|---|---|---|---|---|
| | 1 | 2 | 3 | 4 | 5 | 6 | 7 | Total |
| 1. Sales (tons) | 200 | 300 | 400 | 400 | 400 | 400 | 400 | 2,500 |
| **Skr per kg** | | | | | | | | |
| 2. Sales price | 20.0 | 18.5 | 18.5 | 18.5 | 18.5 | 18.5 | 18.5 | |
| 3. Variable costs | 13.8 | 13.8 | 13.8 | 13.8 | 13.8 | 13.8 | 13.8 | |
| 4. Profit margin | 6.2 | 4.7 | 4.7 | 4.7 | 4.7 | 4.7 | 4.7 | |
| **Thousand Skr** | | | | | | | | |
| 5. Contribution | 1,240 | 1,410 | 1,880 | 1,880 | 1,880 | 1,880 | 1,880 | 12,050 |
| 6. Promotion costs | 1,300 | 750 | 500 | 500 | 500 | 500 | 500 | 4,550 |
| 7. Savings* | 120 | 120 | 120 | 120 | 120 | 120 | 120 | 840 |
| 8. Before-tax profit | 60 | 780 | 1,500 | 1,500 | 1,500 | 1,500 | 1,500 | 8,340 |
| 9. Taxes payable | 30 | 390 | 750 | 750 | 750 | 750 | 750 | 4,170 |
| 10. Net cash flow | 30 | 390 | 750 | 750 | 750 | 750 | 750 | 4,170 |

*These are savings incurred in sales to other markets due to more efficient purchasing and production scheduling (600 tons × Skr200 per ton).

---

**EXHIBIT 11**

---

**ESTIMATED WORKING CAPITAL REQUIRED FOR MANUFACTURE OF XL-4 IN CANADA FOR SALE IN SWEDEN** (Skr Thousand)

| | (1)<br>Inventory<br>at cost | (2)<br>Other current<br>assets less<br>current<br>liabilities | (3)<br>Working<br>capital<br>[(1) + (2)] | (4)<br>Change<br>from<br>previous<br>year | (5)<br>Tax credit<br>[30% of<br>change<br>in (1)] | (6)<br>Net funds<br>required<br>[(4) − (5)] |
|---|---|---|---|---|---|---|
| Year 0 | 500 | 100 | 600 | +600 | 60* | 540 |
| Year 1 | 550 | 150 | 700 | +100 | 0 | 100 |
| Year 2 | 600 | 200 | 800 | +100 | 0 | 100 |
| Years 3+ | 600 | 200 | 800 | 0 | 0 | 0 |
| Total | 600 | 200 | 800 | 800 | 60 | 740 |

*Based on finished goods inventory of Skr200,000 in Sweden.

---

of course an exchange risk associated with these flows, but one that would apply equally to any future dividends from Sweden.[2]

Finally, I must call attention to my position as compared with that of Lavanchy. He and I are agreed on the most important issue—that it would be much more profitable to manufacture in Canada. But we differ on one point. He stresses that we would save Skr120,000 per year on fixed costs if we manufacture total production here, because our existing plant would produce 400 tons more per year, thus lowering cost per ton and depreciation charges per ton. This is not correct. The plant is already built here. There would be no actual money costs one way or the other for our plant under either of three alternatives: produce in Canada, produce in Sweden, or simply not produce additional XL-4 at all. You will notice, therefore, that I do not include any depreciation cost in my calculations.

I hope that this analysis is of help to you in formulating a divisional policy on construction of

---

manufacturing plants around the world. It seems to me that it should be the policy of Roget to construct plants whenever and wherever the group as a whole will gain most benefits, taking into consideration worldwide supply and demand, rather than conditions in any one country or one part of the group. That is, we should produce at the point where the cost of production is lowest.

We in Finance have the highest respect for the Swedish management. Mr. Ekstrom, particularly, is an outstanding manager with great financial expertise himself. In this case, he has simply not had the complete information from our total group. I trust that he will understand that this is not a personal rejection, but one that is for the good of the group as a whole—the parent company and Thorsten's sister companies in other countries.

---

[2]See Exhibit 13 for historical data on the Swedish kroner/Canadian dollar exchange rates and relative inflation rates in both countries. For simplicity, most calculations in the case have been translated to Swedish kroner at a rate of Skr5.5/C$ (prevalent at the time) to facilitate comparisons with the original proposal.

---

**EXHIBIT 12**

---

**ESTIMATED END-OF-LIFE VALUE OF CANADIAN ASSETS**

| | |
|---|---|
| Working capital | Skr800,000 |
| Less payment of deferred tax on special inventory reserves | 60,000 |
| Net value of working capital after 7 years | 740,000 |

```
EXHIBIT 13
```

**EXCHANGE RATES AND RELATIVE INFLATION—CANADA AND SWEDEN (1980–1986)**

| | Exchange rates | | | Inflation rate indexes (1980 = 100) | |
|---|---|---|---|---|---|
| | Skr/US$ | Can$/US$ | Skr/Can$ | Canada | Sweden |
| 1980 | 4.23 | 1.169 | 3.62 | 100.0 | 100.0 |
| 1981 | 5.06 | 1.199 | 4.22 | 112.5 | 112.1 |
| 1982 | 6.28 | 1.234 | 5.09 | 124.6 | 121.7 |
| 1983 | 7.67 | 1.232 | 6.23 | 131.8 | 132.6 |
| 1984 | 8.27 | 1.295 | 6.39 | 137.6 | 143.2 |
| 1985 | 8.60 | 1.366 | 6.30 | 143.0 | 153.7 |
| 1986 (Q1) | 7.48 | 1.404 | 5.28 | 146.9 | 158.9 |
| (Q2) | 7.20 | 1.384 | 5.20 | 148.0 | 159.7 |

# Benetton (B)

Against a backdrop of budding fruit trees and birds singing from the carefully pruned vineyard on the grounds of Villa Minelli, headquarters for the Benetton Group, the company's managing director, Aldo Palmeri, reflected on the challenges that Benetton's rapid growth posed for the company's management in the spring of 1985.

Chief among these was the evolution from entrepreneurial to nonowner management. Although this change had proceeded at a steady pace, it nevertheless was the source of continuing questions. Growth had brought with it the need for additional financing. And recent questions had arisen about the best way of organizing to serve the company's fastest growing and potentially largest national market, the United States. In particular, careful thought was being given to whether to create a separate U.S. subsidiary and the scope of activity for which such a subsidiary might be given responsibility.

## BACKGROUND

The Benetton Group, the principal subsidiary of the INVEP holding company, was founded in 1965 by Luciano and Giuliana Benetton, brother and sister, who decided that a fashion clothing business could be built around Luciano's business skills and Giuliana's ability to create knitted garments with attractive design and bright colors.[1] With early success of these products, two younger brothers, Gilberto and Carlo, were brought into the rapidly growing company. Opening the first shop of their own in only 40 square meters (about 400 square feet) in 1968, the members of the Benetton family rapidly expanded their business over the years, bringing many of their closest friends and former schoolmates from the vicinity of Treviso,

This case was prepared by Professor James L. Heskett of the Harvard Graduate School of Business Administration and Professor Sergio Signorelli of the Istituto Studi Direzionali Spa (ISTUD), with the assistance of Dr. Claudio Pitilino, as the basis for class discussion rather than to illustrate either effective or ineffective handling of an administrative situation. Selected data in the case were based on estimates or are disguised. Copyright © 1985 by the President and Fellows of Harvard College and the Istituto Studi Direzionali SpA. All rights reserved.

[1]For a more complete background, see Case Thirty-Two.

Italy, the family home, into the growing organization.

## Basic Strategy

Financing required by both manufacturing and retailing operations prompted Luciano Benetton to develop an informal network of agents comprised of long-term friends and acquaintances who might find others interested in managing and investing in individual retail shops with them. Although the company initially had owned many of its shops, it gradually had divested itself of all but a handful of retail outlets in "lead" (prestigious) locations. Nevertheless, its shops continued to have distinctive features of relatively small size and simple design, intended to show off the "palette of colors" provided by neatly stacked Benetton garments. Location was carefully controlled, with agents encouraged to locate shops intended for slightly different market segments in clusters in city centers.

Luciano Benetton had also sought innovative ways of achieving low manufacturing costs. He had devised an ingenious method of conditioning wool to make it softer and had converted old outmoded hosiery knitting machines into productive machines for making sweater and jersey materials. Over the years, a growing proportion of work had been delegated to contractors, whose costs were significantly lower than those experienced by Benetton in its own manufacturing facilities. By 1983, payments to contractors for their work were nearly six times the direct labor expense for work performed in Benetton's factories. The roughly 220 contractors with whom the company dealt were nearly all owned by Benetton employees or their relatives, many of whom further subcontracted the work of knitting, assembling, and finishing various garments of both wool and cotton. At the same time, Benetton retained control over more complex operations, knitting intricately patterned material, dyeing as much of its material as its capacity would allow, and inspecting and preparing all garments for shipment in its own factory facilities.

## Early Growth

The Benetton Group, through INVEP, was owned totally by the Benettons. In addition, each of them had maintained an active role in the management of the company. From the very beginning, Luciano Benetton, the oldest, had assumed responsibility for production activities as well as the commercial activities with which he was more familiar, having had experience as a wholesaler who had sold the output of a number of artisans to department stores. His sister, Giuliana, with whom he had formed the company, produced the designs that made the company's products distinctive. By 1985, she presided over a free-lance group of some sixteen designers from her separate offices several miles from Ponzano Veneto, spending a great deal of time in the Ponzano factory coordinating the work of her group with manufacturing management.

When the two younger brothers were invited to join the venture, Gilberto, formerly employed by the Crafts Association of Treviso, was put in charge of administration, and Carlo, the youngest and a draftsman in a small local engineering company, assumed responsibility for the technical function (production). By 1985, Gilberto concentrated his attention on finance and Carlo still maintained an active role in the management of the company's network of seven plants located in Italy, France, and Scotland.

Growth created a number of managerial opportunities at the company. And many of these were filled by friends and acquaintances of the Benettons, often with little formal job definition and a minimal understanding of salary and other terms. Similarly, agents agreeing to establish and stock retail outlets only with Benetton products often did so with no written agreement. And relationships with contractors who produced much of the Benetton garments were often established and maintained with a handshake.

Long-time employees of the company exhibited strong fealty toward the Benettons. This was attributed by various members of the organization to two factors. First, the manner in which Luciano Benetton led the organization was found attractive by many. As one executive put it, "he never commands, he always suggests, and in a way that makes you want to do your best." A second factor, cited by several, was the natural respect paid to the *padrone,* or owner, by the *dirigente,* or professional manager, in the typical Italian organization.

One factor in Benetton's success had been Luciano Benetton's efforts to build an effective retail distribution program. Working through long-term associates with some financial capacity, called agents, he set out to enlist young adults with no previous experience in retailing but at least a small amount of money to invest to become majority partners with agents in retail shops selling Benetton products. Agents took the lead in finding such partners in geographic territories granted by the company. In return for finding new retailers, displaying Benetton products to them, and consolidating orders and passing them on to Benetton, agents received a commission of 4 percent of the value of all goods shipped from Benetton's factories. Instead of charging a franchise fee for the use of its name on their stores, Benetton expected its retailer customers not to carry competing products. In addition, it undertook to finance much of the inventory carried by these young shop owners. The Appendix contains excerpts from an article describing Luciano Benetton's business philosophy.

By 1985, a combination of well-designed products, an innovative retailing strategy, and a carefully coordinated manufacturing and logistics support system had brought the company to the point where its current sales were at the rate of about Lit900 billion per year to nearly 3,000 retail shops, most of them in Europe.[2] In the process, it had become the world's largest purchaser of wool. (See Exhibits 1 and 2 for company financial statements for 1982, 1983, and 1984.)

## ORGANIZATION AND CULTURE

Growth had not been achieved without strain in the company's organization. In addition, growth brought with it the need for additional financial resources. At the time the company was seeking financing in 1981, Luciano Benetton, already searching for additional professional management for his company, was attracted to a highly regarded executive of the Bank of Italy in Rome, Aldo Palmeri. After a period of more than a year during which Palmeri consulted for Benetton, Luciano Benetton convinced Palmeri to take a position as one of two managing directors of the company, primarily responsible for matters of finance. He assumed a position alongside Elio Aluffi, a long-time employee of the company who was made managing director responsible for "internal" operations, including manufacturing, commercial (marketing), and information systems.

From the start, differences in the management approaches of Aluffi and Palmeri were obvious to many. While Palmeri set out to attract other managers from other companies, Aluffi concentrated his efforts on the management of the budgeting process, the development of a new information system connecting Benetton with its retail outlets, and the design and construction of a new automated central warehouse near Ponzano.

By December 1984, Aluffi had left the organization. The reason suggested by one executive was that most of Aluffi's responsibilities had been assumed by others. The projects supervised by Aluffi had experienced delays, prompting the hiring of a U.S. consultant on the management of information systems to review progress. Del Nero, the new director of manufacturing hired in 1982 from another textile manufacturing company, began reporting infor-

---

[2] At the exchange rate early in 1985 of about 2,000 lire to the dollar, this figure approximated $450 million.

| EXHIBIT 1 |
| --- |

**INCOME STATEMENTS FOR THE BENETTON GROUP, 1982, 1983, AND 1984** (Lit Billion)

|  | 1982* | 1983† | 1984† |
| --- | --- | --- | --- |
| Revenues |  |  |  |
| Net sales | n.a. | 559.8 | 711.3 |
| Other revenues | n.a. | 2.4 | 2.7 |
| Total | 401.7 | 562.2† | 714.0 |
| Cost of sales |  |  |  |
| Materials | 134.5 | 195.1 | 252.7 |
| Labor and related costs | 26.4 | 26.0 | 29.6 |
| Outworkers services | n.a. | 141.6 | 170.0 |
| Depreciation | 12.6 | 15.0 | 6.6 |
| Other costs‡ | n.a.‡ | 15.6‡ | 16.8‡ |
| Total | n.a. | 393.3 | 475.8 |
| Gross profit | n.a. | 168.9 | 238.2 |
| Selling, general, and administrative expenses |  |  |  |
| Labor and related costs | n.a. | 22.7 | 22.1 |
| Distribution | n.a. | 23.4 | 22.9 |
| Sales commissions | n.a. | 23.2 | 30.4 |
| Advertising and promotion | n.a. | 14.4 | 20.4 |
| Depreciation | 6.3 | 8.1 | 16.2 |
| Other costs and expenses | n.a. | 26.9 | 31.6 |
| Total | n.a. | 118.7 | 143.6 |
| Income from operations | 47.3 | 50.2 | 94.6 |
| Other (income) expenses |  |  |  |
| Interest income | (3.5) | (8.3) | (11.4) |
| Interest expense | 20.7 | 37.2 | 42.0 |
| Other expense, net | 1.1 | 1.0 | (.9) |
| Total | 18.3 | 29.9 | 29.6 |
| Income before taxes and minority interest | 29.0 | 20.3 | 64.9 |
| Income taxes | 12.6 | 8.6 | 30.8 |
| Income before minority interest | 16.4 | 11.7 | 34.2 |
| Loss of consolidated subsidiaries attributable to minority interest | n.a. | 1.5 | 3.0 |
| Net income for the year | 16.4 | 13.2 | 37.2 |

*Constructed by casewriters.
†*Source:* Published Group statements.
‡Includes royalties paid to INVEP parent of Lit13 billion in 1982 and unstated amounts in 1983 and 1984.
*Note:* Average exchange rates for 1982, 1983, and 1984 were Lit1,300, Lit1,519, and Lit1,757 to $1, respectively.
n.a. = not available.

mally to Palmeri as well as Carlo Benetton. And managers in the commercial function continued working directly with Luciano Benetton. When Aluffi resigned, he was not replaced.

As a result, by the spring of 1985, the senior managers of Benetton were organized in the manner shown in Exhibit 3. Most of the senior functional managers had two reporting relationships, a formal one to Aldo Palmeri and an informal one to a member of the Benetton family.

EXHIBIT 2

## CONSOLIDATED BALANCE SHEET OF THE BENETTON GROUP, DECEMBER 31, 1982, 1983, AND 1984
(Lit Billion)

|  | 1982* | 1983† | 1984† |
|---|---|---|---|
| Current assets |  |  |  |
| Cash | 3.4 | 14.5 | 19.1 |
| Marketable securities | n.a. | 24.7 | 41.1 |
| Accounts receivable (less allowance for doubtful accounts) | 140.1 | 227.2 | 253.2 |
| Inventories | 49.6 | 92.8 | 100.4 |
| Prepayments | n.a. | 4.0 | 7.4 |
| Total | 225.4 | 363.2 | 421.4 |
| Investments and other noncurrent assets |  |  |  |
| Investments and loans to affiliates | n.a. | 5.0 | 4.7 |
| Guarantee deposits | n.a. | 0.9 | 0.7 |
| Total | 8.4 | 5.9 | 5.4 |
| Fixed assets |  |  |  |
| Land and buildings | n.a. | 52.8 | 68.8 |
| Plant, machinery and equipment | n.a. | 37.7 | 64.5 |
| Office equipment, furniture, and leasehold improvements | n.a. | 16.6 | 6.7 |
| Vehicles and aircraft | n.a. | 6.4 | 14.2 |
| Less accumulated depreciation | (22.6) | (46.7) | (66.3) |
| Construction in progress and advances | n.a. | 27.6 | — |
| Total | 49.3 | 94.3 | 87.9 |
| Intangible assets |  |  |  |
| Licenses and trademarks | n.a. | 9.1 | 8.3 |
| Deferred charges | n.a. | 3.9 | 2.9 |
| Total | n.a. | 13.0 | 11.2 |
| Total assets | 283.1 | 476.5 | 525.6 |
| Current liabilities |  |  |  |
| Bank overdrafts | 47.3 | 98.1 | 94.5 |
| Current portion of long-term loans | n.a. | 26.0 | 24.4 |
| Accounts payable | 72.6 | 122.4 | 150.6 |
| Other payables and accruals | n.a. | 18.4 | 21.0 |
| Accrual for exchange losses | 2.0 | 2.0 | 1.7 |
| Reserve for income taxes | 0.3 | 5.1 | 23.9 |
| Total | 139.1 | 272.0 | 316.1 |
| Long-term liabilities |  |  |  |
| Long-term loans, net of current portion | 52.3 | 81.0 | 64.9 |
| Reserve for severance indemnities | 3.7 | 5.9 | 6.9 |
| Total | 56.0 | 86.9 | 71.8 |
| Reserve for capital gains to be reinvested | n.a. | 0.9 | 0.6 |
| Minority interest in consolidated subsidiaries | n.a. | 2.1 | — |
| Stockholders' equity |  |  |  |
| Capital stock | 8.0 | 8.0 | 8.0 |
| Surplus from spinoff and monetary revaluation of assets | n.a. | 81.6 | 81.6 |
| Other reserves and prior years' retained earnings | n.a. | 12.8 | 11.5 |
| Net income for the year | 16.4 | 13.2 | 37.2 |
| Less treasury stock | n.a. | (1.1) | (1.1) |
| Total | 88.0 | 114.5 | 137.1 |
| Total liabilities and stockholders' equity | 283.1 | 476.5 | 525.6 |

*Constructed by casewriters.
†*Source:* Published Group statements.
n.a. = not available.

**EXHIBIT 3**

## TOP MANAGEMENT ORGANIZATION RELATIONSHIPS, BENETTON SpA (GROUP)

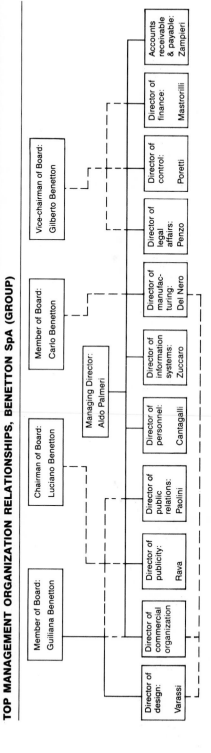

*Source:* Based on casewriters' interpretations. Dotted lines signify informal reporting relationships.

The director of design largely worked with Giuliana Benetton, coordinating efforts with manufacturing and marketing (commercial). Marketing-related functions reported informally to Luciano Benetton, who took primary responsibility for marketing in the absence of a director of commercial activities. Directors of the finance, control, and legal functions all worked informally with Gilberto Benetton. And Carlo Benetton maintained a direct but informal working relationship with the director of manufacturing as well as the managers of several of the company's factories, until recently sharing an office with the manager of the Ponzano plant.

The senior management was responsible to the group's Consiglio d'Administratione (board of directors), comprised of the Benettons, Palmeri, and Angelo Bianchi, a personal advisor to the Benetton family, with Luciano Benetton as chairman. The board met monthly to take up matters concerning the general direction of the firm as well as specific proposals for capital expenditures or projects. For example, it had approved the proposal by Palmeri that the U.S. consultant in information systems be hired. In addition, it was thought that the Benettons themselves met from time to time to reach agreement on such matters as the hiring of their children into the organization (something they had only recently decided to do as two Benetton offspring reached their mid-twenties).

Within the past eight months, a management committee chaired by Palmeri had been formed and met roughly every three weeks. Comprising the directors of the manufacturing, finance, control, personnel, and commercial functions, it had served largely as what one executive termed "a channel of communication." Nevertheless, at one of its recent meetings it had approved the hiring of Hay and Associates to carry out a job evaluation study prior to an overhaul of the company's compensation program.

Of the nine directors reporting directly to Palmeri, Del Nero had been with the firm the longest, approximately 30 months. Paolini, director of public relations, had been hired in 1983 from a newspaper where he was a journalist. Can-

tagalli, director of personnel, had joined Benetton in 1983 from a similar position with Minnesota Mining and Manufacturing in Italy. Mastrorilli, director of finance, Penzo, director of legal affairs, and Rava, director of publicity, all had been hired in 1984. Penzo also had come from Minnesota Mining and Manufacturing, and Rava had been employed by an advertising agency. The most recent arrivals had been the directors of control and information systems. The latter, Zuccaro, had been hired from Zanussi, a large Italian manufacturer of appliances, following the outside consultant's study. Many of these arrivals came from outside the Veneto region.

The position of director of commercial activities had been vacant since Lucio Zotta had been asked to leave the organization in January 1984. During his brief eight-month relationship with the company, Zotta had, however, implemented the reorganization of the commercial function shown in Exhibit 4. It delineated the responsibilities and reporting relationships for area and product managers. The former were responsible for new store development, store management, and retailer credit. The latter engaged primarily in selecting the final product line, negotiating prices with manufacturing, managing service levels provided to company agents and clients (store owners), and advising clients on product selection.

Nearly all the members of the commercial organization had been hired by Luciano Benetton and had been accustomed to working directly with him. He was described by one associate as having built a highly loyal commercial organization that followed "the Benetton line that encouraged people to be aggressive, to try. You can make mistakes if you don't make too many." Several had resented the hiring of Zotta as commercial director. This was exacerbated by what one member of the organization described as Mr. Zotta's management style:

Perhaps reflecting the fact that he came to us from STANDA, a large department store organization headquartered in Milan, his manner was more di-

**EXHIBIT 4**

## COMMERCIAL ORGANIZATION, THE BENETTON GROUP

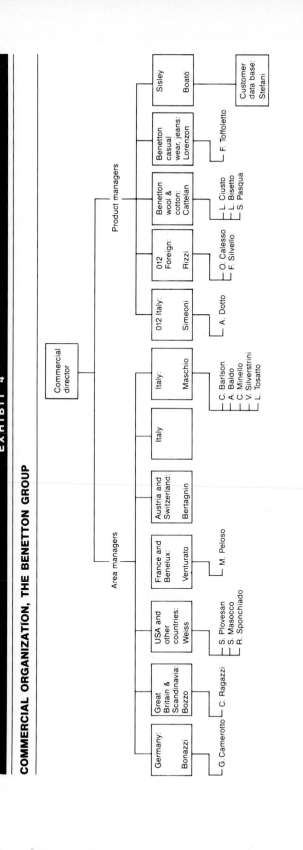

rect than that of the typical Veneto manager. When he said yes or no, you knew he meant it. Like other newcomers, he worked behind closed doors. The owners' doors have always been open to anyone in the company.

Until a new director of commercial activities could be found, Luciano Benetton was once again filling the role.

## DIRECTION AND CONTROL

Much of the strategic planning for the Benetton Group had been carried out in the past by members of the family. Their concurrence had, for example, led to the acquisition of a high-fashion design house, Fiorucci, and a shoe manufacturer, Calza Turificio di Varese, in 1982. The former was thought to add prestige to the Benetton name. The latter, manufacturing a million pairs of shoes per year, was thought to provide a natural product line extension. As Luciano Benetton had put it:

> When we started making trousers, we thought this already might be a different sector. Instead, it was coordinated exactly as we can coordinate the shoes. . . . If the common denominator is clothing, we will also have to produce evening dresses. But we don't because ours is the "casual" market segment comprising clothing without too much elegance for specific hours of the day.[3]

Until his departure, Elio Aluffi had managed the budgeting process out of what one executive termed "his black book." Basically, it consisted of collecting estimates from the field of the number of pieces that might be ordered by stores during the year, estimates from agents and area managers of the number of pieces needed to stock new stores that might be opened during the year, and estimates from product managers of average prices for items to be offered. These data were compared with manufacturing capability, and the budget was developed based on the number of pieces projected for shipment. The process began in July of each year with a final revenue and expense budget developed by December for the following year. The results were described as "typically conservative." Even in 1983, when the company had experienced a downturn in sales as the result of a weak Italian market, sales results had exceeded expectations.

Goals for managers implicitly were tied to the budgeting process. For example, product managers were expected to ship a certain number of pieces for their respective product lines. Area managers were expected to develop a targeted number of new store openings and maintain a low level of bad-debt losses to retailers.

Goals for senior executives were described by several as "self set." For example, when he had joined the organization, Giovanni Cantagalli, director of personnel, had set out with encouragement from the owners, both to reduce the company's payroll and improve relations with the union. Now that both had been achieved, he was developing a program in human resource management that would encompass personal development, job progression, and an improved compensation scheme. The goals of the latter were to bring compensation more closely in line with responsibility and raise salary levels above the average for the area. Under a system in which executives received no bonuses or other incentives, morale was thought to have suffered.

## COORDINATION OF MARKETING AND MANUFACTURING

The reorganization of the commercial function by product and area had raised questions concerning not only roles and relationships of product and area managers but also the process by which commercial and manufacturing activities might be most effectively coordinated. Essentially, two different models had evolved for managing these relationships. Important to an understanding of these two models is a review of the seasonal cycle and the supply chain re-

---

[3] Kenneth Labich, "Benetton Takes on the World," *Fortune*, June 13, 1983, p. 119.

quired to get Benetton's products from design to the retail shops.

## Seasonal Cycle and Supply Chain[4]

Roughly 21 months elapsed from the preparation of clothing designs for a particular selling season to the final payment of commissions to Benetton agents, as shown in Exhibit 5 for the spring-summer season, one of the two major annual selling seasons. Basic steps in the process included the preparation of designs, the production of samples of each of up to 600 items in the line, and the review and elimination of about a fourth of the items in a "prepresentation" meeting process involving Giuliana Benetton, product and manufacturing managers, and several of the company's agents. The remaining items were then produced in small quantities for presentation by members of the design group to agents and by agents to their individual franchisees in a process that extended from mid-May to mid-July. Within two weeks after the collection of the first orders from franchisees by agents in early June, a rough production plan for the season, by fabrics and styles, was "exploded" from the first 5 to 10 percent of total orders. This allowed time for the placement of final orders for purchased threads and garments as well as negotiations with subcontractors for necessary increases or decreases in subcontracted volumes prior to the start of production of so-called basic retail stocks early in July in advance of the company's three- to four-week vacation in August.

As orders for basic stocks were received from agents, they were assigned reserved slots in the rough production plan by fabric, style, color, and individual store. These orders were produced for delivery to stores from early November through late May for a sales season beginning early in January in the stores. They were scheduled so that each store could present 80 to 90 percent of all items (fabrics, styles, and colors

in its basic collection) to its customers at the outset of the selling season. Other items and remaining quantities ordered arrived at the stores during the selling season.

Because Benetton required its clients (store owners) to commit themselves to specific orders seven months in advance of the start of the selling season, it provided several opportunities to clients to adjust the actual items presented to their customers. From August through early December as they gathered more information about color preferences, clients and agents were allowed to specify colors of woven items previously ordered and held in "greggio" (grey form) and not yet dyed to order. Up to 30 percent of total orders for the basic collection could be ordered in this fashion. During this period, Benetton's product managers negotiated with agents to encourage them to concentrate their orders on items achieving the highest order popularity.

A second process, called the "flash collection," involved the addition of about 50 items to each season's product line based on early customer requests for fabric-style-color combinations not found in the store. This occurred for the spring-summer collection in January and required the analysis of requests by Benetton's product and manufacturing managers and a subset of agents prior to the presentation of the flash collection by agents to the stores.

A third process, "reassortment," involved the acceptance of additional orders for rapid delivery later in the selling season, approximately March for the spring-summer collection. Fill-in reassortment orders were processed for store delivery roughly five weeks from the date of their receipt at Benetton. The service was made available only for a small number of items determined through a process of negotiation between Benetton's product managers, its manufacturing management, and agents. Because of its process of dyeing grey garments, Benetton's plant at Ponzano could fill an order within seven days of its receipt from an agent. This practice, occasionally requested by agents through Luciano Benetton and product managers, was not encouraged, because it often resulted in dye

---

[4]Much of this section also appears in Case Thirty-Four.

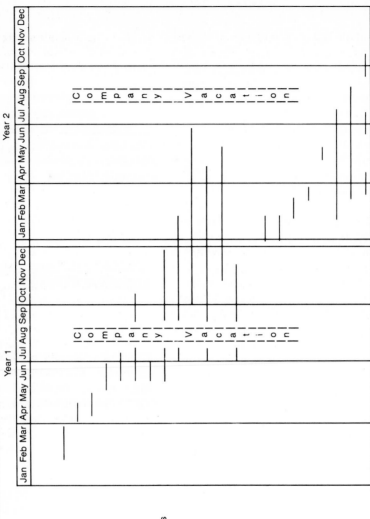

**EXHIBIT 5**

**STEPS IN OPERATING CYCLE, BENETTON GROUP SPRING-SUMMER SEASON**

batches smaller than vat capacity and interfered with long-standing production plans. Because of the need for careful quality control and rapid response when necessary, as much dyeing as possible was concentrated at the Ponzano plant.

The two major collections (spring-summer and fall-winter) were planned so that about 80 percent of a season's total sales volume was represented by the basic collection, less than 10 percent by the flash collection, and less than 10 percent by reassortment. The remaining sales were realized from a small "cruise" collection presented in the spring and a small Christmas collection presented in the fall. In total, sales of the spring-summer collection approximated 40 percent of a typical year's sales volume.

## The Benetton Product Line

The first of two approaches to the management of the supply chain involved the Benetton product line, constituting about 70 percent of the company's sales in pieces. Relationships involved in this approach are shown in a simplified manner by the diagram in Exhibit 6.

A Benetton employee of 13 years from near Treviso who had joined the company at the invitation of Giuliana Benetton when it had a total of three people in the commercial function, described elements of her role as product manager of all Benetton wool and cotton items (excluding only jeans) as follows:

At the outset of a new season, I meet with the designers who present their latest styles and colors. Through the prepresentation process, we eliminate a number of these. At the same time, manufacturing management makes an initial determination of the prices at which each item can be sold, based on production cost and an assumed manufacturing margin, and I then negotiate with them for adjustments in certain of these prices where I think it is necessary to the product line.

As agents present the resulting line to their clients, we test the market on the basis of early orders. As a result of an analysis of these orders, I negotiate with agents for the cancellation of certain items with few sales from the line.

At the time of reassortment we pay particular attention to order patterns in order to be able to advise agents which items they should suggest that their clients reorder. This requires that we coordinate with manufacturing to make sure that they can produce the orders in a five-week cycle and that the number of items for which this is permitted is not too high. At this time of year, I spend a great deal of time talking with our area managers and agents about the priorities with which such orders should be processed. This too requires many discussions with manufacturing.

As Mr. (Luciano) Benetton has correctly pointed out, reassortment is the most critical step in the marketing effort. It has a great impact on the service our clients experience, and its management is very important. . . . I used to spend a great deal of time matching clients with products. With the increase in both clients and products, this has become impossible. It is much more important that we have the right product than that the agents know the market; therefore, we have to have larger collections. . . . When questions arise or I need help with something, I have always been able to turn to Luciano Benetton. . . .

At one time when Benetton offered only woolen garments, this same product manager had been responsible both for area and product management for the entire line. As of spring 1985, she was responsible for items representing about 15 million pieces in annual sales. She continued to maintain close contact with individual clients, especially during the reassortment process, but while this had been accomplished at one time by visits to Italian store sites (in part reflecting her strong preference for speaking Italian), she now had to rely heavily on telephone and telex.

From time to time, questions had arisen concerning the relative responsibilities of product and area managers, particularly around issues of responsibility for and communication about negotiations leading to both the flash collection and reassortment. In order to clarify relationships at one critical moment, Luciano Benetton had made product managers for the Benetton product lines solely responsible for these matters. They had been particularly effective in

EXHIBIT 6

**MANAGEMENT RELATIONSHIPS IN THE SUPPLY CHAIN FOR BENETTON COTTON AND WOOLEN ITEMS**

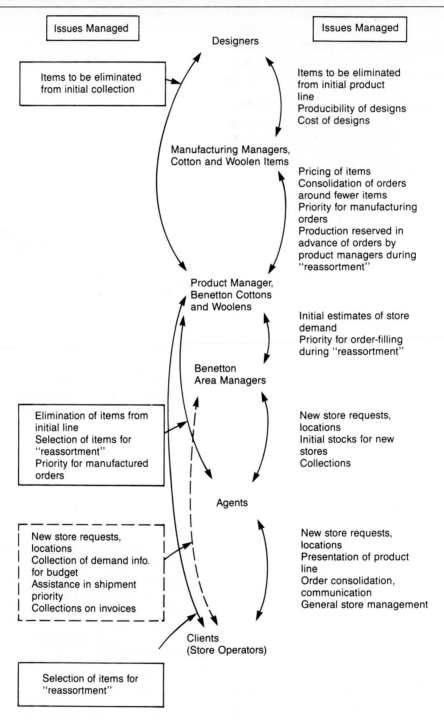

Issues Managed

Issues Managed

Designers

Items to be eliminated from initial collection

Items to be eliminated from initial product line
Producibility of designs
Cost of designs

Manufacturing Managers, Cotton and Woolen Items

Pricing of items
Consolidation of orders around fewer items
Priority for manufacturing orders
Production reserved in advance of orders by product managers during "reassortment"

Product Manager, Benetton Cottons and Woolens

Initial estimates of store demand
Priority for order-filling during "reassortment"

Benetton Area Managers

Elimination of items from initial line
Selection of items for "reassortment"
Priority for manufactured orders

New store requests, locations
Initial stocks for new stores
Collections

Agents

New store requests, locations
Collection of demand info. for budget
Assistance in shipment priority
Collections on invoices

New store requests, locations
Presentation of product line
Order consolidation, communication
General store management

Clients (Store Operators)

Selection of items for "reassortment"

dealing with Benetton's more senior agents on these matters.

Area managers, however, primarily were responsible for the location and timing of new store openings (following what were termed "guidelines" from Luciano Benetton), the development of sales projections on which the budget was based, assistance to agents and store operators in matters of merchandising and order replenishment, and collections of receivables on orders shipped to the stores. All were Italian and based at Ponzano but spent a great deal of time in their respective areas. The area manager for the United States and other countries, described his role as follows:

> Nearly half of my time is spent traveling. I probably spend more time in the United States than anyone else in the company, maybe as much as some of our U.S. agents. Much of this time is spent with agents in going over proposed locations other than the "lead" or "experimental" store locations that Mr. Benetton handles himself. (One example of an experiment was the new store on Fifth Avenue in New York that was nearly ten times larger than the typical Benetton outlet and carried all of the company's lines.) Time spent in the stores helps me assist agents in anticipating problems and balancing stocks between their stores. To assist in this, most of the stores now send me every week a daily sales summary showing units sold by general category of merchandise. Thus far, product managers haven't expressed much interest in the information in this report. . . . I spend time with agents helping them select items to present to each of their stores to ensure that stores located near one another have different "looks." Right now, area managers are doing this on their own initiative. We could use more help from product managers on this task. . . .
>
> Reassortment is another problem. With the growing number of countries in which Benetton sells its products, the number of so-called best sellers is increasing because preferences are not the same. Ideally, product managers should choose a reassortment list for each country based on particular knowledge of the market. But they don't travel, and therefore they are influenced too much by the agents. . . . Because there are five area managers, our suggestions don't come across to

> product managers with one voice. They are sometimes contradictory, so they are not acted on.

Much of this area manager's time recently had been taken up in the development of distribution agreements for Benetton products in Eastern Europe, including the USSR. The day following his interview with the casewriters would be spent in Yugoslavia.

The manager of manufacturing for woolen products and the manager of the Ponzano plant described the impact of trends in the supply chain on their work. (The interview was interrupted for an hour, during which the manager of manufacturing discussed by telephone with Carlo Benetton a technical problem in Benetton's French plant.) According to the manager of manufacturing:

> The reorganization of the commercial function didn't affect us much. We still communicate only with the product managers just as before. What we do notice are trends in product preferences. Now that half of all wool items are multicolored, it has meant that we dye a smaller proportion from the grey garment. With the growth in volume, we wouldn't have been able to handle it otherwise in our dyeing operation. As it is, we are planning to double our dyeing capacity to be able to bring more of our dyeing work in-house. That doesn't necessarily mean that we see a greater use of the reassortment process, with changes in the dyeing schedule that it requires. On the contrary, we would prefer to see the practice diminish in importance.
>
> Of course, we would like to see the product managers exert a greater influence on agents and clients to produce the right balance and concentration of production, especially for reassortment. Recently, we ended up with too many small orders for items and had to cancel orders involving about 300,000 units. We recommended doing that rather than favoring one agent as opposed to another; the commercial department accepted our proposal. Most of the agents adjusted their orders accordingly. Of course, this would not have been necessary if sales could have been concentrated in advance. But this will never happen because Benetton will never constrain the agent. . . .
>
> In general, the business today requires more items and more complicated items to produce. This

makes production planning and time and motion study more difficult. But while we've gone to electronic knitting and sent more and more of our knitting to contractors, our work here has not changed all that much. . . . I spend more of my time on the telephone talking with Carlo Benetton since he moved out of my office and into the Villa (several hundred feet away). That move was necessary because of his increasing responsibility, especially for existing and possible new plant investment outside Italy. . . . (See Exhibit 7 for a chart of organization for Benetton's manufacturing function.)

## The 012 Product Line

The 012 product line for children was managed by a native of the Lombardy region north of Milan who had been a children's department buyer in the Mestre store (near Venice) of the COIN chain of department stores. She was originally hired as a potential area manager, but after spending an orientation period in England, she had nearly decided that the problems of communication with the Ponzano headquarters were so great that she would not take the job when Luciano Benetton suggested that she try her hand as product manager for 012 outside of Italy. At the time, the 012 line represented about 20 percent of total pieces sold by Benetton. Its growth rate had been declining. It was suggested that instead of working with area managers in dealing with agents she work directly with the six agents who specialized in 012 stores. As she put it:

It's important that 012 be separately identified in this process. After all, it represents a small proportion of total company sales. It's quite natural for agents and area managers alike to give it a lower priority when thinking about store management, information feedback, and reassortment. . . . I have to maintain a close contact with each major market. The customer needs and the competition are so different in each one. For example, customers in Germany, England, and the United States are interested in cheap, practical clothing that washes easily. In Italy, children are treated and dressed like princes and princesses.

To some extent, this is true of France as well. . . . You have to travel to these markets to be able to read field reports from agents and actual sales orders accurately. . . .

The process begins for me in discussions with Giuliana Benetton and her assistant in which they share their views of style and fashion with my concerns about markets and competition. I try to bring samples of competitors' styles to these meetings, but not for us to copy. . . . It used to be that manufacturing set the prices based on costs established by the time and methods engineers on a take-it-or-leave-it basis. With the support of Mr. Del Nero (corporate director of manufacturing) we now negotiate prices so that I can have the right number of items at various price levels and still be competitive in each market. In this process, my goal is to produce a net profit for the line of 10 percent, keeping in mind that the stores in each country mark up the merchandise different amounts, ranging from about 85 percent in Italy to 175 percent (including tariffs) in the United States. . . .

But I spend a good deal of my time working with the agents and the stores. After all, if the stores are not successful, we feel it in the long run. As a result, I am particularly interested in the early orders. We have to move fast on those because the 012 line is produced first each season. . . . And then reassortment is always a challenge. When I think the basic collection is poorly bought by the stores, I'll place an order "libero" with manufacturing and then sell the items to agents. If I wait until the clients reorder, it's too late. Last year when that happened, we were unable to fill orders for 200,000 pieces. . . . The goal given to 012 for this year worldwide is 6 million pieces in sales, both in existing stores and those that we plan to open. That's how my performance will be measured.

## The "United Colors of Benetton" Program

Benetton's philosophy had been to develop one product line of sufficient breadth to accommodate the needs of particular markets and stores. The story was told by one executive that an area manager had suggested that a line of outsized garments be produced for his market. Luciano

**EXHIBIT 7**

## CHART OF ORGANIZATION, MANUFACTURING FUNCTION, THE BENETTON GROUP

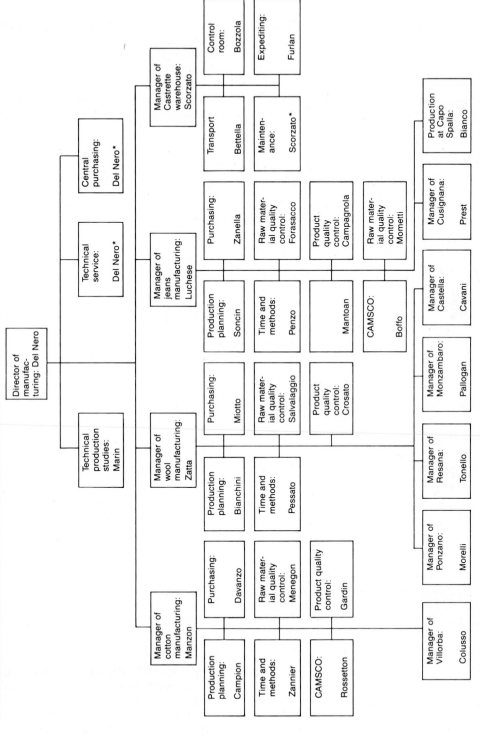

*Provisionally.

**551**

Benetton is said to have remarked that he didn't want that kind of customer wearing a Benetton garment.

Through the process of preselection, the flash collection, and reassortment, it was thought that a single product line could be adjusted to meet the needs of particular markets. But it was thought important that the line have a unity and the Italian design feel provided by the all-Italian core of freelance designers employed by Giuliana Benetton.

The most recent advertising campaign reflected this philosophy. Recommended by the Italian branch of Benetton's U.S.-based advertising agency, it featured a series of panels showing people of various ages and races wearing a variety of colorful Benetton garments under a common headline in English, "The United Colors of Benetton." It was to be used worldwide, primarily in billboard advertising and for shelf-talkers in retail outlets.

## THE U.S. STRATEGY

The rapid growth of the U.S. market following Benetton's decision to enter it in 1982 had raised questions about future strategy for that market.

At the time of entry, the United States had been divided into 20 territories. Existing Benetton agents were then given the opportunity to request one or more territories. In all, 13 agents were awarded the 20 territories. All were European in background and residence, but all agreed to establish and staff small offices in each territory to handle matters concerning store development and order consolidation. It was thought to be much more important that agents understand the Benetton way of doing things than have a knowledge of a specific market.

Initially, an effort was made to establish Benetton departments on a nonexclusive basis in department stores such as Macy's and Associated Dry Goods. But Benetton soon found that the department stores assigned only one person to the department, paid insufficient attention to the product on the shelf, and equated Benet-

ton's casual merchandise with low price, buying primarily the lower-priced items in the line. When sales did not exceed 1,500 pieces per season in most shops, the arrangements were terminated by 1984.

In the meantime, Benetton had launched its own stand-alone stores through its U.S. agents. The lead effort in each major market consisted of Luciano Benetton's careful attention to lead store location and company ownership of the store. One such lead store was established on Fifth Avenue in New York; although only 600 square feet in area, it quickly developed the highest volume of any Benetton store in the world. And it became one of a cluster of stores developed by agents and their clients.

Over time, adjustments had been made in Benetton's policies concerning the U.S. market. For example, its long-standing standard markup of 80 percent of landed cost was found to be too low for the U.S. market. By U.S. law, Benetton could only suggest retail prices to its agents and clients. And the program for payment of invoices had been adjusted to call for 50 percent of payment 60 days after the beginning date of a season and 50 percent after 90 days to reflect sales patterns in the U.S. markets.

Although Giuliana Benetton from time to time personally collected samples from the U.S. market, the company employed no U.S. designers. Nevertheless, acceptance of Benetton's products in the United States was rapid. As shown in Exhibits 8 and 9, store and sales increases were impressive. These had been supported by a supply chain depending on the electronic transmission of orders collected by agents from their regional offices and the use of ocean transport for early shipments and air shipments from Italy for subsequent orders. Benetton had not established a warehouse in the United States.

This had given rise to a number of questions concerning the future strategy for supplying a U.S. market that was variously estimated to be able to support from 800 to 2,000 Benetton stores. Specifically, Palmeri and his staff were weighing the advantages of establishing a separate U.S. subsidiary for Benetton. The necessary analysis

## EXHIBIT 8

**TRENDS IN NUMBER OF RETAIL SHOPS, BENETTON GROUP, BY COUNTRY AND MAJOR BRAND, 1982–1984**

| | Number of shops | | |
|---|---|---|---|
| | **1982** | **1983** | **1984** |
| **Country** | | | |
| Italy | 1,165 | 1,227 | 1,253 |
| France | 283 | 387 | 430 |
| W. Germany | 168 | 233 | 285 |
| United States | 32 | 66 | 190 |
| United Kingdom | 44 | 63 | 85 |
| Spain | 9 | 19 | 61 |
| Canada | 3 | 5 | 17 |
| Other | 213 | 296 | 323 |
| Total | 1,917 | 2,296 | 2,644 |
| **Brand** | | | |
| Benetton | 1,236 | 1,528 | 1,794 |
| 012 | 545 | 625 | 701 |
| Sisley | 136 | 143 | 149 |
| Total | 1,917 | 2,296 | 2,644 |

to support such a decision had not yet been carried out, although in late 1982 it was estimated that the establishment of a plant in the United States might require an investment of perhaps $10 million and labor costs perhaps 50 percent higher than at the Ponzano plant, and a much higher cost for grey garments if they were sourced in the United States in the same manner as in Italy.[5] Nevertheless, such a plant could help Benetton avert the high transport costs and a 35 percent tariff incurred in importing product to the United States from Italy.

The analysis would have to provide a basis for assessing the scope as well as the desirability of such a move. For example, should the subsidiary have any responsibility for product design? Should it have any marketing capability? Or should it continue to rely on the agents, area managers, and product managers currently representing the company? Should it be able to arrange separate financing that would be needed to support U.S. growth? What responsibility should it have for warehousing product in the United States? Should Benetton establish a manufacturing capability in the United States, especially for cotton items for which it found itself less competitive? If so, should such a facility have dyeing capability and operate in much the same fashion as the plant at Ponzano? And how should the U.S. subsidiary relate to its Italian parent, especially at a time when its parent was itself experiencing an evolution in its own organization?

---

[5] For a more extensive discussion of the logistics of supplying the U.S. market, see Case Thirty-Two.

## EXHIBIT 9

**TRENDS IN BENETTON GROUP SHIPMENTS TO ALL MARKETS AND UNITED STATES** (Thousands)

| Year | Total pieces* | Total pieces to U.S.* | Benetton-manufactured pieces shipped to U.S. |
|---|---|---|---|
| 1982 | 26,900 | — | — |
| 1983 | 27,600 | 596† | 541 |
| 1984 | 31,000 | 1,988‡ | 1,818 |
| 1985(e) | 35,000§ | 4,158 | 4,000 |

*Including items such as gloves and scarves not manufactured by Benetton.

†Revenues to the Benetton Group from these shipments were Lit10.706 billion or about $7,048,000 at the average exchange rate for 1983 of Lit1,519 lire to $1.

‡Revenues to the Benetton Group from these shipments were Lit46.253 billion or about $26,295,000 at the average exchange rate for 1984 of Lit1,757 to $1.

§It was estimated that about 45 percent of these pieces would be woolen, 27 percent cotton, and 28 percent other, including jeans.

All these questions were foremost in Palmeri's mind as he prepared for his next meeting of the board as well as a trip to the United States to view its market development first-hand.

# Benetton: Between Armani and Coca-Cola

PONZANO, Italy—At 8:30 one recent June morning, Gianni Tossiti drove up to the sprawling Benetton compound in Ponzano, a small country village 20 miles north of Venice. He announced his name to the guard who stands behind a glass booth at the gate, was let inside and asked to wait. Luciano Benetton, already in his first of many meetings that day, was running a little behind.

Tossiti, who as chairman of F.T.M., a consulting and distributing firm that works with Soprani, Basile and others, heads up a firm that grossed $25 million last year. He is not in general the kind of board chairman who finds it necessary to hightail it to small country villages to snag a deal. But Tossiti, part owner with Benetton in a line of medium- to high-price apparel called Hike, makes the three-hour trip from Milan to Ponzano twice a month to meet with Luciano Benetton.

"I find it tiring to go out there so often, but it's necessary," says Tossiti. "Luciano is a somewhat enigmatic person. He's not a big talker, and he's a bit of a hermit. For him, results are everything."

Benetton, the dark horse of the Italian fashion industry, the man who says that if he weren't in apparel he'd be in the fast-food business, the outsider from Ponzano who early on made it clear he didn't need anybody else's factories, anybody else's financing, PR hype, or help, has the Milan fashion industry coming to him—if he wants it, which he doesn't seem to. To Luciano Benetton, his apparel is industrial first, fashion second.

"We're somewhere between Armani and Coca-Cola," he assesses, laughing slightly.

At age 50, Benetton heads a 20-year-old firm that has broken every rule in the Italian fashion industry

and grossed $400 million last year. A shy, affable man on meeting, Benetton has the look of a Trotskyite professor and the dreams of a Horatio Alger hero. He started his firm out of his home in 1964, selling sweaters designed by his sister, Giuliana, and today he, his two brothers and sister control the largest apparel manufacturing-retailing business in Europe.

The Benetton stores—the little green shops that have sprouted at the rate of one a day across the world—now number 3,000 and sold some 38 million pieces of clothing last year. Benetton wants to open a store in every country in the world, and he's got a good shot at it. In March, he opened in Budapest, in April in Belgrade and in September, he'll open in Prague. Meantime, talks are going on to open next year in Moscow, Beijing, Shanghai.

The master behind this worldwide conversion to "Benettonitis" is a soft-spoken man, with very blue eyes, very white teeth, graying hair that's overdue for a trim and an easy smile that makes him look at least 10 years younger than his 50 years. His way of dressing is casual even for the Benetton crowd: worn, button-down shirts from Brooks Bros. or Paul Stuart, casual slacks and boots.

If the image he conveys of himself doesn't mesh with the big-money seriousness of his firm, the marketing mind behind it does. Benetton considers himself a meditative type and believes that his lack of training and experience allowed him to enter the apparel manufacturing-retailing world with a fresh approach.

He is thoughtful about explaining all of this—in a measured, self-effacing style that reeks with good manners. In fact, Benetton promotes such an easy air of confidence and cordiality that it acts as a shield: He's an intensely private person whose wall of policies is almost impossible to pierce. It is obvious from the empire he has created, however, that his entrepreneurship is laced with grit.

Every now and then, the shark beneath the still water shakes a fin—such as when he talks about the retail revolution he has masterminded. Benetton has consistently held that the company's success is due to its ability to connect directly with the consumer, without the middleman—the retailer—getting in the way.

His well-documented thoughts on the subject are that the traditional store owner with his power to buy only certain products from a manufacturer and with complete control over display and sales had to be "killed—and we killed him." Along this vein, Benetton also believes that an ex-florist or ex-hairdresser is as fit and able to manage a Benetton as an experienced apparel retailer—"if not better."

"Investing in a Benetton store is not like investing in the stock market," he says. "Each person starts with one boutique, and we watch their progress very carefully." While the stores are franchised—and therefore involve no investment on the firm's part in terms of financing or capital—the franchiser enters into a tight agreement with Benetton to follow one of five types of interior design and to purchase only Benetton products—though each store owner may select his own product mix.

Born in 1935 in Treviso, Italy, Benetton never finished school, owing to the fact that his father, a car rental dealer, died when he was 10, and his mother, Rosa, couldn't support him and his younger brothers and sister alone. The town was provincial, employment opportunities slim, and Benetton learned to keep an eye open for a deal or an opportunity. He describes himself as the kind of kid who was never the best on the basketball team but always the captain. . . .

Benetton travels two weeks out of each month: One week is always spent in the U.S. He travels by his Cessna Citation to either France or London, where he boards a Concorde for the trans-Atlantic flight.

When not traveling, Benetton makes his home in Treviso, in an old restored house ("it's small," he insists), part of which dates to the 12th century. He is divorced and lives near his ex-wife and their four children, ages 16 to 23. He says he manages to socialize with old friends "about twice a year." In fashion, he claims a close friendship with partner Elio Fiorucci, but few others.

For relaxation, Benetton enjoys spectator sports, jazz and reflecting on future possibilities, such as launching a U.S. factory, to speed deliveries and sales there.

In spite of the 12-hour days he works, Benetton says he finds plenty of time to relax because "I sleep well, even on buses."

_____

*Source: Women's Wear Daily,* June 26, 1985. Reprinted with permission. Fairchild Publications.

# Heineken— Organizational Issues

Concomitant with the rapid expansion of Heineken's international activities, a number of organizational issues arose in the early 1980s that centered on what should be the proper division of responsibilities between headquarters staff, functional directors, and the management of the operating companies. The increasing complexity and diversity of national subsidiaries and licensees together with the different stakes held by Heineken in each local company made any universal approach to managing these relationships difficult if not unworkable.

It was increasingly obvious that operating companies should be as autonomous and self-reliant as possible in order to exploit to the best of their ability all domestic market opportunities. Since market conditions, competition, and political factors varied enormously among the more than forty countries where Heineken operated, it was widely accepted that no central organization could deal effectively with this diversity.

Nonetheless, Heineken's top management felt that there were a number of issues that must be either directed or closely controlled from Amsterdam. These were not limited to marketing and brand policy; it was argued that major deviations from corporate functional policies from one country to another could entail considerable difficulties for the company's desire to achieve a uniform worldwide corporate image as well as for its effectiveness. Thus the essence of the argument was how best to reconcile these two divergent requirements and foster a willing acceptance by managers, both in the operating companies and at head office, that none could be wholly independent of the others.

## ORGANIZATIONAL EVOLUTION

During the past 20 years, Heineken had lived through a series of structural reorganizations typical of any large company which was both growing rapidly and diversifying its activities on several fronts. In the early 1960s, the company was managed by a three-person executive board (*Raad van Bestuur*) which reported to a larger

This case was written by Professor José de la Torre as a basis for discussion. The generous contribution of many Heineken executives is gratefully acknowledged, but the author retains all responsibility for any errors or misinterpretation of facts. © INSEAD, The European Institute of Business Administration, 1986.

supervisory council composed mainly of external directors. Below the board, in addition to some limited corporate functions, the company was organized into two major groups: Heineken Netherlands was responsible for exports, finance, production and technology, personnel and commercial affairs; while Heineken International handled foreign participations, licensing agreements and international finance. The three managing directors, while having direct supervisory responsibility for different aspects of the business, were jointly accountable for the whole.

After the Amstel merger in 1968, the company was reorganized into three major divisions: commercial, responsible for all Dutch sales; technical, handling all production and technical assistance worldwide; and international, with line authority over exports, licenses, and participations. Given that each member of the board had direct operational responsibility for one division, many minor decisions were constantly pushed up to the board for resolution. Faced with this problem, the company gradually returned to a collegial board management and to a geographic structure whereby all domestic operations—production and sales of beer, soft drinks, and distilled products—were grouped in one division, and the international division retained control over foreign licensing and participations as well as exports from Holland. Four regional groupings—Europe, Asia/Australia, Africa, and Western Hemisphere—were created at this time.

Throughout the 1970s, the company rebalanced its structure in a number of small but meaningful ways. A critical step was to bring the control of exports and foreign participations back to a centralized corporatewide level. The corporate marketing, exports, and technical areas were given worldwide responsibility, and regional subgroups were established within each function. Simultaneously, four overall regional "coordinators" were given strategic and coordinating responsibility for their respective regions of the world (later expanded to five) and were placed under the direct supervision of one of the members of the board. In this fashion,

whenever a decision had to be taken which concerned a specific country or region, the regional coordinator could call on his or her counterparts within the corporate functional staff. The objective of this matrix structure was to balance the need for geographic focus and coordination with the requirement for close control of critical corporate functions. Finally, beginning in 1976, greater autonomy was given to the operating units both in the Netherlands and abroad. Exhibit 1 presents a simplified version of the company's organizational structure in 1983.

## HEINEKEN N.V. AS A SHAREHOLDER

Heineken as a shareholder expected to exercise a primary influence on strategic decisions by its subsidiaries and be entitled to a return on its invested capital. Hence, it was to have the right to full information regarding the local company's financial matters and business conduct. The executive board of Heineken N.V., assisted by corporate staff from its Amsterdam head office, would handle subjects such as investment proposals, plans for the disposition of retained earnings, appraisals of operating company's performance and key executive appointments. A list of specific points for which agreement of Heineken N.V. must be sought or which would be dealt with by the parent company included:

- Major changes in organizational structure
- Approval of operational plans
- Approval of investments
- Acquisition, granting, renewal, or relinquishment of licenses
- Joint operations and/or participation agreements with third parties
- International supply contracts
- Use of corporate brands, trademarks, and patents
- Setting standards for and monitoring the quality of corporate products
- Changes in quality of products outside general specifications
- Activities which could affect other companies in which Heineken had an interest

# EXHIBIT 1

## ORGANIZATIONAL STRUCTURE, 1982

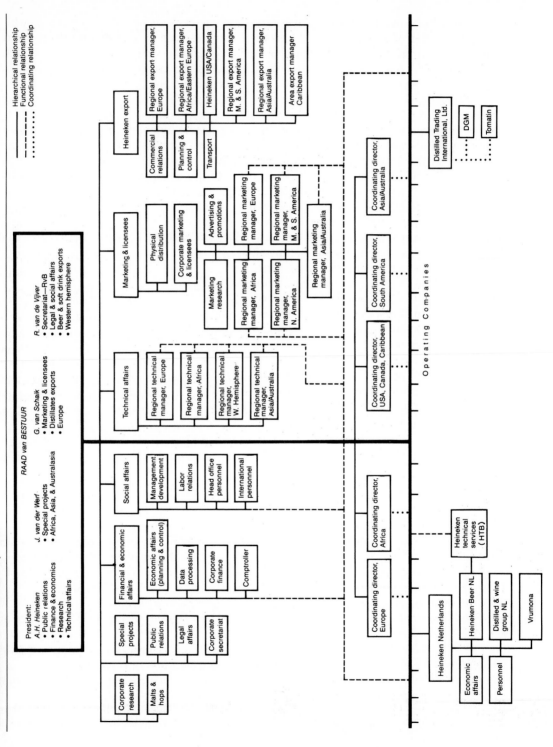

- Deviations from corporate functional policies
- Development of employees for and actual appointment to key positions
- Terms of service of expatriates
- Remuneration, emoluments, and terms of service, and the development and career planning of managers in the higher echelons
- Appraising operating company results and assessing their future broad plans and prospects

## HEINEKEN N.V. AS A SERVICE COMPANY

A second major role of Heineken N.V. was to provide assistance and service which operating companies might require in order to carry out their own as well as any corporate plans within their specific territories. In addition to the purely control activities implied in the various categories listed above, some of which included some service component (e.g., maintenance of quality standards), Heineken viewed its role to include the following areas:

- The management of each operating company was responsible for the achievement of its objectives in both the short and long term. For those policies, however, which it could not establish or evaluate autonomously, local management would decide and request the necessary assistance from Heineken N.V. staff.
- To the extent that the management of an operating company developed experience and expertise in certain areas which might be of value to other companies in which Heineken had an interest, Heineken N.V. would act as a focal point for the collection and dissemination of such knowledge for the benefit of all Heineken companies.
- For policies which the management of operating companies might wish to establish but which they were unable to evaluate fully themselves, either because this required knowledge pertaining to affairs outside their jurisdiction or because it might prejudice the affairs of other Heineken companies, advice must be obtained from Heineken N.V.

## THE ANNUAL PLANNING LETTER AND STRATEGY REVIEW

The major vehicle through which the executive board exercised its control over the activities of operating companies was the annual operational and strategic review of each subsidiary and affiliated company. As described in Case 7, beginning in 1980 a planning letter was prepared by the executive board every year and sent to each operating company. The objectives laid out in the letter would constitute the basis for a detailed 5-year plan (and a 1-year operational plan) prepared by the affiliate and discussed with the board, the regional coordinator, and other key executives, at least once a year.

## REGIONAL COORDINATING DIRECTORS

The executive board had delegated to the regional coordinating directors (RCDs) some of the aspects of the shareholding relationship with the operating companies. The degree of delegation and supervision varied considerably from region to region and, within regions, from company to company. A number of factors contributed to this variation:

- The personalities, management styles and availability of the member of the executive board responsible for that region, the RCD, and the local general manager
- The knowledge and length of service of the RCD as well as the RCD's familiarity with the issues prevalent in the region
- The size and complexity of the operating company
- Heineken's stake in the ownership of the operating company
- The history of relations between the operating company and headquarters

Specifically, RCDs were responsible to the corporate executive board or to one of its members for:

1. Promoting harmony between the operating companies with their local viewpoint, and functional coordinators and other depart-

ments in the head office with their global viewpoints

2. Appraising the operating company from the point of view of a shareholder in terms of the employment of capital already invested and the conduct of the company's operations
3. Reviewing, in cooperation with the relevant functional directors, investment prospects and projects, and agreeing with the operating company on its targets and objectives
4. Advising, in cooperation with the relevant functional directors, on management appointments after assessing past performance and future requirements
5. Keeping fellow coordinating directors and functional directors informed on political and economic affairs for the purpose of their duties
6. Seeing to it that Heineken N.V.'s viewpoint on broad policy, investment prospects, corporate objectives and targets, and staff development and appointment was provided to all affiliates within their region
7. Aiding upon request: (a) corporate functional directors to resolve their own or their staff's differences with operating companies, and (b) general managers to resolve differences between their organization and corporate functional directors or their staff.

As of January 1983, the Heineken world was organized along the following five regions: Europe, Africa, North America and the Caribbean, Central and South America, and Asia/Australia.

## FUNCTIONAL DIRECTORS

In principle, functional directors had no authority outside Heineken's corporate office other than for the promulgation of functional policies and for monitoring the adherence thereto. They were expected not to adopt an authoritative role toward an individual operating company or group of companies. Functional directors "should structure their respective organizations in such a manner that they can adequately support the regional coordinators in providing, as econom-

ically and efficiently as possible, the help and advice that operating companies require." As a result, most functional directors had chosen to structure their staff along geographic lines. Should differences of opinion arise from the interpretation by operating companies of functional policies, it would be the functional director's responsibility to bring these to the attention of the corresponding RCD and/or the Heineken executive board.

Specifically, functional directors were responsible to the executive board for:

1. Providing the executive board with functional advice
2. Initiating functional worldwide targets, objectives, and policies
3. Initiating new ideas and methods of improving performance for use in specific operating companies or throughout Heineken as a whole
4. Providing staff suitable for international service
5. Providing advice and service to: (a) RCDs to assist them in the functional aspects of their work, (b) other units in Heineken corporate office, and (c) operating companies, to assist them in achieving agreed-upon targets and objectives
6. Monitoring the adherence to agreed-upon functional policies
7. Providing operating companies with enough information on the outcome of the appraisal of their business conduct to enable general managers to remedy weaknesses in their companies or to contest the validity of the appraisal

As of January 1983, the principal functional areas at Heineken N.V. were: financial and economic affairs (including planning and control and all data processing activities), social affairs (including management development and industrial relations), marketing and licenses (including physical distribution, marketing research, and advertising and promotions), Heineken export (which handled sales to all countries where Heineken operated, excluding local produc-

---

EXHIBIT 2

**TECHNICAL MANAGEMENT AT HEINEKEN**

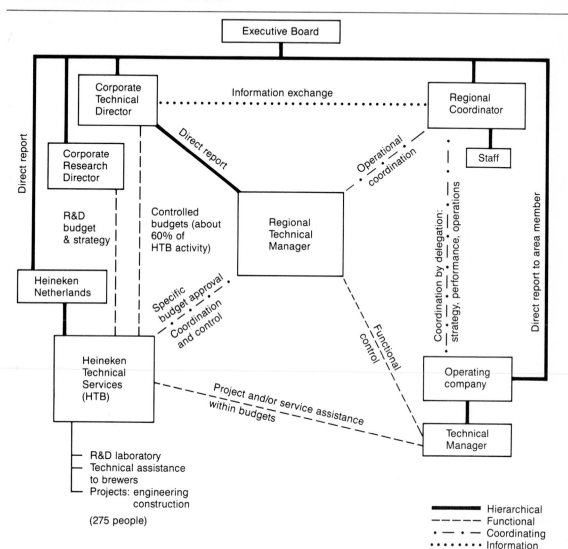

tion), corporate research, and technical affairs. Heineken Technical Services was housed within the Heineken Netherlands operating company, but its services to international subsidiaries were channeled through the corporate office of technical affairs and its regional technical managers.

The offices of special projects (e.g., the ongoing negotiations with China), public relations, legal affairs, and the corporate secretariat were also located at headquarters and reported directly to the executive board.

Since the various corporate functional directors were expected to provide all necessary support to the regions, including day-to-day operational assistance to operating companies as required, the regional coordinating directors would not normally need any staff. Some of the larger and more complex areas, however, whether as a result of the importance of their business or their geographical disparity, might require that the RCD be assisted by one or two qualified professionals. It was not expected, however, that regional coordinating directors would develop their own capability to monitor functional (as opposed to strategic or financial) performance among the various affiliates within their region. They should rely, instead, on the regional functional staff for these purposes.

As an example, Exhibit 2 illustrates the multitude of relationships involved in the technical function and the respective roles of the corporate office of technical affairs, the technical staff in the Netherlands, the operating company's technical management, and the regional coordinating director.

## THE FUTURE

In commenting on the balance of responsibility between headquarters and the operating subsidiaries, a member of the executive board stated:

> In principle we want to decentralize as much as possible; people in the field should be responsible for their contribution. But we are mainly a one-brand, one-product company which limits their freedom in terms of image and price. If you take away brand and advertising policy, financial policy, and the technology for main products, this leaves local managers with responsibility only for day-to-day and local people management issues. Is that enough?
>
> We are struggling with this problem; operating freedom means different things to various people. It is important that we balance centralized controls with the need to maintain local identity and initiative. We have made some progress in enlarging the scope for local managers, but perhaps we need to do more.

# Suji-INS K.K.

Mike Flynn, president of the International Division of Information Network Services Corporation, was undecided as to how he could best approach several delicate issues with his Japanese joint venture partner. He needed to develop an agenda for his trip to Japan, scheduled for the following day. In many ways, he considered this trip of vital importance. For one thing, the problems to be discussed were likely to affect the long-term relationship between his company and the Japanese partner in the management of their joint venture. Moreover, this was his first trip to Japan in the capacity of president of the International Division, and he was anxious to make a good impression and to begin to build a personal relationship with senior executives of the Japanese firm.

Flynn had assumed the position of president several months previously in May of 1988. He was 40 years old and was considered to be one of the most promising executives in the company. After 2 years of military service followed

by business school, he had joined a consulting company for several years prior to accepting a position with Information Network Services Corporation (INS). Prior to his promotion to the presidency of the International Division, he had served as managing director of INS's wholly owned subsidiary in Canada.

INS was a major provider of value added network (VAN) services in the United States. Its principal products included high-speed data communications (packet switching), data base management, transaction processing services, and a variety of industry-specific information services. The company's total sales for 1988 were roughly $250 million, and it had recently established successful presences in the United Kingdom and other European countries. International operations accounted for roughly 25 percent of the company's total sales, and the company's top management felt that international markets represented a major field for future growth.

The company's management recognized that in order to capitalize on the rapidly growing Japanese market, a direct presence was needed. By the mid-1980s, the company began to receive a number of inquiries from major Japanese cor-

This case was written by Professor William H. Davidson on the basis of original research by Professor Michael Yoshiuo at the Harvard Business School. Copyright © 1988 by the University of Southern California.

porations concerning licensing possibilities. INS was particularly interested in the possibility of establishing a joint venture to provide VAN services.

The company, after 2 years of demanding negotiations, was successful in establishing a joint venture in Japan with Suji Company, a leading Japanese telecommunications equipment manufacturer. The arrangement was formalized in the summer of 1987.

Suji was one of the companies that approached INS initially to arrange a licensing agreement involving VAN technology and expertise. It appeared to be an attractive potential partner. Suji was a medium-sized telecommunication equipment vendor that was directly tied to one of the major Japanese industrial groups. The company had only limited sales to Nippon Telegraph and Telephone (NTT), the national telephone company. About half of its sales were exported, and the remainder went largely to other Japanese firms within the same industrial group. Suji had established a reputation for high quality, and its brands were well established.

In the mid-1980s, as the Japanese telecommunications market was deregulated, Suji began to explore opportunities in the telecommunication services market, particularly in paging and mobile phone services. Prior to deregulation, telephone and related services were monopoly markets served only by NTT. Under the terms of the 1984 New Telecommunications Law, other Japanese firms were permitted to offer these services to the general public. VAN services in particular could be initiated simply by notifying the Ministry of Posts and Telecommunications. The Ministry of International Trade and Industry had established several programs to provide incentives for new VAN services, including tax breaks and low-cost loans. Suji's management felt that VAN services would be a major growth area. Suji's management, after some investigation, concluded that the quickest and most efficient way to achieve entry into these markets was through either licensing or a joint venture with a leading U.S. company. Suji's management felt that timing was of partic-ular importance, since its major competitors were also considering expansion into these markets. Suji's expression of interest to INS was timely, as INS had become increasingly interested in Japan. Suji was at first interested in a licensing arrangement, but INS, anxious to establish a permanent presence in Japan, wished to establish a joint venture.

The negotiations concerning this joint venture were difficult in part because it was the first experience of the kind for both companies. INS had virtually no prior experience in Japan, and for Suji this was the first joint venture with a foreign company, although it had engaged in licensing agreements with several U.S. and European firms.

The ownership of the joint venture was divided between the two companies, such that Suji owned two-thirds and INS one-third of its equity. Japanese law limited foreign ownership in telecom services vendors to one-third equity participation. In addition to a predetermined cash contribution, the agreement stipulated that INS was to provide network technology and the Japanese partner was to contribute facilities and network equipment. The joint venture was first to market data communication services and later was to introduce transaction processing services. The services were to be marketed under the joint brands of INS and Suji. The agreement also stipulated that both companies would have equal representation on the board of directors, with four people each, and that Suji would provide the entire personnel for the joint venture from top management down to production workers. Such a practice was quite common among foreign joint ventures in Japan, since, given limited mobility among personnel in large corporations, recruiting would represent a major problem for foreign companies. The companies also agreed that the Japanese partner would nominate the president of the joint venture, subject to approval of the board, and the U.S. company would nominate a person for the position of executive vice president. INS also agreed to supply, for the time being, a technical director on a full-time basis.

INS had four members on the board: Flynn, Jack Rose (INS's nominee for executive vice president of the joint venture), and the chair and the president of INS. Representing the Japanese company were the president and executive vice president of Suji, and two senior executives of the joint venture, the president and vice president for finance.

By the fall of 1988, the venture had initiated tests of its data communication services, and a small sales organization had been built. Although the venture was progressing reasonably well, Flynn had become quite concerned over several issues that had come to his attention during the previous 2 months. The first and perhaps the most urgent of these was the selection of a new president for the joint venture.

The first president had died suddenly about 3 months before at the age of 68. He had been a managing director of the parent company and had been the chief representative in Suji's negotiations with INS. When the joint venture was established, it appeared only natural for him to assume the presidency; INS management had no objection.

About a month after his death, Suji, in accordance with the agreement, nominated Kenzo Satoh as the new president. Flynn, when he heard Satoh's qualifications, concluded that he was not suitable for the presidency of the joint venture. He became even more disturbed when he received further information about how he was selected from Jack Rose, the executive vice president of the joint venture.

Satoh had joined Suji 40 years previously upon graduating from Tokyo University. He had held a variety of positions in the Suji company, but during the previous 15 years, he had served almost exclusively in staff functions. He had been manager of Administrative Services at the company's major plant, manager of the General Affairs Department at the corporate headquarters, and personnel director. When he was promoted to that position, he was admitted to the company's board of directors. His responsibility was then expanded to include overseeing several service-oriented staff departments, including personnel, industrial relations, administrative services, and the legal department.

Flynn was concerned that Satoh had virtually no line experience and could not understand why Suji would propose such a person for the presidency of the joint venture, particularly when it was at a critical stage of development.

Even more disturbing to Mr. Flynn was the manner in which Satoh was selected. This first came to Mr. Flynn's attention when he received a letter from Rose, which included the following description:

By now you have undoubtedly examined the background information forwarded to you regarding Mr. Satoh, nominated by our Japanese partner for the presidency of the joint venture.

I have subsequently learned the manner in which Mr. Satoh was chosen for the position, which I am sure would be of great interest to you. I must point out at the outset that what I am going to describe, though shocking by our standards, is quite commonplace among Japanese corporations; in fact, it is well-accepted.

Before describing the specific practice, I must give you a brief background of the Japanese personnel system. As you know, the major companies follow the so-called lifetime employment where all managerial personnel are recruited directly from universities, and they remain with the company until they reach their compulsory retirement age, which is typically around 57. Career advancement in the Japanese system comes slowly, primarily by seniority. Advancement to middle management is well-paced, highly predictable, and virtually assured for every college graduate. Competence and performance become important as they reach upper middle management and top management. Obviously, not everyone will be promoted automatically beyond middle management, but whatever the degree to which competence and qualifications are considered in career advancement, chronological age is the single most important factor.

A select few within the ranks of upper-middle management will be promoted to top management positions, that is, they will be given memberships in the board of directors. In large Japanese companies, the board typically consists exclusively of full-time operating executives. Suji's board is no exception. Moreover, there is a clear-cut hierarchy among the members. The Suji board consists of the chair of the board, president, executive vice president, three managing directors, five ordinary directors, and two statutory auditors.

Typically, ordinary directors have specific operating responsibilities such as head of a staff department, a plant, or a division. Managing directors are comparable to our group vice presidents. Each will have two or three functional or staff groups or product divisions reporting to them. Japanese commercial law stipulates that the members are to be elected by stockholders for a 2-year term. Obviously, under the system described, the members are designated by the chair of the board or the president and serve at their pleasure. Stockholders have very little voice in the actual selection of the board members. Thus, in some cases, it is quite conceivable that board membership is considered as a reward for many years of faithful and loyal service.

As you are well aware, a Japanese corporation is well known for its paternalistic practices in return for lifetime service, and they do assume obligations, particularly for those in middle management or above, even after they reach their compulsory retirement age, not just during their working careers. Appropriate positions are generally found for them in the company's subsidiaries, related firms, or major suppliers where they can occupy positions commensurate to their last position in the parent corporation for several more years.

A similar practice applies to the board members. Though there is no compulsory retirement age for board members, the average tenure for board membership is usually around 6 years. This is particularly true for those who are ordinary or managing directors. Directorships being highly coveted positions, there must be regular turnover to allow others to be promoted to board membership. As a result, all but a fortunate few who are earmarked as heir apparent to the chair, presidency, or executive vice presidency must be "retired." Since most of these executives are in their late fifties or early sixties, they do not yet wish to retire. Moreover, even among major Japanese corporations, the compensation for top management positions is quite low compared with the U.S. standard, and pension plans being still quite inadequate, they will need respectable positions with a reasonable income upon leaving the company. Thus, it is common practice among Japanese corporations to transfer senior executives of the parent company to the chair or presidency of the company's subsidiaries or affiliated companies. Typically, these people will serve in these positions for several years before they retire. Suji had a dozen subsidiaries, and you might be interested in knowing that every top management position is held by those who have retired from the parent corporation. Such a system is well routinized.

Our friend, Mr. Satoh is clearly not the caliber that would qualify for further advancement in the parent company, and his position must be vacated for another person. Suji's top management must have decided that the presidency of the joint venture was the appropriate position for him to "retire" into. This is the circumstances under which Mr. Satoh has been nominated for our consideration.

When he read this letter, Flynn instructed Rose to indicate to the Suji management that Satoh was not acceptable. Not only did Flynn feel that Satoh lacked the qualifications and experience for the presidency, but he resented the fact that Suji was using the joint venture as a home to accommodate a retired executive. It would be justifiable for Suji to use one of its wholly owned subsidiaries for that purpose, but there was no reason why the joint venture should take him on. On the contrary, the joint venture needed dynamic leadership to establish a viable market position.

In his response to Rose, Flynn suggested as president another person, Takao Toray, marketing manager of the joint venture. Toray was 50 years old and had been transferred to the joint venture from Suji, where he had held a number of key marketing positions, including regional sales manager and assistant marketing director. Shortly after he was appointed to the latter position, Toray was sent to INS headquarters to become acquainted with the company's marketing operations. He spent roughly 3 months in the United States, during which time Flynn met him. Though he had not gone beyond a casual acquaintance, Flynn was much impressed by Toray. He appeared to be dynamic, highly motivated, and pragmatic. Moreover, Toray had a reasonable command of English. While communication was not easy, at least it was possible to have conversations on substantive matters. From what Flynn was able to gather, Toray impressed everyone he saw favorably and gained the confidence of not only the International Division staff but those in the corporate marketing group as well as sales executives in the field.

Flynn was aware that Toray was a little too young to be acceptable to Suji, but he felt that it was critical to press for his appointment for two reasons. First, he was far from convinced of the wisdom of adopting Japanese managerial practices blindly in the joint venture. Some of the Japanese executives he met in New York had told him of the pitfalls and weaknesses of Japanese management practices. He was disturbed over the fact that, as he was becoming familiar with the joint venture, he was finding that in every critical aspect such as organization structure, personnel practices, and decision making, the company was managed as though it were a Japanese company. Rose had had little success in introducing U.S. practices. Flynn had noticed in the past that the joint venture had been consistently slow in making decisions because it engaged in a typical Japanese group-oriented and consensus-based process. He also learned that control and reporting systems were virtually nonexistent. Flynn felt that INS's sophisticated planning and control system should be introduced. It had proved successful in the company's wholly owned European subsidiaries, and there seemed to be no reason why such a system could not improve the operating efficiency of the joint venture. He recalled from his Canadian experience that U.S. management practices, if judiciously applied, could give U.S. subsidiaries abroad a significant competitive advantage over local firms.

Second, Flynn felt that the rejection of Satoh and appointment of Toray might be important as a demonstration to the Japanese partner that Suji-INS was indeed a joint venture and not a subsidiary of the Japanese parent company. He was also concerned that INS had lost the initiative in the management of the joint venture. This move would help INS gain stronger influence over the management of the joint venture.

Rose conveyed an informal proposal along these lines to Suji management. Suji's reaction to Flynn's proposal was swift; they rejected it totally. Suji management was polite, but made it clear that they considered Flynn unfair in judging Mr. Satoh's suitability for the presidency without even having met him. They requested Rose to assure Flynn that their company, as majority owner, indeed had an important stake in the joint venture and certainly would not have recommended Satoh unless it had been convinced of his qualifications. Suji management also told Flynn, through Rose, that the selection of Toray was totally unacceptable because in the Japanese corporate system such a promotion was unheard of and would be detrimental not only to the joint venture but to Toray himself, who was believed to have a promising future in the company.

Flynn was surprised at the tone of Suji's response. He wondered whether it would be possible to establish an effective relationship with the Japanese company. Suji seemed determined to run the venture on their own terms.

Another related issue which concerned Flynn was the effectiveness of Rose as executive vice president. Flynn appreciated the difficulties he faced but began to question Rose's qualifications for his position and his ability to work with Japanese top management. During the last visit, for example, Rose had complained of his inability to integrate himself with the Japanese top management team. He indicated that he felt he was still very much an outsider to the company, not only because he was a foreigner but also because the Japanese executives, having come from the parent company, had known each other and in many cases had worked together for at least 20 years. He also indicated that none of the executives spoke English well enough to achieve effective communication beyond the most rudimentary level and that his Japanese was too limited to be of practical use. In fact, his secretary, hired specifically for him, was the only one with whom he could communicate easily. He also expressed frustration over the fact that his functions were very ill-defined and his experience and competence were not really being well utilized by the Japanese.

Flynn discovered after he assumed the presidency that Mr. Rose had been chosen for this assignment for his knowledge of Japan. Rose graduated from a midwestern university in 1973, and after enlisting in the Army was posted to Japan for 4 years. Upon returning home, he joined INS as a management trainee. In 1984, he became assistant district sales manager in California, Oregon, and Washington. When the company began to search for a candidate for executive vice president for the new joint venture, Rose's name came up as someone who was qualified and available for posting to Japan. Rose, although somewhat ambivalent about the new opportunity at first, soon became persuaded that this would represent a major challenge and opportunity.

Flynn was determined to get a first-hand view of the joint venture during his visit. He had many questions, and he wondered whether he had inherited a problem. He was scheduled to meet with Mr. Ohtomo, executive vice president of Suji Corporation on the day following his arrival. Ohtomo, who had been with Suji for over 40 years, was the senior executive responsible for overseeing the joint venture. Flynn had not met Ohtomo, but he knew that Ohtomo had visited the United States and spoke English reasonably well. He wondered how best to approach and organize his meetings and discussions with Mr. Ohtomo. He also wondered if his planned stay of 1 week would be adequate to achieve his objectives. While practicing with chopsticks, he returned to reading *Theory Z,* a popular book on Japanese management, in the hope of gaining insight for the days ahead.

# Ciba-Geigy— Management Development

On December 18, 1981, Arnold Delage, soon to become Managing Director of Ciba-Geigy's French subsidiary, was looking forward to his dinner meeting in Basel, Switzerland (headquarters to Ciba-Geigy), with the top management of the parent company's Pharma Division. Together they were going to review candidates for the position of Sales and Marketing Manager for the French subsidiary's pharmaceutical business, an important position since this division accounted for nearly a quarter of total French sales and had shown rapid growth in recent years.

Until recently, Delage had been general manager of Ciba-Geigy's French Pharma Division and President of "Laboratories Ciba-Geigy," the pharmaceutical subsidiary of Ciba-Geigy in France, with sales of about Fr700 million. René Lamont, the current Managing Director of Ciba-Geigy France, was scheduled to retire effective at the end of the year, and Delage had been chosen by Ciba-Geigy's top management to succeed him, a selection announced in early December.

Delage had had a successful career with Ciba-Geigy. A Frenchman, he joined Esso-Africa upon graduation from INSEAD in 1965 and worked in Switzerland (Geneva) and in Madagascar, in sales and marketing positions. He was subsequently recruited by Ciba-Geigy and, after a year at Pharma Division's headquarters in Basel, was sent to Hong Kong in a sales and marketing management position. After four years in the Far East he was appointed Marketing Manager in Belgium, where he successfully launched a number of new pharmaceutical products. In 1973, he was promoted to Pharma Division Manager in Belgium, a position he held for three years. Delage was recalled to France in 1976 as Marketing Manager, where he successfully launched a new antirheumatic formulation (Voltarene) and, in 1979, was promoted to Pharma Division Manager. During the last two years he had considerably strengthened the management of the French Pharma division.

Delage's promotion to Managing Director of Ciba-Geigy France had opened the position of Pharma Division Manager within the French subsidiary. Jules Breton, an experienced man-

This case was prepared by Professor Yves Doz with the assistance of Ms. Martine van den Poel, Research Associate. © INSEAD, The European Institute of Business Administration, July 1983.

ager recently hired from Sanofi (a major French pharmaceutical company where he had held the position of President and General Manager of one of its subsidiaries), was promoted to the post. The position of Pharma Marketing Manager therefore became vacant. Delage and Breton presented the candidacy of Pierre Dumont, a Frenchman who had recently been recruited from Specia (another French competitor) to head marketing and sales for the Geigy product line in France. Pharma Division headquarters in Basel had suggested several other candidates. Among them, their preference fell on Michel Malterre, a Swiss national from Montreux, currently heading Pharma marketing in West Africa and based in Abidjan, Ivory Coast.

Such decisions as the appointment of key executives in subsidiary companies were usually the result of joint agreement by divisional management in Basel and the local managing directors and were often debated at the highest levels within the company. A long-standing corporate commitment to human resource and management development ensured that such choices received considerable attention and that all relevant aspects were carefully weighed before a decision was reached.

## THE COMPANY AND ITS ORGANIZATION

Ciba-Geigy resulted from the 1970 merger between two long-standing Basel chemical companies: Ciba (created in 1884) and Geigy (created in 1758). Both companies were active competitors in certain business areas, e.g., dyestuffs, pharmaceuticals, industrial chemicals, and agrochemicals. In other areas, their activities were complementary. Both were strong internationally, although Geigy had a stronger worldwide presence in agro-chemicals and Ciba a wider experience in pharmaceuticals.

The management styles and structures of the two companies, however, differed widely. Ciba was centrally managed by one person, Dr. Kappeli, its chairman. He relied on strong and entrepreneurial division managers to control Ciba's widely diversified activities. In contrast, Geigy had been reorganized in 1968 into a three-dimensional organizational structure where businesses, national subsidiaries, and corporate functions were managed by an Executive Committee regrouping Geigy's top management.

Following the merger, the Geigy structure was retained. By 1980–1981 the structure comprised the following units (see Exhibit 1):

1. Divisional structure covering the seven main product areas: dyestuffs and chemicals, pharmaceuticals, agro-chemicals, plastics and additives, the Airwick consumer products group, the Ilford photographic products group, and the recently constituted electronic equipment products group
2. Geographic structure with 80 group companies organized in a loose administrative way into six main regions: North America, Western Europe, Latin America, Africa/Middle East, Eastern Europe, and Asia/Australia
3. Ten central corporate functions (legal, finance, technology, etc.) at group headquarters in Basel, Switzerland

In general, Ciba-Geigy had a policy of 100 percent ownership of group companies. As a rule, these group companies were responsible for all Ciba-Geigy activities in a given country, for making use of available opportunities for the local development of Ciba-Geigy's business, and for the overall financial results within their territories. The various product divisions and the Executive Committee (*Konzernleitung*) coordinated and integrated the group companies' activities.

*Product divisions* were responsible to the Executive Committee for the worldwide management of their businesses and their overall results. Research and development, production, and marketing of products were specific responsibilities of the divisions. Divisional plans and budgets for the group companies were discussed with headquarters' divisions in Basel and coordinated with group companies' managing directors. Major investment projects in the group

---

EXHIBIT 1

**CORPORATE ORGANIZATION, 1981**

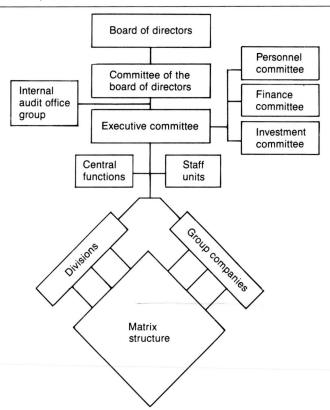

| Central functions | Product divisions | Staff units |
|---|---|---|
| • Research | • Dyestuffs and chemicals | • Central secretariat |
| • Technology, Switzerland | • Pharma | • Regional services |
| • Technology, group | • Agro-chemicals | • Management development |
| • Finance | • Plastics and additives | • Corporate planning |
| • Control and management services | • Airwick group | |
| • Personnel, Switzerland | • Ilford group | |
| • Information and promotion | • Electronic equipment group | |
| • Legal services | | |
| • Commercial services | | |
| • Superannuation fund and property | | |
| • Protection of health and environment | | |

companies were reviewed by the product divisions, which were also responsible for business development on a worldwide basis.

Divisional management also participated in establishing the organizational structure of, and in nominating candidates for top positions in, their corresponding divisions within group companies. Product divisions were managed through divisional management committees reflecting the main functions of a division.

*Group companies* combined all Ciba-Geigy's divisions and functions into one managerial entity in each country. The company believed that this structure allowed Ciba-Geigy to operate locally as a homogeneous unit, consolidate financial results across divisions, and optimize local financial resource utilization. In addition, central administrative functions could serve several local units more economically than if each division had to do so independently. Finally, relations with local government, industry and trade associations, and other national entities could be made more effective.

The group company Managing Director was responsible for the total activity of local units as well as for overall local financial results, but had to operate within the framework of policies and guidelines set from the center and harmonize plans between the various central units (divisions and central functions) and local requirements. The divisional heads within the group companies were administratively responsible to the Managing Director but were also functionally responsible to the corresponding division in Basel.

The *Executive Committee,* in Basel, had 10 members and was responsible for:

- Formulation and implementation of the group policy
- Approval of long-term objectives and strategies, and resource allocation decisions
- Approval of organizational structures and appointment of key managers within the product divisions, central functions, and group companies
- Creation of corporatewide uniform management systems and guidelines (especially for planning, resource allocation, and management information)
- Review of major integrated plans, budgets, and investment projects and decisions on their approval
- Control of the performance of the individual units and evaluation of the business and its results from a corporatewide perspective

Each member of the Executive Committee was overseeing, as a "patron," a number of countries and one or two divisions or central functions, so that all major units were covered. For example, the Executive Committee member responsible for the Pharma Division also had responsibility for the plastics and additives division and the Southeast Asian and Chinese region. Another patron was responsible for the Airwick division, the finance function, Eastern Europe, and Latin America. The Executive Committee met as a group frequently, usually once a week.

The preparation and negotiation of decisions involving several divisions, group companies, and/or central functions could be delegated by the Executive Committee to regional staffs. These provided an intermediate level between the group companies and the Executive Committee, since all 80 or so group companies could not effectively be supervised directly by the individual Executive Committee members.

*Central services* fell into two categories: Executive Committee staffs and corporate functions. They formulated, for the approval of the Executive Committee, opinions, guidelines, and procedures specific to their field, commented on functional plans and budgets to the heads of group companies, and participated in the nomination of group companies' functional executives. Central functions and staffs also placed their specific expertise at the service of group companies.

Two key Executive Committee staff functions were corporate planning and management development (the latter is described below in detail). Recently, planning had acquired more prominence with the redefinition of Ciba-Geigy's businesses into about 30 "corporate segments," and the establishment of a corporate strategic plan drawn from a bottom-up planning process at segment level rather than only at divisional level. The corporate planning staff at

Ciba-Geigy employed only four people and was directly responsible to the Chair of the Executive Committee. Franz Hartmann, its Director, explained the changes in corporate strategy and in the way resources were allocated that had transpired over the past few years:

During the 1960s and early 1970s the resource allocation process in Ciba-Geigy was not very sophisticated. It was rather informal since there were no financial constraints. The real beginning of strategic planning ocurred in 1974, in the sense of it being more than simple operational planning with a longer-term horizon. The 1974–1975 economic crisis was quite helpful to us, because it forced us to put more emphasis on actual strategic thinking and less on number pushing. We introduced a long-term strategic plan and conceded more flexibility in the process, emphasizing key issues and implementation through strategic projects and action plans. The strategic projects involved business entries and exits, new plant construction in foreign countries, etc. . . . In recent years, it became quite clear that the chemical industry was maturing. Some of our businesses were plagued by slow innovation and very intense competition and, therefore, needed different strategies and different managers from those required by businesses that were still growing rapidly.

In 1980 we started to introduce portfolio approaches for the first time. We also faced a trend toward lower profitability and started a "turn-around" program. The program was not only designed to reduce inventories, cut personnel and cut costs but also to strengthen strategic planning and to allocate proper strategic roles and resources to each segment. This reflected the growing differentiation among our businesses and the need to account for different success factors in how and by whom they were managed. For example, the divisions are now moving from worldwide segment strategies to local portfolios. After the merger in 1970, we had needed to integrate operations centrally. Now there is growing delegation in operational matters by the Executive Committee to divisions and group companies.

This segment approach questions the divisional structure. We will need to implement substructural changes to fit the segments and reallocate functional responsibilities within divisions. We are also going to need better managers and more general managers. We are now recruiting MBAs and putting a lot of emphasis on young people and training, sending them abroad early in their careers to take up responsibility. In fact, we have been forced to look outside to find general managers for some of our new activities.

One implication of all this is that there is going to be a lot more internal competition within the firm. Changes are being made in the role of group company managers. Originally, they were mainly administrators and caretakers. The turn-around project has given them more control as they had to play a key role in cost cutting measures and had to make difficult trade-offs among divisions within their companies on issues of employment, investment, plant location, and so on. They are increasingly being asked to contribute to the planning dialogue between local and headquarter division management.

## THE ORIGINS OF MANAGEMENT DEVELOPMENT AT CIBA-GEIGY

Leopold Luthi, a lawyer who joined Geigy in 1951, worked in line management positions in the Agchem division for over 15 years, and later became head of management development for Ciba-Geigy. He explained the early development of the management development (MD) function in the company as follows:

After the 1968 reorganization which gave Geigy its three-dimensional structure a separate staff unit was created called "Executive Development" whose role was to assure a supply of qualified managers for top and line management positions. The unit was to report directly to the Executive Committee, and I was given responsibility for it. The idea was to make management development planning an automatic component of the yearly divisional and regional plans. At the beginning we overestimated the possibility of developing precise instruments of measurement and evaluation from which to derive the development potential. In fact, a formal system would not work. Line managers might comment quite differently on their people according to whether they evaluated current performance or future development potential.

Then, in 1969, the merger with Ciba was announced and everything slowed down for a while.

From 1971 onward, the management development unit took shape and developed rapidly. According to Dr. Luthi:

> The units in Basel and abroad started to work on MD plans, we discussed these plans with them, and we started to present them to the chairman of the Executive Committee and to the unit's patron. One of the early issues was to get comparability of people and profiles on a lateral basis among the units. While in the late 1960s at Geigy we dealt with only 400 people (200 executives and 200 potential executives), after the merger we had about 1,000 executives included in our MD program. At the beginning, the system we developed worked mainly with the executive group within each company where the immediate preoccupation with succession was the highest. We later expanded the process to reach those young men and women of high potential in the organization, and to increase the supply of them over time.

## MANAGEMENT DEVELOPMENT: PURPOSES AND FUNCTIONS IN 1980–1981

By 1980, the management development staff unit at corporate headquarters employed 14 people, roughly half of them working in management education, running and organizing in-house and external training courses, and the other half dealing with succession planning, recruitment, job rotations, MD plans, etc. (see Exhibit 2).

The Central Management Development program focused on some 2,100 employees (2 percent of total employment) of the company, the so-called executives and potential executives. In addition to slightly over 100 senior executives in top management positions, the executives occupied the 1,000 or so most senior management positions in Ciba-Geigy worldwide (400 in Basel and 600 abroad) including Directors, Deputy Directors, and Vice Directors of the parent company, and the top management positions within the group companies. The potential executives, numbering about 1,000, were employees at lower-

and middle-management levels who in the opinion of their supervisors were likely to advance some day to an executive position. The final responsibility for appointments and selection to the list was with line management: the Executive Committee for executive appointments, and with the various group company, divisional, and central functional heads in the case of potential executives.

This corporatewide management development program had several objectives:

1. Planning executive successions for the whole group on the basis of corporate, divisional, and group company MD planning reports.
2. Identification of potential executives and planning their next development steps.
3. Monitoring the quality and age structure of each unit's executive and potential executive population.
4. Setting up career moves and job rotation for both executives and potential executives. [During 1980, for example, 281 job rotations took place, mostly local, with a smaller number of international rotations between headquarters and group companies, as shown in Exhibit 3.]
5. Coordination of the moves of obsolete executives into new positions to give them new incentives and added motivation.
6. The educational development of all executives and potential executives through internal (in-house) and external (business schools) management courses.

As such the role of the MD unit was *conceptual* (policy and system development); *pedagogical* (assignment and coordination of management training activities); and *advisory* (to the Executive Committee). It follows that the three mainstays of Ciba-Geigy's MD program were the MD plans, its training programs, and its role in executive appointments.

**The MD plans** Drawn up every two years by the heads of every group company and every division and function of the parent company, each MD plan showed the current executive

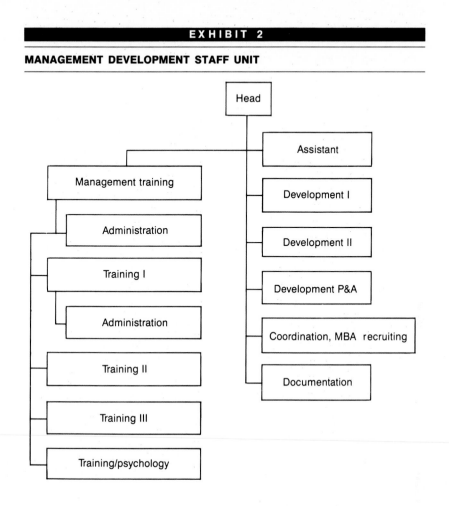

EXHIBIT 2

**MANAGEMENT DEVELOPMENT STAFF UNIT**

positions in the organization, indicated future moves and candidates for job rotations, proposed internal successors and offered positions for outside candidates, showed potential executives, and defined action programs (see Exhibit 4 for examples). Upon receipt of an MD plan, the MD staff at headquarters would first discuss it with the unit head who wrote it, and then present it to the Chair of the Executive Committee and to the appropriate patrons. In the case of an MD plan for a group company, it would also be discussed with each corporate division or function as far as its corresponding local subunit was concerned. Dr. Luthi added:

The way in which the various group companies are handling this question varies a great deal. In the United States and Italy, for example, the local group company's Executive Committee discusses the plan and then holds additional discussions with the various divisional management committees. The whole system permeates the group company. In Mexico they are now going to do a two-day human resource planning meeting in Cuernavaca. One day is going to deal with the strategic plan, and another day with implications in terms of the MD plan. That is good because they can couple the two systems very closely.

Other countries do it with a lot more secrecy. They do not discuss this as a group, only face to

---

**EXHIBIT 3**

**TOTAL JOB ROTATIONS, 1979–1980, AND INTERNATIONAL JOB ROTATIONS, 1980**

| | Total | | | | | |
|---|---|---|---|---|---|---|
| | **1980** | | | **1979** | | |
| | Total | Local | Int'l | Total | Local | Int'l |
| Executives | 96 | 76 | 20 | 66 | 51 | 15 |
| Potential executives | 185 | 154 | 31 | 181 | 156 | 25 |
| Total | 281 | 230 | 51 | 247 | 207 | 40 |

| | International | | | |
|---|---|---|---|---|
| | Total | Headquarters to group company | Group company to headquarters | Group company to group company |
| Executives | 20 | 3 | 8 | 9 |
| Potential executives | 31 | 14 | 5 | 12 |
| Total | 51 | 17 | 13 | 21 |

---

face with the relevant managers. It is very important for us in Basel to have the confidence of line management. Therefore, we have to assure them that each unit's MD plan will be treated with appropriate confidentiality. . . .

A critical element in the successful implementation of our objectives is the full commitment and backing of the Chair of the Executive Committee and its members. The general managers of large group companies come personally to Basel to discuss the management development plan with the Chairman of the Executive Committee, the patrons, and our staff. . . .

Putting full responsibility for MD plans with line managers made the plan adaptive. Rather than try to forecast centrally what managerial profiles would be required, when and in what numbers, the process was designed to develop, cultivate and track a large inventory of diverse people, from which could be extracted those with the skills required for a particular position at any point in time.

**Management Training Programs**  Ciba-Geigy put more emphasis and devoted more resources to management training than most European companies. The main Ciba-Geigy management course

was a two-week program offered to all newly promoted executives of Ciba-Geigy worldwide. Prior to this course many new executives had taken a group orientation course and a basic management course, each one week long. Ciba-Geigy's top management was active in teaching these courses. Senior management seminars were organized every few years in various countries (with a total of 450 participants) to discuss the strategies and profitability of Ciba-Geigy. These in-house central training programs (see Exhibit 5) were the backbone of the company's educational efforts, covering a large number of participants, emphasizing Ciba-Geigy specific topics, and concentrating on general management issues.

Each division, function, or group company had its own more specific and more function-oriented training program with basic management courses. The external training programs at various business schools around the world were viewed as important supporting elements, where the emphasis was on the individual needs of the participant, exposure to other firms and industries, and more general business topics.

**Executive Appointments**   Appointments to all 1,100 executive positions were decided by the Personnel Committee consisting of three members of the Board of Directors and three members of the Executive Committee. The Personnel Committee typically met every Thursday to recommend top appointments; its decisions went next to the full Executive Committee for their approval.

The head of the MD unit met every Monday morning with the Chair of the Executive Committee to review all pending MD matters. From time to time, this Monday meeting dealt with possible crises and reviewed individual cases for both executive and potential executive appointments. The meetings could include other executives as appropriate. Based on the MD plans and numerous discussions with division, function, and group company heads, the MD unit prepared a list of candidates for promotion.[1] Luthi commented:

> Decisions are taken in person-to-person discussions, and not exclusively based on the personnel files of the candidates. Our approach is not only an appraisal of the current job performance but also considers suggestions regarding the job someone could take over in the future. Personal judgments of the line managers on candidates are critical, they know the task and the job and they are the person's direct boss. Yet for any particular promotion someone has to write a broad list of candidates, not only coming from the specific line organization (division), but also from other divisions, other group companies, other functions and eventually from outside Ciba-Geigy. The list is based mainly on the MD plan, but we can put additional candidates of a given background on the list. The process builds on the inventory of suitable candidates.

The product divisions were a centralizing element in MD planning. As they had worldwide profit responsibility and were responsible for

worldwide strategies, they had a strong interest in the quality and choice of the people in the different group companies. Therefore, when a divisional executive in a group company came up for a promotion appointment, the Executive Committee expected the head of the group company and of the parent division to provide a joint proposal.

## MANAGEMENT DEVELOPMENT IN THE PHARMA DIVISION

While some divisions were facing a slowdown in profitability and low growth prospects (see Appendix) the Pharma division was growing rapidly. Divisional management was concerned that there would be a shortage of executives and potential executives to fill future positions. Alfred Steiner had been head of management development for the Pharma division for the past three years, and prior to that a member of the corporate MD staff for seven years. He explained the situation:

> Five years ago a new Pharma division head developed a strategy to branch out more broadly into the health care market, rather than stay exclusively in ethical pharmaceuticals. This diversification led divisional management to become overburdened and to the realization that what the division had as available potential executives was in no way sufficient to staff our needs for the next 5 to 10 years given the new growth targets. In fact, the division realized that it had too few potential executives even for current replacement alone.
>
> Part of the problem was that management development had not been taken seriously and that after the merger we had found ourselves with a top-heavy organization and no new people were recruited. The new division head realized that he couldn't cope with that problem and saw a need for an MD function within the Pharma division. Discussions took place with Dr. Luthi, since this was the first attempt at decentralizing a corporate function.
>
> When I first came to the Pharma division I soon realized that the secretary of the division's management committee had sat down over a weekend to get the MD plan done. The forms were filled

---

[1] For some divisions, such as Pharma, and for positions below that of group company Division Head, the preparation of such lists was often delegated to the divisional MD Manager, in this case A. Steiner.

**EXHIBIT 4**

## MD SUCCESSION CHARTS

(a) Key for MD Planning Signs. (b) MD Chart for Medium to Large Group Company. (c) MD Chart for Large Company. (d) MD Chart for a Small Company.

Management Development
Planning Signs

Key management position: key manager

Key management position which is also an executive position: executive

Key manager with potential for advancement*

Key manager who could assume greater responsibility at the same organizational level*

Key management position which could be abrogated when present holder leaves*

Key management position which is expected to become vacant within the next 5 years*

Potential key manager

Key manager or potential key manager in position outside the organization unit represented by the chart

Possible move (e.g., for successor candidate)

Definite move (i.e., decision already made)

*These descriptions can also be used for key managers in executive positions.

(a)

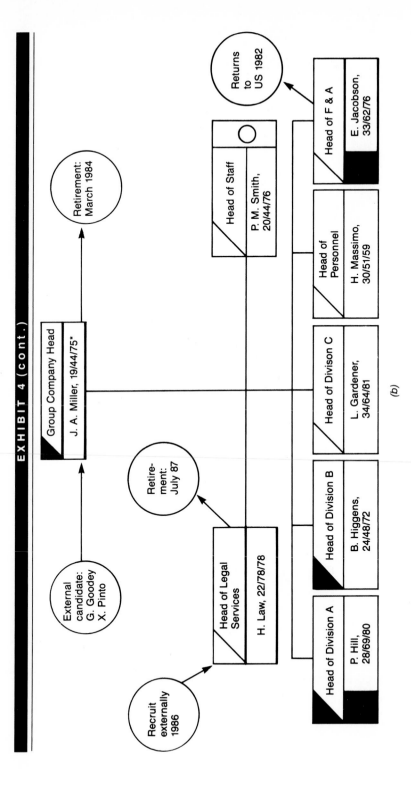

(b)

*Note:* It is suggested that this chart show the top management organization and the succession situation for the company head and for any other key management positions not shown on the divisional/functional charts. The successor situation for the heads of divisions and functions is usually best shown on their respective charts.

*X/Y/Z figures, below names, mean: X, year of birth; Y, year when joined Ciba-Geigy (or the pre-merger companies), and Z, year when appointed to current position. Therefore, Mr. J. A. Miller was born in 1919, joined Ciba-Geigy in 1944, and has been head of the group company since 1975 (in the example given above).

EXHIBIT 4 (cont.)

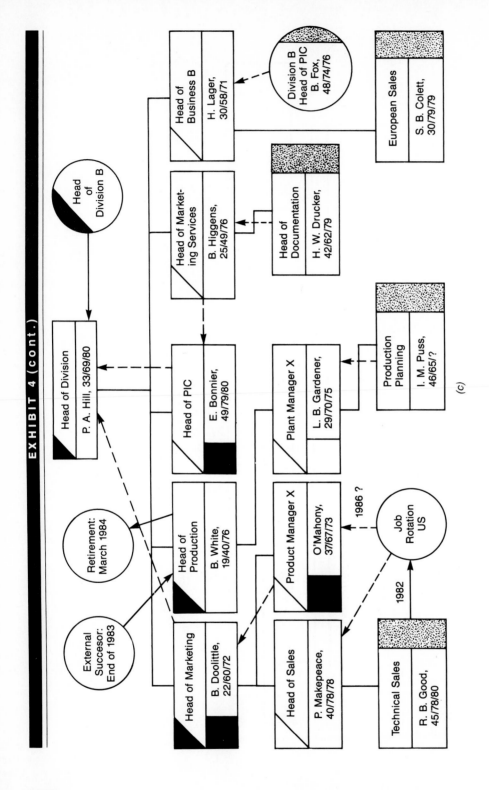

(c)

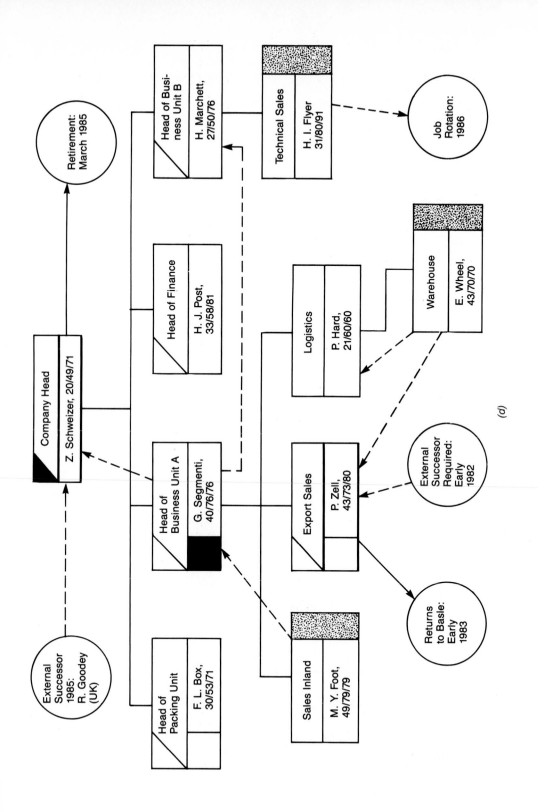

(d)

---

**EXHIBIT 5**

**INTERNAL MANAGEMENT TRAINING AND ORIENTATION PROGRAMS**

---

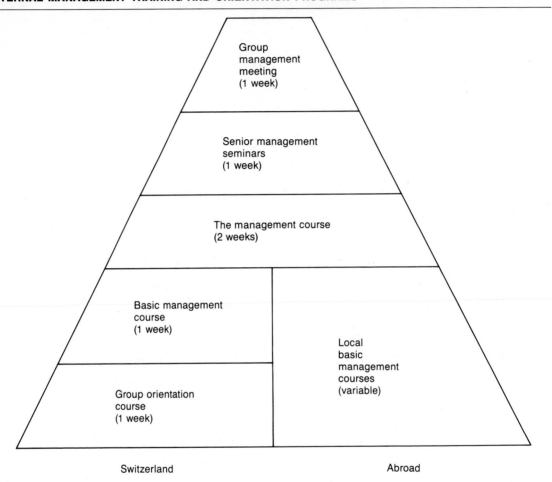

Switzerland

Abroad

in, but not taken very seriously. The official MD planning system was conceived as a corporate instrument with too-restrictive definitions for actual development purposes in critical stages. Potential executives were 35 to 40 years old, but by that age a career is almost over in development potential!

Another problem is that the MD plan reflects today's organizational structure and does not project requirements into the future. The organization is changing constantly, you can't do tomorrow's succession planning based on an inter-

pretation of today's structure. Therefore, it is not a real plan; it remains a mere inventory, not an action program. But at least it shows us who are the potential executives and what they may become.

Steiner set out in 1978 with an action plan for management development in the Pharma division. Several goals were formulated such as achieving an even ratio between executives and potential executives, since currently the former far outnumbered the latter who would eventually be needed to fill an ever-increasing number of executive positions. He also initiated a program to recruit 40 young people each year, mainly MBAs, and put them on a fast-track development. This was a major change from Ciba-Geigy's traditional recruitment policy. A study of the age structure in the Pharma division had revealed that only 24 percent of the potential executives were below age 35. Finally, systematic MD planning was instituted that would account for different profiles of executives needed for the traditional drug business, new business sectors, and acquisitions (see Exhibit 6).

In total the MD unit in Pharma dealt with nearly 600 people, 330 executives and 250 potential executives on a worldwide basis, covering operations in over 60 countries. The MD action plan was specifically tailored to the needs of the Pharma division as Steiner remarked:

> Obviously, what we developed here would not apply to Ciba-Geigy as a whole since other divisions face different management development problems. But we were also in a Catch 22 situation because while the corporate turn-around rationalization plans placed an almost complete ban on recruitment, we were told to go ahead with our strategic recruitment program.
>
> The Pharma division is growing fast but competing head-on with other companies like Hoechst or MSD. If we want to compete successfully for executives, we have to offer salary levels comparable to those offered by our main competitors. Clearly we have a conflict between the salaries our division has to pay and those other divisions

want to pay. Also, as a rule, the most profitable divisions believe that they should have a higher standard of living.

## THE PHARMA DIVISION IN FRANCE

Pharma division operations in France had always been rather autonomous. In the old days, the French Pharma Division had been headed by Dr. Henri d'Encausses, a pharmacist and the Mayor of Gaillardon, a village in Southern France. He gladly entertained visiting executives from headquarters but carefully protected his autonomy. In this he had the implicit support of the company's Managing Director, Antoine Roux, who ran the French subsidiary quite successfully and kept headquarters at bay. Middle managers were caused to think that Basel was trying to influence the group company unduly. Since his thinking was often ahead of that in Basel, Roux maintained his advantage and kept the management of the French company close to his chest.

With the divisional reorganization which followed the merger, tensions grew between Roux and divisional and corporate management in Basel. He was replaced in 1977 by R. Lamont, a French-speaking Swiss national of English origin, who had been head of the French Pharma division since 1974. Lamont was succeeded in this role by Maitre Guillaume, a French lawyer, who was appointed at age 65, and retired in September 30, 1979, upon his replacement by Delage. Lamont was a skillful negotiator who

---

EXHIBIT 6

**PHARMA DIVISION—BUSINESS, STRUCTURE, AND EXECUTIVE ASSUMPTIONS**

| Type of business | Future business structure | Types of executives required |
|---|---|---|
| Traditional drug business (3 pillars) | Same basic structure but trend toward more independent profit center units | Fewer functional managers, more entrepreneurs than in the past |
| New business sectors (e.g., antibiotics, OTC, generics) | Creation of self-contained business units | All-around managers, entrepreneurs |
| Acquisitions | Normally will remain independent units | All-around managers, entrepreneurs |

did much to improve communications between headquarters and the French company.

Neither Lamont nor Guillaume had a strong feeling for management development. They did not have the necessary potential executives to fill new positions and let an enduring weakness develop in their supply of managers. At headquarters the situation was made difficult by a hiring freeze in the early 1970s that led to a scarcity 10 years later of promotable managers age 35 to 40. Following the merger, Ciba-Geigy had found itself with too many managers and with a commitment to its employees that no lay-offs would result from it. Furthermore, some divisions, such as dyestuffs, faced shrinking markets and increasing competition. Pharma, alone, was growing rapidly in France from Fr250 million in sales in 1975, to over Fr700 million by 1981. When Delage came back to France in 1976, for instance, he was the only manager with a marketing background and a good knowledge of English. Lamont and Guillaume had satisfied corporate MD formal requirement by drawing up MD plans when requested, but concrete implementation actions rarely followed these plans, and little was done to recruit and develop potential managers.

Between 1976 and 1981, Delage strengthened the French Pharma Division considerably. First, he spent much time in the field improving the quality of the medical representatives' force, by training, selection, and replacement. He then created two positions of product line managers—one for Ciba products, the other for Geigy's—to provide additional sales and marketing management competence and support. He also replaced several of the weaker product managers. By 1981, the Pharma organization in France (see Exhibit 7), was in much better shape.

## THE CHOICE OF A NEW MARKETING MANAGER

When Lamont retired, Delage was chosen to replace him in competition with a Swiss expatriate. Among many factors in the decision it was felt that national feelings in France would favor a Frenchman to head the local group company. According to the manager of the European region in the Pharma division:

> Delage is a prototype of a successful career within Ciba-Geigy Pharma. He has been successful wherever he was. Delage is the type of person we really like. Among possible candidates he was closest to the ideal profile: a Frenchman to head the French group company, but with good experience of headquarters, several successful assignments abroad, and a clear perspective on relationships with Basel. We want that type of person in key positions abroad. He already was an ideal division manager who understood the Ciba-Geigy philosophy well. There is nothing worse than having key people in group companies who know nobody in Basel, are not known to headquarters, and lack the company culture.

The major issue with Delage's appointment was that he had been division head in France for less than two years and, in reviewing the French MD plan, the Executive Committee had put a hold on him as recently as October 1981. Yet, since no other candidate came close to his profile, he was selected.

Finding a new Pharma division head to replace Delage was more difficult. In 1979, Delage proposed to hire Charles Mortier as Marketing Manager for Pharma-France. Nobody from the French Pharma division was well-qualified for the job, and the only candidate suggested by the corporate MD unit was a Swiss manager from Canada, Paul Aubert. Unfortunately, he came from another division and was not well-known to the Basel Pharma division management. Mortier had a good track record with a U.S. pharmaceutical company in France, where his career progression had been stifled, and he was a seasoned marketing and sales manager. After much discussion, his appointment was agreed to by all parties.

Yet, after a year with Ciba-Geigy, Mortier went back to his former employer. The unexpected dismissal of their marketing manager and a financially attractive offer had hired him back. Soon thereafter, the U.S. company introduced

---

**EXHIBIT 7**

**FRENCH PHARMA DIVISION—SALES AND MARKETING STRUCTURE, 1981**

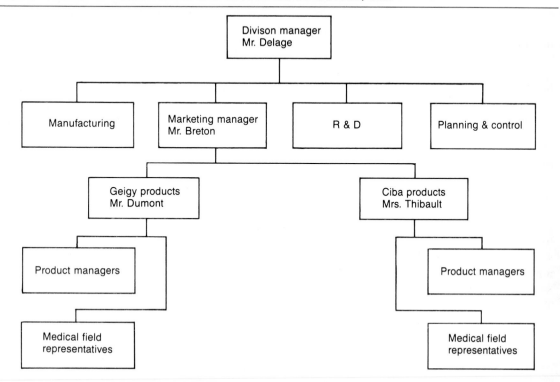

---

a product in direct competition to Ciba-Geigy's very successful Voltarene.

In the spring of 1980, Delage hired Jules Breton from Sanofi to become the new marketing manager.[2] Breton joined Ciba-Geigy by the late summer of 1980 and was more a general manager than a marketing specialist. Over a year later, with Delage's appointment as Managing Director, the opportunity to promote him as division head came. According to Mr. Steiner: "Breton was promoted; there was no better candidate. We are reluctant to go out on the market for division heads. Breton knew the French market and his people." The major difficulty was that Breton had only been with the company a very short time. He did not know headquarters or the Ciba-Geigy culture and was not well-known to headquarters' managers.

Breton and Delage then suggested Dumont as a replacement for Breton as marketing manager. Dumont had been recruited in March 1980 from Specia (a French competitor) to take responsibility for the marketing of the Geigy line of pharmaceutical products. He was a pharmacist (graduated in 1972) with an additional degree in political science (from "Science-Po" in Paris, 1974). In 1975, following military service, he had joined Boehringer-Ingelheim in Reims as product manager for over-the-counter (OTC) drugs. A year later, he joined a Specia subsidiary, overseeing two products which be-

---

[2] In the meantime, Delage had stepped back into the vacant marketing manager's role, spending about 60 percent of his time as division head on marketing and sales issues.

tween them accounted for over 50 percent of the subsidiary's sales. In 1977 he became responsible for all product managers at Specia and was very successful. In 1979 he was offered to head a newly acquired market research subsidiary and to create, for the whole of Specia, a marketing "methodology" unit to advise and assist line managers. Seeing himself more as a line manager, he was not very pleased with the new position when he was approached by an executive placement firm on behalf of Ciba-Geigy in November 1979. Following interviews and discussions with Mortier and Delage, he decided to join Ciba-Geigy.

By the time Dumont came on board, in March 1980, Mortier had left the company, and for the next six months (until Breton actually arrived) the French Pharma Division had no marketing manager. Delage, in addition to his divisional management duties, concentrated most of his attention on the Ciba products, where rapid product line management turnover had created problems. Dumont was immediately given full responsibility for the Geigy product line with very little supervision. This included a marketing and sales force of about 120 people, supported by a service staff of more than 20 people. He handled them successfully, continuing the 20 percent per annum real rate of growth started under Delage. According to Dumont, the quality of the products, the commitment of management, and the financial means of Ciba-Geigy explained that continued success.

In less than one year, Dumont had created a good impression at headquarters. According to the Pharma European regional manager, Dr. Grunwald, "he attended meetings in Basel and left good impressions everywhere; he elicited positive feelings and was known within headquarters."

In spite of this positive view about Dumont among Pharma division management in Basel, headquarters routinely initiated a wider search for candidates. According to Mr. Steiner: "We were suggested 'why not go with Dumont?' by Delage and Breton. Our initial reaction was 'we do not really know Mr. Dumont, he has been

in the company only a few months. Let us look at him. At first sight he is very young—he was born in 1948—but maybe we are getting old?' We then looked into who else we had. Delage knew all of them anyway."

Dumont had been very successful in France and knew both the techniques of marketing and the specific character of the French pharmaceutical markets extremely well. The French pharmaceutical market was considered to be one of the most difficult for foreign competitors, among European markets. France had some strong national competitors, such as Specia, with extensive positions on their domestic market but little international presence. Furthermore, prices were tightly controlled, and complex administrative and political procedures governed the registration of new drugs. In a price inelastic market, margins were slim. In 1981, the new Socialist government in France was about to initiate discussions with foreign pharmaceutical companies with the objective of granting price increases only to those which agreed to increase their local investment and employment levels.

Despite these difficulties the French market was important to Ciba-Geigy and one of the largest national markets for its pharmaceutical products. Among the group companies, France had had the most success with Voltarene, and this product now accounted for a substantial proportion of Ciba-Geigy's sales in France. Steiner and Grunwald drew up a profile of an ideal candidate. According to them, international exposure and headquarters experience were desirable characteristics that Dumont lacked. Together, they drew a more formalized profile to assess candidates (see Exhibit 8). This blank profile would be sent to each senior manager within Ciba-Geigy who knew the candidate.

Steiner started to go through files of possible candidates from outside the French group company. On November 23, 1981, a first list of about 40 candidates was drawn from Steiner's files on 600 Pharma managers, worldwide. He then started to go through these, one by one. The three main criteria used to pare the list were:

EXHIBIT 8

## CANDIDATE PROFILE FORM

| | | Education | | | | Experience | | | | | | Personality | | | | | | | |
|---|---|---|---|---|---|---|---|---|---|---|---|---|---|---|---|---|---|---|---|
| Group Company<br>Division marketing<br>management evaluation grid | Professional Education | MBA or Management Seminars | Knowledge of English | Knowledge of Local Languages | Several Years of Successful Line Management Experience | Pharma Marketing Management | Market Research | Planning & Control | International Management Experience | Local Market Experience | Analytic Skills | Creativity | Overall Management Skills | Leadership Capability | Overall Balance | Development Potential | Career Development Aspect | Availability | |
| Individuals | | | | | | | | | | | | | | | | | | | |

suitability for the position, availability, and career development considerations. The requirement for full "perfect" fluency in French quickly eliminated all but 6 candidates. Only 3 of these could be considered as "genuine" candidates by Steiner and Grunwald. They were submitted to Delage.

Delage quickly brushed aside one candidate who looked perfect on paper but that he knew personally from his previous positions in the Pharma division and whom he did not consider suitable for the position. Another candidate turned out not to be available, having been in his current position only nine months and not being easily replaceable there. This left one possible candidate: Michel Malterre. Malterre, however, had been slotted to go to Greece in 1982 and was not, therefore, technically available.

Malterre, a French-speaking Swiss, born in 1944, was Marketing Manager for Pharma in West Africa. He had started with Ciba in 1970, two months before the merger, as a lawyer working on legal problems resulting from the merger. For the next two years he was legal assistant to the Pharma division's Manager for Planning, Information, and Control in Basel.

During the uprising of Bangladesh against Pakistan in 1971, the International Committee of the Red Cross (Geneva) asked Ciba-Geigy for Malterre's detachment on leave to Bangladesh, where he had worked with the Red Cross prior to his joining Ciba-Geigy. After four months spent organizing medical relief programs there, often flying in helicopters through combat zones, he returned to his job in Basel. The company's Executive Committee was interested in the value of lending executives to nonprofit organizations for humanitarian purposes and asked Malterre to make a detailed presentation of his experience upon his return.

In 1972–1973 Malterre was named product manager for anesthetics in Switzerland, after which he was appointed to the secretariat of the Chair of the Executive Committee. In 1978, he applied for a line job and was sent to the Ivory Coast to market Pharma products. By 1981 he

had been quite successful in developing sales in Africa and had developed good relationships with local health officials and ministers. His MD plan called for his transfer to Greece at the end of 1982.

Headquarters executives were sensitive to various aspects of Malterre's career. According to Grunwald: "Malterre has worked in Pharma, at corporate level and abroad. His big disadvantage is not to be French, but his mother tongue is French. He is well-experienced in the Ciba-Geigy organization and knows the French group company, since most products sold in French West Africa are made in France."

---

**APPENDIX**

# The Ciba-Geigy Organization in 1981

Ciba-Geigy was a leading chemical company with affiliates in over 60 countries on five continents and employing more than 80,000 people worldwide. Switzerland's chemical industry has turned a disadvantage—the country's lack of natural resources—into a strength: specialization in high-quality products. Ciba-Geigy had always assigned central importance to research: Apart from its extensive R&D facilities in Switzerland, the company maintained research units in the United States, United Kingdom, France, West Germany, Italy, Canada, Japan, Indonesia, and Australia. Exhibits 9 through 12 summarize key information about Ciba-Geigy. The company operated through seven product divisions.

## DYESTUFFS AND CHEMICALS DIVISION

Dyestuffs were Ciba-Geigy's first major products and still represented a core field of activity. A variety of colors for the dyeing and printing of wool, silk, cellulosic, and synthetic fibers and blends constituted the division's main product range. The textile chemicals range also included products for pretreatment, whitening agents, dyeing auxiliaries and softeners, mothproofing, as well as finishing auxiliaries that imparted dimensional stability and crease-re-

## EXHIBIT 9

**GROUP SALES** (SFr Millions)

| Operating sector | 1981 | 1980 | Change (%) |
|---|---|---|---|
| Dyestuffs and chemicals | 2,173 | 2,007 | +18 |
| Pharmaceuticals | 3,782 | 3,213 | +18 |
| Agricultural | 3,397 | 2,683 | +27 |
| Plastics and additives | 2,607 | 2,345 | +11 |
| Airwick | 706 | 617 | +14 |
| Ilford | 472 | 619 | −24 |
| Electronic equipment | 462 | 430 | + 7 |
| Group total | 13,599 | 11,914 | +14 |

## EXHIBIT 10

**GROUP FINANCIAL PERFORMANCE** (SFr Millions)

| | 1981 | 1980 |
|---|---|---|
| Group operating profit | 521 | 305 |
| Group operating cash flow | 1,339 | 1,032 |
| Wages, salaries, bonuses, and welfare benefits | 4,095 | 3,719 |
| Research and development expenditures | 1,076 | 937 |
| Capital expenditures | 875 | 853 |
| Insured value of fixed assets at end of year | 14,110 | 14,412 |
| Number of employees at year-end | 80,179 | 81,184 |

## EXHIBIT 11

**GEOGRAPHIC BREAKDOWN OF GROUP SALES AND CAPITAL EXPENDITURES (%)**

| | Sales | | Capital expenditures | |
|---|---|---|---|---|
| | 1981 | 1980 | 1981 | 1980 |
| Europe | 43 | 48 | 65 | 70 |
| (Switzerland) | | | (36) | (41) |
| North America | 29 | 26 | 16 | 16 |
| Latin America | 12 | 11 | 14 | 10 |
| Asia | 10 | 9 | 4 | 2 |
| Africa, Australia, and Oceania | 6 | 6 | 1 | 2 |
| Total | 100 | 100 | 100 | 100 |

---

**EXHIBIT 12**

---

**LOCATION OF MAJOR AFFILIATES**

| Region | Major affiliates and agencies |
| --- | --- |
| Europe | Austria, Belgium, Bulgaria, Czechoslovakia, Denmark, Finland, France, German Democratic Republic, German Federal Republic, Greece, Hungary, Ireland, Italy, Netherlands, Norway, Poland, Portugal, Rumania, Spain, Sweden, Turkey, United Kingdom, U.S.S.R., Yugoslavia |
| North America | Canada, United States |
| Latin America | Argentina, Bolivia, Brazil, Chile, Colombia, Ecuador, Guadaloupe, Guatemala, Mexico, Panama, Paraguay, Peru, Uruguay, Venezuela |
| Africa | Algeria, Angola, Cameroon, Egypt, Ivory Coast, Kenya, Madagascar, Mali, Morocco, Mozambique, Nigeria, Senegal, Somalia, South Africa, Sudan, Tanzania, Uganda, Zaire, Zambia, Zimbabwe |
| Australasia | Australia, Bangladesh, Hong Kong, India, Indonesia, Iran, Iraq, Japan, Kuwait, Lebanon, Malaysia, Pakistan, Philippines, Saudi Arabia, Singapore, South Korea, Syria, Taiwan, Thailand |

*Note:* Headquarters in Basel, Switzerland.

---

sistant, water-repellent, flame-retardant and anti-static properties. Fluorescent whitening agents found further use above all in the detergents and cosmetics industries, as did antimicrobials. Finally, the division offered a broad range of dyes and synthetic tannins for leather and fur and of specialty chemicals that go into the manufacture of paper.

## PHARMACEUTICALS DIVISION

This was Ciba-Geigy's largest division, with five medically important areas of specialization: cardiovascular preparations (particularly in the beta-blockers field); antirheumatics and other anti-inflammatory preparations; psychotropic and neurotropic drugs (e.g., antidepressants and drugs for the treatment of epilepsy); medicines for the treatment of various infectious diseases (such as special antibiotics against tuberculosis); and a more heterogeneous but also significant range of preparations, notably dermatologicals (specially for the treatment of eczema), a new drug against breast cancer, and drugs for coughs and colds.

The Pharma Division was also concerned with developing more effective forms of administering medicines. This effort had already resulted in the Transdermal Therapeutic Systems, which made possible the controlled-rate introduction of certain drugs through the skin and into the bloodstream. Ciba-Geigy

pharmaceutical research was at the same time probing the frontiers of immunology and biotechnology.

## AGRICULTURAL DIVISION

The primary mission of this division was to improve the yield and quality of food crops, livestock, and natural fibers. It was functionally articulated into three branches. Plant protection provided growers with safe, reliable products that served to ensure larger and better harvests, such as herbicides, insecticides, fungicides, and micronutrients. The biotechnical products branch was active in animal health with specialties for the prevention and treatment of disease; in public health with insecticides and disinfectants; and in the protection of stored commodities with insecticides and rodenticides. The seeds branch was engaged principally in the breeding and production of high performance hybrid seeds, above all—though by no means exclusively—for maize and sorghum.

## PLASTICS AND ADDITIVES DIVISION

This division's activities encompassed three important product groups: plastics, pigments, and additives. The plastics range comprised synthetic resins, molding compounds, and high-grade thermoplastic resins for application in electrical and electronic engineering, automotive and aerospace engineering, plastics, metal and wood processing, the construction industry, and paints and coatings. The division also produced resin-impregnated fiber materials, honeycomb materials and honeycomb sandwich panels used in lightweight structures, and fiber-reinforced composites for application in the aerospace and automotive industries. Organic and inorganic pigments and pigment preparations, together with special colors for plastics, paints, printing inks, and synthetic fibers, were important products in numerous branches of industry.

Ciba-Geigy was a major supplier of many additives, a product group which included antioxidants and light and heat stabilizers, fluorescent whiteners, plasticizers for plastics, elastomers and synthetic fibers, ultraviolet curing agents, biocides and other auxiliaries, synthetic lubricant base stocks, fire-resistant hydraulic fluids, antiwear additives and metal passivators for the petroleum industry, corrosion inhibitors, and water treatment chemicals.

## AIRWICK GROUP

Airwick manufactured and marketed a variety of consumer products throughout the world. The household products line included air fresheners, insecticides, carpet, floor and curtain care products, laundry starches and other textile products, and bathroom and kitchen cleaners. The garden products group was derived from Ciba-Geigy's agricultural research, and consisted of insecticides, herbicides, fertilizers, snail bait granules and lawn care products. Personal hygiene products included toothpastes, mouthwashes and breath fresheners, facial and hair preparations and shower and bath products.

## ILFORD GROUP

Ilford was a leading manufacturer of black-and-white photographic materials. It also supplied a broad range of printing and enlarging papers, together with processing chemicals and equipment. In the color photography field, Ilford's specialty was the Cibachrome product line, based on the silver dye-bleach process. This included materials for making enlargements from color slides and for copying documents in color.

## ELECTRONIC EQUIPMENT GROUP

The Gretag/CX group specialized in four sectors of electronics. One was its telecommunications security systems. Another, color measuring instruments, were used for quality control in the graphic arts. Eidophor large-screen television projection was also a major Gretag innovation. Finally, in partnership with CX Corporation of Seattle, Gretag has become a leading manufacturer of equipment for the color photo-finishing industry.

The Mettler group's electronic precision, analytical, micro- and ultramicro-balances were used for weighing and for such industrial applications as determining weight deviations, formula weighing with net total display, determining moisture content, or the counting of small, mass-produced parts. Mettler's micro-processor-controlled automatic titrators and thermal analysis systems simplified quality assurance in the pharmaceutical, food, and plastics industries, among others. Mettler Optic AG was chiefly occupied with micro-lithography and thin-film technology.

# PART TEN

# A Final Series— Managing Strategic Redirection

# The European Paint Industry in 1977

The paint industry was one of the major sectors of the chemical and allied products industries in 1977, accounting for between 12 percent and 15 percent of total chemical output (on a value basis) in most European countries. Annual paint production totaled over 5 million tons in Europe in that year, which was slightly above paint output in the United States and compared with over 1.5 million tons for Japan. In value terms, this production equalled DM14.6 billion (or about $7 billion) in 1977. Total employment in the industry was estimated at almost 120,000 in that year, down some 6,800 from the peak 1973 figure.

This case first discusses the main products and technologies which comprised the industry and which were subject to rapid change during the period under consideration. Second, the principal market segments are described, as well as some of the major characteristics of the distribution system then prevailing. Finally, all major competitors are identified, and the shifting nature of the industry's competitive structure is briefly outlined.

## PRODUCTS AND TECHNOLOGIES

The chief function of paints or their generic equivalent, coatings, is to protect and/or decorate a multitude of different surfaces. In addition to demand for paints of every color and shade, countless performance characteristics were required for the many end-uses in which coatings were employed. All paints were made of three main ingredients: the vehicle (also known as the binder or resin), the pigment, and the solvent. The particular types and combinations of these three components determined the actual properties of the coating and its likely uses.

Only the largest paint manufacturers could justify a resin plant of their own, and, consequently, large amounts of resin were purchased annually by the paint industry. The four main types of resin were: (1) alkyd resins, most commonly made from modified vegetable oils; (2) resins based on other natural products, including some made from vegetable oils; (3) water-based resins (acrylic and vinyl resins); and (4) other synthetic resins.

Pigments consist of organic or inorganic solids that are incorporated into the paint as dis-

This industry note was written by Claire Fortier and André Khodjamirian, research associates, and Professor José de la Torre. It is intended to be used in conjunction with the case series on BOK Finishes. © INSEAD, The European Institute of Business Administration, 1986.

crete particles and whose function is to confer color and opacity as well as to attribute certain properties such as light resistance and flow characteristics to the coating material.

Organic solvents are volatile liquids whose main functions are to dissolve the paint resins and to modify its viscosity. The two most important characteristics of a particular solvent material thus are its power (that is, its ability to dissolve a specific resin) and its rate of evaporation, which, in turn, determines the degree of atmospheric pollution it creates. The major categories of solvents include hydrocarbons, esters, ketones, alcohols, and glycol ethers.

It is the solid content of a paint which determines demand. The overall average solids content of coatings was 46 percent of volume in 1977, with a dramatic increase to 65 percent predicted by 1984. In addition, all technologies available in 1977, except powder coating, generally showed a trend toward higher dry film thicknesses, thereby reducing the number of coats needed to achieve the desired results.

Raw materials accounted for up to 50 percent of total paint product costs and were subject to cyclical price variations. Natural ingredients, notably vegetable-derived oils, had always been prone to sharp price fluctuations as the result of changing world supply and demand conditions or natural phenomena such as variations in climate. Escalating oil prices had caused the prices of commodity chemicals (resins and solvents) to increase substantially over the past few years. Currency changes and legislation concerning environmental protection that may affect the production of certain chemicals also influenced price levels. Large-scale speculative buying by some companies would occasionally exacerbate the situation to the extent that some materials were sold only on an allocation basis. Prices of up to three times normal list prices had been cited by some users as necessary in order to obtain a supply of essential materials at times of heavy or unexpected demand.

## Technological Change

Since its inception, the coatings industry had relied primarily on one technology, that is, low-solids, solvent-based systems, the main exception being water-based architectural paints. As late as 1970, approximately 75 percent of all paints produced used traditional technology. After that time, a number of factors played a major role in changing the basic nature of the product. The advent of environmental awareness, for example, brought pressure to bear on the industry to reduce the pollution risk of its products. California's "Rule 66," implemented in 1967, was the landmark legislation act affecting the coatings industry in the United States. This eventually led to increased concern over pollution from coatings in Europe, particularly on the seriousness of health hazards and environmental risks with regard to the manufacture and application of paints. Three types of pollution can be attributed to operations associated with coatings:

- Air—from the evaporation of solvents in both coating production and application; by far the most serious
- Water—process and waste water discharged into sewers, streams, and lakes
- Solid—solid waste generation typically disposed into landfills

A common factor in the legislation of different countries was their limitation of the emission of organic materials into the air, i.e., solvents and decomposition products that were formed during the drying process. For West Germany the most important guideline was set out in the seventh emission by-law of the North-Rhine Westphalia region whereby the amount of carbon in the exhaust gas of the drying ovens may not exceed 300 mg/ml. In addition, industry norms increasingly required noncontamination of water by soluble binders, either water- or solvent-based. Easy cleaning of the processing equipment and the removal of the paint wastes by safe methods (e.g., by burning) were also part of these requirements. Finally, the market called for increased safety for the paint user, that is, for paints containing minimum toxic constituents.

A second determinant factor in the technological revolution shaking the industry was the major changes in the costs and availability of chemical raw materials that occurred in the 1970s. Rising prices and material shortages motivated the industry to seek alternative product technologies that would minimize these problems. Third, although direct labor contributed only 9 percent of total paint costs, the user's application costs typically consisted of as much as 85 percent labor and only 15 percent materials. Therefore, any reduction in the number of coats and/or application time needed to obtain the required degree of protection could represent a substantial saving to the end user.

In response to these factors, the industry was shifting toward low-solvent, high-solid paints and toward emulsion or water-based paints, which also allowed for better pollution control. A low-solvent content reduced the degree of pollution in application, whereas a high-solid content sometimes also decreased the number of coats that need to be applied without impairing quality.

A plethora of new products were introduced in response to these often conflicting environmental, energy-saving, and product-effectiveness demands. Oil- and/or synthetic-resin-based paints were still the most popular products in 1977, but demand for new products such as higher-solids coatings, powders, and water-based dispersions and emulsions was growing at an average annual rate of 5 percent compared to a rate of 1.5 percent for older technologies. Such technological market segmentation was most pronounced within the industrial paints sector, where seven different technologies were being used:

1. *Solvent systems/low solids:* all types of solvent-based coatings whose solid content was below 70 percent by volume
2. *Solvent systems/high solids:* all types of solvent-based coatings where the solid content was above 70 percent by volume
3. *Two-pack catalyzed systems:* all liquid compositions, with or without solvent or water present, which required the blending of two components or the addition of a catalyst just before use

4. *Emulsions and lactices:* water-based compositions in which the main film-forming ingredient was in a fully polymerized, emulsified state
5. *Water solubles and colloidal dispersions:* all water-borne systems containing film-forming materials of relatively low molecular weight which underwent further polymerization when finally cured—this category included all "electrocoat" systems
6. *Powder coatings:* all systems in which the coating composition was in the form of a powder
7. *Radiation-cured systems:* compositions formulated to be cured by high-energy radiation systems, such as ultraviolet or electron beam

An estimate of market shares (by volume) in the industrial paint sector by technology type, for 1977 and five-year projections, appears in Exhibit 1.

High-solid paints were considered promising as they offered many advantages when compared with conventional systems such as materials savings, reduction of toxic emissions, reduced transport and storage costs, lower insurance costs (due to reduced inflammable solvent content), and often lower curing temperature. Powder coatings, long regarded as having significant potential for the penetration of conventional coating systems, had not been fully successful due mainly to the reluctance of large users to write off their existing investments in conventional spraying installations. Yet, there existed considerable potential savings in direct labor costs in application by substituting powder for liquid coatings. Since these costs represented 40 to 50 percent, on average, and sometimes as high as 75 percent of total user application costs, certain high-volume sectors such as household appliances, the automotive industry, and tubular steel products had undertaken the necessary investments and accounted for almost half of powder coatings demand in 1977.

As material, labor, and energy costs rose in the mid-1970s, new and more efficient means of

**EXHIBIT 1**

**ESTIMATED AND PROJECTED DEMAND BY COATING TECHNOLOGY IN W. EUROPE, 1977 TO 1987** (Percent)

|  | Estimated 1977 | Projected | | |
|---|---|---|---|---|
|  |  | 1980 | 1982 | 1987 |
| Solvent systems under 70% solids | 66 | 57 | 47 | 37 |
| Solvent systems over 70% solids | 6 | 9 | 12 | 15 |
| Two-pack catalyzed systems | 16 | 17 | 18 | 19 |
| Emulsions & lactices | 4 | 5 | 7 | 8 |
| Water solubles & colloidal dispersions | 5 | 7 | 9 | 12 |
| Powder coatings | 2 | 4 | 5 | 6 |
| Radiation-cured systems | 1 | 1 | 2 | 3 |
| Total | 100 | 100 | 100 | 100 |

Source: *Problems or Profit? The European Coatings Industry,* volume 1, Chemical Marketing Services, London, 1977.

application and curing of coatings were being sought and adopted. The pattern of change for each market was nonetheless very diverse, as each had a unique profile in terms of its requirements for technology, product mix, volume, solids content, and dry film thickness.

## Production Volumes and Costs

Until 1973, European production of paints, varnishes, and mastic grew steadily at 4 to 5 percent per annum. Subsequently, the impact of the worldwide economic recession was reflected in a decrease in demand in most countries, limiting total growth of output to less than 2 percent per annum. The most important producing country was West Germany, which manufactured about one-quarter of European production, followed by Italy (16.7 percent), France (15.2 percent), and the United Kingdom (13.8 percent). Together these four countries accounted for over 70 percent of total West European production (see Exhibit 2).

In 1977, about 5.2 million tons of raw materials (of which, two thirds were hydrocarbons), were used for paint production in Europe. Their relative importance was as follows:

|  | Percent of value | Percent of volume |
|---|---|---|
| Solvents | 17.5 | 36.0 |
| Resins | 36.0 | 23.5 |
| Pigments | 42.0 | 19.5 |
| Extenders | 3.5 | 13.0 |
| Water | — | 9.0 |
| Other additives | 1.0 | 1.0 |
|  | 100.0 | 100.0 |

Because of differences in classification, it was not possible to compare the different types of paint produced by country. For Europe as a whole the approximate breakdown in 1977 was 42 percent water and emulsion paints, 23 percent alkyds, 7 percent cellulose-based paints and varnishes, and 28 percent unspecified. In most countries, there was a definite trend away from oil-based toward emulsion paints.

The costs of supplying paint to a given market obviously varied depending on the type of paint and the scale of production. Raw materials averaged about 46 percent of sales in 1977 and direct labor 9 percent. Subject to variations according to product mix and degree of sophistication of the industry, about one-half of all in-

## EXHIBIT 2

### WEST EUROPEAN PRODUCTION OF PAINTS & ALLIED PRODUCTS, 1970 TO 1977

| | 1970 Volume (thousand tons) | 1970 Percent | 1971 (thousand tons) | 1972 (thousand tons) | 1973 (thousand tons) | 1974 (thousand tons) | 1975 (thousand tons) | 1976 (thousand tons) | 1977 Volume (thousand tons) | 1977 Percent | Average annual growth (%) |
|---|---|---|---|---|---|---|---|---|---|---|---|
| Austria | 78 | 2.0 | 84 | 81 | 104 | 105 | 103 | 111 | 115 | 2.3 | 6.1 |
| Belgium | 125 | 3.2 | 130 | 126 | 133 | 120 | 117 | 135 | 137 | 2.7 | 1.6 |
| Denmark | 94 | 2.4 | 100 | 92 | 88 | 84 | 98 | 110 | 114 | 2.3 | 3.1 |
| Finland | 45 | 1.1 | 46 | 53 | 63 | 60 | 68 | 65 | 60 | 1.2 | 4.7 |
| France | 570 | 15.1 | 610 | 648 | 789 | 688 | 675 | 675 | 712 | 14.2 | 3.6 |
| West Germany | 1,146 | 29.2 | 1,192 | 1,301 | 1,363 | 1,169 | 1,207 | 1,245 | 1,265 | 25.2 | 1.7 |
| Greece | 18 | 0.5 | 20 | 18 | 22 | 30 | 30 | 32 | 35 | 0.7 | 10.5 |
| Ireland | 16 | 0.4 | 17 | 18 | 18 | 17 | 15 | 18 | 18 | 0.4 | 2.1 |
| Italy | 412 | 10.5 | 420 | 505 | 550 | 850 | 781 | 925 | 870 | 17.3 | 12.8 |
| Netherlands | 184 | 4.7 | 192 | 193 | 202 | 192 | 190 | 197 | 200 | 4.0 | (1.1) |
| Norway | 56 | 1.4 | 58 | 63 | 66 | 72 | 73 | 75 | 77 | 1.5 | 5.4 |
| Portugal | 30 | 0.8 | 32 | 41 | 44 | 44 | 42 | 63 | 72 | 1.4 | 14.6 |
| Spain | 195 | 5.0 | 208 | 269 | 293 | 328 | 350 | 370 | 1374 | 7.5 | 10.1 |
| Sweden | 152 | 3.9 | 160 | 149 | 155 | 158 | 205 | 206 | 194 | 3.9 | 4.1 |
| Switzerland | 64 | 1.6 | 68 | 77 | 80 | 74 | 68 | 68 | 70 | 1.4 | 1.5 |
| United Kingdom | 715 | 18.2 | 745 | 765 | 744 | 740 | 821 | 680 | 707 | 14.1 | 0.2 |
| Total | 3,920 | 100.0 | 4,082 | 4,402 | 4,714 | 4,731 | 4,843 | 4,975 | 5,020 | 100.0 | 3.6 |

Source: A Profile of the European Paint Industry, 3d & 4th editions, Information Research Ltd., London, 1977 & 1979.

| EXHIBIT 3 | | | |
|---|---|---|---|

**EXFACTORY COSTS FOR TYPICAL, FULL-LINE OPERATION** (Percent)

| | 1973 | 1975 | 1977 |
|---|---|---|---|
| Sales | 100.0 | 100.0 | 100.0 |
| Raw materials & packaging | 44.0 | 49.0 | 46.0 |
| Production costs | 15.0 | 13.0 | 13.0 |
| Margin exworks | 41.0 | 38.0 | 41.0 |
| Direct & indirect selling | 19.0 | 20.0 | 20.0 |
| Advertising | 2.0 | 2.0 | 2.5 |
| R&D | 2.0 | 2.5 | 2.5 |
| Contribution to profit | 18.0 | 13.5 | 16.0 |
| General administration & other | 10.0 | 9.0 | 8.0 |
| Operating income | 8.0 | 4.0 | 8.0 |

*Source:* Industry studies and BOK Finishes internal documents.

dustry employment was in production, of which skilled and semiskilled categories typically accounted for 30 percent each. About 2.5 percent of sales was spent on R&D (globally, but company variations were enormous), and another 22.5 percent on sales, distribution, and advertising. Sales, administration, and technical staff accounted for about 45 percent of total employment. An approximate breakdown of the exfactory cost of a unit volume of paint is given in Exhibit 3 for a typical, full-line operation.

Paint production was invariably a batch process with average batch size often being used as a measure of business activity. Production costs were almost entirely related to batch size; once the proper combination of materials had been selected for the particular application in mind, the actual production process itself was quite simple. One of the most critical stages involved the cleaning of the machinery and tanks between batches to avoid cross-contamination.

As the European paint industry was entering an era of unprecedented technological market segmentation, it also suffered from a degree of overcapacity related to its fragmented nature. Since manufacturers would need to become competent in at least two new types of coating technology, the need to remain profitable during this transition was accompanied by a major ra-

tionalization effort within the industry. Old and inefficient plants were being shut, and new units that might come on stream would have to be larger, more flexible, and more economical. Thus, future trends called for manufacturers to produce a larger number of production batches to meet the increasing variety of customer needs, with a consequent shrinkage in batch sizes. Exhibit 4 provides an overview of this complexity by showing the shares held by each technology type in the main industrial markets.

## Strategic Implications

Profound changes in average solids content, storage stability, application methods, solvent usage, resin selection, average batch size, unit cost, and selling price will be a direct result of this technological revolution. Awareness of its importance dawned on the U.S. industry in the early 1970s and spread to Europe within 3 to 4 years. The systematic evaluation of alternative technologies, whereby large users began to experiment with new products or application methods on production lines and prototype installations, was currently underway in the United States and Europe. The wholesale adoption of new coating technologies and the implied investments in new plant and equipment might

## INDUSTRIAL COATINGS TECHNOLOGY SHARES BY END USE, 1977 (Percent Market Share)

| End use (industrial markets only) | Percent of total market | Solvent systems under 70% solids | Solvent systems over 70% solids (incl. hot melts) | Two-part catalyzed systems (incl. Polyester/Styrene) | Emulsions & lactices | Water solubles & colloidal dispersions (incl. electrocoat) | Powder coatings | Radiation-cured systems |
|---|---|---|---|---|---|---|---|---|
| Wood furniture | 12.9 | 44 | 3 | 42 | 6 | 1 | | 4 |
| Sheet metal products and fittings | 6.3 | 68 | 3 | 8 | | 6 | | 1 |
| Food and beverage cans | 2.1 | 94 | 3 | | 1 | 1 | | 1 |
| Metal containers and closures | 2.2 | 94 | 3 | | | 2 | 1 | |
| Coil coating | 2.5 | 80 | 16 | | 2 | 2 | | |
| Domestic appliances | 1.9 | 78 | 3 | | | 9 | 10 | |
| Motor vehicles—top coats | 5.5 | 94 | 2 | 2 | | 1 | 1 | |
| Motor vehicles—primers | 7.2 | 63 | 3 | 1 | | 32 | 1 | |
| Motor vehicles—components and subassemblies | 2.7 | 44 | 4 | 5 | 6 | 26 | 15 | |
| Motor vehicles—refinishing topcoats | 4.9 | 77 | 2 | 21 | | | | |
| Motor vehicles—refinishing primer surfaces | 2.6 | 64 | 4 | 32 | | 5 | 3 | |
| Machinery | 7.7 | 78 | 6 | 7 | 1 | 2 | 1 | |
| Industrial maintenance | 19.5 | 57 | 12 | 16 | 12 | | | |
| Miscellaneous fabricated metal products | 2.6 | 65 | 11 | 18 | 1 | 2 | 2 | 1 |
| Electrical insulation coatings | 3.2 | 71 | 12 | 15 | 1 | 1 | | |
| Marine finishes | 5.7 | 72 | 9 | 17 | 2 | | | |
| All others | 10.5 | | | | | | | |
| Total | 100.0 | | | | | | | |

Note: The market shares for each end use total 100% horizontally; the percent of total market shown in the first vertical column indicates the relative size of each end use.

Source: Problems or Profit? The European Coating Industry, 1977–1987, volume 1.

peak between 1981 and 1985 in the United States and a few years later in Europe.

Among the strategic implications of these technological changes, the following were considered critical in 1977:

1. Customers would continue to want all their special requirements met, but with at least twice as many different types of coatings; thus the average market size of any specific product was likely to decline.
2. The rising content of solids meant that any given volume would cover larger surfaces, with a resulting decrease in liquid demand and a profound influence on the size and design of future production facilities.
3. Because of these new formulations, packaging stability and storage life would decline, contributing to smaller and more frequent orders, increased inventory losses, and costly laboratory efforts to overcome these problems.
4. Average batch size was a critical determinant of the most efficient size for various tank installations and would directly affect the cost of production labor, color matching, and the justification for automatic raw materials handling and filling equipment.
5. The total number of raw materials which would have to be maintained in inventory at every production facility was likely to increase. The current value of the average pound of inventory would therefore increase at an annual rate appreciably higher than that of inflation.
6. Because no one company would be able to handle successfully all seven technologies, market shares would be redistributed according to these rather than to customers. Although in 1977 most coating purchasers were using no more than two technologies, in a decade's time most would be using at least four.
7. Product pricing was expected to become crucial as raw material and production costs escalated. So far the industry had been largely unsuccessful in passing on rising costs to the consumer. From 1964 to 1973, coatings prices rose at an annual rate of 2.5 percent. While oil prices jumped over 300 percent in 1973–1974, coatings prices increased only at an annual rate of 19 percent; and while oil prices continued to rise 8 percent per annum from 1975 to 1977, coatings prices rose at a 7 percent annual rate.
8. Application efficiency will gain increased importance as a measure of a coating's marketability. The steady shift toward higher-volume solids plus rising raw material costs for every liquid coating will require improving the overall transfer efficiency (that is the percentage ratio of coating deposited on the object relative to the volume sprayed) of the existing spray applications.

## THE MARKET

The consumption of paints and allied products in Europe was 4.7 million tons in 1977, up almost a million tons from the beginning of the decade but down from the 1974 high of 5 million (see Exhibit 5). The largest market was West Germany, which accounted for 22.5 percent of European consumption in 1977. When combined with the next three largest users in order of size— Italy (18.1 percent), France (15.6 percent), and the United Kingdom (13.8 percent)—the four countries accounted for 70 percent of West European consumption. The rankings in terms of per capita consumption were different, however: Sweden led with 23.4 kg followed by Norway and Germany at 20.3 kg, and Denmark at 17.9 kg. The European average was 14.3 kg, which compared with 21.0 kg in the United States and 11.3 kg in Japan. Overall paint consumption in Europe was maturing and was expected to show a declining annual growth rate of 3 to 4 percent in the late 1970s and 2 to 3 percent in the 1980s.

### Market Segments

The paint market could be split into two main groups each covering several subsegments according to end-use as shown below. Exhibit 6 provides a breakdown of the total European paint

## EXHIBIT 5

## WEST EUROPEAN CONSUMPTION OF PAINTS & ALLIED PRODUCTS, 1970 TO 1977

| | 1970 Volume (thousand tons) | 1970 Percent | 1970 Kg per capita | 1971 (thousand tons) | 1972 (thousand tons) | 1973 (thousand tons) | 1974 (thousand tons) | 1975 (thousand tons) | 1976 (thousand tons) | 1977 Volume (thousand tons) | 1977 Percent | 1977 Kg per capita |
|---|---|---|---|---|---|---|---|---|---|---|---|---|
| Austria | 84 | 2.2 | 11.6 | 91 | 90 | 110 | 98 | 97 | 106 | 100 | 2.1 | 14.8 |
| Belgium | 121 | 3.2 | 12.9 | 122 | 124 | 130 | 122 | 115 | 138 | 180 | 3.8 | 13.7 |
| Denmark | 73 | 1.9 | 15.4 | 67 | 69 | 110 | 94 | 91 | 100 | 91 | 1.9 | 17.9 |
| Finland | 49 | 1.3 | 9.8 | 49 | 58 | 65 | 76 | 73 | 70 | 65 | 1.4 | 13.9 |
| France | 726 | 19.2 | 15.0 | 722 | 784 | 830 | 800 | 779 | 742 | 740 | 15.6 | 16.4 |
| West Germany | 1,094 | 28.9 | 18.8 | 1,178 | 1,247 | 1,310 | 1,171 | 1,149 | 1,117 | 1,064 | 22.5 | 20.3 |
| Greece | 19 | 0.5 | 2.4 | 20 | 21 | 22 | 18 | 16 | 49 | 50 | 1.1 | 5.5 |
| Ireland | 22 | 0.6 | 7.7 | 23 | 24 | 25 | 19 | 18 | 26 | 24 | 0.5 | 7.6 |
| Italy | 412 | 10.9 | 8.2 | 485 | 506 | 650 | 899 | 777 | 920 | 857 | 18.1 | 15.5 |
| Netherlands | 153 | 4.0 | 12.6 | 146 | 152 | 210 | 171 | 159 | 166 | 183 | 3.9 | 12.5 |
| Norway | 57 | 1.5 | 15.5 | 54 | 61 | 70 | 73 | 71 | 78 | 81 | 1.7 | 20.3 |
| Portugal | 28 | 0.7 | 3.1 | 37 | 42 | 50 | 42 | 40 | 71 | 77 | 1.5 | 7.2 |
| Spain | 195 | 5.1 | 6.2 | 198 | 270 | 280 | 320 | 320 | 288 | 303 | 6.4 | 10.7 |
| Sweden | 155 | 4.1 | 20.2 | 143 | 156 | 200 | 205 | 194 | 196 | 183 | 3.9 | 23.4 |
| Switzerland | 71 | 1.9 | 12.1 | 74 | 80 | 83 | 100 | 84 | 84 | 89 | 1.9 | 14.2 |
| United Kingdom | 529 | 14.0 | 9.8 | 559 | 600 | 700 | 814 | 769 | 646 | 653 | 13.8 | 13.3 |
| Total | 3,788 | 100.0 | | 3,968 | 4,285 | 4,845 | 5,022 | 4,752 | 4,794 | 4,733 | 100.0 | |

Source: A Profile of the European Paint Industry, 3d & 4th editions, Information Research Ltd., London, 1977 & 1979.

**EXHIBIT 6**

**TOTAL PAINT MARKET BY MAJOR USER CATEGORIES,
1974 to 1977** (Percent of Total)

|  | 1974 | 1975 | 1976 | 1977 |
|---|---|---|---|---|
| Architectural coatings |  |  |  |  |
| Decorative | 36.5 | 36.4 | 36.4 | 37.0 |
| Do-it-yourself | 16.2 | 16.4 | 16.6 | 16.5 |
|  | 52.6 | 52.8 | 53.0 | 53.5 |
| Industrial coatings |  |  |  |  |
| Automotive | 5.3 | 4.8 | 4.4 | 4.7 |
| Car refinishes | 3.3 | 3.4 | 3.6 | 4.0 |
| Wood finishes | 10.3 | 10.4 | 10.1 | 9.8 |
| Coil coating | 0.8 | 0.8 | 0.9 | 1.0 |
| Powder coating | 0.6 | 0.8 | 0.9 | 1.0 |
| Home appliances | 1.3 | 1.2 | 1.2 | 1.3 |
| Marine | 3.1 | 3.1 | 3.1 | 3.3 |
| Other | 22.7 | 22.8 | 22.8 | 21.4 |
|  | 47.4 | 47.2 | 47.0 | 46.5 |
| Total | 100.0 | 100.0 | 100.0 | 100.0 |

*Source: Profile of the European Paint Industry,* 4th edition, Information Research Ltd., London, 1979.

market in terms of these categories. *Architectural coatings* included decorative paints (deco) used by professional painters and trades people and do-it-yourself (DIY) paints for amateurs and hobbies. *Industrial coatings* included the following:

- Automotive: car manufacturers (OEM) and automotive suppliers
- Car refinishes: car and vehicle repairs
- Wood finishes: architectural elements and furniture
- Can and coil coating: endless metal strips
- Anticorrosion: industrial maintenance, piping, etc.
- Marine: ship building and maintenance, offshore platforms
- Home appliances: "white" goods, electrical appliances, etc.
- Aircraft: OEMs and maintenance
- Other industries: machinery, rolling stock, highway signs, etc.

This market segment breakdown varied considerably by country, however, depending on such factors as the level of industrialization and the importance of individual national industries, such as automobile, ship building, and aviation. For example, the architectural market was relatively small (less than 50 percent of the total) in highly industrialized countries such as Belgium, West Germany, and Sweden; it exceeded 60 percent of the total in Ireland and Switzerland, and it was over 70 percent in Greece and Portugal. For all other European countries it oscillated from 53 to 58 percent of the total market. Furthermore, the breakdown of the architectural market between the deco trade and DIY segments differed widely among countries. In Scandinavia, the United Kingdom, and other northern European markets, the DIY segment was relatively more important than in the less developed areas of southern Europe. Exhibit 7 gives an approximate breakdown of consumption for some European countries.

Each market segment could be characterized by the number of suppliers, customers, growth, life cycle, etc. For instance, although the product was basically the same for the deco and DIY

**EXHIBIT 7**

**END-USE BREAKDOWN FOR SELECTED COUNTRIES, 1977** (Percent of Total)

| | Belgium | France | West Germany | Italy | Netherlands | United Kingdom |
|---|---|---|---|---|---|---|
| Architectural (total) | 47.0 | 55.7 | 42.0 | 57.8 | 56.2 | 52.9 |
| Industrial | | | | | | |
| Car refinish | 4.0 | 8.2 | 3.8 | 10.1 | 2.5 | 4.1 |
| Wood finishes | 5.5 | 5.9 | 6.5 | 12.4 | 4.5 | 4.9 |
| Other (including automotive) | 27.0 | 16.7 | 29.2 | 11.3 | 17.9 | 27.9 |
| Marine | } 10.5 | 1.6 | } 12.5 | 1.7 | 6.1 | 6.2 |
| Anticorrosion | | } 11.9 | | 3.6 | } 12.8 | 4.0 |
| Unspecified | 6.0 | | 6.0 | 3.1 | | — |
| Total | 100.0 | 100.0 | 100.0 | 100.0 | 100.0 | 100.0 |

*Source:* Profile of the European Paint Industry, 4th edition, Information Research Ltd., London, May 1979.

markets (both products were susceptible to fashion trends, particularly insofar as color was concerned), they were very different from a distribution point of view. The DIY market offered greater variations across Europe in that shopping habits varied by culture; for instance, in Italy 19 percent of DIY sales were made through specialized DIY outlets, but in the Netherlands only 9 percent of sales were made this way. An overview of the main characteristics of the main market segments follows.

**Decorative and Do-It-Yourself**   The architectural paints market was the largest segment. It was characterized by slow growth and many suppliers, regional, national, and international. Product technology was quite basic, but the product line was wide with huge variations in prices and quality. Critical to success in the deco market was an efficient distribution system, not always easy to realize because of the large number of end users. Technical and marketing image were also considered important and delivery times were extremely short.

The DIY segment was relatively new, growing fastest in areas where labor was either in short supply and/or expensive. There were fewer suppliers in this market than in the deco sector because of the difficulty of obtaining retail shelf space. Promotion and advertising were important in this segment. As the market matured,

and DIY users became more knowledgeable, price sensitivity decreased, and quality took on more importance. For medium-quality paints, large surface outlets were chosen, but as the need for quality increased, the specialist stores gained in importance. One advantage of the segment was its almost inverse relationship to the business cycle: As times got harder, consumers tended to stay at home and maintain their property.

**Automotive and Car Refinishes**   The automotive segment was the most "international" sector of the paint industry as customers tended to be few but large and geographically diversified. Barriers to entry were high because the product was complex and tailor-made, usually at the forefront of paint and application technology. Although the actual cost of the coating was a small fraction of the total cost of the end product, its quality was an essential element affecting product image and, therefore, was crucial to sales. The segment was particularly sensitive to environmental and health issues and also to the business cycle. Despite this and the low growth of the sector, profitability tended to be high. However, a large market share was required to support the necessary R&D effort, and good customer service was essential to maintain that share.

Car refinishing was a small but growing segment of the paint market characterized by a limited number of suppliers but many customers. The keys to this market included effective distribution channels with quick delivery and quality products in a complete assortment of exactly matching colors. Price sensitivity appeared to be quite low, as again materials represented only a small fraction of total end-user cost. Application innovation and the capability to offer assistance in their use were important aspects in selling the product.

**General Industry** This group of users represented a highly fragmented market with almost as many subsegments as there were customer categories or industrial applications. Products were tailored to individual customers or groups of customers to meet specific needs and application possibilities. The keys to success in this market were the ability to segment effectively and deal directly with large customers in any category. Good customer and technical service as well as continuous innovation were required, but price competition from small local suppliers was intensive, especially in the less technology-intensive categories. They included the following:

- The *aircraft finishes* market was very small, highly specialized, and strongly influenced by U.S.-based specifications and know-how. There was a strong need for application support by suppliers, but it was nevertheless a very profitable segment with significant growth.
- *Can and coil coating* consisted of the process of continuously coating metal sheets in the production line. This method of application was growing as a prefabrication step in the building and industrial segments. It was a small but rapidly growing segment, characterized by few suppliers and customers. Profitability was uncertain, however, because of high technical and distribution costs.
- *Marine paints* were likely to show a slow rate of growth; the shipping industry was in recession, and improved paint quality reduced the frequency of repainting of vessels. However, there was a growing market for marine-

resistant paints for off-shore oil rigs and other coastal environments.
- *Anticorrosion paints* were increasingly favored by the construction sector in view of rising costs of steel (need to protect and prolong life) and labor (longer-lasting coatings). This was a technology-intensive segment closely related to the marine segment, yet very fragmented and highly competitive.
- *Texture coatings,* usually resin-based thick films applied in one coat by spraying, were characterized by their long-life decorative properties, excellent impermeability to water, resistance to corrosion and fungi, and good flame-spread resistance, and were finding increasing usage, particularly as wall paints for renovation of buildings. Added advantages included some degree of thermal and acoustical insulation being imparted to the treated surfaces.

A more detailed breakdown of the European and U.S. markets for industrial finishes in 1977 can be found in Exhibit 8. Obviously, this breakdown changed dramatically from country to country. For example:

- In paints for wood furniture, Italy accounted for 23 percent of European demand while the United Kingdom for only 10 percent.

---

**EXHIBIT 8**

**SEGMENT SHARES OF EUROPEAN AND U.S. INDUSTRIAL FINISHES, 1977** (Percent)

|  | Europe | USA |
|---|---|---|
| Protective maintenance | 20.9 | 13.5 |
| Automotive (OEM) | 15.7 | 14.0 |
| Wood furniture | 14.2 | 12.7 |
| Machinery | 7.8 | 9.0 |
| Car refinishes | 7.7 | 5.6 |
| Marine | 5.7 | 2.7 |
| Miscellaneous sheet metal | 5.3 | 1.3 |
| Metal cans & containers | 5.1 | 11.0 |
| Others | 17.6 | 30.2 |
|  | 100.0 | 100.0 |

*Source: Problems or Profit? The European Coatings Industry (1977–1987), volume 1, Chemical Marketing Services, Inc., 1978.*

- In metal containers and coil coating, the United Kingdom represented 38 percent and 30 percent, respectively, of total European demand.
- In appliances, Italy had the largest share of the European demand (30 percent).
- In marine application, Benelux and Scandinavia collectively led with 42 percent of total European usage.

## Distribution

There were several methods of distribution of paint in Western Europe, the relative importance of these varying by segment, country, and region. The three main methods were the use of wholesalers, direct sales to major customers, and the establishment of company-owned outlets. There were also a considerable number of different types of retail outlets of varying importance which stocked paints.

The traditional and favored method of selling to the deco market was through wholesalers. In Belgium and the United Kingdom, for example, sales through wholesalers were estimated to account for around 60 percent of the total segment volume, with corresponding levels of 45 percent in France and 40 percent in the Netherlands. By contrast, only 10 percent of deco sales in West Germany were attributed to wholesalers, this low level being due to the presence of large and extensive networks of local depots operated by the major paint manufacturers, selling directly to major users and retailers. Wholesalers usually earned a gross margin of 20 to 30 percent on their sales.

Wholesalers were generally independent companies and operated on a local and/or regional basis. Four major types of wholesalers could be identified:

1. Specialized paint wholesalers, with paint accounting for over 50 percent of turnover
2. Specialized wall paper wholesalers, with paint accounting for up to 10 percent of sales
3. Wholesalers offering a wide range of hardware supplies
4. Wholesalers specializing in a comprehensive range of building materials

Many of these wholesalers were also involved in contracting and retailing. Of equal importance in many countries were direct sales to contractors, which accounted for 40 percent of sales in France, 25 percent in Belgium and the United Kingdom, and 30 percent in the Netherlands. Retail paint outlets for the DIY segment varied significantly by country as shown in Exhibit 9.

In the industrial paints sector, manufacturers often sold directly to the users, particularly in the case of the automotive and shipbuilding industries. Large automotive companies were, in fact, very closely linked with the paint manu-

---

**E X H I B I T  9**

**DISTRIBUTION OF DIY PAINTS BY TYPE OF OUTLET, SELECTED COUNTRIES** (Percent)

|  | Belgium | France | W. Germany | Netherlands | United Kingdom |
|---|---|---|---|---|---|
| Department stores | 14 | 4 | 2 | 29 | 7 |
| Specialist paint and hardware shops | 22 | 20 | 40 | 40 | 44 |
| Wallpaper shops | 8 | — | — | 16 | — |
| Large DIY shops | — | 22 | — | — | 10 |
| Hardware shops | 9 | 10 | 5 | 7 | 10 |
| Variety shops | 44 | 24 | 3 | 6 | 10 |
| Supermarkets and hypermarkets | 7 | 24 | 35 | 4 | 16 |
| Others | 2 | — | 15 | 8 | 3 |
| Total | 100 | 100 | 100 | 100 | 100 |

Source: Profile of the European Paint Industry, Information Research Ltd., London, 1979.

facturer in the research and development of new paint and application technology.

The relative importance of the international trade of paints in Europe is shown in Exhibit 10. It can be seen that some of the larger exporters of paint also imported significant amounts of similar material.

## INDUSTRY STRUCTURE

The European paint industry was highly fragmented with many small-sized companies operating in most countries. In general, however, each national market was dominated by a few large companies which tended to operate also on an international basis and had other interests besides paint manufacture. The total number of paint manufacturers in Europe was not accurately known. The frequent incidence of mergers and acquisitions prevalent over the past several years had effectively reduced the number of companies in this industry. Yet a large number of small (often with fewer than 10 employees) family-owned firms continued to operate in local or regional markets, primarily but not exclusively in decorative paints.

Exhibit 11 shows the number and concentration of paint manufacturers in Western Europe in 1971 and 1977. The eleven most important firms in the industry had estimated consolidated sales of DM105 billion in 1977, of which anywhere between 2.5 and 60 percent were in coatings. Exhibit 12 provides an estimate of the coatings sales of this group for 1977. A brief description of these and other European coatings companies appears below.

### Hoechst

The largest company in the world involved in the production of paint, Hoechst's 1977 total sales were DM23.3 billion, of which 7.3 percent, or almost DM1.8 billion, were in paints. An additional 10.5 percent of sales were in synthetic resins and pigments. Although 33 percent of the group's sales were made in W. Germany, Hoechst had operations worldwide. Total profits for the group in 1977 equalled DM304 million with a return on equity of 5.7 percent.

Hoechst's coating activities began in 1969 as the company integrated forward. Their coatings division consisted of two groups: Dr. Kurt Herberts & Co. GmbH (W. Germany), which had managerial responsibility for the European continent, and Berger, Jenson & Nicholson Ltd. (BJ&N) which was based in Britain and managed activities in the rest of the world. In Western Europe, Herberts had operations in W. Germany, the Netherlands, Switzerland, Austria, Belgium, France, Italy, and Spain, while BJ&N handled the U.K. and Scandinavian affiliates. Hoechst had a leading position in the quality segments. However, profitability had been continually low due to its large range of general industry products, which were marketed in all segments.

Hoechst's strategy consisted of obtaining high market shares in R&D-intensive chemicals and related products, forward integration based on captive use of successful existing products, and an accent on internationalization. Hoechst appeared to concentrate efforts on proprietary products (automotive OEM and car refinishes segments) and on market-oriented innovation, that is, a search for new products and new processes responsive to changes in customer needs.

### BASF

BASF, like Hoechst, was a highly diversified chemical company, with a range of activities encompassing basic petrochemicals, agricultural products, plastics, chemicals, consumer goods, and pigments, dyes, and related products. On 1977 group sales of DM21.1 billion, BASF realized a profit of DM388 million. Although it maintained operations worldwide, 66 percent of sales were made in the EEC. It was difficult to determine accurately what percentage of sales was attributable to paints, as coatings were included in the consumer products group along with such other products as pharmaceuticals. One reliable estimate was that ap-

## EXHIBIT 10

### INTERNATIONAL TRADE IN PAINTS AND VARNISHES, 1973 TO 1977

| | Value (DM million) | | | | | | | | | Percentage of domestic production volume | | | | | |
| | Exports | | | Imports | | | Net trade | | | Exports | | | Imports | | |
| | 1973 | 1975 | 1977 | 1973 | 1975 | 1977 | 1973 | 1975 | 1977 | 1973 | 1975 | 1977 | 1973 | 1975 | 1977 |
|---|---|---|---|---|---|---|---|---|---|---|---|---|---|---|---|
| Austria | 38.2 | 61.9 | n.a. | 28.8 | 40.4 | 60.0 | 9.3 | 21.5 | — | 15.0 | 15.6 | 14.2 | 8.0 | 8.9 | 10.8 |
| Belgium/Luxembourg | 93.7 | 110.1 | 152.6 | 92.4 | 97.2 | 156.8 | 1.3 | 12.9 | (4.2) | 23.0 | 28.8 | 29.2 | 23.0 | 23.0 | 29.6 |
| Denmark | 67.5 | 103.5 | 126.5 | 37.4 | 67.6 | 76.5 | 30.1 | 35.9 | 50.0 | 27.0 | 28.5 | 34.6 | 14.0 | 21.9 | 21.6 |
| Finland | 4.8 | 8.1 | 22.4 | 24.6 | 42.1 | 40.2 | 19.8 | (34.0) | (17.8) | 4.0 | 4.1 | 11.0 | 13.0 | 12.1 | 16.9 |
| France | 95.0 | 200.9 | 194.0 | 150.3 | 240.5 | 244.0 | 55.3 | (39.6) | (50.0) | 4.0 | 6.6 | 7.5 | 7.0 | 10.6 | 10.5 |
| W. Germany | 374.9 | 440.8 | 662.6 | 119.8 | 149.5 | 214.0 | 255.0 | 291.3 | 448.6 | 8.0 | 8.1 | 19.6 | 3.0 | 3.3 | 5.6 |
| Greece | 1.6 | n.a. | n.a. | 19.2 | 33.5 | 43.9 | 17.6 | — | — | 0.5 | 1.4 | 6.6 | 33.0 | 30.0 | 25.5 |
| Ireland | n.a. | n.a. | n.a. | n.a. | n.a. | 23.9 | — | — | — | n.a. | 1.3 | 11.1 | n.a. | 11.3 | 12.0 |
| Italy | 32.0 | 51.4 | 89.5 | 54.7 | 57.9 | 86.9 | 22.7 | (6.5) | 2.6 | 2.0 | 7.7 | 3.7 | 3.0 | 1.5 | 2.2 |
| Netherlands | 208.3 | 214.4 | 307.1 | 89.7 | 121.4 | 126.5 | 118.5 | 93.0 | 180.6 | 36.0 | 32.3 | 33.3 | 14.0 | 17.9 | 20.6 |
| Norway | 28.0 | 39.4 | 48.1 | 23.0 | 30.7 | 56.9 | 5.1 | 8.7 | (8.8) | 17.0 | 17.4 | 21.0 | 13.0 | 11.9 | 26.0 |
| Portugal | 3.2 | n.a. | 4.6 | 3.2 | n.a. | 22.6 | — | — | (18.0) | 3.6 | 2.3 | 4.6 | 3.0 | 5.4 | 5.0 |
| Spain | 8.8 | 7.2 | 23.6 | 16.3 | 20.3 | 67.7 | 7.5 | (13.1) | (44.1) | 1.0 | 1.9 | 2.5 | 1.0 | 0.9 | 2.3 |
| Sweden | 41.1 | 86.1 | 87.0 | 59.3 | 95.0 | 110.6 | 18.1 | (8.9) | (23.6) | 12.0 | 17.8 | 20.5 | 12.0 | 11.8 | 15.1 |
| Switzerland | 23.5 | 12.6 | 14.7 | 57.1 | 77.4 | 105.9 | 33.6 | (64.8) | (91.2) | 6.0 | 4.8 | 5.3 | 19.0 | 27.4 | 31.6 |
| United Kingdom | 136.0 | 246.3 | 191.4 | 34.4 | 59.9 | 59.0 | 102.5 | 186.4 | 132.4 | 9.0 | 10.1 | 10.2 | 1.0 | 1.6 | 1.7 |

Source: Profile of the European Paint Industry, 3d & 4th editions, Information Research Ltd., London, 1977–1979.

**NUMBER AND CONCENTRATION OF PAINT MANUFACTURERS IN WESTERN EUROPE, 1971 AND 1977**

| | 1971 | | 1977 | |
|---|---|---|---|---|
| | Number of paint manufacturers | Market share of largest companies (%) | Number of paint manufacturers | Market share of largest companies (%) |
| Austria | 50 | 63 (3 cos.) | 50 | 50 (3 cos.) |
| Belgium | 90 | 45 (6 cos.) | 70 | 73 (6 cos.) |
| Denmark | 30 | 71 (5 cos.) | 30 | 71 (3 cos.) |
| Finland | 7 | 55 (3 cos.) | 6 | 73 (3 cos.) |
| France | 390 | 31 (3 cos.) | 235 | 40 (5 cos.) |
| | | 43 (6 cos.) | | 72 (50 cos.) |
| West Germany | 340 | 29 (2 cos.) | 250 | 28 (6 cos.) |
| | | 43 (5 cos.) | | 48 (5 cos.) |
| Italy | 260 | 45 (6 cos.) | 235 | 28 (6 cos.) |
| | | 95 (20 cos.) | | 95 (20 cos.) |
| Netherlands | 120 | 65 (2 cos.) | 100 | 69 (2 cos.) |
| | | 84 (8 cos.) | | 90 (5 cos.) |
| Norway | 18 | 80 (4 cos.) | 35 | 80 (1 co.) |
| Portugal | 49 | 89 (5 cos.) | 60 | 82 (4 cos.) |
| Spain | 600 | 63 (6 cos.) | 350 | 73 (6 cos.) |
| Sweden | 50 | 43 (5 cos.) | 150 | 82 (4 cos.) |
| Switzerland | 95 | 75 (5 cos.) | 100 | 64 (5 cos.) |
| United Kingdom | 490 | 39 (2 cos.) | 285 | 32 (2 cos.) |
| | | 62 (4 cos.) | | 57 (4 cos.) |
| Total | 2,589 | | 1,956 | |

*Note:* These figures exclude the large numbers of very small family firms, often with fewer than 10 employees and producing paint of indifferent quality.

*Source: Profile of the European Paint Industry,* 1st and 4th editions, Information Research Limited, London, 1973 and 1979.

proximately 14 percent of company sales were in coatings.

BASF paint operations came under the umbrella of BASF Farben & Fasern AG, with subsidiaries in W. Germany, the United Kingdom, Spain, France, Switzerland, and Italy. Like Hoechst, the division's emphasis was on the high-quality end of the range and on product innovation, but efforts were concentrated on strategically important segments (especially automotive and car refinishes) and certain geographic areas (W. Europe, United Kingdom, N. America, Japan, and Latin America). This, combined with an objective of obtaining and maintaining market leadership, had led the company to acquire strong positions in the profitable automotive and car refinish sectors. However,

its activities in the general industry sector remained unsatisfactory.

## ICI

After Hoechst, ICI was the second largest manufacturer of paints and Europe's third largest in terms of total sales. The company's total turnover in 1977 was £4.7 billion, on which profits of £534 million were realized. Paint sales accounted for almost 9 percent of this total (£409 million) and contributed £11 million (2 percent) to total profits. Based in the United Kingdom (38 percent of total sales), other European markets accounted for an additional 18 percent of sales. ICI was Britain's largest manufacturer of architectural paints but also competed in the

**EXHIBIT 12**

**LARGEST EUROPEAN COMPETITORS** (DM Million)

| | Total sales | Coatings sales | Percent |
|---|---|---|---|
| Europe | | | |
| Hoechst (D) | 23,298 | 1,800 | 7.7 |
| BASF (D) | 21,150 | 900 | 13.7 |
| ICI (GB) | 18,824 | 1,690 | 9.0 |
| Petrofina (B) | 14,179 | 354* | 2.5 |
| Akzo (NL) | 9,848 | 890 | 9.0 |
| Courtaulds- | | | |
| International Paint (UK) | 6,360 | 865 | 13.6 |
| BOK (B) | 5,780 | 632 | 10.9 |
| CdF (F) | 2,320 | 208 | 9.0 |
| Reed-Crown (UK) | 1,983 | 380* | 19.1 |
| Nobel Bozel (F) | 1,043 | 350* | 31.6 |
| Jotun (N) | 273 | 180 | 66.0 |
| United States | | | |
| Du Pont | 21,900 | 1,310 | 6.0 |
| PPG | 4,721 | 1,086 | 23.0 |
| Inmont† | 1,239 | 620 | 50.0 |

*Includes other products as well as paint.
†1976 figures.
*Note:* Conversion rate 1977: DM 2.32 = $1.
*Source:* Company annual reports and estimates from other sources.

industrial and automotive sectors. With the 1975 acquisition of Hermann Wiederhold, the company established a modest foothold on the German market.

ICI's strategy appeared to emphasize the character of a technology-oriented chemical group. In paints, the focus was on innovation and international expansion through exports and local production, with the accent on the European continent. The company also stressed production efficiency and cost reduction, and was committed to maintaining strong positions in existing profitable markets with divestment when necessary.

## Akzo

Akzo was a Dutch-based group of companies with operations in more than 50 countries. Its product range included man-made fibers, commodity and specialty chemicals, coatings, pharmaceuticals, consumer and miscellaneous industrial products. Business activities were organized in a divisional structure according to product groups. On total 1977 sales of D$f$10.4 billion, the company earned an operating income of D$f$420 million. Of this total, Akzo Coatings contributed sales of D$f$975 million (9 percent of total sales) and made an operating income of D$f$45 million (10.7 percent of total profits). Akzo Coatings operated through three major companies in the Netherlands (Sikkens), France (Astral), and Germany (Lesonal). Akzo was present in most market segments and had a relatively strong position in the car refinish market.

## International Paint

International Paint (IP) was the coatings division of Courtaulds, a diversified multinational textile firm. Of Courtaulds 1977–1978 sales of £1.6 billion, £214 million (or 13.6 percent) were made by IP. In that year, IP realized a profit of £18.7 million, contributing 22 percent to Courtaulds total profit. IP was well diversified geographically, with 27 percent of sales made in the

United Kingdom, 25 percent in the rest of Europe, 24 percent in the Americas, and 15 percent in Australasia. The group was the world's largest supplier of marine paints and marketed industrial finishes for all major industries, decorative paints, and allied products. IP's strategy had been to concentrate on highly technical products (e.g., industrial specialties, automotive, and car refinishes).

## BOK

BOK was a diversified Belgian chemical firm with a strong base on the high end of the specialty chemicals market. Its main product areas covered pharmaceuticals, industrial chemicals, plastics, and coatings, as well as a large and growing activity in processed foods. With annual sales of nearly BF90 billion, its finishes division accounted for BF9.75 billion, or about 11 percent of group sales.

The parent company operated worldwide and had affiliates in more than 40 countries. Its consumer products (coatings and process foods), however, were nearly limited to the European market. BOK Finishes operated through major subsidiaries in Belgium, Holland, France, Germany, Italy, and the United Kingdom. Although highly diversified in terms of market segments, the company had strong positions in the car refinish and architectural markets.

## Nobel-Bozel

Another diversified firm, Nobel-Bozel was based in France and was active in electrometallurgy, explosives, construction materials, plastics, and paints. Total 1977 sales amounted to Fr2.2 billion, on which a loss of Fr233 million was reported. Nobel-Bozel's main paint interests included Cie des Vernis Valentine and Société Duco, both French companies. Valentine held a license to manufacture Jotun's (see below) marine paints in France.

## Petrofina

Petrofina, a large oil production and distribution multinational based in Belgium, was somewhat less diversified than its competitors. Of total 1977 sales of BF219 billion, only BF19.5 billion or 9 percent came from their chemical, paint, and other activities. Paint sales, grouped under Sigma Coatings, with operations in Belgium and Holland, were estimated to account for approximately 2.5 percent of the total. Consolidated profits for that year were BF6.4 billion.

## Crown

Crown Paints was one of four companies making up the Decorative Products division of Reed International, a diversified multinational pulp and paper manufacturer based in the United Kingdom. Reed's total sales in 1977 were £1.5 billion with profits of £96 million. Sales of the decorative products division were £285 million with profits of £2.9 million. The British market accounted for 56 percent of total sales, and an additional 8 percent came from continental Europe.

## CdF Chimie

CdF Chimie, a member of the Charbonnages de France Group, was a large diversified chemical firm that was rather limited in geographic scope, with more than 60 percent of its sales in France. In 1977, CdF Chimie reported a loss of Fr68 million on sales of Fr4.9 billion. Paint division sales in the same year accounted for approximately 9 percent of the total, or Fr431 million. The main paint subsidiaries of CdF Chimie included Helic (van Cauwenberghe and Les Peintures de la Seine), Ripolin-Georget-Freitag, and the recently acquired AVI. Helic supplied mainly the general industry market, and AVI activities were limited almost exclusively to the DIY sector. The more diversified RGF sold to the decorative, DIY, anticorrosion, and general industry segments. Like their mother company, these firms had only limited international sales while maintaining a strong base in their home market.

## Jotun

Jotungruppen, formed in 1972 by the merger of the four largest Norwegian paint manufacturers,

**EXHIBIT 13**

## PROFILES OF MAJOR EUROPEAN PAINT COMPANIES

| Country and company | Estimated sales ($ million) | Local market share (%) | Number of international affiliates | | |
|---|---|---|---|---|---|
| | | | Europe | N. America | Rest of world |
| **Austria** | | | | | |
| Stollack A.G. (Hoechst) | 35.0 | 30.0 | — | — | — |
| Ing. Egon. Wildschek | 15.5 | 13.5 | — | — | — |
| Brunal-Austria (BOK) | 8.5 | 7.0 | — | — | |
| Wegscheider | 7.5 | 6.5 | — | — | 1 |
| **Belgium** | | | | | |
| BOK Finishes | 52.0 | 35.0 | 8 | — | 5 |
| Levis | 36.0 | 23.0 | 6 | — | 1 |
| Trimetal Paint Co. | 16.0 | 12.0 | 3 | — | — |
| Du Pont de Nemours | 15.0 | 11.0 | — | — | — |
| Keyn Frères SA | 14.0 | 9.5 | 2 | — | — |
| **Denmark** | | | | | |
| Sadolin & Holmblad | 46.5 | 39.0 | 7 | — | 7 |
| Dyrup & Co. | 22.5 | 18.8 | 3 | — | 2 |
| Hempel | 16.5 | 13.0 | 8 | 2 | 8 |
| **Finland** | | | | | |
| Tikkurilan | 36.5 | 38.0 | 1 | — | — |
| Teknos-Maalit | 17.7 | 20.0 | — | — | — |
| Winter | 15.0 | 15.2 | — | — | — |
| **France** | | | | | |
| Valentine-Duco (Nobel Bozel) | 140.0 | 16.2 | 8 | — | — |
| Ripolin (CdF Chimie) | 60.0 | 7.8 | 3 | — | — |
| Corona (PPG) | 56.0 | 6.5 | 1 | — | — |
| Astral (AKZO) | 56.0 | 6.5 | 1 | — | 2 |
| Sofravel (BOK) | 52.0 | 6.0 | — | — | 6 |
| **West Germany** | | | | | |
| BASF | 210.0 | 17.5 | 4 | — | 1 |
| Hoechst | 128.0 | 10.5 | 8 | — | — |
| H. Wiederhold (ICI) | 104.0 | 9.0 | 2 | — | — |
| Lesonal (AKZO) | 79.5 | 6.5 | — | — | — |
| Brunal (BOK) | 53.0 | 4.5 | 1 | — | — |
| D. Amphibolin Werke | 48.0 | 4.0 | 4 | — | — |
| **Italy** | | | | | |
| Max Meyer | 64.0 | 8.0 | — | — | — |
| IVI (Fiat) | 63.2 | 7.9 | 1 | — | — |
| Duco (Montedison) | 40.0 | 5.0 | — | — | — |
| Savid | 20.0 | 2.5 | — | — | — |
| BOK-Siver | 20.0 | 2.5 | — | — | — |
| Boero | 20.0 | 2.5 | — | — | — |
| **Netherlands** | | | | | |
| Sikkens (Akzo) | 80.0 | 36.0 | 2 | — | — |
| Sigma Coatings (Petrofina) | 73.5 | 33.0 | 5 | — | 3 |
| Brink/Molyn | 20.0 | 9.0 | — | — | — |
| BOK Netherlands | 18.0 | 7.5 | — | — | — |
| Wagemakers (Hoechst) | 17.5 | 6.2 | 1 | — | — |
| **Norway** | | | | | |
| Jotungruppen | 67.8 | 80.0 | 9 | 1 | 3 |

**EXHIBIT 13 (cont.)**

**PROFILES OF MAJOR EUROPEAN PAINT COMPANIES**

| Country and company | Estimated sales ($ million) | Local market share (%) | Number of international affiliates | | |
|---|---|---|---|---|---|
| | | | Europe | N. America | Rest of world |
| Portugal | | | | | |
| Robbialac (Hoechst) | 18.9 | 41.0 | — | — | — |
| Ind. do Norte | 8.0 | 17.5 | — | — | — |
| Valentine (F) | 7.2 | 15.6 | — | — | — |
| Spain | | | | | |
| Protocolor | 50.0 | 17.5 | — | — | — |
| Ind. Titan | 40.0 | 15.0 | — | — | — |
| Urruzola (BASF) | 37.5 | 12.0 | — | — | — |
| Valentine (F) | 34.5 | 10.5 | — | — | — |
| Ripolin (F) | 33.0 | 10.0 | — | — | 1 |
| Bruguer | 25.0 | 7.5 | — | — | — |
| P. Gabriel (BOK) | 22.5 | 6.7 | — | — | — |
| Lacas y Pinturas (Du Pont) | 20.0 | 6.0 | — | — | — |
| Sweden | | | | | |
| Wilhelm Becker | 76.5 | 35.0 | 6 | — | — |
| NN & S (Bayer) | 44.1 | 20.0 | 3 | — | — |
| Alfort & Cronholm | 41.5 | 18.8 | — | — | — |
| Switzerland | | | | | |
| Dr. A. Landolt | 22.5 | 17.5 | — | — | — |
| Sieg. Keller | 21.0 | 16.5 | 6 | — | — |
| W. Mäder | 15.4 | 13.0 | — | — | — |
| Jallut | 14.0 | 11.0 | 1 | — | — |
| United Kingdom | | | | | |
| ICI | 137.0 | 16.0 | 1 | 1 | 5 |
| BJ & N (Hoechst) | 123.0 | 15.5 | 4 | — | 10 |
| Crown (Reed) | 101.3 | 12.5 | 5 | — | 3 |
| International Paint | 96.0 | 12.5 | 11 | 2 | 11 |
| MacPherson | 56.5 | 5.0 | 1 | — | 3 |
| Ault & Wiberg | 25.5 | 3.5 | 1 | 1 | — |

Source: *A Profile of the European Paint Industry,* Information Research Ltd., London, 1977.

dominated the paint industry in Norway. Total sales in 1977 were Kr695 million, of which decorative and maintenance paints were 38 percent; industrial paints, 6 percent; and marine coatings, 22 percent. A loss of Kr1.7 million was recorded for that year, but this was attributable in part to a fire which destroyed their main manufacturing plant in 1976. It was estimated that this group accounted for some 80 percent of total sales in the Norwegian market, strongest in the marine and industrial paint sectors. The group had very limited interests in the rest of Europe but was expanding in areas such as the Middle East.

## Du Pont

Du Pont, one of the largest chemical companies in the world, had sales in 1977 of $9.4 billion with profits of $545 million. Coatings represented around 5 to 6 percent of total sales. The company was known as a leading U.S. supplier of automotive topcoats and car refinishes and had longstanding ties with the industry leader,

EXHIBIT 14

**SELECTED CHARACTERISTICS OF SOME OF THE LARGEST COATING SUPPLIERS**

| | Product mix | | | | | Geographic mix | | | | R&D potential |
|---|---|---|---|---|---|---|---|---|---|---|
| | Deco/DIY | Automotive | Car refinish | Marine/ anticorrosives | Other industries* | N. America | Europe | Japan | Rest of world | |
| Hoechst (BJN/Herberts) | 3 | 3 | 3 | 2 | 2 | — | 3 | — | 3 | 3 |
| ICI | 3 | 2 | 2 | 1 | 1 | — | 2 | — | 3 | 3 |
| Sherwin Williams | 2 | 1 | 2 | — | 2 | 3 | — | — | 1 | 1 |
| Du Pont | 2 | 3 | 2 | — | 1 | 3 | 1 | — | 1 | 3 |
| PPG | 3 | 3 | 2 | 2 | 2 | 3 | 2 | — | 1 | 3 |
| Akzo Coatings | 3 | 2 | 3 | 1 | 1 | — | 3 | 1 | 2 | 2 |
| BASF | 2 | 3 | 3 | 1 | 2 | 1–2 | 3 | — | 2 | 3 |
| International Paint | 1 | 1 | — | 3 | 1 | 1–2 | 3 | 1 | 3 | 1 |
| BOK Finishes | 2 | 2 | 2 | 1 | 2 | — | 3 | — | 1 | 2 |
| SCM (Glidden) | 2 | — | — | — | 2 | 2 | — | — | 1 | 2 |
| Kansai Paint | 2 | 3 | 2 | 2 | 2 | — | — | 3 | 1 | 2 |
| Nippon Paint | 2 | 2 | 1 | 2 | 2 | — | — | 3 | 1 | 2 |
| Inmont | — | 3 | 2 | — | 1 | 3 | 1–2 | — | 1 | 2 |

1 = small position
2 = significant position
3 = strong or leading position
*Includes general industry, coil coating, aviation, electro insulation, powders, etc.
*Source:* Internal documents.

General Motors. Its image was that of quality and reliability as a supplier. Du Pont had a limited presence in Europe, with only two production plants in Belgium and Spain. The company's strategy was to improve its position in the U.S. decorative/DIY segments as well as in the European car refinish market.

## PPG

PPG was incorporated in 1883 as Pittsburgh Plate Glass Company and entered the coatings market in 1900. PPG had subsidiaries or held shares in companies in France (Peintures Corona S.A.), Italy (Italver-Pittsburgh Paints SpA), Germany, Spain, Belgium, and Mexico. PPG Coatings & Resins Division sales in 1977 were $593 million; 80 percent were in coatings and represented around 23 percent of total corporate sales. Earnings of the division amounted to $55 million, contributing 19 percent to corporate earnings. The division's strategy consisted of a growing penetration of profitable industrial markets, an emphasis on advanced technology, and a continued refinement of trade paint sales and distribution techniques (color machines, use of computers, etc.). PPG's "cathodic electrode-position" primer system for the automotive market had been a major success in recent years.

## Inmont

Incorporated in Ohio in 1928 as The International Printing Ink Corporation, the company made a number of acquisitions through the years and adopted the Inmont name in 1969. Inmont moved into Europe by acquiring operations in Italy and Germany in the 1970s. Last published figures for Inmont as a separate entity were in 1976 (it was acquired by Carrier in 1977): Corporate sales were $534 million with profits of $20 million. Over 50 percent of the business was in coatings, most of it in automotive OEM and car refinishes. The company's strategy was known to emphasize product development, customer service, and aggressive marketing to these segments.

Two other large U.S.-based paint companies were Glidden and Sherwin-Williams, although they operated almost exclusively in the architectural paint markets and were present only in the Western Hemisphere. Exhibits 13 and 14 provide additional information concerning companies in the industry.

# BOK Finishes

BOK Finishes was the coatings division of BOK N.V., a diversified multinational firm active in a variety of chemical fields and based in Belgium. In 1977, the division's total sales were BF9.75 billion and operating income BF0.5 billion, representing 11 percent and 15 percent, respectively, of the parent company's total sales and profits.

## FORMATION OF BOK

The BOK group was established in 1960 as a result of a series of mergers that characterized the Belgian (and European) chemical industry in the postwar period. The first of these was the merger of Oostende Chemische Groep with Belgische Pharmaceutieke in 1952, intended to create a diversified chemical firm then known as

This case was written by Claire Fortier and André Khodjamirian, research associates, and Professor José de la Torre as a basis for discussion. The generous contribution of many executives from a European chemical firm that wishes to remain anonymous is gratefully acknowledged. All names, places, and financial figures, as well as some events, have been disguised to preserve confidentiality. © INSEAD, The European Institute of Business Administration, 1986.

Belpharm-Oostende. In 1956, the board of Belpharm-Oostende decided to enter the coatings market in order to realize an opportunity for forward integration of the company's activities in resins and additives as well as to take advantage of the expected further concentration in the coatings industry that would result from increased levels of technology.

A major consulting firm was employed by the company, which was advised to proceed in two steps. First, an acquisition of a Belgian paint company was recommended for expertise in the coating business and its requirements. Second, expansion to other major markets, particularly, Britain, France, and Germany, via acquisition was to follow shortly. Finally, the consultants recommended that entry not be limited to the industrial coatings market but that architectural paints be included. A list of candidates was prepared and presented to the board. In 1958, as a consequence of this process, Belpharm-Oostende acquired Van Houdt & Co., a full-line Belgian manufacturer of paints with operations mainly in Belgium and Holland and a small volume of sales in other European markets.

The second step in the strategy was delayed by the complex negotiations and implementation of the 1960 merger of Belpharm-Oostende with Koninklijke Chemische Fabrieken (KCF), a diversified group with activities in chemical fibers, plastics, processed foods, and consumer products. KCF brought needed managerial and marketing skills to the merger, plus a more international orientation, which had to be melded with the technical and research culture that prevailed at Belpharm-Oostende. The resulting company was renamed BOK and reorganized into eight major divisions, including a finishes and coatings group as part of a specialty chemicals division. Eventually, BOK Finishes was established as a separate division of BOK, N.V., and the original expansion strategy was implemented with the acquisition of the German coatings company Brunal in 1970 and the French company Sofravel in 1971.

## VAN HOUDT

The history of Van Houdt began in 1806 with the establishment of a varnish cooking plant by Willem Van Houdt in Antwerp. Through the initiative of Dr. Johannes Wouters, later appointed joint managing director, a paint laboratory was created in the mid-1920s followed a few years later by a synthetic resin laboratory. During this period the reputation of Van Houdt was established by its high-quality Stralend decorative paints as well as its automotive and aircraft finishes.

A period of unprecedented expansion followed in the postwar years. Van Houdt's stated policy in the early 1950s was "to manufacture bulk and specialty products of such high quality that this will be the decisive factor in purchasing them. This will assure continuity to the business and guarantee employment to the workers." The *1954 Annual Report* gave an indication of how they proposed to meet these objectives: "through cooperation with specialized manufacturers . . . to raise technical performance and bring down the cost per unit of output."

This objective and the wish to cover different segments of the coatings market led to the ac-quisition of Zonneschijn, a specialized manufacturer of do-it-yourself (DIY) paints, in 1954. A unit manufacturing marine and anticorrosion paints was also formed that year with licensed Danish technology. Van Houdt had achieved a minor position in the automotive finishes sector, mainly supplying paint for some of the cars produced or assembled in the Benelux area, and it expanded into the aviation coatings market with know-how obtained from a British specialist in the field. In 1963 an agreement relating to advanced automotive topcoats was concluded with a major U.S. company. Also in that year, Rubens Colors, a well-known producer of artists' colors and associated products, and Weerts, a firm with an excellent reputation for its stains and adhesives, were acquired.

During these years, Van Houdt strengthened its position outside the home market through exports, license agreements, and the establishment of a number of foreign manufacturing units. Van Houdt Peintures (France) was incorporated in 1954; Van Houdt GmbH (W. Germany), in 1955; and Siver SpA, (Italy) in 1958. By 1959, the first year after its acquisition by Belpharm-Oostende, aggregate foreign sales accounted for some 40 percent of Van Houdt's group sales. In 1964, the acquisition of the West German firm F. Mahler Lackfabriken, a specialized manufacturer of wall paints, constituted a further step toward a broader European base.

An analysis of Van Houdt's operations carried out by a consulting firm in 1965 highlighted the production-site orientation of the company, the result of numerous acquisitions of small firms over the years. Van Houdt set out to refocus its attention in terms of market segments, and a long period of rationalization of the company's activities followed. A reorganization of BOK's activities in that same year led to the creation of a separate division, BOK Finishes, under the leadership of K. Verhulst, who had previously been in charge of the resin department of BOK's specialty chemicals division. One of the board members of BOK was given functional responsibility for overseeing the new division's development.

## BRUNAL

Brunal traced its history to the late nineteenth century and the creation of a small paint firm in Mannheim by a former pharmacist, Bruno Anger. Eventually, other partners joined the firm; employment grew rapidly in the postwar years, reaching 633 in 1958 and nearly doubling again to 1,200 by 1970. From 1958 to 1971, the total plant site was enlarged sixfold, and warehousing facilities were established in Munich, Nuremberg, Cologne, and Hamburg. In 1960, a subsidiary was created to supply the Austrian affiliates of the company's major West German customers. It also served as a springboard for commercial activities in Eastern Europe. Further expansion came in the form of the acquisition in 1964 of a manufacturer of industrial coatings for bicycles, machinery, rolling stock, and other industrial products.

The development of the company was closely bound to technological progress in the field of paints. By the end of the nineteenth century, industrial paints already occupied an important place in the company's line of products, but it was not until the 1930s, when new resins were introduced, that they surpassed the company's decorative paints in volume of sales. In terms of quality, the company's paints equalled if not exceeded those of the biggest producers, thanks to the high professional standard of its development laboratory. Over the years, the company specialized more and more in the manufacture of industrial and automotive coatings, all research being carried on in-house. Eventually automotive finishes became the leading product group, with the company holding a major market share in West Germany, including such big customers as Volkswagen, NSU, and Opel. Moreover, sizeable quantities were exported to car producers in Hungary, Iran, Yugoslavia, and Poland. After 1958, when the company decided to enter the car refinishes segment, Brunal soon captured a moderate share of the West German market. The Volkswagen contract was later to result in the acquisition of a controlling share in Gonsalvez & Santos, a Bra-

zilian paint manufacturer that supplied Volkswagen's local automotive operations.

During this period of phenomenal growth, little attention was paid to the development of an organization or to support staff services. The time was ripe for consolidation. In 1968, a broker informed Brunal's management that Van Houdt was interested in a merger. The negotiations were long and complex, but in 1970 a final agreement was reached by which Brunal joined the newly formed BOK Finishes Group.

## SOFRAVEL

In 1865, the Ripoud brothers opened a drugstore in Paris to manufacture paint and varnish products. Their reputation spread quickly, and in 1875 branches were opened in Basel, Amsterdam, and Brussels. With the takeover of the Société des Produits Chimiques de St. Germain in 1911, the company acquired a new trade name and changed its own name to Société Française de Vernis et Lacques (Sofravel). By the end of the 1930s, the company ranked first in the French decorative paints market and marketed industrial coatings and automotive finishes.

During the late nineteenth and early twentieth centuries business was expanded to North Africa through importers who were eventually taken over by the Ripoud brothers. This resulted in the establishment of both selling and manufacturing operations in several African countries, which contributed consistently to Sofravel's earnings. Although started as manufacturers of decorative paints, these subsidiaries subsequently expanded into the general industry, car refinishes, and automotive sectors with the latter two accounting for a high percentage of sales.

By the end of the 1940s, Sofravel had regained its leadership position in the decorative market but was meeting growing competition in other segments. In order to consolidate its industrial infrastructure, broaden its geographical markets, and diversify operations, a number of key decisions were made. These included adopting a direct selling approach in the car refinishes market and becoming a major supplier of paints to the navy and merchant marines. Entry into the general industry sector was less successful.

In the late 1950s, Sofravel obtained a contract to supply one of the first and biggest dipping tanks in the Citroën plant at Levallois, a success that soon opened doors to other products for this customer. In order to shorten the interval between the conception of new technologies and their practical application, Sofravel supplemented its own development effort with agreements with foreign manufacturers. The 1960s saw a continuation of this cross-licensing policy as a means of acquiring new expertise and of commercially exploiting the company's own developments.

A big boost was given the company in 1964 when it acquired Figier Société des Peintures et Vernis, one of the big names in the French paint industry. The acquisition of Figier added many new customers in the decorative paints, general industry, and automotive sectors and brought Sofravel a complete network of wholesalers of decorative paints. In 1967, the purchase of an Italian company, Delfina, enabled Sofravel to supply its Italian coil-coating customers locally. In this same year a license agreement in the field of coil coating was concluded with a major U.S. supplier enabling Sofravel to make rapid advances in this and many other fields. Lastly, the year 1969 saw the acquisition of La Maison, a French decorative paints manufacturer supplying large supermarkets and discount stores. In early 1971, Sofravel was the third largest French paint company when it joined BOK Finishes.

## POSTMERGER STRUCTURE

Following these mergers, the need for a new organizational structure was recognized. Verhulst, then president of BOK Finishes, identified the main question: "How do we unite our individual group companies with their own specific characteristics into a single business operation without losing their identities and val-

ues?'' Consequently, in late 1971, an external consultant was commissioned to propose such a plan for all three companies and their subsidiaries.

The basic principle underlying the new organizational structure was "the formation of a coherent and internationally strong group of coatings activities enabling BOK to realize maximum synergistic benefits from the acquisition of the individual companies, while maintaining the basic strengths of the individual working companies." The report identified two principal types of markets: those with a local focus and those with a transborder focus. Included in the first group were the decorative, DIY, car refinishes, and general industry segments. These were felt to require a differentiated, national marketing and sales approach. However, markets for "major industrial coatings," i.e., automotive, coil and can coatings, marine paints and aviation paints, were felt to have a more international character.

Insofar as R&D were concerned, again two major activities were identified: applied research and more fundamental research or major product-development projects. Applied research needs were seen to be dictated more by the technical demands of the customers of a particular working company, and therefore the need for central guidance of such activities was considered to be limited. In contrast, more fundamental research with a longer-term focus should be executed where the right skills and activities were available, and the results could, in principle, be applied throughout the whole division.

Opportunities for synergy in production were seen to be found primarily in the joint manufacturing of similar products that were until then being produced in uneconomically small batches. This was particularly the case for car refinishes. Eventually, the consultants suggested that after a process of market evaluation and subsequent product standardization, even larger benefits would ensue.

As a result of this analysis four organizational principles were outlined:

1. Overall strategy was to be determined at the divisional level. Division management, in addition to specifying financial goals, would also state a series of operational objectives related to specific markets, e.g., geographical coverage, individual market segments to be served in each geographic area, required market shares by country and/or segment, and required technology.
2. Strong local management would be retained, with responsibility for local operations being borne by the operating companies. Division staff would only be relied on for specialized expertise and international know-how.
3. Activities with a transborder focus, i.e., where effective marketing, research, and production required deployment of resources for more than just one national company, would not be left completely to the responsibility of individual local managements; such activities would require central programming or management.
4. Recognizing the need for overall coordination in a decentralized structure, management systems would be put in place to ensure long-term consistency of local policies and strategies within overall division objectives and policies and to achieve a maximum exchange of locally available expertise and know-how.

The new organization, based on the above principles, contained the following main elements:

1. An *executive committee*—composed of the presidents of Sofravel, Brunal, and Van Houdt and three other top-echelon executives under the chair of the division president—was the highest authority for all basic policy and strategic decisions for the division. Its role was to determine the overall objectives, strategies, and policies for the division; to ratify the plans and budgets of the operating companies and their affiliates; and to monitor the overall performance of the division. The first executive committee was constituted as follows:

K. Verhulst: president, BOK Finishes
G. Gumber: country president, West Germany (Brunal)
H. Baeyens: country president, Benelux (Van Houdt)
F. de Castelnau: country president, France (Sofravel)
Ch. Meynckens: manager, marketing coordination
G. Smeets: manager, finance
J. P. Verbeek: manager, research and development

2. The *country presidents* for the Benelux, France, and Germany represented the top-line management authority for the operating company(ies) assigned to them. As such, each president decided on all strategies, plans, and budgets regarding the marketing activities that fell within the scope of the operating companies (i.e, the decorative, DIY, car refinish, and local industrial coatings markets) and retained responsibility for local production, research, and other support functions. In addition the country presidents had to ensure that their respective companies effectively carried out assigned activities in the market for major industrial coatings. All presidents were ultimately responsible for their company's profitability and reported directly to the board of BOK, N.V. through the functionally responsible board member.
3. The *division research manager* was responsible for all major development and fundamental research projects and programs carried out in the various local laboratories and provided functional leadership, i.e., advice and guidance, over all other research activities. In the execution of this task the division research manager was supported by the *research steering group,* consisting of local research managers, but no direct-line authority over local research managers was implied.
4. The *coordinating committee for major industries* was composed of the various commercial managers of Sofravel, Brunal, and Van Houdt responsible for all major indus-

trial coatings markets (automotive, coil coatings, etc.) and the division research manager, under the chairmanship of the division president. The coordinating committee had responsibility for managing all divisional activities in these markets, including evaluating strategies, plans, and budgets, and for assigning the responsibility for serving major industrial customers (particularly the automotive companies) or special industries to specific executives in the operating companies. The committee had overall responsibility for the profitability of these markets.

5. The manager of the *marketing coordination group* provided divisionwide functional leadership for all activities in the decorative, do-it-yourself, and car refinishes markets, and for all sales promotion and publicity activities. In addition the manager was directly responsible for the decorative and DIY activities in Germany and Italy and in this capacity had the authority of a country president. The marketing coordination manager was assisted by one coordinator for each of the three market sectors. The group acted in a purely advisory capacity in formulating local marketing and sales programs and attempted to stimulate product standardization and the transfer of know-how between companies.

6. Additional support staff at the divisional level included the *manager of finance and general staff services,* the *head of the personnel policy department,* as well as a *manager of non-paint activities* (essentially laminates and resin production). The latter was subsequently also named to the executive committee.

In implementing this divisional structure (see Exhibits 1 to 3), it was intended that the central staff be as international as possible. However, notwithstanding the choice of English as the official language, there was a strong Flemish bias. The two non-Flemish members of the executive committee (Gumber and de Castelnau) spoke very little English and were obligated to participate at committee meetings through an as-sistant or by using interpreters. Furthermore, divisional staff were housed in a separate office at Van Houdt's main plant near Antwerp, from where regular contact was maintained with BOK corporate staff in Brussels. Thus, most business outside formal executive committee meetings was conducted in Flemish.

In addition to restructuring the central staff, the new structure also meant certain changes at the operating company level. In France, it was decided that Sofravel should assume the overall responsibility for all BOK Finishes activities in France, integrating Van Houdt (France) and Figier into its lines. In Germany, Brunal assumed overall responsibility for all car repair paint activities in that country, and Van Houdt (Belgium) retained responsibility for its own decorative-DIY markets. In Holland, Van Houdt absorbed the activities of both Sofravel and Brunal in that country. In Italy, Sofravel retained control over its affiliate Delfina, operating mainly in the coil coatings and automotive markets, and Siver (Societa Italiana de Vernici) reported directly to Van Houdt and dealt mainly in the decorative and car refinish market. In 1972, a third Italian company was acquired, Rapole SpA, and all three companies were put under one umbrella holding organization (BOK Siver SpA), which reported directly to Antwerp. Nonetheless, strong product development and technical linkage remained between each operating unit and its former parent.

Laboratories in all countries were assessed in order to identify particular strengths and were designated "centers of excellence" for one or more areas. Accordingly, the Sofravel laboratory became the center for coil coatings research and, jointly with Van Houdt, for anti-corrosion paints; Van Houdt was given the lead for car refinishes and decorative/DIY paints; and Brunal for automotive finishes. No laboratory was assigned exclusive responsibility for general industrial coatings research, and it was assumed that activities in this field would continue to be carried out by the three units based on their specific market and product mix.

The implementation of this international or-

EXHIBIT 1

**ORGANIZATION OF BOK FINISHES DIVISION, 1971**

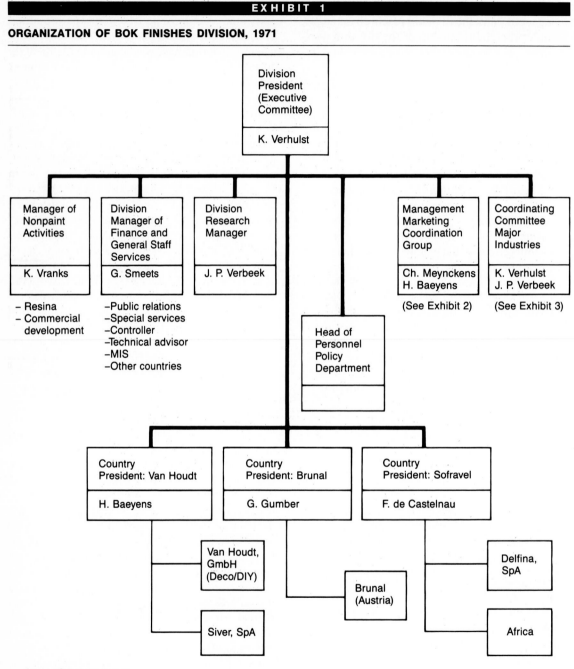

*Source:* Company records.

**EXHIBIT 2**

**ORGANIZATIONAL RELATIONSHIPS, MARKETING COORDINATION GROUP, 1971**

Division President

Management Marketing Coordination Group — Ch. Meynckens, H. Baeyens

Marketing Coordinator, Decorative

Marketing Coordinator, Do-It-Yourself

Marketing Coordinator, Car Repair

Publicity Coordination

Technical Assistant

Country President, Van Houdt

Country President, Brunal

Country President, Sofravel

Commercial Manager, Belgium

Commercial Manager, Holland

Commercial Manager, Car Repair

Commercial Manager, Decorative, Do-It-Yourself (wholesaler sales)

Commercial Manager, Decorative, Do-It-Yourself (direct sales)

*Source:* Company records.

623

**ORGANIZATIONAL RELATIONSHIPS, COORDINATING COMMITTEE MAJOR INDUSTRIES, 1971**

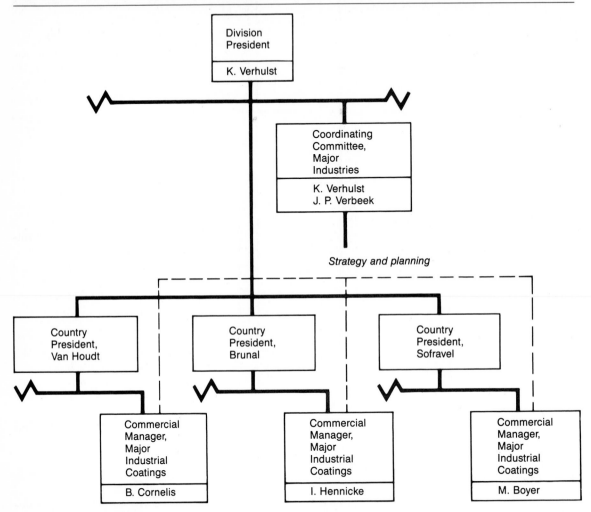

Source: Company records.

ganizational structure was a major task occupying much of the division's attention in 1972 and 1973. All three companies were going through a period of rationalization and modernization. Van Houdt was turning away from its plant site orientation toward a market focus. Brunal, a highly technical company, was thrown somewhat into disarray when its president, Dr. Holzapfel, left in 1970 as set out in the merger agreement. Dr. Holzapfel, a trained chemist, had been something of an autocrat, running a very centralized operation. He knew all of his 1,000 employees by name and was very popular but took all decisions himself and personally attended to all major customers. With his departure, many of these contacts were lost and had to be reestablished. Support staff services were almost nonexistent at Brunal; there was not even a personnel manager. By contrast, the former president of Sofravel had not been very popular with his staff. He never met with more than one of his subordinates at a time, thus creating an uncooperative atmosphere in the company. Trained in finance and production, he had paid no attention to the marketing side of the business, and marketing strategies were all but nonexistent upon his departure in 1971.

## EARLY RESULTS

By late 1973 the organizational restructuring had been essentially completed. In evaluating this process, Verhulst commented later: "Looking back, we can say that we reached several of our goals, but—quite obviously—not all our wishes could be fulfilled. Where are we now? Well, today's reality shows a different picture. Our business environment has changed drastically. . . . The oil crisis has left its impact, and all possible efforts have now to be made to regain an acceptable profitability level."

Divisional attention was directed to two new themes: innovation and diversification. Until 1973, BOK Finishes grew steadily at a rate better than the average industry growth and with improved profitability. However, with the advent of the oil crisis and the consequent slump in production and consumption of paints, especially in the industrial sector, heavy competition in the field of decorative paints and the unprecedented increase in raw material costs, profitability suffered a sharp setback. One primary reason for the profit crisis was the company's inability to fully absorb increased costs in higher selling prices. Despite the facts that raw material costs had increased by 40 percent and paint prices had virtually remained constant through the 1960s, customers balked at more than marginal price increases.

Following the mergers and reorganization, group sales increased by almost 70 percent, compared to only 20 percent for the industry, during the 1972 to 1977 period. However, operating income did not keep pace. It fluctuated from a high of 6.7 percent of sales in 1972 to a low of 2.7 percent in 1975, recovering to 5.5 percent in 1977. Return on investment (ROI), after falling from 4 percent in 1973 to 2.7 percent in 1975, reached its highest level in 1977 at 8.9 percent but was still short of the division's goal of achieving an ROI of at least 10 percent (after taxes). See Exhibit 4 for more details on the division's financial performance from 1972 to 1977.

During the same period, the parent company also had its share of problems. BOK, N.V. sales had increased in value only 10.8 percent since 1973. Total operating income decreased from BF17.6 billion to only BF12.4 billion, and a net loss of BF11.7 billion was reported in 1977. The finishes division contribution to sales increased slightly from 9 percent to 11 percent, and contribution to operating income increased from 3.5 percent to 15 percent, reflecting the deteriorating performance of BOK's other activities rather than the outstanding performance of the finishes division.

BOK Finishes' management identified several key strategic objectives for the future:

- Achieve at least 8 percent ROI on European business and a higher ROI on overseas activities, for an average over 10 percent.
- Reduce working capital in relation to sales from the current 31 percent to about 26 percent of sales.
- Achieve a sales volume growth level of about 4 percent per annum.
- Be the innovative leader in car repair.
- Develop a stronger position in automotive.
- Penetrate further in DIY activities.
- Concentrate on, and upgrade, color and design know-how.
- Generate related new business up to about BF1 billion by 1982.
- Put as much emphasis as possible on the utilization of high technology.
- Improve organizational effectiveness, motivation, and communication by using advance management techniques.

Exhibits 5 and 6 show the historical evolution of sales and contribution to profits by sector and

EXHIBIT 4

## FINANCIAL STATEMENTS, 1972 TO 1977 (BF Million)

| | 1972 Volume | 1972 Percent of sales | 1973 | 1974 | 1975 | 1976 | 1977 Volume | 1977 Percent of sales |
|---|---|---|---|---|---|---|---|---|
| Sales | 5,789 | 100.0 | 6,402 | 7,732 | 8,366 | 9,413 | 9,749 | 100.0 |
| Raw materials and packaging | 2,524 | 43.6 | 2,844 | 3,716 | 4,062 | 4,484 | 4,482 | 46.0 |
| Production costs | 885 | 15.3 | 975 | 1,033 | 1,114 | 1,214 | 1,316 | 13.5 |
| Gross margin | 2,380 | 41.1 | 2,583 | 2,983 | 3,192 | 3,715 | 3,951 | 40.5 |
| Expenses | | | | | | | | |
| Direct selling | 222 | 3.8 | 257 | 288 | 315 | 369 | 382 | 3.9 |
| Indirect selling | 978 | 16.9 | 1,172 | 1,344 | 1,517 | 1,629 | 1,741 | 17.9 |
| Advertising | 136 | 2.3 | 171 | 176 | 182 | 216 | 228 | 2.3 |
| Research | 174 | 3.0 | 208 | 229 | 240 | 281 | 297 | 3.0 |
| Licenses | — | | — | — | 141† | 111† | 10 | 0.1 |
| | 1,510 | 26.1 | 1,808 | 2,037 | 2,268 | 2,507 | 2,657 | 27.2 |
| Contribution to profit | 870 | 15.0 | 776 | 946 | 924 | 1,207 | 1,294 | 13.3 |
| Administration | 403 | 7.0 | 424 | 474 | 500 | 544 | 564 | 5.8 |
| Other expenses | 20 | 0.3 | 25 | 138 | 120 | 45 | 117 | 1.2 |
| Divisional research | 55 | 1.0 | 54 | 77 | 75 | 89 | 78 | 0.8 |
| Operating income | 392 | 6.7 | 273 | 257 | 229 | 530 | 535 | 5.5 |
| ROI income* | 212 | 3.7 | 156 | 174 | 134 | 415 | 465 | 4.8 |
| Net income† | 206 | 3.6 | 7 | (17) | (52) | 41 | 85 | 0.9 |
| Current assets | 2,944 | 50.9 | 3,382 | 4,125 | 4,277 | 4,474 | 4,702 | 48.2 |
| Fixed assets | 1,926 | 33.3 | 1,964 | 2,147 | 2,175 | 1,985 | 2,020 | 20.7 |
| Current liabilities | 1,229 | 21.2 | 1,418 | 1,428 | 1,524 | 1,608 | 1,692 | 17.4 |
| Net invested capital | 3,642 | 62.9 | 3,928 | 4,844 | 4,927 | 4,851 | 5,030 | 51.6 |
| Return on investment (%) | — | — | 4.0% | 3.6% | 2.7% | 8.3% | 8.9% | — |
| No. of employees | — | — | 3871 | 4156 | 4065 | 4147 | 4101 | — |
| Personnel cost | — | — | 1804 | 2149 | 2325 | 2583 | 2738 | 28.1 |
| Depreciation | — | — | 193 | 210 | 209 | 210 | 203 | 2.1 |

*Net of earned interest, taxes, and earnings of nonconsolidated affiliates.
†After interest payments, extraordinary items, and intracorporate transfers.
Source: Company records.

| EXHIBIT 5 |
| --- |

**RESULTS PER MARKET SECTOR, 1973 TO 1977**

|  | 1973 | 1974 | 1975 | 1976 | 1977 |
| --- | --- | --- | --- | --- | --- |
| **Sales per sector (BF million)** | | | | | |
| Decorative | 1,505 | 1,638 | 1,674 | 1,774 | 1,783 |
| Do-it-yourself | 920 | 1,084 | 1,232 | 1,284 | 1,382 |
| Automotive | 903 | 873 | 991 | 1,161 | 1,123 |
| Car refinishes | 679 | 785 | 877 | 1,034 | 1,204 |
| General industries | 654 | 719 | 656 | 722 | 722 |
| Export | 209 | 289 | 360 | 431 | 546 |
| Marine | 118 | 178 | 238 | 214 | 232 |
| Coil coating | 75 | 91 | 118 | 151 | 148 |
| Road marking | 74 | 94 | 68 | 86 | 84 |
| Aviation | 54 | 80 | 87 | 88 | 91 |
| Other paint products | 25 | 27 | 51 | 56 | 79 |
| Rubens (artist paints) | 225 | 263 | 287 | 314 | 336 |
| Non-European markets | 382 | 899 | 1,081 | 1,325 | 1,404 |
| Nonpaint products | 578 | 712 | 646 | 771 | 615 |
| Total | 6,402 | 7,732 | 8,366 | 9,413 | 9,749 |
| **Contribution to profit per sector (% of sales)** | | | | | |
| Decorative | 11.0 | 10.4 | 7.2 | 8.7 | 8.8 |
| Do-it-yourself | 13.4 | 11.2 | 10.6 | 9.7 | 10.3 |
| Automotive | 12.9 | 8.6 | 13.9 | 19.5 | 19.5 |
| Car refinishes | 15.2 | 16.5 | 12.2 | 13.7 | 14.7 |
| General industries | 2.9 | 6.8 | 4.0 | 6.0 | 8.1 |
| Export | 7.9 | 10.8 | 12.6 | 16.5 | 15.1 |
| Marine | 0.1 | 4.1 | 11.4 | 10.0 | 4.5 |
| Coil coating | 12.4 | 7.2 | 9.7 | 7.6 | 3.5 |
| Road marking | 18.3 | 20.4 | 14.3 | 15.8 | 15.0 |
| Aviation | 15.6 | 21.9 | 20.3 | 21.1 | 24.2 |
| Others | 8.0 | 7.4 | (93.0) | (69.1) | 4.2 |
| Rubens (artist) | 1.7 | 6.4 | 3.9 | 6.4 | 4.9 |
| Non-European markets | 25.9 | 22.0 | 21.8 | 22.4 | 20.9 |
| Nonpaint products | 12.9 | 14.3 | 12.4 | 12.8 | 16.2 |
| Total | 12.1 | 12.2 | 10.9 | 12.8 | 13.3 |

*Source:* Company records.

geographic unit, respectively, from 1973 to 1977. Exhibit 7 provides greater detail about the amount of research expenditures allocated by divisional staff, but performed by the operating companies, as well as total divisional overheads. Finally, Exhibit 8 presents the division's assessment as to where each segment was located in the market attractiveness/competitive position matrix for 1977.

## PERFORMANCE IMPROVEMENT EXERCISE (PIE)

Recognition of changing external conditions, the unsatisfactory profit picture, and the general organizational malaise felt by many prompted a new review of the organizational structure which began in 1977. In introducing the performance improvement exercise (PIE), as it became known,

EXHIBIT 6

## OPERATING RESULTS BY GEOGRAPHIC AREA, 1973 TO 1977

| | 1973 | 1974 | 1975 | 1976 | 1977 |
|---|---|---|---|---|---|
| **Sales (BF million)** | | | | | |
| Van Houdt (Benelux)* | 1,963 | 2,339 | 2,431 | 2,633 | 2,875 |
| Van Houdt (Germany)† | 556 | 541 | 592 | 688 | 674 |
| Brunal (Germany/Austria) | 1,186 | 1,153 | 1,282 | 1,579 | 1.707 |
| Sofravel (France)‡ | 1,204 | 1,422 | 1,646 | 1,672 | 1,625 |
| BOK Siver (Italy)§ | 298 | 389 | 363 | 403 | 435 |
| International¶ | 382 | 899 | 1,081 | 1,325 | 1,404 |
| Other activities** | 820 | 989 | 970 | 1,141 | 1,030 |
| Total | 6,402 | 7,732 | 8,366 | 9,413 | 9,749 |
| **Contributions to profits (% of sales)** | | | | | |
| Van Houdt (Benelux)* | 12.7 | 11.7 | 9.5 | 12.3 | 13.6 |
| Van Houdt (Germany)† | 8.6 | 5.4 | 2.7 | 3.9 | 5.8 |
| Brunal (Germany/Austria) | 9.4 | 6.3 | 9.0 | 14.5 | 17.0 |
| Sofravel (France)‡ | 11.0 | 13.3 | 13.9 | 11.9 | 7.2 |
| BOK Siver (Italy)§ | 10.4 | 15.9 | 12.4 | 12.9 | 11.0 |
| International¶ | 25.9 | 22.0 | 21.9 | 22.3 | 20.9 |
| Other activities** | 12.6 | 12.0 | 4.7 | 7.0 | 11.6 |
| Total | 12.1 | 12.2 | 10.9 | 12.8 | 13.3 |

*Includes sales of Sofravel products in the Benelux area and Van Houdt's subsidiaries in the United Kingdom and Spain.

†Only Van Houdt's deco/DIY sales are included, since their car refinish business in Germany was transferred to Brunal (and accounts for about 55 percent of the total German car refinish business).

‡Does not include Sofravel brand sales outside of France nor its African subsidiaries.

§All products irrespective of original source.

¶Africa, Mexico, Brazil, and the Philippines.

**Mainly Rubens and Resina.

EXHIBIT 7

## DIVISIONAL RESEARCH AND OVERHEADS, 1973 TO 1977 (BF Million)

| | 1973 | 1974 | 1975 | 1976 | 1977 |
|---|---|---|---|---|---|
| Divisional research | | | | | |
| Van Houdt | 20.4 | 31.8 | 27.6 | 33.2 | 27.1 |
| Brunal | 4.4 | 8.0 | 10.6 | 12.8 | 10.9 |
| Sofravel | 14.5 | 18.1 | 20.0 | 24.8 | 16.4 |
| Resina | 13.8 | 18.2 | 16.5 | 20.1 | 19.1 |
| Administration (Antwerp) | 6.9 | 7.5 | 8.0 | 8.5 | 4.5 |
| Subtotal | 53.6 | 77.2 | 74.9 | 89.0 | 78.1 |
| Total coatings R&D | 261.2 | 306.6 | 328.8 | 381.4 | 384.2 |
| Divisional overhead | n.a. | 80.0 | 92.0 | 91.0 | 96.9 |

n.a. = not available.

*Note:* The "divisional" research figures above represent only that proportion of R&D work performed by the operating companies on divisionwide projects. These were generally of an innovative nature and had to have, by definition, an international interest, even though the actual work was assigned to one of the national laboratories.

Total coatings R&D expenditures were much higher, as indicated in Exhibit 4. This total included all development and support conducted by the group companies on their own accord for specific local applications.

*Source:* Company records.

EXHIBIT 8

**BUSINESS SEGMENT PORTFOLIO POSITIONING, 1977**

Attractiveness of the business

|  |  | H | M | L | Total |
|---|---|---|---|---|---|
| **Strength of BOK Finishes competitive position** | **H** | Africa 8<br>Car refinishes 12<br>Coil 2<br>DIY 15 | Automotive 13 |  | 50 |
|  | **M** | Brazil 7<br>Resins 5<br>Anticorrosives 1 | Decorative 18<br>Other 2 | General industries 8<br>Marine 1 | 42 |
|  | **L** | Rubens 3 |  | Bulk resins 5 | 8 |
|  | **Total** | 53 | 33 | 14 | 100% |

*Note:* Figures in the matrix indicate percent of sales for each business segment relative to total divisional sales.
*Source:* Company records.

Verhulst stated: "... an organization has to be reviewed every 5–6 years. ... We want to have a very effective organization. So, our first target is to match the organization to its needs."

To that end, BOK Finishes embarked on PIE, which was intended to clarify and, where necessary, adapt the divisional organization structure to the new prevailing conditions. But, according to Mr. Verhulst: "Our preference continues for an organizational structure of the division based primarily on decentralized country management over an organizational set-up based on centralized product management. This implies centralized policy direction based on explicit strategy concepts, and a decentralized operation administration based on operating standards and goals."

The areas reserved for divisional competence

were to be limited to the "development of divisional strategies and plans, the allocation of resources between local organizations, and an overall control of local activities." Furthermore, Verhulst emphasized that, "Control will be exercised under an approach of loose delegation. This means that intervention in current local operations is expected to be minimal."

Nonetheless, there was wide recognition by senior divisional managers that some sacrifices of local autonomy were necessary, as one of them indicated:

An important strategic objective of the Finishes Division is the exploitation of economies of scale. We realize very well that this is not an easy job. In certain fields, e.g., research, it is quite clear that we can profit from a joint approach. This applies particularly to the automotive industry where we must try not to duplicate our research activities.

What about market sectors such as car refinishes, decorative, do-it-yourself and general industry? Some people think that the realization of economies of scale will be hampered by our decentralized organization. We think that flexible units can stimulate each other and take advantage of their mutual strength.

Experience has proved already that our decentralized organization is no real obstacle for this. Take for example the car refinishes sector where a common product assortment has been realized. Furthermore, the total-service package, including mixing machines, viewers, color documentation, etc. is an international one. Even a common market approach in several countries will become reality through the so-called Key Accounts Project.

The decorative/DIY sector shows another example. With the Rainbow Project we will reach a real European approach: one mixing machine system, one product assortment, one color collection. It is evident that for such operations we can really profit from the economies of scale.

## THE NEW ORGANIZATION

As a result of PIE a number of important changes were proposed for the organization. First among these, the executive committee was to be re-placed by a *board of management* (BOM), composed of the division president, two vice-presidents, and the three country presidents. In restyling the board, a formal system for holding division/group–company meetings was to be put in place by which it was hoped that the operating companies could bring specific issues of division-company importance to be aired and decided at the highest level. As the new organizational manual stated:

In this Board of Management all basic decisions on BOK Finishes' objectives and strategies will be prepared, discussed and made, taking into account the various views of all members. With this new Board of Management, BOK Finishes will have a better balanced top compared to the former Executive Committee in which five members from divisional headquarters in Antwerp and three country presidents were present. This also reinforces the concept of management by consensus rather than by majority.

Within the BOM, the *president* would have overall responsibility for setting objectives for the three country presidents and the general manager of Resina (the newly reorganized resin and laminates production unit) as well as for the two vice-presidents and the central staff; the president was also directly responsible for special strategic issues, automotive group policy, and for general BOK duties. One *vice-president* would oversee all major international activities outside the area of influence of Van Houdt, Brunal, and Sofravel and would be responsible for marketing and product-group coordination and new business development. The second *vice-president* would focus on technical matters, innovation, and new business planning, and oversee resin production and manpower development. The *country presidents* would be accountable for the operations of each group of companies under their command, with responsibility for profits and for ensuring compliance with all divisional plans touching their respective areas.

A second major innovation was the creation of an *automotive policy group* (APG) to replace

EXHIBIT 9

## NEW ORGANIZATIONAL STRUCTURE, 1978

Board
of
Management

| President (1) |
| Vice-president (2) |
| Vice-president (3) |

K. Verhulst
Ch. Meynckens
L. Gerrits
F. de Castelnau
G. Gumber
D. Hanssens

Secretariat

(1) Resins Development & Special Projects: K. Vrancks

(1) Automotive Development & Raw Materials: F. Janssens *

(1) Finance Planning & Control Systems: G. Leynen

(1) Personnel & Organization
(3) Manpower Development: A. Goyens

(3) R&D, Engineering & Production: Vacant

(2) Marketing & Product Group Coordination: J. Brun *

(1) Country President, France—Sofravel, Africa: F. de Castelnau

(1) General Manager, Resina: R. Maas

(2) General Manager, BOK Siver (Italy): J. Alger

(1) Country President, W. Germany/Austria: G. Gumber

P. Gabriel, Spain

Manila Paints, Philippines

(1) Country President, Benelux: D. Hanssens

(2) Coordinator Internationalization

Copimex, Mexico

Gonsalves & Santos, Brazil

*See Exhibit 10.
Note: (1), (2), and (3) denote reporting lines.
Source: Company records.

631

**EXHIBIT 10**

**AUTOMOTIVE PRODUCT GROUP AND STEERING COMMITTEES**

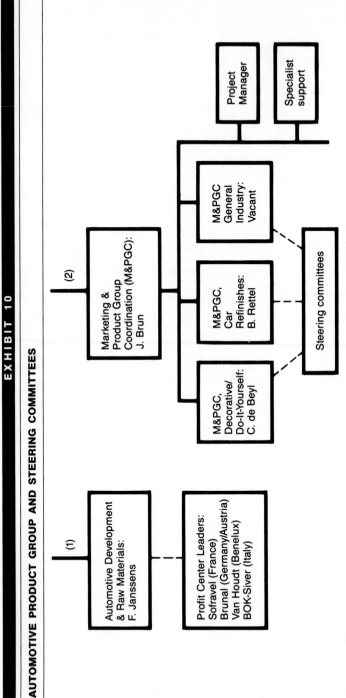

*Source:* Company records.

the coordinating committee for major industries and of a number of *steering committees* with competence for specific product segments. The APG would be accountable directly to the president for all automotive policy. Chaired by the "functional manager for automotive development" (a new post), the APG would include one representative from each main group "having the highest authority with respect to automotive affairs."

Equally, four steering committees were created to deal with research, car refinishes, decorative, and DIY. The actual authority of each committee was left vague, but most were expected to act in an advisory capacity. The objectives of these steering committees were to coordinate marketing activities of the various operating companies as well as to encourage economies of scale and transfer of technical know-how and research. The market segment steering committees would consist of representatives of the particular segment from each of the operating companies involved in that seg-

ment, as well as the manager of the specialist research center with responsibility for that segment. The chairman of each committee would be named by the BOM and would be responsible to the BOM through the "manager for marketing and product-group coordination."

Exhibits 9 and 10 summarize the new organizational structure as resulting from the performance improvement exercise. Verhulst commented on the future as follows:

> One can easily create a very sophisticated theoretical organization structure. Its functioning in practice, however, depends entirely on its acceptance by people. We believe that we have many well qualified people throughout our organization on whom we can rely fully. We also believe that within this new organization structure a greater involvement of all concerned will become a reality.
>
> We have not only clarified our organization but also created conditions for the improvement of working relationships.

# BOK Finishes— Automotive Products

In the early 1970s, the automotive finishes segment of the paint market was becoming increasingly international. Customers were few in number, but each represented high sales potential, and many had international production and technological links. Automotive manufacturers generally relied on many outside sources for their component purchases and demanded technical sophistication. Thus, suppliers of automotive original equipment (OEM) paints relied on a highly trained sales force, at ease with modern marketing techniques and capable of assisting with a multitude of specific and complex customer requirements.

All three core companies within BOK Finishes—Sofravel (France), Van Houdt (Belgium), and Brunal (Germany)—were producers of automotive finishes. Brunal was a major sup-

plier to Opel (GM) and Volkswagen; Van Houdt, to Ford and DAF-Volvo; Sofravel to Peugeot, Talbot, and Citroën; and Delfina (a sister company of Sofravel in Italy) to Alfa Romeo. Under the postmerger structure, competition between companies for the same customer was to be avoided, and the markets were divided by country, with two exceptions. As Van Houdt was supplying Ford throughout Europe, it maintained the Ford account in Germany, and, for the same reasons, Brunal continued to supply Opel in Belgium. In keeping with this strategy, Van Houdt relinquished its contacts with Peugeot in France, an account that was to be serviced by Sofravel.

## THE AUTOMOTIVE INDUSTRY

The number of cars produced worldwide rose by around 1.5 percent per annum between 1973 and 1977, and the average growth for the following 5 years was not expected to exceed 1 to 2 percent per annum. This was partly due to the gradual saturation of traditional markets in countries where car ownership had reached high levels, as well as the impact of higher fuel prices and economic recession in the industrial coun-

This case was written by André Khodjamirian, research associate, and Professor José de la Torre as a basis for discussion. The generous contributions of many executives from a European chemical firm that prefers to remain anonymous are gratefully acknowledged. All names, places, and financial figures, as well as some events, have been disguised to preserve the confidentiality of the data. © INSEAD—The European Institute of Business Administration, 1986.

tries. World production of motor vehicles had reached the figure of 41 million units in 1977, of which 16 million (39 percent) were manufactured in Europe. Considering passenger cars only, about 11 million units were produced by the top 13 European automakers (see Exhibits 1 and 2 for more details). Simultaneously, the share of imported cars had gone from 2.2 percent of European demand in 1970 to 8 percent (750,000 vehicles) in 1977. Total exports by the European automotive industry to non-European countries amounted to 1.4 million cars in 1977. Over 30 percent of these were German exports to the United States, and an additional 10 percent consisted of French exports to Africa. BOK forecasts showed a gradual increase in car imports and a decrease in exports in the future.

The automotive industry had experienced a long period of relative technological maturity: Basic motor vehicle designs dated back to the 1910s, mass production to the 1920s, and front-wheel drive, four-wheel independent suspension, and monopiece bodies to the mid-1930s. Most recent changes had occurred after the energy crisis and included innovations such as the increased use of plastic-based materials to obtain improved rust resistance and lighter weight in car bodies. New engine designs increased the use of electronics aimed at improved performance and reduced maintenance.

With growing emphasis on lighter and more rust-resistant bodies, and with the increasing use of plastics, the quality/quantity relationship of car paints was expected to change. Furthermore, the growing tendency for assembly units to be located near the markets to be served (e.g., Ford, GM, Renault, and Fiat setting up assembly or manufacturing plants in Belgium, Spain, Portugal, and East European countries) was also affecting the industry suppliers. Industry concentration had also increased during the past decade, and auto manufacturers were becoming

---

### EXHIBIT 1

**MOTOR VEHICLE PRODUCTION, INCLUDING COMMERCIAL VEHICLES** (Thousands)

| Year | United States | Canada | U.S. & Canada total | Europe | Asia | Other | World total |
|------|------|------|------|------|------|------|------|
| 1977 | 12,703 | 1,775 | 14,478 | 15,979 | 8,604 | 1,888 | 40,949 |
| 1976 | 11,498 | 1,640 | 13,138 | 15,316 | 7,927 | 1,960 | 38,346 |
| 1975 | 8,987 | 1,424 | 10,411 | 13,590 | 7,016 | 1,982 | 32,998 |
| 1974 | 10,071 | 1,525 | 11,596 | 14,513 | 6,640 | 1,985 | 34,733 |
| 1973 | 12,682 | 1,575 | 14,256 | 15,700 | 7,180 | 1,781 | 38,918 |
| 1972 | 11,311 | 1,430 | 12,741 | 14,836 | 6,384 | 1,584 | 35,545 |
| 1971 | 10,672 | 1,347 | 12,018 | 13,956 | 6,000 | 1,450 | 33,424 |
| 1970 | 8,284 | 1,187 | 9,471 | 13,154 | 5,365 | 1,276 | 29,267 |
| 1969 | 10,205 | 1,326 | 11,532 | 12,367 | 4,753 | 1,158 | 29,810 |
| 1968 | 10,820 | 1,150 | 11,971 | 11,241 | 4,164 | 980 | 28,356 |
| 1967 | 9,024 | 940 | 9,943 | 9,969 | 3,217 | 894 | 24,023 |
| 1966 | 10,396 | 872 | 11,269 | 10,364 | 2,357 | 862 | 24,852 |
| 1965 | 11,138 | 847 | 11,984 | 9,549 | 1,947 | 787 | 24,267 |
| 1964 | 9,308 | 671 | 9,979 | 9,216 | 1,770 | 762 | 21,727 |
| 1963 | 9,109 | 631 | 9,740 | 8,640 | 1,340 | 653 | 20,373 |
| 1962 | 8,197 | 505 | 8,702 | 7,598 | 1,048 | 651 | 17,999 |
| 1961 | 6,653 | 387 | 7,040 | 6,582 | 1,092 | 514 | 15,228 |
| 1960 | 7,905 | 398 | 8,303 | 6,824 | 811 | 550 | 16,488 |
| 1955 | 9,204 | 452 | 9,656 | 3,742 | 168 | 62 | 13,628 |
| 1950 | 8,006 | 391 | 8,397 | 2,128 | 32 | 20 | 10,577 |

*Source:* Motor Vehicle Manufacturers Association of the United States.

**EXHIBIT 2**

**MOTOR VEHICLE PRODUCTION, 1975**

| Manufacturers | Passenger cars | Commercial vehicles | Total production, 1975 | Rank production total |
|---|---|---|---|---|
| General Motors—U.S. | 3,679,260 | 970,270 | 4,649,530 | 1 |
| Ford—U.S. | 1,808,038 | 692,200 | 2,500,238 | 2 |
| Toyota | 1,714,836 | 621,217 | 2,336,053 | 3 |
| Nissan* | 1,532,731 | 572,003 | 2,104,734 | 4 |
| VW-Audi-NSU | 1,255,448 | 71,651 | 1,327,099 | 5 |
| Fiat-OM-Autobianchi-Lancia | 1,123,752 | 107,957 | 1,231,709 | 6 |
| Chrysler—U.S. | 902,902 | 319,694 | 1,222,596 | 7 |
| Renault-Saviem-Berliet | 1,042,261 | 146,025 | 1,188,286 | 8 |
| Leyland Ltd. | 605,141 | 133,057 | 738,198 | 9 |
| Opel | 655,877 | 1,662 | 657,539 | 10 |
| Peugeot | 563,821 | 80,164 | 643,985 | 11 |
| Toyo Kogyo | 387,411 | 255,203 | 642,614 | 12 |
| Ford Werke† | 606,973 | 27,563 | 634,536 | 13 |
| Citroën | 548,451 | 50,377 | 598,828 | 14 |
| General Motors—Canada | 407,247 | 190,343 | 597,590 | 15 |
| Mercedes-Hanomag-Henschel | 356,477 | 178,852 | 535,329 | 16 |
| Mitsubishi | 288,846 | 231,392 | 520,238 | 17 |
| VW do Brazil | 291,672 | 210,908 | 502,580 | 18 |
| Ford—Canada | 325,513 | 155,411 | 480,924 | 19 |
| American Motors | 323,796 | 139,906 | 463,702 | 20 |
| Ford—U.K. | 329,648 | 129,111 | 458,759 | 21 |
| Honda | 328,107 | 85,646 | 413,753 | 22 |
| Chrysler—France | 383,169 | 24,783 | 407,952 | 23 |
| Seat | 328,806 | 3,272 | 332,078 | 24 |
| Volvo—DAF | 285,000 | 31,615 | 316,615 | 25 |
| Chrysler—Canada | 261,275 | 24,715 | 285,990 | 26 |
| Daihatsu | 92,123 | 165,551 | 257,674 | 27 |
| Chrysler—U.K. | 226,612 | 19,211 | 245,823 | 28 |
| Isuzu | 64,735 | 180,086 | 244,821 | 29 |
| BMW | 217,458 | 0 | 217,458 | 30 |

*Nissan: Nissan and Nissan Diesel.
†Ford Werke, Cologne-Köln, and Genk. (Production Genk, Belgium, 1975: 221,411.)
*Note:* Manufacturers' figures from the professional associations.
*Source:* OECD, Addendum 2 to DSTI/IND/80.46—*Automobile Industry, Statistical Index.*

conscious of the benefits that cooperative agreements in different markets could offer (e.g., the mergers of Fiat-Lancia in Italy and Peugeot-Citroën in France; common engine sourcing of Peugeot, Renault, and Volvo; joint model design of the Chrysler Horizon [Europe]/Omni [U.S.] model). Such agreements invariably affected the relationships that existed between the auto manufacturers and their principal suppliers.

## BOK AND THE EUROPEAN AUTOMOTIVE MARKETS

Van Houdt had started working toward a Europewide presence (the Netherlands in 1954, West Germany in 1955, and Italy in 1958) when the Common Market was formed in 1958. In the Benelux countries, Van Houdt's paints and stoving enamels were used by public transport companies and vehicle body manufacturers. Although Van Houdt enjoyed a leading position with the supply of topcoats to Ford of Europe (25 percent of that company's total consumption), its overall market share in the Benelux market had suffered a slight decline since the early 1970s.

BOK Finishes was committed to the concept that product innovation was essential to maintain or strengthen its position in the automotive finishes market. An example of this was the development by Van Houdt of a next-generation acrylic enamel, both for metallic and nonmetallic topcoats.[1] This had been the main factor behind Van Houdt's success at Ford. Brunal had made a number of major product improvements in the field of primers and fillers. And Sofravel's introduction of highly fashionable colors had helped their position with Citroën, but only as a supplier of nonmetallic topcoats.

BOK had not always taken advantage of every important product development, however. A case in point was the company's failure to capitalize on the rising demand for better rustproofing of cars. In 1975, Sofravel and Rennoil, a U.S. petroleum company, formed a joint venture, Sofren, to market in France two corrosion-resistant steel-coating systems developed by Rennoil. During the same period, PPG (the U.S. market leader) launched a new primer system called "cathodic electro-deposition" that was soon to capture a major share of the world's automotive primer market. The license to use this technology was made available by PPG to major European paint manufacturers. BOK's management, in spite of Brunal's vehement arguments that it purchase the license, preferred to wait for Sofren's development, and the license was purchased by BASF (Glasurit). Industry observers believed that failing to purchase this advanced primer-coating process was a major setback for BOK in automotive coatings.

Another example was Brunal's and Sofrav-

el's weak positions in metallic topcoats. One BOK executive stated that, "in general there was insufficient awareness among the operating companies of the shift in topcoats from traditional to metallics. Both marketing and research were much too involved in solving day-to-day problems. Moreover, the cooperation between the laboratories was not always what it should be. There remained a reluctance to accept someone else's findings; . . . they were 'not invented here.' "

The German market for automotive paint was shared mainly by BASF, Hoechst, Akzo, and BOK Finishes (with Van Houdt and Brunal). Prior to the takeover by BOK, Brunal followed the strategy laid down by its co-owner and director, Dr. Holtzapfel, who believed that success was to be found by concentrating on special activities, a policy encouraged by the lack of sufficient R&D resources for diversification at that time. Among its past achievements, Brunal pioneered the application of stoving enamels for the 1938 D.K.W. Super Sport, the first German motor car using that coating process. Company historians were proud to recall that ". . . the first Bosch refrigerator, and its countless successors, gleamed with a Brunal finish." Automotive coatings became the company's leading product group, winning them a major share of the German market by supplying Volkswagen, NSU, Auto Union, and Opel. Furthermore, the company started exporting automotive coatings, and its brand became well known in many markets outside Western Europe. As one former Brunal executive said: "In the automotive paint business, you need to have the automotive 'smell.' Brunal had that quality and most of our customers trusted us. We had the privilege of maintaining friendly relations with our clients. An automotive manufacturer needs a supplier that can solve their problems."

In the mid-1960s, the French automotive paints market amounted to 1,500 tons a year. The leading brands, Sofravel, Van Houdt, and PPG, shared about 50 percent of the market. The rapid growth of the industry resulted in an increase of the total market to 4,000 tons by 1974 as well

---

[1] See Appendix for a glossary of technical terms used in defining different automotive paints.

as a larger market share for Sofravel (20 percent of automotive paints). At the time of the merger with BOK, both Sofravel and Van Houdt brands were supplied to the French automobile industry in France. Sofravel was supplying Citroën and Talbot (Chrysler), and Van Houdt had agreements with Peugeot. Renault was the only French auto manufacturer to have its own integrated paint-producing facility.

It was generally believed that the strained relations that existed between Sofravel and BOK following the merger had braked the development of the Sofravel and Van Houdt brands in the French automotive market. Unnecessary competition between them and an unclear brand policy discouraged the sales force and confused customers. As one BOK executive later put it:

> Paint companies have a naturally tough time selling their products because, by developing ways to be more efficient with paint, they actually contribute to less paint consumption per car. In fact, we expect paint usage to drop to 12 kg per car in the 1980s, down from the actual 15.5 kg. This means that in order to remain competitive a paint company should do everything to benefit from available conditions and make sure that once a customer becomes a "regular," it should remain so for as long as possible.
>
> Mr. de Castelnau [Sofravel's president] was so involved in protecting Sofravel's "freedom" from the Belgians that he often overlooked this basic business common sense.

Following the acquisition of a 40 percent share in Copimex (Mexico) in 1972, the Italian operations (then consisting of a Van Houdt subsidiary manufacturing high-quality professional paints and Delfina, a manufacturer of industrial coatings and major supplier to Alfa Romeo) were expanded by the acquisition of Rapole SpA of Naples. Alfa Romeo had been induced by the government's *Mezzogiorno* development plan to build a large assembly plant in Naples and was looking for local paint suppliers. Although Rapole was a manufacturer of decorative paints, it met Van Houdt's requirements for local capacity, and a production line geared to the needs

of Alfa Romeo Sud (Alfasud) was set up at Rapole, with technical assistance from Delfina.

Given the size and importance of Britain's auto industry, BOK Finishes set an objective to acquire a position in the U.K. market. In 1976, a sales company, Van Houdt U.K., was created to promote the sale and distribution of Van Houdt car refinishes and specialty decorative paints. However, automotive enamels were supplied to the United Kingdom directly from the Van Houdt Belgium operation. It was felt that no major auto manufacturer would be happy dealing through a sales office and that it was necessary to maintain direct contact through qualified sales personnel. This was also the case in Sweden, where all automotive product sales were handled by Van Houdt Belgium directly.

Exhibit 3 shows the sales of BOK automotive finishes in the 1973–1977 period, and Exhibit 4 shows relative market shares of all paint manufacturers among major auto firms in Europe for 1973 and 1977.

## THE FORD OF SPAIN EPISODE

Anticipating the growth of automotive assembly plants in Spain, BOK Finishes had periodically considered acquiring local paint-manufacturing facilities. Early in 1975, BOK Finishes was approached by P. Gabriel, head of Gabriel S.A. The company was a major supplier to SEAT, the Spanish auto manufacturer, then 35 percent owned by Fiat. It produced automotive finishes under license from IVI, an Italian paint manufacturer belonging to the Fiat group. Gabriel had been asked by Ford to supply automotive coatings for Ford's new assembly plant in Valencia, and Ford had suggested that Gabriel contact Van Houdt for a possible production license of the latter's automotive finishes. These initial contacts led to Van Houdt's acquisition of Gabriel S.A. later that year.

Ford of Spain, following a standard auto industry practice of not relying on a single supplier, was buying part of its local automotive paint requirements from Urruzola (a subsidiary

**EXHIBIT 3**

**AUTOMOTIVE PAINT SALES AND CONTRIBUTION TO PROFITS (CTP), 1973–1977***

| | 1973 | | 1974 | | 1975 | | 1976 | | 1977 | |
|---|---|---|---|---|---|---|---|---|---|---|
| | Sales | CTP | Sales | CTP | Sales | CTP | Sales | CTP | Sales | CTP |
| Van Houdt (Benelux) | 204 | 10.1 | 190 | 4.3 | 214 | 10.1 | 243 | 13.4 | 237 | 14.9 |
| Brunal | 550 | 13.3 | 487 | 7.0 | 555 | 11.1 | 697 | 21.6 | 679 | 22.3 |
| Sofravel | 97 | 18.6 | 97 | 12.3 | 127 | 24.5 | 137 | 18.1 | 101 | 7.9 |
| Delfina | 52 | 8.9 | 66 | 24.9 | 69 | 25.5 | 58 | 24.6 | 75 | 26.2 |
| Export | — | — | 32 | 12.4 | 25 | 21.8 | 26 | 15.1 | 30 | 13.5 |
| Total | 903 | 12.9 | 873 | 8.6 | 990 | 13.9 | 1,161 | 19.5 | 1,123 | 19.5 |

*Sales figures are in BF million, and CTP figures are percentages of sales.
*Source:* Company records.

# EXHIBIT 4

## MARKET SHARE BY CUSTOMER—EUROPE

| | 1973 | | | | 1977 | | | |
|---|---|---|---|---|---|---|---|---|
| | | | Topcoats | | | | Topcoats | |
| | Primers | Fillers | Nonmetallic (60%) | Metallic (40%) | Primers | Fillers | Nonmetallic (40%) | Metallic (60%) |
| Ford consumption, tons | 3750 | 3750 | 3750 | 3750 | 4200 | 4200 | 3500 | 4900 |
| **Ford market share, %** | | | | | | | | |
| Akzo | — | — | 20 | 20 | 10 | — | 20 | 25 |
| BASF | — | — | 5 | 5 | — | — | 10 | 20 |
| BOK | — | 20 | 20 | 10 | — | 20 | 25 | 25 |
| Hoechst | 60 | — | 10 | 15 | 60 | — | 10 | 15 |
| ICI | 20 | — | — | 10 | 20 | — | 5 | 5 |
| Inmont | 20 | — | 10 | — | 10 | — | 5 | — |
| PPG | — | — | — | — | — | — | — | — |
| Others | — | 80 | 35 | 40 | — | 80 | 25 | 10 |
| Captive | — | — | — | — | — | — | — | — |
| G.M. consumption, tons | 3600 | 3600 | 3600 | 3360 | 3750 | 3750 | 3125 | 4375 |
| **G.M. market share, %** | | | | | | | | |
| Akzo | 10 | 15 | 20 | 20 | 20 | 20 | 15 | 15 |
| BASF | 15 | 10 | 10 | 10 | 10 | 15 | 25 | 25 |
| BOK | 30 | 20 | 20 | 20 | 30 | 25 | 10 | 10 |
| Hoechst | 20 | 15 | 20 | 25 | 20 | 10 | 15 | 20 |
| ICI | 5 | 5 | 10 | 10 | — | 5 | 10 | 10 |
| Inmont | 5 | 10 | 5 | 10 | 10 | 5 | 10 | 15 |
| PPG | — | — | — | — | — | — | — | — |
| Others | 15 | 25 | 15 | 5 | 10 | 20 | 15 | 5 |
| Captive | — | — | — | — | — | — | — | — |
| Volkswagen & Audi consumption, tons | 3360 | 3360 | 3640 | 2744 | 4800 | 4800 | 4000 | 5600 |
| **VW & Audi market, %** | | | | | | | | |
| Akzo | — | — | — | — | — | 5 | 10 | 40 |
| BASF | 20 | 10 | 15 | 30 | 20 | 30 | 35 | 20 |
| BOK | 20 | 10 | 20 | 20 | 20 | 25 | 20 | 40 |
| Hoechst | 20 | 15 | 20 | 25 | — | 30 | 35 | — |
| ICI | 10 | 15 | — | 15 | — | — | — | — |
| Inmont | — | — | — | — | — | 10 | — | — |
| PPG | — | — | — | — | — | — | 5 | — |
| Others | — | — | 45 | 10 | — | — | — | — |
| Captive | 50 | 50 | — | — | 60 | — | — | — |

**Peugeot**

| Peugeot consumption, tons | 1950 | 1950 | 2437 | 1137 | 2100 | 2100 | 2450 | 1470 |
|---|---|---|---|---|---|---|---|---|
| Peugeot market share, % | | | | | | | | |
| Akzo | — | — | 20 | — | — | — | 10 | — |
| BASF | — | — | — | — | — | — | 10 | 20 |
| BOK | — | — | 20 | — | 20 | 20 | 15 | — |
| Hoechst | — | — | — | — | — | — | 20 | — |
| ICI | — | — | — | — | — | — | — | — |
| Inmont | 20 | 40 | 20 | — | — | 35 | 20 | — |
| PPG | 40 | 40 | 10 | 80 | 80 | 35 | 15 | 70 |
| Others | 40 | 20 | 30 | 20 | — | 10 | 10 | 10 |
| Captive | — | — | — | — | — | — | — | — |

**Citroën**

| Citroën consumption, tons | 2250 | 2250 | 2812 | 1312 | 2400 | 2400 | 2800 | 1470 |
|---|---|---|---|---|---|---|---|---|
| Citroën market share, % | | | | | | | | |
| Akzo | 10 | 15 | 20 | 15 | — | 20 | 30 | — |
| BASF | — | — | — | — | — | — | — | 40 |
| BOK | 20 | 20 | 25 | 25 | 20 | 20 | 30 | — |
| Hoechst | — | — | — | — | — | 20 | — | — |
| ICI | — | — | — | — | — | — | — | — |
| Inmont | 20 | 30 | 25 | — | 10 | 20 | 20 | — |
| PPG | 50 | 35 | 20 | 45 | 60 | 20 | 5 | 60 |
| Others | — | — | 10 | 15 | 10 | — | 15 | — |
| Captive | — | — | — | — | — | — | — | — |

**Renault**

| Renault consumption, tons | 4350 | 4350 | 5437 | 2537 | 4500 | 4500 | 5250 | 3150 |
|---|---|---|---|---|---|---|---|---|
| Renault market share, % | | | | | | | | |
| Akzo | — | — | 10 | 10 | — | — | — | 10 |
| BASF | — | — | — | — | — | — | — | 20 |
| BOK | — | 10 | 10 | 15 | — | — | 20 | — |
| Hoechst | — | — | — | 20 | — | — | — | 30 |
| ICI | — | — | — | — | — | — | — | — |
| Inmont | — | — | 10 | 35 | — | — | — | 20 |
| PPG | — | 10 | 10 | — | — | 10 | 10 | — |
| Others | — | — | — | 20 | — | — | — | 20 |
| Captive | 100 | 80 | 60 | — | 100 | 90 | 70 | — |

*Source: Company records.*

of BASF) and Inmont, as well as from Gabriel. Normally, Ford's business wold have been shared almost evenly between the three suppliers, but according to a Van Houdt executive: "BOK Finishes made all the mistakes that could have been made. To start with, Gabriel was using Van Houdt's technology and Ford was Van Houdt's major European automotive finishes customer, yet not one representative of Van Houdt was named to the board of Gabriel."

Instead, G. Smeets, vice president of finance and executive committee member responsible for "other countries" at BOK Finishes, and M. Boyer, commercial manager of major industries for Sofravel, represented BOK on Gabriel's board. Boyer's nomination rested on the fact that Citroën, a major Sofravel customer, had a plant in Spain, and it was felt that there was an opportunity for Gabriel to get some of Citroën's Spanish business. Gabriel, however, did not succeed in developing the Citroën account nor did it maintain the service level to which Ford was accustomed.

In response to Ford's complaints, BOK approached Van Houdt in order to improve the situation. B. Cornelis, then Van Houdt's commercial manager for major industries, was in no mood to help, having been shunted aside in the beginning. Instead, he sent two lower-level technical men to Spain, one of whom Van Houdt had been trying to get rid of for some years. By 1977, the competition had taken the lion's share of the business, and Ford was threatening to abandon Gabriel altogether.

## COORDINATING POLICY:
## THE BRUNAL PERSPECTIVE

The creation after the mergers of the coordinating committee for major industries was intended to deal with the issue of a unified approach to the critical issue of customer relations in the automotive sector. In spite of the fact that Brunal had been designated as the "center of excellence" for automotive finishes, Brunal management felt that they had been forced to "play catch-up" to the market throughout the early 1970s. This, they felt, was a consequence of centralizing decision making in Belgium rather than allowing Brunal to continue to innovate. One German executive described the situation as follows:

> Brunal has always been the innovator but now that our hands are tied, thanks to BOK Finishes, we are losing our competitive advantage. . . . In 1938, for example, we helped redesign the back window of the early Beetles in order to facilitate the adherence of paint around the frame. That sort of cooperation between automotive manufacturers and paint companies was relatively unheard of at the time.
>
> Another example of our ability to respond to market needs was the development of slow-bake enamels. The temperature required to cure paint used to be about 170°C. This consumed quite a lot of energy which became very expensive after 1974. Seeing the problem we developed a binder system for surfacers and topcoats that would cure at considerably lower temperatures, say 130–140°C. Yet we never proceeded beyond the laboratory stage. Divisional management stopped development work on the product for reasons that were never made clear to us. This was doubly frustrating as the use of plastic in automotive parts increased. Brunal's lower curing temperature paint would have been compatible with plastic developments in the industry.

The major complaint of H. Klauss, then director of automotive paints at Brunal, was that BOK had created a bureaucratic process for getting resources allocated to different activities. Since, in his view, Belgium did not want to show favoritism and had limited resources, it did not always support projects that Klauss felt were critical to Brunal's long-term success in the automotive industry. A typical case, he argued, was BOK Finishes' refusal in 1975 to purchase the PPG license for the cathodic electro-deposition primer. Glasurit then moved ahead with it, and Brunal lost market share. Klauss felt that the damage to Brunal's reputation as a technological innovator had been considerable: "We are still recovering from it."

Another Brunal executive cited problems in

account management that resulted from unclear lines of authority in the automotive sector:

At one point in the early 1970s there were some possibilities to develop business at Ford in Germany, but because we were asked to focus on some automotive manufacturers and not on others, the Ford account was neglected. Our emphasis [at Brunal] was to be placed on Volkswagen, where account relations were already strong, and to try to develop new accounts with other German companies such as Mercedes Benz and BMW. In addition, our Belgian friends decided to centralize the R&D decisions about automotive in Belgium, even though Brunal had been the innovator in automotive and would continue to execute most of the work.

For these two reasons we missed an opportunity which we have regretted ever since. Brunal was strong in topcoats and in undercoats, but did not have a position in Ford. Van Houdt had the account with Ford for undercoats, but would not draw on the expertise of Brunal for topcoats, so they were unable to get the topcoat business with Ford Germany. It was a stupid situation. Van Houdt had access to the account but not the technology. We had the products but were denied access to the account. In the end, we both lost.

Klauss felt that there was little hope that things would improve as long as Belgium would call the shots:

Mr. Verhulst is a very technology-oriented man; too much so for my taste. In this business you have to have a feeling for the automotive. Sales are based on trust between the paint people and the automotive people. It is personalities working together. Yes, you have to have the technology, but you also have to realize when the automotive manufacturers have a problem, even before they know it, and then you have to create a solution for them. That requires a close relationship with your customers. It is trust that leads to friendship, that leads to sales. Verhulst does not appreciate that.

## COMPETITION

BOK's main competitors in the European automotive field were Hoechst, BASF, Akzo, PPG, and ICI (see Exhibit 5). Hoechst (mainly Herberts) had the highest market share with a strong position in topcoats and primers, in particular in Germany, Sweden, Italy, and the Benelux. BASF (Glasurit) was strong in topcoats, particularly in Germany, Spain, Sweden, and the Benelux. Akzo had a good position in topcoats in Italy, the Netherlands, and Germany. PPG (Corona) had a strong position in primers, surfacers, and topcoats and was particularly strong in France. ICI had a good position in primers and topcoats, especially in the United Kingdom. Global market shares in 1978 in automotive paint for the major world producers were estimated by BOK Finishes as shown in Exhibit 6.

It was becoming increasingly clear to industry observers that future opportunities existed in markets outside Western Europe, North America, and Japan, where conditions for growth were particularly favorable. Although there were 540 cars per 1,000 inhabitants in the United States and 332 in the EEC, the world average was only 79 cars per 1,000. Furthermore, as rationalization and mergers in the auto industry continued, the need for component manufacturers (coating suppliers among them) to adopt a worldwide approach was increasingly felt.

## R&D AND MANUFACTURING POLICY

The automotive sector was ". . . very technical and specifications oriented, where products need to be of very high quality and made specially to customer specifications." Sofravel, Brunal, Van Houdt, and Delfina each had separate research labs, based on the specific needs of their respective markets. Brunal, a highly technical company with extensive experience in supplying paint to automotive manufacturers, was named the "center of excellence" for R&D and manufacturing in the automotive sector after the acquisition of BOK. Officially, technical information was exchanged freely between group companies, and BOK Finishes executives felt that a certain level of synergy was being achieved. In reality, the need for common action was not

**EXHIBIT 5**

## MAJOR COMPETITORS AND MARKET SHARES FOR EUROPEAN AUTOMOTIVE PAINTS, 1974–1978 (%)

| | Total European market share | | | Market shares by major BOK market areas, 1977 | | | | |
|---|---|---|---|---|---|---|---|---|
| | 1974 | 1975 | 1978(e) | Van Houdt (Benelux, UK) | Brunal (Germany, Austria) | Sofravel (France) | BOK-Siver (Italy) | Gabriel (Spain) |
| Hoechst | 12 | 14 | 17 | 18 | 28 | 5 | 14 | 11 |
| BASF | 8 | 13 | 16 | 14 | 24 | 6 | 8 | 33 |
| Akzo | 14 | 13 | 11 | 14 | 16 | 8 | 7 | — |
| BOK Finishes | 7 | 10 | 9 | 8 | 12 | 6 | 4 | 20 |
| PPG | 7 | 9 | 9 | — | 2 | 28 | 10 | — |
| Renault (in-house) | 11 | 11 | 7 | 15 | — | 30 | 13 | — |
| Inmont | 12 | 10 | 7 | 18 | 3 | 6 | — | — |
| ICI | 5 | 4 | 4 | — | 3 | — | — | — |
| Nobel Bozel | — | 2 | 4 | — | — | 9 | 7 | 5 |
| IVI | — | 2 | 3 | — | — | 0 | 20 | — |
| VW (in-house) | — | 4 | 3 | — | 8 | — | — | — |
| Du Pont | — | 1 | 2 | — | 3 | 2 | — | 2 |
| Valentine | — | 1 | 2 | — | — | — | — | 20 |
| Others | 14 | 6 | 6 | 13 | 1 | 0 | 17 | 9 |
| Total market | 100 | 100 | 100 | 100 | 100 | 100 | 100 | 100 |
| Market area as a percent of European total | | | | 18 | 34 | 23 | 16 | 9 |

*Source:* Company records.

| EXHIBIT 6 |
|---|

**WORLD MARKET SHARES IN AUTOMOTIVE OEM PAINTS, 1978 (%)**

|  | N. America | W. Europe | Japan | Global |
|---|---|---|---|---|
| Du Pont (U.S.) | 32 | 2 | — | 14 |
| PPG (U.S.) | 24 | 9 | — | 11 |
| Kansai (J) | — | — | 43 | 9 |
| Hoechst (D) | — | 17 | — | 8 |
| BASF (D) | — | 16 | — | 8 |
| Inmont (U.S.) | 16 | 3 | — | 7 |
| Akzo (NL) | — | 11 | — | 6 |
| Nippon (J) | — | — | 29 | 5 |
| BOK (B) | — | 9 | — | 4 |
| All others | 28 | 33 | 28 | 28 |
| Total | 100 | 100 | 100 | 100 |

felt in the operating companies. As one Brunal executive explained:

> We have no cross manufacturing in the automotive sector. Only once did we do that, and it involved a special kind of base coat which was used by more than one auto manufacturer in Europe. You see, the technical requirements of our business make joint manufacture and joint research unfeasible. We work together with our customers and help them develop their paint requirements. We try to solve their problems and, since they are usually unique, each one of us (the operating companies) needs to have a personalized approach. . . . We may try to move towards increased centralized R&D, but that will be only possible if the auto industry also moves in the direction of standardized specifications and the much talked-about "world car." At present, the main automotive research center is here in Mannheim. Montmorency (Sofravel) and Antwerp (Van Houdt) have their own labs, but they obviously can have access to our knowledge whenever they need.

To avoid duplication and improve cooperation and coordination, the newly formed Automotive Product Group (see below) recommended centralization of automotive product development in the 1978–1982 strategic plan. Location of such efforts at Brunal (Mannheim) was advised, except for electro-deposition coatings to be kept at Sofravel for the time being.

Although production would normally continue to be carried out at the local level, the APG recommended that new product lines might be produced at one location only and shipped across national boundaries.

## STRATEGIC OBJECTIVES FOR 1978–1982

The 1978–1982 strategic objectives for the automotive sector called for improving BOK's competitive position from a "major" to a "leading" supplier to the European automotive industry. This implied major efforts to "develop a number of products/systems, increase the level of marketing and technical support, and organize for international project coordination and product promotion."

In spite of the low-growth forecast for European car production, important substitutions might take place in coatings products and systems, and still more innovations were expected in the years ahead. The growth of the automotive industry outside Western Europe, North America, and Japan offered new opportunities for international coatings suppliers. If accompanied by further rationalization and mergers in the West European car industry, the need for a worldwide approach would become more obvious. BOK's main competitors in Europe had improved their respective positions because of the availability of new systems, and they would threaten BOK's product assortment within a few years. However, BOK had considerable technical and marketing how-how, a superior degree of internationalization within Europe, and was considered a strong and reliable supplier by its current customers. The following market share objectives were proposed for Western Europe (in percentages):

|  | 1977 | 1984 | 1989 |
|---|---|---|---|
| Primers | 8 | 10 | 10 |
| Surfacers | 12 | 15 | 23 |
| Topcoats (solid) | 15 | 15 | 21 |
| Topcoats (metallic) | 6 | 12 | 18 |
| Average, all main products | 9 | 13 | 18 |

Accordingly, BOK Finishes should:

- Increase its R&D effort by about 60 percent
- Initiate exploratory R&D activities to develop concepts for new generation products/systems
- Improve product introduction in the market and the transfer of BOK project know-how to local staff
- Evaluate the ability of local organizations to react more quickly to current requirements
- Develop a more sophisticated information, planning, and control system on a worldwide basis

Targeted profit contributions by major company are shown in Exhibit 7.

## ORGANIZATION

Under the postmerger structure, responsibility for the automotive segment was placed with the Coordinating Committee Major Industries (CCMI). Composed of the division research manager and the commercial managers of major industrial finishes of Sofravel, Brunal, and Van Houdt, the CCMI was chaired by the division president, Verhulst. The CCMI had an overall coordinating function over the "major industries" sector, and decisions were carried out in the operating companies by the respective local commercial managers or the division research manager. The country presidents were responsible for the execution of and performance against plans and budgets decided by the CCMI and could take corrective action when necessary. In actual practice, the CCMI had no direct functional influence and operated more at a staff level.

The various organizational changes that occurred in BOK in the 1971–1976 period (see BOK Finishes, Case Forty) led to the creation of steering committees for other market segments. For the automotive segment, however, a divisional "automotive development" executive (Functional Manager, Automotive Development and Raw Materials) was appointed, whose principal activity was defined as: "Establishing

---

**EXHIBIT 7**

**CONTRIBUTION TO PROFIT, ACTUAL (1977), AND TARGETS**

| | Contribution to profits (% of sales) | | | |
|---|---|---|---|---|
| | Actual 1977 | Target 1979 | Target 1982 | Target ROI (%) 1981–1988 |
| Van Houdt | 14.9 | 13.1 | 16.0 | 13.8 |
| Brunal | 22.3 | 18.2 | 22.6 | 25.1 |
| Sofravel | 7.9 | 5.5 | 12.5 | 12.5 |
| Delfina | 26.2 | 24.0 | 25.6 | 25.1 |

*Source:* Company records.

EXHIBIT 8

**DECISION-MAKING PROCESS**

| | Local | | | | Divisional | | |
|---|---|---|---|---|---|---|---|
| | Product committee, automotive | Country president | Automotive policy group | Automotive development | Research & development | President | Board of management |
| Optimalization of commercial benefit | | | | | | | |
| Development of innovative work; products/processes/applications | P/A | | P/A | P/A/R | A | D | Ap |
| Maintenance of technological base | | | | | | | |
|   Country scope | P/A | D | | A | A | | Ap |
|   Division scope | | | A | P/R | | D | |
| Organization/staffing/appraisal of automotive depts of group companies | P/A | D | | P/A | | | |
| Corrective actions for divisional projects | A | | (A) | P/R | A | D | (Ap) |
| Priorities/strategies for major international customers | | | A | P/R | | | D |
| Tactics for major international customers | A/D | (Ap) | (A) | P/R | | | |
| Visits to customers/automotive industry | | | | | | | |
|   Within group company region | D | | | P | | | |
|   Outside group company region | P | | | D | | | |
| Mutual sales support | P/A | D | R | P/A | | | (Ap) |
| Trends in auto industry | A | | D | P/R | | | |
| Trends in new and existing products | A | | D | P/R | | | |
| Commercialization of products, developed by other group companies | P/A | | D | P/A/R | (A) | | |
| Allocation of customers | P/A | Ap | D | P/A | | | (Ap) |
| Strategy for automotive development | | | | | | | |
| Divisional strategic plan for automotive development | | | A | P/R | A | D | |
| Local operational plans for automotive and related products | P/R | D | | A/C | | | Ap |
| Consistency of operational plan in relation to strategic plan | A | | | P/R | | D | Ap |

EXHIBIT 8 (cont.)

| | Local | | | | Divisional | | |
|---|---|---|---|---|---|---|---|
| | Product committee, automotive | Country president | Automotive policy group | Automotive development | Research & development | President | Board of management |
| Incorporation of divisional projects in operational plans | A | | A | P/R | | D | |
| Development of automotive markets in new countries | | | A | P/R | A | D | Ap |
| Research programs for automotive development | | | | | | | |
| Research programs with divisional scope | | | A | P/R | A | D | (Ap) |
| Procedures for the way of interchange of know-how | | | R | P | A | | D |
| Implementation of research findings in local commercial activities | R | D | | P | A (local) | | |
| Licensing | | | | | | | |
| Granting and taking licenses | | | A | P/R | A | D | Ap |
| Potential clients for licenses | | | A | P/R | A | D | Ap |
| Potential licenses to be taken | | | A | P/R | A | D | Ap |
| Price and conditions of licenses | | | | | | | |
| Division scope | A | A | A | P/R | A | D | Ap |
| Local scope | P/R | D | | A | (A) | Ap | |
| Emergency situations—production allocation | A | A | | P/R | A | | D |

Note: P = proposes, A = advises, R = recommends, D = decides, Ap = approves.
Source: Company records.

the optimal commercial benefit of BOK Finishes' total technological base in the automotive industries, both in and outside Europe, and submitting objectives derived from it to the Board of Management.''

This divisional executive, F. Janssens, was accountable to the division president, had ''functional authority over automotive managers of the group companies with respect to the execution of division-related activities,'' and would act as chair to the automotive policy group (APG) and any related ''automeetings.'' The APG was composed of ''one representative per group company, having the highest authority with respect to automotive affairs.'' Meetings were to be held four times a year, and, besides dealing with matters of current interest in the automotive sector, APG members had to ensure that ''decisions regarding the coordination of automotive activities are executed in a manner which promotes communication, avoids duplications, and optimizes the overall automotive effort of the division.'' Exhibit 8 provides more details on the decision-making process in the automotive segment.

---

**APPENDIX**

# Glossary of Coating Terms

## COATING SYSTEMS FOR CAR BODIES

**Primer**  The primer consists of the first coatings layer on the pretreated steel body, used for corrosion resistance and adhesion between steel and other coatings. Applied by a type of ''electro-deposition process'' called ''anaphoresis,'' which sometimes involved dipping the car body into a tank. Color generally unimportant.

**Surfacer**  The surfacer consists of the second layer, intended to give a smooth surface by covering imperfections of the steel and to add extra mechanical strength. Applied by electrostatic spraying. Color generally unimportant.

**Topcoat**  The topcoat consists of the outer layer, giving the desired color, gloss, and smoothness to the body. Mechanical and chemical properties are important. Applied by electrostatic spraying. The main resin systems in the late seventies were alkyd enamels, for general purposes, and acrylic enamels, which improved gloss and weather resistance.

Topcoats were supplied in two appearance configurations: solid colors, i.e., pigmented, without metallic look; and metallics. The latter could be applied by a colored metallic base coat and a transparent topcoat for improved gloss and resistance (the so-called two-coat system).

## OTHER AUTOMOTIVE COATINGS

**Fillers**  Fillers are coatings to hide metal defects and to increase corrosion resistance.

**Coatings for car components such as chassis, engine, gearbox, axles, fuel tanks, wheels**  For these coatings mechanical and weathering resistance is important and color is not. Generally applied by spraying or dipping.

**Special underbody coatings for mechanical and chemical protection**  Often based on PVC compounds, these coatings increase protection of parts that are exposed to flying stones on the road. Applied by spraying.

**Protective waxes**  These are used to avoid damage to new cars during transportation or storage. Applied by spraying.

# BOK Finishes— Car Refinishes

Throughout the early 1960s, the three main BOK Finishes' companies had been active in the European car refinishes market with their own brands: Van Houdt in the Benelux, Verluz (Sofravel's brand) in France, and Brunal in Germany. The major automotive markets at that time were characterized by strong national orientation in car-buying habits: the French normally bought French-made cars, and so did the Italians and Germans generally prefer their own automobiles. Equally, automotive manufacturers tended to buy their paint requirements from local suppliers. This state of affairs was reflected in the car refinishes sector, where the wholesale trade preferred the same suppliers that worked with the national OEMs. But the increase in car exports among European countries

This case was prepared by André Khodjamirian, research associate, and Professor José de la Torre as a basis for discussion. The generous contributions of many executives from a European chemical firm that prefers to remain anonymous are gratefully acknowledged. All names, places, and financial figures, as well as some events, have been disguised to preserve the confidentiality of the data. © INSEAD—The European Institute of Business Administration, 1986.

that accelerated throughout the 1970s forced the makers of car refinishes to follow, and various "local" brands became available in neighboring countries to meet the needs for a more diverse product inventory.

In the wake of the 1977 profit improvement exercise, BOK's management believed that there was a pressing need to review current company policies and future strategy in the car refinishes sector in order to improve performance in such key markets as Germany, France, the Netherlands, and Italy.

## GENERAL MARKET CHARACTERISTICS

The market sector known as "car refinishes" included all paints (primers, fillers, and topcoats), thinners, and related products used for the repair and finishing of vehicles, such as passenger cars and commercial vehicles, other than the automotive OEMs. Main customer groups consisted of car-spray specialists (both big and small), franchised and independent garages, and fleet owners. A separate subsegment was that of trucks and buses, small-scale production (essentially customizing and finishing) of commercial vehicles.[1] Total market size was influenced by factors such as size of the carpark (the total stock of vehicles in circulation at any point in time), habits of car owners, local weather conditions, type of paint used and original paint systems on the car, and the structure of insurance formalities and warranties. The importance of the carpark, coupled with replacement habits, were key determinants of market size.

In the 1963–1973 period the passenger carpark worldwide grew by an average of 6 percent per annum from 117 million in 1963 to 220 million in 1973. This large increase was stimulated by the continuing growth of incomes and the relatively low cost of driving. After 1973, the annual growth decreased to around 3 percent as a consequence of lower incomes, rising costs of driving (fuel in particular), and saturation levels being attained in several developed countries. It was forecast that this lower growth pattern would continue into the 1980s. Developed countries, where 80 percent of the total cars in the world were concentrated, could expect an annual growth of 1.5 percent in their carpark, while growth was forecast to be around 5 percent per annum in the less developed markets. In 1977, the total world carpark was estimated to be around 250 million cars.

The OECD countries[2] accounted for around 93 percent of total world automotive demand in the 1960s. This figure had dropped to 87 percent in 1974 and was expected to amount to no more than 76 percent by 1990. The number of cars in circulation in Europe in 1977 represented around 36 percent of the worldwide carpark, comparable in size to the U.S. market. Most international makes of cars were available in Europe, and every year car manufacturers launched new models, adapted in style and color to prevailing trends. See Exhibits 1 to 3 for details.

The total West European car refinishes market was estimated to be around 200,000 tons of paint and related products per year, and a typical car refinishing paint supplier had to service up to 12,000 different shades of color. The majority of end users in the European market were small businesses with an average of 3.5 employees per spraying workshop. They could be classified according to how well organized and well equipped their workshops were. In addition, there were a number of different "types" of workshops as follows:

- Car-spray specialist: A workshop that specialized in the spraying of cars, without carrying out any repairs on the body.
- Car-body repair shop: A workshop equipped to carry out both the repair of the car's body and its subsequent painting.
- Car dealer: Franchised distributor that maintained a car-spray workshop as part of its business.
- Garage: A freelance operation, dealing mainly in car repair and maintenance and a sideline spraying workshop.
- Refinishing workshop of commercial vehicles: Usually involved in truck/bus custom and special bodies.
- Commercial vehicle producer: Small-scale commercial vehicle manufacture.

The relative importance of these end users varied according to each market. BOK Finishes' management believed that European markets could be grouped into four major categories (see Exhibit 4) as follows:

- Underdeveloped: low car density, not very diversified car population, mostly primitive bodyshops, local manufacturers of car refinishes, sometimes international suppliers via import. Type of finishes: dominant use of thermoplastic air-drying (nitrocellulose, acrylics) products. See the Appendix for a glossary of technical terms and product types.
- Developing: growing car density, diversifying

---

[1]Commercial vehicles were not always delivered to the customer as a complete truck, bus, or van, but often as semifinished products (either a bare chassis or with a driver's cabin) to smaller independent companies which, in turn, finished the vehicle to the customer's requirements.

[2]The 24 industrial countries comprising the Organization for Economic Cooperation and Development, mainly Western Europe, North America, Japan, Australia, and New Zealand.

## MOTORIZATION (PASSENGER CARS) IN WESTERN EUROPE, 1970–2000

| | Car stock | | | | | | Number of cars per 1,000 persons | | | Percent of households with a car | | |
| | Units (thousands) | | | Average annual growth rate (%) | | | | | | | | |
| | 1970 | 1985 | 2000 | 1970–1985 | 1985–2000 | 1970–2000 | 1970 | 1985 | 2000 | 1970 | 1985 | 2000 |
|---|---|---|---|---|---|---|---|---|---|---|---|---|
| EEC | 54,062 | 88,550 | 107,904 | 3.3 | 1.3 | 2.3 | 215 | 328 | 381 | 50.3 | 64.6 | 69.6 |
| Belgium | 2,060 | 3,378 | 4,088 | 3.4 | 1.3 | 2.3 | 214 | 328 | 380 | 50.2 | 64.6 | 67.7 |
| Denmark | 1,077 | 1,722 | 2,087 | 3.2 | 1.3 | 2.2 | 218 | 325 | 381 | 47.5 | 61.0 | 66.4 |
| France | 12,035 | 19,779 | 23,960 | 3.4 | 1.3 | 2.3 | 237 | 339 | 382 | 54.8 | 65.3 | 72.2 |
| Germany | 12,963 | 19,899 | 22,895 | 2.4 | 0.9 | 1.7 | 230 | 330 | 383 | 48.7 | 60.9 | 66.6 |
| Ireland | 354 | 1,032 | 1,630 | 7.4 | 3.1 | 5.2 | 120 | 305 | 375 | 34.7 | 65.4 | 70.4 |
| Italy | 10,171 | 18,425 | 23,305 | 4.0 | 1.6 | 2.8 | 189 | 318 | 377 | 49.4 | 67.8 | 70.8 |
| Luxembourg | 91 | 122 | 144 | 2.0 | 1.1 | 1.5 | 268 | 340 | 400 | 59.2 | 65.0 | 70.0 |
| Netherlands | 2,509 | 4,723 | 6,089 | 4.3 | 1.7 | 3.0 | 192 | 321 | 377 | 48.9 | 64.5 | 69.1 |
| United Kingdom | 11,802 | 19,470 | 23,706 | 3.4 | 1.3 | 2.4 | 213 | 330 | 382 | 50.3 | 65.7 | 69.6 |
| Other industrialized countries | 2,545 | 4,691 | 5,501 | 4.2 | 1.1 | 2.6 | 186 | 323 | 366 | 44.5 | 61.0 | 66.2 |
| Austria | 1,165 | 2,424 | 2,755 | 5.0 | 0.9 | 2.9 | 157 | 314 | 346 | 39.3 | 60.9 | 65.4 |
| Switzerland | 1,380 | 2,271 | 2,746 | 3.4 | 1.3 | 2.3 | 220 | 334 | 388 | 50.7 | 61.2 | 67.0 |
| Developing countries | 3,800 | 19,543 | 29,320 | 11.5 | 2.7 | 7.0 | 54 | 227 | 302 | 17.8 | 53.2 | 63.0 |
| Greece | 226 | 2,206 | 3,417 | 16.4 | 3.0 | 9.5 | 26 | 231 | 335 | 9.2 | 53.4 | 66.8 |
| Portugal | 459 | 2,930 | 3,933 | 13.2 | 2.0 | 7.4 | 53 | 293 | 348 | 20.0 | 65.1 | 68.7 |
| Spain | 2,350 | 10,998 | 15,260 | 10.8 | 2.2 | 6.4 | 70 | 282 | 346 | 23.3 | 62.2 | 68.1 |
| Turkey in Europe | 44 | 625 | 1,590 | 19.4 | 6.4 | 12.7 | 14 | 139 | 265 | 5.6 | 43.7 | 65.3 |
| Yugoslavia | 721 | 2,784 | 5,120 | 9.4 | 4.1 | 6.8 | 45 | 120 | 200 | 13.4 | 34.8 | 49.3 |

*Source:* OECD—*Interfutures Report*, February 1978.

EXHIBIT 2

**WORLD DEMAND FOR PASSENGER CARS, 1960–1990**

| | Actual | | | Projected | | |
|---|---|---|---|---|---|---|
| | 1960 | 1970 | 1974 | 1980 | 1985 | 1990 |
| Total demand | 11,584 | 24,143 | 27,477 | 36,080 | 42,530 | 47,990 |
| (thousand units) | | | | | | |
| OECD | 10,715 | 21,951 | 24,018 | 30,570 | 34,360 | 36,510 |
| North America | 6,585 | 10,751 | 11,273 | 12,750 | 14,400 | 14,800 |
| Western Europe | 3,713 | 8,434 | 9,498 | 12,740 | 14,430 | 15,630 |
| Japan | 159 | 2,256 | 2,670 | 4,300 | 4,600 | 5,100 |
| Oceania | 258 | 510 | 577 | 780 | 930 | 980 |
| Other regions | 869 | 2,192 | 3,459 | 5,510 | 8,170 | 11,480 |
| Eastern Europe | 257 | 743 | n.a. | 2,100 | 2,900 | 3,900 |
| Latin America | 276 | 785 | n.a. | 2,060 | 3,360 | 4,900 |
| Other Asia | 117 | 315 | n.a. | 680 | 1,000 | 1,450 |
| Africa | 219 | 349 | n.a. | 670 | 910 | 1,230 |
| Total demand (%) | | | | | | |
| OECD | 92.5 | 90.9 | 87.4 | 84.7 | 80.8 | 76.1 |
| North America | 56.8 | 44.5 | 41.0 | 35.3 | 33.9 | 30.8 |
| Western Europe | 32.1 | 34.9 | 34.6 | 35.3 | 33.9 | 32.6 |
| Japan | 1.4 | 9.3 | 9.7 | 11.9 | 10.8 | 10.6 |
| Oceania | 2.2 | 2.1 | 2.1 | 2.2 | 2.2 | 2.0 |
| Other regions | 7.5 | 9.1 | 12.6 | 15.3 | 19.2 | 23.9 |
| Eastern Europe | 2.2 | 3.1 | n.a. | 5.8 | 6.8 | 8.1 |
| Latin America | 2.4 | 3.3 | n.a. | 5.7 | 7.9 | 10.2 |
| Other Asia | 1.0 | 1.3 | n.a. | 1.9 | 2.4 | 3.0 |
| Africa | 1.9 | 1.4 | n.a. | 1.9 | 2.1 | 2.6 |
| Replacement | | | | | | |
| demand (% of total) | 47.9 | 49.1 | 56.2 | 64.5 | 71.5 | 75.0 |
| OECD | 50.3 | 52.8 | 62.3 | 70.9 | 79.5 | 84.8 |
| North America | 66.4 | 66.6 | 71.9 | 80.0 | 84.0 | 87.8 |
| Western Europe | 23.7 | 43.4 | 57.1 | 66.6 | 77.3 | 82.6 |
| Japan | 28.9 | 22.9 | 40.8 | 58.1 | 73.9 | 84.3 |
| Oceania | 34.9 | 49.6 | 60.5 | 62.8 | 73.1 | 79.6 |
| Other regions | 18.8 | 12.5 | 13.2 | 28.9 | 37.5 | 43.7 |
| Eastern Europe | 22.6 | 11.6 | n.a. | 23.8 | 34.5 | 43.6 |
| Latin America | 17.0 | 5.7 | n.a. | 23.3 | 34.5 | 40.8 |
| Other Asia | — | 10.8 | n.a. | 36.8 | 40.0 | 44.8 |
| Africa | 37.4 | 30.9 | n.a. | 53.7 | 54.9 | 54.5 |

n.a. = not available.
*Source:* OECD—*Interfutures Report,* February 1978.

car population, bodyshops with spraying booth, local manufacturers of car refinishes, international suppliers often present via import or licenses and occasional subsidiaries. Type of finishes: mainly air-drying (nitrocellulose, acrylics) products.

- Developed: high car density, rather complex car population, well-equipped bodyshops, some with low-bake ovens, international suppliers present via operating companies. Type of finishes: mainly alkyds requiring cure processes.
- Advanced: high car density, complex car pop-

**EXHIBIT 3**

**MOTOR VEHICLES PER 1,000 PEOPLE, 1967 AND 1977**

| Country | 1967 | 1977 | Average annual growth rate (%) |
|---|---|---|---|
| North & Central America | 369 | 481 | 2.7 |
| Oceania* | 295 | 397 | 3.0 |
| Europe | 104 | 181 | 5.2 |
| South America | 37 | 73 | 7.0 |
| Asia | 9 | 19† | 7.8 |
| Africa | 12 | 18 | 4.1 |

*Includes Australia, New Zealand, and surrounding area.
†The figure for Japan for 1977 was 297.
*Source:* Automobile Manufacturing Association, *Automobile Facts and Figures, 1970 and 1977.*

ulation, well-equipped bodyshops with low-bake facilities, international suppliers dominate, growing do-it-yourself activity. Type of finishes: mainly two-packs.

## BOK FINISHES' CAR REFINISHES ACTIVITIES

In 1965, Van Houdt executives in Antwerp decided that the car refinishes sector needed to be treated as a separate business. Prior to that time, car refinishes had been considered as part of two sectors: the automotive, for technical development aspects, and the decorative/do-it-yourself in terms of marketing. Following this decision, a small department was formed, called "coordination, car refinishes." This department consisted of three persons, M. J. Brugge as head of marketing services, H. Franken, a "color expert" whose job was to gather all existing colors in the automotive and car refinishes sectors, and one staff member.

Distribution was restructured in various major markets, such as Belgium, Holland, and France, to accommodate the new objectives. The first long-term plan for car refinishes was made for the Belgian market in 1967. In 1969, it was decided to concentrate on the German market, as BOK's main competitors, Herberts (Hoechst), Glasurit (BASF), and Sikkens (Akzo) were getting increasingly visible in car refinishes

in Germany and in other European countries. Van Houdt started putting together a distribution network by setting up its own depots, since getting existing distributors interested in non-German products was no easy task.

BOK management felt that a few elements were instrumental in the success of the company's international strategy in this product area. The first was the introduction in 1968 of a Van Houdt brand called Poly-Gloss, a two-pack acrylic enamel which constituted a first-of-a-kind product to be marketed systematically in Germany. The two-pack concept was a spin-off of BOK's R&D activities in automotive OEM products. It allowed paint shops greater flexibility in paint application, shorter drying time, and better gloss characteristics than the traditional one-pack method.

The two-pack system allowed BOK to offer satisfactory results in matching or "imitating" the high-gloss metallic paintwork provided by the OEM car manufacturers and to distinguish itself from other suppliers of car refinishes. According to a BOK executive:

It took our competitors three years to introduce a similar process, and by that time we had made great advances in our product development. Later, we found out that the two-pack concept was also adaptable to single-coat as well as thermo-hardening metallics. This really made the paint-shop operators happy as they had finally found a multi-

**EXHIBIT 4**

**STAGE OF MARKET DEVELOPMENT, 1977**

= Developing    = Developed    = Advanced

*Source:* Company records.

purpose product that made their job so much easier. . . . We understood that in order to be successful in car refinishes, a company needed to be innovative in products and systems.

The second element in helping develop the market as well as BOK's own position was, as an executive called it, "the mixing-machine phenomenon." Until the late 1960s, only factory-made, ready-mixed colors were available on the market. With the growing number of cars and colors on the road, paint distributors and shops were faced with the need of stocking large numbers of colors, some obsolete, which resulted in frequent logistical problems and high costs. Major American paint companies such as Dupont and Inmont first introduced the mixing-machine concept in France and other European countries. BOK, realizing the obvious advantages of this technique, developed its own mixing machines in the early 1970s, which met with immediate success. Distributors were pleased to be able to "mix and sell" paint to the paint shops with quicker turnaround times and at lower investments in inventory. Later, the larger car-spraying specialists and paint shops, by installing mixing-machines on their own premises, could offer even faster and more flexible service to their customers who often needed quick and "invisible" repairs on their cars' bodywork.

A by-product of the mixing-machine concept was the introduction by Brunal in Germany of the Lack-Punkt program in 1974. In consisted essentially of reaching small-scale car refinishers through selected auto parts and accessory shops and retailers. This form of distribution was aimed at those customers, mostly non-professionals and do-it-yourselfers, who were less likely to shop in specialized and professional paint shops, and thus would allow BOK to increase market coverage with little or no additional sales and technical support. It was described as: ". . . a passive distribution point, focused on the small professional workshops, the bunglers and do-it-yourselfers, where we could offer a limited professional product range and an 'easy to apply' package. It was a 'shop-in-a-shop' point of sale promotion, aimed at the 'convenience' market segment."

The Key Account Program was another innovative decision by Van Houdt in 1974. Following the oil shock, small and medium-size businesses were confronted with the consequences of a deteriorating economic climate, such as reduced market growth, flat sales volume, higher financial costs, and lower incomes for the car-refinishing shops. These developments encouraged BOK to target the more professional and potentially profitable car-refinishing shops. The program consisted of a cooperative agreement between BOK and a selected number of paint shops in Belgium, Holland, and Germany. The objective was to assist the "key account" in developing its business and, as a BOK executive expressed it, "to ensure the short- and long-term profitability and development of a number of key bodyshops and, consequently, of the best customers for BOK's car refinishes."

BOK would provide them, against a fixed yearly fee of BF40,000–50,000, managerial and technical training, consulting, and promotional and information programs designed to help the owners of the paint shops to develop from simple craftspeople to more professional managers. BOK management felt that these services were generally well received in the marketplace.

## THE SITUATION IN THE LATE 1970s

BOK's total car refinishes volume in Europe was 17,200 tons in 1977, which represented a total market share of about 9 percent. This volume had grown by an average of 3.3 percent per year in the 1973–1977 period, and sales had grown by 16.2 percent in the same period. Approximately 45 percent of this volume was distributed through wholesalers, 30 percent through importers, and 25 percent directly or through BOK Finishes' own depots which were concentrated in the Benelux, Germany, and Austria. Throughout this period the car refinishes activity represented 10 to 12 percent of total BOK

Finishes' sales and averaged about 13.5 percent of the division's total contribution to profits.

While the European car refinishes market had similar product needs, application methods, and repair processes, the structure of competition varied significantly across borders. The northern countries such as Germany, the Benelux, Scandinavia, Switzerland, and Austria were considered "advanced" according to the classification above. Generally, these markets were characterized by larger, more specialized units, a greater use of two-pack and similar higher-technology products, and greater relative importance of direct distribution methods. However, the market structures in France, Italy, Spain, and the United Kingdom were relatively more fragmented and artisanal, would employ less sophisticated products and methods (e.g., air drying), and would rely on many wholesalers and distributors for market coverage.

Exhibit 5 summarizes the main characteristics associated with the major markets for car refinishes in Europe. The data, which although imperfect and inexact can be considered the best available, point to the large variations that existed in market structure and competitive conditions among countries. For example, the proportion of do-it-yourself car repair was high in certain "advanced" countries (e.g., the Netherlands) as well as "developing" countries such as the United Kingdom. Equally, a high proportion of wholesale trade could be associated with highly fragmented wholesalers as in the United Kingdom (over 700) and Italy (2,800), or with highly concentrated distribution networks as in Switzerland. Furthermore, the definition of what constituted a "specialized" workshop varied from country to country and encompassed enormous variations in the average size of these establishments.

Competitive structures varied as well. In northern European countries, over 60 percent of the market was shared by BASF, Hoechst, Akzo, and BOK Finishes, whereas in southern Europe, local suppliers, although threatened by the large companies, still maintained a respectable share of the market. Exhibit 6 provides available information on relative market shares.

In their strategic analysis of the car refinishes business, BOK's management identified several factors that were in their estimation liable to influence the company's future position in that market and which needed further examination:

- The growth of the potential market would be limited by a slowdown in carpark expansion, speed limits caused by energy conservation, higher fuel prices, the use of smaller cars, and a tendency to delay repair of small damages by car owners.
- Insurance companies were expected to increase their control over car repair activities by standardizing systems and prices.
- Car manufacturers would influence the repair market by gradually switching to water-thinnable topcoats and, at a later stage, to powder coatings, which would introduce constraints in the development of adequate repair systems. It was also expected that they would increase their activity in car repairs directly by attracting clients to their dealer-operated paint shops, particularly in the "developed and advanced" markets.
- The competitive advantage of BOK Finishes would be eroded by the introduction of two-pack systems similar to BOK's Poly-Gloss by Hoechst, BASF, and Akzo, as well as the provision of mixing machines to wholesalers and paint shops by most of the competition.
- Rising labor costs would cause a growth in do-it-yourself activities, and increased environmental awareness would encourage governments to impose rules for the production of less polluting refinishing products.

## DISTRIBUTION AND BRAND POLICY

It was clear to management that the role of the distributor was very important in the car refinishes business. Given the nature of the market and customer needs, the distributor was a key element in offering a service consisting mainly

EXHIBIT 5

## MARKET CHARACTERISTICS, 1977

| Countries by stage of development | Market size | | | No. of workshops, size & type | | | Type of paint used (%) | | | | Distribution (%) | |
|---|---|---|---|---|---|---|---|---|---|---|---|---|
| | Tons | % DIY | Total | Largest (% no./% tons) | Smallest (% no./% tons) | Specialist (%) | Two-pack | Base/clear | Synth. | Air dry | Direct/depot | Wholesalers |
| Advanced | | | | | | | | | | | | |
| Netherlands | 6,000 | 21 | 1,400 | 18/23 | 41/7 | 60 | 40 | 25 | 25 | 5 | 52 | 45 |
| Germany | 36,000 | 8 | 8,500 | 8/40 | 26/4 | 50 | 55 | 26 | 19 | — | 55 | 33 |
| Austria | 3,600 | 9 | 1,590 | 13/23 | 53/15 | 50 | 42 | 16 | 31 | 11 | 10 | 90 |
| Switzerland | 3,100 | 3 | 750 | 33/35 | −/12 | 80 | 50 | 21 | 16 | 8 | 5 | 95 |
| Sweden | 4,200 | n.a. | 2,000 | n.a. | n.a. | 70 | n.a. | n.a. | n.a. | n.a. | n.a. | 70 |
| Denmark | 2,500 | n.a. | 1,000 | 35/n.a. | n.a. | 80 | 55 | 16 | 29 | — | 50 | 50 |
| Developed | | | | | | | | | | | | |
| France | 28,000 | 10 | 28,800 | 2/10 | 86/65 | 25 | 15 | 6 | 63 | 15 | 5 | 95 |
| Belgium | 7,800 | 6 | 5,000 | 2/5 | 82/27 | 60 | 28 | 19 | 25 | 20 | 40 | 60 |
| Developing | | | | | | | | | | | | |
| UK | 40,000 | 9 | 20,000 | 5/13 | 33/24 | 30 | 10 | 2 | 23 | 64 | 5 | 85 |
| Italy | 40,000 | — | 19,300 | 6/19 | 80/50 | 90 | 10 | 6 | 16 | 62 | 5 | 95 |
| Spain | 10,000 | — | 7,500 | 5/8 | 28/7 | 95 | 2 | 5 | 72 | 21 | 30 | 70 |
| Other | | | | | | | | | | | | |
| Norway | 2,000 | — | 620 | 11/n.a. | 56/n.a. | 50 | 47 | 24 | 19 | 9 | 30 | 70 |
| Finland | 1,900 | — | 950 | 16/43 | 63/29 | 60 | 70 | 15 | 15 | — | 30 | 70 |

n.a. = not available.

EXHIBIT 6

**MAJOR COMPETITORS AND MARKET SHARES IN CAR REFINISHES, 1977 AND 1982 (PROJECTIONS)**

| | Hoechst | BASF | Akzo | BOK | ICI | Inmont | PPG | Dupont | Local suppliers |
|---|---|---|---|---|---|---|---|---|---|
| **Current shares, % (1977)** | | | | | | | | | |
| Belgium | 3 | 12 | 18 | 32 | — | 4 | — | 25 | 6 |
| Netherlands | 23 | 4 | 38 | 12 | — | — | — | 5 | 18 |
| France | 12 | 8 | 6 | 10 | — | 16 | 15 | — | 33 |
| Germany | 28 | 25 | 11 | 14 | 3 | 3 | — | 2 | 14 |
| Italy | 7 | 7 | 12 | 7 | — | — | 4 | 3 | 60 |
| United Kingdom | 12 | 5 | 2 | 2 | 28 | — | 3 | — | 48 |
| Austria/Switzerland | 27 | 21 | 12 | 18 | — | — | — | 6 | 13 |
| Spain | 5 | 32 | — | 9 | — | 5 | — | 4 | 50 |
| Scandinavia | 30 | 15 | 15 | 5 | — | — | — | 10 | 20 |
| W. Europe | 15 | 13 | 10 | 9 | 7 | 5 | 4 | 4 | 33 |
| **Projected shares, % (1982)** | | | | | | | | | |
| Belgium | 5 | 15 | 20 | 35 | — | 5 | — | 20 | — |
| Netherlands | 20 | 10 | 40 | 20 | — | — | — | 5 | 5 |
| France | 15 | 10 | 15 | 15 | <5 | 15 | 15 | <5 | 10 |
| Germany | 30 | 30 | 15 | 20 | — | <5 | — | — | — |
| Italy | 10 | 10 | 15 | 15 | — | <5 | 5 | <5 | 40 |
| United Kingdom | 15 | 10 | 5 | 5 | 25 | 5 | — | — | 35 |
| Austria/Switzerland | 30 | 25 | 10 | 20 | — | — | <5 | <5 | 10 |
| Spain | 10 | 35 | 10 | 15 | — | — | — | 5 | 25 |
| Scandinavia | 35 | 20 | 20 | 5 | — | 5 | — | 10 | 5 |
| W. Europe | 18 | 17 | 14 | 13 | 6 | 5 | 4 | 4 | 19 |

*Source:* Company records.

of: (1) quick delivery of refinishing products in large or small quantities; (2) personal selling approach and customer assistance; and (3) a broad assortment of products, especially paint colors. Besides sales through distributors, the company needed to maintain direct relationships with major clients, which entailed having a qualified and specialized sales force. Furthermore, distributors needed to be supported in their sales efforts by increased attention to the requirements of their territory, their client structure, pricing policies, etc. Exhibit 7 shows the market segmentation and distribution pattern as seen by BOK management.

Establishing long-term relationships with distributors was considered critical to safeguarding a market position in all paint-related segments. EEC rules allowed for exclusive distribution agreements but did not provide for absolute territorial protection. A company could expect its exclusive distributors to abide by certain buying arrangements, engage in promotional programs, refrain from manufacturing or distributing competitive products, or actively promoting sales outside their assigned territory. However, a company was limited in controlling parallel import activities or resale prices.

In 1974, BOK Finishes still marketed the three original brands (Brunal, Verluz, and Van Houdt) of car refinishes in Europe. (See Exhibit 8 for details on performance by company and major markets.) At the outset, each brand covered a relatively defined geographic area, but developments in the auto industry affected the regional segmentation of the brands such that while maintaining their regional character, the three brands tended to cross borders in Europe and began to acquire an end-user segmentation. Van Houdt was primarily aimed at the key accounts and big end-user clientele, Brunal served the smaller professional and nonprofessional segments, and Verluz did not seem to have a particular segment identification.

Shortly after the merger, Sofravel underwent several top management upheavals until the arrival of F. de Castelnau in 1972. His management style contrasted with that of BOK, and this became the source of periodic problems,

---

**MARKET SEGMENTATION AND DISTRIBUTION PATTERN**

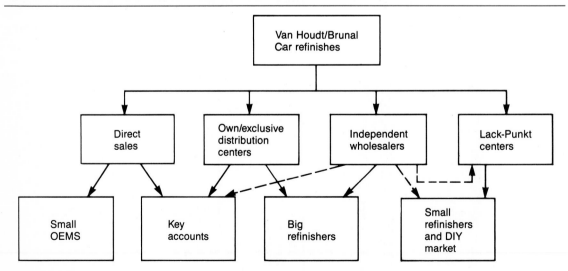

*Source:* Company records.

## EXHIBIT 8

**CAR REFINISHES SALES AND CONTRIBUTION TO PROFITS (CTP), 1973–1977***

| | 1973 | | 1974 | | 1975 | | 1976 | | 1977 | |
|---|---|---|---|---|---|---|---|---|---|---|
| | Sales | CTP | Sales | CTP | Sales | CTP | Sales | CTP | Sales | CTP |
| Van Houdt (Benelux) | 253 | 22.1 | 300 | 24.3 | 297 | 14.8 | 336 | 19.0 | 381 | 14.4 |
| Sofravel† | 132 | 7.6 | 147 | 10.6 | 169 | 4.8 | 175 | 7.2 | 170 | 4.8 |
| BOK-Siver | 8 | 14.0 | 10 | 19.9 | 10 | 11.9 | 29 | 9.9 | 52 | 5.7 |
| Van Houdt (Germany) | 134 | 10.0 | 171 | 10.0 | 218 | 8.6 | 277 | 9.9 | 322 | 16.9 |
| Brunal | 142 | 14.4 | 157 | 13.9 | 184 | 19.0 | 217 | 16.0 | 268 | 20.5 |
| Total | 669 | 15.2 | 785 | 16.5 | 878 | 10.9 | 1,034 | 13.7 | 1,204 | 14.7 |

*Sales figures are in BF million and CTP figures are percentage of sales.
†From 1976 onward, includes only sales of the Van Houdt brand.
*Source:* Company records.

especially at the marketing level. De Castelnau believed in "total autonomy" for his company and resisted any dominating or "big-parent" approach from BOK. In 1972, a group of Sofravel car refinish salespeople and their manager resigned in protest against the company's brand policy, or "lack of it" as described by a Sofravel executive. At the time, the company had a 12 percent market share in the French car refinishes segment. Having lost many of their best sales representatives, Sofravel scrambled to hire and train new people. In retrospect, a Sofravel executive said: "This may have been why the early integration efforts in car refinishes was relatively smooth. All the old timers were gone, and the new sales staff had none of the old 'company pride'; they were willing to cooperate with the people from Van Houdt to an extent that was not true in other business segments."

Things were not to remain smooth for long, however. Competition soon became fierce between the Van Houdt and Verluz sales representatives as they tried to push their brands on the market. The battle meant that resources were squandered in duplicate efforts, and market share was gradually lost. Finally, in 1975, the Verluz brand was dropped, and Van Houdt remained as the only BOK car refinishes product in France with only 10 percent of the market.

In Germany, however, the brand differentiation between Brunal and Van Houdt seemed to work better. Separate sales forces resulted in some unavoidable conflicts, but the natural segmentation which developed allowed both brands to grow rapidly to the point where by 1977 they jointly controlled over 20 percent of the market. Most of the promotional emphasis, nonetheless, was given to the Van Houdt key account programs, which, although it achieved significant results in market share, generated some resentment among Brunal management. One manager commented: "The company (BOK Finishes) is oversold on this portfolio idea of allocating resources to different businesses. It often means giving a large share of the available funds to a 'sick child' when you have three other healthy ones at home. The end result is that the healthy children soon become sick too."

## R&D AND MANUFACTURING POLICY

The car refinishes sector had been traditionally a technical off-shoot of the automotive OEM business. After Van Houdt decided to treat it as a separate business, management realized that car refinish R&D activities could no longer be fully dependent on the automotive sector. Furthermore, developments in the market, (e.g., the popularity of mixing machines), increased the need for a "universal" product approach. Although automotive OEM paint products were of very high technical quality and were made specially to customer specifications, car refinish products needed to strike a balance between good quality (i.e., observance of current technical specifications) and ease of application, that is, they had to be "user friendly" as one BOK executive liked to point out.

Experience had shown that in Brunal, where car refinishes R&D activities had been kept as a subdepartment to the automotive R&D labs, the results were not always positive. As one former Brunal executive recalled: "I remember a period when one of our automotive customers had struck a particularly difficult problem with his paint application methods. As we were their main supplier, we naturally mobilized our lab personnel to help. This problem lasted almost a year, and, in the meantime, activities in car refinishes research came to a complete standstill. It was only when we found out that our products were declining in competitiveness that we understood that we could not sacrifice car refinishes research for automotive."

Car refinishes products were manufactured with little or no distinction to brands, and the main objective was to benefit from economies of scale. Accordingly, Brunal and Van Houdt brands could be manufactured in either location for sale in any country. Sofravel's car refinishes had not been fully integrated with Van Houdt or Brunal products until the brand was dropped in 1975. Production was scheduled separately for both sites at Mannheim and Antwerp and would be balanced according to market and other criteria. Antwerp, however, was considered the "center of excellence" for car refinish products, and major R&D and manufacturing activities took place at that location.

## STRATEGIC OBJECTIVES FOR 1978–1982

The 1978–1982 strategic objectives for car refinishes outlined an overall need to become ". . . the innovative leader in products and systems, meeting environmental trends and requirements." The plan specifically stressed, "to remain in and/or improve the positions of car refinish products in Germany, Austria, Italy, Switzerland, Greece, Yugoslavia and the Benelux; restore profitability in France and improve market position in Scandinavia; develop the operations in the U.K.; and develop a plan for Eastern Europe."

It also called for an improvement of the company's position in markets outside Europe, particularly the existing operations in South America, Africa, and the Philippines. Activities in the U.S., Japanese, and Middle Eastern markets were to be developed as well through integrated export/licensing plans.

R&D efforts were to be channeled further into the development of higher solids, necessary to meet the ever-increasing pollution awareness issue. Color and design know-how was to be improved, and a next generation of mixing machines was to be developed. Finally, the key account program in Germany and the Benelux was to be developed further and introduced to other countries.

In view of the forecast growth for the 1978–1982 period (3 percent per annum in volume terms, with more developed markets growing at only 2 percent), target profit contributions and return on investment are given in Exhibit 9.

## ORGANIZATION

The various organizational changes that occurred in BOK in the 1971–1977 period led to the creation of steering committees for different market segments. The basic function of the car refinishes steering committee was to "advise on marketing input with regard to the strategic plan," including project evaluation and long-term product development, and to "ensure optimal exploitation of market economies of scale." The latter responsibility covered such initiatives as identifying, proposing, and controlling projects common to all operating companies; submitting proposals for the concentration of specific activities in one company; encouraging exchanges of know-how and experience; and proposals for

---

**EXHIBIT 9**

**CONTRIBUTION TO PROFIT, ACTUAL (1977), AND TARGETS**

| | Contribution to profits (% of sales) | | | Target ROI (%) 1981–1988 |
|---|---|---|---|---|
| | Actual 1977 | Target 1979 | Target 1982 | |
| Van Houdt (Benelux) | 14.4 | 15.0 | 15.0 | 15.0 |
| Brunal | 20.5 | 20.0 | 20.0 | 14.0 |
| Van Houdt (Germany) | 16.9 | 16.0 | 16.0 | 14.0 |
| Sofravel | 4.8 | 12.0 | 15.0 | 8.0 |
| BOK-Siver | 5.7 | 12.0 | 15.0 | 15.0 |

*Source:* Company records.

---

**EXHIBIT 10**

---

**DECISION-MAKING PREROGATIVES—
CAR REFINISHES STEERING COMMITTEE**

| Activity | Responsibility |
| --- | --- |
| Strategy—Divisional strategic marketing plan | Advise |
| Market development | |
|   Procedures for market information exchange | Advise |
|   Common projects | |
|     Identification | Propose/Decide |
|     Corrective actions | Recommend/Decide |
|     Output | Recommend/Decide |
|   Common activities | |
|     Identification | Propose/Decide |
|     Nomination of liaison | Propose/Decide |
|     Corrective actions | Recommend/Decide |
|     Budget, incl. cost sharing | Advise |
|   Priorities setting short-term product development | Propose/Decide |
|   Coordination procedures | Advise |
| Divisional projects | |
|   Terms of reference | Advise |
|   Local commercial activities as result of research findings | Advise |
| Licensing | |
|   Granting and taking licenses | Advise |
|   Price and conditions | Advise |
| Resource utilization—Short-term product allocation | Advise |

*Source:* Company records.

---

taking or granting of licenses, brand policy, short-term production allocation among units, etc. These activities were to be carried out within the framework of the strategic plan for car refinishes and the organizational reality of BOK Finishes, and meetings were to be held at least three times a year.

The members of the car refinishes steering committee consisted of the senior car refinishes product group executive for each group company or his or her equivalent (nominated by the corresponding country president), the manager of the car refinishes specialist research center at Antwerp, and the divisonal marketing coordinator for car refinishes. A chair would be appointed by the board of management (BOM) from among these members or by bringing someone else from outside the group. The steering committee would be accountable to the di-

visional board of management, and minutes of meetings were to be sent to the BOM and a selected number of divisional managers. Exhibit 10 shows the decision-making prerogatives of the car refinishes steering committee in greater detail.

---

**APPENDIX**

# Glossary of Coating Terms

## COATING SYSTEMS FOR CAR BODIES

**Primer** The primer consists of the first coatings layer on the steel body, used for corrosion resistance and adhesion between steel and other coatings. Color generally unimportant.

**Surfacer** The surfacer consists of the second layer, intended to give a smooth surface by covering imperfections of the steel and to add extra mechanical strength. Applied sometimes in combination with a putty. Color generally unimportant.

**Topcoat** The topcoat consists of the outer layer, giving the desired color, gloss, and smoothness to the body. Mechanical and chemical properties are important. The main resin systems in the late seventies were:

- *Nitrocellulose:* An air-drying process of old vintage and low technical level

- *Acrylic:* An air-drying improved process
- *Alkyd enamels:* Cured in an oven at moderate temperatures so as not to damage the car's interior
- *Two-pack systems:* A hardener added to the paint prior to application, also cured at moderate temperatures

Topcoats were supplied in two appearance configurations:

- *Solid colors:* Pigmented, without metallic look
- *Metallics:* Which could be applied by a colored metallic base coat and a transparent topcoat for improved gloss and resistance (the so-called two-coat system)

# BOK Finishes— Decorative/Do-It-Yourself Markets

Before BOK Finishes moved in, we had a family atmosphere around here. We certainly didn't have the problems we had later. . . . Working relationships were positive; morale was positive. Afterwards, it was all different.

So claimed Mr. Didier, a Sofravel executive who survived the transition:

It was true that there was no long-term planning, no budgeting . . . but the company was profitable. After BOK moved in, we had "professional management"; we had budgets; we had plans. But we also had so many meetings that we never accomplished anything. . . .

They promised that Mr. de Vitry [Sofravel's president at the time of the merger] would be able to continue managing the way he always had— that BOK's role was only to provide help when it was needed. We were supposed to remain an in-

dependent company, which is the way it should be since we, as Frenchmen, understand the French market better than they ever could. What do the Belgians know about the French market?

J. Mollerius, a Belgian executive and an internal consultant to BOK, sat quietly as he pondered these comments about Sofravel before the BOK acquisition. When he finally responded, his exasperation showed:

The only reason that Sofravel was profitable in 1974 and 1975 was thanks to the oil crisis. If it hadn't been for that, Sofravel would not have been able to raise their prices, which the customers tolerated because the cost of raw materials had increased. Otherwise, they would have had terrible years. If BOK hadn't come in when they did, Sofravel would be in worse shape today. . . .

It is true that there were some problems with the integration of the two companies that we did not foresee, but a lot of it boils down to the differences in cultures between the French and the Flemish. We didn't have the same problems with the Germans . . . they were more than willing to accept our help in developing a product that would do well against their strong competitors. The French just couldn't deal with a "little, unimportant country" like Belgium controlling a French company in France with her glorious history! That, by the

This case was prepared by Visiting Professor Deborah Smith Cook and Professor José de la Torre as a basis of discussion. The generous contributions of many executives from a European chemical firm that wishes to remain anonymous are gratefully acknowledged. All names, places, and financial figures, as well as some events, have been disguised to preserve the confidentiality of the data. © INSEAD—The European Institute of Business Administration, 1986.

way, is a rough quote of what one of them said at our first meeting. How do we overcome attitudes like that?

Both men were convinced that the fault of the poorly managed integration lay with the other side. The conflict was particularly acute in the decorative/do-it-yourself (deco/DIY) group of products and in car refinishes, since these two segments had the most overlap in Sofravel, Van Houdt, and Brunal. By the end of 1977, however, management in all operating companies were trying to find ways to resolve these conflicts and improve performance in the deco/DIY segment.

## PRODUCT CHOICE

Decorative/DIY (also known as architectural paints) was the largest sector of the paint industry. It consisted of paints and related products that were used for protection and decoration of real estate property and which were applied either by professional painting contractors or by private people. These paints were composed mainly of conventional solvent-based gloss paints (with oil and/or resin as the vehicle, or binder) and water-based emulsions. Architectural paints varied considerably from country to country. Some factors that influenced the choice of a particular type of paint were the following:

- Climatic conditions: Paints that were produced to give a good external performance in the Mediterranean areas may fail in the colder, more humid areas of Northern Europe. Countries with a wide variation of climate over a small area, such as Switzerland or France, had to have a wider range of products available, as well as different vehicles.
- Conservatism: The inherent conservatism of the construction industry (to which architectural paints were related) in most countries, but particularly in the Netherlands and the United Kingdom, made changes in binders more difficult to introduce.
- Availability of materials: The availability or,

conversely, the lack of availability of certain raw materials might make certain types of paints sell better in some areas. For example, the wide availability of styrene/acrylic emulsion in Germany had had an influence on the local paint market resulting in a cheaper paint with a lower level of performance.
- Type of substrate (building materials): In Scandinavia, wooden houses were more common than anywhere else. In southern Germany, a plaster of lime, cement, and sand was frequently used, but in northern Germany and the Benelux most homes were built of unplastered, unpainted bricks. All these materials required different paints.
- Availability, skill, and cost of craftsmen also influenced the rate of acceptance of new paints.
- Fashion: Color preferences varied widely by region from southern France to Germany to Scandinavia, as did preference for flat paints versus enamels.

The deco/DIY segment was also characterized by a low rate of technical innovation. Some of the major product introductions since the early 1930s included:

- Replacement of natural resins by synthetic resins/alkyds (1935)
- Breakthrough of waterborne dispersions for wall paints (1950)
- Market acceptance of translucent systems (1960)
- Growth of waterborne dispersions and trend toward higher solids (1975)

## VOLUME AND END-USERS

Deco/DIY comprised about 55 to 60 percent of total paint consumption. The DIY volume alone accounted for between 5 percent to 40 percent of total paint consumption, depending on many factors, including the stage of development of the country, local habits, and the cost of labor. Exhibits 1 and 2 show the pattern of consumption of deco/DIY paints for the major European markets. In 1973, DIY constituted about 40 percent of the market in Scandinavia and the United

---

**EXHIBIT 1**

---

**MAJOR MARKETS, 1973 AND 1977: GERMANY, FRANCE, UNITED KINGDOM, ITALY, BENELUX, AUSTRIA, SWITZERLAND** (Thousand Tons)

| | 1973 | 1977 |
|---|---|---|
| Decorative | | |
|   Wallpaints | 1350 | 1000 |
|   Transparent wood finishes | 20 | 30 |
|   Opaque wood finishes | 250 | 230 |
|   Other products (putties, steel, concrete) | 180 | 180 |
|     Total decorative | 1800 | 1440 |
| DIY | | |
|   Wallpaints | 300 | 330 |
|   Transparent wood finishes | 15 | 25 |
|   Opaque wood finishes | 105 | 115 |
|   Other products (See decorative) | 10 | 10 |
|     Total DIY | 430 | 480 |

*Source:* Company records.

---

Kingdom; 25 percent in Germany, France, and Benelux; 10 percent in Austria and Switzerland; and 5 percent in Italy.

Total paint consumption in the deco/DIY sector peaked around 1973. Prior to 1973, consumption had increased about 5 to 10 percent per year, primarily due to a sustained postwar boom in new construction; afterward, it began to decrease gradually. Based on projections of continued expansion in building construction, a number of paint companies built up capacity. This was the case in particular for emulsion wall paints, which accounted for about 75 percent of total consumption. Solvent-based wood and steel coatings were not influenced as much by these market changes.

Painting contractors dominated demand for the deco segment. They could be subdivided into three categories: small (fewer than 5 employees), medium (between 5 and 20 employees), and large (more than 20 employees). The breakdown of the market group was as follows:

| | 1973 | 1977 |
|---|---|---|
| Small contractors | 40% | 40% |
| Medium contractors | 25 | 30 |
| Large contractors | 35 | 30 |

Identifying potential end users in the DIY area was a little more difficult since there were approximately 350 million inhabitants in the relevant geographic area, and approximately 70 to 80 million households. The architectural coatings market was also characterized by complex decision-making patterns. In the decorative segment there were at least four separate decision makers. The building contractor may or may not specify the paint to be used if the architect had not already done so. The painting contractor may be able to select the paint, or the property owner may reserve the right to specify the product. The DIY market was also dispersed. The homeowner or the tenant could specify the paint, and either the husband or wife (or both) could be involved in the decision. Identifying the decision maker was critical if the advertising and distribution strategies were to be effective.

General market trends were toward more diversified constructions, smaller-scale projects, fewer towerblocks, and more adaptation to the needs of the final purchaser. The construction industry overall was expected to stabilize or experience very low rates of growth. Furthermore, materials that did not need to be painted would be increasingly used in new construction, particularly in offices, government buildings (e.g.,

EXHIBIT 2

**EUROPEAN CONSUMPTION OF ARCHITECTURAL PAINTS, 1977**

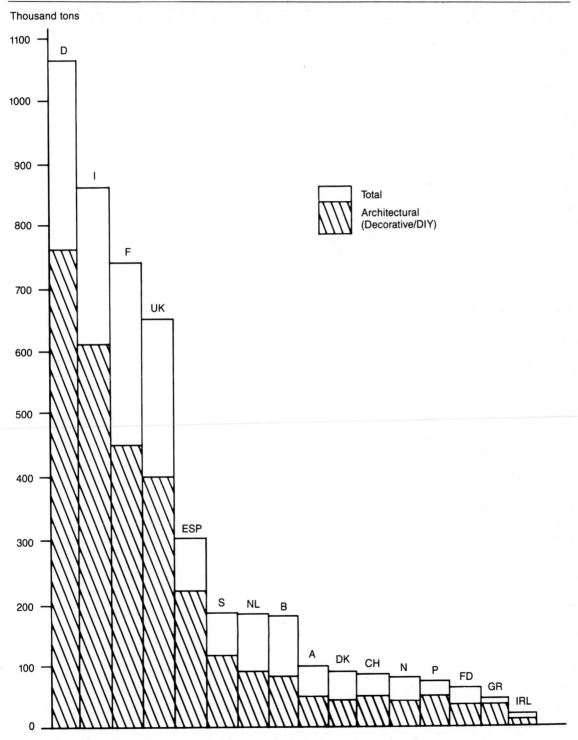

Thousand tons

Legend:
- Total
- Architectural (Decorative/DIY)

Source: *A Profile of the European Paint Industry,* Information Research Ltd, 1977.

schools and hospitals), and multistory buildings. Renovations, rehabilitations, and remodeling were also expected to continue to increase in importance.

Individuals increasingly felt the need for greater use of color and decoration in their personal surroundings to offset the "greyness" of the external environment. Consumers, faced with lower growth in disposable income, would also demand greater price-to-quality value. As professional painting became more and more expensive, there would be a further shift to the DIY segment. Finally, there seemed to be less need for differences between professional and nonprofessional applications from a product quality and formulation point of view.

## SELLING AND DISTRIBUTION

As illustrated in Exhibit 3, there were three main methods of distribution in the European decorative market, the relative importance of which varied from country to country: directly to the painting contractor, through independent

wholesalers, and through a manufacturer's own outlets. For the DIY segment, there existed a considerable number of different types of retail outlets of varying importance, such as specialty retailers (sometimes also acting as contractors) and new retail forms (e.g., superstores and hypermarkets). Selling directly to contractors constituted the normal method of selling throughout Europe, favored by the majority of small paint companies. These contractors were generally independent enterprises and operated on a local or regional basis. Larger paint manufacturers tended to favor distribution through wholesalers and/or the use of their own depots. There were four types of wholesalers:

- Specialized paint wholesalers with paint accounting for 50 percent of turnover
- Specialized wallpaper wholesalers with paint accounting for 10 to 20 percent of turnover
- Wholesalers offering a wide range of *droguerie* (variety store) items
- Wholesalers specializing in a wide range of building materials

---

**EXHIBIT 3**

**TYPICAL DISTRIBUTION CHANNELS**

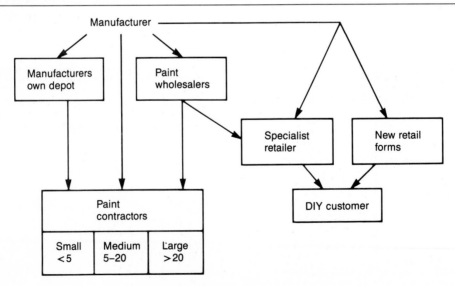

The volume of sales through these outlets varied considerably by country. In Belgium and the United Kingdom, sales through wholesalers accounted for 60 percent of the total; in France it was 45 percent; and in the Netherlands it was 40 percent. By contrast, only 10 percent of the sales volume in West Germany was attributed to wholesalers, primarily due to the large number of manufacturer depots. Of equal importance was the variation in direct sales to contractors, which accounted for about 40 percent of sales in France, 25 percent in Belgium and the United Kingdom, and 30 percent in the Netherlands.

Direct sales were generally made to large accounts, and indirect buyers tended to be medium or small firms and even individual tradespeople. This breakdown was seen to be quite stable over time. Large enterprises required good technical assistance and low prices, squeezing the middleman's margins. Direct selling to the thousands of small painting contractors tended to be unprofitable because of the time involved and the number of depots required to service the contractors properly. Serving the contractors through wholesalers had an additional advantage in that the wholesalers were able to supply a certain measure of credit to their local customers. Yet, France was the only country where the wholesale sector for deco increased in importance, mainly because of backward integration, where some wholesalers started their own paint production.

Both direct and indirect selling channels were utilized in the DIY sector as well. Some companies, particularly in the United Kingdom, had their own retail outlets in addition to using the traditional wholesalers. However, there was little indication that this trend would increase in popularity, since the great majority of paint companies had no experience in retailing. Direct sales were usually made to the large surface discount and department stores as well as to major specialist retailers such as paint and wallpaper centers. These large scale outlets had various forms in different countries: hypermarkets in France, department stores in the United Kingdom, and *Bau und Heimwerkermaerkte* in Germany. Wholesalers looked after the more traditional outlets in less populated areas as well as the smaller retailers (see Exhibit 4). The breakdown of distribution channels by percentage of volume is shown in Exhibit 5.

Selling and distribution costs were quite high in this segment as shown in Exhibit 6 for a typical deco/DIY manufacturer supplying mainly through the wholesaler channel.

There were several promotional strategies utilized by the industry, which varied substantially in their relative importance from country to country. The biggest variations could be seen in the amount of advertising dollars spent on

---

### EXHIBIT 4

**SALES COMPARISON OF DIFFERENT RETAIL OUTLETS, 1977 (%)**

|  | Belgium | France | W. Germany | Netherlands | United Kingdom |
|---|---|---|---|---|---|
| Department stores | 3 | 5 | — | 19 | 10 |
| Specialist stores | 25 | 33 | 60 | 40 | 45 |
| Hardware shops | 10 | 3 | 5 | 7 | 18 |
| Variety stores | 45 | 50 | 55 | 6 | — |
| Supermarkets/hypermarkets | 7 | 8 | — | 4 | 12 |
| Wallpaper shops | 8 | — | — | 16 | — |
| Others | 2 | 1 | — | 8 | 15 |
|  | 100 | 100 | 100 | 100 | 100 |

*Source:* Company records.

---

**EXHIBIT 5**

---

**VOLUME OF SALES BY CHANNEL OF DISTRIBUTION (%)**

| Decorative | | | Do-it-yourself | | |
|---|---|---|---|---|---|
| Channel | 1973 | 1977 | Channel | 1973 | 1977 |
| Direct | 45 | 50 | Traditional paint stores | 80 | 70 |
| Through wholesalers | 55 | 50 | Large scale outlets | 20 | 30 |
| | 100 | 100 | | 100 | 100 |

*Source:* Company records.

press and television. Total industry expenditures in the United Kingdom in 1974 were over $6 million, of which 75 percent was for television advertising; $5 million was spent in West Germany, with only 25 percent on television advertising. In contrast, advertising expenditures in France and the Benelux countries were well below $1 million annually.

For both deco and DIY markets, single-brand and multibrand policies were applied by different companies in different countries. When the outlets for both segments were the same, one-brand policies seemed to dominate. But in the case of multiple distribution channels, it was generally believed that a multibrand strategy was necessary. Manufacturers selling directly to the professional decorative market would not distribute the same brand through wholesalers to

the DIY segment. In addition, retailers preferred not to depend on one supplier and to be able to offer an extended choice to clients, thereby profiting from the reputation of each brand. Although a single brand would have permitted more effective advertising, the extensive distribution necessary to turn awareness into sales could not be realized in this way.

Variations in the price/quality relationship sought by different customers also suggested multiple brands. The chart in Exhibit 7 summarizes the industry's view on how the market divided on this issue. The large price disparities normally found between the large surface discounters and local retailers could be attributed to these differences.

## COMPETITION

Competition was intense in the deco/DIY market. There were approximately 2,000 regional paint manufacturers who were strongly represented in Germany, France, and Italy which produced over 50 percent of the total consumption of architectural coatings. In addition there were another 100 national and international manufacturers. In Germany, France, and Italy, the regional suppliers had the largest share of the market, and they typically used direct channels of distribution on a local or regional basis. In the United Kingdom and Benelux, a smaller number of larger suppliers had a more dominant position and tended to rely on wholesalers and/or their own depots.

---

**EXHIBIT 6**

---

**SELLING AND DISTRIBUTION COSTS FOR TYPICAL DECO/DIY MANUFACTURER AS PERCENT OF SALES**

| | |
|---|---|
| Sales | 100 |
| Raw materials | 45 |
| Gross margin | 55 |
| Manufacturing costs | 10 |
| Margin exworks | 45 |
| Selling and distribution costs | 24 |
| Advertising costs | 6 |
| R&D | 2 |
| Contribution to profit | 13 |

*Source:* Company records.

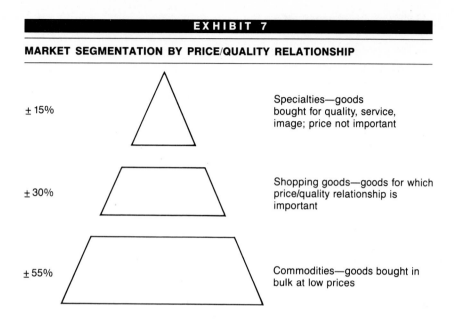

**EXHIBIT 7**

**MARKET SEGMENTATION BY PRICE/QUALITY RELATIONSHIP**

± 15% — Specialties—goods bought for quality, service, image; price not important

± 30% — Shopping goods—goods for which price/quality relationship is important

± 55% — Commodities—goods bought in bulk at low prices

The wave of mergers which characterized the industry from 1965 to 1973 involved mainly multinational raw-materials companies engaged in forward integration strategies. Since 1973, the number and size of suppliers had not changed very much, but competition became more intense due to the shrinking market and existing overcapacity. This was particularly true for wall paints, where many smaller, mainly regional, operating companies generally specialized. Resins for wall paints (emulsions) were produced by a small number of large suppliers which also provided the necessary paint "know-how" to their customers. It was therefore difficult to obtain a technical proprietary position in this segment.

The main suppliers for the deco/DIY area and their relative market shares (when available) are shown in Exhibit 8.

## THE FRENCH DECO/DIY MARKET: THE SOFRAVEL STORY

BOK Finishes had an excellent base from which to launch a multibrand strategy in France. The Sofravel brand was strong in rural areas with good direct distribution to traditional retailers. The Figier brand was strong in Paris and Lyon and was sold primarily through wholesalers. Figier also had an image of superior varnishes. Finally, La Maison was distributed directly to large surface outlets as an economy brand, and Van Houdt sold to wholesalers under the brand name Zonneschijn ("sunshine"), the "Flemish" paint.

Under the postmerger reorganization, the industrial paints activities of Figier were transferred to Sofravel, since they no longer fit the new Figier/Van Houdt focus on the wholesaler channel. A major problem arose, however, over Van Houdt's stake in the French car refinishes market. BOK Finishes management felt that Van Houdt's strong position vis-à-vis wholesalers would be weakened were it to give up its brand in the car refinishes segment. Consequently, it was agreed that Van Houdt and Sofravel would maintain their own independent car refinishes departments. The dual organization for decorative/DIY and car refinishes meant that close cooperation between Sofravel and Figier/Van Houdt was required, particularly in terms of product range, new product introduction, pric-

---

**EXHIBIT 8**

**MAIN COMPETITION AND MARKET SHARES, 1977**

| Country | Company | Market share (%) | Trend |
|---------|---------|------------------|-------|
| Belgium | Levis | 22 | + |
| | BOK Finishes (Van Houdt) | 18 | − |
| | Petrofina (Sigma) | 7 | + |
| | Akzo (Sikkens) | 6 | 0 |
| | Hoechst, DAW | 4–5 | 0 |
| Holland | Petrofina (Sigma) | 21 | + |
| | Akzo (Sikkens) | 16 | 0 |
| | BOK Finishes (Van Houdt) | 10 | + |
| | Hoechst | 7 | + |
| | DAW, Levis, Brink Molijn | 4–5 | − |
| W. Germany | DAW | 9 | + |
| | BASF (Glasurit) | 7 | + |
| | Akzo (Sikkens) | 5 | − |
| | Hoechst (Herberts) | 4 | + |
| | BOK Finishes (Van Houdt) | 3 | − |
| | ICI (Wiederhold) | 2 | − |
| France | CDF | 13 | − |
| | La Seigneurie | 10 | + |
| | IPA | 7 | + |
| | BOK (Sofravel, Van Houdt) | 6 | − |
| | Akzo (Astral) | 5 | 0 |
| | BASF, DAW, Levis, Gauthier | 2–4 | 0 |
| United Kingdom | ICI | 20 | + |
| | Hoechst (Berger) | 20 | − |
| | Reed (Crown), Akzo (Sikkens), Donald Mac Pherson | 5–10 | 0 |
| Italy | Max Meyer, DAW, Akzo, Duco, BOK | n.a. | |

n.a. = not available.
*Source:* Company records.

---

ing policies, potential duplicate coverage of clients, and general exchange of information regarding new sales points.

To facilitate this coordination, the responsibility for all activities in France, including Figier/Van Houdt, as well as Delfina in Italy and operations in Western Africa, was delegated to Sofravel. Mr. de Vitry, a former part-owner of Sofravel, was named president-director general (PDG) of the Sofravel group after the merger. Shortly after the reorganization, however, he left the company, and after a brief interim period, F. de Castelnau was appointed his successor in 1972.

A marketing committee composed of de Castelnau and the three commercial directors (Sofravel, Figier/Van Houdt, and Delfina) was established. Sofravel's commercial organization, based on a series of regional distribution centers, would be replaced by a vertical market segment structure with separate lines of authority for the decorative, DIY, car refinishes, and marine segments. Administration and commercial as well as other common staff functions would be separated.

Sofravel's operations in the decorative and DIY segments had not been particularly profitable; local or regional warehouses operated with a great deal of autonomy, which made a national commercial strategy difficult to implement. Under the new policy, Sofravel would attempt to rationalize its warehouses, aim at more profitable clients, and improve the efficiency of its sales force. Sofravel's first task was to evaluate their current customers and to identify those that fit with their new objectives. For example, almost 50 percent of Sofravel's direct accounts in the decorative segment consisted of tradespeople who could be better served by wholesalers, the domain then allocated to Figier/Van Houdt. Equally, approximately 85 percent of their clients in the DIY sector were small retailers in rural zones. The Sofravel commercial director was assigned the responsibility to inform the new Figier/Van Houdt organization whenever Sofravel deleted accounts which could be profitably served by the Figier/Van Houdt group.

A. Figier (formerly the owner of the company bearing his name which had been acquired by Sofravel in 1964) was named marketing director for all Sofravel product groups and made responsible for general sales policy, product and warehouse profitability, and coordination of the administrative and commercial functions of all Sofravel's activities, including the decorative, DIY, car refinish, and marine segments. Commercial directors were appointed for each of the segments and given responsibility for the segment's profitability and sales force. A distribution manager was named to manage physical distribution and to control inventory and warehouse expenses. At the time of the reorganization, the Figier/Van Houdt personnel were moved to the downtown Paris offices of Sofravel.

## INTEGRATION PROBLEMS

The integration of the Sofravel operations into the BOK Finishes structure had been fraught with problems, Mollerius admitted. The issue recently had come to a head when a corporate personnel administrator who was supposed to give advice about personnel practices to Sofravel was banned from setting foot on Sofravel property. He was accused of being a BOK "spy," and "eavesdropper," and he was not allowed to talk to any Sofravel employees.

Language was one of the biggest problems. A number of BOK executives did not speak French properly, and very few of the French spoke any Flemish. English was declared the common business language, but only two members of Sofravel's board of management and one of the members of its marketing committee (Figier) spoke English. One consequence of the language barrier was that the merger only occurred at the top levels where all three languages were spoken or where translators were available. There was such an atmosphere of mistrust, however, that even the translators were viewed suspiciously: "I would go to these meetings as a translator since I am half Flemish and half French, and a BOK employee working in France, but I think that no one fully trusted me. People would accuse me of not telling them everything that was said!"

Cultural differences accounted for some of the conflict. Although Mollerius thought that Sofravel had deliberately kept alive "French chauvinism" and refused to be integrated, he admitted that Van Houdt had added fuel to the fire by not recognizing the differences between the French and the Benelux markets. Style differences in terms of sales and management approaches were categorized in terms of "Flemish" and "French." BOK did initiate cross-cultural training to ease the tension and facilitate communication and coordination, but it was generally viewed as a waste of time.

Regular meetings were also established with representatives from each operating company and headquarters for each function or position, for instance among personnel managers. One manager's response to these was: "It was a good opportunity to go to Paris and have some nice dinners . . . nice chats with other people . . . but we didn't really do anything, or discuss anything. If someone brought up an issue about compensation and how it was done in their organization, we would all say that's nice, but it won't work in our organization. Still, it was a good try." The meetings were eventually dropped.

De Castelnau did not agree with BOK's strategy, and he did not want to be another branch of a Belgian company. He argued that BOK had acquired them under false pretenses, since BOK had agreed that Sofravel would remain independent and that BOK would only provide assistance when wanted. He was particularly offended by the division of Sofravel's operations and the loss of their broad-based R&D department. He was not happy with the Flemish style of management, stating that it was too blunt and not well-suited for the French market. A number of Sofravel employees supported de Castelnau and stayed with the company. Other key members of the management team left to join competitors or to form their own businesses. Figier, the marketing director, eventually left and went into real estate because of a clash with de Castelnau.

Mollerius knew that the dual sales forces were not working well. There had been evidence recently to suggest that the Sofravel sales force was only promoting the Sofravel brand, despite the fact that the Van Houdt paint might be better suited for a specific application. The Van Houdt sales group was guilty of the same offense. In addition, many potential customers were not being served because leads were not given to the appropriate group. The result was lost sales overall.

One other aspect in need of coordination was manufacturing capacity. The four main operating companies had 11 plants among them, some making small amounts of deco/DIY products (see Exhibit 9). Although economies of scale were not large and product diversity was significant, management felt that there was room for improvement. As far as R&D was concerned, expenditures were small (less than 2 percent of sales) compared to automotive or car refinishes.

## STRATEGIC OBJECTIVES FOR 1978–1982

The main strategic objectives for the DIY area were clear: (1) obtain a greater than 14 percent ROI; (2) defend the leading position in paints in Belgium, and improve positions in France, Italy, and Holland; (3) concentrate on better segments in Germany; (4) improve profitability everywhere by rationalization of customers, products, brands, and services; and (5) improve customer control and customer mix.

---

### EXHIBIT 9

**CAPACITY UTILIZATION FOR DECORATIVE/DIY PRODUCTION** (Tons)

| Plant and location | Total capacity | Output decorative/DIY |
|---|---|---|
| Belgium 1 | 33,000 | 6,300 |
| Belgium 2 | 11,000 | 800 |
| Belgium 3 | 7,500 | 6,200 |
| Holland 1 | 6,000 | 5,000 |
| Holland 2 | 5,000 | 5,000 |
| W. Germany 1 | 4,150 | 400 |
| W. Germany 2 | 19,000 | 16,250 |
| Austria | 2,000 | 600 |
| France | 37,000 | 24,000 |
| N. Italy | 6,000 | 3,450 |
| S. Italy | 5,000 | 3,500 |

*Source:* Company records.

EXHIBIT 10

## SALES AND CONTRIBUTION TO PROFITS (CTP) FOR DECORATIVE/DIY PAINTS, 1973-1977*

| | 1973 | | 1974 | | 1975 | | 1976 | | 1977 | |
|---|---|---|---|---|---|---|---|---|---|---|
| | Sales | CTP | Sales | CTP | Sales | CTP | Sales | CTP | Sales | CTP |
| **Decorative** | | | | | | | | | | |
| Van Houdt (B) | 248.8 | 16.9 | 272.5 | 12.5 | 259.7 | 5.2 | 276.4 | 15.2 | 297.6 | 14.6 |
| Van Houdt (NL) | 134.0 | 16.6 | 153.3 | 15.4 | 152.5 | 9.2 | 169.4 | 8.4 | 190.2 | 16.6 |
| Sofravel (B) | 42.0 | (2.5) | 53.6 | 1.8 | 50.0 | 0.2 | 43.7 | (7.4) | 47.2 | 0.1 |
| Van Houdt GmbH (D)† | 533.3 | 10.0 | 504.0 | 6.1 | 552.2 | 2.8 | 605.2 | 3.5 | 599.9 | 6.0 |
| Sofravel (F) | 230.0 | 11.1 | 277.1 | 13.2 | 306.5 | 13.4 | 288.9 | 9.6 | 268.0 | 3.5 |
| Figier/Van Houdt (F) | 114.0 | 7.1 | 115.0 | 10.9 | 134.4 | 12.9 | 152.2 | 15.1 | 148.1 | 13.0 |
| BOK Siver SpA (I)‡ | 161.4 | 13.2 | 202.3 | 15.4 | 198.5 | 8.2 | 216.3 | 13.6 | 203.2 | 7.6 |
| Total§ | 1,463.5 | 11.7 | 1,596.2 | 10.8 | 1,673.6 | 7.2 | 1,773.5 | 8.7 | 1,783.0 | 8.8 |
| **Do-it-Yourself** | | | | | | | | | | |
| Van Houdt (B) | 542.1 | 16.1 | 618.7 | 11.0 | 654.9 | 8.1 | 691.9 | 8.9 | 718.8 | 13.4 |
| Van Houdt (NL) | 42.2 | 1.3 | 61.5 | (1.5) | 67.9 | 8.0 | 66.3 | 1.7 | 75.0 | 3.9 |
| Van Houdt GmbH (D) | 25.4 | (21.1) | 39.9 | (3.7) | 42.5 | 3.2 | 55.0 | 10.2 | 76.4 | 3.7 |
| Sofravel (F) | 158.3 | 14.4 | 183.6 | 16.2 | 225.7 | 14.5 | 221.7 | 11.6 | 227.3 | 9.3 |
| Figier (F) | 118.2 | 13.3 | 136.8 | 15.8 | 187.2 | 16.8 | 182.9 | 13.4 | 184.5 | 7.6 |
| La Maison (F) | 34.1 | 7.7 | 43.8 | 10.7 | 53.8 | 11.6 | 63.6 | 9.0 | 99.9 | 4.4 |
| Total¶ | 920.4 | 13.4 | 1,084.3 | 11.2 | 1,234.1 | 10.6 | 1,283.9 | 9.7 | 1,381.8 | 10.3 |

*Sales figures are in BF million, and CTP figures are percentages of sales.
†Includes small amounts (less than BF2 million per year) of Brunal decorative products.
‡Includes some DIY sales.
§Includes "others" in Europe, but not plastic compounds.
¶Includes small quantities sold in other European markets.

In the decorative market, at least a 10 percent ROI was desired. The objectives were to concentrate on better segments in all geographic areas, to rationalize products and customer lines continuously, and to develop and introduce a European mixing system and other new products.

Exhibit 10 shows sales and contribution to profits by country and brand group for both deco and DIY segments for 1973 to 1977.

## ORGANIZATION

A steering committee for both the decorative and DIY segments existed in BOK Finishes. For both, their principal activities were to: (1) recommend marketing inputs to the strategic plan including project evaluation and long-term product development; (2) identify, propose, and control "common" projects across national boundaries; (3) submit proposals for concentration of resources on specific common activities within the group; (4) facilitate exchange of know-how and experience between companies; (5) initiate and prepare, if necessary, changes in brand policy; and (6) arbitrate short-term product development. These activities were to be carried out "within the constraints of the BOK Finishes Strategic Plan and the current organizational reality."

Meetings were to be held three times a year. Members were nominated by the board of management and consisted of representatives of Van Houdt, Brunal, Sofravel, the manager of the specialist R&D center for decorative (or DIY), the function marketing and product group coordinator, and other invited participants for special projects. The steering committee was accountable through the functional manager to BOK Finishes' board of management.